Customer Support Information

Plunkett's Energy Industry Almanac 2011

Please register your book immediately...

if you did not purchase it directly from Plunkett Research, Ltd. This will enable us to fulfill your requests for assistance. Also, it will enable us to notify you of future editions.

Your purchase includes access to Book Data and Exports online

As a book purchaser, you can register for free, 1-year, 1-seat online access to the latest data for your book's industry trends, statistics and company profiles. This includes tools to export company data. We are migrating from our former CD-ROMs, for supplemental data and export tools, to the web. Simply send us this registration form, and we will send you a user name and password. In this manner, you will have access to our continual updates during the year. Certain restrictions apply.

____ YES, please register me as a purchaser of the book.
I did not buy it directly from Plunkett Research, Ltd.

____ YES, please register me for free online access. I am the actual, original purchaser. (Proof of purchase may be required.)

Customer Name ____

Title ____

Organization ____

Address ____

City ______________________ State ________ Zip ____________

Country (if other than USA) ____________________________________

Phone ______________________ Fax ______________________

E-mail ____

Return to: Plunkett Research, Ltd.
Attn: Registration
P.O. Drawer 541737, Houston, TX 77254-1737 USA
713.932.0000 · Fax 713.932.7080 · www.plunkettresearch.com
customersupport@plunkettresearch.com

* Purchasers of used books are not eligible to register. Use of online access is subject to the terms of the end user license agreement.

PLUNKETT'S ENERGY INDUSTRY ALMANAC 2011

The Only Comprehensive Guide to the Energy & Utilities Industry

Jack W. Plunkett

Published by:
Plunkett Research, Ltd., Houston, Texas
www.plunkettresearch.com

PLUNKETT'S ENERGY INDUSTRY ALMANAC 2011

Editor and Publisher:
Jack W. Plunkett

Special Thanks to:
BP plc, *BP Statistical Reviews*
U.S. Department of Energy, and the editors and analysts at the *Energy Information Administration*
U.S. Energy Information Administration
U.S. National Science Foundation

Plunkett Research, Ltd.
P. O. Drawer 541737, Houston, Texas 77254 USA
Phone: 713.932.0000 Fax: 713.932.7080
www.plunkettresearch.com

Published by:
Plunkett Research, Ltd.
P. O. Drawer 541737
Houston, Texas 77254-1737

Phone: 713.932.0000
Fax: 713.932.7080
Internet: www.plunkettresearch.com

ISBN13 # 978-1-59392-186-6
(eBook Edition # 978-1-59392-529-1)

Disclaimer of liability for use and results of use:

The editors and publishers assume no responsibility for your own success in making an investment or business decision, in seeking or keeping any job, in succeeding at any firm or in obtaining any amount or type of benefits or wages. Your own results and the job stability or financial stability of any company depend on influences outside of our control. All risks are assumed by the reader. Investigate any potential employer or business relationship carefully and carefully verify past and present finances, present business conditions and the level of compensation and benefits currently paid. Each company's details are taken from sources deemed reliable; however, their accuracy is not guaranteed. The editors and publishers assume no liability, beyond the actual payment received from a reader, for any direct, indirect, incidental or consequential, special or exemplary damages, and they do not guarantee, warrant nor make any representation regarding the use of this material. Trademarks or tradenames are used without symbols and only in a descriptive sense, and this use is not authorized by, associated with or sponsored by the trademarks' owners. Ranks and ratings are presented as an introductory and general glance at corporations, based on our research and our knowledge of businesses and the industries in which they operate. The reader should use caution.

PLUNKETT'S ENERGY INDUSTRY ALMANAC 2011

CONTENTS

Continued on next page

Continued from previous page

A Short Energy Industry Glossary

10-K: An annual report filed by publicly held companies. It provides a comprehensive overview of the company's business and its finances. By law, it must contain specific information and follow a given form, the "Annual Report on Form 10-K." The U.S. Securities and Exchange Commission requires that it be filed within 90 days after fiscal year end. However, these reports are often filed late due to extenuating circumstances. Variations of a 10-K are often filed to indicate amendments and changes. Most publicly held companies also publish an "annual report" that is not on Form 10-K. These annual reports are more informal and are frequently used by a company to enhance its image with customers, investors and industry peers.

3-D Seismic Surveying: An enhancement of seismic imaging from the standard two-dimensional view to a three-dimensional view. Three-dimensional seismic images have greater resolution and help delineate oil and gas reservoirs hidden by complex faulting. See also "Seismic Surveying."

4-D Seismic Surveying: Adds the dimension of time to 3-D seismic surveying.

Air-Conditioning and Refrigeration Institute (ARI): A U.S. trade association representing manufacturers of more than 90% of North American produced central air conditioning and commercial refrigeration equipment.

Alcohol: The family name of a group of organic chemical compounds composed of carbon, hydrogen and oxygen. The series of molecules vary in chain length and are composed of a hydrocarbon plus a hydroxyl group. Alcohols include methanol and ethanol. Alcohol is frequently used in fuel, organic solvents, anti-freeze and beverages. Also see "Ethanol."

Alternating Current (AC): An electric current that reverses its direction at regularly recurring intervals, usually 50 or 60 times per second.

American Petroleum Institute (API): A trade association for the petrochemical industry.

Amorphous Silicon: An alloy of silica and hydrogen, with a disordered, noncrystalline internal atomic arrangement, that can be deposited in thin layers (a few micrometers in thickness) by a number of deposition methods to produce thin-film photovoltaic cells on glass, metal or plastic substrates.

Anthracite Coal: Anthracite, or hard coal, is the highest rank of economically usable coal. It is jet black with a high luster. The moisture content is generally less than 15%. It usually has a high fixed carbon and ash content and is low in volatile matter. It is a non-coking coal.

APAC: Asia Pacific Advisory Committee. A multi-country committee representing the Asia and Pacific region.

Applied Research: The application of compounds, processes, materials or other items discovered during basic research to practical uses. The goal is to move discoveries along to the final development phase.

ARI: See "Air-Conditioning and Refrigeration Institute (ARI)."

ASEAN: Association of Southeast Asian Nations. A regional economic development association established in 1967 by five original member countries: Indonesia, Malaysia, Philippines, Singapore, and Thailand. Brunei joined on 8 January 1984, Vietnam on 28 July 1995, Laos and Myanmar on 23 July 1997, and Cambodia on 30 April 1999.

Asphalt (Natural): A natural mineral pitch, tar or bitumen composed principally of hydrocarbons; a natural bituminous rock that is dark colored, comparatively hard and nonvolatile. Does not include asphalt, bitumen, tar or other substances, derived from petroleum processing.

Authority for Expenditure (AFE): A standard industry procedure in which a formal written estimate is generated outlining in advance the cost of drilling a given well, both as a dry hole and as a completed well.

Barrel (Petroleum): A unit of volume equal to 42 U.S. gallons.

Barrels of Oil Equivalent (BOE): A measure of the energy of non-oil fuels. For example, a BOE of natural gas is roughly 6,000 cubic feet. The measure is derived by assessing the amount of a fuel required to generate the same heat content as a typical barrel of oil.

Barrels of Oil per Day (BOPD): A standard measurement for volume of oil production.

Basic Research: Attempts to discover compounds, materials, processes or other items that may be largely or entirely new and/or unique. Basic research may start with a theoretical concept that has yet to be proven. The goal is to create discoveries that can be moved along to applied research. Basic research is sometimes referred to as "blue sky" research.

Bbl: See "Barrel (Petroleum)."

Bcf: One billion cubic feet.

Bcfe: One billion cubic feet of natural gas equivalent.

Benchmark Crude Oil: An established variety of crude oil used by a country as the standard of comparison in documenting the properties of other oils and in setting prices. West Texas Intermediate is the U.S. benchmark. Brent is the benchmark in the U.K.

Binary Cycle Generation: A method of geothermal electricity generation where lower-temperature geothermal sources are tapped. The geothermal steam source is used to heat another liquid that has a lower boiling point, which then drives the turbine. Also see "Flash Steam Generation."

Biodiesel: A fuel derived when glycerin is separated from vegetable oils or animal fats. The resulting byproducts are methyl esters (the chemical name for biodiesel) and glycerin which can be used in soaps and cleaning products. It has lower emissions than petroleum diesel and is currently used as an additive to that fuel since it helps with lubricity.

Bioenergy: Useful, renewable energy produced from organic matter, which may either be used directly as a fuel or processed into liquids and gases. See "Biomass."

Bioethanol: A fuel produced by the fermentation of plant matter such as corn. Fermentation is enhanced through the use of enzymes that are created through biotechnology. Also, see "Ethanol."

Biomass: Organic, non-fossil material of biological origin constituting a renewable energy source. The biomass can be burnt as fuel in a system that creates steam to turn a turbine, generating electricity. For example, biomass can include wood chips and agricultural crops.

Biorefinery: A refinery that produces fuels from biomass. These fuels may include bioethanol (produced from corn or other plant matter) or biodiesel (produced from plant or animal matter).

Bit (Drill Bit): The cutting device connected to the bottom end of a drill, used to bore through rock formations in drilling.

Bitumen: A naturally occurring viscous mixture, mainly of hydrocarbons heavier than pentane, that may contain sulfur compounds. Also, see "Tar Sands (Oil Sands)."

Bituminous Coal: The most common coal, bituminous coal is dense and black, often with well-defined bands of bright and dull materials. Its moisture content is usually less than 20%. It is used for generating electricity, making coke and space heating.

Black Liquor: A byproduct of the paper production process that can be used as a source of energy.

Black Oil: Oil containing relatively high percentages of long, heavy and nonvolatile hydrocarbons.

Blowout: A sudden, uncontrolled flow of fluid from a well.

Blowout Preventer (BOP): A safety device installed to allow closure of a well should it begin a blowout, and to control escape of pressurized fluids during drilling and related operations. A blowout preventer stack is mounted on top of a well and consists of a series of rams and spools for closing down a wellhead.

Borehole: A hole resulting from the drilling (boring) of a well.

Borehole Compensated Sonic Log (BHCS): A borehole compensated sonic log is generated using two sets of alternately pulsed transmitters, with measurements then averaged in order to compensate for erroneous results due to irregularities in borehole size and tilting of the measuring device.

Bottomhole Assembly: The drill collars, sub pipe and adapters and bit installed at the bottom of a drill.

BPL: See "Broadband Over Power Lines (BPL)."

BPO: See "Business Process Outsourcing (BPO)."

Branding: A marketing strategy that places a focus on the brand name of a product, service or firm in order to increase the brand's market share, increase sales, establish credibility, improve satisfaction, raise the profile of the firm and increase profits.

BRIC: An acronym representing Brazil, Russia, India and China. The economies of these four countries are seen as some of the fastest growing in the world. A 2003 report by investment bank Goldman Sachs is often credited for popularizing the term; the report suggested that by 2050, BRIC economies will likely outshine those countries which are currently the richest in the world.

British Thermal Unit (Btu): The quantity of heat needed to raise the temperature of 1 pound of water by 1 degree Fahrenheit at or near 39.2 degrees Fahrenheit.

Broadband Over Power Lines (BPL): Refers to the use of standard electric power lines to provide fast Internet service. Internet data is converted into radio frequency signals, which are not affected by electricity. Subscribers utilize special modems.

B-to-B, or B2B: See "Business-to-Business."

B-to-C, or B2C: See "Business-to-Consumer."

Bulk Terminal: A facility, used primarily for the storage and/or marketing of petroleum products, which has a total bulk storage capacity of 50,000 barrels or more and/or receives petroleum products by tanker, barge or pipeline.

Business Process Outsourcing (BPO): The process of hiring another company to handle business activities. BPO is one of the fastest-growing segments in the offshoring sector. Services include human resources management, billing and purchasing and call centers, as well as many types of customer service or marketing activities, depending on the industry involved. Also, see “Knowledge Process Outsourcing (KPO).”

Business-to-Business: An organization focused on selling products, services or data to commercial customers rather than individual consumers. Also known as B2B.

Business-to-Consumer: An organization focused on selling products, services or data to individual consumers rather than commercial customers. Also known as B2C.

Butane: A normally gaseous straight-chain or branch-chain hydrocarbon (C_4H_{10}), extracted from natural gas or refinery gas streams. It includes isobutane and normal butane.

Butanol (Biobutanol): Butyl alcohol, sometimes used as a solvent. In the form of biobutanol, it is an ethanol substitute, generally derived from sugar beets to be used as a fuel additive.

CAFTA-DR: See “Central American-Dominican Republic Free Trade Agreement (CAFTA-DR).”

CANDU Reactor: A pressurized heavy-water, natural-uranium power reactor designed by a consortium of Canadian government and private industry participants. CANDU utilizes natural, unenriched uranium oxide as fuel. Because unenriched uranium is cheaper, this kind of reactor is attractive to developing countries. The fuel is contained in hundreds of tubes that are pressure resistant. This means that a tube can be refueled while the reactor is operating. CANDU is a registered trademark of the CANDU consortium.

Cap and Trade: A system in which governments attempt to reduce carbon emissions by major industry. First, an overall “cap” is placed, by government regulation, on total carbon emissions for particular companies and/or their industries. The "trade" part of cap and trade allows companies that operate efficiently on a carbon basis, and thereby emit a lower amount of carbon than law allows, to sell or trade the unused part of their carbon allowances to firms that are less efficient.

Capacity Factor: The ratio of the electrical energy produced by a generating unit for a certain period of time to the electrical energy that could have been produced at continuous full-power operation during the same period.

Captive Offshoring: Used to describe a company-owned offshore operation. For example, Microsoft owns and operates significant captive offshore research and development centers in China and elsewhere that are offshore from Microsoft's U.S. home base. Also see “Offshoring.”

Carbon Capture and Storage: See “Carbon Sequestration.”

Carbon Sequestration (CCS): The absorption and storage of CO_2 from the atmosphere by the roots and leaves of plants; the carbon builds up as organic matter in the soil. In the energy industry, carbon sequestration refers to the process of isolating and storing carbon dioxide (a so-called greenhouse gas). One use is to avoid releasing carbon dioxide into the air when burning coal at a coal-fired power plant. Instead, the carbon dioxide is stored in the ground or otherwise stored in a permanent or semi-permanent fashion. Other uses include the return to the ground of carbon dioxide that is produced at natural gas wells, and the introduction of carbon dioxide into oil wells in order to increase internal pressure and production. This process is also known as carbon capture and storage (CCS).

Cased Hole Log: A wireline logging device installed in a well that has been successfully cased. Cased hole logs enable engineers to analyze and monitor the characteristics and movements of a given well.

Casing: A steel pipe with a large diameter that supports the walls or sides of the borehole to prevent them from caving in.

Casinghead: A fitting attached to the top of the casing in an oil or gas well that regulates the flow of oil or gas, allowing the pumping of oil from the well.

Cast Silicon: Crystalline silicon obtained by pouring pure molten silicon into a vertical mold and adjusting the temperature gradient along the mold volume during cooling to obtain slow, vertically advancing crystallization of the silicon. The polycrystalline ingot thus formed is composed of large, relatively parallel, interlocking crystals. The cast ingots are sawed into wafers for further fabrication into photovoltaic cells. Cast-silicon wafers and ribbon-silicon sheets fabricated into cells are usually referred to as polycrystalline photovoltaic cells.

CCS: See “Carbon Sequestration (CCS).”

Cement: A mineral growth that bonds the surfaces of elastic sediments, or a composite powder that hardens when mixed with water used to bind casing to the walls of a well.

Central American-Dominican Republic Free Trade Agreement (CAFTA-DR): A trade agreement signed into law in 2005 that aimed to open up the Central American and Dominican Republic markets to American goods. Member nations include Guatemala, Nicaragua, Costa Rica, El Salvador, Honduras and the Dominican Republic. Before the law was signed, products from those countries could enter the U.S. almost tariff-free, while American goods heading into those countries faced stiff tariffs. The goal of this agreement was to create U.S. jobs while at the same time offering the non-U.S. member citizens a chance for a better quality of life through access to U.S.-made goods.

CHP: See "Combined Cycle."

Christmas Tree: An intricate assemblage of pipe connections, gauges, fittings and valves/controls located at the top of a casing of a flowing oil well. The Christmas tree controls the flow of the well.

CIS: See "Commonwealth of Independent States (CIS)."

Climate Change (Greenhouse Effect): A theory that assumes an increasing mean global surface temperature of the Earth caused by gases (sometimes referred to as greenhouse gases) in the atmosphere (including carbon dioxide, methane, nitrous oxide, ozone and chlorofluorocarbons). The greenhouse effect allows solar radiation to penetrate the Earth's atmosphere but absorbs the infrared radiation returning to space.

Coal: A black or brownish-black solid, combustible substance formed by the partial decomposition of vegetable matter without access to air. The ranks of coal, which include anthracite, sub-anthracite, bituminous, sub-bituminous and lignite, are based on fixed carbon, volatile matter, coking and coking properties, and heating value. Coal rank includes the progressive alteration, or coalification, from lignite to anthracite.

Coalbed Methane (CBM): A natural methane gas that is found in coal seams, while traditional natural gas deposits are trapped in porous rock formations. A small amount of CBM is already produced successfully in the Rocky Mountain region of the U.S.

Cogeneration: See "Combined Heat and Power (CHP) Plant."

Coiled Tubing Unit: An industrial device that feeds flexible steel tubing from a reel, enabling technicians to run equipment down a well. The tubing, typically measuring 1¼ inches in diameter, is passed through a pipe straightener before it enters the well.

Coke (Coal): In general, coke is made from bituminous coal (or blends of bituminous coals) from which the volatile constituents are driven off by baking in an oven at temperatures as high as 2,000 degrees Fahrenheit, so that the fixed carbon and ash are fused together. Coke is hard and porous, has a gray submetallic luster and is strong enough to support a load of iron ore in a blast furnace. It is used both as a fuel and as a reducing agent in smelting iron ore in a blast furnace.

Combined Cycle: An electric generating technology in which electricity is produced from otherwise lost waste heat exiting from one or more gas (combustion) turbines. The exiting heat is routed to a conventional boiler or to a heat recovery steam generator for utilization by a steam turbine in the production of electricity. Such designs increase the efficiency of the electric generating unit. This process is also known as cogeneration or "combined heat and power" (CHP).

Combined Heat and Power (CHP) Plant: A facility that generates power via combined cycle technology. See "Combined Cycle."

Commonwealth of Independent States (CIS): An organization consisting of 11 former members of the Soviet Union: Russia, Ukraine, Armenia, Moldova, Georgia, Belarus, Kazakhstan, Uzbekistan, Azerbaijan, Kyrgyzstan and Tajikistan. It was created in 1991. Turkmenistan recently left the Commonwealth as a permanent member, but remained as an associate member. The Commonwealth seeks to coordinate a variety of economic and social policies, including taxation, pricing, customs and economic regulation, as well as to promote the free movement of capital, goods, services and labor.

Compressor: A device to increase gas pressure capable of causing the flow of gas.

Concentrated Solar Power (CSP): The use of solar thermal collectors to absorb solar heat and then heat water, oil or other substances with that energy. A good example is the Stirling Engine, which uses focused solar energy to heat liquid hydrogen in a closed-loop system. Expanding hydrogen gas creates pressure on pistons within the engine, which turns at a steady 1,800 RPM. The engine then powers an electric generator. CSP technologies include the use of parabolic troughs that focus solar energy, and the use of "solar towers" to attract and gather solar heat.

Concession Agreement: A contractual arrangement between a company and a government, in which the company receives exclusive rights to explore, drill and produce energy resources, at its own expense, within an agreed area of the country, in exchange for payment of negotiated bonuses, royalties and taxes to the government.

Condensate (Lease): A liquid recovered from natural gas at the well or at small gas/oil separators in the field. Consists primarily of pentanes and heavier hydrocarbons. Also called field condensate. Does not include plant condensate.

Condensate (Plant-Petroleum): A light hydrocarbon liquid, consisting mostly of pentanes and heavier hydrocarbons, recovered by condensation of hydrocarbon vapors at natural gas liquids processing plants.

Consumer Price Index (CPI): A measure of the average change in consumer prices over time in a fixed market basket of goods and services, such as food, clothing and housing. The CPI is calculated by the U.S. Federal Government and is considered to be one measure of inflation.

Contango: A condition in futures markets where future contracts, generally for a commodity, trade at higher prices than the current spot month price.

Continental Shelf: The shallow transitional boundary running from the ocean's shore to a depth of roughly 450 feet, after which an abrupt change occurs in slope and depth. Continental shelf environments are the most typical sites of offshore drilling and production.

Continental Slope: The area between the continental shelf and the deep ocean floor, which has become increasingly targeted for oil and gas exploration using various deepwater techniques and devices.

Conventional Thermal Electricity Generation: Electricity generated by an electric power plant using coal, petroleum or gas as its source of energy.

Crude Oil: A mixture of hydrocarbons that exists in liquid form at atmospheric pressure after passing through surface separating facilities. Included are lease condensate and liquid hydrocarbons produced from tar sands, Gilsonite and oil shale. Drip gases are also included, but topped crude oil (residual) and other unfinished oils are excluded. Liquids produced at natural gas processing plants and mixed with crude oil are likewise excluded where identifiable.

CSP: See "Concentrated Solar Power (CSP)."

Customer Relationship Management (CRM): Refers to the automation, via sophisticated software, of business processes involving existing and prospective customers. CRM may cover aspects such as sales (contact management and contact history), marketing (campaign management and telemarketing) and customer service (call center history and field service history). Well known providers of CRM software include Salesforce, which delivers via a Software as a Service model (see "Software as a Service (Saas)"), Microsoft and Siebel, which as been acquired by Oracle.

Decline Curve: A graphic representation of projected oil production over time.

Deepwater Well: An offshore well drilled in more than 1,000 feet of water depth.

Demand Chain: A similar concept to a supply chain, but with an emphasis on the end user.

Depletion (Economic): The reduction in value of a mineral deposit as it is depleted through production.

Depletion (Physical): The consumption of a mineral deposit by production of the mineral to the point that its deposits are no longer available.

Deregulation: See "Regulated Business (Utility Companies)."

Development: The phase of research and development (R&D) in which researchers attempt to create new products from the results of discoveries and applications created during basic and applied research.

Direct Current (DC): An electric current that flows in a constant direction. The magnitude of the current does not vary or has a slight variation.

Directional Drilling: Involves the intentional inclination of a well away from vertical in order to optimize production and enable drilling in challenging environments. Sometimes referred to as slant drilling, the process has generated public controversy over related attempts to extract oil from under the Great Lakes and was cited by Iraq as one of its grievances with the emirs of Kuwait, leading to its invasion of the country in the early 1990s. Also called deviation drilling.

Distributed Power Generation: A method of generating electricity at or near the site where it will be consumed, such as the use of small, local generators or fuel cells to power individual buildings, homes or neighborhoods. Distributed power is thought by many analysts to offer distinct advantages. For example, electricity generated in this manner is not reliant upon the grid for distribution to the end user.

Distribution System: The portion of an electric system that is dedicated to delivering electric energy to an end user.

Distributor: An individual or business involved in marketing, warehousing and/or shipping of products manufactured by others to a specific group of end users. Distributors do not sell to the general public. In order to develop a competitive advantage, distributors often focus on serving one industry or one set of niche clients. For example, within the medical industry, there are major distributors that focus on providing pharmaceuticals, surgical supplies or dental supplies to clinics and hospitals.

Division Orders: A standard form used to assign distribution of production-related revenues and to assess costs to royalty and working-interest owners.

Downstream: The segment of the oil and gas business involved in the secondary and final phases of the use of production from wells. That is, the post-well delivery of oil and gas through the pipeline to the refinery and processing plants and/or to the final customers. Downstream is the opposite of upstream. See "Upstream."

Drilling Line: Also known as the hoisting line, this wire rope is composed of braided steel cable wound around a fiber or steel core and is used to position equipment on a drilling rig.

Drilling Mud: See "Mud (Drilling Mud)."

Dry Hole: Any well that fails to produce oil or gas in commercially viable quantities. A dry hole might flow water, gas or oil, but at levels insufficient to justify production. Sometimes referred to as a duster.

Electric Power Industry: The privately, publicly, federally and cooperatively owned electric utilities of the United States taken as a whole. Does not include special-purpose electric facilities.

Electric Power System: An individual electric power entity.

Electric Utility: A corporation, person, agency, authority or other legal entity or instrumentality that owns and/or operates facilities within the United States for the generation, transmission, distribution or sale of electric energy primarily for use by the public.

Electronic Data Interchange (EDI): An accepted standard format for the exchange of data between various companies' networks. EDI allows for the transfer of e-mail as well as orders, invoices and other files from one company to another.

EMEA: The region comprised of Europe, the Middle East and Africa.

Emission: The release or discharge of a substance into the environment. Generally refers to the release of gases or particulates into the air.

Energy: The capacity for doing work as measured by the capability of doing work (potential energy) or the conversion of this capability to motion (kinetic energy). Most of the world's convertible energy comes from fossil fuels that are burned to produce heat that is then used as a transfer medium to mechanical or other means in order to accomplish tasks.

Energy Information Administration (EIA): An independent agency within the U.S. Department of Energy, the Energy Information Administration (EIA) develops surveys, collects energy data and does analytical and modeling analyses of energy issues.

Energy Intensity: The amount of energy needed for a nation to produce a unit of GDP (gross domestic product, a measure of economic output).

Enhanced Oil Recovery (EOR): Any enhancement of oil recovery methods, most typically involving flooding depleted reservoirs with water or gas in order to recover any remaining oil.

Enterprise Resource Planning (ERP): An integrated information system that helps manage all aspects of a business, including accounting, ordering and human resources, typically across all locations of a major corporation or organization. ERP is considered to be a critical tool for management of large organizations. Suppliers of ERP tools include SAP and Oracle.

ERP: See "Enterprise Resource Planning (ERP)."

Ethanol: A clear, colorless, flammable, oxygenated hydrocarbon, also called ethyl alcohol. In the U.S., it is used as a gasoline octane enhancer and oxygenate in a 10% blend called E10. Ethanol can be used in higher concentrations (such as an 85% blend called E85) in vehicles designed for its use. It is typically produced chemically from ethylene or biologically from fermentation of various sugars from carbohydrates found in agricultural crops and cellulose residues from crops or wood. Grain ethanol production is typically based on corn or sugarcane. Cellulosic ethanol production is based on agricultural waste, such as wheat stalks, that has been treated with enzymes to break the waste down into component sugars.

EU: See "European Union (EU)."

EU Competence: The jurisdiction in which the EU can take legal action.

European Community (EC): See "European Union (EU)."

European Union (EU): A consolidation of European countries (member states) functioning as one body to facilitate trade. Previously known as the European Community (EC), the EU expanded to include much of

Eastern Europe in 2004, raising the total number of member states to 25. In 2002, the EU launched a unified currency, the Euro. See europa.eu.int.

Exempt Wholesale Generator (EWG): A non-utility electricity generator that is not a qualifying facility under the Public Utility Regulatory Policies Act of 1978.

Expansion-Gas Drive: A reservoir drive mechanism, also known as a volumetric drive, in which the initial production of a reservoir triggers a related reduction in pressure that, in turn, enables the gas to expand and produce energy sufficient to force the gas through surrounding rocks.

Exploration and Production (E&P): See "Upstream."

Exploratory Well: A well drilled to find and produce oil and gas in an area previously considered unproductive, to find a new reservoir in a known field (i.e., one previously producing oil or gas in another reservoir) or to extend the limit of a known oil or gas reservoir.

Fast Reactor: An advanced technology nuclear reactor that uses a fast fission process utilizing fast neutrons that would split some of the U-258 atoms as well as transuranic isotopes. The goal is to use nuclear material more efficiently and safely in the production of nuclear energy.

Federal Energy Regulatory Commission (FERC): A quasi-independent regulatory agency within the Department of Energy having jurisdiction over interstate electricity sales, wholesale electricity rates, hydro-electric licensing, natural gas pricing, oil pipeline rates and gas pipeline certification.

Federal Power Act: Regulates licensing of non-federal hydroelectric projects, as well as the interstate transmission of electrical energy and rates for its sale at wholesale in interstate commerce. It was enacted in 1920 and amended in 1935.

Federal Power Commission: The predecessor agency of the FERC, abolished when the Department of Energy was created.

Fishing: The process of retrieving a foreign object (such as a tool or pipe) from a well in order to restore normal functionality.

Fishing String: A length of connected hollow tubes used to lower an attached fishing tool to the bottom of a well.

Flash Steam Generation: The most common type of hydroelectric power generation technique. Flash steam describes a system where a high temperature geothermal steam source can be used to directly drive a turbine. Also see "Binary Cycle Generation."

Flat Plate Pumped: A medium-temperature solar thermal collector that typically consists of a metal frame, glazing, absorbers (usually metal) and insulation and that uses a pump liquid as the heat-transfer medium. Its predominant use is in water heating applications.

Float Collar: A special one-way coupling device inserted just above the bottom of the casing. The collar contains a check valve that permits fluid to flow downward but not return upward, preventing drilling mud from entering the casing and avoiding backflow of cement.

Flow Cell Battery: A massive electricity storage device based on a series of modules. Each module contains a large number of fuel cells. The flow cell battery technology receives electricity from a generating or transmission source, conditions it into appropriate format via transformers and stores it in the fuel cell modules using sophisticated technology. On a large scale, a flow cell battery has the ability to store enough electricity to power a small city. In the U.S., a large flow cell battery installation can be found at the Columbus Air Force Base in Mississippi. Leading flow cell technology companies include Regenesys Technologies in Swindon, England, and VRB Power Systems in Vancouver, Canada.

FOB (Free On Board) Price: The price actually charged at the producing country's port of loading. The reported price includes deductions for any rebates and discounts or additions of premiums where applicable and should be the actual price paid with no adjustment for credit terms.

Formation Density Compensated Log (FDC): A standard porosity tool that uses gamma rays to log the characteristics of a typically uncased hole, composed of two sets of detectors to compensate for the presence of mud and borehole irregularities. Also called a gamma-gamma log.

Fossil Fuel: Any naturally occurring organic fuel, such as petroleum, coal or natural gas.

Frac: See "Fracing (fraccing)."

Fracing (fraccing): A hydraulic fracturing method that uses injected fluids to break open reservoir rock and stimulate flow. The fluid carries suspended propping agents or "proppants" (such as sand grains, aluminum pellet and glass beads) in order to keep the newly formed pathways open and permeable.

Fractionating: Separation of crude oil into various products by means of controlled heating and evaporation, according to the characteristic boiling point of each component.

Fracturing: See Fracing (fraccing)."

Fuel Cell: An environmentally friendly electrochemical engine that generates electricity using hydrogen and oxygen as fuel, emitting only heat and water as byproducts.

Fumarole: A vent from which steam or gases issue; a geyser or spring that emits gases.

Fusion: See "Nuclear Fusion."

Futures Contract: An agreement to buy or sell a specified number of shares of a particular stock or commodity in a designated future month, at a price agreed upon by both buyer and seller. Futures contracts are frequently traded on the futures market. They differ from options in that options offer the right to buy or sell, while futures contracts bind the buyer and seller to an actual transaction.

Gas Hydrates: Gas hydrates are solid particles of methane (which is normally found in gas form) and water molecules in a crystalline form. They are widely found in many parts of the world, including the U.S., South Korea, India and China, often offshore. Gas hydrates have immense potential as a source of energy and may possibly exist in much larger quantities than all other known forms of fossil fuels. Unfortunately, they are not stable except under high pressure. Gas hydrate reserves could be very expensive and difficult to develop as a commercial source of energy. Nonetheless, today's very high prices for oil and gas may eventually make them a viable energy source.

Gas Injection: A production enhancement technique in which natural gas is injected into oil reservoirs, thereby maintaining reservoir pressure and continuing the flow of oil to operating wells.

Gas Turbine: Typically consists of an axial-flow air compressor and one or more combustion chambers where liquid or gaseous fuel is burned. The hot gases are passed to the turbine, in which they expand to drive the generator and are then used to run the compressor.

Gas Turbine Plant: A plant in which the prime mover is a gas turbine.

Gas Well: A well completed for the production of natural gas from one or more gas zones or reservoirs. (Wells producing both crude oil and natural gas are classified as oil wells.)

Gasification: Any chemical or heat process used to convert a feedstock to a gaseous fuel.

Gasohol: A blend of finished motor gasoline containing alcohol (generally ethanol but sometimes methanol) at a concentration of 10% or less by volume. Data on gasohol that has at least 2.7% oxygen, by weight, and is intended for sale inside carbon monoxide non-attainment areas are included in data on oxygenated gasoline.

Gas-to-Liquids (GTL): A special process that converts natural gas into liquids that can be burnt as fuel. Major investments by ExxonMobil and others in the nation of Qatar, which contains massive natural gas reserves, will create an immense GTL plant capable of making up to 750,000 of GTL daily. The product will be GTL diesel, a very low emission alternative to standard diesel fuel.

GDP: See "Gross Domestic Product (GDP)."

Generating Unit: Any combination of physically connected generators, reactors, boilers, combustion turbines or other prime movers operated together to produce electric power.

Generation (Electricity): The process of producing electric energy; also, the amount of electric energy produced, expressed in watt-hours (Wh).

Geophysicist: A professional who applies the principles of physics to the field of geology. Geophysicists are involved in exploration for oil, gas, coal, geothermal and other underground energy sources.

Geothermal Electric Power Generation: Electricity derived from heat found under the earth's surface. Also see "Flash Steam Generation," "Binary Cycle Generation" and "Hot Dry Rock Geothermal Energy Technology (HDR)."

Geothermal Plant: A plant in which the prime mover is a steam turbine. The turbine is driven either by steam produced from hot water or by natural steam that derives its energy from heat found in rocks or fluids at various depths beneath the surface of the earth. The energy is extracted by drilling and/or pumping.

GHG: See "Greenhouse Gas (GHG)."

Gigawatt: Equal to one billion watts of power. It is also equal to one million kilowatts or 1,000 megawatts.

Global Warming: An increase in the near-surface temperature of the Earth. Global warming has occurred in the distant past as the result of natural influences, but the term is most often used to refer to a theory that warming occurs as a result of increased use of hydrocarbon fuels by man. See "Climate Change (Greenhouse Effect)."

Globalization: The increased mobility of goods, services, labor, technology and capital throughout the world. Although globalization is not a new development, its pace has increased with the advent of new technologies, especially in the areas of telecommunications, finance and shipping.

Green Pricing: In the case of renewable electricity, green pricing represents a market solution to the various problems associated with regulatory valuation of the non-market benefits of renewables. Green pricing programs allow electricity customers to express their willingness to pay for renewable energy development through direct payments on their monthly utility bills.

Greenhouse Gas (GHG): See "Climate Change (Greenhouse Effect)."

Grid (The): In the U.S., the networks of local electric lines that businesses and consumers depend on every day are connected with and interdependent upon a national series of major lines collectively called "the grid." The grid is divided into three major regions: the East, West and Texas regions. The regions are also known as "interconnects." In total, the grid consists of about 200,000 miles of high-voltage backbone lines and millions of miles of smaller local lines.

Gross Domestic Product (GDP): The total value of a nation's output, income and expenditures produced with a nation's physical borders.

Gross National Product (GNP): A country's total output of goods and services from all forms of economic activity measured at market prices for one calendar year. It differs from Gross Domestic Product (GDP) in that GNP includes income from investments made in foreign nations.

Group of Eight (G8): The eight major industrial countries, including the United States, Japan, Germany, France, the United Kingdom, Italy, Russia and Canada, whose leaders meet at annual economic summits to coordinate economic policies. The group was formerly known as the G7, before Russia was admitted in June 2002.

Heat Pump: A year-round heating and air-conditioning system employing a refrigeration cycle.

High-Temperature Collector: A solar thermal collector designed to operate at a temperature of 180 degrees Fahrenheit or higher.

Hot Dry Rock Geothermal Energy Technology (HDR): A technique that drills holes into the ground until rock of a suitably high temperature is reached. Pipes are then installed in a closed loop. Water is pumped down one pipe, where it is heated to extraordinarily high temperatures, and then is pumped up the other pipes as steam. The resulting steam shoots up to the surface, which drives a turbine to power an electric generating plant. As the steam cools, it returns to a liquid state which is then is pumped back into the ground. The technology was developed by the Los Alamos National labs in New Mexico.

Hydraulic Fracturing: See Facing (fraccing)." Sometimes called hydrofracture.

Hydraulic Pump: An artificial lift method used to raise oil to the surface once reservoir pressure has diminished to the point where the well no longer produces by means of natural energy. This system employs a surface pump to inject power oil into the well, which in turn drives a pump connected to a sucker-rod pump at the bottom of the well.

Hydrocarbons: Organic compounds of hydrogen and carbon. Mixtures including various hydrocarbons include crude oil, natural gas, natural gas condensate and methane.

Hydroelectric Energy: The production of electricity from kinetic energy in flowing water.

Hydroelectric Plant: An electric generating plant in which the turbine generators are driven by falling water, typically located at a dam or major waterfall.

Hydroelectric Power Generation: Electricity generated by an electric power plant whose turbines are driven by falling water. It includes electric utility and industrial generation of hydroelectricity, unless otherwise specified. Generation is reported on a net basis, i.e., on the amount of electric energy generated after deducting the energy consumed by station auxiliaries and the losses in the transformers that are considered integral parts of the station.

ICE: Intercontinental Exchange. An electronic futures and commodities exchange headquartered in Atlanta, Georgia, focused on energy markets.

IEEE: The Institute of Electrical and Electronic Engineers. The IEEE sets global technical standards and acts as an authority in technical areas including computer engineering, biomedical technology, telecommunications, electric power, aerospace and consumer electronics, among others. www.ieee.org.

Improved Oil Recovery: Any of the conventional methods of secondary recovery (in which water is injected into a reservoir in order to move remaining oil toward producing wells) or enhanced oil recovery methods that are used to optimize production from increasingly depleted reservoirs.

Independent (Oil Company): Any domestic oil company that is not one of the major international oil companies such as BP, ExxonMobil or Royal Dutch/Shell. It also refers to any U.S. oil company that is not part of the 18 to 20 largest integrated oil companies in the United States.

Independent Power Producer: A corporation, person, agency, authority or other legal entity or instrumentality that owns electric generating capacity and is a wholesale electric producer without a designated franchised service area.

Independent System Operator (ISO): One of many independent, nonprofit organizations created by many states in the U.S. during the deregulation of the electricity industry. Its function is to ensure that electric generating companies have equal access to the power grid. It may be replaced by larger Regional Transmission Organizations (RTOs), which would each cover a major area of the U.S.

Induction Log: Measures conductivity or resistivity by generating magnetic fields that in turn cause receiver coils to induce signals at low conductivities proportional to the surrounding formation. Induction logging is often combined with other measuring devices, and can safely be used in nonconductive borehole fluids that preclude the use of other logging techniques. It is utilized in uncased drilling sites.

Infrastructure: 1) The equipment that comprises a system. 2) Public-use assets such as roads, bridges, sewers and other assets necessary for public accommodation and utilities. 3) The underlying base of a system or network.

Initial Public Offering (IPO): A company's first effort to sell its stock to investors (the public). Investors in an up-trending market eagerly seek stocks offered in many IPOs because the stocks of newly public companies that seem to have great promise may appreciate very rapidly in price, reaping great profits for those who were able to get the stock at the first offering. In the United States, IPOs are regulated by the SEC (U.S. Securities Exchange Commission) and by the state-level regulatory agencies of the states in which the IPO shares are offered.

Interconnects: See "Grid (The)."

Investor-Owned Electric Utility: A class of utility that is investor-owned and organized as a tax-paying business.

ISO: See "Independent System Operator (ISO)."

ISO 9000, 9001, 9002, 9003: Standards set by the International Organization for Standardization. ISO 9000, 9001, 9002 and 9003 are the highest quality certifications awarded to organizations that meet exacting standards in their operating practices and procedures.

IT-Enabled Services (ITES): The portion of the Information Technology industry focused on providing business services, such as call centers, insurance claims processing and medical records transcription, by utilizing the power of IT, especially the Internet. Most ITES functions are considered to be back-office procedures. Also, see "Business Process Outsourcing (BPO)."

ITES: See "IT-Enabled Services (ITES)."

Jack-Up Rig: A mobile, self-elevating drilling platform that can be used in water depths of 20 to 250 feet.

Jet Fuel (Kerosene-Type): A quality kerosene product with an average gravity of 40.7 degrees API, and a 10% distillation temperature of 400 degrees Fahrenheit. A relatively low freezing-point distillate of the kerosene type, it is used primarily for commercial turbojet and turboprop aircraft engines.

Jet Fuel (Naphtha-Type): A fuel in the heavy naphtha boiling range with an average gravity of 52.8 degrees API and 20 to 90% distillation temperatures of 290 degrees to 470 degrees Fahrenheit. This type of fuel is used for turbojet and turboprop aircraft engines, primarily by the military. Excludes ram-jet and petroleum rocket fuels.

Joule: The meter-kilogram-second unit of work or energy, equal to the work done by a force of one Newton when its point of application moves through a distance of one meter in the direction of the force; equivalent to 107 ergs and one watt-second.

Just-in-Time (JIT) Delivery: Refers to a supply chain practice whereby manufacturers receive components on or just before the time that they are needed on the assembly line, rather than bearing the cost of maintaining several days' or weeks' supply in a warehouse. This adds greatly to the cost-effectiveness of a manufacturing plant and puts the burden of warehousing and timely delivery on the supplier of the components.

Kerogen: See "Oil Shale (Shale Oil)."

Kerosene: Light hydrocarbon distillates in the distillation range of 150 degrees to 280 degrees Centigrade (300 degrees to 550 degrees Fahrenheit). Includes vaporizing oil for use in reciprocating engines (primarily tractors), lamp oil, kerosene and heating oil.

Kilowatt (kW): One thousand watts.

Kilowatthour (kWh): One thousand watt-hours.

Knowledge Process Outsourcing (KPO): The use of outsourced and/or offshore workers to perform business tasks that require judgment and analysis. Examples include such professional tasks as patent research, legal research, architecture, design, engineering, market research, scientific research, accounting and tax return preparation. Also, see "Business Process Outsourcing (BPO)."

LAC: An acronym for Latin America and the Caribbean.

Landed Cost: Represents the dollar-per-barrel price of crude oil at the port of discharge. Includes charges associated with the purchase, transporting and insuring of cargo from the purchase point to the port of discharge.

Does not include charges incurred at the discharge port (e.g., import tariffs or fees, wharfage charges and demurrage).

Landman: A person who negotiates the purchase of leases, generally an agent or an employee of an oil company.

LDCs: See "Least Developed Countries (LDCs)."

Lease (Oil and Gas): The exclusive contractual rights to explore for and develop minerals on a property owned by a mineral rights owner.

Least Developed Countries (LDCs): Nations determined by the U.N. Economic and Social Council to be the poorest and weakest members of the international community. There are currently 50 LDCs, of which 34 are in Africa, 15 are in Asia Pacific and the remaining one (Haiti) is in Latin America. The top 10 on the LDC list, in descending order from top to 10th, are Afghanistan, Angola, Bangladesh, Benin, Bhutan, Burkina Faso, Burundi, Cambodia, Cape Verde and the Central African Republic. Sixteen of the LDCs are also Landlocked Least Developed Countries (LLDCs) which present them with additional difficulties often due to the high cost of transporting trade goods. Eleven of the LDCs are Small Island Developing States (SIDS), which are often at risk of extreme weather phenomenon (hurricanes, typhoons, Tsunami); have fragile ecosystems; are often dependent on foreign energy sources; can have high disease rates for HIV/AIDS and malaria; and can have poor market access and trade terms.

Levelized Cost: The present value of the total cost of building and operating a generating plant over its economic life, converted to equal annual payments. Costs are levelized in real dollars (i.e., adjusted to remove the impact of inflation).

Lifting Costs: Expenses related to lifting oil from a producing reservoir in a well up to the surface.

Lignite: The lowest rank of coal. Lignite is a young coal that is brownish-black in color and has high moisture content, sometimes as high as 45%, and a high ash content. It tends to disintegrate when exposed to the weather. The heat content of lignite is usually less than 5700 Kcal/kg.

Liquefied Natural Gas (LNG): Natural gas that is liquefied by reducing its temperature to -260 degrees Fahrenheit at atmospheric pressure. The volume of the LNG is 1/600 that of the gas in its vapor state. LNG requires special processing and transportation. First, the natural gas must be chilled in order for it to change into a liquid state. Next, the LNG is put on specially designed ships where extensive insulation and refrigeration maintain the cold temperature. Finally, it is offloaded at special receiving facilities where it is converted, via regasification, into a state suitable for distribution via pipelines.

Liquefied Petroleum Gases (LPG): See "Liquefied Refinery Gases (LRG)."

Liquefied Refinery Gases (LRG): Liquefied petroleum fractionated from refinery or still gases. Through compression and/or refrigeration, they are retained in the liquid state. The reported categories are ethane/ethylene, propane/propylene, normal butane/butylene and isobutene. Excludes still gas used for chemical or rubber manufacture, which is reported as petrochemical feedstock, as well as liquefied petroleum gases intended for blending into gasoline, which are reported as gasoline blending components.

Liquid Collector: A medium-temperature solar thermal collector, employed predominantly in water heating, which uses pumped liquid as the heat-transfer medium.

LNG: See "Liquefied Natural Gas (LNG)."

Load (Electric): The amount of electric power delivered or required at any specific point or points on a system. The requirement originates at the energy-consuming equipment of the consumers.

Log (Petroleum): A record of the activities related to the drilling and completion of oil and gas wells.

Logging (Wireline): The lowering of a sensing device into the borehole on the end of an electric cable, which then logs information about the borehole.

LOHAS: Lifestyles of Health and Sustainability. A marketing term that refers to consumers who choose to purchase and/or live with items that are natural, organic, less polluting, etc. Such consumers may also prefer products powered by alternative energy, such as hybrid cars.

Low-Temperature Collectors: Metallic or nonmetallic solar thermal collectors that generally operate at temperatures below 110 degrees Fahrenheit and use pumped liquid or air as the heat-transfer medium. They usually contain no glazing and no insulation, and they are often made of plastic or rubber, although some are made of metal.

Lubricants (Greases): Mixtures of lubricating oils that contain substances that reduce their ability to flow.

Lubricants (Lubricating Oils): Substances used to reduce friction between bearing surfaces. Petroleum lubricants may be produced either from distillates or residues. Other substances may be added to impart or improve certain required properties. Lubricants include all grades of lubricating oils from spindle oil to cylinder oil and those used in greases.

M3 (Measurement): Cubic meters.

Major Oil Company: Traditionally refers to the large integrated international companies such as British Petroleum (BP), ExxonMobil, Chevron and ConocoPhillips.

Marginal Cost: The change in cost associated with a unit change in quantity supplied or produced.

Marketing: Includes all planning and management activities and expenses associated with the promotion of a product or service. Marketing can encompass advertising, customer surveys, public relations and many other disciplines. Marketing is distinct from selling, which is the process of sell-through to the end user.

Mbbl: One thousand barrels.

Mcf: One thousand cubic feet.

Mcfe: One thousand cubic feet of natural gas equivalent, using the ratio of six Mcf of natural gas to one Bbl of crude oil, condensate and natural gas liquids.

Medium-Temperature Collectors: Solar thermal collectors designed to operate in the temperature range of 140 degrees to 180 degrees Fahrenheit, but that can also operate at a temperature as low as 110 degrees Fahrenheit. The collector typically consists of a metal frame, metal absorption panels with integral flow channels (attached tubing for liquid collectors or integral ducting for air collectors) and glazing and insulation on the sides and back.

Megawatt (MW): One million watts.

Megawatthour (MWh): One million watt-hours.

Metallurgical Coke: A strong, hard coke produced mainly for use in the iron and steel industry, where it serves as a chemical agent and source of energy. It is used mainly in blast furnaces to absorb the oxygen contained in iron oxides and provide energy for smelting. A portion of its potential energy is captured in the gases generated in the smelting process, then recycled in the form of blast furnace gas to provide additional energy inside or outside the smelting process. Metallurgical coke is also used to some extent as a domestic fuel and as raw material for the manufacture of gas.

Methane: A colorless, odorless, flammable hydrocarbon gas (CH_4); the major component of natural gas. It is also an important source of hydrogen in various industrial processes. Also, see "Coalbed Methane (CBN)."

Methanol: A light, volatile alcohol (CH_3OH) eligible for motor gasoline blending. It is also used as a feedstock for synthetic textiles, plastics, paints, adhesives, foam, medicines and more.

Microbial Enhanced Oil Recovery (MEOR): An oil field recovery technology that creates microbes that biologically generate CO_2 and chemicals with cleaning agents that help flush oil out of rock.

Microturbine: A small, scaled-down turbine engine that may be fueled by natural gas, methane or other types of gas.

Mineral Interests: The rights of ownership to gas, oil or other minerals as they naturally occur at or below a tract of land. Also known as "mineral rights."

Mineral Rights: See "Mineral Interests."

Mmbtu: One million British thermal units.

Mmcf: One million cubic feet.

Mmcfe: One million cubic feet of natural gas equivalent.

MOX Fuel (Mixed Oxide Fuel): A method of reprocessing spent nuclear material. Surplus plutonium is mixed with uranium to fabricate MOX fuel for use in a commercial nuclear power plant. Traditionally, fuel for commercial nuclear power plants is made of low-enriched uranium. MOX fuel contains 5 percent plutonium. European countries such as the United Kingdom, Germany, Belgium and France have been fabricating MOX fuel for many years. Commercial MOX-fueled light water reactors are used in France, the United Kingdom, Germany, Switzerland, and Belgium. In the U.S., MOX fuel was fabricated and used in several commercial reactors in the 1970's as part of a development program.

Mud (Drilling Mud): A mixture of one or two liquid phases (water, oil and related emulsions) with clay that circulates during drilling in order to cool and lubricate the bit, remove material from the borehole and bring traces of fluids to the surface. The characteristic qualities of the drilling mud can be engineered to provide specific indicators to surface workers.

NAFTA: See "North American Free Trade Agreement (NAFTA)."

Nanotechnology: The science of designing, building or utilizing unique structures that are smaller than 100 nanometers (a nanometer is one billionth of a meter). This involves microscopic structures that are no larger than the width of some cell membranes.

Natural Gas: A mixture of hydrocarbon compounds, primarily methane and small quantities of various nonhydrocarbons, existing in a gaseous phase or in solution with crude oil in natural underground reservoirs at reservoir conditions.

Natural Gas Field Facility: A field facility designed to process natural gas produced from more than one lease for the purpose of recovering condensate from a stream of natural gas. Some field facilities are designed to recover propane, normal butane, pentanes plus, etc., and to control the quality of natural gas to be marketed.

Natural Gas Liquids: Those hydrocarbons in natural gas that are separated from the gas as liquids through the process of absorption, condensation or other methods in gas processing or cycling plants. Generally such liquids consist of propane and heavier hydrocarbons and are commonly referred to as lease condensate, natural gasoline and liquefied petroleum gases. Natural gas liquids include natural gas plant liquids (primarily ethane, propane, butane and isobutane) and lease condensate (primarily pentanes produced from natural gas at lease separators and field facilities). See "Condensate (Lease)."

Net Generation: Gross generation minus plant use from all electric utility-owned plants. The energy required for pumping at a pumped-storage plant is regarded as plant use and must be deducted from the gross generation.

Net Summer Capability: The steady hourly output that generating equipment is expected to supply to system load exclusive of auxiliary power, as demonstrated by tests at the time of summer peak demand.

Non-Regulated Business: See "Regulated Business (Utility Companies)."

Nonutility Power Producer: A corporation, person, agency, authority or other legal entity or instrumentality that owns electric generating capacity and is not an electric utility.

North American Free Trade Agreement (NAFTA): A trade agreement signed in December 1992 by U.S. President George H. W. Bush, Canadian Prime Minister Brian Mulroney and Mexican President Carlos Salinas de Gortari. The agreement eliminates tariffs on most goods originating in and traveling between the three member countries. It was approved by the legislatures of the three countries and had entered into force by January 1994. When it was created, NAFTA formed one of the largest free-trade areas of its kind in the world.

Nuclear Electric Power Generation: Electricity generated by nuclear reactors of various types, such as heavy water, light water and boiling water. Generation is reported on a net basis and excludes energy that is used by the electric power plant for its own operating purposes and not for commercial use.

Nuclear Fuel: Fissionable materials that have been enriched to such a composition that, when placed in a nuclear reactor, they will support a self-sustaining fission chain reaction, producing heat in a controlled manner for process use.

Nuclear Fusion: An atomic energy-releasing process in which light weight atomic nuclei, which might be hydrogen or deuterium, combine to form heavier nuclei, such as helium. The result is the release of a tremendous amount of energy in the form of heat. As of 2007, nuclear fusion had yet to be made practical as a commercial energy source, but several well-funded efforts are attempting to do so.

Nuclear Power Plant: A facility in which heat produced in a reactor by the fission of nuclear fuel is used to drive a steam turbine.

Nuclear Reactor: An apparatus in which the nuclear fission chain can be initiated, maintained and controlled so that energy is released at a specific rate.

NYMEX: New York Mercantile Exchange, Inc. (NYMEX Exchange). The company is a major provider of financial services to the energy and metals industries including the trading of energy futures and options contracts. It is owned by the CME Group.

Octane Rating: A number used to indicate motor gasoline's antiknock performance in motor vehicle engines. The two recognized laboratory engine test methods for determining the antiknock rating, or octane rating, of gasoline are the research method and the motor method. To provide a single number as guidance to the customer, the antiknock index (R + M)/2, which is the average of the research and motor octane numbers, was developed.

OECD: See "Organisation for Economic Co-operation and Development (OECD)."

Offshoring: The rapidly growing tendency among U.S., Japanese and Western European firms to send knowledge-based and manufacturing work overseas. The intent is to take advantage of lower wages and operating costs in such nations as China, India, Hungary and Russia. The choice of a nation for offshore work may be influenced by such factors as language and education of the local workforce, transportation systems or natural resources. For example, China and India are graduating high numbers of skilled engineers and scientists from their universities. Also, some nations are noted for large numbers of workers skilled in the English language, such as the Philippines and India. Also see "Captive Offshoring" and "Outsourcing."

Ohm: The unit of measurement of electrical resistance; the resistance of a circuit in which a potential difference of one volt produces a current of one ampere.

Oil Shale (Shale Oil): Sedimentary rock that contains kerogen, a solid, waxy mixture of hydrocarbon compounds. Heating the rock to very high temperatures will convert the kerogen to a vapor, which can then be condensed to form a slow flowing heavy oil that can later be refined or used for commercial purposes. The United States contains vast amounts of oil shale deposits, but so far it has been considered not economically feasible to produce from them on a large scale.

Onshoring: The opposite of "offshoring." Providing or maintaining manufacturing or services within or nearby a company's domestic location. Sometimes referred to as reshoring.

OPEC: Organization of Petroleum Exporting Countries. Current members are Algeria, Indonesia, Iran, Iraq, Kuwait, Libya, Nigeria, Qatar, Saudi Arabia, United Arab Emirates and Venezuela. (Ecuador withdrew from OPEC on December 31, 1992, and Gabon withdrew on December 31, 1994.)

Operation and Maintenance (O&M) Cost: Expenses associated with operating a facility (e.g., supervising and engineering expenses) and maintaining it, including labor, materials and other direct and indirect expenses incurred for preserving the operating efficiency or physical condition of utility plants that are used for power production, transmission and distribution of energy.

Organisation for Economic Co-operation and Development (OECD): A group of more than 30 nations that are strongly committed to the market economy and democracy. Some of the OECD members include Japan, the U.S., Spain, Germany, Australia, Korea, the U.K., Canada and Mexico. Although not members, Estonia, Israel and Russia are invited to member talks; and Brazil, China, India, Indonesia and South Africa have enhanced engagement policies with the OECD. The Organisation provides statistics, as well as social and economic data; and researches social changes, including patterns in evolving fiscal policy, agriculture, technology, trade, the environment and other areas. It publishes over 250 titles annually; publishes a corporate magazine, the OECD Observer; has radio and TV studios; and has centers in Tokyo, Washington, D.C., Berlin and Mexico City that distributed the Organisation's work and organizes events.

Outsourcing: The hiring of an outside company to perform a task otherwise performed internally by the company, generally with the goal of lowering costs and/or streamlining work flow. Outsourcing contracts are generally several years in length. Companies that hire outsourced services providers often prefer to focus on their core strengths while sending more routine tasks outside for others to perform. Typical outsourced services include the running of human resources departments, telephone call centers and computer departments. When outsourcing is performed overseas, it may be referred to as offshoring. Also see "Offshoring."

Ozone: A molecule made up of three atoms of oxygen. It occurs naturally in the stratosphere and provides a protective layer shielding the Earth from harmful ultraviolet radiation. In the troposphere, it is a chemical oxidant, a greenhouse gas and a major component of photochemical smog.

Ozone-Depleting Substances: Gases containing chlorine that are being controlled because they deplete ozone. They are thought to have some indeterminate impact on greenhouse gases.

Packer: A rubber-like cylinder that is used to seal a well at a given level. A packer is often equipped with a flowmeter, forcing the flow of fluid through a monitoring device providing data to the surface.

Paraffin (Oil): A light-colored, wax-free oil obtained by pressing paraffin distillate.

Paraffin-Base Crude Oil: Crude oil containing little or no asphalt, yielding at the refinery a high percentage of paraffin, lubricating oil and kerosene.

Passive Solar: A system in which solar energy (heat from sunlight) alone is used for the transfer of thermal energy. Heat transfer devices that depend on energy other than solar are not used. A good example is a passive solar water heater on the roof of a building.

Pay: The part of a formation producing or capable of producing oil, gas or another viable product. See "Pay Zone."

Pay Sand: A sandstone formation that produces gas or oil.

Pay Zone: A vertical measure denoting the portion of a well producing gas or oil.

Peak Watt: A manufacturer's unit indicating the amount of power a photovoltaic cell or module will produce at standard test conditions (normally 1,000 watts per square meter and 25 degrees Celsius).

Pebble-Bed Modular Reactor (PBMR): A nuclear reactor technology that utilizes tiny silicon carbide-coated uranium oxide granules sealed in "pebbles" about the size of oranges, made of graphite. Helium is used as the coolant and energy transfer medium. This containment of the radioactive material in small quantities has the potential to achieve an unprecedented level of safety. This technology may become popular in the development of new nuclear power plants.

Persian Gulf: The countries that comprise the Persian Gulf region are: Bahrain, Iran, Iraq, Kuwait, Qatar, Saudi Arabia and the United Arab Emirates.

Petrochemical Feedstocks: Products from petroleum refineries and natural gas liquids processing plants to be processed further at a petrochemical plant. Includes products primarily in the naphtha range, still gas (refinery gas) and liquefied gases for petrochemical use.

Petroleum: A generic term applied to oil and oil products in all forms, such as crude oil, lease condensate, unfinished oils, refined petroleum products, natural gas plants and liquids, and nonhydrocarbon compounds blended into finished petroleum products.

Petroleum Geologist: A geologist specializing in research and analysis that supports the exploration and production of petroleum resources.

Petroleum Products: Products obtained from the processing of crude oil, unfinished oils, natural gas liquids and other miscellaneous hydrocarbon compounds. Includes aviation gasoline, motor gasoline, naphtha-type jet fuel, kerosene-type jet fuel, kerosene, distillate fuel oil, residual fuel oil, ethane, liquefied petroleum gases, petrochemical feedstocks, special naphthas, lubricants, paraffin wax, petroleum coke, asphalt and road oil, still gas and other products.

Petroleum Stocks: Primary stocks of crude oil and petroleum products held in storage at (or in) leases, refineries, natural gas processing plants, pipelines, tankfarms and bulk terminals that can store at least 50,000 barrels of petroleum products or that can receive petroleum products by tanker, barge or pipeline.

Photovoltaic (PV) Cell: An electronic device consisting of layers of semiconductor materials fabricated to form a junction (adjacent layers of materials with different electronic characteristics) and electrical contacts, capable of converting incident light directly into electricity (direct current). Photovoltaic technology works by harnessing the movement of electrons between the layers of a solar cell when the sun strikes the material.

Photovoltaic (PV) Module: An integrated assembly of interconnected photovoltaic cells designed to deliver a selected level of working voltage and current at its output terminals, packaged for protection against environment degradation and suited for incorporation in photovoltaic power systems.

Pipeline (Natural Gas): A continuous pipe conduit, complete with such equipment as valves, compressor stations, communications systems and meters, for transporting natural gas and/or supplemental gaseous fuels from one point to another, usually from a point in or beyond the producing field or processing plant to another pipeline or to points of utilization. Also refers to a company operating such facilities.

Pipeline (Petroleum): Crude oil and product pipelines (including interstate, intrastate and intracompany pipelines) used to transport crude oil and petroleum products, respectively, within the 50 states and the District of Columbia.

Plugged and Abandoned (P&A): A term describing a dry hole or depleted site that has been fitted with a cement plug to close the well.

Porosimeter: A device used to measure porosity.

Porosity: Percentage of rock or soil that is void of solid material.

Power (Electrical): The rate at which energy is transferred. A volt ampere, an electric measurement unit of power, is equal to the product of one volt and one ampere. This is equivalent to one watt for a direct current system. A unit of apparent power is separated into real and reactive power. Real power is the work-producing part of apparent power that measures the rate of supply of energy and is denoted in kilowatts.

PPP: See "Purchasing Power Parity (PPP) or Point-to-Point Protocol (PPP)."

Primary Recovery: The production of oil from a reservoir into the well under natural occurrences. Oil flows from a reservoir into the well under natural conditions (the first phase in oil production).

Prime Mover: The motive force that drives an electric generator.

Producing Gas-Oil Ratio: A ratio derived from the cubic foot measure of natural gas produced by a well relative to each barrel of oil produced.

Production Casing: The last section of casing to be set in a well, the production casing is the smallest diameter and longest string of tubulars to be installed.

Propane: A normally gaseous straight-chain hydrocarbon (C3H8). Propane is a colorless paraffinic gas that boils at a temperature of –43.67 degrees Fahrenheit. It is extracted from natural gas or refinery gas streams.

Proppant: Sand or other materials used during fracing to help stabilize a pay zone. See "Fracing (fraccing)."

Prospect: The hypothetical location of naturally occurring, commercially exploitable oil and gas at a clearly defined underground location.

Proved Reserves (Crude Oil, Natural Gas or Coal): The estimated quantities of all crude oil, natural gas or coal which geological and engineering data demonstrate with reasonable certainty to be recoverable in future years from known reservoirs or seams under existing economic and operating conditions.

Public Utility: An enterprise providing essential public services, such as electric, gas, telephone, water and sewer services, under legally established monopoly conditions.

Public Utility District (PUD): A municipal corporation organized to provide electric service to both incorporated cities and towns and unincorporated rural areas. Public utility districts operate in six states.

Public Utility Regulatory Policies Act of 1978 (PURPA): A part of the National Energy Act. PURPA contains measures designed to encourage the conservation of energy, more efficient use of resources and equitable rates. Principal among these were suggested retail rate reforms and new incentives for production of electricity by cogenerators and users of renewable resources.

Publicly Owned Electric Utility: A class of ownership found in the electric power industry. This group includes those utilities operated by municipalities and state and federal power agencies.

Pumped-Storage Hydroelectric Plant: A plant that usually generates electric energy during peak load periods by using water previously pumped into an elevated storage reservoir during off-peak periods, when excess generating capacity is available to do so. When additional generating capacity is needed, the water can be released from the reservoir through a conduit to turbine generators located in a power plant at a lower level.

Purchasing Power Parity (PPP): Currency conversion rates that attempt to reflect the actual purchasing power of a currency in its home market, as opposed to examining price levels and comparing an exchange rate. PPPs are always given in the national currency units per U.S. dollar.

PV: See "Photovoltaic (PV) Cell."

Qualifying Facility (QF): A cogeneration or small power production facility that meets certain ownership, operating and efficiency criteria established by the Federal Energy Regulatory Commission (FERC) pursuant to the Public Utility Regulatory Policies Act of 1978 (PURPA).

R&D: Research and development. Also see "Applied Research" and "Basic Research."

Rate Base: The value of property upon which a utility is permitted to earn a specified rate of return as established by a regulatory authority. The rate base generally represents the value of property used by the utility in providing service.

Ratemaking Authority: A utility commission's legal authority to fix, modify, approve or disapprove rates, as determined by the powers given to the commission by a state or federal legislature.

Refiner: A firm or the part of a firm that refines products or blends and substantially changes products; refines liquid hydrocarbons from oil and gas field gases; or recovers liquefied petroleum gases incident to petroleum refining and sells those products to resellers, retailers or ultimate consumers. Includes gas plant operators.

Refinery: An installation that manufactures finished petroleum products from crude oil, unfinished oils, natural gas liquids, other hydrocarbons and alcohol.

Refuse-Derived Fuel (RDF): Fuel processed from municipal solid waste that can be in shredded, fluff or dense pellet forms.

Regional Transmission Organization (RTO): See "Independent System Operator (ISO)."

Regulated Business (Utility Companies): The business of providing natural gas or electric service to customers under regulations and at prices set by government regulatory agencies. Generally, utilities have been required to operate at set prices and profit ratios because they have been granted monopoly or near-monopoly status to serve a given geographic market. Under deregulation, utility companies are being granted greater flexibility to set prices and to enter new geographic markets. At the same time, consumers gain the right to choose among several different utilities providers.

Renewable Energy Resources: Energy resources that are naturally replenishing but flow-limited. They are virtually inexhaustible in duration but limited in the amount of energy that is available per unit of time. Renewable energy resources include biomass, hydro, geothermal, solar, wind, ocean thermal, wave action and tidal action.

Reseller: A firm (other than a refiner) that carries on the trade or business of purchasing refined petroleum products and reselling them to purchasers other than ultimate consumers.

Reserves (Oil, Gas or Coal): Recoverable, unproduced resources contained in a given formation. Reserves are categorized as developed or undeveloped, and as proved, unproved, probable or possible. Also see "Proved Reserves (Crude Oil, Natural Gas or Coal)."

Reservoir: A subsurface deposit of gas, oil or condensate, typically contained in a porous rock formation of limestone, dolomite or sandstone.

Resistivity (R): Measures a material's characteristic resistance to the flow of electrical current. Resistivity is the reciprocal of conductivity. It is denoted by the symbol R.

Return on Investment (ROI): A measure of a company's profitability, expressed in percentage as net profit (after taxes) divided by total dollar investment.

Royalty and Royalty Interest (Oil and Gas): A specified percentage of the oil and gas produced at a property to which the royalty owner is entitled without bearing an investment in exploration or the costs of such production. The ownership of a "royalty interest" entitles the owner to receive royalty payments.

RTO: See "Regional Transmission Organization (RTO)."

Rural Electrification Administration (REA): A lending agency of the U.S. Department of Agriculture. It makes self-liquidation loans to qualified borrowers to finance electric and telephone service to rural areas. The REA also finances the construction and operation of generating plants, electric transmission and distribution lines, or systems for the furnishing of initial and continued adequate electric services to persons in rural areas not receiving central station service.

Saas: See "Software as a Service (Saas)."

Salt Dome: A common type of rock formation, in which a dome is formed by the intrusion of salt into overlying sediments.

SeaBed Logging (SBL): Controlled source electromagnetic sounding that can improve the accuracy in detecting and characterizing hydrocarbon reservoirs in deepwater areas.

Secondary Recovery: The second phase of oil production. Involves activities to waterflood or re-pressurize the reservoir to recover more of the remaining oil. (Additional phases include primary recovery and tertiary recovery. See "Tertiary Recovery.")

Seismic: Petroleum exploration methodologies that use seismic surveying and related analysis to identify petroleum traps in sub-surface formations.

Seismic Surveying: The recording of echoes reflected to the surface from pulses of sound sent down into the earth. Used to determine underground geological structures.

Semi-Submersible Rig: An offshore drilling rig that floats with its lower hull between 55 and 90 feet below the surface. It is held in position by anchors or by a computer-controlled thruster system.

Shot Hole: Drilling through surface sediments to form a shallow hole in hard sedimentary rocks creates a shot hole, in which explosives can be detonated as part of a related seismic survey.

Silicon: A semiconductor material made from silica, purified for photovoltaic applications.

Single-Crystal Silicon (Czochralski): An extremely pure form of crystalline silicon produced by the Czochralski method of dipping a single crystal seed into a pool of molten silicon under high-vacuum conditions and slowly withdrawing a solidifying single-crystal boule rod of silicon. The boule is sawed into thin wafers and fabricated into single-crystal photovoltaic cells.

Small Power Producer: A producer that generates electricity by using renewable energy (wood, waste, conventional hydroelectric, wind, solar or geothermal) as a primary energy source. Fossil fuels can be used, but renewable resources must provide at least 75% of the total energy input. It is part of the Public Utility Regulatory Policies Act, a small power producer. See "Nonutility Power Producer."

Smart Buildings: Buildings or homes that have been designed with interconnected electronic and electrical systems which can be controlled by computers. Advantages include the ability to turn appliances and systems on or off remotely or on a set schedule, leading to greatly enhanced energy efficiency.

Software as a Service (SaaS): Refers to the practice of providing users with software applications that are hosted on remote servers and accessed via the Internet. Excellent examples include the CRM (Customer Relationship Management) software provided in SaaS format by Salesforce. An earlier technology that operated in a similar, but less sophisticated, manner was called ASP or Application Service Provider.

Solar Energy: Energy produced from the sun's radiation for the purposes of heating or electric generation. Also, see "Photovoltaic (PV) Cell," "Concentrated Solar Power (CSP)" and "Passive Solar."

Solar Thermal Collector: A device designed to receive solar radiation and convert it into thermal energy. Normally, a solar thermal collector includes a frame, glazing and an absorber, together with the appropriate insulation. The heat collected by the solar thermal collector may be used immediately or stored for later use. Typical use is in solar hot water heating systems. Also, see "Passive Solar" and "Concentrated Solar Power (CSP)."

Solar Tower: See "Concentrated Solar Power (CSP)."

Sonic Amplitude Log: A well log that uses sound attenuation to detect fractures in a formation.

Sonic Log: A sonic, or acoustic, log records the travel time of a compression wave through a well and surrounding formation, providing data useful in calculating porosity and aiding lithology-related analysis.

Spot Price: The price for a one-time market transaction for immediate delivery to the specific location where the commodity is purchased "on the spot," at current market rates.

Standard Cubic Foot (SCF): A regulated measure of natural gas volumes, based on a standardized surface temperature of 60 degrees Fahrenheit and surface pressure of 14.65 psi.

Steam-Electric Plant (Conventional): A plant in which the prime mover is a steam turbine. The steam used to drive the turbine is produced in a boiler where fossil fuels are burned.

Stratigraphic Column: Shows the vertical composition of successive strata, or rock layers, in a given formation.

Stripper Oil Well: A well that produces no more than 10 barrels of oil per day, making it barely profitable.

Structural Map: A contour map detailing elevations of sub-surface rock layers, calibrated either in linear measure of feet or meters, or in time measure based on seismic surveys.

Subsea Completion: A finished well, including casing and wellhead components, in which the wellhead equipment is installed on the bottom of the ocean.

Subsidiary, Wholly-Owned: A company that is wholly controlled by another company through stock ownership.

Substation: Facility equipment that switches, changes or regulates electric voltage.

Sucker-Rod Pumping System: An artificial lift method in which a surface pump drives a sucker-rod pump at the bottom of the well in order to recover additional oil. See "Hydraulic Pump."

Superconductivity: The ability of a material to act as a conductor for electricity without the gradual loss of electricity over distance (due to resistance) that is normally associated with electric transmission. There are two types of superconductivity. "Low-temperature" superconductivity (LTS) requires that transmission cable be cooled to -418 degrees Fahrenheit. Even newer technologies are creating a so-called "high-temperature" superconductivity (HTS) that requires cooling to a much warmer -351 degrees Fahrenheit.

Supply Chain: The complete set of suppliers of goods and services required for a company to operate its business. For example, a manufacturer's supply chain may include providers of raw materials, components, custom-made parts and packaging materials.

Switching Station: Facility equipment used to tie together two or more electric circuits through switches. The switches are selectively arranged to permit a circuit to be disconnected, or to change the electric connection between the circuits.

Syngas: The synthetic creation of gas to be used as a fuel, typically from coal. See "Gasification."

System (Electric): See "Transmission System (Electric)."

Take-or-Pay Contract: An agreement, generally long-term, whereby a gas purchaser (such as a pipeline transmission company) agrees to purchase a minimum annual amount of gas from the producer or pays the producer for the minimum amount, even if no gas is physically transferred.

Tank Farm: An installation used by gathering and trunk pipeline companies, crude oil producers and terminal operators to store crude oil.

Tar Sands (Oil Sands): Sands that contain bitumen, which is a tar-like crude oil substance that can be processed and refined into a synthetic light crude oil. Typically, tar sands are mined from vast open pits where deposits are softened with blasts of steam. The Athabasca sands in Alberta, Canada and the Orinoco sands in Venezuela contain vast amounts of tar sands. The Athabasca sands are now producing commercially in high volume.

Tax Royalty Participation Contract: See "Concession Agreement."

Tertiary Recovery: Methods used to increase production from oil fields. Tertiary methods may include the injection of CO_2, steam injection, or the use of special chemicals. Often, such methods are used in existing fields where production has started to decline under normal production. Other recovery stages are defined as "primary" which is a field that flows normally with little additional effort, and "secondary" which often involves waterflooding.

Time Slice: A flat section generated from a 3-D seismic survey, establishing the relative position of various seismic reflectors at a specific time.

Time to Depth Conversion: A translation process to recalibrate seismic records from time measures in millisecond units to linear measures of depth in feet or meters.

Tokamak: A reactor used in nuclear fusion in which a spiral magnetic field inside doughnut-shaped tube is used to confine high temperature plasma produced during fusion. See "Nuclear Fusion."

Toluene: A basic aromatic compound derived from petroleum. It is the most common hydrocarbon purchased for use in increasing octane. Toluene is also used to produce phenol and TNT.

Transformer: An electrical device for changing the voltage of an alternating current.

Transmission (Electricity): The movement or transfer of electric energy over an interconnected group of lines and associated equipment between points of supply and points at which it is transformed for delivery to consumers or delivered to other electric systems. Transmission is considered to end when the energy is transformed for distribution to the consumer.

Transmission System (Electric): An interconnected group of electric transmission lines and associated equipment for moving or transferring electric energy in bulk between points of supply and points at which it is transformed for delivery to consumers or delivered to other electric systems.

True Vertical Depth (TVD): The depth of a given point in a well when measured straight down from horizontal, disregarding inclination of the borehole.

Tubing Head: A flanged fitting made of forged or cast steel set at the top of the wellhead to support the tubing string in the well and to seal off pressure between the exterior casing and the interior tubing.

Tubing Packer: A piece of equipment that temporarily seals off the space between the casing and tubing inside an oil or gas well.

Turbine: A machine for generating rotary mechanical power from the energy of a stream of fluid (such as water, steam or hot gas). Turbines convert the kinetic energy of fluids to mechanical energy through the principles of impulse and reaction or a mixture of the two.

Ultimate Oil Recovery: The total amount of oil that can be recovered from a reservoir using primary, secondary (including waterflood) and tertiary enhanced recovery techniques.

Ultradeepwater Well: An offshore well drilled in more than 5,000 feet of water depth.

Unfinished Oils: All oils that require further processing, except those requiring only mechanical blending.

Upstream: The segment of the oil and gas exploration and production business involved in the initial phases of production (i.e., finding a prospect, drilling, producing and maintaining the well). Upstream is the opposite of downstream. See "Downstream."

Uranium: A heavy, naturally radioactive, metallic element (atomic number 92). Its two principally occurring isotopes are uranium-235 and uranium-238. Uranium-235 is indispensable to the nuclear industry, because it is the only isotope existing in nature to any appreciable extent that is fissionable by thermal neutrons. Uranium-238 is also important, because it absorbs neutrons to produce a radioactive isotope that subsequently decays to plutonium-239, another isotope that is fissionable by thermal neutrons.

Value Added Tax (VAT): A tax that imposes a levy on businesses at every stage of manufacturing based on the value it adds to a product. Each business in the supply chain pays its own VAT and is subsequently repaid by the next link down the chain; hence, a VAT is ultimately paid by the consumer, being the last link in the supply chain, making it comparable to a sales tax. Generally, VAT only applies to goods bought for consumption within a given country; export goods are exempt from VAT, and purchasers from other countries taking goods back home may apply for a VAT refund.

Velocity Analysis: The coordinated measurement of seismic data from one source with multiple receivers at varied distances in order to compute seismic velocity through different portions of a formation.

Vertical Integration: A business model in which one company owns many (or all) of the means of production of the many goods that comprise its product line. For example, founder Henry Ford designed Ford Motor Company's early River Rogue plant so that coal, iron ore and other needed raw materials arrived at one end of the plant and were processed into steel, which was then converted on-site into finished components. At the final stage of the plant, completed automobiles were assembled.

Vertical Seismic Profiling (VSP): A method used to measure seismic velocities of various strata in a well. It utilizes a seismic source positioned at the surface and a borehole instrument that records measurements at specific depths.

Waste Energy (Waste-to-Energy): The use of garbage, biogases, industrial steam, sewerage gas or industrial, agricultural and urban refuse ("biomass") as a fuel or power source used in turning turbines to generate electricity or as a method of providing heat.

Waterflood: Techniques that involve the injection of water into an underproducing or depleted reservoir in order to move oil toward producing wells.

Watt (Electric): The electrical unit of power equal to the power dissipated by a current of one ampere flowing across a resistance of one ohm.

Watt (Thermal): A unit of power in the metric system, expressed in terms of energy per second, equal to the work done at a rate of one joule per second.

Watthour (Wh): An electrical energy unit equal to one watt of power supplied to, or taken from, an electric circuit steadily for one hour.

Well: A hole drilled in the Earth for the purpose of finding or producing crude oil or natural gas or for providing services related to the production of crude oil or natural gas. Wells are classified as oil wells, gas wells, dry holes, stratigraphic test wells or service wells. The latter two types of wells are counted for Federal Reporting System data reporting. Oil wells, gas wells and dry holes are classified as exploratory wells or development wells. Exploratory wells are subclassified as new-pool wildcats, deeper-pool tests, shallow-pool tests and outpost (extersion) tests. Well classifications reflect the status of wells after drilling has been completed.

Well Log: An individual or composite record of survey activity relating to a given well. See "Logging (Wireline)."

Well Servicing Unit: Truck-mounted equipment generally used for downhole services after a well is drilled. Services include well completions and recompletions, maintenance, repairs, workovers and well plugging and abandonments. Jobs range from minor operations, such as pulling the rods and rod pumps out of an oil well, to major workovers, such as milling out and repairing collapsed casing. Well depth and characteristics determine the type of equipment used.

Well Shooting: A method of depth measurement in which a sensor is propelled down a well to transmit seismic waves back to the surface.

Well Stimulation: Methods, such as hydraulic fracturing, which increase permeability of a reservoir and increase flow to producing wells.

Wellhead: The point at which the crude oil (and/or natural gas) exits the ground. Following historical precedent, the volume and price for crude oil production are labeled as wellhead, even though the cost and volume are now generally measured at the lease boundary. In the context of domestic crude price data, the term wellhead is the generic term used to reference the production site or lease property.

Wheeling Service: The movement of electricity from one system to another over transmission facilities of intervening systems. Wheeling service contracts can be established between two or more systems.

Wildcat: An exploration well, usually drilled to a reservoir from which no oil or gas has been produced previously.

Wind Energy: Energy present in wind motion that can be converted to mechanical energy for driving pumps, mills and electric power generators. Wind pushes against sails, vanes or blades radiating from a central rotating shaft.

Wind Power Plant: A group of wind turbines interconnected to a common utility system through a system of transformers, distribution lines and (usually) one substation. Operation, control and maintenance functions are often centralized through a network of computerized monitoring systems, supplemented by visual inspection. This is a term commonly used in the United States. In Europe, it is called a generating station.

Wind Turbine: A system in which blades (windmills) collect wind power to propel a turbine that generates electricity.

Wireless Sensor Network (WSN): Consists of a grouping of remote sensors that transmit data wirelessly to a receiver that is collecting data into a database. Special controls may alert the network's manager to changes in the environment, traffic or hazardous conditions. Long-term collection of data from remote sensors can be used to establish patterns and make predictions. The use of WSNs is growing rapidly, in such applications as environmental monitoring, agriculture, military intelligence, surveillance, factory automation, home automation and traffic control.

Wireline (in oil field services): See "Logging (Wireline)."

Working Interest (WI): An interest resulting from an oil and gas lease, by which the working-interest owner is entitled to a certain percentage of revenues from production. For example, a 100% working interest entitles the working-interest owner to exclusively explore for oil and gas in a tract of land, while also paying 100% of the cost of oil or gas production.

World Trade Organization (WTO): One of the only globally active international organizations dealing with the trade rules between nations. Its goal is to assist the free flow of trade goods, ensuring a smooth, predictable supply of goods to help raise the quality of life of member citizens. Members form consensus decisions that are then ratified by their respective parliaments. The WTO's conflict resolution process generally emphasizes interpreting existing commitments and agreements, and discovers how to ensure trade policies to conform to those agreements, with the ultimate aim of avoiding military or political conflict.

WTO: See "World Trade Organization (WTO)."

Xylene: An aromatic hydrocarbon commonly used as an industrial solvent. It is also used in producing aviation fuel, resins, and dyes.

ZigBee: May become the ultimate wireless control system for home and office lighting and entertainment systems. The ZigBee Alliance is an association of companies working together to enable reliable, cost-effective, low-power, wirelessly networked monitoring and control products based on an open global standard, 802.15.4 entertainment systems.

INTRODUCTION

PLUNKETT'S ENERGY INDUSTRY ALMANAC, the tenth edition of our guide to the energy field, is designed to be used as a general source for researchers of all types.

The data and areas of interest covered are intentionally broad, from the various types of businesses involved in energy and utilities, to advances in nuclear power and renewable energy sources, to an in-depth look at the major firms (which we call "THE ENERGY 500") within the many industry sectors that make up the energy arena, from upstream and downstream oil and gas companies, to coal producers, oil field services and utilities companies.

This reference book is designed to be a general source for researchers. It is especially intended to assist with market research, strategic planning, employment searches, contact or prospect list creation and financial research, and as a data resource for executives and students of all types.

PLUNKETT'S ENERGY INDUSTRY ALMANAC takes a rounded approach for the general reader. This book presents a complete overview of the entire energy field (see "How To Use This Book"). For example, advances in oil shale and tar sands production are discussed, as well as the deregulation of the utilities industry, volatility in the price of oil, gas and coal, extremely deep offshore wells and production in Russia.

THE ENERGY 500 is our unique grouping of the biggest, most successful corporations in all segments of the energy and utilities industry. Tens of thousands of pieces of information, gathered from a wide variety of sources, have been researched and are presented in a unique form that can be easily understood. This section includes thorough indexes to THE ENERGY 500, by geography, industry, sales, brand names, subsidiary names and many other topics. (See Chapter 4.)

Especially helpful is the way in which PLUNKETT'S ENERGY INDUSTRY ALMANAC enables readers who have no business background to readily compare the financial records and growth plans of large energy companies and major industry groups. You'll see the mid-term financial record of each firm, along with the impact of earnings, sales and strategic plans on each company's potential to fuel growth, to serve new markets and to provide investment and employment opportunities.

No other source provides this book's easy-to-understand comparisons of growth, expenditures, technologies, corporations and many other items of great importance to people of all types who may be studying this, one of the largest industries in the world today.

By scanning the data groups and the unique indexes, you can find the best information to fit your personal research needs. The major growth companies in energy are profiled and then ranked using several different groups of specific criteria. Which firms are the biggest employers? Which companies earn the most profits? These things and much more are easy to find.

In addition to individual company profiles, an overview of energy markets and trends is provided. This book's job is to help you sort through easy-to-understand summaries of today's trends in a quick and effective manner.

Whatever your purpose for researching the energy field, you'll find this book to be a valuable guide. Nonetheless, as is true with all resources, this volume has limitations that the reader should be aware of:

- Financial data and other corporate information can change quickly. A book of this type can be no more current than the data that was available as of the time of editing. Consequently, the financial picture, management and ownership of the firm(s) you are studying may have changed since the date of this book. For example, this almanac includes the most up-to-date sales figures and profits available to the editors as of late 2010. That means that we have typically used corporate financial data as of the end of 2009.

- Corporate mergers, acquisitions and downsizing are occurring at a very rapid rate. Such events may have created significant change, subsequent to the publishing of this book, within a company you are studying.

- Some of the companies in THE ENERGY 500 are so large in scope and in variety of business endeavors conducted within a parent organization, that we have been unable to completely list all subsidiaries, affiliations, divisions and activities within a firm's corporate structure.

- This volume is intended to be a general guide to a vast industry. That means that researchers should look to this book for an overview and, when conducting in-depth research, should contact the specific corporations or industry associations in question for the very latest changes and data. Where possible, we have listed contact names, toll-free telephone numbers and Internet addresses for the companies, government agencies and industry associations involved so that the reader may get further details without unnecessary delay.

- Tables of industry data and statistics used in this book include the latest numbers available at the time of printing, generally through the end of 2009. In a few cases, the only complete data available was for earlier years.

- We have used exhaustive efforts to locate and fairly present accurate and complete data. However, when using this book or any other source for business and industry information, the reader should use caution and diligence by conducting further research where it seems appropriate. We wish you success in your endeavors, and we trust that your experience with this book will be both satisfactory and productive.

Jack W. Plunkett
Houston, Texas
November 2010

HOW TO USE THIS BOOK

The two primary sections of this book are devoted first to the energy industry as a whole and then to the "Individual Data Listings" for THE ENERGY 500. If time permits, you should begin your research in the front chapters of this book. Also, you will find lengthy indexes in Chapter 4 and in the back of the book.

THE ENERGY INDUSTRY

Glossary: A short list of energy industry terms.

Chapter 1: Major Trends Affecting the Energy Industry. This chapter presents an encapsulated view of the major trends that are creating rapid changes in the energy industry today.

Chapter 2: Energy Industry Statistics. This chapter presents in-depth statistics on production, usage, reserves and more.

Chapter 3: Important Energy Industry Contacts – Addresses, Telephone Numbers and Internet Sites. This chapter covers contacts for important government agencies, energy organizations and trade groups. Included are numerous important Internet sites.

THE ENERGY 500

Chapter 4: THE ENERGY 500: Who They Are and How They Were Chosen. The companies compared in this book were carefully selected from the energy industry, largely in the United States. 222 of the firms are based outside the U.S. For a complete description, see THE ENERGY 500 indexes in this chapter.

Individual Data Listings:

Look at one of the companies in THE ENERGY 500's Individual Data Listings. You'll find the following information fields:

Company Name:

The company profiles are in alphabetical order by company name. If you don't find the company you are seeking, it may be a subsidiary or division of one of the firms covered in this book. Try looking it up in the Index by Subsidiaries, Brand Names and Selected Affiliations in the back of the book.

Ranks:

Industry Group Code: An NAIC code used to group companies within like segments. (See Chapter 4 for a list of codes.)

Ranks Within This Company's Industry Group: Ranks, within this firm's segment only, for annual sales and annual profits, with 1 being the highest rank.

Business Activities:

A grid arranged into six major industry categories and several sub-categories. A "Y" indicates that the firm operates within the sub-category. A complete Index by Industry is included in the beginning of Chapter 4.

Types of Business:

A listing of the primary types of business specialties conducted by the firm.

Brands/Divisions/Affiliations:

Major brand names, operating divisions or subsidiaries of the firm, as well as major corporate affiliations—such as another firm that owns a significant portion of the company's stock. A complete Index by Subsidiaries, Brand Names and Selected Affiliations is in the back of the book.

Contacts:

The names and titles up to 27 top officers of the company are listed, including human resources contacts.

Address:

The firm's full headquarters address, the headquarters telephone, plus toll-free and fax numbers where available. Also provided is the World Wide Web site address.

Financials:

<u>Annual Sales (2010 or the latest fiscal year available to the editors, plus up to four previous years):</u> These are stated in thousands of dollars (add three zeros if you want the full number). This figure represents consolidated worldwide sales from all operations. 2010 figures may be estimates.

<u>Annual Profits (2010 or the latest fiscal year available to the editors, plus up to four previous years):</u> These are stated in thousands of dollars (add three zeros if you want the full number). This figure represents consolidated, after-tax net profit from all operations. 2010 figures may be estimates.

<u>Stock Ticker, International Exchange, Parent Company</u>: When available, the unique stock market symbol used to identify this firm's common stock for trading and tracking purposes is indicated. Where appropriate, this field may contain "private" or "subsidiary" rather than a ticker symbol. If the firm is a publicly-held company headquartered outside of the U.S., its international ticker and exchange are given. If the firm is a subsidiary, its parent company is listed.

<u>Total Number of Employees:</u> The approximate total number of employees, worldwide, as of the end of 2009 (or the latest data available to the editors).

Apparent Salaries/Benefits:

(The following descriptions generally apply to U.S. employers only.)

A "Y" in appropriate fields indicates "Yes."

Due to wide variations in the manner in which corporations report benefits to the U.S. Government's regulatory bodies, not all plans will have been uncovered or correctly evaluated during our effort to research this data. Also, the availability to employees of such plans will vary according to the qualifications that employees must meet to become eligible. For example, some benefit plans may be available only to salaried workers—others only to employees who work more than 1,000 hours yearly. Benefits that are available to employees of the main or parent company may not be available to employees of the subsidiaries. In addition, employers frequently alter the nature and terms of plans offered.

NOTE: Generally, employees covered by wealth-building benefit plans do not *fully* own ("vest in") funds contributed on their behalf by the employer until as many as five years of service with that employer have passed. All pension plans are voluntary—that is, employers are not obligated to offer pensions.

<u>Pension Plan:</u> The firm offers a pension plan to qualified employees. In this case, in order for a "Y" to appear, the editors believe that the employer offers a defined benefit or cash balance pension plan (see discussions below).The type and generosity of these plans vary widely from firm to firm. Caution: Some employers refer to plans as "pension" or "retirement" plans when they are actually 401(k) savings plans that require a contribution by the employee.

- <u>Defined Benefit Pension Plans</u>: Pension plans that do not require a contribution from the employee are infrequently offered. However, a few companies, particularly larger employers in high-profit-margin industries, offer defined benefit pension plans where the employee is guaranteed to receive a set pension benefit upon retirement. The amount of the benefit is determined by the years of service with the company and the employee's salary during the later years of employment. The longer a person works for the employer, the higher the retirement benefit. These defined benefit plans are funded entirely by the employer. The benefits, up to a reasonable limit, are guaranteed by the Federal Government's Pension Benefit Guaranty Corporation. These plans are not portable—if you leave the company, you cannot transfer your benefits into a different plan. Instead, upon retirement you will receive the benefits that vested during your service with the company. If your employer offers a pension plan, it must give you a summary plan description within 90 days of the date you join the plan. You can also request a summary annual report of the plan, and once every 12 months you may request an individual benefit statement accounting of your interest in the plan.

- Defined Contribution Plans: These are quite different. They do not guarantee a certain amount of pension benefit. Instead, they set out circumstances under which the employer will make a contribution to a plan on your behalf. The most common example is the 401(k) savings plan. Pension benefits are not guaranteed under these plans.
- Cash Balance Pension Plans: These plans were recently invented. These are hybrid plans—part defined benefit and part defined contribution. Many employers have converted their older defined benefit plans into cash balance plans. The employer makes deposits (or credits a given amount of money) on the employee's behalf, usually based on a percentage of pay. Employee accounts grow based on a predetermined interest benchmark, such as the interest rate on Treasury Bonds. There are some advantages to these plans, particularly for younger workers: a) The benefits, up to a reasonable limit, are guaranteed by the Pension Benefit Guaranty Corporation. b) Benefits are portable—they can be moved to another plan when the employee changes companies. c) Younger workers and those who spend a shorter number of years with an employer may receive higher benefits than they would under a traditional defined benefit plan.

ESOP Stock Plan (Employees' Stock Ownership Plan): This type of plan is in wide use. Typically, the plan borrows money from a bank and uses those funds to purchase a large block of the corporation's stock. The corporation makes contributions to the plan over a period of time, and the stock purchase loan is eventually paid off. The value of the plan grows significantly as long as the market price of the stock holds up. Qualified employees are allocated a share of the plan based on their length of service and their level of salary. Under federal regulations, participants in ESOPs are allowed to diversify their account holdings in set percentages that rise as the employee ages and gains years of service with the company. In this manner, not all of the employee's assets are tied up in the employer's stock.

Savings Plan, 401(k): Under this type of plan, employees make a tax-deferred deposit into an account. In the best plans, the company makes annual matching donations to the employees' accounts, typically in some proportion to deposits made by the employees themselves. A good plan will match one-half of employee deposits of up to 6% of wages. For example, an employee earning $30,000 yearly might deposit $1,800 (6%) into the plan. The company will match one-half of the employee's deposit, or $900. The plan grows on a tax-deferred basis, similar to an IRA. A very generous plan will match 100% of employee deposits. However, some plans do not call for the employer to make a matching deposit at all. Other plans call for a matching contribution to be made at the discretion of the firm's board of directors. Actual terms of these plans vary widely from firm to firm. Generally, these savings plans allow employees to deposit as much as 15% of salary into the plan on a tax-deferred basis. However, the portion that the company uses to calculate its matching deposit is generally limited to a maximum of 6%. Employees should take care to diversify the holdings in their 401(k) accounts, and most people should seek professional guidance or investment management for their accounts.

Stock Purchase Plan: Qualified employees may purchase the company's common stock at a price below its market value under a specific plan. Typically, the employee is limited to investing a small percentage of wages in this plan. The discount may range from 5 to 15%. Some of these plans allow for deposits to be made through regular monthly payroll deductions. However, new accounting rules for corporations, along with other factors, are leading many companies to curtail these plans—dropping the discount allowed, cutting the maximum yearly stock purchase or otherwise making the plans less generous or appealing.

Profit Sharing: Qualified employees are awarded an annual amount equal to some portion of a company's profits. In a very generous plan, the pool of money awarded to employees would be 15% of profits. Typically, this money is deposited into a long-term retirement account. Caution: Some employers refer to plans as "profit sharing" when they are actually 401(k) savings plans. True profit sharing plans are rarely offered.

Highest Executive Salary: The highest executive salary paid, typically a 2010 amount (or the latest year available to the editors) and typically paid to the Chief Executive Officer.

Highest Executive Bonus: The apparent bonus, if any, paid to the above person.

Second Highest Executive Salary: The next-highest executive salary paid, typically a 2010 amount (or the latest year available to the editors) and typically paid to the President or Chief Operating Officer.

Second Highest Executive Bonus: The apparent bonus, if any, paid to the above person.

Other Thoughts:

Apparent Women Officers or Directors: It is difficult to obtain this information on an exact basis, and employers generally do not disclose the data in a public way. However, we have indicated what our best efforts reveal to be the apparent number of women who either are in the posts of corporate officers or sit on the board of directors. There is a wide variance from company to company.

Hot Spot for Advancement for Women/Minorities: A "Y" in appropriate fields indicates "Yes." These are firms that appear either to have posted a substantial number of women and/or minorities to high posts or that appear to have a good record of going out of their way to recruit, train, promote and retain women or minorities. (See the Index of Hot Spots For Women and Minorities in the back of the book.) This information may change frequently and can be difficult to obtain and verify. Consequently, the reader should use caution and conduct further investigation where appropriate.

Growth Plans/ Special Features:

Listed here are observations regarding the firm's strategy, hiring plans, plans for growth and product development, along with general information regarding a company's business and prospects.

Locations:

A "Y" in the appropriate field indicates "Yes."

Primary locations outside of the headquarters, categorized by regions of the United States and by international locations. A complete index by locations is also in the front of this chapter.

Chapter 1

MAJOR TRENDS AFFECTING THE ENERGY INDUSTRY

Major Trends Affecting the Energy Industry:

1) Energy Industry Introduction

There is a broad, global focus today on energy as an economic, geopolitical and strategic resource. In addition, there is a greater focus than ever before on the impact of energy consumption on the environment. Worldwide, investment in the development and implementation of clean, renewable energy technologies and conservation will be a major priority of governments and industry, subject to fluctuations in the economy and the price of crude oil and natural gas. The emphasis will vary widely from nation to nation, ranging from cleaner ways to burn the world's immense stores of coal; to the construction of advanced-technology nuclear generating plants that are exponentially safer than older models (with China leading the way in nuclear implementation); to the use of advanced, more cost-effective renewable technologies based on solar, wind and wave power.

Nonetheless, with the exception of hydroelectric power, renewable energy sources remain vastly more costly to implement than fossil fuel-based generators (primarily coal and natural gas). This means that they require significant government subsidies, loan guarantees or incentives in order to cover the capital costs. As governments in developed economies in Europe, along with the United States, continue to struggle with large deficits and debts, their willingness to back costly renewable energy projects may be dampened significantly. Japan, on the other hand, while facing economic challenges of its own, will maintain a keen interest in alternative energy sources, since it has essentially no fossil fuel supplies of its own.

The most important emerging nations are investing heavily in alternative energy sources, while continuing to use large quantities of fossil fuels. China leads the world in investment in new nuclear plants, and it is installing vast numbers of wind turbines. India is likewise planning multiple new nuclear plants. Brazil continues to be a leader in the low cost production and use of ethanol as a transportation fuel, while developing the world's most important new offshore oil and gas fields at a rapid clip.

The financial crisis of 2008-09 put a damper on the growth of energy consumption. In the United States, for example, consumption of electricity and oil declined significantly from 2007 peaks. Total energy consumption in America dropped by 6.9% in 2009 compared to 2007. In fact, analysts at BP report that global primary energy consumption dropped by 1.1% during 2009, the largest drop since 1980. This is clear evidence that the Great Recession made consumers more cost conscious while slowing down industrial and transportation use of energy. The drop in electricity demand in the U.S. means there is less urgency, at least for the short term, to build new electric plants, which may delay the start of expensive new nuclear facilities.

Emerging economies will continue to burn a lot of coal and fossil fuels. This is where the growth in consumption is essentially unavoidable, in rapidly rising economies such as India and China. Total Chinese energy consumption rose by 7.0% in 2008, despite the global recession, and rose by another 8.7% in 2009. In contrast, consumption in all of Europe fell by 6% in 2009. China's primary energy consumption grew to be 19.5% of the world's total, in 2009, equal to that of the U.S. India's consumption grew 6.6% in 2009, to 4.2% of total world consumption. (These figures are from BP.)

The global energy numbers:

Oil: According to the latest data available from analysts at energy giant BP, the world produced 79.9 million barrels of oil daily in 2009, down 2.6% from 2008. This includes unconventional petroleum output from such sources as oil shale, oil sands and natural gas liquids. However, it does not include alternative sources such as biomass and coal derivatives. Consumption in 2009 averaged 84.0 million barrels of oil per day, down by 1.7% from 2008. (In the U.S., consumption of oil fell by 4.9% to 18.6 million barrels daily, accounting for 21.7% of global consumption in 2009, down from 23.9% in the peak year of 2007. China, excluding Hong Kong, accounted for 10.4%, while India accounted for 3.8% of global consumption.)

Proven reserves worldwide totaled 1.333 trillion barrels at the end of 2009, up slightly from the previous year (not including oil sands). OPEC member nations hold 77.2% of those reserves. The addition of BP's estimate of Canadian oil sands, at 143.3 billion proven barrels, increases the world's total proven reserves to 1.476 trillion barrels.

Natural Gas: According to BP, global production of natural gas was 2,987 billion cubic meters in 2009, down 2.1% from the previous year. Production in the U.S. increased by 3.5%, to 593.4 billion cubic meters, a 2.1% share of the world's total.

Global consumption was 2,940 billion cubic meters, down by 2.1% over the previous year. (The U.S. consumed 22.0% of that total. Europe and Eurasia consumed 35.9%.)

Proven reserves totaled 187.49 trillion cubic meters: enough to last several decades at today's consumption rates. Massive discoveries of natural gas in shale formations in the U.S. and elsewhere are rapidly altering the gas industry. Likewise, vast investments in LNG infrastructure are enabling international shipment of gas from production areas to major markets, particularly to China.

Coal: Analysts at BP estimate that global production of coal was 3,408 million tons of oil equivalents in 2009, up 2.4% over the previous year. Consumption was 3,278 billion tons, virtually unchanged from the previous year.

The largest emerging nations are hooked on coal. China, excluding Hong Kong, accounted for 46.9% of the world's consumption, up from 42.6% during the previous year. India accounted for only 6.9% of global consumption, but its usage was up 7.5% over the previous year. The U.S., where much of electric generation is fired by coal, used only 17.1%, and American consumption was down 11.5% over the previous year, thanks to a weak economy and to electricity utilities switching to natural gas as a fuel for generators. Europe and Eurasia used 13.9%, and consumption was down 11.4% over 2008.

Global coal reserves are massive, at 826,001 million tons or enough to last about 250 years at today's consumption rates. The U.S. holds 28.9% of those reserves, Europe and Eurasia 33.0%, China 13.9% and Australia 9.2%.

America's energy numbers:

In the U.S., the Department of Energy estimates oil production was 5.3 million barrels per day from 526,000 wells during 2009. While production in many of America's largest fields, such as the North Slope in Alaska, is down substantially, investments in offshore production and enhanced recovery in older fields has paid off. Nonetheless, total production is down dramatically from the 1985 peak of 8.97 million barrels of oil per day. (Part of the problem is that Alaskan production peaked in 1988 at 2.0 million barrels daily, and had dropped to 685,000 barrels daily by 2008.)

However, as the nation's natural gas industry has been growing, and new production has ensued thanks to wells in shale, the total production picture has improved dramatically when "natural gas plant liquids," or oil that is stripped from natural gas during processing, are included. Under this view, total oil production was 7,196 barrels daily in 2009 (including 1,886 barrels of natural gas liquids), up 5.1% from the previous year.

America's use of petroleum has led to an increase in annual net petroleum imports from 3,161 thousand barrels per day in 1970 to 9,700 thousand barrels per day in 2009. This figure has been dropping steadily since a 2005 peak.

Meanwhile, only 148 refineries operate in America as of 2009, down by about 50% from 1980. These remaining refineries have invested heavily in additional capacity. However, America also imports substantial quantities of finished refinery products, including gasoline.

Total American consumption of energy of all types was 94,578,267 billion BTUs in 2009, having grown about 50% since 1970. However, 2009 consumption represented a significant drop of more than 6% from the 2007 peak of 101,599,750 billion BTUs.

In terms of BTUs consumed, use by Americans soared from 227 million BTUs per year per capita in 1950 to 331 million BTUs by 1970, but has remained relatively flat ever since. That is, while the number of automobiles and aircraft per capita has grown dramatically; along with vast growth in the percentage of homes and buildings that are air conditioned; combined with tremendous increases in the number of appliances, computers and entertainment devices per person; efficiency has grown to the extent that the energy consumption of an average American declined from a peak in 2000 of 351 million BTUs yearly, to only 308 million in 2009.

While America's economy and population have been growing, energy use per unit of economic output has fallen dramatically. On an inflation-adjusted basis, energy consumption per dollar of GDP dropped from 17.99 thousand BTUs in 1970 to only 7.28 thousand BTUs in 2009.

According to the U.S. Department of Energy, electric generation in America as of 2008 used the following ratio of fuels: coal 44.95% (down from 48.5% the previous year); nuclear 20.09% (up from 19.6%); natural gas 23.45% (up from 21.6%); and renewables, which includes hydroelectric, wind and solar, at 10.52% (up from 9.0%). Most of that "renewable" energy source is hydroelectric, which America has used for decades. Other sources such as solar and wind are growing rapidly, but at only about 3.59% of total generation, they clearly have a long way to go to make a significant impact.

U.S. consumers have shown a true sea change in their preferences and priorities as a result of higher energy prices, and the era of the gas-guzzling, giant family truck or SUV as a standard is over. Meanwhile, consumers and businesses alike are increasingly willing to invest more in the initial cost of green buildings, high-efficiency appliances and equipment and energy-saving vehicles, with the promise of lower energy costs for daily operation.

Thanks to the development of advanced technologies for producing gas from America's immense shale formations, available gas reserves are growing at a rapid rate, with no end in sight. This trend is revolutionizing the gas industry, while keeping natural gas prices at very modest levels.

Oil Prices and Total Reserves:

Ever since William Hart dug America's first successful gas well in Fredonia, New York in 1821, and "Colonel" Edwin Drake drilled the first true U.S. oil well in the state of Pennsylvania in 1859, the ability of oil and natural gas to power electric generation plants, transportation, homes and industry has created both immense economic advances and significant controversy. Many times it has been assumed that the world would quickly run out of oil. In 1939, the U.S. Department of the Interior warned that America's oil reserves totaled only enough to fuel the nation for about 13 years. Similar misjudgments were announced on a regular basis in the mid to late 1900s by the federal government and by a continuing stream of respected reports and books by various authors. In fact, rather than becoming scarcer over time, energy, including oil and gas, became much more plentiful. Energy prices can fluctuate wildly. Nonetheless, over much of history the trend has often been lower prices on an inflation-adjusted basis, when a combination of advancing technologies, determined entrepreneurs and alternative sources exponentially expanded the total amount of energy and reserves available for consumption. The breakthrough in shale gas in recent years is a perfect example.

An estimate of crude oil resources on a global basis, published by Cambridge Energy Research Associates in 2006, was 4.82 trillion barrels—enough to take care of the world's needs for more than 100 years. This number included oil shale and other sources that are relatively difficult to tap. Technologies will continue to be enhanced, enabling the recovery of significant portions of these resources, as long as the market price of energy is high enough to justify necessary investments in technology, exploration, development, production and distribution.

There have long been periods of major fluctuations in price for oil, coal and natural gas. Energy consumers of all types, from residential consumers to transportation firms to industrial plants, have seen oil and gas prices swing wildly, and they have often suffered the economic effects of greatly increased energy costs. Strong global demand for energy combined with political strife in many oil exporting nations could easily lead to a long-term period of relatively high market prices, both for crude oil and natural gas. The price of Arabian light crude oil rose from about $1.85 per barrel in 1972 to about $40 in 1981 during an "energy crisis," the peak price for many years to come. Adjusted for inflation, that $40 barrel of oil would have been $100 or so in 2009 dollars.

More recently, during 1986 and again in 1998, the price of a barrel of oil plummeted to about $10 in a short period of time. However, prices generally rose from 2003 through early 2008. In the fall of 2005, the post-Hurricane Katrina price of a barrel of light U.S. crude oil peaked just shy of $70 as the extent of the damage to production became apparent. The price of natural gas more than doubled from June through October 2005, rising from about $6 to nearly $16 per million BTUs for spot market prices, compared to $4.59 on average during July 2010.

In mid-2006, the price of light U.S. crude peaked at about $80. By late 2007, it had neared $100. By mid-2008 it was over $145, but plummeted quickly into the $60s when the global financial crisis of 2008 slowed economies worldwide. Another significant factor in the price of a barrel of oil is the value of the U.S. dollar relative to other currencies. During much of 2009-10, the dollar was in a lengthy slide in value, causing the price of oil (which is valued in U.S. dollars on world markets) to rise. Of course, the value of the dollar is not the sole factor regulating the price of a barrel of oil, but it is a very important contributing factor.

Recent high prices for oil and gas put a new emphasis on production from alternative (or "unconventional") oil sources such as tar sands in Canada and oil shale in the U.S. These fields are significantly more expensive to produce than conventional fields. Meanwhile, offshore exploration and production will continue to be emphasized in many parts of the world, with sophisticated rigs drilling ever deeper to tap massive reservoirs, using technologies that enable the rigs to go to depths undreamed of 20 years ago. Vast new investments in very deep offshore wells in the Gulf of Mexico brought significant new production to the American market. However, it remains to be seen what the effect on new drilling and production will be from stringent new federal regulations applied to offshore operations in 2010. Meanwhile, outside the U.S., the industry is investing quickly and heavily in deep wells offshore of Africa, Brazil and elsewhere.

Consumers and business organizations alike are attempting to insulate themselves from high energy costs. Many are reacting with new conservation efforts. For example, Toyota's hybrid-powered automobiles have been a huge success. Greatly enhanced building materials and appliances that provide much greater energy efficiency are becoming standard in developed nations. Meanwhile, the growing industrial base and middle class in many parts of the globe, particularly India and China, are putting new strains on energy supplies while energy emissions are creating new environmental concerns.

In 1892, Thomas Alva Edison established the Pearl Street Station in New York City—the world's first central electric power station. By the 1920s, electricity was in common use in American buildings and homes, and millions of automobiles were clogging American streets.

A significant portion of oil consumption is used as fuel for transportation, including cars, aircraft and trucks. There is no end in sight to the need for power and fuel in developed and emerging economies such as the U.S., the European Union, Japan, India and China. Although the world has made an immense investment in electric supply infrastructure, as much as one-third of the world's population either has no access to, or cannot afford, a steady supply of electricity.

Fuels for electric generation vary widely around the globe, but coal, oil and natural gas are common sources. In Europe, a large ratio of electricity is generated by nuclear plants, especially in France, and massive investments are being made in European solar and wind generation. As 2010 drew to a close, a looming question was whether America and major nations in Europe will resume construction of nuclear generation plants. New, advanced generation nuclear technologies can provide much greater operating efficiencies with vastly increased safety over the plants constructed in earlier years.

2) The U.S. Electric Grid Needs Significant New Investment

In the U.S., the networks of local electric lines that businesses and consumers depend on every day are connected with and interdependent upon a national network of major lines collectively called "the grid." The grid is divided into three major regions, named East, West and Texas. The regions are also known as "interconnects." In total, the grid consists of about 200,000 miles of high-voltage backbone lines and millions of miles of smaller local lines.

The grid is one of the most reliable electricity delivery platforms in the world, but it is far from perfect, and deregulation of the electricity industry created intense problems. Unfortunately, much of this grid was designed and constructed with technology developed in the 1950s and 1960s, and it was never intended to carry the amazing amount of power that today's electricity-hungry Americans consume. Simply put, the grid is out of date. For example, while electric consumption zoomed ahead by about 35% during the 1990s, the transmission capacity of the grid grew by only about 15%.

When a local utility system needs more power than it is generating, it can draw upon the grid. (In fact, many utility companies in America have no generating capacity at all and draw all of their power from the grid as they resell it to end users.) Conversely, when a generating system is producing more power than is needed locally, it can push power into the grid for other areas to use.

Since electricity cannot be easily stored in large volume for future use, the grid is absolutely vital in smoothing out the fluctuations that occur in supply and demand. Unfortunately, the grid suffers from a long list of inadequacies. For example, about 7% of the energy pushed into the grid is lost during transmission. Also, the grid has bottlenecks, or distribution squeezes, particularly in densely populated areas like New York City and San Francisco. This means that utilities cannot always get all of the electricity they need to meet local demand, and blackouts or shortages occur.

In addition to these mounting problems, the grid is suffering from old age. As electricity demand increases significantly, the grid is going to have serious difficulty delivering as needed. Possible solutions include: 1) greater use of energy conservation; 2) construction of additional high-voltage lines; and 3) use of "distributed power"—that is, smaller generating plants (such as fuel cells or microturbines) that generate electricity close to the source where it is needed, thereby bypassing the need for the grid.

The Electric Power Research Institute (EPRI) and other industry experts put the cost of overall grid improvements at as much as $100 billion over a period of up to 10 years, a huge increase from today's level of investment. At the same time, the payoff for energy consumers would be significantly higher than the cost. By some estimates, a state of the art smart grid could reduce power consumption in the U.S. by 10% while reducing the need for new power plants and cutting greenhouse gas emissions substantially.

3) Proposals for U.S. Electricity Grid Enhancements include a "Smart Grid," Regional Transmission Organizations (RTOs) and Technologies such as Flow Cell Batteries

Proposed solutions to the U.S. electricity grid's problems range from reorganization to massive investments in advanced computerization to barely proven technologies. Some engineers promote the use of immense, high-capacity batteries called "flow cell batteries" to store enough excess electricity to make the grid much more flexible and reliable. The use of large-scale storage systems scattered around the grid would mean that generating companies could create excess power during periods of slow demand, store that electricity and then sell it through the grid a few hours later when demand picks up. It would also mean that spikes in demand, such as the demand caused by air conditioners turned on during an extremely hot summer afternoon, could be served quickly by drawing on stored power. A few of these large battery energy storage systems are already in place in Japan, Australia, Alaska and Utah. Others are being tested in several locations worldwide.

Battery systems such as these not only add reliability to an electricity grid system, they also lower costs and improve efficiency. For example, wholesale power can be purchased at night, when demand and energy prices are low, and then sold the next day during peak hours for a premium.

SPOTLIGHT: Battery Energy Storage Systems
For more information on battery energy storage systems, check the following company web sites:

ABB	www.abb.com
Prudent Energy	www.pdenergy.com
Telepower Australia	www.telepower.com.au
A123 Systems	www.a123systems.com

Other super-capacity storage technologies include flywheels, pumped hydro storage and compressed air energy storage. (A lack of efficient, large-scale storage systems has also been one of the factors holding back the development of solar power.) For additional thoughts along these lines, visit the Electricity Storage Association at www.electricitystorage.org.

Superconductive wires also hold promise over the long-term. (See "Superconductivity Comes of Age.") Meanwhile, shorter-term solutions to the grid's inadequacies are needed, as evidenced by the massive Northeastern U.S. blackout of August 2003. Multiple changes could vastly increase the reliability and efficiency of the grid. Currently, the grid is something of a free-for-all. Thousands of utility companies utilize it, but there is little communication among those companies regarding their real-time operating status. At the same time, regulation of the grid desperately needs to be revamped. Companies that transmit via the grid and that might be interested in investing in grid infrastructure currently must deal with a quagmire of competing interests. The grid's three interconnects are broken down into about 120 control areas, but operators of those control areas have very little authority beyond making requests (but not demands) of utilities participating within those areas.

U.S. state and federal agencies are making efforts to increase the grid's efficiency and enforce compliance to regulatory standards. After the massive blackout of August 2003, a joint U.S.-Canadian taskforce was created that stipulated 46 recommendations for improvement to the monitoring of transmission lines and for use of the grid. Each recommendation has since been implemented. These recommendations included the establishment of Independent System Operators (ISOs), which are independent, nonprofit organizations. ISOs ensure that electric generating companies have equal access to the power grid. They may be replaced by larger Regional Transmission Organizations (RTOs), which would each cover a major area of the U.S. The North American Electric Reliability Corporation (NERC), www.nerc.com, is now responsible for enforcing mandatory reliability standards on utilities. NERC fines are levied when performance falls below those standards.

The utilities industry is pushing its own vision of the grid's future, via the respected Electric Power Research Institute (EPRI, www.epri.com), an organization of members representing more than 90% of the electricity generated and delivered in the U.S. EPRI envisions creating an environment in which utilities are encouraged to invest heavily in new transmission technologies. Part of its plan is aimed at developing constant communication among the systems pushing power to, and pulling power from, the grid. EPRI hopes the grid will become a self-repairing, intelligent, digital electricity delivery system. As a result, a systems breakdown in one area might be compensated for by users or producers elsewhere, aborting potential blackout situations. The total investment required would be more than $100 billion.

Another part of its technology platform is based on making the grid "smarter," by using state of the art digital switches and sensors to monitor and manage the grid—a vast improvement over today's equipment. This smart grid would incorporate sensors throughout the entire delivery system, employ instant communications and computing power and use solid-state power electronics to sense and, where needed, control power flows and resolve disturbances instantly. The upgraded system would have the ability to read and diagnose problems. It would be self-repairing, by automatically isolating affected areas and re-routing power to keep the rest of the system running. Another advantage of this smart grid is that it would be able to seamlessly integrate an array of locally installed, distributed power sources, such as fuel cells and solar power, with traditional central-station power generation.

Internet Research Tip:
For the latest in research regarding generation and distribution of power by electric utility companies, see the Palo Alto, California-based **Electric Power Research Institute** (EPRI) at my.epri.com.

Also, the GridWise Alliance, www.gridwise.org, is a consortium of public and private utility and energy companies that supports a stronger electricity grid. Members include General Electric (GE), IBM, the Tennessee Valley Authority and the U.S. Department of Energy.

In 2009, a new transmission link was proposed that would connect the Eastern, Western and Texas grids. Called the Tres Amigas superstation, the project would be located in Clovis, New Mexico, and would use superconducting cable to convert different kinds of current from each region into a common direct current for transmission. (Superconductivity is created by cooling transmission cable to as low as minus 418 degrees Fahrenheit, thus enabling the system to transmit electricity with almost none of the power loss associated with standard cables.) The current would be converted again to the necessary type to match the destination grid. Tres Amigas is spearheaded by Tres Amigas LLC, run by Phil Harris, the former CEO of PJM Interconnection LLC, a major grid-running concern. American Superconductor Corporation will provide planning services as well as the superconducting cable. The Clovis location is less than 100 miles from substations in each of the existing grids, and would be especially useful in transmitting power generated from renewable sources in out-of-the-way areas. The greater connectivity afforded by the superstation could promote the development of new energy sources. Despite the $1 billion cost for the venture, Tres Amigas had moved ahead with construction planning and had been granted approval from the Federal Energy Regulatory Commission (FERC) to offer transmission services at negotiated rates, with construction to begin as early as 2012.

New smart utility meters are beginning to be installed at consumers' locations in major U.S. markets that transmit usage data to utilities, display price fluctuations and alert utilities to service interruptions instantaneously. The meters save utilities the cost of employing meter readers and promote conservation since homeowners can plan activities such as washing clothes or charging plug-in devices at night when prices are lower. Homes with solar panels can use the smart meters to measure and sell excess power back to the utility. There's even the ability, for homeowners willing to participate, for utilities to remotely adjust air conditioning and heating systems to cheaper settings when demand is high. Homeowners can adjust settings remotely as well.

Internet Research Tip: Smart Meters
For an excellent explanation of smart meters, how they work and how they save energy, see CenterPoint Energy's Energy InSight web page:
www.centerpointenergy.com/services/electricity/residential/smartmeters

In October 2009, U.S. President Obama announced grants totaling $3.4 billion (part of the $862 billion economic stimulus package) to be provided to 100 companies including utilities, manufacturers, cities and other agencies in 49 states. The funds, which are being matched by grant money from private sources totaling an additional $4.7 billion, would be used to pay for approximately 18 million smart meters, 700 automated substations and 200,000 smart transformers. Working together, these systems promise higher efficiency, reliability and sustainability. However, as of mid-2010, only $107.5 million of the $3.4 billion had been spent, according to the U.S. Department of Energy (DOE). Since state regulators must okay new initiatives undertaken by utilities, a number of roadblocks have slowed the process, in some cases leaving utilities with precious little time to lock in funds promised by the government. For example, Baltimore Gas & Electric, a subsidiary of Constellation Energy Group, was rejected by the Maryland Public Service Commission when it proposed smart grid improvements in June 2010. The DOE responded by extending its deadline for state approval which was eventually granted.

San Francisco, California and Dallas, Texas are two examples of metro areas where smart meters are being installed. In San Francisco, Pacific Gas & Electric (PG&E) plans to install as many as 10 million advanced electric and gas meters by 2012. In Dallas, Oncor Electric Delivery Co. plans to install 3 million meters. The San Francisco project is budgeted at about $2.3 billion. On a national basis, 15.6 million smart meters had been installed by mid-

2010, with another 37.8 million expected to be installed by 2015, according to FERC.

Proponents of smart meters claim that their efficiencies will offset the high installation costs. PG&E estimated that about 70% of its initial investment will be recouped due to savings in maintenance crew costs. Widespread use of the meters creates a smarter network, as their powerful technology allows communication to flow from utilities to consumers and back again.

The meters also have detractors. Power companies have received complaints from customers claiming that their bills are higher due to the meters showing falsely high readings. In several states, class action lawsuits have been filed. In some cases, manufacturers are blaming a lack of consumer education with regard to reading and using the meters. In others, a fast rollout of the new meters caused problems when old billing systems incurred erroneous charges when interfacing with the new equipment.

Technology firms are hoping to cash in on the federal funds-supported smart meter initiative. According to research firm IDC Energy Insights, North American utilities were projected to spend $17.5 billion on computer software, hardware and communications services related to intelligent grid technology between 2010 and 2013. Companies including ABB, Cisco Systems, Ambient Corp., IBM and Microsoft are all promoting new products that support smart grid needs. ABB, for example, specializes in high-voltage direct current links (HVDC) that are ideally suited for transmitting power over long distances. Likewise, appliance manufacturers such as General Electric, Whirlpool and LG are developing new, smart products that turn themselves off when electricity demand is high (and most expensive) and back on when demand falls.

SPOTLIGHT: Ray Bell's Smart Meter

Silicon Valley entrepreneur Ray Bell has a serious entry in the smart meter market with his advanced technology concept. In addition to measuring power usage, the Bell meter acts as an Internet router, monitoring energy usage remotely and noting problems instantaneously. Better yet, the meters communicate via WiMax for extra-long range wireless transmission. Bell signed a deal with General Electric to license his wireless interface and network software, which GE uses in manufacturing the meters and marketing them to utilities. Intel Capital (the capital arm of Intel, which is a manufacturer of WiMax chip sets) is another investor in Bell's startup company, Grid Net, www.grid-net.com. The global market opportunity is vast. New smart units cost between $125 and $300 each. Bell and GE face competition from Washington state-based Itron, among others, but Grid Net's GE and Intel-backed credentials place it in the forefront of the smart meter market.

4) Superconductivity Comes of Age

Superconductivity is based on the concept of using super-cooled cable to distribute electricity over distance, with little of the significant loss of electric power incurred during traditional transmission over copper wires. It is one of the most promising technologies for upgrading the ailing electricity grid.

Superconductivity dates back to 1911, when a Dutch physicist determined that the element mercury, when cooled to minus 452 degrees Fahrenheit, has virtually no electrical resistance. That is, it lost zero electric power when used as a means to distribute electricity from one spot to another. Two decades later, in 1933, a German physicist named Walther Meissner discovered that superconductors have no interior magnetic field. This property enabled superconductivity to be put to commercial use by 1984, when magnetic resonance imaging machines (MRIs) were commercialized for medical imaging.

In 1986, IBM researchers K. Alex Muller and Georg Bednorz paved the path to superconductivity at slightly higher temperatures using a ceramic alloy as a medium. Shortly thereafter, a team led by University of Houston physicist Paul Chu created a ceramic capable of superconductivity at temperatures high enough to encourage true commercialization.

In May 2001, the Danish city of Copenhagen established a first when it implemented a 30-meter-long "high temperature" superconductivity (HTS) cable in its own energy grids. Other small but successful implementations have occurred in the U.S.

Internet Research Tip:
For an easy-to-understand overview of superconductivity and its many current and future applications, visit the Superconductivity Technology Center of the Los Alamos National Labs:
www.lanl.gov/orgs/mpa/mpastc.shtml

Today, the Holy Grail for researchers is a quest for materials that will permit superconductivity at temperatures above the freezing point, even at room temperature. There are two types of superconductivity: "low-temperature" superconductivity (LTS), which requires temperatures lower than minus 328 degrees Fahrenheit; and "high-temperature" superconductivity (HTS), which operates at any temperature higher than that. The former type requires the use of liquid helium to maintain these excessively cold temperatures, while the latter type can reach the required temperatures with much cheaper liquid nitrogen. Liquid nitrogen is pumped through HTS cable assemblies, chilling thin strands of ceramic material that can carry electricity with no loss of power as it travels through the super-cooled cable. HTS wires are capable of carrying more than 130 times the electrical current of conventional copper wire of the same dimension. Consequently, the weight of such cable assemblies can be one-tenth the weight of old-fashioned copper wire.

While cable for superconductivity is both exotic and expensive, the cost is plummeting as production ramps up, and the advantages can be exceptional. Increasing production to commercial levels at an economic cost, as well as producing lengths suitable for transmission purposes remain among the largest hurdles for the superconductor industry. Applications that are currently being implemented include use in electric transmission bottlenecks and in expensive engine systems such as those found in submarines.

Another major player in HTS components is Sumitomo Electric Industries, the largest cable and wire manufacturer in Japan. The firm has begun commercial production of HTS wire at a facility in Osaka. In addition, Sumitomo has developed electric motors based on HTS coil. The superconducting motors are much smaller and lighter than conventional electric motors, at about 90% less volume and 80% less weight.

Another leading firm, American Superconductor (www.amsc.com), is doing well enough that it grew its workforce by 40% during 2010, to a global total of 1,000. While the firm is based in Devens, Massachusetts, it received 94% of its revenues from foreign sources as of 2010. The company is selling technology to wind turbine makers, enabling them to design full 10 megawatt class superconductor wind turbines that will operate with higher efficiency than traditional models. It is also participating in advanced-technology electric transmission projects. For example, in collaboration of LS Cable in Korea, it is supplying technology for over 30 miles of superconducting cable systems for the Korean electric grid, starting in late 2010.

Advanced-generation HTS cable has been developed at American Superconductor, utilizing multiple coatings on top of a 100-millimeter substrate, a significant improvement over its earlier 40-millimeter technology. The goal is to achieve the highest level of alignment of the atoms in the superconductor material resulting in higher electrical current transmission capacity. This will increase manufacturing output while increasing efficiency. This is a convergence of nanotechnology with superconductivity, since it deals with materials at the atomic level. The company is well set up to increase production as demand increases.

Leading Firms in Superconductivity Technology:
Sumitomo Electric Industries, Ltd., www.sei.co.jp
American Superconductor, www.amsc.com
Nexans, www.nexans.com
SuperPower, Inc., www.superpower-inc.com

5) New Drilling Methods Increase Natural Gas Supply/Shale Gas Is Abundant

Natural gas supplies a significant portion of America's energy needs by heating buildings, running factories and providing energy to power plants that generate about 23% of the electricity used in the U.S. Environmental concerns about burning coal to generate electricity, even when using the latest clean technologies, have made it difficult to gain a license for the construction of new coal-fired power plants. Gas, on the other hand, is the fossil fuel of choice from a clean air point-of-view. Consequently, a reliable and reasonably priced supply of natural gas is absolutely vital to the U.S. economy. In addition, natural gas is used heavily by industry, as raw material in the manufacture of fertilizers, plastics and many other items.

From the 1980s through the early '90s, natural gas prices in the range of $1.50 to $2.00 per MMBTU (million Btu) were common. Lately, however, prices are much higher. The Henry Hub price per MMBTU is considered the base price for natural gas in the U.S. (The Henry Hub is a major gas-gathering site.) In 2003, the average Henry Hub price was up to $5.80. Prices in 2007 through 2010 have varied widely, often running $3.50 to $7.00. As of mid-2010, prices were about $4.50, which was below the price needed by many operators in order to earn good profits on new wells, which tend to be in shale. New gas wells in shale require an investment of up to $3.5 million each. However, the vast new quantities of gas being discovered and brought into production are depressing market prices for natural gas.

The most important development is the use of better technologies to get natural gas from shale. The gas industry has known for decades that shale holds high quantities of gas, but it was previously too difficult or too expensive to produce. First of all, the shale tends to lie deep in the ground, typically around 5,000 feet, where the gas permeates rock rather than lying in an easily accessed pool. In the 1990s, a technique was perfected that drills multiple long, horizontal holes, all reaching out from one drilling site, and then uses high-pressure water streams to fracture the shale, thus releasing gas. Drilling can extend from the drilling site for one mile or more in any direction. After the initial penetration is complete, the large drilling rig is removed and a process called hydrofracturing is done in which millions of gallons of water are forced down the well into the shale. This process, also called "fracking" or "fraccing," creates fractures in the shale, opening up access to the gas. When the water is pumped back out, the gas that was trapped in the shale is released into the pipe.

Although it has been produced in substantial quantity for only a few years, shale gas (now produced in numerous important fields across America in addition to the large Barnett field in Texas) already accounted for about 20% of America's natural gas supply by 2010. By some estimates it could account for 50% by 2035. There are multiple reasons why this is important: First, this shale gas is a domestic supply, not at all reliant on imports. Next, natural gas is easy to distribute. A massive pipeline and urban supply system is already in place. Finally, natural gas has about one-half the carbon impact of coal, and it is relatively easy and inexpensive for electric power plants to switch from relying on coal as a fuel to using gas. Numerous shale gas areas are widespread across America. For example, there is the massive Marcellus shale field and the adjacent Utica and Devonian, running from New York southwest through several states to Kentucky and Tennessee. The New Albany is being actively explored in Illinois and Indiana; the Fayetteville is in Arkansas; and the Bakken and Gammon are in the Dakotas and Montana, to name just a few of the known fields. Tax revenues from shale gas production will soon help to bail out the budgets of many state governments. Depending on whom you ask, shale discoveries have boosted U.S. reserves to between 2,000 and 3,000 trillion cubic feet (TCF), much more than a 100-year supply. (Meanwhile, even more gas is on the way. New pipelines are planned to bring conventional Alaskan gas to the lower 48 states, while massive fields of gas await a resumption of exploration in the prolific Gulf of Mexico.)

While the U.S. already has more than 20 known shale areas of significance, shale zones also exist in many other nations. Several fields are already being explored in Canada. This new production in shale is generating tens of thousands of jobs and billions of dollars in revenues for energy companies and for state tax collectors. ExxonMobil is exploring 250,000 acres it has leased in British Columbia, Canada in an area known as the Horn River Basin. In the U.S., ExxonMobil has agreed to acquire a leading shale gas producer, XTO Energy, for $31 billion. In 2010, CNOOC, the Chinese National Offshore Oil Corp., agreed to pay $2.2 billion for a one-third interest in a South Texas shale project owned by Chesapeake Energy.

European firms are extremely interested in shale production. Norway's StatOilHydro bought a significant interest in leases owned by U.S. leader Chesapeake Energy in 2009. Engineers from other countries such as Italy and Norway are studying American gas extraction techniques to expand their own proven natural gas reserves. Greater reliance on natural gas could profoundly impact global oil consumption. U.S. production companies are taking action in foreign prospects. ExxonMobil, for example, drilled several new gas wells in Germany in 2009 and it has shale gas projects as far afield as Poland, while Devon Energy, in partnership with French oil firm Total, is seeking approval to drill in France. To a large extent, Europe currently relies on gas imported from Russia.

On the demand side, new gas-fired power plants were built to the extent that electric generation consumes vastly more gas than it did in the '90s. At the same time, it has become fashionable for new homes to rely heavily on gas-fired heating and appliances. Meanwhile, U.S. producers are using advanced technologies in an attempt to get the most out of aging gas fields, and new wells both onshore and offshore are bringing in new production. The North Slope in Alaska produces immense quantities of gas, but much of it is currently re-injected into oil wells in order to increase oil production. Conservatively speaking, known gas reserves in the North Slope total 35 trillion cubic feet, although some analysts believe reserves may eventually be as high as 235 trillion cubic feet. New pipelines are being planned to bring Alaska's gas to the lower 48 states.

State of the art technologies used to successfully get natural gas from shale are also being used to develop new crude oil production in the U.S. In the Eagle Ford Shale in South Texas, for example, substantial numbers of new shale oil wells are currently being developed.

Another side effect of the boom in shale gas production, and resulting low market prices for gas, is a bust in the LNG business. During the early to mid 2000s, a handful of firms invested billions of dollars in new LNG (liquefied natural gas) processing plants in America, intended to offload imported gas from foreign fields for U.S. markets. They were encouraged by high demand for this relatively clean fuel, and spot prices that reached nearly $16 in 2005. However, the bounty of new shale gas production has devastated LNG prospects in America. By 2010, without the new shale gas wells, there would have been a constant stream of LNG ships offloading needed gas into American markets at high prices. This would have made America's energy bill vastly higher, while making its balance of trade look even worse.

6) Coalbed Methane Looks Promising

A promising alternative gas technology is coalbed methane, or CBM. (Traditional natural gas consists of about 80% methane.) CBM is a natural methane gas that is found in coal seams, while traditional natural gas deposits are trapped in porous rock formations. Since coal is found in abundance throughout much of the world, CBM could eventually be an important energy source.

A small amount of CBM is already produced successfully in the Rocky Mountain regions of the U.S. Meanwhile, Canada is producing small amounts as well, and it is seriously studying the potential of producing a large amount of CBM in coal areas of Alberta. U.S. coalbed methane resources could total 100 trillion cubic feet of economically recoverable CBM out of an estimated total of 700 trillion cubic feet in place. CBM already accounts for about 8% of U.S. natural gas production as of 2009. CBM exploration costs are relatively low, and recent high market prices for natural gas may encourage this industry to accelerate.

7) Demand for Natural Gas Leads to Massive New Pipeline Projects

In 2009, as many as 3,000 additional miles of pipeline were constructed, spread across about 43 pipeline projects and costing almost $9.9 billion. The largest project completed in 2009 was the Rockies Express-East pipeline system which extends 639 miles.

Two proposed pipeline projects are competing to build a line to connect Alaska's North Slope, with its estimated 35 trillion cubic feet of gas reserves, to the lower 48 states. One is the massive, $35 billion pipeline project called "Denali" after the famous mountain that dominates Alaska's landscape. ConocoPhillips and BP PLC, both major producers of oil and gas on the North Slope in Alaska, have begun design of this pipeline, proposed to run from Alaska to Alberta, Canada and on to a final destination near Chicago for a total of 3,500 miles. In October 2010, Denali concluded its "open seasons "in the U.S. and Canada. This is a process in which shippers are invited to make bids as to what they would be willing to pay to have their gas transported via the pipeline. The firms hope to begin moving gas through the pipe as early as 2020.

Meanwhile, a major Canada-based company, TransCanada, proposes a new 48-inch diameter pipe that would parallel the existing trans-Alaska oil pipeline to a point near Fairbanks, Alaska. It would then follow the Alaska Highway, continuing through British Columbia, to link up with the Alberta Hub on TransCanada's pipeline grid in northwestern Alberta. As of mid-2009, ExxonMobil had announced its participation in the project with TransCanada, dealing a significant blow to the Denali project and to BP and ConocoPhillips. The project had its own open season in early 2010, and at that time TransCanada and ExxonMobil announced that costs to complete the pipeline were expected to be between 23% and 58% more than initially projected.

Various entities have been attempting to gain financing and support for new Alaskan gas pipelines for several years. These two proposals have serious potential to succeed. However, numerous engineering, regulatory and financial hurdles remain. Battles over environmental impact will be particularly onerous.

A less ambitious, but nonetheless extremely important, gas pipeline will deliver gas out of Rocky Mountain fields to consumers in the upper Midwest and Eastern U.S. The 1,679-mile, $4.4 billion Rockies Express ("REX") pipeline is being built by Kinder Morgan Energy Partners LP, ConocoPhillips and Sempra Pipelines & Storage, a unit of Sempra Energy. It is the largest gas pipeline built in the U.S. in more than 20 years, with a capacity of as much as 2 billion cubic feet of gas daily. The western segment ("REX West"), to Audrain County, Missouri, went into full service in May 2008. The eastern segment ("REX East"), which terminates in Ohio, began full service as of late 2009. An extension to the project has been proposed which would add an additional 375 miles, stretching the endpoint from Clarington, Ohio to Princeton, New Jersey.

Meanwhile, the Canadian Government is considering a plan to encourage the development of a $7 billion (Canadian dollars) MacKenzie Pipeline to carry natural gas produced in the Northwest Territories. It could be a major supply of energy to the oil sands operations of Alberta. However, the project has hit numerous snags, including environmental issues, high construction costs, and low market prices for natural gas. If it finally gets underway, the $16.2 billion project would run from the Mackenzie Delta on the Beaufort Sea to Canadian and U.S. markets. Partners in the 1,220-kilometer pipeline include Imperial Oil, Aboriginal Pipeline, Royal Dutch Shell, ConocoPhillips and ExxonMobil.

Outside the U.S., additional pipeline projects are in the planning stages. Turkey, Austria, Hungary, Romania and Bulgaria are working together on the $11.8 billion Nabucco project which would run 2,051 miles from Austria southeast to Turkey and then east to the Caspian Sea. The pipeline would have an annual capacity of 8 billion cubic meters and a maximum of 31 billion cubic meters, or 5% of the EU's consumption. If funded, the project is scheduled for a construction start in 2011 and completion in 2014. In early 2009, the EU committed $279 million in seed money. Supply negotiations were underway in late 2010 with Azerbaijan's Shah Deniz gas field, but may be compromised by competition from Russia's proposed South Stream pipeline. South Stream would transport natural gas from the Black Sea to Bulgaria, where it would branch off in two directions, one towards southern Italy and the other through Hungary into Austria. South Stream AG, a joint venture between Italy's Eni SpA and Russia's OAO Gazprom, Electricite de France and another joint venture between Gazprom and Bulgargaz of Bulgaria are among the companies that are slated to build and operate the pipeline, which will have an annual capacity of 63 billion cubic meters. The project is expected to be completed as early as 2015.

Another project on the drawing board is Nord Stream, a pipeline that would deliver natural gas from Russia to Germany, bypassing Ukraine, which has historically been the site of major pipelines and currently delivers most of the Russian natural gas used in the EU. In late 2009, the project was green-lighted by both Sweden and Finland to pass through their economic zones in the Baltic Sea (Denmark had already given its approval). The new pipeline would come at a fortuitous time, since there have been disruptions in supply from Russia due to pricing disputes between Moscow and the Ukraine, as well as Ukraine's difficulties in paying for the gas it obtains from Russia. Nord Stream is backed by a consortium primarily led by OAO Gazprom, Russia's state-owned gas supplier. Other partners in the project are German-based BASF/Wintershall AG and E.On Rhurgas AG and the Netherlands' NV Nederlandse Gasunie. The project would include two parallel pipelines, each 760 miles long.

8) LNG Imports and New Projects Offer Increased Supply/Floating LNG Plants May Change the Industry

One way to distribute natural gas to high-demand markets like China and Japan is through LNG (liquefied natural gas). However, due to the necessity of special handling, bringing that supply to market in major quantities requires advanced technology and huge capital outlays. First, the natural gas must be chilled to minus 259 degrees Fahrenheit, in order for it to change into a liquid state. Next, the LNG is put on specially designed ships where extensive insulation and refrigeration maintain the cold temperature. Finally, it is offloaded at special receiving facilities where it is warmed and converted back into a gaseous state ("gasification") suitable for distribution via pipelines.

Offshore gasification facilities, far from onshore residences, sometimes have a better chance at regulatory approval. These plants can receive LNG, heat it to the extent that it resumes gaseous form and then pipe it to an onshore terminal. One such project in the U.S., called Energy Bridge, is located 116 miles off the coast of Louisiana and uses adapted oil technology to send the product back to shore.

LNG facilities are immense engineering projects that take many years and serious financial commitments to complete. Nonetheless, by 2009 America had significant gasification facilities, with 5.2 trillion cubic feet of yearly capacity, according to the Department of Energy (DOE).

In 2007, the U.S. received 770 billion cubic feet of LNG. Imports in 2008 fell to 350 billion cubic feet, with 500 billion cubic feet projected for 2009, according to the EIA. Prices in the U.S. for natural gas were falling in much of 2009 due to excess supply, however, the U.S. maintains some of the world's largest storage capacity for LNG, making it a "market of last resort" for LNG shippers. At one time, LNG looked like it would become an important source for America's gas needs, but abundant domestic gas from shale has changed the picture dramatically.

Historically, the vast majority of all liquid natural gas exports to the United States came from a single LNG processing plant in Trinidad and Tobago, a Caribbean island nation near the coast of Venezuela. This facility, Atlantic LNG, was built with investments from BP, BG Group and Repsol.

On the receiving side, the special terminals in the U.S. dedicated to LNG were previously limited to four on the mainland and one in Puerto Rico (a paltry number when compared to the 25 terminals in Japan). Many of these plants have been expanded in recent years.

Optimistic forecasts of demand brought about significant investment in new terminals in Louisiana and Texas. A small company called Cheniere Energy (www.cheniere.com), with assistance from ExxonMobil and Sempra Energy, completed three new LNG terminals. Two of the completed terminals are in Louisiana and one is in Texas. The Sabine Pass facility, on the Texas/Louisiana border, completed construction and began operation in mid-2009, at a total cost of $1.55 billion.

In October 2009, Sempra Energy completed an LNG receiving and regasification terminal near Lake Charles, Louisiana at a cost of nearly $1 billion. Sempra also completed a plant on the west coast of Mexico, called the *Energia Costa Azul*, in May 2008. At a cost of about $875 million, the terminal includes 45 miles of new gas pipeline to connect with existing infrastructure to deliver gas throughout Northern Mexico and California.

Most of the world's LNG is shipped to Asia, where market prices are significantly higher than in the rest of the world. Currently, major exporters of LNG include Qatar, Russia and Iran. Additional sources include Algeria, Malaysia, Nigeria, Oman, the Australia region, and Trinidad and Tobago.

The global LNG market is partly dominated by two firms in Qatar; Qatargas and RasGas. This is partly due to Qatar's ownership of one of the world's largest conventional natural gas reservoirs, the offshore North Field. In May 2009, Qatargas completed the largest LNG import terminal in Europe at South Hook on the Welsh coast. The new terminal could supply about one-fifth of the U.K.'s natural gas. Qatar also welcomes foreign oil and gas firms, especially ExxonMobil, which owns the RasGas gas liquification facility there in partnership with Qatar Petroleum. At a cost of $20 billion, RasGas added 31.2 million tons of LNG to annual capacity. ExxonMobil is also building one of the world's largest petrochemical plants at Qatar.

A revolutionary new floating gas plant concept is underway off the northwestern coast of Australia. Royal Dutch Shell signed a contract in 2009 with a consortium comprised of Korea's Samsung Heavy Industries Co. and France's Technip SA to build a $5 billion floating facility that will be about 500 yards long and 82 yards wide (larger than an aircraft carrier). By processing LNG offshore, previously stranded reserves that were too remote to be feasible can be tapped. In Australia alone, the government estimates that there were 140 trillion cubic feet of stranded gas reserves in 2009, worth about $890 billion. When complete, the facility can produce up to 3.7 million tons of LNG per year. Once an underwater field is exhausted, the floating plant can be deployed elsewhere. Other floating plant projects are on the drawing board, including Japan's Inpex Holdings, Inc.'s plant in the Timor Sea in Indonesia and Australia's Santos Ltd. plans to work on a plant in a joint venture with French-based company GDF Suez SA.

ExxonMobil is also extremely active in gas/LNG production in the Australia area. In 2009, China signed a multi-year contract with ExxonMobil, valued at $41 billion, for the delivery of LNG from the Gorgon project, a vast natural gas and LNG facility jointly owned by ExxonMobil, Chevron and Royal Dutch Shell.

With demand from the U.S. not meeting expectations, where will new LNG production go? Markets in Japan, China and India continue to grow. Japan is already a huge importer of LNG, there being few alternatives for the transport of gas to the island nation.

China plans to become a major importer of LNG and has completed several terminals along the

Chinese coast. Total Chinese consumption of gas is expected to grow threefold from 2010 through 2020, and LNG will be a major component.

SPOTLIGHT: BG Group plc

2009 Revenues:	$14.7 billion
2009 Profits:	$4.5 billion
Employees:	6,191

This rapidly growing British company is at the forefront of LNG development. BG has delivered cargoes to 18 out of the world's 19 importing nations. Its liquefication operations are in Egypt and Trinidad and Tobago. In addition, BG owns and operates regasification facilities in the U.S., U.K., Chile and Italy. 2010 saw BG Group selling off most of its power plants. In March, the firm agreed to sell its three U.S. power plants to Energy Capital Partners for total considerations of $450 million. In April, BG agreed to sell its 50% stake in the Seabank Power Limited combined-cycle gas turbine power plant located in the U.K. In July of the same year, the group agreed to sell Premier Power Limited, a subsidiary operating a power plant in Northern Ireland, and in September, it agreed to sell its interests in two power plants in the Philippines. As for acquisitions, the company entered into a joint venture agreement with its U.S. shale partner, EXCO Resources, Inc., to acquire certain producing assets in the Appalachian region in May 2010.

9) Russia, Brazil and West Africa Play Increasingly Important Roles in Oil and Gas/Israel Develops Major Gas Fields

OPEC (the Organization of Petroleum Exporting Countries) nations are slowly losing some of their dominance in oil production, as output of crude oil in Russia, Brazil and Africa has become very significant. Russia's crude output reached a record estimated 9.97 million barrels daily in August 2009 (following a downturn in 2008 during which output fell for the first time in a decade)—making Russia a powerhouse in crude production on a level similar to Saudi Arabia. Production costs remain relatively low in many Russian fields.

Russia holds among the world's largest reserves of conventional oil and natural gas. Geographically speaking, Russia is perfectly located to feed increasing demand in China for oil and gas and quite capable of supplying Japan, which has no major petroleum sources of its own. Meanwhile, Russia is a vital supplier of natural gas to European nations, via an extensive network of pipelines. At one time, Western companies were clamoring to cooperate with their Russian peers in exploration and in constructing vast new pipelines to deliver Russian oil and gas to thirsty markets. However, in 2006 the Russian government became much less accommodating to the investment interests of foreign oil firms, and forced some companies out of their positions in major Russian projects. As of late 2010, this was still the case, with state-run Rosneft leading the pack. It remains to be seen whether Russian energy development will become largely a local effort or an effort of global cooperation.

The west coast of Africa is another of the world's petroleum wildcards. Wells offshore Nigeria and Angola are already spouting immense quantities of oil and gas. New activity is promising offshore Senegal, the Ivory Coast, Equatorial Guinea, Ghana, Gabon and Namibia. Deepwater wells are also being drilled off South Africa. Eventually, deepwater tracts offshore of Africa will account for a significant portion of the world's oil production, primarily in Libya, Nigeria, Algeria and Angola. This can be good news for the Unites States for two reasons. First, major American oil firms have been able to invest in African exploration and production in a big way. Second, that production is finding its way to American consumers—a large and rapidly growing portion of U.S. oil imports are flowing from this part of Africa. Europe is also benefitting from this nearby production.

By 2009, Africa was producing 9.7 million barrels daily (compared to its 2007 record high of 10.2 million barrels per day). Nigeria alone produces about 2.1 million barrels of oil daily. Its output is highly desirable light crude that is low in sulfur content. Unfortunately, Nigeria's politics are in a volatile state, with rebel troops often fighting the government for control. Nigeria was the biggest oil producer in Africa in 2009, producing 2.06 million barrels per day, followed by Algeria at 1.81 million, Angola at 1.78 million and Libya at 1.65 million.

Off the African coast, companies like ExxonMobil, Royal Dutch/Shell and Chevron are drilling deep, technologically advanced wells. Total depth of new wells is frequently in the 12,000- to 15,000-foot range, including 4,000 to 6,000 feet of water. Oil corporation Total has signed important agreements to operate offshore of Nigeria.

Many of the world's poorest countries are in Africa, and they have an opportunity to benefit hugely from this new oil production, in both royalties and fees earned by their governments and in jobs created for their people. However, there is great concern that newfound wealth will be misused.

Consequently, major oil firms and agencies such as the World Bank and the United Nations are cooperating in unique ways in an attempt to ensure that the billions of dollars of economic activity to be created will clearly benefit local populations. For example, the São Tomé measure, which was signed into law in 2004 by an island nation off the east coast of Africa, requires transparent accounting of oil revenue and creates an investment fund that will kick in when the oil is tapped out. Meanwhile, political strife in Nigeria and other oil-producing African nations can lead to production interruptions and may cause foreign firms to think twice about further investments here.

Meanwhile, Brazil has become a major contender in oil production. Already a global leader in the production and use of ethanol (for fuel in cars and trucks), Brazil has proven to have immense oil reserves offshore in deep water. While the potential for production is excellent, costs of producing from Brazil's offshore fields is very high. This cost structure will create long-term challenges. By 2009, Brazil was producing 2.02 million barrels of oil per day, compared to Venezuela's 2.43 million.

Mammoth new oil and gas fields hold promise in many parts of the world. For example, from the fall of 2007 through the spring of 2008, Petrobras, Brazil's government-controlled oil company, announced the discovery of three mega-giant oilfields offshore, including a major gas deposit named Jupiter, off the coast of the state of Rio de Janeiro, and an immense new oil discovery about 155 miles offshore of the state of Sao Paulo in the Santos Basin. This is close to the major offshore find known as Tupi, which was discovered in 2006 in the Santos Basin. Combined, these finds turned Brazil into an offshore oil and gas giant almost overnight. Tupi ranked as the world's largest find since 2000 and the biggest in the Western Hemisphere in 30 years. The Santos Basin is a vast area in very deep water. There, oil reservoirs lie under a thick layer of salt, which creates technical challenges due to heat, pressure and potential movement of the salt structure. Tupi may hold between 5 billion and 8 billion barrels of oil, and the latest Santos Basin discovery may hold as much as 33 billion barrels. Drilling a single well in the Santos Basin requires an investment of about $250 million. These wells have an average depth of about 22,000 feet, including 7,000 feet of water. Under the water is the 6,500-foot-thick, corrosive layer of salt. When a drill bit finally penetrates the salt, it can access a pool of oil estimated to run from 250 to 400 feet thick. The total Santos Basin covers about 1,000 square miles. The exploration and production challenges here are similar to those faced on a regular basis in the Gulf of Mexico. Oil and gas fields in Brazil are so promising that Petrobras has set a stunning $224 billion investment budget for the 2010-2014 period.

As a nation, Brazil was a net importer of oil until recent years, which led it to be a successful pioneer in the commercialization of ethanol, made on a very cost-effective basis from local sugar cane. Now, Brazil has leased up many of the world's rigs that are capable of deep water operation. Petrobras is among the world's largest producers of oil drilled in waters deeper than 1,000 feet. According to consultant PFC Energy, Petrobras pumped 20% of all deep water oil in 2009. Brazil could easily become one of the world's leading oil exporters, if it can manage exploration and production costs effectively.

Seismic surveys of the Leviathan prospect, located about 84 miles offshore of the northern coast of Israel, may hold 16 trillion cubic feet of natural gas, making it one of the world's most promising offshore fields. Should the surveys prove true (analysts estimate a 50% chance of success), the find would position Israel as an exporter of natural gas for the first time, in addition to supplying the country's domestic needs for 100 years. Noble Energy, Inc. of Texas is leading the drilling activity there. Leviathan lies next to the Tamar, a field discovered in 2009 which has the potential of holding 8 trillion cubic feet of gas.

10) Companies Use New Technologies for Enhanced Oil and Gas Recovery

Even as demand decreased during the global economic recession of 2008-2009, oil companies continued to look for ways to expand their production capabilities. The problem is that extraction and development costs can be extremely high. The direct cost of extraction (sometimes referred to as "lifting costs") varies widely around the world's oil fields. For example, Pemex in Mexico was spending $4.30 per barrel in 2006, which rose to $10.60 per barrel by mid-2010. "Finding Costs" are a separate expense. This represents the cost of exploring for and developing fields prior to production.

Today, sophisticated methods are used to enhance and prolong oil field production. However, such methods can be expensive. "Tertiary recovery" methods may include the injection of CO_2, steam injection, or the use of special chemicals. Other recovery stages are defined as "primary recovery," which is a field that flows normally with little additional effort, and "secondary recovery," a term which often is used to describe enhanced recovery via waterflooding.

By the 1970s, drillers began mixing water with carbon dioxide (CO_2) and injecting it into wells. The CO_2 dissolves in oil and causes it to expand, making it easier to force out of the ground. It also makes oil less viscous and easier to pump. Houston-based oil pipeline company Kinder Morgan, Inc. has used the process with remarkable success. The firm acquired an oil field in Texas' long-established Permian Basin in 2000. Production in the field had dropped to 8,500 barrels per day. With the use of CO_2, Kinder Morgan produced as much as 31,000 barrels per day from that field.

Likewise, Anadarko is investing $684 million for long-term operations at its Salt Creek oil field in Casper, Wyoming. CO_2 injection was predicted to boost Salt Creek's production from about 5,000 barrels per day to 30,000 barrels by 2010.

A related technology, called MEOR (microbial enhanced oil recovery), creates microbes that biologically generate CO_2 and chemicals with cleaning agents that help flush oil out of rock. It is hoped that the microbes, which multiply very quickly, will penetrate into rock and naturally transform heavy oil into easily obtained sweet crude. The U.S. Department of Energy is funding a number of MEOR research products. MEOR is already used to treat heavy oil deposits in Venezuela, China, Indonesia and the U.S.

Another new technology is the use of steam injection which heats rock and thins viscous liquids including crude oil. Steam injection is expensive, so geologists are using sensors to detect temperatures far below ground at likely drilling sites. The sensors detect where the steam is most needed, saving drilling effort and costs with better targeting. Chevron is using the technology to pump more oil from its prolific Kern River field in southern California. The company drilled 660 observation wells equipped with the sensors in 2009, and Chevron officials believe the process has saved the firm $300 million in drilling costs while prolonging the life of the field. While most fields drilled around the world often yield about 30% of the oil contained there, Chevron hopes to tap 80% of Kern River's oil.

Yet another sensor technology assisting geologists and producers utilizes tiny carbon clusters called nanoreporters. Roughly 30,000 times smaller than a human hair, the nanoclusters react to the temperature, pressure and other factors in the rock, soil and liquid around them. By injecting nanoreporters into potential drilling sites and measuring their chemical changes, geologists may have better indications of where to drill. Research on the technology is currently underway at Rice University, funded by Marathon Oil, ConocoPhillips, Royal Dutch Shell and BP. Researchers at Rice hoped to begin field tests in 2010.

However, one of the most important developments in exploration is the horizontal well. Today's drillers are able to literally bend the drilling effort so that it branches out horizontally from the rig. This means that one rig can be used to create many horizontal holes around it. This also means that fields can be made commercially productive that we unusable before. For example, in the extremely productive Barnett Shale in Texas, much of the drilling activity has been within the urban Fort Worth area. Horizontal drilling has enabled producers to drill under houses, under commercial buildings and under streets to open up large areas of shale filled with gas. Horizontal wells are also used both onshore and offshore for oil production in a very cost-effective manner.

As of November 2010, 3,165 drilling rigs were active worldwide, up significantly from the previous year's total of 2,271. Of that count, 1,668 were in the U.S., up from 1,044 a year earlier, due to growing activity in drilling for both oil and gas in shale. These numbers are from oil field services giant Baker Hughes.

Exploration and production expenses skyrocketed from 2003 through mid-2008, due to increased demand for everything from steel pipe to oil-drilling services to transportation infrastructure. Higher oil prices led to higher drilling activity and higher fees by oil field services firms. This type of boom always leads to shortages of rigs, workers and materials. Deepwater drilling ships were in particularly short supply. When oil plummeted from about $145 per barrel to less than $70 in the fall of 2008, drilling prospects changed considerably for some firms, depending on the nature of the field being explored and the long-term vision of the company investing in the wells.

For example, Canadian tar sands production costs had risen so quickly and so high by 2008 that it was difficult to make a profit when market prices fell below $70 per barrel. In the fall of 2008, Royal Dutch Shell announced that it would postpone a major expansion of its tar sands activity, hoping that facilities development costs will drop in the mid-term due to lowering demand. Extremely deep offshore wells face the same dilemma, where observers believe that market prices of $80 or more per barrel are required to make some fields profitable.

A major firm, Marathon Oil, announced that it would reduce capital investment by about 15% for 2009. However, other majors, such as ExxonMobil, plan to continue with their investment programs. ExxonMobil invested $27.1 billion in capital projects during 2009 and planned $28 billion for 2010. Such firms have long-term investment programs that have been underway or in planning stages for years.

Some small to mid-size production companies recently had been aggressively drilling based on an assumption that prices would remain above $100. More than a few were in financial trouble when prices per barrel dropped. On the other hand, major oil companies on the scale of ExxonMobil and BP have much deeper pockets and long-term investment strategies. These giant companies have long experienced rapid ups and downs in market prices, and they are investing for the long-haul. The major companies will likely take advantage of their deep pockets to acquire smaller firms that are in debt. Oil isn't the only market to swing drastically. Prices for natural gas dropped in 2008 through much of 2009. This means that companies that had been drilling aggressively on the assumption that gas prices would remain high have been forced to put on the brakes.

11) Advances in Technology Lead to New Gains in Exploration and Production/Electromagnetic Technology Looks Promising

In the same way that the InfoTech revolution has increased productivity everywhere from the factory floor to the supermarket to the business office, leading-edge technology is shaking up the energy industry. Both onshore and offshore, the use of advanced seismic technologies and horizontal drilling with pinpoint accuracy are drastically improving drilling results. Offshore, subsea templates that allow both drilling and production of dozens of wells, as much as 15 miles apart, from one underwater structure provide finding and lifting efficiencies undreamed of a few years ago. Pipeline and transport systems are advancing at the same time. For example, it is now common to deliver oil from a subsea well straight to a pipeline system without ever bringing it to the ocean's surface.

Geophysicists are using high-powered computer workstations to analyze seismic data in three-dimensional, color-coded views that show oil- and gas-producing structures never seen before. Drilling success rates are up substantially. An enhanced 4-D system adds the dimension of time to geologists' seismic view of evolving underground formations. Exploration companies utilizing 3-D and 4-D seismic data typically find productive wells more than 70% of the time, compared to 40% with conventional methods.

Many of these technologies, however, are only refinements of techniques that were discovered many years ago. One very promising technology uses electromagnetic waves (instead of sound) to map features of the earth far below the surface. Instead of mapping density and solidity, as sound does, electromagnetic waves map resistance to electricity. Because oil has a fairly unique electromagnetic signature, maps made with these waves can be incredibly accurate. Electromagnetic exploration is currently in a period of rapid commercialization. This technology works well in salt water, so it is appearing in deep-sea explorations. However, some firms are performing airborne electromagnetic surveys aboard aircraft. ExxonMobil is one of the first innovators of this technology, calling it Remote Reservoir Resistivity Mapping, or R3M. Another, much smaller company, ElectroMagnetic GeoServices AS (www.emgs.com), has developed its own version of electromagnetic exploration called marine EM that promises to make this new field very competitive. The Norway-based firm was awarded a $2 million contract in late 2010 to conduct logging service for an underwater area on the Filipino shelf for Shell Philippines Exploration.

12) Extension of Offshore Drilling into Extreme Water Depths Continues/Deepwater Horizon Accident Impacts Gulf Drilling

Since the first offshore well was drilled in shallow water 10 miles off the Louisiana coastline in 1947, offshore oil and gas production has been of rapidly growing importance in the U.S. and many other nations worldwide. Today, the average oil well in the Gulf of Mexico flows over 30,000 barrels of oil daily—100 times the rate of flow of an average onshore U.S. well. Newer, extremely deep-water wells flow at even greater rates. The U.S. Energy Information Administration projected that about 14% of crude oil production in the lower 48 states in 2010 would come from four deepwater wells in the Gulf of Mexico. The Gulf of Mexico already produces from approximately 4,000 American platforms. According to the U.S. Minerals Management Service, 1.88 million barrels of oil per day will be produced there in 2013, compared to 1.14 million barrels per day in 2008. On a global basis, deepwater fields provided

7.8% of the world's supply of oil in 2010, up from 2.2% in 2000, according to Deutsche Bank.

In the aftermath of the explosion of BP's Deepwater Horizon well in the Gulf of Mexico, the Obama Administration placed a moratorium on deepwater drilling off the U.S. coast that lasted for several months. The federal government also placed stringent new requirements on offshore drillers. The result has been a significant slowdown in exploration. A number of industry analysts believe that Brazil hired deepwater rigs away from the U.S. Gulf during the uncertainty. Since there are only a limited number of sophisticated rigs capable of operating in extremely deep water, this could be a serious setback for the U.S.

For example, Royal Dutch Shell, one of the biggest producers of oil and gas in the Gulf, states that its Gulf of Mexico production for the first nine months of 2010 was 230,000 barrels of oil equivalent daily; 10,000 barrels a day lower than it would have been without the moratorium, according to the firm's management. That's a loss of $70,000 per day worth of production. The firm further stated in late 2010 that it was expecting 220,000 average daily production in the Gulf for 2011, 40,000 barrels below previous forecasts, due to the moratorium, and that 2012 could be even worse.

Mars, a floating platform off the coast of Louisiana, is one of the major production sites in the Gulf. (Production is from up to 24 wells that are attached to the platform for gathering purposes and maintenance.) It was jointly developed by Shell (71.5%) and BP Amoco (28.5%). Shell Deepwater Production, Inc. is the operator. Mars is an excellent example of modern offshore technology. It utilizes a Tension Leg Platform (TLP) that weighs about 36,500 tons. The platform is over 3,250 feet tall from the seabed to the top of the drilling rig. It is designed to stand up to hurricane force winds of 140 mph or more, and waves of 70 feet. Over 100 workers can live onboard at any one time, coming and going via helicopter, while supply ships keep a stream of necessary materials on hand. Oil production is sent via an underwater pipeline to Louisiana in a 116 mile trip. Gas production is sent 55 miles to a separate facility. Mars is so big that it represented about 5% of all U.S. Gulf of Mexico production when Hurricane Katrina slammed into it in 2005. The hurricane caused extensive damage topside; aerial photos of Mars showed something that looked like a giant collapsed factory, with broken cranes and a collapsed rig tower. Shell quickly repaired Mars, improved the platform's safety precautions and restored production ahead of schedule.

Historically, it took one very deep water project to set off today's drilling activity. The former Coastal Corporation (later acquired by El Paso Corporation) was one of the first to attempt an extreme-depth offshore well. The steel pipe used to perform the drilling collapsed at 16,000 feet, since pressure on offshore equipment increases dramatically with every 1,000 feet of depth. The company developed new technology and shortly thereafter drilled a second well to a depth of 18,400 feet. Extremely high rates of production from this well encouraged other firms to drill deep.

Technological advances have further extended possible well depths to six miles. One example of these wells is the Tonga #1 well in the Gulf of Mexico. Completed in December 2003 by Schlumberger and ChevronTexaco, the well reaches an astounding depth of 31,825 feet, or slightly less than six miles. Another well, Unocal's St. Malo, found oil by drilling through water and rock to a depth of 35,966 feet. The latest record as of 2008 is ExxonMobil's 39,222 foot well at the Sakhalin-1 oil project near an island off eastern Russia, seven miles offshore.

In 2009, BP announced a new discovery in its Tiber prospect about 200 miles offshore of the Louisiana coast. Estimated to hold 3 billion barrels of oil, Tiber lies beneath almost two miles (10,560 feet) of water. Tiber is one of at least 12 recent discoveries in the Gulf of Mexico at extreme depths made possible by advances in deepwater drilling technology. In early 2010, yet another new discovery, this one by Royal Dutch Shell, was made below 7,217 feet of water. Located off the Mississippi coast, the find may hold more than 100 million barrels of oil.

Deep water hubs for natural gas are also reaching new depths. For example, the Independence Hub off the coast of Louisiana in the Gulf of Mexico, regulates gas flow from wells on the Gulf floor, two miles below. Attached to the wells by cables called umbilicals, the hub sends data, electricity and chemicals such as antifreeze to keep droplets of water from freezing and slowing the flow of natural gas to the wells below. The wells are capped by heads that regulate flow and pressure. Flow lines transport gas from the wells back to the hub for transmission via the Independence Trail pipeline to the mainland. Ten different gas fields feed the Independence Hub, collectively extracting 1 billion cubic feet of natural gas per day.

The April 2010 explosion of BP's Deepwater Horizon floating rig caused the deaths of 11 people and approximately 4.9 million barrels of oil to leak into the Gulf of Mexico. The devastating accident resulted in the Obama Administration's imposition of a six-month ban on drilling in water deeper than 500 feet. Those six months cost an estimated 23,000 jobs as rigs were shut down and support services idled. As the ban came to an end in October 2010, there was still a question of permitting to be decided.

New legislation regarding offshore drilling requires stricter environmental reviews, greater federal involvement in rig operations and drilling company CEOs to personally certify compliance. Oil and gas companies must also hire outside auditors to certify the reliability of blowout preventers. The preventers must be equipped with two sets of blind shear rams, which are pincer-like clamps that cut through drill pipe to shut off the flow of oil. As of late 2010, only 16 of the 33 floating rigs in the Gulf of Mexico were equipped with these kinds of preventers. Refitting or replacing them will be expensive and some rig platforms are not large enough to hold them.

In addition to upgrading equipment, drilling companies must have a cleanup plan ready in the event of another disaster. To that end, Exxon Mobil Corp., Chevron Corp., Royal Dutch Shell PLC and ConocoPhillips announced a $1 billion joint venture to create a rapid-response system capable of containing up to 100,000 barrels per day (the Deepwater Horizon spilled up to 60,000 barrels per day). The nonprofit venture, to be called the Marine Well Containment Co., and will be available to any drilling company with the assets to afford the billions necessary to pay for use of the system and the crews necessary to man it. Exxon estimates the system could be ready by 2012.

Prior to the Deepwater Horizon debacle, a shortage of rigs capable of drilling at such extreme depths was a serious problem. Entering into a long-term contract for a rig was extremely difficult and costly. Because of the shortage, rental rates had been prohibitive, and waiting times were lengthy. As of mid-2009, drilling costs for deepwater rigs in the Gulf of Mexico reached approximately $500,000 to $600,000 per day, compared to $150,000 per day in 2002. More rigs are being constructed and entering the market, but many of them are already under contract for several years of drilling. Today, post Deepwater Horizon, new rigs more easily pass stringent safety requirements, which is the good news. The bad news is that permitting issues may make existing wells slow to restart and new wells difficult to begin. Some drilling companies have expressed concern that the U.S. lost a number of existing rigs during the federal ban to wells off the coast of Brazil.

In total, offshore reserves near America's Atlantic, Pacific and Gulf Coasts might reach 86 billion barrels or more, if widespread exploration was allowed. Meanwhile, watch for extensive, extremely deep exploration in other parts of the world, including offshore Brazil, the west coast of Africa, parts of Asia and the Arctic Circle, to capitalize on the technology developed for use in the Gulf of Mexico.

Petrobras, Brazil's state-controlled oil company, is building its first floating production, storage and offloading facility in the Gulf of Mexico. Called an FPSO, these facilities resemble oil tankers in appearance and have been in use for a number of years in other parts of the world including the North Sea, the North Atlantic, the Mediterranean and the Indian Ocean. Each FPSO can process up to 150,000 barrels of oil per day and 6 million cubic meters of gas per day. The Petrobras vessel was built in Singapore and arrived in the Gulf in early 2010 where it serves the Cascade and Chinook fields. In late 2010, Petrobras and several partner companies signed contracts worth $3.46 billion with Engevix Engenharia SA, a Brazilian shipbuilder. The contract is for the construction of eight FPSO hulls for delivery between 2013 and 2015.

In addition to the challenges posed by deep water activity, which cover everything from shifting pressure zones, extreme temperatures and drills required to pass quickly from water to sand to rock, oil and gas companies face the scarcity of deep water drilling rigs. The September 2010 international offshore rig count was 317, up 43 from the 274 counted in September 2009. (Most of the offshore rigs are not capable of working in extreme depths.) Natural gas activity in the South China Sea and off Malaysia, Indonesia and Vietnam will further stress the demand for equipment and know-how.

13) OPEC Continues to Have Major Influence

Several mitigating circumstances deeply influence the day-to-day market prices of oil and natural gas. Among them are weather; economic crises, such as the depression that occurred in most Asian nations starting in August 1997 (leading to a dramatic drop in demand for oil in those nations); political events, such as the 1978 revolution in Iran (which led to the overthrow of the Shah and caused that nation to cut oil exports by 75%), or embargoes such as one that limited oil exports from Iraq after the Persian Gulf War of 1990; and disruptions in the supply system, such as hurricanes, fires, wars, terrorism or other disasters that temporarily shut down major production areas. Since oil is priced in U.S. dollars per barrel on international markets, changes in the value of the dollar relative to other currencies also have a significant role in pricing. The global economic crisis of 2008-09 had profound effects on oil and natural gas prices, as a significant slowdown in global economic activity lowered both demand and prices for oil.

Through the years, day-to-day market trends in oil prices will always be influenced by economic growth or decline among oil-consuming nations, oil field production and discovery, political risks and the effectiveness of the OPEC cartel in controlling a significant portion of the world's oil supply. OPEC (the Organization of Petroleum Exporting Countries) was created in 1960 when several major oil-producing nations banded together, eventually wresting control of their oil production away from foreign oil companies in a highly effective effort to increase their national incomes. (Ecuador, one of the largest producers in South America, had dropped out at one time but rejoined in 2007. Indonesia dropped out in 2008 because of the high cost of membership dues.) The organization evolved into a true cartel, attempting to control prices by adding or withdrawing oil from the market by restricting the production allowed for each member nation. In reality, the production and reserves of one nation, Saudi Arabia, are so vast and such a significant market factor that OPEC has relied on the Saudis to follow the production rules while many other members have cheated, far exceeding their stated production quotas.

OPEC has not always been effective. Historically, frequent breakdowns in discipline within OPEC have led to a collapse of oil prices. The cartel's success in controlling prices has been largely hit-or-miss, and OPEC member nations watched helplessly as prices fell in 1997. By 1998, plummeting oil prices devastated the economy of Saudi Arabia, as that nation's economic output shrank by 2% and its budget deficits soared to nearly 10% of GDP. (The damage created by low oil prices was not at all limited to OPEC members. The after-tax profits of the six leading U.S. oil companies fell by 90% during the fourth quarter of 1998 compared to the same period the previous year.) Clearly, OPEC was in a bind, and its production controls and political wrangling were ineffective. The price of oil per barrel of Arab light crude sank to the $10 range by the beginning of 1999, after holding in the $40s during parts of the late 1970s and early 1980s, and ranging from about $17 to $21 from the mid-1980s through 1996.

OPEC Member Countries	
Algeria	Libya
Angola	Nigeria
Ecuador	Qatar
Iran	Saudi Arabia
Iraq	United Arab Emirates
Kuwait	Venezuela

While OPEC has enjoyed various levels of success and failure in its lengthy history, current market trends show that the organization has become more effective. In the early 2000s, even during a global economic slowdown, it managed to manipulate supply effectively to help in keeping market prices high. The Energy Intelligence Agency (EIA) reported OPEC's net export revenues of $571 billion in 2009. For 2010 and 2011, the EIA forecast earnings of $748 billion and $840 billion respectively. Nigeria's earnings especially were at risk as of late 2009 due to political unrest and repeated attacks on oil installations in the Niger Delta. Today, OPEC is a difficult partnership among nations with various agendas and political perspectives.

In late 2008 and on into 2009, demand weakened as consumers adopted conservation efforts due to high fuel prices and a faltering economy. 2008's freefall in oil prices from historic highs spurred OPEC to cut production by 1.5 million barrels per day in late October. World consumption of oil declined slightly in early 2009, due to the global economic recession, but rebounded later in the year. The International Energy Agency projected demand to rise from an average of 84.6 million barrels per day in 2009 to 86.6 million barrels per day in 2010 and 87.9 million in 2011.

14) Energy Demand Climbs in India and China/Nuclear, Hydro and Gas Projects Grow

China is by far the fastest-growing major economy in the world. As of 2009, it surpassed the U.S. and became the world's biggest power consumer. The International Energy Agency (IEA) reported that China consumed 2.25 billion tons of oil equivalent (which represents crude oil, nuclear power, coal, natural gas and renewable sources) in

2009, or 4% more than America's 2.17 billion tons. China's consumption has grown at a staggering rate. As recently as 10 years ago, its consumption rate was only half that of the U.S.

China is industrializing and modernizing at a very rapid rate. As a result, its demand for energy is booming, due both to a rise in its industrial base and to rapidly growing middle and upper classes that are clamoring for automobiles, larger houses and other energy-guzzling items such as TVs and home computers. China's petroleum consumption in 2009 (not including Hong Kong) equaled 10.4% of total global consumption, up from 9.6% the previous year. (In comparison, U.S., consumption of oil fell by 4.9% to 18.6 million barrels daily in 2009, accounting for 21.7% of global consumption, down from 23.9% in the peak year of 2007.) China weathered the global economic recession relatively well, further increasing energy demand.

More electricity means a greater need for an infrastructure system to handle transmission and distribution. In the spring of 2010, Chinese government officials announced plans to upgrade the nation's electricity network with advanced equipment and digital technology to create a smart grid similar to that proposed in the U.S. A number of foreign companies, including General Electric, Siemens and LS Industrial Systems, are vying for lucrative contracts. They, along with State Grid Corp. of China, are focusing their efforts in the city of Yangzhou, where a smart grid demonstration facility has already been built. Analysts estimate that China will spend between $60 billion and $100 billion on the project over the next decade.

China has a modest amount of oil production of its own, including its largest area, the 40-year-old Daqing Field, where production has fallen since its peak in 1997. By 1993, China's rapid industrial growth forced it to become a net importer of oil, and it now depends highly on foreign oil. In late 2009, ExxonMobil completed construction in China of a $4.5 billion refinery and petrochemical plant, one of the largest facilities in the firm's global operations.

Today, much of China's oil imports come from the Middle East. Like many other nations, it is working hard to improve its oil security and move away from reliance on OPEC. As a result, China is investing heavily in oil fields and projects from South America to Indonesia to Kazakhstan to Russia. China National Offshore Oil Corp. International Limited (CNOOC), for example, has properties in production or under development in Indonesia, Australia and Nigeria.

China is also importing heavily from Canada and investing in Canadian ventures. Trade between the two countries doubled from 2000 through 2006. China's state-controlled CNOOC owns 17% of Canadian oil sands company MEG Energy. Meanwhile, in August 2009, the Chinese entered into one of the largest contracts in the history of the energy business by agreeing to purchase $41 billion in LNG over an extended period of time, to be produced at an ExxonMobil project in Australia.

By 2009 China had become the world's largest automobile market, surpassing the U.S. in terms of units purchased each year. China's government is trying to head off growing automobile pollution and gasoline consumption problems. It has imposed strict new mileage standards for automobiles, stricter than those in place in the U.S. Electric vehicles may quickly become popular in China, thanks in part to the growing success of BYD Company Ltd., a Chinese battery and automobile manufacturer that is partly owned by America's Berkshire Hathaway, which is led by respected investor Warren Buffett. Now is definitely the time to plan ahead for China's energy future and lay the groundwork for widespread alternative and renewable power sources, as the country continues to rapidly grow its economy. The Chinese government has called for 15% of all its energy needs to be supplied by renewable sources by 2020, up from about 7.5% in 2007. It remains to be seen whether it can meet this goal. However, it is building large numbers of wind turbine and solar plants.

Also, one of China's prime renewable sources is hydroelectric power. Already one of the world's largest producers of such power, China plans to triple its output by 2020, to 300 gigawatts, taking advantage of massive rivers that flow through the center of the nation. China is also investing heavily in solar, wind and biomass projects. It is home to companies that are highly competitive in the manufacture and installation of solar and wind power systems. The country doubled its total wind energy capacity between 2005 and 2009.

China's economic development has been more rapid than India's. Its reliance on manufacturing industries creates large and rapidly growing demands on electric production. In addition, its population is about 300 million larger than India's. As of late 2010, China had 12 nuclear reactors in operation and at least 24 under construction, with many more on the drawing board. The goal is to increase nuclear power generation capacity from 8.7 million kilowatts to 40 million kilowatts by 2020. A host of international energy and construction companies are involved in Chinese projects, including Westinghouse and General Electric.

Meanwhile, China relies very heavily on coal for generation. Unfortunately, its coal-fired plants are very heavy polluters, adding to China's already great dilemma with industrial pollution. Adoption of clean coal technologies, such as relatively easy to install scrubbers, would be an immense help. As of 2009, as much as 80% of China's electricity was supplied by domestic coal. China holds massive coal reserves. While this is good news for China's economy, it's very harmful to the environment. China's burning of coal is one of the world's largest sources of carbon dioxide emissions.

Several initiatives are in place to partner Chinese coal mines with international energy companies to create synthetic gas from coal. Royal Dutch Shell and South Africa's Sasol are working on projects with China's Shenhua Group that were planned for completion in 2012. Shenhua Group also completed a $1.5 billion coal-to-oil facility in 2008, which can convert coal into as much as 22,000 barrels of crude-oil-type fuel per day. Moreover, Shenhua Group is part of a consortium of power and coal companies called GreenGen, which plans to build an even cleaner-burning integrated gasification combined cycle (IGCC) plant that will include carbon capture and storage technology by 2015.

However, energy demands are so great that the nation forged ahead with the construction or expansion of relatively low-tech coal-fired power plants, increasing its carbon emissions and further adding to pollution problems in the past decade. Not all the newly constructed plants are low-tech. The Chinese are also rapidly building more efficient coal plants that use steam heated to extreme temperatures. The most efficient new plants convert up to 44% of the energy in coal into electricity. The most efficient plants in the U.S. achieve only 40% efficiency because the steam temperatures are kept at a lower level. China's commitment to building more plants with high-specification emission control systems, despite the higher cost, is making it one of the world's top markets for advanced coal-fired plants, according to the IEA.

China and the U.S. combined already account for about 40% of the world's greenhouse gas emissions. Under current practices, China's emissions could grow to twice those of the United States by 2030, according to IEA estimates. The same source estimates that overall energy efficiency is so low in China that it consumes about three times the U.S. level of BTUs per dollar of economic output as of 2009.

India's federal government promised electrical access to all Indians by 2012, which may be an optimistic goal. The government is seeking private sector investment and promoting competition for lucrative power plant contracts. The government is actively promoting construction of coal-fired plants, nuclear plants and renewable energy.

India has long been plagued by power shortages. In fiscal 2006, the power supply deficit exceeded 12.8% of peak demand, according to the Indian Ministry of Power. Recently, about 50% of the population was without any kind of reliable electricity.

Indian power utility Reliance Energy Ltd. announced an $11-billion coal-based power plant in the state of Orissa. (India is one of the world's major coal producers.) Another project, a $2.53-billion, 3,500 megawatt natural gas plant in the state of Uttar Pradesh, has also been announced. It would capitalize on the 2002 discovery of sizeable deposits of natural gas off India's east coast. Both of these plants would be among the largest of their types in the world.

A primary focus for India's development will be nuclear power generation. The U.S.-India Nuclear Energy Accord, passed by the U.S. Congress in late 2006, affords India access to U.S. civil nuclear technology. India has a stated goal of producing 20,000 megawatts of nuclear power by 2020. In September 2008, India signed an agreement similar to the U.S.-India Accord with France, opening the door for industry leader AREVA Group. India's lower and upper houses of parliament both passed a civilian nuclear bill in late 2010 which is expected to green light the agreement into operation. As of 2010, India had 19 nuclear power reactors in operation, according to the World Nuclear Association. Meanwhile, two Russian firms are helping to build a new Indian reactor. Contracts have already been signed for four new Westinghouse advanced-technology nuclear reactors, and several more nuclear plants will likely follow. In addition to the construction of new power plants, infrastructure such as transmission lines must be modernized.

Analysts at BP estimate that India accounted for 4.2% of the world's primary energy consumption, while China at 19.5% equaled the level of the U.S., also at 19.5% (2009 numbers). Continued economic growth in China recently pushed its consumption past that of the U.S., while the growth rate of India was likewise expected to boost its consumption steadily.

15) Canada's Oil Sands Production Reaches 1.49 Million Barrels per Day, But Operating Costs Are High

The oil sands (also referred to as "tar sands") found in Canada, Venezuela and other locations throughout the world were historically regarded as unrecoverable assets by many members of the energy industry. However, through a combination of decades of work, starting in the 1970s, and a rise in oil prices, the process of turning oil sands into crude oil has become a viable business. According to the EIA, Canada is the largest exporter of oil to the U.S. (providing 22% of total imports). Including tar sands, it has 179 billion barrels of oil and gas reserves, ranking second in the world behind Saudi Arabia.

In the Athabasca field in the province of Alberta, Canada (due north of Montana on the U.S./Canada border), immense cranes wield vast scoops of oil sands. These scoops dump the sands into monstrous trucks nearly as tall as three-story buildings. The trucks burn 50 gallons of diesel per hour as they lumber along, each hauling 360-ton loads of tar-laden soil to giant tumblers and superheated cookers. A mixture of oil and sand with the texture of tar results, which morphs into heavy crude oil. This labor-intensive work is turning the black dirt of Athabasca into one of the greatest sources of oil in the world. Additional Alberta fields are in the Peace River and Cold Lake regions. That's the good news. The bad news is that tar sands are incredibly dirty and pollution producing.

The process and the technology used in oil sands has been a long time in coming. By 2003, a collection of startups and joint ventures, including major oil company partners, managed to streamline the process of mining, transportation and processing these oil sands so that the cost of turning two tons of tar sand into a barrel of crude oil was about $25. The price of harvesting the oil sands was still high, but it became an acceptable cost to help supply the voracious energy needs of the U.S.

Unfortunately, the oil sands industry became something of a victim of its own success. Billions of dollars were poured into new facilities to mine and convert the sands to usable crude. Thousands of people were hired and moved to remote areas where workers were scarce, and housing and other services were even scarcer. Costs soared quickly, to the extent that the newest oil sands operations need lofty market values per barrel of oil in order to operate profitably.

Oil sands contain bitumen, which is a tar-like crude oil substance that can be processed and refined into a synthetic crude oil. Typically, oil sands are mined from vast open pits where deposits are softened with blasts of steam. The tar-like product that is mined from the sands is processed to yield synthetic light crude.

At oil sands mines, natural gas is often used both to run large electric generating plants and to generate steam that is used to loosen deep deposits. However, the fact that large quantities of natural gas are used creates potential problems. First, this high-volume oil sands production is beginning to use a large portion of Canada's natural gas output. Next, when natural gas prices rise significantly, oil sands production becomes less viable in economic terms. Fortunately, new technologies have the potential to greatly reduce the use of natural gas in this process.

The oil sands industry is evolving, and the introduction of new energy sources and new technologies for these plants will take many years. One solution under consideration is the construction of a small nuclear generating plant in the oil sands region. The late-2008 slump in oil prices deflated the oil sands boom, and prices for building and operating these plants declined as a result.

How much of this mineral-rich black dirt is there? In Canada alone, where most of the oil sands projects are located, there may be as much as 1 trillion barrels of oil equivalent.

Despite falling overall demand for oil in 2009 due to the global economic crisis, production from Canada's oil sands rose 14% to 1.49 million barrels per day, according to a report from the Alberta Energy Resources Conservation Board. Production is expected to reach 3.2 million barrels per day by 2019. Future production growth depends on whether oil prices remain high and environmental concerns are managed. The surprising rise in production in 2009 is largely due to a number of small companies choosing to forge ahead with new projects, taking advantage of lower development costs brought about by the recession. New production in 2009 included the Horizon Oil Sands mining venture owned by Canadian Natural Resources Ltd. and the Long Lake in situ project owned by Nexen, Inc.

The costs for developing a new oil sands operation had become so high by 2008 that market prices of at least $80 per barrel of crude could be required to justify the investment. At one time, Canadian and international energy companies were planning to invest almost $87 billion in oil sands development from 2005 through 2016. By 2008, costs had risen so steeply that even those figures were not sufficient to cover the facilities that were planned. The recession was also an obvious blow, during which 70% of proposed investment was put on hold, at least temporarily. This decrease in demand took some pressure off construction and development prices. Meanwhile, lower natural gas prices also benefitted operations. The Canadian Association of Petroleum Producers estimates that Canada's oil sands production could reach 6 million barrels daily by 2030, an amount equal to more than one-half of Saudi Arabia's current production, but growth in production will depend to a large extent on market prices along with the industry's ability to control production costs as well as environmental damage. Massive oil sands deposits also exist in Venezuela.

SPOTLIGHT: Oil Sands Operations at Suncor Energy

Suncor Energy, www.suncor.com, is a unit of Sunoco with a history of production in the Alberta, Canada oil sands since 1967. Today, it has about 6,500 employees, and a wide variety of energy activities including natural gas, wind power, ethanol production and downstream operations. For the third quarter of 2010, it estimated oil sands production at 306,600 barrels per day, compared to 305,300 barrels per day in the same quarter in 2009. Capital spending in 2009 was $4.2 billion, following $8.0 billion in 2008. For 2010, the firm has a $5.5 billion capital spending plan, with $1.5 billion earmarked for growth in its oil sands operations.

Long term, the firm plans a $20.6 billion expansion to oil sands capacity, in a project called "Voyageur." When fully implemented, the Voyageur project will give Suncor an oil sands capacity of 550,000 barrels per day. In early 2009, Suncor acquired Petro-Canada. This will add significant new businesses to Suncor, including retailing, refining and conventional oil production.

16) Oil Shale Technologies Draw New Investment

While the U.S. has much smaller oil sands deposits than those of Canada, it is rich in a different unconventional oil formation: oil shale. Oil shale is a rock formation containing the oil precursor kerogen, which can be processed into synthetic oil of very high quality, similar to sweet crude. Oil shale yields between 15 and 50 gallons of oil per ton of rock. Vast reserves are in the Green River Formation in the Western U.S., including parts of Colorado, Wyoming and Utah. The state of Ohio also contains large reserves. Oil shale poses huge implications for American consumption and for the world's energy industry as a whole. For example, an area known as the Bakken Formation in North Dakota and Montana was estimated to hold between 3 billion and 4.3 billion barrels of oil by the United States Geological Survey. While oil shale deposits can be found outside the U.S., including in China, the American deposits are of gargantuan size. By some estimates, U.S. shale may hold an astonishing 2 trillion barrels of oil equivalent.

During the 1970s, after the oil embargo crisis, the federal government strongly encouraged both energy conservation and alternative production. In 1979, it established the U.S. Synthetic Fuels Corp., endowing it with billions of dollars for research and development of new fuels. As a result, major oil companies attempted to commercialize oil shale, but those efforts were largely abandoned by the 1980s as oil prices fell. There were also concerns about environmental damage from shale mining, and there were many technical hurdles to face. Commercial production seemed impossible. By 1985, Congress killed the Synthetic Fuels Corp.

Today, producing oil from shale remains a major challenge, but the immense oil needs of Americans combined with fluctuating prices for petroleum means that oil shale will receive a new look by the industry. As long as the price of crude oil remains above $40, oil shale production may become attractive. For example, Shell Exploration & Production has a well-advanced test site in Colorado where it is attempting to perfect a technology that warms the kerogen while in the ground, by using heated rods that are sunk into layers of shale and then pumping out the resulting liquid. The system is called the In Situ Conversion Process (ICP). (See www.shell.us/home/content/usa/aboutshell/projects_locations/mahogany/technology for details.) ExxonMobil is researching similar technology called Electrofrac which cracks shale deposits with hydraulic pumps and then pours in electrolytic fluid to separate the kerogen from the rock. Shale deposits can be deep—up to hundreds of feet below the surface. Shell's technology is moving ahead rapidly, with more than 200 oil shale development patents filed, it is the firm's biggest R&D investment. Shell has even announced that it will work with the government of China to develop shale deposits there.

Other firms seek to "mine" the rock and then process the oil from the shale using high heat in furnaces. There are vast ecological problems with this method, however, as the process is very similar to strip mining.

This mining of kerogen-rich oil shale is quite different from the production of conventional oil reserves from shale formations. The recent enhancements to drilling and production for natural gas trapped in shale have led to a major boost in the production of conventional oil trapped in shale as well.

17) Coal Is Abundant/Clean Coal and Coal Gasification Technologies Have Promise

In 2009, global production of coal was 3.41 billion tons of oil equivalent, up from 3.32 billion tons in 2008, according to BP plc. While coal is an abundant resource in many parts of the world, it is generally burned in a manner that creates significant amounts of air pollution. On a global scale, coal produces more carbon dioxide than any other fossil source. "Clean coal" technologies are in the works, but such technologies are expensive and beyond the economic reach of emerging economies.

In the U.S., coal comes from several different regions. The Northern Appalachian area of the Eastern U.S. and the Illinois Basin in the Midwest produce coal that is high in sulfur, which produces more pollutants. In contrast are the enormous stores of coal in Wyoming and Montana, which burn at lower temperatures and produce less energy than high-sulfur coal, but create less pollution. In existing mines, the U.S. has about 250 billion tons of recoverable coal. Combined with coal seams outside of mines, the U.S. has 500 billion tons of recoverable coal.

According to BP, world consumption of coal was up by 46% from 1998 through 2008. The largest increases, in terms of millions of tons used, were found in large economies like China (more than doubling in that period), India (up by 76.8%), Japan (up by 36.9%), and the U.S. (up by 27.5%). However, as demand for energy fell during the global economic recession, coal consumption fell slightly from a global total of 3.286 million tons of oil equivalent in 2008 to 3.278 in 2009.

As of 2010, a number of U.S. utilities were turning away from coal in favor of less polluting fuels such as natural gas. This is due partly to stricter emissions regulations now placed on coal-burning plants. Texas-based Calpine announced plans to buy 19 power plants from Pepco Holdings, Inc. for $1.65 billion. The bulk of the plants burn natural gas, and Calpine is planning to convert its coal burning concerns in New Jersey and Delaware to gas also. North Carolina utility Progress Energy plans to close 11 coal burning plants by 2017.

High-sulfur coal is now easier to sell in some markets, since advanced filtering units called scrubbers are in use by a growing number of electric generating companies. Scrubbers are multistory facilities that are built adjacent to smokestacks. They capture sulfur as the coal exhaust billows through the smokestack and sequester it for storage before it can be cleaned. Progress Energy is spending $1 billion on the technology for three of its newer coal-burning plants, which generate enough revenue to justify the expense.

Multiple clean coal technologies are in development. For example, scientists at the University of Texas are developing a new technology that blasts sound waves into the flue ducts of coal-fired power plants. The noise, which registers at more than 150 decibels (about as loud as a jet engine at takeoff) causes tiny ash particles in the emission stream to vibrate and stick to larger ones, thereby making larger particles that are easier to capture by pollution control equipment like scrubbers.

Yet another technology to reduce emissions is the use of photosynthesis to capture exhaust gases, such as CO_2, from power plants. A company called GS CleanTech (now a part of GreenShift Corporation, www.greenshift.com) developed a CO_2 Bioreactor that converts a concentrated supply of carbon dioxide into oxygen and biomass in the form of algae, which can then be converted into fuel. Competitor GreenFuel Technologies (www.greenfuelonline.com) uses a different method of recycling carbon dioxide from flue gases, achieving the same end result: algae. An early test of GreenFuel's reactor at the Massachusetts Institute of Technology promised the removal of 75% of the carbon dioxide in the exhaust sampled. The biggest company in this field is Synthetic Genomics, www.syntheticgenomics.com, which received a massive investment from ExxonMobil.

Coal-gasification plants could become a trend for electric generation plant construction over the long term. However, costs remain a significant obstacle. Such plants use a process that first converts coal into a synthetic gas, later burning that gas to power the electric generators. The steam produced in the process is further used to generate electricity. The process is called Integrated Gasification Combined Cycle (IGCC). While these plants are much more expensive to construct than traditional coal-burning plants, they produce much less pollution. Since the coal isn't actually burnt, these plants can use lower-cost coal that is high in sulfur. In addition, such plants reduce the amount of mercury emitted from the use of coal by as much as 95%. Two existing "demonstration" plants use IGCC technology, built and operated with federal subsidies. They are located in Mulbery, Florida and West Terre Haute, Indiana. Japan has constructed a demonstration plant, the Nakoso Power Station at Iwaki City.

American Electric Power (AEP), a Columbus, Ohio electric utility, reached an agreement in late 2005 with General Electric and Bechtel to design an IGCC plant. The first such plant may eventually be built at a New Haven, West Virginia location. AEP also announced interest in building a similar plant in Ohio. GE, Siemens and Mitsubishi are among major corporations active in IGCC technology as well.

An additional step that can be added to IGCC plants is the capture or "sequestration" of carbon dioxide. The technology to do so already exists. For example, Norway's Statoil has used it for years at its natural-gas wells in the North Sea. The sequestered carbon dioxide can be pumped underground. Fortunately, carbon dioxide can be used in oil and gas wells to enhance recovery in a process known as CO_2 flooding. As of 2004, about one-half of the world's CO_2 floods were in the Permian Basin of Texas and New Mexico, according to the Department of Energy (DOE). These floods sit near large, natural reservoirs of CO_2. The DOE estimated that U.S. oil production using CO_2 flooding could multiply fourfold by 2020.

Internet Research Tip: Carbon Capture and Sequestration
For an excellent discussion of carbon capture and sequestration technologies, research and demonstration projects, see the U.S. Department of Energy's web site for the NETL (National Energy Technology Laboratory) www.netl.doe.gov/technologies/carbon_seq/index.html.

South African fuel company Sasol Ltd. has had success in making liquid fuel from coal that powers gasoline, diesel and jet engines. The Nazi party first used the technology, which is called Fischer-Tropsch after the German scientists who developed it, during World War II. In the decades since then, the technology has been refined and improved to the point that Sasol provides 28% of South Africa's fuel needs and is expanding with gas-to-liquids plants in Qatar and Nigeria.

While clean coal technologies, such as carbon capture and sequestration, are viable alternatives to traditional coal use, multiple challenges remain, particularly in terms of the cost of equipment and operation. Dallas, Texas-based utility company TXU planned to build 11 coal-burning plants in Texas by 2011 hoping to avoid costly restrictions on coal plant emissions and/or enjoy "allowances" due to the fact that the plants are to be built before the restrictions take effect. However, in 2007, eight of the 11 plants were scrapped when private investors acquired TXU for $45 billion. The reason? Traditional plants emit too much carbon dioxide and clean coal technology is too expensive.

In the U.S., recent federal stimulus funding includes money for carbon capture and sequestration research and demonstration. FutureGen Alliance, www.futuregenalliance.org, a project involving a utilities consortium funded by subsidies from the U.S. government, hopes to build a plant in Mattoon, Illinois to test cutting-edge techniques for converting coal to gas, capturing and storing pollutants and burning gas for power. Originally endorsed by President Bush, the project lost its government support in early 2008 when estimated costs almost doubled to $1.8 billion. By late 2008, efforts were being made to save the project in the U.S. Senate. In June 2009, the Obama administration's new Secretary of Energy indicated support for the project, subject to further review. By late 2010, FutureGen Alliance signed an agreement with the DOE to build the FutureGen 2.0 CO_2 pipeline network and CO_2 storage site.

18) Conservation and Alternative Energy Lead to Technology Investment and Innovation

In the U.S., emphasis on alternative energy and conservation has a varied history. Nearly 40 years ago, the 1973 oil trade embargo staged by Persian Gulf producers, which limited the supply of petroleum to the U.S., created an instant interest in energy conservation. Thermostats were turned to more efficient levels, solar water heating systems sprouted on the rooftops of American homes (including a system that was used for a few years at the White House) and tax credits were launched by various government agencies to encourage investment in more efficient systems that would utilize less oil, gasoline and/or electricity. Meanwhile, American motorists crawled through lengthy lines at filling stations trying to top off their tanks during the horrid days of gasoline rationing.

While some consumers maintained a keen interest in alternative and conservative energy methods from an environmentally-friendly point of view, most Americans quickly forgot about energy conservation when the prices of gasoline and electricity plummeted during the 1980s and 1990s. Gasoline prices as low as 99 cents per gallon were common. As advancing technology made oil exploration and production much more efficient, a global, low commodity price trend kept market prices under control. As a result, Americans returned to ice-cold air-conditioned rooms and purchased giant, gas-guzzling SUVs, motor homes and motorboats. The median newly constructed American single-family home built in 1972 contained 1,520 square feet; in 2006, it contained 2,495 square feet. More square footage means more lights, air conditioning and heating to power. (However, the recent recession saw the average size of the new U.S. home declining.) Meanwhile, federal and state regulators made efforts to force automobile engines and industrial plants to operate in a cleaner mode, largely through the use of advanced technologies, while requiring gasoline refiners to adopt an ever-widening web of additives and standards that would create cleaner-burning fuels.

Fortunately, the first energy crisis in the early 1970s did lead to the use of technology to create significant efficiencies in some areas. For example, prior to that time, as much as 40% of a typical household's natural gas consumption was for pilot lights burning idly in case a stove or furnace was needed. Today, electric pilots create spark ignition on demand. Likewise, today's refrigerators use about one-third the electricity of models built in 1970. Many other appliances and electrical devices have become much more efficient. While the number of electricity-burning personal computers proliferated, computer equipment makers rapidly adopted energy-saving PC technologies.

Today, oil and gas prices and environmental concerns have combined with a frugal mindset enhanced by the global economic crisis to create a renewed interest in all things energy-efficient. Smaller cars, high-efficiency homes and even solar power are once again part of popular culture. Sales of gas-guzzling SUVs have slowed to a crawl while the demand for hybrid vehicles has been strong. At the same time, renewable energy sources and cleaner-burning fuels are of great appeal to the large number of consumers who have developed a true interest in protecting the environment. For example, surveys have shown that some consumers would be willing to pay somewhat more for electricity if they knew it was coming from non-polluting, renewable sources.

Many U.S. consumers are looking forward to a choice of plug-in electric vehicles. Meanwhile, some municipalities, such as the City of Seattle, are investing in buses and other vehicles that are hybrids or run on alternative fuels.

An energy-saving lighting standard in the U.S. may phase out common incandescent light bulbs by 2016 and replace them with compact fluorescent lights (CFL). Many other nations are doing the same thing. Australia began phasing out old-fashioned bulbs entirely with a national ban beginning in 2009. GE is a big maker of CFL bulbs, which use 75% less energy than incandescent bulbs and last six times longer. At the same time, manufacturers are also working to reduce prohibitive costs of light-emitting diodes (LEDs), which have tremendous potential to save billions of dollars in electricity costs while greatly reducing pollution.

In 2009, electricity production through renewable sources remained miniscule in the United States, despite massive federal and state subsidies for wind and solar projects. Wind, solar and other non-hydro sources accounted for only 3.59% of electric generation, while hydro-electric accounted for 6.93%. (Renewables include hydropower, solar, geothermal and wind, as well as biomass, waste-to-energy and alcohol).

There are powerful government subsidies and incentives available to firms involved in energy efficiency technologies and services. Recent federal economic stimulus money has focused to a large extent on alternative and renewable energy, energy conservation, "smart" electric metering, and advanced automobile battery technology.

The city of Austin, Texas has passed a resolution to develop 20% of its electricity from renewables by 2020. California is the leading U.S. state in terms of solar power generation. The California Public Utilities Commission okayed the creation of the largest solar-power program in the U.S. in early 2006. Utility customers are to spend $2.86 billion through 2017 to subsidize the installation of 3,000 megawatts of new solar capacity. Meanwhile, venture capital investors have been swarming around energy entrepreneurs, backing everything from advance solar cell manufacturing facilities to smart meter technology.

Outside of the U.S., major initiatives in Germany, the United Kingdom, Japan and a handful of other countries spur technology research and implementation of renewable power. Japanese firms, notably Sharp, Sanyo and Kyocera, have massive solar power research and development initiatives underway, as do several firms in China. These Asian companies are significant competitors to American manufacturers of solar equipment. Consumers in Japan are encouraged to invest in solar power by government incentives, and the Japanese Government's strategy is to get 38% of the nation's total power needs from renewable sources by 2020—a logical goal for a country with high energy demands and major dependence on foreign supplies of fossil fuels. Japan is a major producer of wind power.

Germany has been investing in both wind and solar power, and it is an innovative manufacturer in these industries. It is one of the world's largest producers of wind power. Through powerful incentives that include rebates and payment for excess power, German consumers and companies alike have been building nonstop.

19) The Industry Takes a New Look at Nuclear Power

The first man-made nuclear fission reaction was achieved in 1938, unlocking atomic power both for destructive and creative purposes. In 1951, the first usable electricity was created via the energy produced by a nuclear reactor, thanks largely to research conducted in the Manhattan Project that developed the first atomic weapons during World War II.

By the 1970s, nuclear power was in widespread use, in the U.S. and abroad, as a source of electricity. As of 2009, nuclear power provided about 20.1% of the electricity generated in the U.S. (up from 19.6% in 2008), created by 104 licensed nuclear reactors, according to the Nuclear Energy Institute. The U.S. Department of Energy predicted that 1,000 nuclear plants will be running worldwide by 2050, up from 439 in 2008. This prediction may be in jeopardy in part due to the global economic recession of 2008 and 2009. Demand for electricity in America dropped as economic belts were tightened, falling more than 4% from 2007 to 2009. As of late 2010, as many as seven new American reactor projects had been deferred due to funding problems. Exelon suspended plans to build a twin reactor in Texas, while Constellation Energy abandoned a new project in Maryland after the federal government refused to reduce an $880 million fee to guarantee the $7.6 billion loan necessary to build the plant.

The potential for accidents, meltdowns and other disasters has never been far from the minds of many consumers (after all, for many of us the first image that comes to mind upon hearing the word "nuclear" is a nuclear bomb). The 1979 Three Mile Island nuclear power plant accident in the U.S. led to the cancellation of scores of nuclear projects across the nation. This trend was later reinforced by the disaster at Chernobyl in what was then the Soviet Union. Regulatory agencies took an even harder line on U.S. nuclear power plants, and the popular movie *The China Syndrome* highlighted the terrifying possibility of human error and hubris leading to a nuclear power plant meltdown on the California coast. As of late 2010, only two new nuclear plants looked relatively solid in the U.S. Southern Company's project slated for a site near Waynesboro, Georgia was waiting for final regulatory approval (a process which could take a year or more); and Scana Corporation's subsidiary South Carolina Electric & Gas Company had received approval but was competing for a loan guarantee with NRG Energy, which hopes to build its own plant in Texas.

The nation of France was an early adopter of nuclear power. The French approved a single, very cost-effective nuclear plant design and built it over and over again around the nation. France currently gets nearly 80% of its electricity from nuclear sources. Many other nations create significant portions of their power from nuclear plants, including Belgium, Germany, Sweden, South Korea, Switzerland and Japan. For example, South Korea's electricity demand is expected to increase by 40% from 2006 to 2030. In order to meet that demand, it will have to add from nine to 13 new reactors.

SPOTLIGHT: AREVA Group
2009 Sales: $18.6 billion
2009 Profits: $668 million
Employees: 75,000
Headquarters: Paris, France

AREVA Group was created through the merger of AREVA T&D, COGEMA and FRAMATOME ANP, which combined the French Government's interests in several nuclear power and information technology businesses. The CEA (Commissariat a l'Energie Atomique), the French atomic energy commission, owns 79% of the company. The firm has manufacturing facilities in over 43 countries and a sales network in over 100 countries. AREVA operates in five divisions: mining; front-end; reactors and services; back-end; and renewable energy. The mining division handles the uranium ore exploration, mining and processing operations of the company, with mines located in Canada, Kazakhstan and Niger. Through the front-end division, and wholly-owned subsidiary AREVA NC, the company manages concentration, conversion and enrichment of uranium ore, as well as nuclear fuel design and fabrication. The reactors and services division offers design and construction services for nuclear reactors and other non-carbon dioxide emitting power generation systems. Through AREVA NP, 34%-owned by Siemens, the firm designs and constructs nuclear power plants and research reactors and offers instrumentation and control, modernization and maintenance services, components manufacture and the supply of nuclear fuel. The back-end division provides treatment and recycling of used fuel, as well as cleanup of nuclear facilities. The renewable energy division invests in and develops sites for wind energy, bioenergy, solar power and hydrogen power, as well as energy storage.

In March 2010, AREVA acquired Ausra, Inc., a pioneer in concentrated solar power (solar thermal). In May 2010, the firm received a conditional $2 billion loan from the U.S. Department of Energy for the development of a nuclear enrichment facility in Idaho. In June of that year, the company finalized the sale of its energy transmission and distribution division to Alstom and Schneider Electric. AREVA was recently awarded a contract by the Tennessee Valley Authority (TVA) for engineering and development work toward the completion of a nuclear power plant in northern Alabama.

In the late 1990s, the U.S. Nuclear Regulatory Commission (NRC) began to extend nuclear reactor license periods from 40 years to 60 years, thereby greatly extending the life of existing reactors. Nuclear technology has progressed significantly since most U.S. reactors were built in the late 1960s and early 1970s. Modifications made to existing reactors, such as key systems upgrades, digitization and high-efficiency mechanization, are helping many sites qualify for NRC relicensing. For example, a typical U.S. nuclear plant is online 90% of the time today, compared to less than 50% in the 1970s.

New Nuclear Reactor Construction in the U.S., Europe and Asia: The most recent reactor in the U.S. was built in 1996 at Watts Bar in Tennessee, after 23 years of planning and licensing and an investment of $7 billion. (Engineering giant Bechtel has been selected to complete Unit 2 at Watts Bar, which had been sitting in an incomplete state for years. The project will cost $2.5 billion and be online as early as 2012, with generating capacity to serve 650,000 homes.)

Estimates of final costs for a new, 1,000-megawatt unit in the United States range from $6 to $12 billion, depending on whom you ask. However, the history of nuclear reactor construction is littered with cost overruns, delays and complications. What is needed for renewed development in the U.S. and Europe is a focus on standardized, advanced technology designs that can be built over and over again. This would hopefully streamline the regulatory process, reduce financial risks and encourage investment. New construction is unlikely anywhere in the world without substantial government guarantees and assistance. The fact that nuclear power can dramatically reduce a nation's carbon emissions is a big plus.

The manufacture of advanced-technology reactors on a large scale in America could do a great deal to boost the nation's beleaguered manufacturing sector. Thanks to growing interest in nuclear development in the U.S., AREVA has announced a joint venture with Northrop Grumman in which they may jointly manufacture reactor equipment at Northrop's Newport News, Virginia shipyard. They plan to build a 300,000 square foot engineering and manufacturing facility at a cost of about $360 million that will employ 500 workers.

Outside the U.S., there are new plants under planning or construction in nations ranging from Italy, where Enel SpA and EDF will form a joint venture to construct four new plants valued at 16 billion Euros, to the United Arab Emirates (UAE) which has a dramatic, $41 billion nuclear development plan designed to meet electricity demand projected to double by 2020. India, which had 17 nuclear plants operating as of 2010, has firm plans to build at least six additional plants over the near term. Even the green-leaning nation of Germany wants to drop an existing law that requires that all 17 of its nuclear plants (providing 23% of the nation's electricity as of 2008) must be shut down by 2022.

In a bill signed by former President Bush in August 2005, the U.S. federal government offers several incentives for the construction of new reactors, including $18.5 billion in new federal financing assistance to be granted by the Department of Energy for nuclear site construction. In 2010, President Obama requested an additional $36 billion in federal loans for new plant construction as part of the 2011 budget.

Nuclear Waste and Uranium Reprocessing: The controversial Yucca Mountain nuclear waste repository project in Nevada was intended to create a permanent location for America's nuclear waste. It was designed to store waste 1,000 feet underground above another 1,000 feet of solid rock. Supporters maintain that one central depository is far safer than the current method of storing waste underwater near each reactor site. Waste would be transported to a central repository by truck and rail, and it would be sealed in armored casks designed to withstand puncturing and exposure to fire or water. However, the Obama Administration vowed to end development of the site, which has sucked up $13 billion in federal funds to date, and little further construction is expected for the near term. The proposed 2011 federal budget calls for the elimination of funding for the project.

Technology Spotlight: TerraPower

A unique, private technology research firm based in Bellevue, Washington, Intellectual Ventures www.intellectualventures.com, has proposed a revolutionary nuclear reactor concept it calls TerraPower. This technology would use a new class of reactor called TWR or traveling-wave reactor that would solve the current nuclear waste problem. TWRs would use today's stockpiles of depleted uranium from power plants as its primary fuel source. The TWR would essentially be a reactor-reprocessor. Traditional reactors rely on uranium-235, and their operation leaves a more common uranium-238 as waste.

Every year or two, traditional reactors must be opened and refueled, and the "spent" uranium-238 waste is stockpiled. Millions of pounds of it are now in storage. A TWR could be fed that uranium-238, which it would convert into a desirable fuel, plutonium-239. Similar conversion of U-238 has already been proven, but present technologies for reprocessing into plutonium are expensive and complicated. TWR could represent a significant step forward while reducing the potential of diverting plutonium to use in atomic weapons.

Another underground disposal site project is in Finland at the Olkiluoto Nuclear Power Plant. The proposed waste site will store spent fuel rods in iron canisters sealed in copper shells to resist corrosion. The canisters will be placed in holes surrounded by clay far below ground. The project is slated for completion in 2020.

The alternative to the storage of nuclear waste is reprocessing, in which spent fuel is dissolved in nitric acid. The resulting substance is then separated into uranium, plutonium and unusable waste. The positive side of reprocessing is the recycling of uranium for further nuclear power generation. Surplus plutonium can be mixed with uranium to fabricate MOX (mixed oxide fuel) for use in a commercial nuclear power plant. MOX fuel contains 5% plutonium. Commercial MOX-fueled light water reactors are used in France, the United Kingdom, Germany, Switzerland and Belgium. In the U.S., MOX fuel was fabricated and used in several commercial reactors in the 1970s as part of a development program. The negative side of reprocessing is that the resulting plutonium may be used for nuclear weapons. Additionally, environmentalists are extremely concerned about the potentially high levels of radioactivity produced during reprocessing and the transportation of reprocessed waste.

Safer New Nuclear Power Technologies: New technologies may eventually enable construction of nuclear generating plants that are less expensive to build and much safer to operate than those of previous generations. Although nuclear power plants are far more costly to construct than plants producing energy from fossil fuels, they may have lower operating costs. At one time, the Electric Power Research Institute (EPRI) projected that new reactors will be capable of producing electricity at about $49 per megawatt hour, compared to $55 per megawatt hour for gasified coal and $65 per megawatt hour for energy made from pulverized coal at plants that sequester carbon dioxide. However, fluctuating prices of oil, natural gas, coal and uranium make long term operating costs hard to predict.

PBMR, Ltd. (www.pbmr.co.za), is a pioneer in "pebble-bed modular reactor" (PBMR) technology. It is based in South Africa, where at one point the firm hoped to build a working reactor. However, funding was never definite and the company is attempting to regroup. Earlier, scientists in Germany operated a 15-megawatt prototype PBMR from 1967 to 1988. Pebble-bed technology utilizes tiny silicon carbide-coated uranium oxide granules sealed in "pebbles" about the size of oranges, made of graphite. Helium is used as the coolant and energy transfer medium. This containment of the radioactive material in small quantities has the potential to achieve an unprecedented level of safety. However, multiple challenges remain, partly stemming from the fact that PBMRs operate at very high temperatures. For several years, various efforts around the world have attempted to create viable high-temperature, gas-cooled reactors similar to this.

In 2008, PBMR, Ltd. said that it created its first enriched uranium-coated particles, 14,000 of which are contained in one of its "pebbles." In September 2009, the firm announced that it had manufactured its first complete pebbles, each containing 9.6% enriched uranium. Sixteen pebbles were shipped to Russia for two years of irradiation tests to demonstrate the fuel's integrity under reactor conditions. Successful tests would mean that the fuel is ready to be used in a demonstration reactor.

The world's most promising pebble bed project is being carried out at the Tsinghua Institute of Nuclear and New Energy Technology in China. China actually has a working model that was completed, tested and brought on line in 2000-2004. Even though this test prototype generates a relatively minute 10 megawatts, it is theoretically only a matter of scaling up the design to create a commercially viable project. The best part of the Chinese design is modularity. Future, full-size sites will consist of small 100-megawatt reactors that can be grouped and chained into a single plant, making a more distributed energy model possible, where capacity can be upscaled as needed. The Chinese appear to be solving the high temperature problem by operating the reactors at a relatively low 750 degrees Celsius. Cooling is being considered using steam cycle technology as an alternative to helium. A 200-megawatt pebble bed plant may come on line in China as early as 2011. The test site, in Shandong, could eventually house up to 18 reactors. It remains to be seen whether the Chinese can create a commercially-viable reactor in this manner, but this is a serious effort that looks promising. Success could have a great impact on global nuclear development.

Other nuclear technologies will be used elsewhere in China. In December 2006, Westinghouse, a major maker of nuclear power plants (and owned by Toshiba in Japan), announced a multi-billion dollar deal to sell four new nuclear plants, its AP1000 model, to China. The deal includes work to be performed by U.S. engineering giant Shaw Group, Inc. AREVA Group also has a deal with China for two reactors and approximately 20 years worth of atomic fuel.

Westinghouse, like competitor GE, is focusing on an advanced, water-cooled reactor technology. The world's first AP1000 plant began construction in March 2009 at Sanmen, in the Shejiang province of China. China is expected to have more than 100 reactors by 2030, up from 11 in 2009, a nine-fold increase.

The AP1000 is considered a generation 3+ reactor technology. Advanced generation reactors feature higher operating efficiency, greater safety and design that uses fewer pumps and other moving parts in order to simplify construction and operation, and make emergency responses more dependable. "Passive" safety systems are built-in that require no outside support, such as external electric power and human action, to kick in. For example, the AP1000 features systems for passive core cooling, passive leak containment cooling and leak containment isolation. Passive systems rely on the use of gravity, natural circulation and/or compressed gas in order to react to emergencies.

In the U.S. a consortium called NuStart Energy was founded in 2004 by energy companies including Duke Energy, Entergy Nuclear, Exelon, FLP Group, Progress Energy, SCANA, Southern Company and the Tennessee Valley Authority (TVA), as well as reactor builders Westinghouse and General Electric. The consortium's mission is to demonstrate the feasibility of obtaining Construction and Operating Licenses (COLs) from the NRC so that utility firms will be encouraged to move ahead with new projects. NuStart (www.nustartenergy.com) is also committed to promoting the use of advanced technology and engineering design for new reactors in the U.S.

Several COLs are likely to be under processing at once in the near future. For example, in September 2008, Entergy, a major U.S. utility and a member of NuStart, filed a 13,000-page COL with the Nuclear

Regulatory Commission seeking authorization to build an additional reactor at the Mississippi site of Entergy's present River Bend Station, a GE reactor that came on line in 1986. Once the NRC accepts an application, it takes 36 to 42 months to complete a comprehensive review.

However, in America as of 2010, the recent drop in electricity consumption and the difficulty of obtaining long term financing was putting a damper on new nuclear projects, while projects soared ahead full speed in China, the UAE and other nations. In October 2010, Constellation Energy announced it would pull out of a joint venture with France's EDF to build a new $10 billion nuclear plant in Maryland. Constellation stated that the federal government's intention to charge an $880 million fee for loan guarantees (a fee equal to 11.6% of the proposed loans) made the project unviable.

The long term future of nuclear plant design may be exemplified by the work of Babcock & Wilcox. This company was founded decades ago as a manufacturer of boilers and it has a lengthy history of making components, such as pressure vessels, for the energy industry. It has adapted its technology base in order to design an innovative nuclear generation concept, the mPower modular reactor. It is a low cost, high efficiency design of compact size. The engineers leading the project were focused on one concept: to create a reactor pressure vessel, the core of the unit, that can be built at a factory and be small enough to fit on a railroad car for delivery to the final site. This overcomes the massive, custom engineering and construction challenges that typically drive the cost of a site-built nuclear plant to more than $6 billion, and the time required for completion to several years. One modular unit from Babcock & Wilcox could be installed in relatively short order, and could power a single large industrial complex or a few thousand homes. Several of these small, low-cost units could be combined at one site to create power stations of enough overall capacity to power a small city. The air-cooled design is described as passively safe. The firm already has a lengthy history in the nuclear field, as it builds reactors for the U.S. Navy.

Several other firms are pursuing the mini-reactor business, including Westinghouse and NuScale Power. Santa Fe, New Mexico-based Hyperion Power Generation hopes to be able to sell a small reactor, suitable to power about 20,000 American homes, for only $50 million. Hyperion is utilizing technology that originated more than 50 years ago at the nearby Los Alamos Labs. Competitor Toshiba hopes to install a test unit of its "4S" (super safe, small and simple) mini-reactor in a remote village in Alaska in the near future.

SPOTLIGHT: Fusion Power

As opposed to nuclear fission, nuclear fusion is the reaction when two light atomic nuclei fuse together, forming a heavier nucleus. That nucleus releases energy. So far, fusion power generators burn more energy than they create. However, that may change with the construction of the International Thermonuclear Experimental Reactor (ITER) in Southern France. To be completed in 2016 at a cost of about $11.7 billion, the reactor is a pilot project to show the world the feasibility of full-scale fusion power.

SPOTLIGHT: Hyperion Power Generation

Santa Fe, New Mexico startup Hyperion Power Generation (HPG, www.hyperionpowergeneration.com) is working on utilizing technology from nearby Los Alamos National Laboratory for a nuclear battery. The unit, which is a little less than five feet wide, can produce more than 25 megawatts for five years, or enough to power about 25,000 homes. The battery runs on uranium hydride which, in addition to providing fuel, regulates power output so the possibility of a meltdown is almost nil. There are no moving parts, and the unit can be buried underground for additional safety. The company claims that the cost of each unit will be far less than the price for building and operating a natural gas plant with the same capacity. HPG has backing from venture capital firm Altira. In late 2010, Hyperion announced an agreement with Savannah River National Laboratory that could lead to the construction of a small modular nuclear reactor at the U.S. Department of Energy's Savannah River Site in South Carolina.

20) Ethanol Production Soared, But a Market Glut May Slow Expansion

High gasoline prices, effective lobbying by agricultural and industrial interests and a growing interest in cutting reliance on imported oil put a high national focus on bioethanol in America in recent years. Corn and other organic materials, including agricultural waste, can be converted into ethanol through the use of engineered bacteria and superenzymes manufactured by biotechnology firms. This trend has given a boost to the biotech, agriculture and alternative energy sectors. At present, corn is almost the exclusive source for bioethanol in America. This is a shift of a crop from use in the food chain to use in the energy chain that is unprecedented in all of agricultural history—a shift that is having profound effects on prices for consumers, livestock growers (where corn has long been a traditional animal feed) and food processors.

In addition to the use of ethanol in cars and trucks, the chemicals industry, faced with daunting increases in petrochemicals costs, has a new appetite for bioethanol. In fact, bioethanol can be used to create plastics—an area that consumes vast quantities of oil in America and around the globe. Archer Daniels Midland is constructing a plant in Clinton, Iowa that will produce 50,000 tons of plastic per year through the use of biotechnology to convert corn into polymers.

Ethanol is an alcohol produced by a distilling process similar to that used to produce liquors. A small amount of ethanol is added to much of the gasoline sold in America, and most U.S. autos are capable of burning "E10," a gasoline blend that contains 10% ethanol. E85 is an 85% ethanol blend that may grow in popularity due to a shift in automotive manufacturing. Although only about 2,233 of the 170,000 U.S. service stations sold E85 as of the middle of 2010, there may be an increase in demand for ethanol in the U.S. due to mandates by the U.S. government calling for reduced dependence on oil.

Yet, despite the millions of vehicles on the road that can run on E85 and billions of dollars in federal subsidies to participating refiners, many oil companies seem unenthusiastic about the adoption of the higher ethanol mix. E85 requires separate gasoline pumps, trucks and storage tanks, as well as substantial cost to the oil companies (the pumps alone cost about $200,000 per gas station to install). The plants needed to create ethanol cost $500 million or more to build. Many drivers who have tried filling up with E85 once revert to regular unleaded when they find as much as a 25% loss in fuel economy when burning the blend.

Ethanol is a very popular fuel source in Brazil. In fact, Brazil is one of the world's largest producers of ethanol, which provides a significant amount of the fuel used in Brazil's cars. This is due to a concerted effort by the government to reduce dependency on petroleum product imports. After getting an initial boost due to government subsidies and fuel tax strategies beginning in 1975, Brazilian producers developed methods (typically using sugar cane) that enable them to produce ethanol at moderate cost. The fact that Brazil's climate is ideally suited for sugarcane is a great asset. Also, sugar cane can be converted with one less step than corn, which is the primary source for American ethanol. Brazilian automobiles are typically equipped with engines that can burn pure ethanol or a blend of gasoline and ethanol. Brazilian car manufacturing plants operated by Ford, GM and Volkswagen all make such cars.

In America, partly in response to the energy crisis of the 1970s, Congress instituted federal ethanol production subsidies in 1979. Corn-based grain ethanol production picked up quickly, and federal subsidies have amounted to several billion dollars. The size of these subsidies and environmental concerns about the production of grain ethanol produced a steady howl of protest from observers through the years. Nonetheless, the Clean Air Act of 1990 further boosted ethanol production by increasing the use of ethanol as an additive to gasoline. Meanwhile, the largest producers of ethanol, such as Archer Daniels Midland (ADM), have reaped significant subsidies from Washington for their output. Between 2005 and 2009, the federal government spent $17 billion in tax credits. For 2010, the budget calls for another $5.4 billion.

The U.S. Energy Act of 2005 specifically required that oil refiners mix 7.5 billion gallons of renewable fuels such as ethanol in the nation's gasoline supply by 2012. Ethanol production in the U.S. reached 10.75 billion gallons in 2009, compared to 3.8 billion in 2005, according to the U.S. Energy Information Administration (EIA). Iowa, Illinois, Nebraska, Minnesota and South Dakota are the biggest producers, in that order. Although grain farmers and ethanol producers enjoyed high prices at the onset, a glut of ethanol supply eventually caused market prices to plummet. Next, the Energy Independence and Security Act of 2007 called for even more ethanol production, with a goal of 36 billion gallons per year by 2022 including 21 billion gallons to come from cellulosic and advanced biofuel sources. However, environmental concerns, the sizeable investments needed to construct ethanol refineries and questions about the advisability of using a food grain as a source for fuel made these goals unattainable using existing technologies. In addition, the automobile industry expects a significant amount of market share to slowly shift to electric or hybrid-electric vehicles over the long term, which will reduce dependency on liquid fuels, such as gasoline and ethanol. The Renewable Fuel Standard of 2010 reduced ethanol requirements to 15 billion gallons of the 36 billion gallons of renewable fuel that must be used for transport by 2022.

More recently, some of the largest ethanol production companies have suffered severe financial problems. Notably, VeraSun filed for bankruptcy protection in late 2008, citing high corn prices and difficulty in obtaining trade credit. The Iowa-based company operated 14 ethanol plants in the Midwestern U.S. (Valero, a leading petroleum refiner, purchased some of VeraSun's plants.) The 2008-2009 plummet in the price of crude oil made ethanol look much less attractive from a cost point-of-view. Meanwhile, ethanol factories have generally encountered great difficulty when seeking profitability in the U.S., despite immense federal government support. New plant construction projects have been cancelled or put on hold, and it is looking very unlikely that the industry can meet the production goals set by congressional mandates.

Traditional grain ethanol is typically made from corn or sugarcane. In contrast to grain ethanol, "cellulosic" ethanol is typically made from agricultural waste like corncobs, wheat husks, stems, stalks and leaves, which are treated with specially engineered enzymes to break the waste down into its component sugars. The sugars (or sucrose) are used to make ethanol. Since agricultural waste is plentiful, turning it into energy seems a good strategy. Cellulosic ethanol can also be made from certain types of plants and grasses.

The trick to cellulosic ethanol production is the creation of efficient enzymes to treat the agricultural waste. The U.S. Department of Energy is investing heavily in research, along with major companies such as Dow Chemical, DuPont and Cargill. Another challenge lies in efficient collection and delivery of cellulosic material to the refinery. It may be more costly to make cellulosic ethanol than to make it from corn. In any event, the U.S. remains far behind Brazil in cost-efficiency, as Brazil's use of sugar cane refined in smaller, nearby biorefineries creates ethanol at much lower costs per gallon.

Iogen, a Canadian biotechnology company, makes just such an enzyme and has been operating a test plant to determine how economical the process may be. The company hopes to construct a $300-million, large-scale biorefinery with a potential output of 50 million gallons per year. Its pilot plant in Ottawa utilizes wheat straw and corn stalks. In mid-2009, a Shell gasoline station in Ottawa, Canada became the first retail outlet in that nation to sell a blend of gasoline that features 10% cellulosic ethanol.

In the U.S., the Department of Energy has selected six proposed new cellulosic ethanol refineries to receive a total of $385 million in federal funding. If completed, these six refineries are expected to produce 130 million gallons of ethanol yearly. Iogen's technology will be used in one of the refineries, to be located in Shelley, Idaho. Partners in the refinery include Royal Dutch Shell.

Meanwhile, the Canadian government plans to support the Canadian biofuel industry with up to 500 million Canadian dollars for construction of next-generation plants. Iogen is expected to receive part of those funds for construction of a commercial scale cellulosic ethanol plant.

In the U.S., BP and Verenium announced plans in February 2009 to form a joint venture to build, on a commercial scale, a cellulosic ethanol plant in Highlands County, Florida. In July 2010, BP Biofuels North America acquired Verenium's cellulosic biofuels business and became the sole investor in the new plant. The plant is expected to cost $300 million and have the capacity to produce 36 million gallons of ethanol yearly from agricultural waste.

Other companies, such as Syngenta, DuPont and Ceres, are genetically engineering crops so that they can be more easily converted to ethanol or other energy producing products. Syngenta, for example, is testing a bio-engineered corn that contains the enzyme amylase. Amylase breaks down the corn's starch into sugar, which is then fermented into ethanol. The refining methods currently used with traditional corn crops add amylase to begin the process.

Environmentalists are concerned that genetically engineering crops for use in energy-related yields will endanger the food supply through cross-pollination with traditional plants. Monsanto is focusing on conventional breeding of plants with naturally higher fermentable starch content as an alternative to genetic engineering.

Another concern relating to ethanol use is that its production is not as energy efficient as that of biodiesel made from soybeans. According to a study at the University of Minnesota, the farming and processing of corn grain for ethanol yields only 25% more energy than it consumes compared to 93% for biodiesel. Likewise, greenhouse gas emissions savings are greater for biodiesel. According to one estimate, producing and burning ethanol results in 12% fewer greenhouse gas emissions than burning gasoline, while producing and burning biodiesel results in a 41% reduction compared to making and burning regular diesel fuel. A 2009 vote by Illinois' Air Resources Board requires the use of "lower carbon intensity" fuels starting in 2011, which may have a negative long term effect on the use of ethanol.

Global warming concerns were heightened in 2009 by a report by the International Council for Science (ICSU) that concluded that the production of biofuels, including ethanol, has hurt rather than helped the fight against climate change. The report cites findings by a scientist at the Max Planck Institute for Chemistry in Germany that biofuels expand the harmful effects of a gas called nitrous oxide, which may be 300 times worse for global warming than carbon dioxide. The amounts of nitrous oxide released when farming biofuel crops such as corn may negate any advantage gained by reduced carbon dioxide emissions.

In addition, ethanol production requires enormous amounts of water. To produce one gallon of ethanol, up to four gallons of water are consumed by ethanol refineries. Add in the water needed to grow the corn in the first place, and the number grows to as much as 1,700 gallons of water for each gallon of ethanol.

Other concerns regarding the use of corn to manufacture ethanol include the fact that a great deal of energy is consumed in planting, reaping and transporting the corn in trucks. Also, high demand for corn for use in biorefineries has, from time-to-time, dramatically driven up the cost per bushel, creating burdens on consumers.

As of mid-2009, new technology was being tested that would produce ethanol from corn cobs that have been stripped of edible kernels. Poet, a South Dakota-based producer of ethanol that operates 26 plants in seven U.S. states, is constructing a plant in Emmetsburg, Iowa that will be one of the first in the U.S. to produce ethanol on a large scale using a non-food source. The plant is slated for completion in 2011.

Novozymes, a Danish bioindustrial product manufacturer, has developed an enzyme blend containing an agent called GH-61 that has the potential to speed chemical reactions. Enzymes containing GH-61 may reduce production costs to the extent that producing ethanol can be competitive on a price basis with fossil fuels. Novozymes says that the cost of the enzyme, called Cellic, is about 50 cents per gallon, or less than a third of the projected $1.90 per gallon total cost (naturally, the retail price per gallon would be higher). Poet's Emmetsburg plant will utilize the substance in its ethanol production.

Another potential for ethanol production plants is to retool them to produce other kinds of biochemicals. For example, Houston, Texas startup Glycos Biotechnologies, Inc. is developing an add-on process to use glycerin, a by-product of ethanol, to make chemicals suitable for use in fabrics, insulation and food stuffs. Other firms pursuing similar avenues include Genomatica, Inc., Gevo, Inc. and Myriant Technologies LLC.

SPOTLIGHT: Biofuels

Corn is far from the only source of cellulose for creating biofuels.

Municipal/Agricultural Waste: Cheaply produced, but in limited supply compared to the billions of gallons of fuel needed in the market place.

Wood: Easily harvested and in somewhat healthy supply, however cellulose is more difficult to extract from wood than from other biosources.

Algae: The slimy green stuff does have the potential for high yields per acre, but the process for distilling its cellulose is complex, requiring a source of carbon dioxide to permeate the algae.

Grasses/Wheat: Including switchgrass, miscanthus, sugar cane and wheat straw, the supply would be almost limitless. The challenge here is creating efficient methods for harvesting and infrastructure for delivering it to biorefineries.

Vegetable Oils: Including soybean, canola, sunflower, rapeseed, palm or hemp. It is difficult to keep production costs of these oils low.

SPOTLIGHT: Algae Draws Major Investment

Algae's potential as a source of biofuel got a big boost from an unlikely source in 2009. ExxonMobil announced plans to invest $300 million or more in San Diego, California-based Synthetic Genomics, a company headed by genome pioneer Craig Venter. Dr. Venter is studying ways in which an ideal species of algae can be developed for a unique culturing process. This process induces algae to release their oil (naturally stored as a foodstuff for the organisms), which can then be manipulated so that the oxygen molecules in the oil are disposed of, leaving a pure hydrocarbon suitable for use as biofuel. Another plus to Venter's process is that carbon dioxide claimed from industrial plant exhaust is used in the culturing process and then released in the atmosphere. This does not make algae biofuel production carbon neutral, but it does utilize carbon dioxide twice before it's released. Should the study go well, ExxonMobil has pledged an additional $300 million in funding to further develop the process to an industrial scale.

21) New Refineries May Create Surplus Capacity

The last time a new refinery was opened in America was 1976. That's not to say that refining capacity hasn't changed—in fact, while many refineries have closed, the 150 remaining refineries have added significant capacity. Meanwhile, the U.S. has an emergency Strategic Petroleum Reserve of about 726 million barrels, but that reserve holds crude—there is no emergency reserve of refined fuels such as gasoline.

There are many difficult challenges to developing new plants in the U.S. The first is the "not in my backyard" factor. Consumers want a reliable supply of refined oil, but they don't want a refinery in the neighborhood.

The next problem is investment. To build a refinery requires a massive investment of capital. In the past, refinery profits have been sporadic and profit margins have often been low. The prospect of low or no profits doesn't encourage investment. However, profitability of any kind is compromised when some refiners don't produce enough of their own crude oil to refine and must buy it at widely fluctuating prices.

A third problem lies in environmental concerns. U.S. environmental standards require that refineries produce a dizzying variety of refined gasoline to meet emissions standards that are set for certain locations and certain times of year. This complicates both refinery design and operation. Meanwhile, vast regulatory barriers have been erected that make it all but impossible to pass the environmental impact tests necessary to build a new refinery. One stalwart firm, Arizona Clean Fuels Yuma, has been trying for years to build a new refinery in Arizona. The company submitted its initial permit application in 1999, only to spend the next decade embroiled in permit negotiations, financing hurdles and legal disputes with a nearby Native American tribe with ancestral ties to the originally proposed refinery site. Existing plants have invested more than $50 billion since 1993 in order to meet increasingly complex environmental regulations. The list of new requirements is endless, while the investment requirements continue unabated.

Finally, there is the varying nature of crude itself. American oil fields luckily tend to contain light sweet crude. Such crude is light in viscosity and low in sulfur, making it is relatively easy to refine. Sweet crude is the most desirable type of raw oil and thus is the highest priced. It is scarce in quantity on the market. What is available in abundance is heavy sour crude. Heavy crude is thicker and lower in desirability. It sells for considerably less per barrel than sweet crude—as much as a 30% discount is not uncommon. Heavy crude is produced in vast quantity in Mexico, Saudi Arabia and elsewhere. The problem is that American refineries are generally equipped in a manner that makes it difficult to impossible for them to process the heavy crude, and heavy crude contains high quantities of sulfur that must be dealt with in an environmentally acceptable manner. Refining heavy crude is more complex and more costly.

Nonetheless, some U.S. refiners make excellent profits from their ability to process cheaper, lower quality crude. They enjoy fat profit margins from these plants because their raw feedstock of heavy crude costs less. Additional refiners may be encouraged to refit for handling heavy crude, despite the fact that refitting can cost from $250 million to $800 million. These refits may make plants more flexible, but they won't boost total refining capacity in the U.S.

A hugely ambitious project was announced in 2008. Saudi Aramco and Royal Dutch Shell are spending about $7 billion to double the size of the Motiva refinery in Port Arthur, Texas, capable of refining heavy crude. The refinery will grow to a 600,000 barrel per day capacity. It will be one of the largest refineries in America. The new production capacity will enable the refinery to produce 23 million gallons daily of gasoline, diesel and aviation fuel. Originally scheduled for completion in 2010, the refinery expansion is expected to be complete by early 2012.

To paint a broader picture of the American refining situation, a little history is in order. In 1981, there were 325 refineries in the U.S., with a combined capacity of 18.6 million barrels per day. More than one-half of these refineries have been closed due to historically low profit margins and the vast investments that would have been needed for them to meet evolving environmental standards. While the number of refineries has dwindled, the capacity of remaining refineries has been steadily enhanced at great investment. Nonetheless, America is depending to some extent on imported refined products in order to survive.

By 1992, America's refining capacity had declined to about 15 million barrels per day. As of mid-2009, plant expansion had pushed U.S. refining capacity to about 17.7 million barrels per day.

Meanwhile, massive investments are being made in new petrochemical and refinery plants in China, the Middle East and India. Saudi Arabia is vastly increasing the size of its petrochemicals facilities, often in partnership with leading global oil companies. In India, one of the world's largest refinery complexes was completed in December 2008. Reliance Industries Ltd., invested $6 billion to double its Jamnagar refinery near the Pakistani border, which is now producing at full capacity of 580,000 barrels per day. Approximately 60% of new refinery construction is in Asia and the Middle East, predominantly in China, India, Saudi Arabia, Vietnam, Indonesia, Kuwait and Japan. One of the leaders in the investment in new refineries is Saudi Aramco.

As new refineries come on line, capacity will increase significantly. According to BP, worldwide capacity was 90.6 million barrels per day as of the end of 2009, an increase of 2.2% over 2008. Despite the increase in capacity, demand for refined products fell during the global economic crisis of 2008-2009, and most industry analysts forecast that demand will be slow to rebound as global economies begin to strengthen. Over the long term, a trend toward smaller, more efficient automobiles will also have a strong effect on U.S. gasoline consumption. Eventually, a large number of cars will be gasoline/electric hybrids or plug-in electric vehicles.

Meanwhile, U.S. oil refiner Sunoco closed its Eagle Point refinery in Westville, New Jersey in October 2009 due to poor refining profit margins and growing competition from new refineries in Europe and the Middle East. About the same time, Valero Energy (the largest U.S. independent refiner by volume) slashed operations at its refinery in Delaware and announced plans to close its Aruba facility indefinitely.

Chapter 2

ENERGY INDUSTRY STATISTICS

Tables and Charts:

I. Overview of the Energy Industry

Contents:

Global Energy Overview: 2008-2009

(Latest Years Available)

	North America	South & Central America	Europe & Eurasia	Middle East	Africa	Asia Pacific	Total World
Petroleum							
Production (thousand barrels daily)							
2008	13,169	6,678	17,572	26,182	10,219	8,175	81,995
2009	13,388	6,760	17,702	24,357	9,705	8,036	79,948
Consumption (thousand barrels daily)							
2008	23,795	5,681	20,193	6,864	3,045	25,662	85,239
2009	22,826	5,653	19,372	7,146	3,082	25,998	84,077
Proved Reserves (thousand million barrels)							
2008	73.4	198.9	137.2	753.7	127.5	41.7	1,332.4
2009	73.3	198.9	136.9	754.2	127.7	42.2	1,333.1
Natural Gas							
Production (billions of cubic meters)							
2008	801.8	157.1	1,086.3	383.4	214.3	417.9	3,060.8
2009	813.0	151.6	973.0	407.2	203.8	438.4	2,987.0
Consumption (billions of cubic meters)							
2008	822.0	141.0	1,138.5	331.8	96.1	481.4	3,010.8
2009	810.9	134.7	1,058.6	345.6	94.0	496.6	2,940.4
Proved Reserves (trillion cubic meters)							
2008	9.18	7.32	62.26	75.82	14.71	16.00	185.28
2009	9.16	8.06	63.09	76.18	14.76	16.24	184.49
Coal							
Production (million tonnes oil equivalent)							
2008	637.5	57.1	452.6	1.0	144.5	2,044.2	3,336.9
2009	578.1	52.9	420.4	1.0	143.0	2,213.3	3,408.6
Consumption (million tonnes oil equivalent)							
2008	602.1	24.0	516.7	9.2	111.1	2,023.4	3,286.4
2009	531.3	22.5	456.4	9.2	107.3	2,151.6	3,278.3
Proved Reserves (millions of tonnes)							
2009	246,097	15,006	272,246	1,386	32,013	259,253	826,001
Nuclear							
Consumption (millions of tonnes oil equivalent)							
2008	215.9	4.8	276.8	0.0	3.0	119.7	620.2
2009	212.7	4.7	265.0	0.0	2.7	125.3	610.5
Hydro-Electric							
Consumption (millions of tonnes oil equivalent)							
2008	159.7	154.4	181.0	2.8	22.3	211.1	731.4
2009	158.3	158.4	182.0	2.4	22.0	217.1	740.3

Note: Proved reserves of oil are generally taken to be those quantities that geological and engineering information indicates with reasonable certainty can be recovered in the future from known reservoirs under existing economic and operating conditions. North America data in this table does not include the Canadian oil sands.

Source: BP, *Statistical Review of World Energy*, June 2010
Plunkett Research, Ltd.
www.plunkettresearch.com

U.S. Energy Industry Overview

Energy Production	72,970,019	Bil. Btu*	2009	DOE
By Fossil Fuels	56,859,891	Bil. Btu*	2009	DOE
By Renewable Energy Power Sources	7,760,850	Bil. Btu*	2009	DOE
By Nuclear	8,349,279	Bil. Btu*	2009	DOE
U.S. Energy Consumption	94,578,267	Bil. Btu*	2009	DOE
U.S. Energy Consumption per Person	308	Mil. Btu*	2009	DOE
Share of U.S. Oil Consumption for Transportation	72	%	2009	DOE
Energy Imports	29,781,081	Bil. Btu*	2009	DOE
Energy Exports	6,931,896	Bil. Btu*	2009	DOE
Crude Oil Production	5.310	MMBD	2009	DOE
Number of Operable Refineries	148		2009	DOE
Number of Oil Wells	526,000		2009	DOE
Average Oil Well Productivity	10.1	Bbl/Well/Day	2009	DOE
U.S. Strategic Petroleum Reserve Size	727 Million	Barrels	2009	DOE
Dry Natural Gas Production	20,955,000	Mcf	2009	DOE
Coal Production	1,107,280,000	Short Tons	2009	DOE
Electricity Net Generation	3,953.1	Bil. KWh	2009	DOE
From Coal (44.95%)	1,764.5	Bil. KWh	2009	DOE
From Petroleum (0.99%)	38.8	Bil. KWh	2009	DOE
From Gas (23.45%)	920.4	Bil. KWh	2009	DOE
From Nuclear (20.09%)	788.7	Bil. KWh	2009	DOE
From Hydro-Electric (6.93%)	272.1	Bil. KWh	2009	DOE
From Other Renewables (3.59%)	141.1	Bil. KWh	2009	DOE
Average U.S. Retail Price of Electricity, All Sectors	9.89	Cents/KWh	2009	DOE
U.S. Share of the World's Total Petroleum Consumption	21.7	%	2009	BP
U.S. Share of the World's Coal Reserves	28.9	%	2009	BP
U.S. Share of the World's Natural Gas Reserves	3.7	%	2009	BP
U.S. Share of the World's Petroleum Reserves	2.1	%	2009	BP
Primary Energy by Source				
Petroleum	37.4	%	2009	DOE
Natural Gas	24.8	%	2009	DOE
Coal	20.9	%	2009	DOE
Renewable Energy	8.1	%	2009	DOE
Nuclear Electric Power	8.8	%	2009	DOE

*Reserves that can be commercially recovered.

DOE = U.S. Department of Energy

BP = BP Statistical Review of World Energy

Btu = British Thermal Unit = 0.252 kilocalories

MMBD = millions of barrels per day

Bbl = barrel = 42 U.S. gallons

Mcf = million cubic feet

KWh = Kilowatt-Hour = 860 kilocalories

U.S. Energy Overview: Selected Years, 1970-2009

(In Billions of Btus; Latest Year Available)

	1970	1980	1990	2000	2007	2008	2009
Production							
Fossil Fuels Production[1]	59,186,071	59,007,873	58,559,602	57,366,013	56,447,084	57,613,054	56,859,891
Nuclear Energy Consumed by the Electric Power Sector	239,347	2,739,169	6,104,350	7,862,349	8,455,364	8,427,297	8,349,279
Renewable Energy Production[2]	4,075,857	5,485,420	6,206,027	6,257,018	6,705,528	7,380,699	7,760,850
Total Energy Production	63,501,275	67,232,462	70,869,979	71,485,380	71,607,975	73,421,316	72,970,019
Imports							
Petroleum Imports[3]	7,469,646	14,658,259	17,117,225	24,531,405	28,762,140	27,643,804	25,159,511
Total Energy Imports[4]	8,341,615	15,796,247	18,817,264	28,973,190	34,685,121	32,951,874	29,781,081
Exports							
Coal Exports	1,935,500	2,420,518	2,772,273	1,527,552	1,506,648	2,070,504	1,514,832
Total Energy Exports[5]	2,632,135	3,694,770	4,752,479	4,005,875	5,447,587	7,015,849	6,931,896
Consumption							
Fossil Fuels Consumption[6]	63,522,269	69,984,251	72,333,123	84,732,454	86,245,934	83,496,114	73,368,135
Nuclear Energy Consumed by the Electric Power Sector	239,347	2,739,169	6,104,350	7,862,349	8,455,364	8,427,297	8,349,279
Renewable Energy Consumption[2]	4,075,857	5,485,420	6,206,062	6,259,661	6,719,160	7,366,122	7,743,759
Total Energy Consumption[7]	67,844,161	78,280,238	84,651,424	98,969,664	101,527,089	99,401,914	94,578,267

Note: Totals may not equal sum of components due to independent rounding.

[1] Coal, natural gas (dry), crude oil and natural gas plant liquids.

[2] End-use consumption, electric utility and non-utility electricity net generation.

[3] Crude oil and petroleum products. Includes imports into the Strategic Petroleum Reserve.

[4] Also includes natural gas, coal, coal coke, fuel ethanol and electricity.

[5] Also includes natural gas, petroleum, coal coke, and electricity.

[6] Coal, coal coke net imports, natural gas and petroleum.

[7] Also includes electricity net imports.

Source: U.S. Department of Energy, Energy Information Administration
Plunkett Research, Ltd.
www.plunkettresearch.com

Primary Energy Flow by Source & Sector, U.S.: 2009

(Latest Year Available; Total Energy: Approximately 94.6 Quadrillion Btu)

Consumption by Source

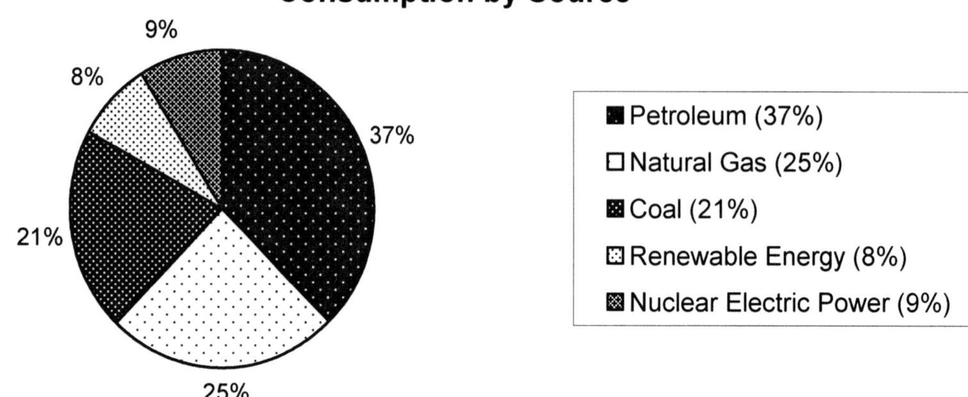

Consumption by Sector

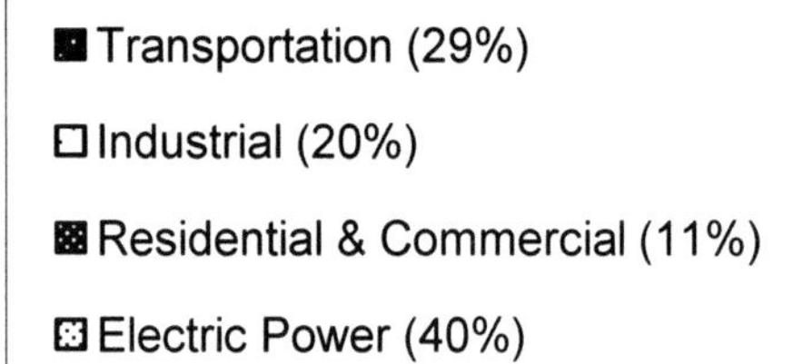

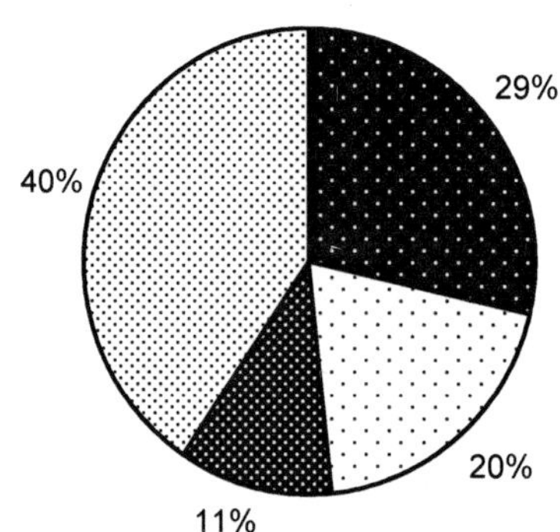

Notes: Sum of components may not equal 100 percent due to independent rounding.

Petroleum: Does not include biofuels that have been blended with petroleum, which are included in "Renewable Energy."

Natural Gas: Excludes supplemental gaseous fuels.

Coal: Includes less than 0.1 quadrillion Btu of coal coke net exports.

Renewable Energy: Includes conventional hydroelectric power, geothermal, solar/PV, wind, and biomass.

Industrial: Includes industrial combined-heat-and-power (CHP) and industrial electricity-only plants.

Residential & Commercial: Includes commercial combined-heat-and-power (CHP) and commercial electricity-only plants.

Electric Power: Includes electricity-only and combined-heat-and-power (CHP) plants whose primary business is to sell electricity, or electricity and heat, to the public.

Source: U.S. Department of Energy, U.S. Energy Information Administration
Plunkett Research, Ltd.
www.plunkettresearch.com

Energy Consumption by Source & Sector, U.S.: 2009

(By Percent; Latest Year Available; Total Energy: 94.6 Quadrillion Btu)

Sector, by Source	
Petroleum[1]: 35.3 Quad. Btu	
Transportation	72
Industrial	22
Residential & Commercial	5
Electric Power	1
Natural Gas[2]: 23.4 Quad. Btu	
Transportation	3
Industrial	32
Residential & Commercial	35
Electric Power	30
Coal[3]: 19.7 Quad. Btu	
Industrial	7
Residential & Commercial	< 1
Electric Power	93
Nuclear Electric Power: 8.3 Quad. Btu	
Electric Power	100
Renewable Energy[4]: 7.7 Quad. Btu	
Transportation	12
Industrial	26
Residential & Commercial	9
Electric Power	53

Source, by Sector	
Transportation: 27.0 Quad. Btu	
Petroleum	94
Natural Gas	3
Renewable Energy	3
Industrial[5]: 18.8 Quad. Btu	
Petroleum	41
Natural Gas	40
Coal	7
Renewable Energy	11
Residential & Commercial[6]: 10.6 Quad. Btu	
Petroleum	17
Natural Gas	76
Coal	1
Renewable Energy	7
Electric Power[7]: 38.3 Quad. Btu	
Petroleum	1
Natural Gas	18
Coal	48
Renewable Energy	11
Nuclear Electric Power	22

Note: Sum of components may not equal 100 percent due to independent rounding.

[1] Does not include biofuels that have been blended with petroleum, which are included in "Renewable Energy."

[2] Excludes supplemental gaseous fuels.

[3] Includes less than 0.1 quadrillion Btu of coal coke net exports.

[4] Conventional hydroelectric power, geothermal, solar/PV, wind, and biomass.

[5] Includes industrial combined-heat-and-power (CHP) and industrial electricity-only plants.

[6] Includes commercial combined-heat-and-power (CHP) and commercial electricity-only plants.

[7] Electricity-only and combined-heat-and-power (CHP) plants whose primary business is to sell electricity, or electricity and heat, to the public.

Source: U.S. Department of Energy, U.S. Energy Information Administration
Plunkett Research, Ltd.
www.plunkettresearch.com

Energy Consumption & Expenditures Indicators, U.S.: Selected Years, 1950-2009

(Latest Year Available)

Year	Energy Consumption	Energy Consumption per Person	Energy Expenditures	Energy Expenditures per Person	Gross Domestic Product (GDP)	Energy Expenditures as Share of GDP	Gross Domestic Product (GDP)	Energy Consumption per Dollar of GDP
	*Quadrillion Btu**	*Mil. Btu**	*Mil. Nominal US$*	*Nominal US$*	*Bil. Nominal US$*	*Percent*	*Bil. Chained (2005) US$*	*Thousand Btu per Chained (2005) US$*
1950	34.62	227	NA	NA	293.7	NA	2,006.0	17.26
1955	40.21	242	NA	NA	414.7	NA	2,500.3	16.08
1960	45.09	250	NA	NA	526.4	NA	2,830.9	15.93
1965	54.02	278	NA	NA	719.1	NA	3,610.1	14.96
1970	67.84	331	82,911	404	1,038.3	8.0	4,269.9	15.89
1975	72.00	333	171,846	796	1,637.7	10.5	4,879.5	14.76
1980	78.12	344	374,346	1,647	2,788.1	13.4	5,839.0	13.38
1985	76.49	321	438,184	1,842	4,217.5	10.4	6,849.3	11.17
1990	84.65	339	472,539	1,893	5,800.5	8.1	8,033.9	10.54
1991	84.61	334	470,559	1,860	5,992.1	7.9	8,015.1	10.56
1992	85.96	335	475,587	1,854	6,342.3	7.5	8,287.1	10.37
1993	87.60	337	491,168	1,890	6,667.4	7.4	8,523.4	10.28
1994	89.26	339	504,204	1,916	7,085.2	7.1	8,870.7	10.06
1995	91.17	342	514,049	1,930	7,414.7	6.9	9,093.7	10.03
1996	94.17	350	559,954	2,079	7,838.5	7.1	9,433.9	9.98
1997	94.76	348	566,785	2,079	8,332.4	6.8	9,854.3	9.62
1998	95.18	345	525,738	1,906	8,793.5	6.0	10,283.5	9.26
1999	96.81	347	556,509	1,994	9,353.5	5.9	10,779.8	8.98
2000	98.97	351	687,587	2,437	9,951.5	6.9	11,226.0	8.82
2001	96.32	338	694,515	2,436	10,286.2	6.8	11,347.2	8.49
2002	97.85	340	661,902	2,300	10,642.3	6.2	11,553.0	8.47
2003	98.13	338	754,668	2,599	11,142.1	6.8	11,840.7	8.29
2004	100.31	342	869,112	2,966	11,867.8	7.3	12,263.8	8.18
2005	100.45	340	1,045,465	3,535	12,638.4	8.3	12,638.4	7.95
2006	99.79	334	1,158,483	3,880	13,398.9	8.6	12,976.2	7.69
2007	101.53	337	1,233,058	4,089	14,077.6	8.8	13,254.1	7.66
2008	99.40	327	NA	NA	14,441.4	NA	13,312.2	7.47
2009	94.58	308	NA	NA	14,256.3	NA	12,987.4	7.28

Note: Expenditures include taxes where data are available.

NA = Not available. * Btu = British Thermal Unit.

Source: U.S. Department of Energy, Energy Information Administration

Plunkett Research, Ltd.

www.plunkettresearch.com

Energy Imports, U.S.: Selected Years, 1950-2009

(In Billions of Btus; Latest Year Available)

	Coal	Coal Coke	Natural Gas	Petroleum			Bio-fuels[3]	Elec-tricity	Total
				Crude Oil[1]	Petroleum Products[2]	Total			
1950	9,132	10,862	0	1,056,154	830,142	1,886,296	NA	6,596	1,912,887
1955	8,425	3,125	11,269	1,690,834	1,060,671	2,751,505	NA	15,583	2,789,908
1960	6,551	3,125	161,094	2,196,380	1,802,314	3,998,694	NA	18,163	4,187,626
1965	4,600	2,232	470,999	2,654,379	2,747,586	5,401,965	NA	12,140	5,891,935
1970	900	3,794	846,224	2,813,732	4,655,914	7,469,646	NA	21,051	8,341,615
1975	23,500	45,111	977,786	8,720,912	4,226,634	12,947,546	NA	38,446	14,032,389
1980	29,840	16,343	1,006,432	11,194,854	3,463,406	14,658,259	NA	85,373	15,796,247
1985	48,810	14,334	951,614	6,813,508	3,795,708	10,609,216	NA	156,595	11,780,570
1990	67,485	18,972	1,550,646	12,766,330	4,530,895	17,117,225	NA	62,936	18,817,264
1991	84,745	29,338	1,798,139	12,553,444	3,794,330	16,347,774	NA	74,829	18,334,826
1992	95,069	52,030	2,161,017	13,253,408	3,714,306	16,967,714	NA	96,377	19,372,208
1993	204,524	53,444	2,397,117	14,749,427	3,760,170	18,509,597	869	106,992	21,272,544
1994	221,746	82,782	2,681,563	15,339,528	3,903,514	19,243,042	994	159,795	22,389,924
1995	236,828	94,736	2,900,710	15,669,254	3,211,347	18,880,600	1,379	146,216	22,260,469
1996	202,882	63,042	3,002,036	16,341,399	3,942,893	20,284,292	1,115	148,410	23,701,776
1997	187,169	77,847	3,063,039	17,875,688	3,864,481	21,740,169	303	146,823	25,215,350
1998	218,092	95,083	3,224,555	18,916,158	3,991,733	22,907,891	235	134,820	26,580,676
1999	227,233	79,955	3,664,386	18,935,152	4,197,772	23,132,924	310	147,449	27,252,257
2000	312,816	93,769	3,868,580	19,782,784	4,748,621	24,531,405	413	165,797	28,972,779
2001	494,682	62,645	4,068,409	20,347,647	5,050,346	25,397,993	1,542	131,363	30,156,633
2002	421,886	80,402	4,103,803	19,920,301	4,753,137	24,673,438	2,113	125,490	29,407,132
2003	626,099	68,423	4,042,343	21,060,345	5,158,059	26,218,404	1,542	103,706	31,060,518
2004	682,000	170,450	4,365,022	22,082,229	6,113,608	28,195,837	13,141	116,725	33,543,175
2005	761,509	87,519	4,449,560	22,090,819	7,155,956	29,246,774	12,630	151,928	34,709,920
2006	906,149	100,886	4,290,938	22,084,624	7,076,991	29,161,615	67,755	145,663	34,673,006
2007	908,671	61,008	4,722,771	21,913,503	6,848,637	28,762,140	55,168	175,362	34,685,121
2008	855,192	89,354	4,083,839	21,448,357	6,195,447	27,643,804	85,130	194,554	32,951,874
2009	565,963	8,606	3,841,792	19,805,970	5,353,541	25,159,511	26,320	178,890	29,781,081

NA = Not Available.

[1] Crude oil and lease condensate. Includes imports into the Strategic Petroleum Reserve, which began in 1977.

[2] Petroleum products, unfinished oils, pentanes plus, and gasoline blending components. Does not include biofuels.

[3] Fuel ethanol (including denaturant) and biodiesel.

Source: U.S. Energy Information Administration
Plunkett Research, Ltd.
www.plunkettresearch.com

Energy Exports, U.S.: Selected Years, 1950-2009

(In Billions of Btus; Latest Year Available)

	Coal	Coal Coke	Natural Gas	Petroleum			Bio-fuels[3]	Elec-tricity	Total
				Crude Oil[1]	Petroleum Products[2]	Total			
1950	877,294	13,590	20,756	191,800	487,721	679,521	NA	598	1,591,760
1955	1,464,521	13,169	32,115	67,112	706,887	773,999	NA	1,705	2,285,508
1960	1,023,170	8,754	11,729	17,905	413,229	431,133	NA	2,689	1,477,475
1965	1,376,486	20,683	26,968	6,363	385,811	392,173	NA	12,622	1,828,933
1970	1,935,500	61,454	71,977	28,948	519,893	548,841	NA	14,363	2,632,135
1975	1,761,300	31,570	73,692	12,447	426,899	439,345	NA	17,344	2,323,252
1980	2,420,518	51,361	49,365	608,623	550,929	1,159,552	NA	13,974	3,694,770
1985	2,438,129	27,826	55,876	432,175	1,225,220	1,657,395	NA	16,940	4,196,166
1990	2,772,273	14,186	87,105	229,987	1,593,879	1,823,866	NA	55,048	4,752,479
1991	2,853,670	19,642	132,087	245,833	1,881,865	2,127,698	NA	7,863	5,140,959
1992	2,681,926	17,410	220,175	188,343	1,819,439	2,007,783	NA	9,644	4,936,938
1993	1,962,467	26,338	142,426	207,837	1,907,219	2,115,056	NA	12,082	4,258,368
1994	1,878,801	24,453	163,517	208,916	1,778,600	1,987,516	NA	6,858	4,061,144
1995	2,318,168	33,678	155,814	200,152	1,790,696	1,990,849	NA	12,361	4,510,870
1996	2,368,031	40,226	155,080	233,224	1,825,433	2,058,657	NA	11,266	4,633,260
1997	2,193,135	31,397	158,733	227,986	1,872,116	2,100,102	NA	30,619	4,513,987
1998	2,091,677	27,999	160,756	232,592	1,739,580	1,972,172	NA	46,596	4,299,200
1999	1,525,108	22,270	164,395	249,580	1,705,120	1,954,700	NA	48,525	3,714,999
2000	1,527,552	28,421	245,178	106,442	2,047,685	2,154,127	NA	50,598	4,005,875
2001	1,265,220	33,381	377,011	42,839	1,995,576	2,038,415	211	56,207	3,770,444
2002	1,032,088	19,642	520,363	19,117	2,023,029	2,042,146	298	53,895	3,668,430
2003	1,117,147	17,906	686,041	26,320	2,123,817	2,150,138	588	81,802	4,053,621
2004	1,253,129	32,711	861,825	56,741	2,150,114	2,206,856	662	78,128	4,433,311
2005	1,273,227	43,326	735,158	67,390	2,373,208	2,440,599	1,103	67,527	4,560,939
2006	1,263,672	40,077	730,474	52,194	2,694,314	2,746,508	4,435	82,814	4,867,980
2007	1,506,648	35,811	829,856	58,034	2,913,798	2,971,833	34,710	68,730	5,447,587
2008	2,070,504	48,583	1,014,776	60,691	3,652,692	3,713,383	86,430	82,173	7,015,849
2009	1,514,832	32,414	1,080,918	92,711	4,115,292	4,208,002	33,934	61,795	6,931,896

NA = Not Available

[1] Crude oil and lease condensate.

[2] Petroleum products, unfinished oils, pentanes plus, and gasoline blending components. Does not include biofuels.

[3] Biodiesel only.

Source: U.S. Energy Information Administration

Plunkett Research, Ltd.

www.plunkettresearch.com

Total Energy Imports, Net Energy Imports & Petroleum Imports, U.S.: 1970-2009

(In Quadrillion Btus; Latest Year Available)

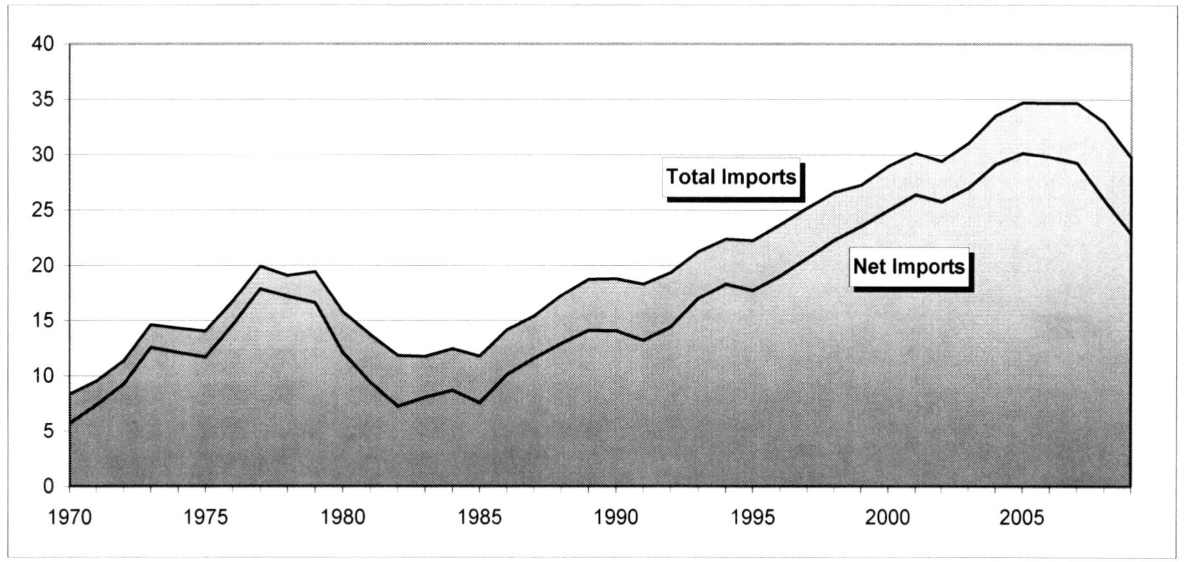

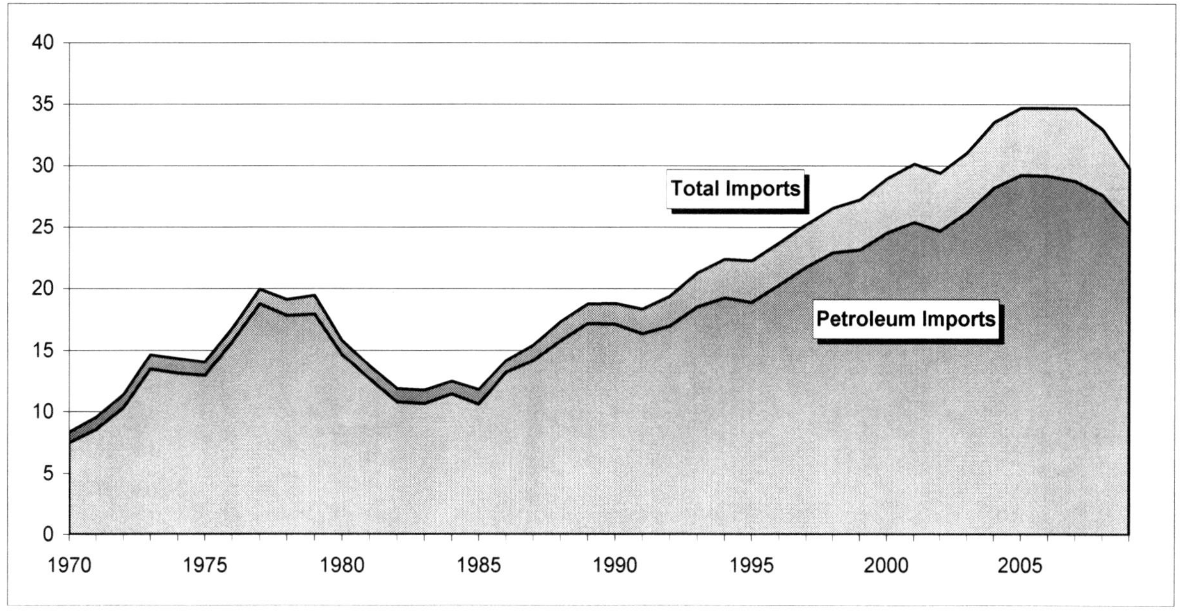

Note = Net imports equal imports minus exports. Negative numbers would indicate exports greater than imports.

Source: U.S. Energy Information Administration
Plunkett Research, Ltd.
www.plunkettresearch.com

Federal R&D & R&D Plant Funding for Energy, U.S.: Fiscal Years 2009-2011

(In Millions of US$)

Funding Category and Agency	2009 Actual	2009 ARRA*	2010 Prelim.	2011 Proposed	% Change (2010-11)
Total	2,234	1,560	2,392	2,549	6.6
Department of Energy	2,095	1,560	2,266	2,421	6.8
Energy programs	2,095	1,175	2,266	2,148	-5.2
Energy efficiency and renewable energy	850	1,116	996	1,031	3.5
Electricity delivery and energy reliability	75	10	122	144	18.0
Fossil energy	540	49	511	458	-10.4
Nuclear energy	630	0	637	515	-19.2
ARPA-E	0	385	0	273	NA
Nuclear Regulatory Commission	101	0	81	78	-3.7
Tennessee Valley Authority	18	0	17	20	17.6
U.S. Department of Agriculture (Biomass R&D)	20	0	28	30	7.1

ARPA-E = Advanced Research Projects Agency-Energy. NA = Not Available.

* For total FY 2009 amounts, sum FY 2009 Actual and FY 2009 ARRA (funds appropriated through the American Recovery and Reinvestment Act of 2009).

Note: Detail may not add to total because of rounding. Percentage change calculated on unrounded data.

Source: U.S. National Science Foundation
Plunkett Research, Ltd.
www.plunkettresearch.com

U.S. Department of Energy
Funding for Scientific Research: 2009-2011

(In Thousands of US$)

Area of Scientific Research	2009 Current Appropriation	2009 Current Recovery*	2010 Current Appropriation	2011 Congressional Request
Energy Programs	**17,772,671**	**31,588,000**	**10,334,351**	**11,353,690**
Energy Efficiency & Renewable Energy	**2,156,865**	**16,771,907**	**2,242,500**	**2,355,473**
Hydrogen and Fuel Cell Technologies	164,638	42,967	174,000	137,000
Biomass & Biorefinery Systems R&D	214,245	777,138	220,000	220,000
Solar Energy	172,414	115,963	247,000	302,398
Wind Energy	54,370	106,932	80,000	122,500
Geothermal Technology	43,322	393,106	44,000	55,000
Water Power	39,082	31,667	50,000	40,488
Vehicle Technologies	267,143	109,249	311,365	325,302
Building Technologies	138,113	319,186	222,000	230,698
Industrial Technologies	88,196	212,854	96,000	100,000
Federal Energy Management Program	22,000	22,388	32,000	42,272
Electricity Delivery & Energy Reliability	134,629	4,495,712	171,982	185,930
Nuclear Energy	791,444	0	786,637	824,052
Fuel Cycle Research & Development	0	0	136,000	201,000
Fossil Energy Programs	**1,097,003**	**3,398,607**	**951,133**	**760,358**
Fossil Energy Research & Development	863,104	3,398,607	672,383	586,583
Coal	681,264	3,388,607	404,000	403,850
Clean Coal Power Initiative	288,174	0	0	0
Fuels & Power Systems	393,090	3,388,607	404,000	403,850
Innovations for existing plants	48,600	0	52,000	65,000
Combined cycle	63,409	0	63,000	55,000
Advanced turbines	27,216	0	32,000	31,000
Carbon sequestration	145,800	0	154,000	143,000
Fuels	24,300	0	25,000	12,000
Fuel cells	56,376	0	50,000	50,000
Advanced research	27,389	0	28,000	47,850
Naval Petroleum & Oil Shale Reserves	19,099	0	23,627	23,614
Strategic Petroleum Reserve	226,586	0	243,823	138,861
Northeast Home Heating Oil Reserve	9,800	0	11,300	11,300
Science	**4,813,470**	**1,632,918**	**4,903,710**	**5,121,437**
High Energy Physics	775,868	232,390	810,483	829,000
Proton accelerator-based physics	401,368	107,990	434,167	439,262
Electron accelerator-based physics	32,030	1,400	27,427	24,707
Non-accelerator physics	101,138	4,445	99,625	88,539
Theoretical physics	66,148	5,975	66,962	69,524
Advanced technology R&D	175,184	112,580	182,302	189,968
Nuclear Physics	500,307	154,800	535,000	562,000
Biological & Environmental Research	585,176	165,653	604,182	626,900
Basic Energy Sciences	1,535,765	555,406	1,636,500	1,835,000
Other				
Uranium Enrichment D&D Fund	535,503	390,000	573,850	730,498
Energy Information Administration	110,595	0	110,595	128,833
Non-Defense Environmental Cleanup	261,819	483,000	254,673	225,163

* Represents funding from the American Recovery and Reinvestment Act of 2009.

Source: U.S. Department of Energy, Office of Science
Plunkett Research, Ltd.
www.plunkettresearch.com

Approximate Energy Unit Conversion Factors

Crude oil[1]

	To convert into:				
	tonnes[2]	kilolitres	barrels	US gallons	tonnes/year
From	**Multiply by:**				
Tonnes[2]	1	1.165	7.33	307.86	–
Kilolitres	0.8581	1	6.2898	264.17	–
Barrels	0.1364	0.159	1	42	–
US gallons	0.00325	0.0038	0.0238	1	–
Barrels per day	–	–	–	–	49.8

[1] Based on worldwide average gravity. [2] tonnes = metric tons

Products

	To convert:			
	barrels to tonnes	tonnes to barrels	kilolitres to tonnes	tonnes to kilolitres
From	**Multiply by:**			
Liquefied Petroleum Gas (LPG)	0.086	11.6	0.542	1.844
Gasoline	0.118	8.5	0.740	1.351
Kerosene	0.128	7.8	0.806	1.240
Gas oil/diesel	0.133	7.5	0.839	1.192
Fuel oil	0.149	6.7	0.939	1.065

Natural Gas (NG) and Liquefied Natural Gas (LNG)

	To convert to:					
	billion cubic meters NG	billion cubic feet NG	million tonnes oil equivalent	million tonnes LNG	trillion British thermal units	million barrels oil equivalent
From	**Multiply by:**					
1 billion cubic meters NG	1	35.3	0.90	0.74	35.7	6.60
1 billion cubic feet NG	0.028	1	0.025	0.021	1.01	0.19
1 million tonnes oil equivalent	1.111	39.2	1	0.82	39.7	7.33
1 million tonnes LNG	1.36	48.0	1.22	1	48.6	8.97
1 trillion British thermal units	0.028	0.99	0.025	0.021	1	0.18
1 million barrels oil equivalent	0.15	5.35	0.14	0.11	5.41	1

Units

1 metric tonne = 2204.62 lb.	1 kilocalorie (kcal) = 4.187 kJ = 3.968 Btu
= 1.1023 short tons	1 kilojoule (kJ) = 0.239 kcal = 0.948 Btu
1 kilolitre = 6.2898 barrels	1 British thermal unit (Btu) = 0.252 kcal = 1.055 kJ
1 kilolitre = 1 cubic meter	1 kilowatt-hour (kWh) = 860 kcal = 3600 kJ = 3412 Btu

Calorific equivalents:
One tonne of oil equivalent equals approximately:

Heat units	10 million kilocalories	**Solid fuels**	1.5 tonnes of hard coal
	42 gigajoules		3 tonnes of lignite
	40 million Btu	**Gaseous fuels**	See Natural gas and LNG table
		Electricity	12 megawatt-hours

Note: One million tonnes of oil or oil equivalent produces about 4,400 gigawatt-hours (= 4.4. terawatt-hours) of electricity in a modern power station.

Source: BP, *Statistical Review of Energy,* June 2010
Plunkett Research, Ltd.
www.plunkettresearch.com

II. Electricity

Contents:

Electricity Overview, U.S.: Selected Years, 1950-2009

(In Millions of Kilowatt-Hours; Latest Year Available)

Year	Net Generation				Imports[1]	Exports[1]	T & D[5] Losses and Unaccounted For[6]	End Use		
	Electric Power Sector[2]	Commercial Sector[3]	Industrial Sector[4]	Total				Retail Sales[7]	Direct Use[8]	Total
1950	329,141	NA	4,946	334,088	1,933	147	44,430	291,443	NA	291,443
1955	547,038	NA	3,261	550,299	4,567	500	57,618	496,748	NA	496,748
1960	755,549	NA	3,607	759,156	5,323	788	75,616	688,075	NA	688,075
1965	1,055,252	NA	3,134	1,058,386	3,558	3,699	104,455	953,789	NA	953,789
1970	1,531,868	NA	3,244	1,535,111	6,170	4,209	144,772	1,392,300	NA	1,392,300
1975	1,917,649	NA	3,106	1,920,755	11,268	5,083	179,849	1,747,091	NA	1,747,091
1980	2,286,439	NA	3,161	2,289,600	25,021	4,096	216,077	2,094,449	NA	2,094,449
1985	2,469,841	NA	3,161	2,473,002	45,895	4,965	189,959	2,323,974	NA	2,323,974
1990	2,901,322	5,837	130,830	3,037,988	18,445	16,134	203,216	2,712,555	124,529	2,837,084
1995	3,194,230	8,232	151,025	3,353,487	42,854	3,623	228,755	3,013,287	150,677	3,163,963
1996	3,284,141	9,030	151,017	3,444,188	43,497	3,302	230,617	3,101,127	152,638	3,253,765
1997	3,329,375	8,701	154,097	3,492,172	43,031	8,974	224,380	3,145,610	156,239	3,301,849
1998	3,457,416	8,748	154,132	3,620,295	39,513	13,656	221,056	3,264,231	160,866	3,425,097
1999	3,529,982	8,563	156,264	3,694,810	43,215	14,222	240,086	3,312,087	171,629	3,483,716
2000	3,637,529	7,903	156,673	3,802,105	48,592	14,829	243,511	3,421,414	170,943	3,592,357
2001	3,580,053	7,416	149,175	3,736,644	38,500	16,473	201,564	3,394,458	162,649	3,557,107
2002	3,698,458	7,415	152,580	3,858,452	36,779	15,796	247,785	3,465,466	166,184	3,631,650
2003	3,721,159	7,496	154,530	3,883,185	30,390	23,972	227,576	3,493,734	168,295	3,662,029
2004	3,808,360	8,270	153,925	3,970,555	34,210	22,898	265,918	3,547,479	168,470	3,715,949
2005	3,902,192	8,492	144,739	4,055,423	44,527	19,791	269,175	3,660,969	150,016	3,810,984
2006	3,908,077	8,371	148,254	4,064,702	42,691	24,271	266,277	3,669,919	146,927	3,816,845
2007	4,005,343	8,273	143,128	4,156,745	51,396	20,144	264,183	3,764,561	159,254	3,923,814
2008	3,974,349	7,926	137,113	4,119,388	57,021	24,083	245,881	3,732,962	173,481	3,906,443
2009	3,814,298	7,638	131,174	3,953,111	52,430	18,111	245,945	3,575,450	166,034	3,741,484

NA = Not Available

[1] Electricity transmitted across U.S. borders.

[2] Electricity-only and combined-heat-and-power (CHP) plants within the NAICS 22 category whose primary business is to sell electricity, or electricity and heat, to the public. Through 1988, data are for electric utilities only; beginning in 1989, data are for electric utilities and independent power producers.

[3] Commercial combined-heat-and-power (CHP) and commercial electricity-only plants.

[4] Industrial combined-heat-and-power (CHP) and industrial electricity-only plants. Through 1988, data are for industrial hydroelectric power only.

[5] Transmission and distribution losses (electricity losses that occur between the point of generation and delivery to the customer).

[6] Data collection frame differences and nonsampling error.

[7] Electricity retail sales to ultimate customers by electric utilities and, beginning in 1996, other energy service providers.

[8] Use of electricity that is 1) self-generated, 2) produced by either the same entity that consumes the power or an affiliate, and 3) used in direct support of a service or industrial process located within the same facility or group of facilities that house the generating equipment. Direct use is exclusive of station use.

Source: U.S. Department of Energy, Energy Information Administration
Plunkett Research, Ltd.
www.plunkettresearch.com

Total Electrical Power Generation by Fuel Type, U.S.: 1980-1st 7 Months of 2010

(Thousands of Megawatt Hours; Latest Year Available)

Year	Coal[1]	Petroleum[2]	Natural Gas	Other Gases[3]	Nuclear Energy	Conventional Hydroelectric Power	Other Renewables[4]	Other[5]	Total
1980	1,161,562	245,994	346,240	NA	251,116	279,182	5,073	NA	2,289,600
1981	1,203,203	206,421	345,777	NA	272,674	263,845	5,686	NA	2,297,973
1982	1,192,004	146,797	305,260	NA	282,773	312,374	4,843	NA	2,244,372
1983	1,259,424	144,499	274,098	NA	293,677	335,291	6,075	NA	2,313,446
1984	1,341,681	119,808	297,394	NA	327,634	324,311	7,741	NA	2,419,465
1985	1,402,128	100,202	291,946	NA	383,691	284,311	9,325	NA	2,473,002
1986	1,385,831	136,585	248,508	NA	414,038	294,005	10,308	NA	2,490,471
1987	1,463,781	118,493	272,621	NA	455,270	252,856	10,775	NA	2,575,288
1988	1,540,653	148,900	252,801	NA	526,973	226,101	10,300	NA	2,707,411
1989	1,583,779	164,518	352,629	7,862	529,355	271,977	14,593	3,830	2,967,306
1990	1,594,011	126,621	372,765	10,383	576,862	292,866	15,434	3,616	3,037,988
1991	1,590,623	119,752	381,553	11,336	612,565	288,994	15,966	4,739	3,073,799
1992	1,621,206	100,154	404,074	13,270	618,776	253,088	16,138	3,720	3,083,882
1993	1,690,070	112,788	414,927	12,956	610,291	280,494	16,789	3,487	3,197,191
1994	1,690,694	105,901	460,219	13,319	640,440	260,126	15,535	3,667	3,247,522
1995	1,709,426	74,554	496,058	13,870	673,402	310,833	73,965	4,104	3,353,487
1996	1,795,196	81,411	455,056	14,356	674,729	347,162	75,796	3,571	3,444,188
1997	1,845,016	92,555	479,399	13,351	628,644	356,453	77,183	3,612	3,492,172
1998	1,873,516	128,800	531,257	13,492	673,702	323,336	77,088	3,571	3,620,295
1999	1,881,087	118,061	556,396	14,126	728,254	319,536	79,423	4,024	3,694,810
2000	1,966,265	111,221	601,038	13,955	753,893	275,573	80,906	4,794	3,802,105
2001	1,903,956	124,880	639,129	9,039	768,826	216,961	70,769	11,906	3,736,644
2002	1,933,130	94,567	691,006	11,463	780,064	264,329	79,109	13,527	3,858,452
2003	1,973,737	119,406	649,908	15,600	763,733	275,806	79,487	14,045	3,883,185
2004	1,978,301	121,145	710,100	15,252	788,528	268,417	83,067	14,232	3,970,555
2005	2,012,873	122,225	760,960	13,464	781,986	270,321	87,329	12,821	4,055,423
2006	1,990,511	64,166	816,441	14,177	787,219	289,246	96,525	12,974	4,064,702
2007	2,016,456	65,739	896,590	13,453	806,425	247,510	105,238	12,231	4,156,745
2008	1,985,801	42,242	882,981	11,707	806,208	254,831	126,212	11,692	4,119,388
2009	1,764,486	38,827	920,378	10,698	788,745	272,131	141,115	11,078	3,953,111
2010* (Jan-July)	1,090,955	23,029	548,058	6,560	466,905	159,747	93,627	6,604	2,393,612

* Year to date, through July. NA = Not available.

[1] Anthracite, bituminous, subbituminous, lignite, waste coal, and coal synfuel.

[2] Petroleum liquids including distillate fuel oil, residual fuel oil, jet fuel, kerosene, and waste oil; and petroleum coke.

[3] Blast furnace gas, propane gas, and other manufactured and waste gases derived from fossil fuels.

[4] Includes wind; solar thermal and photovoltaic; wood and wood-derived fuels; geothermal; and other biomass. Category realignments are responsible for the dramatic increase in 1995.

[5] Non-biogenic municipal solid waste, batteries, chemicals, hydrogen, pitch, purchased steam, sulfur, tire-derived fuel, and miscellaneous technologies.

Source: U.S. Department of Energy, Energy Information Administration
Plunkett Research, Ltd.
www.plunkettresearch.com

Average Retail Prices of Electricity Sold by U.S. Electric Utilities: Selected Years 1960-2009

(In Cents per Kilowatt-Hour; Latest Year Available)

Year	Residential		Commercial[1]		Industrial[2]		Other/ Transportation[3]		Total Average	
	Nominal[4]	Real[5]	Nominal[4]	Real[5]	Nominal[4]	Real[5]	Nominal[4]	Real[5]	Nominal[4]	Real[5]
1960	2.60	14.00	2.40	12.90	1.10	5.90	1.90	10.20	1.80	9.70
1970	2.20	9.10	2.10	8.60	1.00	4.10	1.80	7.40	1.70	7.00
1980	5.40	11.30	5.50	11.50	3.70	7.80	4.80	10.10	4.70	9.80
1990	7.83	10.84	7.34	10.17	4.74	6.57	6.40	8.86	6.57	9.10
2000	8.24	9.30	7.43	8.38	4.64	5.23	6.56	7.40	6.81	7.68
2001	8.58	9.46	7.92	8.74	5.05	5.57	7.20	7.94	7.29	8.04
2002	8.44	9.16	7.89	8.57	4.88	5.30	6.75	7.33	7.20	7.82
2003	8.72	9.27	8.03	8.53	5.11	5.43	7.54	8.01	7.44	7.91
2004	8.95	9.25	8.17	8.44	5.25	5.43	7.18	7.42	7.61	7.86
2005	9.45	9.45	8.67	8.67	5.73	5.73	8.57	8.57	8.14	8.14
2006	10.40	10.07	9.46	9.16	6.16	5.97	9.54	9.24	8.90	8.62
2007	10.65	10.03	9.65	9.09	6.39	6.02	9.70	9.13	9.13	8.60
2008	11.26	10.38	10.36	9.55	6.83	6.30	10.74	9.90	9.74	8.98
2009	11.55	10.52	10.21	9.30	6.84	6.23	11.17	10.18	9.89	9.01

Notes: Data represent revenue from electricity retail sales divided by electricity retail sales. Through 1979, data are for Classes A and B privately owned electric utilities only. For 1980-1982, data are for selected Class A utilities whose electric operating revenues were $100 million or more during the previous year. For 1983, data are for a selected sample of electric utilities. Beginning in 1984, data are for a census of electric utilities. Beginning in 1996, data also include energy service providers selling to retail customers.

[1] Commercial sector. For 1960-2002, prices exclude public street and highway lighting, interdepartmental sales, and other sales to public authorities.

[2] Industrial sector. For 1960-2002, prices exclude agriculture and irrigation.

[3] The category "Other" was changed to "Transportation" in 2003. It reflects sales to public street and highway lighting, other sales to public authorities, sales to railroads and railways, and interdepartmental sales.

[4] In dollars not adjusted for inflation.

[5] In chained (2005) dollars, calculated by using gross domestic product implicit price deflators.

Source: U.S. Department of Energy, Energy Information Administration
Plunkett Research, Ltd.
www.plunkettresearch.com

III. Fossil Fuels & Nuclear Energy

Contents:

Energy Production by Fossil Fuels & Nuclear Power, U.S.: Selected Years, 1950-2009

(In Billions of Btus; Latest Year Available)

Year	Fossil Fuels					Nuclear Electric Power	Total[2]
	Coal	Natural Gas (Dry)	Crude Oil[1]	Natural Gas Plant Liquids	Total		
1950	14,060,135	6,232,975	11,446,729	822,828	32,562,667	0	35,540,385
1955	12,369,608	9,344,668	14,409,682	1,239,721	37,363,680	0	40,147,667
1960	10,817,398	12,656,133	14,934,611	1,460,974	39,869,116	6,026	42,803,761
1965	13,055,285	15,775,441	16,521,381	1,882,795	47,234,902	43,164	50,676,101
1970	14,607,064	21,665,670	20,401,210	2,512,128	59,186,072	239,347	63,501,275
1975	14,989,315	19,640,343	17,729,318	2,374,297	54,733,273	1,899,798	61,356,565
1980	18,597,726	19,907,600	18,248,917	2,253,630	59,007,873	2,739,169	67,232,462
1985	19,325,166	16,980,380	18,992,407	2,240,771	57,538,724	4,075,563	67,799,166
1990	22,487,548	18,326,155	15,571,185	2,174,714	58,559,602	6,104,350	70,869,979
1991	21,636,424	18,228,736	15,700,826	2,305,740	57,871,727	6,422,132	70,531,332
1992	21,694,132	18,375,100	15,222,866	2,362,961	57,655,059	6,479,206	70,126,437
1993	20,335,654	18,584,037	14,494,391	2,408,002	55,822,084	6,410,499	68,493,804
1994	22,202,083	19,348,014	14,102,561	2,390,979	58,043,637	6,693,877	70,890,723
1995	22,129,550	19,082,245	13,886,754	2,441,583	57,540,133	7,075,436	71,316,338
1996	22,790,148	19,344,268	13,722,899	2,529,910	58,387,225	7,086,674	72,638,657
1997	23,309,614	19,393,795	13,658,020	2,495,207	58,856,635	6,596,992	72,630,769
1998	24,045,199	19,613,280	13,235,130	2,420,459	59,314,068	7,067,809	73,036,802
1999	23,295,084	19,340,704	12,451,046	2,527,649	57,614,483	7,610,256	71,903,053
2000	22,735,478	19,661,518	12,358,101	2,610,916	57,366,013	7,862,349	71,485,380
2001	23,547,080	20,165,568	12,281,564	2,547,136	58,541,347	8,028,853	71,882,553
2002	22,732,237	19,438,838	12,163,319	2,559,168	56,893,563	8,145,429	70,931,450
2003	22,093,652	19,633,303	12,026,027	2,346,260	56,099,243	7,958,858	70,196,814
2004	22,852,099	19,074,254	11,503,152	2,465,850	55,895,355	8,221,985	70,352,355
2005	23,185,189	18,556,015	10,962,615	2,333,842	55,037,660	8,160,810	69,591,871
2006	23,789,510	19,021,706	10,801,102	2,355,836	55,968,153	8,215,414	70,957,207
2007	23,492,742	19,824,741	10,721,012	2,408,589	56,447,084	8,455,364	71,607,975
2008	23,851,368	20,833,789	10,508,538	2,419,358	57,613,054	8,427,297	73,421,316
2009	21,578,333	21,499,836	11,241,142	2,540,580	56,859,891	8,349,297	72,970,019

Note: Totals may not equal sum of components due to independent rounding.

[1] Includes lease condensate.

[2] This total includes generation from renewable sources such as hydro-electric, geothermal, solar, wind and biomass.

Source: U.S. Department of Energy, Energy Information Administration

Plunkett Research, Ltd.

www.plunkettresearch.com

Petroleum Overview, U.S.: Selected Years, 1950-2009

(In Thousands of Barrels per Day; Latest Year Available)

Year	Petroleum Production[1]			Petroleum Trade			Stock Change[2]	Adjust-ments[3]	Petroleum Products Supplied
	Crude Oil	Natural Gas Plant Liquids	Total	Imports[4]	Exports	Net Imports			
1950	5,407	499	5,906	850	305	545	-56	-51	6,458
1955	6,807	771	7,578	1,248	368	880	<1	-37	8,455
1960	7,035	929	7,965	1,815	202	1,613	-83	-8	9,797
1965	7,804	1,210	9,014	2,468	187	2,281	-8	-10	11,512
1970	9,637	1,660	11,297	3,419	259	3,161	103	-16	14,697
1975	8,375	1,633	10,007	6,056	209	5,846	32	41	16,322
1980	8,597	1,573	10,170	6,909	544	6,365	140	64	17,056
1985	8,971	1,609	10,581	5,067	781	4,286	-103	200	15,726
1990	7,355	1,559	8,914	8,018	857	7,161	107	338	16,988
1991	7,417	1,659	9,076	7,627	1,001	6,626	-10	287	16,714
1992	7,171	1,697	8,868	7,888	950	6,938	-68	386	17,033
1993	6,847	1,736	8,582	8,620	1,003	7,618	151	422	17,237
1994	6,662	1,727	8,388	8,996	942	8,054	15	523	17,718
1995	6,560	1,762	8,322	8,835	949	7,886	-246	496	17,725
1996	6,465	1,830	8,295	9,478	981	8,498	-151	528	18,309
1997	6,452	1,817	8,269	10,162	1,003	9,158	143	487	18,620
1998	6,252	1,759	8,011	10,708	945	9,764	239	495	18,917
1999	5,881	1,850	7,731	10,852	940	9,912	-422	567	19,519
2000	5,822	1,911	7,733	11,459	1,040	10,419	-69	532	19,701
2001	5,801	1,868	7,670	11,871	971	10,900	325	501	19,649
2002	5,746	1,880	7,626	11,530	984	10,546	-105	527	19,761
2003	5,681	1,719	7,400	12,264	1,027	11,238	56	478	20,034
2004	5,419	1,809	7,228	13,145	1,048	12,097	209	564	20,731
2005	5,178	1,717	6,895	13,714	1,165	12,549	145	513	20,802
2006	5,102	1,739	6,841	13,707	1,317	12,390	60	522	20,687
2007	5,064	1,783	6,847	13,468	1,433	12,036	-148	653	20,680
2008	4,950	1,784	6,734	12,915	1,802	11,114	195	852	19,498
2009	5,310	1,886	7,196	11,726	2,026	9,700	112	186	18,686

[1] Crude oil production on leases, and natural gas plant liquids (liquefied petroleum gases, pentanes plus, and a small amount of finished petroleum products) production at natural gas processing plants. Excludes what was previously classified as "Field Production" of finished motor gasoline, motor gasoline blending components, and other hydrocarbons and oxygenates; these are now included in "Adjustments."

[2] A negative number indicates a decrease in stocks and a positive number indicates an increase. Includes crude oil stocks in the Strategic Petroleum Reserve, but excludes distillate fuel oil stocks in the Northeast Heating Oil Reserve.

[3] An adjustment for crude oil, finished motor gasoline, motor gasoline blending components, fuel ethanol, and distillate fuel oil.

[4] Includes crude oil imports for the Strategic Petroleum Reserve, which began in 1977.

Source: U.S. Department of Energy, Energy Information Administration
Plunkett Research, Ltd.
www.plunkettresearch.com

Crude Oil Production & Oil Well Productivity, U.S.: Selected Years, 1955-2009

(In Thousands of Barrels per Day Unless Otherwise Noted; Latest Year Available)

	Geographic Location		Site		Type		Total Petroleum Production	Oil Well Productivity	
	48 States[1]	Alaska	Onshore	Offshore	Crude Oil	Lease Con-densate[2]		Producing Wells[3] *(thous.)*	Average Daily Productivity[4] *(barrels per well)*
1955	6,807	0	6,645	162	6,807	NA	6,807	524	13.0
1960	7,034	2	6,716	319	7,035	NA	7,035	591	11.9
1965	7,774	30	7,140	665	7,804	NA	7,804	589	13.2
1970	9,408	229	8,060	1,577	9,180	457	9,637	531	18.1
1975	8,183	191	7,012	1,362	8,007	367	8,375	500	16.8
1980	6,980	1,617	7,562	1,034	8,210	386	8,597	548	15.7
1985	7,146	1,825	7,722	1,250	8,971	NA	8,971	647	13.9
1986	6,814	1,867	7,426	1,254	8,680	NA	8,680	623	13.9
1987	6,387	1,962	7,153	1,196	8,349	NA	8,349	620	13.5
1988	6,123	2,017	6,949	1,191	8,140	NA	8,140	612	13.3
1989	5,739	1,874	6,486	1,127	7,613	NA	7,613	603	12.6
1990	5,582	1,773	6,273	1,082	7,355	NA	7,355	602	12.2
1991	5,618	1,798	6,245	1,172	7,417	NA	7,417	614	12.1
1992	5,457	1,714	5,953	1,218	7,171	NA	7,171	594	12.1
1993	5,264	1,582	5,606	1,241	6,847	NA	6,847	584	11.7
1994	5,103	1,559	5,291	1,370	6,662	NA	6,662	582	11.4
1995	5,076	1,484	5,035	1,525	6,560	NA	6,560	574	11.4
1996	5,071	1,393	4,902	1,562	6,465	NA	6,465	574	11.3
1997	5,156	1,296	4,803	1,648	6,452	NA	6,452	573	11.3
1998	5,077	1,175	4,560	1,692	6,252	NA	6,252	562	11.1
1999	4,832	1,050	4,132	1,750	5,881	NA	5,881	546	10.8
2000	4,851	970	4,049	1,773	5,822	NA	5,822	534	10.9
2001	4,839	963	3,879	1,923	5,801	NA	5,801	530	10.9
2002	4,761	984	3,743	2,003	5,746	NA	5,746	529	10.9
2003	4,706	974	3,668	2,012	5,681	NA	5,681	513	11.1
2004	4,510	908	3,536	1,883	5,419	NA	5,419	510	10.6
2005	4,314	864	3,466	1,712	5,178	NA	5,178	498	10.4
2006	4,361	741	3,401	1,701	5,102	NA	5,102	497	10.3
2007	4,342	722	3,407	1,657	5,064	NA	5,064	500	10.1
2008	4,268	683	3,580	1,371	4,950	NA	4,950	526	9.4
2009	4,665	645	3,442	1,868	5,310	NA	5,310	526	10.1

Note: Totals may not equal sum of components due to independent rounding.

[1] United States excluding Alaska and Hawaii.

[2] For 1955-1967 and 1983-2008, "Lease Condensate" is included in "Crude Oil."

[3] As of December 31.

[4] Through 1976, average productivity is based on the average number of producing wells. Beginning in 1977, average productivity is based on the number of wells producing at end of year.

Source: U.S. Department of Energy, Energy Information Administration
Plunkett Research, Ltd.
www.plunkettresearch.com

Crude Oil Domestic First Purchase Prices, U.S.: Selected Years, 1960-2009

(In US$ per Barrel; Latest Year Available)

	Alaska North Slope		California		Texas		U.S. Average	
	Nominal[1]	Real[2]	Nominal[1]	Real[2]	Nominal[1]	Real[2]	Nominal[1]	Real[2]
1960	—	—	—	—	—	—	2.88	15.49
1970	—	—	—	—	—	—	3.18	13.08
1980	16.87	35.33	23.87	49.99	21.84	45.74	21.59	45.21
1981	23.23	44.48	26.80	51.32	35.06	67.13	31.77	60.83
1982	19.92	35.95	24.58	44.36	31.77	57.33	28.52	51.47
1983	17.69	30.71	22.61	39.25	29.35	50.95	26.19	45.47
1984	17.91	29.97	22.09	36.96	28.87	48.31	25.88	43.30
1985	16.98	27.58	22.14	35.96	26.80	43.52	24.09	39.12
1986	6.45	10.25	11.90	18.91	14.73	23.40	12.51	19.88
1987	10.83	16.72	13.92	21.49	17.55	27.10	15.40	23.78
1988	8.43	12.58	10.97	16.38	14.71	21.96	12.58	18.78
1989	12.00	17.26	14.06	20.22	17.81	25.62	15.86	22.81
1990	15.23	21.09	17.81	24.67	22.37	30.98	20.03	27.74
1991	11.57	15.48	13.72	18.35	19.04	25.47	16.54	22.12
1992	11.73	15.33	13.55	17.70	18.32	23.94	15.99	20.89
1993	10.84	13.86	12.11	15.48	16.19	20.70	14.25	18.22
1994	9.77	12.23	12.12	15.17	14.98	18.76	13.19	16.51
1995	11.12	13.64	14.00	17.17	16.38	20.09	14.62	17.93
1996	15.32	18.44	16.72	20.12	20.31	24.44	18.46	22.22
1997	14.84	17.55	15.78	18.66	18.66	22.07	17.23	20.38
1998	8.47	9.91	9.55	11.17	12.28	14.36	10.87	12.71
1999	12.46	14.36	14.08	16.23	17.29	19.93	15.56	17.93
2000	23.62	26.65	24.82	28.00	28.60	32.26	26.72	30.14
2001	18.18	20.06	20.11	22.18	23.41	25.82	21.84	24.09
2002	19.37	21.03	21.87	23.74	23.77	25.80	22.51	24.44
2003	23.78	25.27	26.43	28.09	29.13	30.96	27.56	29.29
2004	33.03	34.13	34.47	35.62	38.79	40.08	36.77	38.00
2005	47.05	47.05	47.08	47.08	52.61	52.61	50.28	50.28
2006	56.86	55.07	57.34	55.53	61.31	59.38	59.69	57.81
2007	63.69	59.96	65.07	61.26	68.30	64.30	66.52	62.63
2008	90.10	83.05	90.47	83.40	96.85	89.28	94.04	86.69
2009	54.41	49.57	56.12	51.13	57.40	52.29	56.39	51.37

Note: Prices are for the marketed first sales price of domestic crude oil.

[1] In dollars not adjusted for inflation.

[2] In chained (2005) dollars, calculated by using gross domestic product implicit price deflators.

Source: U.S. Department of Energy, Energy Information Administration

Plunkett Research, Ltd.

www.plunkettresearch.com

Landed Costs of U.S. Crude Oil Imports from Selected Countries: Selected Years, 1975-2009

(In Nominal US$ per Barrel; Latest Year Available)

	Persian Gulf	Selected OPEC[2] Countries					Selected Non-OPEC Countries						
	Persian Gulf Nations[1]	Kuwait	Nigeria	Saudi Arabia	Venezuela	Total OPEC[2]	Canada	Colombia	Mexico	Norway	United Kingdom	Total Non-OPEC	Average Imports
1975	12.64	W	12.70	12.50	12.36	12.70	12.84	NA	12.61	12.80	NA	12.70	12.70
1980	30.59	W	37.15	29.80	25.92	33.56	30.11	W	31.77	36.82	35.68	33.99	33.67
1985	22.50	NA	28.96	24.72	24.43	26.86	25.71	NA	25.63	28.32	28.36	26.53	26.67
1990	20.55	17.01	23.33	21.82	20.31	21.23	20.48	22.34	19.64	21.11	22.65	20.98	21.13
1991	17.34	18.48	21.39	17.22	15.92	18.08	17.16	19.55	15.89	21.44	21.37	17.93	18.02
1992	17.58	16.99	20.78	17.48	15.13	17.81	17.04	18.46	15.60	20.90	20.63	17.67	17.75
1993	15.26	14.23	18.73	15.40	13.39	15.68	15.27	16.54	14.11	18.99	17.92	15.78	15.72
1994	15.00	14.49	17.21	15.11	13.12	15.08	14.83	15.80	14.09	17.09	16.64	15.29	15.18
1995	16.78	16.47	18.25	16.84	14.81	16.61	16.65	17.45	16.19	18.06	17.91	16.95	16.78
1996	20.45	20.32	21.95	20.49	18.59	20.14	19.94	22.02	19.64	21.34	20.88	20.47	20.31
1997	17.44	17.03	20.64	17.52	16.35	17.73	17.63	19.71	17.30	20.26	20.64	18.45	18.11
1998	11.18	11.00	14.14	11.16	10.16	11.46	11.62	13.26	11.04	13.83	13.55	12.22	11.84
1999	17.37	16.77	17.63	17.48	15.58	16.94	17.54	18.09	16.12	19.06	18.26	17.51	17.23
2000	26.77	26.28	30.04	26.58	26.05	27.29	26.69	29.68	26.03	30.13	29.26	27.80	27.53
2001	20.73	19.66	26.55	20.98	19.81	21.52	20.72	25.88	19.37	25.77	25.32	22.17	21.82
2002	24.13	23.04	26.45	24.77	21.93	23.83	22.98	25.28	22.09	26.60	26.35	23.97	23.91
2003	27.54	26.82	31.07	27.50	25.70	27.70	26.76	30.55	25.48	30.51	30.62	27.68	27.69
2004	36.53	35.89	40.95	37.11	33.79	36.84	34.51	39.03	32.25	39.92	39.28	35.29	36.07
2005	49.68	48.36	57.55	50.31	47.87	51.36	44.73	53.42	43.47	56.23	55.28	47.31	49.29
2006	58.92	57.64	68.26	59.19	57.37	61.21	53.90	62.13	53.76	64.39	67.44	57.14	59.11
2007	69.83	66.01	78.01	70.78	66.13	71.14	60.38	70.91	62.31	71.66	72.47	63.96	67.97
2008	93.59	86.35	104.83	94.75	90.76	95.49	90.00	93.43	85.97	104.13	96.95	90.59	93.33
2009	61.99	60.96	67.59	62.03	57.70	61.73	57.59	58.35	57.35	58.95	63.53	58.55	60.12

Notes: This table reports landed costs of crude oil imports only; it does not account for refined petroleum products imported into the United States. Totals may not equal sum of components due to independent rounding.

W = Data withheld to avoid disclosure of individual company data. NA = Not available, or no data reported.

[1] Bahrain, Iran, Iraq, Kuwait, Qatar, Saudi Arabia, United Arab Emirates and the Neutral Zone (between Kuwait and Saudi Arabia).

[2] OPEC = Organization of Petroleum Exporting Countries. On this table, "Total OPEC" for all years includes Algeria, Iran, Iraq, Kuwait, Libya, Nigeria, Qatar, Saudi Arabia, United Arab Emirates, and Venezuela; for 1973-2008, also includes Indonesia; for 1973-1992 and beginning in 2008, also includes Ecuador; for 1974-1995, also includes Gabon; and beginning in 2007, also includes Angola. Data for all countries not included in "Total OPEC" are included in "Total Non-OPEC."

Source: U.S. Department of Energy, Energy Information Administration
Plunkett Research, Ltd.
www.plunkettresearch.com

Value of U.S. Crude Oil Imports from Selected Countries: 1980-2009

(In Thousands of Nominal US$; Latest Year Available)

	1980	1990	2000	2005	2006	2007	2008	2009
Persian Gulf Nations[1]	**16,878,614**	**13,505,727**	**23,604,207**	**40,024,841**	**46,454,413**	**53,904,780**	**80,143,831**	**37,774,598**
Total OPEC[2] Countries	**47,458,069**	**27,226,010**	**45,387,718**	**90,276,191**	**106,870,946**	**139,901,007**	**189,234,920**	**98,374,348**
Kuwait	W	492,303	2,532,525	4,000,823	3,759,684	4,211,834	6,506,732	4,120,225
Nigeria	11,436,256	6,675,320	9,616,915	22,619,337	25,848,014	30,857,168	35,365,344	19,012,459
Saudi Arabia	13,638,596	9,517,731	14,820,184	26,527,809	30,733,579	37,385,217	52,138,651	22,388,736
Venezuela	1,476,144	4,933,502	11,663,523	21,680,993	23,923,347	27,720,373	34,526,828	20,326,441
Total Non-OPEC	**17,395,806**	**18,232,797**	**46,006,816**	**91,898,220**	**111,427,072**	**108,964,623**	**144,951,251**	**100,445,979**
Canada	2,198,090	4,802,888	13,165,003	26,667,266	35,457,253	41,614,439	64,438,380	40,734,328
Colombia	0	1,140,256	3,452,110	3,045,047	3,207,772	3,552,520	6,080,051	5,407,528
Mexico	5,894,638	4,936,416	12,506,608	24,689,004	30,938,934	32,035,066	37,340,210	22,949,979
Norway	1,941,408	736,275	3,333,975	2,443,418	2,311,408	1,453,121	1,134,913	1,315,469
United Kingdom	2,264,217	1,279,657	3,111,274	4,512,009	3,187,956	3,674,505	2,762,881	2,410,138
Total Crude Oil Imports	**64,853,875**	**45,458,807**	**91,394,534**	**182,174,411**	**218,298,018**	**248,865,630**	**334,186,171**	**198,820,327**

Notes: Crude oil import volumes used to calculate values in this table are for the 50 States and the District of Columbia. Totals may not equal sum of components due to independent rounding.

W = Data withheld to avoid disclosure of individual company data.

[1] Bahrain, Iran, Iraq, Kuwait, Qatar, Saudi Arabia, United Arab Emirates and the Neutral Zone (between Kuwait and Saudi Arabia).

[2] OPEC = Organization of Petroleum Exporting Countries. On this table, "Total OPEC" for all years includes Algeria, Iran, Iraq, Kuwait, Libya, Nigeria, Qatar, Saudi Arabia, United Arab Emirates, and Venezuela; for 1973-2008, also includes Indonesia; for 1973-1992 and beginning in 2008, also includes Ecuador; for 1974-1995, also includes Gabon; and beginning in 2007, also includes Angola. Data for all countries not included in "Total OPEC" are included in "Total Non-OPEC."

Source: U.S. Department of Energy, Energy Information Administration

Plunkett Research, Ltd.

www.plunkettresearch.com

Petroleum Imports by Country of Origin, U.S.: Selected Years, 1960-2009

(In Thousands of Barrels; Latest Year Available)

	1960	1970	1980	1990	2000	2006	2007	2008	2009
Total Petroleum Imports	664,111	1,248,062	2,528,703	2,926,395	4,194,086	5,003,082	4,915,957	4,726,994	4,279,908
From Selected OPEC[1] Countries									
Total Persian Gulf Nations[2]	**NA**	**44,083**	**555,922**	**717,425**	**910,598**	**807,172**	**789,607**	**867,559**	**620,938**
Persian Gulf Nations as Share of Total Imports (%)	NA	3.5	22.0	24.5	21.7	16.1	16.1	18.4	14.5
Total OPEC[3]	**451,342**	**472,250**	**1,573,815**	**1,568,093**	**1,904,188**	**2,013,603**	**2,182,607**	**2,179,305**	**1,747,055**
OPEC as Share of Total Imports (%)	68.0	37.8	62.2	53.6	45.4	40.2	44.4	46.1	40.8
Iraq	7,927	0	10,328	189,105	226,804	201,866	176,709	229,300	164,125
Nigeria	NA	NA	313,816	291,959	328,079	406,662	413,932	361,659	293,568
Saudi Arabia	30,786	10,858	461,365	488,818	575,274	534,143	541,987	559,750	369,488
Venezuela	333,589	361,155	176,135	373,989	565,865	517,947	496,684	435,029	393,426
From Selected Non-OPEC Countries									
Total Non-OPEC Countries	**212,769**	**775,812**	**954,888**	**1,358,302**	**2,289,898**	**2,989,479**	**2,733,350**	**2,547,689**	**2,532,853**
Brazil	416	909	1,187	17,874	18,840	70,281	73,039	94,519	112,183
Canada	44,076	279,733	166,361	340,858	661,351	858,839	895,976	912,263	899,370
Mexico	5,808	15,439	195,103	275,594	502,509	622,408	559,304	476,366	450,525
Russia[5]	0	1,081	260	16,411	26,382	134,646	151,074	170,264	202,216
United Kingdom	6	3,951	64,271	69,021	133,799	99,330	101,181	85,512	89,283

Notes: The country of origin for refined petroleum products may not be the country of origin for the crude oil from which the refined products were produced. For example, refined products imported from refineries in the Caribbean may have been produced from Middle East crude oil. Data include any imports for the Strategic Petroleum Reserve, which began in 1977. Totals may not equal sum of components due to independent rounding.

[1] OPEC = Organization of Petroleum Exporting Countries.

[2] Bahrain, Iran, Iraq, Kuwait, Qatar, Saudi Arabia, the UAE, and the Neutral Zone (between Kuwait and Saudi Arabia).

[3] On this table, "Total OPEC" for all years includes Iran, Iraq, Kuwait, Saudi Arabia and Venezuela; beginning in 1961, also includes Qatar; beginning in 1962, also includes Libya; for 1962-2008, also includes Indonesia; beginning in 1967, also includes United Arab Emirates; beginning in 1969, also includes Algeria; beginning in 1971, also includes Nigeria; for 1973-1992 and beginning in 2008, also includes Ecuador; for 1975-1994, also includes Gabon; and beginning in 2007, also includes Angola. Data for all countries not included in "Total OPEC" are included in "Total Non-OPEC."

[4] Nigeria joined OPEC in 1971. Prior to that year, Nigeria is included in "Total Non-OPEC."

[5] Through 1992, may include imports from republics other than Russia in the former U.S.S.R.

Source: U.S. Department of Energy, Energy Information Administration

Plunkett Research, Ltd.

www.plunkettresearch.com

Refinery Capacity & Utilization in the U.S.: Selected Years, 1960-2009

(Latest Year Available)

	1960	1970	1980	1990	2000	2004	2005	2006	2007	2008	2009
Number of Operable Refineries	309	276	319	205	158	149	148	149	149	150	150
Crude Oil Refining Capacity on Jan. 1st *(in thousands of barrels per day)*	9,843	12,021	17,988	15,572	16,512	16,894	17,125	17,339	17,443	17,594	17,672
Crude Oil Gross Input to Distillation Units *(in millions of barrels)*	3,088.6	4,203.6	5,049.3	4,967.6	5,599.4	5,776.7	5,686.1	5,694.6	5,639.2	5,499.8	5,343.6
Operable Refineries Utilization Percent *(%)*[1]	85.1	92.6	75.4	87.1	92.6	92.8	90.6	89.7	88.5	85.3	82.8

[1]Through 1980, utilization is calculated by dividing gross input to distillation units by one-half of the current year January 1 capacity and the following year January 1 capacity. Beginning in 1981, utilization is calculated by dividing gross input to distillation units by the annual average capacity.

Source: U.S. Department of Energy, Energy Information Administration

Plunkett Research, Ltd.

www.plunkettresearch.com

Refiner Sales Prices & Refiner Profit Margins for Selected Petroleum Products, U.S.: Selected Years, 1990-2009

(In Nominal Cents per Gallon, Excluding Taxes; Latest Year Available)

Product	1990	1995	2000	2004	2005	2006	2007	2008	2009
Sales Prices to Resellers[1]									
Aviation Gasoline	106.3	97.5	133.0	162.7	207.6	249.0	275.8	334.2	248.0
Motor Gasoline	78.6	62.6	96.3	128.8	167.0	196.9	218.2	258.6	176.7
Leaded Regular	75.4	NA	NA	NA	NA	NA	NA	NA	NA
Unleaded Regular	75.8	59.3	94.2	126.9	165.4	195.0	216.1	257.0	174.7
Unleaded Midgrade	81.4	67.0	101.3	134.0	170.8	201.6	224.5	261.0	178.4
Premium	87.4	72.2	105.5	140.8	178.9	211.7	235.7	274.6	195.8
Kerosene	83.9	58.0	96.9	127.1	175.7	200.7	224.9	285.1	184.4
Jet Fuel, Kerosene-Type	77.3	53.9	88.0	120.8	172.3	196.1	217.1	302.0	171.9
No. 1 Distillate	83.8	62.5	101.9	128.9	180.1	204.4	243.0	271.2	205.0
No. 2 Distillate	69.5	53.0	89.6	117.8	172.0	199.1	219.0	297.0	170.7
No. 2 Fuel Oil	69.7	51.1	88.6	112.5	162.3	183.4	207.2	274.5	165.7
No. 2 Diesel Fuel	69.4	53.8	89.8	118.7	173.7	201.2	220.3	299.4	171.3
No. 4 Fuel[2]	59.0	46.3	77.8	103.3	137.7	139.5	155.1	21537.0	156.1
Residual Fuel Oil	41.3	36.3	56.6	68.1	97.1	113.6	135.0	186.6	134.2
Sulfur ≤ 1%[3]	47.2	38.3	62.7	76.4	111.5	120.2	140.6	191.8	133.7
Sulfur > 1%	37.2	33.8	51.2	60.1	84.2	108.5	131.4	184.3	134.4
Propane (Consumer Grade)	38.6	34.4	59.5	75.1	93.3	103.1	119.4	143.7	92.1
Sales Prices to End Users[1]									
Aviation Gasoline	112.0	100.5	130.6	181.9	223.1	268.2	284.9	327.3	244.2
Motor Gasoline	88.3	76.5	110.6	143.5	182.9	212.8	234.5	277.5	188.8
Leaded Regular	83.1	NA	NA	NA	NA	NA	NA	NA	NA
Unleaded Regular	84.9	71.7	107.3	140.4	180.2	209.9	231.5	274.8	185.6
Unleaded Midgrade	92.1	80.8	116.8	149.9	189.3	221.3	243.8	287.9	199.7
Premium	98.5	89.0	124.2	159.6	199.2	232.0	255.2	296.5	212.1
Kerosene	92.3	58.9	112.3	116.0	195.7	224.4	226.3	328.3	267.5
Jet Fuel, Kerosene-Type	76.6	54.0	89.9	120.7	173.5	199.8	216.5	305.2	170.4
No. 1 Distillate	81.9	62.0	98.8	126.2	183.2	213.7	228.6	298.3	214.1
No. 2 Distillate	72.6	56.0	93.4	123.5	177.7	209.1	226.6	314.3	184.0
No. 2 Fuel Oil	73.4	56.2	92.7	117.3	170.5	198.2	224.1	298.6	196.2
No. 2 Diesel Fuel	72.5	56.0	93.5	124.3	178.6	209.6	226.7	315.0	183.4
No. 4 Fuel[2]	62.2	50.5	76.9	101.7	W	W	W	W	W
Residual Fuel Oil	44.4	39.2	60.2	13.9	104.8	121.8	137.4	196.4	134.1
Sulfur ≤ 1%[3]	50.5	43.6	70.8	83.5	116.8	134.2	143.6	214.4	141.3
Sulfur > 1%	40.0	37.7	56.6	69.2	97.4	117.3	135.0	188.9	130.6
Propane (Consumer Grade)	74.5	49.2	60.3	83.9	108.9	135.8	148.9	189.2	122.0
Refiner Margins[4]									
Motor Gasoline	25.7	21.6	29.0	40.8	47.4	53.5	56.4	33.0	35.6
Jet Fuel, Kerosene-Type	24.4	12.9	20.7	32.8	52.7	52.7	55.3	76.4	30.8
No. 2 Distillate	16.6	12.0	22.3	29.8	52.4	55.7	57.2	71.4	29.6
Residual Fuel Oil	-11.6	-4.8	-10.7	-19.9	-22.5	-29.8	-26.8	-39.0	-6.9
Composite	22.1	18.1	26.1	36.7	48.4	53.0	55.3	45.3	32.9

NA = Not Available. W = Value withheld to avoid disclosure of individual company data.

[1] Sales for resale (wholesale sales) are those made to purchasers who are other than ultimate consumers. Sales to end users are those made directly to the ultimate consumer, including bulk customers, such as agriculture, industry, and utilities, as well as residential and commercial customers.

[2] Includes No. 4 fuel oil and No. 4 diesel fuel.

[3] Sulfur content by weight.

[4] In this table, refiner margin is the difference between the composite refiner acquisition price of crude oil and the price to resellers.

Source: U.S. Department of Energy, Energy Information Administration
Plunkett Research, Ltd.
www.plunkettresearch.com

Petroleum Consumption by the Transportation Sector, U.S.: Selected Years, 1950-2009

(In Thousands of Barrels per Day; Latest Year Available)

Year	Aviation Gasoline	Distillate Fuel Oil	Jet Fuel[1]		Liquefied Petroleum Gases	Lubricants	Motor Gasoline[2]	Residual Fuel Oil	Total
			KT	Total					
1950	108	226	0	[1]	2	64	2,433	524	3,356
1955	192	372	0	154	9	70	3,221	440	4,458
1960	161	418	91	371	13	68	3,736	367	5,135
1965	120	514	334	602	23	67	4,374	336	6,036
1970	55	738	718	967	32	66	5,589	332	7,778
1975	39	998	782	992	31	70	6,512	310	8,951
1980	35	1,311	845	1,062	13	77	6,441	608	9,546
1985	27	1,491	1,005	1,218	21	71	6,667	342	9,838
1990	24	1,722	1,340	1,522	16	80	7,080	443	10,888
1991	23	1,694	1,296	1,471	15	71	7,042	447	10,763
1992	22	1,728	1,310	1,454	14	72	7,125	465	10,881
1993	21	1,785	1,357	1,469	14	74	7,367	393	11,124
1994	21	1,896	1,480	1,527	24	77	7,487	385	11,417
1995	21	1,973	1,497	1,514	13	76	7,674	397	11,668
1996	20	2,096	1,575	1,578	11	73	7,772	370	11,921
1997	22	2,198	1,598	1,599	10	78	7,883	310	12,099
1998	19	2,263	1,623	1,622	13	81	8,128	294	12,420
1999	21	2,352	1,675	1,673	10	82	8,336	290	12,765
2000	20	2,422	1,725	1,725	8	81	8,370	386	13,012
2001	19	2,489	1,656	1,655	10	74	8,435	255	12,938
2002	18	2,536	1,621	1,614	10	73	8,662	295	13,208
2003	16	2,665	1,578	1,578	12	68	8,733	249	13,321
2004	17	2,783	1,630	1,630	14	69	8,887	321	13,720
2005	19	2,858	1,679	1,679	20	68	8,948	365	13,957
2006	18	3,017	1,633	1,633	20	67	9,029	395	14,178
2007	17	3,037	1,622	1,622	16	69	9,093	433	14,287
2008	15	2,833	1,539	1,539	28	64	8,834	400	13,712
2009	14	2,606	1,396	1,396	29	58	8,831	342	13,277

[1] Through 1951, naphtha-type jet fuel is included in the products from which jet fuel was blended: in 1952, 71 percent gasoline, 17 percent kerosene, and 12 percent distillate fuel oil. Beginning in 1952, includes naphtha-type jet fuel. Beginning in 1957, also includes kerosene-type jet fuel. Beginning in 2005, includes kerosene-type jet fuel only. KT = Kerosene Type.

[2] Finished motor gasoline. Through 1963, also includes special naphthas. Beginning in 1993, also includes ethanol blended into motor gasoline.

Source: U.S. Department of Energy, Energy Information Administration

Plunkett Research, Ltd.

www.plunkettresearch.com

Retail Motor Gasoline & On-Highway Diesel Fuel Prices, U.S.: Selected Years, 1950-2009

(In Dollars per Gallon; Latest Year Available)

Year	Motor Gasoline by Grade								Regular Motor Gasoline by Area Type (Nominal)			On-Highway Diesel Fuel (Nominal)
	Leaded Regular		Unleaded Regular		Unleaded Premium		All Grades		Conventional Gasoline Areas[1]	Reformulated Gasoline Areas[2]	All Areas	
	Nominal	Real[3]	Nominal	Real[3]	Nominal	Real[3]	Nominal	Real[3]				
1950	0.27	1.85	NA	NA	NA	NA	NA	NA	NA	NA	NA	NA
1955	0.29	1.75	NA	NA	NA	NA	NA	NA	NA	NA	NA	NA
1960	0.31	1.67	NA	NA	NA	NA	NA	NA	NA	NA	NA	NA
1965	0.31	1.57	NA	NA	NA	NA	NA	NA	NA	NA	NA	NA
1970	0.36	1.47	NA	NA	NA	NA	NA	NA	NA	NA	NA	NA
1975	0.57	1.69	NA	NA	NA	NA	NA	NA	NA	NA	NA	NA
1980	1.19	2.49	1.25	2.61	NA	NA	1.22	2.56	NA	NA	NA	NA
1985	1.12	1.81	1.20	1.95	1.34	2.18	1.20	1.94	NA	NA	NA	NA
1990	1.15	1.59	1.16	1.61	1.35	1.87	1.22	1.69	NA	NA	NA	NA
1995	NA	NA	1.15	1.41	1.34	1.64	1.21	1.48	1.10	1.16	1.11	1.11
1996	NA	NA	1.23	1.48	1.41	1.70	1.29	1.55	1.19	1.28	1.22	1.24
1997	NA	NA	1.23	1.46	1.42	1.68	1.29	1.53	1.19	1.25	1.20	1.20
1998	NA	NA	1.06	1.24	1.25	1.46	1.12	1.30	1.02	1.08	1.03	1.04
1999	NA	NA	1.17	1.34	1.36	1.56	1.22	1.41	1.12	1.20	1.14	1.12
2000	NA	NA	1.51	1.70	1.69	1.91	1.56	1.76	1.46	1.54	1.48	1.49
2001	NA	NA	1.46	1.61	1.68	1.83	1.53	1.69	1.38	1.50	1.42	1.40
2002	NA	NA	1.36	1.47	1.56	1.69	1.44	1.56	1.31	1.41	1.35	1.32
2003	NA	NA	1.59	1.69	1.78	1.89	1.64	1.74	1.52	1.66	1.56	1.51
2004	NA	NA	1.88	1.94	2.07	2.14	1.92	1.99	1.81	1.94	1.85	1.81
2005	NA	NA	2.30	2.30	2.49	2.49	2.34	2.34	2.24	2.34	2.27	2.40
2006	NA	NA	2.59	2.51	2.81	2.72	2.64	2.55	2.53	2.65	2.57	2.71
2007	NA	NA	2.80	2.64	3.03	2.86	2.85	2.68	2.77	2.86	2.80	2.89
2008	NA	NA	3.27	3.01	3.52	3.24	3.32	3.06	3.21	3.31	3.25	3.80
2009	NA	NA	2.35	2.14	2.61	2.38	2.40	2.19	2.32	2.43	2.35	2.47

NA = Not Available. Nominal = Not adjusted for inflation.

[1] Any area that does not require the sale of reformulated gasoline. For 1993-2000, includes data collected for oxygenated areas.

[2] "Reformulated Gasoline Areas" are ozone nonattainment areas designated by the Environmental Protection Agency that require the use of reformulated gasoline. For 1995-2000, includes data collected for combined oxygenated and reformulated areas.

[3] In chained (2005) dollars, calculated by using gross domestic product implicit price deflators.

Source: U.S. Department of Energy, Energy Information Administration
Plunkett Research, Ltd.
www.plunkettresearch.com

Top World Oil Reserves by Country: 2009

(End of Period; Latest Year Available)

Rank	Country	Proven Reserves (in Billions of Barrels)	Share of Total (%)
1	Saudi Arabia	264.6	19.8
2	Venezuela	172.3	12.9
3	Iran	137.6	10.3
4	Iraq	115.0	8.6
5	Kuwait	101.5	7.6
6	United Arab Emirates	97.8	7.3
7	Russian Federation	74.2	5.6
8	Libya	44.3	3.3
9	Kazakhstan	39.8	3.0
10	Nigeria	37.2	2.8
11	Canada*	33.2	2.5
12	United States	28.4	2.1
13	Qatar	26.8	2.0
14	China	14.8	1.1
15	Angola	13.5	1.0
16	Brazil	12.9	1.0
17	Algeria	12.2	0.9
18	Mexico	11.7	0.9
19	Norway	7.1	0.5
20	Azerbaijan	7.0	0.5

Note: Proved reserves of oil are generally taken to be those quantities that geological and engineering information indicates with reasonable certainty can be recovered in the future from known reservoirs under existing economic and operating conditions.

* Canadian proved reserves on this table include an official estimate of 27.1 billion barrels for oil sands currently "under active development," and do not include an additional 143.3 billion barrels of oil sands reserves not under active development, which if included would put the overall Canadian total at 176.5 billion barrels.

Source: BP, *Statistical Review of World Energy*, June 2010

Plunkett Research, Ltd.

www.plunkettresearch.com

Top World Oil Producers: 2009

(In Thousands of Barrels per Day; Latest Year Available)

Rank	Country	Production
1	Russia	9,934
2	Saudi Arabia	9,765
3	United States	9,156
4	Iran	4,177
5	China	3,996
6	Canada	3,294
7	Mexico	3,001
8	United Arab Emirates	2,795
9	Brazil	2,577
10	Kuwait	2,496
11	Venezuela	2,471
12	Iraq	2,400
13	Norway	2,350
14	Nigeria	2,211
15	Algeria	2,126

Note: Includes crude oil, lease condensates, natural gas plant liquids, other liquids, and refinery processing gain.

Source: U.S. Department of Energy, Energy Information Administration
Plunkett Research, Ltd.
www.plunkettresearch.com

Top World Oil Net Exporters: 2008

(In Thousands of Barrels per Day; Latest Year Available)

Rank	Country	Net Exports
1	Saudi Arabia	8,030
2	Russia	7,017
3	United Arab Emirates	2,475
4	Iran	2,342
5	Norway	2,338
6	Kuwait	2,288
7	Nigeria	2,062
8	Venezuela	1,957
9	Algeria	1,905
10	Angola	1,709
11	Libya	1,575
12	Iraq	1,524
13	Mexico	1,361
14	Kazakhstan	1,204
15	Canada	1,116

Note: Includes crude oil, lease condensates, natural gas plant liquids, other liquids, and refinery processing gain.

Source: U.S. Department of Energy, Energy Information Administration
Plunkett Research, Ltd.
www.plunkettresearch.com

Top World Oil Net Importers: 2008

(In Thousands of Barrels per Day; Latest Year Available)

Rank	Country	Net Imports
1	United States	12,224
2	Japan	4,903
3	China	3,670
4	Germany	2,325
5	South Korea	2,210
6	India	1,964
7	France	1,897
8	Spain	1,583
9	Italy	1,519
10	Taiwan	950
11	The Netherlands	905
12	Singapore	898
13	Turkey	644
14	Belgium	629
15	Thailand	602

Note: Includes crude oil, lease condensates, natural gas plant liquids, other liquids, and refinery processing gain.

Source: U.S. Department of Energy, Energy Information Administration
Plunkett Research, Ltd.
www.plunkettresearch.com

Top World Oil Consumers: 2009

(In Thousands of Barrels per Day; Latest Year Available)

Rank	Country	Consumption
1	United States	18,771
2	China	8,200
3	Japan	4,367
4	India	2,980
5	Russia	2,850
6	Brazil	2,460
7	Germany	2,440
8	Saudi Arabia	2,430
9	South Korea	2,185
10	Canada	2,151
11	Mexico	2,084
12	France	1,828
13	Iran	1,809
14	United Kingdom	1,667
15	Italy	1,528

Note: Includes consumption of petroleum products and direct combustion of crude oil.

Source: U.S. Department of Energy, Energy Information Administration
Plunkett Research, Ltd.
www.plunkettresearch.com

Coal Overview, U.S.: Selected Years, 1950-2009

(In Short Tons; Latest Year Available)

Year	Production[1]	Waste Coal[2]	Imports	Exports	Stock Change[3]	Losses and Unaccounted For[4]	Consumption
1950	560,388,000	NA	365,000	29,360,000	(5)	9,462,414	494,101,770
1955	490,838,000	NA	337,000	54,429,000	(5)	-6,292,456	447,012,195
1960	434,329,000	NA	262,000	37,981,000	(5)	1,722,211	398,081,359
1965	526,954,000	NA	184,000	51,032,000	(5)	2,244,341	471,965,119
1970	612,661,000	NA	36,000	71,733,000	(5)	6,633,150	523,230,708
1975	654,641,000	NA	940,000	66,309,000	32,154,048	-5,522,480	562,640,432
1980	829,700,000	NA	1,193,582	91,741,902	25,595,070	10,826,875	702,729,735
1985	883,638,117	NA	1,952,418	92,679,860	-27,933,579	2,795,595	818,048,659
1990	1,029,075,527	3,338,950	2,699,395	105,803,889	26,542,128	-1,729,713	904,497,568
1991	995,983,881	3,950,350	3,389,792	108,968,594	-946,765	-3,924,611	899,226,805
1992	997,544,933	6,287,340	3,802,767	102,516,199	-2,996,804	460,847	907,654,798
1993	945,424,286	8,136,520	8,180,976	74,519,334	-51,943,327	-4,915,510	944,081,285
1994	1,033,504,293	8,226,780	8,869,854	71,358,614	23,616,696	4,339,718	951,285,899
1995	1,032,973,772	8,560,960	9,473,101	88,547,298	-275,428	632,189	962,103,774
1996	1,063,855,513	8,777,550	8,115,265	90,472,643	-17,456,081	1,410,995	1,006,320,771
1997	1,089,931,788	8,095,640	7,486,776	83,544,831	-11,253,272	3,678,189	1,029,544,456
1998	1,117,535,167	8,689,800	8,723,683	78,047,646	24,228,347	-4,430,162	1,037,102,819
1999	1,100,431,428	8,683,370	9,089,333	58,475,842	23,988,167	-2,906,419	1,038,646,541
2000	1,073,611,561	9,088,580	12,512,623	58,488,793	-48,308,620	937,716	1,084,094,875
2001	1,127,688,806	10,085,275	19,787,299	48,666,038	41,630,103	7,119,707	1,060,145,532
2002	1,094,283,061	9,052,496	16,875,429	39,601,241	10,214,972	4,040,200	1,066,354,573
2003	1,071,752,573	10,015,882	25,043,970	43,013,508	-26,659,114	-4,402,812	1,094,860,843
2004	1,112,098,870	11,298,837	27,280,004	47,997,895	-11,461,854	6,887,131	1,107,254,539
2005	1,131,498,099	13,351,970	30,460,349	49,942,211	-9,701,713	9,092,308	1,125,977,612
2006	1,162,749,659	14,409,295	36,245,976	49,647,269	42,642,131	8,823,765	1,112,291,765
2007	1,146,635,345	14,076,027	36,346,847	59,163,103	5,811,551	4,085,436	1,127,998,129
2008	1,171,808,669	14,145,556	34,207,679	81,519,115	12,354,461	5,739,885	1,120,548,443
2009	1,072,751,787	12,434,598	22,638,515	59,096,951	33,710,797	14,593,513	1,000,423,639

NA = Not available.

[1] Beginning in 2001, includes a small amount of refuse recovery (coal recaptured from a refuse mine and cleaned to reduce the concentration of noncombustible materials).

[2] Waste coal (including fine coal, coal obtained from a refuse bank or slurry dam, anthracite culm, bituminous gob, and lignite waste) consumed by the electric power and industrial sectors. Beginning in 1989, waste coal supplied is counted as a supply-side item to balance the same amount of waste coal included in "Consumption."

[3] A negative value indicates a decrease in stocks; a positive value indicates an increase.

[4] "Losses and Unaccounted For" is calculated as the sum of production, imports, and waste coal supplied, minus exports, stock change and consumption.

[5] Through 1973, stock change is included in "Losses and Unaccounted For."

Source: U.S. Department of Energy, Energy Information Administration

Plunkett Research, Ltd.

www.plunkettresearch.com

Natural Gas Production, U.S.: Selected Years, 1950-2009

(In Billions of Cubic Feet; Latest Year Available)

Year	Gross Withdrawals				Repressuring	NH[1] Gases Removed	Vented & Flared	Marketed Production	Extraction Loss[2]	Dry Gas Production
	From Gas Wells	From Oil Wells	Coal-bed Wells	Total						
1950	5,603	2,876	NA	7,547	1,273	NA	854	5,420	224	5,195
1955	7,842	3,878	NA	11,720	1,541	NA	774	9,405	377	9,029
1960	10,853	4,234	NA	15,088	1,754	NA	563	12,771	543	12,228
1965	13,524	4,440	NA	17,963	1,604	NA	319	16,040	753	15,286
1970	18,595	5,192	NA	23,786	1,376	NA	489	21,921	906	21,014
1975	17,380	3,723	NA	21,104	861	NA	134	20,109	872	19,236
1980	17,573	4,297	NA	21,870	1,365	199	125	20,180	777	19,403
1985	14,535	5,071	NA	19,607	1,915	326	95	17,270	816	16,454
1990	16,054	5,469	NA	21,523	2,489	289	150	18,594	784	17,810
1991	16,018	5,732	NA	21,750	2,772	276	170	18,532	835	17,698
1992	16,165	5,967	NA	22,132	2,973	280	168	18,712	872	17,840
1993	16,691	6,035	NA	22,726	3,103	414	227	18,982	886	18,095
1994	17,351	6,230	NA	23,581	3,231	412	228	19,710	889	18,821
1995	17,282	6,462	NA	23,744	3,565	388	284	19,506	908	18,599
1996	17,737	6,376	NA	24,114	3,511	518	272	19,812	958	18,854
1997	17,844	6,369	NA	24,213	3,492	599	256	19,866	964	18,902
1998	17,729	6,380	NA	24,108	3,427	617	103	19,961	938	19,024
1999	17,590	6,233	NA	23,823	3,293	615	110	19,805	973	18,832
2000	17,726	6,448	NA	24,174	3,380	505	91	20,198	1,016	19,182
2001	18,129	6,371	NA	24,501	3,371	463	97	20,570	954	19,616
2002	17,795	6,146	NA	23,941	3,455	502	99	19,885	957	18,928
2003	17,882	6,237	NA	24,119	3,548	499	98	19,974	876	19,099
2004	17,885	6,084	NA	23,970	3,702	654	96	19,517	927	18,591
2005	17,472	5,985	NA	23,457	3,700	711	119	18,927	876	18,051
2006	17,996	5,539	NA	23,535	3,265	731	129	19,410	906	18,504
2007	17,065	5,818	1,780	24,664	3,663	661	143	20,196	930	19,266
2008	18,011	5,845	1,898	25,754	3,639	710	167	21,240	953	20,286
2009	18,881	5,186	2,110	26,177	3,439	686	159	21,893	938	20,955

NA = Not available

Notes: Beginning with 1965 data, all volumes are shown on a pressure base of 14.73 p.s.i.a. at 60° F. For prior years, the pressure base was 14.65 p.s.i.a. at 60° F. Totals may not equal sum of components due to independent rounding.

[1] NH Gases = Non-hydrocarbon Gases.

[2] Volume reduction resulting from the removal of natural gas plant liquids, which are transferred to petroleum supply.

Source: U.S. Department of Energy, Energy Information Administration

Plunkett Research, Ltd.

www.plunkettresearch.com

Natural Gas Prices Paid, by Sector, U.S.: Selected Years, 1970-2009

(In US$ per Thousand Cubic Feet; Latest Year Available)

Year	Residential			Commercial[1]			Industrial[2]			Vehicle Fuel[3]		Electric Power[4]		
	Prices			Prices			Prices			Prices		Prices		
	Nominal[5]	Real[6]	% of Sector[7]	Nominal[5]	Real[6]	% of Sector[7]	Nominal[5]	Real[6]	% of Sector[7]	Nominal[5]	Real[6]	Nominal[5]	Real[6]	% of Sector[7]
1970	1.09	4.48	NA	0.77	3.17	NA	0.37	1.52	NA	NA	NA	0.29	1.19	NA
1975	1.71	5.09	NA	1.35	4.02	NA	0.96	2.86	NA	NA	NA	0.77	2.29	96.1
1980	3.68	7.71	NA	3.39	7.10	NA	2.56	5.36	NA	NA	NA	2.27	4.75	96.9
1985	6.12	9.94	NA	5.50	8.93	NA	3.95	6.41	68.8	NA	NA	3.55	5.77	94.0
1990	5.80	8.03	99.2	4.83	6.69	86.6	2.93	4.06	35.2	3.39	4.70	2.38	3.30	76.8
1991	5.82	7.78	99.2	4.81	6.43	85.1	2.69	3.60	32.7	3.96	5.30	2.18	2.92	79.3
1992	5.89	7.70	99.1	4.88	6.38	83.2	2.84	3.71	30.3	4.05	5.29	2.36	3.08	76.5
1993	6.16	7.87	99.1	5.22	6.67	83.9	3.07	3.92	29.7	4.27	5.46	2.61	3.34	74.1
1994	6.41	8.03	99.1	5.44	6.81	79.3	3.05	3.82	25.5	4.11	5.15	2.28	2.85	73.4
1995	6.06	7.43	99.0	5.05	6.19	76.7	2.71	3.32	24.5	3.98	4.88	2.02	2.48	71.4
1996	6.34	7.63	99.0	5.40	6.50	77.6	3.42	4.12	19.4	4.34	5.22	2.69	3.24	68.4
1997	6.94	8.21	98.8	5.80	6.86	70.8	3.59	4.25	18.1	4.44	5.25	2.78	3.29	68.0
1998	6.82	7.98	97.7	5.48	6.41	67.0	3.14	3.67	16.1	4.59	5.37	2.40	2.81	63.7
1999	6.69	7.71	95.2	5.33	6.14	66.1	3.12	3.60	18.8	4.34	5.00	2.62	3.02	58.3
2000	7.76	8.75	92.6	6.59	7.43	63.9	4.45	5.02	19.8	5.54	6.25	4.38	4.94	50.5
2001	9.63	10.62	92.4	8.43	9.30	66.0	5.24	5.78	20.8	6.60	7.28	4.61	5.09	40.2
2002	7.89	8.57	97.9	6.63	7.20	77.4	4.02	4.36	22.7	5.10	5.54	3.68	3.99	83.9
2003	9.63	10.23	97.5	8.40	8.93	78.2	5.89	6.26	22.1	6.19	6.58	5.57	5.92	91.2
2004	10.75	11.11	97.7	9.43	9.74	78.0	6.53	6.75	23.7	7.16	7.40	6.11	6.31	89.8
2005	12.70	12.70	98.2	11.34	11.34	82.1	8.56	8.56	24.1	9.14	9.14	8.47	8.47	91.3
2006	13.73	13.30	98.1	12.00	11.62	80.8	7.87	7.62	23.4	8.72	8.45	7.11	6.89	93.4
2007	13.08	12.31	98.0	11.34	10.68	80.4	7.68	7.23	22.2	8.50	8.01	7.31	6.88	92.2
2008	13.89	12.80	97.9	12.23	11.27	79.9	9.67	8.91	20.5	11.75	10.83	9.26	8.54	101.1
2009	11.97	10.90	98.0	9.75	8.88	72.9	5.27	4.80	17.7	NA	NA	4.89	4.45	101.2

[1] Commercial sector, including commercial combined-heat-and-power (CHP) and commercial electricity-only plants.

[2] Industrial sector, including industrial combined-heat-and-power (CHP) and industrial electricity-only plants.

[3] Much of the natural gas delivered for vehicle fuel represents deliveries to fueling stations that are used primarily or exclusively by fleet vehicles. Thus, the prices are often those associated with the operation of fleet vehicles.

[4] Electricity-only and combined-heat-and-power (CHP) plants within the NAICS 22 category whose primary business is to sell electricity, or electricity and heat, to the public. Through 2001, data are for electric utilities only; beginning in 2002, data are for electric utilities and independent power producers.

[5] In dollars not adjusted for inflation.

[6] In chained (2005) dollars, calculated by using gross domestic product implicit price deflators.

[7] The percentage of the sector's consumption for which price data are available.

Source: U.S. Department of Energy, Energy Information Administration
Plunkett Research, Ltd.
www.plunkettresearch.com

The 15 Largest Nuclear Power Plants in the U.S.: 2009

(Latest Year Available)

	Name of Plant	State	Operating Utility	Capacity[1] (Net MW)	Capacity Factor[2]	1st Year Operative
1	Palo Verde-3	AZ	Arizona Public Service Company	1,317	83%	1988
2	Palo Verde-2	AZ	Arizona Public Service Company	1,314	83%	1986
3	Palo Verde-1	AZ	Arizona Public Service Company	1,311	101%	1986
4	South Texas-1	TX	STP Nuclear Operating Co.	1,280	90%	1988
5	South Texas-2	TX	STP Nuclear Operating Co.	1,280	101%	1989
6	Grand Gulf-1	MS	System Energy Resources, Inc.	1,259	100%	1985
7	Perry-1	OH	FirstEnergy Corp.	1,245	70%	1987
8	Seabrook-1	NH	FPL Energy Seabrook, Inc.	1,245	81%	1990
9	Comanche Peak-1	TX	Luminant	1,209	100%	1990
10	Callaway-1	MO	Union Electric Company	1,190	98%	1984
11	Susquehanna-1	PA	PPL Susquehanna, LLC	1,185	101%	1983
12	Braidwood-1	IL	Exelon Generation	1,178	95%	1988
13	Waterford-3	LA	Entergy Louisiana	1,176	87%	1985
14	Salem-1	NJ	PSEG Power, LLC	1,174	99%	1977
15	Byron-1	IL	Exelon Generation	1,164	94%	1985

MW = Megawatts.

[1] Summer Capacity (Net): The maximum output, excluding electricity used for station's internal operations, expressed in Megawatts (electricity). Note that nuclear power can also be expressed in Megawatts (thermal).

[2] Capacity Factor: The ratio of power actually generated to the maximum potential generation, expressed as a percent. The factor is calculated by multiplying the summer capacity by the number of hours in a day (24) by the number of days in a year (365 or 366). That total is then divided into the amount of actual generation and multiplied by 100 to get a percent.

Source: U.S. Department of Energy, Energy Information Administration
Plunkett Research, Ltd.
www.plunkettresearch.com

IV. Renewable Energy

Contents:

Energy Production by Renewable Energy, U.S.: Selected Years, 1950-2009

(In Billions of Btus; Latest Year Available)

Year	Renewable Energy						Total, Renewable & Non-Renewable
	Conventional Hydroelectric Power	Geothermal	Solar/PV	Wind	Biomass	Total Renewable	
1950	1,415,411	NA	NA	NA	1,562,307	2,977,718	35,540,384
1955	1,359,844	NA	NA	NA	1,424,143	2,783,987	40,147,667
1960	1,607,975	774	NA	NA	1,319,870	2,928,619	42,803,762
1965	2,059,077	4,197	NA	NA	1,334,761	3,398,036	50,676,101
1970	2,633,547	11,347	NA	NA	1,430,962	4,075,857	63,501,275
1975	3,154,607	70,153	NA	NA	1,498,734	4,723,494	61,356,565
1980	2,900,144	109,776	NA	NA	2,475,500	5,485,420	67,232,462
1985	2,970,192	198,282	111	60	3,016,233	6,184,878	67,799,166
1990	3,046,391	335,801	59,718	29,007	2,735,110	6,206,027	70,869,979
1991	3,015,943	346,247	62,688	30,796	2,781,798	6,237,473	70,531,332
1992	2,617,436	349,309	63,886	29,863	2,931,678	5,992,172	70,126,437
1993	2,891,613	363,716	66,458	30,987	2,908,446	6,261,220	68,493,804
1994	2,683,457	338,108	68,548	35,560	3,027,535	6,153,209	70,890,723
1995	3,205,307	293,893	69,857	32,630	3,099,082	6,700,769	71,316,338
1996	3,589,656	315,529	70,833	33,440	3,155,301	7,164,759	72,638,657
1997	3,640,458	324,959	70,236	33,581	3,107,908	7,177,141	72,630,769
1998	3,297,054	328,303	69,787	30,853	2,928,929	6,654,925	73,036,802
1999	3,267,575	330,919	68,793	45,894	2,965,132	6,678,315	71,903,053
2000	2,811,116	316,796	66,388	57,057	3,005,661	6,257,018	71,485,380
2001	2,241,858	311,264	65,454	69,617	2,624,160	5,312,354	71,882,553
2002	2,689,017	328,308	64,391	105,334	2,705,408	5,892,458	70,931,450
2003	2,824,533	330,554	63,620	114,571	2,805,435	6,138,713	70,196,814
2004	2,690,078	341,082	64,500	141,749	2,997,605	6,235,014	70,352,355
2005	2,702,942	342,576	66,131	178,088	3,103,664	6,393,401	69,591,871
2006	2,869,035	342,876	72,222	263,738	3,225,769	6,773,640	70,957,207
2007	2,446,389	348,730	80,943	340,503	3,488,962	6,705,528	71,607,975
2008	2,511,108	360,432	96,657	545,548	3,867,220	7,380,966	73,421,316
2009	2,681,578	373,361	108,562	697,278	3,900,070	7,760,850	72,970,019

NA = Not available

Note: Most data are estimates. Totals may not equal sum of components due to independent rounding.

Source: U.S. Department of Energy, Energy Information Administration

Plunkett Research, Ltd.

www.plunkettresearch.com

Renewable Energy Consumption by Source: Selected Years, 1950-2009

(In Billions of Btus; Latest Year Available)

Year	Hydroelectric Power[1]	Biomass[2]	Geothermal[3]	Solar[4]	Wind[5]	Total
1950	1,415,411	1,562,307	NA	NA	NA	2,977,718
1960	1,607,975	1,319,870	774	NA	NA	2,928,619
1970	2,633,547	1,430,962	11,347	NA	NA	4,075,857
1980	2,900,144	2,475,500	109,776	NA	NA	5,485,420
1990	3,046,391	2,735,145	335,801	59,718	29,007	6,206,062
1995	3,205,307	3,101,207	293,893	69,857	32,630	6,702,894
1996	3,589,656	3,156,852	315,529	70,833	33,440	7,166,310
1997	3,640,458	3,105,279	324,959	70,236	33,581	7,174,512
1998	3,297,054	2,927,554	328,303	69,787	30,853	6,653,551
1999	3,267,575	2,963,358	330,919	68,793	45,894	6,676,540
2000	2,811,116	3,008,305	316,796	66,388	57,057	6,259,661
2001	2,241,858	2,622,428	311,264	65,454	69,617	5,310,622
2002	2,689,017	2,700,694	328,308	64,391	105,334	5,887,744
2003	2,824,533	2,807,264	330,554	63,620	114,571	6,140,541
2004	2,690,078	3,009,831	341,082	64,500	141,749	6,247,240
2005	2,702,942	3,116,597	342,576	66,131	178,088	6,406,334
2006	2,869,035	3,276,606	342,876	72,222	263,738	6,824,477
2007	2,446,389	3,502,595	358,730	80,943	340,503	6,719,160
2008	2,511,108	3,852,376	360,432	96,657	545,548	7,366,122
2009	2,681,578	3,882,980	373,361	108,562	697,278	7,743,759

[1] Conventional hydroelectric net generation (converted to Btu using the fossil-fueled plants heat rate).

[2] Includes energy from wood and wood-derived fuels; municipal solid waste from biogenic sources, landfill gas, sludge waste, agricultural byproducts and other biomass (through 2000, also includes non-renewable waste such as municipal solid waste from non-biogenic sources, and tire-derived fuels); and fuel ethanol and biodiesel consumption, plus losses and co-products from the production of fuel ethanol and biodiesel.

[3] Geothermal electricity net generation (converted to Btu using the geothermal energy plants heat rate), and geothermal heat pump and direct use energy.

[4] Solar thermal and photovoltaic electricity net generation (converted to Btu using the fossil-fueled plants heat-rate), and solar thermal direct use energy.

[5] Wind electricity net generation (converted to Btu using the fossil-fueled plants heat rate).

Source: U.S. Department of Energy, Energy Information Administration

Plunkett Research, Ltd.

www.plunkettresearch.com

Renewable Energy Consumption in the Residential, Commercial & Industrial Sectors: 2003-2009

(In Billions of Btus; Latest Year Available)

	2003	2004	2005	2006	2007	2008	2009
Residential Sector							
Biomass (Wood[1])	400,000	410,000	430,000	390,000	430,000	450,000	430,000
Geothermal[2]	13,000	14,000	15,900	18,300	22,000	26,400	32,800
Solar[3]	58,151	58,736	60,628	67,186	74,896	88,140	100,600
Total	471,151	482,736	506,528	475,486	526,896	564,540	563,400
Commercial Sector[4]							
Hydroelectric[5]	740	1,052	860	927	764	591	679
Biomass	101,287	105,319	104,778	102,290	102,355	109,328	124,720
Wood[1]	71,435	70,327	69,649	64,729	69,428	72,983	71,824
Waste[6]	29,028	34,237	34,249	36,309	30,960	32,214	33,857
Fuel Ethanol[7]	824	755	880	1,251	1,967	2,131	2,383
Geothermal[2]	11,000	12,000	13,600	14,000	14,400	14,800	16,700
Total	113,026	118,371	119,238	117,216	117,519	124,720	125,443
Industrial Sector							
Hydroelectric[5]	43,242	32,556	31,951	28,756	15,715	16,514	18,328
Biomass	1,678,865	1,816,565	1,836,924	1,896,634	1,943,987	2,031,192	1,996,721
Wood[1]	1,363,315	1,475,735	1,451,729	1,472,379	1,413,086	1,343,874	1,216,854
Waste[6]	142,439	131,930	148,248	129,562	144,363	143,624	159,851
Fuel Ethanol[7]	4,456	6,287	6,846	9,673	9,846	11,652	13,026
Geothermal[2]	3,400	3,800	4,300	4,400	4,700	5,000	4,200
Total	1,725,507	1,852,921	1,873,175	1,929,789	1,964,403	2,052,706	2,019,249

Notes: All values are estimated, except for commercial sector hydroelectric power and waste. Totals may not equal sum of components due to independent rounding.

[1] Wood and wood-derived fuels.

[2] Geothermal heat pump and direct use energy.

[3] Solar thermal direct use energy and photovoltaic electricity net generation (converted to Btu using the fossil-fueled plants heat rate). Includes a small amount of commercial sector use.

[4] Including commercial/industrial combined-heat-and-power (CHP) and commercial/industrial electricity-only plants.

[5] Conventional hydroelectricity net generation (converted to BTU using the fossil-fueled plants heat rate).

[6] Municipal solid waste from biogenic sources, landfill gas, sludge waste, agricultural byproducts, and other biomass. Through 2000, also includes non-renewable waste (municipal solid waste from non-biogenic sources, and tire-derived fuels).

[7] The fuel ethanol (minus denaturant) portion of motor fuels, such as E10, consumer by these sectors.

Source: U.S. Department of Energy, Energy Information Administration
Plunkett Research, Ltd.
www.plunkettresearch.com

Renewable Energy Consumption in the Transportation & Electric Power Sectors: 2003-2009

(In Billions of Btus; Latest Year Available)

	2003	2004	2005	2006	2007	2008	2009
Transportation Sector							
Fuel Ethanol[1]	228,215	286,452	327,611	441,952	557,105	786,288	879,041
Biodiesel[2]	1,727	3,429	11,589	33,249	45,699	40,294	43,312
Total	229,942	289,881	339,200	475,201	602,804	826,582	922,353
Electric Power Sector[3]							
Hydroelectric[4]	2,780,551	2,656,470	2,670,131	2,839,353	2,429,909	2,494,003	2,662,571
Biomass	397,170	388,066	405,695	412,482	423,447	435,274	425,842
Wood[5]	167,290	165,189	184,973	181,815	185,956	177,348	172,707
Waste[6]	229,880	222,877	220,722	230,667	237,492	257,926	253,136
Geothermal[7]	303,154	311,282	308,776	306,176	307,630	314,232	319,661
Solar[8]	5,469	5,764	5,502	5,036	6,047	8,516	7,961
Wind[9]	114,571	141,749	178,088	263,738	340,503	545,548	697,278
Total	3,600,915	3,503,331	3,568,193	3,826,785	3,507,537	3,797,574	4,113,315

[1] The ethanol portion of motor fuels (such as E10 and E85) consumed by the transportation sector.

[2] Either a diesel fuel substitute or diesel fuel additive or extender.

[3] The electric power sector comprises electricity only and combined heat and power (CHP) plants within the NAICS 22 category whose primary business is to sell electricity, or electricity and heat, to the public.

[4] Conventional hydroelectricity net generation (converted to Btu using the fossil-fueled plants heat rate).

[5] Wood and wood-derived fuels.

[6] Municipal solid waste from biogenic sources, landfill gas, sludge waste, agricultural byproducts, and other biomass. Through 2000, also includes non-renewable waste (municipal solid waste from non-biogenic sources, and tire-derived fuels).

[7] Geothermal electricity net generation (converted to Btu using the geothermal energy plants heat rate).

[8] Solar thermal and photovoltaic electricity net generation (converted to Btu using the fossil-fueled plants heat rate).

[9] Wind electricity net generation (converted to Btu using the fossil-fueled plants heat rate).

Source: U.S. Department of Energy, Energy Information Administration
Plunkett Research, Ltd.
www.plunkettresearch.com

Chapter 3

IMPORTANT ENERGY INDUSTRY CONTACTS

Addresses, Telephone Numbers and Web Sites

Contents:

I. Accountants & CPAs Associations

Council of Petroleum Accountants Societies, Inc. (COPAS)
3900 E. Mexico Ave., Ste. 602
Denver, CO 80210 US
Phone: 303-300-1131
Fax: 303-300-3733
Toll Free: 877-992-6727
E-mail Address: *Execdir@copas.org*
Web Address: www.copas.org
The Council of Petroleum Accountants Societies, Inc. (COPAS) provides a forum for discussing and solving the variety of problems related to accounting for oil and gas. COPAS also provides valuable educational materials related to oil and gas accounting.

II. Agriculture Industry Associations

Brazilian Sugarcane Industry Association
Av Brigadeiro Faria Lima, 217, 9th Fl.
Sao Paulo, SP 01452-000 Brazil
Phone: 55-11-3093-4949
Fax: 55-11-3812-1416
Web Address: unica.com.br
The Brazilian Sugarcane Industry Association (Uniao da Industria de Cana-de-Acucar, or UNICA), created in 1997, is the country's largest trade association representing producers of sugar, ethanol and bioelectricity. Its member companies are responsible for approximately 50% of Brazil's ethanol production and 60% of the country's sugar production. UNICA maintains a number of international offices, including one in Washington D.C.

III. Alternative Energy-Biomass

CEDER-CIEMAT
Altos de Lubia, Soria
Lubia, 42290 Spain
Phone: 975-281013
Fax: 975-281051
E-mail Address: *ceder@ciemat.es*
Web Address:
www.ciemat.es/portal.do?IDM=197&NM=3
The CEDER (Centre for the Development of Renewable Energy Sources) is a unit of Spain's CIEMAT (Research Centre for Energy, Environment and Technology). CEDER focuses on biomass energy.

IV. Alternative Energy-Clean Coal

Center for Energy and Economic Development (CEED)
333 John Carlyle St., Ste. 530
Alexandria, VA 22314 US
Phone: 703-684-6292
E-mail Address:
info@cleancoalusa.org
Web Address: www.ceednet.org
The Center for Energy and Economic Development (CEED) is a nonprofit organization that promotes clean coal electricity generation.

V. Alternative Energy-Ethanol

Renewable Fuels Association (RFA)
1 Massachusetts Ave. NW, Ste. 820
Washington, DC 20001 US
Phone: 202-289-3835
E-mail Address: *info@ethanolrfa.org*
Web Address: www.ethanolrfa.org
The Renewable Fuels Association (RFA) is a trade organization representing the ethanol industry. It publishes a wealth of useful information, including a listing of biorefineries and monthly U.S. fuel ethanol production and demand.

VI. Alternative Energy-Fuel Cells

Fuel Cell Today
Orchard Rd.
Royston
Hertfordshire, SG8 5HE UK
E-mail Address:
info@fuelcelltoday.com
Web Address: www.fuelcelltoday.com
Fuel Cell Today is an Internet portal that provides news, commentary and information on the fuel cell industry.

Fuel Cells 2000
1100 H St. NW, Ste. 800
Washington, DC 20005 US
Phone: 202-785-4222
Fax: 202-785-4313
E-mail Address: *marlee@fuelcells.org*
Web Address: www.fuelcells.org
Fuel Cells 2000, run by the Breakthrough Technologies Institute (BTI), is a site devoted to preparing and sharing information on fuel cells, an efficient energy source.

United States Fuel Cell Council (USFCC)
1100 H St. NW, Ste. 800
Washington, DC 20005 US
Phone: 202-293-5500
Fax: 202-785-4313
E-mail Address:
germain@fuelcells.org
Web Address: www.usfcc.com
The United States Fuel Cell Council (USFCC) is an industry association dedicated to fostering the commercialization of fuel cells in the U.S. Members include the world's leading fuel cell developers, manufacturers, suppliers and customers.

VII. Alternative Energy-Hydroelectric

International Journal on Hydropower & Dams
123 Westmead Rd.
Sutton, Surrey SM1 4JH UK
Phone: 44-0-20-8643-5133
Fax: 44-0-20-8643-8200
E-mail Address: *ami@hydropower-dams.com*

Web Address:
www.hydropower-dams.com
The International Journal on Hydropower & Dams is an online journal with detailed information about the hydropower segment of the energy industry.

National Hydropower Association (NHA)
1 Massachusetts Ave. NW, Ste. 850
Washington, DC 20001 US
Phone: 202-682-1700
Fax: 202-682-9478
E-mail Address: *help@hydro.org*
Web Address: www.hydro.org
The National Hydropower Association (NHA) is the only national trade association dedicated exclusively to representing the interests of the hydropower industry. Its members span the breadth of the industry and all related fields.

VIII. Alternative Energy-Storage

Electricity Storage Association
830 Claremont Dr.
Morgan Hill, CA 95037 US
Phone: 614-716-1269
E-mail Address:
info@electricitystorage.org
Web Address:
www.electricitystorage.org
The Electricity Storage Association promotes the development and commercialization of improved energy storage delivery systems for use by electricity suppliers and their customers. Its web site provides information on advanced storage technologies such as flywheels, pumped hydro storage, flow cell batteries and compressed air energy storage.

IX. Alternative or Renewable Energy-General

Alliance to Save Energy (ASE)
1850 M St. NW, Ste. 600
Washington, DC 20036 US
Phone: 202-857-0666
Fax: 202-331-9588
E-mail Address: *info@ase.org*
Web Address: www.ase.org
The Alliance to Save Energy (ASE) promotes energy-efficiency worldwide to achieve a healthier economy, a cleaner environment and energy security.

American Council for an Energy-Efficient Economy (ACEEE)
529 14th St. NW, Ste. 600
Washington, DC 20045-1000 US
Phone: 202-507-4000
Fax: 202-429-2248
E-mail Address: *info@aceee.org*
Web Address: www.aceee.org
The American Council for an Energy-Efficient Economy (ACEEE) is a nonprofit organization dedicated to advancing energy-efficiency as a means of promoting both economic prosperity and environmental protection.

American Council on Renewable Energy (ACORE)
1600 K St., Ste. 700
Washington, DC 20006 US
Phone: 202-393-0001
Fax: 202-393-0606
E-mail Address: *info@acore.org*
Web Address: www.acore.org
The American Council On Renewable Energy (ACORE) is a nonprofit organization focused on accelerating the adoption of renewable energy technologies into the mainstream of American society. With an interest in trade, finance and policy, ACORE promotes all renewable energy options for the production of electricity, hydrogen, fuels and end-use energy.

Business Council for Sustainable Energy (BCSE)
1629 I St. NW, Ste. 501
Washington, DC 20002 US
Phone: 202-785-0507
Fax: 202-785-0514
E-mail Address: *bcse@bcse.org*
Web Address: www.bcse.org
The Business Council for Sustainable Energy (BCSE) strives to realize goals for the nation's economic, environmental and national security. The Council focuses on the promotion of clean energy technologies as solutions to certain environmental challenges.

Center for Energy Efficiency and Renewable Technologies (CEERT)
1100 11th St., Ste. 311
Sacramento, CA 95814 US
Phone: 916-442-7785
Fax: 916-447-2940
Toll Free: 877-758-4462
E-mail Address: *info@ceert.org*
Web Address: www.ceert.org
The Center for Energy Efficiency and Renewable Technologies (CEERT) provides technical support to environmental advocates and clean technology developers.

Chinese Renewable Energy Industries Association (CREIA)
Xicheng District
A4 Chegongzhuang St., Wuhua Plz., Ste. A2106
Beijing, 100044 China
Phone: 86-10-68002617-18
Fax: 86-10-68002674
E-mail Address: *creia@creia.net*
Web Address: www.creia.net
The Chinese Renewable Energy Industries Association (CREIA) was established in 2000 under official government sanction to promote the use of renewable energy sources within China.

Interstate Renewable Energy Council
P.O. Box 1156
Latham, NY 12110 US
Phone: 518-458-6059
E-mail Address: *info@irecusa.org*
Web Address: www.irecusa.org
Interstate Renewable Energy Council (IREC), formed in 1982 as a nonprofit organization, supports market-oriented services promoting renewable energy, aimed at education, coordination, procurement, the adoption and implementation of uniform guidelines and standards, workforce development, and consumer protection.

Renewable Energy & Energy Efficiency Partnership (REEEP)
Vienna International Ctr.
Rm. D1732, Wagramerstrasse 5
Vienna, A-100 Austria
Phone: 43 1 26026-3425
Fax: 43 1 21346-3425
E-mail Address: *info@reeep.org*
Web Address: www.reeep.org

The Renewable Energy and Energy Efficiency Partnership (REEEP) is a global, public-private partnership that structures policy and regulatory initiatives for clean energy, and facilitates financing for energy projects. Backed by more than 200 national governments, businesses, development banks and NGOs, REEEP hopes to contribute to international, national and regional policy dialogues. Its aim is to accelerate the integration of renewables into the energy mix and to advocate energy efficiency as a path to improved energy security and reduced carbon emissions, ensuring socio-economic benefits.

Renewable Energy Policy Project (REPP)
1612 K St. NW, Ste. 202
Washington, DC 20006 US
Phone: 202-293-2898
Fax: 202-293-5857
E-mail Address: *gsterzinger@repp.org*
Web Address: www.crest.org
The Renewable Energy Policy Project (REPP) is devoted to creating policy tools and disseminating information on public policy about alternative energy.

Sustainable Energy Association of Singapore (SEAS)
2 Bukit Merah Central
18-02 SPRING Bldg.
159835 Singapore
Phone: 65-6338-8578
Fax: 65-276-4257
Web Address: www.seas.com
The Sustainable Energy Association of Singapore (SEAS) represents the interests of companies in renewable energy, carbon trading, energy efficiency, clean development mechanism projects and their financial institutions.

X. Alternative or Renewable Energy-Geothermal

GeoExchange Heat Pump Consortium (GHPC)
1050 Connecticut Ave. NW, Ste. 1000
Washington, DC 20036 US
Phone: 202-558-7175
Fax: 202-558-6759
Toll Free: 1-888-255-4436
E-mail Address: *info@ghpc.org*
Web Address: www.geoexchange.org
GeoExchange Heat Pump Consortium (GHPC) offers information on how geothermal heating and cooling can provide energy efficiency and reliability in the field of interior climate control.

Geothermal Resources Council (GRC)
2001 2nd St., Ste. 5
Davis, CA 95617 US
Phone: 530-758-2360
Fax: 530-758-2839
E-mail Address: *crobinson@geothermal.org*
Web Address: www.geothermal.org
The Geothermal Resources Council (GRC) is an association that encourages the development of geothermal resources and provides information on geothermal energy.

XI. Alternative or Renewable Energy-Solar

American Solar Energy Society (ASES)
2400 Central Ave., Ste. A
Boulder, CO 80301 US
Phone: 303-443-3130
Fax: 303-443-3212
E-mail Address: *ases@ases.org*
Web Address: www.ases.org
The American Solar Energy Society (ASES) is committed to advancing the use of solar energy to benefit citizens and the global environment, promoting widespread solar energy use in the near future and long-term.

International Solar Energy Society (ISES)
Wiesentalstr. 50
Villa Tannheim
Freiburg, 79115 Germany
Phone: 49-761-4506-0
Fax: 49-761-45906-99
E-mail Address: *hq@ises.org*
Web Address: www.ises.org
The International Solar Energy Society (ISES) is an international group promoting the advancement of renewable energy technology, implementation and education worldwide.

Solar Electric Power Association
1341 Connecticut Ave. NW, Ste. 401
Washington, DC 20036 US
Phone: 202-857-0898
Fax: 202-559-2035
E-mail Address: *info@solarelectricpower.org*
Web Address: www.solarelectricpower.org
The Solar Electric Power Association is a nonprofit organization consisting of more than 100 companies and associations in eight countries.

Solar Energy Industries Association (SEIA)
805 15th St. NW, Ste. 510
Washington, DC 20005 US
Phone: 202-682-0556
Fax: 202-682-7779
E-mail Address: *info@seia.org*
Web Address: www.seia.org
Solar Energy Industries Association (SEIA) operates a web site that provides news for the solar energy industry, links to related products and companies and solar energy statistics.

Solar Platform of Almeria (PSA)
N-340A, Almeria, Spain
Phone: 950-38-79-90
Fax: 950-38-79-91
E-mail Address: *info@psa.es*
Web Address: www.psa.es
The Solar Platform of Almeria (Plataforma Solar de Almería), a dependency of Spain's Center for Energy, Environment and Technological Research (CIEMAT), is the largest center for research, development and testing of concentrating solar power (CSP) technologies in Europe. PSA activities form an integral part of the CIEMAT Department of Renewable Energies as one of its lines of R&D.

XII. Alternative or Renewable Energy-Wind

American Wind Energy Association (AWEA)
1501 M St. NW, Ste. 1000
Washington, DC 20005 US
Phone: 202-383-2500
Fax: 202-383-2505
E-mail Address: *windmail@awea.org*
Web Address: www.awea.org

The American Wind Energy Association (AWEA) promotes wind energy as a clean source of electricity worldwide. Its website provides excellent resources for research, including an online library, discussions of legislation, and descriptions of wind technologies.

Canadian Wind Energy Association (CanWEA)
170 Laurier Ave. W, Ste. 810
Ottawa, ON K1P 5V5 Canada
Phone: 613-234-8716
Fax: 613-234-5642
Toll Free: 800-922-6932
E-mail Address: *info@canwea.ca*
Web Address: www.canwea.ca
The Canadian Wind Energy Association (CanWEA) is a nonprofit trade association that promotes the development of wind energy.

European Wind Energy Association (EWEA)
63-65 Rue d'Arlon
Brussels, B-1040 Belgium
Phone: 32-2-546-1940
Fax: 32-2-546-1944
E-mail Address: *ewea@ewea.org*
Web Address: www.ewea.org
The European Wind Energy Association (EWEA) co-ordinates international policy, communications, research and analysis from its headquarters in Brussels. EWEA manages European programs, hosts events and supports the needs of its members.

Indian Wind Energy Association
Opp. Asian Games Village, August Kranti Marg
PHD House, 3rd Fl.
New Delhi, 110 016 India
Phone: 91-11-26523042
E-mail Address: *manish@inwea.org*
Web Address: www.inwea.org
The Indian Wind Energy Association was organized to promote and develop wind power in India.

XIII. Automotive Industry Resources

DieselNet
Ecopoint Inc., P.O. Box 47055
Mississauga, ON L5K 2R2 Canada
Phone: 905-990-0775
Fax: 905-990-0776
E-mail Address: *consult2@dieselnet.com*
Web Address: www.dieselnet.com
DieselNet is an online information service on diesel emissions, emission control, diesel engines, fuels and more. Ecopoint Inc. owns and publishes the site.

XIV. Canadian Government Agencies-Energy

Canadian Nuclear Safety Commission (CNSC)
280 Slater St., Ste. B
Ottawa, ON K1P 5S9 Canada
Phone: 613-995-5894
Fax: 613-995-5086
Toll Free: 800-668-5284
E-mail Address: *info@cnsc-ccsn.gc.ca*
Web Address: www.nuclearsafety.gc.ca
The Canadian Nuclear Safety Commission (CNSC) regulates nuclear power plants, nuclear research facilities and the use of nuclear materials in Canada.

National Energy Board (NEB)
444 7th Ave. SW
Calgary, AB T2P 0X8 Canada
Phone: 403-292-4800
Fax: 403-292-5503
Toll Free: 800-899-1265
E-mail Address: *info@neb-one.gc.ca*
Web Address: www.neb-one.gc.ca
The National Energy Board (NEB) is the Canadian government body responsible for the regulation of oil and natural gas pipeline traffic and construction, international power line construction and the export of oil, electricity and gas, as well as oil and gas activities within the country.

XV. Canadian Government Agencies-General

Canadian Polar Commission
360 Albert St., Ste. 1710
Ottawa, ON K1R 7X7 Canada
Phone: 613-943-8605
Fax: 613-943-8607
Toll Free: 888-765-2701
E-mail Address: *mail@polarcom.gc.ca*
Web Address: www.polarcom.gc.ca
The Canadian Polar Commission promotes and distributes research in the Polar regions.

XVI. Careers-First Time Jobs/New Grads

Black Collegian Online (The)
140 Carondelet St.
New Orleans, LA 70130 US
Phone: 504-523-0154
Web Address: www.black-collegian.com
The Black Collegian Online features listings for job and internship opportunities, as well as other tools for students of color; it is the web site of The Black Collegian Magazine, published by IMDiversity, Inc. The site includes a list of the top 100 minority corporate employers and an assessment of job opportunities.

CollegeGrad.com, Inc.
234 E. College Ave., Ste. 200
State College, PA 16801 US
Phone: 262-375-6700
Toll Free: 1-800-991-4642
Web Address: www.collegegrad.com
CollegeGrad.com, Inc. offers in-depth resources for college students and recent grads seeking entry-level jobs.

Job Web
Nat'l Association of Colleges & Employers (NACE)
62 Highland Ave.
Bethlehem, PA 18017-9085 US
Phone: 610-868-1421
Fax: 610-868-0208
Toll Free: 800-544-5272
E-mail Address: *editors@jobweb.com*
Web Address: www.jobweb.com
Job Web, owned and sponsored by National Association of Colleges and Employers (NACE), displays job openings and employer descriptions. The site also offers a database of career fairs, searchable by state or keyword, with contact information.

MBAjobs.net
Fax: 413-556-8849
E-mail Address: *contact@mbajobs.net*
Web Address: www.mbajobs.net
MBAjobs.net is a unique international service for MBA students and graduates, employers, recruiters and

business schools. The MBAjobs.net service is provided by WebInfoCo.

MonsterTRAK
11845 W. Olympic Blvd., Ste. 500
Los Angeles, CA 90064 US
Toll Free: 800-999-8725
E-mail Address:
trakstudent@monster.com
Web Address:
www.college.monster.com
MonsterTRAK provides information about internships and entry-level jobs.

National Association of Colleges and Employers (NACE)
62 Highland Ave.
Bethlehem, PA 18017-9085 US
Phone: 610-868-1421
Fax: 610-868-0208
Toll Free: 800-544-5272
E-mail Address:
mcollins@naceweb.org
Web Address: www.naceweb.org
The National Association of Colleges and Employers (NACE) is a premier U.S. organization representing college placement offices and corporate recruiters who focus on hiring new grads.

XVII. Careers-General Job Listings

Career Exposure, Inc.
805 SW Broadway, Ste. 2250
Portland, OR 97205 US
Phone: 503-221-7779
Fax: 503-221-7780
E-mail Address: *lisam@mackenzie-marketing.com*
Web Address:
www.careerexposure.com
Career Exposure, Inc. is an online career center and job placement service, with resources for employers, recruiters and job seekers.

CareerBuilder, Inc.
200 N. LaSalle St., Ste. 1100
Chicago, IL 60601 US
Phone: 773-527-3600
Toll Free: 800-638-4212
Web Address: www.careerbuilder.com
CareerBuilder, Inc. focuses on the needs of companies and also provides a database of job openings. The site has 1.5 million jobs posted by 300,000 employers, and receives an average 23 million unique visitors monthly. The company also operates online career centers for 150 newspapers, 1,000 partners and other online portals such as America Online. Resumes are sent directly to the company, and applicants can set up a special e-mail account for job-seeking purposes. CareerBuilder is primarily a joint venture between three newspaper giants: The McClatchy Company (which recently acquired former partner Knight Ridder), Gannett Co., Inc. and Tribune Company. In 2007, Microsoft acquired a minority interest in CareerBuilder, allowing the site to ally itself with MSN.

CareerOneStop
Toll Free: 877-348-0502
E-mail Address:
info@careeronestop.org
Web Address: www.careeronestop.org
CareerOneStop is operated by the employment commissions of various state agencies. It contains job listings in both the private sector and in government. CareerOneStop is sponsored by the U.S. Department of Labor. It includes a wide variety of useful career resources and workforce information.

HotJobs
45 W. 18th St., 6th Fl.
New York, NY 10011 US
Phone: 646-351-5300
Web Address:
www.hotjobs.yahoo.com
HotJobs, designed for experienced professionals, employers and job seekers, is a Monster-owned site that provides company profiles, a resume posting service and a resume workshop. The site allows posters to block resumes from being viewed by certain companies and provides a notification service of new jobs.

JobCentral
DirectEmployers Association, Inc.
9002 N. Purdue Rd., Quad III, Ste. 100
Indianapolis, IN 46268 US
Phone: 317-874-9000
Fax: 317-874-9100
Toll Free: 866-268-6206
E-mail Address: *info@jobcentral.com*
Web Address: www.jobcentral.com
JobCentral, operated by the nonprofit DirectEmployers Association, Inc., links users directly to hundreds of thousands of job opportunities posted on the sites of participating employers, thus bypassing the usual job search sites. This saves employers money and allows job seekers to access many more job opportunities.

LaborMarketInfo
Employment Dev. Dept.
Labor Market Info. Div.
800 Capitol Mall, MIC 83
Sacramento, CA 95814 US
Phone: 916-262-2162
Fax: 916-262-2352
Toll Free: 800-480-3287
Web Address:
www.labormarketinfo.edd.ca.gov
LaborMarketInfo, formerly the California Cooperative Occupational Information System, is geared to providing job seekers and employers a wide range of resources, namely the ability to find, access and use labor market information and services. It provides demographical statistics for employment on both a local and regional level, as well as career searching tools for California residents. The web site is sponsored by California's Employment Development Office.

Recruiters Online Network
947 Essex Ln.
Medina, OH 44256 US
Phone: 888-364-4667
Fax: 888-237-8686
E-mail Address:
info@recruitersonline.com
Web Address:
www.recruitersonline.com
The Recruiters Online Network provides job postings from thousands of recruiters, Careers Online Magazine, a resume database, as well as other career resources.

True Careers, Inc.
Web Address: www.truecareers.com
True Careers, Inc. offers job listings and provides an array of career resources. The company also offers a search of over 2 million scholarships. It is partnered with CareerBuilder.com,

which powers its career information and resume posting functions.

USAJOBS
U.S. Office of Personnel Management
1900 E St. NW
Washington, DC 20415 US
Phone: 202-606-1800
Web Address: usajobs.opm.gov
USAJOBS, a program of the U.S. Office of Personnel Management, is the official job site for the U.S. Federal Government. It provides a comprehensive list of U.S. government jobs, allowing users to search for employment by location; agency; type of work, using the Federal Government's numerical identification code, the General Schedule (GS) Series; or by senior executive positions. It also has a special veterans' employment section; an information center, offering resume and interview tips and other useful information such as hiring trends and a glossary of Federal terms; and allows users to create a profile and post a resume.

Wall Street Journal - CareerJournal
Wall Street Journal
200 Liberty St.
New York, NY 10281 US
Phone: 212-416-2000
Toll Free: 800-568-7625
E-mail Address:
onelinejournal@wsj.com
Web Address:
cj.careercast.com/careers/jobsearch
The Wall Street Journal's CareerJournal, an executive career site, features a job database with thousands of available positions; career news and employment related articles; and advice regarding resume writing, interviews, networking, office life and job hunting.

XVIII. Careers-Job Reference Tools

NewsVoyager
4401 Wilson Blvd., Ste. 900
Arlington, VA 22203-1867 US
Phone: 571-366-1000
Fax: 571-366-1195
E-mail Address: *sally.clarke@naa.org*
Web Address: www.newsvoyager.com
NewsVoyager, a service of the Newspaper Association of America (NAA), links individuals to local, national and international newspapers. Job seekers can search through thousands of classified sections.

Vault.com, Inc.
75 Varick St., 8th Fl.
New York, NY 10013 US
Phone: 212-366-4212
E-mail Address:
feedback@staff.vault.com
Web Address: www.vault.com
Vault.com, Inc. is a comprehensive career web site for employers and employees, with job postings and valuable information on a wide variety of industries. Vault gears many of its features toward MBAs. The site has been recognized by Forbes and Fortune Magazines.

XIX. Chemicals Industry Associations

American Chemical Society (ACS)
1155 16th St. NW
Washington, DC 20036 US
Phone: 202-872-4600
Fax: 202-776-8258
Toll Free: 800-227-5558
E-mail Address: *help@acs.org*
Web Address: www.acs.org
The American Chemical Society (ACS) is a nonprofit organization aimed at promoting the understanding of chemistry and chemical sciences. It represents a wide range of disciplines including chemistry, chemical engineering and other technical fields.

China Petroleum & Chemical Industry Association (CPCIA)
Asian Games Village
Bldg. 16 Qu 4 Anhuili
Beijing, 100723 China
Phone: 86-10-8488-5056
Fax: 86-10-8488-5087
E-mail Address: *bgs@cpcia.org.cn*
Web Address: www.cpcia.org
The China Petroleum & Chemical Industry Association (CPCIA) is a non-government and nonprofit association composed of regional and local associations including the China Polyurethane Industry Association.

Korea Petrochemical Industry Association (KPIA)
Yeonji-Dong, Jongno-Gu
6th Fl. Yeojundo-Bldg., 1-1
Seoul, 110-738 Korea
Phone: 82-2-744-0116
Fax: 82-2-743-1887
E-mail Address: *kpia@kpia.or.kr*
Web Address: www.kpia.or.kr
The Korea Petrochemical Industry Association (KPIA) is a leading Korean association focused on the petrochemicals sector. It is especially dedicated to developing safe practices, promoting international cooperation and general research and development in the industry.

Singapore Chemical Industry Council (SCIC)
120 Lower Delta Rd.
10-12 Cendex Ctr.
169208 Singapore
Phone: 65-6278-9576
E-mail Address: *secretariat@scic.sg*
Web Address: www.scic.sg
The Singapore Chemical Industry Council (SCIC) is the official body representing the chemical industry of Singapore in the private sector. Its membership comprises key companies, logistics service providers and traders.

XX. Chemicals Industry Resources

Chemical Cluster Singapore
120 Lower Delta Rd.
10-12 Cendex Ctr.
169208 Singapore
E-mail Address: *secretariat@scic.sg*
Web Address:
www.chemindustry.org.sg
The Singapore Chemical Industry Council (SCIC) hosts the Chemical Cluster Singapore website which provides press releases; environment and saftey information; directories; and links to tenders, buyers and sellers.

ICIS.com
Quadrant House
The Quadrant
Sutton, Surrey SM2 5AS UK
Phone: 44 20 8652 3335
Fax: 44 20 8652 3924
E-mail Address: *csc@icis.com*

Web Address: www.icis.com/v2/magazine/home.aspx
ICIS.com is an online market intelligence site for the chemical and energy industries.

XXI. Construction Resources-Energy Efficient Buildings

Energy Efficiency Programme Office (E2PO)
140 Hill St.
5th Storey, MICA Bldg.
Singapore, 179369 Singapore
Fax: 65-6235-2611
Toll Free: 800-225-5632
E-mail Address: *contact_NEA@nea.gov.sg*
Web Address: www.e2singapore.gov.sg
To drive energy efficiency improvement in Singapore, the Energy Efficiency Programme Office (E2PO) has been established. The website includes information about energy programs, publications, incentives and development opportunities for power generation, industry, transport, green buildings and the public sector of Singapore.

XXII. Corporate Information Resources

bizjournals.com
120 W. Morehead St., Ste. 400
Charlotte, NC 28202 US
Web Address: www.bizjournals.com
Bizjournals.com is the online media division of American City Business Journals, the publisher of dozens of leading city business journals nationwide. It provides access to research into the latest news regarding companies small and large.

Business Wire
44 Montgomery St.
39th Fl.
San Francisco, CA 94104 US
Phone: 415-986-4422
Fax: 415-788-5335
Toll Free: 800-227-0845
Web Address: www.businesswire.com
Business Wire offers news releases, industry- and company-specific news, top headlines, conference calls, IPOs on the Internet, media services and access to tradeshownews.com and BW Connect On-line through its informative and continuously updated web site.

Edgar Online, Inc.
50 Washington St., 11th Fl.
Norwalk, CT 06854 US
Phone: 203-852-5666
Fax: 203-852-5667
Toll Free: 800-416-6651
Web Address: www.edgar-online.com
Edgar Online, Inc. is a gateway and search tool for viewing corporate documents, such as annual reports on Form 10-K, filed with the U.S. Securities and Exchange Commission.

PR Newswire Association LLC
810 7th Ave., 32nd Fl.
New York, NY 10019 US
Phone: 201-360-6700
Toll Free: 800-832-5522
E-mail Address: *information@prnewswire.com*
Web Address: www.prnewswire.com
PR Newswire Association LLC provides comprehensive communications services for public relations and investor relations professionals ranging from information distribution and market intelligence to the creation of online multimedia content and investor relations web sites. Users can also view recent corporate press releases. The Association is owned by United Business Media plc.

Silicon Investor
100 W. Main
P.O. Box 29
Freeman, MO 64746 US
E-mail Address: *admin_dave@techstocks.com*
Web Address: siliconinvestor.advfn.com
Silicon Investor is focused on providing information about technology companies. The company's web site serves as a financial discussion forum and offers quotes, profiles and charts.

XXIII. Economic Data & Research

Eurostat
Phone: 32-2-299-9696
Toll Free: 80-0-6789-1011
Web Address: www.epp.eurostat.ec.europa.eu
Eurostat is the European Union's service that publishes a wide variety of comprehensive statistics on European industries, populations, trade, agriculture, technology, environment and other matters.

India Brand Equity Foundation (IBEF)
249-F Sector 18
Udyog Vihar Phase IV
Gurgaon, Haryana 122015 India
Phone: 91-124-4014060
Fax: 91-124-4013873
E-mail Address: *ceo@ibef.org*
Web Address: www.ibef.org
India Brand Equity Foundation (IBEF) is a public-private partnership between the Ministry of Commerce and Industry, Government of India, and the Confederation of Indian Industry. The Foundation's primary objective is to build positive economic perceptions of India globally. It aims to effectively present the India business perspective and leverage business partnerships in a globalizing market-place.

National Bureau of Statistics (China)
57, Yuetan Nanjie, Sanlihe
Xicheng District
Beijing, 100826 China
Fax: 86-10-68782000
E-mail Address: *info@stats.gov.cn*
Web Address: www.stats.gov.cn/english
The National Bureau of Statistics of China provides statistics and economic data regarding China's economic and social issues.

Organization for Economic Co-operation and Development (OECD)
2 rue André Pascal
Cedex 16
Paris, F-75775 France
Phone: 33-145-24-8200
Fax: 33-145-24-8500
Web Address: www.oecd.org

The Organization for Economic Co-operation and Development (OECD) publishes detailed economic, government, population, social and trade statistics on a country-by-country basis for over 30 nations representing the world's largest economies. Sectors covered range from industry, labor, technology and patents, to health care, environment and globalization.

Statistics Canada
150 Tunney's Pasture Driveway
Ottawa, ON K1A 0T6 Canada
Phone: 613-951-8116
Fax: 613-951-0581
Toll Free: 800-263-1136
Web Address: www.statcan.gc.ca
A complete portal to Canadian economic data and statistics.

STAT-USA/Internet
STAT-USA, HCHB
U.S. Dept. of Commerce, Rm. 4885
Washington, DC 20230 US
Phone: 202-482-1986
Fax: 202-482-2164
Toll Free: 800-782-8872
E-mail Address: *statmail@esa.doc.gov*
Web Address: www.stat-usa.gov
STAT-USA/Internet offers daily economic news, statistical releases and databases relating to export and trade, as well as the domestic economy. It is provided by STAT-USA, which is an agency in the Economics & Statistics Administration of the U.S. Department of Commerce. The site mainly consists of two main databases, the State of the Nation (SOTN), which focuses on the current state of the U.S. economy; and the Global Business Opportunities (GLOBUS) & the National Trade Data Bank (NTDB), which deals with U.S. export opportunities, global political/socio-economic conditions and other world economic issues.

XXIV. Emissions Cap and Trade Associations

International Emissions Trading Association (IETA)
24, Rue Merle dAubigne
Geneva, 1207 Switzerland
Phone: 41 22 737 05 00
Fax: 41 22 737 05 08
E-mail Address: *info@ieta.org*
Web Address: www.ieta.org
IETA is a leading association in the carbon emissions cap and trade industry. It sponsors research, publications and conferences on a worldwide basis.

UK Emissions Trading Group (ETG)
8 Duncannon St.
Golden Cross House
London, WC2N 4JF UK
Phone: 020 7484 5274
E-mail Address:
John.Craven@etg.uk.com
Web Address: www.uketg.com
The business-led UK Emissions Trading Group (ETG) offers a forum for discussion and resolution of all aspects of emissions trading and enables communication to take place between commerce and industry, and the UK Government.

XXV. Energy Associations-Coal

American Coal Foundation
101 Constitution Ave. NW, Ste. 525 E.
Washington, DC 20001-2133 US
Phone: 202-463-9785
Fax: 202-463-9786
E-mail Address: *info@teachcoal.org*
Web Address: www.teachcoal.org
The American Coal Foundation was created to develop, produce and disseminate coal-related educational materials and programs designed for teachers and students.

Coal Association of Canada
205-9th Ave. SE, Ste. 150
Calgary, AB T2G 0R3 Canada
Phone: 403-262-1544
Fax: 403-265-7604
Toll Free: 800-910-2625
E-mail Address: *info@coal.ca*
Web Address: www.coal.ca
The Coal Association of Canada represents members of the Canadian coal industry.

Kentucky Coal Association
340 S. Broadway, Ste. 100
Lexington, KY 40508-2553 US
Phone: 859-233-4743
Fax: 859-233-4745
E-mail Address:
kca@kentuckycoal.com
Web Address: www.kentuckycoal.org
The Kentucky Coal Association represents members of the coal industry in Kentucky.

West Virginia Coal Association
P.O. Box 3923
Charleston, WV 25309 US
Phone: 304-342-4153
Fax: 304-342-7651
Web Address: www.wvcoal.com
The West Virginia Coal Association represents members of the coal industry in West Virginia.

Wyoming Coal division of the Wyoming Mining Association
P. O. Box 866
Cheyenne, WY 82003 US
Phone: 307-635-0331
Fax: 307-778-6240
E-mail Address: *wma@vcn.com*
Web Address: www.wma-minelife.com
The Wyoming Mining Association operates web pages dedicated to the state's extensive coal production industry.

XXVI. Energy Associations-Electric Power

American Public Power Association (APPA)
1875 Connecticut Ave. NW, Ste. 1200
Washington, DC 20009-5715 US
Phone: 202-467-2900
Fax: 202-467-2910
E-mail Address: *mrufe@appanet.org*
Web Address: www.appanet.org
The American Public Power Association (APPA) is a nonprofit service organization for the country's community-owned electric utilities, dedicated to advancing the public policy interests of its members and their consumers.

Edison Electric Institute (EEI)
701 Pennsylvania Ave. NW
Washington, DC 20004-2696 US
Phone: 202-508-5000
E-mail Address: *feedback@eei.org*
Web Address: www.eei.org
The Edison Electric Institute (EEI) is an association of U.S. shareholder-owned electric companies as well as worldwide affiliates and industry

associates. Its web site provides energy news and a link to Electric Perspectives magazine.

Electric Power Research Institute (EPRI)
3420 Hillview Ave.
Palo Alto, CA 94304 US
Phone: 650-855-2121
Fax: 704-595-2871
Toll Free: 800-313-3774
E-mail Address: *askepri@epri.com*
Web Address: www.energysearch.com
Electric Power Research Institute (EPRI) is a leader in creating technology and solving tough environmental problems.

Electric Power Service Provider Association
1401 New York Ave. NW
11th Fl.
Washington, DC 20005-2110 US
Phone: 202-628-8200
Fax: 202-628-8260
Web Address: www.epsa.org
The Electric Power Service Provider Association promotes the interests of the electric power generation and distribution industry.

Institute of Public Utilities
Michigan State University
W157 Owen Graduate Hall
East Lansing, MI 48825-1109 US
Phone: 517-355-1876
Fax: 517-355-1854
E-mail Address: *ipu@msu.edu*
Web Address: www.ipu.msu.edu
The Institute of Public Utilities is committed to a mission of supporting informed, effective and efficient utility regulation by providing educational programs and applied research to the regulatory policy community.

National Rural Electric Cooperative Association (NRECA)
4301 Wilson Blvd.
Arlington, VA 22203-1860 US
Phone: 703-907-5500
E-mail Address:
Patrick.lavigne@nreca.coop
Web Address: www.nreca.coop
The National Rural Electric Cooperative Association (NRECA) is the national service organization dedicated to representing the interests of consumer-owned cooperative electric utilities and the consumers they serve.

Public Utility Research Center (PURC)
University of Florida, 205 Matherly Hall
P.O. Box 117142
Gainesville, FL 32611-7142 US
Phone: 352-392-6148
Fax: 352-392-7796
E-mail Address:
purcecon@cba.ufl.edu
Web Address:
bear.cba.ufl.edu/centers/purc
Public Utility Research Center (PURC) provides international training and strategic research in public utility regulation, market rules, and infrastructure management in the energy, telecommunications, and water industries.

Western Energy Institute (WEI)
827 NE Oregon St.
Portland, OR 97232-2172 US
Phone: 503-231-1994
Fax: 503-231-2595
E-mail Address:
himes@westernenergy.org
Web Address: www.westernenergy.org
The Western Energy Institute (WEI) serves the electric and gas industries throughout the western U.S. and Canada.

Women's International Network of Utility Professionals (WINUP)
P.O. Box 817
Fergus Falls, MN 56538-0817 US
Phone: 218-731-1659
E-mail Address: *tdrexler@otpco.com*
Web Address: www.winup.org
The Women's International Network of Utility Professionals (WINUP) provides networking and support for women in the utility industry.

XXVII. Energy Associations-International

International Association for Energy Economics (IAEE)
28790 Chagrin Blvd., Ste. 350
Cleveland, OH 44122 US
Phone: 216-464-5365
Fax: 216-464-2737
E-mail Address: *iaee@iaee.org*
Web Address: www.iaee.org
The International Association for Energy Economics (IAEE) provides members with an opportunity to exchange ideas and information relevant to professionals involved in energy economics.

International Energy Agency (IEA)
9 rue de la Federation
Paris Cedex 15, 75739 France
Phone: 33-1-40-57-65-00
Fax: 33-1-40-57-65-59
E-mail Address: *info@iea.org*
Web Address: www.iea.org
The International Energy Agency (IEA) is the energy forum for its members' countries and is committed to taking joint measures to meet oil supply emergencies. It shares energy information, coordinates energy policies and helps in the development of national energy programs.

XXVIII. Energy Associations-Natural Gas

American Gas Association (AGA)
400 N. Capitol St. NW, Ste. 450
Washington, DC 20001 US
Phone: 202-824-7000
E-mail Address: *rshelby@aga.org*
Web Address: www.aga.org
The American Gas Association (AGA) represents a large number of natural gas providers, advocating for these companies and providing a broad range of programs and services for members.

Canadian Gas Association (CGA)
350 Sparks St., Ste. 80
Ottawa, ON K1R 7S8 Canada
Phone: 613-748-0057
Fax: 613-748-9078
E-mail Address: *info@cga.ca*
Web Address: www.cga.ca
The Canadian Gas Association (CGA) is a trade organization representing natural gas distribution companies, transmission companies and related equipment manufacturers and service providers in Canada and the U.S.

GAS Association of Singapore
111 Somerset Rd. 10-05
Singapore Power Bldg.
238164 Singapore

Phone: 65-6823-8648
Fax: 65-6823-8699
E-mail Address: *info@gas.org.sg*
Web Address: www.gas.org.sg
The Gas Association of Singapore represents professionals in the gas and gas related industries in Singapore.

Gas Processing Association Canada (GPAC)
900-6th Ave. SW
Calgary, AB T2P 3K2 Canada
Phone: 403-705-0223
Fax: 403-263-6886
E-mail Address: *info@gpacanada.com*
Web Address: www.gpacanada.com
The Gas Processing Association Canada (GPAC), formed by the merger of the Canadian Gas Processing Association and the Canadian Gas Processing Suppliers Association, aims to serve the needs of natural gas processors, suppliers and relevant industry associations and entities affected by the hydrocarbon processing industry.

Gas Processors Association (GPA)
6526 E. 60th St.
Tulsa, OK 74145 US
Phone: 918-493-3872
Fax: 918-493-3875
Web Address: www.GPAglobal.org
The Gas Processors Association (GPA) is an organization of companies involved in the natural gas processing industry. The association sets product standards, publishes industry statistics and is an educational resource.

Gas Technology Institute (GTI)
1700 S. Mount Prospect Rd.
Des Plaines, IL 60018-1804 US
Phone: 847-768-0500
Fax: 847-768-0501
E-mail Address:
businessdevelopmentinfo@gastechnology.org
Web Address: www.gastechnology.org
The Gas Technology Institute (GTI) is a not-for-profit research and development organization, and works to develop and deploy technologies related to affordable energy production, sustainable energy development and the efficient use of energy resources. Its network of partners, investors and clients includes state and federal government agencies; natural gas utilities and pipeline companies; industrial companies; electric utilities; independent power producers; technology developers; and national laboratories. In addition to its Illinois headquarters (which houses 28 specialized laboratories working on various advanced energy technologies), GTI also maintains smaller offices and facilities in locations including Houston, Texas; Sacramento, California; and Washington D.C.

Interstate Natural Gas Association of America (INGAA)
10 G St. NE, Ste. 700
Washington, DC 20002 US
Phone: 202-216-5900
Fax: 202-216-0870
E-mail Address: *webinfo@ingaa.org*
Web Address: www.ingaa.org
The Interstate Natural Gas Association of America (INGAA) represents interstate and interprovincial natural gas pipeline companies as a voice on important issues concerning natural gas pipeline companies. It also provides expertise and information services.

National Propane Gas Association (NPGA)
1150 17th St. NW, Ste. 310
Washington, DC 20036-4623 US
Phone: 202-466-7200
Fax: 202-466-7205
E-mail Address: *info@npga.org*
Web Address: www.npga.org
The National Propane Gas Association (NPGA) is a national trade association that strives for safe and increased use of propane and for a more positive environment for propane production.

Natural Gas Supply Association (NGSA)
805 15th St. NW, Ste. 510
Washington, DC 20005 US
Phone: 202-326-9300
Fax: 202-326-9330
Web Address: www.ngsa.org
The Natural Gas Supply Association (NGSA) represents domestic producers and marketers of natural gas.

Propane Gas Association of Canada (PGAC)
800, 717-7th Ave. SW
Calgary, AB T2P 0Z3 Canada
Phone: 403-543-6500
Fax: 403-543-6508
Toll Free: 877-784-4636
E-mail Address: *info@propanegas.ca*
Web Address: www.propanegas.ca
The Propane Gas Association of Canada (PGAC) is a nonprofit organization dedicated to the development of a safe and environmentally-friendly propane industry in Canada.

XXIX. Energy Associations-Nuclear

Canadian Nuclear Association
130 Albert St., Ste. 1610
Ottawa, ON K1P 5G4 Canada
Phone: 613-237-4262
Fax: 613-237-0989
E-mail Address: *elstonm@cna.ca*
Web Address: www.cna.ca
The Canadian Nuclear Association is a nonprofit organization that promotes nuclear power in Canada.

China Atomic Energy Authority
China Atomic Energy Authority
Beijing, 100037 China
E-mail Address:
webmaster@caea.gov.cn
Web Address: www.caea.gov.cn
The China Atomic Energy Authority is involved in developing policies and regulations and the development programming, planning and industrial standards for peaceful uses of nuclear energy.

International Atomic Energy Agency (IAEA)
Wagramer Strasse 5
P.O. Box 100
Vienna, A-1400 Austria
Phone: 431-2600-0
Fax: 431-2600-7
E-mail Address:
official.mail@iaea.org
Web Address: www.iaea.org
The International Atomic Energy Agency (IAEA) focuses on global nuclear energy developments.

Nuclear Energy Institute (NEI)
1776 I St. NW, Ste. 400
Washington, DC 20006-3708 US
Phone: 202-739-8000

Fax: 202-785-4019
E-mail Address: *webmasterp@nei.org*
Web Address: www.nei.org
The Nuclear Energy Institute (NEI) is a policy organization for the national nuclear technologies industry.

XXX. Energy Associations-Oil Field Services/Drilling

Association of Well Head Equipment Manufacturers
P.O. Box 1166
Bellaire, TX 77402 US
E-mail Address: *pres@awhem.org*
Web Address: www.awhem.org
The Association of Well Head Equipment Manufacturers provides technical consulting to national and international standards bodies and serves to influence value-added standardization of well head and related equipment in a positive manner.

Canadian Association of Oilwell Drilling Contractors (CAODC)
800, 540-5 Ave. SW
Calgary, AB T2P 0M2 Canada
Phone: 403-264-4311
Fax: 403-263-3796
E-mail Address: *info@caodc.ca*
Web Address: www.caodc.ca
The Canadian Association of Oilwell Drilling Contractors (CAODC) is a trade association that represents drilling and rig services contractors throughout Canada. The web site provides members with the latest information in the Canadian oil and gas exploration industry.

International Association of Geophysical Contractors (IAGC)
2550 North Loop W., Ste. 104
Houston, TX 77092 US
Phone: 713-957-8080
Fax: 713-957-0008
E-mail Address: *iagc@iagc.org*
Web Address: www.iagc.org
The International Association of Geophysical Contractors (IAGC) is the international trade association representing the industry that provides geophysical services to the oil and gas industry.

National Association of Energy Service Companies (NAESCO)
1615 M St. NW, Ste. 800
Washington, DC 20036 US
Phone: 202-822-0950
Fax: 202-822-0955
E-mail Address: *info@naesco.org*
Web Address: www.naesco.org
The National Association of Energy Service Companies (NAESCO) provides an opportunity for energy service companies to meet with industry peers to discuss issues relative to the energy services industry's growth and future direction.

National Association of Steel Pipe Distributors (NASPD)
1501 E. Mockingbird Ln., Ste. 307
Victoria, TX 77904 US
Phone: 361-574-7878
Fax: 832-201-9479
E-mail Address: *info@naspd.com*
Web Address: www.naspd.com
The National Association of Steel Pipe Distributors (NASPD) represents the steel pipe and tubular products distribution industry.

Petroleum Equipment Suppliers Association (PESA)
9225 Katy Fwy., Ste. 310
Houston, TX 77024 US
Phone: 713-932-0168
Fax: 713-932-0497
E-mail Address: *webmaster@pesa.org*
Web Address: www.pesa.org
The Petroleum Equipment Suppliers Association (PESA) is an organization of equipment manufacturers, well site service providers and supply companies serving the drilling and production segments of the petroleum industry.

XXXI. Energy Associations-Oil Sands

Oil Sands Developers Group
613A - 8600 Franklin Ave.
Fort McMurray, ALB T9H 4GB Canada
Phone: 780-790-1999
Fax: 780-790-1971
E-mail Address: *info@oilsandsdevelopers.ca*
Web Address: www.oilsands.cc
On behalf of its members, the group works closely with oil sands operators and developers, related industries, governments, Aboriginal peoples, and other organizations active in the Athabasca oil sands deposit region to define and address regional issues related to oil sands development.

XXXII. Energy Associations-Other

Alliance for Energy & Economic Growth
1615 H St. NW
Washington, DC 20062 US
Phone: 202-463-3130
Fax: 202-887-3445
E-mail Address: *info@yourenergyfuture.org*
Web Address: www.yourenergyfuture.org
The Alliance for Energy & Economic Growth is a broad alliance of interests that develop, deliver and consume energy from all sources. The alliance strives to help build an agreement for a strategy that balances supply and demand so that America's economy is fueled and the quality of life is supported.

American Association of Blacks in Energy
1625 K St. NW, Ste. 450
Washington, DC 20006 US
Phone: 202-371-9530
Fax: 202-371-9218
E-mail Address: *info@aabe.org*
Web Address: www.aabe.org
The American Association of Blacks in Energy is dedicated to ensuring the input of African Americans and other minorities in discussions and developments of energy policies, regulations, research and development technologies and environmental issues.

International Coiled Tubing Association (ICoTA)
P.O. Box 1082
Montgomery, TX 77356 US
Phone: 936-520-1549
Fax: 832-201-9977
E-mail Address: *ababin@icota.com*
Web Address: www.icota.com
The International Coiled Tubing Association (ICoTA) is a nonprofit,

member organization that works to improve communication and promotion of technical awareness within the coiled tubing industry.

National Association of State Energy Officials (NASEO)
1414 Prince St., Ste. 200
Alexandria, VA 22314 US
Phone: 703-299-8800
Fax: 703-299-6208
E-mail Address: *energy@naseo.org*
Web Address: www.naseo.org
The National Association of State Energy Officials (NASEO) provides a forum for energy officials, policymakers and others to trade information and discuss issues with regional and national implications.

National Oil Recyclers Association (NORA)
5965 Amber Ridge Rd.
Haymarket, VA 20169 US
Phone: 703-753-4277
Fax: 703-753-2445
E-mail Address: *sparker@noranews.org*
Web Address: www.noranews.org
The National Oil Recyclers Association (NORA) promotes proper recycling of used oil, oil filters, used antifreeze and other automotive and industrial materials to protect health and environment through education and the development of legislation and regulations.

New England Fuel Institute (NEFI)
20 Summer St.
Watertown, MA 02472 US
Phone: 617-924-1000
Fax: 617-924-5962
Web Address: www.nefi.com
The New England Fuel Institute (NEFI) provides information about the fuel oil business in New England.

Society of Energy Professionals International
300-425 Bloor St. E
Toronto, ON M4W 3R4 Canada
Phone: 416-979-2709
Fax: 416-979-5794
E-mail Address: *society@society.on.ca*
Web Address: www.thesociety.ca
The Society of Energy Professionals International is an independent trade union representing professionals in the energy industry within Ontario, Canada.

U.S. Energy Association (USEA)
1300 Pennsylvania Ave. NW, Ste. 550, Mailbox 142
Washington, DC 20004-3022 US
Phone: 202-312-1230
Fax: 202-682-1682
Web Address: www.usea.org
The U.S. Energy Association (USEA) represents the interests of the U.S. energy sector by increasing understanding in domestic and international energy issues. USEA is the U.S. member committee of the World Energy Counsel (WEC).

Women's Council on Energy and the Environment (WCEE)
P.O. Box 33211
Washington, DC 20033 US
Phone: 703-351-7850
Fax: 202-318-2506
E-mail Address: *info@wcee.org*
Web Address: www.wcee.org
The Women's Council on Energy and the Environment (WCEE) is dedicated to promoting professional and educational opportunities for women in the fields of energy and environment in the Washington, D.C. area.

XXXIII. Energy Associations-Petroleum, Exploration, Production, etc.

Alaska Oil & Gas Association
121 W. Fireweed Ln., Ste. 207
Anchorage, AK 99503 US
Phone: 907-272-1481
Fax: 907-279-8114
E-mail Address: *info@aoga.org*
Web Address: www.aoga.org
The Alaska Oil & Gas Association is a trade association that provides a forum for communication regarding oil and gas issues in Alaska.

American Association of Professional Landmen (AAPL)
4100 Fossil Creek Blvd.
Fort Worth, TX 76137 US
Phone: 817-847-7700
Fax: 817-847-7704
E-mail Address: *aapl@landman.org*
Web Address: www.landman.org
The American Association of Professional Landmen (AAPL) promotes the highest standards of performance for all land professionals and seeks to advance their stature and to encourage sound stewardship of energy and mineral resources.

American Petroleum Institute (API)
1220 L St. NW
Washington, DC 20005-4070 US
Phone: 202-682-8000
Web Address: www.api.org
American Petroleum Institute (API) represents U.S. oil and gas industries and its web site includes in-depth sections for energy consumers and energy professionals.

American Petroleum Institute-Delta API Chapter
P.O. Box 50110
New Orleans, LA 70150 US
E-mail Address: *bwaring@ocsbbs.com*
Web Address: www.api-delta.org
The American Petroleum Institute-Delta API Chapter acts as an umbrella organization to serve all aspects of the oil and gas industry. It actively supports the community and surrounding area of New Orleans.

American Petroleum Institute-Houston API Chapter
7170 Cherry Park Dr.
Houston, TX 77095 US
Phone: 281-861-7484
Fax: 281-463-0050
E-mail Address: *preynolds@signa.net*
Web Address: www.api-houston.org
The American Petroleum Institute-Houston API Chapter is a nonprofit organization that provides a forum for discussion of energy-related matters and promotes education and personal interaction to improve the energy industry.

Association of the German Petroleum Industry (MWV)
Steindamm 55
Hamburg, 20099 Germany
Phone: 49 (0) 40 24849 0
Fax: 49 (0) 40 24849 253
Web Address: www.mwv.de
Association of the German Petroleum Industry (MWV) promotes the interests of its member companies as well as

collects and publishes statistics regarding the industry.

Australian Institute of Petroleum
24 Marcus Clarke St.
Level 2
Canberra City, ACT 2601 Australia
Phone: 02-6247-3044
Fax: 02-6247-3844
E-mail Address: *aip@aip.com.au*
Web Address: www.aip.com.au
The Australian Institute of Petroleum, a globally recognized representative of Australia's petroleum industry, strives to develop a better Australian petroleum industry and provides responsible, professional and principled representation of the industry.

Canadian Association of Petroleum Producers (CAPP)
350 7th Ave. SW, Ste. 2100
Calgary, AB T2P 3N9 Canada
Phone: 403-267-1100
Fax: 403-261-4622
E-mail Address: *communication@capp.ca*
Web Address: www.capp.ca
Canadian Association of Petroleum Producers (CAPP) is committed to improving the economic well-being and sustainability of the Canadian upstream petroleum industry.

China Energy Association (CEA)
7th of Nanlishi St.
Xicheng District
Beijing, 100045 China
Phone: 86-010-68051807
Fax: 86-010-68051799
E-mail Address: *znx18303@126.com*
Web Address: www.zhnx.org.cn
The China Energy Association (CEA) is a membership organization that represents the energy sources sector and energy industry. The organization publishes the Energy Resource World magazine.

Domestic Petroleum Council (DPC)
101 Constitution Ave. NW, Ste. 800
Washington, DC 20001-2133 US
Phone: 202-544-4300
E-mail Address: *info@dpcusa.org*
Web Address: www.dpcusa.org
The Domestic Petroleum Council (DPC) is a representative for large U.S. independent natural gas and crude oil exploration and production companies. It strives for more responsible exploration, development and production to better meet the needs of consumers and to fuel the economy.

Independent Petroleum Association of America (IPAA)
1201 15th St. NW, Ste. 300
Washington, DC 20005 US
Phone: 202-857-4722
Fax: 202-857-4799
E-mail Address: *rcarter@ipaa.org*
Web Address: www.ipaa.org
The Independent Petroleum Association of America (IPAA) provides a forum for the exploration and production segment of the independent oil and natural gas business. It also provides information on the domestic exploration and production industry.

International Association of Drilling Contractors (IADC)
10370 Richmond Ave., Ste. 760
Houston, TX 77042 US
Phone: 713-292-1945
Fax: 713-292-1946
E-mail Address: *info@iadc.org*
Web Address: www.iadc.org
The International Association of Drilling Contractors (IADC) represents the worldwide oil and gas drilling industry and promotes commitment to safety, preservation of the environment and advances in drilling technology.

International Association of Oil & Gas Producers (OGP)
209-215 Blackfriars Rd.
London, SEI 8NL UK
Phone: 44-0-20-7633-0272
Fax: 44-0-20-7633-2350
E-mail Address: *reception@ogp.org.uk*
Web Address: www.ogp.org.uk
The International Association of Oil & Gas Producers (OGP) provides engineering, environmental, health, safety and personal competence and communications support for the international oil and gas industry in the areas of exploration and production.

International Petroleum Industry Environmental Conservation Association (IPIECA)
209-215 Blackfriars Rd., 5th Fl.
London, SE1 8NL UK
Phone: 44-020-7633-2388
Fax: 44-020-7633-2389
E-mail Address: *info@ipieca.org*
Web Address: www.ipieca.org
The International Petroleum Industry Environmental Conservation Association (IPIECA) works for the petroleum industry by developing and promoting solutions to global environmental issues.

Louisiana Mid-Continent Oil & Gas Association (LMOGA)
801 North Blvd., Ste. 201
Baton Rouge, LA 70802 US
Phone: 225-387-3205
Fax: 225-344-5502
E-mail Address: *info@lmoga.com*
Web Address: www.lmoga.com
The Louisiana Mid-Continent Oil & Gas Association (LMOGA) represents all sectors of the oil and gas industry in Louisiana and the Gulf of Mexico.

Mid-Continent Oil & Gas Association of Oklahoma
6701 N. Broadway, Ste. 300
Oklahoma, OK 73116 US
Phone: 405-843-5741
Web Address: www.okmoga.com
The Mid-Continent Oil & Gas Association of Oklahoma strives to solve problems and provide a unified voice for the advancement and improvement of the oil and gas industry.

National Association of Royalty Owners (NARO)
15 W. 6th St., Ste. 2626
Tulsa, OK 74119 US
Phone: 918-794-1660
Fax: 918-794-1662
Toll Free: 800-558-0557
E-mail Address: *NARO@NARO-us.org*
Web Address: www.naro-us.org
The National Association of Royalty Owners (NARO) remains the only national organization promoting the rights, responsibilities and definitions of citizens that own the natural resources in our country.

National Ocean Industries Association (NOIA)
1120 G St. NW, Ste. 900
Washington, DC 20005 US
Phone: 202-347-6900
Fax: 202-347-8650
E-mail Address: *mkearns@noia.org*
Web Address: www.noia.org
The National Ocean Industries Association (NOIA) represents all facets of the domestic offshore petroleum industry and strives to secure access to the nation's offshore hydrocarbon resources so that they may be developed, produced and supplied in an environmentally conscious manner.

National Petroleum Council (NPC)
1625 K St. NW, Ste. 600
Washington, DC 20006 US
Phone: 202-393-6100
Fax: 202-331-8539
E-mail Address: *info@npc.org*
Web Address: www.npc.org
The National Petroleum Council (NPC) web site offers a comprehensive look at the federally charted, privately funded advisory committee and its operations.

New Mexico Oil & Gas Association (NMOGA)
203 E. Santa Fe Ave.
Santa Fe, NM 87505 US
Phone: 505-982-2568
Fax: 505-985-1904
Toll Free: 866-982-1809
Web Address: www.nmoga.org
The New Mexico Oil & Gas Association (NMOGA) is a private, nonprofit organization dedicated to promoting the welfare of the oil and gas industry of New Mexico and the conservation and environmentally responsible development of oil and gas resources within the state.

North Dakota Petroleum Council
120 N. 3rd St., Ste. 200
Bismarck, ND 58502 US
Phone: 701-223-6380
Fax: 701-222-0006
E-mail Address: *ndpc@ndoil.org*
Web Address: www.ndoil.org
The North Dakota Petroleum Council provides a voice for the oil industry in North Dakota.

Oil and Gas UK
232-242 Vauxhall Bridge Rd., 2nd Fl.
London, SW1V 1AU UK
Phone: 44-020-7802-2400
Fax: 44-020-7802-2401
E-mail Address: *info@oilandgasuk.co.uk*
Web Address: www.oilandgas.org.uk
The United Kingdom Offshore Operators Association (UKOOA) is the representative organization for the U.K. offshore oil and gas industry.

Permian Basin Petroleum Association (PBPA)
415 W. Wall
Midland, TX 79701 US
Phone: 432-684-6345
Fax: 432-684-7836
E-mail Address: *allison@pbpa.info*
Web Address: www.pbpa.info
The Permian Basin Petroleum Association (PBPA) is the voice of the Permian Basin oil and gas community, serving the Permian Basin of Texas and New Mexico.

Petroleum Association of Wyoming (PAW)
951 Werner Ct., Ste. 100
Casper, WY 82601 US
Phone: 307-234-5333
Fax: 307-266-2189
E-mail Address: *paw@pawyo.org*
Web Address: www.pawyo.org
The Petroleum Association of Wyoming (PAW) strives to better Wyoming's oil and gas industry and public welfare.

Petroleum Equipment Institute (PEI)
6514 E. 69 St.
Tulsa, OK 74133-1729 US
Phone: 918-494-9696
Fax: 918-491-9895
Web Address: www.pei.org
The Petroleum Equipment Institute (PEI) is the leading authority and information source for the petroleum marketing and liquid handling equipment industry.

Petroleum Industry Research Foundation (PIRINC)
1031 31st St. NW
Washington, DC 20007-4401 US
Phone: 202-944-3339
Fax: 202-944-9830
E-mail Address: *benm@eprinc.org*
Web Address: www.pirinc.org
The Petroleum Industry Research Foundation (PIRINC) is internationally known for providing objective analysis of energy issues and studying energy economics with a special focus on oil.

Petroleum Services Association of Canada (PSAC)
800 6th Ave. SW, Ste. 1150
Calgary, AB T2P 3G3 Canada
Phone: 403-264-4195
Fax: 403-263-7174
E-mail Address: *info@psac.ca*
Web Address: www.psac.ca
The Petroleum Services Association of Canada (PSAC) is the national association of Canadian oil field service, supply and manufacturing companies.

Texas Independent Producers and Royalty Owners Association (TIPRO)
919 Congress Ave., Ste. 1000
Austin, TX 78701 US
Phone: 512-477-4452
Fax: 512-476-8070
E-mail Address: *ahaynes@tipro.org*
Web Address: www.tipro.org
The Texas Independent Producers and Royalty Owners Association (TIPRO) provides legislative and public representation, important information and opportunities to develop business relationships for independent oil and gas operators, working interest owners and other businesses in the energy industry.

Texas Oil & Gas Association (TXOGA)
304 W. 13th St.
Austin, TX 78701 US
Phone: 512-478-6631
Fax: 512-472-3859
E-mail Address: *bennis@txoga.org*
Web Address: www.txoga.org
The Texas Oil & Gas Association (TXOGA) is a petroleum trade association for oil and gas industry professionals in Texas.

Western States Petroleum Association (WSPA)
1415 L St., Ste. 600

Sacramento, CA 95814 US
Phone: 916-498-7750
Fax: 916-444-5745
Web Address: www.wspa.org
The Western States Petroleum Association (WSPA) strives to supply precise information about industry issues and to provide a discussion for different ideas on petroleum matters.

World Petroleum Council (WPC)
1 Duchess St., 4th Fl., Ste. 1
London, W1W 6AN UK
Phone: 44-0-20-7637-4995
Fax: 44-020-7637-4973
E-mail Address: *ulrike@world-petroleum.org*
Web Address: www.world-petroleum.org
The World Petroleum Council (WPC) sponsors the World Petroleum Congress, which provides an opportunity for discussions of the issues facing the worldwide oil industry.

XXXIV. Energy Associations-Pipelines

Association of Oil Pipe Lines
1808 I St. NW
Washington, DC 20006 US
Phone: 202-408-7970
Fax: 202-280-1949
E-mail Address: *rdobre@aopl.org*
Web Address: www.aopl.org
The Association of Oil Pipe Lines is an information source for the public, the media and the pipeline industry. It represents common carrier crude and product petroleum pipelines before Congress and regulatory agencies and in the federal courts.

Canadian Energy Pipeline Association (CEPA)
1860, 205–5th Ave. SW
Calgary, AB T2P 2V7 Canada
Phone: 403-221-8777
Fax: 403-221-8760
E-mail Address: *info@cepa.com*
Web Address: www.cepa.com
The Canadian Energy Pipeline Association (CEPA) is the trade association representing the Canadian transmission pipeline industry.

XXXV. Energy Associations-Refining

Canadian Petroleum Products Institute (CPPI)
1000-275 Slater
Ottawa, ON K1P 5H9 Canada
Phone: 613-232-3709
Fax: 613-236-4280
Web Address: www.cppi.ca
The Canadian Petroleum Products Institute (CPPI) is an association of Canadian companies involved in the refining, distribution and marketing of petroleum products. The Institute represents the views of its members on business, environmental, health and safety issues.

Europia
Blvd. du Souverain 165, 3rd Fl.
Brussels, B-1160 Belgium
Phone: 32-2-566-91-00
Fax: 32-2-566-91-11
E-mail Address: *info@europia.com*
Web Address: www.europia.com
Europia, the European government affairs organization of the oil refining and marketing industry, represents the problems of its members for institutions of the European Union and other European industrial and commercial organizations.

Independent Lubricant Manufacturers Association (ILMA)
400 N. Columbus St., Ste. 201
Alexandria, VA 22314 US
Phone: 703-684-5574
Fax: 703-836-8503
E-mail Address: *ilma@ilma.org*
Web Address: www.ilma.org
The Independent Lubricant Manufacturers Association (ILMA) strives to improve the role of independent lubricant manufacturers in a universal, competitive marketplace.

National Petrochemical & Refiners Association (NPRA)
1899 L St. NW, Ste. 1000
Washington, DC 20036-3896 US
Phone: 202-457-0480
Fax: 202-457-0486
E-mail Address: *info@npra.org*
Web Address: www.npra.org
The National Petrochemical & Refiners Association (NPRA) gathers and distributes information and statistics regarding petroleum refining and petrochemical manufacturing industries.

XXXVI. Energy Education Resources

Arctic National Wildlife Refuge (ANWR)
425 8th St. NW, Ste. 540
Washington, DC 20004 US
Phone: 202-248-4468
Fax: 202-248-6123
Web Address: www.anwr.org
Arctic National Wildlife Refuge (ANWR), located in the Coastal Plain, is believed to have the potential to hold billions of recoverable barrels of oil and gas. This web site is promotes the authorization to lease and develop this area.

California Energy Commission-Energy Quest
1516 9th St., MS-29
Sacramento, CA 95814 US
Phone: 916-654-4989
Fax: 916-654-4420
E-mail Address: *mediaoffice@energy.state.ca.us*
Web Address: www.energyquest.ca.gov
Energy Quest is an educational web site that teaches children about energy.

Canadian Centre for Energy Information
800-6 Ave. SW, Ste. 1600
Calgary, AB T2P 3G3 Canada
Phone: 403-263-7722
Fax: 403-237-6286
Toll Free: 877-606-4636
Web Address: www.centreforenergy.com
The Canadian Centre for Energy Information provides conferences, workshops and other activities, as well as informational publications designed to inform the public about issues affecting the Canadian energy industry.

Chevron's Energy Information for Kids
Web Address: www.chevroncars.com/learn

Chevron's Energy Information for Kids is a web site providing energy information geared for children.

National Energy Education Development (NEED)
8408 Kao Cir.
Manassas, VA 20110 US
Phone: 703-257-1117
Fax: 703-257-0037
E-mail Address: *info@need.org*
Web Address: www.need.org
National Energy Education Development (NEED) is devoted to developing and disseminating hands-on energy education programs to schools nationwide.

National Ocean Industries Association-About Offshore Oil & Gas
1120 G St. NW, Ste. 900
Washington, DC 20005 US
Phone: 202-347-6900
Fax: 202-347-8650
E-mail Address: *mkearns@noia.org*
Web Address:
www.noia.org/website/article.asp?id=122
The National Ocean Industries Association provides information about offshore oil and gas, petroleum and natural gas through this web page.

Society of Petroleum Engineers-Reference Material
222 Palisades Creek Dr.
Richardson, TX 75080 US
Phone: 972-952-9393
Fax: 972-952-9435
Toll Free: 800-45-6863
E-mail Address: *service@spe.org*
Web Address: www.spe.org/spe-app/spe/industry/reference/index.htm
The Society of Petroleum Engineers offers a Reference Materials web page that provides a sophisticated E&P Industry search engine, a glossary of industry terminology, unite conversion tools, engineering tools, an oil and gas information resource and a wide range of links to other resources.

XXXVII. Energy Industry Resources

Baker Hughes Incorporated
2929 Allen Pkwy., Ste. 2100
Houston, TX 77019-2118 US
Phone: 713-439-8600
Fax: 713-439-8699
E-mail Address:
info@bakerhughes.com
Web Address: www.bakerhughes.com
Baker Hughes' web site is the home of the firm's famous drilling rig count. Their site includes historical and global data concerning drilling, formation evaluation, completion and production products and services.

BP Statistical Review of World Energy
1 St. James Sq.
London, SW1Y 4PD UK
Phone: 44-20-7496-4000
Fax: 44-20-7496-4630
E-mail Address: *sr@bp.com*
Web Address:
www.bp.com/worldenergy
BP Statistical Review of World Energy, a publication of BP p.l.c., is an excellent source of the worlds current and historical energy trends.

Canadian Energy Research Institute (CERI)
3512-33 St. NW, Ste. 150
Calgary, AB T2L 2A6 Canada
Phone: 403-282-1231
Fax: 403-284-4181
E-mail Address: *mmasri@ceri.ca*
Web Address: www.ceri.ca
The Canadian Energy Research Institute (CERI) represents various Canadian governmental departments, the University of Calgary and over 100 private sector energy-related companies. It seeks to provide analysis of energy economics and related government issues in the fields of energy production, transportation and consumption.

Defense Energy Support Center (DESC)
Phone: 703-767-4357
E-mail Address: *hqhelpdesk@dla.mil*
Web Address: www.desc.dla.mil
The Defense Energy Support Center (DESC) is focused on designing an energy program that moves the Department of Defense out of the management of energy infrastructure and into the management of energy products. DESC also grants electricity services contracts to the DoD and the Federal Civilian Agency.

Earth Sciences and Resources Institute
1233 Washington St., Ste. 300
Columbia, SC 29208 US
Phone: 803-978-7550
Fax: 803-978-7528
E-mail Address:
cpeterson@esri.sc.edu
Web Address: www.esri.sc.edu
The Earth Sciences and Resources Institute is a free-standing environmental and petroleum geology research institute operating out of the University of South Carolina.

ElectricNet
5340 Fryling Rd., Ste. 101
Erie, PA 19510 US
E-mail Address:
info@vertmarkets.com
Web Address: www.electricnet.com
ElectricNet is a gateway to valuable industry information pertinent to those who design, manufacture, construct, startup, test, repair, service, calibrate, maintain or sell electrical equipment, power apparatus, plant electrical facilities or generation, transmission or distribution equipment or systems.

Energy Central
2821 S. Parker Rd., Ste. 1105
Aurora, CO 80014 US
Phone: 303-782-5510
Fax: 303-782-5331
Toll Free: 800-459-2233
E-mail Address:
service@energycentral.com
Web Address: www.energycentral.com
Energy Central provides a large number of news releases related to the energy industry as well as other industry information.

Energy Charter Secretariat
Boulevard de la Woluwe, 56
Brussels, B-1200 Belgium
Phone: 32 2 775 98 00
Fax: 32 2 775 98 01
E-mail Address: *info@encharter.org*
Web Address: www.encharter.org
The Energy Charter Treaty, an international agreement, plays an important role as part of an effort to build a legal foundation for energy

security, based on the principles of open, competitive markets and sustainable development. The group holds conferences and publishes excellent reports on such topics as LNG, renewable energy and investments. More than 50 nations are members.

Energy Market Authority (EMA)
111 Somerset Rd., 15-05
238164 Singapore
Phone: 65-6835-8000
Fax: 65-6835-8020
Web Address: www.ema.gov.sg
The Energy Market Authority (EMA) promotes competition in the electricity and piped gas industry and maintains the security and reliability of the power system. EMA is a statutory board under the Ministry of Trade and Industry that regulates the electricity and gas industry and district cooling services in designated areas of Singapore.

Energy Security Analysis, Inc. (ESAI)
301 Edgewater Pl., Ste. 640
Wakefield, MA 01880 US
Phone: 781-245-2036
Fax: 781-245-8706
E-mail Address: *kcooper@esai.com*
Web Address: www.esai.com
Energy Security Analysis, Inc. (ESAI) has a site that provides full-service energy research and analysis on both regional and global energy markets.

Hydrocarbononline
5340 Fryling Rd., Ste. 101
Erie, PA 16510 US
E-mail Address: *info@vertmarkets.com*
Web Address: www.hydrocarbononline.com
Hydrocarbononline is a site offering information on oil refining and hydrocarbon processing, a careers page, breaking news in the petroleum and chemicals industries, product news and more.

India Energy Portal (IEP)
Lodhi Rd.
Darbari Seth Block, IHC Complex
New Delhi, 110 003 India
Phone: 91-11-2468-2100
Fax: 91-11-2468-2144
E-mail Address: *mailbox@teri.res.in*
Web Address: www.indiaenergyportal.org
The India Energy Portal (IEP), built upon public-private partnership, provides access to information and knowledge on various aspects of energy.

National Energy Policy (NEP) Initiative
Phone: 970-927-7334
E-mail Address: *comments@nepinitiative.org*
Web Address: www.nepinitiative.org
National Energy Policy (NEP) Initiative is a non-governmental, nonpartisan, foundation-funded project designed to support the development of a stakeholder-based national energy policy. The group is being administered by two nonprofit organizations, the Rocky Mountain Institute and the Consensus Building Institute.

ODS-Petrodata
3200 Wilcrest Dr., Ste. 170
Houston, TX 77042 US
Phone: 832-463-3000
Fax: 832-463-3100
E-mail Address: *tmarsh@ods-petrodata.com*
Web Address: www.ods-petrodata.com
ODS-Petrodata provides users with data, information and market intelligence on the upstream oil and marine construction industries.

Offshore Technology
55-57 N. Wharf Rd.
London, W2 1LA UK
Phone: 44-207-915-9957
Fax: 44-207-915-9958
E-mail Address: *offshore@spgmedia.com*
Web Address: www.offshore-technology.com
Offshore Technology produces online and print resources with latest news, detailed information and breakdown of products and services available to professionals in the offshore oil and gas industry.

Oil & Gas Journal Online
1455 West Loop S, Ste. 400
Houston, TX 77027 US
Phone: 713-963-6220
Fax: 713-963-6228
E-mail Address: *trippw@pennwell.com*
Web Address: ogj.pennnet.com
Oil & Gas Journal Online, produced by PennWell Petroleum Group, is an online portal containing useful global energy news and information.

OilOnline
1635 W. Alabama
Houston, TX 77006 US
Phone: 713-831-1768
Fax: 713-523-7804
E-mail Address: *robg@oilonline.com*
Web Address: www.oilonline.com
OilOnline provides online exploration and production information for the oil industry.

Petro Pages
1100 NASA Rd. One
Houston, TX 77058 US
Phone: 281-957-0048
Fax: 866-430-0239
E-mail Address: *webmaster@petropages.com*
Web Address: www.petropages.com
Petro Pages offers information about jobs, products, services and suppliers for the petroleum and process industries.

Petroleum Place, Inc.
216 16th St., Ste. 1700
Denver, CO 80202 US
Phone: 303-390-9400
Fax: 303-390-9401
Web Address: www.petroleumplace.com
Petroleum Place features extensive oil and gas business and consultants directories, listings of oil and gas properties and prospects for sale, online discussion groups, a powerful directory search engine and a careers section.

Pipeline Industry Directory
Scientific Surveys Ltd.
P.O. Box 21
Beaconsfield, Bucks HP9 1NS UK
Phone: 44-1494-675139
Fax: 44-1494-670155
E-mail Address: *info@scientificsurveys.com*
Web Address: www.pipedir.com

The Pipeline Industry Directory is a reference source for companies and organizations in the oil, gas, water, wastewater and associated pipeline industries worldwide.

Power Online
5340 Fryling Rd., Ste. 101
Erie, PA 16510 US
E-mail Address:
info@vertmarkets.com
Web Address: www.poweronline.com
Power Online is an energy industry web site offering a global newswire and energy job postings, as well as a Web Resource Center link.

Refining Connection (The)
P.O. Box 218275
Houston, TX 77218 US
Phone: 281-589-6600
Fax: 281-589-7335
E-mail Address:
info@refiningonline.com
Web Address:
www.refiningonline.com
The Refining Connection, a service of Astron International, Inc., is an online refining resource that provides unite conversion tools, information on steam properties, line pressure drop calculators, Internet bulletins, a scientific calculator and various other software.

Rigzone
5870 Hwy 6 N., Ste. 107
Houston, TX 77084 US
Phone: 281-345-4040
Fax: 281-345-4848
Toll Free: 800-503-0925
E-mail Address: *support@rigzone.com*
Web Address: www.rigzone.com
Rigzone provides oil and gas industry news, events and information, offshore reports, rig updates, a company and products database and directory, careers, a classifieds marketplace, and more.

WorldOil.com
2 Greenway Plz., Ste. 1020
Houston, TX 77046 US
Phone: 713-529-4301
Fax: 713-520-4433
E-mail Address:
rusty.meador@worldoil.com
Web Address: www.worldoil.com
Worldoil.com is an Internet business that serves the oil field services industry. The web site includes a catalog of products and services, a magazine, an information center of breaking industry news and an industry directory.

XXXVIII. Engineering Indices

Engineering Library
Cornell University
Carpenter Hall
Ithaca, NY 14853 US
Phone: 607-255-5933
Fax: 607-255-0278
E-mail Address:
engranswers@cornell.edu
Web Address:
www.astech.library.cornell.edu/ast/engr
Cornell University's Engineering Library web site has a number of resources concerning engineering research.

XXXIX. Engineering, Research & Scientific Associations

American Association for the Advancement of Science (AAAS)
1200 New York Ave. NW
Washington, DC 20005 US
Phone: 202-326-6400
E-mail Address: *webmaster@aaas.org*
Web Address: www.aaas.org
The American Association for the Advancement of Science (AAAS) is the world's largest scientific society and the publisher of Science magazine. It is an international nonprofit organization dedicating to advancing science.

American Association of Petroleum Geologists (AAPG)
1444 S. Boulder Ave.
Tulsa, OK 74119 US
Phone: 918-584-2555
Fax: 918-560-2665
Toll Free: 800-364-2274
E-mail Address: *lnation@aapg.org*
Web Address: www.aapg.org
The American Association of Petroleum Geologists (AAPG) is an international geological organization that supports educational and scientific programs and projects related to geosciences.

American Geophysical Union (AGU)
2000 Florida Ave. NW
Washington, DC 20009 US
Phone: 202-777-7483
Fax: 202-328-0566
Toll Free: 800-966-2481
E-mail Address:
development@agu.org.
Web Address: www.agu.org
The American Geophysical Union (AGU) is an international scientific community that performs research and provides information about the interdisciplinary field of geophysics.

American Institute of Chemical Engineers (AIChE)
3 Park Ave.
New York, NY 10016-5991 US
Phone: 203-702-7660
Fax: 203-775-5177
Toll Free: 800-242-4363
E-mail Address: *xpress@aiche.org*
Web Address: www.aiche.org
The American Institute of Chemical Engineers (AIChE) provides leadership in advancing the chemical engineering profession. The organization, which is comprised of 40,000 members from 93 countries, provides informational resources to chemical engineers.

American Institute of Mining, Metallurgical and Petroleum Engineers (AIME)
8307 Shaffer Pkwy.
Littleton, CO 80127 US
Phone: 303-948-4255
Fax: 303-948-4260
E-mail Address: *aime@aimehq.org*
Web Address: www.aimehq.org
The American Institute of Mining, Metallurgical and Petroleum Engineers (AIME) is a trade association devoted to the science of the production and use of minerals, metals, energy sources and materials.

American National Standards Institute (ANSI)
1819 L St. NW, 6th Fl.
Washington, DC 20036 US
Phone: 202-293-8020
Fax: 202-293-9287
E-mail Address: *info@ansi.org*

Web Address: www.ansi.org
The American National Standards Institute (ANSI) is a private, nonprofit organization that administers and coordinates the U.S. voluntary standardization and conformity assessment system. Its mission is to enhance both the global competitiveness of U.S. business and the quality of life by promoting and facilitating voluntary consensus standards and conformity assessment systems and safeguarding their integrity.

American Nuclear Society (ANS)
555 N. Kensington Ave.
La Grange Park, IL 60526 US
Phone: 708-352-6611
Fax: 708-352-0499
Toll Free: 800-323-3044
Web Address: www.ans.org
The American Nuclear Society (ANS) is a nonprofit organization unifying professional activities within the nuclear science and technology fields. ANS seeks to promote the awareness and understanding of the application of nuclear science and technology.

American Society for Testing & Materials (ASTM)
100 Barr Harbor Dr.
P.O. Box C700
West Conshohocken, PA 19428 US
Phone: 610-832-9500
Fax: 610-832-9555
E-mail Address: *service@astm.org*
Web Address: www.astm.org
The American Society for Testing & Materials (ASTM) provides and develops voluntary consensus standards and related technical information, and services that promote public health and safety. It also contributes to the reliability of materials, as well as provides technical standards for industries worldwide.

American Society of Civil Engineers (ASCE)
1801 Alexander Bell Dr.
Reston, VA 20191-4400 US
Phone: 703-295-6300
Fax: 703-295-6222
Toll Free: 800-548-2723
Web Address: www.asce.org
The American Society of Civil Engineers (ASCE) is a leading professional organization serving civil engineers. It ensures safer buildings, water systems and other civil engineering works by developing technical codes and standards.

Association of Consulting Chemists and Chemical Engineers (ACC&CE)
P.O. Box 297
Sparta, NJ 07871 US
Phone: 973-729-6671
Fax: 973-729-7088
E-mail Address: *info@chemconsult.org*
Web Address: www.chemconsult.org
The Association of Consulting Chemists and Chemical Engineers (ACC&CE) was founded in 1928 by a group of distinguished chemists. The association exists to advance the practices of consulting chemists and chemical engineers.

Chinese Hydraulic Engineering Society (CHES)
2-2 BaiGuang Rd.
Beijing, 100053 China
Phone: 86-1063202163
Fax: 86-1063202154
E-mail Address: *Ches@mwr.gov.cn*
Web Address: www.ches.org.cn
The Chinese Hydraulic Engineering Society (CHES) aims to promote hydraulic engineering professionals and the water resources sciences and technologies. CHES has 31 regional socieites in China.

CIEMAT
Avda. Complutense 22
Madrid, 28040 Spain
Phone: 91-346-60-00
Fax: 91-346-60-05
E-mail Address: *contacto@ciemat.es*
Web Address: www.ciemat.es
The CIEMAT, a unit of Spain's Ministry of Education and Science, is a public research agency. Its areas of focus include solar energy, biomass energy, wind energy, environment, basic research, fusion by magnetic confinement, nuclear safety, and technology transfer. Primary operations include PSA, the Solar Platform of Almeria, where concentrating solar power (CSP) is researched; CEDER, the Centre for the Development of Renewable Energy Sources; and CETA-CIEMAT, a center for information technology research.

European Association of Geoscientists & Engineers (EAGE)
P.O. Box 59
Db Houten, 3990 The Netherlands
Phone: 31-88-995-5055
Fax: 31-30-6343524
E-mail Address: *eage@eage.org*
Web Address: www.eage.org
EAGE is a professional association for geoscientists and engineers. It is a European-based organization with a worldwide membership providing a global network of commercial and academic professionals to all members. The association is truly multi-disciplinary and international in form and pursuits.

IEEE Oceanic Engineering Society (OES)
15 Rocky Brook Rd.
Cranbury, NJ 08512 US
Phone: 609-865-6797
E-mail Address: *elcreed@ieee.org*
Web Address: www.oceanicengineering.org
The IEEE Oceanic Engineering Society (OES) is the division of the IEEE that deals with electrical engineering at sea, including unmanned submarines and offshore oil platforms.

Industrial Research Institute (IRI)
2200 Clarendon Blvd., Ste. 1102
Arlington, VA 22201 US
Phone: 703-647-2580
Fax: 703-647-2581
E-mail Address: *information@iriinc.org*
Web Address: www.iriinc.org
The Industrial Research Institute (IRI) is a nonprofit organization of over 200 leading industrial companies, representing industries such as aerospace, automotive, chemical, computers and electronics, which carry out industrial research efforts in the U.S. manufacturing sector. IRI helps members improve research and development capabilities.

Institute of Electrical and Electronics Engineers (IEEE)
3 Park Ave., 17th Fl.
New York, NY 10016-5997 US
Phone: 212-419-7900
Fax: 212-752-4929
E-mail Address: *ieeeusa@ieee.org*
Web Address: www.ieee.org
The Institute of Electrical and Electronics Engineers (IEEE) is a nonprofit, technical professional association of more than 375,000 individual members in approximately 160 countries. The IEEE sets global technical standards and acts as an authority in technical areas ranging from computer engineering, biomedical technology and telecommunications, to electric power, aerospace and consumer electronics.

Institute of Industrial Engineers (IIE)
3577 Parkway Ln., Ste. 200
Norcross, GA 30092 US
Phone: 770-449-0460
Fax: 770-441-3295
Toll Free: 800-494-0460
E-mail Address: *execoffice@iienet.org*
Web Address: www.iienet2.org
The Institute of Industrial Engineers (IIE) is dedicated to the professional needs of industrial engineers.

Institute of Marine Engineering, Science and Technology (IMarEST)
80 Coleman St.
London, EC2R 5BJ UK
Phone: 44-0-20-7382-2600
Fax: 44-0-20-7382-2670
E-mail Address: *info@imarest.org*
Web Address: www.imarest.org
The Institute of Marine Engineering, Science and Technology (IMarEST) works to promote the development of marine engineering, science and technology.

Institution of Mechanical Engineers-UK
1 Birdcage Walk
Westminster
London, SW1H 9JJ UK
Phone: 44(0)20-7222-7899
Fax: 44(0)20-7222-4557
E-mail Address: *membership@imeche.org*
Web Address: www.imeche.org
Institution of Mechanical Engineers represents the mechanical engineering profession in UK. The UK has the sixth largest manufacturing industry in the world and this association recognizes engineering professionals in this field. In addition, its other major themes are the energy, environment and transport industries as well as hosting educational opportunities for engineers.

International Petroleum Technology Institute (IPTI)
11757 Katy Fwy., Ste. 865
Houston, TX 77079 US
Phone: 281-493-3491
Fax: 281-493-3493
E-mail Address: *irelandm@asme.org*
Web Address: www.asme-ipti.org
The International Petroleum Technology Institute (IPTI) is the division of the ASME concerned with the special engineering needs of the petroleum industry.

International Society for Measurement and Control (ISA)
67 Alexander Dr.
Research Triangle Park, NC 27709 US
Phone: 919-549-8411
Fax: 919-549-8288
E-mail Address: *info@isa.org*
Web Address: www.isa.org
The International Society for Measurement and Control (ISA) is a nonprofit organization which serves the professional development and credential needs of control system engineers, instrument technicians and others within the field of measurement and control.

International Standards Organization (ISO)
1 ch. de la Voie-Creuse
Case Postale 56
Geneva 20, CH-1211 Switzerland
Phone: 41-22-749-01-11
Fax: 41-22-733-34-30
E-mail Address: *central@iso.org*
Web Address: www.iso.org
The International Standards Organization (ISO) is a global consortium of national standards institutes from 157 countries. The established International Standards are designed to make products and services more efficient, safe and clean.

Marine Technology Society (MTS)
5565 Sterrett Pl., Ste. 108
Columbia, MD 21044 US
Phone: 410-884-5330
Fax: 410-884-9060
E-mail Address: *membership@mtsociety.org*
Web Address: www.mtsociety.org
The Marine Technology Society (MTS) is an organization devoted to marine science and technical knowledge.

Minerals, Metals & Materials Society (TMS)
184 Thorn Hill Rd.
Warrendale, PA 15086-7514 US
Phone: 724-776-9000
Fax: 724-776-3770
Toll Free: 800-759-4867
E-mail Address: *webmaster@tms.org*
Web Address: www.tms.org
The Minerals Metals & Materials Society (TMS) is an organization of professionals and students involved in metallurgy and material engineering, promoting the exchange of information, education and technology transference.

Research in Germany, German Academic Exchange Service (DAAD)
Kennedyallee 50
Bonn, 53175 Germany
Phone: 49(0)228 882 - 0
Fax: 49(0)228 882 - 660
Web Address: www.research-in-germany.de
The Research in Germany portal, German Academic Exchange Service (DAAD), is an information platform and contact point for those looking to find out more about Germany's research landscape and its latest research achievements. The portal is an initiative of the Federal Ministry of Education and Research.

Royal Society (The)
6-9 Carlton House Ter.
London, SW1Y 5AG UK
Phone: 44-20-7451-2500
Fax: 44-20-7930-2170
E-mail Address: *info@royalsociety.org*
Web Address: www.royalsoc.ac.uk

The Royal Society is the UK's leading scientific organization. It operates as a national academy of science, supporting scientists, engineers, technologists and research. On its website, you will find a wealth of data about the research and development initiatives of its fellows and foreign members.

Society of Exploration Geophysicists (SEG)
8801 S. Yale, Ste. 500
Tulsa, OK 74137-3575 US
Phone: 918-497-5500
Fax: 918-497-5557
E-mail Address: *membership@seg.org*
Web Address: www.seg.org
The Society of Exploration Geophysicists (SEG) promotes the science of geophysics. The website provides access to their foundation, online publications and employment and education services.

Society of Manufacturing Engineers (SME)
1 SME Dr.
Dearborn, MI 48121 US
Phone: 313-425-3000
Fax: 313-425-3412
Toll Free: 800-733-4763
E-mail Address: *communications@sme.org*
Web Address: www.sme.org
The Society of Manufacturing Engineers (SME) a leading professional organization serving engineers in the manufacturing industries.

Society of Naval Architects and Marine Engineers (SNAME)
601 Pavonia Ave.
Jersey City, NJ 07306 US
Phone: 201-798-4800
Fax: 201-798-4975
Toll Free: 800-798-2188
E-mail Address: *ldavis@sname.org*
Web Address: www.sname.org
The Society of Naval Architects and Marine Engineers (SNAME) is an internationally recognized nonprofit, professional society of members serving the maritime and offshore industries and their suppliers.

Society of Petroleum Engineers (SPE)
222 Palisades Creek Dr.
Richardson, TX 75080-2040 US
Phone: 972-952-9393
Fax: 972-952-9435
Toll Free: 800-456-6863
E-mail Address: *service@spe.org*
Web Address: www.spe.org
The Society of Petroleum Engineers (SPE) helps connect engineers in the oil and gas industry with ideas, answers, resources and technological information.

World Federation of Engineering Organizations
Maison de l'UNESCO 1
rue Miollis
Paris, Cedex 15 F-75732 France
Phone: 33-1-45-68-48-46
Fax: 33-1-45-68-48-65
E-mail Address: *tl.fmoi@unesco.org*
Web Address: www.wfeo.org
World Federation of Engineering Organizations (WFEO) is an international non-governmental organization that represents major engineering professional societies in over 90 nations. It has several standing committees including engineering and the environment, technology, communications, capacity building, education, energy and women in engineering.

XL. Environmental & Ecological Organizations

Center for Clean Air Policy (CCAP)
750 First St. NE, Ste. 940
Washington, DC 20002 US
Phone: 202-408-9260
Fax: 202-408-8896
E-mail Address: *communications@ccap.org*
Web Address: www.ccap.org
The Center for Clean Air Policy (CCAP) promotes and applies solutions to key environmental and energy problems.

Environment Canada
351 St. Joseph Blvd.
Place Vincent Massey, 8th Fl.
Gatineau, QC K1A 0H3 Canada
Phone: 819-997-2800
Fax: 819-994-1412
Toll Free: 800 668-6767
E-mail Address: *enviroinfo@ec.gc.ca*
Web Address: www.ec.gc.ca
Environment Canada is the Canadian government's natural environment preservation department.

Foundation for Clean Air Progress
601 Pennsylvania Ave. NW
N. Bldg., Ste. 540
Washington, DC 20004 US
E-mail Address: *info@cleanairprogress.org*
Web Address: www.cleanairprogress.org
The Foundation for Clean Air Progress (FCAP) is an organization that provides public education and information about air quality progress.

German Federal Environmental Foundation
Deutsche Bundesstiftung Umwelt
An der Bornau 2
Osnabruck, 49090 Germany
Phone: 0541 96330
Fax: 0541 9633190
E-mail Address: *info@dbu.de*
Web Address: www.dbu.de
The German Federal Environmental Foundation's projects and activities concentrate on environmental technology and research, nature conservation, environmental communication and cultural assets. It is an initiative of the German Government.

Pew Center on Global Climate Change
2101 Wilson Blvd., Ste. 550
Arlington, VA 22201 US
Phone: 703-516-4146
Fax: 703-841-1422
Web Address: www.pewclimate.org
The Pew Center on Global Climate Change was established in 1998 as a nonprofit, non-partisan and independent organization. The Center's mission is to provide credible information, straight answers, and innovative solutions in the effort to address global climate change.

XLI. Financial Industry Resources

SNL Financial
1 SNL Plz., P.O. Box 2124
Charlottesville, VA 22902 US
Phone: 434-977-1600
Fax: 434-977-4466
Toll Free: 866-296-3743
E-mail Address: *support@snl.com*
Web Address: www.snl.com
SNL Financial provides industry-specific research and statistics in the banking, financial services, insurance, real estate and energy sectors.

XLII. Gasoline Retailing Associations

Florida Petroleum Marketers Association (FPMA)
209 Office Plaza Dr.
Tallahassee, FL 32301 US
Phone: 850-877-5178
Fax: 850-877-5864
Toll Free: 800-523-9166
Web Address: www.fpma.org
The Florida Petroleum Marketers Association (FPMA) represents the petroleum and convenience store industry in Florida. Its web site includes Internet resources, government news, general industry news and updated information.

Indiana Petroleum Marketers and Convenience Store Association (IPCA)
101 W. Washington St., Ste. 805E
Indianapolis, IN 46204 US
Phone: 317-633-4662
Fax: 317-630-1827
E-mail Address: *kransdell@ipca.org*
Web Address: www.ipca.org
The Indiana Petroleum Marketers and Convenience Store Association (IPCA) represents Indiana's petroleum marketers, lube oil dealers and convenience store and truck stop operators.

Kentucky Petroleum Marketers Association (KPMA)
622 Shelby St.
Frankfort, KY 40601 US
Phone: 502-875-3738
Fax: 502-875-4515
E-mail Address: *kpma@kpma.net*
Web Address: www.kpma.net
The Kentucky Petroleum Marketers Association (KPMA) is a nonprofit trade association providing information relevant to retail petroleum sales for all segments of the petroleum industry in the state of Kentucky.

Louisiana Oil Marketers and Convenience Stores Association (LOMCSA)
2431 S. Acadian Trwy., Ste. 230
Baton Rouge, LA 70808 US
Phone: 225-926-8300
Fax: 225-926-7722
E-mail Address: *lomcsa@lomcsa.com*
Web Address: www.lomcsa.com
The Louisiana Oil Marketers and Convenience Stores Association (LOMCSA) is a nonprofit organization that represents the business interests of independent distributors of petroleum products in Louisiana.

Maine Oil Dealers Association (MODA)
25 Greenwood Rd.
P.O. Box 249
Brunswick, ME 04011-0249 US
Phone: 207-729-5298
Fax: 207-721-9227
E-mail Address: *jamie@meoil.com*
Web Address: www.meoil.com
The Maine Oil Dealers Association (MODA) is a member organization that represents the petroleum industry in Maine.

Missouri Petroleum Marketers and Convenience Store Association (MPCA)
205 E. Capitol Ave., Ste. 200
Jefferson City, MO 65101 US
Phone: 573-635-7117
Fax: 573-635-3575
E-mail Address: *mpca@mpca.org*
Web Address: www.mpca.org
The Missouri Petroleum Marketers and Convenience Store Association (MPCA) is dedicated to serving the interests of convenience stores across Missouri.

Ohio Petroleum Marketers & Convenience Store Association (OPMCA)
4242 Tuller Rd., Unit B
Dublin, OH 43017 US
Phone: 614-792-5212
Fax: 614-792-1706
E-mail Address: *info@opmca.org*
Web Address: www.opmca.org
The Ohio Petroleum Marketers & Convenience Store Association (OPMCA) is dedicated to serving the interests of retail petroleum marketers, independent refineries, truck stops, retail chains and convenience stores throughout Ohio.

Petroleum Marketers Association of America (PMAA)
1901 N. Ft. Myer Dr., Ste. 500
Arlington, VA 22209-1604 US
Phone: 703-351-8000
Fax: 703-351-9160
E-mail Address: *info@pmaa.org*
Web Address: www.pmaa.org
The Petroleum Marketers Association of America (PMAA) is a federation of 42 state and regional trade associations.

Society of Independent Gasoline Marketers of America (SIGMA)
3930 Pender Dr., Ste. 340
Fairfax, VA 22030 US
Phone: 703-709-7000
Fax: 703-709-7007
E-mail Address: *sigma@sigma.org*
Web Address: www.sigma.org
The Society of Independent Gasoline Marketers of America (SIGMA) represents chain retailers and marketers of motor fuel, ensuring a free and unencumbered economic environment.

XLIII. Hybrid & Electric Vehicles

Electric Drive Transportation Association (EDTA)
1101 Vermont Ave. NW, Ste. 401
Washington, DC 20005 US
Phone: 202-408-0774
E-mail Address:
info@electricdrive.org
Web Address: www.electricdrive.org
The Electric Drive Transportation Association (EDTA) is an industry association working to advance electric vehicle transportation technologies and supporting infrastructure through policy, information and market development initiatives.

XLIV. Industry & Market Research

Forrester Research
400 Technology Sq.
Cambridge, MA 02139 US
Phone: 617-613-6000
Fax: 617-613-5200
Toll Free: 866-367-7378
Web Address: www.forrester.com
Forrester Research identifies and analyzes emerging trends in technology and their impact on business. Among the firm's specialties are the financial services, retail, health care, entertainment, automotive and information technology industries.

Marketresearch.com
11200 Rockville Pike, Ste. 504
Rockville, MD 20852 US
Phone: 240-747-3000
Fax: 240-747-3004
Toll Free: 800-298-5699
E-mail Address:
customerservice@marketresearch.com
Web Address:
www.marketresearch.com
Marketresearch.com is a leading broker for professional market research and industry analysis. Users are able to search the company's database of research publications including data on global industries, companies, products and trends.

Plunkett Research, Ltd.
P.O. Drawer 541737
Houston, TX 77254-1737 US
Phone: 713-932-0000
Fax: 713-932-7080
E-mail Address:
customersupport@plunkettresearch.com
Web Address:
www.plunkettresearch.com
Plunkett Research, Ltd. is a leading provider of market research, industry trends analysis and business statistics. Since 1985, it has served clients worldwide, including corporations, universities, libraries, consultants and government agencies. At the firm's web site, visitors can view product information and pricing and access a great deal of basic market information on industries such as financial services, infotech, e-commerce, health care and biotech.

XLV. Maritime Associations

Association of Singapore Marine Industries (ASMI)
20 Science Park Rd.
02-04/05 TeleTech Park
117674 Singapore
Phone: 65-6872-0030
Fax: 65-6872-5747
E-mail Address: *asmi@pacific.net.sg*
Web Address: www.asmi.com
The Association of Singapore Marine Industries (ASMI) is a nonprofit trade association which promotes the interests of a wide cross-section of the Singapore ship repair, shipbuilding, rig building and marine industry in Singapore.

XLVI. MBA Resources

MBA Depot
Phone: 512-499-8728
Web Address: www.mbadepot.com
MBA Depot is an online community for MBA professionals.

XLVII. Patent Organizations

U.S. Patent and Trademark Office
U.S. Patent and Trademark Office
Office of Public Affairs
P. O. Box 1450
Alexandria, VA 22313-1450 US
Phone: 571-272-1000
Fax: 571-273-8300
Toll Free: 800-786-9199
E-mail Address: *usptoinfo@uspto.gov*
Web Address: www.uspto.gov
The U.S. Patent and Trademark Office (PTO) administers patent and trademark laws for the U.S. and enables registration of patents and trademarks.

XLVIII. Research & Development, Laboratories

Applied Research Laboratories (ARL)
Applied Research Laboratories
University of Texas at Austin, 10000 Burnet Rd.
Austin, TX 78758 US
Phone: 512-835-3200
Fax: 512-835-3259
E-mail Address:
WebContactUs@arlut.utexas.edu
Web Address: www.arlut.utexas.edu
Applied Research Laboratories (ARL) at the University of Texas at Austin provides research programs dedicated to improving the military capability of the United States in applications of acoustics, electromagnetic and information technology.

Argonne National Laboratory, Nuclear Engineering Division (ANL)
9700 S. Cass Ave.
Argonne, IL 60439-4814 US
Phone: 630-252-4780
E-mail Address: *neinfo@anl.gov*
Web Address: www.td.anl.gov
The Argonne National Laboratory-Nuclear Engineering Division (ANL) is engaged in research and development in the applied nuclear technology fields. These focuses include nuclear-related technologies such as nonproliferation, environmental remediation, fusion power and new initiatives.

Commonwealth Scientific and Industrial Research Organization (CSRIO)
CSIRO Enquiries, Bag 10
Clayton South, Victoria 3169 Australia
Phone: 61-3-9545-2176
Fax: 61-3-9545-2175
E-mail Address: *enquiries@csiro.au*
Web Address: www.csiro.au
The Commonwealth Scientific and Industrial Research Organization (CSRIO) is Australia's national science agency and a leading international research agency. CSRIO performs research in Australia over a broad range of areas including agriculture, minerals and energy, manufacturing, communications, construction, health and the environment.

Council of Scientific & Industrial Research (CSIR)
2 Rafi Marg
Anusandhan Bhawan
New Delhi, 110 001 India
Phone: 011-23710618
Fax: 011-23713011
E-mail Address: *itweb@csir.res.in*
Web Address: www.csir.res.in

The Council of Scientific & Industrial Research (CSIR) is a government-funded organization that promotes research and development initiatives in India. It operates in the fields of energy, biotechnology, space, science and technology.

Hanford Nuclear Site
825 Jadwin Ave., Ste. 1
Richland, WA 99352 US
Phone: 509-376-7411
E-mail Address: *Webmaster@rl.gov*
Web Address: www.hanford.gov
The Hanford Nuclear Site is designed to solve critical problems related to the environment, energy production and use, U.S. economic competitiveness and national security.

Helmholtz Association
AhrstraBe 45
Bonn, 53175 Germany
Phone: 49 228 30818-0
Fax: 49 228 30818-30
E-mail Address: *org@helmholtz.de*
Web Address: www.helmholtz.de/en
The Helmholtz Association is a community of 16 scientific-technical and biological-medical research centers. Helmholtz Centers perform top-class research in strategic programs in six core fields: energy, earth and environment, health, key technologies, structure of matter, aeronautics, space and transport.

Idaho National Laboratory (INL)
1765 N. Yellowstone Hwy.
P.O. Box 1625
Idaho Falls, ID 83415 US
Phone: 208-526-0111
Toll Free: 866-495-7440
Web Address: www.inl.gov
Idaho National Laboratory (INL) is a multidisciplinary, multiprogram laboratory that specializes in developing nuclear energy with research concerning the environment, energy, science and national defense.

Indira Gandhi Institute of Development Research
Gen. A. K. Vaidya Marg
Goregaon (E)
Mumbai, 400 065 India
Phone: 022-2840-0919
Fax: 022-2840-2752
E-mail Address: *nachane@igidr.ac.in*
Web Address: www.igidr.ac.in
The Indira Gandhi Institute of Development Research (IGIDR) focuses on research of the economic, technological, social, political and ecological aspects of development and the influence of international trading, financial and economic systems on countries. It also includes an examination of energy, technology and environmental problems in global setting.

Leibniz Association of German Research Institutes (WGL)
Postfach 12 01 69, D-53043
Eduard-Pfluger-Str. 55
Bonn, D-53113 Germany
Phone: 49-228-30815-0
Fax: 49-228-30815-55
E-mail Address: *wgl@wgl.de*
Web Address: www.leibniz-gemeinschaft.de
The Leibniz Association of German Research Institutes (WGL) is a research organization that comprises over 80 institutes. WGL works on international interdisciplinary research and acts as a bridge between traditional research and customer oriented applications. The association focuses on scientific excellence and social relevance.

Los Alamos National Laboratory (LANL)
Bikini Atoll Rd., SM 30
P.O. Box 1663
Los Alamos, NM 87545 US
Phone: 505-665-4400
Fax: 505-665-4411
Toll Free: 888-841-8256
E-mail Address: *community@lanl.gov*
Web Address: www.lanl.gov
The Los Alamos National Laboratory (LANL), a national energy lab in New Mexico, was originally built as a work site for the team that designed the first atomic bomb during World War II. Currently, it provides a continual stream of research in physics and energy matters. Much of that research is put to use in the commercial sector.

Max Planck Society (MPG)
P.O. Box 10 10 62
Munchen, 80084 Germany
Phone: 49 (89) 2108 - 0
Fax: 49 (89) 2108 - 1111
Web Address: www.mpg.de
The Max Planck Society (MPG) currently maintains 80 institutes, research units, and working groups that are devoted to basic research in the natural sciences, life sciences, social sciences, and the humanities. Max Planck Institutes work largely in an interdisciplinary setting and in close cooperation with universities and research institutes in Germany and abroad.

National Renewable Energy Laboratory (NREL)
1617 Cole Blvd.
Golden, CO 80401-3393 US
Phone: 303-275-3000
E-mail Address: *public_affairs@nrel.gov*
Web Address: www.nrel.gov
The National Renewable Energy Laboratory (NREL) reduces nuclear danger, transfers applied environmental technology to government and non-government entities and forms economic and industrial alliances.

National Research Council Canada (NRC)
NRC Communications & Corp. Rel.
1200 Montreal Rd., Bldg. M-58
Ottawa, ON K1A 0R6 Canada
Phone: 613-993-9101
Fax: 613-952-9907
Toll Free: 877-672-2672
E-mail Address: *info@nrc-cnrc.gc.ca*
Web Address: www.nrc-cnrc.gc.ca
National Research Council Canada (NRC) is a government organization of 20 research institutes that carry out multidisciplinary research with partners in industries and sectors key to Canada's economic development.

Oak Ridge National Laboratory (ORNL)
P.O. Box 2008
1 Bethel Valley Rd.
Oak Ridge, TN 37831 US
Phone: 865-574-4160
Fax: 865-574-0595
E-mail Address: *strohlhf@ornl.gov*
Web Address: www.ornl.gov

The Oak Ridge National Laboratory (ORNL) is a multiprogram science and technology laboratory managed for the U.S. Department of Energy by U.T.-Battelle, LLC. It conducts basic and applied research and development to create scientific knowledge and technological solutions.

Sandia National Laboratories
1515 Eubank SE
Albuquerque, NM 87123 US
Phone: 505-845-0011
E-mail Address:
webmaster@sandia.gov
Web Address: www.sandia.gov
Sandia National Laboratories is a national security laboratory operated for the U.S. Department of Energy by the Sandia Corporation. It designs all -nuclear components for the nation's nuclear weapons and performs a wide variety of energy research and development projects.

Savannah River Site (SRS)
Washington Savannah River Company
2131 S. Centennial Avenue SE
Aiken, SC 29803 US
Phone: 803.952.9583
Fax: 803-952-9523
E-mail Address: *will.callicott@srs.gov*
Web Address: www.srs.gov
The Savannah River Site (SRS) is a nuclear fuel storage and production site that works to protect the people and the environment of the U.S. through safe, secure, cost-effective management of the country's nuclear weapons stockpile and nuclear materials. While the site is owned by the U.S. Department of Energy, it is operated by Washington Savannah River Company, LLC (WSRC), a wholly-owned subsidiary of Washington Group International.

SRI International
333 Ravenswood Ave.
Menlo Park, CA 94025-3493 US
Phone: 650-859-2000
E-mail Address: *ellie.javadi@sri.com*
Web Address: www.sri.com
SRI International is a nonprofit organization offering a wide range of services, including engineering services, information technology, pure and applied physical sciences, product development, pharmaceutical discovery, biopharmaceutical discovery and policy issues. SRI conducts research for commercial and governmental customers.

The Fraunhofer-Gesellschaft (FhG)
Fraunhofer-Gesellschaft zur Forderung der angewandten Forschung e.V.
Postfach 20 07 33
Munchen, 80007 Germany
Phone: 49-89-1205-0
Fax: 49-89-1205-7531
Web Address: www.fraunhofer.de
The Fraunhofer-Gesellschaft (FhG) institute focuses on research in health, security, energy, communication, the environment and mobility. FhG includes over 80 research units in 40 locations in Germany. Two-thirds of its projects are derived from industry contracts.

XLIX. Science & Technology Resources

Technology Review
1 Main St., 7th Fl.
Cambridge, MA 02142 US
Phone: 617-475-8000
Fax: 617-475-8042
Toll Free: 800-877-5230
Web Address:
www.technologyreview.com
Technology Review, an MIT enterprise, publishes tech industry news, covers innovation and writes in-depth articles about research, development and cutting-edge technologies.

L. Stocks and Financial Markets Data

Bloomberg LP
731 Lexington Ave.
New York, NY 10022 US
Phone: 212-318-2000
Fax: 917-369-5000
Web Address: www.bloomberg.com
Bloomberg LP is one of the world's premier providers of archived financial information online.

LI. Technology Transfer Associations

Association of University Technology Managers (AUTM)
111 Deer Lake Rd., Ste. 100
Deerfield, IL 60015 US
Phone: 847-559-0846
Fax: 847-480-9282
E-mail Address: *info@autm.net*
Web Address: www.autm.net
The Association of University Technology Managers (AUTM) is a nonprofit professional association whose members belong to over 350 research institutions, universityies, teaching hospitals, government agencies and corporations from 45 countries. The association's mission is to advance the field of technology transfer, and enhance members' ability to bring academic and nonprofit research to people around the world.

Federal Laboratory Consortium for Technology Transfer
950 North Kings Highway, Ste. 208
Cherry Hill, NJ 08304 US
Phone: 856-667-7727
Fax: 856-667-8009
E-mail Address:
flcmso@federallabs.org
Web Address: www.federallabs.org
In keeping with the aims of the Federal Technology Transfer Act of 1986 and other related legislation, the Federal Laboratory Consortium (FLC) works to facilitate the sharing of research results and technology developments between federal laboratories and the mainstream U.S. economy. FLC affiliates include federal laboratories, large and small businesses, academic and research institutions, state and local governments, and various federal agencies. The group has regional support offices and local contacts throughout the U.S.

Licensing Executives Society (U.S.A. and Canada), Inc.
1800 Diagonal Rd., Ste. 280
Alexandria, VA 22314 US
Phone: 703-836-3106
Fax: 703-836-3107
E-mail Address: *info@les.org*
Web Address: www.lesusacanada.org

Licensing Executives Society (U.S.A. and Canada), Inc., established in 1965, is a professional association composed of about 5,000 members who work in fields related to the development, use, transfer, manufacture and marketing of intellectual property. Members include executives, lawyers, licensing consultants, engineers, academic researchers, scientists and government officials. The society is part of the larger Licensing Executives Society International, Inc. (same headquarters address), with a worldwide membership of some 12,000 members in 30 national societies, representing approximately 80 countries.

The State Science and Technology Institute
5015 Pine Creek Dr.
Westerville, OH 43081 US
Phone: 614-901-1690
Fax: 614-901-1696
Web Address: www.ssti.org
The State Science and Technology Institute (SSTI) is a national nonprofit group that serves as a resource for technology-based economic development. In addition to the information on its web site, the Institute publishes a free weekly digest of news and issues related to technology-based economic development efforts, as well as a members-only publication listing application information, eligibility criteria and submission deadlines for a variety of funding oportunities, federal and otherwise.

LII. Trade Associations-General

BUSINESSEUROPE
168 Ave. de Cortenbergh
Brussels, 1000 Belgium
Phone: 32-0-2-237-65-11
Fax: 32-0-2-231-14-45
E-mail Address:
main@businesseurope.eu
Web Address: www.businesseurope.eu
BUSINESSEUROPE is a major European trade federation that operates in a manner similar to a chamber of commerce. Its members are the central national business federations of the 34 countries throughout Europe from which they come. Companies cannot become direct members of BUSINESSEUROPE, though there is a support group which offers the opportunity for firms to encourage BUSINESSEUROPE objectives in various ways.

LIII. Trade Associations-Global

World Trade Organization (WTO)
Centre William Rappard
Rue de Lausanne 154
Geneva 21, CH-1211 Switzerland
Phone: 41-22-739-51-11
Fax: 41-22-731-42-06
E-mail Address: *enquiries@wto.og*
Web Address: www.wto.org
The World Trade Organization (WTO) is a global organization dealing with the rules of trade between nations. To become a member, nations must agree to abide by certain guidelines. Membership increases a nation's ability to import and export efficiently.

LIV. Trade Resources

BrazilBiz
Web Address: www.brazilbiz.com.br
The BrazilBiz web site serves as a clearinghouse of general contact information for Brazilian companies; registration on the site is free, and allows users to search within the BrazilBiz database for firms across a range of industries.

LV. U.S. Government Agencies

Bureau of Economic Analysis (BEA)
1441 L St. NW
Washington, DC 20230 US
Phone: 202-606-9900
E-mail Address:
customerservice@bea.gov
Web Address: www.bea.gov
The Bureau of Economic Analysis (BEA), an agency of the U.S. Department of Commerce, is the nation's economic accountant, preparing estimates that illuminate key national, international and regional aspects of the U.S. economy.

Bureau of Labor Statistics (BLS)
2 Massachusetts Ave. NE
Washington, DC 20212-0001 US
Phone: 202-691-5200
Web Address: stats.bls.gov
The Bureau of Labor Statistics (BLS) is the principal fact-finding agency for the Federal Government in the field of labor economics and statistics. It is an independent national statistical agency that collects, processes, analyzes and disseminates statistical data to the American public, U.S. Congress, other federal agencies, state and local governments, business and labor. The BLS also serves as a statistical resource to the Department of Labor.

Bureau of Ocean Energy Management, Regulation and Enforcement (BOEMRE)
1849 C St. NW
Washington, DC 20240 US
Phone: 202-208-3985
E-mail Address:
BOEMPublicAffairs@BOEMRE.GOV
Web Address: www.boemre.gov
The Department of the Interior's (DOI), Bureau of Ocean Energy Management, Regulation and Enforcement (BOEMRE), is the federal agency responsible for overseeing the development of energy and mineral resources on the outer continental shelf, including offshore oil and gas production. (This bureau replaced the former Minerals Management Service in 2010.)

Energy Information Administration (EIA)
1000 Independence Ave. SW
Washington, DC 20585 US
Phone: 202-586-8800
E-mail Address: *infoctr@eia.doe.gov*
Web Address: www.eia.doe.gov
The Energy Information Administration (EIA) is a vast source of useful information on every branch of the industry. It is operated by the U.S. Department of Energy (DOE). The site includes links to a number of other helpful energy industry web sites.

Federal Energy Regulatory Commission (FERC)
888 First St. NE
Washington, DC 20426 US
Phone: 202-502-6088
Toll Free: 866-208-3372
E-mail Address: *customer@ferc.gov*

Web Address: www.ferc.gov
The Federal Energy Regulatory Commission (FERC) regulates and oversees energy industries in the economic, environmental and safety interests of the American pubic.

National Institute of Standards and Technology (NIST)
100 Bureau Dr., Stop 1070
Gaithersburg, MD 20899-1070 US
Phone: 301-975-6478
E-mail Address: *inquiries@nist.gov*
Web Address: www.nist.gov
The National Institute of Standards and Technology (NIST) is an agency of the U.S. Department of Commerce's Technology Administration. It works with various industries to develop and apply technology, measurements and standards.

National Science Foundation (NSF)
4201 Wilson Blvd.
Arlington, VA 22230 US
Phone: 703-292-5111
Toll Free: 800-877-8339
E-mail Address: *info@nsf.gov*
Web Address: www.nsf.gov
The National Science Foundation (NSF) is an independent U.S. government agency responsible for promoting science and engineering. The foundation provides grants and funding for research.

Occupational Safety and Health Administration (OSHA)
200 Constitution Ave. NW
Washington, DC 20210 US
Phone: 202-693-1999
Fax: 410-865-2068
Toll Free: 800-321-6742
Web Address: www.osha.gov
The Occupational Safety and Health Administration (OSHA), regulates safety within the workplace. Its web site provides an abundance of information on laws and regulations, safety and health, statistics, compliance assistance and news. OSHA is a unit of the U.S. Department of Labor.

Office of Fossil Energy
1000 Independence Ave. SW
Washington, DC 20585 US
Phone: 202-586-5000
Fax: 202-586-4403
Toll Free: 800-342-5363
E-mail Address:
The.Secretary@hq.doe.gov
Web Address: www.fe.doe.gov
The Office of Fossil Energy, an office within the U.S. Department of Energy (DOE), studies and reports on the latest developments in advanced fossil fuel technology.

U.S. Census Bureau
4600 Silver Hill Rd.
Washington, DC 20233-8800 US
Phone: 301-763-4636
Fax: 301-457-3670
Toll Free: 800-923-8282
E-mail Address: *pio@census.gov*
Web Address: www.census.gov
The U.S. Census Bureau is the official collector of data about the people and economy of the U.S. Founded in 1790, it provides official social, demographic and economic information.

U.S. Department of Commerce (DOC)
1401 Constitution Ave. NW
Washington, DC 20230 US
Phone: 202-482-2000
E-mail Address: *cgutierrez@doc.gov*
Web Address: www.commerce.gov
The U.S. Department of Commerce (DOC) regulates trade and provides valuable economic analysis of the economy.

U.S. Department of Energy (DOE)
1000 Independence Ave. SW
Washington, DC 20585 US
Phone: 202-586-5000
Fax: 202-586-4403
Toll Free: 800-342-5363
E-mail Address:
the.secretary@hq.doe.gov
Web Address: www.energy.gov
U.S. Department of Energy (DOE) web site is the best way to gain information from the U.S. Government regarding its many agencies, bureaus and operations in energy. Through the site, users can gain access to government agencies such as Los Alamos National Laboratory, the strategic oil reserves and the agencies that regulate nuclear, geothermal and other types of power.

U.S. Department of Labor (DOL)
Frances Perkins Bldg.
200 Constitution Ave. NW
Washington, DC 20210 US
Toll Free: 866-487-2365
Web Address: www.dol.gov
The U.S. Department of Labor (DOL) is the government agency responsible for labor regulations. This site provides tools to help citizens find out whether companies are complying with family and medical-leave requirements.

U.S. Environmental Protection Agency (EPA) On-road Vehicles and Engines
Office of Transportation and Air Quality (6401A)
1200 Pennsylvania Ave. NW
Washington, DC 20460 US
Phone: 202-564-1682
E-mail Address:
otaqpublicweb@epa.gov
Web Address:
www.epa.gov/otaq/hwy.htm
The U.S. Environmental Protection Agency (EPA) On-road Vehicles and Engines site, part of the EPA's Office of Transportation and Air Quality (OTAQ), provides details about the best and worst cars and trucks in terms of exhaust emissions. Its web site allows people to instantly check the emission rating of any vehicle. The site also contains information about industry emission trends and goals.

U.S. Geological Survey (USGS)
12201 Sunrise Valley Dr.
Reston, VA 20192 US
Phone: 703-648-4000
Toll Free: 888-275-8747
Web Address: www.usgs.gov
The U.S. Geological Survey (USGS) conducts research on geography, geology, biology and related hazards and benefits in the United States.

U.S. Nuclear Regulatory Commission (NRC)
11555 Rockville Pike
Rockville, MD 20852 US
Phone: 301-415-7000
Fax: 301-415-3716
Toll Free: 800-368-5642
Web Address: www.nrc.gov
The U.S. Nuclear Regulatory Commission (NRC) is an independent

agency established by Congress to ensure adequate protection of public health and safety, common defense and security and the environment in use of nuclear materials in the United States.

U.S. Securities and Exchange Commission (SEC)
100 F St. NE
Washington, DC 20549 US
Phone: 202-551-6000
Toll Free: 888-732-6585
E-mail Address: *publicinfo@sec.gov*
Web Address: www.sec.gov
The U.S. Securities and Exchange Commission (SEC) is a nonpartisan, quasi-judicial regulatory agency responsible for administering federal securities laws. These laws are designed to protect investors in securities markets and ensure that they have access to disclosure of all material information concerning publicly traded securities. Visitors to the web site can access the EDGAR database of corporate financial and business information.

U.S. Trade Representative (USTR)
600 17th St. NW
Washington, DC 20508 US
Phone: 202-395-7360
E-mail Address: *contactustr@ustr.eop.gov*
Web Address: www.ustr.gov
The U.S. Trade Representative (USTR) is the nation's chief trade negotiator and the principal trade policy advisor to the President.

Yucca Mountain Project
U.S. Department of Energy, Office of Civilian Radioactive Waste Management
1551 Hillshire Dr.
Las Vegas, NV 89134 US
Fax: 702-295-5222
Toll Free: 800-225-6972
Web Address: www.ocrwm.doe.gov/ym_repository/index.shtml
The Yucca Mountain Project, located underneath Yucca Mountain in Nevada and established by the U.S. Department of Energy (DOE), is a controversial and incomplete site designed to be a long term radioactive waste depository. If completed, it will accept waste from nuclear power and national defense sites to be stored in a single, underground facility that is designed to safely hold the materials for at least 10,000 years.

LVI. Waste Industry Associations

Air & Waste Management Association
420 Fort Duquesne Blvd.
1 Gateway Ctr., 3rd Fl.
Pittsburgh, PA 15222-1435 US
Phone: 412-232-3444
Fax: 412-232-3450
Toll Free: 800-270-3444
E-mail Address: *info@awma.org*
Web Address: www.awma.org
The Air & Waste Management Association provides training, information and networking opportunities to environmental professionals worldwide.

LVII. Water Resources Associations

American Water Resources Association (AWRA)
P.O. Box 1626
Middleburg, VA 20118 US
Phone: 540-687-8390
Fax: 540-687-8395
E-mail Address: *info@awra.org*
Web Address: www.awra.org
The American Water Resources Association (AWRA) represents the interests of professionals involved in water resources.

Chapter 4

THE ENERGY 500: WHO THEY ARE AND HOW THEY WERE CHOSEN

Includes Indexes by Company Name, Industry & Location, And a Complete Table of Sales, Profits and Ranks

The companies chosen to be listed in PLUNKETT'S ENERGY INDUSTRY ALMANAC comprise a unique list. THE ENERGY 500 (the actual count is 518 companies) were chosen specifically for their dominance in the many facets of the energy industry in which they operate. Complete information about each firm can be found in the "Individual Profiles," beginning at the end of this chapter. These profiles are in alphabetical order by company name.

THE ENERGY 500 includes leading companies from all parts of the United States as well as many other nations, and from all energy and related industry segments: exploration, production, distribution, retailing and special services relating to the industry.

Simply stated, the list contains 518 of the largest, most successful, fastest growing firms in the energy and related industries in the world. To be included in our list, the firms had to meet the following criteria:

1) Generally, these are corporations based in the U.S., however, the headquarters of 222 firms are located in other nations.
2) Prominence, or a significant presence, in energy and supporting fields. (See the following Industry Codes section for a complete list of types of businesses that are covered).
3) The companies in THE ENERGY 500 do not have to be exclusively in the energy field.
4) Financial data and vital statistics must have been available to the editors of this book, either directly from the company being written about or from outside sources deemed reliable and accurate by the editors. A small number of companies that we would like to have included are not listed because of a lack of sufficient, objective data.

INDEXES TO THE ENERGY 500, AS FOUND IN THIS CHAPTER AND IN THE BACK OF THE BOOK:

INDUSTRY LIST, WITH CODES

This book refers to the following list of unique industry codes, based on the 2007 NAIC code system (NAIC is used by many analysts as a replacement for older SIC codes because NAIC is more specific to today's industry sectors, see www.census.gov/NAICS). Companies profiled in this book are given a primary NAIC code, reflecting the main line of business of each firm.

Energy

Fuel Mining & Extraction

211111 Oil & Natural Gas Exploration & Production
21211 Coal Mining
213111 Petroleum-Drilling Oil & Gas Wells Support
213112 Oil Field Services

Utilities

221 Utilities-Electric & Gas
2211 Utilities-Electric
2213 Utilities-Water
221111 Utilities-Hydroelectric
221113 Utilities-Nuclear Generation
221121 Utilities-Electric, Wholesale Generation
221210 Utilities-Gas

Petroleum-Refining & Manufacturing

324110 Petroleum Refineries
324199 Other Petrochemical & Coal Products Manufacturing
325110 Petrochemicals Manufacturing

Financial Services

Banking, Credit & Finance

522220 Financing--Business

Stocks & Investments

523140 Commodity & Futures Brokerage
523910 Venture Capital/Private Equity Investments

Insurance

524126 Insurance--Property & Casualty, Specialty, Surety

InfoTech

Computers & Electronics Manufacturing

33411 Computer Networking & Related Equipment, Manufacturing
3345 Instrument Manufacturing, including Measurement, Control, Test & Navigational

Manufacturing

Chemicals

325 Chemicals, Manufacturing

Energy

325188 Nuclear Fuels & Other Inorganic Chemicals

Fabricated Metals

331210 Steel Pipe Manufacturing

Machinery & Manufacturing Equipment

333 Machinery, Manufacturing
33313 Machinery-Mining & Oil & Gas Field, Manufacturing
33361 Turbine & Turbine Generator Set Unit Manufacturing

Electrical Equipment, Appliances, Tools

335 Electrical Equipment, Manufacturing

Mining

212 Mining (Except Oil & Gas)

Retailing

Gasoline Stations

447110 Gasoline Stations

Nonstore Retailers

454312 Bottled Gas Dealers, Retail

Services

Construction

237 Construction, Heavy & Civil Engineering
2389 Construction--Other Special Trade Contractors

Consulting & Professional Services

541330 Engineering Services
541360 Surveying & Mapping--Geophysical
541690 Consulting--Scientific & Technical
541712 Research & Development-Physical, Engineering & Life Sciences

Telecommunications

Telecommunications Equipment

334220 Radio & Wireless Communication, Manufacturing

Transportation

Air

481111 Air Transportation

Ships

483111 Shipping-Deep Sea

Wholesale Distribution-Other

Distribution-Nondurable Goods

424710 Petroleum Bulk Stations & Terminals Distribution
486 Petroleum Products (except Bulk Stations/Terminals) Distribution & Pipelines

INDEX OF RANKINGS WITHIN INDUSTRY GROUPS

Company	Industry Code	2009 Sales (U.S. $ thousands)	Sales Rank	2009 Profits (U.S. $ thousands)	Profits Rank
Air Transportation-Charter Services					
BRISTOW GROUP	481211	1,133,803	1	124,308	1
CHC HELICOPTER CORP	481211				
PHI INC	481211	487,175	2	12,968	2
Bottled Gas Dealers, Retail					
AMERIGAS PARTNERS LP	454312	2,260,095	2	224,643	2
BLUE RHINO LLC	454312				
FERRELLGAS PARTNERS LP	454312	2,069,522	3	52,046	4
INERGY LP	454312	1,570,600	4	101,400	3
UGI CORP	454312	5,737,800	1	258,500	1
Chemicals, Manufacturing					
BASF SE	325	67,557,500	1	1,879,080	1
DOW CHEMICAL COMPANY	325	44,875,000	2	336,000	2
EVONIK INDUSTRIES AG	325	16,030,300	4	294,220	3
MITSUBISHI CHEMICAL HOLDINGS CORPORATION	325	31,926,400	3	-737,270	4
Coal Mining					
ALLIANCE RESOURCE PARTNERS LP	21211	1,231,031	12	192,157	8
ANGLO AMERICAN PLC	21211	20,858,000	2	2,425,000	2
ARCH COAL INC	21211	2,576,081	10	42,169	10
CHINA SHENHUA ENERGY COMPANY LTD	21211	18,198,600	3	4,756,360	1
CLOUD PEAK ENERGY INC	21211	1,398,200	11	381,701	7
CONSOL ENERGY INC	21211	4,621,875	5	539,717	5
DRUMMOND COMPANY INC	21211	2,850,000	8		
MASSEY ENERGY COMPANY	21211	2,691,159	9	104,433	9
OXBOW CORPORATION	21211	3,700,000	6		
PEABODY ENERGY CORP	21211	6,012,400	4	463,000	6
RHINO RESOURCE PARTNERS	21211				
UK COAL PLC	21211	511,250	13	-206,280	12
WESTMORELAND COAL CO	21211	443,368	14	-29,162	11
XSTRATA PLC	21211	22,732,000	1	661,000	3
YANZHOU COAL MINING CO LTD	21211	2,967,100	7	605,400	4
Commodity & Futures Brokerage					
TENASKA INC	523140	7,904,000	1		
Computer Networking & Related Equipment, Manufacturing					
SILVER SPRING NETWORKS	33411				
Construction, Heavy & Civil Engineering					
BECHTEL GROUP INC	237	30,800,000	1		
BLACK & VEATCH HOLDING CO	237	2,700,000	7		
CHICAGO BRIDGE & IRON COMPANY NV	237	4,556,503	6	174,289	4
FLUOR CORP	237	21,990,300	2	732,875	1
FOSTER WHEELER AG	237	5,056,334	5	361,358	3
LAYNE CHRISTENSEN CO	237	1,008,063	8	26,534	7
MATRIX SERVICE COMPANY	237	689,720	9	30,589	6
RELIANCE POWER LIMITED	237	85,970	10	64,010	5

Company	Industry Code	2009 Sales (U.S. $ thousands)	Sales Rank	2009 Profits (U.S. $ thousands)	Profits Rank
SEMBCORP INDUSTRIES LTD	237	6,870,650	4	490,010	2
SHAW GROUP INC	237	7,279,690	3	14,995	8
Construction--Other Special Trade Contractors					
ACERGY SA	2389	2,208,800	1	265,700	1
Consulting--Scientific & Technical					
AMERESCO INC	541690				
Electrical Equipment, Manufacturing					
ABB (INDIA) LTD	335	1,439,510	8	115,260	8
ABB LTD	335	31,795,000	3	2,901,000	3
ALSTOM SA	335	27,831,200	4	1,647,090	4
AREVA GROUP	335	18,657,500	6	667,670	6
BSST LLC	335				
COOPER INDUSTRIES PLC	335	5,069,600	7	439,100	7
GE ENERGY INFRASTRUCTURE	335	37,134,000	2	6,842,000	1
POWERSECURE INTERNATIONAL INC	335	102,540	9	2,793	9
SCHNEIDER ELECTRIC SA	335	21,457,000	5	1,157,560	5
SIEMENS AG	335	113,842,000	1	3,404,080	2
WESTINGHOUSE ELECTRIC CO	335				
Engineering Services					
ATOMIC ENERGY OF CANADA	541330	387,890	4	-399,500	5
ENGLOBAL CORP	541330	343,462	5	1,233	4
KBR INC	541330	12,105,000	1	290,000	2
MCDERMOTT INTERNATIONAL	541330	6,193,077	2	387,056	1
WILLBROS GROUP INC	541330	1,259,818	3	19,640	3
Financing--Business					
POWER FINANCE CORP LTD	522220	506,390	1	425,470	1
Gasoline Stations					
SUSSER HOLDINGS CORP	447110	3,307,308	1	2,068	1
Instrument Manufacturing, including Measurement, Control, Test & Navigational					
ELSTER GROUP SE	3345				
SIEMENS METERING SERVICES	3345				
Insurance--Property & Casualty, Specialty, Surety					
LOEWS CORPORATION	524126	14,117,000	1	564,000	1
Machinery, Manufacturing					
MITSUBISHI CORP	333	67,854,600		4,083,990	
Machinery, Mining & Oil & Gas Field, Manufacturing					
CAMERON INTERNATIONAL	33313	5,223,245	1	475,519	1
CE FRANKLIN LTD	33313	419,960	4	6,050	5
DRIL-QUIP INC	33313	240,204	6	105,141	3
JOY GLOBAL INC	33313	3,598,314	2	454,650	2
LUFKIN INDUSTRIES INC	33313	521,359	3	22,026	4
TESCO CORPORATION	33313	356,478	5	-5,265	6
Mining (Except Oil & Gas)					
CAMECO CORPORATION	212	2,239,310	2	1,063,460	2
RIO TINTO GROUP	212	41,825,000	1	4,872,000	1
Nuclear Fuels & Other Inorganic Chemicals					
USEC INC	325188	2,036,800	1	58,500	1

Company	Industry Code	2009 Sales (U.S. $ thousands)	Sales Rank	2009 Profits (U.S. $ thousands)	Profits Rank
Oil & Natural Gas Exploration & Production					
ABU DHABI NATIONAL OIL CO	211111				
ADAMS RESOURCES & ENERGY	211111	1,943,128	72	4,149	72
ADDAX PETROLEUM INC	211111				
AERA ENERGY LLC	211111				
ANADARKO PETROLEUM CORP	211111	9,000,000	50	-103,000	88
APACHE CORP	211111	8,614,826	51	-284,398	100
APCO OIL AND GAS INTERNATIONAL INC	211111	72,716	110	23,527	68
ATLAS ENERGY INC	211111	1,587,602	75	-84	73
ATLAS ENERGY RESOURCES	211111				
BARNWELL INDUSTRIES INC	211111	32,178	113	-24,362	77
BERRY PETROLEUM CO	211111	574,712	94	54,030	67
BG GROUP PLC	211111	14,737,200	41	3,128,380	22
BHP BILLITON	211111	50,800,000	22	6,338,000	14
BOLT TECHNOLOGY CORP	211111	48,876	111	10,501	70
BP PLC	211111	239,272,000	3	16,759,000	4
BREITBURN ENERGY PARTNERS LP	211111	204,862	101	-107,257	89
CABOT OIL & GAS CORP	211111	879,276	81	148,343	60
CALLON PETROLEUM CO	211111	101,259	108	54,419	65
CAMAC INTERNATIONAL CORP	211111				
CANADIAN NATURAL RESOURCES LTD	211111	9,810,410	47	1,528,340	34
CANADIAN OIL SANDS TRUST	211111	2,688,140	67	417,880	50
CARRIZO OIL & GAS INC	211111	114,079	106	-204,845	96
CEYLON PETROLEUM CORP (CPC)	211111				
CHENIERE ENERGY INC	211111	181,126	103	-161,490	94
CHESAPEAKE ENERGY CORP	211111	7,702,000	55	-5,805,000	109
CHEVRON CORPORATION	211111	171,636,000	7	10,483,000	10
CHINA NATIONAL PETROLEUM CORP (CNPC)	211111	179,545,000	6	18,952,200	3
CHINA PETROLEUM & CHEMICAL (SINOPEC)	211111	196,769,000	4	9,433,420	11
CIMAREX ENERGY CO	211111	1,009,794	78	-311,943	101
CLAYTON WILLIAMS ENERGY	211111	255,961	98	-117,415	90
CNOOC LIMITED	211111	15,384,400	39	4,312,160	18
CNX GAS CORPORATION	211111	683,400	87	164,500	58
CONOCOPHILLIPS COMPANY	211111	149,341,000	9	4,858,000	17
CONTINENTAL RESOURCES INC	211111	626,211	89	71,338	64
DENBURY RESOURCES INC	211111	889,150	80	-75,156	83
DEVON ENERGY CORP	211111	8,015,000	54	-2,479,000	108
DORCHESTER MINERALS LP	211111	43,631	112	21,681	69
ECOPETROL SA	211111	15,769,900	37	2,661,850	26
ENCANA CORP	211111	11,114,000	46	1,862,000	28
ENERGY PARTNERS LTD	211111	191,600	102	-57,100	82
ENI SPA	211111	106,284,000	11	5,576,830	15
EOG RESOURCES INC	211111	4,786,959	59	546,627	46
EXCO RESOURCES INC	211111	585,835	93	-496,804	103
EXXON MOBIL CORPORATION (EXXONMOBIL)	211111	301,500,000	1	19,280,000	2
FOREST OIL CORPORATION	211111	767,830	85	-923,133	106
FORMOSA PETROCHEMICAL CORP (FPCC)	211111	19,968,500	33	1,231,300	37

Company	Industry Code	2009 Sales (U.S. $ thousands)	Sales Rank	2009 Profits (U.S. $ thousands)	Profits Rank
GAIL (INDIA) LIMITED	211111	5,334,870	57	611,460	45
GALP ENERGIA SGPS SA	211111	14,909,100	40	428,970	49
GAZPROM (OAO)	211111	95,472,800	14	24,884,600	1
GOODRICH PETROLEUM CORP	211111	110,426	107	-257,033	99
HARVEST NATURAL RESOURCES INC	211111	181	114	-3,107	74
HELMERICH & PAYNE INC	211111	1,894,038	73	353,545	55
HESS CORPORATION	211111	29,614,000	26	740,000	42
HUNT CONSOLIDATED INC	211111				
HUSKY ENERGY INC	211111	14,607,700	42	1,372,200	36
IMPERIAL OIL LIMITED	211111	21,292,000	31	1,579,000	33
INPEX CORPORATION	211111	12,166,800	44	1,640,030	32
JOHN WOOD GROUP PLC	211111	4,927,100	58	163,200	59
JSC GAZPROM NEFT	211111	24,166,000	28	3,081,000	23
KOREA GAS CORPORATION	211111	16,655,600	36	204,420	57
KUWAIT PETROLEUM CORP	211111	65,000,000	20		
LUKOIL (OAO)	211111	81,083,000	17	7,011,000	12
MARATHON OIL CORP	211111	54,139,000	21	1,463,000	35
MCMORAN EXPLORATION CO	211111	435,435	96	-204,889	97
MDU RESOURCES GROUP INC	211111	4,176,501	61	-123,274	91
MESA ENERGY HOLDINGS INC	211111				
MURPHY OIL CORPORATION	211111	18,918,181	34	837,621	40
NEWFIELD EXPLORATION CO	211111	1,338,000	76	-542,000	104
NEXEN INC	211111	8,268,750	52	476,830	47
NIGERIAN NATIONAL PETROLEUM CORPORATION	211111				
NOBLE ENERGY INC	211111	2,313,000	68	-131,000	92
NOVATEK OAO	211111	2,921,040	66	845,680	39
OAO TATNEFT	211111	12,349,400	43	1,765,600	31
OCCIDENTAL PETROLEUM	211111	15,403,000	38	2,927,000	25
OGX PETROLEO E GAS PARTICIPACOES SA	211111	127,500	104	6,380	71
OIL & NATURAL GAS CORP LTD	211111	22,143,300	30	4,163,670	19
OIL SEARCH LTD	211111	512,200	95	133,700	62
OMV AKTIENGESELLSCHAFT	211111	22,565,900	29	720,030	43
PENN VIRGINIA CORP	211111	815,137	84	-77,368	84
PENN WEST ENERGY TRUST	211111	2,280,510	69	-138,910	93
PETROBRAS ARGENTINA SA	211111	3,021,500	65	233,450	56
PETROCHINA COMPANY	211111	149,107,000	10	15,124,200	7
PETROLEO BRASILEIRO SA (PETROBRAS)	211111	103,523,000	12	16,421,100	5
PETROLEOS DE VENEZUELA SA (PDVSA)	211111	90,000,000	15		
PETROLEOS MEXICANOS (PEMEX)	211111	85,000,000	16		
PETROLEUM DEVELOPMENT CORPORATION	211111	254,800	99	-79,300	85
PETRONAS (PETROLIAM NASIONAL BERHAD)	211111	79,590,800	18	15,815,700	6
PETROQUEST ENERGY INC	211111	218,875	100	-90,190	86
PIONEER NATURAL RESOURCES COMPANY	211111	1,711,516	74	-52,106	80
PLAINS EXPLORATION AND PRODUCTION COMPANY	211111	1,187,130	77	136,305	61
POLSKI KONCERN NAFTOWY ORLEN SA (PKN ORLEN GROUP)	211111	20,809,900	32	400,860	52

Company	Industry Code	2009 Sales (U.S. $ thousands)	Sales Rank	2009 Profits (U.S. $ thousands)	Profits Rank
PREMIER OIL PLC	211111	617,900	90	113,000	63
PRIMEENERGY CORPORATION	211111	89,992	109	-22,665	76
PT PERTAMINA (PERSERO)	211111				
PTT EXPLORATION AND PRODUCTION PCL	211111	4,031,900	62	744,580	41
PTT PCL	211111	48,814,700	23	1,832,580	30
QATAR PETROLEUM	211111				
QUESTAR CORPORATION	211111	3,038,000	64	395,900	53
QUICKSILVER RESOURCES INC	211111	832,725	82	-545,239	105
RANGE RESOURCES CORP	211111	907,341	79	-53,870	81
ROSNEFT (OAO)	211111	35,431,000	24	6,514,000	13
ROYAL DUTCH SHELL (SHELL GROUP)	211111	278,188,000	2	12,718,000	8
SANDRIDGE ENERGY INC	211111	591,044	92	-1,773,332	107
SANTOS LTD	211111	2,214,500	70	440,670	48
SAUDI ARAMCO (SAUDI ARABIAN OIL CO)	211111	190,000,000	5		
SHELL CANADA LIMITED	211111				
SHELL OIL CO	211111	100,000,000	13		
SM ENERGY COMPANY	211111	832,201	83	-99,370	87
SONATRACH	211111				
SOUTHWESTERN ENERGY CO	211111	2,145,779	71	-35,792	78
STATOIL ASA	211111	79,003,700	19	3,004,650	24
STONE ENERGY CORP	211111	714,356	86	-211,708	98
SUNCOR ENERGY INC	211111	24,559,700	27	1,104,610	38
SURGUTNEFTEGAS (OJSC)	211111	17,117,700	35	3,779,160	20
SWIFT ENERGY CO	211111	370,445	97	-39,076	79
SYNCRUDE CANADA LTD	211111				
TALISMAN ENERGY INC	211111	6,179,580	56	416,930	51
TARGA RESOURCES PARTNERS LP	211111	3,950,000	63	54,200	66
TNK-BP	211111	34,753,000	25	4,973,000	16
TOTAL SA	211111	152,376,000	8	11,476,400	9
TRANSOCEAN INC	211111	11,556,000	45	3,170,000	21
ULTRA PETROLEUM CORP	211111	666,762	88	-451,053	102
VAALCO ENERGY INC	211111	115,298	105	-4,144	75
W&T OFFSHORE INC	211111	610,996	91	-187,919	95
WILLIAMS COMPANIES INC	211111	8,255,000	53	361,000	54
WINTERSHALL AG	211111				
WOODSIDE PETROLEUM LTD	211111	4,418,850	60	1,852,020	29
XTO ENERGY INC	211111	9,064,000	48	2,019,000	27
YPF SA	211111	9,032,000	49	686,000	44
Oil Field Support Services					
ARCTIC SLOPE REGIONAL	213112				
BASIC ENERGY SERVICES INC	213112	526,627	23	-253,538	26
BJ SERVICES COMPANY	213112	4,121,897	7	149,943	12
BOOTS & COOTS INTERNATIONAL LLC	213112				
CARBO CERAMICS INC	213112	341,872	26	52,810	17
CHINA OILFIELD SERVICES LTD (COSL)	213112	2,752,080	8	470,340	5
EXTERRAN HOLDINGS INC	213112	2,715,601	9	-545,407	27
FLINT ENERGY SERVICES LTD	213112	1,794,370	13	44,460	18
FURMANITE CORP	213112	275,940	27	-2,830	20

Company	Industry Code	2009 Sales (U.S. $ thousands)	Sales Rank	2009 Profits (U.S. $ thousands)	Profits Rank
GLOBAL INDUSTRIES LTD	213112	914,348	19	73,731	14
HALLIBURTON COMPANY	213112	14,675,000	2	1,155,000	3
HELIX ENERGY SOLUTIONS GROUP INC	213112	1,461,687	14	156,054	11
KEY ENERGY SERVICES INC	213112	1,078,665	18	-156,121	25
NATIONAL OILWELL VARCO INC	213112	12,712,000	4	1,469,000	2
NEWPARK RESOURCES INC	213112	490,275	25	-20,573	21
OCEANEERING INTERNATIONAL	213112	1,822,081	12	292,116	8
OIL STATES INTERNATIONAL	213112	2,108,250	11	59,612	16
PETROLEUM GEO SERVICES	213112	1,350,200	17	165,800	10
RPC INC	213112	587,863	22	-22,745	22
SAIPEM SPA	213112	14,365,200	3	1,021,700	4
SCHLUMBERGER LIMITED	213112	22,702,000	1	3,134,000	1
SMITH INTERNATIONAL INC	213112	8,218,559	6	148,469	13
SUBSEA 7 INC	213112	2,439,278	10	412,200	6
SUPERIOR ENERGY SERVICES	213112	1,449,300	15	-102,323	23
TEAM INC	213112	497,559	24	22,911	19
TECHNIP	213112	8,773,380	5	231,510	9
TETRA TECHNOLOGIES INC	213112	878,877	20	68,804	15
TIDEWATER INC	213112	1,390,835	16	406,898	7
TRICO MARINE SERVICES INC	213112	642,200	21	-145,266	24
WESTERNGECO	213112				
Other Petrochemical & Coal Products Manufacturing					
DAKOTA GASIFICATION CO	324199				
HEADWATERS INC	324199	666,676	1	-415,550	1
Petrochemicals Manufacturing					
BRASKEM SA	325110	7,605,480	5	501,740	3
LYONDELLBASELL INDUSTRIES	325110	30,828,000	3	-2,865,000	5
RELIANCE INDUSTRIES LTD (RELIANCE GROUP)	325110	31,792,300	2	3,320,500	1
REPSOL YPF SA	325110	60,084,800	1	1,981,350	2
SINOPEC SHANGHAI PETROCHEMICAL	325110	7,759,160	4	234,260	4
Petroleum Bulk Stations & Terminals Distribution					
APEX OIL COMPANY INC	424710	3,560,000	6		
COLONIAL GROUP INC	424710	3,800,000	5		
DUNCAN ENERGY PARTNERS	424710	979,300	7	45,800	4
GLOBAL PARTNERS LP	424710	5,818,411	2	34,134	5
GULF OIL LIMITED PARTNERSHIP	424710				
NUSTAR ENERGY LP	424710	3,855,871	4	224,875	2
PAA NATURAL GAS STORAGE	424710	72,200	8	24,000	6
SUNOCO LOGISTICS PARTNERS	424710	5,429,677	3	250,362	1
WORLD FUEL SERVICES CORP	424710	11,295,177	1	117,139	3
Petroleum Products (except Bulk Stations/Terminals) Distribution & Pipelines					
AEGEAN MARINE PETROLEUM NETWORK INC	486	2,470,960	14	48,525	14
CENTER OIL COMPANY	486				
COSMO OIL CO LTD	486	37,547,400	2	-1,012,330	21
CROSSTEX ENERGY LP	486	1,459,090	16	104,406	12
DCP MIDSTREAM LLC	486				

Company	Industry Code	2009 Sales (U.S. $ thousands)	Sales Rank	2009 Profits (U.S. $ thousands)	Profits Rank
EL PASO CORP	486	4,631,000	12	-474,000	20
ENBRIDGE ENERGY PARTNERS	486	5,731,800	9	316,600	9
ENBRIDGE INC	486	11,920,400	6	1,493,640	1
ENERGY TRANSFER PARTNERS	486	5,417,295	11	791,542	5
ENOGEX LLC	486	851,000	20	66,000	13
ENTERPRISE PRODUCTS PARTNERS LP	486	25,510,900	3	1,155,100	3
GENESIS ENERGY LP	486	1,435,360	17	8,063	18
GETTY PETROLEUM MARKETING	486				
GREAT LAKES GAS TRANSMISSION COMPANY	486				
HUNTING PLC	486	582,300	21	46,440	15
IDEMITSU KOSAN CO LTD	486	41,602,900	1	36,400	17
KINDER MORGAN ENERGY PARTNERS LP	486	7,003,400	7	1,283,800	2
MAGELLAN MIDSTREAM PARTNERS LP	486	1,014,171	19	226,205	11
NEDERLANDSE GASUNIE NV	486				
ONEOK PARTNERS LP	486	6,474,491	8	434,356	7
PETROBRAS DISTRIBUIDORA	486				
PLAINS ALL AMERICAN PIPELINE	486	18,520,000	5	580,000	6
ROYAL VOPAK NV	486	1,426,470	18	385,930	8
SHV HOLDINGS NV	486				
SMF ENERGY CORPORATION	486	199,249	23	-2,339	19
SPECTRA ENERGY CORP	486	4,552,000	13	923,000	4
TEXAS GAS TRANSMISSION LLC	486				
TRANSAMMONIA INC	486	5,490,000	10		
TRANSMONTAIGNE INC	486				
TRANSPORTADORA DE GAS DEL SUR SA	486	403,890	22	45,020	16
TRUMAN ARNOLD COMPANIES	486	2,300,000	15		
ULTRAPAR PARTICIPACOES SA	486	19,379,000	4	250,420	10
US VENTURES INC	486				
Petroleum Refineries					
ALON USA ENERGY INC	324110	3,915,732	26	-115,156	21
ARABIAN AMERICAN DEVELOPMENT CO	324110	117,587	30	6,627	18
BANGCHAK PETROLEUM PCL	324110	3,636,820	28	251,790	9
BHARAT PETROLEUM CORPORATION LTD	324110	29,160,400	8	135,330	14
CALTEX AUSTRALIA LIMITED	324110	15,026,500	15	266,050	8
CITGO PETROLEUM CORP	324110				
COMPANIA ESPANOLA DE PETROLEOS SA (CEPSA)	324110	22,762,500	10	462,730	4
CROWN CENTRAL PETROLEUM	324110				
ERGON INC	324110	3,830,000	27		
FORTUM COMPANY	324110	7,628,840	19	1,841,590	1
FRONTIER OIL CORPORATION	324110	4,237,213	23	-83,760	20
GS CALTEX CORP	324110	22,629,600	12	566,240	2
GS HOLDINGS CORP	324110	30,955,300	7	438,250	5
HELLENIC PETROLEUM SA	324110	9,484,040	17	245,500	10
HINDUSTAN PETROLEUM CORP	324110	27,766,000	9	162,950	13
HOLLY CORP	324110	4,834,268	22	53,269	16
INDIAN OIL CORP LTD	324110	61,575,500	4	559,260	3

Company	Industry Code	2009 Sales (U.S. $ thousands)	Sales Rank	2009 Profits (U.S. $ thousands)	Profits Rank
JX HOLDINGS INC	324110				
JX NIPPON MINING & METALS CORPORATION	324110	45,079,100	5	-452,380	26
KOCH INDUSTRIES INC	324110	100,000,000	1		
KOCHI REFINERIES LTD	324110				
MARATHON PETROLEUM CO	324110				
MOTIVA ENTERPRISES LLC	324110				
PAKISTAN STATE OIL CO LTD	324110	7,150,060	21	-78,170	19
PETRON CORP	324110	4,149,660	24	99,620	15
PTT AROMATICS AND REFINING	324110	7,587,240	20	308,150	7
RED APPLE GROUP INC	324110	4,020,000	25		
RELIANCE PETROLEUM LTD	324110	783,630	29	17,900	17
SHOWA SHELL SEKIYU KK	324110	21,865,900	13	-622,930	27
SINCLAIR OIL CORP	324110				
SK HOLDINGS CO LTD	324110	68,720,100	2	224,950	11
S-OIL CORPORATION	324110	14,029,200	16	183,540	12
SUNOCO INC	324110	31,312,000	6	-329,000	24
TESORO CORP	324110	16,872,000	14	-140,000	22
THAI OIL PCL	324110	9,427,690	18	400,130	6
TONENGENERAL SEKIYU KK	324110	22,708,900	11	-233,550	23
TOTAL UK LIMITED	324110				
UNITED REFINING COMPANY	324110				
VALERO ENERGY CORP	324110	68,144,000	3	-352,000	25
Petroleum--Drilling Oil & Gas Wells Support					
ABBOT GROUP LIMITED	213111				
ATWOOD OCEANICS INC	213111	586,507	16	250,745	9
BAKER HUGHES INC	213111	9,664,000	1	421,000	5
CHESAPEAKE MIDSTREAM PARTNERS LP	213111				
DIAMOND OFFSHORE DRILLING	213111	3,631,284	4	1,376,219	2
ENSCO PLC	213111	1,945,900	7	779,400	4
ENSIGN ENERGY SERVICES	213111	1,087,810	11	119,910	11
HERCULES OFFSHORE INC	213111	742,851	14	-91,734	16
NABORS INDUSTRIES LTD	213111	3,503,431	5	-85,888	15
NOBLE CORPORATION	213111	3,640,784	3	1,678,642	1
PARKER DRILLING COMPANY	213111	752,910	13	9,267	12
PATTERSON-UTI ENERGY INC	213111	781,946	12	-38,290	13
PRECISION DRILLING CORP	213111	1,171,830	10	158,240	10
PRIDE INTERNATIONAL INC	213111	1,594,200	9	285,800	7
ROWAN COMPANIES INC	213111	1,770,180	8	367,504	6
SEADRILL LIMITED	213111	3,253,900	6	1,353,100	3
UNIT CORP	213111	709,898	15	-55,500	14
WEATHERFORD INTERNATIONAL LTD	213111	8,826,933	2	253,766	8
Radio & Wireless Communication, Manufacturing					
ITRON INC	334220	1,687,447	1	-2,249	1
Research & Development--Physical, Engineering & Life Sciences					
FUEL TECH INC	541712	71,397	1	-2,306	1
Shipping-Deep Sea					
AP MOLLER-MAERSK A/S	483111	48,522,000	1	-1,024,000	6

Company	Industry Code	2009 Sales (U.S. $ thousands)	Sales Rank	2009 Profits (U.S. $ thousands)	Profits Rank
BW GAS LIMITED	483111				
FRONTLINE LTD	483111	1,133,286	4	102,701	3
GULFMARK OFFSHORE INC	483111	388,871	6	50,583	4
MITSUI OSK LINES LTD	483111	20,745,700	2	1,411,960	1
SEACOR HOLDINGS INC	483111	1,711,338	3	145,103	2
TSAKOS ENERGY NAVIGATION	483111	444,926	5	30,175	5
Steel Pipe Manufacturing					
TENARIS SA	331210	8,149,320	1	1,207,599	1
Surveying & Mapping--Geophysical					
CGGVERITAS	541360	3,118,460	1	-361,530	3
DAWSON GEOPHYSICAL CO	541360	243,995	3	10,222	1
GEOKINETICS INC	541360	510,966	2	-5,011	2
SEITEL INC	541360				
Turbine & Turbine Generator Set Unit Manufacturing					
ENERCON GMBH	33361				
Utilities-Electric					
ALABAMA POWER COMPANY	2211				
AMERICAN ELECTRIC POWER COMPANY INC (AEP)	2211	13,489,000	14	1,356,000	9
ARIZONA PUBLIC SERVICE CO	2211				
BANGOR HYDRO-ELECTRIC CO	2211				
BLACK HILLS CORP	2211	1,269,578	41	81,555	41
CALPINE CORPORATION	2211	6,564,000	25	149,000	36
CENTRAIS ELETRICAS BRASILEIRAS SA (ELETROBRAS)	2211	15,524,500	12	101,580	39
CEZ AS	2211	10,798,200	19	2,937,940	5
CHEUNG KONG INFRASTRUCTURE HOLDING	2211	295,530	47	718,250	20
CHUBU ELECTRIC POWER CO	2211	27,850,780	6	-210,470	46
CLP HOLDINGS LIMITED	2211	6,536,590	26	1,057,350	13
COMMONWEALTH EDISON CO	2211				
COMPANHIA DE TRANSMISSAO DE ENERGIA ELETRICA PAULISTA (CTEEP)	2211	967,080	44	487,040	23
DETROIT EDISON COMPANY	2211				
DPL INC	2211	1,588,900	38	229,100	31
EDISON INTERNATIONAL	2211	12,361,000	17	945,000	16
EDP - ENERGIAS DE PORTUGAL	2211	14,963,400	13	1,256,130	10
ELECTRICITY GENERATING AUTHORITY OF THAILAND	2211	12,569,300	16	1,174,990	11
ELETROBRAS PARTICIPACOES	2211				
ELETROPAULO METROPOLITANA ELECTRICIDADE DE SAO PAULO	2211				
ENDESA SA	2211	30,574,100	4	4,235,780	2
ENEL SPA	2211	82,128,400	1	6,964,190	1
FIRSTENERGY CORP	2211	12,967,000	15	990,000	14
GEORGIA POWER COMPANY	2211				
GLOW ENERGY PCL	2211	1,157,380	43	140,450	37
GREAT PLAINS ENERGY INC	2211	1,965,000	36	150,000	35
HAWAIIAN ELECTRIC INDUSTRIES INC	2211	2,018,623	35	83,011	40
HONGKONG ELECTRIC HOLDINGS LIMITED	2211	1,341,090	40	864,000	17
IBERDROLA SA	2211	30,499,200	5	3,507,440	4

Company	Industry Code	2009 Sales (U.S. $ thousands)	Sales Rank	2009 Profits (U.S. $ thousands)	Profits Rank
ITC HOLDINGS CORP	2211	621,015	46	130,900	38
KANSAI ELECTRIC POWER CO	2211	30,615,400	3	-96,540	45
KOREA ELECTRIC POWER	2211	27,171,400	7	-77,310	44
LIGHT SA	2211	3,168,680	31	355,920	25
NATIONAL THERMAL POWER	2211				
NEXTERA ENERGY INC	2211	15,643,000	11	1,615,000	7
ONCOR ELECTRIC DELIVERY	2211	2,690,000	33	320,000	27
ONTARIO POWER GENERATION	2211	5,599,060	27	621,450	21
PACIFICORP	2211	4,457,000	28	542,000	22
PINNACLE WEST CAPITAL	2211	3,297,101	30	68,330	42
POWER GRID CORPORATION OF INDIA LTD	2211	1,444,270	39	365,750	24
PROGRESS ENERGY INC	2211	9,885,000	21	761,000	18
PUBLIC POWER CORPORATION	2211	8,550,930	22	983,080	15
PUERTO RICO ELECTRIC POWER AUTHORITY	2211				
RATCHABURI ELECTRICITY GENERATING HOLDING PCL	2211	1,188,130	42	226,520	32
RELIANCE INFRASTRUCTURE	2211	2,721,170	32	292,761	28
SHIKOKU ELECTRIC POWER CO	2211	7,043,240	24	322,750	26
SOUTHERN CALIFORNIA EDISON COMPANY	2211	9,965,000	20	1,371,000	8
SOUTHERN COMPANY	2211	15,743,000	10	1,643,000	6
TAMPA ELECTRIC COMPANY	2211				
TATA POWER	2211	3,713,330	29	257,320	30
TENAGA NASIONAL BERHAD (TNB)	2211	8,426,700	23	268,700	29
TENNESSEE VALLEY AUTHORITY (TVA)	2211	11,300,000	18	726,000	19
TOHOKU ELECTRIC POWER CO	2211	20,420,980	9	-352,090	47
TOKYO ELECTRIC POWER COMPANY INC	2211	52,356,100	2	1,103,720	12
TRANSALTA CORP	2211	2,684,340	34	175,400	33
UIL HOLDINGS CORPORATION	2211	896,550	45	54,317	43
VATTENFALL AB	2211	26,515,400	8	3,606,430	3
VIRGINIA ELECTRIC AND POWER COMPANY	2211				
WESTAR ENERGY	2211	1,858,231	37	175,075	34
Utilities-Electric & Gas					
AES CORPORATION	221	14,119,000	10	658,000	18
ALLEGHENY ENERGY INC	221	3,426,800	35	394,100	25
ALLIANT ENERGY CORP	221	3,432,800	34	129,700	41
AMEREN CORP	221	7,090,000	26	612,000	19
AMEREN ILLINOIS COMPANY	221				
ATCO LTD	221	3,007,250	39	274,040	31
ATLANTIC CITY ELECTRIC CO	221				
AVISTA CORPORATION	221	1,512,565	48	87,071	46
BALTIMORE GAS AND ELECTRIC COMPANY	221	3,579,000	33	90,700	45
CENTERPOINT ENERGY INC	221	8,281,000	21	372,000	27
CENTRICA PLC	221	31,910,700	3	1,226,270	12
CH ENERGY GROUP INC	221	931,589	52	43,484	48
CMS ENERGY CORP	221	6,205,000	28	220,000	35
COGENTRIX ENERGY LLC	221				

Company	Industry Code	2009 Sales (U.S. $ thousands)	Sales Rank	2009 Profits (U.S. $ thousands)	Profits Rank
COMPANHIA PARANAENSE DE ENERGIA - COPEL	221	3,304,160	37	603,740	20
CONSOLIDATED EDISON INC	221	13,032,000	12	868,000	16
CONSTELLATION ENERGY GROUP	221	15,598,800	8	4,443,400	3
CONSUMERS ENERGY CO	221				
DELMARVA POWER AND LIGHT COMPANY	221				
DIRECT ENERGY	221				
DOMINION RESOURCES INC	221	15,131,000	9	1,287,000	11
DTE ENERGY COMPANY	221	8,014,000	23	532,000	21
DUKE ENERGY CORP	221	12,731,000	13	1,075,000	14
DYNEGY INC	221	2,468,000	42	-1,247,000	50
E.ON AG	221	105,614,000	1	11,159,500	1
E.ON UK PLC	221				
E.ON US LLC	221				
EDISON MISSION GROUP	221				
ELECTRABEL SA	221				
EMERA INC	221	1,408,350	49	168,850	39
ENERGY FUTUREHOLDINGS CORP (TXU)	221	9,550,000	17		
EPCOR UTILITIES INC	221				
EXELON CORPORATION	221	17,318,000	7	2,707,000	4
GAS NATURAL SDG SA	221	18,251,900	6	1,465,890	9
INTEGRYS ENERGY GROUP INC	221	7,499,800	25	-68,800	49
MANITOBA HYDRO-ELECTRIC	221	2,233,770	44	281,580	30
MIDAMERICAN ENERGY HOLDINGS CO	221	11,200,000	15		
MIRANT CORP	221	2,309,000	43	494,000	22
NATIONAL GRID PLC	221	25,165,100	5	1,525,300	7
NATIONAL GRID USA	221				
NEW YORK STATE ELECTRIC & GAS CORP	221				
NIAGARA MOHAWK POWER	221				
NISOURCE INC	221	6,649,400	27	217,700	36
NORTHEAST UTILITIES	221	5,439,430	29	330,033	29
NORTHERN INDIANA PUBLIC SERVICE COMPANY	221				
NORTHWESTERN CORP	221	1,141,910	51	73,420	47
NRG ENERGY INC	221	8,952,000	19	942,000	15
NSTAR	221	3,050,044	38	253,248	33
NV ENERGY INC	221	3,585,798	32	182,936	38
OGE ENERGY CORP	221	2,869,700	40	258,300	32
PEPCO HOLDINGS INC	221	9,259,000	18	235,000	34
PG&E CORPORATION	221	13,399,000	11	2,299,000	5
PNM RESOURCES INC	221	1,647,744	47	124,316	42
PPL CORPORATION	221	7,556,000	24	426,000	23
PUBLIC SERVICE ENTERPRISE GROUP (PSEG)	221	12,406,000	14	1,592,000	6
PUGET HOLDINGS LLC	221				
ROCHESTER GAS AND ELECTRIC CORP	221				
RRI ENERGY INC	221	1,825,000	46	403,000	24
RWE AG	221	59,530,700	2	4,538,420	2
RWE NPOWER	221				

Company	Industry Code	2009 Sales (U.S. $ thousands)	Sales Rank	2009 Profits (U.S. $ thousands)	Profits Rank
SAN DIEGO GAS & ELECTRIC COMPANY	221				
SCANA CORPORATION	221	4,237,000	30	348,000	28
SCOTTISH AND SOUTHERN ENERGY PLC	221	25,424,200	4	1,503,310	8
SCOTTISHPOWER UK PLC	221				
SEMPRA ENERGY	221	8,106,000	22	1,119,000	13
TECO ENERGY INC	221	3,310,500	36	213,900	37
TRANSCANADA CORP	221	8,688,740	20	1,337,330	10
UNISOURCE ENERGY CORP	221	1,394,424	50	104,258	44
VECTREN CORPORATION	221	2,088,900	45	133,100	40
WGL HOLDINGS INC	221	2,706,856	41	120,373	43
WISCONSIN ENERGY CORP	221	4,127,900	31	382,400	26
XCEL ENERGY INC	221	9,644,303	16	680,887	17
Utilities-Electric, Wholesale Generation					
ABU DHABI NATIONAL ENERGY COMPANY PJSC (TAQA)	221121	4,588,040	2	49,540	3
CPFL ENERGIA SA	221121	6,215,040	1	756,730	1
LS POWER ASSOCIATES LP	221121				
TRACTEBEL ENERGIA SA	221121	2,083,230	3	675,840	2
Utilities-Gas					
AGL RESOURCES INC	221210	2,317,000	9	249,000	7
ATMOS ENERGY CORP	221210	4,969,080	5	190,978	8
EQT CORPORATION	221210	1,269,827	17	156,929	10
GAZ METRO LIMITED PARTNERSHIP	221210	2,121,980	11	149,460	11
GDF SUEZ SA	221210	103,150,000	1	5,779,180	1
HONG KONG AND CHINA GAS CO LTD	221210	1,593,410	16	667,590	4
LACLEDE GROUP INC	221210	1,895,198	13	64,247	16
METROGAS SA	221210	271,110	18	-19,760	18
MICHIGAN CONSOLIDATED GAS COMPANY	221210				
NATIONAL FUEL GAS CO	221210	2,057,852	12	100,708	14
NEW JERSEY RESOURCES CORPORATION	221210	2,592,460	8	27,242	17
NICOR INC	221210	2,652,100	7	135,500	12
ONEOK INC	221210	11,111,600	4	894,600	3
OSAKA GAS CO LTD	221210	14,726,890	3	400,040	6
PIEDMONT NATURAL GAS COMPANY INC	221210	1,638,116	15	122,824	13
SNAM RETE GAS SPA	221210	3,447,690	6	1,026,730	2
SOUTHERN CALIFORNIA GAS COMPANY	221210				
SOUTHERN UNION COMPANY	221210	2,179,018	10	170,897	9
SOUTHWEST GAS CORP	221210	1,893,824	14	87,482	15
TOKYO GAS CO LTD	221210	16,940,428	2	425,591	5
Utilities-Hydroelectric					
BRITISH COLUMBIA HYDRO AND POWER AUTHORITY	221111	4,033,830	3	345,840	3
HYDRO ONE INC	221111	4,732,220	2	468,830	2
HYDRO-QUEBEC	221111	12,303,400	1	3,027,460	1
PORTLAND GENERAL ELECTRIC COMPANY	221111	1,804,000	4	89,000	4
Utilities-Nuclear Generation					
BRITISH ENERGY GROUP PLC	221113				
ELECTRICITE DE FRANCE SA (EDF)	221113	85,630,500	1	5,040,810	1

Company	Industry Code	2009 Sales (U.S. $ thousands)	Sales Rank	2009 Profits (U.S. $ thousands)	Profits Rank
ENTERGY CORP	221113	10,745,650	2	1,251,050	2
UNISTAR NUCLEAR ENERGY	221113				
Utilities-Water					
UNITED UTILITIES GROUP PLC	2213	4,014,360	1	295,800	1
Venture Capital/Private Equity Investments					
ESSAR GROUP LTD	523910				

ALPHABETICAL INDEX

ELECTRICITY GENERATING AUTHORITY OF THAILAND
ELETROBRAS PARTICIPACOES SA
ELETROPAULO METROPOLITANA ELECTRICIDADE DE SAO PAULO SA
ELSTER GROUP SE
EMERA INC
ENBRIDGE ENERGY PARTNERS LP
ENBRIDGE INC
ENCANA CORP
ENDESA SA
ENEL SPA
ENERCON GMBH
ENERGY FUTUREHOLDINGS CORP (TXU)
ENERGY PARTNERS LTD
ENERGY TRANSFER PARTNERS LP
ENGLOBAL CORP
ENI SPA
ENOGEX LLC
ENSCO PLC
ENSIGN ENERGY SERVICES INC
ENTERGY CORP
ENTERPRISE PRODUCTS PARTNERS LP
EOG RESOURCES INC
EPCOR UTILITIES INC
EQT CORPORATION
ERGON INC
ESSAR GROUP LTD
EVONIK INDUSTRIES AG
EXCO RESOURCES INC
EXELON CORPORATION
EXTERRAN HOLDINGS INC
EXXON MOBIL CORPORATION (EXXONMOBIL)
FERRELLGAS PARTNERS LP
FIRSTENERGY CORP
FLINT ENERGY SERVICES LTD
FLUOR CORP
FOREST OIL CORPORATION
FORMOSA PETROCHEMICAL CORP (FPCC)
FORTUM COMPANY
FOSTER WHEELER AG
FRONTIER OIL CORPORATION
FRONTLINE LTD
FUEL TECH INC
FURMANITE CORP
GAIL (INDIA) LIMITED
GALP ENERGIA SGPS SA
GAS NATURAL SDG SA
GAZ METRO
GAZPROM (OAO)
GDF SUEZ SA
GE ENERGY INFRASTRUCTURE
GENESIS ENERGY LP
GEOKINETICS INC
GEORGIA POWER COMPANY
GETTY PETROLEUM MARKETING
GLOBAL INDUSTRIES LTD
GLOBAL PARTNERS LP
GLOW ENERGY PCL
GOODRICH PETROLEUM CORP
GREAT LAKES GAS TRANSMISSION COMPANY
GREAT PLAINS ENERGY INC
GS CALTEX CORP
GS HOLDINGS CORP
GULF OIL LIMITED PARTNERSHIP
GULFMARK OFFSHORE INC
HALLIBURTON COMPANY
HARVEST NATURAL RESOURCES INC
HAWAIIAN ELECTRIC INDUSTRIES INC
HEADWATERS INC
HELIX ENERGY SOLUTIONS GROUP INC
HELLENIC PETROLEUM SA
HELMERICH & PAYNE INC
HERCULES OFFSHORE INC
HESS CORPORATION
HINDUSTAN PETROLEUM CORPORATION LTD
HOLLY CORP
HONG KONG AND CHINA GAS CO LTD (THE)
HONGKONG ELECTRIC HOLDINGS LIMITED
HUNT CONSOLIDATED INC
HUNTING PLC
HUSKY ENERGY INC
HYDRO ONE INC
HYDRO-QUEBEC
IBERDROLA SA
IDEMITSU KOSAN CO LTD
IMPERIAL OIL LIMITED
INDIAN OIL CORP LTD
INERGY LP
INPEX CORPORATION
INTEGRYS ENERGY GROUP INC
ITC HOLDINGS CORP
ITRON INC
JOHN WOOD GROUP PLC
JOY GLOBAL INC
JSC GAZPROM NEFT
JX HOLDINGS INC
JX NIPPON MINING & METALS CORPORATION
KANSAI ELECTRIC POWER COMPANY INC
KBR INC
KEY ENERGY SERVICES INC
KINDER MORGAN ENERGY PARTNERS LP
KOCH INDUSTRIES INC
KOCHI REFINERIES LTD
KOREA ELECTRIC POWER CORPORATION
KOREA GAS CORPORATION
KUWAIT PETROLEUM CORPORATION
LACLEDE GROUP INC (THE)
LAYNE CHRISTENSEN COMPANY
LIGHT SA
LOEWS CORPORATION
LS POWER ASSOCIATES LP
LUFKIN INDUSTRIES INC
LUKOIL (OAO)
LYONDELLBASELL INDUSTRIES
MAGELLAN MIDSTREAM PARTNERS LP
MANITOBA HYDRO-ELECTRIC
MARATHON OIL CORP
MARATHON PETROLEUM COMPANY LLC
MASSEY ENERGY COMPANY
MATRIX SERVICE COMPANY
MCDERMOTT INTERNATIONAL INC
MCMORAN EXPLORATION CO
MDU RESOURCES GROUP INC
MESA ENERGY HOLDINGS INC
METROGAS SA
MICHIGAN CONSOLIDATED GAS COMPANY
MIDAMERICAN ENERGY HOLDINGS CO
MIRANT CORP
MITSUBISHI CHEMICAL HOLDINGS CORPORATION
MITSUBISHI CORP
MITSUI OSK LINES LTD
MOTIVA ENTERPRISES LLC
MURPHY OIL CORPORATION
NABORS INDUSTRIES LTD
NATIONAL FUEL GAS CO
NATIONAL GRID PLC
NATIONAL GRID USA
NATIONAL OILWELL VARCO INC
NATIONAL THERMAL POWER CORP LTD
NEDERLANDSE GASUNIE NV
NEW JERSEY RESOURCES CORPORATION
NEW YORK STATE ELECTRIC & GAS CORP
NEWFIELD EXPLORATION CO
NEWPARK RESOURCES INC
NEXEN INC
NEXTERA ENERGY INC
NIAGARA MOHAWK POWER CORPORATION
NICOR INC
NIGERIAN NATIONAL PETROLEUM CORPORATION
NISOURCE INC
NOBLE CORPORATION
NOBLE ENERGY INC
NORTHEAST UTILITIES
NORTHERN INDIANA PUBLIC SERVICE COMPANY
NORTHWESTERN CORPORATION
NOVATEK OAO
NRG ENERGY INC
NSTAR
NUSTAR ENERGY LP
NV ENERGY INC
OAO TATNEFT
OCCIDENTAL PETROLEUM CORP
OCEANEERING INTERNATIONAL INC
OGE ENERGY CORP

OGX PETROLEO E GAS PARTICIPACOES SA
OIL & NATURAL GAS CORP LTD
OIL SEARCH LTD
OIL STATES INTERNATIONAL INC
OMV AKTIENGESELLSCHAFT
ONCOR ELECTRIC DELIVERY COMPANY
ONEOK INC
ONEOK PARTNERS LP
ONTARIO POWER GENERATION INC
OSAKA GAS CO LTD
OXBOW CORPORATION
PAA NATURAL GAS STORAGE LP
PACIFICORP
PAKISTAN STATE OIL CO LTD
PARKER DRILLING COMPANY
PATTERSON-UTI ENERGY INC
PEABODY ENERGY CORP
PENN VIRGINIA CORP
PENN WEST ENERGY TRUST
PEPCO HOLDINGS INC
PETROBRAS DISTRIBUIDORA SA
PETROBRAS ARGENTINA SA
PETROCHINA COMPANY
PETROLEO BRASILEIRO SA (PETROBRAS)
PETROLEOS DE VENEZUELA SA (PDVSA)
PETROLEOS MEXICANOS (PEMEX)
PETROLEUM DEVELOPMENT CORPORATION
PETROLEUM GEO SERVICES ASA
PETRON CORP
PETRONAS (PETROLIAM NASIONAL BERHAD)
PETROQUEST ENERGY INC
PG&E CORPORATION
PHI INC
PIEDMONT NATURAL GAS COMPANY INC
PINNACLE WEST CAPITAL CORPORATION
PIONEER NATURAL RESOURCES COMPANY
PLAINS ALL AMERICAN PIPELINE
PLAINS EXPLORATION AND PRODUCTION COMPANY
PNM RESOURCES INC
POLSKI KONCERN NAFTOWY ORLEN SA (PKN ORLEN GROUP)
PORTLAND GENERAL ELECTRIC COMPANY
POWER FINANCE CORPORATION LIMITED
POWER GRID CORPORATION OF INDIA LTD
POWERSECURE INTERNATIONAL INC
PPL CORPORATION
PRECISION DRILLING CORPORATION
PREMIER OIL PLC
PRIDE INTERNATIONAL INC
PRIMEENERGY CORPORATION
PROGRESS ENERGY INC
PT PERTAMINA (PERSERO)
PTT AROMATICS AND REFINING PCL
PTT EXPLORATION AND PRODUCTION PCL
PTT PCL
PUBLIC POWER CORPORATION SA
PUBLIC SERVICE ENTERPRISE GROUP (PSEG)
PUERTO RICO ELECTRIC POWER AUTHORITY
PUGET HOLDINGS LLC
QATAR PETROLEUM
QUESTAR CORPORATION
QUICKSILVER RESOURCES INC
RANGE RESOURCES CORP
RATCHABURI ELECTRICITY GENERATING HOLDING PCL
RED APPLE GROUP INC
RELIANCE INDUSTRIES LTD (RELIANCE GROUP)
RELIANCE INFRASTRUCTURE LTD
RELIANCE PETROLEUM LTD
RELIANCE POWER LIMITED
REPSOL YPF SA
RHINO RESOURCE PARTNERS
RIO TINTO GROUP
ROCHESTER GAS AND ELECTRIC CORP
ROSNEFT (OAO)
ROWAN COMPANIES INC
ROYAL DUTCH SHELL (SHELL GROUP)
ROYAL VOPAK NV
RPC INC
RRI ENERGY INC
RWE AG
RWE NPOWER
SAIPEM SPA
SAN DIEGO GAS & ELECTRIC COMPANY
SANDRIDGE ENERGY INC
SANTOS LTD
SAUDI ARAMCO (SAUDI ARABIAN OIL CO)
SCANA CORPORATION
SCHLUMBERGER LIMITED
SCHNEIDER ELECTRIC SA
SCOTTISH AND SOUTHERN ENERGY PLC
SCOTTISHPOWER UK PLC
SEACOR HOLDINGS INC
SEADRILL LIMITED
SEITEL INC
SEMBCORP INDUSTRIES LTD
SEMPRA ENERGY
SHAW GROUP INC (THE)
SHELL CANADA LIMITED
SHELL OIL CO
SHIKOKU ELECTRIC POWER COMPANY INC
SHOWA SHELL SEKIYU KK
SHV HOLDINGS NV
SIEMENS AG
SIEMENS METERING SERVICES LTD
SILVER SPRING NETWORKS
SINCLAIR OIL CORP
SINOPEC SHANGHAI PETROCHEMICAL
SK HOLDINGS CO LTD
SM ENERGY COMPANY
SMF ENERGY CORPORATION
SMITH INTERNATIONAL INC
SNAM RETE GAS SPA
S-OIL CORPORATION
SONATRACH
SOUTHERN CALIFORNIA EDISON COMPANY
SOUTHERN CALIFORNIA GAS COMPANY
SOUTHERN COMPANY (THE)
SOUTHERN UNION COMPANY
SOUTHWEST GAS CORP
SOUTHWESTERN ENERGY CO
SPECTRA ENERGY CORP
STATOIL ASA
STONE ENERGY CORPORATION
SUBSEA 7 INC
SUNCOR ENERGY INC
SUNOCO INC
SUNOCO LOGISTICS PARTNERS LP
SUPERIOR ENERGY SERVICES INC
SURGUTNEFTEGAS (OJSC)
SUSSER HOLDINGS CORPORATION
SWIFT ENERGY CO
SYNCRUDE CANADA LTD
TALISMAN ENERGY INC
TAMPA ELECTRIC COMPANY
TARGA RESOURCES PARTNERS LP
TATA POWER
TEAM INC
TECHNIP
TECO ENERGY INC
TENAGA NASIONAL BERHAD (TNB)
TENARIS SA
TENASKA INC
TENNESSEE VALLEY AUTHORITY (TVA)
TESCO CORPORATION
TESORO CORP
TETRA TECHNOLOGIES INC
TEXAS GAS TRANSMISSION LLC
THAI OIL PCL
TIDEWATER INC
TNK-BP
TOHOKU ELECTRIC POWER CO INC
TOKYO ELECTRIC POWER COMPANY INC (THE)
TOKYO GAS CO LTD
TONENGENERAL SEKIYU KK
TOTAL SA
TOTAL UK LIMITED
TRACTEBEL ENERGIA SA
TRANSALTA CORP
TRANSAMMONIA INC
TRANSCANADA CORP
TRANSMONTAIGNE INC
TRANSOCEAN INC

TRANSPORTADORA DE GAS DEL SUR SA
TRICO MARINE SERVICES INC
TRUMAN ARNOLD COMPANIES
TSAKOS ENERGY NAVIGATION LTD
UGI CORP
UIL HOLDINGS CORPORATION
UK COAL PLC
ULTRA PETROLEUM CORP
ULTRAPAR PARTICIPACOES SA
UNISOURCE ENERGY CORPORATION
UNISTAR NUCLEAR ENERGY LLC
UNIT CORP
UNITED REFINING COMPANY
UNITED UTILITIES GROUP PLC
US VENTURE INC
USEC INC
VAALCO ENERGY INC
VALERO ENERGY CORP
VATTENFALL AB
VECTREN CORPORATION
VIRGINIA ELECTRIC AND POWER COMPANY
W&T OFFSHORE INC
WEATHERFORD INTERNATIONAL LTD
WESTAR ENERGY
WESTERNGECO
WESTINGHOUSE ELECTRIC COMPANY LLC
WESTMORELAND COAL CO
WGL HOLDINGS INC
WILLBROS GROUP INC
WILLIAMS COMPANIES INC (THE)
WINTERSHALL AG
WISCONSIN ENERGY CORP
WOODSIDE PETROLEUM LTD
WORLD FUEL SERVICES CORP
XCEL ENERGY INC
XSTRATA PLC
XTO ENERGY INC
YANZHOU COAL MINING CO LTD
YPF SA

INDEX OF U.S. HEADQUARTERS LOCATION BY STATE

To help you locate members of the firms geographically, the city and state of the headquarters of each company are in the following index.

ALABAMA
ALABAMA POWER COMPANY; Birmingham
DRUMMOND COMPANY INC; Birmingham

ALASKA
ARCTIC SLOPE REGIONAL CORP; Anchorage

ARIZONA
ARIZONA PUBLIC SERVICE COMPANY; Phoenix
PINNACLE WEST CAPITAL CORPORATION; Phoenix
UNISOURCE ENERGY CORPORATION; Tucson

ARKANSAS
MURPHY OIL CORPORATION; El Dorado

CALIFORNIA
AERA ENERGY LLC; Bakersfield
BECHTEL GROUP INC; San Francisco
BREITBURN ENERGY PARTNERS LP; Los Angeles
BSST LLC; Irwindale
CHEVRON CORPORATION; San Ramon
EDISON INTERNATIONAL; Rosemead
EDISON MISSION GROUP; Irvine
OCCIDENTAL PETROLEUM CORP; Los Angeles
PG&E CORPORATION; San Francisco
SAN DIEGO GAS & ELECTRIC COMPANY; San Diego
SEMPRA ENERGY; San Diego
SILVER SPRING NETWORKS; Redwood City
SOUTHERN CALIFORNIA EDISON COMPANY; Rosemead
SOUTHERN CALIFORNIA GAS COMPANY; Los Angeles

COLORADO
BERRY PETROLEUM CO; Denver
CIMAREX ENERGY CO; Denver
DCP MIDSTREAM LLC; Denver
FOREST OIL CORPORATION; Denver
PETROLEUM DEVELOPMENT CORPORATION; Denver
SM ENERGY COMPANY; Denver
TRANSMONTAIGNE INC; Denver
WESTMORELAND COAL CO; Colorado Springs

CONNECTICUT
BOLT TECHNOLOGY CORP; Norwalk
NORTHEAST UTILITIES; Hartford
PRIMEENERGY CORPORATION; Stamford
UIL HOLDINGS CORPORATION; New Haven

DELAWARE
DELMARVA POWER AND LIGHT COMPANY; Wilmington

DISTRICT OF COLUMBIA
PEPCO HOLDINGS INC; Washington
WGL HOLDINGS INC; Washington

FLORIDA
NEXTERA ENERGY INC; Juno Beach
OXBOW CORPORATION; West Palm Beach
SEACOR HOLDINGS INC; Ft. Lauderdale
SMF ENERGY CORPORATION; Fort Lauderdale
TAMPA ELECTRIC COMPANY; Tampa
TECO ENERGY INC; Tampa
WORLD FUEL SERVICES CORP; Miami

GEORGIA
AGL RESOURCES INC; Atlanta
COLONIAL GROUP INC; Savannah
GE ENERGY INFRASTRUCTURE; Atlanta
GEORGIA POWER COMPANY; Atlanta
MIRANT CORP; Atlanta
RPC INC; Atlanta
SOUTHERN COMPANY (THE); Atlanta

HAWAII
BARNWELL INDUSTRIES INC; Honolulu
HAWAIIAN ELECTRIC INDUSTRIES INC; Honolulu

ILLINOIS
AMEREN ILLINOIS COMPANY; Peoria
COMMONWEALTH EDISON COMPANY; Chicago
EXELON CORPORATION; Chicago
FUEL TECH INC; Warrenville
INTEGRYS ENERGY GROUP INC; Chicago
NICOR INC; Naperville

INDIANA
NISOURCE INC; Merrillville
NORTHERN INDIANA PUBLIC SERVICE COMPANY; Merrillville
VECTREN CORPORATION; Evansville

IOWA
MIDAMERICAN ENERGY HOLDINGS CO; Des Moines

KANSAS
BLACK & VEATCH HOLDING COMPANY; Overland Park
FERRELLGAS PARTNERS LP; Overland Park
KOCH INDUSTRIES INC; Wichita
LAYNE CHRISTENSEN COMPANY; Mission Woods
WESTAR ENERGY; Topeka

KENTUCKY
E.ON US LLC; Louisville
RHINO RESOURCE PARTNERS; Lexington
TEXAS GAS TRANSMISSION LLC; Owensboro

LOUISIANA
ENERGY PARTNERS LTD; New Orleans
ENTERGY CORP; New Orleans
GLOBAL INDUSTRIES LTD; Carlyss
MCMORAN EXPLORATION CO; New Orleans
PETROQUEST ENERGY INC; Lafayette
PHI INC; Lafayette
SHAW GROUP INC (THE); Baton Rouge
STONE ENERGY CORPORATION; Lafayette
SUPERIOR ENERGY SERVICES INC; New Orleans
TIDEWATER INC; New Orleans

MAINE
BANGOR HYDRO-ELECTRIC COMPANY; Bangor

MARYLAND
BALTIMORE GAS AND ELECTRIC COMPANY; Baltimore
CONSTELLATION ENERGY GROUP; Baltimore
CROWN CENTRAL PETROLEUM LLC; Baltimore
UNISTAR NUCLEAR ENERGY LLC; Baltimore
USEC INC; Bethesda

MASSACHUSETTS
AMERESCO INC; Framingham
GLOBAL PARTNERS LP; Waltham
GULF OIL LIMITED PARTNERSHIP; Framingham
NATIONAL GRID USA; Westborough

NSTAR; Boston

MICHIGAN
CMS ENERGY CORP; Jackson
CONSUMERS ENERGY COMPANY; Jackson
DETROIT EDISON COMPANY (THE); Detroit
DOW CHEMICAL COMPANY (THE); Midland
DTE ENERGY COMPANY; Detroit
ITC HOLDINGS CORP; Novi
MICHIGAN CONSOLIDATED GAS COMPANY; Detroit

MINNESOTA
XCEL ENERGY INC; Minneapolis

MISSISSIPPI
CALLON PETROLEUM COMPANY; Natchez
ERGON INC; Jackson

MISSOURI
AMEREN CORP; St. Louis
APEX OIL COMPANY INC; Clayton
ARCH COAL INC; St. Louis
CENTER OIL COMPANY; St. Louis
GREAT PLAINS ENERGY INC; Kansas City
INERGY LP; Kansas City
LACLEDE GROUP INC (THE); St. Louis
PEABODY ENERGY CORP; St. Louis

NEBRASKA
TENASKA INC; Omaha

NEVADA
NV ENERGY INC; Las Vegas
SOUTHWEST GAS CORP; Las Vegas

NEW JERSEY
ATLANTIC CITY ELECTRIC COMPANY; Mays Landing
NEW JERSEY RESOURCES CORPORATION; Wall
NRG ENERGY INC; Princeton
PUBLIC SERVICE ENTERPRISE GROUP (PSEG); Newark

NEW MEXICO
PNM RESOURCES INC; Albuquerque

NEW YORK
CH ENERGY GROUP INC; Poughkeepsie
CONSOLIDATED EDISON INC; New York
GETTY PETROLEUM MARKETING; East Meadow
HESS CORPORATION; New York
LOEWS CORPORATION; New York
LS POWER ASSOCIATES LP; New York
NATIONAL FUEL GAS CO; Williamsville
NEW YORK STATE ELECTRIC & GAS CORP; Binghamton
NIAGARA MOHAWK POWER CORPORATION; Syracuse
RED APPLE GROUP INC; New York
ROCHESTER GAS AND ELECTRIC CORP; Rochester
TRANSAMMONIA INC; New York

NORTH CAROLINA
BLUE RHINO LLC; Winston-Salem
COGENTRIX ENERGY LLC; Charlotte
DUKE ENERGY CORP; Charlotte
PIEDMONT NATURAL GAS COMPANY INC; Charlotte
POWERSECURE INTERNATIONAL INC; Wake Forest
PROGRESS ENERGY INC; Raleigh

NORTH DAKOTA
DAKOTA GASIFICATION COMPANY; Bismarck
MDU RESOURCES GROUP INC; Bismarck

OHIO
AMERICAN ELECTRIC POWER COMPANY INC (AEP); Columbus
DPL INC; Dayton
FIRSTENERGY CORP; Akron
MARATHON PETROLEUM COMPANY LLC; Findlay

OKLAHOMA
ALLIANCE RESOURCE PARTNERS LP; Tulsa
APCO OIL AND GAS INTERNATIONAL INC; Tulsa
CHESAPEAKE ENERGY CORP; Oklahoma City
CHESAPEAKE MIDSTREAM PARTNERS LP; Oklahoma City
CONTINENTAL RESOURCES INC; Enid
DEVON ENERGY CORPORATION; Oklahoma City
ENOGEX LLC; Oklahoma City
HELMERICH & PAYNE INC; Tulsa
MAGELLAN MIDSTREAM PARTNERS LP; Tulsa
MATRIX SERVICE COMPANY; Tulsa
OGE ENERGY CORP; Oklahoma City
ONEOK INC; Tulsa
ONEOK PARTNERS LP; Tulsa
SANDRIDGE ENERGY INC; Oklahoma City
UNIT CORP; Tulsa
WILLIAMS COMPANIES INC (THE); Tulsa

OREGON
PACIFICORP; Portland
PORTLAND GENERAL ELECTRIC COMPANY; Portland

PENNSYLVANIA
ALLEGHENY ENERGY INC; Greensburg
AMERIGAS PARTNERS LP; King of Prussia
ATLAS ENERGY INC; Moon Township
ATLAS ENERGY RESOURCES LLC; Moon Township
CNX GAS CORPORATION; Canonsburg
CONSOL ENERGY INC; Canonsburg
EQT CORPORATION; Pittsburgh
PENN VIRGINIA CORP; Radnor
PPL CORPORATION; Allentown
SUNOCO INC; Philadelphia
SUNOCO LOGISTICS PARTNERS LP; Philadelphia
UGI CORP; King of Prussia
UNITED REFINING COMPANY; Warren
WESTINGHOUSE ELECTRIC COMPANY LLC; Monroeville

SOUTH CAROLINA
SCANA CORPORATION; Columbia

SOUTH DAKOTA
BLACK HILLS CORP; Rapid City
NORTHWESTERN CORPORATION; Sioux Falls

TENNESSEE
TENNESSEE VALLEY AUTHORITY (TVA); Knoxville

TEXAS
ADAMS RESOURCES & ENERGY INC; Houston
ALON USA ENERGY INC; Dallas
ANADARKO PETROLEUM CORPORATION; The Woodlands
APACHE CORP; Houston
ARABIAN AMERICAN DEVELOPMENT CO; Sugarland
ATMOS ENERGY CORPORATION; Dallas
ATWOOD OCEANICS INC; Houston
BAKER HUGHES INC; Houston
BASIC ENERGY SERVICES INC; Midland
BJ SERVICES COMPANY; Houston
BOOTS & COOTS INTERNATIONAL LLC; Houston
BRISTOW GROUP (THE); Houston
CABOT OIL & GAS CORP; Houston
CALPINE CORPORATION; Houston
CAMAC INTERNATIONAL CORP; Houston

CAMERON INTERNATIONAL CORPORATION; Houston
CARBO CERAMICS INC; Houston
CARRIZO OIL & GAS INC; Houston
CENTERPOINT ENERGY INC; Houston
CHENIERE ENERGY INC; Houston
CITGO PETROLEUM CORPORATION; Houston
CLAYTON WILLIAMS ENERGY INC; Midland
CONOCOPHILLIPS COMPANY; Houston
CROSSTEX ENERGY LP; Dallas
DAWSON GEOPHYSICAL COMPANY; Midland
DENBURY RESOURCES INC; Plano
DIAMOND OFFSHORE DRILLING INC; Houston
DORCHESTER MINERALS LP; Dallas
DRIL-QUIP INC; Houston
DUNCAN ENERGY PARTNERS LP; Houston
DYNEGY INC; Houston
EL PASO CORP; Houston
ENBRIDGE ENERGY PARTNERS LP; Houston
ENERGY FUTUREHOLDINGS CORP (TXU); Dallas
ENERGY TRANSFER PARTNERS LP; Dallas
ENGLOBAL CORP; Houston
ENTERPRISE PRODUCTS PARTNERS LP; Houston
EOG RESOURCES INC; Houston
EXCO RESOURCES INC; Dallas
EXTERRAN HOLDINGS INC; Houston
EXXON MOBIL CORPORATION (EXXONMOBIL); Irving
FLUOR CORP; Irving
FRONTIER OIL CORPORATION; Houston
FURMANITE CORP; Richardson
GENESIS ENERGY LP; Houston
GEOKINETICS INC; Houston
GOODRICH PETROLEUM CORP; Houston
GREAT LAKES GAS TRANSMISSION COMPANY; Houston
GULFMARK OFFSHORE INC; Houston
HALLIBURTON COMPANY; Houston
HARVEST NATURAL RESOURCES INC; Houston
HELIX ENERGY SOLUTIONS GROUP INC; Houston
HERCULES OFFSHORE INC; Houston
HOLLY CORP; Dallas
HUNT CONSOLIDATED INC; Dallas
KBR INC; Houston
KEY ENERGY SERVICES INC; Houston
KINDER MORGAN ENERGY PARTNERS LP; Houston
LUFKIN INDUSTRIES INC; Lufkin
MARATHON OIL CORP; Houston
MCDERMOTT INTERNATIONAL INC; Houston
MESA ENERGY HOLDINGS INC; Dallas
MOTIVA ENTERPRISES LLC; Houston
NATIONAL OILWELL VARCO INC; Houston
NEWFIELD EXPLORATION CO; Houston
NEWPARK RESOURCES INC; The Woodlands
NOBLE ENERGY INC; Houston
NUSTAR ENERGY LP; San Antonio
OCEANEERING INTERNATIONAL INC; Houston
OIL STATES INTERNATIONAL INC; Houston
ONCOR ELECTRIC DELIVERY COMPANY; Dallas
PAA NATURAL GAS STORAGE LP; Houston
PARKER DRILLING COMPANY; Houston
PATTERSON-UTI ENERGY INC; Houston
PIONEER NATURAL RESOURCES COMPANY; Irving
PLAINS ALL AMERICAN PIPELINE; Houston
PLAINS EXPLORATION AND PRODUCTION COMPANY; Houston
PRIDE INTERNATIONAL INC; Houston
QUICKSILVER RESOURCES INC; Fort Worth
RANGE RESOURCES CORP; Fort Worth
ROWAN COMPANIES INC; Houston
RRI ENERGY INC; Houston
SCHLUMBERGER LIMITED; Houston
SEITEL INC; Houston
SHELL OIL CO; Houston
SMITH INTERNATIONAL INC; Houston
SOUTHERN UNION COMPANY; Houston
SOUTHWESTERN ENERGY CO; Houston
SPECTRA ENERGY CORP; Houston
SUSSER HOLDINGS CORPORATION; Corpus Christi
SWIFT ENERGY CO; Houston
TARGA RESOURCES PARTNERS LP; Houston
TEAM INC; Alvin
TESCO CORPORATION; Houston
TESORO CORP; San Antonio
TETRA TECHNOLOGIES INC; The Woodlands
TRICO MARINE SERVICES INC; The Woodlands
TRUMAN ARNOLD COMPANIES; Texarkana
ULTRA PETROLEUM CORP; Houston
VAALCO ENERGY INC; Houston
VALERO ENERGY CORP; San Antonio
W&T OFFSHORE INC; Houston
WILLBROS GROUP INC; Houston
XTO ENERGY INC; Fort Worth

UTAH

HEADWATERS INC; South Jordan
QUESTAR CORPORATION; Salt Lake City
SINCLAIR OIL CORP; Salt Lake City

VIRGINIA

AES CORPORATION (THE); Arlington
DOMINION RESOURCES INC; Richmond
MASSEY ENERGY COMPANY; Richmond
VIRGINIA ELECTRIC AND POWER COMPANY; Richmond

WASHINGTON

AVISTA CORPORATION; Spokane
ITRON INC; Liberty Lake
PUGET HOLDINGS LLC; Bellevue

WISCONSIN

ALLIANT ENERGY CORP; Madison
JOY GLOBAL INC; Milwaukee
US VENTURE INC; Appleton
WISCONSIN ENERGY CORP; Milwaukee

WYOMING

CLOUD PEAK ENERGY INC; Gillette

INDEX OF NON-U.S. HEADQUARTERS LOCATION BY COUNTRY

POWER FINANCE CORPORATION LIMITED; New Delhi
POWER GRID CORPORATION OF INDIA LTD; Gurgaon
RELIANCE INDUSTRIES LTD (RELIANCE GROUP); Mumbai
RELIANCE INFRASTRUCTURE LTD; Mumbai
RELIANCE PETROLEUM LTD; Mumbai
RELIANCE POWER LIMITED; Navi Mumbai
TATA POWER; Mumbai

INDONESIA
PT PERTAMINA (PERSERO); Jakarta

IRELAND
COOPER INDUSTRIES PLC; Dublin

ITALY
ENEL SPA; Rome
ENI SPA; Rome
SAIPEM SPA; Milan
SNAM RETE GAS SPA; Milan

JAPAN
CHUBU ELECTRIC POWER CO INC; Nagoya
COSMO OIL CO LTD; Tokyo
IDEMITSU KOSAN CO LTD; Tokyo
INPEX CORPORATION; Tokyo
JX HOLDINGS INC; Tokyo
JX NIPPON MINING & METALS CORPORATION; Tokyo
KANSAI ELECTRIC POWER COMPANY INC; Osaka
MITSUBISHI CHEMICAL HOLDINGS CORPORATION; Tokyo
MITSUBISHI CORP; Tokyo
MITSUI OSK LINES LTD; Tokyo
OSAKA GAS CO LTD; Osaka
SHIKOKU ELECTRIC POWER COMPANY INC; Takamatsu
SHOWA SHELL SEKIYU KK; Tokyo
TOHOKU ELECTRIC POWER CO INC; Miyagi
TOKYO ELECTRIC POWER COMPANY INC (THE); Tokyo
TOKYO GAS CO LTD; Tokyo
TONENGENERAL SEKIYU KK; Tokyo

KOREA
GS CALTEX CORP; Seoul
GS HOLDINGS CORP; Seoul
KOREA ELECTRIC POWER CORPORATION; Seoul
KOREA GAS CORPORATION; Gyeonggi-do
SK HOLDINGS CO LTD; Seoul
S-OIL CORPORATION; Seoul

KUWAIT
KUWAIT PETROLEUM CORPORATION; Safat

LUXEMBOURG
TENARIS SA; Luxembourg

MALAYSIA
PETRONAS (PETROLIAM NASIONAL BERHAD); Kuala Lumpur
TENAGA NASIONAL BERHAD (TNB); Kuala Lumpur

MEXICO
PETROLEOS MEXICANOS (PEMEX); Mexico City

NIGERIA
NIGERIAN NATIONAL PETROLEUM CORPORATION; Garki Abuja

NORWAY
BW GAS LIMITED; Oslo
PETROLEUM GEO SERVICES ASA; Lysaker
STATOIL ASA; Stavanger

PAKISTAN
PAKISTAN STATE OIL CO LTD; Karachi

PAPUA NEW GUINEA
OIL SEARCH LTD; Port Moresby

PHILIPPINES
PETRON CORP; Manila

POLAND
POLSKI KONCERN NAFTOWY ORLEN SA (PKN ORLEN GROUP); Plock

PORTUGAL
EDP - ENERGIAS DE PORTUGAL SA; Lisbon
GALP ENERGIA SGPS SA; Lisbon

PUERTO RICO
PUERTO RICO ELECTRIC POWER AUTHORITY; San Juan

QATAR
QATAR PETROLEUM; Doha

RUSSIA
GAZPROM (OAO); Moscow
JSC GAZPROM NEFT; Moscow
LUKOIL (OAO); Moscow
NOVATEK OAO; Yamalo-Nenets
OAO TATNEFT; Tatarstan
ROSNEFT (OAO); Moscow
SURGUTNEFTEGAS (OJSC); Tyumenskaya
TNK-BP; Moscow

SAUDI ARABIA
SAUDI ARAMCO (SAUDI ARABIAN OIL CO); Dhahran

SINGAPORE
SEMBCORP INDUSTRIES LTD; Singapore

SPAIN
COMPANIA ESPANOLA DE PETROLEOS SA (CEPSA); Madrid
ENDESA SA; Madrid
GAS NATURAL SDG SA; Barcelona
IBERDROLA SA; Bilbao
REPSOL YPF SA; Madrid
SCOTTISHPOWER UK PLC; Bilbao

SRI LANKA
CEYLON PETROLEUM CORP (CPC); Colombo

SWEDEN
VATTENFALL AB; Stockholm

SWITZERLAND
ABB LTD; Zurich
ADDAX PETROLEUM INC; Geneva
FOSTER WHEELER AG; Geneva
NOBLE CORPORATION; Baar
TRANSOCEAN INC; Vernier
WEATHERFORD INTERNATIONAL LTD; Geneva
XSTRATA PLC; Zug

TAIWAN
FORMOSA PETROCHEMICAL CORP (FPCC); Taipei

THAILAND
BANGCHAK PETROLEUM PCL (THE); Bangkok
ELECTRICITY GENERATING AUTHORITY OF THAILAND; Bang Kruai
GLOW ENERGY PCL; Bangkok
PTT AROMATICS AND REFINING PCL; Bangkok
PTT EXPLORATION AND PRODUCTION PCL; Bangkok
PTT PCL; Bangkok
RATCHABURI ELECTRICITY GENERATING HOLDING PCL; Bangkok
THAI OIL PCL; Bangkok

THE NETHERLANDS
CHICAGO BRIDGE & IRON COMPANY NV; The Hague
LYONDELLBASELL INDUSTRIES; Rotterdam
NEDERLANDSE GASUNIE NV; Groningen

ROYAL DUTCH SHELL (SHELL GROUP); The Hague
ROYAL VOPAK NV; Rotterdam
SHV HOLDINGS NV; Utrecht

UNITED ARAB EMIRATES

ABU DHABI NATIONAL ENERGY COMPANY PJSC (TAQA); Abu Dhabi
ABU DHABI NATIONAL OIL COMPANY; Abu Dhabi

UNITED KINGDOM

ABBOT GROUP LIMITED; Aberdeen
ACERGY SA; London
ANGLO AMERICAN PLC; London
BG GROUP PLC; Reading
BHP BILLITON; London
BP PLC; London
BRITISH ENERGY GROUP PLC; East Kilbride
CENTRICA PLC; Windsor
E.ON UK PLC; Coventry
ENSCO PLC; London
HUNTING PLC; London
JOHN WOOD GROUP PLC; Aberdeen
NATIONAL GRID PLC; London XO
PREMIER OIL PLC; London
RIO TINTO GROUP; London
RWE NPOWER; Swindon
SCOTTISH AND SOUTHERN ENERGY PLC; Perth
SIEMENS METERING SERVICES LTD; Camberley
TOTAL UK LIMITED; Watford
UK COAL PLC; Doncaster
UNITED UTILITIES GROUP PLC; Great Sankey
WESTERNGECO; Gatwick Airport

VENEZUELA

PETROLEOS DE VENEZUELA SA (PDVSA); Caracas

INDEX BY REGIONS OF THE U.S. WHERE THE FIRMS HAVE LOCATIONS

WEST

TESORO CORP
TETRA TECHNOLOGIES INC
TIDEWATER INC
TOKYO ELECTRIC POWER COMPANY INC (THE)
TOTAL SA
TRANSALTA CORP
TRANSCANADA CORP
TRANSMONTAIGNE INC
TRUMAN ARNOLD COMPANIES
UGI CORP
ULTRA PETROLEUM CORP
UNIT CORP
VALERO ENERGY CORP
WEATHERFORD INTERNATIONAL LTD
WESTINGHOUSE ELECTRIC COMPANY LLC
WESTMORELAND COAL CO
WILLIAMS COMPANIES INC (THE)
WORLD FUEL SERVICES CORP
XCEL ENERGY INC
XSTRATA PLC
XTO ENERGY INC

SOUTHWEST

ABBOT GROUP LIMITED
ACERGY SA
ADAMS RESOURCES & ENERGY INC
AES CORPORATION (THE)
AGL RESOURCES INC
ALLIANCE RESOURCE PARTNERS LP
ALON USA ENERGY INC
ALSTOM SA
AMERESCO INC
AMERICAN ELECTRIC POWER COMPANY INC (AEP)
AMERIGAS PARTNERS LP
ANADARKO PETROLEUM CORPORATION
AP MOLLER-MAERSK A/S
APACHE CORP
APCO OIL AND GAS INTERNATIONAL INC
APEX OIL COMPANY INC
ARABIAN AMERICAN DEVELOPMENT CO
ARCH COAL INC
ARCTIC SLOPE REGIONAL CORP
ARIZONA PUBLIC SERVICE COMPANY
ATLAS ENERGY INC
ATMOS ENERGY CORPORATION
ATWOOD OCEANICS INC
BAKER HUGHES INC
BASF SE
BASIC ENERGY SERVICES INC
BECHTEL GROUP INC
BERRY PETROLEUM CO
BG GROUP PLC
BHP BILLITON
BJ SERVICES COMPANY
BLACK & VEATCH HOLDING COMPANY
BLACK HILLS CORP
BLUE RHINO LLC
BOLT TECHNOLOGY CORP
BOOTS & COOTS INTERNATIONAL LLC
BP PLC
BRASKEM SA
BREITBURN ENERGY PARTNERS LP
BRISTOW GROUP (THE)
CABOT OIL & GAS CORP
CALLON PETROLEUM COMPANY
CALPINE CORPORATION
CAMAC INTERNATIONAL CORP
CAMERON INTERNATIONAL CORPORATION
CARBO CERAMICS INC
CARRIZO OIL & GAS INC
CENTERPOINT ENERGY INC
CENTRICA PLC
CGGVERITAS
CHENIERE ENERGY INC
CHESAPEAKE ENERGY CORP
CHESAPEAKE MIDSTREAM PARTNERS LP
CHEVRON CORPORATION
CHICAGO BRIDGE & IRON COMPANY NV
CIMAREX ENERGY CO
CITGO PETROLEUM CORPORATION
CLAYTON WILLIAMS ENERGY INC
COLONIAL GROUP INC
CONOCOPHILLIPS COMPANY
CONSTELLATION ENERGY GROUP
CONTINENTAL RESOURCES INC
COOPER INDUSTRIES PLC
CROSSTEX ENERGY LP
DAWSON GEOPHYSICAL COMPANY
DCP MIDSTREAM LLC
DENBURY RESOURCES INC
DEVON ENERGY CORPORATION
DIAMOND OFFSHORE DRILLING INC
DIRECT ENERGY
DOMINION RESOURCES INC
DORCHESTER MINERALS LP
DOW CHEMICAL COMPANY (THE)
DRIL-QUIP INC
DUNCAN ENERGY PARTNERS LP
DYNEGY INC
EDISON INTERNATIONAL
EDISON MISSION GROUP
EL PASO CORP
ELSTER GROUP SE
ENBRIDGE ENERGY PARTNERS LP
ENBRIDGE INC
ENCANA CORP
ENERGY FUTUREHOLDINGS CORP (TXU)
ENERGY PARTNERS LTD
ENERGY TRANSFER PARTNERS LP
ENGLOBAL CORP
ENI SPA
ENOGEX LLC
ENSCO PLC
ENSIGN ENERGY SERVICES INC
ENTERGY CORP
ENTERPRISE PRODUCTS PARTNERS LP
EOG RESOURCES INC
ERGON INC
ESSAR GROUP LTD
EXCO RESOURCES INC
EXELON CORPORATION
EXTERRAN HOLDINGS INC
EXXON MOBIL CORPORATION (EXXONMOBIL)
FERRELLGAS PARTNERS LP
FLINT ENERGY SERVICES LTD
FLUOR CORP
FOREST OIL CORPORATION
FOSTER WHEELER AG
FRONTIER OIL CORPORATION
FURMANITE CORP
GDF SUEZ SA
GE ENERGY INFRASTRUCTURE
GENESIS ENERGY LP
GEOKINETICS INC
GLOBAL INDUSTRIES LTD
GOODRICH PETROLEUM CORP
GULFMARK OFFSHORE INC
HALLIBURTON COMPANY
HARVEST NATURAL RESOURCES INC
HEADWATERS INC
HELIX ENERGY SOLUTIONS GROUP INC
HELMERICH & PAYNE INC
HERCULES OFFSHORE INC
HESS CORPORATION
HOLLY CORP
HUNT CONSOLIDATED INC
HUNTING PLC
IBERDROLA SA
INERGY LP
INPEX CORPORATION
INTEGRYS ENERGY GROUP INC
JOHN WOOD GROUP PLC
KBR INC
KEY ENERGY SERVICES INC
KINDER MORGAN ENERGY PARTNERS LP
KOCH INDUSTRIES INC
KUWAIT PETROLEUM CORPORATION
LACLEDE GROUP INC (THE)
LAYNE CHRISTENSEN COMPANY
LOEWS CORPORATION
LS POWER ASSOCIATES LP
LUFKIN INDUSTRIES INC
LYONDELLBASELL INDUSTRIES
MAGELLAN MIDSTREAM PARTNERS LP
MARATHON OIL CORP
MARATHON PETROLEUM COMPANY LLC
MATRIX SERVICE COMPANY
MCDERMOTT INTERNATIONAL INC
MCMORAN EXPLORATION CO
MDU RESOURCES GROUP INC
MESA ENERGY HOLDINGS INC

MIDAMERICAN ENERGY HOLDINGS CO
MIRANT CORP
MITSUI OSK LINES LTD
MOTIVA ENTERPRISES LLC
MURPHY OIL CORPORATION
NABORS INDUSTRIES LTD
NATIONAL FUEL GAS CO
NATIONAL OILWELL VARCO INC
NEWFIELD EXPLORATION CO
NEWPARK RESOURCES INC
NEXEN INC
NEXTERA ENERGY INC
NISOURCE INC
NOBLE CORPORATION
NOBLE ENERGY INC
NRG ENERGY INC
NUSTAR ENERGY LP
OCCIDENTAL PETROLEUM CORP
OCEANEERING INTERNATIONAL INC
OGE ENERGY CORP
OIL STATES INTERNATIONAL INC
ONCOR ELECTRIC DELIVERY COMPANY
ONEOK INC
ONEOK PARTNERS LP
OXBOW CORPORATION
PAA NATURAL GAS STORAGE LP
PARKER DRILLING COMPANY
PATTERSON-UTI ENERGY INC
PENN VIRGINIA CORP
PETROLEO BRASILEIRO SA (PETROBRAS)
PETROLEOS DE VENEZUELA SA (PDVSA)
PETROLEOS MEXICANOS (PEMEX)
PETROLEUM GEO SERVICES ASA
PETROQUEST ENERGY INC
PHI INC
PINNACLE WEST CAPITAL CORPORATION
PIONEER NATURAL RESOURCES COMPANY
PLAINS ALL AMERICAN PIPELINE
PLAINS EXPLORATION AND PRODUCTION COMPANY
PNM RESOURCES INC
POWERSECURE INTERNATIONAL INC
PRECISION DRILLING CORPORATION
PRIDE INTERNATIONAL INC
PRIMEENERGY CORPORATION
QUESTAR CORPORATION
QUICKSILVER RESOURCES INC
RANGE RESOURCES CORP
ROWAN COMPANIES INC
ROYAL DUTCH SHELL (SHELL GROUP)
ROYAL VOPAK NV
RPC INC
RWE AG
SAIPEM SPA
SANDRIDGE ENERGY INC
SAUDI ARAMCO (SAUDI ARABIAN OIL CO)
SCHLUMBERGER LIMITED
SEACOR HOLDINGS INC
SEADRILL LIMITED
SEITEL INC
SEMPRA ENERGY
SHAW GROUP INC (THE)
SHELL OIL CO
SIEMENS AG
SINCLAIR OIL CORP
SK HOLDINGS CO LTD
SM ENERGY COMPANY
SMF ENERGY CORPORATION
SMITH INTERNATIONAL INC
SOUTHERN CALIFORNIA EDISON COMPANY
SOUTHERN UNION COMPANY
SOUTHWEST GAS CORP
SOUTHWESTERN ENERGY CO
SPECTRA ENERGY CORP
STATOIL ASA
STONE ENERGY CORPORATION
SUNOCO INC
SUNOCO LOGISTICS PARTNERS LP
SUPERIOR ENERGY SERVICES INC
SUSSER HOLDINGS CORPORATION
SWIFT ENERGY CO
TALISMAN ENERGY INC
TARGA RESOURCES PARTNERS LP
TEAM INC
TECHNIP
TENARIS SA
TENASKA INC
TESCO CORPORATION
TESORO CORP
TETRA TECHNOLOGIES INC
TEXAS GAS TRANSMISSION LLC
TIDEWATER INC
TOTAL SA
TRANSALTA CORP
TRANSAMMONIA INC
TRANSMONTAIGNE INC
TRANSOCEAN INC
TRICO MARINE SERVICES INC
TRUMAN ARNOLD COMPANIES
TSAKOS ENERGY NAVIGATION LTD
UGI CORP
ULTRA PETROLEUM CORP
UNISOURCE ENERGY CORPORATION
UNIT CORP
VAALCO ENERGY INC
VALERO ENERGY CORP
W&T OFFSHORE INC
WEATHERFORD INTERNATIONAL LTD
WESTAR ENERGY
WESTERNGECO
WESTINGHOUSE ELECTRIC COMPANY LLC
WESTMORELAND COAL CO
WILLBROS GROUP INC
WILLIAMS COMPANIES INC (THE)
WOODSIDE PETROLEUM LTD
WORLD FUEL SERVICES CORP
XCEL ENERGY INC
XTO ENERGY INC

MIDWEST

ABU DHABI NATIONAL ENERGY COMPANY PJSC (TAQA)
AES CORPORATION (THE)
ALLIANCE RESOURCE PARTNERS LP
ALLIANT ENERGY CORP
AMEREN CORP
AMEREN ILLINOIS COMPANY
AMERESCO INC
AMERICAN ELECTRIC POWER COMPANY INC (AEP)
AMERIGAS PARTNERS LP
AP MOLLER-MAERSK A/S
APEX OIL COMPANY INC
ARCH COAL INC
ARCTIC SLOPE REGIONAL CORP
ATLAS ENERGY INC
ATLAS ENERGY RESOURCES LLC
ATMOS ENERGY CORPORATION
AVISTA CORPORATION
BAKER HUGHES INC
BASF SE
BASIC ENERGY SERVICES INC
BECHTEL GROUP INC
BJ SERVICES COMPANY
BLACK & VEATCH HOLDING COMPANY
BLACK HILLS CORP
BLUE RHINO LLC
BP PLC
BREITBURN ENERGY PARTNERS LP
CABOT OIL & GAS CORP
CALPINE CORPORATION
CAMECO CORPORATION
CAMERON INTERNATIONAL CORPORATION
CENTER OIL COMPANY
CENTERPOINT ENERGY INC
CHESAPEAKE ENERGY CORP
CHEVRON CORPORATION
CHICAGO BRIDGE & IRON COMPANY NV
CIMAREX ENERGY CO
CITGO PETROLEUM CORPORATION
CMS ENERGY CORP
CNX GAS CORPORATION
COGENTRIX ENERGY LLC
COMMONWEALTH EDISON COMPANY
CONOCOPHILLIPS COMPANY
CONSTELLATION ENERGY GROUP
CONSUMERS ENERGY COMPANY
CONTINENTAL RESOURCES INC
COOPER INDUSTRIES PLC
DAKOTA GASIFICATION COMPANY
DAWSON GEOPHYSICAL COMPANY
DCP MIDSTREAM LLC
DETROIT EDISON COMPANY (THE)
DIRECT ENERGY
DOMINION RESOURCES INC

DOW CHEMICAL COMPANY (THE)
DPL INC
DTE ENERGY COMPANY
DUKE ENERGY CORP
DYNEGY INC
E.ON AG
EDISON INTERNATIONAL
EDISON MISSION GROUP
EDP - ENERGIAS DE PORTUGAL SA
EL PASO CORP
ELSTER GROUP SE
ENBRIDGE ENERGY PARTNERS LP
ENBRIDGE INC
ENCANA CORP
ENERGY TRANSFER PARTNERS LP
ENGLOBAL CORP
ENTERPRISE PRODUCTS PARTNERS LP
EOG RESOURCES INC
EQT CORPORATION
ERGON INC
EXCO RESOURCES INC
EXELON CORPORATION
EXTERRAN HOLDINGS INC
EXXON MOBIL CORPORATION (EXXONMOBIL)
FERRELLGAS PARTNERS LP
FIRSTENERGY CORP
FLINT ENERGY SERVICES LTD
FLUOR CORP
FOSTER WHEELER AG
FRONTIER OIL CORPORATION
FUEL TECH INC
FURMANITE CORP
GE ENERGY INFRASTRUCTURE
GREAT LAKES GAS TRANSMISSION COMPANY
GREAT PLAINS ENERGY INC
HEADWATERS INC
HELMERICH & PAYNE INC
HESS CORPORATION
IDEMITSU KOSAN CO LTD
INERGY LP
INTEGRYS ENERGY GROUP INC
ITC HOLDINGS CORP
ITRON INC
JOHN WOOD GROUP PLC
JOY GLOBAL INC
KEY ENERGY SERVICES INC
KINDER MORGAN ENERGY PARTNERS LP
KOCH INDUSTRIES INC
LACLEDE GROUP INC (THE)
LAYNE CHRISTENSEN COMPANY
LOEWS CORPORATION
LS POWER ASSOCIATES LP
LYONDELLBASELL INDUSTRIES
MAGELLAN MIDSTREAM PARTNERS LP
MARATHON OIL CORP
MARATHON PETROLEUM COMPANY LLC
MATRIX SERVICE COMPANY
MCDERMOTT INTERNATIONAL INC
MDU RESOURCES GROUP INC
MICHIGAN CONSOLIDATED GAS COMPANY
MIDAMERICAN ENERGY HOLDINGS CO
MIRANT CORP
MITSUI OSK LINES LTD
MURPHY OIL CORPORATION
NABORS INDUSTRIES LTD
NATIONAL OILWELL VARCO INC
NEXTERA ENERGY INC
NICOR INC
NISOURCE INC
NOBLE ENERGY INC
NORTHERN INDIANA PUBLIC SERVICE COMPANY
NORTHWESTERN CORPORATION
NRG ENERGY INC
NUSTAR ENERGY LP
OCCIDENTAL PETROLEUM CORP
OIL STATES INTERNATIONAL INC
ONEOK INC
ONEOK PARTNERS LP
OXBOW CORPORATION
PAA NATURAL GAS STORAGE LP
PATTERSON-UTI ENERGY INC
PEABODY ENERGY CORP
PHI INC
PIONEER NATURAL RESOURCES COMPANY
PLAINS ALL AMERICAN PIPELINE
PPL CORPORATION
PRIMEENERGY CORPORATION
PUBLIC SERVICE ENTERPRISE GROUP (PSEG)
QUESTAR CORPORATION
RHINO RESOURCE PARTNERS
ROYAL DUTCH SHELL (SHELL GROUP)
RRI ENERGY INC
RWE AG
SCHLUMBERGER LIMITED
SEACOR HOLDINGS INC
SHAW GROUP INC (THE)
SHELL OIL CO
SIEMENS AG
SINCLAIR OIL CORP
SMITH INTERNATIONAL INC
SOUTHERN UNION COMPANY
SUNOCO INC
SUNOCO LOGISTICS PARTNERS LP
TARGA RESOURCES PARTNERS LP
TEAM INC
TECO ENERGY INC
TENARIS SA
TENASKA INC
TESORO CORP
TEXAS GAS TRANSMISSION LLC
TRANSAMMONIA INC
TRANSMONTAIGNE INC
TRUMAN ARNOLD COMPANIES
UGI CORP
UNITED REFINING COMPANY
US VENTURE INC
USEC INC
VALERO ENERGY CORP
VECTREN CORPORATION
WEATHERFORD INTERNATIONAL LTD
WESTAR ENERGY
WESTINGHOUSE ELECTRIC COMPANY LLC
WESTMORELAND COAL CO
WILLBROS GROUP INC
WILLIAMS COMPANIES INC (THE)
WISCONSIN ENERGY CORP
XCEL ENERGY INC
XTO ENERGY INC

SOUTHEAST

ADAMS RESOURCES & ENERGY INC
AES CORPORATION (THE)
AGL RESOURCES INC
ALABAMA POWER COMPANY
ALON USA ENERGY INC
AMERESCO INC
AMERICAN ELECTRIC POWER COMPANY INC (AEP)
AMERIGAS PARTNERS LP
ANADARKO PETROLEUM CORPORATION
AP MOLLER-MAERSK A/S
APACHE CORP
APEX OIL COMPANY INC
ARCTIC SLOPE REGIONAL CORP
ATLAS ENERGY INC
ATLAS ENERGY RESOURCES LLC
ATMOS ENERGY CORPORATION
BAKER HUGHES INC
BASF SE
BASIC ENERGY SERVICES INC
BECHTEL GROUP INC
BG GROUP PLC
BJ SERVICES COMPANY
BLACK & VEATCH HOLDING COMPANY
BLACK HILLS CORP
BLUE RHINO LLC
BOOTS & COOTS INTERNATIONAL LLC
BREITBURN ENERGY PARTNERS LP
BRISTOW GROUP (THE)
CABOT OIL & GAS CORP
CALLON PETROLEUM COMPANY
CALPINE CORPORATION
CAMERON INTERNATIONAL CORPORATION
CARBO CERAMICS INC
CARRIZO OIL & GAS INC
CENTERPOINT ENERGY INC
CENTRICA PLC
CHENIERE ENERGY INC
CHESAPEAKE ENERGY CORP
CHEVRON CORPORATION
CHICAGO BRIDGE & IRON COMPANY NV
CIMAREX ENERGY CO
CITGO PETROLEUM CORPORATION
CLAYTON WILLIAMS ENERGY INC
COGENTRIX ENERGY LLC
COLONIAL GROUP INC

CONOCOPHILLIPS COMPANY
CONSTELLATION ENERGY GROUP
CONTINENTAL RESOURCES INC
COOPER INDUSTRIES PLC
CROWN CENTRAL PETROLEUM LLC
DCP MIDSTREAM LLC
DENBURY RESOURCES INC
DIAMOND OFFSHORE DRILLING INC
DIRECT ENERGY
DOMINION RESOURCES INC
DOW CHEMICAL COMPANY (THE)
DRIL-QUIP INC
DRUMMOND COMPANY INC
DUKE ENERGY CORP
DUNCAN ENERGY PARTNERS LP
DYNEGY INC
EDISON INTERNATIONAL
EL PASO CORP
ELSTER GROUP SE
ENBRIDGE ENERGY PARTNERS LP
ENBRIDGE INC
ENCANA CORP
ENERGY PARTNERS LTD
ENGLOBAL CORP
ENSCO PLC
ENTERGY CORP
ENTERPRISE PRODUCTS PARTNERS LP
EOG RESOURCES INC
EQT CORPORATION
ERGON INC
EXCO RESOURCES INC
EXTERRAN HOLDINGS INC
EXXON MOBIL CORPORATION (EXXONMOBIL)
FERRELLGAS PARTNERS LP
FLUOR CORP
FOREST OIL CORPORATION
FOSTER WHEELER AG
FURMANITE CORP
GE ENERGY INFRASTRUCTURE
GENESIS ENERGY LP
GEORGIA POWER COMPANY
GLOBAL INDUSTRIES LTD
GOODRICH PETROLEUM CORP
GULFMARK OFFSHORE INC
HALLIBURTON COMPANY
HEADWATERS INC
HELIX ENERGY SOLUTIONS GROUP INC
HELMERICH & PAYNE INC
HERCULES OFFSHORE INC
HESS CORPORATION
HUNT CONSOLIDATED INC
INERGY LP
INTEGRYS ENERGY GROUP INC
JOHN WOOD GROUP PLC
KBR INC
KEY ENERGY SERVICES INC
KINDER MORGAN ENERGY PARTNERS LP
KOCH INDUSTRIES INC
LAYNE CHRISTENSEN COMPANY
LOEWS CORPORATION
LS POWER ASSOCIATES LP
LYONDELLBASELL INDUSTRIES
MAGELLAN MIDSTREAM PARTNERS LP
MARATHON OIL CORP
MARATHON PETROLEUM COMPANY LLC
MCDERMOTT INTERNATIONAL INC
MCMORAN EXPLORATION CO
MDU RESOURCES GROUP INC
MIDAMERICAN ENERGY HOLDINGS CO
MIRANT CORP
MITSUI OSK LINES LTD
MOTIVA ENTERPRISES LLC
MURPHY OIL CORPORATION
NABORS INDUSTRIES LTD
NATIONAL FUEL GAS CO
NATIONAL OILWELL VARCO INC
NEWPARK RESOURCES INC
NEXTERA ENERGY INC
NICOR INC
NISOURCE INC
NOBLE CORPORATION
NRG ENERGY INC
NUSTAR ENERGY LP
OCCIDENTAL PETROLEUM CORP
OCEANEERING INTERNATIONAL INC
OGE ENERGY CORP
OIL STATES INTERNATIONAL INC
OXBOW CORPORATION
PAA NATURAL GAS STORAGE LP
PARKER DRILLING COMPANY
PATTERSON-UTI ENERGY INC
PENN VIRGINIA CORP
PETROQUEST ENERGY INC
PHI INC
PIEDMONT NATURAL GAS COMPANY INC
PLAINS ALL AMERICAN PIPELINE
PLAINS EXPLORATION AND PRODUCTION COMPANY
POWERSECURE INTERNATIONAL INC
PRIDE INTERNATIONAL INC
PRIMEENERGY CORPORATION
QUESTAR CORPORATION
RANGE RESOURCES CORP
ROWAN COMPANIES INC
ROYAL DUTCH SHELL (SHELL GROUP)
ROYAL VOPAK NV
RPC INC
RRI ENERGY INC
RWE AG
SEACOR HOLDINGS INC
SEITEL INC
SEMPRA ENERGY
SHAW GROUP INC (THE)
SHELL OIL CO
SIEMENS AG
SM ENERGY COMPANY
SMF ENERGY CORPORATION
SMITH INTERNATIONAL INC
SOUTHERN COMPANY (THE)
SOUTHERN UNION COMPANY
SOUTHWESTERN ENERGY CO
STONE ENERGY CORPORATION
SUBSEA 7 INC
SUNOCO INC
SUPERIOR ENERGY SERVICES INC
SWIFT ENERGY CO
TAMPA ELECTRIC COMPANY
TARGA RESOURCES PARTNERS LP
TEAM INC
TECHNIP
TECO ENERGY INC
TENARIS SA
TENNESSEE VALLEY AUTHORITY (TVA)
TETRA TECHNOLOGIES INC
TEXAS GAS TRANSMISSION LLC
TIDEWATER INC
TRANSAMMONIA INC
TRANSMONTAIGNE INC
TRUMAN ARNOLD COMPANIES
UGI CORP
UNIT CORP
UNITED REFINING COMPANY
USEC INC
VALERO ENERGY CORP
W&T OFFSHORE INC
WEATHERFORD INTERNATIONAL LTD
WESTINGHOUSE ELECTRIC COMPANY LLC
WILLBROS GROUP INC
WILLIAMS COMPANIES INC (THE)
WOODSIDE PETROLEUM LTD
WORLD FUEL SERVICES CORP
XTO ENERGY INC

NORTHEAST

ABB LTD
AEGEAN MARINE PETROLEUM NETWORK INC
AES CORPORATION (THE)
AGL RESOURCES INC
ALLEGHENY ENERGY INC
ALLIANCE RESOURCE PARTNERS LP
ALSTOM SA
AMERESCO INC
AMERICAN ELECTRIC POWER COMPANY INC (AEP)
AMERIGAS PARTNERS LP
AP MOLLER-MAERSK A/S
APEX OIL COMPANY INC
ARCH COAL INC
ARCTIC SLOPE REGIONAL CORP
AREVA GROUP
ATLANTIC CITY ELECTRIC COMPANY
ATLAS ENERGY INC
ATLAS ENERGY RESOURCES LLC
ATMOS ENERGY CORPORATION
ATOMIC ENERGY OF CANADA LIMITED
BAKER HUGHES INC

BALTIMORE GAS AND ELECTRIC COMPANY
BANGOR HYDRO-ELECTRIC COMPANY
BASF SE
BECHTEL GROUP INC
BG GROUP PLC
BHP BILLITON
BJ SERVICES COMPANY
BLACK & VEATCH HOLDING COMPANY
BLUE RHINO LLC
BOLT TECHNOLOGY CORP
BP PLC
CABOT OIL & GAS CORP
CALPINE CORPORATION
CAMERON INTERNATIONAL CORPORATION
CARRIZO OIL & GAS INC
CENTER OIL COMPANY
CENTRICA PLC
CH ENERGY GROUP INC
CHESAPEAKE ENERGY CORP
CHEVRON CORPORATION
CHICAGO BRIDGE & IRON COMPANY NV
CHINA PETROLEUM & CHEMICAL (SINOPEC)
CHUBU ELECTRIC POWER CO INC
CITGO PETROLEUM CORPORATION
CMS ENERGY CORP
CNX GAS CORPORATION
COGENTRIX ENERGY LLC
COLONIAL GROUP INC
CONOCOPHILLIPS COMPANY
CONSOL ENERGY INC
CONSOLIDATED EDISON INC
CONSTELLATION ENERGY GROUP
COOPER INDUSTRIES PLC
CROWN CENTRAL PETROLEUM LLC
DAWSON GEOPHYSICAL COMPANY
DCP MIDSTREAM LLC
DELMARVA POWER AND LIGHT COMPANY
DIRECT ENERGY
DOMINION RESOURCES INC
DOW CHEMICAL COMPANY (THE)
DPL INC
DYNEGY INC
E.ON US LLC
EDISON INTERNATIONAL
EDISON MISSION GROUP
EL PASO CORP
ELECTRICITE DE FRANCE SA (EDF)
ELSTER GROUP SE
EMERA INC
ENBRIDGE ENERGY PARTNERS LP
ENBRIDGE INC
ENCANA CORP
ENERGY TRANSFER PARTNERS LP
ENGLOBAL CORP
ENI SPA
EOG RESOURCES INC
EPCOR UTILITIES INC
EQT CORPORATION
ERGON INC
ESSAR GROUP LTD
EXCO RESOURCES INC
EXELON CORPORATION
EXTERRAN HOLDINGS INC
EXXON MOBIL CORPORATION (EXXONMOBIL)
FERRELLGAS PARTNERS LP
FIRSTENERGY CORP
FLUOR CORP
FOSTER WHEELER AG
FUEL TECH INC
FURMANITE CORP
GAZ METRO
GDF SUEZ SA
GE ENERGY INFRASTRUCTURE
GETTY PETROLEUM MARKETING
GLOBAL PARTNERS LP
GULF OIL LIMITED PARTNERSHIP
GULFMARK OFFSHORE INC
HEADWATERS INC
HESS CORPORATION
HUNT CONSOLIDATED INC
HYDRO-QUEBEC
IBERDROLA SA
IDEMITSU KOSAN CO LTD
INERGY LP
INTEGRYS ENERGY GROUP INC
ITRON INC
JOHN WOOD GROUP PLC
KBR INC
KEY ENERGY SERVICES INC
KINDER MORGAN ENERGY PARTNERS LP
KOCH INDUSTRIES INC
LAYNE CHRISTENSEN COMPANY
LOEWS CORPORATION
LS POWER ASSOCIATES LP
LUFKIN INDUSTRIES INC
LUKOIL (OAO)
LYONDELLBASELL INDUSTRIES
MAGELLAN MIDSTREAM PARTNERS LP
MARATHON OIL CORP
MARATHON PETROLEUM COMPANY LLC
MASSEY ENERGY COMPANY
MATRIX SERVICE COMPANY
MCDERMOTT INTERNATIONAL INC
MDU RESOURCES GROUP INC
MESA ENERGY HOLDINGS INC
MIDAMERICAN ENERGY HOLDINGS CO
MIRANT CORP
MITSUBISHI CHEMICAL HOLDINGS CORPORATION
MITSUI OSK LINES LTD
MOTIVA ENTERPRISES LLC
MURPHY OIL CORPORATION
NATIONAL FUEL GAS CO
NATIONAL GRID PLC
NATIONAL GRID USA
NATIONAL OILWELL VARCO INC
NEW JERSEY RESOURCES CORPORATION
NEW YORK STATE ELECTRIC & GAS CORP
NEXTERA ENERGY INC
NIAGARA MOHAWK POWER CORPORATION
NISOURCE INC
NORTHEAST UTILITIES
NRG ENERGY INC
NSTAR
NUSTAR ENERGY LP
OCCIDENTAL PETROLEUM CORP
OCEANEERING INTERNATIONAL INC
OXBOW CORPORATION
PATTERSON-UTI ENERGY INC
PENN VIRGINIA CORP
PEPCO HOLDINGS INC
PETROLEO BRASILEIRO SA (PETROBRAS)
PETROLEOS DE VENEZUELA SA (PDVSA)
PETROLEUM DEVELOPMENT CORPORATION
PG&E CORPORATION
PHI INC
PIEDMONT NATURAL GAS COMPANY INC
PLAINS ALL AMERICAN PIPELINE
POWERSECURE INTERNATIONAL INC
PPL CORPORATION
PRIMEENERGY CORPORATION
PROGRESS ENERGY INC
PUBLIC SERVICE ENTERPRISE GROUP (PSEG)
RANGE RESOURCES CORP
RED APPLE GROUP INC
RHINO RESOURCE PARTNERS
ROCHESTER GAS AND ELECTRIC CORP
ROYAL DUTCH SHELL (SHELL GROUP)
ROYAL VOPAK NV
RPC INC
RRI ENERGY INC
RWE AG
SAUDI ARAMCO (SAUDI ARABIAN OIL CO)
SCANA CORPORATION
SCHLUMBERGER LIMITED
SEACOR HOLDINGS INC
SHAW GROUP INC (THE)
SHELL OIL CO
SIEMENS AG
SK HOLDINGS CO LTD
SMF ENERGY CORPORATION
SMITH INTERNATIONAL INC
SONATRACH
SOUTHERN UNION COMPANY
SPECTRA ENERGY CORP
STATOIL ASA
STONE ENERGY CORPORATION
SUNOCO INC
SUNOCO LOGISTICS PARTNERS LP
SUPERIOR ENERGY SERVICES INC

INDEX OF FIRMS WITH INTERNATIONAL OPERATIONS

ELECTRICITE DE FRANCE SA (EDF)
ELECTRICITY GENERATING AUTHORITY OF THAILAND
ELETROBRAS PARTICIPACOES SA
ELETROPAULO METROPOLITANA ELECTRICIDADE DE SAO PAULO SA
ELSTER GROUP SE
EMERA INC
ENBRIDGE ENERGY PARTNERS LP
ENBRIDGE INC
ENCANA CORP
ENDESA SA
ENEL SPA
ENERCON GMBH
ENGLOBAL CORP
ENI SPA
ENSCO PLC
ENSIGN ENERGY SERVICES INC
EOG RESOURCES INC
EPCOR UTILITIES INC
ERGON INC
ESSAR GROUP LTD
EVONIK INDUSTRIES AG
EXTERRAN HOLDINGS INC
EXXON MOBIL CORPORATION (EXXONMOBIL)
FERRELLGAS PARTNERS LP
FLINT ENERGY SERVICES LTD
FLUOR CORP
FOREST OIL CORPORATION
FORMOSA PETROCHEMICAL CORP (FPCC)
FORTUM COMPANY
FOSTER WHEELER AG
FRONTLINE LTD
FUEL TECH INC
FURMANITE CORP
GAIL (INDIA) LIMITED
GALP ENERGIA SGPS SA
GAS NATURAL SDG SA
GAZ METRO
GAZPROM (OAO)
GDF SUEZ SA
GE ENERGY INFRASTRUCTURE
GEOKINETICS INC
GLOBAL INDUSTRIES LTD
GLOW ENERGY PCL
GREAT LAKES GAS TRANSMISSION COMPANY
GS CALTEX CORP
GS HOLDINGS CORP
GULFMARK OFFSHORE INC
HALLIBURTON COMPANY
HARVEST NATURAL RESOURCES INC
HEADWATERS INC
HELIX ENERGY SOLUTIONS GROUP INC
HELLENIC PETROLEUM SA
HELMERICH & PAYNE INC
HERCULES OFFSHORE INC
HESS CORPORATION
HINDUSTAN PETROLEUM CORPORATION LTD
HONG KONG AND CHINA GAS CO LTD (THE)
HONGKONG ELECTRIC HOLDINGS LIMITED
HUNT CONSOLIDATED INC
HUNTING PLC
HUSKY ENERGY INC
HYDRO ONE INC
HYDRO-QUEBEC
IBERDROLA SA
IDEMITSU KOSAN CO LTD
IMPERIAL OIL LIMITED
INDIAN OIL CORP LTD
INPEX CORPORATION
INTEGRYS ENERGY GROUP INC
ITRON INC
JOHN WOOD GROUP PLC
JOY GLOBAL INC
JSC GAZPROM NEFT
JX HOLDINGS INC
JX NIPPON MINING & METALS CORPORATION
KANSAI ELECTRIC POWER COMPANY INC
KBR INC
KOCH INDUSTRIES INC
KOCHI REFINERIES LTD
KOREA ELECTRIC POWER CORPORATION
KOREA GAS CORPORATION
KUWAIT PETROLEUM CORPORATION
LAYNE CHRISTENSEN COMPANY
LIGHT SA
LOEWS CORPORATION
LUFKIN INDUSTRIES INC
LUKOIL (OAO)
LYONDELLBASELL INDUSTRIES
MANITOBA HYDRO-ELECTRIC
MARATHON OIL CORP
MATRIX SERVICE COMPANY
MCDERMOTT INTERNATIONAL INC
MDU RESOURCES GROUP INC
METROGAS SA
MIDAMERICAN ENERGY HOLDINGS CO
MITSUBISHI CHEMICAL HOLDINGS CORPORATION
MITSUBISHI CORP
MITSUI OSK LINES LTD
MURPHY OIL CORPORATION
NABORS INDUSTRIES LTD
NATIONAL FUEL GAS CO
NATIONAL GRID PLC
NATIONAL OILWELL VARCO INC
NATIONAL THERMAL POWER CORP LTD
NEDERLANDSE GASUNIE NV
NEWFIELD EXPLORATION CO
NEWPARK RESOURCES INC
NEXEN INC
NEXTERA ENERGY INC
NIGERIAN NATIONAL PETROLEUM CORPORATION
NOBLE CORPORATION
NOBLE ENERGY INC
NOVATEK OAO
NRG ENERGY INC
NUSTAR ENERGY LP
OAO TATNEFT
OCCIDENTAL PETROLEUM CORP
OCEANEERING INTERNATIONAL INC
OGX PETROLEO E GAS PARTICIPACOES SA
OIL & NATURAL GAS CORP LTD
OIL SEARCH LTD
OIL STATES INTERNATIONAL INC
OMV AKTIENGESELLSCHAFT
ONEOK PARTNERS LP
ONTARIO POWER GENERATION INC
OSAKA GAS CO LTD
OXBOW CORPORATION
PAKISTAN STATE OIL CO LTD
PARKER DRILLING COMPANY
PATTERSON-UTI ENERGY INC
PEABODY ENERGY CORP
PENN WEST ENERGY TRUST
PETROBRAS DISTRIBUIDORA SA
PETROBRAS ARGENTINA SA
PETROCHINA COMPANY
PETROLEO BRASILEIRO SA (PETROBRAS)
PETROLEOS DE VENEZUELA SA (PDVSA)
PETROLEOS MEXICANOS (PEMEX)
PETROLEUM GEO SERVICES ASA
PETRON CORP
PETRONAS (PETROLIAM NASIONAL BERHAD)
PIONEER NATURAL RESOURCES COMPANY
PLAINS ALL AMERICAN PIPELINE
POLSKI KONCERN NAFTOWY ORLEN SA (PKN ORLEN GROUP)
POWER FINANCE CORPORATION LIMITED
POWER GRID CORPORATION OF INDIA LTD
PPL CORPORATION
PRECISION DRILLING CORPORATION
PREMIER OIL PLC
PRIDE INTERNATIONAL INC
PT PERTAMINA (PERSERO)
PTT AROMATICS AND REFINING PCL
PTT EXPLORATION AND PRODUCTION PCL
PTT PCL
PUBLIC POWER CORPORATION SA
PUERTO RICO ELECTRIC POWER AUTHORITY
QATAR PETROLEUM
QUICKSILVER RESOURCES INC
RATCHABURI ELECTRICITY GENERATING HOLDING PCL
RED APPLE GROUP INC
RELIANCE INDUSTRIES LTD (RELIANCE GROUP)

RELIANCE INFRASTRUCTURE LTD
RELIANCE PETROLEUM LTD
RELIANCE POWER LIMITED
REPSOL YPF SA
RIO TINTO GROUP
ROSNEFT (OAO)
ROWAN COMPANIES INC
ROYAL DUTCH SHELL (SHELL GROUP)
ROYAL VOPAK NV
RWE AG
RWE NPOWER
SAIPEM SPA
SANTOS LTD
SAUDI ARAMCO (SAUDI ARABIAN OIL CO)
SCHLUMBERGER LIMITED
SCHNEIDER ELECTRIC SA
SCOTTISH AND SOUTHERN ENERGY PLC
SCOTTISHPOWER UK PLC
SEACOR HOLDINGS INC
SEADRILL LIMITED
SEITEL INC
SEMBCORP INDUSTRIES LTD
SEMPRA ENERGY
SHAW GROUP INC (THE)
SHELL CANADA LIMITED
SHELL OIL CO
SHIKOKU ELECTRIC POWER COMPANY INC
SHOWA SHELL SEKIYU KK
SHV HOLDINGS NV
SIEMENS AG
SIEMENS METERING SERVICES LTD
SILVER SPRING NETWORKS
SINCLAIR OIL CORP
SINOPEC SHANGHAI PETROCHEMICAL
SK HOLDINGS CO LTD
SMITH INTERNATIONAL INC
SNAM RETE GAS SPA
S-OIL CORPORATION
SONATRACH
SPECTRA ENERGY CORP
STATOIL ASA
SUBSEA 7 INC
SUNCOR ENERGY INC
SUNOCO INC
SUPERIOR ENERGY SERVICES INC
SURGUTNEFTEGAS (OJSC)
SYNCRUDE CANADA LTD
TALISMAN ENERGY INC
TARGA RESOURCES PARTNERS LP
TATA POWER
TEAM INC
TECHNIP
TECO ENERGY INC
TENAGA NASIONAL BERHAD (TNB)
TENARIS SA
TENASKA INC
TESCO CORPORATION
TESORO CORP
TETRA TECHNOLOGIES INC
THAI OIL PCL
TIDEWATER INC
TNK-BP
TOHOKU ELECTRIC POWER CO INC
TOKYO ELECTRIC POWER COMPANY INC (THE)
TOKYO GAS CO LTD
TONENGENERAL SEKIYU KK
TOTAL SA
TOTAL UK LIMITED
TRACTEBEL ENERGIA SA
TRANSALTA CORP
TRANSAMMONIA INC
TRANSCANADA CORP
TRANSOCEAN INC
TRANSPORTADORA DE GAS DEL SUR SA
TRICO MARINE SERVICES INC
TSAKOS ENERGY NAVIGATION LTD
UGI CORP
UK COAL PLC
ULTRAPAR PARTICIPACOES SA
UNITED REFINING COMPANY
UNITED UTILITIES GROUP PLC
VAALCO ENERGY INC
VALERO ENERGY CORP
VATTENFALL AB
WEATHERFORD INTERNATIONAL LTD
WESTAR ENERGY
WESTERNGECO
WESTINGHOUSE ELECTRIC COMPANY LLC
WILLBROS GROUP INC
WILLIAMS COMPANIES INC (THE)
WINTERSHALL AG
WOODSIDE PETROLEUM LTD
WORLD FUEL SERVICES CORP
XSTRATA PLC
XTO ENERGY INC
YANZHOU COAL MINING CO LTD
YPF SA

Individual Profiles On Each Of THE ENERGY 500

ABB (INDIA) LTD

www.abb.co.in

Industry Group Code: 335 **Ranks within this company's industry group:** Sales: 8 Profits: 8

Exploration/Production:		Refining/Retailing:		Utilities:		Alternative Energy:		Specialty Services:		Energy Mktg./Other Svcs.	
Exploration:		Refining:		Electric Utility:		Waste/Solar/Other:		Consulting/Eng.:	Y	Energy Marketing:	
Production:		Retailing:		Gas Utility:		Thermal/Steam:		Seismic:		Equipment/Machinery:	Y
Coal Production:		Convenience Stores:		Pipelines:		Wind:		Drilling:		Oil Field Services:	
		Chemicals:		Water:		Hydro:		InfoTech:	Y	Air/Shipping Transportation:	
						Fuel Cells:		Specialty Services:	Y		

TYPES OF BUSINESS:

Electrical Equipment, Manufacturing
Automation Technologies
Electric Substations
Process Automation Equipment
Electric Generation Equipment
Robotics

BRANDS/DIVISIONS/AFFILIATES:

ABB Ltd.
Metsys Engineering & Consultancy Pvt. Limited

CONTACTS: *Note: Officers with more than one job title may be intentionally listed here more than once.*

Biplab Majumder, Managing Dir.
Amlan Dutta Majumdar, CFO
N. Venu, Head-Mktg. & Front End Sales
Ramesh S. Shankar, Head-Human Resources
Madhav Vemuri, Head-Corp. Research
Madhav Vemuri, Head-Global Eng. & Svcs.
David Huegin, Head-Legal & Compliance
Juliane Lenzner, Head-Comm.
Juliane Lenzner, Head-Investor Rel.
Amlan Dutta Majumdar, Sr. VP-Finance
B Gururaj, Sec.
R. Narayanan, Head-Discrete Automation & Motion Div.
Prakash Nayak, Head-Power Systems
Pitamber Shivnani, Head-Power Prod.
Gary Steel, Chmn.
Prakash Nayak, Head-Global Svcs.

Phone: 91-80-229-49150	**Fax:** 91-80-229-49148
Toll-Free:	
Address: 49 Race Course Rd., 2nd Fl., Eastern Wing, Bangalore, 560 001 India	

GROWTH PLANS/SPECIAL FEATURES:

ABB (India) Ltd., a member of the ABB Group, is an India-based provider of power and automation technologies. ABB's operations in India include 14 manufacturing facilities, approximately 18 marketing offices, eight service centers, three logistics warehouses and a network of over 800 channel partners. The company operates in five divisions; power systems, power products, discrete automation and motion, process automation and low voltage products. The power systems division engineers and produces grid systems, power generation systems, network management solutions and substations. The division also offers automation, control and protection systems and related services for power transmission and distribution networks, power plants and water pumping stations. Customers include central, state and private power utilities as well as industry clients. The power products division supplies power transmission and distribution products and services, serving electric, gas and water utilities, as well as industrial and commercial customers. Product offerings include circuit breakers, air and gas insulated switchgear, instrument transformers, disconnectors, reactive power compensators, power and distribution transformers and a range of distribution products. The discrete automation and motion segment includes products and systems targeted at discrete manufacturing applications, such as robotics and programmable logic controllers, and providing motion in plants, such as motors and drives. This segment incorporates the former operations of the robotics division. The process automation division provides industry-specific solutions for plant automation and electrification, energy management, process and asset optimization, analytical measurement and telecommunication. Major industries served include oil and gas, metals and minerals, pulp and paper, chemicals and pharmaceuticals. Comprising the operations of the low voltage products unit are businesses producing low-voltage electrical equipment sold on the wholesale and original equipment manufacturers markets. In September 2010, ABB India acquired Metsys Engineering and Consultancy Pvt. Limited., which provides technical solutions to the steel industry domestically and in emerging markets.

FINANCIALS: **Sales and profits are in thousands of dollars—add 000 to get the full amount. 2010 Note: Financial information for 2010 was not available for all companies at press time.**

2010 Sales: $	2010 Profits: $	**U.S. Stock Ticker: Subsidiary**
2009 Sales: $1,439,510	2009 Profits: $115,260	**Int'l Ticker: 500002** Int'l Exchange: Bombay-BSE
2008 Sales: $1,248,610	2008 Profits: $103,520	Employees: 6,496
2007 Sales: $899,880	2007 Profits: $71,650	Fiscal Year Ends: 12/31
2006 Sales: $	2006 Profits: $	Parent Company: ABB LTD

SALARIES/BENEFITS:

Pension Plan:	ESOP Stock Plan:	Profit Sharing:	Top Exec. Salary: $	Bonus: $
Savings Plan:	Stock Purch. Plan:		Second Exec. Salary: $	Bonus: $

OTHER THOUGHTS:

Apparent Women Officers or Directors:
Hot Spot for Advancement for Women/Minorities:

LOCATIONS: ("Y" = Yes)

West:	Southwest:	Midwest:	Southeast:	Northeast:	International:
					Y

ABB LTD

www.abb.com

Industry Group Code: 335 **Ranks within this company's industry group:** Sales: 3 Profits: 3

Exploration/Production:		Refining/Retailing:		Utilities:		Alternative Energy:		Specialty Services:		Energy Mktg./Other Svcs.	
Exploration:		Refining:		Electric Utility:		Waste/Solar/Other:		Consulting/Eng.:	Y	Energy Marketing:	
Production:		Retailing:		Gas Utility:		Thermal/Steam:		Seismic:		Equipment/Machinery:	Y
Coal Production:		Convenience Stores:		Pipelines:		Wind:	Y	Drilling:		Oil Field Services:	
		Chemicals:		Water:		Hydro:	Y	InfoTech:	Y	Air/Shipping Transportation:	
						Fuel Cells:		Specialty Services:	Y		

TYPES OF BUSINESS:

Diversified Engineering Services
Power Transmission & Distribution Systems
Control & Automation Technology Products
Industrial Robotics
Energy Trading Software

BRANDS/DIVISIONS/AFFILIATES:

Vectek Electronics
Sinai Engineering Corp.
ABB (Thailand) Ltd
ABB (India) Ltd
Polovodice a.s.
Ventyx

CONTACTS:

Note: Officers with more than one job title may be intentionally listed here more than once.

Joseph Hogan, CEO
Michel Demare, CFO/Head-Global Markets
Brice Koch, Head-Mktg. & Customer Solutions
Gary Steel, Head-Human Resources
Peter Terwiesch, Head-Group R&D
Diane de Saint Victor, General Counsel/Head-Legal & Compliance
Clarissa Haller, Head-Group Corp. Comm.
Michael Gerber, Head-Investor Rel.
Ulrich Spiesshofer, Head-Automation & Motion Prod. Div.
Bernhard Jucker, Head-Power Prod. Div.
Veli-Matti Reinikkala, Head-Process Automation Div.
Anders Jonsson, Head-Global Footprint & Cost Program
Hubertus von Grunberg, Chmn.
Sergio Gomes, Head-South American Oper.
John Walker, Head-Supply Chain Mgmt.

Phone: 41-43-317-7111	**Fax:** 41-43-317-4420
Toll-Free:	
Address: Affolternstrasse 44, Zurich, CH-8050 Switzerland	

GROWTH PLANS/SPECIAL FEATURES:

ABB, Ltd. is a global leader in power and automation technologies for utility and industrial companies. The company provides a broad range of products, systems, solutions and services that improve power grid reliability, increase industrial productivity and enhance energy efficiency. The firm operates in approximately 100 countries, and divides its business into five divisions: power products; power systems; low voltage products; discrete automation and motion; and process automation. The power products segment manufactures and sells high to medium voltage switchgear and apparatus, circuit breakers for various current and voltage levels and power and distribution transformers. The power systems division's solutions include engineering of grid systems, power generation systems, network management solutions and substations. Comprising the operations of the low voltage products unit are businesses producing low-voltage electrical equipment sold on the wholesale and original equipment manufacturers markets. The discrete automation and motion segment includes products and systems targeted at discrete manufacturing applications, such as robotics and programmable logic controllers, and providing motion in plants, such as motors and drives. This segment incorporates the former operations of the robotics division. The process automation segment offers plant automation and electrification, energy management, process and asset optimization, analytical measurement and telecommunications for such industries as metals and minerals; pharmaceuticals; oil and gas; pulp and paper; chemicals; and petrochemicals. In October 2009, the company entered the North American market by acquiring the Canadian firm Sinai Engineering Corp. In March 2010, ABB agreed to acquire the semiconductor business of Polovodice a.s., which operates in the Czech Republic. In May 2010, the firm announced plans to construct a cable factory in the U.S. Also in May, ABB agreed to acquire Ventyx, a leading software provider to the global energy, utility, communications and other industries. In July 2010, the company increased its ownership share in ABB India to 75%.

FINANCIALS:

Sales and profits are in thousands of dollars—add 000 to get the full amount. 2010 Note: Financial information for 2010 was not available for all companies at press time.

2010 Sales: $	2010 Profits: $	**U.S. Stock Ticker: ABB**
2009 Sales: $31,795,000	2009 Profits: $2,901,000	**Int'l Ticker: ABBN** Int'l Exchange: Zurich-SWX
2008 Sales: $34,912,000	2008 Profits: $3,118,000	Employees: 117,000
2007 Sales: $29,183,000	2007 Profits: $3,757,000	Fiscal Year Ends: 12/31
2006 Sales: $23,281,000	2006 Profits: $1,390,000	Parent Company:

SALARIES/BENEFITS:

Pension Plan:	ESOP Stock Plan:	Profit Sharing:	Top Exec. Salary: $1,981,704	Bonus: $944,280
Savings Plan:	Stock Purch. Plan:		Second Exec. Salary: $1,251,606	Bonus: $1,524,037

OTHER THOUGHTS:

Apparent Women Officers or Directors: 2
Hot Spot for Advancement for Women/Minorities:

LOCATIONS: ("Y" = Yes)

West:	Southwest:	Midwest:	Southeast:	Northeast:	International:
				Y	Y

ABBOT GROUP LIMITED

www.kcadeutag.com

Industry Group Code: 213111 **Ranks within this company's industry group:** Sales: Profits:

Exploration/Production:		**Refining/Retailing:**		**Utilities:**		**Alternative Energy:**		**Specialty Services:**		**Energy Mktg./Other Svcs.**	
Exploration:		Refining:		Electric Utility:		Waste/Solar/Other:		Consulting/Eng.:	Y	Energy Marketing:	
Production:		Retailing:		Gas Utility:		Thermal/Steam:		Seismic:		Equipment/Machinery:	Y
Coal Production:		Convenience Stores:		Pipelines:		Wind:		Drilling:	Y	Oil Field Services:	Y
		Chemicals:		Water:		Hydro:		InfoTech:		Air/Shipping Transportation:	
						Fuel Cells:		Specialty Services:			

TYPES OF BUSINESS:

Drilling Oil & Gas Wells Support
Well & Engineering Services

BRANDS/DIVISIONS/AFFILIATES:

KCA Deutag
Bentec
First Reserve Corporation
RDS
International Drilling Technology Company LLC
LLC Bentec Drilling and Oilfield Systems

CONTACTS: *Note: Officers with more than one job title may be intentionally listed here more than once.*

Holger Temmen, CEO
Brian Taylor, COO
Daniel Wiest, CFO
Ross Richardson, Dir.-Human Resources & Training
Ian MacKenzie, Dir.-Technical Svcs.
Neil Stevenson, Dir.-Bus. Dev. & Commercial
Alex Christou, Mgr.-Corp. Comm.
Mark Walker, Dir.-Finance
Ian MacKenzie, Dir.-Projects & Bus. Excellence

Phone: 44-1224-299-600	**Fax:** 44-1224-230-403
Toll-Free:	
Address: Minto Dr., Altens Industrial Estate, Aberdeen, ABI2 3LW UK	

GROWTH PLANS/SPECIAL FEATURES:

Abbot Group Limited is a wholly-owned subsidiary of First Reserve Corporation, a private equity firm focused on energy acquisitions. The company, through its operating subsidiaries, provides drilling and related well and engineering services to the energy industry worldwide. Its primary operating subsidiary, KCA Deutag, offers a full range of production drilling services, both onshore and offshore, along with engineering, rig design and construction services. KCA Deutag has operations around the globe, including Europe and Eurasia (with a strong presence in the Caspian region), the Middle East, North Africa, West Africa, Siberia, Kazakhstan, the North Sea and far Eastern Russia. It is a leading offshore platform drilling contractor in the North Sea and the Caspian region and one of the largest international land drilling contractors outside the Americas. KCA Deutag operates a fleet of over 60 land rigs, 30 managed offshore platforms, the North Sea's only modular drilling and well workover rig and 10 mobile offshore drilling units, including three wholly-owned and one managed jack-up rig, and four part-owned and three managed self-erect tenders. RDS, is KCA Deitag's engineering division, that specializes in project and site engineering management; concept screening and engineering; detail and front end engineering design; procurement of equipment; and survey of drilling facilities. The group's second subsidiary, Bentec, provides onshore and offshore drilling facility design, fabrication, installation and project management. Bentec also offers engineering and repair services, drilling equipment and systems services. In addition, Bentec has two other subsidiaries: International Drilling Technology Co. LLC, which specializes in maintenance and repair of all types of drilling rigs and oilfield equipment; and LLC Bentec Drilling and Oilfield Systems, which operates in Tyumen, Russia. Clients of the company include ExxonMobil, BP, Nexen, CNR International, StatoilHydro, Talisman, Sakhalin Energy Investment Company, Lundin Chevron and Total.

FINANCIALS: **Sales and profits are in thousands of dollars—add 000 to get the full amount. 2010 Note: Financial information for 2010 was not available for all companies at press time.**

2010 Sales: $	2010 Profits: $	**U.S. Stock Ticker: Private**
2009 Sales: $	2009 Profits: $	**Int'l Ticker:** Int'l Exchange:
2008 Sales: $	2008 Profits: $	Employees:
2007 Sales: $1,542,243	2007 Profits: $50,720	Fiscal Year Ends: 12/31
2006 Sales: $1,162,890	2006 Profits: $30,679	Parent Company: FIRST RESERVE CORPORATION

SALARIES/BENEFITS:

Pension Plan:	ESOP Stock Plan:	Profit Sharing:	Top Exec. Salary: $411,222	Bonus: $
Savings Plan:	Stock Purch. Plan:		Second Exec. Salary: $352,476	Bonus: $115,534

OTHER THOUGHTS:

Apparent Women Officers or Directors:
Hot Spot for Advancement for Women/Minorities:

LOCATIONS: ("Y" = Yes)

West:	Southwest:	Midwest:	Southeast:	Northeast:	International:
	Y				Y

ABU DHABI NATIONAL ENERGY COMPANY PJSC (TAQA)

www.taqa.ae

Industry Group Code: 221121 **Ranks within this company's industry group:** Sales: 2 Profits: 3

Exploration/Production:		Refining/Retailing:		Utilities:		Alternative Energy:		Specialty Services:		Energy Mktg./Other Svcs.	
Exploration:	Y	Refining:		Electric Utility:	Y	Waste/Solar/Other:		Consulting/Eng.:		Energy Marketing:	
Production:	Y	Retailing:		Gas Utility:		Thermal/Steam:		Seismic:		Equipment/Machinery:	
Coal Production:		Convenience Stores:		Pipelines:		Wind:		Drilling:		Oil Field Services:	
		Chemicals:		Water:	Y	Hydro:		InfoTech:		Air/Shipping Transportation:	
						Fuel Cells:		Specialty Services:	Y		

TYPES OF BUSINESS:

Electricity Generation
Water Desalinization
Oil & Gas Exploration and Production
Gas Storage & Pipelines

BRANDS/DIVISIONS/AFFILIATES:

TAQA North
TAQA Bratani
DSM Energie Holding B.V.
Suncor Energy Oil and Gas Partnership

CONTACTS: *Note: Officers with more than one job title may be intentionally listed here more than once.*

Abdulla Saif Al Nuaimi, CEO
Doug Fraser, CFO
Yasser El Zein, Group VP-Tech.
Francois Duquette, Interim General Counsel
Johanna Kornelius, Head-Strategic Planning
Sucharita Sethi, Group VP-Corp. Comm.
Tanis Thacker, Head-Investor Rel.
Ryan Wong, Group VP/Treas.
Carl Sheldon, Gen. Mgr.
Frank Perez, Exec. Officer/Head-Global Power
Klaus Reinisch, Head-Midstream & Portfolio Optimization
Jan Willem van Hoogstraten, Managing Dir.-TAQA Energy
Hamad Al-Hurr Al-Suwaidi, Chmn.
Leo Koot, Managing Dir.-TAQA Bratani

Phone: 971-02-691-4900 **Fax:** 971-02-641-3286
Toll-Free:
Address: ADWEA Research Centre, 7th Fl., Jawazat St., Abu Dhabi, UAE

GROWTH PLANS/SPECIAL FEATURES:

Abu Dhabi National Energy Company PJSC (TAQA) is a United Arab Emirates-based power generation and water desalinization company. TAQA operates in 13 markets across four continents, with six independent water and power producers in Abu Dhabi. The firm has three segments: Downstream, which contributed 46% of the firm's 2009 total revenues; midstream, 2%; and upstream operations, 52%. The downstream segment is managed by TAQA generation, which supplies 98% of Abu Dhabi's power and water. Other locales for downstream implementation include Morocco, Saudi Arabia, Ghana and India. The upstream operations are provided by international subsidiaries. TAQA North is among the top 12 energy companies in Canada and specializes in oil, gas and coalbed methane exploration. TAQA Bratani operates exploration and production blocks in the North Sea. TAQA Bratani also operates the Brent pipeline system in the North Sea. Together TAQA North, Bratani and Energy have proved plus probable reserves of 574.4 million barrels of oil equivalent (MMBOE). The midstream operations segment, also based in the Netherlands and Canada, stores natural gas and transports oil resources. One of the company's major interests in this segment is the Canada-Chicago Alliance pipeline. In October 2009, the company acquired the assets of DSM Energie Holding B.V., which included interests in several gas pipelines and 20 producing oil and gas fields in the North Sea. In June 2010, TAQA North acquired a portion of the property assets belonging to Suncor Energy Oil and Gas Partnership in west central Alberta. In September 2010, TAQA Bratani acquired additional interests in the North Sea at the Otter Field Development Area.

FINANCIALS: **Sales and profits are in thousands of dollars—add 000 to get the full amount. 2010 Note: Financial information for 2010 was not available for all companies at press time.**

2010 Sales: $	2010 Profits: $	**U.S. Stock Ticker:**
2009 Sales: $4,588,040	2009 Profits: $49,540	**Int'l Ticker: TAQA** Int'l Exchange: Abu Dhabi-ADSM
2008 Sales: $4,574,170	2008 Profits: $496,790	Employees:
2007 Sales: $2,269,130	2007 Profits: $281,600	Fiscal Year Ends: 12/31
2006 Sales: $	2006 Profits: $	Parent Company:

SALARIES/BENEFITS:

Pension Plan:	ESOP Stock Plan:	Profit Sharing:	Top Exec. Salary: $	Bonus: $
Savings Plan:	Stock Purch. Plan:		Second Exec. Salary: $	Bonus: $

OTHER THOUGHTS:

Apparent Women Officers or Directors: 1
Hot Spot for Advancement for Women/Minorities:

LOCATIONS: ("Y" = Yes)

West:	Southwest:	Midwest:	Southeast:	Northeast:	International:
		Y			Y

ABU DHABI NATIONAL OIL COMPANY

www.adnoc.ae

Industry Group Code: 211111 **Ranks within this company's industry group:** Sales: Profits:

Exploration/Production:		Refining/Retailing:		Utilities:		Alternative Energy:		Specialty Services:		Energy Mktg./Other Svcs.	
Exploration:	Y	Refining:	Y	Electric Utility:		Waste/Solar/Other:		Consulting/Eng.:		Energy Marketing:	
Production:	Y	Retailing:		Gas Utility:		Thermal/Steam:		Seismic:		Equipment/Machinery:	
Coal Production:		Convenience Stores:		Pipelines:		Wind:		Drilling:	Y	Oil Field Services:	Y
		Chemicals:	Y	Water:		Hydro:		InfoTech:		Air/Shipping Transportation:	Y
						Fuel Cells:		Specialty Services:			

TYPES OF BUSINESS:

Oil & Gas Exploration & Production
Drilling Services
Oil & Gas Processing & Refining
Maritime Transportation
Refined Products Distribution
Chemicals & Petrochemicals Manufacturing

BRANDS/DIVISIONS/AFFILIATES:

Ruwais Fertilizer Industries (FERTIL)
Abu Dhabi Company for Onshore Oil Operations
Zakum Development Company (ZADCO)
National Drilling Company (NDC)
Abu Dhabi Petroleum Ports Operating Co. (IRSHAD)
Abu Dhabi Gas Liquefaction Co. Ltd. (ADGAS)
Abu Dhabi Oil Refining Company (TAKREER)
Abu Dhabi Marine Operating Company

CONTACTS:

Note: Officers with more than one job title may be intentionally listed here more than once.

Yousef Omair Bin Yousef, CEO
Khalifa Bin Zayed Al Nahyan, Chmn.-Supreme Petroleum Council
Yousef Omair Bin Yousef, Sec. Gen.-Supreme Petroleum Council

Phone: 971-2-602-0000	Fax: 971-2-602-3389
Toll-Free:	
Address: P.O. Box 898, Abu Dhabi, UAE	

GROWTH PLANS/SPECIAL FEATURES:

Abu Dhabi National Oil Company (ADNOC) specializes in the marketing and distribution of petroleum products within the United Arab Emirates (U.A.E.). The Supreme Petroleum Council (SPC), part of the U.A.E. government, oversees and formulates the implementation of the petroleum policies of Abu Dhabi, including ADNOC's activities. The company produces approximately 2.7 million barrels of oil per day. It also controls around 196 trillion cubic feet of natural gas reserves. Since 1971, ADNOC has substantially broadened its activities beyond exploration and production to include oil refining and gas processing as well as chemical and petrochemical production. It also offers support services for the oil and gas industry and engages in maritime transportation. In the U.A.E., ADNOC operates over 170 filling stations and offers re-fueling services for airlines and shipping companies. Additionally, the company owns its own lubricants blending, filling and packaging plant; two LPG (liquefied petroleum gas) bottling plants; and three vessels that supply gasoline and oil to the Abu Dhabi Islands. The firm's oil fields include Upper Zakum (the largest field), Umm Al-Dalkh, Satah and Ruwais. The firm operates largely through its 14 subsidiaries: Abu Dhabi Company for Onshore Oil Operations (ADCO); Zakum Development Company (ZADCO); National Drilling Company (NDC); Abu Dhabi Petroleum Ports Operating Company (IRSHAD); Abu Dhabi Gas Liquefaction Company Limited (ADGAS); Abu Dhabi Oil Refining Company (TAKREER); Ruwais Fertilizer Industries (FERTIL); Abu Dhabi Polymers Company Limited (BOROUGE); Abu Dhabi National Oil Company Distribution (ADNOCD); Abu Dhabi Marine Operating Company (ADMA-OPCO); Abu Dhabi Gas Industries Ltd. (GASCO); National Gas Shipping Company (NGSCO); Abu Dhabi National Tanker Company (ADNATCO); and ESNAAD, which means support in Arabic language. In July 2009, the firm signed an agreement with ConocoPhillips to jointly share the cost of the Shah gas field development project.

FINANCIALS:

Sales and profits are in thousands of dollars—add 000 to get the full amount. 2010 Note: Financial information for 2010 was not available for all companies at press time.

2010 Sales: $	2010 Profits: $	**U.S. Stock Ticker: Government-Owned**
2009 Sales: $	2009 Profits: $	**Int'l Ticker:** Int'l Exchange:
2008 Sales: $	2008 Profits: $	Employees:
2007 Sales: $	2007 Profits: $	Fiscal Year Ends: 12/31
2006 Sales: $	2006 Profits: $	Parent Company:

SALARIES/BENEFITS:

Pension Plan:	ESOP Stock Plan:	Profit Sharing:	Top Exec. Salary: $	Bonus: $
Savings Plan:	Stock Purch. Plan:		Second Exec. Salary: $	Bonus: $

OTHER THOUGHTS:

Apparent Women Officers or Directors:
Hot Spot for Advancement for Women/Minorities:

LOCATIONS: ("Y" = Yes)

West:	Southwest:	Midwest:	Southeast:	Northeast:	International:
					Y

ACERGY SA

www.acergy-group.com

Industry Group Code: 2389 **Ranks within this company's industry group:** Sales: 1 Profits: 1

Exploration/Production:		Refining/Retailing:		Utilities:		Alternative Energy:		Specialty Services:		Energy Mktg./Other Svcs.	
Exploration:		Refining:		Electric Utility:		Waste/Solar/Other:		Consulting/Eng.:	Y	Energy Marketing:	
Production:		Retailing:		Gas Utility:		Thermal/Steam:		Seismic:		Equipment/Machinery:	Y
Coal Production:		Convenience Stores:		Pipelines:		Wind:		Drilling:		Oil Field Services:	Y
		Chemicals:		Water:		Hydro:		InfoTech:		Air/Shipping Transportation:	
						Fuel Cells:		Specialty Services:			

TYPES OF BUSINESS:

Offshore Platform Construction
Pipeline Construction
Offshore Support Services
Design Services
Oil Field Services

BRANDS/DIVISIONS/AFFILIATES:

NKT Flexibles
Seaway Heavy Lifting
Sapura-Acergy
Sonamet
Stanislav Yudin
Acergy M.S. Limited
Subsea 7, Inc.

CONTACTS:

Note: Officers with more than one job title may be intentionally listed here more than once.

Jean Cahuzac, CEO
Bruno Chabas, COO
Simon Crowe, CFO
Mark Preece, VP-Mktg. & Bus. Dev.
Keith Tipson, Sr. VP-Human Resources
Allen Leatt, CTO
Allen Leatt, Sr. VP-Eng.
Johan Rasmussen, General Counsel/Sr. VP
Jean-Luc Laloe, Sr. VP-Corp. Dev.
Karen Menzel, Group Mgr.-Investor Rel.
Andy Culwell, VP-Health, Safety, Environment & Quality
Gael Cailleaux, VP-Offshore Resources
Olivier Carre, Sr. VP-Territory II
Oyvind Mikaelsen, Sr. VP-Territory I
Peter Mason, Chmn.

Phone: 44--8210-5500	**Fax:** 44-8210-5501
Toll-Free:	
Address: 200 Hammersmith Rd., London, W6 7DL UK	

GROWTH PLANS/SPECIAL FEATURES:

Acergy S.A., formerly Stolt Offshore S.A., is a U.K.-based company that offers contract seabed-to-surface engineering and construction for the offshore oil and gas production industry throughout the world. The company provides products and services from flowline and pipeline construction to subsea wells, umbilicals, risers and fixed or floating platforms. Acergy manages its marine assets through a global asset organization based in Aberdeen, U.K. and operates in two territories: Territory I is composed of the Northern European, Canadian, Southeast Asian and Middle Eastern operations; and Territory II, which includes activities in Africa, the Mediterranean, North America and Mexico and South America. Territory II represented 61% of the firm's revenue in 2009. The majority of the firm's activities fall into the areas of engineering, procurement, installation, and commissioning (EPIC) project delivery. Within the restraints of these activities, the company can be further branched into several additional types including deepwater operations; inspection, maintenance and repair; and conventional field development. The deepwater division provides design, installation and commissioning of subsea infrastructure, umbilical, riser and flowline systems. Inspection, maintenance and repair services includes both diver and remotely operated vehicle inspection as well as maintenance and repair services that keep oil and gas fields producing at a desired level. The conventional field development division focuses on hydrocarbon extraction and field development problems. In September 2010, Acergy received anti-trust clearance from the U.S. Federal Trade Commission and the Norwegian Competition Authority in regards to its proposed merger transaction with Subsea 7, Inc.

FINANCIALS:

Sales and profits are in thousands of dollars—add 000 to get the full amount. 2010 Note: Financial information for 2010 was not available for all companies at press time.

2010 Sales: $	2010 Profits: $	**U.S. Stock Ticker: ACGY**
2009 Sales: $2,208,800	2009 Profits: $265,700	**Int'l Ticker: ACY** Int'l Exchange: Oslo-OBX
2008 Sales: $2,522,400	2008 Profits: $307,200	Employees: 6,385
2007 Sales: $2,406,300	2007 Profits: $134,500	Fiscal Year Ends: 11/30
2006 Sales: $2,124,200	2006 Profits: $236,700	Parent Company:

SALARIES/BENEFITS:

Pension Plan:	ESOP Stock Plan:	Profit Sharing:	Top Exec. Salary: $2,100,000	Bonus: $
Savings Plan:	Stock Purch. Plan:		Second Exec. Salary: $111,499	Bonus: $

OTHER THOUGHTS:

Apparent Women Officers or Directors: 1
Hot Spot for Advancement for Women/Minorities:

LOCATIONS: ("Y" = Yes)

West:	Southwest:	Midwest:	Southeast:	Northeast:	International:
	Y				Y

ADAMS RESOURCES & ENERGY INC

www.adamsresources.com

Industry Group Code: 211111 **Ranks within this company's industry group:** Sales: 72 Profits: 72

Exploration/Production:		**Refining/Retailing:**		**Utilities:**		**Alternative Energy:**		**Specialty Services:**		**Energy Mktg./Other Svcs.**	
Exploration:	Y	Refining:		Electric Utility:		Waste/Solar/Other:		Consulting/Eng.:		Energy Marketing:	Y
Production:	Y	Retailing:		Gas Utility:		Thermal/Steam:		Seismic:		Equipment/Machinery:	
Coal Production:		Convenience Stores:		Pipelines:	Y	Wind:		Drilling:	Y	Oil Field Services:	
		Chemicals:	Y	Water:		Hydro:		InfoTech:		Air/Shipping Transportation:	Y
						Fuel Cells:		Specialty Services:	Y		

TYPES OF BUSINESS:

Oil & Gas Marketing
Oil & Gas Exploration & Production
Oil Trucking & Storage
Rail & Marine Transport Services
Machinery Servicing & Lubricants

BRANDS/DIVISIONS/AFFILIATES:

GulfMark Energy, Inc.
Ada Resources, Inc.
Adams Resources Marketing Ltd.
Service Transport Company
Adams Resources Exploration Corp.

CONTACTS:

Note: Officers with more than one job title may be intentionally listed here more than once.

K. S. Adams, Jr., CEO
Frank T. Webster, COO
Frank T. Webster, Pres.
Richard B. Abshire, CFO/VP
Tony Grant, Pres., Adams Resources Mktg., Ltd.
David B. Hurst, Corp. Sec.
Sharon C. Davis, Treas./Chief Acct. Officer
James L. Smith, Pres., Ada Resources, Inc.
Claude H. Lewis, Pres., Service Transport Co.
Geoffrey L. Griffith, Pres., GulfMark Energy, Inc.
K. S. Adams, Jr., Chmn.

Phone: 713-881-3600 **Fax:** 713-881-3491
Toll-Free:
Address: 4400 Post Oak Pkwy., Ste. 2700, Houston, TX 77027 US

GROWTH PLANS/SPECIAL FEATURES:

Adams Resources & Energy, Inc. (AR&E) is Texas-based energy firm. The company is engaged in crude oil, natural gas and petroleum product marketing; tank truck transportation of liquid chemicals; and oil and gas exploration and production. AR&E operates through five subsidiaries: GulfMark Energy, Inc.; Adams Resources Marketing, Ltd.; Ada Resources, Inc.; Service Transport Company; and Adams Resources Exploration Corp. GulfMark Energy purchases crude oil and arranges sales and deliveries to refineries and other customers. The subsidiary purchases about 65,000 barrels per day of crude oil at the wellhead or lease level; operates 101 tractor-trailer rigs; and maintains more than 50 pipeline inventory locations or injection stations. GulfMark Energy maintains roughly 200,000 barrels of storage capacity at certain dock facilities for the access of waterborne markets for its products. Adams Resources Marketing, Ltd. is a wholesale purchaser, distributor and marketer of natural gas; it purchases approximately 400 million cubic feet of natural gas per day at the wellhead and pipeline pooling point from 60 independent producers. Ada Resources, Inc. is a marketer of branded and unbranded refined petroleum products, such as lubricants and motor fuel. Lubricants include passenger car motor oils, as well as industrial oils and greases; motor fuel sales include automotive gasoline, conventional diesel and biodiesel. Service Transport Company transports liquid chemicals on a for-hire basis throughout the U.S. and Canada. It operates a satellite-linked fleet of approximately 262 truck tractors and 416 tank trailers. Adams Resources Exploration Corp. explores and develops domestic oil and gas properties, primarily along the Gulf Coast of Texas and Louisiana; it holds interest in 325 wells.

FINANCIALS:

Sales and profits are in thousands of dollars—add 000 to get the full amount. 2010 Note: Financial information for 2010 was not available for all companies at press time.

2010 Sales: $	2010 Profits: $	**U.S. Stock Ticker: AE**
2009 Sales: $1,943,128	2009 Profits: $4,149	**Int'l Ticker:** Int'l Exchange:
2008 Sales: $4,159,672	2008 Profits: $-5,572	Employees: 679
2007 Sales: $2,636,222	2007 Profits: $17,056	Fiscal Year Ends: 12/31
2006 Sales: $2,246,603	2006 Profits: $10,483	Parent Company:

SALARIES/BENEFITS:

Pension Plan:	ESOP Stock Plan:	Profit Sharing:	Top Exec. Salary: $399,807	Bonus: $77,000
Savings Plan:	Stock Purch. Plan:		Second Exec. Salary: $245,336	Bonus: $47,250

OTHER THOUGHTS:

Apparent Women Officers or Directors: 1
Hot Spot for Advancement for Women/Minorities:

LOCATIONS: ("Y" = Yes)

West:	Southwest:	Midwest:	Southeast:	Northeast:	International:
	Y		Y		

ADDAX PETROLEUM INC

www.addaxpetroleum.com

Industry Group Code: 211111 **Ranks within this company's industry group:** Sales: Profits:

Exploration/Production:		Refining/Retailing:		Utilities:		Alternative Energy:		Specialty Services:		Energy Mktg./Other Svcs.	
Exploration:	Y	Refining:		Electric Utility:		Waste/Solar/Other:		Consulting/Eng.:		Energy Marketing:	
Production:	Y	Retailing:		Gas Utility:		Thermal/Steam:		Seismic:		Equipment/Machinery:	
Coal Production:		Convenience Stores:		Pipelines:		Wind:		Drilling:		Oil Field Services:	
		Chemicals:		Water:		Hydro:		InfoTech:		Air/Shipping Transportation:	
						Fuel Cells:		Specialty Services:			

TYPES OF BUSINESS:

Oil & Gas Exploration
Oil and Gas Development

BRANDS/DIVISIONS/AFFILIATES:

China Petrochemical Corporation
Sinopec Group (The)

CONTACTS:

Note: Officers with more than one job title may be intentionally listed here more than once.

Xianliang Geng, CEO
James Pearce, COO
Michael Ebsary, CFO
David Codd, Chief Legal Officer/Corp. Sec.
Jean Claude Gandur, Vice Chmn.

Phone: 41-22-702-9400 | **Fax:** 41-22-702-9590

Toll-Free:

Address: 16, av. Eugene-Pittard, P.O. Box 265, Geneva, CH-1211 Switzerland

GROWTH PLANS/SPECIAL FEATURES:

Addax Petroleum, named for a desert antelope native to the sub-Saharan regions in which the company operates, is an oil and gas exploration and production company headquartered in Geneva, Switzerland. The firm is a subsidiary of China Petrochemical Corporation (Sinopec Group). The company's interests are primarily in the Middle East and Africa, specifically Nigeria, Gabon, Cameroon, the Kurdistan region of Iraq and the Joint Development Zone (JDZ) located between Nigeria and the Republic of Sao Tome and Principe. Addax's Nigerian operations encompass seven company-operated properties (five offshore and one onshore), of which four are 100% owned, one is majority owned and two are minority owned. The Gabon operations include six onshore production sharing contracts (PSCs), as well as four offshore PSCs and one technical evaluation agreement covering five offshore properties. The Cameroon operations consist of two offshore license areas: a 60% interest in a shallow water exploration property, Ngosso, and a 100% interest in the Iroko license area. In the Kurdistan region of Iraq, the company's interests comprise a 45% interest in the Taq Taq onshore license area and a PSC for the Sangaw North license area. The company has interests in four prospective exploration blocks in the JDZ. The company averages 136,500 barrels of oil production per day, with proved plus probable reserves totaling approximately 536.7 million Boe (barrels of oil equivalent). In August 2009, Sinopec Group acquired Addax Petroleum in a transaction valued at approximately $7.3 billion.

FINANCIALS:

Sales and profits are in thousands of dollars—add 000 to get the full amount. 2010 Note: Financial information for 2010 was not available for all companies at press time.

2010 Sales: $ | 2010 Profits: $
2009 Sales: $ | 2009 Profits: $
2008 Sales: $ | 2008 Profits: $
2007 Sales: $2,830,000 | 2007 Profits: $482,000
2006 Sales: $1,651,621 | 2006 Profits: $243,100

U.S. Stock Ticker: Subsidiary
Int'l Ticker: Int'l Exchange:
Employees:
Fiscal Year Ends: 12/31
Parent Company: CHINA PETROCHEMICAL CORPORATION

SALARIES/BENEFITS:

Pension Plan: | ESOP Stock Plan: | Profit Sharing: | Top Exec. Salary: $1,802,970 | Bonus: $1,893,119
Savings Plan: | Stock Purch. Plan: | | Second Exec. Salary: $832,140 | Bonus: $748,926

OTHER THOUGHTS:

Apparent Women Officers or Directors:
Hot Spot for Advancement for Women/Minorities:

LOCATIONS: ("Y" = Yes)

West:	Southwest:	Midwest:	Southeast:	Northeast:	International:
					Y

AEGEAN MARINE PETROLEUM NETWORK INC

www.ampni.com

Industry Group Code: 486 **Ranks within this company's industry group:** Sales: 14 Profits: 14

Exploration/Production:		Refining/Retailing:		Utilities:		Alternative Energy:		Specialty Services:		Energy Mktg./Other Svcs.	
Exploration:		Refining:		Electric Utility:		Waste/Solar/Other:		Consulting/Eng.:		Energy Marketing:	
Production:		Retailing:		Gas Utility:		Thermal/Steam:		Seismic:		Equipment/Machinery:	
Coal Production:		Convenience Stores:		Pipelines:		Wind:		Drilling:		Oil Field Services:	
		Chemicals:		Water:		Hydro:		InfoTech:		Air/Shipping Transportation:	Y
						Fuel Cells:		Specialty Services:	Y		

TYPES OF BUSINESS:

Marine Fuel Logistics
Marine Fuel Delivery
Marine Fuel Technical Support
Marine Lubricants

BRANDS/DIVISIONS/AFFILIATES:

Alfa Marine Lubricants
Aegean Bunkering (Singapore) Pte. Ltd.
Aegean Bunkering Gibraltar Ltd.
Aegean Marine Petroleum S.A.
Aegean Bunkering Jamaica Ltd.
Verbeke Bunkering N.V.
Portland Bunkers International Limited
Shell Las Palmas

CONTACTS:

Note: Officers with more than one job title may be intentionally listed here more than once.

E. Nikolas Tavlarios, Pres.
Spyros Gianniotis, CFO
Spyros Fokas, General Counsel/Corp. Sec.
Dimitris Melisanidis, Head-Corp. Dev.
Gregory Robolakis, Gen. Mgr.-Aegean Marine Petroleum S.A.
Nick Hondos, Gen. Mgr.-Aegean Bunkering Svcs. Inc.
Peter C. Georgiopoulos, Chmn.

Phone: 30-210-458-6200	Fax:
Toll-Free:	
Address: 42 Hatzikiriakou Ave., Piraeus, 185 38 Greece	

GROWTH PLANS/SPECIAL FEATURES:

Aegean Marine Petroleum Network, Inc. is a marine fuel logistics company that supplies and markets refined marine fuel and lubricants to ships in port and at sea. Aegean purchases its marine fuel from refineries and major oil producers before reselling and delivering its fuels, using its bunkering tankers, to virtually all types of ocean-going vessels and many types of coastal vessels. These include tankers, container ships, drybulk carriers, cruise ships, reefers, LNG/LPG, car carriers and ferries. Other customers include marine fuel traders and brokers. The firm operates through service centers in Greece, Gibraltar, United Arab Emirates, Belgium, Canada, the U.S., Jamaica, Mexico, Trinidad and Tobago, Singapore, Morocco, the U.K. and West Africa. It owns a fleet of 65 bunkering vessels, including about 37 double hull tankers. The company also owns five floating oil storage tankers and six bunkering tankers. Aegean also markets marine lubricants under the Alfa Marine Lubricants brand. The firm operates primarily through subsidiaries Aegean Marine Petroleum S.A.; Aegean Bunkering Gibraltar Ltd.; Aegean Bunkering Jamaica Ltd.; Aegean Bunkering (Singapore) Pte. Ltd.; Aegean Bunkering (Ghana) Limited; Bunkers at Sea NV; ICS Petroleum Ltd.; and Portland Bunkers International Limited. In June 2009, the company announced the acquisition of a double-hull barge, with an approximant carrying capacity of 2,588 dwt that will be utilized in the Vancouver markets. The company also announced in June that it had launched operations in Trinidad and Tobago, and in August commenced operations in Tangiers, Morocco. During 2009 and early 2010, the company acquired 17 double-hull bunkering vessels, with expectations to receive another seven tankers. In March 2010, Aegean acquired Verbeke Bunkering N.V., a marine fuel supplier in the Antwerp-Rotterdam-Amsterdam region of Europe. In July 2010, the firm acquired the Shell Las Palmas terminal in the Canary Islands.

FINANCIALS:

Sales and profits are in thousands of dollars—add 000 to get the full amount. 2010 Note: Financial information for 2010 was not available for all companies at press time.

2010 Sales: $	2010 Profits: $
2009 Sales: $2,470,960	2009 Profits: $48,525
2008 Sales: $2,777,972	2008 Profits: $39,915
2007 Sales: $1,352,873	2007 Profits: $27,738
2006 Sales: $803,812	2006 Profits: $24,225

U.S. Stock Ticker: ANW
Int'l Ticker: Int'l Exchange:
Employees: 909
Fiscal Year Ends: 12/31
Parent Company:

SALARIES/BENEFITS:

Pension Plan:	ESOP Stock Plan:	Profit Sharing:	Top Exec. Salary: $	Bonus: $
Savings Plan:	Stock Purch. Plan:		Second Exec. Salary: $	Bonus: $

OTHER THOUGHTS:

Apparent Women Officers or Directors:
Hot Spot for Advancement for Women/Minorities:

LOCATIONS: ("Y" = Yes)

West:	Southwest:	Midwest:	Southeast:	Northeast:	International:
				Y	Y

AERA ENERGY LLC

www.aeraenergy.com

Industry Group Code: 211111 **Ranks within this company's industry group:** Sales: Profits:

Exploration/Production:		Refining/Retailing:		Utilities:		Alternative Energy:		Specialty Services:		Energy Mktg./Other Svcs.	
Exploration:	Y	Refining:		Electric Utility:		Waste/Solar/Other:		Consulting/Eng.:		Energy Marketing:	
Production:	Y	Retailing:		Gas Utility:		Thermal/Steam:		Seismic:		Equipment/Machinery:	
Coal Production:		Convenience Stores:		Pipelines:		Wind:		Drilling:		Oil Field Services:	
		Chemicals:		Water:		Hydro:		InfoTech:		Air/Shipping Transportation:	
						Fuel Cells:		Specialty Services:	Y		

TYPES OF BUSINESS:

Oil & Gas Production
Real Estate Development
Soil Management Products & Services
Dust Control Products

BRANDS/DIVISIONS/AFFILIATES:

Shell Oil Co
Exxon Mobil Corporation (ExxonMobil)
Aera Energy Services Co
Vista Del Verde
Coles Levee Ecosystem Preserve
Toll Brothers Inc

CONTACTS:

Note: Officers with more than one job title may be intentionally listed here more than once.

Gaurdie E. Banister Jr., CEO
Gaurdie E. Banister Jr., Pres.
Kate Shae, CFO
David Walker, CIO

Phone: 661-665-5000	**Fax:** 661-665-5169
Toll-Free:	
Address: 10000 Ming Ave., Bakersfield, CA 93311 US	

GROWTH PLANS/SPECIAL FEATURES:

Aera Energy, LLC is a joint venture between affiliates of Exxon Mobil and Royal Dutch Shell. The company is one of California's largest oil and gas producers, with proved reserves of over 750 million barrels of oil equivalent (MBOE) and approximately 25% share of the state's oil production. Aera owns properties from the Los Angeles Basin to just south of San Francisco, which together produce approximately 156,000 barrels of oil and 46 million cubic feet of natural gas per day. The firm's primary oilfield is in Kern County, one of the largest oil-producing counties in the U.S. The firm also produces light oil from the Kern area diatomite formation. In addition, Aera maintains four offshore platforms near Long Beach and Huntington Beach. Subsidiary Aera Energy Services Company provides for the firm's workforce needs. The Coles Levee Ecosystem Preserve, owned by Aera in cooperation with the California Department of Fish and Game, is located in San Joaquin Valley and provides educational and conservation resources. The company is also involved in a partnership with Toll Brothers, Inc. to develop a golf course and residential planned community called Vista Del Verde in Yorba Linda, California. Vista del Verde is part of a larger Aera ownership totaling more than 4,000 acres in Orange and Los Angeles Counties. These lands will provide additional real estate development opportunities as the firm seeks to phase out its oil production operations over the next several years.

The company offers its employees an 9/80 work schedule; medical, dental and vision; 401(k); company sponsored training program; tuition assistance; and life insurance.

FINANCIALS:

Sales and profits are in thousands of dollars—add 000 to get the full amount. 2010 Note: Financial information for 2010 was not available for all companies at press time.

2010 Sales: $	2010 Profits: $	**U.S. Stock Ticker: Joint Venture**
2009 Sales: $	2009 Profits: $	**Int'l Ticker:** Int'l Exchange:
2008 Sales: $	2008 Profits: $	Employees:
2007 Sales: $	2007 Profits: $	Fiscal Year Ends: 12/31
2006 Sales: $	2006 Profits: $	Parent Company:

SALARIES/BENEFITS:

Pension Plan: Y	ESOP Stock Plan:	Profit Sharing:	Top Exec. Salary: $	Bonus: $
Savings Plan: Y	Stock Purch. Plan:		Second Exec. Salary: $	Bonus: $

OTHER THOUGHTS:

Apparent Women Officers or Directors: 1
Hot Spot for Advancement for Women/Minorities:

LOCATIONS: ("Y" = Yes)

West:	Southwest:	Midwest:	Southeast:	Northeast:	International:
Y					

AES CORPORATION (THE)

www.aes.com

Industry Group Code: 221 **Ranks within this company's industry group:** Sales: 10 Profits: 18

Exploration/Production:		Refining/Retailing:		Utilities:		Alternative Energy:		Specialty Services:		Energy Mktg./Other Svcs.	
Exploration:		Refining:		Electric Utility:	Y	Waste/Solar/Other:		Consulting/Eng.:		Energy Marketing:	Y
Production:		Retailing:		Gas Utility:		Thermal/Steam:		Seismic:		Equipment/Machinery:	
Coal Production:		Convenience Stores:		Pipelines:		Wind:	Y	Drilling:		Oil Field Services:	
		Chemicals:		Water:		Hydro:		InfoTech:		Air/Shipping Transportation:	
						Fuel Cells:		Specialty Services:			

TYPES OF BUSINESS:

Utilities-Electricity
Wind Generation
Contract Power Generation

BRANDS/DIVISIONS/AFFILIATES:

Indianapolis Power & Light
AES Wind Generation
AES Solar Energy LLC
AES Ballylumford Holdings Limited
China Investment Corporation
AES Eletropaulo
AES Kievoblenergo
AES Rivneenergo

CONTACTS: *Note: Officers with more than one job title may be intentionally listed here more than once.*

Paul T. Hanrahan, CEO
Andres Gluski, COO/Exec. VP
Paul T. Hanrahan, Pres.
Victoria Harker, CFO/Exec. VP
Rita Trehan, VP-Human Resources & Internal Comm.
Elizabeth Hackenson, CIO/Sr. VP
Brian Miller, General Counsel/Exec. VP/Corp. Sec.
Gardner W. Walkup, VP-Strategy
Meghan Dotter, Dir.-External Comm.
Ahmed Pasha, VP-Investor Rel.
Andrew M. Vesey, Exec. VP/Pres., Latin America & Africa
Ned Hall, Exec. VP/Pres., North America
Richard Santoroski, Exec. VP/Chief Risk Officer
Philip Odeen, Chmn.
Andres Gluski, Interim Pres., Asia, Europe & Middle East

Phone: 703-522-1315	**Fax:** 703-528-4510
Toll-Free:	
Address: 4300 Wilson Blvd., 11th Fl., Arlington, VA 22203 US	

GROWTH PLANS/SPECIAL FEATURES:

The AES Corporation, through its subsidiaries, operates in the global power industry in 31 countries on five continents. It has a total capacity of roughly 40,300 Megawatts (MW) and over 2,200 MW under construction in six countries. AES operates two primary business lines: power generation and utilities. Utilities operations (55% of the firm's revenues) consist of 14 distribution companies in seven countries that serve over 11 million customers. The segment has integrated utilities in the U.S. through Indianapolis Power & Light and in Cameroon through Sonel; additionally, it has distribution companies in Brazil through AES Eletropaulo and AES Sul; in Chile through AES Gener; and in the Ukraine through AES Kievoblenergo and AES Rivneenergo. AES's generation business (45% of revenues) generates approximately 34,000 MW and sells electricity to wholesale customers through 99 power generation plants in 26 countries. It also has roughly 1,900 MW of capacity under construction in four countries. AES is expanding its wind, solar and other alternative energy operations. The firm's wind power business, AES Wind Generation, has 30 facilities in four countries with a total capacity of over 1,400 MW. Joint venture AES Solar Energy LLC (with Riverstone Holdings, LLC) has nine plants in Spain with an output capacity of 33 MW of solar power. In September 2009, AES opened new plants in Jordan, Chile and China. In December 2009, the firm agreed to sell its operations in Oman and Pakistan for approximately $200 million. In early 2010, AES Wind Generation began operating a new wind farm in Pennsylvania and acquired U.K.-based Your Energy Ltd. In March 2010, China Investment Corporation acquired roughly 15% ownership of AES. In April 2010, AES agreed to sell its 55% interest in Ras Laffan to partner Qatar Electricity and Water Company. In August 2010, subsidiary AES Ballylumford Holdings Limited acquired North Ireland-based Premier Power Limited.

FINANCIALS: **Sales and profits are in thousands of dollars—add 000 to get the full amount. 2010 Note: Financial information for 2010 was not available for all companies at press time.**

2010 Sales: $	2010 Profits: $	**U.S. Stock Ticker: AES**
2009 Sales: $14,119,000	2009 Profits: $658,000	**Int'l Ticker:** Int'l Exchange:
2008 Sales: $15,358,000	2008 Profits: $1,234,000	Employees: 27,000
2007 Sales: $13,014,000	2007 Profits: $-95,000	Fiscal Year Ends: 12/31
2006 Sales: $11,509,000	2006 Profits: $247,000	Parent Company:

SALARIES/BENEFITS:

Pension Plan: Y	ESOP Stock Plan:	Profit Sharing: Y	Top Exec. Salary: $1,014,000	Bonus: $4,031,500
Savings Plan: Y	Stock Purch. Plan:		Second Exec. Salary: $670,000	Bonus: $1,521,070

OTHER THOUGHTS:

Apparent Women Officers or Directors: 5
Hot Spot for Advancement for Women/Minorities: Y

LOCATIONS: ("Y" = Yes)

West:	Southwest:	Midwest:	Southeast:	Northeast:	International:
Y	Y	Y	Y	Y	Y

AGL RESOURCES INC

www.aglresources.com

Industry Group Code: 221210 **Ranks within this company's industry group:** Sales: 9 Profits: 7

Exploration/Production:		**Refining/Retailing:**		**Utilities:**		**Alternative Energy:**		**Specialty Services:**		**Energy Mktg./Other Svcs.**	
Exploration:		Refining:		Electric Utility:		Waste/Solar/Other:		Consulting/Eng.:		Energy Marketing:	Y
Production:		Retailing:		Gas Utility:	Y	Thermal/Steam:		Seismic:		Equipment/Machinery:	
Coal Production:		Convenience Stores:		Pipelines:	Y	Wind:		Drilling:		Oil Field Services:	
		Chemicals:		Water:		Hydro:		InfoTech:		Air/Shipping Transportation:	
						Fuel Cells:		Specialty Services:			

TYPES OF BUSINESS:

Utilities-Electricity & Natural Gas
Retail Energy Marketing
Natural Gas Storage
Conduit & Fiber Infrastructure

BRANDS/DIVISIONS/AFFILIATES:

SouthStar Energy Services LLC
Sequent Energy Management LP
LNG Distribution Company

CONTACTS:

Note: Officers with more than one job title may be intentionally listed here more than once.

John W. Somerhalder II, CEO
John W. Somerhalder II, Pres.
Andrew W. Evans, CFO/Exec. VP
Donna N. Peeples, Chief Mktg. Officer/VP-Corp. Comm.
Melanie M. Platt, Sr. VP-Human Resources & Mktg.
Joseph A. Surber, III, CIO/VP
Ralph Cleveland, Exec. VP-Eng.
Paul R. Shlanta, General Counsel/Exec. VP/Chief Compliance Officer
Ralph Cleveland, Exec. VP-Oper.
Melanie M. Platt, Sr. VP-Comm.
, Dir.-Investor Rel. & Corp. Dev.
Bryan E. Seas, Chief Acct. Officer/Controller/Sr. VP
Steve Cave, VP-Finance
Hank Linginfelter, Exec. VP-Utility Oper.
Suzanne Sitherwood, Sr. VP-Southern Oper.
Dana A. Grams, Pres., Pivotal Energy Dev.
John W. Somerhalder II, Chmn.
Jay Sutton, VP-Supply Chain & Eng. Svcs.

Phone: 404-584-4000	**Fax:** 404-584-3714
Toll-Free: 866-757-6646	
Address: 10 Peachtree Place NE, Atlanta, GA 30309 US	

GROWTH PLANS/SPECIAL FEATURES:

AGL Resources, Inc. is an energy services holding company that sells, distributes, transports and stores natural gas. The company's principal business is the distribution of natural gas in six states: Florida, Georgia, Maryland, New Jersey, Tennessee and Virginia. The firm, one of the largest distributors of natural gas in the southeastern and mid-Atlantic regions of the U.S., serves more than 2.3 million end-use customers. AGL Resources operates in four segments: distribution, retail energy, wholesale services and energy investments. The distribution segment includes the company's six natural gas local distribution utilities, which construct, manage and maintain intrastate natural gas pipelines and distribution facilities. The retail energy operations segment consists of SouthStar Energy Services LLC, a joint venture engaged in retail natural gas marketing primarily in Georgia, of which 85% is owned by the company. The wholesale services segment consists of Sequent Energy Management, L.P., a subsidiary involved in asset management and optimization, storage and transportation services and wholesale marketing. The energy investments division includes a number of businesses related and complementary to the firm's primary business. The most significant of these is its natural gas storage business, which develops, acquires and operates high-deliverability salt-dome and other storage assets in the Gulf Coast region of the U.S. In addition, AGL Resources owns and operates a small telecommunications business that constructs and operates conduit and fiber infrastructure. In July2010, the firm sold its dark-fiber telecommunications unit, AGL Networks, to Zayo Group, LLC. Also in July 2010, AGL Resources agreed to establish a 50-50 joint venture with El Paso Corporation. The joint venture, named Southeast LNG Distribution Company, will transport liquefied natural gas (LNG) across the southeastern portion of the U.S. for distribution to the heavy-duty transportation industry.

The firm offers employees medical, dental, vision and life insurance; disability insurance; flexible spending accounts; and adoption assistance.

FINANCIALS:

Sales and profits are in thousands of dollars—add 000 to get the full amount. 2010 Note: Financial information for 2010 was not available for all companies at press time.

2010 Sales: $	2010 Profits: $	**U.S. Stock Ticker: AGL**
2009 Sales: $2,317,000	2009 Profits: $249,000	**Int'l Ticker:** Int'l Exchange:
2008 Sales: $2,800,000	2008 Profits: $217,000	Employees: 2,469
2007 Sales: $2,494,000	2007 Profits: $211,000	Fiscal Year Ends: 12/31
2006 Sales: $2,621,000	2006 Profits: $212,000	Parent Company:

SALARIES/BENEFITS:

Pension Plan: Y	ESOP Stock Plan:	Profit Sharing:	Top Exec. Salary: $821,154	Bonus: $2,169,901
Savings Plan: Y	Stock Purch. Plan: Y		Second Exec. Salary: $457,692	Bonus: $658,349

OTHER THOUGHTS:

Apparent Women Officers or Directors: 10
Hot Spot for Advancement for Women/Minorities: Y

LOCATIONS: ("Y" = Yes)

West:	Southwest:	Midwest:	Southeast:	Northeast:	International:
	Y		Y	Y	

ALABAMA POWER COMPANY

www.alabamapower.com

Industry Group Code: 2211 **Ranks within this company's industry group:** Sales: Profits:

Exploration/Production:		**Refining/Retailing:**		**Utilities:**		**Alternative Energy:**		**Specialty Services:**		**Energy Mktg./Other Svcs.**	
Exploration:		Refining:		Electric Utility:	Y	Waste/Solar/Other:	Y	Consulting/Eng.:		Energy Marketing:	
Production:		Retailing:		Gas Utility:		Thermal/Steam:	Y	Seismic:		Equipment/Machinery:	
Coal Production:		Convenience Stores:		Pipelines:		Wind:		Drilling:		Oil Field Services:	
		Chemicals:		Water:		Hydro:	Y	InfoTech:		Air/Shipping Transportation:	
						Fuel Cells:		Specialty Services:	Y		

TYPES OF BUSINESS:

Electric Utility
Hydroelectric Power
Nuclear Power
Appliance & Electronics Retail
Steam Service
Wholesale Electricity
Online Services
Outdoor Lighting

BRANDS/DIVISIONS/AFFILIATES:

Southern Company (The)
Georgia Power
Gulf Power
Mississippi Power
Southern Power
Southern Nuclear
SouthernLINC Wireless
Southern Telecom

CONTACTS:

Note: Officers with more than one job title may be intentionally listed here more than once.

Charles D. McCrary, CEO
Charles D. McCrary, Pres.
Phil Raymond, CFO/Exec. VP
Kathleen King, CIO
Ted McCullough, Sr. Prod. Officer/Sr. VP
Patrick Wylie, Dir.-Corp. Comm.
Phil Raymond, Treas.
Greg Barker, Sr. VP-Mktg. & Econ. Dev.

Phone: 205-257-1000	**Fax:** 205-257-2445
Toll-Free:	
Address: 600 N. 18th St., Birmingham, AL 35291 US	

GROWTH PLANS/SPECIAL FEATURES:

Alabama Power Company is a subsidiary of The Southern Company, one of the U.S.'s largest generators of electricity. The firm is engaged in the generation and purchase of electricity, as well as the distribution and sale of electricity to over 4.4 million customers in southern and mid-Alabama. Residential customers make up 84.4% of those, with commercial and industrial making up 15.2% and 0.4% respectively. It also wholesales electricity to 15 municipally owned electric distribution systems and two rural cooperative associations. The company operates more than 78,000 miles of transmission and distribution lines throughout a 44,500-square-mile service area. Alabama Power has a combined generating capacity of approximately 13 million kilowatts (kW) from its 24 facilities. These facilities utilize a range of fuel sources, including coal (68.86% of generation), nuclear (18.78%), gas/oil (8.23%) and hydroelectric (4.13%). In addition, the company sells and cooperates with dealers in promoting the sale of appliances, electronics and accessories through its web site to customers within its service area. The company also supplies steam service in downtown Birmingham.

The company offers its employees medical, dental and group and dependent life insurance; prescription drug coverage; single and family mental health and substance abuse treatment; accident and sickness insurance; flexible spending accounts; a health and wellness program; AD&D coverage; an employee assistance program; tuition assistance; and credit union membership and services.

FINANCIALS:

Sales and profits are in thousands of dollars—add 000 to get the full amount. 2010 Note: Financial information for 2010 was not available for all companies at press time.

2010 Sales: $	2010 Profits: $	**U.S. Stock Ticker: Subsidiary**
2009 Sales: $	2009 Profits: $	**Int'l Ticker:** Int'l Exchange:
2008 Sales: $	2008 Profits: $	Employees:
2007 Sales: $5,360,000	2007 Profits: $	Fiscal Year Ends: 12/31
2006 Sales: $5,014,700	2006 Profits: $542,500	Parent Company: SOUTHERN COMPANY (THE)

SALARIES/BENEFITS:

Pension Plan:	ESOP Stock Plan:	Profit Sharing:	Top Exec. Salary: $	Bonus: $808,636
Savings Plan:	Stock Purch. Plan:		Second Exec. Salary: $	Bonus: $

OTHER THOUGHTS:

Apparent Women Officers or Directors: 1
Hot Spot for Advancement for Women/Minorities:

LOCATIONS: ("Y" = Yes)

West:	Southwest:	Midwest:	Southeast:	Northeast:	International:
			Y		

ALLEGHENY ENERGY INC

www.alleghenyenergy.com

Industry Group Code: 221 **Ranks within this company's industry group:** Sales: 35 Profits: 25

Exploration/Production:		Refining/Retailing:		Utilities:		Alternative Energy:		Specialty Services:		Energy Mktg./Other Svcs.	
Exploration:		Refining:		Electric Utility:	Y	Waste/Solar/Other:		Consulting/Eng.:	Y	Energy Marketing:	Y
Production:		Retailing:		Gas Utility:	Y	Thermal/Steam:		Seismic:		Equipment/Machinery:	
Coal Production:		Convenience Stores:		Pipelines:		Wind:		Drilling:		Oil Field Services:	
		Chemicals:		Water:		Hydro:	Y	InfoTech:		Air/Shipping Transportation:	
						Fuel Cells:		Specialty Services:			

TYPES OF BUSINESS:

Utilities-Electricity & Natural Gas
Electrical Generation
Wholesale Energy
Energy Infrastructure
Energy Facility Management

BRANDS/DIVISIONS/AFFILIATES:

Monongahela Power Company
Potomac Edison Company (The)
West Penn Power Company
PATH LLC
TrAIL Company
AE Supply Company, LLC
Allegheny Generating Company

CONTACTS:

Note: Officers with more than one job title may be intentionally listed here more than once.

Paul J. Evanson, CEO
Paul J. Evanson, Pres.
Kirk R. Oliver, CFO/Sr. VP
Edward Dudzinski, VP-Human Resources & Security
Rick C. Arthur, Jr., CIO/VP
George J. Farah, VP-Eng., Construction & Support Svcs.
David M. Feinberg, General Counsel/Sec./VP
Daniel C. McIntire, VP-Generation Oper.
Eric S. Gleason, VP-Corp. Dev. & Quality
Aldie Warnock, VP-External Affairs
William F. (Rick) Wahl III, Chief Acct. Officer/Controller/VP
Rodney L. Dickens, Pres., Allegheny Power
Bruce M. Sedlock, VP-Corp Planning & Taxes
Barry E. Pakenham, VP/Treas.
David C. Cannon, Jr., VP-Environment, Health & Safety
Paul J. Evanson, Chmn.

Phone: 724-837-3000	**Fax:**
Toll-Free: 800-255-3443	
Address: 800 Cabin Hill Dr., Greensburg, PA 15601 US	

GROWTH PLANS/SPECIAL FEATURES:

Allegheny Energy, Inc. (AE) is an integrated energy business that generates and delivers electricity to more than 1.5 million customers in Pennsylvania, West Virginia, Maryland and Virginia through its various subsidiaries. The company operates through two business segments: Regulated Operations and Merchant Generation. The Regulated Operations segment consists of a group of public utility companies that operate under the name Allegheny Power. These companies are Monongahela Power Company; The Potomac Edison Company; and West Penn Power Company. Also included in this segment is TrAIL Company, which was established to finance and manage a transmission expansion project involving the construction of new transmission lines, including TrAIL, a 500 kilovolt (kV) transmission line. Another company in this segment is PATH LLC, formed to oversee the construction of the PATH line, a 765 kV transmission network. The Merchant Generation segment includes AE Supply Company LLC and its subsidiary Allegheny Generating Company (AGC), 41% owned by Monongahela Power Company. AE Supply owns, operates and manages electric generation facilities, and also purchases and sells energy and energy-related commodities. AE Supply markets its electric generation capacity in different markets, with the majority of its generation capacity supplying AE subsidiaries. In February 2010, the firm agreed to be acquired by FirstEnergy Corp. for $4.7 billion. In June 2010, the company sold its distribution operations in Virginia to Rappahannock Electric Cooperative and Shenandoah Valley Electric Cooperative.

Employees are offered medical, dental and vision insurance; disability coverage; tuition assistance; flexible spending accounts; a 401(k) savings plan; a retirement plan; life insurance; and tuition assistance.

FINANCIALS:

Sales and profits are in thousands of dollars—add 000 to get the full amount. 2010 Note: Financial information for 2010 was not available for all companies at press time.

2010 Sales: $	2010 Profits: $	**U.S. Stock Ticker: AYE**
2009 Sales: $3,426,800	2009 Profits: $394,100	**Int'l Ticker:** Int'l Exchange:
2008 Sales: $3,385,900	2008 Profits: $395,400	Employees: 4,383
2007 Sales: $3,307,000	2007 Profits: $412,200	Fiscal Year Ends: 12/31
2006 Sales: $3,121,500	2006 Profits: $319,300	Parent Company:

SALARIES/BENEFITS:

Pension Plan: Y	ESOP Stock Plan:	Profit Sharing:	Top Exec. Salary: $1,200,000	Bonus: $1,918,500
Savings Plan: Y	Stock Purch. Plan:		Second Exec. Salary: $525,000	Bonus: $350,000

OTHER THOUGHTS:

Apparent Women Officers or Directors: 2
Hot Spot for Advancement for Women/Minorities:

LOCATIONS: ("Y" = Yes)

West:	Southwest:	Midwest:	Southeast:	Northeast:	International:
				Y	

Note: Financial information, benefits and other data can change quickly and may vary from those stated here.

ALLIANCE RESOURCE PARTNERS LP

www.arlp.com

Industry Group Code: 21211 **Ranks within this company's industry group:** Sales: 12 Profits: 8

Exploration/Production:		**Refining/Retailing:**		**Utilities:**		**Alternative Energy:**		**Specialty Services:**		**Energy Mktg./Other Svcs.**	
Exploration:		Refining:		Electric Utility:		Waste/Solar/Other:		Consulting/Eng.:		Energy Marketing:	
Production:		Retailing:		Gas Utility:		Thermal/Steam:		Seismic:		Equipment/Machinery:	
Coal Production:	Y	Convenience Stores:		Pipelines:		Wind:		Drilling:		Oil Field Services:	
		Chemicals:		Water:		Hydro:		InfoTech:		Air/Shipping Transportation:	
						Fuel Cells:		Specialty Services:	Y		

TYPES OF BUSINESS:

Coal Mining
Coal Production
Coal Marketer
Coal Support Services

BRANDS/DIVISIONS/AFFILIATES:

Alliance Resource Operating Partners, LP
Alliance Resource Management GP, LLC
Alliance Resource GP, LLC
Warrior Coal, LLC
Alliance Resource Hodlings, Inc.
Webster County Coal, LLC
Matrix Design Group, LLC
METS 2.1

CONTACTS:

Note: Officers with more than one job title may be intentionally listed here more than once.

Joseph W. Craft, III, CEO
Thomas M. Wynne, COO/Sr. VP
Joseph W. Craft, III, Pres.
Brian L. Cantrell, CFO/Sr. VP
Robert G. Sachse, Exec. VP-Mktg.
R. Eberley Davis, General Counsel/Sr. VP/Sec.
Charles R. Wesley, Exec. VP
John P. Neafsey, Chmn.

Phone: 918-295-7600 **Fax:**
Toll-Free:
Address: 1717 S. Boulder Ave., Tulsa, OK 74119 US

GROWTH PLANS/SPECIAL FEATURES:

Alliance Resource Partners, L.P. (ARLP) is a diversified coal producer and marketer to major U.S. utilities and industrial users. The firm has approximately 647.2 million tons of reserves located in Illinois, Indiana, Kentucky, Maryland, Pennsylvania and West Virginia. ALRP maintains nine underground mining complexes in five states and a coal loading terminal on the Ohio River at Mt. Vernon, Indiana. Alliance operates in three primary regions: The Illinois Basin; Central Appalachian; and Northern Appalachian. The firm produces a diverse range of steam coals with varying sulfur and heat contents, which enables it to satisfy a broad range of customer specifications. The Illinois Basin operation, which supplied over 80% of the firm's coal production, has six mining complexes in which continuous mining units employ room-and-pillar mining techniques. The central Appalachian operation has two mining complexes that produce low-sulfur coal. The northern Appalachian operation has one mining complex, which utilizes a longwall miner for the majority of the coal extraction as well as continuous mining units used to prepare the mine for the future longwall mining operation areas. Alliance also develops and markets additional services including ash and scrubber sludge removal, coal yard maintenance and arranging alternate transportation services. Through subsidiary Matrix Design Group, LLC, the company provides mine equipment and products for itself and other third-party outfits, including the METS 2.1 tracking and communication system. In 2009, the firm produced 25.8 million tons of coal, of which nearly 92% was sold to electric utilities.

FINANCIALS:

Sales and profits are in thousands of dollars—add 000 to get the full amount. 2010 Note: Financial information for 2010 was not available for all companies at press time.

2010 Sales: $	2010 Profits: $	**U.S. Stock Ticker: ARLP**
2009 Sales: $1,231,031	2009 Profits: $192,157	**Int'l Ticker:** Int'l Exchange:
2008 Sales: $1,156,549	2008 Profits: $134,176	Employees: 3,090
2007 Sales: $1,033,334	2007 Profits: $170,390	Fiscal Year Ends: 12/31
2006 Sales: $967,557	2006 Profits: $172,927	Parent Company:

SALARIES/BENEFITS:

Pension Plan: Y	ESOP Stock Plan:	Profit Sharing:	Top Exec. Salary: $341,267	Bonus: $
Savings Plan: Y	Stock Purch. Plan:		Second Exec. Salary: $280,148	Bonus: $220,000

OTHER THOUGHTS:

Apparent Women Officers or Directors: 1
Hot Spot for Advancement for Women/Minorities:

LOCATIONS: ("Y" = Yes)

West:	Southwest:	Midwest:	Southeast:	Northeast:	International:
	Y	Y		Y	

ALLIANT ENERGY CORP

www.alliantenergy.com

Industry Group Code: 221 **Ranks within this company's industry group:** Sales: 34 Profits: 41

Exploration/Production:		Refining/Retailing:		Utilities:		Alternative Energy:		Specialty Services:		Energy Mktg./Other Svcs.	
Exploration:		Refining:		Electric Utility:	Y	Waste/Solar/Other:		Consulting/Eng.:	Y	Energy Marketing:	Y
Production:		Retailing:		Gas Utility:	Y	Thermal/Steam:		Seismic:		Equipment/Machinery:	
Coal Production:		Convenience Stores:		Pipelines:		Wind:	Y	Drilling:		Oil Field Services:	
		Chemicals:		Water:		Hydro:		InfoTech:		Air/Shipping Transportation:	Y
						Fuel Cells:		Specialty Services:	Y		

TYPES OF BUSINESS:

Utilities-Electricity & Natural Gas
Energy Marketing
Rail & Barge Transportation
Environmental Consulting
Energy Planning & Procurement Services

BRANDS/DIVISIONS/AFFILIATES:

Alliant Energy Resources, Inc.
RMT, Inc.
Wisconsin Power and Light Co.
Interstate Power and Light Co.
Alliant Energy Transportation
Williams Bulk Transfer
Cedar Rapids and Iowa Railway
IEI Barge Services

CONTACTS:

Note: Officers with more than one job title may be intentionally listed here more than once.

William D. Harvey, CEO
Eliot G. Protsch, COO/Sr. Exec. VP
William D. Harvey, Pres.
Patricia Kampling, CFO/Exec. VP/Treas.
Barbara J. Swan, Chief Admin. Officer
Barbara J. Swan, General Counsel/Exec. VP
Thomas L. Aller, Sr. VP-Energy Resource Dev.
Peggy Howard Moore, VP-Finance
Dundeana K. Doyle, Sr. VP-Energy Delivery
Thomas L. Aller, Pres., Interstate Power & Light Co.
John O. Larsen, Sr. VP-Generation
William D. Harvey, Chmn.

Phone: 608-458-3311 **Fax:** 608-458-0100
Toll-Free: 800-255-4268
Address: 4902 North Biltmore Ln., Madison, WI 53707 US

GROWTH PLANS/SPECIAL FEATURES:

Alliant Energy Corp. operates as a public utility holding company. Through its subsidiaries, it provides electricity and natural gas to approximately 1 million electric customers and 412,000 natural gas customers throughout Iowa, Wisconsin and Minnesota. The company has a service territory of over 56,000 square miles along with 8,000 miles of natural gas pipeline. This infrastructure allows the company to generate more than 31 million megawatt-hours (MWh) of electricity each year. Alliant's total assets are in excess of $9 billion. The company's primary subsidiaries include Interstate Power and Light; Wisconsin Power and Light; Alliant Energy Resources; RMT, Inc.; and Alliant Energy Transportation. Interstate Power and Light is a public utility engaged principally in the generation and distribution of electric energy; and the distribution and transportation of natural gas in Iowa and southern Minnesota. Wisconsin Power and Light is a public utility that distributes electricity and natural gas to southern and central Wisconsin. Alliant Energy Resources manages a small portfolio of wholly-owned subsidiaries and additional investments through two distinct platforms: non-regulated generation and other non-regulated investments. RMT, Inc. assists clients with meeting environmental regulatory needs at the state and federal level. It is currently constructing the Kahuku Wind facility on the island of Oahu. Alliant Energy Transportation provides freight, rail and barge transportation solutions through its subsidiaries Williams Bulk Transfer, Cedar Rapids and Iowa Railway and IEI Barge Services. In April 2010, Wisconsin Power and Light agreed to purchase the 25% interest in Edgewater Generating Station owned by Wisconsin Electric Power Company.

The company offers employees medical, dental and vision insurance; life insurance; disability insurance; 401(k); tuition reimbursement; paid apprenticeship program; adoption assistance; employee discount program; and a wellness program.

FINANCIALS:

Sales and profits are in thousands of dollars—add 000 to get the full amount. 2010 Note: Financial information for 2010 was not available for all companies at press time.

2010 Sales: $	2010 Profits: $	**U.S. Stock Ticker: LNT**
2009 Sales: $3,432,800	2009 Profits: $129,700	**Int'l Ticker:** Int'l Exchange:
2008 Sales: $3,681,700	2008 Profits: $288,000	Employees: 4,957
2007 Sales: $3,437,600	2007 Profits: $425,300	Fiscal Year Ends: 12/31
2006 Sales: $3,359,400	2006 Profits: $315,700	Parent Company:

SALARIES/BENEFITS:

Pension Plan:	ESOP Stock Plan:	Profit Sharing:	Top Exec. Salary: $832,000	Bonus: $
Savings Plan: Y	Stock Purch. Plan:		Second Exec. Salary: $594,846	Bonus: $

OTHER THOUGHTS:

Apparent Women Officers or Directors: 4
Hot Spot for Advancement for Women/Minorities: Y

LOCATIONS: ("Y" = Yes)

West:	Southwest:	Midwest:	Southeast:	Northeast:	International:
		Y			Y

ALON USA ENERGY INC

www.alonusa.com

Industry Group Code: 324110 **Ranks within this company's industry group:** Sales: 26 Profits: 21

Exploration/Production:		Refining/Retailing:		Utilities:		Alternative Energy:		Specialty Services:		Energy Mktg./Other Svcs.	
Exploration:		Refining:	Y	Electric Utility:		Waste/Solar/Other:		Consulting/Eng.:		Energy Marketing:	
Production:		Retailing:	Y	Gas Utility:		Thermal/Steam:		Seismic:		Equipment/Machinery:	
Coal Production:		Convenience Stores:	Y	Pipelines:		Wind:		Drilling:		Oil Field Services:	
		Chemicals:		Water:		Hydro:		InfoTech:		Air/Shipping Transportation:	
						Fuel Cells:		Specialty Services:	Y		

TYPES OF BUSINESS:

Petroleum Products Refining & Marketing
Asphalt Production
Convenience Stores

BRANDS/DIVISIONS/AFFILIATES:

ALON Israel Oil Co., Ltd.
FINA
7-Eleven

CONTACTS:

Note: Officers with more than one job title may be intentionally listed here more than once.

Jeff D. Morris, CEO
Joseph Isreal, COO
Paul Eisman, Pres.
Shai Even, CFO/Sr. VP
Claire A. Hart, Sr. VP
Joseph A. Concienne, Sr. VP-Refining
Michael Oster, Sr. VP-Mergers & Acquisitions
David Wiessman, Exec. Chmn.
Alan Moret, Sr. VP-Supply

Phone: 972-367-3600	**Fax:** 972-367-3725
Toll-Free:	
Address: 7616 LBJ Freeway, Ste. 300, Dallas, TX 75251-7030 US	

GROWTH PLANS/SPECIAL FEATURES:

Alon USA Energy, Inc. is an independent refiner and marketer of petroleum products operating primarily in the South Central, Southwestern and Western regions of the U.S. The company operates in three segments: refining and unbranded marketing; asphalt; and retail and branded marketing. The refining and unbranded marketing segment includes three sour and heavy crude oil refineries located in Big Spring, Texas, and Paramount and Long Beach, California; and a light sweet crude oil refinery in Krotz Springs, Louisiana. These four refineries have a combined throughput capacity of roughly 240,000 barrels per day. The facilities refine crude oil into petroleum products, including various grades of gasoline, diesel fuel, jet fuel, petrochemicals, petrochemical feedstocks and asphalt. The asphalt segment was developed to maximize the value of the additional amount of vacuum tower bottoms produced after making gasoline and distillate products from crude oils. The division markets asphalt produced at Alon's California refineries in the refining and marketing segment and asphalt produced by the company's fifth refinery, located in Willbridge, Oregon. This segment also operates the Oregon refinery. This refinery is an asphalt topping refinery located on 42 acres; it has a crude oil throughput capacity of 12,000 barrels per days. It processes primarily heavy crude oil, with roughly 70% of its production sold as asphalt products. The retail and branded marketing segment operates more than 308 owned and leased convenience stores operating primarily in West and Central Texas and New Mexico. The convenience stores typically offer various grades of gasoline, diesel fuel, food and tobacco products, non-alcoholic and alcoholic beverages and general merchandise to the public under the 7-Eleven and FINA brand names. Alon Israel Oil Co., Ltd., owns roughly 76% of the company. In June 2010, Alon USA acquired a refinery in Bakersfield, California, from Big West of California LLC.

FINANCIALS:

Sales and profits are in thousands of dollars—add 000 to get the full amount. 2010 Note: Financial information for 2010 was not available for all companies at press time.

2010 Sales: $	2010 Profits: $	**U.S. Stock Ticker: ALJ**
2009 Sales: $3,915,732	2009 Profits: $-115,156	**Int'l Ticker:** Int'l Exchange:
2008 Sales: $5,156,706	2008 Profits: $82,883	Employees: 2,825
2007 Sales: $4,542,151	2007 Profits: $103,936	Fiscal Year Ends: 12/31
2006 Sales: $3,093,890	2006 Profits: $157,368	Parent Company:

SALARIES/BENEFITS:

Pension Plan:	ESOP Stock Plan:	Profit Sharing:	Top Exec. Salary: $333,100	Bonus: $
Savings Plan:	Stock Purch. Plan:		Second Exec. Salary: $313,100	Bonus: $400,000

OTHER THOUGHTS:

Apparent Women Officers or Directors:
Hot Spot for Advancement for Women/Minorities:

LOCATIONS: ("Y" = Yes)

West:	Southwest:	Midwest:	Southeast:	Northeast:	International:
Y	Y		Y		

ALSTOM SA

www.alstom.com

Industry Group Code: 335 **Ranks within this company's industry group:** Sales: 4 Profits: 4

Exploration/Production:		**Refining/Retailing:**		**Utilities:**		**Alternative Energy:**		**Specialty Services:**		**Energy Mktg./Other Svcs.**	
Exploration:		Refining:		Electric Utility:		Waste/Solar/Other:	Y	Consulting/Eng.:	Y	Energy Marketing:	
Production:		Retailing:		Gas Utility:		Thermal/Steam:	Y	Seismic:		Equipment/Machinery:	Y
Coal Production:		Convenience Stores:		Pipelines:		Wind:	Y	Drilling:		Oil Field Services:	
		Chemicals:		Water:		Hydro:	Y	InfoTech:		Air/Shipping Transportation:	
						Fuel Cells:		Specialty Services:	Y		

TYPES OF BUSINESS:

Equipment-Electric Power Distribution
Energy & Transport Infrastructure
Power Plant Machinery
Rail Transport Services
Rail Transport Manufacturing
Technical Consulting & Power Plant Refurbishment

BRANDS/DIVISIONS/AFFILIATES:

Alstom Power
Alstom Transport
Alstom Grid
Areva
Transmashholding
Amstar Surface Technology Ltd.
BrightSource Energy, Inc.

CONTACTS: *Note: Officers with more than one job title may be intentionally listed here more than once.*

Patrick Kron, CEO
Nicolas Tissot, CFO
Patrick Dubert, Sr. VP-Human Resources
Philippe Joubert, Exec. VP/Pres., Power Systems Sector
Philippe Mellier, Exec. VP/Pres., Transport Sector
Henri Poupart-Lafarge, Exec. VP/Pres., Grid Sector
Patrick Kron, Chmn.

Phone: 33-1-41-49-20-00 **Fax:** 33-1-41-49-24-85
Toll-Free:
Address: 3 Ave. Andre Malraux, Levallois-Perret, 75795 France

GROWTH PLANS/SPECIAL FEATURES:

Alstom S.A., is a world leader in integrated power plant, power production services, air quality control systems and rail transport systems with operations in over 70 countries. The company divides its activities into three sectors: Transport, power generation and transmission. Alstom Transport develops and markets a complete range of systems, equipment and services for the railway market. Alstom offers rolling stock for high speed and very high speed trains, regional and commuter trains, locomotives, freight cars, metros, trams and tram-trains. The transport division has contracts to build or has built railway cars and equipment for transit systems across the globe, from Russia, China and India to Brazil, Italy and New York, among others. The power generation segment, operating as Alstom Power, designs, manufactures, supplies and services products and systems for the power generation sector. Its products and services include boilers, turbines (gas, hydroelectric and steam), turbogenerators, air quality control systems, product retrofitting and control systems. It also provides refurbishment and maintenance of existing plants as well as turnkey solutions for range of fossil fuel-based and renewable energy power generation facilities. Alstom's transmission business, operating under the moniker Alstom Grid, was acquired in June 2010 from Areva. This segment offers multiple products, systems, automation and after-sale services for electricity power grids. In March 2010, the firm acquired a 25% capital interest in Russia's largest railway equipment manufacturer Transmashholding. In May, Alstom entered the solar energy market with an investment in BrightSource Energy, Inc., which designs, builds and operates solar thermal power plants. In June, along with the acquisition of Areva's transmission segment, the company acquired Amstar Surface Technology Ltd., specializing in the production of thermal spray coatings, and also opened a turbine manufacturing facility in Chattanooga, Tennessee. In July 2010, Alstom signed an agreement with the Iraqi government for the development and modernization of Iraq's electricity infrastructure.

FINANCIALS: **Sales and profits are in thousands of dollars—add 000 to get the full amount. 2010 Note: Financial information for 2010 was not available for all companies at press time.**

2010 Sales: $	2010 Profits: $	**U.S. Stock Ticker:**
2009 Sales: $27,831,200	2009 Profits: $1,647,090	**Int'l Ticker: ALSO** Int'l Exchange: Paris-Euronext
2008 Sales: $21,980,400	2008 Profits: $1,107,600	Employees: 81,500
2007 Sales: $21,880,300	2007 Profits: $686,800	Fiscal Year Ends: 3/31
2006 Sales: $20,656,000	2006 Profits: $275,700	Parent Company:

SALARIES/BENEFITS:

Pension Plan:	ESOP Stock Plan:	Profit Sharing:	Top Exec. Salary: $1,484,610	Bonus: $1,812,200
Savings Plan:	Stock Purch. Plan:		Second Exec. Salary: $	Bonus: $

OTHER THOUGHTS:

Apparent Women Officers or Directors:
Hot Spot for Advancement for Women/Minorities:

LOCATIONS: ("Y" = Yes)

West:	Southwest:	Midwest:	Southeast:	Northeast:	International:
	Y			Y	Y

AMEREN CORP

www.ameren.com

Industry Group Code: 221 **Ranks within this company's industry group:** Sales: 26 Profits: 19

Exploration/Production:		Refining/Retailing:		Utilities:		Alternative Energy:		Specialty Services:		Energy Mktg./Other Svcs.	
Exploration:		Refining:		Electric Utility:	Y	Waste/Solar/Other:	Y	Consulting/Eng.:		Energy Marketing:	Y
Production:		Retailing:		Gas Utility:	Y	Thermal/Steam:	Y	Seismic:		Equipment/Machinery:	
Coal Production:		Convenience Stores:		Pipelines:		Wind:		Drilling:		Oil Field Services:	
		Chemicals:		Water:		Hydro:	Y	InfoTech:		Air/Shipping Transportation:	
						Fuel Cells:		Specialty Services:	Y		

TYPES OF BUSINESS:

Utilities-Electricity & Natural Gas
Electrical Generation & Distribution
Natural Gas Purchasing & Distribution
Investment Services
Energy Marketing

BRANDS/DIVISIONS/AFFILIATES:

AmerenUE
AmerenCIPS
AmerenCILCO
AmerenEnergy Resources
AmerenEnergy Resources Generating Company
Ameren Missouri
Ameren Transmission Company
Ameren Illinois Company

CONTACTS:

Note: Officers with more than one job title may be intentionally listed here more than once.

Thomas R. Voss, CEO
Thomas R. Voss, Pres.
Martin J. Lyons, Jr., CFO/Sr. VP
Andrew M. Serri, Pres., Ameren Energy Mktg.
Steven R. Sullivan, General Counsel/Sr. VP/Corp. Sec.
Richard J. Mark, Sr. VP-Ameren Missouri Customer Oper.
Michael Moehn, Sr. VP-Corp. Planning & Bus. Risk Mgmt.
Karen Foss, Sr. VP-Comm. & Brand Mgmt.
Adam C. Heflin, Chief Nuclear Officer/Sr. VP
Scott A. Cisel, CEO/Pres., Ameren Illinois
Charles D. Nusland, CEO/Pres., AmerenEnergy Resources
Thomas R. Voss, Exec. Chmn.

Phone: 314-621-3222 **Fax:** 314-554-3801
Toll-Free:
Address: 1901 Chouteau Ave., St. Louis, MO 63166-6149 US

GROWTH PLANS/SPECIAL FEATURES:

Ameren Corporation is a public utility holding company operating through two principal subsidiaries: Ameren Missouri and Ameren Illinois. Ameren Missouri (formerly AmerenUE), located in St. Louis, Missouri, operates a rate-regulated electric generation, transmission and distribution business. It supplies electricity to approximately 1.2 million customers and natural gas to over 125,000 customers in both Missouri and Illinois. Ameren's other primary operating subsidiary, Ameren Illinois, is principally engaged in the generation, transmission, distribution and sale of electric energy to 1.2 million customers, and the purchase, distribution, transportation and sale of natural gas to approximately 813,000 customers in Illinois. Ameren Illinois combines the operations of AmerenIP; AmerenCIPS; and AmerenCILCO. The firm's other subsidiaries include AmerenEnergy Resources, an integrated energy commodity company that offers services to non-rate-regulated generation, development and marketing companies; Ameren Energy Marketing, the power marketer for Ameren Energy Resources and other subsidiaries; AmerenEnergy Generating, a non-regulated generation company with more than 4,600 megawatts of generating capacity; and Ameren Services, which supplies administrative support to Ameren and its various companies. Ameren's combined energy capacity of 16,900 megawatts is generated from coal-fired plants, more than a dozen combustion turbine facilities, three hydroelectric plants and one nuclear facility. In August 2010, Ameren created a new subsidiary dedicated to electric transmission infrastructure investment, to be named Ameren Transmission Company. In October 2010, the firm completed the reorganization of its Illinois business, combining the operations of legacy subsidiaries AmerenIP; AmerenCILCO; and AmerenCIPS into Ameren Illinois Company.

Ameren offers employees medical, dental and vision insurance; flexible work schedules; an employee assistance program; educational assistance program; and a retirement plan after five years of service.

FINANCIALS:

Sales and profits are in thousands of dollars—add 000 to get the full amount. 2010 Note: Financial information for 2010 was not available for all companies at press time.

2010 Sales: $	2010 Profits: $	**U.S. Stock Ticker: AEE**
2009 Sales: $7,090,000	2009 Profits: $612,000	**Int'l Ticker:** Int'l Exchange:
2008 Sales: $7,839,000	2008 Profits: $605,000	Employees: 9,780
2007 Sales: $7,562,000	2007 Profits: $618,000	Fiscal Year Ends: 12/31
2006 Sales: $6,895,000	2006 Profits: $547,000	Parent Company:

SALARIES/BENEFITS:

Pension Plan: Y	ESOP Stock Plan:	Profit Sharing:	Top Exec. Salary: $660,733	Bonus: $484,604
Savings Plan: Y	Stock Purch. Plan: Y		Second Exec. Salary: $616,667	Bonus: $272,715

OTHER THOUGHTS:

Apparent Women Officers or Directors: 1
Hot Spot for Advancement for Women/Minorities:

LOCATIONS: ("Y" = Yes)

West:	Southwest:	Midwest:	Southeast:	Northeast:	International:
		Y			

AMEREN ILLINOIS COMPANY

www.ameren.com/sites/aiu

Industry Group Code: 221 **Ranks within this company's industry group:** Sales: Profits:

Exploration/Production:		**Refining/Retailing:**		**Utilities:**		**Alternative Energy:**		**Specialty Services:**		**Energy Mktg./Other Svcs.**	
Exploration:		Refining:		Electric Utility:	Y	Waste/Solar/Other:		Consulting/Eng.:		Energy Marketing:	
Production:		Retailing:		Gas Utility:	Y	Thermal/Steam:		Seismic:		Equipment/Machinery:	
Coal Production:		Convenience Stores:		Pipelines:	Y	Wind:		Drilling:		Oil Field Services:	
		Chemicals:		Water:		Hydro:		InfoTech:		Air/Shipping Transportation:	
						Fuel Cells:		Specialty Services:			

TYPES OF BUSINESS:

Utilities-Electricity & Natural Gas
Natural Gas Storage & Distribution

BRANDS/DIVISIONS/AFFILIATES:

Ameren Corporation
AmerenIP
AmerenCILCO
AmerenCIPS

CONTACTS: *Note: Officers with more than one job title may be intentionally listed here more than once.*

Scott A. Cisel, CEO
Scott A. Cisel, Pres.
Ronald D. Pate, VP-Oper.
Stan E. Ogden, VP-Public Rel. & Customer Service
Craig D. Nelson, Sr. VP-Financial Svcs. & Regulatory Affairs
Scott A. Glaeser, VP-Gas & Electric Tech. Svcs.
D. Scott Wiseman, VP-Regulatory Affairs

Phone: 309-677-5271	**Fax:** 217-424-6758
Toll-Free: 800-755-5000	
Address: 300 Liberty St., Peoria, IL 61602 US	

GROWTH PLANS/SPECIAL FEATURES:

Ameren Illinois Company, a subsidiary of Ameren Corp., is an electric and natural gas supplier in the state of Illinois. The company brings together the combined operations of AmerenCISP, AmerenIP and AmerenCLICO. It serves approximately 1.2 million electric customers and 813,000 natural gas customers in all or part of 85 of Illinois' 102 counties. The company operates through 18,000 miles of gas main distribution lines, 45,000 circuit miles of electrical line and seven underground gas storage fields with 15 billion cubic feet of total working capacity. It serves its customers by purchasing long-term power agreements through various providers. In October 2010, Ameren Illinois was formed by combining the operations of AmerenCISP, AmerenIP and AmerenCLICO.

Ameren Illinois offers its employees medical, dental and vision; flexible spending account; an employee assistance program; a pension plan; a savings investment plan; long-term disability and life insurance; tuition assistance; a stock purchase plan; and credit union membership.

FINANCIALS: **Sales and profits are in thousands of dollars—add 000 to get the full amount. 2010 Note: Financial information for 2010 was not available for all companies at press time.**

2010 Sales: $	2010 Profits: $	**U.S. Stock Ticker: Subsidiary**
2009 Sales: $	2009 Profits: $	**Int'l Ticker:** Int'l Exchange:
2008 Sales: $	2008 Profits: $	Employees:
2007 Sales: $	2007 Profits: $	Fiscal Year Ends: 12/31
2006 Sales: $	2006 Profits: $	Parent Company: AMEREN CORP

SALARIES/BENEFITS:

Pension Plan: Y	ESOP Stock Plan:	Profit Sharing:	Top Exec. Salary: $	Bonus: $986,000
Savings Plan: Y	Stock Purch. Plan: Y		Second Exec. Salary: $	Bonus: $

OTHER THOUGHTS:

Apparent Women Officers or Directors:
Hot Spot for Advancement for Women/Minorities:

LOCATIONS: ("Y" = Yes)

West:	Southwest:	Midwest:	Southeast:	Northeast:	International:
		Y			

AMERESCO INC

www.ameresco.com

Industry Group Code: 541690 **Ranks within this company's industry group:** Sales: Profits:

Exploration/Production:		Refining/Retailing:		Utilities:		Alternative Energy:		Specialty Services:		Energy Mktg./Other Svcs.	
Exploration:		Refining:		Electric Utility:		Waste/Solar/Other:	Y	Consulting/Eng.:	Y	Energy Marketing:	
Production:		Retailing:		Gas Utility:		Thermal/Steam:		Seismic:		Equipment/Machinery:	
Coal Production:		Convenience Stores:		Pipelines:		Wind:		Drilling:		Oil Field Services:	
		Chemicals:		Water:		Hydro:		InfoTech:		Air/Shipping Transportation:	
						Fuel Cells:		Specialty Services:	Y		

TYPES OF BUSINESS:

Energy Consulting
Landfill Gas-to-Energy Generation
Solar Power Technology
Cogeneration

BRANDS/DIVISIONS/AFFILIATES:

Ameresco Canada
Ameresco Enertech
Ameresco E-Three
AmerescoSolutions
Quantum Engineering and Development, Inc.

CONTACTS: *Note: Officers with more than one job title may be intentionally listed here more than once.*

George P. Sakellaris, CEO
George P. Sakellaris, Pres.
Andrew B. Spence, CFO/VP
David J. Corrsin, General Counsel/Exec. VP/Corp. Sec.
David J. Anderson, Exec. VP-Bus. Dev.
CarolAnn Hibbard, Dir.-Media Rel.
Andrew Spence, Dir.-Investor Rel.
Michael T. Bakas, Sr. VP-Renewable Energy
Joseph P. DeManche, Exec. VP/Gen. Mgr.-Federal Oper.
William J. Cunningham, Sr. VP-Corp. Gov't Rel.
Kevin A. Derrington, Exec. VP/Gen. Mgr.-Federal Oper.
George P. Sakellaris, Chmn.
Mario Iusi, Pres., Ameresco Canada

Phone: 508-661-2200	**Fax:** 508-661-2201
Toll-Free: 866-263-7372	
Address: 111 Speen St., Ste. 410, Framingham, MA 01701 US	

GROWTH PLANS/SPECIAL FEATURES:

Ameresco, Inc. is an independent efficiency consulting company that helps corporations decrease operating expenses, upgrade and maintain facilities and stabilize operating costs. From 38 offices in the U.S. and Canada, the company works with corporate customers and surrounding utilities to negotiate lower electricity costs, with individual subsidiaries focusing on particular regional markets. Ameresco Canada, formerly part of DukeSolutions, Inc., serves institutional, commercial and industrial energy users in Canada. The company estimates that Ameresco Canada has assisted its clients in reducing green house gas emissions by approximately 4.5 million tons. AmerescoSolutions, also formerly part of DukeSolutions, focuses on federal government clients and has national contracts with the U.S. Departments of Defense and Energy. Ameresco Enertech, formerly LG&E Enertech, focuses on primary education, higher education, industrial and commercial facilities within Tennessee and Kentucky. Ameresco E-Three, which stands for Energy Efficient Expertise, is an energy consulting and services company with offices in Nevada serving the western states. The company went public in July 2010. In August 2010, the firm acquired Quantum Engineering and Development, Inc., an energy service company active in Oregon and Washington.

FINANCIALS: **Sales and profits are in thousands of dollars—add 000 to get the full amount. 2010 Note: Financial information for 2010 was not available for all companies at press time.**

2010 Sales: $	2010 Profits: $	**U.S. Stock Ticker: AMRC**
2009 Sales: $	2009 Profits: $	**Int'l Ticker:** Int'l Exchange:
2008 Sales: $	2008 Profits: $	Employees:
2007 Sales: $	2007 Profits: $	Fiscal Year Ends: 12/31
2006 Sales: $	2006 Profits: $	Parent Company:

SALARIES/BENEFITS:

Pension Plan:	ESOP Stock Plan:	Profit Sharing:	Top Exec. Salary: $	Bonus: $
Savings Plan:	Stock Purch. Plan:		Second Exec. Salary: $	Bonus: $

OTHER THOUGHTS:

Apparent Women Officers or Directors:
Hot Spot for Advancement for Women/Minorities:

LOCATIONS: ("Y" = Yes)

West:	Southwest:	Midwest:	Southeast:	Northeast:	International:
Y	Y	Y	Y	Y	Y

AMERICAN ELECTRIC POWER COMPANY INC (AEP) www.aep.com

Industry Group Code: 2211 **Ranks within this company's industry group:** Sales: 14 Profits: 9

Exploration/Production:		Refining/Retailing:		Utilities:		Alternative Energy:		Specialty Services:		Energy Mktg./Other Svcs.	
Exploration:		Refining:		Electric Utility:	Y	Waste/Solar/Other:		Consulting/Eng.:		Energy Marketing:	Y
Production:		Retailing:		Gas Utility:		Thermal/Steam:		Seismic:		Equipment/Machinery:	
Coal Production:		Convenience Stores:		Pipelines:		Wind:	Y	Drilling:		Oil Field Services:	
		Chemicals:		Water:		Hydro:		InfoTech:		Air/Shipping Transportation:	Y
						Fuel Cells:		Specialty Services:			

TYPES OF BUSINESS:

Utilities-Electricity
Natural Gas Power Generation
Nuclear Power Generation
Coal Transport-Barge & Rail
Energy Trading
Coal Power Generation
Solar Power Generation

BRANDS/DIVISIONS/AFFILIATES:

AEP Ohio
AEP Texas Central Company
Appalachian Power
Indiana Michigan Power
Kentucky Power
Public Service Company of Oklahoma
Southwestern Electric Power Company
AEP Texas North Company

CONTACTS: *Note: Officers with more than one job title may be intentionally listed here more than once.*

Michael G. Morris, CEO
Carl English, COO
Michael G. Morris, Pres.
Brian Tierney, CFO/Exec. VP
Michael Miller, General Counsel/Sr. VP/Sec.
Todd Busby, Sr. VP-Commercial Oper.
Pat D. Hemlepp, Dir.-Corp. Media Rel.
Bette Jo Rozsa, Managing Dir.-Investor Rel.
Charles E. Zebula, Treas./Sr. VP
Robert Powers, Pres., AEP Utilities
Susan Tomasky, Pres., AEP Transmission
Barbara Radous, Sr. VP-Shared Svcs.
Nick Akins, Exec. VP-Generation
Michael G. Morris, Chmn.

Phone: 614-716-1000	**Fax:** 614-716-1823
Toll-Free:	
Address: 1 Riverside Plz., Columbus, OH 43215-2372 US	

GROWTH PLANS/SPECIAL FEATURES:

American Electric Power Company, Inc. (AEP) is a holding company based in Ohio. The firm serves roughly 5.2 million customers through 12 utility subsidiaries: Ohio Power Company; Appalachian Power Company; Indiana Michigan Power; Kentucky Power; Kingsport Power Company; Columbus Southern Power Company; AEP Texas Central Company; AEP Texas North Company; AEP Generating Company; Wheeling Power Company; Public Service Company of Oklahoma; and Southwestern Electric Power Company. AEP's generating and transmission facilities comprise a 39,000-mile network spanning 11 states. It also owns 215,800 miles of distribution lines. The company's transmission system serves roughly 10% of the electrical demand in the Eastern Interconnection in the U.S. and eastern Canada; and approximately 11% of the electrical demand for Electric Reliability Council of Texas. AEP owns approximately 80 generating stations in the U.S., with 73% based on coal, 16% natural gas and 8% nuclear. These generating stations have a power capacity of approximately 38,000 megawatts. The company also owns approximately 697 barges, 18 towboats and 9,000 rail cars. AEP holds interest in two terminal facilities: the Cook Coal Terminal on the Ohio River and the International Marine Terminal in New Orleans. These terminals have a combined 32 million tons per year transfer capability. Operations in Ohio account for the largest percentage of the firm's revenue (approximately 33%). In November 2009, Southwestern Electric Power Company agreed to acquire the transmission and distribution operations of Valley Electric Membership Corporation for roughly $94 million.

FINANCIALS: **Sales and profits are in thousands of dollars—add 000 to get the full amount. 2010 Note: Financial information for 2010 was not available for all companies at press time.**

2010 Sales: $	2010 Profits: $	**U.S. Stock Ticker: AEP**
2009 Sales: $13,489,000	2009 Profits: $1,356,000	**Int'l Ticker:** Int'l Exchange:
2008 Sales: $14,440,000	2008 Profits: $1,380,000	Employees: 21,673
2007 Sales: $13,380,000	2007 Profits: $1,089,000	Fiscal Year Ends: 12/31
2006 Sales: $12,622,000	2006 Profits: $1,002,000	Parent Company:

SALARIES/BENEFITS:

Pension Plan:	ESOP Stock Plan:	Profit Sharing:	Top Exec. Salary: $1,254,808	Bonus: $
Savings Plan: Y	Stock Purch. Plan:		Second Exec. Salary: $552,115	Bonus: $

OTHER THOUGHTS:

Apparent Women Officers or Directors: 5
Hot Spot for Advancement for Women/Minorities: Y

LOCATIONS: ("Y" = Yes)

West:	Southwest:	Midwest:	Southeast:	Northeast:	International:
	Y	Y	Y	Y	

AMERIGAS PARTNERS LP

www.amerigas.com

Industry Group Code: 454312 **Ranks within this company's industry group:** Sales: 2 Profits: 2

Exploration/Production:		**Refining/Retailing:**		**Utilities:**		**Alternative Energy:**		**Specialty Services:**		**Energy Mktg./Other Svcs.**	
Exploration:		Refining:		Electric Utility:		Waste/Solar/Other:		Consulting/Eng.:		Energy Marketing:	
Production:		Retailing:	Y	Gas Utility:		Thermal/Steam:		Seismic:		Equipment/Machinery:	Y
Coal Production:		Convenience Stores:		Pipelines:		Wind:		Drilling:		Oil Field Services:	
		Chemicals:		Water:		Hydro:		InfoTech:		Air/Shipping Transportation:	Y
						Fuel Cells:		Specialty Services:	Y		

TYPES OF BUSINESS:

Propane Distribution
Retail Propane Sales
Propane Services
Wholesale Propane Sales

BRANDS/DIVISIONS/AFFILIATES:

AmeriGas Propane, Inc.
UGI Corp.
Amerigas Propane, L.P.
AmeriGas Eagle Propane, L.P.

CONTACTS:

Note: Officers with more than one job title may be intentionally listed here more than once.

Eugene Bissell, CEO
Eugene Bissell, Pres.
Jerry Sheridan, CFO/VP-Finance
Andrew J. Peyton, VP-Sales & Mktg.
William Katz, VP-Human Resources
Richard W. Fabrizio, CIO/VP
Robert Knauss, General Counsel/Corp. Sec./VP
Kevin Rumbelow, VP-Oper. Support
William Stanczak, Chief Acct. Officer/Controller
Robert W. Krick, VP/Treas.
Joseph B. Powers, VP-AmeriGas Cylinder Exchange
William G. Robey, VP-Sales Oper.
John S. Iannarelli, VP-Midwest Oper.
Lon Greenberg, Chmn.
David Lugar, VP-Supply & Logistics

Phone: 610-337-7000	**Fax:** 610-992-3259
Toll-Free:	
Address: 460 N. Gulph Rd., King of Prussia, PA 19406 US	

GROWTH PLANS/SPECIAL FEATURES:

AmeriGas Partners, L.P. markets propane, propane equipment and related services. The company serves over 1.3 million customers from approximately 1,200 locations in all 50 states, selling more than 1 billion gallons of retail propane annually. The firm serves residential, industrial, commercial, agricultural, motor fuel and wholesale customers. In 2009, retail accounts constituted approximately 89% of the firm's sales, with wholesale accounts making up 11% of sales. Residential customers represented 41% of sales; commercial/industrial customers, 36%; motor fuel customers, 13%; transport customers, 5%; and agricultural customers, 5%. The company's business is conducted primarily through its subsidiary, AmeriGas Propane, L.P. and that company's subsidiary, AmeriGas Eagle Propane, L.P. General partner, AmeriGas Propane, Inc., which has an effective 44% ownership interest in the firm, is a wholly-owned subsidiary of UGI Corporation. It is responsible for managing the operations of AmeriGas Partners, L.P. In addition to selling propane, the firm sells propane-related products and exchanges pre-filled portable tanks for empty ones, through its ACE program; sells, installs and services propane appliances, including heating systems; and installs and services propane fuel systems for motor vehicles. The company also operates as an interstate carrier of propane in 48 states and the Canadian provinces of British Columbia and Quebec.

AmeriGas offers its employees medical, prescription and dental plans; a 401(k); and tuition reimbursement.

FINANCIALS:

Sales and profits are in thousands of dollars—add 000 to get the full amount. 2010 Note: Financial information for 2010 was not available for all companies at press time.

2010 Sales: $	2010 Profits: $	**U.S. Stock Ticker: APU**
2009 Sales: $2,260,095	2009 Profits: $224,643	**Int'l Ticker:** Int'l Exchange:
2008 Sales: $2,815,189	2008 Profits: $158,019	Employees: 5,950
2007 Sales: $2,277,375	2007 Profits: $190,784	Fiscal Year Ends: 9/30
2006 Sales: $2,119,266	2006 Profits: $91,158	Parent Company:

SALARIES/BENEFITS:

Pension Plan:	ESOP Stock Plan:	Profit Sharing:	Top Exec. Salary: $1,067,975	Bonus: $1,591,643
Savings Plan: Y	Stock Purch. Plan:		Second Exec. Salary: $648,202	Bonus: $821,800

OTHER THOUGHTS:

Apparent Women Officers or Directors:
Hot Spot for Advancement for Women/Minorities:

LOCATIONS: ("Y" = Yes)

West:	Southwest:	Midwest:	Southeast:	Northeast:	International:
Y	Y	Y	Y	Y	

ANADARKO PETROLEUM CORPORATION

www.anadarko.com

Industry Group Code: 211111 **Ranks within this company's industry group:** Sales: 50 Profits: 88

Exploration/Production:		Refining/Retailing:		Utilities:		Alternative Energy:		Specialty Services:		Energy Mktg./Other Svcs.	
Exploration:	Y	Refining:		Electric Utility:		Waste/Solar/Other:		Consulting/Eng.:		Energy Marketing:	
Production:	Y	Retailing:		Gas Utility:		Thermal/Steam:		Seismic:	Y	Equipment/Machinery:	
Coal Production:	Y	Convenience Stores:		Pipelines:		Wind:		Drilling:	Y	Oil Field Services:	
		Chemicals:		Water:		Hydro:		InfoTech:		Air/Shipping Transportation:	
						Fuel Cells:		Specialty Services:			

TYPES OF BUSINESS:

Oil & Gas Exploration & Production
Field Services
Drilling Technology
Mineral Exploration
Coal-Bed Methane Production

BRANDS/DIVISIONS/AFFILIATES:

Anadarko Energy Services Company
Anadarko Algeria Company LLC
Kerr-McGee Corporation
Western Gas Resources, Inc.

CONTACTS: *Note: Officers with more than one job title may be intentionally listed here more than once.*

James T. Hackett, CEO
R.A. Walker, COO
James T. Hackett, Pres.
Robert G. Gwin, CFO/Sr. VP-Finance
David C. Bretches, VP-Mktg. & Minerals
Julia A. Struble, VP-Human Resources
Robert D. Abendschein, VP-Exploration & Prod.
Mario M. Coll, III, CIO/VP-IT
Robert K. Reeves, Chief Admin. Officer/Sr. VP
Robert K. Reeves, General Counsel
James J. Kleckner, VP-Oper.
Katie Jackson, VP-Corp. Dev.
John M. Colglazier, VP-Comm.
John M. Colglazier, VP-Investor Rel.
M. Cathy Douglas, Chief Acct. Officer/VP
Danny J. Rea, VP-Midstream
Gregory M. Pensabene, VP-Gov't Rel.
Douglas P. Hazlett, VP-Exploration
James T. Hackett, Chmn.
Frank J. Patterson, VP-Int'l Exploration

Phone: 832-636-1000 **Fax:** 832-636-8220
Toll-Free: 800-800-1101
Address: 1201 Lake Robbins Dr., The Woodlands, TX 77380 US

GROWTH PLANS/SPECIAL FEATURES:

Anadarko Petroleum Corporation is one of the world's largest independent oil and gas exploration and production companies, holding approximately 2.3 billion barrels of oil equivalent (BOE) of proved reserves, consisting of 7.8 trillion cubic feet of natural gas and 1 billion barrels of crude oil, condensate and natural gas liquids (NGL). The company has an ownership interest in 4,264 productive oil wells and 26,942 productive gas wells. The company's production activities are located primarily in Louisiana, Texas, the U.S. mid-continent area, Alaska, Canada and offshore in the Gulf of Mexico. The company is also active in Brazil, Algeria, Indonesia, China, West Africa and Mozambique. The firm's domestic and international operations lie in field services, producer services, market services and financial services. The midstream segment includes gathering, compression and processing operations. The company actively markets natural gas, oil and natural gas liquids and owns and operates gas-gathering systems in its core producing areas. In addition to traditional drilling, the company is engaged in carbon dioxide-enhanced oil recovery, as well as coal-bed methane production and the production of minerals including coal and soda ash. The company has several subsidiaries, including Anadarko Energy Services Company; Anadarko Algeria Company, LLC; Western Gas Holdings LLC; Kerr-McGee Oil; and Western Gas Resources, Inc.

Employees are offered medical, dental and vision insurance; an employee assistance program; life insurance; business travel accident insurance; disability coverage; flexible spending accounts; a retirement plan; a 401(k) plan; adoption assistance; and educational assistance.

FINANCIALS: **Sales and profits are in thousands of dollars—add 000 to get the full amount. 2010 Note: Financial information for 2010 was not available for all companies at press time.**

2010 Sales: $	2010 Profits: $	**U.S. Stock Ticker: APC**
2009 Sales: $9,000,000	2009 Profits: $-103,000	**Int'l Ticker:** Int'l Exchange:
2008 Sales: $15,162,000	2008 Profits: $3,260,000	Employees: 4,300
2007 Sales: $16,416,000	2007 Profits: $3,778,000	Fiscal Year Ends: 12/31
2006 Sales: $10,116,000	2006 Profits: $4,746,000	Parent Company:

SALARIES/BENEFITS:

Pension Plan: Y	ESOP Stock Plan:	Profit Sharing:	Top Exec. Salary: $1,567,500	Bonus: $3,749,460
Savings Plan: Y	Stock Purch. Plan:		Second Exec. Salary: $685,192	Bonus: $1,260,754

OTHER THOUGHTS:

Apparent Women Officers or Directors: 4
Hot Spot for Advancement for Women/Minorities: Y

LOCATIONS: ("Y" = Yes)

West:	Southwest:	Midwest:	Southeast:	Northeast:	International:
Y	Y		Y		Y

ANGLO AMERICAN PLC

www.angloamerican.com

Industry Group Code: 21211 **Ranks within this company's industry group:** Sales: 2 Profits: 2

Exploration/Production:		Refining/Retailing:		Utilities:		Alternative Energy:		Specialty Services:		Energy Mktg./Other Svcs.	
Exploration:		Refining:		Electric Utility:		Waste/Solar/Other:		Consulting/Eng.:		Energy Marketing:	
Production:		Retailing:		Gas Utility:		Thermal/Steam:		Seismic:		Equipment/Machinery:	
Coal Production:	Y	Convenience Stores:		Pipelines:		Wind:		Drilling:		Oil Field Services:	
		Chemicals:		Water:		Hydro:		InfoTech:		Air/Shipping Transportation:	
						Fuel Cells:		Specialty Services:	Y		

TYPES OF BUSINESS:

Mining-Metals & Minerals
Coal Mining
Platinum Mining
Steel Manufacturing
Diamond Mining

BRANDS/DIVISIONS/AFFILIATES:

Anglo Platinum
De Beers SA
Anglo Coal
Anglo Base Metals
Anglo Industrial Minerals
Tarmac Limited
Anglo Ferrous Metals
Copebras

CONTACTS: *Note: Officers with more than one job title may be intentionally listed here more than once.*

Cynthia Carroll, CEO
Rene Medori, Group Dir.-Finance
Mervyn Walker, Group Dir.-Human Resources
Brian Beamish, Group Dir.-Tech. & Mining
Peter Whitcutt, Group Dir.-Strategy & Bus. Dev.
Mervyn Walker, Group Dir.-Comm.
Nick von Schirnding, Head-Investor & Corp. Affairs
Seamus French, CEO-Metallurgical Coal
Walter De Simoni, CEO-Anglo Nickel
Ian Cockerill, CEO-Anglo Coal
David Weston, Group Dir.-Bus. Performance & Projects
Sir John Parker, Chmn.
Godfrey Gomwe, Exec. Dir.-Anglo American South Africa Ltd.

Phone: 44-20-7968-8888 **Fax:** 44-20-7968-8500
Toll-Free:
Address: 20 Carlton House Terrace, London, SW1Y 5AN UK

GROWTH PLANS/SPECIAL FEATURES:

Anglo American plc is a global mining group with interests in the extraction of platinum, gold, diamonds, coal, base metals, industrial minerals and ferrous metals. Wholly-owned subsidiary Anglo Platinum, located in South Africa, produces approximately 39% of the global platinum supply. It owns two refineries, one each for base and precious metals, three smelters and five mines. In addition to platinum it also extracts base metals such as nickel, cobalt sulfate and copper. The firm has a 45% interest in De Beers Investments, owner of De Beers S.A., one of the largest diamond producers in the world. De Beers has 15 active mines, spanning across Botswana, Canada, Namibia, South Africa and Tanzania. Wholly-owned subsidiary Anglo Coal has eight wholly-owned mines and interests in five other mines in Venezuela, Colombia, Australia and Africa. Subsidiary Anglo Base Metals has interests in 14 mines in Chile, Brazil, Venezuela, South Africa, Namibia and Ireland, which mine copper, silver, molybdenum, titanium dioxide, lead and other metals. Subsidiary Anglo Industrial Minerals operates through Copebras and Tarmac. Tarmac produces crushed rock, asphalt, sand, gravel, concrete and other construction materials for markets in the U.K., Europe and the Middle East. Copebras produces phosphate fertilizers, sodium tripolyphosphate and phosphoric acid in Brazil. Subsidiary Anglo Ferrous Metals mines iron ore, vanadium and manganese and produces carbon steel. In line with an announcement made in October 2009, the company has made a number of divestitures of certain non-core operations in 2010. These include the sale of its majority interest in the Peace River Coal Limited Partnership in April; the disposal of Tarmac's French and Belgian building materials business, Tarmac Materiaux de Construction in May; the divestment of its zinc portfolio, also in May; and the liquidation of undeveloped coal assets in Australia during July.

FINANCIALS: **Sales and profits are in thousands of dollars—add 000 to get the full amount. 2010 Note: Financial information for 2010 was not available for all companies at press time.**

2010 Sales: $	2010 Profits: $	**U.S. Stock Ticker: AAUK**
2009 Sales: $20,858,000	2009 Profits: $2,425,000	**Int'l Ticker: AAL** Int'l Exchange: London-LSE
2008 Sales: $26,311,000	2008 Profits: $5,215,000	Employees: 107,000
2007 Sales: $25,470,000	2007 Profits: $5,290,000	Fiscal Year Ends: 12/31
2006 Sales: $33,072,000	2006 Profits: $6,922,000	Parent Company:

SALARIES/BENEFITS:

Pension Plan:	ESOP Stock Plan:	Profit Sharing:	Top Exec. Salary: $1,763,945	Bonus: $594,926
Savings Plan:	Stock Purch. Plan:		Second Exec. Salary: $1,108,290	Bonus: $374,228

OTHER THOUGHTS:

Apparent Women Officers or Directors: 2
Hot Spot for Advancement for Women/Minorities: Y

LOCATIONS: ("Y" = Yes)

West:	Southwest:	Midwest:	Southeast:	Northeast:	International:
					Y

AP MOLLER-MAERSK A/S

www.maersk.com

Industry Group Code: 483111 **Ranks within this company's industry group:** Sales: 1 Profits: 6

Exploration/Production:		Refining/Retailing:		Utilities:		Alternative Energy:		Specialty Services:		Energy Mktg./Other Svcs.	
Exploration:		Refining:		Electric Utility:		Waste/Solar/Other:		Consulting/Eng.:		Energy Marketing:	
Production:	Y	Retailing:		Gas Utility:		Thermal/Steam:		Seismic:		Equipment/Machinery:	
Coal Production:		Convenience Stores:		Pipelines:		Wind:		Drilling:	Y	Oil Field Services:	Y
		Chemicals:		Water:		Hydro:		InfoTech:		Air/Shipping Transportation:	Y
						Fuel Cells:		Specialty Services:	Y		

TYPES OF BUSINESS:

Deep Sea Freight Transportation
Logistics Services
Oil & Gas Production
Trucking
Supermarkets
Aviation Services
Shipyards

BRANDS/DIVISIONS/AFFILIATES:

A.P. Moller-Maersk Group
Firm A.P. Moller (The)
Maersk Line
Maersk Tankers
Maersk Drilling
Maersk Olie og Gas AS
Dansk Supermarked A/S
Star Air A/S

CONTACTS: *Note: Officers with more than one job title may be intentionally listed here more than once.*

Nils S. Andersen, CEO
Trond O. Westlie, CFO
Stephen Fraser, Head-Group IT
Klaus Rud Sejling, Head-Group Strategy
Henrik Lund, Head-Investor Rel.
Jesper Cramon, Head- Group Acct.
Eivind Kolding, CEO-Container Bus.
Claus V. Hemmingsen, CEO-Maersk Drilling
Soren Skou, CEO-Maersk Tankers
Jakob Thomasen, CEO-Maersk Oil
Michael P. Rasmussen, Chmn.

Phone: 45-3363-3363	**Fax:** 45-3363-4108
Toll-Free:	
Address: Esplanaden 50, Copenhagen, DK-1098 Denmark	

GROWTH PLANS/SPECIAL FEATURES:

A.P. Moller-Maersk A/S forms the core of the A.P. Moller-Maersk Group, a Danish conglomerate of companies. The primary businesses of A.P. Moller-Maersk relate to container and tanker shipping, offshore drilling activities; oil and gas production; retail and banking; and management of shipyards, aviation and other industrial companies. Subsidiaries engaged in container shipping, including Maersk Line, are supported by companies providing agency and terminal services, logistics management and transfers. Maersk Tankers, with 225 vessels, provides deep sea transport of crude oil, natural gas and other refined oil products, while regional companies, such as Norfolkline B.V., oversee door-to-door transport and roll-on/roll-off ferry services. The firm's drilling and oilfield activities include contract drilling through Maersk Drilling, management of floating oil and gas production rigs through Maersk FPSOs and through Maersk LNG the company operates a fleet of liquefied natural gas carriers. Maersk Olie og Gas AS (Maersk Oil) has an oil production volume of roughly 600,000 barrels per day primarily at operations in the North Sea, offshore Qatar, Algeria and Kazakhstan. The company has other exploration and production assets in the Middle East, Africa, South America and the Gulf of Mexico. Retail operations include the firm's 68% ownership of Dansk Supermarked A/S, which controls Fotex and Bilka supermarkets and F. Salling department stores. The group also owns a 20% interest in Danske Bank A/S, a leading Danish bank. Maersk operates shipyards in Denmark, Germany and the Baltic States, and is also involved in the production of refrigerated containers, industrial machines and plastics. Star Air A/S and Martinair Holland N.V oversee passenger and cargo aviation services across Europe. In May 2010, the firm sold its Premier Technical Plastics, Inc., a US subsidiary producing plastics in Texas, Arkansas and Louisiana, to McCalmont Industries LLC. In July 2010, Maersk Tankers agreed to collaborate with Hyundai Heavy Industries and Det Norske Veritas on the design of tankers for transporting carbon dioxide gas.

FINANCIALS: **Sales and profits are in thousands of dollars—add 000 to get the full amount. 2010 Note: Financial information for 2010 was not available for all companies at press time.**

2010 Sales: $	2010 Profits: $	**U.S. Stock Ticker:**
2009 Sales: $48,522,000	2009 Profits: $-1,024,000	**Int'l Ticker: MAERSKA** Int'l Exchange: Copenhagen-CSE
2008 Sales: $61,211,000	2008 Profits: $3,462,000	Employees:
2007 Sales: $51,218,000	2007 Profits: $3,422,000	Fiscal Year Ends: 12/31
2006 Sales: $43,743,000	2006 Profits: $2,723,000	Parent Company:

SALARIES/BENEFITS:

Pension Plan:	ESOP Stock Plan:	Profit Sharing:	Top Exec. Salary: $	Bonus: $
Savings Plan:	Stock Purch. Plan:		Second Exec. Salary: $	Bonus: $

OTHER THOUGHTS:

Apparent Women Officers or Directors: 1
Hot Spot for Advancement for Women/Minorities:

LOCATIONS: ("Y" = Yes)

West:	Southwest:	Midwest:	Southeast:	Northeast:	International:
Y	Y	Y	Y	Y	Y

APACHE CORP

www.apachecorp.com

Industry Group Code: 211111 **Ranks within this company's industry group:** Sales: 51 Profits: 100

Exploration/Production:		Refining/Retailing:		Utilities:		Alternative Energy:		Specialty Services:		Energy Mktg./Other Svcs.	
Exploration:	Y	Refining:		Electric Utility:		Waste/Solar/Other:		Consulting/Eng.:		Energy Marketing:	
Production:	Y	Retailing:		Gas Utility:		Thermal/Steam:		Seismic:		Equipment/Machinery:	
Coal Production:		Convenience Stores:		Pipelines:		Wind:		Drilling:		Oil Field Services:	
		Chemicals:		Water:		Hydro:		InfoTech:		Air/Shipping Transportation:	
						Fuel Cells:		Specialty Services:			

TYPES OF BUSINESS:

Oil & Gas Exploration & Production

BRANDS/DIVISIONS/AFFILIATES:

Apache Canada Ltd.
DEK Energy Company
Apache Energy Ltd.
Apache North America, Inc.
Apache Overseas, Inc.

CONTACTS:

Note: Officers with more than one job title may be intentionally listed here more than once.

G. Steven Farris, CEO
John A. Crum, Co-COO
Roger B. Plank, Pres.
Janine J. McArdle, VP-Oil & Gas Mktg.
Margery M. Harris, VP-Human Resources
Michael S. Bahorich, CTO/Exec. VP
Kregg Olson, Sr. VP-Corp. Reservoir Eng.
P. Anthony Lannie, General Counsel/Sr. VP
David L. French, VP-Bus. Dev.
Thomas P. Chambers, VP-Investor Rel. & Planning
Matthew W. Dundrea, Treas./VP
John A. Crum, Pres., North America
Jon A. Jeppesen, Sr. VP-Gulf Coast Region
Rodney J. Eichler, Co-COO
Sarah B. Teslik, Sr. VP-Policy & Governance
G. Steven Farris, Chmn.
Rodney J. Eichler, Pres., Int'l

Phone: 713-296-6000 **Fax:** 713-296-6496
Toll-Free: 800-272-2434
Address: 2000 Post Oak Blvd., Ste. 100, Houston, TX 77056-4400 US

GROWTH PLANS/SPECIAL FEATURES:

Apache Corp. is an independent energy company that explores, develops and produces natural gas, crude oil and natural gas liquids around the world. In North America, Apache's exploration and production interests are focused on the Gulf of Mexico; the Anadarko Basin of western Oklahoma; the Permian Basin of western Texas and New Mexico; the Texas-Louisiana Gulf Coast; East Texas; and the Western Sedimentary basin of Canada. Internationally, Apache has exploration and production interests in Egypt, Australia, Argentina, Chile and the U.K. sector of the North Sea. In 2009, crude oil and liquids provided 48% of the firm's production and 71% of its revenue. Natural gas accounted for the remaining 50% of production and 28% of revenues. Apache's estimated proved reserves were balanced at 55% natural gas and 45% crude oil and liquids. Although the company treats all operations as one line of business, interests in many of its properties are through subsidiaries, such as Apache Canada Ltd.; DEK Energy Company; Apache Energy Ltd.; Apache North America, Inc.; and Apache Overseas, Inc. Apache's Canadian natural gas operations have been growing significantly in recent years due to several acquisitions and discoveries. Growth strategies in the U.S. focus on exploiting and expanding established areas, while growth abroad is a mix of exploration and exploitation. In April 2010, the company agreed to buy Mariner Energy, Inc. for $2.7 billion. In June 2010, Apache acquired the Gulf of Mexico Shelf assets of Devon Energy Corp. for $105 billion. Also in June 2010, the firm agreed to purchase certain assets from BP, Inc., including oil and gas operations in the Texas Permian Basin, New Mexico and Egypt.

Employees of Apache receive health and medical benefits; life insurance; disability coverage; education assistance; alternative work schedules; and flexible spending accounts.

FINANCIALS:

Sales and profits are in thousands of dollars—add 000 to get the full amount. 2010 Note: Financial information for 2010 was not available for all companies at press time.

2010 Sales: $	2010 Profits: $	**U.S. Stock Ticker: APA**
2009 Sales: $8,614,826	2009 Profits: $-284,398	**Int'l Ticker:** Int'l Exchange:
2008 Sales: $12,389,750	2008 Profits: $711,954	Employees: 3,452
2007 Sales: $9,999,752	2007 Profits: $2,806,678	Fiscal Year Ends: 12/31
2006 Sales: $8,309,131	2006 Profits: $2,546,771	Parent Company:

SALARIES/BENEFITS:

Pension Plan: Y	ESOP Stock Plan:	Profit Sharing:	Top Exec. Salary: $1,387,500	Bonus: $2,500,000
Savings Plan: Y	Stock Purch. Plan:		Second Exec. Salary: $578,598	Bonus: $525,000

OTHER THOUGHTS:

Apparent Women Officers or Directors: 5
Hot Spot for Advancement for Women/Minorities: Y

LOCATIONS: ("Y" = Yes)

West:	Southwest:	Midwest:	Southeast:	Northeast:	International:
	Y		Y		Y

APCO OIL AND GAS INTERNATIONAL INC

www.apcooilandgas.com

Industry Group Code: 211111 **Ranks within this company's industry group:** Sales: 110 Profits: 68

Exploration/Production:		Refining/Retailing:		Utilities:		Alternative Energy:		Specialty Services:		Energy Mktg./Other Svcs.	
Exploration:	Y	Refining:		Electric Utility:		Waste/Solar/Other:		Consulting/Eng.:		Energy Marketing:	
Production:	Y	Retailing:		Gas Utility:		Thermal/Steam:		Seismic:		Equipment/Machinery:	
Coal Production:		Convenience Stores:		Pipelines:		Wind:		Drilling:		Oil Field Services:	
		Chemicals:		Water:		Hydro:		InfoTech:		Air/Shipping Transportation:	
						Fuel Cells:		Specialty Services:			

TYPES OF BUSINESS:

Oil & Gas Exploration & Production

BRANDS/DIVISIONS/AFFILIATES:

Williams Group (The)
Apco Argentina S.A.
Petrolifera Petroleum Ltd.
TC Oil and Services Ltd.

CONTACTS:

Note: Officers with more than one job title may be intentionally listed here more than once.

Ralph A. Hill, CEO
Thomas Bueno, COO
Thomas Bueno, Pres.
Landy L. Fullmer, CFO
Michael Kyle, VP-Bus. Dev.
Thomas Bueno, Dir.-Investor Rel.
Landy L. Fullmer, Chief Acct. Officer/Controller
Ernesto Hermo, Country Mgr.-Sucursal Argentina
Ralph A. Hill, Chmn.

Phone: 918-573-2164	**Fax:** 918-573-6546
Toll-Free:	
Address: 1 Williams Ctr., 35th Fl., Tulsa, OK 74172 US	

GROWTH PLANS/SPECIAL FEATURES:

Apco Oil and Gas International, Inc., formerly Apco Argentina, Inc., is engaged in oil and natural gas exploration, production and development in Argentina. The company's core assets lay in the Neuquen basin located between the provinces of Rio Negro and Neuquen in Argentina. It holds a majority share of these fields with 52.79%. In recent years, the company has expanded its operation further out to include adjacent lands, giving the company a majority share in a combined 388,000 gross acres of drilling fields. In 2009, these tracts of land produced a daily output in excess of 12,300 barrels of oil equivalent (BOE). The company holds 53% of a joint venture with Petrolera and Pecom Energia S.A., which grants them the right to pump oil from the Entre Lomas concession in Argentina until 2026. The Entre Lomas venture in southwest Argentina is Apco's principal business. The company also owns a 1.5% participation in a joint venture that performs oil and gas exploration and development in the Acambuco concession, located in northwest Argentina. In addition, Apco has a 42% interest in a third venture engaged in oil exploration and development in the Canadon Ramirez concession in southern Argentina; a 53% interest in the Agua Amarga exploration permit in the Rio Negro province; and a 26% interest in concessions located in Tierra del Fuego. Collectively, Apco's proved reserves total 11.9 million barrels of oil and 67.8 billion cubic feet of natural gas. The company is 69%-owned by The Williams Company, Inc. In December 2009, Apco entered into two farm-in agreements to expand its activities into Colombia, acquiring a 50% interest in the Turpial contract in the Middle Magdellena basin from Petrolifera Petroleum Ltd. and a 20% interest in the Llanos 32 contract located in the Llanos basin from TC Oil and Services Ltd.

FINANCIALS:

Sales and profits are in thousands of dollars—add 000 to get the full amount. 2010 Note: Financial information for 2010 was not available for all companies at press time.

2010 Sales: $	2010 Profits: $	**U.S. Stock Ticker: APAGF**
2009 Sales: $72,716	2009 Profits: $23,527	**Int'l Ticker:** Int'l Exchange:
2008 Sales: $69,116	2008 Profits: $23,793	Employees: 21
2007 Sales: $62,506	2007 Profits: $31,349	Fiscal Year Ends: 12/31
2006 Sales: $58,215	2006 Profits: $22,391	Parent Company:

SALARIES/BENEFITS:

Pension Plan: Y	ESOP Stock Plan:	Profit Sharing:	Top Exec. Salary: $503,654	Bonus: $566,473
Savings Plan:	Stock Purch. Plan:		Second Exec. Salary: $173,504	Bonus: $108,478

OTHER THOUGHTS:

Apparent Women Officers or Directors:
Hot Spot for Advancement for Women/Minorities:

LOCATIONS: ("Y" = Yes)

West:	Southwest:	Midwest:	Southeast:	Northeast:	International:
	Y				Y

APEX OIL COMPANY INC

www.apexoil.com

Industry Group Code: 424710 **Ranks within this company's industry group:** Sales: 6 Profits:

Exploration/Production:		Refining/Retailing:		Utilities:		Alternative Energy:		Specialty Services:		Energy Mktg./Other Svcs.	
Exploration:		Refining:		Electric Utility:		Waste/Solar/Other:		Consulting/Eng.:		Energy Marketing:	Y
Production:		Retailing:	Y	Gas Utility:		Thermal/Steam:		Seismic:		Equipment/Machinery:	
Coal Production:		Convenience Stores:		Pipelines:		Wind:		Drilling:		Oil Field Services:	
		Chemicals:	Y	Water:		Hydro:		InfoTech:		Air/Shipping Transportation:	Y
						Fuel Cells:		Specialty Services:	Y		

TYPES OF BUSINESS:

Petroleum Product Terminals
Petroleum Product Sales & Distribution
Petroleum Storage
Marine Towing Services
Oil Trading
Recreational Resort Operation

BRANDS/DIVISIONS/AFFILIATES:

Apex Towing Company
Petroleum Fuel & Terminal Company
Clark Oil Trading Company
Enjet Incorporated
Shanty Creek Resort & Club

CONTACTS: *Note: Officers with more than one job title may be intentionally listed here more than once.*

P. Anthony Novelly, CEO
Edwin Wahl, Pres.
Julie Cook, Dir.-Human Resources & Benefits
Dave Paul, Dir.-IT
Mary Hockle, Dir.-Legal Dept.
John L. Hank, Jr., VP/Treas.

Phone: 314-889-9600	**Fax:** 314-854-8539
Toll-Free:	
Address: 8235 Forsyth Blvd., Ste. 400, Clayton, MO 63105 US	

GROWTH PLANS/SPECIAL FEATURES:

Apex Oil Company, Inc. provides wholesale sales, storage and distribution of petroleum products and custom marine bunkers, made to specification. Petroleum products offered by Apex include conventional and reformulated gasoline (RFG); clear and dyed diesel fuel; high and low sulfur dyed fuel oil; ranges and blends of heavy oil; PG asphalt binder; flux asphalt; different grades of kerosene; dyed kerosene; biodiesel; and marine bunkers made to specification. Nationwide locations include terminals along the East Coast and Gulf Coast as well as locations in California and the Midwest. The company also services Holland, Monaco and Bermuda. Apex's subsidiaries and affiliates include Apex Towing Company, a tug and barge company; Petroleum Fuel and Terminal Company, which provides storage and truck racks in the U.S.; Clark Oil Trading Company; Enjet Incorporated, which markets, blends and stores carbon black feedstock oils, fuel oils, refinery feedstocks and petrochemical feedstocks; and Shanty Creek Resort & Club, a country club in Bellaire, Michigan with three separate village concepts containing four championship golf courses, 49 downhill skiing slopes on two mountains, 19 miles of Nordic ski trails, dining, entertainment, a fitness center, a wellness spa and a full-service conference and banquet center.

FINANCIALS: **Sales and profits are in thousands of dollars—add 000 to get the full amount. 2010 Note: Financial information for 2010 was not available for all companies at press time.**

2010 Sales: $	2010 Profits: $	**U.S. Stock Ticker: Private**
2009 Sales: $3,560,000	2009 Profits: $	**Int'l Ticker:** Int'l Exchange:
2008 Sales: $2,640,000	2008 Profits: $	Employees: 700
2007 Sales: $	2007 Profits: $	Fiscal Year Ends: 8/31
2006 Sales: $1,430,000	2006 Profits: $	Parent Company:

SALARIES/BENEFITS:

Pension Plan:	ESOP Stock Plan:	Profit Sharing:	Top Exec. Salary: $	Bonus: $
Savings Plan:	Stock Purch. Plan:		Second Exec. Salary: $	Bonus: $

OTHER THOUGHTS:

Apparent Women Officers or Directors: 2
Hot Spot for Advancement for Women/Minorities: Y

LOCATIONS: ("Y" = Yes)

West:	Southwest:	Midwest:	Southeast:	Northeast:	International:
Y	Y	Y	Y	Y	Y

ARABIAN AMERICAN DEVELOPMENT CO

arabianamericandev.com

Industry Group Code: 324110 **Ranks within this company's industry group:** Sales: 30 Profits: 18

Exploration/Production:		Refining/Retailing:		Utilities:		Alternative Energy:		Specialty Services:		Energy Mktg./Other Svcs.	
Exploration:		Refining:	Y	Electric Utility:		Waste/Solar/Other:		Consulting/Eng.:		Energy Marketing:	
Production:		Retailing:		Gas Utility:		Thermal/Steam:		Seismic:		Equipment/Machinery:	
Coal Production:		Convenience Stores:		Pipelines:	Y	Wind:		Drilling:		Oil Field Services:	
		Chemicals:	Y	Water:		Hydro:		InfoTech:		Air/Shipping Transportation:	
						Fuel Cells:		Specialty Services:			

TYPES OF BUSINESS:

Petroleum Refining
Pipelines
Mining-Copper, Gold, Silver & Zinc
Specialty Petrochemicals

BRANDS/DIVISIONS/AFFILIATES:

American Shield Refining Company
Texas Oil & Chemical Co. II, Inc.
South Hampton Resources, Inc.
Gulf State Pipe Line Company, Inc.
Pioche-Ely Valley Mines, Inc.
Al Masane
Al Masani Al Kobra Mining Company

CONTACTS: *Note: Officers with more than one job title may be intentionally listed here more than once.*

Nicholas N. Carter, CEO
Nicholas Carter, Pres.
Mark Williamson, VP-Mktg.
Charles W. Goehringer, Jr., General Counsel
Connie J. Cook, Chief Acct. Officer/Treas.
Hatem El Khalidi, Chmn.

Phone: 409-385-8300	Fax:
Toll-Free:	
Address: 1600 Hwy 6 S., Ste. 240, Sugarland, TX 77478 US	

GROWTH PLANS/SPECIAL FEATURES:

Arabian American Development Co. is an independent refiner of specialty petrochemicals in Texas and Mexico and a developer of mineral properties in Saudi Arabia and the U.S. The company operates through several direct and indirect subsidiaries. Its primary U.S. subsidiary is American Shield Refining Company, owner of Texas Oil and Chemical Co. II, Inc. (TOCCO). TOCCO is the parent of South Hampton Resources, Inc., which, in turn, operates Gulf State Pipe Line Company, Inc. South Hampton Refining Company owns and operates a specialty petrochemical products refinery in Texas that produces solvents, additives, blowing agents and cooling agents. It also owns 69 storage tanks with nearly 225,000 barrels total capacity; 106 acres of developed and undeveloped land; and a truck and rail loading facility. Gulf State Pipe Line owns and operates three 8-inch pipelines connecting the South Hampton facility to its loading terminal as well as to a natural gas line and a third party operated marine terminal. Arabian American's Saudi Arabian activities consist of a 41% stake in Al Masani Al Kobra Mining Company (AMAK). Its primary asset in Saudi Arabia is the 17-square-mile Al Masane mining project, which is under a 30-year lease set to expire in 2023. The mine has an estimated 7 million tons of mineralized materials, consisting of approximately 1.4% copper, 5.3% zinc, 1.2 grams per tonne (g/t) gold and 40.2 g/t silver. The company also owns 55% of Nevada-based Pioche-Ely Valley Mines, Inc., which doesn't conduct any substantial business activities. In September 2010, the firm completed the expansion of its South Hampton Resources facility with the addition of a new isomerization unit that will provide more flexibility in converting C5 Normal Pentane into Isopentane.

FINANCIALS: **Sales and profits are in thousands of dollars—add 000 to get the full amount. 2010 Note: Financial information for 2010 was not available for all companies at press time.**

2010 Sales: $	2010 Profits: $	**U.S. Stock Ticker: ARSD**
2009 Sales: $117,587	2009 Profits: $6,627	**Int'l Ticker:** Int'l Exchange:
2008 Sales: $154,630	2008 Profits: $-10,731	Employees: 140
2007 Sales: $108,638	2007 Profits: $7,771	Fiscal Year Ends: 12/31
2006 Sales: $98,502	2006 Profits: $7,875	Parent Company:

SALARIES/BENEFITS:

Pension Plan:	ESOP Stock Plan:	Profit Sharing:	Top Exec. Salary: $234,837	Bonus: $42,552
Savings Plan: Y	Stock Purch. Plan:		Second Exec. Salary: $227,500	Bonus: $32,652

OTHER THOUGHTS:

Apparent Women Officers or Directors: 1
Hot Spot for Advancement for Women/Minorities:

LOCATIONS: ("Y" = Yes)

West:	Southwest:	Midwest:	Southeast:	Northeast:	International:
	Y				Y

ARCH COAL INC

www.archcoal.com

Industry Group Code: 21211 **Ranks within this company's industry group:** Sales: 10 Profits: 10

Exploration/Production:		**Refining/Retailing:**		**Utilities:**		**Alternative Energy:**		**Specialty Services:**		**Energy Mktg./Other Svcs.**	
Exploration:		Refining:		Electric Utility:		Waste/Solar/Other:		Consulting/Eng.:		Energy Marketing:	
Production:		Retailing:		Gas Utility:		Thermal/Steam:		Seismic:		Equipment/Machinery:	
Coal Production:	Y	Convenience Stores:		Pipelines:		Wind:		Drilling:		Oil Field Services:	
		Chemicals:		Water:		Hydro:		InfoTech:		Air/Shipping Transportation:	
						Fuel Cells:		Specialty Services:			

TYPES OF BUSINESS:

Coal Mining

BRANDS/DIVISIONS/AFFILIATES:

Arch Western Resources, LLC
Thunder Basin Coal Company, LLC
Arch of Wyoming, LLC
Canyon Fuel Company, LLC
Triton Coal Company
Trailblazer Energy Center
Great Northern Properties Limited Partnership

CONTACTS: *Note: Officers with more than one job title may be intentionally listed here more than once.*

Steven F. Leer, CEO
John W. Eaves, COO
John W. Eaves, Pres.
John T. Drexler, CFO/Sr. VP
David N. Warnecke, VP-Mktg. & Trading
Sheila B. Feldman, VP-Human Resources
David E. Hartley, CIO/VP
Robert G. Jones, General. Counsel/Sec./Sr. VP-Law
Paul A. Lang, Sr. VP-Oper.
C. Henry Besten, Jr., Sr. VP-Strategic Dev.
Deck S. Slone, VP-Public & Gov't Affairs
Deck S. Slone, VP-Investor Rel.
John W. Lorson, Chief Acct. Officer/VP
Robert W. Shanks, Pres., Eastern Oper.
James E. Florczak, Treas.
Anthony S. Bumbico, VP-Safety
David B. Peugh, VP-Bus. Dev.
Steven F. Leer, Chmn.

Phone: 314-994-2700	**Fax:** 314-994-2878
Toll-Free:	
Address: 1 City Place Dr., Ste. 300, St. Louis, MO 63141 US	

GROWTH PLANS/SPECIAL FEATURES:

Arch Coal, Inc. is one of the largest coal producers in the U.S., generating approximately 16% of America's total coal supply through 19 active mines in seven states. The majority of the coal is sold to producers of electric power, steel producers and industrial facilities. In 2009, the firm sold 126.1 million tons of pro forma coal, which provided U.S. utilities with fuel to produce approximately 12.7% of the nation's electricity. The company concentrates its business on low sulfur coal, which constitutes 79.8% of its proven and probable coal reserves. It controls a domestic reserve base of 3.2 billion tons, which is made up of 84% low in sulfur and 77% meets the requirements of the Clean Air Act. Arch Coal operates in Wyoming's Powder River Basin; the Central Appalachian region in Virginia, West Virginia and Kentucky; and the Western Bituminous region in Utah and Colorado. The firm invests in research and development of clean coal, as well as coal conversion technologies such as coal to diesel fuel and coal to natural gas. Company subsidiaries include Triton Coal Company; Canyon Fuel Company, LLC; Arch of Wyoming, Inc.; and Thunder Basin Coal Company, LLC. In October 2009, the firm acquired Rio Tinto's Jacobs Ranch mine. In November 2009, Arch Coal signed a coal lease comprising all of Great Northern Properties Limited Partnership's coal resources in the Otter Creek Tracts located in southeastern Montana, granting the company rights to mine 9,600 acres of land containing 731 million tons of sub-bituminous coal reserves. In March 2010, the firm acquired a 35% stake in the power plant Trailblazer Energy Center being developed in Texas, which will supply 600 megawatts of energy and act as a source of carbon dioxide for enhanced oil recovery.

Employee benefits include medical, dental and vision insurance; life and disability insurance; a 401(k); and educational assistance.

FINANCIALS: **Sales and profits are in thousands of dollars—add 000 to get the full amount. 2010 Note: Financial information for 2010 was not available for all companies at press time.**

2010 Sales: $	2010 Profits: $	**U.S. Stock Ticker: ACI**
2009 Sales: $2,576,081	2009 Profits: $42,169	**Int'l Ticker:** Int'l Exchange:
2008 Sales: $2,983,806	2008 Profits: $354,330	Employees: 4,601
2007 Sales: $2,413,644	2007 Profits: $174,929	Fiscal Year Ends: 12/31
2006 Sales: $2,500,431	2006 Profits: $260,553	Parent Company:

SALARIES/BENEFITS:

Pension Plan: Y	ESOP Stock Plan:	Profit Sharing:	Top Exec. Salary: $850,000	Bonus: $624,800
Savings Plan: Y	Stock Purch. Plan:		Second Exec. Salary: $535,000	Bonus: $314,600

OTHER THOUGHTS:

Apparent Women Officers or Directors: 2
Hot Spot for Advancement for Women/Minorities: Y

LOCATIONS: ("Y" = Yes)

West:	Southwest:	Midwest:	Southeast:	Northeast:	International:
Y	Y	Y		Y	

ARCTIC SLOPE REGIONAL CORP

www.asrc.com

Industry Group Code: 213112 **Ranks within this company's industry group:** Sales: Profits:

Exploration/Production:		Refining/Retailing:		Utilities:		Alternative Energy:		Specialty Services:		Energy Mktg./Other Svcs.	
Exploration:	Y	Refining:	Y	Electric Utility:		Waste/Solar/Other:		Consulting/Eng.:	Y	Energy Marketing:	Y
Production:	Y	Retailing:	Y	Gas Utility:		Thermal/Steam:		Seismic:	Y	Equipment/Machinery:	Y
Coal Production:	Y	Convenience Stores:		Pipelines:		Wind:		Drilling:	Y	Oil Field Services:	Y
		Chemicals:		Water:		Hydro:		InfoTech:		Air/Shipping Transportation:	
						Fuel Cells:		Specialty Services:	Y		

TYPES OF BUSINESS:

Energy Services
Petroleum Refining, Distribution & Marketing
Engineering & Construction Services
Geological & Geophysical Services
Communications Installation Services
Drilling, Exploration & Production Services
Financial Services
Tourism & Hospitality Services

BRANDS/DIVISIONS/AFFILIATES:

ASRC Energy Services
Petro Star Inc
ASRC Federal Holding Company
ASRC Construction Holding Company

CONTACTS:

Note: Officers with more than one job title may be intentionally listed here more than once.

Rex A. Rock, Sr., CEO
Rex A. Rock, Sr., Pres.
Kristin Mellinger, CFO
Debbie Akpik, Dir.-Shareholder Hire & Career Dev.
Tina Wolgemuth, Dir.-Shareholder Admin.
Angela Cox, Dir.-Foundation & Endowment Dev.
Crawford Patkotak, Treas.
Crawford Patkotak, VP-Shareholder & Community Programs
Patsy Aamodt, Dir.-Community Program
Mary Sage, Mgr.-Arctic Education Foundation
George Kaleak Sr, Second VP
Jacob Adams, Chmn.

Phone: 907-339-6000 **Fax:** 907-339-6028
Toll-Free: 800-770-2772
Address: 3900 C St., Ste. 801, Anchorage, AK 99503-5963 US

GROWTH PLANS/SPECIAL FEATURES:

Arctic Slope Regional Corp. (ASRC) is an Alaska Native-owned company, representing the business interests of the Arctic Slope Inupiat, specifically the eight villages of Barrow, Nuiqsut, Point Lay, Wainwright, Point Hope, Atqasuk, Kaktovik and Anaktuvuk Pass. The company owns over 5 million acres of land, which includes approximately 11.1% of the world's known coal reserves; oil leases in the Arctic National Wildlife Refuge and the Colville River Delta; potential unexplored zinc, lead and silver deposits; and gravel deposits. ASRC Energy Services, a subsidiary, provides construction, project management and maintenance for energy and industrial projects in Alaska, Louisiana and Canada. It offers oil and gas services; module fabrication; geological and geophysical services; drilling, exploration and production services; well stimulation and testing; and onshore and offshore facilities design. It also supplies construction, maintenance, fiber-optic cable and communications installation services to clients in Alaska and the continental U.S. Through ASRC Construction Holding Company and its subsidiaries, the company offers consulting, engineering and design services to enterprise and government agencies throughout Alaska, specializing in remote construction. It also offers construction services from feasibility studies to procurement, fabrication, transportation and installation. Petro Star, Inc. is ASRC's petroleum refining, distribution and marketing network, providing fuel and lubricants to consumers and military and commercial aviation clients. ASRC Federal Holding Company is the firm's technical services segment, offering operations and maintenance of radar, utility environmental and logistical support systems; buildings and structures; communications and electronic systems; information technology; security and fire protection systems; transportation facilities; and aerospace engineering and computer support services. ASRC's other businesses engage in construction, financing, local fuel distribution, automotive parts, snow machine sales/repairs, tourism/hospitality, cable television and wireless service.

FINANCIALS:

Sales and profits are in thousands of dollars—add 000 to get the full amount. 2010 Note: Financial information for 2010 was not available for all companies at press time.

2010 Sales: $	2010 Profits: $	**U.S. Stock Ticker: Private**
2009 Sales: $	2009 Profits: $	**Int'l Ticker:** Int'l Exchange:
2008 Sales: $2,920,000	2008 Profits: $	Employees: 9,000
2007 Sales: $1,777,500	2007 Profits: $207,700	Fiscal Year Ends: 12/31
2006 Sales: $1,700,500	2006 Profits: $196,100	Parent Company:

SALARIES/BENEFITS:

Pension Plan:	ESOP Stock Plan:	Profit Sharing:	Top Exec. Salary: $	Bonus: $
Savings Plan:	Stock Purch. Plan:		Second Exec. Salary: $	Bonus: $

OTHER THOUGHTS:

Apparent Women Officers or Directors: 6
Hot Spot for Advancement for Women/Minorities: Y

LOCATIONS: ("Y" = Yes)

West:	Southwest:	Midwest:	Southeast:	Northeast:	International:
Y	Y	Y	Y	Y	Y

AREVA GROUP

www.arevagroup.com

Industry Group Code: 335 **Ranks within this company's industry group:** Sales: 6 Profits: 6

Exploration/Production:		Refining/Retailing:		Utilities:		Alternative Energy:		Specialty Services:		Energy Mktg./Other Svcs.	
Exploration:	Y	Refining:		Electric Utility:		Waste/Solar/Other:	Y	Consulting/Eng.:	Y	Energy Marketing:	Y
Production:	Y	Retailing:		Gas Utility:		Thermal/Steam:	Y	Seismic:		Equipment/Machinery:	Y
Coal Production:		Convenience Stores:		Pipelines:		Wind:	Y	Drilling:		Oil Field Services:	
		Chemicals:		Water:		Hydro:	Y	InfoTech:		Air/Shipping Transportation:	
						Fuel Cells:		Specialty Services:	Y		

TYPES OF BUSINESS:

Nuclear Power Generation Equipment
Nuclear Power Plant Design, Construction & Maintenance
Electrical Transmission & Distribution Products
Electrical & Electronic Interconnect Systems
Uranium Mining & Processing
Forged Steel Equipment
Solar Thermal Technology (CSP)

BRANDS/DIVISIONS/AFFILIATES:

AREVA T&D
AREVA NC
AREVA NP
Commissariat a l'Energie Atomique (CEA)
IFASTAR
PN Rotor GmbH

CONTACTS: *Note: Officers with more than one job title may be intentionally listed here more than once.*

Anne Lauvergeon, CEO
Gerald Arbola, COO
Alain Pierre-Raynaud, CFO
Dominique Mockly, Sr. VP-Mktg.
Philippe Vivien, Sr. Exec. VP-Human Resources
Alain Bucaille, Sr. VP-Research & Innovation
Ahmed Bennour, Mgr.-Info. Sys. & Svcs.
Joel Pijselman, Sr. VP-Industrial
Pierre Charrenton, Sr. VP-Corp. Legal Dept.
Jean Huby, Sr. VP-Strategy, Mergers & Acquisitions
Jacques-Emmanuel Saulnier, Sr. VP-Comm.
Isabelle Coupey, VP-Investor Rel. & Financial Comm.
Alain-Pierre Raynaud, Dir.-Finance
Didier Benedetti, COO-AREVA NC, Research
Luc Oursel, Pres./CEO-AREVA NP
Benoit Bazire, CEO-AREVA TA
Josseline de Clausade, Sr. VP-Compliance
Jean-Cyril Spinetta, Chmn.
Dominique Mockly, Sr. VP-Int'l Bus. Dev.
Patrick Champalaune, Sr. VP-Purchasing

Phone: 33-1-34-96-00-00	**Fax:** 33-1-34-96-00-01
Toll-Free:	
Address: 33 rue La Fayette, Paris, 75442 France	

GROWTH PLANS/SPECIAL FEATURES:

AREVA Group is a leading producer of nuclear reactors. The CEA (Commissariat a l'Energie Atomique), the French atomic energy commission, owns 79% of the company. The company has manufacturing facilities in over 43 countries and a sales network in over 100. AREVA operates in five divisions: mining; front-end; reactors and services; back-end; and renewable energy. The mining division handles the uranium ore exploration, mining and processing operations of the company, with mines located in Canada, Kazakhstan and Niger. Through the front-end division, and wholly-owned subsidiary AREVA NC, the company manages concentration, conversion and enrichment of uranium ore, as well as nuclear fuel design and fabrication. The reactors and services division offers design and construction services for nuclear reactors and other non-carbon dioxide emitting power generation systems. Through AREVA NP, 34%-owned by Siemens, the firm designs and constructs nuclear power plants and research reactors and offers instrumentation and control, modernization and maintenance services, components manufacture and the supply of nuclear fuel. The back-end division provides treatment and recycling of used fuel, as well as cleanup of nuclear facilities. The renewable energy division invests in and develops sites for wind energy, bioenergy, solar power and hydrogen power, as well as energy storage. In March 2010, AREVA acquired Ausra, Inc., a pioneer in concentrated solar power (solar thermal). In May 2010, the firm received a conditional $2 billion loan from the U.S. Department of Energy for the development of a nuclear enrichment facility in Idaho. In June 2010, the company finalized the sale of its energy transmission and distribution division to Alstom and Schneider Electric. In October 2010, AREVA was awarded a contract by the Tennessee Valley Authority (TVA) for engineering and development work toward the completion of a nuclear power plant in northern Alabama.

FINANCIALS: **Sales and profits are in thousands of dollars—add 000 to get the full amount. 2010 Note: Financial information for 2010 was not available for all companies at press time.**

2010 Sales: $	2010 Profits: $	**U.S. Stock Ticker: ARVCF**
2009 Sales: $18,657,500	2009 Profits: $667,670	**Int'l Ticker: CEI** Int'l Exchange: Paris-Euronext
2008 Sales: $17,404,900	2008 Profits: $658,640	Employees: 75,414
2007 Sales: $15,768,900	2007 Profits: $1,166,500	Fiscal Year Ends: 12/31
2006 Sales: $14,331,600	2006 Profits: $856,200	Parent Company:

SALARIES/BENEFITS:

Pension Plan:	ESOP Stock Plan:	Profit Sharing:	Top Exec. Salary: $	Bonus: $
Savings Plan:	Stock Purch. Plan:		Second Exec. Salary: $	Bonus: $

OTHER THOUGHTS:

Apparent Women Officers or Directors: 3
Hot Spot for Advancement for Women/Minorities: Y

LOCATIONS: ("Y" = Yes)

West:	Southwest:	Midwest:	Southeast:	Northeast:	International:
				Y	Y

ARIZONA PUBLIC SERVICE COMPANY

www.aps.com

Industry Group Code: 2211 **Ranks within this company's industry group:** Sales: Profits:

Exploration/Production:		Refining/Retailing:		Utilities:		Alternative Energy:		Specialty Services:		Energy Mktg./Other Svcs.	
Exploration:		Refining:		Electric Utility:	Y	Waste/Solar/Other:	Y	Consulting/Eng.:		Energy Marketing:	Y
Production:		Retailing:		Gas Utility:		Thermal/Steam:	Y	Seismic:		Equipment/Machinery:	
Coal Production:		Convenience Stores:		Pipelines:		Wind:	Y	Drilling:		Oil Field Services:	
		Chemicals:		Water:		Hydro:		InfoTech:		Air/Shipping Transportation:	
						Fuel Cells:		Specialty Services:			

TYPES OF BUSINESS:

Utilities-Electricity & Natural Gas
Energy Trading & Marketing
Nuclear Power Generation

BRANDS/DIVISIONS/AFFILIATES:

Pinnacle West Capital Corporation
Palo Verde Nuclear Power Plant
Sundance Generating Station
Navajo Generating Station

CONTACTS: *Note: Officers with more than one job title may be intentionally listed here more than once.*

Donald E. Brandt, CEO
Donald G. Robinson, COO
Donald G. Robinson, Pres.
James R. Hatfield, CFO/Sr. VP
Pat Dinkel, VP-Power Mktg. & Resource Planning
Lori Sundberg, VP-Human Resources & Ethics
Kenneth C. Bohlen, CIO/VP
John Hesser, VP-Eng., Palo Verde Nuclear Station
David P. Falck, General Counsel/Exec. VP/Sec.
Bob Bement, VP-Oper., Palo Verde Nuclear Station
Warren Kotzmann, VP-Strategic Initiatives & Risk
Denise R. Danner, Chief Acct. Officer/VP/Controller
Randy Edington, Chief Nuclear Officer/Exec. VP
Tammy McLeod, Chief Customer Officer/VP
Jeff Guldner, VP-Rates & Regulation
Mark A. Schiavoni, Sr. VP-Fossil Generation
William J. Post, Chmn.
Barbara M. Gomez, VP-Supply Chain Mgmt.

Phone: 602-371-7171	**Fax:** 602-250-3007
Toll-Free: 800-253-9405	
Address: 400 N. 5th St., Phoenix, AZ 85004 US	

GROWTH PLANS/SPECIAL FEATURES:

Arizona Public Service Company (APS), the principal subsidiary of Pinnacle West Capital Corp., is one of the largest electricity providers in Arizona. The company serves approximately 1.1 million customers across the state, excluding the Tucson metropolitan area and approximately half of the Phoenix metropolitan area. APS operates 5,870 miles of transmission lines and 28,000 miles of distribution lines and generates 6,160 megawatts (MW) at predominately fossil fuel-based plants. It also operates and owns a 29% stake in the Palo Verde Nuclear Generation Station, the leading power producer in the U.S. The firm has two business segments: regulated electricity and marketing and trading. The regulated electricity segment consists of traditional regulated retail and wholesale electricity businesses and related activities, including electricity generation, transmission and distribution. The marketing and trading division is in charge of generating, selling and delivering electricity to wholesale customers in the U.S. It also markets, hedges and trades in electricity, fuels and emission allowances and credits. The company's Solana Generating Station, currently under development, is expected to have enough capacity to serve 70,000 customers. In April 2010, the firm received approval for its Flagstaff community power project, which proposes to install company-owned solar panels on customer rooftops, creating a neighborhood renewable power plant. In July 2010, APS entered a long-term power purchase agreement with Perrin Ranch Wind LLC for 100% of the energy produced at its 99 MW Perrin Ranch Wind Energy Center. In August 2010, the company announced construction plans for a 15 MW photovoltaic power plant, which it will own and operate. In September 2010, it announced plans for another solar plant to be constructed 70 miles southwest of Phoenix.

The company offers its employees medical and dental insurance; a 401(k) plan; life insurance; tuition reimbursement; short- and long-term disability insurance; a stock purchase plan; and an employee discount program.

FINANCIALS: **Sales and profits are in thousands of dollars—add 000 to get the full amount. 2010 Note: Financial information for 2010 was not available for all companies at press time.**

2010 Sales: $	2010 Profits: $	**U.S. Stock Ticker: Subsidiary**
2009 Sales: $	2009 Profits: $	**Int'l Ticker:** Int'l Exchange:
2008 Sales: $	2008 Profits: $	Employees:
2007 Sales: $2,936,277	2007 Profits: $283,940	Fiscal Year Ends: 12/31
2006 Sales: $2,658,513	2006 Profits: $269,730	Parent Company: PINNACLE WEST CAPITAL CORPORATION

SALARIES/BENEFITS:

Pension Plan:	ESOP Stock Plan:	Profit Sharing:	Top Exec. Salary: $	Bonus: $
Savings Plan: Y	Stock Purch. Plan: Y		Second Exec. Salary: $	Bonus: $

OTHER THOUGHTS:

Apparent Women Officers or Directors: 4
Hot Spot for Advancement for Women/Minorities: Y

LOCATIONS: ("Y" = Yes)

West:	Southwest:	Midwest:	Southeast:	Northeast:	International:
	Y				

ATCO LTD

www.atco.com

Industry Group Code: 221 **Ranks within this company's industry group:** Sales: 39 Profits: 31

Exploration/Production:		Refining/Retailing:		Utilities:		Alternative Energy:		Specialty Services:		Energy Mktg./Other Svcs.	
Exploration:		Refining:		Electric Utility:	Y	Waste/Solar/Other:		Consulting/Eng.:	Y	Energy Marketing:	
Production:		Retailing:		Gas Utility:	Y	Thermal/Steam:		Seismic:		Equipment/Machinery:	Y
Coal Production:		Convenience Stores:		Pipelines:	Y	Wind:		Drilling:		Oil Field Services:	
		Chemicals:		Water:		Hydro:		InfoTech:		Air/Shipping Transportation:	
						Fuel Cells:		Specialty Services:	Y		

TYPES OF BUSINESS:

Utilities-Electricity & Natural Gas
Natural Gas Transportation & Storage
Power Distribution & Transmission
IT & Management Services
Logistics Services
Travel Services
Construction
Noise Reduction Services

BRANDS/DIVISIONS/AFFILIATES:

Canadian Utilities Ltd
ATCO Electric
ATCO Pipelines
ATCO Midstream
ATCO Frontec
ATCO Gas
ATCO I-Tek
ATCO Power

CONTACTS:

Note: Officers with more than one job title may be intentionally listed here more than once.

Nancy C. Southern, CEO
Nancy C. Southern, Pres.
Brian R. Bale, CFO/Sr. VP
Carson J. Ackroyd, VP-Mktg.
Erhard M. Kiefer, VP-Human Resources & Corp. Svcs.
Siegfried W. Kiefer, CIO/Managing Dir.-Utilities
Susan R. Werth, Chief Admin. Officer/Sr. VP
Patricia Spruin, Corp. Sec./VP-Admin.
Bob Myles, Sr. VP-Corp. Dev. & Planning
Carson J. Ackroyd, VP-Corp. Comm.
Paul G. Wright, VP-Finance/Controller/Treas.
Kevin P. Hunt, VP-Internal Audit & Risk Mgmt.
Robert C. Neumann, VP/Controller
Ian D. Hargrave, VP-Project Dev.
Harry Wilmot, Pres./COO-ATCO Structures & Logistics
Ronald D. Southern, Chmn.

Phone: 403-292-7500 **Fax:** 403-292-7532
Toll-Free:
Address: 909 11th Ave. SW, Ste. 1400, Calgary, AB T2R 1N6 Canada

GROWTH PLANS/SPECIAL FEATURES:

ATCO Ltd. operates utilities, generates power and provides industrial services, as well as other services. The firm primarily operates in the Canadian market, but also maintains activities in over 100 countries. The firm's business is divided into four operational segments: utilities, energy, structures and logistics and uncategorized. Canadian Utilities, Ltd., the firm's main operating subsidiary, manages all the utilities segment subsidiaries including ATCO Gas, ATCO Electric and ATCO Pipelines. ATCO Gas distributes natural gas to nearly 1 million customers throughout Alberta; ATCO Electric serves approximately 207,000 customers in Alberta, the Northwest Territories and Yukon; and ATCO Pipelines transports natural gas throughout Alberta via 5,320 miles of pipeline. The energy segment consists of ATCO Power, ATCO Midstream and ATCO Energy Solutions. ATCO Power operates 19 power generation plants in Canada, the U.K. and Australia. ATCO Midstream works with natural gas producers to gather, process and store natural gas and extract liquids from it. ATCO Energy Solutions provides infrastructure solutions including pipelines, water and wastewater treatment and hydrocarbon storage to industrial and municipal customers. ATCO Structures and Logistics brings together three divisions; ATCO Frontec, ATCO Structures and ATCO Noise Management. ATCO Frontec provides electronic systems installation; integration and management; logistics; infrastructure management; airport management; and operation and integrated security services worldwide. ATCO Structures constructs manufactured housing and commercial buildings, and ATCO Noise Management provides noise-reduction services to industrial and institutional clients. Key customers of this division include NATO, NORAD and The Canadian Department of Defense. Lastly, under the uncategorized segment fall ATCO Travel, a corporate and personal travel management service, and ATCO I-Tek, which offers billing, customer care and information technology services to clients throughout Canada. In 2010, ATCO opened several new facilities including, a power plant in Western Australia and operating facilities in Perth and Edmonton.

FINANCIALS:

Sales and profits are in thousands of dollars—add 000 to get the full amount. 2010 Note: Financial information for 2010 was not available for all companies at press time.

2010 Sales: $	2010 Profits: $	**U.S. Stock Ticker:**
2009 Sales: $3,007,250	2009 Profits: $274,040	**Int'l Ticker: ACO** Int'l Exchange: Toronto-TSX
2008 Sales: $3,035,820	2008 Profits: $252,400	Employees:
2007 Sales: $2,727,700	2007 Profits: $235,800	Fiscal Year Ends: 12/31
2006 Sales: $2,689,200	2006 Profits: $194,600	Parent Company:

SALARIES/BENEFITS:

Pension Plan: Y	ESOP Stock Plan:	Profit Sharing:	Top Exec. Salary: $	Bonus: $1,177,859
Savings Plan:	Stock Purch. Plan:		Second Exec. Salary: $	Bonus: $

OTHER THOUGHTS:

Apparent Women Officers or Directors: 5
Hot Spot for Advancement for Women/Minorities: Y

LOCATIONS: ("Y" = Yes)

West:	Southwest:	Midwest:	Southeast:	Northeast:	International:
					Y

ATLANTIC CITY ELECTRIC COMPANY

www.atlanticcityelectric.com

Industry Group Code: 221 **Ranks within this company's industry group:** Sales: Profits:

Exploration/Production:		**Refining/Retailing:**		**Utilities:**		**Alternative Energy:**		**Specialty Services:**		**Energy Mktg./Other Svcs.**	
Exploration:		Refining:		Electric Utility:	Y	Waste/Solar/Other:		Consulting/Eng.:		Energy Marketing:	
Production:		Retailing:		Gas Utility:		Thermal/Steam:		Seismic:		Equipment/Machinery:	
Coal Production:		Convenience Stores:		Pipelines:		Wind:		Drilling:		Oil Field Services:	
		Chemicals:		Water:		Hydro:		InfoTech:		Air/Shipping Transportation:	
						Fuel Cells:		Specialty Services:			

TYPES OF BUSINESS:

Utilities-Electricity

BRANDS/DIVISIONS/AFFILIATES:

Pepco Holdings Inc

CONTACTS:

Note: Officers with more than one job title may be intentionally listed here more than once.

Joseph M. Rigby, Pres./CEO-Pepco Holdings, Inc.

Phone: 202-872-2000 **Fax:**
Toll-Free: 800-642-3780
Address: 5100 Harding Hwy., Mays Landing, NJ 08330 US

GROWTH PLANS/SPECIAL FEATURES:

Atlantic City Electric Company (ACE), a subsidiary of Pepco Holdings, Inc., is an electrical utility firm engaged in the transmission and distribution of electricity. The firm's primary service area service area consists of Gloucester, Camden, Burlington, Ocean, Atlantic, Cape May, Cumberland and Salem counties in southern New Jersey. This service area provides electrical service to 547,000 customers in a 2,700 square mile region with an approximate population of 1.1 million. Atlantic City Electric maintains a distribution network consisting of more than 11,000 miles of transmission and distribution lines. ACE delivers approximately 9.659 megawatt hours of electricity to its customers per year. Roughly 45% of this energy is delivered to commercial customers, 45% to residential customers and 10% to industrial customers. ACE relies entirely on purchases from third-party electricity-generating sources. The firm also offers basic generation services (BGS) to retail customers that choose not to purchase electricity from a competitive supplier. It offers two types of BGS: BGS-Fixed Price, which is supplied to smaller residential and commercial customers at seasonally-adjusted fixed prices; and BGS-Commercial and Industrial Energy Price, which is offered to larger customers at hourly PJM RTO real-time market prices for a one-year term. In May 2010, ACE introduced the Energy Wise Rewards Program, which reduces electrical usage through the use of central air conditioner compressor cycling.

Pepco Holdings Inc. offers employees benefits including medical, dental and vision packages; life and disability coverage; healthcare and dependent care reimbursement accounts; transportation reimbursement accounts; a 401(k) retirement savings plan; and tuition reimbursement.

FINANCIALS:

Sales and profits are in thousands of dollars—add 000 to get the full amount. 2010 Note: Financial information for 2010 was not available for all companies at press time.

2010 Sales: $	2010 Profits: $	**U.S. Stock Ticker: Subsidiary**
2009 Sales: $	2009 Profits: $	**Int'l Ticker:** Int'l Exchange:
2008 Sales: $	2008 Profits: $	Employees:
2007 Sales: $1,542,500	2007 Profits: $60,100	Fiscal Year Ends: 12/31
2006 Sales: $1,373,300	2006 Profits: $62,700	Parent Company: PEPCO HOLDINGS INC

SALARIES/BENEFITS:

Pension Plan: Y	ESOP Stock Plan:	Profit Sharing:	Top Exec. Salary: $	Bonus: $
Savings Plan: Y	Stock Purch. Plan:		Second Exec. Salary: $	Bonus: $

OTHER THOUGHTS:

Apparent Women Officers or Directors:
Hot Spot for Advancement for Women/Minorities:

LOCATIONS: ("Y" = Yes)

West:	Southwest:	Midwest:	Southeast:	Northeast:	International:
				Y	

ATLAS ENERGY INC

www.atlasenergy.com

Industry Group Code: 211111 **Ranks within this company's industry group:** Sales: 75 Profits: 73

Exploration/Production:		**Refining/Retailing:**		**Utilities:**		**Alternative Energy:**		**Specialty Services:**		**Energy Mktg./Other Svcs.**	
Exploration:	Y	Refining:		Electric Utility:		Waste/Solar/Other:		Consulting/Eng.:		Energy Marketing:	
Production:	Y	Retailing:		Gas Utility:		Thermal/Steam:		Seismic:		Equipment/Machinery:	
Coal Production:		Convenience Stores:		Pipelines:		Wind:		Drilling:		Oil Field Services:	
		Chemicals:		Water:		Hydro:		InfoTech:		Air/Shipping Transportation:	
						Fuel Cells:		Specialty Services:			

TYPES OF BUSINESS:

Natural Gas Development & Production
Natural Gas Production
Natural Gas Transportation
Oil Production

BRANDS/DIVISIONS/AFFILIATES:

Atlas Pipeline Partners L.P.
Atlas Energy, Inc.
Lightfoot Capital Partners L.P.
Atlas Pipeline Holdings L.P.

CONTACTS:

Note: Officers with more than one job title may be intentionally listed here more than once.

Edward Cohen, CEO
Richard D. Weber, Pres.
Matthew Jones, CFO/Exec. VP
Lisa Washington, Chief Legal Officer/Sr. VP/Sec.
Daniel Herz, Sr. VP-Corp. Dev.
Brian Begley, VP-Investor Rel.
Sean McGrath, Chief Acct. Officer
Eugene N. Dubay, Exec. VP/Pres. & CEO-Atlas Pipeline Partners L.P.
Freddie M. Kotek, Exec. VP
Jeff Kupfer, Sr. VP
Edward Cohen, Chmn.

Phone: 412-262-2830	**Fax:** 412-262-7430
Toll-Free:	
Address: 1550 Coraopolis Heights Rd., Moon Township, PA 15108 US	

GROWTH PLANS/SPECIAL FEATURES:

Atlas Energy, Inc. is one of the largest producers of natural gas in the U.S. The firm was formed in 2009 following the merger of Atlas America, Inc. and Atlas Energy Resources, LCC. The company's primary focus is on oil and natural gas exploration and production, specifically in northern Michigan's Antrim Shale, the Appalachian Basin and the Illinois Basin. In 2009, Atlas' total production of oil and natural gas was 36.9 billion cubic feet equivalent (bcfe). The company has proved gas reserves of 1 trillion cubic feet (Tcf); along with approximately 9,500 miles of interstate natural gas gathering systems. Atlas Energy owns interest in several companies, including Atlas Pipeline Partners L.P.; Lightfoot Capital Partners, L.P.; and Atlas Pipeline Holdings L.P. Atlas Pipeline Holdings owns and operates the general partner of Atlas Pipeline Partners L.P. Atlas Pipeline Partners primarily focuses on the transmission, gathering and processing of natural gas in the areas of Oklahoma, Arkansas, Kansas and Texas. It owns and operates eight active gas processing plants and treating facilities; 7,900 miles of interstate gas gathering pipeline; and a 565-mile interstate natural gas pipeline. Lightfoot Capital Partners, L.P. has an investment strategy that focuses on new MLPs (master limited partnerships), or infusing existing MLPs with needed equity or structured debt. This is done with the intent to acquire assets in areas such as coal and infrastructure. In November 2010, the firm agreed to be acquired by Chevron Corporation for $3.2 billion.

Atlas offers employees benefits including medical, dental, vision and prescription drug coverage; life insurance; short- and long-term disability; a 401(k); an employee assistance program; paid time off; and tuition reimbursement.

FINANCIALS:

Sales and profits are in thousands of dollars—add 000 to get the full amount. 2010 Note: Financial information for 2010 was not available for all companies at press time.

2010 Sales: $	2010 Profits: $	**U.S. Stock Ticker: ATLS**
2009 Sales: $1,587,602	2009 Profits: $- 84	**Int'l Ticker:** Int'l Exchange:
2008 Sales: $2,098,845	2008 Profits: $-485,589	Employees: 872
2007 Sales: $1,161,782	2007 Profits: $-58,140	Fiscal Year Ends: 12/31
2006 Sales: $	2006 Profits: $	Parent Company:

SALARIES/BENEFITS:

Pension Plan:	ESOP Stock Plan:	Profit Sharing:	Top Exec. Salary: $938,846	Bonus: $2,500,000
Savings Plan: Y	Stock Purch. Plan:		Second Exec. Salary: $676,923	Bonus: $2,000,000

OTHER THOUGHTS:

Apparent Women Officers or Directors: 1
Hot Spot for Advancement for Women/Minorities:

LOCATIONS: ("Y" = Yes)

West:	Southwest:	Midwest:	Southeast:	Northeast:	International:
	Y	Y	Y	Y	

ATLAS ENERGY RESOURCES LLC

www.atlasenergyresources.com

Industry Group Code: 211111 **Ranks within this company's industry group:** Sales: Profits:

Exploration/Production:		Refining/Retailing:		Utilities:		Alternative Energy:		Specialty Services:		Energy Mktg./Other Svcs.	
Exploration:	Y	Refining:		Electric Utility:		Waste/Solar/Other:		Consulting/Eng.:		Energy Marketing:	
Production:	Y	Retailing:		Gas Utility:		Thermal/Steam:		Seismic:		Equipment/Machinery:	
Coal Production:		Convenience Stores:		Pipelines:		Wind:		Drilling:	Y	Oil Field Services:	
		Chemicals:		Water:		Hydro:		InfoTech:		Air/Shipping Transportation:	
						Fuel Cells:		Specialty Services:	Y		

TYPES OF BUSINESS:

Natural Gas Production & Development
Oil Production & Development
Tax-Advantage Investment Partnerships

BRANDS/DIVISIONS/AFFILIATES:

Atlas Pipeline Holdings LP
Atlas Pipeline Partners L.P
Lightfoot Capital Partners LP
Lightfoot Capital Partners GP LLC

CONTACTS:

Note: Officers with more than one job title may be intentionally listed here more than once.

Edward E. Cohen, CEO
Richard D. Weber, COO
Richard D. Weber, Pres.
Matthew A. Jones, CFO/Exec. VP
Frank P. Carolas, Sr. VP-Geology
Lisa Washington, Chief Legal Officer/Sec./Sr. VP
Daniel Herz, Sr. VP-Corp. Dev.
Brian Begley, VP-Investor Rel.
Sean P. McGrath, Chief Acct. Officer
Eugene N. Dubay, Pres./CEO-Atlas Pipeline Partners LP
Freddie M. Kotek, Exec. VP
Jeff Kupfer, Sr. VP
Edward E. Cohen, Chmn.

Phone: 412-262-2830 | **Fax:** 412-262-7430
Toll-Free:
Address: 1550 Corapolis Heights Rd., 3rd Fl., Moon Township, PA 15108 US

GROWTH PLANS/SPECIAL FEATURES:

Atlas Energy Resources LLC, a subsidiary of Atlas Energy, Inc., focuses on the development and production of natural gas in the Appalachian Basin region of the U.S., and to a lesser extent, oil in western New York, eastern Ohio, western Pennsylvania and Tennessee. The firm provides services as an operator and drilling contractor, which includes drilling, completing, and operating the wells. The company utilizes horizontal shale drilling and vertical multi-stage fracturing drilling. Currently, the firm operates more than 10,000 oil and gas wells in Pennsylvania, Ohio, Tennessee and New York, which are all situated within the Appalachian Basin. Additionally, Atlas Energy has operating teams in other areas of the U.S., primarily in Michigan's Antrim Shale. The firm holds acreages with roughly 1.0 trillion cubic feet equivalent, of which 40% was proved undeveloped reserves. The company also sponsors and manages tax-advantage investment partnerships, in which it co-invests, to finance the exploitation and development of its acreage. Atlas Energy Resources, LLC is a wholly-owned subsidiary of Atlas Energy, Inc., formerly Atlas America. Atlas Energy Resources was originally formed to own and operate substantially all of the natural gas and oil assets and the investment partnership management business of Atlas America, Inc.

The company has a comprehensive benefits package including; medical plan choices; dental and vision coverage; life insurance and prescription drug coverage; a 401(k) plan; short and long term disability coverage; an employee assistance program as well as health advocate services; paid time off; and tuition reimbursement.

FINANCIALS:

Sales and profits are in thousands of dollars—add 000 to get the full amount. 2010 Note: Financial information for 2010 was not available for all companies at press time.

2010 Sales: $	2010 Profits: $	**U.S. Stock Ticker: Subsidiary**
2009 Sales: $	2009 Profits: $	**Int'l Ticker:** Int'l Exchange:
2008 Sales: $787,400	2008 Profits: $142,779	Employees: 602
2007 Sales: $577,897	2007 Profits: $117,504	Fiscal Year Ends: 12/31
2006 Sales: $320,982	2006 Profits: $58,182	Parent Company: ATLAS ENERGY INC

SALARIES/BENEFITS:

Pension Plan:	ESOP Stock Plan:	Profit Sharing:	Top Exec. Salary: $210,000	Bonus: $600,000
Savings Plan: Y	Stock Purch. Plan:		Second Exec. Salary: $150,000	Bonus: $500,000

OTHER THOUGHTS:

Apparent Women Officers or Directors: 4
Hot Spot for Advancement for Women/Minorities: Y

LOCATIONS: ("Y" = Yes)

West:	Southwest:	Midwest:	Southeast:	Northeast:	International:
		Y	Y	Y	

ATMOS ENERGY CORPORATION

www.atmosenergy.com

Industry Group Code: 221210 **Ranks within this company's industry group:** Sales: 5 Profits: 8

Exploration/Production:		Refining/Retailing:		Utilities:		Alternative Energy:		Specialty Services:		Energy Mktg./Other Svcs.	
Exploration:		Refining:		Electric Utility:		Waste/Solar/Other:		Consulting/Eng.:	Y	Energy Marketing:	Y
Production:		Retailing:		Gas Utility:	Y	Thermal/Steam:		Seismic:		Equipment/Machinery:	
Coal Production:		Convenience Stores:		Pipelines:	Y	Wind:		Drilling:		Oil Field Services:	
		Chemicals:		Water:		Hydro:		InfoTech:		Air/Shipping Transportation:	
						Fuel Cells:		Specialty Services:	Y		

TYPES OF BUSINESS:

Utilities-Natural Gas
Pipelines & Storage Facilities
Natural Gas Marketing
Risk Management
Generation Plant Developing
Gas Supply Management

BRANDS/DIVISIONS/AFFILIATES:

Atmos Energy Marketing
Atmos Pipeline and Storage, LLC.
Atmos Energy Holdings

CONTACTS:

Note: Officers with more than one job title may be intentionally listed here more than once.

Kim R. Cocklin, CEO
Kim R. Cocklin, Pres.
Fred E. Meisenheimer, CFO/Sr. VP/Treas.
Michael E. Haefner, Sr. VP-Human Resources
Richard Gius, CIO/VP
Louis P. Gregory, General Counsel/Sr. VP
Conrad E. Gruber, VP-Strategic Planning
Verlon R. Aston, Jr., VP-Public & Gov't Affairs
Susan K. Giles, VP-Investor Rel.
Christopher T. Forsythe, VP/Controller
Kenneth M. Malter, VP-Gas Supply & Svcs.
John A. Paris, Pres., Mid-Tex Div.
Tom S. Hawkins, Jr., Pres., Louisiana Div.
Richard A. Erskine, Pres., Atmos Pipeline-Texas
Robert W. Best, Exec. Chmn.

Phone: 972-934-9227 **Fax:** 972-855-3040
Toll-Free: 888-286-6700
Address: 5430 LBJ Fwy., 3 Lincoln Center, Ste. 1800, Dallas, TX 75240 US

GROWTH PLANS/SPECIAL FEATURES:

Atmos Energy Corporation is one of the largest pure natural gas distributors in the U.S., supplying approximately 3.2 million residential, commercial, industrial and agricultural and public-authority customers in 12 states. The company owns and operates one of the largest interstate gas lines in the U.S., and is one of the largest natural gas distributors in Texas, Mississippi and Louisiana. Its low average distribution and maintenance cost per consumer has allowed the company to build an extensive customer base. The company is organized into four operating segments: natural gas distribution; regulated transmission and storage; natural gas marketing; and pipeline storage. The natural gas distribution segment consists of natural gas sales to consumers throughout a 12 state area. The regulated transmission and storage segment operates the company's Atmos Pipeline and Storage, LLC subsidiary and is responsible for the movement and storage of natural gas from the Mid-Texas division to the company's five major reservoirs. The natural gas marketing operations are conducted primarily through Atmos Energy Marketing and consist of the company's natural gas marketing and non-utility operations in 22 states. These operations include procuring and trading gas supplies; arranging for gas transportation and management services; managing company-owned gas storage and pipeline assets; and constructing/leasing small electric generating plants for industrial customers and municipalities. The pipeline storage segment provides storage services to select natural gas distributors and certain third parties, through subsidiary Atmos Energy Holdings, Inc.

Atmos offers its employees medical, dental and vision; 401(k); employee wellness program; life insurance; flexible spending accounts; AD&D; and home and auto insurance.

FINANCIALS:

Sales and profits are in thousands of dollars—add 000 to get the full amount. 2010 Note: Financial information for 2010 was not available for all companies at press time.

2010 Sales: $	2010 Profits: $	**U.S. Stock Ticker: ATO**
2009 Sales: $4,969,080	2009 Profits: $190,978	**Int'l Ticker:** Int'l Exchange:
2008 Sales: $7,221,305	2008 Profits: $180,331	Employees: 4,691
2007 Sales: $5,898,431	2007 Profits: $168,492	Fiscal Year Ends: 9/30
2006 Sales: $6,152,363	2006 Profits: $147,737	Parent Company:

SALARIES/BENEFITS:

Pension Plan: Y	ESOP Stock Plan:	Profit Sharing:	Top Exec. Salary: $848,844	Bonus: $657,000
Savings Plan: Y	Stock Purch. Plan:		Second Exec. Salary: $537,328	Bonus: $337,000

OTHER THOUGHTS:

Apparent Women Officers or Directors: 2
Hot Spot for Advancement for Women/Minorities: Y

LOCATIONS: ("Y" = Yes)

West:	Southwest:	Midwest:	Southeast:	Northeast:	International:
Y	Y	Y	Y	Y	

ATOMIC ENERGY OF CANADA LIMITED

www.aecl.ca

Industry Group Code: 541330 **Ranks within this company's industry group:** Sales: 4 Profits: 5

Exploration/Production:		Refining/Retailing:		Utilities:		Alternative Energy:		Specialty Services:		Energy Mktg./Other Svcs.	
Exploration:		Refining:		Electric Utility:	Y	Waste/Solar/Other:	Y	Consulting/Eng.:		Energy Marketing:	
Production:		Retailing:		Gas Utility:		Thermal/Steam:	Y	Seismic:		Equipment/Machinery:	Y
Coal Production:		Convenience Stores:		Pipelines:		Wind:		Drilling:		Oil Field Services:	
		Chemicals:		Water:		Hydro:		InfoTech:		Air/Shipping Transportation:	
						Fuel Cells:		Specialty Services:	Y		

TYPES OF BUSINESS:

Nuclear Reactor Design
Nuclear Waste Management
Research & Laboratories
Medical Isotopes & Diagnostics
Engineering Services
Nuclear Power Plant Construction

BRANDS/DIVISIONS/AFFILIATES:

CANDU
MACSTOR
Advanced CANDU Reactor (ACR)
Team CANDU
Chalk River Laboratories
Canadian Neutron Centre (The)
National Research Universal (NRU)
National Research Council (The)

CONTACTS: *Note: Officers with more than one job title may be intentionally listed here more than once.*

Hugh MacDiarmid, CEO
Ken Petrunik, COO/Exec. VP
Hugh MacDiarmid, Pres.
Kent Harris, CFO/Sr. VP
Ala Alizadeh, VP-Mktg.
Beth Medhurst, Sr. VP-Human Resources
William Kupferschmidt, VP-R&D
Andre Robillard, CIO/VP
Anthony De Vuono, CTO/Sr. VP
Jerry Hopwood, VP-Prod. Dev.
Joseph Lau, VP-Eng. & Technical Delivery
Jonathan Lundy, General Counsel/Corp. Sec./Sr. VP
Ramzi Fawaz, Sr. VP-Oper.
Ala Alizadeh, VP-Bus. Dev.
George Bothwell, Sr. VP-External Rel. & Comm.
Georgina Kossivas, VP-Finance
Bill Pilkington, Sr. VP-Nuclear Laboratories
Michael Robins, Sr. VP-Restructuring
Earnest (Hank) Drumhiller, Chief Nuclear Officer/VP
Richard V. Cote, VP-Commercial
Glenna Carr, Chmn.
Tracy Greig, VP-Supply Chain

Phone: 905-823-9040 **Fax:** 905-823-7565
Toll-Free: 866-513-2325
Address: 2251 Speakman Dr., Mississauga, ON L5K 1B2 Canada

GROWTH PLANS/SPECIAL FEATURES:

Atomic Energy of Canada, Ltd. (AECL) is a global technology and engineering company that provides research and development, nuclear services, design, engineering, construction management, specialist technology, 3D kinematic simulation, waste management and decommissioning to the nuclear industry. The company constructs Canada Deuterium Uranium (CANDU) nuclear power plants and provides reactor services and technical support to operating CANDU reactors. Approximately 48 CANDU reactors are in use or under construction on four continents; reactors of this type supply approximately 15% of Canada's nuclear power. In Ontario, the firm's nuclear power contributes approximately 51% of the total electricity supply; in New Brunswick, 30% and in Quebec, 3% from CANDU nuclear. AECL also designs and builds MACSTOR (Modular Air Cooled Storage) used-fuel storage facilities. AECL operates nuclear laboratories that perform research; produce isotopes used in nuclear medicine and other applications; store and manage nuclear wastes; and decommission nuclear facilities. The NRU (National Research Universal) research reactor at AECL's Chalk River Laboratories has been the primary source of radio-isotopes produced for use in nuclear medicine. AECL's research reactors are also used for neutron beam research, inspection tools, nuclear power industry support and other research and training. Team CANDU, formed by AECL and four leading nuclear technology and engineering companies plan to develop a turnkey service and competitive solutions for building nuclear power plants in Ontario. Recent developments of AECL include The Canadian Neutron Centre (CNC), which is conceptual replacement for the NRU. It is being coordinated by AECL, the National Research Council and relevant government departments; and the Advanced CANDU Reactor (ACR), which is Generation III+ 1200 MWe (MegaWatt energy) class heavy water reactor. In recent years, AECL discontinued development of the MAPLE (Multipurpose Applied Physics Lattice Experimental) reactors because of problems with power. The MAPLE reactors program was a short-term answer for the production of medical isotopes.

FINANCIALS: **Sales and profits are in thousands of dollars—add 000 to get the full amount. 2010 Note: Financial information for 2010 was not available for all companies at press time.**

2010 Sales: $	2010 Profits: $	**U.S. Stock Ticker: Government-Owned**
2009 Sales: $387,890	2009 Profits: $-399,500	**Int'l Ticker:** Int'l Exchange:
2008 Sales: $442,170	2008 Profits: $-228,860	Employees: 4,891
2007 Sales: $549,728	2007 Profits: $11,760	Fiscal Year Ends: 3/31
2006 Sales: $324,060	2006 Profits: $50,270	Parent Company:

SALARIES/BENEFITS:

Pension Plan: Y	ESOP Stock Plan:	Profit Sharing:	Top Exec. Salary: $	Bonus: $
Savings Plan:	Stock Purch. Plan:		Second Exec. Salary: $	Bonus: $

OTHER THOUGHTS:

Apparent Women Officers or Directors: 7
Hot Spot for Advancement for Women/Minorities: Y

LOCATIONS: ("Y" = Yes)

West:	Southwest:	Midwest:	Southeast:	Northeast:	International:
				Y	Y

ATWOOD OCEANICS INC

www.atwd.com

Industry Group Code: 213111 **Ranks within this company's industry group:** Sales: 16 Profits: 9

Exploration/Production:		Refining/Retailing:		Utilities:		Alternative Energy:		Specialty Services:		Energy Mktg./Other Svcs.	
Exploration:		Refining:		Electric Utility:		Waste/Solar/Other:		Consulting/Eng.:	Y	Energy Marketing:	
Production:	Y	Retailing:		Gas Utility:		Thermal/Steam:		Seismic:		Equipment/Machinery:	
Coal Production:		Convenience Stores:		Pipelines:		Wind:		Drilling:	Y	Oil Field Services:	
		Chemicals:		Water:		Hydro:		InfoTech:		Air/Shipping Transportation:	
						Fuel Cells:		Specialty Services:			

TYPES OF BUSINESS:

Oil & Gas Drilling Support
Offshore Drilling
Consulting

BRANDS/DIVISIONS/AFFILIATES:

Atwood Oceanics Australia Pty. Ltd.
Atwood Oceanics Pacific Limited
Atwood Oceanics Malta Ltd.
Atwood Oceanics Pacific Ltd.
Atwood Eagle
Atwood Hunter
Atwood Falcon
Atwood Southern Cross

CONTACTS: *Note: Officers with more than one job title may be intentionally listed here more than once.*

Robert J.Saltiel, CEO
Robert J.Saltiel, Pres.
James M. Holland, CFO
Glen P. Kelley, Sr. VP-Mktg.
Luis A. Jimenez, Dir.-Human Resources
Barry Smith, VP-Tech. Svcs.
Glen P. Kelley, Sr. VP-Admin.
James M. Holland, Sec./Sr. VP
Alan Quintero, Sr. VP-Oper.
Michael Campelll, Controller
Ronnie L. Hall, VP-Oper.

Phone: 281-749-7800 **Fax:** 281-492-7871
Toll-Free:
Address: 15835 Park Ten Place Dr., Ste. 200, Houston, TX 77084 US

GROWTH PLANS/SPECIAL FEATURES:

Atwood Oceanics, Inc. is engaged in the international contract drilling of exploratory and development oil and gas wells. These services are located in offshore areas and include related support, management and consulting offerings. Approximately 97% of its sales come from overseas operations in offshore Southeast Asia, offshore Africa, offshore Australia, the Black Sea and the U.S. Gulf of Mexico. The company has many subsidiaries, among them Atwood Oceanics Australia Pty. Ltd. in Australia; Atwood Oceanics Pacific Ltd. in the Cayman Islands; Atwood Oceanics Pacific Limited in Malaysia; and Atwood Oceanics Malta Ltd. in Malta. Atwood's fleet currently consists of nine active, wholly-owned drilling units: Atwood Eagle, Atwood Hunter and Atwood Falcon, three semi-submersibles capable of drilling in up to 5,000 feet of water; the Atwood Southern Cross, a semi-submersible capable of drilling in up to 2,000 feet of water; the Atwood Beacon, Vicksburg and Atwood Aurora 400-,300- and 350-foot cantilever jack-ups, respectively; the Seahawk, a semi-submersible, 600-foot self-erecting tender-assist rig; and the Richmond, a 70-foot submersible. In addition to the owned rigs, the company also manages two modern, self-contained platform rigs.

Atwood Oceanics offers health and dental care, life insurance, long-term disability and retirement plans.

FINANCIALS: **Sales and profits are in thousands of dollars—add 000 to get the full amount. 2010 Note: Financial information for 2010 was not available for all companies at press time.**

2010 Sales: $	2010 Profits: $	**U.S. Stock Ticker: ATW**
2009 Sales: $586,507	2009 Profits: $250,745	**Int'l Ticker:** Int'l Exchange:
2008 Sales: $526,604	2008 Profits: $215,438	Employees: 1,000
2007 Sales: $403,037	2007 Profits: $139,024	Fiscal Year Ends: 9/30
2006 Sales: $276,625	2006 Profits: $86,122	Parent Company:

SALARIES/BENEFITS:

Pension Plan:	ESOP Stock Plan:	Profit Sharing:	Top Exec. Salary: $498,000	Bonus: $531,000
Savings Plan: Y	Stock Purch. Plan:		Second Exec. Salary: $292,000	Bonus: $255,000

OTHER THOUGHTS:

Apparent Women Officers or Directors:
Hot Spot for Advancement for Women/Minorities:

LOCATIONS: ("Y" = Yes)

West:	Southwest:	Midwest:	Southeast:	Northeast:	International:
	Y				Y

AVISTA CORPORATION

www.avistacorp.com

Industry Group Code: 221 **Ranks within this company's industry group:** Sales: 48 Profits: 46

Exploration/Production:		Refining/Retailing:		Utilities:		Alternative Energy:		Specialty Services:		Energy Mktg./Other Svcs.	
Exploration:		Refining:		Electric Utility:	Y	Waste/Solar/Other:		Consulting/Eng.:	Y	Energy Marketing:	Y
Production:		Retailing:		Gas Utility:	Y	Thermal/Steam:	Y	Seismic:		Equipment/Machinery:	
Coal Production:		Convenience Stores:		Pipelines:		Wind:		Drilling:		Oil Field Services:	
		Chemicals:		Water:		Hydro:	Y	InfoTech:		Air/Shipping Transportation:	
						Fuel Cells:	Y	Specialty Services:			

TYPES OF BUSINESS:

Utilities-Electricity & Natural Gas
Fuel Cells
e-Business & Consulting Services
Energy Marketing
Resource Management
Community Investment Management

BRANDS/DIVISIONS/AFFILIATES:

ReliOn
Advantage IQ
Avista Energy
Avista Utilities
Avista Development
Relion Inc

CONTACTS:

Note: Officers with more than one job title may be intentionally listed here more than once.

Scott L. Morris, CEO
Scott L. Morris, Pres.
Mark Thies, CFO/Sr. VP
Karen S. Feltes, Sr. VP-Human Resources/Corp. Sec.
James M. Kensok, CIO/VP
Marian Durkin, General Counsel/Sr. VP/Chief Compliance Officer
Jason Lang, Mgr.-Investor Rel.
Jason Thackston, VP-Finance
Christy Burmeister-Smith, Controller/Principal Acct. Officer/VP
Dennis P. Vermillion, Sr. VP/Pres., Avista Utilities
Jeffery D. Heggedahl, Pres./CEO-Advantage IQ
Don Kopczynski, VP-Transmission & Dist. Oper., Avista Utilities
Scott L. Morris, Chmn.

Phone: 509-495-8090	Fax: 509-777-5075
Toll-Free:	
Address: 1411 E. Mission Ave., Spokane, WA 99220-3727 US	

GROWTH PLANS/SPECIAL FEATURES:

Avista Corporation generates, transmits and distributes electricity and natural gas in the U.S. Pacific Northwest. The firm operates through two business segments: Avista Utilities and Advantage IQ. Avista Utilities manages the regulated utility business operations, which include generating, transmitting and delivering electricity, natural gas and related services to customer in California, Idaho, Montana, Oregon and Washington. Avista Utilities also engages in wholesale purchases and sales of electricity and natural gas. In total, the segment supplies retail electric service to approximately 356,000 customers and retail natural gas service to roughly 316,000 customers in its five state service area. The firm's generation capacity is 1,776 megawatts, with 56% generated from hydroelectric sources and 44% from thermal resources. Advantage IQ, Avista's indirect subsidiary, partners with multi-site companies across North America to assess sustainable utility expense management solutions. Advantage IQ's services include strategic management and the processing, payment and auditing of water/sewer, telecom, waste, energy and lease bills. The firm engages in other businesses indirectly, including sheet metal fabrication, venture fund investments and real estate investments, as well as certain natural gas storage facilities held by Avista Energy, Inc.

FINANCIALS:

Sales and profits are in thousands of dollars—add 000 to get the full amount. 2010 Note: Financial information for 2010 was not available for all companies at press time.

2010 Sales: $	2010 Profits: $	**U.S. Stock Ticker: AVA**
2009 Sales: $1,512,565	2009 Profits: $87,071	**Int'l Ticker:** Int'l Exchange:
2008 Sales: $1,676,763	2008 Profits: $73,620	Employees:
2007 Sales: $1,417,757	2007 Profits: $38,475	Fiscal Year Ends: 12/31
2006 Sales: $1,506,311	2006 Profits: $72,941	Parent Company:

SALARIES/BENEFITS:

Pension Plan: Y	ESOP Stock Plan:	Profit Sharing:	Top Exec. Salary: $630,001	Bonus: $582,026
Savings Plan: Y	Stock Purch. Plan:		Second Exec. Salary: $314,998	Bonus: $194,009

OTHER THOUGHTS:

Apparent Women Officers or Directors: 6
Hot Spot for Advancement for Women/Minorities: Y

LOCATIONS: ("Y" = Yes)

West:	Southwest:	Midwest:	Southeast:	Northeast:	International:
Y		Y			

BAKER HUGHES INC

www.bakerhughes.com

Industry Group Code: 213111 **Ranks within this company's industry group:** Sales: 1 Profits: 5

Exploration/Production:		Refining/Retailing:		Utilities:		Alternative Energy:		Specialty Services:		Energy Mktg./Other Svcs.	
Exploration:		Refining:		Electric Utility:		Waste/Solar/Other:		Consulting/Eng.:		Energy Marketing:	
Production:		Retailing:		Gas Utility:		Thermal/Steam:		Seismic:		Equipment/Machinery:	Y
Coal Production:		Convenience Stores:		Pipelines:		Wind:		Drilling:	Y	Oil Field Services:	Y
		Chemicals:	Y	Water:		Hydro:		InfoTech:	Y	Air/Shipping Transportation:	
						Fuel Cells:		Specialty Services:	Y		

TYPES OF BUSINESS:

Oil & Gas Drilling Support Services
Specialty Chemicals
Process Equipment
Geophysical Services
Drilling Fluids
Drill Bits
Data Management

BRANDS/DIVISIONS/AFFILIATES:

Tricone
BJ Services Company
Oilpump Services
Iraqi South Oil Company

CONTACTS: *Note: Officers with more than one job title may be intentionally listed here more than once.*

Chad C. Deaton, CEO
Martin S. Craighead, COO
Martin S. Craighead, Pres.
Peter A. Ragauss, CFO/Sr. VP
Didier Charreton, VP-Human Resources
Clifton Triplett, CIO/VP
Derek Mathieson, Pres., Tech.
Derek Mathieson, Pres., Prod.
Alan R. Crain, General Counsel/Sr. VP
Rusty McNicoll, Pres., Integrated Oper.
David E. Emerson, VP-Corp. Dev.
Gary R. Flaharty, VP-Investor Rel.
Alan J. Keifer, Controller/VP
John A. O'Donnell, Pres., Western Hemisphere
Sandra E. Alford, Corp. Sec.
Chad C. Deaton, Chmn.
Belgacem Chariag, VP/Pres., Eastern Hemisphere Oper.
Arthur Soucy, VP-Supply Chain

Phone: 713-439-8600 **Fax:** 713-439-8699
Toll-Free:
Address: 2929 Allen Pkwy., Ste. 2100, Houston, TX 77019-2118 US

GROWTH PLANS/SPECIAL FEATURES:

Baker Hughes, Inc. is a major supplier of wellbore-related products and technology services and a provider of drilling, formation evaluation, completion and production products and services to the oil and natural gas industry. The firm operates through two main segments: drilling and evaluation, and completion and production. The drilling and evaluation segment provides products and services used to drill and evaluate oil and natural gas wells, as well as consulting services for the analysis of oil and gas reservoirs. The products and services in this segment include wireline formation evaluation and wireline completion services; data management, processing and analysis services; and real-time drilling, measurement-while-drilling and logging-while-drilling services. Additionally, the firm provides drilling and completion fluids and related services, and is a leading provider of Tricone roller cone drill bits and ream-while-drilling and casing drilling technology. The completion and production segment provides equipment and services used through the productive life of oil and natural gas wells. Baker Hughes' completion and production segment includes equipment for the workover, finishing and completion of wells; oilfield specialty chemicals and chemical technology solutions for petroleum production, transportation and refining; and electric submersible pumps and progressing cavity pumps. Baker Hughes maintains over 2,800 on and offshore rigs worldwide, maintaining more than 1,000 service locations in 90 countries. In April 2010, the company acquired BJ Services Company, a leading pressure pumping, well completion, production enhancement and pipeline services firm. In June 2010, the firm acquired Siberia-based Oilpump Services, an electrical submersible pumping (ESP) system service company. In the same month, Baker Hughes agreed to supply services to PetroChina Tarim Oilfield Co. at its Tarim oilfield in northwest China. In August 2010, the company signed a strategic alliance with the Iraqi South Oil Company to provide technical services for its wireline logging department.

FINANCIALS: **Sales and profits are in thousands of dollars—add 000 to get the full amount. 2010 Note: Financial information for 2010 was not available for all companies at press time.**

2010 Sales: $	2010 Profits: $	**U.S. Stock Ticker: BHI**
2009 Sales: $9,664,000	2009 Profits: $421,000	**Int'l Ticker:** Int'l Exchange:
2008 Sales: $11,864,000	2008 Profits: $1,635,000	Employees: 34,400
2007 Sales: $10,428,200	2007 Profits: $1,513,900	Fiscal Year Ends: 12/31
2006 Sales: $9,027,400	2006 Profits: $2,419,000	Parent Company:

SALARIES/BENEFITS:

Pension Plan:	ESOP Stock Plan:	Profit Sharing:	Top Exec. Salary: $1,155,000	Bonus: $1,517,962
Savings Plan:	Stock Purch. Plan:		Second Exec. Salary: $618,622	Bonus: $585,149

OTHER THOUGHTS:

Apparent Women Officers or Directors: 2
Hot Spot for Advancement for Women/Minorities: Y

LOCATIONS: ("Y" = Yes)

West:	Southwest:	Midwest:	Southeast:	Northeast:	International:
Y	Y	Y	Y	Y	Y

BALTIMORE GAS AND ELECTRIC COMPANY

www.bge.com

Industry Group Code: 221 **Ranks within this company's industry group:** Sales: 33 Profits: 45

Exploration/Production:		**Refining/Retailing:**		**Utilities:**		**Alternative Energy:**		**Specialty Services:**		**Energy Mktg./Other Svcs.**	
Exploration:		Refining:		Electric Utility:	Y	Waste/Solar/Other:		Consulting/Eng.:		Energy Marketing:	
Production:		Retailing:		Gas Utility:	Y	Thermal/Steam:		Seismic:		Equipment/Machinery:	
Coal Production:		Convenience Stores:		Pipelines:		Wind:		Drilling:		Oil Field Services:	
		Chemicals:		Water:		Hydro:		InfoTech:		Air/Shipping Transportation:	
						Fuel Cells:		Specialty Services:			

TYPES OF BUSINESS:

Utilities-Electricity & Natural Gas
Distribution & Transmission Lines

BRANDS/DIVISIONS/AFFILIATES:

Constellation Energy Group
PJM Interconnectio, LLC

CONTACTS:

Note: Officers with more than one job title may be intentionally listed here more than once.

Kenneth W. DeFontes, Jr., CEO
Kenneth W. DeFontes, Jr., Pres.
Kevin Hadlock, CFO
Robert Gould, VP-Mktg.
David Vosvick, VP-Human Resources
Richard Burchfield, VP-IT Applications
Daniel Gahagan, General Counsel/VP
A. Christopher Burton, Sr. VP-Gas & Electric Oper.
Mark Case, Sr. VP-Strategy & Regulatory Affairs
Robert Gould, Chief Comm. Officer/VP-Corp. Comm.
Jeannette Mills, Sr. VP-Customer Rel. & Account Svcs.
Carol Dodson, Sr. VP-Asset Mgmt. Svcs.
Brian Daschbach Sr., Sr. VP-Integrated Field Svcs.
Stephen Woerner, Sr. VP
Thomas Valenti, Sr. VP-Logistics Mgmt. Svcs.

Phone: 410-685-0123	**Fax:** 410-712-9323
Toll-Free: 800-685-0123	
Address: 7225 Windsor Blvd., Baltimore, MD 21244 US	

GROWTH PLANS/SPECIAL FEATURES:

Baltimore Gas and Electric Company (BGE), a subsidiary of Constellation Energy, is a regulated electric and gas public utility serving Baltimore City and 10 central Maryland counties. It transmits and distributes electricity to over 1.2 million business and residential customers and distributes natural gas to more than 630,000 customers. Overall, the firm's electric service spans more than 2,300 square miles, and its natural gas service covers 800 square miles. The company only delivers energy produced by neighboring utility systems. The company maintains approximately 250 substations and more than 1,300 circuit miles of electrical transmission lines and over 22,500 circuit miles of overhead and underground distribution lines. Under the PJM Tariff and various agreements, BGE and other market participants can use regional transmission facilities for energy, capacity, and ancillary services transactions including emergency assistance. In addition to providing its residential natural gas customers with storage, distribution and livery services, BGE also provides customers with meter reading, billing, emergency response, regular maintenance and balancing services. The company is a member of PJM Interconnection, LLC; the independent system operator in Maryland, Pennsylvania, New Jersey and Delaware. BGE also has large volumes of propane under contract for the operation of its propane air facility and is capable of liquefying sufficient volumes of natural gas during the summer months for operations of its liquefied natural gas facility during peak winter periods. In August 2010, the firm was awarded $200 million federal stimulus grant from the Department of Energy to implement a smart grid throughout Central Maryland. Reducing the customer's cost on the project by 80%.

Employees of the firm are offered medical, dental and vision plans; short and long term disability; life insurance; flexible spending accounts; educational assistance; auto and home insurance discounts; adoption assistance; a travel reimbursement incentive program; alternate work schedules and onsite medical facilities.

FINANCIALS:

Sales and profits are in thousands of dollars—add 000 to get the full amount. 2010 Note: Financial information for 2010 was not available for all companies at press time.

2010 Sales: $	2010 Profits: $	**U.S. Stock Ticker: Subsidiary**
2009 Sales: $3,579,000	2009 Profits: $90,700	**Int'l Ticker:** Int'l Exchange:
2008 Sales: $3,703,700	2008 Profits: $51,500	Employees: 10,200
2007 Sales: $3,418,500	2007 Profits: $139,900	Fiscal Year Ends: 12/31
2006 Sales: $3,015,400	2006 Profits: $170,300	Parent Company: CONSTELLATION ENERGY GROUP

SALARIES/BENEFITS:

Pension Plan: Y	ESOP Stock Plan:	Profit Sharing:	Top Exec. Salary: $	Bonus: $475,780
Savings Plan: Y	Stock Purch. Plan:		Second Exec. Salary: $	Bonus: $

OTHER THOUGHTS:

Apparent Women Officers or Directors: 3
Hot Spot for Advancement for Women/Minorities: Y

LOCATIONS: ("Y" = Yes)

West:	Southwest:	Midwest:	Southeast:	Northeast:	International:
				Y	

BANGCHAK PETROLEUM PCL (THE)

www.bangchak.co.th

Industry Group Code: 324110 **Ranks within this company's industry group:** Sales: 28 Profits: 9

Exploration/Production:		Refining/Retailing:		Utilities:		Alternative Energy:		Specialty Services:		Energy Mktg./Other Svcs.	
Exploration:		Refining:	Y	Electric Utility:		Waste/Solar/Other:	Y	Consulting/Eng.:		Energy Marketing:	
Production:		Retailing:	Y	Gas Utility:		Thermal/Steam:		Seismic:		Equipment/Machinery:	
Coal Production:		Convenience Stores:	Y	Pipelines:		Wind:		Drilling:		Oil Field Services:	
		Chemicals:	Y	Water:		Hydro:		InfoTech:		Air/Shipping Transportation:	
						Fuel Cells:		Specialty Services:			

TYPES OF BUSINESS:

Petroleum Refineries
Fuel Service Stations
Fuel & Industrial Products
Auto Services
Convenience Stores

BRANDS/DIVISIONS/AFFILIATES:

Bangchak Biofuel Company Limited
Bangchak Green Net Company Limited
Lemongreen
Bai Chak
Green Series
Inthanin Coffee House
Fuel Pipeline Transportation Co. Ltd.
ASEAN Potash Mining plc

CONTACTS: *Note: Officers with more than one job title may be intentionally listed here more than once.*

Anusorn Sangnimnaun, Pres.
Yodphot Wongrukmit, Exec. VP-Mktg.
Watcharapong Saisuk, VP-Solar Farm Project
Wattana Opanon-amata, Sr. Exec. VP-IT
Wattana Opanon-amata, Sr. Exec. VP-Admin.
Anusorn Sangnimnaun, Sec.
Bundit Sapianchai, Exec. VP-Corp. Bus. Dev. & Strategy
Chavewan Kiatchokechaikul, VP-Corp. Comm. & Community Rel.
Surachai Kositareewong, Exec. VP-Finance & Acct.
Vichien Usanachote, Sr. Exec. VP-Refinery Bus.
Pongchai Chaichirawiwat, Sr. VP/Managing Dir.-Bangchak Biofuel Co. Ltd.
Thanachit Makaranond, VP-Refinery Technique
Krairit Nilkuha, Chmn.

Phone: 0-2335-4999	**Fax:** 0-2335-4009
Toll-Free:	
Address: 210 Sukhumvit 64, Prakanong, Bangkok, 10260 Thailand	

GROWTH PLANS/SPECIAL FEATURES:

The Bangchak Petroleum PCL is a Thailand-based refiner of crude oil products, with a processing capacity of 120,000 barrels per day. The company obtains its oil from East Asia and the Middle East, as well as domestically; selling its products to 1,100 service stations in Thailand, industrial plants, airlines, car companies and construction businesses. The company's retail division includes 507 standard service stations and 546 community service stations. The service stations offer several types of renewable fuel, such as Gasohol 95, unleaded gasoline consisting of 95% octane with a combination of gasoline and ethanol; Gasohol Superfast 91, containing a cleansing compound called Super Clean for Super Save (SCSS); and PowerD B5, containing biodiesel B5. The firm sells a variety of other fuels, lubricants and industrial products. In addition, Bangchak stations offer a family of services under the Green Series, which consist of auto care; car washing and waxing; and tire services. The service stations also host Inthanin Coffee Houses, which sell snacks, coffee and other beverages. The company also operates convenience stores under the names Lemongreen and Bai Chak, which offer oil change and carwash services. Subsidiaries include Bangchak Biofuel Company Limited, which produces alternative energy sources in Thailand, and Bangchak Green Net Company Limited, which manages the firm's service stations and products. The company also has investment interests in two related companies; Fuel Pipeline Transportation Co. Ltd., in which Bangchak has an 11.4% interest and ASEAN Potash Mining plc, in which the firm has a 6.6% interest.

FINANCIALS: **Sales and profits are in thousands of dollars—add 000 to get the full amount. 2010 Note: Financial information for 2010 was not available for all companies at press time.**

2010 Sales: $	2010 Profits: $	**U.S. Stock Ticker:**
2009 Sales: $3,636,820	2009 Profits: $251,790	**Int'l Ticker: BCP** Int'l Exchange: Bangkok-BAK
2008 Sales: $3,810,440	2008 Profits: $-22,150	Employees:
2007 Sales: $2,804,610	2007 Profits: $52,090	Fiscal Year Ends: 12/31
2006 Sales: $	2006 Profits: $	Parent Company:

SALARIES/BENEFITS:

Pension Plan: Y	ESOP Stock Plan:	Profit Sharing:	Top Exec. Salary: $	Bonus: $
Savings Plan:	Stock Purch. Plan:		Second Exec. Salary: $	Bonus: $

OTHER THOUGHTS:

Apparent Women Officers or Directors: 3
Hot Spot for Advancement for Women/Minorities: Y

LOCATIONS: ("Y" = Yes)

West:	Southwest:	Midwest:	Southeast:	Northeast:	International:
					Y

BANGOR HYDRO-ELECTRIC COMPANY

www.bhe.com

Industry Group Code: 2211 **Ranks within this company's industry group:** Sales: Profits:

Exploration/Production:		**Refining/Retailing:**		**Utilities:**		**Alternative Energy:**		**Specialty Services:**		**Energy Mktg./Other Svcs.**	
Exploration:		Refining:		Electric Utility:	Y	Waste/Solar/Other:		Consulting/Eng.:		Energy Marketing:	
Production:		Retailing:		Gas Utility:		Thermal/Steam:		Seismic:		Equipment/Machinery:	
Coal Production:		Convenience Stores:		Pipelines:		Wind:		Drilling:		Oil Field Services:	
		Chemicals:		Water:		Hydro:		InfoTech:		Air/Shipping Transportation:	
						Fuel Cells:		Specialty Services:	Y		

TYPES OF BUSINESS:

Utilities-Electricity & Natural Gas
Credit Union

BRANDS/DIVISIONS/AFFILIATES:

Emera, Inc.
Bangor Hydro Federal Credit Union
New England Power Pool

CONTACTS:

Note: Officers with more than one job title may be intentionally listed here more than once.

Robert Hanf, CEO
Gerard Chasse, COO
Gerard Chasse, Pres.
Robert Lysaght, VP-Human Resources
Kim Wadleigh, VP-Info. & Support Svcs.
Karen Redford, VP-Legal & Regulatory Affairs
Dan McCarthy, Mgr.-Field Oper.
Susan E. Faloon, Comm. Officer
Peter Dawes, VP-Finance/Treas.
David Keep, Key Account Exec.
Robert Lysaght, VP-Customer Oper.
Rick Manning, Dir.-Transmission
Lisa Martin, Mgr.-Transmission Dev.
Chris Huskilson, Chmn.
Kim Wadleigh, VP-Dist. Oper.

Phone: 207-945-5621 **Fax:** 207-973-2813
Toll-Free: 800-499-6600
Address: 21 Telcom Dr., Bangor, ME 04401 US

GROWTH PLANS/SPECIAL FEATURES:

Bangor Hydro-Electric (BHE), a subsidiary of Emera, Inc., is a regulated electric utility engaged in the purchase, transmission and distribution of electricity and other energy-related services in the state of Maine. Based in the city of Bangor with additional divisions in Lincoln, Ellsworth and Machias, it is one of the largest electric utilities in the state, serving a population of about 117,000 customers over an area of 5,275 square miles in the counties of Penobscot, Hancock, Washington, Waldo, Piscataquis and Aroostook (coastal Maine). The company's transmission system is composed of approximately 800 miles of transmission lines and 4,350 miles of distribution lines. After divesting its generation facilities due to regulatory changes within Maine, BHE now acquires capacity and energy through contracts with other utilities and generating facilities. Revenues from the distribution of electricity represent approximately 47% of the firm's total operating income, while transmission generates 40% and Stranded cost recovery income the remaining 13%. The company is a member of the New England Power Pool, an alliance of 100 utility companies producing and transmitting power in the New England States. It also operates Bangor Hydro Federal Credit Union, a full service credit union offering savings accounts, checking accounts, share accounts, home equity loans and automobile loans.

The firm offers an employee benefits package that includes health and life insurance; a 401(k) savings plan; medical and dependent care reimbursement accounts; tuition reimbursement; AD&D; and an employee assistance program.

FINANCIALS:

Sales and profits are in thousands of dollars—add 000 to get the full amount. 2010 Note: Financial information for 2010 was not available for all companies at press time.

2010 Sales: $	2010 Profits: $	**U.S. Stock Ticker: Subsidiary**
2009 Sales: $	2009 Profits: $	**Int'l Ticker:** Int'l Exchange:
2008 Sales: $	2008 Profits: $	Employees:
2007 Sales: $	2007 Profits: $	Fiscal Year Ends: 12/31
2006 Sales: $	2006 Profits: $	Parent Company: EMERA INC

SALARIES/BENEFITS:

Pension Plan: Y	ESOP Stock Plan:	Profit Sharing:	Top Exec. Salary: $	Bonus: $6,564
Savings Plan: Y	Stock Purch. Plan:		Second Exec. Salary: $	Bonus: $

OTHER THOUGHTS:

Apparent Women Officers or Directors: 4
Hot Spot for Advancement for Women/Minorities: Y

LOCATIONS: ("Y" = Yes)

West:	Southwest:	Midwest:	Southeast:	Northeast:	International:
				Y	

BARNWELL INDUSTRIES INC

www.brninc.com

Industry Group Code: 211111 **Ranks within this company's industry group:** Sales: 113 Profits: 77

Exploration/Production:		Refining/Retailing:		Utilities:		Alternative Energy:		Specialty Services:		Energy Mktg./Other Svcs.	
Exploration:	Y	Refining:		Electric Utility:		Waste/Solar/Other:		Consulting/Eng.:		Energy Marketing:	
Production:	Y	Retailing:		Gas Utility:		Thermal/Steam:		Seismic:		Equipment/Machinery:	
Coal Production:		Convenience Stores:		Pipelines:		Wind:		Drilling:	Y	Oil Field Services:	
		Chemicals:		Water:	Y	Hydro:		InfoTech:		Air/Shipping Transportation:	
						Fuel Cells:		Specialty Services:	Y		

TYPES OF BUSINESS:

Oil & Gas Exploration & Production
Real Estate Development
Water Systems
Drilling Support

BRANDS/DIVISIONS/AFFILIATES:

Barnwell of Canada, Limited
Kaupulehu Developments
Water Resources International, Inc.
Kaupulehu 2007, LLP

CONTACTS: *Note: Officers with more than one job title may be intentionally listed here more than once.*

Morton H. Kinzler, CEO
Alexander C. Kinzler, COO
Alexander C. Kinzler, Pres.
Russell M. Gifford, CFO/Exec. VP/Treas./Corp. Sec.
Alexander C. Kinzler, General Counsel
Mark A. Murashige, Corp. Controller/VP
Morton H. Kinzler, Chmn.

Phone: 808-531-8400	**Fax:** 808-531-7181
Toll-Free:	
Address: 1100 Alakea St., Ste. 2900, Honolulu, HI 96813 US	

GROWTH PLANS/SPECIAL FEATURES:

Barnwell Industries, Inc. and its subsidiaries are principally engaged in exploration, development, production and sale of oil and natural gas in Canada. The company is divided into four business segments: oil and natural gas, land investment, residential real estate and contract drilling. The oil and natural gas segment encompasses Barnwell of Canada, Limited, an exploration and development company in Alberta, Canada. The company has proved reserves of approximately 1.3 million barrels of oil and 20.36 billion cubic feet of natural gas. Barnwell's land investment segment's operations are carried out by Hawaii-based Kaupulehu Developments, of which Barnwell owns 77.6%. Kaupulehu owns leasehold rights to roughly 1,000 acres of land. The residential real estate segment operated by 80% owned Kaupulehu 2007, LLP, acquires house lots for investment and develops luxury residences for sale. Barnwell's contracted drilling segment includes subsidiary Water Resources International, based in Hawaii. It specializes in the exploration and development of groundwater resources, including drilling wells and installing and repairing water pumping systems for government, commercial and private clients in Hawaii. Water Resources owns and operates three portable rotary drill rigs, a rotary drill/workover rig, pump installation and servicing equipment and maintains drilling materials and pump inventory.

FINANCIALS: **Sales and profits are in thousands of dollars—add 000 to get the full amount. 2010 Note: Financial information for 2010 was not available for all companies at press time.**

2010 Sales: $	2010 Profits: $	**U.S. Stock Ticker: BRN**
2009 Sales: $32,178	2009 Profits: $-24,362	**Int'l Ticker:** Int'l Exchange:
2008 Sales: $65,644	2008 Profits: $11,732	Employees: 47
2007 Sales: $47,436	2007 Profits: $3,516	Fiscal Year Ends: 9/30
2006 Sales: $57,960	2006 Profits: $14,637	Parent Company:

SALARIES/BENEFITS:

Pension Plan:	ESOP Stock Plan:	Profit Sharing:	Top Exec. Salary: $694,271	Bonus: $
Savings Plan:	Stock Purch. Plan:		Second Exec. Salary: $595,833	Bonus: $

OTHER THOUGHTS:

Apparent Women Officers or Directors: 5
Hot Spot for Advancement for Women/Minorities: Y

LOCATIONS: ("Y" = Yes)

West:	Southwest:	Midwest:	Southeast:	Northeast:	International:
Y					Y

BASF SE

www.basf.com

Industry Group Code: 325 **Ranks within this company's industry group:** Sales: 1 Profits: 1

Exploration/Production:		Refining/Retailing:		Utilities:		Alternative Energy:		Specialty Services:		Energy Mktg./Other Svcs.	
Exploration:	Y	Refining:	Y	Electric Utility:		Waste/Solar/Other:		Consulting/Eng.:		Energy Marketing:	
Production:	Y	Retailing:	Y	Gas Utility:		Thermal/Steam:		Seismic:		Equipment/Machinery:	
Coal Production:		Convenience Stores:		Pipelines:		Wind:		Drilling:		Oil Field Services:	
		Chemicals:	Y	Water:		Hydro:		InfoTech:		Air/Shipping Transportation:	
						Fuel Cells:		Specialty Services:			

TYPES OF BUSINESS:

Chemicals Manufacturing
Agricultural Products
Oil & Gas Production
Plastics
Coatings
Nanotechnology Research
Nutritional Products
Agricultural Biotechnology

BRANDS/DIVISIONS/AFFILIATES:

Wintershall AG
BASF Canada
BASF Future Business GMBH
Sorex Holdings Ltd
Ciba Holding AG
BASF AG
STYROLUTION

CONTACTS:

Note: Officers with more than one job title may be intentionally listed here more than once.

Jurgen Hambrect, CEO
Kurt W. Bock, CFO
Harald Schwager, Exec. Dir.-Human Resources
Stefan Marcinowski, Exec. Dir.-Specialty Chemicals Research Div.
Kurt W. Bock, Exec. Dir.-Info. Svcs.
Andreas Kreimeyer, Exec. Dir.-Chemicals Research & Eng.
Magdalena Moll, Sr. VP-Investor Rel.
Hans-Ulrich Engel, Exec. Dir.-Oil & Gas Div.
John Feldmann, Exec. Dir.-Construction & Performance Chemicals
Stefan Marcinowski, Exec. Dir.-Crop Protection
Walter Dissinger, Pres., Nutrition & Health Div.
Juergen Hambrecht, Chmn.
Martin Brudermueller, Exec. Dir.-Asia Pacific Div.
Hans-Ulrich Engel, Exec. Dir.-Procurement & Logistics

Phone: 49-621-60-0	**Fax:** 49-621-60-42525
Toll-Free:	
Address: 38 Carl-Bosch St., Ludwigshafen, 67056 Germany	

GROWTH PLANS/SPECIAL FEATURES:

BASF SE, formerly BASF AG, is a chemical manufacturing company that serves customers in more than 170 countries. The firm operates in six business segments: chemicals; plastics; performance products; agricultural solutions; functional solutions; and oil and gas. The chemicals segment manufactures inorganic, petrochemical and intermediate chemicals for the pharmaceutical, construction, textile and automotive industries. The plastics segment manufactures polystyrene and performance polymers for the manufacturing and packaging industries. The performance products segment produces pigments, inks, printing supplies, coatings and polymers for the automotive, oil, packaging, textile, detergent, sanitary care, construction and chemical industries. BASF also employs chemical nanotechnology to produce pigments used to color coatings, paints, plastics and sunscreen. The firm's agricultural solutions segment produces genetically engineered plants, nutritional supplements, herbicides, fungicides and insecticides for use in agriculture, public health and pest control. The functional solutions segment develops automotive and industrial catalysts; construction chemicals; and coatings and refinishes for the automotive and construction markets. The oil and gas segment, operated through Wintershall AG, focuses on petroleum and natural gas exploration and production in North America, Asia, Europe, the Middle East and Africa. The company is one of the world's leading R&D firms, with 8,000 employees working in research in 70 sites worldwide, employing a research budget equal to $1.8 billion yearly. In June 2010, the company agreed to purchase Cognis Deutschland GmbH & Co KG, a specialty chemicals company, for approximately $ 4.1 billion. In August 2010, with the aforementioned acquisition agreement with Cognis, the firm announced the separation of its Care Chemicals division into two discrete units: Nutrition & Health and Personal Care. In October 2010, BASF revealed plans to establish an umbrella company, STYROLUTION, in which to conglomerate its styrenics activities.

U.S. employees are offered medical, dental and vision insurance; life insurance; disability coverage; an employee savings plan; tuition reimbursement; adoption assistance; and a supplier discount.

FINANCIALS:

Sales and profits are in thousands of dollars—add 000 to get the full amount. 2010 Note: Financial information for 2010 was not available for all companies at press time.

2010 Sales: $	2010 Profits: $	**U.S. Stock Ticker: BASFY**
2009 Sales: $67,557,500	2009 Profits: $1,879,080	**Int'l Ticker: BAS** Int'l Exchange: Frankfurt-Euronext
2008 Sales: $83,990,800	2008 Profits: $3,925,610	Employees: 96,924
2007 Sales: $78,122,600	2007 Profits: $5,479,950	Fiscal Year Ends: 12/31
2006 Sales: $69,448,400	2006 Profits: $4,575,330	Parent Company:

SALARIES/BENEFITS:

Pension Plan:	ESOP Stock Plan:	Profit Sharing:	Top Exec. Salary: $1,532,893	Bonus: $2,124,987
Savings Plan:	Stock Purch. Plan:		Second Exec. Salary: $982,371	Bonus: $1,063,144

OTHER THOUGHTS:

Apparent Women Officers or Directors: 3
Hot Spot for Advancement for Women/Minorities: Y

LOCATIONS: ("Y" = Yes)

West:	Southwest:	Midwest:	Southeast:	Northeast:	International:
Y	Y	Y	Y	Y	Y

BASIC ENERGY SERVICES INC

www.basicenergyservices.com

Industry Group Code: 213112 **Ranks within this company's industry group:** Sales: 23 Profits: 26

Exploration/Production:		Refining/Retailing:		Utilities:		Alternative Energy:		Specialty Services:		Energy Mktg./Other Svcs.	
Exploration:		Refining:		Electric Utility:		Waste/Solar/Other:		Consulting/Eng.:	Y	Energy Marketing:	
Production:		Retailing:		Gas Utility:		Thermal/Steam:		Seismic:		Equipment/Machinery:	Y
Coal Production:		Convenience Stores:		Pipelines:		Wind:		Drilling:	Y	Oil Field Services:	Y
		Chemicals:		Water:		Hydro:		InfoTech:		Air/Shipping Transportation:	
						Fuel Cells:		Specialty Services:	Y		

TYPES OF BUSINESS:

Oil & Gas Well Support Service
Contract Drilling Services

BRANDS/DIVISIONS/AFFILIATES:

Azurite Leasing Company LLC
Azurite Services Company
Freestone Disposal L.P.
Team Snubbing Services, Inc.
Rocky Mountain Cementers, Inc.
New Tech Systems, Inc.
Taylor Rig, LLC

CONTACTS: *Note: Officers with more than one job title may be intentionally listed here more than once.*

Ken V. Huseman, CEO
Ken V. Huseman, Pres.
Alen Krenek, CFO/Sr. VP
Doug Rogers, VP-Mktg.
Jim Tyner, VP-Human Resources
Lars Crotwell, VP-IT
Alan Krenek, Sr. VP/Sec.
Alan Krenek, Sr. VP/Treas.
Mark Rankin, VP-Risk Mgmt.
Bobby Adkins, VP-Rental & Fishing Tool Div.
Lynn Wigington, VP-Permian Basin Region
Steve McCoy, VP-Contract Drilling
Steven A. Webster, Chmn.

Phone: 432-620-5500	**Fax:**
Toll-Free:	
Address: 400 W. Illinois, Ste. 800, Midland, TX 79701 US	

GROWTH PLANS/SPECIAL FEATURES:

Basic Energy Services, Inc. (BES) is a well servicing contractor that provides services to oil and gas drilling and production companies. BES provides services during the entire life cycle of a well, from the initial drilling to the final abandonment of the site. The company provides services to over 2,000 oil and gas companies in approximately 100 service points around the country. It is one of the largest well servicing contractors in the U.S., with a service area that focuses primarily on the major oil and gas producing regions, including Texas, Oklahoma, Louisiana, Arkansas, Kansas, New Mexico and the Rocky Mountain states. The company operates in four distinct segments. These segments include well servicing, which constituted 30% of the company's 2009 revenue, operates a fleet of 405 well servicing rigs and related equipment; the fluid service segment (41%) operates a fleet of 791 fluid service trucks that aid in transport and disposal of materials to and from well sites; completion and remedial services segment (26%) operates the pressure pumping units fleet designed to configure underbalanced drilling operations; and the contract drilling segment (3%) operates nine drilling rigs that are contracted out to initiate production of a well. The investment firm DLJ Merchant Banking Partners III, L.P. owns 44.4% of BES. In December 2009, BES acquired Team Snubbing Services, Inc. In March 2010, it acquired Rocky Mountain Cementers, Inc. In April 2010, Basic acquired New Tech Systems, Inc. In May 2010, the firm acquired the assets of Taylor Rig, LLC, adding its operations to the well servicing segment.

FINANCIALS: **Sales and profits are in thousands of dollars—add 000 to get the full amount. 2010 Note: Financial information for 2010 was not available for all companies at press time.**

2010 Sales: $	2010 Profits: $	**U.S. Stock Ticker: BAS**
2009 Sales: $526,627	2009 Profits: $-253,538	**Int'l Ticker:** Int'l Exchange:
2008 Sales: $1,004,942	2008 Profits: $68,238	Employees: 3,800
2007 Sales: $877,173	2007 Profits: $87,733	Fiscal Year Ends:
2006 Sales: $	2006 Profits: $	Parent Company:

SALARIES/BENEFITS:

Pension Plan:	ESOP Stock Plan:	Profit Sharing:	Top Exec. Salary: $510,000	Bonus: $
Savings Plan:	Stock Purch. Plan:		Second Exec. Salary: $282,661	Bonus: $

OTHER THOUGHTS:

Apparent Women Officers or Directors:
Hot Spot for Advancement for Women/Minorities:

LOCATIONS: ("Y" = Yes)

West:	Southwest:	Midwest:	Southeast:	Northeast:	International:
Y	Y	Y	Y		

BECHTEL GROUP INC

www.bechtel.com

Industry Group Code: 237 **Ranks within this company's industry group:** Sales: 1 Profits:

Exploration/Production:		Refining/Retailing:		Utilities:		Alternative Energy:		Specialty Services:		Energy Mktg./Other Svcs.	
Exploration:		Refining:		Electric Utility:		Waste/Solar/Other:		Consulting/Eng.:	Y	Energy Marketing:	
Production:		Retailing:		Gas Utility:		Thermal/Steam:		Seismic:		Equipment/Machinery:	
Coal Production:		Convenience Stores:		Pipelines:		Wind:		Drilling:		Oil Field Services:	Y
		Chemicals:		Water:		Hydro:		InfoTech:		Air/Shipping Transportation:	
						Fuel Cells:		Specialty Services:	Y		

TYPES OF BUSINESS:

Engineering, Construction & Project Management Services
Civic Engineering
Outsourcing
Financial Services
Atomic Propulsion Systems Engineering
Airport Construction
Electric Power Plant Construction
Nuclear Power Plant Construction

BRANDS/DIVISIONS/AFFILIATES:

CONTACTS:

Note: Officers with more than one job title may be intentionally listed here more than once.

Riley P. Bechtel, CEO
Bill Dudley, COO
Bill Dudley, Pres.
Peter Dawson, CFO
John MacDonald, Dir.-Human Resources
Geir Ramleth, Dir.-Info. Systems
Geir Ramleth, Dir.-Tech.
Michael Bailey, General Counsel
Jim Jackson, Pres., Oil, Gas & Chemicals
Mike Adams, Pres., Civil
Scott Ogilvie, Pres., Bechtel Systems & Infrastructure, Inc.
Andy Greig, Pres., Mining & Metals
Riley P. Bechtel, Chmn.
David Hammerle, Mgr.-Contracts & Procurement

Phone: 415-768-1234	Fax: 415-768-9038
Toll-Free:	
Address: 50 Beale St., San Francisco, CA 94105-1895 US	

GROWTH PLANS/SPECIAL FEATURES:

Bechtel Group, Inc., founded in 1906 by Warren A. Bechtel, is one of the world's largest engineering companies. The privately-owned firm offers engineering, construction and project management services, with a broad project portfolio including road and rail systems, airports and seaports, nuclear power plants, petrochemical facilities, mines, defense and aerospace facilities, environmental cleanup projects, telecommunication networks, pipelines and oil fields development. The firm has participated in such notable endeavors as the construction of the Hoover Dam, the creation of the Bay Area Rapid Transit system in San Francisco, the massive James Bay Hydroelectric Project in Quebec and the quelling of oil field fires in Kuwait following the Persian Gulf War. Bechtel also constructed the Trans-Alaska Oil Pipeline, covering 800 miles between the Prudhoe Bay oil field and Valdez. Bechtel has also been contracted to develop the New Doha International Airport in Qatar, Iraq. An 11-year, multi-billion-dollar project, the new airport will be designed to accommodate six Airbus A380-800's, the largest passenger aircraft in the world. In December 2009, Bechtel formed a strategic alliance with Calera Corporation to jointly build facilities using carbon capture technology that reduces emissions.

FINANCIALS:

Sales and profits are in thousands of dollars—add 000 to get the full amount. 2010 Note: Financial information for 2010 was not available for all companies at press time.

2010 Sales: $	2010 Profits: $	**U.S. Stock Ticker: Private**
2009 Sales: $30,800,000	2009 Profits: $	**Int'l Ticker:** Int'l Exchange:
2008 Sales: $31,400,000	2008 Profits: $	Employees: 44,000
2007 Sales: $27,000,000	2007 Profits: $	Fiscal Year Ends: 12/31
2006 Sales: $20,500,000	2006 Profits: $	Parent Company:

SALARIES/BENEFITS:

Pension Plan:	ESOP Stock Plan:	Profit Sharing:	Top Exec. Salary: $	Bonus: $
Savings Plan:	Stock Purch. Plan:		Second Exec. Salary: $	Bonus: $

OTHER THOUGHTS:

Apparent Women Officers or Directors: 4
Hot Spot for Advancement for Women/Minorities: Y

LOCATIONS: ("Y" = Yes)

West:	Southwest:	Midwest:	Southeast:	Northeast:	International:
Y	Y	Y	Y	Y	Y

BERRY PETROLEUM CO

www.bry.com

Industry Group Code: 211111 **Ranks within this company's industry group:** Sales: 94 Profits: 67

Exploration/Production:		Refining/Retailing:		Utilities:		Alternative Energy:		Specialty Services:		Energy Mktg./Other Svcs.	
Exploration:	Y	Refining:		Electric Utility:		Waste/Solar/Other:		Consulting/Eng.:		Energy Marketing:	
Production:	Y	Retailing:		Gas Utility:		Thermal/Steam:		Seismic:		Equipment/Machinery:	
Coal Production:		Convenience Stores:		Pipelines:		Wind:		Drilling:		Oil Field Services:	
		Chemicals:		Water:		Hydro:		InfoTech:		Air/Shipping Transportation:	
						Fuel Cells:		Specialty Services:			

TYPES OF BUSINESS:

Oil & Gas Exploration & Production

BRANDS/DIVISIONS/AFFILIATES:

CONTACTS:

Note: Officers with more than one job title may be intentionally listed here more than once.

Robert F. Heinemann, CEO
Michael Duginski, COO/Exec. VP
Robert F. Heinemann, Pres.
David D. Wolf, CFO/Exec. VP
Walter B. Ayers, VP-Human Resources
Bruce S. Kelso, Chief Geoscientist
Kenneth A Olson., Corp. Sec.
George W. Ciotti, VP-Corp. Dev.
Todd Crabtree, Investor Rel.
Shawn M. Canaday, VP-Finance/Treas.
Dan G. Anderson, VP-Rocky Mountain & Mid-Continent Prod.
G.Timothy Crawford, VP-California Prod.
Jamie L. Wheat, Controller
Martin H. Young, Jr., Chmn.

Phone: 303-999-4400	**Fax:**
Toll-Free:	
Address: 1999 Broadway, Ste. 3700, Denver, CO 80202 US	

GROWTH PLANS/SPECIAL FEATURES:

Berry Petroleum Co. produces, develops, acquires, exploits and explores for crude oil and natural gas. It is headquartered in Denver Colorado and maintains regional offices in Bakersfield, California; and Plano, Texas. The company's principal reserves and producing properties are located in the San Joaquin Valley in Los Angeles and Ventura County in California, the Uinta Basin in Utah, the Piceance Basin in Colorado, and the Permian Basin and Cotton Valley in Texas. The firm owns three cogeneration facilities which supply steam that Berry uses for thermal recovery of its oil reserves. Berry's Midway-Sunset field facility utilizes cyclic steam recovery methods to reduce oil viscosity, enabling the oil to flow more efficiently to the surface. In 2009, Berry held 235 million barrels of oil equivalent (MMBOE) in proved reserves. The firm's most recent figures, factoring in the acquisition of the Permian basin locations, place the total reserves at an estimated 246 million. Approximately 35% of Berry's production and proved reserves come from the Rocky Mountain region; 48% from California; and 17% from Texas. Berry markets its crude oil production to competing buyers, including independent marketing, pipeline and oil refining companies. The company's current proved reserves consist of 55% crude oil and 45% natural gas. In January 2010, Berry purchased Wolfberry Oil Assets in the Permian Basin for $126 million; an acquisition it anticipates will increase the company's yearly production by 1,300 barrels of oil equivalent per day (BOE/d) from an estimated 130 distinct drilling locations. The company has plans for further development in all of its properties in 2010, including drilling 100 diatomite wells in the San Joaquin Valley and opening up 150 additional drilling locations in the Permian Basin.

Berry Petroleum offers its employees health and dental insurance; a 529 college savings plan; and a section 125 tax reduction plan.

FINANCIALS:

Sales and profits are in thousands of dollars—add 000 to get the full amount. 2010 Note: Financial information for 2010 was not available for all companies at press time.

2010 Sales: $	2010 Profits: $	**U.S. Stock Ticker: BRY**
2009 Sales: $574,712	2009 Profits: $54,030	**Int'l Ticker:** Int'l Exchange:
2008 Sales: $750,517	2008 Profits: $133,529	Employees: 243
2007 Sales: $547,427	2007 Profits: $129,928	Fiscal Year Ends: 12/31
2006 Sales: $486,338	2006 Profits: $107,943	Parent Company:

SALARIES/BENEFITS:

Pension Plan:	ESOP Stock Plan:	Profit Sharing:	Top Exec. Salary: $600,000	Bonus: $1,184,500
Savings Plan: Y	Stock Purch. Plan:		Second Exec. Salary: $320,000	Bonus: $404,830

OTHER THOUGHTS:

Apparent Women Officers or Directors:
Hot Spot for Advancement for Women/Minorities:

LOCATIONS: ("Y" = Yes)

West:	Southwest:	Midwest:	Southeast:	Northeast:	International:
Y	Y				

BG GROUP PLC

www.bg-group.com

Industry Group Code: 211111 **Ranks within this company's industry group:** Sales: 41 Profits: 22

Exploration/Production:		**Refining/Retailing:**		**Utilities:**		**Alternative Energy:**		**Specialty Services:**		**Energy Mktg./Other Svcs.**	
Exploration:	Y	Refining:	Y	Electric Utility:		Waste/Solar/Other:		Consulting/Eng.:		Energy Marketing:	Y
Production:	Y	Retailing:	Y	Gas Utility:		Thermal/Steam:		Seismic:		Equipment/Machinery:	
Coal Production:		Convenience Stores:		Pipelines:		Wind:		Drilling:		Oil Field Services:	
		Chemicals:		Water:		Hydro:		InfoTech:		Air/Shipping Transportation:	Y
						Fuel Cells:		Specialty Services:			

TYPES OF BUSINESS:

Oil & Gas Exploration & Production
Natural Gas Transportation & Distribution
Natural Gas Storage
Power Generation Plants
Gas Marketing

BRANDS/DIVISIONS/AFFILIATES:

Pure Energy Resources Limited
EXCO Resources Inc
Queensland Gas Company, Ltd.
Premier Power Limited
Comgas
Gujarat Gas Company Limited
Mahanagar Gas Limited
MetroGas

CONTACTS:

Note: Officers with more than one job title may be intentionally listed here more than once.

Frank Chapman, CEO
Ashley Almanza, CFO
Robert Booker, Exec. VP-Human Resources
Graham Vinter, General Counsel
Edel McCaffrey, Head-Media Rel.
John Grant, Exec. VP-Policy & Corp. Affairs
Jorn Berget, Exec. VP/Managing Dir.-BG Advance
Chirs Finlayson, Exec. VP/Managing Dir.-Europe & Central Asia
Sami Iskander, Exec. VP/Mgr.-Africa, Middle East & Asia
Robert P. Wilson, Chmn.
Martin Houston, Exec. VP/Managing Dir.-Americas & Global LNG

Phone: 44-118-935-3222	**Fax:** 44-118-935-3484
Toll-Free:	
Address: 100 Thames Valley Park Dr., Reading, Berkshire RG6 1PT UK	

GROWTH PLANS/SPECIAL FEATURES:

BG Group plc, operating in 27 countries, is engaged in the exploration, development, production, transmission, distribution and supply of natural gas. The company is divided into four business segments: exploration and production; liquefied natural gas; transmission and distribution; and power generation. The company's exploration and production division develops, produces and markets gas and oil in 12 countries. In 2009, the firm produced nearly 235 million barrels of oil equivalent and increased its reserves and resources to approximately 14.94 billion barrels of oil equivalent. BG Group's liquefied natural gas (LNG) division develops and operates infrastructure for the procurement, transport and sale of LNG, as well as LNG liquefaction and regasification facilities. The company's transmission and distribution division aims to develop new markets, transport gas to them and distribute that gas to power generating, industrial, commercial and residential customers. BG Group owns interests in distribution companies in Brazil (Comgas), India (Gujarat Gas Company Limited and Mahanagar Gas Limited), Argentina and Uruguay (MetroGas) and a pipeline in Kazakhstan. BG Group's power generation division manages a portfolio of gas-fired power plants in the U.K., Italy, Malaysia and Australia. In March 2010, the firm agreed to sell its three U.S. power plants to Energy Capital Partners for total considerations of $450 million. In April 2010, BG agreed to sell its 50% stake in the Seabank Power Limited combined-cycle gas turbine power plant located in the U.K. In May 2010, the company entered into a joint venture agreement with its U.S. shale partner, EXCO Resources, Inc., to acquire certain producing assets in the Appalachian region. In July of the same year, the group agreed to sell Premier Power Limited, a subsidiary operating a power plant in Northern Ireland, and in September 2010, it agreed to sell its interests in two power plants in the Philippines.

FINANCIALS:

Sales and profits are in thousands of dollars—add 000 to get the full amount. 2010 Note: Financial information for 2010 was not available for all companies at press time.

2010 Sales: $	2010 Profits: $	**U.S. Stock Ticker: BRGYY**
2009 Sales: $14,737,200	2009 Profits: $3,128,380	**Int'l Ticker: BG** Int'l Exchange: London-LSE
2008 Sales: $18,132,500	2008 Profits: $4,512,200	Employees: 6,191
2007 Sales: $16,430,000	2007 Profits: $3,460,000	Fiscal Year Ends: 12/31
2006 Sales: $15,034,133	2006 Profits: $4,119,987	Parent Company:

SALARIES/BENEFITS:

Pension Plan:	ESOP Stock Plan:	Profit Sharing:	Top Exec. Salary: $1,811,409	Bonus: $3,081,232
Savings Plan:	Stock Purch. Plan:		Second Exec. Salary: $1,089,840	Bonus: $1,062,066

OTHER THOUGHTS:

Apparent Women Officers or Directors: 1
Hot Spot for Advancement for Women/Minorities:

LOCATIONS: ("Y" = Yes)

West:	Southwest:	Midwest:	Southeast:	Northeast:	International:
	Y		Y	Y	Y

BHARAT PETROLEUM CORPORATION LTD www.bharatpetroleum.in

Industry Group Code: 324110 **Ranks within this company's industry group:** Sales: 8 Profits: 14

Exploration/Production:		Refining/Retailing:		Utilities:		Alternative Energy:		Specialty Services:		Energy Mktg./Other Svcs.	
Exploration:	Y	Refining:	Y	Electric Utility:		Waste/Solar/Other:		Consulting/Eng.:		Energy Marketing:	
Production:	Y	Retailing:	Y	Gas Utility:		Thermal/Steam:		Seismic:		Equipment/Machinery:	
Coal Production:		Convenience Stores:	Y	Pipelines:	Y	Wind:		Drilling:		Oil Field Services:	
		Chemicals:	Y	Water:		Hydro:		InfoTech:		Air/Shipping Transportation:	
						Fuel Cells:		Specialty Services:	Y		

TYPES OF BUSINESS:

Petroleum Products
Jet Fuel
Refining
Petrochemicals & Lubricants
Oil Change Shops
Gas Stations

BRANDS/DIVISIONS/AFFILIATES:

Kochi Refinery Limited
Numaligarh Refinery Limited
Bazaar
In & Out
Bharatgas
Bharat PetroResources Ltd.

CONTACTS: *Note: Officers with more than one job title may be intentionally listed here more than once.*

S. Radhakrishnan, Managing Dir.
Vinod Giri, Gen. Mgr.-Corp. Mktg.
S. P. Gathoo, Exec. Dir.-Human Resources Svcs.
S. P. Mathur, Exec. Dir.-Eng. & Projects
S. V. Kulkarni, Corp. Sec.
Brij Pal Singh, Gen. Mgr.-Retail Oper.
P. S. Bhargava, Exec. Dir.-Planning
S. Krishnamurti, Exec. Dir.-Corp. Affairs
S. K. Joshi, Dir.-Finance
S. Ramesh, Exec. Dir.-Lubes
D. M. Reddy, Exec. Dir.-Industrial & Commercial
R. K. Singh, Dir.-Refineries
S. B. Bhattacharya, Gen. Mgr.-Aviation
S. Radhakrishnan, Chmn.
R. Mehra, Exec. Dir.-Int'l Trade
Arun Kumar Singh, Chief Procurement Officer

Phone: 91-22-2271-3000 **Fax:** 91-22-2271-3874
Toll-Free:
Address: Bharat Bhavan, 4 & 6 Currimbhoy Rd., Ballard Est., Mumbai, 400 001 India

GROWTH PLANS/SPECIAL FEATURES:

Bharat Petroleum Corporation, Ltd. (BPCL), formerly Burmah Shell Refineries, Ltd., is one of India's top petroleum companies. The government of India is the firm's majority shareholder. BPCL is organized in six business units: refinery; retail; LPG (Liquefied Petroleum Gas); lubricants; industrial and commercial; and aviation. The refinery segment operates a refinery in Mumbai with a throughput capacity of 12.75 million tons of crude oil per year; the Kochi Refinery, with a throughput of 8.6 million tons per year; and owns 61.35% of Numaligarh Refinery Limited, which specializes in kerosene and diesel and has a throughput of roughly 3.3 million tons per year. The retail segment operates over 6,550 retail gasoline and diesel outlets, as well as almost 1,010 kerosene dealers and convenience stores under the Bazaar and In & Out brand names. The firm markets LPG under the Bharatgas name through physical distribution and online orders to 28 million households. The lubricant business unit, with manufacturing plants in Mumbai, Kolkata, Delhi and Chennai, offers a full range of automotive engine, gear, transmission and specialty oils as well as greases. BPCL's industrial and commercial segment provides bulk petroleum products, including fuel oils, solvents and bitumen, to approximately 8,000 industrial customers. The firm's aviation unit operates jet fueling stations and aviation lubricants in 10 international airports and 30 domestic airports. The company's wholly-owned subsidiary Bharat PetroResources Ltd. was formed in order to manage BPCL's activities in the upstream exploration and production sector, which has exploration blocks in India as well as Australia, Brazil, East Timor, Indonesia, Mozambique and the U.K. BPCL is also party to a number of joint ventures involved in a diverse mix of activities, from LNG importing and distribution to investment in renewable fuel development.

FINANCIALS: **Sales and profits are in thousands of dollars—add 000 to get the full amount. 2010 Note: Financial information for 2010 was not available for all companies at press time.**

2010 Sales: $	2010 Profits: $	**U.S. Stock Ticker:**
2009 Sales: $29,160,400	2009 Profits: $135,330	**Int'l Ticker: 500547** Int'l Exchange: Bombay-BSE
2008 Sales: $23,754,800	2008 Profits: $377,870	Employees: 14,016
2007 Sales: $21,016,400	2007 Profits: $458,090	Fiscal Year Ends: 3/31
2006 Sales: $17,651,700	2006 Profits: $157,700	Parent Company:

SALARIES/BENEFITS:

Pension Plan: Y	ESOP Stock Plan:	Profit Sharing:	Top Exec. Salary: $	Bonus: $
Savings Plan:	Stock Purch. Plan:		Second Exec. Salary: $	Bonus: $

OTHER THOUGHTS:

Apparent Women Officers or Directors: 5
Hot Spot for Advancement for Women/Minorities: Y

LOCATIONS: ("Y" = Yes)

West:	Southwest:	Midwest:	Southeast:	Northeast:	International:
					Y

BHP BILLITON

www.bhpbilliton.com

Industry Group Code: 211111 **Ranks within this company's industry group:** Sales: 22 Profits: 14

Exploration/Production:		**Refining/Retailing:**		**Utilities:**		**Alternative Energy:**		**Specialty Services:**		**Energy Mktg./Other Svcs.**	
Exploration:	Y	Refining:	Y	Electric Utility:		Waste/Solar/Other:		Consulting/Eng.:		Energy Marketing:	
Production:	Y	Retailing:		Gas Utility:		Thermal/Steam:		Seismic:		Equipment/Machinery:	
Coal Production:	Y	Convenience Stores:		Pipelines:		Wind:		Drilling:		Oil Field Services:	
		Chemicals:		Water:		Hydro:		InfoTech:		Air/Shipping Transportation:	
						Fuel Cells:		Specialty Services:			

TYPES OF BUSINESS:

Oil & Gas Exploration & Production
Aluminum Exploration & Production
Metallurgical Coal Exploration & Production
Nickel Exploration & Production
Diamond Exploration & Production
Base Metals Exploration & Production
Iron Ore Exploration & Production
Energy Coal Exploration & Production

BRANDS/DIVISIONS/AFFILIATES:

BHP Billiton Ltd
Anglo Potash, Ltd.
Rio Tinto, Ltd.
BHP Billiton Mitsubishi Alliance
New Hope Corp., Ltd.
Athabasca Potash, Inc.
PT Adaro Energy TBK

CONTACTS: *Note: Officers with more than one job title may be intentionally listed here more than once.*

Marius Kloppers, CEO
Ian Ashby, COO
Ian Ashby, Pres.
Alex Vanselow, CFO
Mike Henry, Pres., Mktg.
Karen Wood, Chief People Officer
Alberto Calderon, Chief Commercial Officer
Marcus Randolph, CEO-Ferrous & Coal
J. Michael Yeager, CEO-Petroleum
Andrew Mackenzie, CEO-Non-Ferrous
Jacques Nasser, Chmn.
Peter Beaven, Pres., Base Metals

Phone: 44-20-7802-4000 **Fax:** 44-20-7802-4111
Toll-Free:
Address: Neathhouse Place, Victoria, London, SW1V 1BH UK

GROWTH PLANS/SPECIAL FEATURES:

BHP Billiton, a dual-listed company doing business as BHP Billiton plc in the U.K. and BHP Billiton Ltd. in Australia, is one of the world's largest diversified natural resources companies. Its discovery, development and conversion operations focus in numerous major natural resource markets: alumina and aluminum, copper, coal, iron ore, nickel, manganese, oil, gas and uranium, as well as gold, zinc, lead, silver and diamonds. The company's major production operations are in Australia, the Americas and southern Africa. BHP Billiton divides its operations into nine business units: petroleum, aluminum, base metals, diamonds and specialty products, stainless steel materials, iron ore, manganese, metallurgical coal and energy coal. The petroleum business unit produced 158.6 million barrels of oil equivalent in 2009. The aluminum segment has a total production capacity of approximately 1.3 metric tons per annum. Through operations in Chile, Australia and Peru, the company's base metals segment mines copper, silver, lead, uranium and zinc. The diamonds and specialty products segment encompasses BHP's diamonds and titanium minerals businesses. The stainless steel materials segment primarily provides nickel to the stainless steel industry. The company's iron ore operations are based in the Pilbara region of Australia. The manganese segment produces ores, alloys and metals. The metallurgical coal segment produces hard coking coals for the steel industry. The energy coal unit provides thermal coal for use in the electric power generation and other industries. In December 2009, the company sold its Ravensthorpe Nickel Operation to First Quantum Minerals Australia Pty Ltd. In March 2010, BHP acquired Athabasca Potash, Inc., including the Burr project and various additional potash exploration properties in Saskatchewan, Canada. In May 2010, the company formed a joint venture for its Indonesian Coal Project with a subsidiary of PT Adaro Energy TBK. In August 2010, offered to acquire the Potash Corporation of Saskatchewan, Inc. in a deal valued at $40 billion.

FINANCIALS: **Sales and profits are in thousands of dollars—add 000 to get the full amount. 2010 Note: Financial information for 2010 was not available for all companies at press time.**

2010 Sales: $	2010 Profits: $	**U.S. Stock Ticker: BBL**
2009 Sales: $50,800,000	2009 Profits: $6,338,000	**Int'l Ticker: BLT** Int'l Exchange: London-LSE
2008 Sales: $60,122,000	2008 Profits: $15,962,000	Employees: 40,990
2007 Sales: $48,076,000	2007 Profits: $13,163,000	Fiscal Year Ends: 6/30
2006 Sales: $31,850,000	2006 Profits: $10,350,000	Parent Company:

SALARIES/BENEFITS:

Pension Plan:	ESOP Stock Plan:	Profit Sharing:	Top Exec. Salary: $2,038,885	Bonus: $2,330,527
Savings Plan:	Stock Purch. Plan:		Second Exec. Salary: $1,183,092	Bonus: $1,336,407

OTHER THOUGHTS:

Apparent Women Officers or Directors: 3
Hot Spot for Advancement for Women/Minorities: Y

LOCATIONS: ("Y" = Yes)

West:	Southwest:	Midwest:	Southeast:	Northeast:	International:
	Y			Y	Y

Note: Financial information, benefits and other data can change quickly and may vary from those stated here.

BJ SERVICES COMPANY

www.bjservices.com

Industry Group Code: 213112 **Ranks within this company's industry group:** Sales: 7 Profits: 12

Exploration/Production:		Refining/Retailing:		Utilities:		Alternative Energy:		Specialty Services:		Energy Mktg./Other Svcs.	
Exploration:		Refining:		Electric Utility:		Waste/Solar/Other:		Consulting/Eng.:		Energy Marketing:	
Production:		Retailing:		Gas Utility:		Thermal/Steam:		Seismic:		Equipment/Machinery:	Y
Coal Production:		Convenience Stores:		Pipelines:		Wind:		Drilling:		Oil Field Services:	Y
		Chemicals:		Water:		Hydro:		InfoTech:		Air/Shipping Transportation:	
						Fuel Cells:		Specialty Services:	Y		

TYPES OF BUSINESS:

Oil & Gas Drilling Support Services
Casing & Tubular Services
Pipeline & Industrial Commissioning
Oilfield Equipment Sales
Specialty Chemical Services
Stimulation Services
Cement Services

BRANDS/DIVISIONS/AFFILIATES:

Baker Hughes Inc
Innicor Subsurface Technologies, Inc.

CONTACTS:

Note: Officers with more than one job title may be intentionally listed here more than once.

John A. O'Donnell, Pres.
Chad C. Deaton, Chmn./CEO-Baker Hughes, Inc.

Phone: 713-462-4239	**Fax:** 713-895-5851
Toll-Free:	
Address: 4601 Westway Park Blvd., Houston, TX 77041 US	

GROWTH PLANS/SPECIAL FEATURES:

BJ Services Company, a subsidiary of Baker Hughes Inc., is a provider of pressure pumping and other oilfield services. The company provides its services both on land and offshore on a 24-hour-a-day, on-call basis through facilities in approximately 200 locations worldwide. It conducts operations through four principal segments: U.S./Mexico Pressure Pumping Services, International Pressure Pumping Services, Canada Pressure Pumping Services and the Oilfield Services Group. The firm's pressure pumping services include cementing and stimulation services. Cementing services seal off a wellbore to prevent fluid loss, to isolate fluids behind cement casing or to provide structural support. Stimulation services include fracturing, which enhances natural gas and oil production by opening up, or fracturing, a well with specialized fluids, pumped in at pressures up to 20,000 p.s.i.; acidizing, which utilizes corrosives to open up a well; sand control, which utilizes gravel as a filter to keep sand out of a wellbore during drilling; nitrogen services, which use nitrogen to displace fluids in pressure pumping operations; coiled tubing services, which include injecting a flexible steel pipe into a well for various well-servicing applications; and general service tools and technical personnel, which the firm generally rents. The oilfield services division provides casing and tubular services, process and pipeline services, chemical services, completion tools and completion fluids in the U.S. and select international markets. In April 2010, the firm was acquired by Baker Hughes, Inc. in a stock and cash transaction worth $5.5 billion.

BJ Services offers its employees health and dental plans, a stock purchase plan, a 401(k) plan and educational assistance.

FINANCIALS:

Sales and profits are in thousands of dollars—add 000 to get the full amount. 2010 Note: Financial information for 2010 was not available for all companies at press time.

2010 Sales: $	2010 Profits: $	**U.S. Stock Ticker: Subsidiary**
2009 Sales: $4,121,897	2009 Profits: $149,943	**Int'l Ticker:** Int'l Exchange:
2008 Sales: $5,359,077	2008 Profits: $609,365	Employees: 14,400
2007 Sales: $4,730,493	2007 Profits: $753,640	Fiscal Year Ends: 9/30
2006 Sales: $4,367,864	2006 Profits: $804,610	Parent Company: BAKER HUGHES INC

SALARIES/BENEFITS:

Pension Plan: Y	ESOP Stock Plan:	Profit Sharing:	Top Exec. Salary: $1,141,669	Bonus: $575,000
Savings Plan: Y	Stock Purch. Plan: Y		Second Exec. Salary: $600,001	Bonus: $242,000

OTHER THOUGHTS:

Apparent Women Officers or Directors: 2
Hot Spot for Advancement for Women/Minorities: Y

LOCATIONS: ("Y" = Yes)

West:	Southwest:	Midwest:	Southeast:	Northeast:	International:
Y	Y	Y	Y	Y	Y

BLACK & VEATCH HOLDING COMPANY

www.bv.com

Industry Group Code: 237 **Ranks within this company's industry group:** Sales: 7 Profits:

Exploration/Production:		**Refining/Retailing:**		**Utilities:**		**Alternative Energy:**		**Specialty Services:**		**Energy Mktg./Other Svcs.**	
Exploration:		Refining:		Electric Utility:		Waste/Solar/Other:		Consulting/Eng.:	Y	Energy Marketing:	
Production:		Retailing:		Gas Utility:		Thermal/Steam:		Seismic:		Equipment/Machinery:	
Coal Production:		Convenience Stores:		Pipelines:		Wind:		Drilling:		Oil Field Services:	
		Chemicals:		Water:		Hydro:		InfoTech:		Air/Shipping Transportation:	
						Fuel Cells:		Specialty Services:	Y		

TYPES OF BUSINESS:

Construction, Heavy & Civil Engineering
Infrastructure & Energy Services
Environmental & Hydrologic Engineering
Consulting Services
IT Services
Power Plant Engineering and Construction
LNG and Gas Processing Plant Engineering

BRANDS/DIVISIONS/AFFILIATES:

BV Solutions Group, Inc.
Fortegra
B&V China
B&V Corporation
B&V Construction, Inc.
B&V Europe
BV Solutions Group, Inc.
B&V International Co.

CONTACTS: *Note: Officers with more than one job title may be intentionally listed here more than once.*

Leonard C. Rodman, CEO
Leonard C. Rodman, Pres.
Karen L. Daniel, CFO
John G. Voeller, CTO
Howard G. Withey, Chief Admin. Officer
Daniel W. McCarthy, Pres./CEO-B&V Water
Leonard C. Rodman, Chmn.

Phone: 913-458-2000	**Fax:** 913-458-2934
Toll-Free:	
Address: 11401 Lamar Ave., Overland Park, KS 66211 US	

GROWTH PLANS/SPECIAL FEATURES:

Black & Veatch Holding Company (B&V) is a leading engineering, consulting and construction company specializing in infrastructure development for the energy, water and telecommunications, federal, management consulting and environmental markets. The company is employee-owned and operates over 100 offices worldwide. B&V provides its clients with conceptual and preliminary engineering services, engineering design, procurement, construction, financial management, asset management, information technology, environmental, security design and consulting, and management consulting services. The firm's energy market services include energy engineering and construction services for cogeneration, coal, nuclear and renewable energy sources; energy services, such as asset optimization, strategic market analysis, asset valuation and asset addition; gas, oil and chemical construction and consulting services for natural gas processing, sulfur recovery, LNG, petroleum refining, petrochemicals and cogeneration; and power delivery services for substations, overhead transmission, underground transmission, power system studies and distributed generation. B&V's water sector provides a broad range of water and environmental study, consulting, design, design-build and construction management services to utilities, agencies and industrial clients in the Americas, Europe and Asia Pacific. It develops water treatment facilities, distribution systems for potable water and wastewater collection systems and provides water reclamation and reuse consulting services. The company's information market services include telecommunications services, A&E services, integrated networks, federal and state government networks, as well as offerings through BV Solutions Group, Inc., a wholly-owned IT service provider subsidiary. In January 2010, the company was contracted by Thames Water to modify the Mogden Sewage Treatment Works in London. Also in January 2010, the company was contracted to redesign the Davyhulme Wastewater Treatment Works, which is one of the largest in the U.K. In March 2010, the company acquired Enspiria Solutions, which provides smart grid solutions.

The company offers employees private medical insurance; income protection; an employee assistance program; a pension program; and life insurance.

FINANCIALS: **Sales and profits are in thousands of dollars—add 000 to get the full amount. 2010 Note: Financial information for 2010 was not available for all companies at press time.**

2010 Sales: $	2010 Profits: $	**U.S. Stock Ticker: Private**
2009 Sales: $2,700,000	2009 Profits: $	**Int'l Ticker:** Int'l Exchange:
2008 Sales: $3,200,000	2008 Profits: $	Employees: 8,600
2007 Sales: $3,200,000	2007 Profits: $	Fiscal Year Ends: 12/31
2006 Sales: $1,800,000	2006 Profits: $	Parent Company:

SALARIES/BENEFITS:

Pension Plan:	ESOP Stock Plan:	Profit Sharing:	Top Exec. Salary: $	Bonus: $
Savings Plan:	Stock Purch. Plan:		Second Exec. Salary: $	Bonus: $

OTHER THOUGHTS:

Apparent Women Officers or Directors: 2
Hot Spot for Advancement for Women/Minorities: Y

LOCATIONS: ("Y" = Yes)

West:	Southwest:	Midwest:	Southeast:	Northeast:	International:
Y	Y	Y	Y	Y	Y

BLACK HILLS CORP

www.blackhillscorp.com

Industry Group Code: 2211 **Ranks within this company's industry group:** Sales: 41 Profits: 41

Exploration/Production:		Refining/Retailing:		Utilities:		Alternative Energy:		Specialty Services:		Energy Mktg./Other Svcs.	
Exploration:	Y	Refining:		Electric Utility:	Y	Waste/Solar/Other:		Consulting/Eng.:		Energy Marketing:	Y
Production:	Y	Retailing:		Gas Utility:	Y	Thermal/Steam:		Seismic:		Equipment/Machinery:	
Coal Production:	Y	Convenience Stores:		Pipelines:		Wind:		Drilling:		Oil Field Services:	
		Chemicals:		Water:		Hydro:		InfoTech:		Air/Shipping Transportation:	
						Fuel Cells:		Specialty Services:			

TYPES OF BUSINESS:

Utilities-Electricity & Natural Gas
Coal Production
Oil & Natural Gas Exploration & Production

BRANDS/DIVISIONS/AFFILIATES:

Black Hills Energy
Black Hills Power
Cheyenne Light, Fuel & Power
Colorado Natural Gas
Kansas Natural Gas
Wyodak Resources Development Corp.
Black Hills Exploration and Production, Inc.
Enserco

CONTACTS:

Note: Officers with more than one job title may be intentionally listed here more than once.

David R. Emery, CEO
David R. Emery, Pres.
Anthony S. Cleberg, CFO/Exec. VP
Robert A. Myers, Sr. VP-Human Resources
Scott A. Buchholz, CIO/Sr. VP
Steven J. Helmers, General Counsel/Sr. VP/Chief Compliance Officer
Richard W. Kinzley, Sr. VP-Strategic Planning & Dev.
Lynnette K. Wilson, Sr. VP-Comm.
Lynnette K. Wilson, Sr. VP-Investor Rel.
Garner M. Anderson, Treas./VP/Chief Risk Officer
Kyle D. White, VP-Regulatory & Corp. Affairs
Linden R. Evans, Pres./COO-Utilities
Jeffrey B. Berzina, Controller/VP
Roxann R. Basham, VP-Governance/Corp. Sec.
David R. Emery, Chmn.
Perry S. Krush, VP-Supply Chain

Phone: 605-721-1700	**Fax:** 605-348-4748
Toll-Free:	
Address: 625 9th St., Rapid City, SD 57701 US	

GROWTH PLANS/SPECIAL FEATURES:

Black Hills Corporation is an energy company operating west and mid-west regions of the U.S. The firm divides its business in two segments: utilities and non-regulated energy. The utilities group conducts business in two divisions: electric utilities and gas utilities. Through Black Hills Power, the group engages in the generation, transmission and distribution of electricity to roughly 63,500 customers in South Dakota, Wyoming and Montana. Through Cheyenne Light, Fuel & Power, the group engages in the distribution of electric and natural gas and serves approximately 39,800 electric and 33,900 natural gas customers in Cheyenne, Wyoming area. Other gas utilities operated by the company and doing business as Black Hills Energy include Colorado Natural Gas, Kansas Natural Gas, Nebraska Natural Gas and Iowa Natural Gas. The non-regulated energy group conducts business in four divisions: oil and gas, which develops and produces natural gas and crude oil through Black Hills Exploration and Production, Inc.; power generation, which engages in the production and sale of electric capacity and energy through a diversified portfolio of generating plants; coal mining, which, through Wyodak Resources Development Corp., mines and sells coal at the company's coal mine located near Gillette, Wyoming; and energy marketing, which, through Enserco, engages in the marketing of coal, natural gas and crude oil primarily in the Western portion of the U.S. and in Canada. Black Hills also holds a number of power generation plants in Colorado, Wyoming and South Dakota, which produce over 1,000 megawatts (MW) of energy.

Employees are offered medical, dental and vision insurance; flexible spending accounts; a 401(k) plan; pension plans; annual incentive bonus plans; disability coverage; life insurance; travel and accident insurance; an employee assistance plan; tuition reimbursement; a computer purchase program; and scholarships for employees' children.

FINANCIALS:

Sales and profits are in thousands of dollars—add 000 to get the full amount. 2010 Note: Financial information for 2010 was not available for all companies at press time.

2010 Sales: $	2010 Profits: $	**U.S. Stock Ticker: BKH**
2009 Sales: $1,269,578	2009 Profits: $81,555	**Int'l Ticker:** Int'l Exchange:
2008 Sales: $1,005,790	2008 Profits: $105,080	Employees: 2,171
2007 Sales: $574,838	2007 Profits: $98,772	Fiscal Year Ends: 12/31
2006 Sales: $656,882	2006 Profits: $81,019	Parent Company:

SALARIES/BENEFITS:

Pension Plan: Y	ESOP Stock Plan:	Profit Sharing:	Top Exec. Salary: $564,000	Bonus: $221,088
Savings Plan: Y	Stock Purch. Plan:		Second Exec. Salary: $351,000	Bonus: $98,280

OTHER THOUGHTS:

Apparent Women Officers or Directors: 4
Hot Spot for Advancement for Women/Minorities: Y

LOCATIONS: ("Y" = Yes)

West:	Southwest:	Midwest:	Southeast:	Northeast:	International:
Y	Y	Y	Y		

BLUE RHINO LLC

www.bluerhino.com

Industry Group Code: 454312 **Ranks within this company's industry group:** Sales: Profits:

Exploration/Production:		Refining/Retailing:		Utilities:		Alternative Energy:		Specialty Services:		Energy Mktg./Other Svcs.	
Exploration:		Refining:		Electric Utility:		Waste/Solar/Other:		Consulting/Eng.:		Energy Marketing:	
Production:		Retailing:	Y	Gas Utility:		Thermal/Steam:		Seismic:		Equipment/Machinery:	
Coal Production:		Convenience Stores:		Pipelines:		Wind:		Drilling:		Oil Field Services:	
		Chemicals:		Water:		Hydro:		InfoTech:		Air/Shipping Transportation:	
						Fuel Cells:		Specialty Services:	Y		

TYPES OF BUSINESS:

Propane Cylinder Exchange, Distribution
Patio Heaters
Barbecue Products
Lawn & Garden Products
Mosquito Control Products

BRANDS/DIVISIONS/AFFILIATES:

Ferrellgas Partners LP
Uniflame
Endless Summer
SceeterVac

CONTACTS:

Note: Officers with more than one job title may be intentionally listed here more than once.

Tod D. Brown, Pres.
William M. Dull, CFO/VP
Chris Hartley, VP-Mktg.
Robert S. Travatello, CIO/VP
D. Scott Coward, General Counsel

Phone: 336-659-6900 **Fax:** 336-659-6726
Toll-Free: 800-258-7466
Address: 470 W. Hanes Mill Rd., Ste. 200, Winston-Salem, NC 27105 US

GROWTH PLANS/SPECIAL FEATURES:

Blue Rhino LLC, a subsidiary of propane retailer Ferrellgas Partners, LP, is a leading provider of propane cylinder exchange in the U.S. The company has cylinder exchange displays at over 41,000 retail locations in 50 states and Puerto Rico, including major retailers Circle K, ExxonMobil, Home Depot, K-mart, Kroger, Lowe's, Sears, SuperAmerica, Wal-Mart and Winn-Dixie. Blue Rhino establishes partnerships with retailers and independent distributors to provide consumers with a nationally branded product as an alternative to a traditional grill cylinder refill. Cylinder exchange allows consumers to exchange empty grill cylinders for clean, safe, precision-filled cylinders, rather than having their own tanks refilled. Customers can buy Blue Rhino cylinders without having an empty tank to exchange. Blue Rhino also sells carbon dioxide (CO_2) tanks, in 9- and 20-ounce sizes, as well as CO_2 tank refill services, for use in pneumatic power tools and paintball equipment. In addition to its cylinder exchange service, the firm offers an array of outdoor products through Blue Rhino Global Sourcing, LLC, including Uniflame, Endless Summer and SkeeterVac branded barbecue grills, outdoor heaters, fireplaces, firepits, mosquito traps and other outdoor accessories. The company also has an extensive recycling program that collects discarded propane tanks from recycling facilities to refurbish and put them back into use.

The company offers its employees medical, dental and vision insurance; life insurance; flexible spending accounts; AD&D; a 401(k) plan; an employee stock ownership plan; and an employee discount program.

FINANCIALS:

Sales and profits are in thousands of dollars—add 000 to get the full amount. 2010 Note: Financial information for 2010 was not available for all companies at press time.

2010 Sales: $	2010 Profits: $	**U.S. Stock Ticker: Private**
2009 Sales: $	2009 Profits: $	**Int'l Ticker:** Int'l Exchange:
2008 Sales: $	2008 Profits: $	Employees:
2007 Sales: $	2007 Profits: $	Fiscal Year Ends: 7/31
2006 Sales: $	2006 Profits: $	Parent Company: FERRELLGAS PARTNERS LP

SALARIES/BENEFITS:

Pension Plan:	ESOP Stock Plan: Y	Profit Sharing:	Top Exec. Salary: $	Bonus: $459,600
Savings Plan: Y	Stock Purch. Plan:		Second Exec. Salary: $	Bonus: $

OTHER THOUGHTS:

Apparent Women Officers or Directors:
Hot Spot for Advancement for Women/Minorities:

LOCATIONS: ("Y" = Yes)

West:	Southwest:	Midwest:	Southeast:	Northeast:	International:
Y	Y	Y	Y	Y	Y

BOLT TECHNOLOGY CORP

www.bolt-technology.com

Industry Group Code: 211111 **Ranks within this company's industry group:** Sales: 111 Profits: 70

Exploration/Production:		Refining/Retailing:		Utilities:		Alternative Energy:		Specialty Services:		Energy Mktg./Other Svcs.	
Exploration:		Refining:		Electric Utility:		Waste/Solar/Other:		Consulting/Eng.:		Energy Marketing:	
Production:		Retailing:		Gas Utility:		Thermal/Steam:		Seismic:		Equipment/Machinery:	Y
Coal Production:		Convenience Stores:		Pipelines:		Wind:		Drilling:		Oil Field Services:	
		Chemicals:		Water:		Hydro:		InfoTech:		Air/Shipping Transportation:	
						Fuel Cells:		Specialty Services:			

TYPES OF BUSINESS:

Marine Oil & Gas Equipment
Geophysical Equipment
Industrial Clutches

BRANDS/DIVISIONS/AFFILIATES:

A-G Geophysical Products, Inc.
Real Time Systems Inc

CONTACTS:

Note: Officers with more than one job title may be intentionally listed here more than once.

Raymond M. Soto, CEO
Raymond M. Soto, Pres.
Joseph Espeso, CFO
Joseph Mayerick, Jr., Sr. VP-Mktg.
William C. Andrews, VP-Admin. & Compliance
William C. Andrews, Corp. Sec.
Joseph Espeso, Sr. VP-Investor Rel.
Joseph Espeso, Sr. VP-Finance
Michael C. Hedger, Pres., A-G Geophysical Products, Inc.
Raymond M. Soto, Chmn.

Phone: 203-853-0700	**Fax:** 203-854-9601
Toll-Free:	
Address: 4 Duke Pl., Norwalk, CT 06854 US	

GROWTH PLANS/SPECIAL FEATURES:

Bolt Technology Corporation (Bolt) develops, manufactures and sells marine seismic energy sources (air guns) and replacement parts for global oil and gas exploration. Bolt operates in two business divisions: geophysical equipment and industrial clutches. The geophysical equipment segment develops, manufactures and sells seismic energy source components used by the marine seismic industry including marine air guns; underwater electrical connectors and cables, air gun signature hydrophones and pressure transducers; source array synchronization and management systems; and sea floor data logging systems used in electromagnetic imaging for oil and gas exploration. Subsidiaries operating in this segment include A-G Geophysical Products, Inc., which develops, manufactures and sells underwater cables, connectors, hydrophones and seismic source monitoring systems, and Real Time Systems Inc., which develops, manufactures and sells air gun controllers/synchronizers, data loggers and auxiliary equipment. The industrial clutch segment manufactures and sells mechanical and pneumatic clutches through subsidiary, Custom Products Corporation. The company has two types of marine air guns: long-life marine air guns and Annular Port Air Guns (APG gun). The long-life marine air gun maximizes the period between routine maintenance and is advantageous in designing 3-D surveys. The APG gun maximizes operating efficiency and acoustic output through a configuration that permits the implementation of simplified multi-gun arrays. These air guns make up a significant portion of annual revenue. In recent years, the company sold Custom Products Corporation, for $5.25 million to A&A Manufacturing Co., Inc.

FINANCIALS:

Sales and profits are in thousands of dollars—add 000 to get the full amount. 2010 Note: Financial information for 2010 was not available for all companies at press time.

2010 Sales: $31,485	2010 Profits: $4,954	**U.S. Stock Ticker: BOLT**
2009 Sales: $48,876	2009 Profits: $10,501	**Int'l Ticker:** Int'l Exchange:
2008 Sales: $61,635	2008 Profits: $14,569	Employees: 123
2007 Sales: $46,929	2007 Profits: $10,607	Fiscal Year Ends: 6/30
2006 Sales: $29,393	2006 Profits: $4,845	Parent Company:

SALARIES/BENEFITS:

Pension Plan:	ESOP Stock Plan:	Profit Sharing:	Top Exec. Salary: $370,000	Bonus: $240,000
Savings Plan:	Stock Purch. Plan:		Second Exec. Salary: $220,500	Bonus: $95,000

OTHER THOUGHTS:

Apparent Women Officers or Directors:
Hot Spot for Advancement for Women/Minorities:

LOCATIONS: ("Y" = Yes)

West:	Southwest:	Midwest:	Southeast:	Northeast:	International:
	Y			Y	Y

Note: Financial information, benefits and other data can change quickly and may vary from those stated here.

BOOTS & COOTS INTERNATIONAL LLC

www.bootsandcoots.com

Industry Group Code: 213112 **Ranks within this company's industry group:** Sales: Profits:

Exploration/Production:		Refining/Retailing:		Utilities:		Alternative Energy:		Specialty Services:		Energy Mktg./Other Svcs.	
Exploration:		Refining:		Electric Utility:		Waste/Solar/Other:		Consulting/Eng.:	Y	Energy Marketing:	
Production:		Retailing:		Gas Utility:		Thermal/Steam:		Seismic:		Equipment/Machinery:	Y
Coal Production:		Convenience Stores:		Pipelines:		Wind:		Drilling:		Oil Field Services:	Y
		Chemicals:		Water:		Hydro:		InfoTech:		Air/Shipping Transportation:	
						Fuel Cells:		Specialty Services:	Y		

TYPES OF BUSINESS:

Drilling Oil & Gas Wells Support
Well Control Services
Emergency Response Services
Insurance
Contingency Planning

BRANDS/DIVISIONS/AFFILIATES:

Boots & Coots International Well Control, Inc.
Halliburton Company
SafeGuard

CONTACTS:

Note: Officers with more than one job title may be intentionally listed here more than once.

Jerry Winchester, CEO
Dewitt H. Edwards, COO/Exec. VP
Jerry Winchester, Pres.
Cary Baetz, CFO
John Wright, Sr. VP-Tech.
Mickie Theriot, VP-Mfg. & Global Assets
Brian Keith, Corp. Sec.
Allen Duke, Sr. VP-Global Bus. Dev. & Delivery
Jennifer Tweeton, Dir.-Corp. Comm.
Jennifer Tweeton, Dir.-Investor Rel.
William Bulcher, Controller/VP
John Garner, VP-Response
Danny Clayton, VP-Well Control
Leonard R. Goin, VP-HWO & Snubbing Svcs.
Mike Clark, VP-Pressure Control
Doug Swanson, Chmn.
Paul Esteves, VP-Europe & Africa

Phone: 281-931-8884 | **Fax:** 281-931-8302
Toll-Free: 800-256-9688
Address: 7908 N. Sam Houston Pkwy. W., 5th Fl., Houston, TX 77064 US

GROWTH PLANS/SPECIAL FEATURES:

Boots & Coots, LLC, formerly Boots & Coots International Well Control, Inc. and now a subsidiary of Halliburton Company, provides a suite of integrated pressure control and related services to onshore and offshore oil and gas exploration and development companies, principally in North America, South America, North Africa, West Africa and the Middle East. The company operates in three segments: pressure control, well intervention and equipment services. The pressure control segment consists of prevention and risk management services, as well as response services, which includes snubbing and emergency services utilized in the case of an oil and gas fire or blowout. Products and services include well control, which offers critical and non-critical event response, and SafeGuard, which provides dedicated risk management and emergency response services. Other services include engineering services; firefighting equipment sales and services; specialized drilling engineering; and inspections. The well intervention segment consists of services that are designed to enhance production for oil and gas operators and reduce the number and severity of critical well events such as oil and gas well fires, blowouts or other losses of control at the well. Products and services include hydraulic workover/snubbing, which provides various well intervention solutions involving workovers, well drilling, well completions and plugging and abandonment services. The equipment services segment consists of renting pressure control equipment and providing services that are designed to enhance production and safety for oil and gas operators drilling under high pressure and high temperature circumstances. Products and services include frac trees, manifolds, hydraulic chokes, sand traps and command centers. In September 2010, the firm was acquired by Halliburton Company and now operates as part of Halliburton's completion and production division.

FINANCIALS:

Sales and profits are in thousands of dollars—add 000 to get the full amount. 2010 Note: Financial information for 2010 was not available for all companies at press time.

2010 Sales: $	2010 Profits: $	**U.S. Stock Ticker: Subsidiary**
2009 Sales: $	2009 Profits: $	**Int'l Ticker:** Int'l Exchange:
2008 Sales: $209,237	2008 Profits: $21,819	Employees: 693
2007 Sales: $105,296	2007 Profits: $7,891	Fiscal Year Ends: 12/31
2006 Sales: $97,030	2006 Profits: $11,165	Parent Company: HALLIBURTON COMPANY

SALARIES/BENEFITS:

Pension Plan:	ESOP Stock Plan:	Profit Sharing:	Top Exec. Salary: $370,000	Bonus: $166,500
Savings Plan:	Stock Purch. Plan:		Second Exec. Salary: $275,000	Bonus: $103,125

OTHER THOUGHTS:

Apparent Women Officers or Directors: 1
Hot Spot for Advancement for Women/Minorities:

LOCATIONS: ("Y" = Yes)

West:	Southwest:	Midwest:	Southeast:	Northeast:	International:
Y	Y		Y		Y

BP PLC

www.bp.com

Industry Group Code: 211111 **Ranks within this company's industry group:** Sales: 3 Profits: 4

Exploration/Production:		**Refining/Retailing:**		**Utilities:**		**Alternative Energy:**		**Specialty Services:**		**Energy Mktg./Other Svcs.**	
Exploration:	Y	Refining:	Y	Electric Utility:		Waste/Solar/Other:	Y	Consulting/Eng.:		Energy Marketing:	
Production:	Y	Retailing:	Y	Gas Utility:		Thermal/Steam:		Seismic:		Equipment/Machinery:	
Coal Production:		Convenience Stores:	Y	Pipelines:	Y	Wind:	Y	Drilling:		Oil Field Services:	
		Chemicals:		Water:		Hydro:	Y	InfoTech:		Air/Shipping Transportation:	
						Fuel Cells:		Specialty Services:			

TYPES OF BUSINESS:

Oil & Gas Exploration & Production
Refining
Renewable & Alternative Energy
Lubricants
Natural Gas
Photovoltaic Modules
Gas Stations & Convenience Stores

BRANDS/DIVISIONS/AFFILIATES:

TNK-BP
Aral
am/pm
ARCO
Castrol
Hydrogen Energy international LLC
BP Solar
BP Alternative Energy

CONTACTS:

Note: Officers with more than one job title may be intentionally listed here more than once.

Robert Dudley, CEO
Byron E. Grote, CFO
Iain C. Conn, CEO-Mktg. & Refining
Sally Bott, Dir.-Human Resources
Andy Inglis, CEO-Exploration & Production
Andy G. Inglis, CEO-Exploration & Prod.
Rupert Bondy, Group General Counsel
Fergus MacLeod, Dir.-Investor Rel.
Steve Westwell, Exec. VP
Carl-Henric Svanberg, Chmn.
Lamar McKay, Pres./Chmn.-BP America

Phone: 44-2074-96-4000	**Fax:** 44-20-7496-4630
Toll-Free:	
Address: 1 St. James's Sq., London, SW1Y 4PD UK	

GROWTH PLANS/SPECIAL FEATURES:

BP plc is one of the world's largest integrated oil companies, with reserves of 18.3 billion barrels of oil and gas equivalent and daily production of about 3.8 million barrels of oil equivalent. Its core brands include BP, Aral, am/pm, ARCO, Castrol and Wild Bean Cafe. The company operates through three segments: Exploration and Production (E&P); Refining and Marketing (R&M); and Alternative Energy. E&P, active in 30 countries, manages BP's upstream activities, including oil and gas exploration, field development and production; and midstream activities, including the management of crude oil and natural gas pipelines, processing and export terminals and liquefied natural gas (LNG) processing facilities. R&M focuses on refining, marketing and transporting crude oil and petroleum products (including gasoline, gasoil, marine and aviation fuels, heating fuels, liquefied petroleum gas, lubricants and bitumen) to wholesale and retail customers. BP owns, fully or partially, 16 refineries and operates about 22,400 gas stations under the BP, Amoco and ARCO brands. This segment also includes the firm's aromatics and acetyls businesses. Alternative Energy processes and markets biofuels, such as ethanol and biodiesel; manages the company's solar, wind and gas-fired power businesses; and conducts biofuel research. BP operates in over 80 countries worldwide. In 2010, a major deepwater Gulf of Mexico well on which BP is the operator and majority owner blew out, creating a massive oil spill and significant liabilities for the firm. As a result, BP announced a change of CEO and it has been selling assets in order to raise cash. In August 2010, the company announced it had made payments of $400 million to claimants from the oil spill, including residents, businesses and localities in the affected areas. In September 2010, the company sealed the well after five months of oil spilling into the Gulf of Mexico.

FINANCIALS:

Sales and profits are in thousands of dollars—add 000 to get the full amount. 2010 Note: Financial information for 2010 was not available for all companies at press time.

2010 Sales: $	2010 Profits: $	**U.S. Stock Ticker: BP**
2009 Sales: $239,272,000	2009 Profits: $16,759,000	**Int'l Ticker: BP** Int'l Exchange: London-LSE
2008 Sales: $361,143,000	2008 Profits: $21,666,000	Employees: 80,300
2007 Sales: $284,365,000	2007 Profits: $21,169,000	Fiscal Year Ends: 12/31
2006 Sales: $270,602,000	2006 Profits: $22,286,000	Parent Company:

SALARIES/BENEFITS:

Pension Plan: Y	ESOP Stock Plan:	Profit Sharing:	Top Exec. Salary: $1,842,150	Bonus: $2,394,890
Savings Plan: Y	Stock Purch. Plan:		Second Exec. Salary: $1,372,044	Bonus: $2,056,519

OTHER THOUGHTS:

Apparent Women Officers or Directors: 3
Hot Spot for Advancement for Women/Minorities: Y

LOCATIONS: ("Y" = Yes)

West:	Southwest:	Midwest:	Southeast:	Northeast:	International:
Y	Y	Y		Y	Y

BRASKEM SA

www.braskem.com.br

Industry Group Code: 325110 **Ranks within this company's industry group:** Sales: 5 Profits: 3

Exploration/Production:		Refining/Retailing:		Utilities:		Alternative Energy:		Specialty Services:		Energy Mktg./Other Svcs.	
Exploration:		Refining:		Electric Utility:		Waste/Solar/Other:		Consulting/Eng.:		Energy Marketing:	
Production:		Retailing:		Gas Utility:		Thermal/Steam:		Seismic:		Equipment/Machinery:	
Coal Production:		Convenience Stores:		Pipelines:		Wind:		Drilling:		Oil Field Services:	
		Chemicals:	Y	Water:		Hydro:		InfoTech:		Air/Shipping Transportation:	
						Fuel Cells:		Specialty Services:			

TYPES OF BUSINESS:

Petrochemicals
Polymers

BRANDS/DIVISIONS/AFFILIATES:

Pequiven
Petroquimica Triunfo SA
Camacari Industrial Complex
Southern Petrochemical Complex

CONTACTS:

Note: Officers with more than one job title may be intentionally listed here more than once.

Bernardo Afonso de Almeida Gradin, CEO
Carlos J. F. de Souza Filho, CFO
Enio Augusto Pereira e Silva, VP-Human Resources
Victor Manuel Martins Pais, Exec. VP-Tech. & Innovation
Mauricio Roberto de Carvalho Ferro, General Counsel/Exec. VP
Carlos J. F. de Souza Filho, Exec. VP-Investor Rel.
Manoel Carnauba Cortez, Exec. VP-Basic Petrochemicals
Marcelo Lyra do Amaral, VP-Institutional Rel.
Luiz de Mendonca, Exec. VP-Polymers
Marcelo Bahia Odebrecht, Chmn.
Roberto P. P. Ramos, VP-Internationalization Bus. Unit
Victor Manuel Martins Pais, Exec. VP-Supply & Quality

Phone: 55-11-3576-9999	**Fax:** 55-11-3576-9017
Toll-Free:	
Address: 8501 Ave. das Nacoes Unidas, Sao Paulo, 05425-070 Brazil	

GROWTH PLANS/SPECIAL FEATURES:

Braskem S.A. is a petrochemical company and one of the largest Brazilian-owned private sector industrial companies. The company produces a diversified portfolio of petrochemical products, with a strategic focus on polyethylene, polypropylene and PVC (polyvinyl chloride). Braskem maintains integrated first and second generation petrochemical production facilities, with 18 plants in Brazil. Braskem operates in three business units: basic products, polymers and international business development. The basic products unit produces olefins, such as ethylene, polymer and chemical grade propylene, butadiene, isoprene and butene-1; and aromatics, such as benzene, toluene, para-xylene and ortho-xylene. The products of the company's basic petrochemicals unit are used primarily in the manufacture of intermediate second-generation petrochemical products, including those manufactured by Braskem's other business units. The polymers unit makes high-density, low-density and linear low-density polyethylene and polypropylene; PVC; ethylene; dichloride; chlorine; and caustic soda. The grades of PVC produced are used in the manufacture of pipes and fittings, laminated sheets, synthetic leather, flooring, cable insulation, electrical conduit, packaging applications, flooring materials, bottles, window frames and plastic films. The international business development unit handles the firm's internationalization operations. This segment has a development partnership with Venezuelan state-owned petrochemical company Pequiven; it is also responsible for prospecting and evaluating new opportunities in Bolivia, Peru, Mexico and other countries in the Americas. Braskem is in the process of building a green polyethylene production unit at the firm's Southern Petrochemical Complex near Triunfo, in the state of Rio Grande do Sul. In April 2009, the firm acquired Petroquimica Triunfo S.A. In August 2009, the company opened two new ETBE (a bioadditive for gasoline made from renewable raw material) production plants at its Camacari Industrial Complex. In January 2010, Braskem acquired petroleum firm Quattor. In February 2010, the company acquired the polypropylene operations of Sunoco Chemicals, Inc. from Sunoco, Inc. for $350 million.

FINANCIALS:

Sales and profits are in thousands of dollars—add 000 to get the full amount. 2010 Note: Financial information for 2010 was not available for all companies at press time.

2010 Sales: $	2010 Profits: $	**U.S. Stock Ticker: BAK**
2009 Sales: $7,605,480	2009 Profits: $501,740	**Int'l Ticker: BRKM3** Int'l Exchange: Sao Paulo-SAO
2008 Sales: $9,159,300	2008 Profits: $-1,271,000	Employees: 4,700
2007 Sales: $8,997,700	2007 Profits: $317,100	Fiscal Year Ends: 12/31
2006 Sales: $6,626,300	2006 Profits: $51,700	Parent Company:

SALARIES/BENEFITS:

Pension Plan:	ESOP Stock Plan:	Profit Sharing:	Top Exec. Salary: $	Bonus: $
Savings Plan:	Stock Purch. Plan:		Second Exec. Salary: $	Bonus: $

OTHER THOUGHTS:

Apparent Women Officers or Directors:
Hot Spot for Advancement for Women/Minorities:

LOCATIONS: ("Y" = Yes)

West:	Southwest:	Midwest:	Southeast:	Northeast:	International:
	Y				Y

BREITBURN ENERGY PARTNERS LP

www.breitburn.com

Industry Group Code: 211111 **Ranks within this company's industry group:** Sales: 101 Profits: 89

Exploration/Production:		Refining/Retailing:		Utilities:		Alternative Energy:		Specialty Services:		Energy Mktg./Other Svcs.	
Exploration:	Y	Refining:		Electric Utility:		Waste/Solar/Other:		Consulting/Eng.:		Energy Marketing:	Y
Production:	Y	Retailing:		Gas Utility:		Thermal/Steam:		Seismic:		Equipment/Machinery:	
Coal Production:		Convenience Stores:		Pipelines:		Wind:		Drilling:		Oil Field Services:	
		Chemicals:		Water:		Hydro:		InfoTech:		Air/Shipping Transportation:	
						Fuel Cells:		Specialty Services:			

TYPES OF BUSINESS:

Oil & Gas Exploration & Production

BRANDS/DIVISIONS/AFFILIATES:

BreitBurn Corporation

GROWTH PLANS/SPECIAL FEATURES:

BreitBurn Energy Partners, L.P. (BBEP) acquires, produces, exploits and develops oil and natural gas containing properties in the U.S. The firm's general partner, BreitBurn GP, LLC, has sole responsibility for the company's management and its operations, which are conducted through its operating subsidiaries. The company operates in California, Michigan, Indiana, Kentucky, Wyoming and Florida. The company has proved reserves of approximately 111.3 million barrels of oil equivalent (MMBoe), of which approximately 65% is natural gas and 35% is crude oil. The company operates substantially all of the wells in which it has an interest, but does not own any other oilfield equipment or drill rigs. BBEP chooses to operate in mature fields that have shown long-lived production. Most of them have been producing for more than 70 years and one for more than 100 years. Its strategy is to make use of remaining oil reserves in extant oil and gas fields. In 2009, the firm's production levels totaled 6.52 MMBoe.

CONTACTS:

Note: Officers with more than one job title may be intentionally listed here more than once.

Halbert S. Washburn, CEO
Mark L. Pease, COO/Exec. VP
Randall H. Breitenbrach, Pres.
James G. Jackson, CFO/Exec. VP
Gregory C. Brown, General Counsel/Exec. VP
Chris E. Williamson, VP-Prod. Oper. & Western Div.
W. Jackson Washburn, Sr. VP-Bus. Dev.
Gloria Chu, Dir.-Investor Rel.
Lawrence C. Smith, Controller/VP
David D. Baker, VP-Eastern Div.
Bruce D. McFarland, Treas./VP
Thurmon Andress, Managing Dir.-BreitBurn Mgmt.
Chirs E. Williamson, Sr. VP-Western Div.
John R. Butler, Jr., Chmn.

Phone: 213-225-5900 **Fax:** 213-225-5916
Toll-Free:
Address: 515 S. Flower St., Ste. 4800, Los Angeles, CA 90071 US

FINANCIALS:

Sales and profits are in thousands of dollars—add 000 to get the full amount. 2010 Note: Financial information for 2010 was not available for all companies at press time.

2010 Sales: $	2010 Profits: $	**U.S. Stock Ticker: BBEP**
2009 Sales: $204,862	2009 Profits: $-107,257	**Int'l Ticker:** Int'l Exchange:
2008 Sales: $802,403	2008 Profits: $378,236	Employees: 370
2007 Sales: $74,991	2007 Profits: $-60,357	Fiscal Year Ends: 12/31
2006 Sales: $133,047	2006 Profits: $49,919	Parent Company:

SALARIES/BENEFITS:

Pension Plan: Y	ESOP Stock Plan:	Profit Sharing:	Top Exec. Salary: $425,000	Bonus: $442,000
Savings Plan:	Stock Purch. Plan:		Second Exec. Salary: $425,000	Bonus: $442,000

OTHER THOUGHTS:

Apparent Women Officers or Directors: 1
Hot Spot for Advancement for Women/Minorities:

LOCATIONS: ("Y" = Yes)

West:	Southwest:	Midwest:	Southeast:	Northeast:	International:
Y	Y	Y	Y		

BRISTOW GROUP (THE)

www.bristowgroup.com

Industry Group Code: 481211 **Ranks within this company's industry group:** Sales: 1 Profits: 1

Exploration/Production:		Refining/Retailing:		Utilities:		Alternative Energy:		Specialty Services:		Energy Mktg./Other Svcs.	
Exploration:		Refining:		Electric Utility:		Waste/Solar/Other:		Consulting/Eng.:		Energy Marketing:	
Production:		Retailing:		Gas Utility:		Thermal/Steam:		Seismic:		Equipment/Machinery:	
Coal Production:		Convenience Stores:		Pipelines:		Wind:		Drilling:		Oil Field Services:	
		Chemicals:		Water:		Hydro:		InfoTech:		Air/Shipping Transportation:	Y
						Fuel Cells:		Specialty Services:	Y		

TYPES OF BUSINESS:

Helicopter Services for the Energy Industry
Military Training Services
Emergency Services & Support
Production Management Services
Search & Rescue Services

BRANDS/DIVISIONS/AFFILIATES:

Bristow Helicopters, Inc.
Bristow Academy, Inc.
Bristow Caribbean Limited

CONTACTS:

Note: Officers with more than one job title may be intentionally listed here more than once.

William E. Chiles, CEO
William E. Chiles, Pres.
Jonathan Baliff, CFO/Sr. VP
Hilary Ware, Sr. VP-Admin.
Randall A. Stafford, General Counsel/VP/Corp. Sec.
Richard D. Burman, Sr. VP-Oper.
Mark Frank, VP-Planning & Mgmt. Info
Linda McNeill, Contact-Investor Rel.
Joseph A. Baj, Treas./VP
Mark B. Duncan, Sr. VP-Commercial
Thomas C. Knudson, Chmn.

Phone: 713-267-7600 **Fax:** 713-267-7620
Toll-Free:
Address: 2000 W. Sam Houston Pkwy. S., Ste. 1700, Houston, TX 77042 US

GROWTH PLANS/SPECIAL FEATURES:

The Bristow Group is one of the largest providers of helicopter services to the worldwide offshore energy industry. The company has major operations in the U.S. Gulf of Mexico and the North Sea, in addition to operations in most of the other major offshore oil and gas producing regions of the world, including Nigeria, Australia and Latin America. Bristow provides helicopter services to a broad base of major, independent, international and national energy companies, which charter its helicopters to transport personnel between onshore bases and offshore platforms, drilling rigs and other installations. The company conducts its business in one segment, Helicopter Services, which is broken into five divisions: North America, Europe, West Africa, Australia and Other International. The North America business unit includes seven operating facilities in the U.S. Gulf of Mexico and three operating facilities in Alaska. The Europe division consists of three bases in the U.K., one base in the Netherlands and three bases in Norway. The company's Europe operations are managed out of facilities in Aberdeen, Scotland. The West Africa business unit's aircraft is operated in Nigeria, with 10 operational bases. The Other International division operates in Brazil, Egypt, India, Malaysia, Mexico, Russia, Trinidad and Turkmenistan. In Brazil, the firm owns a 42.5% interest in Lider, a leading provider of helicopter and executive aviation services. In Egypt, the company owns a 25% interest in Petroleum Air Services, which provides helicopter and fixed wing transportation to the offshore energy industry. In Trinidad, the company owns a 40% interest in Bristow Caribbean Limited, a joint venture with a local partner. In Turkmenistan, the company operates two aircraft through its 51% interest in Turkmenistan Helicopters Limited. The firm's fleet consists of 594 aircraft.

The company offers employees medical, dental and life insurance; disability coverage; pension plans; and bonus programs.

FINANCIALS:

Sales and profits are in thousands of dollars—add 000 to get the full amount. 2010 Note: Financial information for 2010 was not available for all companies at press time.

2010 Sales: $
2009 Sales: $1,133,803
2008 Sales: $1,012,764
2007 Sales: $843,595
2006 Sales: $709,901

2010 Profits: $
2009 Profits: $124,308
2008 Profits: $103,992
2007 Profits: $74,172
2006 Profits: $57,809

U.S. Stock Ticker: BRS
Int'l Ticker: Int'l Exchange:
Employees: 3,569
Fiscal Year Ends: 3/31
Parent Company:

SALARIES/BENEFITS:

Pension Plan: Y
Savings Plan:
ESOP Stock Plan:
Stock Purch. Plan:
Profit Sharing:
Top Exec. Salary: $749,999 Bonus: $1,050,000
Second Exec. Salary: $454,997 Bonus: $448,384

OTHER THOUGHTS:

Apparent Women Officers or Directors: 2
Hot Spot for Advancement for Women/Minorities: Y

LOCATIONS: ("Y" = Yes)

West:	Southwest:	Midwest:	Southeast:	Northeast:	International:
	Y		Y		Y

BRITISH COLUMBIA HYDRO AND POWER AUTHORITY

www.bchydro.com

Industry Group Code: 221111 **Ranks within this company's industry group:** Sales: 3 Profits: 3

Exploration/Production:		**Refining/Retailing:**		**Utilities:**		**Alternative Energy:**		**Specialty Services:**		**Energy Mktg./Other Svcs.**	
Exploration:		Refining:		Electric Utility:	Y	Waste/Solar/Other:		Consulting/Eng.:	Y	Energy Marketing:	Y
Production:		Retailing:		Gas Utility:		Thermal/Steam:		Seismic:		Equipment/Machinery:	
Coal Production:		Convenience Stores:		Pipelines:		Wind:		Drilling:		Oil Field Services:	
		Chemicals:		Water:		Hydro:	Y	InfoTech:		Air/Shipping Transportation:	
						Fuel Cells:		Specialty Services:			

TYPES OF BUSINESS:

Electric Utility
Hydroelectric Power Generation & Distribution
Thermal Power Generation
Testing, Consulting & Research Services
Wholesale Electricity

BRANDS/DIVISIONS/AFFILIATES:

BC Hydro
Powerex Corp.
Powertech Labs, Inc.
BC Transmission Corp.

CONTACTS:

Note: Officers with more than one job title may be intentionally listed here more than once.

David Cobb, CEO
David Cobb, Pres.
Charles Reid, CFO/Exec. VP-Finance
Debbie Nagle, Chief Human Resources Officer
Don Stuckert, CIO
Donna Leclair, CTO
David Facey, Corp. Sec.
Leigh Ann Shoji-Lee, Sr. VP-Field Oper.
Trish Pekeles, Exec Dir-Strategy/Bus. Transformation/Partnerships
Renee Smith-Valade, Sr. VP-Comm.
Cheryl Yaremko, Chief Acct. Officer
Chirs O'Riley, Exec. VP-Generation
Bev Van Ruyven, Exec. VP/Deputy CEO
Teresa Conway, CEO/Pres., Powerex Corp.
Susan Yurkovich, Exec. VP-Site C
Dan Doyle, Chmn.
Trish Pekeles, Exec. Dir.-Procurement

Phone: 604-224-9376	**Fax:**
Toll-Free: 800-224-9376	
Address: 333 Dunsmuir St., Vancouver, BC V6B 5R3 Canada	

GROWTH PLANS/SPECIAL FEATURES:

British Columbia Hydro and Power Authority (BC Hydro), owned by the regional government, is one of the largest electric utilities in Canada. It has two wholly-owned subsidiaries: Powerex Corp., a leading buyer and seller of wholesale electric energy in western Canada and the western U.S.; and Powertech Labs, Inc., which provides testing, consulting and research services to the electric and natural gas industries, their customers and suppliers. BC Hydro's primary business activities are the generation and distribution of electricity to more than 1.8 million residential and business customers in its service territory, representing 95% of British Columbia's population. Of BC Hydro's 11,345 MW of total installed generating capacity, 90% is at the firm's 31 hydroelectric generating facilities, many of which are concentrated in the Peace and Columbia River basins. The GM Shrum and Peace Canyon generating stations on the Peace River produce about 25% of BC Hydro's electricity requirements. Other major power generating areas include the Columbia River, home for the Mica Dam, the Revelstoke Dam and the Duncan Dam; and four generating stations on the Kootenay River. Besides hydroelectric plants, the firm also operates three natural gas powered generating facilities, which account for 9.2% of its installed capacity: the 950 MW Burrard Thermal Generating Station, the 47 MW Fort Nelson plant and the 46 MW Prince Rupert Generating Station. The firm receives the remainder of its power (0.4%) through purchases from third-party producers, most of which operate diesel power plants. BC Hydro's transmission assets are maintained, operated and planed by BC Transmission Corp. In all, this transmission system comprises over 11,000 miles of transmission lines operating at voltages from 60-500 kilovolts, and more than 35,500 miles of distribution lines. Due to the Clean Energy Act passed in B.C. in April 2010, BC Transmission Corp.'s operations were consolidated into BC Hydro.

FINANCIALS:

Sales and profits are in thousands of dollars—add 000 to get the full amount. 2010 Note: Financial information for 2010 was not available for all companies at press time.

2010 Sales: $	2010 Profits: $	**U.S. Stock Ticker: Government-Owned**
2009 Sales: $4,033,830	2009 Profits: $345,840	**Int'l Ticker:** Int'l Exchange:
2008 Sales: $3,848,010	2008 Profits: $292,470	Employees:
2007 Sales: $4,026,820	2007 Profits: $390,497	Fiscal Year Ends: 3/31
2006 Sales: $4,316,710	2006 Profits: $255,253	Parent Company:

SALARIES/BENEFITS:

Pension Plan: Y	ESOP Stock Plan:	Profit Sharing:	Top Exec. Salary: $321,466	Bonus: $105,496
Savings Plan:	Stock Purch. Plan:		Second Exec. Salary: $256,950	Bonus: $122,104

OTHER THOUGHTS:

Apparent Women Officers or Directors: 13
Hot Spot for Advancement for Women/Minorities: Y

LOCATIONS: ("Y" = Yes)

West:	Southwest:	Midwest:	Southeast:	Northeast:	International:
					Y

BRITISH ENERGY GROUP PLC

www.british-energy.com

Industry Group Code: 221113 **Ranks within this company's industry group:** Sales: Profits:

Exploration/Production:		Refining/Retailing:		Utilities:		Alternative Energy:		Specialty Services:		Energy Mktg./Other Svcs.	
Exploration:		Refining:		Electric Utility:		Waste/Solar/Other:	Y	Consulting/Eng.:	Y	Energy Marketing:	
Production:		Retailing:		Gas Utility:		Thermal/Steam:		Seismic:		Equipment/Machinery:	
Coal Production:		Convenience Stores:		Pipelines:		Wind:	Y	Drilling:		Oil Field Services:	
		Chemicals:		Water:		Hydro:		InfoTech:		Air/Shipping Transportation:	
						Fuel Cells:		Specialty Services:			

TYPES OF BUSINESS:

Nuclear Power Stations
Wind Energy

BRANDS/DIVISIONS/AFFILIATES:

British Energy Generation
Lewis Wind Power
British Energy Direct
Electricite de France SA (EDF)
District Energy

CONTACTS:

Note: Officers with more than one job title may be intentionally listed here more than once.

Andrew Spurr, Managing Dir.
Thomas Kusterer, CFO
David Akers, Dir.-Human Resources
Stuart Crooks, CTO
Jean McDonald, General Counsel
Alain Peckre, Dir.-Operational Support & Continuous Improvement
Rob Guyler, Dir.-Finance
Mark Gorry, Dir.-Safety & Tech.
Brian Cowell, Chief Nuclear Officer Region I
Matt Sykes, Chief Nuclear Officer Region II
Peter Prozesky, Chief Nuclear Officer Region III

Phone: 44-1355-846000 **Fax:** 44-1355-846001
Toll-Free:
Address: GSO Business Park, East Kilbride, G74 5PG UK

GROWTH PLANS/SPECIAL FEATURES:

British Energy Group plc (BEG), a subsidiary of French energy company Electricite de France S.A. (EDF), generates and supplies electricity to over 5.5 million businesses and residential costumers throughout the U.K. The company's generation capacity is supplied by eight nuclear power stations with a combined capacity of 9,000 megawatts (MW), which are owned and operated by the group's subsidiary, British Energy Generation. Seven of these power stations operate as gas-cooled reactors, while the eighth station operates as a pressurized water reactor. The firm's alternative energy portfolio, managed by British Energy Renewables, includes a 50% interest in the Lewis Wind Power project, which is planning to build the world's largest onshore wind farm on Scotland's Isle of Lewis. British Energy sells its power to the large industrial and commercial energy market through its direct supply business, British Energy Direct. Subsidiary British Energy Power & Energy Trading manages the firm's energy trading in the U.K. Another subsidiary, District Energy, operates four modern, natural-gas-fueled power plants, which produce 10 MW of energy to help meet peak demands and provide backup power. In April 2010, EDF transferred ownership of the Eggborough coal-fired power station in northern England, which previously served as a secondary, back-up generation facility for BEG, to the bondholders of Eggborough.

British Energy offers employees a benefits package that includes paid vacation, paid subscription fees for professional institutions, a pension plan and relocation assistance.

FINANCIALS:

Sales and profits are in thousands of dollars—add 000 to get the full amount. 2010 Note: Financial information for 2010 was not available for all companies at press time.

2010 Sales: $	2010 Profits: $	**U.S. Stock Ticker: Subsidiary**
2009 Sales: $	2009 Profits: $	**Int'l Ticker:** Int'l Exchange:
2008 Sales: $4,160,300	2008 Profits: $495,800	Employees: 6,121
2007 Sales: $5,900,000	2007 Profits: $920,000	Fiscal Year Ends: 3/31
2006 Sales: $4,941,660	2006 Profits: $1,210,160	Parent Company: ELECTRICITE DE FRANCE SA (EDF)

SALARIES/BENEFITS:

Pension Plan: Y	ESOP Stock Plan:	Profit Sharing:	Top Exec. Salary: $	Bonus: $472,208
Savings Plan:	Stock Purch. Plan:		Second Exec. Salary: $	Bonus: $

OTHER THOUGHTS:

Apparent Women Officers or Directors:
Hot Spot for Advancement for Women/Minorities:

LOCATIONS: ("Y" = Yes)

West:	Southwest:	Midwest:	Southeast:	Northeast:	International:
					Y

BSST LLC

www.bsst.com

Industry Group Code: 335 **Ranks within this company's industry group:** Sales: Profits:

Exploration/Production:		Refining/Retailing:		Utilities:		Alternative Energy:		Specialty Services:		Energy Mktg./Other Svcs.	
Exploration:		Refining:		Electric Utility:		Waste/Solar/Other:		Consulting/Eng.:		Energy Marketing:	
Production:		Retailing:		Gas Utility:		Thermal/Steam:		Seismic:		Equipment/Machinery:	Y
Coal Production:		Convenience Stores:		Pipelines:		Wind:		Drilling:		Oil Field Services:	
		Chemicals:		Water:		Hydro:		InfoTech:		Air/Shipping Transportation:	
						Fuel Cells:		Specialty Services:			

TYPES OF BUSINESS:

Thermoelectric Systems Manufacturing
Waste Heat Recovery Technology

BRANDS/DIVISIONS/AFFILIATES:

Amerigon Inc
5N Plus, Inc.
ZT Plus

CONTACTS:

Note: Officers with more than one job title may be intentionally listed here more than once.

Lon E. Bell, CEO
Lon E. Bell, Pres.
Dan Coker, Pres./CEO-Amerigon, Inc.

Phone: 626-593-4515	**Fax:** 626-815-7441
Toll-Free:	
Address: 5462 Irwindale Ave., Irwindale, CA 91706 US	

GROWTH PLANS/SPECIAL FEATURES:

BSST LLC is the research and development subsidiary of Amerigon, Inc. The firm develops more efficient, effective and practical thermoelectric systems and products for its parent company and other companies in the automotive, computer, consumer, industrial electronics, medical, military and telecommunications industries. BSST focuses on the following applications: personal microclimate conditioning of individuals; thermal management solutions for electronic components and assemblies in confined spaces; thermal management and stable storage solutions for biomedical temperature-sensitive materials; stand-alone telecommunications installation cooling systems; cooled or heated automobile seats and therapy bed pads; and commercially and militarily viable thermal to electrical energy conversion. The company also develops power generation and waste heat recovery projects for military and commercial customers. BSST holds 16 U.S. patents, 24 foreign patents, 29 pending U.S. patents and 46 pending foreign patents. In March 2010, the firm bought the 50% interest in ZT Plus, its joint venture with 5N Plus, Inc., held by 5N. ZT Plus was formed in September 2009 with the intention of discovering and testing new materials possessing greater thermoelectric efficiency.

BSST offers its employees health, dental and vision coverage; flexible spending accounts; dependent care reimbursement accounts; disability and life insurance; a 401(k) plan; and tuition reimbursement.

FINANCIALS:

Sales and profits are in thousands of dollars—add 000 to get the full amount. 2010 Note: Financial information for 2010 was not available for all companies at press time.

2010 Sales: $	2010 Profits: $	**U.S. Stock Ticker: Subsidiary**
2009 Sales: $	2009 Profits: $	**Int'l Ticker:** Int'l Exchange:
2008 Sales: $	2008 Profits: $	Employees:
2007 Sales: $	2007 Profits: $	Fiscal Year Ends:
2006 Sales: $	2006 Profits: $	Parent Company: AMERIGON INC

SALARIES/BENEFITS:

Pension Plan:	ESOP Stock Plan:	Profit Sharing:	Top Exec. Salary: $222,000	Bonus: $78,000
Savings Plan: Y	Stock Purch. Plan:		Second Exec. Salary: $	Bonus: $

OTHER THOUGHTS:

Apparent Women Officers or Directors: 1
Hot Spot for Advancement for Women/Minorities:

LOCATIONS: ("Y" = Yes)

West:	Southwest:	Midwest:	Southeast:	Northeast:	International:
Y					

BW GAS LIMITED

www.bwgas.com

Industry Group Code: 483111 **Ranks within this company's industry group:** Sales: Profits:

Exploration/Production:		Refining/Retailing:		Utilities:		Alternative Energy:		Specialty Services:		Energy Mktg./Other Svcs.	
Exploration:		Refining:		Electric Utility:		Waste/Solar/Other:		Consulting/Eng.:		Energy Marketing:	
Production:		Retailing:		Gas Utility:		Thermal/Steam:		Seismic:		Equipment/Machinery:	
Coal Production:		Convenience Stores:		Pipelines:		Wind:		Drilling:		Oil Field Services:	
		Chemicals:		Water:		Hydro:		InfoTech:		Air/Shipping Transportation:	Y
						Fuel Cells:		Specialty Services:	Y		

TYPES OF BUSINESS:

Natural Gas Transportation
LNG Tankers

BRANDS/DIVISIONS/AFFILIATES:

World Nordic ApS
BW Fleet Management
BW Gas Limited
Marubeni Corporation

CONTACTS:

Note: Officers with more than one job title may be intentionally listed here more than once.

Andreas Sohmen-Pao, CEO
Clarence Lui, CFO
Rebekah France, Sr. VP-Human Resources
Sverre Prytz, Sr. VP-Strategy & Projects
Janice Wong, Dir.-Comm.
Morten Steen Martinsen, Exec. VP-Fleet Mgmt.
Lars V. Mathiasen, Sr. VP-Commercial Gas
Billy Chiu, Sr. VP-Commercial Tankers
Helmut Sohmen, Chmn.

Phone: 47-2212-0505	**Fax:** 47-2212-0500
Toll-Free:	
Address: Drammensveien 106, Oslo, 0204 Norway	

GROWTH PLANS/SPECIAL FEATURES:

BW Gas Limited is a holding company for BW Gas ASA (BW Gas, formerly Bergesen Worldwide Gas ASA). Through BW Gas, the firm is a leading owner and operator of seagoing gas carriers. The company operates in two business areas: liquefied natural gas (LNG) shipping and liquefied petroleum gas (LPG) shipping. BW Gas's fleet consists of very large gas carriers (VLGC), with a capacity exceeding 2.4 million cubic feet (Mmcf); large gas carriers (LGC), with capacities ranging from 1.7-2.4 Mmcf; and medium gas carriers (MGC), with capacities ranging from 0.7-1.4 Mmcf. The VLGC mainly carry LPG such as butane and propane, but can also carry other clean petroleum products; the LGC and MGC carry both LPG and ammonia. BW Gas has a fleet of 57 vessels, 44 of which are LPG vessels and 13 are LNG vessels. The entire fleet falls under the guidance of BW Fleet Management (BWFM), which is responsible for the management of all vessels associated with BW Gas. Aside from its Norwegian headquarters, the company has offices in Bermuda, Cyprus, Singapore, the Philippines, India, Latvia, Russia and China. In October 2010, the firm agreed to sell a 49% joint venture interest in eight of its LNG carriers to Japan's Marubeni Corporation.

The various benefits and perks BW offers its employees include pensions, insurance, cabins in Norway and Sweden, sports facilities, a company doctor and treatment at Volvat Medical Centers in Norway.

FINANCIALS:

Sales and profits are in thousands of dollars—add 000 to get the full amount. 2010 Note: Financial information for 2010 was not available for all companies at press time.

2010 Sales: $	2010 Profits: $	**U.S. Stock Ticker:**
2009 Sales: $	2009 Profits: $	**Int'l Ticker: BWGAS** Int'l Exchange: Oslo-OBX
2008 Sales: $682,300	2008 Profits: $173,700	Employees:
2007 Sales: $704,100	2007 Profits: $-420,900	Fiscal Year Ends: 12/31
2006 Sales: $729,900	2006 Profits: $223,700	Parent Company:

SALARIES/BENEFITS:

Pension Plan: Y	ESOP Stock Plan:	Profit Sharing:	Top Exec. Salary: $	Bonus: $
Savings Plan:	Stock Purch. Plan:		Second Exec. Salary: $	Bonus: $

OTHER THOUGHTS:

Apparent Women Officers or Directors: 2
Hot Spot for Advancement for Women/Minorities:

LOCATIONS: ("Y" = Yes)

West:	Southwest:	Midwest:	Southeast:	Northeast:	International:
					Y

CABOT OIL & GAS CORP

www.cabotog.com

Industry Group Code: 211111 **Ranks within this company's industry group:** Sales: 81 Profits: 60

Exploration/Production:		Refining/Retailing:		Utilities:		Alternative Energy:		Specialty Services:		Energy Mktg./Other Svcs.	
Exploration:	Y	Refining:		Electric Utility:		Waste/Solar/Other:		Consulting/Eng.:		Energy Marketing:	Y
Production:	Y	Retailing:		Gas Utility:		Thermal/Steam:		Seismic:		Equipment/Machinery:	
Coal Production:		Convenience Stores:		Pipelines:	Y	Wind:		Drilling:		Oil Field Services:	
		Chemicals:		Water:		Hydro:		InfoTech:		Air/Shipping Transportation:	
						Fuel Cells:		Specialty Services:			

TYPES OF BUSINESS:

Oil & Gas Exploration & Production
Gas Gathering & Storage
Gas Pipelines

BRANDS/DIVISIONS/AFFILIATES:

CONTACTS:

Note: Officers with more than one job title may be intentionally listed here more than once.

Dan O. Dinges, CEO
Dan O. Dinges, Pres.
Scott C. Schroeder, CFO/VP
Jeffrey W. Hutton, VP-Mktg.
Abraham D. Garza, VP-Human Resources
Robert G. Drake, VP-Info. Svcs.
G. Kevin Cunningham, General Counsel
Todd M. Roemer, Controller
Lisa A. Machesney, Corp. Sec.
Robert G. Drake, VP-Oper. Acct.
Matt Reid, VP/Regional Mgr.-South Region
Phil Stalnaker, VP/Regional Mgr.-North Region
Dan O. Dinges, Chmn.

Phone: 281-589-4600	**Fax:** 281-589-4828
Toll-Free:	
Address: 1200 Enclave Pkwy., Houston, TX 77077 US	

GROWTH PLANS/SPECIAL FEATURES:

Cabot Oil & Gas Corp. is a company engaged in the development, exploitation and exploration of oil and gas properties in the U.S. The company primarily conducts its operations in the Appalachian Basin; the onshore Gulf Coast region, including south and east Texas and north Louisiana; the Rocky Mountains; and the Anadarko Basin. The firm operates in two regions: north and south. The north region's operations include activities in Pennsylvania and West Virginia, as well as Cabot's Rocky Mountain activities, concentrated in the Green River and Washakie Basins in Wyoming and the Paradox Basin in Colorado. The south region includes the firm's operations in Louisiana and Texas and its mid-continent operations, concentrated in the Anadarko Basin in southwest Kansas, Oklahoma and the Texas panhandle. In addition to its exploration activities, Cabot operates a number of gas gathering and transmission pipeline systems that consist of approximately 3,500 miles of pipeline. Cabot has proved reserves totaling nearly 2 trillion cubic feet equivalent, of which approximately 98% of reserves and 95% of production quantity is natural gas. In 2009, the company drilled 143 gross wells with a success rate of 95%.

FINANCIALS:

Sales and profits are in thousands of dollars—add 000 to get the full amount. 2010 Note: Financial information for 2010 was not available for all companies at press time.

2010 Sales: $	2010 Profits: $	**U.S. Stock Ticker: COG**
2009 Sales: $879,276	2009 Profits: $148,343	**Int'l Ticker:** Int'l Exchange:
2008 Sales: $945,791	2008 Profits: $211,290	Employees: 567
2007 Sales: $732,170	2007 Profits: $167,423	Fiscal Year Ends: 12/31
2006 Sales: $761,988	2006 Profits: $321,175	Parent Company:

SALARIES/BENEFITS:

Pension Plan: Y	ESOP Stock Plan:	Profit Sharing:	Top Exec. Salary: $575,000	Bonus: $948,750
Savings Plan:	Stock Purch. Plan:		Second Exec. Salary: $413,000	Bonus: $930,000

OTHER THOUGHTS:

Apparent Women Officers or Directors: 1
Hot Spot for Advancement for Women/Minorities:

LOCATIONS: ("Y" = Yes)

West:	Southwest:	Midwest:	Southeast:	Northeast:	International:
Y	Y	Y	Y	Y	

CALLON PETROLEUM COMPANY

www.callon.com

Industry Group Code: 211111 **Ranks within this company's industry group:** Sales: 108 Profits: 65

Exploration/Production:		Refining/Retailing:		Utilities:		Alternative Energy:		Specialty Services:		Energy Mktg./Other Svcs.	
Exploration:	Y	Refining:		Electric Utility:		Waste/Solar/Other:		Consulting/Eng.:		Energy Marketing:	
Production:		Retailing:		Gas Utility:		Thermal/Steam:		Seismic:		Equipment/Machinery:	
Coal Production:		Convenience Stores:		Pipelines:		Wind:		Drilling:		Oil Field Services:	
		Chemicals:		Water:		Hydro:		InfoTech:		Air/Shipping Transportation:	
						Fuel Cells:		Specialty Services:			

TYPES OF BUSINESS:

Oil & Gas Exploration & Development

BRANDS/DIVISIONS/AFFILIATES:

CONTACTS:

Note: Officers with more than one job title may be intentionally listed here more than once.

Fred L. Callon, CEO
B.F. Weatherly, CFO/Exec. VP
Stephen F. Woodcock, VP-Exploration
H. Clark Smith, CIO
Gregory Hepguler, Sr. Reservoir Engineer
Robert A. Mayfield, Corp. Sec.
Gary Newberry, Sr. VP-Oper.
Rodger W. Smith, Treas./VP
Mitzi P. Conn, Controller
Eric Williams, Mgr.-Financial Reporting
John Beddo, Superintendent-Drilling & Prod.
Fred L. Callon, Chmn.

Phone: 601-442-1601	Fax: 601-446-1410
Toll-Free:	
Address: 200 N. Canal St., Natchez, MS 39120 US	

GROWTH PLANS/SPECIAL FEATURES:

Callon Petroleum Company acquires, develops, explores and operates oil and gas properties onshore in Louisiana and Texas and the offshore waters of the Gulf of Mexico. The firm has estimated net proved reserves of 6.5 billion barrels of oil and over 19.1 billion cubic feet of natural gas. Oil constitutes approximately 67% on an equivalent basis of its total estimated proved reserves. Approximately 66% of the total estimated proved reserves are proved developed reserves. The company's interest in deepwater discoveries includes the Medusa and Habanero fields. While the firm has traditionally focused on exploration and production operations in the Gulf of Mexico, its current strategy is to shift focus to the acquisition and development of lower risk, longer life onshore oil and gas properties, as well as to increase the number of wells it owns. In September 2009, Callon acquired a 70% interest in a 577-acre unit in the Haynesville Shale resource play in Bossier Parish, Louisiana, for $3 million. In October 2009, the company acquired interest in 22 producing wells in located in Crockett, Ector, Midland and Upton Counties in Texas from Ambrose Energy I, Ltd., a subsidiary of ExL Petroleum, LP, for $16.25 million. The estimated total proved reserves of these wells is 1.6 million barrels of oil equivalent. In June 2010, the firm began drilling operations at its first Haynesville Shale well in Louisiana.

FINANCIALS:

Sales and profits are in thousands of dollars—add 000 to get the full amount. 2010 Note: Financial information for 2010 was not available for all companies at press time.

2010 Sales: $	2010 Profits: $	**U.S. Stock Ticker: CPE**
2009 Sales: $101,259	2009 Profits: $54,419	**Int'l Ticker:** Int'l Exchange:
2008 Sales: $141,312	2008 Profits: $-438,893	Employees: 72
2007 Sales: $170,768	2007 Profits: $15,194	Fiscal Year Ends: 12/31
2006 Sales: $182,268	2006 Profits: $40,560	Parent Company:

SALARIES/BENEFITS:

Pension Plan:	ESOP Stock Plan:	Profit Sharing:	Top Exec. Salary: $464,520	Bonus: $696,780
Savings Plan:	Stock Purch. Plan:		Second Exec. Salary: $364,000	Bonus: $546,000

OTHER THOUGHTS:

Apparent Women Officers or Directors: 1
Hot Spot for Advancement for Women/Minorities:

LOCATIONS: ("Y" = Yes)

West:	Southwest:	Midwest:	Southeast:	Northeast:	International:
	Y		Y		

CALPINE CORPORATION

www.calpine.com

Industry Group Code: 2211 **Ranks within this company's industry group:** Sales: 25 Profits: 36

Exploration/Production:		Refining/Retailing:		Utilities:		Alternative Energy:		Specialty Services:		Energy Mktg./Other Svcs.	
Exploration:		Refining:		Electric Utility:	Y	Waste/Solar/Other:		Consulting/Eng.:	Y	Energy Marketing:	Y
Production:		Retailing:		Gas Utility:	Y	Thermal/Steam:	Y	Seismic:		Equipment/Machinery:	Y
Coal Production:		Convenience Stores:		Pipelines:	Y	Wind:		Drilling:		Oil Field Services:	
		Chemicals:		Water:		Hydro:		InfoTech:		Air/Shipping Transportation:	
						Fuel Cells:		Specialty Services:	Y		

TYPES OF BUSINESS:

Utilities-Electricity
Electrical Generation
Engineering & Support Services
Power Plant Construction
Geothermal Power Generation
Turbine Support Services & Engineering
Energy Asset Management
Energy Marketing & Trading

BRANDS/DIVISIONS/AFFILIATES:

Calpine Canada
Calpine Merchant Services
Calpine Power Company
Calpine Power Services
Calpine Construction Finance Company
Conectiv Energy

CONTACTS:

Note: Officers with more than one job title may be intentionally listed here more than once.

Jack A. Fusco, CEO
Jack A. Fusco, Pres.
Zamir Rauf, CFO/Exec. VP
Dennis Fishback, CIO/Sr. VP
W. Thaddeus Miller, Chief Legal Officer/Exec. VP/Corp. Sec.
Larry B. Leverett, Sr. VP-Commercial Oper.
Jim D. Deidiker, Chief Acct. Officer/Sr. VP
Gary M. Germeroth, Chief Risk Officer/Exec. VP
Thad Hill, Chief Commercial Officer/Exec. VP
John Adams, Sr. VP-Power Oper.
Sarah Novosel, Sr. VP-Gov't Affairs

Phone: 713-830-2000 **Fax:** 713-830-2001
Toll-Free:
Address: 717 Texas Ave., Ste. 1000, Houston, TX 77002 US

GROWTH PLANS/SPECIAL FEATURES:

Calpine Corporation is an independent wholesale power generation company primarily engaged in the ownership and operation of natural gas-fired and geothermal power plants throughout North America. The firm is one of the largest publically traded independent wholesale energy companies in the U.S. The company operates in 21 U.S. states and several Canadian provinces with a total of 93 natural gas-fired and geothermal power plants that have a combined capacity of 29,000 megawatts (MW) of energy. Calpine generates roughly 40% of the geothermal power produced in the U.S. at The Geysers facility in California. The firm operates through multiple subsidiaries that run a variety of energy services, including Calpine Canada, which operates power plants in three provinces and manages the Calpine Power Income Fund; Calpine Merchant Services, which manages Calpine's power generation assets; Calpine Power Company, which manages the operations of the company's fleet of power plants; Calpine Power Services, which provides program management and operating services to third parties; and Calpine Construction Finance Company, which manages the construction of power plants. The company also operates NewSouth Energy, which manages marketing and communications for Calpine's assets in southern states. NewSouth also offers green energy options for its customers. In October 2009, the company announced the completion of its Otay Mesa Energy Center outside of San Diego, California. The plant will produce 600 MW of energy for customers of San Diego Gas & Electric. In July 2010, the firm acquired Conectiv Energy from Pepco Holdings Inc., including Conectiv's electric generation business consisting of 19 power plants with a total generating capacity of 4,490 MW.

The company offers its employees medical, dental and vision insurance; flexible spending accounts; short and long term disability; AD&D; an employee assistance plan; a 401(k); adoption assistance; bereavement and family care leave; and tuition assistance.

FINANCIALS:

Sales and profits are in thousands of dollars—add 000 to get the full amount. 2010 Note: Financial information for 2010 was not available for all companies at press time.

2010 Sales: $	2010 Profits: $	**U.S. Stock Ticker: CPN**
2009 Sales: $6,564,000	2009 Profits: $149,000	**Int'l Ticker:** Int'l Exchange:
2008 Sales: $9,937,000	2008 Profits: $10,000	Employees: 2,046
2007 Sales: $7,970,000	2007 Profits: $2,693,000	Fiscal Year Ends: 12/31
2006 Sales: $6,937,000	2006 Profits: $-1,764,907	Parent Company:

SALARIES/BENEFITS:

Pension Plan:	ESOP Stock Plan:	Profit Sharing:	Top Exec. Salary: $1,015,269	Bonus: $1,636,824
Savings Plan: Y	Stock Purch. Plan: Y		Second Exec. Salary: $723,366	Bonus: $1,119,673

OTHER THOUGHTS:

Apparent Women Officers or Directors: 1
Hot Spot for Advancement for Women/Minorities:

LOCATIONS: ("Y" = Yes)

West:	Southwest:	Midwest:	Southeast:	Northeast:	International:
Y	Y	Y	Y	Y	Y

CALTEX AUSTRALIA LIMITED

www.caltex.com.au

Industry Group Code: 324110 **Ranks within this company's industry group:** Sales: 15 Profits: 8

Exploration/Production:		Refining/Retailing:		Utilities:		Alternative Energy:		Specialty Services:		Energy Mktg./Other Svcs.	
Exploration:		Refining:	Y	Electric Utility:		Waste/Solar/Other:		Consulting/Eng.:		Energy Marketing:	Y
Production:		Retailing:	Y	Gas Utility:		Thermal/Steam:		Seismic:		Equipment/Machinery:	
Coal Production:		Convenience Stores:	Y	Pipelines:	Y	Wind:		Drilling:		Oil Field Services:	
		Chemicals:	Y	Water:		Hydro:		InfoTech:		Air/Shipping Transportation:	
						Fuel Cells:		Specialty Services:			

TYPES OF BUSINESS:

Petroleum Refining
Pipelines
Gas Stations
Convenience Stores
Chemicals & Lubricants
Fuel Wholesaling & Distribution

BRANDS/DIVISIONS/AFFILIATES:

Chevron Corporation
Caltex
Ampol
Star Mart
Star Shop
Calstores

CONTACTS:

Note: Officers with more than one job title may be intentionally listed here more than once.

Julian Segal, CEO/Managing Dir.
Simon Hepworth, CFO
Andy Walz, Gen. Mgr.-Mktg.
Simon Willshire, Gen. Mgr.-Human Resources
Helen Conway, General Counsel/Corp. Sec.
Mike McMenamin, Gen. Mgr.-Strategy, Planning & Dev.
Frank Topham, Mgr.-Media & Gov't Affairs
Fran Van Reyk, Mgr.-Investor Rel.
Gary Smith, Gen. Mgr.-Refining
Elizabeth Bryan, Chmn.
Ken James, Gen. Mgr.-Supply & Dist.

Phone: 61-2-9250-5000	**Fax:** 61-2-9250-5742
Toll-Free:	
Address: 2 Market St., Level 24, Sydney, NSW 2000 Australia	

GROWTH PLANS/SPECIAL FEATURES:

Caltex Australia Limited, 50%-owned by Chevron Corporation, is Australia's leading refiner, distributor and marketer of fuels and lubricants. The company owns and operates two fuel refineries, one at Kurnell in Sydney and the other at Lytton in Brisbane, with a combined capacity of 9.2 million gallons per day (gpd). It also has a 158,500-gpd lubricating oil refinery at Kurnell. Caltex owns and operates the longest multi-product pipeline in Australia, stretching more than 125 miles from the Kurnell refinery in Sydney to the Wickham terminal in Newcastle. The firm also manufactures and markets specialty products such as bitumen, gases and waxes. Caltex markets petroleum products through three principal channels of distribution: retail, wholesale and commercial. Its retail division comprises a national service station network, convenience store network and distributor network. The national service station network includes approximately 2,000 Caltex and Ampol gas stations, of which 756 are owned or leased by the company. The remaining sites are owned or leased and operated by franchises, distributors and independent resellers. Caltex's convenience store network contains almost 500 convenience stores, of which 90 sites are fully owned and operated by Calstores, the firm's retail operating arm. Caltex's distributor network currently has 64 distributors that supply approximately 1,100 services stations and many small businesses, especially those located in rural areas, such as farms and smaller transport operators. The company owns or leases 88 depots that are licensed to distributors and used for the storage of petroleum products. As with its gas stations, Caltex's distributor network includes Caltex and Ampol branded sites.

FINANCIALS:

Sales and profits are in thousands of dollars—add 000 to get the full amount. 2010 Note: Financial information for 2010 was not available for all companies at press time.

2010 Sales: $	2010 Profits: $	**U.S. Stock Ticker:**
2009 Sales: $15,026,500	2009 Profits: $266,050	**Int'l Ticker: CTX** Int'l Exchange: Sydney-ASX
2008 Sales: $19,770,000	2008 Profits: $29,000	Employees:
2007 Sales: $16,979,800	2007 Profits: $575,600	Fiscal Year Ends: 12/31
2006 Sales: $16,412,900	2006 Profits: $414,700	Parent Company:

SALARIES/BENEFITS:

Pension Plan: Y	ESOP Stock Plan:	Profit Sharing:	Top Exec. Salary: $1,063,434	Bonus: $321,021
Savings Plan:	Stock Purch. Plan:		Second Exec. Salary: $660,699	Bonus: $184,243

OTHER THOUGHTS:

Apparent Women Officers or Directors: 3
Hot Spot for Advancement for Women/Minorities: Y

LOCATIONS: ("Y" = Yes)

West:	Southwest:	Midwest:	Southeast:	Northeast:	International:
					Y

CAMAC INTERNATIONAL CORP

www.camacholdings.com

Industry Group Code: 211111 **Ranks within this company's industry group:** Sales: Profits:

Exploration/Production:		Refining/Retailing:		Utilities:		Alternative Energy:		Specialty Services:		Energy Mktg./Other Svcs.	
Exploration:	Y	Refining:	Y	Electric Utility:		Waste/Solar/Other:		Consulting/Eng.:		Energy Marketing:	Y
Production:	Y	Retailing:		Gas Utility:		Thermal/Steam:		Seismic:		Equipment/Machinery:	
Coal Production:		Convenience Stores:		Pipelines:		Wind:		Drilling:		Oil Field Services:	
		Chemicals:		Water:		Hydro:		InfoTech:		Air/Shipping Transportation:	
						Fuel Cells:		Specialty Services:	Y		

TYPES OF BUSINESS:

Oil & Gas Exploration & Production
Oil Refining & Marketing
Oil & Gas Industry Services
Insulation
Coating Systems
School Bus Operations

BRANDS/DIVISIONS/AFFILIATES:

Allied Energy Corporation USA
Allied Energy Colombia Corporation
Allied Energy Plc Nigeria
Oceanic Consultations Nigeria Limited
Oceanic Consultations USA
CAMAC International Trading

CONTACTS: *Note: Officers with more than one job title may be intentionally listed here more than once.*

Kase L. Lawal, CEO
Alex Loftus, COO/Exec. VP
Kamoru Lawal, Pres.
Kamorou A. Lawal, CFO/Exec. VP
Segun Omidele, Sr. VP-Exploration & Prod.
Jean-Michel Malek, General Counsel/Sr. VP
Abiola Lawal, Chief Strategy Officer/Sr. VP
Lino Punzalan, Controller/VP
Kase L. Lawal, Chmn.

Phone: 713-965-5100 **Fax:** 713-965-5128
Toll-Free:
Address: 1330 Post Oak Blvd., Ste. 2200, Houston, TX 77056 US

GROWTH PLANS/SPECIAL FEATURES:

CAMAC International Corp. focuses on oil and gas exploration, production, engineering and refining. The company controls major energy assets in Colombia, England, Nigeria and South Africa. CAMAC operates primarily through six business units: Allied Energy Corporation USA (AECU); Allied Energy Colombia Corporation (AECC); Allied Energy Plc. Nigeria (AEPN); Oceanic Consultations Nigeria Limited (OCNL); Oceanic Consultations USA (OCU); and CAMAC International Trading (CIT). AECU is engaged in the exploration of oil and gas as well as the development and production of assets. While the majority of these assets are derived from Africa, AECU also has interests in other international locations. AECC holds a 44,000 acre oil and gas lease in the Tubara region of north Colombia and is currently evaluating the appraisal and development of hydrocarbon resources. AEPN is engaged in upstream oil and gas exploration and production activities in Nigeria. It owns an interest in four offshore Nigerian oil mining leases located in the Oyo field. The field has an estimated 40,000 barrels of proven reserves and up to one million barrels of recoverable reserves. OCNL is a Lagos, Nigeria-based professional engineering and project management corporation, specializing in providing services to the oil and gas exploration and production industry. OCU operates as an engineering consultant, project manager and procurement agent to oil and gas exploration, production, storage and transportation companies. CIT trades and delivers physical crude oil and refined products to international energy markets. CIT maintains purchase and sale contracts for the trading of approximately 120,000 barrels of crude oil per day.

CAMAC is one of the largest African-American-owned businesses in the U.S.

FINANCIALS: Sales and profits are in thousands of dollars—add 000 to get the full amount. 2010 Note: Financial information for 2010 was not available for all companies at press time.

2010 Sales: $	2010 Profits: $	**U.S. Stock Ticker: Private**
2009 Sales: $	2009 Profits: $	**Int'l Ticker:** Int'l Exchange:
2008 Sales: $2,430,000	2008 Profits: $	Employees: 300
2007 Sales: $	2007 Profits: $	Fiscal Year Ends: 12/31
2006 Sales: $1,490,000	2006 Profits: $	Parent Company:

SALARIES/BENEFITS:

Pension Plan:	ESOP Stock Plan:	Profit Sharing:	Top Exec. Salary: $	Bonus: $
Savings Plan:	Stock Purch. Plan:		Second Exec. Salary: $	Bonus: $

OTHER THOUGHTS:

Apparent Women Officers or Directors: 1
Hot Spot for Advancement for Women/Minorities:

LOCATIONS: ("Y" = Yes)

West:	Southwest:	Midwest:	Southeast:	Northeast:	International:
	Y				Y

CAMECO CORPORATION

www.cameco.com

Industry Group Code: 212 **Ranks within this company's industry group:** Sales: 2 Profits: 2

Exploration/Production:		Refining/Retailing:		Utilities:		Alternative Energy:		Specialty Services:		Energy Mktg./Other Svcs.	
Exploration:	Y	Refining:	Y	Electric Utility:		Waste/Solar/Other:	Y	Consulting/Eng.:		Energy Marketing:	Y
Production:		Retailing:		Gas Utility:		Thermal/Steam:		Seismic:		Equipment/Machinery:	
Coal Production:		Convenience Stores:		Pipelines:		Wind:		Drilling:		Oil Field Services:	
		Chemicals:		Water:		Hydro:		InfoTech:		Air/Shipping Transportation:	
						Fuel Cells:		Specialty Services:	Y		

TYPES OF BUSINESS:

Uranium Exploration & Production
Uranium Marketing & Fuel Services
Nuclear Power Generation
Gold Mining

BRANDS/DIVISIONS/AFFILIATES:

Zircatec Precision Industries
Bruce Power Limited Partnership
Centerra Gold, Inc.
UEM, Inc.
Cameco Global Exploration II, Ltd.
Kintyre Uranium Exploration Project

CONTACTS: *Note: Officers with more than one job title may be intentionally listed here more than once.*

Gerald W. Grandey, CEO
Bob Steane, COO/Sr. VP
Tim Gitzel, Pres.
O. Kim Goheen, CFO/Sr. VP
George B. Assie, Sr. VP-Mktg.
Gary M. S. Chad, Sr. VP-Governance, Legal & Regulatory Affairs/Sec.
George B. Assie, Sr. VP-Bus. Dev.
Rachelle Girard, Dir.-Investor Rel.
Grant Issac, Sr. VP-Corp. Svcs.
Victor J. Zaleschuk, Chmn.

Phone: 306-956-6203	**Fax:** 306-956-6201
Toll-Free:	
Address: 2121 11th St. W., Saskatoon, SK S7M 1J3 Canada	

GROWTH PLANS/SPECIAL FEATURES:

Cameco Corporation, based in Saskatoon, Saskatchewan, Canada, is one of the world's largest uranium producers, accounting for roughly 15-20% of the world's uranium production. The company's mining and conversion facilities in North America provide fuel to many of the western world's nuclear power plants. Cameco's operations are divided into three segments: quality uranium; fuel services; and electricity generation. Its uranium assets include two operating mines in northern Saskatchewan, two in the U.S. and one mine in Kazakhstan, as well as exploration projects in Australia. The Saskatchewan facilities represent one of the world's largest high-grade reserves and low-cost operations with 480 million pounds of proven and provable reserves that have ore grades nearly 100 times the world average. The company's fuel services division includes Zircatec Precision Industries, one of two Canadian suppliers of finished fuel for the Candu reactors. As one of the only conversion suppliers, Cameco owns or controls 35% of the western world's capacity to produce the uranium hexafluoride required to produce fuel for light water reactors. It is also one of the world's only commercial producers of natural uranium dioxide. The firm produces electricity through its Bruce Power Limited Partnership. The company owns 32% interest in four Bruce B nuclear reactors. In December 2009, the company disposed of the entirety of its interest in Centerra Gold, Inc.

FINANCIALS: **Sales and profits are in thousands of dollars—add 000 to get the full amount. 2010 Note: Financial information for 2010 was not available for all companies at press time.**

2010 Sales: $	2010 Profits: $	**U.S. Stock Ticker: CCJ**
2009 Sales: $2,239,310	2009 Profits: $1,063,460	**Int'l Ticker: CCO** Int'l Exchange: Toronto-TSX
2008 Sales: $2,339,649	2008 Profits: $280,966	Employees:
2007 Sales: $2,354,550	2007 Profits: $442,919	Fiscal Year Ends: 12/31
2006 Sales: $1,758,557	2006 Profits: $360,710	Parent Company:

SALARIES/BENEFITS:

Pension Plan:	ESOP Stock Plan:	Profit Sharing:	Top Exec. Salary: $976,911	Bonus: $941,236
Savings Plan:	Stock Purch. Plan:		Second Exec. Salary: $553,697	Bonus: $351,864

OTHER THOUGHTS:

Apparent Women Officers or Directors: 2
Hot Spot for Advancement for Women/Minorities:

LOCATIONS: ("Y" = Yes)

West:	Southwest:	Midwest:	Southeast:	Northeast:	International:
Y		Y			Y

CAMERON INTERNATIONAL CORPORATION

www.c-a-m.com

Industry Group Code: 33313 **Ranks within this company's industry group:** Sales: 1 Profits: 1

Exploration/Production:		Refining/Retailing:		Utilities:		Alternative Energy:		Specialty Services:		Energy Mktg./Other Svcs.	
Exploration:		Refining:		Electric Utility:		Waste/Solar/Other:		Consulting/Eng.:		Energy Marketing:	
Production:		Retailing:		Gas Utility:		Thermal/Steam:		Seismic:		Equipment/Machinery:	Y
Coal Production:		Convenience Stores:		Pipelines:		Wind:		Drilling:		Oil Field Services:	Y
		Chemicals:		Water:		Hydro:		InfoTech:		Air/Shipping Transportation:	
						Fuel Cells:		Specialty Services:			

TYPES OF BUSINESS:

Oil Field Machinery
Gas Turbines, Compressors & Engines
Oil Field Services
Pressure & Flow Control Equipment

BRANDS/DIVISIONS/AFFILIATES:

Cooper Cameron Corporation
Cameron
Camrod
IC
McEvoy
NATCO Group, Inc.
SBS
Tundra

CONTACTS: *Note: Officers with more than one job title may be intentionally listed here more than once.*

Jack B. Moore, CEO
John D. Carne, COO/Exec. VP
Jack B. Moore, Pres.
Charles M. Sledge, CFO/VP
Ed Will, VP-Mktg. & Strategy
John Bartos, VP-Tech. & Dev.
William C. Lemmer, General Counsel/Sr. VP
Stephen P. Tomlinson, VP-Oper. Support
Hal J. Goldie, VP-Global Bus. Dev.
R. Scott Amann, VP-Investor Rel.
Christopher A. Krummel, Chief Acct. Officer/Controller/VP
Robert J. Rajeski, VP/Pres., Compression Systems
Joseph H. Mongrain, VP/Pres., Process & Compression Systems
John Carne, Sr. VP/Pres., Drilling & Prod. Systems
H. Keith Jennings, Treas./VP
Sheldon R. Erikson, Chmn.

Phone: 713-513-3300	**Fax:** 713-513-3456
Toll-Free:	
Address: 1333 West Loop S., Ste. 1700, Houston, TX 77027 US	

GROWTH PLANS/SPECIAL FEATURES:

Cameron International Corporation, formerly Cooper Cameron Corporation, is an international provider of flow equipment products, systems and services to oil, gas and processing industries. The firm is also a leading manufacturer of centrifugal air compressors, integral and separable gas compressors and turbochargers. The company operates in three segments: drilling and production systems; valves and measurement; and compression systems. The drilling and production systems products include surface and subsea production systems; blowout preventers (BOPs); drilling and production control systems; oil and gas separation equipment; gas conditioning units; membrane separation systems; water processing systems; block valves; gate valves; actuators; chokes; wellheads; drilling riser; and aftermarket parts and services. The division's products are marketed under the brand names Cameron, Camrod, IC, McEvoy, Precision, SBS, Tundra, Willis and WKM. The valves and measurement segment's products include ball valves, butterfly valves, Orbit valves, double block and bleed valves, globe valves and aftermarket parts and services. Measurement products include totalizers, turbine meters, flow computers, chart recorders, sampling systems and ultrasonic flow meters. The segment markets its products under various brand names, including Demco, Navco, Nutron, Techno, Wheatley and WKM. Lastly, the compression systems segment produces reciprocating and integrally geared centrifugal compression equipment and aftermarket parts and services. It markets its products under various brand names, including Ajax, Superior, Cooper-Bessemer, CSI, Texcentric and Enterprise. In April 2010, Cameron acquired NATCO Group, Inc., a process equipment provider.

FINANCIALS: **Sales and profits are in thousands of dollars—add 000 to get the full amount. 2010 Note: Financial information for 2010 was not available for all companies at press time.**

2010 Sales: $	2010 Profits: $	**U.S. Stock Ticker: CAM**
2009 Sales: $5,223,245	2009 Profits: $475,519	**Int'l Ticker:** Int'l Exchange:
2008 Sales: $5,848,877	2008 Profits: $593,726	Employees: 18,100
2007 Sales: $4,666,368	2007 Profits: $500,860	Fiscal Year Ends: 12/31
2006 Sales: $3,742,907	2006 Profits: $317,816	Parent Company:

SALARIES/BENEFITS:

Pension Plan:	ESOP Stock Plan:	Profit Sharing:	Top Exec. Salary: $900,000	Bonus: $4,500,000
Savings Plan:	Stock Purch. Plan:		Second Exec. Salary: $540,000	Bonus: $1,662,000

OTHER THOUGHTS:

Apparent Women Officers or Directors: 1
Hot Spot for Advancement for Women/Minorities:

LOCATIONS: ("Y" = Yes)

West:	Southwest:	Midwest:	Southeast:	Northeast:	International:
Y	Y	Y	Y	Y	Y

CANADIAN NATURAL RESOURCES LTD

www.cnrl.com

Industry Group Code: 211111 **Ranks within this company's industry group:** Sales: 47 Profits: 34

Exploration/Production:		Refining/Retailing:		Utilities:		Alternative Energy:		Specialty Services:		Energy Mktg./Other Svcs.	
Exploration:	Y	Refining:		Electric Utility:		Waste/Solar/Other:		Consulting/Eng.:		Energy Marketing:	
Production:	Y	Retailing:	Y	Gas Utility:		Thermal/Steam:		Seismic:		Equipment/Machinery:	Y
Coal Production:		Convenience Stores:		Pipelines:	Y	Wind:		Drilling:		Oil Field Services:	
		Chemicals:		Water:		Hydro:		InfoTech:		Air/Shipping Transportation:	
						Fuel Cells:		Specialty Services:	Y		

TYPES OF BUSINESS:

Oil & Gas Exploration & Production
Pipelines
Oil Sands Extraction
Generation Facilities
Surplus Equipment Sales

BRANDS/DIVISIONS/AFFILIATES:

CanNat Energy Inc.
CNR (ECHO) Resources Inc.
CNR International (U.K.), Ltd.
CNR Petro Resources Limited
CNR International (Olowi) Limited
Horizon Construction Management Ltd.
CNR International Cote d'Ivoire SARL
CNR International (U.K.) Investments Limited

CONTACTS:

Note: Officers with more than one job title may be intentionally listed here more than once.

Tim S. McKay, COO
Steve W. Laut, Pres.
Douglas A. Proll, CFO
Real M. Cusson, Sr. VP-Mktg.
Timothy G. Reed, VP-Human Resources
Paul M. Mendes, General Counsel/VP-Legal
Scott G. Stauth, VP-Field Oper.
Allen M. Knight, Sr. VP-Int'l & Corp. Dev.
Corey B. Bieber, VP-Investor Rel. & Finance
Douglas A. Proll, Sr. VP-Finance
Tim Hamilton, VP-Dev. Oper.
Philip A. Keele, VP-Mining
Ron K. Laing, VP-Commercial Oper.
Reno G. Laseur, VP-Upgrading
Allan P. Markin, Chmn.
James A. Edens, VP/Managing Dir.-CNR Int'l (U.K.) Ltd.

Phone: 403-517-6700 **Fax:** 403-517-7350
Toll-Free:
Address: 855 Second St. SW, Ste. 2500, Calgary, AB T2P 4J8 Canada

GROWTH PLANS/SPECIAL FEATURES:

Canadian Natural Resources Ltd. (CNR), one of North America's largest energy companies, is engaged in the exploration, development, production, marketing and sale of crude oil, natural gas liquids (NGLs), natural gas and bitumen. It operates primarily in the Western Canadian Sedimentary Basin, the U.K. sector of the North Sea and Offshore West Africa. CNR owns approximately 80% of known Canadian natural gas assets, within four natural gas areas of western Canada. In 2009, the company's average daily production totaled 355,500 barrels of crude oil and NGLs and 1.32 billion cubic feet of natural gas. CNR's midstream assets include 100% ownership in the ECHO pipeline; 62% of the Pelican Lake Pipeline; and 15% of the Cold Lake Pipeline systems, which transport 75% of the company's heavy oil production to international pipelines. The company also owns 50% of an 84-megawatt cogeneration plant that supplies power to its steam generation facilities. In addition, the firm owns the Athabasca Oil Sands leases in northern Alberta where the Horizon Oil Sands Project is located. The Horizon Oil Sands are estimated to contain approximately 16 billion barrels of oil in place and six to eight billion barrels of mineable reserves and contingent resources. First production on the location commenced in early 2009.

The company offers its employees production bonuses; medical, dental and vision coverage; a contribution savings plan; educational reimbursement; and a wellness program. In addition, the majority of employees at Canadian Natural Resources are shareholders.

FINANCIALS:

Sales and profits are in thousands of dollars—add 000 to get the full amount. 2010 Note: Financial information for 2010 was not available for all companies at press time.

2010 Sales: $	2010 Profits: $	**U.S. Stock Ticker: CNQ**
2009 Sales: $9,810,410	2009 Profits: $1,528,340	**Int'l Ticker: CNQ** Int'l Exchange: Toronto-TSX
2008 Sales: $13,693,200	2008 Profits: $4,822,020	Employees: 4,132
2007 Sales: $11,368,349	2007 Profits: $2,387,435	Fiscal Year Ends: 12/31
2006 Sales: $8,922,400	2006 Profits: $2,226,800	Parent Company:

SALARIES/BENEFITS:

Pension Plan:	ESOP Stock Plan:	Profit Sharing:	Top Exec. Salary: $537,570	Bonus: $977,400
Savings Plan:	Stock Purch. Plan: Y		Second Exec. Salary: $366,525	Bonus: $136,836

OTHER THOUGHTS:

Apparent Women Officers or Directors: 4
Hot Spot for Advancement for Women/Minorities: Y

LOCATIONS: ("Y" = Yes)

West:	Southwest:	Midwest:	Southeast:	Northeast:	International:
					Y

Note: Financial information, benefits and other data can change quickly and may vary from those stated here.

CANADIAN OIL SANDS TRUST

www.cos-trust.com

Industry Group Code: 211111 **Ranks within this company's industry group:** Sales: 67 Profits: 50

Exploration/Production:		**Refining/Retailing:**		**Utilities:**		**Alternative Energy:**		**Specialty Services:**		**Energy Mktg./Other Svcs.**	
Exploration:		Refining:	Y	Electric Utility:		Waste/Solar/Other:		Consulting/Eng.:		Energy Marketing:	
Production:	Y	Retailing:		Gas Utility:		Thermal/Steam:		Seismic:		Equipment/Machinery:	
Coal Production:		Convenience Stores:		Pipelines:		Wind:		Drilling:		Oil Field Services:	
		Chemicals:		Water:		Hydro:		InfoTech:		Air/Shipping Transportation:	
						Fuel Cells:		Specialty Services:	Y		

TYPES OF BUSINESS:

Oil Sands Production
Investment Trust
Refining

BRANDS/DIVISIONS/AFFILIATES:

Syncrude Canada, Ltd.

CONTACTS:

Note: Officers with more than one job title may be intentionally listed here more than once.

Marcel R. Coutu, CEO
Trevor R. Roberts, COO
Marcel R. Coutu, Pres.
Ryan M. Kubik, CFO
Scott W. Arnold, Sustainability Officer
Trudy M. Curran, General Counsel/Corp. Sec.
Darren Hardy, VP-Oper.
Siren Fisekci, VP-Corp. Rel.
Siren Fisekci, VP-Investor Rel.
Robert P. Dawson, Treas.
Laureen C. DuBois, Co-Controller
Allen R. Hagerman, Exec. VP-Special Projects
Philip D. Birkby, Co-Controller
C. E. Shultz, Chmn.

Phone: 403-218-6200 **Fax:** 403-218-6201
Toll-Free:
Address: 2500 First Canadian Centre, 350-7th Ave. SW, Calgary, AB T2P 3N9 Canada

GROWTH PLANS/SPECIAL FEATURES:

Canadian Oil Sands Trust is an investment trust that generates income from its working interest in Syncrude Canada, Ltd. Syncrude's operations include mining, extraction, upgrading and utilities; its primary business relates to its oil sands activities. Syncrude's oil sands holdings, located in Alberta, account for roughly 15% of Canada's total oil production. Syncrude's oil production capacity is approximately 350,000 barrels per day (bpd), and is expected to surpass 500,000 bpd after 2016 as part of an ongoing expansion plan. Oil sand is composed of sand, bitumen, mineral-rich clays and water. Bitumen, in its raw state, is a black, asphalt-like oil that is as thick as molasses. It requires extensive treatment and processing to make it transportable by pipeline and usable by conventional refineries. Syncrude surface mines oil sand, extracts bitumen and upgrades it into sweet light crude oil. Syncrude leases over 102,000 hectares in the Athabasca Oil Sands deposit. Syncrude's proved plus probable reserves are 5.1 billion barrels, of which Canadian Oil Sands Trust's share is approximately 1.9 billion barrels. Canadian Oil Sands estimates that all of Syncrude's high quality resources can be accessed through surface mining. Canadian Oil Sands Trust owns a 36.7% interest in Syncrude. Other investors in Syncrude include Imperial Oil Resources, with 25%; Petro-Canada Oil and Gas, 12%; Conoco-Phillips Oil Sand Partnership II, 9%; Nexen Oil Sands Partnership, 7%; Murphy Oil Company, Ltd., 5%; and Mocal Energy Limited, 5%. In April 2010, shareholders of the trust approved the planned conversion of the company into a corporation.

Syncrude offers its employees medical, dental and vision; tuition assistance; 401(k); relocation assistance; employee career development; performance based bonuses; and an employee discount program.

FINANCIALS:

Sales and profits are in thousands of dollars—add 000 to get the full amount. 2010 Note: Financial information for 2010 was not available for all companies at press time.

2010 Sales: $	2010 Profits: $	**U.S. Stock Ticker: COSWF**
2009 Sales: $2,688,140	2009 Profits: $417,880	**Int'l Ticker:** Int'l Exchange:
2008 Sales: $4,187,870	2008 Profits: $1,403,950	Employees: 5,277
2007 Sales: $3,055,000	2007 Profits: $698,400	Fiscal Year Ends: 12/31
2006 Sales: $2,289,645	2006 Profits: $785,183	Parent Company:

SALARIES/BENEFITS:

Pension Plan: Y	ESOP Stock Plan:	Profit Sharing:	Top Exec. Salary: $781,920	Bonus: $733,929
Savings Plan: Y	Stock Purch. Plan:		Second Exec. Salary: $342,090	Bonus: $239,463

OTHER THOUGHTS:

Apparent Women Officers or Directors: 4
Hot Spot for Advancement for Women/Minorities: Y

LOCATIONS: ("Y" = Yes)

West:	Southwest:	Midwest:	Southeast:	Northeast:	International:
					Y

CARBO CERAMICS INC

www.carboceramics.com

Industry Group Code: 213112 **Ranks within this company's industry group:** Sales: 26 Profits: 17

Exploration/Production:		Refining/Retailing:		Utilities:		Alternative Energy:		Specialty Services:		Energy Mktg./Other Svcs.	
Exploration:		Refining:		Electric Utility:		Waste/Solar/Other:		Consulting/Eng.:	Y	Energy Marketing:	
Production:		Retailing:		Gas Utility:		Thermal/Steam:		Seismic:		Equipment/Machinery:	Y
Coal Production:		Convenience Stores:		Pipelines:		Wind:		Drilling:		Oil Field Services:	Y
		Chemicals:		Water:		Hydro:		InfoTech:	Y	Air/Shipping Transportation:	
						Fuel Cells:		Specialty Services:	Y		

TYPES OF BUSINESS:

Drilling Supplies
Hydraulic Fracturing Proppants
Hydraulic Fracture Diagnostic & Design Services
Reservoir Diagnostics
Fracture Simulation Software

BRANDS/DIVISIONS/AFFILIATES:

CARBOHSP
CARBOPROP
CARBOLITE
CARBOECONOPROP
CARBOTAG
StrataGen Engineering
FracproPT
BBL Falcon Industries, Ltd

CONTACTS:

Note: Officers with more than one job title may be intentionally listed here more than once.

Gary Kolstad, CEO
Gary Kolstad, Pres.
Ernesto Bautista, III, CFO/VP
David G. Gallagher, VP-Mktg. & Sales
R. Sean Elliott, General Counsel/Sec./Chief Compliance Officer
Mark Edmunds, VP-Oper.
William Morris, Chmn.

Phone: 281-921-6400	**Fax:** 281-921-6401
Toll-Free:	
Address: 575 N. Dairy Ashford, Ste. 300, Houston, TX 77079 US	

GROWTH PLANS/SPECIAL FEATURES:

Carbo Ceramics, Inc. is a leading worldwide provider of ceramic proppants for use in hydraulic fracturing of oil and natural gas wells. The firm is one of the largest suppliers of this specialized product in the world. Proppants are granular structures, such as ceramic or sand, contained in the liquids that companies use to fracture the inside of an oil or natural gas well in order to increase the flow of hydrocarbons. The proppant slips into the fractures in order to hold them open after the high-pressure pumping stops, keeping the cracks wide enough for natural gas or oil to slip through. Ceramic proppants are usually on the higher-end of the cost range due to greater strength and more uniform size and shape. The Proppant unit has five main products: CARBOHSP and CARBOPROP, high-strength products designed for use in deep gas wells; and CARBOLITE, CARBOHYDROPROP and CARBOECONOPROP, lighter-weight products designed for use in gas wells of moderate depth and oil wells. The company also offers CARBOTAG, a patent pending process of adding chemical markers to proppants during production that allow an operator to identify the precise well or fracture stage that is failing and allowing the flow of proppant back to the surface. Other well solutions include the firm's FracproPT fracture simulation software, which aids in the design and modeling of fractures. The firm provides consulting services to drilling and exploration companies through StrataGen Engineering. In October 2009, the company acquired the assets of BBL Falcon Industries, Ltd., a provider of spill prevention and containment systems.

FINANCIALS:

Sales and profits are in thousands of dollars—add 000 to get the full amount. 2010 Note: Financial information for 2010 was not available for all companies at press time.

2010 Sales: $	2010 Profits: $	**U.S. Stock Ticker: CRR**
2009 Sales: $341,872	2009 Profits: $52,810	**Int'l Ticker:** Int'l Exchange:
2008 Sales: $387,828	2008 Profits: $110,316	Employees: 741
2007 Sales: $299,996	2007 Profits: $53,870	Fiscal Year Ends: 12/31
2006 Sales: $283,829	2006 Profits: $54,253	Parent Company:

SALARIES/BENEFITS:

Pension Plan:	ESOP Stock Plan:	Profit Sharing: Y	Top Exec. Salary: $500,000	Bonus: $418,430
Savings Plan: Y	Stock Purch. Plan:		Second Exec. Salary: $267,038	Bonus: $201,241

OTHER THOUGHTS:

Apparent Women Officers or Directors:
Hot Spot for Advancement for Women/Minorities:

LOCATIONS: ("Y" = Yes)

West:	Southwest:	Midwest:	Southeast:	Northeast:	International:
Y	Y		Y		Y

CARRIZO OIL & GAS INC

www.crzo.net

Industry Group Code: 211111 **Ranks within this company's industry group:** Sales: 106 Profits: 96

Exploration/Production:		**Refining/Retailing:**		**Utilities:**		**Alternative Energy:**		**Specialty Services:**		**Energy Mktg./Other Svcs.**	
Exploration:	Y	Refining:		Electric Utility:		Waste/Solar/Other:		Consulting/Eng.:		Energy Marketing:	Y
Production:	Y	Retailing:		Gas Utility:		Thermal/Steam:		Seismic:		Equipment/Machinery:	
Coal Production:		Convenience Stores:		Pipelines:		Wind:		Drilling:		Oil Field Services:	
		Chemicals:		Water:		Hydro:		InfoTech:		Air/Shipping Transportation:	
						Fuel Cells:		Specialty Services:			

TYPES OF BUSINESS:

Oil & Gas Exploration & Production

BRANDS/DIVISIONS/AFFILIATES:

Avista Capital Partners
Reliance Industries Ltd.
Sumitomo Corp.

CONTACTS:

Note: Officers with more than one job title may be intentionally listed here more than once.

S. P. Johnson, IV, CEO
Brad Fisher, COO/VP
S. P. Johnson, IV, Pres.
Paul F. Boling, CFO/VP/Corp. Sec.
Michelle Bailey, Dir.-Human Resources
Gregory E. Evans, VP-Exploration & Dev.
Gerry Morton, General Counsel
Gerry Morton, VP-Bus. Dev.
Richard Hunter, VP-Investor Rel.
David Pitts, Chief Acct. Officer
Richard H. Smith, VP-Land
Andrew R. Agosto, VP-Bus. Dev.
Steven A. Webster, Chmn.

Phone: 713-328-1000	**Fax:** 713-328-1035
Toll-Free:	
Address: 1000 Louisiana St., Ste. 1500, Houston, TX 77002 US	

GROWTH PLANS/SPECIAL FEATURES:

Carrizo Oil & Gas, Inc. is engaged in the exploration, development, production and transportation of natural gas and oil. The company operates onshore in proven oil- and gas-producing zones along the Gulf Coast, primarily in the Barnett Shale area in north Texas; and the Marcellus Shale play in Pennsylvania, New York, West Virginia and Virginia. The firm also explores for, develops and produces natural gas and oil in onshore Gulf Coast areas in Texas, Louisiana and Alabama, primarily in the Miocene, Wilcox, Frio and Vicksburg trends. Carrizo utilizes 3-D seismic-driven exploratory and development drilling and horizontal drilling and hydraulic-fracturing technologies to evaluate resource prospects. The company currently has licenses for over 13,784 square miles of 3-D seismic data for processing and evaluation. The company has participated in the drilling of over 780 gross wells, with an apparent success rate of 85% overall and 100% in the Barnett Shale. Carrizo leases approximately 52,166 acres in the Barnett Shale and over 106,800 acres in the Marcellus Shale. Carrizo also has licenses to explore in the U.K. North Sea. Other shale plays the firm has interests in include Fayetteville in Arkansas; Camp Hill Field in Texas; Floyd/Neal in Mississippi; and the New Albany in Kentucky and Illinois. The firm has approximately 601.87 billion cubic feet of natural gas equivalent in proved reserves. In December 2009, the firm sold a working interest in a portion of its assets in the Barnett Shale core area to Sumitomo Corp. In September 2010, Carrizo entered into a joint venture with a subsidiary of Reliance Industries Ltd. covering 104,400 gross acres in the Marcellus Shale play, in which Carrizo will retain a 40% operating interest.

Carrizo offers its employees health, dental and vision insurance; life and long-term disability insurance; flexible spending accounts; parking and public transportation subsidies; and a 401(k) plan.

FINANCIALS:

Sales and profits are in thousands of dollars—add 000 to get the full amount. 2010 Note: Financial information for 2010 was not available for all companies at press time.

2010 Sales: $	2010 Profits: $	**U.S. Stock Ticker: CRZO**
2009 Sales: $114,079	2009 Profits: $-204,845	**Int'l Ticker:** Int'l Exchange:
2008 Sales: $216,677	2008 Profits: $-45,047	Employees: 111
2007 Sales: $125,789	2007 Profits: $15,469	Fiscal Year Ends: 12/31
2006 Sales: $82,945	2006 Profits: $18,248	Parent Company:

SALARIES/BENEFITS:

Pension Plan:	ESOP Stock Plan:	Profit Sharing:	Top Exec. Salary: $432,000	Bonus: $
Savings Plan: Y	Stock Purch. Plan:		Second Exec. Salary: $300,000	Bonus: $

OTHER THOUGHTS:

Apparent Women Officers or Directors: 1
Hot Spot for Advancement for Women/Minorities:

LOCATIONS: ("Y" = Yes)

West:	Southwest:	Midwest:	Southeast:	Northeast:	International:
	Y		Y	Y	Y

CE FRANKLIN LTD

www.cefranklin.com

Industry Group Code: 33313 **Ranks within this company's industry group:** Sales: 4 Profits: 5

Exploration/Production:		**Refining/Retailing:**		**Utilities:**		**Alternative Energy:**		**Specialty Services:**		**Energy Mktg./Other Svcs.**	
Exploration:		Refining:		Electric Utility:		Waste/Solar/Other:		Consulting/Eng.:	Y	Energy Marketing:	
Production:		Retailing:		Gas Utility:		Thermal/Steam:		Seismic:		Equipment/Machinery:	Y
Coal Production:		Convenience Stores:		Pipelines:		Wind:		Drilling:		Oil Field Services:	
		Chemicals:		Water:		Hydro:		InfoTech:		Air/Shipping Transportation:	
						Fuel Cells:		Specialty Services:	Y		

TYPES OF BUSINESS:

Oil & Gas Machinery Manufacturing
Production Equipment
Consulting Services
Procurement & Inventory Management Services

BRANDS/DIVISIONS/AFFILIATES:

CEF Tubulars
IPSCO Inc
Dura
Grove/TK
Nutron
Balon
Argus
PK-Smith

CONTACTS: *Note: Officers with more than one job title may be intentionally listed here more than once.*

Michael West, CEO
Michael West, Pres.
Mark Schweitzer, CFO/VP
Tim Ritchie, VP-Sales
Rod Tatham, VP-Oper.
Merv Day, VP-Bus. Dev.
Mike Boyles, VP-Brand Dev., Mktg. & Comm.
Jim Baumgartner, VP-Commercial Strategies
Ron Koper, VP-Bus. Effectiveness
Brent Greenwood, VP-Tubular & Contracts
Robert McClinton, Chmn.

Phone: 403-531-5600 **Fax:** 403-234-7698
Toll-Free:
Address: 300 5th Ave. SW, Ste. 1900, Calgary, AB T2P 3C4 Canada

GROWTH PLANS/SPECIAL FEATURES:

CE Franklin, Ltd. is a leading supplier of pipe, valves, flanges, fittings, production equipment, tubular products and other general industrial supplies to the oil and gas industry in Canada. The company distributes similar products to the oil sands, refining and petrochemical industries and non-oilfield related industries, such as forestry and mining. The firm also offers a full suite of inventory procurement and management services across its 49 Canadian service centers. In addition, it provides sales, marketing, product expertise, logistics, invoicing, credit and collection and other business services through its corporate office in Calgary. The company distributes over 25,000 products from over 2,000 suppliers. Products sold by CE Franklin include tubulars, Dura-branded products, industrial products, valves and valve automation products. Subsidiary CEF Tubulars offers casing, tubing, line pipe, coatings and other complementary products to customers in the energy industry. IPSCO, Inc. manufactures the company's ERW casing, tubing and line pipe. CE Franklin is the exclusive distributor of Dura products in Canada, offering bottom hole pump products, as well as pump tracking, repair and inventory management services. The company's industrial products division provides materials and logistics to industries including pulp and paper; oil and gas; mining and mine processing; petro-chem; waste and water treatment; gas transmission and distribution; and power and utilities. CE Franklin sells a variety of valve brands, including Grove/TK, Nutron, Balon, Argus, PK-Smith, Navco, MA Stewart and Anderson Greenwood/Century. Valve automation products include Leeden, Rotork and Bettis brands, as well as accessory products. In 2009, 83% of the firm's sales were oilfield products, 15% were oil sands products and the remaining 2% were production services.

FINANCIALS: **Sales and profits are in thousands of dollars—add 000 to get the full amount. 2010 Note: Financial information for 2010 was not available for all companies at press time.**

2010 Sales: $	2010 Profits: $	**U.S. Stock Ticker: CFK**
2009 Sales: $419,960	2009 Profits: $6,050	**Int'l Ticker: CFT** Int'l Exchange: Toronto-TSX
2008 Sales: $447,961	2008 Profits: $17,796	Employees: 497
2007 Sales: $475,321	2007 Profits: $13,830	Fiscal Year Ends: 12/31
2006 Sales: $544,100	2006 Profits: $22,500	Parent Company:

SALARIES/BENEFITS:

Pension Plan:	ESOP Stock Plan:	Profit Sharing:	Top Exec. Salary: $395,847	Bonus: $136,836
Savings Plan:	Stock Purch. Plan:		Second Exec. Salary: $283,446	Bonus: $73,305

OTHER THOUGHTS:

Apparent Women Officers or Directors:
Hot Spot for Advancement for Women/Minorities:

LOCATIONS: ("Y" = Yes)

West:	Southwest:	Midwest:	Southeast:	Northeast:	International:
					Y

CENTER OIL COMPANY

www.centeroil.com

Industry Group Code: 486 **Ranks within this company's industry group:** Sales: Profits:

Exploration/Production:		Refining/Retailing:		Utilities:		Alternative Energy:		Specialty Services:		Energy Mktg./Other Svcs.	
Exploration:		Refining:		Electric Utility:		Waste/Solar/Other:		Consulting/Eng.:		Energy Marketing:	Y
Production:		Retailing:		Gas Utility:		Thermal/Steam:		Seismic:		Equipment/Machinery:	
Coal Production:		Convenience Stores:		Pipelines:		Wind:		Drilling:		Oil Field Services:	
		Chemicals:		Water:		Hydro:		InfoTech:		Air/Shipping Transportation:	Y
						Fuel Cells:		Specialty Services:			

TYPES OF BUSINESS:

Oil Products Distribution & Trading
Oil Distribution Terminals
Land- & Water-Based Transportation

BRANDS/DIVISIONS/AFFILIATES:

Center Marketing Company

CONTACTS:

Note: Officers with more than one job title may be intentionally listed here more than once.

Gary R. Parker, Pres.
Rob Kraeger, Mgr.-Sales
Eric Pitts, Mgr.-IT
Michael C. Aufdenspring, General Counsel/Corp. Sec.
Jerry Jost, Mgr.-Oper. & Scheduling
Richard I. Powers, Treas.
Joseph Beck, Controller
Brian Skoff, Mgr.-Finance
Todd Garland, Assistant Mgr.-Finance

Phone: 314-682-3500 **Fax:** 314-682-3599
Toll-Free:
Address: 600 Mason Ridge Ctr. Dr., 2nd. Fl., St. Louis, MO 63141-8557 US

GROWTH PLANS/SPECIAL FEATURES:

Center Oil Company distributes gasoline and other refined petroleum products throughout the U.S. The company owns or has interests in terminals in St. Louis, Missouri; Hartford and Chillicothe, Illinois; Madison, Wisconsin; Indianapolis, Indiana; Cleveland and Toledo, Ohio; Selma, North Carolina; Newark, New Jersey; and Baltimore, Maryland. Central Oil's terminals have a combined capacity of roughly 2.62 million barrels. Among the firm's primary terminal facilities are the Cleveland facility, with a 647,000 barrel capacity; the Newark facility, with a 500,000 barrel capacity; the Toledo facility, with a 207,000 barrel capacity; the Norfolk facility, with a 200,000 barrel capacity; and the Madison facility, with a 150,000 barrel capacity. All of Center Oil's terminals serve its subsidiary, Center Marketing Company, which wholesales refined oil products to end users throughout the area in which the firm maintains inventory. All of the company's terminals have loading facilities to accommodate multiple trucks. Center Oil also markets its products through pipeline transportation and energy storage company Kinder Morgan; the Texas Eastern pipeline system; the Magellan pipeline system; the Kaneb pipeline; and 36 terminals in 10 states. The company utilizes a fleet of ships, barges and trucks to complete its network. Center Oil sells on commitment bases, either by loads per day or by volume over a specified time period.

FINANCIALS:

Sales and profits are in thousands of dollars—add 000 to get the full amount. 2010 Note: Financial information for 2010 was not available for all companies at press time.

2010 Sales: $	2010 Profits: $	**U.S. Stock Ticker: Private**
2009 Sales: $	2009 Profits: $	**Int'l Ticker:** Int'l Exchange:
2008 Sales: $	2008 Profits: $	Employees:
2007 Sales: $	2007 Profits: $	Fiscal Year Ends: 12/31
2006 Sales: $5,400,000	2006 Profits: $	Parent Company:

SALARIES/BENEFITS:

Pension Plan:	ESOP Stock Plan:	Profit Sharing:	Top Exec. Salary: $	Bonus: $
Savings Plan:	Stock Purch. Plan:		Second Exec. Salary: $	Bonus: $

OTHER THOUGHTS:

Apparent Women Officers or Directors: 4
Hot Spot for Advancement for Women/Minorities: Y

LOCATIONS: ("Y" = Yes)

West:	Southwest:	Midwest:	Southeast:	Northeast:	International:
		Y		Y	

CENTERPOINT ENERGY INC

www.centerpointenergy.com

Industry Group Code: 221 **Ranks within this company's industry group:** Sales: 21 Profits: 27

Exploration/Production:		**Refining/Retailing:**		**Utilities:**		**Alternative Energy:**		**Specialty Services:**		**Energy Mktg./Other Svcs.**	
Exploration:		Refining:		Electric Utility:	Y	Waste/Solar/Other:		Consulting/Eng.:		Energy Marketing:	Y
Production:		Retailing:		Gas Utility:	Y	Thermal/Steam:		Seismic:		Equipment/Machinery:	
Coal Production:		Convenience Stores:		Pipelines:	Y	Wind:		Drilling:		Oil Field Services:	
		Chemicals:		Water:		Hydro:		InfoTech:		Air/Shipping Transportation:	
						Fuel Cells:		Specialty Services:	Y		

TYPES OF BUSINESS:

Utilities-Electricity & Natural Gas
Gas Marketing
Pipelines
Field Services
Management Services

BRANDS/DIVISIONS/AFFILIATES:

CenterPoint Houston
CenterPoint Energy Intrastate Pipeline, Inc.
CenterPoint Energy Services, Inc.
CenterPoint Energy Resources Corp.

CONTACTS:

Note: Officers with more than one job title may be intentionally listed here more than once.

David M. McClanahan, CEO
David M. McClanahan, Pres.
Gary L. Whitlock, CFO/Exec. VP
Rick Zapalac, Sr. VP-Eng. & Gas Oper.
Scott Rozzell, General Counsel/Corp. Sec./Exec. VP
Joseph B. McGoldrick, Pres., Gas Oper.
Jim M. Dumler, Sr. VP-CenterPoint Energy, Inc.
Wayne Stinnett, Jr., Pres., CenterPoint Energy Services
Thomas R. Standish, Pres., Regulated Oper.
C. Gregory Harper, Sr. VP/Group Pres., Pipelines & Field Svcs.
Milton Carroll, Chmn.

Phone: 713-207-1111	**Fax:** 713-207-3169
Toll-Free: 800-231-6406	
Address: 1111 Louisiana St., Houston, TX 77002 US	

GROWTH PLANS/SPECIAL FEATURES:

CenterPoint Energy, Inc. (CNP), with approximately $19 billion in assets, is one of the largest combined electricity and natural gas providers in the U.S., serving over 5 million customers across six states. CenterPoint's largest operations are in the Houston metropolitan area. The firm delivers around 69 kilovolts of electricity to retail electric customers throughout its service territory. Through a host of subsidiaries, the company operates in the following business segments: electric transmission and distribution; natural gas distribution; competitive natural gas sales and services; interstate pipelines; field services; and other operations. The company's electricity operations, comprising electric transmission and distribution services, are conducted through subsidiary CenterPoint Houston, which services approximately 2.1 million customers. CenterPoint Houston delivers electricity on behalf of 80 providers over 3,700 miles of transmission lines and 47,000 miles of distribution lines. CenterPoint's natural gas distribution segment engages in regulated intrastate natural gas sales to, and natural gas transportation for, approximately 3.2 million residential, commercial and industrial customers. It is operated by CenterPoint Energy Resources Corp. The competitive natural gas sales and service segment offers variable and fixed-priced physical natural gas supplies primarily to commercial and industrial customers and electric and gas utilities through CenterPoint Energy Services, Inc. and its subsidiary, CenterPoint Energy Intrastate Pipeline LLC. CenterPoint's interstate pipeline segment operates interstate natural gas pipelines with gas transmission lines primarily located in Arkansas, Illinois, Louisiana, Missouri, Oklahoma and Texas. The company's field services segment operates gas gathering, treating and processing facilities, and also provides operating and technical services and remote data monitoring and communication services. The company's other operations include office buildings and other real estate used in business operations.

Employees of CenterPoint are offered medical, dental and vision insurance; life, disability and accident insurance; a 401(k) plan; and a retirement plan.

FINANCIALS:

Sales and profits are in thousands of dollars—add 000 to get the full amount. 2010 Note: Financial information for 2010 was not available for all companies at press time.

2010 Sales: $	2010 Profits: $	**U.S. Stock Ticker: CNP**
2009 Sales: $8,281,000	2009 Profits: $372,000	**Int'l Ticker:** Int'l Exchange:
2008 Sales: $11,322,000	2008 Profits: $447,000	Employees: 8,810
2007 Sales: $9,623,000	2007 Profits: $399,000	Fiscal Year Ends: 7/31
2006 Sales: $9,319,000	2006 Profits: $432,000	Parent Company:

SALARIES/BENEFITS:

Pension Plan: Y	ESOP Stock Plan:	Profit Sharing:	Top Exec. Salary: $1,060,000	Bonus: $954,000
Savings Plan: Y	Stock Purch. Plan:		Second Exec. Salary: $505,000	Bonus: $435,563

OTHER THOUGHTS:

Apparent Women Officers or Directors: 2
Hot Spot for Advancement for Women/Minorities: Y

LOCATIONS: ("Y" = Yes)

West:	Southwest:	Midwest:	Southeast:	Northeast:	International:
	Y	Y	Y		

CENTRAIS ELETRICAS BRASILEIRAS SA (ELECTROBRAS)

www.eletrobras.gov.br

Industry Group Code: 2211 **Ranks within this company's industry group:** Sales: Profits:

Exploration/Production:		**Refining/Retailing:**		**Utilities:**		**Alternative Energy:**		**Specialty Services:**		**Energy Mktg./Other Svcs.**	
Exploration:		Refining:		Electric Utility:	Y	Waste/Solar/Other:		Consulting/Eng.:		Energy Marketing:	
Production:		Retailing:		Gas Utility:		Thermal/Steam:		Seismic:		Equipment/Machinery:	
Coal Production:		Convenience Stores:		Pipelines:		Wind:		Drilling:		Oil Field Services:	
		Chemicals:		Water:		Hydro:		InfoTech:		Air/Shipping Transportation:	
						Fuel Cells:		Specialty Services:			

TYPES OF BUSINESS:

Energy Generation
Energy Transmission
Energy Distribution

BRANDS/DIVISIONS/AFFILIATES:

Companhia de Geracao Termica de Energia Eletrica
Eletrosul
Centrais Eletricas do Norte do Brasil SA
Eletrobas Termonuclear SA
Electric Power Research Center (The)
Eletrobras Participacoes SA
Companhia de Eletricidade do Acre
Companhia Energetica de Alagoas

CONTACTS:

Note: Officers with more than one job title may be intentionally listed here more than once.

Jose A.M. Lopes, CEO
Astrogildo F. Quental, CFO
Ubirajara R. Meira, CTO
Valter L. Cardeal de Souza, Dir.-Eng.
Valter L. Cardeal de Souza, Dir.-Planning
Astrogildo F. Quental, Chief Investor Rel. Officer
Miguel Colasuonno, Managing Dir.
Marcio P. Zimmermann, Chmn.
Flavio Decat de Moura, Dir.-Dist.

Phone: 55-21-2514-5151	**Fax:**
Toll-Free:	
Address: 409 Presidente Vargas Ave., 13th Fl., Rio de Janeiro, RJ 20071-003 Brazil	

GROWTH PLANS/SPECIAL FEATURES:

Centrais Electricas Brasileiras S.A. (Eletrobras) is a Brazilian holding company whose subsidiaries are principally engaged in the hydroelectric, nuclear and fossil fuel electric power industry. Eletrobras is involved in electric power generation and transmission systems in Brazil through six subsidiaries: Eletrosul; Centrais Eletricas do Norte do Brasil S.A. (Eletronorte); Companhia Hidro Eletrica do Sao Francisco (Chesf); Furnas Centrais Eletricas S.A.; Companhia de Geracao Termica de Energia Eletrica (CGTEE); and Eletrobas Termonuclear S.A. (Eletronuclear). In addition, the firm holds 50% ownership of renewable energy generator Itaipu Binacional; and controlling interest in the Electric Power Research Center and Eletrobras Participacoes S.A. In total, the group has a generating capacity of approximately 39,413 megawatts (MW) and generates roughly 38% of the total power used in Brazil. Its system includes over 37,282 miles of transmission lines and 190 substations that have a transformation capacity of roughly 160,000 megavolt amperes (MVA). Eletrobras is involved in energy distribution through its controlling interest in the following companies: Companhia de Eletricidade do Acre; Companhia Energetica de Alagoas (Ceal); Amazonas Energia; Companhia Energetica do Piaui (Cepisa); Centrais Eletricas de Rondonia S.A.(Ceron); and Boa Vista Energia. In May 2009, Eletrobras openED a new office in Lima, Peru. In August 2009, Eletronuclear opened two new nuclear facilities in Recife, Brazil.

FINANCIALS:

Sales and profits are in thousands of dollars—add 000 to get the full amount. 2010 Note: Financial information for 2010 was not available for all companies at press time.

2010 Sales: $	2010 Profits: $	**U.S. Stock Ticker:**
2009 Sales: $	2009 Profits: $	**Int'l Ticker: ELET6** Int'l Exchange: Sao Paulo-SAO
2008 Sales: $	2008 Profits: $	Employees:
2007 Sales: $	2007 Profits: $	Fiscal Year Ends: 12/31
2006 Sales: $	2006 Profits: $	Parent Company:

SALARIES/BENEFITS:

Pension Plan:	ESOP Stock Plan:	Profit Sharing:	Top Exec. Salary: $	Bonus: $
Savings Plan:	Stock Purch. Plan:		Second Exec. Salary: $	Bonus: $

OTHER THOUGHTS:

Apparent Women Officers or Directors: 2
Hot Spot for Advancement for Women/Minorities:

LOCATIONS: ("Y" = Yes)

West:	Southwest:	Midwest:	Southeast:	Northeast:	International:
					Y

CENTRICA PLC

www.centrica.co.uk

Industry Group Code: 221 **Ranks within this company's industry group:** Sales: 3 Profits: 12

Exploration/Production:		Refining/Retailing:		Utilities:		Alternative Energy:		Specialty Services:		Energy Mktg./Other Svcs.	
Exploration:		Refining:		Electric Utility:	Y	Waste/Solar/Other:		Consulting/Eng.:		Energy Marketing:	Y
Production:	Y	Retailing:		Gas Utility:	Y	Thermal/Steam:		Seismic:		Equipment/Machinery:	Y
Coal Production:		Convenience Stores:		Pipelines:		Wind:	Y	Drilling:		Oil Field Services:	
		Chemicals:		Water:		Hydro:		InfoTech:		Air/Shipping Transportation:	
						Fuel Cells:		Specialty Services:	Y		

TYPES OF BUSINESS:

Utilities-Electricity & Natural Gas
Telecommunications Services
Energy Storage
Heating & Gas Appliance Installation & Maintenance
Gas Production
Energy Marketing
Home Security Systems
Wind Generation

BRANDS/DIVISIONS/AFFILIATES:

British Gas
Scottish Gas
Nwy Prydain
Centrica Energy
Centrica Storage
British Energy Group plc

CONTACTS:

Note: Officers with more than one job title may be intentionally listed here more than once.

Sam H. Laidlaw, CEO
Nick Luff, Dir.-Finance
Anne Minto, Dir.-Human Resources
Grant Dawson, General Counsel/Company Sec.
Catherine May, Dir.-Corp. Affairs
Phil Bentley, Managing Dir.-British Gas Svcs.
Mark Hanafin, Managing Dir.-Centrica Energy
Roger M. Carr, Chmn.
Chris Weston, Managing Dir.-North America

Phone: 44-1753-494-000 **Fax:** 44-1753-494-001
Toll-Free:
Address: Millstream, Maidenhead Rd., Windsor, SL4 5GD UK

GROWTH PLANS/SPECIAL FEATURES:

Centrica plc is a leading supplier of natural gas and electricity in the U.K. Through British Gas, the company provides natural gas (under the British Gas, Scottish Gas and Nwy Prydain brands) and electricity to business and residential customers. Its British Gas Business division develops products and services tailored for its commercial customers. Through its HomeCare brand, British Gas is a leading domestic central heating and gas appliance installation company. It also provides maintenance and breakdown coverage for central heating and gas appliances, plumbing and drains, home electrics and kitchen appliances. Through Centrica Energy, the company sources the gas and electricity to supply customers through its own upstream gas production and electricity generation facilities, as well as through wholesale and gas trading activities. Through Centrica Storage, the firm provides gas storage services for a wide range of customers, including other businesses within the group. In North America, Centrica is active in the energy supply sector through its Direct Energy subsidiary, which owns and operates approximately 4,500 natural gas wells in the Canadian province of Alberta, as well as maintaining several gas-fired power plants and wind power purchase agreements in the U.S. Centrica operates in the Netherlands through the Oxxio brand; in Germany through Centrica Energie; and in Norway through its interest in the Statfjord oil and gas field. The company also has license blocks in Egypt and Nigeria, and another in Trinidad. In August 2009, Centrica acquired oil and gas producer Venture Productions for an estimated $2 billion. In June 2010, the firm's Direct Energy subsidiary acquired Clockwork Home Services, Inc. for $183 million. In October 2010, Direct Energy acquired certain Canadian natural gas assets from Suncor Energy for approximately $367.5 million.

The company offers its employees a pension plan, flexible spending account, childcare allowances and private medical vouchers.

FINANCIALS:

Sales and profits are in thousands of dollars—add 000 to get the full amount. 2010 Note: Financial information for 2010 was not available for all companies at press time.

2010 Sales: $	2010 Profits: $	**U.S. Stock Ticker:**
2009 Sales: $31,910,700	2009 Profits: $1,226,270	**Int'l Ticker: CNA** Int'l Exchange: London-LSE
2008 Sales: $30,352,600	2008 Profits: $-199,050	Employees: 32,817
2007 Sales: $26,769,720	2007 Profits: $2,475,940	Fiscal Year Ends: 12/31
2006 Sales: $32,310,300	2006 Profits: $-301,600	Parent Company:

SALARIES/BENEFITS:

Pension Plan: Y	ESOP Stock Plan:	Profit Sharing:	Top Exec. Salary: $1,468,026	Bonus: $1,456,795
Savings Plan:	Stock Purch. Plan:		Second Exec. Salary: $975,475	Bonus: $956,222

OTHER THOUGHTS:

Apparent Women Officers or Directors: 4
Hot Spot for Advancement for Women/Minorities: Y

LOCATIONS: ("Y" = Yes)

West:	Southwest:	Midwest:	Southeast:	Northeast:	International:
	Y		Y	Y	Y

CEYLON PETROLEUM CORP (CPC)

www.ceypetco.gov.lk

Industry Group Code: 211111 **Ranks within this company's industry group:** Sales: Profits:

Exploration/Production:		Refining/Retailing:		Utilities:		Alternative Energy:		Specialty Services:		Energy Mktg./Other Svcs.	
Exploration:	Y	Refining:	Y	Electric Utility:		Waste/Solar/Other:		Consulting/Eng.:		Energy Marketing:	
Production:		Retailing:		Gas Utility:		Thermal/Steam:		Seismic:		Equipment/Machinery:	
Coal Production:		Convenience Stores:		Pipelines:		Wind:		Drilling:		Oil Field Services:	
		Chemicals:		Water:		Hydro:		InfoTech:		Air/Shipping Transportation:	
						Fuel Cells:		Specialty Services:			

TYPES OF BUSINESS:

Oil Refining & Marketing
Oil Imports
Petrochemicals
Oil Sales
Oil Distribution
Oil Exploration

BRANDS/DIVISIONS/AFFILIATES:

Ceypetco Agro
Ceypetco Aviation

GROWTH PLANS/SPECIAL FEATURES:

Ceylon Petroleum Corp. (CPC) is a Sri Lankan government-owned importer, exporter, seller, supplier and distributor of petroleum products. The firm offers agricultural chemicals via Ceypetco Agro; aviation refueling services via Ceypetco Aviation; and oil refining with a capacity of 51,000 barrels per day. The company's products include unleaded gasoline, diesel, several grades of furnace oil, naphtha and liquefied petroleum gas (LPG). Ceypetco Agro's products include insecticides, herbicides and fungicides. To a lesser extent, CPC is also involved in oil exploration, having drilled seven exploratory wells and conducted several seismic surveys in Sri Lanka both on and offshore. CPC supplies Sri Lanka through a network of 800 dealers.

CONTACTS:

Note: Officers with more than one job title may be intentionally listed here more than once.

D.H.S. Jayawardena, Managing Dir.
R.T.A. Dabare, Acting Deputy Gen. Mgr.-Finance
D.S.L. Muhamdiramge, Mgr.-Retail Mktg.
S.W.Gamage, Deputy Gen. Mgr.-Human Resources
H.Samarawickrama, Mgr.-Eng.
S.W.Gamage, Deputy Gen. Mgr.-Admin.
G. De Fonseka, Chief Legal Officer
R. Wickramasinghe, Deputy Gen. Mgr.-Planning & Dev.
B.C. Jayawardana, Mgr.-Refinery
A. Lambiyas, Mgr.-Agro Chemicals
P.H.N. Samarasinghe, Corp. Sec.
M.R.S.P. Samarasinghe, Mgr.-Security & Investigation
D.H.S. Jayawardena, Chmn.
H. Seneviratne, Mgr.-Supplies

Phone: 94-11-247-3644 **Fax:** 94-11-247-3979
Toll-Free:
Address: No.109, Rotunda Tower, Galle Rd., Colombo, Sri Lanka

FINANCIALS:

Sales and profits are in thousands of dollars—add 000 to get the full amount. 2010 Note: Financial information for 2010 was not available for all companies at press time.

2010 Sales: $	2010 Profits: $	**U.S. Stock Ticker: Government-Owned**
2009 Sales: $	2009 Profits: $	**Int'l Ticker:** Int'l Exchange:
2008 Sales: $	2008 Profits: $	Employees:
2007 Sales: $	2007 Profits: $	Fiscal Year Ends:
2006 Sales: $	2006 Profits: $	Parent Company:

SALARIES/BENEFITS:

Pension Plan:	ESOP Stock Plan:	Profit Sharing:	Top Exec. Salary: $	Bonus: $
Savings Plan:	Stock Purch. Plan:		Second Exec. Salary: $	Bonus: $

OTHER THOUGHTS:

Apparent Women Officers or Directors: 4
Hot Spot for Advancement for Women/Minorities: Y

LOCATIONS: ("Y" = Yes)

West:	Southwest:	Midwest:	Southeast:	Northeast:	International:
					Y

CEZ AS

www.cez.cz

Industry Group Code: 2211 **Ranks within this company's industry group:** Sales: 19 Profits: 5

Exploration/Production:		Refining/Retailing:		Utilities:		Alternative Energy:		Specialty Services:		Energy Mktg./Other Svcs.	
Exploration:		Refining:	Y	Electric Utility:	Y	Waste/Solar/Other:	Y	Consulting/Eng.:		Energy Marketing:	
Production:	Y	Retailing:		Gas Utility:	Y	Thermal/Steam:	Y	Seismic:		Equipment/Machinery:	
Coal Production:		Convenience Stores:		Pipelines:		Wind:	Y	Drilling:		Oil Field Services:	
		Chemicals:		Water:		Hydro:	Y	InfoTech:		Air/Shipping Transportation:	
						Fuel Cells:		Specialty Services:	Y		

TYPES OF BUSINESS:

Electricity Generation & Distribution
Heat Generation & Distribution

BRANDS/DIVISIONS/AFFILIATES:

CEZ Trade Albania
CEZ International Finance
CEZ Group
CEZ Prodej, s.r.o.

CONTACTS:

Note: Officers with more than one job title may be intentionally listed here more than once.

Martin Roman, CEO
Daniel Benes, COO
Martin Novak, CFO
Alan Svoboda, Chief Sales Officer
Hana Krbcova, Chief Personnel Officer
Ivan Lapin, Chief Admin. Officer
Vladimir Schmaz, Dir.-Mergers & Acquisitions
Peter Bodnar, Chief Investment Officer
Vladimir Hlavinka, Chief Prod. Officer
Martin Roman, Chmn.
Tomas Pleskac, CEO-Int'l Div.
Jiri Kudrnac, Chief Dist. Officer

Phone: 420-2-11041111	**Fax:** 420-2-11042001
Toll-Free:	
Address: Duhova 2/1444, Prague, 140 53 Czech Republic	

GROWTH PLANS/SPECIAL FEATURES:

CEZ a.s. is a Czech company engaged in the production, sale and related maintenance and support of electricity and heat generation. The firm, through its CEZ Group subsidiary, is also engaged in telecommunications, informatics, nuclear research, planning, construction and maintenance of energy facilities, mining raw materials, and processing energy by-products. CEZ a.s. serves approximately 7 million customers in the Czech Republic, Bulgaria and Poland and is capable of generating over 60,000 GWh of electricity via 33 hydropower plants, 18 coal power plants, two nuclear power plants, three wind farms, seven solar power generating facilities and one combined cycle and gas-fired power plant. The company has a considerable international presence through its nearly 120 subsidiaries and associates. The bulk of the company's activities are concentrated in Eastern Europe with operations in Poland, Bulgaria, Romania, Turkey, Germany and Hungary. In November 2009, CEZ began operating a photovoltaic power plant in southern Moravia. Covering an area roughly the size of 10 soccer fields, the facility has an installed power capacity of 3.73 megawatts. In January 2010, the firm, through subsidiary CEZ Prodej, s.r.o., began supplying natural gas to end consumers in the Czech Republic. In June 2010, the company completed the first phase of the Fantanele-Cogealac wind farm in Romania, initiating a preliminary 139 wind turbines of a planned 240.

FINANCIALS:

Sales and profits are in thousands of dollars—add 000 to get the full amount. 2010 Note: Financial information for 2010 was not available for all companies at press time.

2010 Sales: $	2010 Profits: $	**U.S. Stock Ticker:**
2009 Sales: $10,798,200	2009 Profits: $2,937,940	**Int'l Ticker: CEZ** Int'l Exchange: Frankfurt-Euronext
2008 Sales: $9,842,180	2008 Profits: $2,578,300	Employees: 30,768
2007 Sales: $7,650,000	2007 Profits: $1,330,000	Fiscal Year Ends: 12/31
2006 Sales: $7,472,100	2006 Profits: $1,384,900	Parent Company:

SALARIES/BENEFITS:

Pension Plan:	ESOP Stock Plan:	Profit Sharing:	Top Exec. Salary: $	Bonus: $
Savings Plan:	Stock Purch. Plan:		Second Exec. Salary: $	Bonus: $

OTHER THOUGHTS:

Apparent Women Officers or Directors:
Hot Spot for Advancement for Women/Minorities:

LOCATIONS: ("Y" = Yes)

West:	Southwest:	Midwest:	Southeast:	Northeast:	International:
					Y

CGGVERITAS

www.cggveritas.com

Industry Group Code: 541360 **Ranks within this company's industry group:** Sales: 1 Profits: 3

Exploration/Production:		Refining/Retailing:		Utilities:		Alternative Energy:		Specialty Services:		Energy Mktg./Other Svcs.	
Exploration:		Refining:		Electric Utility:		Waste/Solar/Other:		Consulting/Eng.:	Y	Energy Marketing:	
Production:		Retailing:		Gas Utility:		Thermal/Steam:		Seismic:	Y	Equipment/Machinery:	Y
Coal Production:		Convenience Stores:		Pipelines:		Wind:		Drilling:		Oil Field Services:	Y
		Chemicals:		Water:		Hydro:		InfoTech:	Y	Air/Shipping Transportation:	
						Fuel Cells:		Specialty Services:			

TYPES OF BUSINESS:

Seismic Data Acquisition & Processing
Seismic Data Library
Quest Geo Solutions Limited

BRANDS/DIVISIONS/AFFILIATES:

Metrolog
Sercel
Petrobras

CONTACTS:

Note: Officers with more than one job title may be intentionally listed here more than once.

Jean-Georges Malcor, CEO
Lionel Lhommet, Exec. VP-Geomarkets & Global Mktg.
Gilles Garczynski, Exec. VP-Human Resources
Colin Murdoch, Exec. VP-Processing, Imaging & Reservoir Div.
Thierry Brizard, Exec. VP-Tech.
Gerard Chambovet, Exec. VP/Gen. Sec.
Dominique Robert, Exec. VP-Global Oper. Excellence
Thierry Le Roux, Exec. VP-Bus. Dev.
Stephane-Paul Frydman, Exec. VP-Finance & Strategy
Stephen Midenet, Exec. VP-Land Div.
Pascal Rouiller, Exec. VP-Equipment Div./CEO-Sercel
Benoit Ribadeau-Dumas, Exec. VP-Marine Div.
Robert Brunck, Chmn.

Phone: 33-16-447-4500	**Fax:** 33-16-447-3431
Toll-Free:	
Address: Tour Maine Montparnasse 33 Ave., Du Maine BP 191, Paris, I0 75015 France	

GROWTH PLANS/SPECIAL FEATURES:

CGGVeritas provides seismic survey planning and design, seismic data acquisition, data processing, multi-client data surveys and information services to the oil and gas industry. The firm operates up to 30 land and marine crews in North and South America and the Middle East and has a fleet of 21 vessels, with 14 high capacity 3D vessels, four mid capacity 3D vessels and three 2D vessels. The firm acquires seismic data in land, marsh, swamp, tidal and marine environments; processes data acquired by its own crews and crews of other operators; and provides comprehensive data management, mapping services and products. Oil and gas companies utilize seismic data to determine suitable locations for drilling exploratory wells and, increasingly, for reservoir management of oil and gas reserves. The company works both on a contractual basis and on a non-exclusive basis for multiple customers. On a contract basis, CGGVeritas acquires and processes data for a single client who pays the company to conduct the survey and is given sole use of the acquired data. The company also acquires and processes data for its own library for multiple clients. In response to the high cost of individual research, the firm has built a large library of surveys consisting of approximately 124,300 line miles of 2D data and 130,500 square miles of 3D data, as well as a marine data library that includes surveys in the Gulf of Mexico and other areas. Through subsidiary Sercel, the company provides geophysical equipment, including seismic acquisition systems and specialized equipment in the land and marine seismic markets. In June 2010, the firm entered a technology cooperation agreement with Brazil's Petrobras for geophysics research to be carried out at a new CGGVeritas Technology Center in Rio de Janeiro.

The company offers its employees tuition reimbursement, training programs, service and safety awards, credit union membership, a performance appraisal plan and the opportunity to work overseas.

FINANCIALS:

Sales and profits are in thousands of dollars—add 000 to get the full amount. 2010 Note: Financial information for 2010 was not available for all companies at press time.

2010 Sales: $	2010 Profits: $	**U.S. Stock Ticker: CGV**
2009 Sales: $3,118,460	2009 Profits: $-361,530	**Int'l Ticker:** Int'l Exchange:
2008 Sales: $3,825,590	2008 Profits: $489,590	Employees: 7,509
2007 Sales: $3,751,100	2007 Profits: $387,900	Fiscal Year Ends: 7/31
2006 Sales: $2,100,800	2006 Profits: $248,200	Parent Company:

SALARIES/BENEFITS:

Pension Plan:	ESOP Stock Plan:	Profit Sharing: Y	Top Exec. Salary: $724,360	Bonus: $
Savings Plan: Y	Stock Purch. Plan: Y		Second Exec. Salary: $557,200	Bonus: $

OTHER THOUGHTS:

Apparent Women Officers or Directors: 1
Hot Spot for Advancement for Women/Minorities:

LOCATIONS: ("Y" = Yes)

West:	Southwest:	Midwest:	Southeast:	Northeast:	International:
	Y				Y

CH ENERGY GROUP INC

www.chenergygroup.com

Industry Group Code: 221 **Ranks within this company's industry group:** Sales: 52 Profits: 48

Exploration/Production:		Refining/Retailing:		Utilities:		Alternative Energy:		Specialty Services:		Energy Mktg./Other Svcs.	
Exploration:		Refining:		Electric Utility:	Y	Waste/Solar/Other:	Y	Consulting/Eng.:	Y	Energy Marketing:	Y
Production:		Retailing:		Gas Utility:	Y	Thermal/Steam:		Seismic:		Equipment/Machinery:	
Coal Production:		Convenience Stores:		Pipelines:		Wind:		Drilling:		Oil Field Services:	
		Chemicals:		Water:		Hydro:		InfoTech:		Air/Shipping Transportation:	
						Fuel Cells:		Specialty Services:	Y		

TYPES OF BUSINESS:

Utilities-Electricity & Natural Gas
Retail & Wholesale Energy Marketing
Energy Management Services
Fuel Distribution Services
Alternative Energy Ventures

BRANDS/DIVISIONS/AFFILIATES:

Central Hudson Gas & Electric Corporation
Central Hudson Enterprises Corporation
Griffith Energy Services, Inc.
CH-Auburn Energy LLC
CH-Greentree LLC
CH-Lyonsdale LLC
CH Shirley Wind LLC

CONTACTS: *Note: Officers with more than one job title may be intentionally listed here more than once.*

Steven V. Lant, CEO
Steven V. Lant, Pres.
Christopher M. Capone, CFO/Exec. VP
Joseph J. Devirgilio, Jr., Exec. VP-Corp. Svcs. & Admin.
John E. Gould, General Counsel/Exec. VP
Denise D. VanBuren, VP-Corp. Comm./Corp. Sec.
Kimberly J. Wright, VP-Acct./Controller
Stacey A. Renner, Treas.
Christopher M. Capone, Pres., Central Hudson Enterprises Corp.
Joseph J. DeVirgilio, Jr., Exec. VP
Joseph A. Koczko, Assistant Sec.
Steven V. Lant, Chmn.

Phone: 845-452-2000	**Fax:**
Toll-Free:	
Address: 284 South Ave., Poughkeepsie, NY 12601 US	

GROWTH PLANS/SPECIAL FEATURES:

CH Energy Group is a holding company for two wholly-owned subsidiaries: Central Hudson Gas & Electric Corporation (Central Hudson) and Central Hudson Enterprises Corporation (CHEC). Through these subsidiaries, the company serves more than 450,000 customers. Central Hudson is a regulated natural gas and electric utility that purchases, sells at wholesale and distributes electricity and natural gas to approximately 374,000 customers in a 2,600-square-mile service area covering eight counties of New York State's Mid-Hudson River Valley. CHEC, through its subsidiaries, markets petroleum products and related services to retail and wholesale customers; and provides service and maintenance of energy conservation measures and generation systems for private businesses, institutions, and government entities. It also participates in cogeneration, wind generation, biomass energy projects, landfill gas projects and alternate fuel and energy production projects in New Jersey, New Hampshire, New York, Wisconsin and Pennsylvania, and a corn-ethanol plant in Nebraska. CHEC's subsidiaries include Griffith Energy Service, Inc.; CH-Auburn Energy LLC; CH-Greentree LLC; CH-Lyonsdale LLC; CH Shirley Wind LLC; and others. Griffith Energy Services is an energy services company engaged in fuel distribution, including heating oil, gasoline, diesel fuel, kerosene, and propane, and the installation and maintenance of heating, ventilating, and air conditioning equipment. CHEC's other subsidiaries consist of the company's equity interest in several electric generating plants, wind projects and other renewable energy projects and partnerships. In November 2009, Griffith Energy Services sold its divisions serving certain markets in Rhode Island, Connecticut and Pennsylvania to Superior Plus, based in Canada.

FINANCIALS: **Sales and profits are in thousands of dollars—add 000 to get the full amount. 2010 Note: Financial information for 2010 was not available for all companies at press time.**

2010 Sales: $	2010 Profits: $	**U.S. Stock Ticker: CHG**
2009 Sales: $931,589	2009 Profits: $43,484	**Int'l Ticker:** Int'l Exchange:
2008 Sales: $1,139,201	2008 Profits: $35,081	Employees:
2007 Sales: $1,196,757	2007 Profits: $42,636	Fiscal Year Ends: 12/31
2006 Sales: $993,433	2006 Profits: $43,084	Parent Company:

SALARIES/BENEFITS:

Pension Plan:	ESOP Stock Plan:	Profit Sharing:	Top Exec. Salary: $525,000	Bonus: $472,650
Savings Plan:	Stock Purch. Plan:		Second Exec. Salary: $309,000	Bonus: $152,669

OTHER THOUGHTS:

Apparent Women Officers or Directors: 4
Hot Spot for Advancement for Women/Minorities: Y

LOCATIONS: ("Y" = Yes)

West:	Southwest:	Midwest:	Southeast:	Northeast:	International:
				Y	

CHC HELICOPTER CORP

www.chc.ca

Industry Group Code: 481211 **Ranks within this company's industry group:** Sales: Profits:

Exploration/Production:		Refining/Retailing:		Utilities:		Alternative Energy:		Specialty Services:		Energy Mktg./Other Svcs.	
Exploration:		Refining:		Electric Utility:		Waste/Solar/Other:		Consulting/Eng.:		Energy Marketing:	
Production:		Retailing:		Gas Utility:		Thermal/Steam:		Seismic:		Equipment/Machinery:	
Coal Production:		Convenience Stores:		Pipelines:		Wind:		Drilling:		Oil Field Services:	
		Chemicals:		Water:		Hydro:		InfoTech:		Air/Shipping Transportation:	Y
						Fuel Cells:		Specialty Services:	Y		

TYPES OF BUSINESS:

Helicopter Charter Service
Air Ambulance Services
Search & Rescue Services
Helicopter Repair & Overhaul
Aerospace Components Manufacturing
Helicopter Support Services

BRANDS/DIVISIONS/AFFILIATES:

Heli-One
CHC Composites
First Reserve
EEA Helicopters

CONTACTS: *Note: Officers with more than one job title may be intentionally listed here more than once.*

William Amelio, CEO
William Amelio, Pres.
Frederick Davis, CFO/Sr. VP
Rick O. Green, CIO/VP
Martin Lockyer, VP-Legal Svcs./Corp. Sec.
Christine Baird, Pres., Global Oper.
Michael Nagel, Dir.-Bus. Dev.
Andrew Huige, Mgr.-Comm.
John Hanbury, Treas.
G. Blake Fizzard, VP-Financial Structuring
Annette Cusworth, VP-Financial Svcs.
Neil Calvert, Pres., Heli-One
Greg Wyght, VP-Safety & Quality
Tilmann Gabriel, Pres., European Oper.

Phone: 604-276-7500	**Fax:** 604-279-2474
Toll-Free:	
Address: 4740 Agar Dr., Richmond, BC V7B 1A3 Canada	

GROWTH PLANS/SPECIAL FEATURES:

CHC Helicopter Corp. (CHC) is leading offshore helicopter service company serving oil and gas companies around the world. CHC is a wholly-owned subsidiary of the investment firm First Reserve. The company maintains a fleet of 233 (123 medium, 107 heavy, three light) helicopters and 19 fixed-wing aircraft, which transport workers and material to offshore rigs. CHC organizes its operations into three divisions: CHC Global Operations; CHC European Operations; and Heli-One. Through these divisions the company provides its customers with aircraft, pilots, maintenance, insurance, logistics support and training. CHC has operations in more than 30 countries, including most emerging and expanding offshore markets. In addition, it provides non-military helicopter services to the United Nations. The company's European Operations service 55% of the market in the North Sea, the largest offshore market in the world. Through its Heli-One division the company provides helicopter related support services such as leasing, logistics, maintenance, engineering, inventory management and safety equipment to independent customers worldwide. The Heli-One division is also a leading provider of global air ambulance and search and rescue helicopter services. CHC Global Operations is based in Vancouver, and operates approximately 150 helicopters and fixed-wing aircraft that provide service to nearly every petroleum market in the world. Among the company's partially and wholly-owned subsidiaries are EEA Helicopter Operations and CHC Composites. EEA Helicopters is a Dutch company of which CHC is a minority holders; EEA is the largest helicopter provider in the North Sea. CHC Composites, based in Newfoundland, maintains the only purpose-built facility in North America for building advanced composite and bonded metal components for the aerospace industry; CHC Composites is a wholly-owned subsidy of CHC.

The company provides its employees with medical coverage; flexible spending account; tuition assistance; a pension account; and an employee assistance program.

FINANCIALS: **Sales and profits are in thousands of dollars—add 000 to get the full amount. 2010 Note: Financial information for 2010 was not available for all companies at press time.**

2010 Sales: $	2010 Profits: $	**U.S. Stock Ticker: Subsidiary**
2009 Sales: $	2009 Profits: $	**Int'l Ticker: FLY** Int'l Exchange: Toronto-TSX
2008 Sales: $	2008 Profits: $	Employees:
2007 Sales: $1,029,700	2007 Profits: $29,500	Fiscal Year Ends: 4/30
2006 Sales: $892,361	2006 Profits: $80,010	Parent Company: FIRST RESERVE CORPORATION

SALARIES/BENEFITS:

Pension Plan:	ESOP Stock Plan:	Profit Sharing:	Top Exec. Salary: $	Bonus: $2,739,204
Savings Plan:	Stock Purch. Plan:		Second Exec. Salary: $	Bonus: $

OTHER THOUGHTS:

Apparent Women Officers or Directors: 1
Hot Spot for Advancement for Women/Minorities:

LOCATIONS: ("Y" = Yes)

West:	Southwest:	Midwest:	Southeast:	Northeast:	International:
					Y

CHENIERE ENERGY INC

www.cheniere.com

Industry Group Code: 211111 **Ranks within this company's industry group:** Sales: 103 Profits: 94

Exploration/Production:		Refining/Retailing:		Utilities:		Alternative Energy:		Specialty Services:		Energy Mktg./Other Svcs.	
Exploration:	Y	Refining:		Electric Utility:		Waste/Solar/Other:		Consulting/Eng.:		Energy Marketing:	Y
Production:	Y	Retailing:		Gas Utility:		Thermal/Steam:		Seismic:		Equipment/Machinery:	
Coal Production:		Convenience Stores:		Pipelines:	Y	Wind:		Drilling:	Y	Oil Field Services:	
		Chemicals:		Water:		Hydro:		InfoTech:		Air/Shipping Transportation:	Y
						Fuel Cells:		Specialty Services:	Y		

TYPES OF BUSINESS:

Liquid Natural Gas Receiving Terminals
Natural Gas Pipelines
Liquid Natural Gas & Natural Gas Marketing
Oil & Gas Exploration & Development
Conversion of Gas to LNG
LNG Export

BRANDS/DIVISIONS/AFFILIATES:

Cheniere Marketing, Inc.
Cheniere Pipeline, LLC
Sabine Pass LNG
Creole Trail Pipeline
Cheniere Energy Partners L.P.
LNG Development L.P.

CONTACTS:

Note: Officers with more than one job title may be intentionally listed here more than once.

Charif Souki, CEO
Charif Souki, Pres.
Meg Gentle, CFO/Sr. VP
Davis Thames, Sr. VP-Mktg.
Ann Raden, VP-Human Resources
Scott Abshire, CIO/VP
Darron Granger, VP-Eng. & Construction
Ann Raden, VP-Admin.
Timothy J. Neumann, General Counsel/VP
Patricia Outtrim, VP-Gov't & Regulatory Affairs
Katie Pipkin, VP-Investor Rel. & Finance
Jerry Smith, Chief Acct. Officer/VP
Graham A. McArthur, Treas./VP
Anne V. Vaughan, Corp. Sec./Asst. General Counsel
R. Keith Teague, Sr. VP-Asset Group
Charif Souki, Chmn.
Jean Abiteboul, Sr. VP-Int'l

Phone: 713-375-5000 **Fax:** 713-375-6000
Toll-Free:
Address: 700 Milam St., Ste. 800, Houston, TX 77002 US

GROWTH PLANS/SPECIAL FEATURES:

Cheniere Energy, Inc. develops, constructs, owns and operates a network of three onshore liquid natural gas (LNG) receiving terminals and related natural gas pipelines along the Gulf Coast of the U.S. The company operates in three segments: LNG receiving terminal, natural gas pipeline and LNG and natural gas marketing. Through the LNG receiving terminal segment, Cheniere focuses on development efforts of three LNG receiving terminals: Sabine Pass LNG in western Cameron Parish, Louisiana; Corpus Christi LNG near Corpus Christi, Texas; and Creole Trail LNG in central Cameron Parish, Louisiana. The natural gas pipeline segment, through subsidiary Grand Cheniere Pipeline, LLC, develops natural gas pipelines that provide access to North American natural gas markets for customers in the Sabine Pass, Corpus Christi and Creole Trail LNG receiving terminals. The LNG and natural gas marketing segment, operating as Cheniere Marketing, Inc., is designed to purchase LNG from international suppliers, arrange its transportation to the company's receiving terminals, utilize the reserve capacity to revaporize LNG and finally, to transport and sell it on the North American market. The firm also has oil and gas exploration, development and exploitation activities, with interests in 15 active wells and three non-producing wells. In April 2010, Cheniere agreed to sell its 30% limited partner interest in Freeport LNG Development L.P. to Zachry American Infrastructure, LLC for net proceeds of $104 million. In September 2010, the firm announced that its Cheniere Energy Partners LP subsidiary received regulatory approval to export LNG from its Louisiana terminal. Along with importing and regasifiying LNG at its Sabine Pass facility, Cheniere would receive gas produced in North America, convert it to LNG and export it to other nations.

Employees are offered medical, dental and vision insurance; disability coverage; life insurance; and a 401(k) plan.

FINANCIALS:

Sales and profits are in thousands of dollars—add 000 to get the full amount. 2010 Note: Financial information for 2010 was not available for all companies at press time.

2010 Sales: $	2010 Profits: $	**U.S. Stock Ticker: LNG**
2009 Sales: $181,126	2009 Profits: $-161,490	**Int'l Ticker:** Int'l Exchange:
2008 Sales: $7,144	2008 Profits: $-372,959	Employees: 98
2007 Sales: $ 647	2007 Profits: $-181,777	Fiscal Year Ends: 12/31
2006 Sales: $2,371	2006 Profits: $-145,853	Parent Company:

SALARIES/BENEFITS:

Pension Plan:	ESOP Stock Plan:	Profit Sharing:	Top Exec. Salary: $722,794	Bonus: $1,080,000
Savings Plan: Y	Stock Purch. Plan:		Second Exec. Salary: $328,266	Bonus: $299,030

OTHER THOUGHTS:

Apparent Women Officers or Directors: 6
Hot Spot for Advancement for Women/Minorities: Y

LOCATIONS: ("Y" = Yes)

West:	Southwest:	Midwest:	Southeast:	Northeast:	International:
	Y		Y		Y

CHESAPEAKE ENERGY CORP

www.chk.com

Industry Group Code: 211111 **Ranks within this company's industry group:** Sales: 55 Profits: 109

Exploration/Production:		Refining/Retailing:		Utilities:		Alternative Energy:		Specialty Services:		Energy Mktg./Other Svcs.	
Exploration:	Y	Refining:		Electric Utility:		Waste/Solar/Other:		Consulting/Eng.:		Energy Marketing:	
Production:	Y	Retailing:		Gas Utility:		Thermal/Steam:		Seismic:		Equipment/Machinery:	
Coal Production:		Convenience Stores:		Pipelines:		Wind:		Drilling:		Oil Field Services:	
		Chemicals:		Water:		Hydro:		InfoTech:		Air/Shipping Transportation:	
						Fuel Cells:		Specialty Services:			

TYPES OF BUSINESS:

Oil & Gas Exploration & Production

BRANDS/DIVISIONS/AFFILIATES:

Chesapeake Energy Marketing, Inc.
Chesapeake Midstream
Compass Manufacturing LLC
Diamond Y Enterprise, Inc.
MidCon Compression LLC
Chesapeake Midstream Partners LLC

CONTACTS: *Note: Officers with more than one job title may be intentionally listed here more than once.*

Aubrey K. McClendon, CEO
Steven C. Dixon, COO
Marcus C. Rowland, CFO/Exec. VP
James C. Johnson, Sr. VP-Energy Mktg.
Martha A. Burger, Sr. VP-Human & Corp. Resources
Jeffrey L. Mobley, Sr. VP-Research
Cathy L. Tompkins, CIO/Sr. VP-IT
Jeffrey A. Fisher, Sr. VP-Prod.
Henry J. Hood, General Counsel/Sr. VP-Land & Legal
Steven C. Dixon, Exec. VP-Oper. & Geosciences
Thomas S. Price, Jr., Sr. VP-Corp. Dev. & Gov't Rel.
Jim Gipson, Dir.-Media Rel.
Jeffrey L. Mobley, Sr. VP-Investor Rel.
Jennifer M. Grigsby, Treas./Sr. VP/Corp. Sec.
J. Mike Stice, CEO-Chesapeake Midstream Partners LP
Douglas J. Jacobson, Exec. VP-Acquisitions & Divestitures
Stephen W. Miller, Sr. VP-Drilling
Michael A. Johnson, Chief Acct. Officer/Controller/Sr. VP-Acct.
Aubrey K. McClendon, Chmn.

Phone: 405-935-8000	**Fax:** 405-843-0573
Toll-Free: 877-245-1427	
Address: 6100 N. Western Ave., Oklahoma City, OK 73118 US	

GROWTH PLANS/SPECIAL FEATURES:

Chesapeake Energy Corp. is one of the leading producers of natural gas in the U.S. The company owns interests in about 44,100 producing oil and natural gas wells that are currently producing roughly 2.4 billion cubic feet equivalent (bcfe) per day, 93% of which is natural gas. The firm's operations focus on developing and acquiring gas reserves in six primary natural gas shale plays: the Barnett Shale in the Fort Worth Basin of north-central Texas; the Haynesville and Bossier Shales in northwestern Louisiana and East Texas; the Fayetteville Shale in the Arkoma Basin of central Arkansas; the Marcellus Shale in the northern Appalachian Basin of West Virginia, Pennsylvania and New York; and the Eagle Ford Shale in South Texas. Chesapeake Energy has about 14.25 trillion cubic feet equivalent of proved reserves, of which 95% are natural gas, 58% are proved developed and all of which are onshore. During 2009, through its drilling activities, the company drilled 1,212 gross operated wells and participated in over 994 wells operated by other companies. The success rate was 99% for operates wells and 98% for non-operated wells. Chesapeake Energy's subsidiaries include Chesapeake Energy Marketing, Inc.; Chesapeake Midstream; Compass Manufacturing LLC, which provides gas compression packages; Diamond Y Enterprise, Inc., a field transportation services company; and MidCon Compression LLC, which supplies natural gas compressors. In September 2009, the firm agreed to form a joint venture, Chesapeake Midstream Partners LLC, with Global Infrastructure Partners on some of Chesapeake's midstream assets. In October 2010, CNOOC Limited agreed to purchase a 33.3% stake in the company's oil and natural gas acres in the Eagle Ford Shale project.

The company offers its employees medical, dental and life insurance; a 401(k) plan; short- and long-term disability insurance; employee stock grants; and on-site health and dental center, on-site fitness center and on-site restaurants.

FINANCIALS: **Sales and profits are in thousands of dollars—add 000 to get the full amount. 2010 Note: Financial information for 2010 was not available for all companies at press time.**

2010 Sales: $	2010 Profits: $	**U.S. Stock Ticker: CHK**
2009 Sales: $7,702,000	2009 Profits: $-5,805,000	**Int'l Ticker:** Int'l Exchange:
2008 Sales: $11,629,000	2008 Profits: $723,000	Employees: 8,200
2007 Sales: $7,800,000	2007 Profits: $1,451,000	Fiscal Year Ends: 12/31
2006 Sales: $7,325,595	2006 Profits: $2,003,323	Parent Company:

SALARIES/BENEFITS:

Pension Plan:	ESOP Stock Plan:	Profit Sharing:	Top Exec. Salary: $975,000	Bonus: $1,951,000
Savings Plan: Y	Stock Purch. Plan:		Second Exec. Salary: $860,000	Bonus: $3,764,125

OTHER THOUGHTS:

Apparent Women Officers or Directors: 3
Hot Spot for Advancement for Women/Minorities: Y

LOCATIONS: ("Y" = Yes)

West:	Southwest:	Midwest:	Southeast:	Northeast:	International:
	Y	Y	Y	Y	

CHESAPEAKE MIDSTREAM PARTNERS LP

www.chesapeakemidstream.com

Industry Group Code: 213111 **Ranks within this company's industry group:** Sales: Profits:

Exploration/Production:		**Refining/Retailing:**		**Utilities:**		**Alternative Energy:**		**Specialty Services:**		**Energy Mktg./Other Svcs.**	
Exploration:	Y	Refining:		Electric Utility:		Waste/Solar/Other:		Consulting/Eng.:		Energy Marketing:	
Production:	Y	Retailing:		Gas Utility:		Thermal/Steam:		Seismic:		Equipment/Machinery:	
Coal Production:		Convenience Stores:		Pipelines:	Y	Wind:		Drilling:		Oil Field Services:	
		Chemicals:		Water:		Hydro:		InfoTech:		Air/Shipping Transportation:	
						Fuel Cells:		Specialty Services:			

TYPES OF BUSINESS:

Natural Gas Gathering Systems

BRANDS/DIVISIONS/AFFILIATES:

Global Infrastructure Partners
Chesapeake Energy Corp

CONTACTS:

Note: Officers with more than one job title may be intentionally listed here more than once.

J. Mike Stice, CEO
Robert S. Purgason, COO
David C. Shiels, CFO

Phone: 405-935-1500 **Fax:**
Toll-Free:
Address: 777 NW Grand Blvd., Oklahoma City, OK 73118 US

GROWTH PLANS/SPECIAL FEATURES:

Chesapeake Midstream Partners, L.P. is a limited partnership formed to own, operate, develop and acquire natural gas gathering systems and other midstream energy assets. The firm was recently formed by Global Infrastructure Partners and Chesapeake Energy Corporation. The company is primarily focused on natural gas gathering, the first segment of midstream energy infrastructure that connects natural gas produced at the wellhead to third-party takeaway pipelines. Chesapeake Midstream Partners provides gathering, treating and compression services to Chesapeake Energy and Total S.A. (its primary customers) and other third-party producers under long-term, fixed-fee contracts. Its systems, which gather roughly 1.6 billion cubic feet of natural gas per day, consist of approximately 2,900 miles of gathering pipelines, servicing approximately 4,000 natural gas wells. The firm's gathering systems operate in the Barnett Shale region in north-central Texas and the Mid-Continent region, which includes the Anadarko, Arkoma, Delaware and Permian Basins. The company generates approximately 75% of its operating income in the Barnett Shale region, where it services approximately 1,700 wells. In the Mid-Continent region, from which the firm derives 25% of its operating income, Chesapeake Midstream has an enhanced focus on the unconventional resources located in the Colony Granite Wash and Texas Panhandle Granite Wash plays of the Anadarko Basin.

The firm offers employees life, disability, health and dental insurance; a stock grant; a 401(k); and paid personal, sick and vacation time off.

FINANCIALS:

Sales and profits are in thousands of dollars—add 000 to get the full amount. 2010 Note: Financial information for 2010 was not available for all companies at press time.

2010 Sales: $	2010 Profits: $	**U.S. Stock Ticker: CHKM**
2009 Sales: $	2009 Profits: $	**Int'l Ticker:** Int'l Exchange:
2008 Sales: $	2008 Profits: $	Employees:
2007 Sales: $	2007 Profits: $	Fiscal Year Ends: 12/31
2006 Sales: $	2006 Profits: $	Parent Company:

SALARIES/BENEFITS:

Pension Plan:	ESOP Stock Plan: Y	Profit Sharing:	Top Exec. Salary: $	Bonus: $
Savings Plan: Y	Stock Purch. Plan:		Second Exec. Salary: $	Bonus: $

OTHER THOUGHTS:

Apparent Women Officers or Directors: 1
Hot Spot for Advancement for Women/Minorities:

LOCATIONS: ("Y" = Yes)

West:	Southwest:	Midwest:	Southeast:	Northeast:	International:
	Y				

CHEUNG KONG INFRASTRUCTURE HOLDINGS LTD

www.cki.com.hk

Industry Group Code: 2211 **Ranks within this company's industry group:** Sales: 47 Profits: 20

Exploration/Production:		**Refining/Retailing:**		**Utilities:**		**Alternative Energy:**		**Specialty Services:**		**Energy Mktg./Other Svcs.**	
Exploration:		Refining:		Electric Utility:	Y	Waste/Solar/Other:		Consulting/Eng.:	Y	Energy Marketing:	
Production:		Retailing:		Gas Utility:	Y	Thermal/Steam:		Seismic:		Equipment/Machinery:	
Coal Production:		Convenience Stores:		Pipelines:		Wind:		Drilling:		Oil Field Services:	
		Chemicals:		Water:	Y	Hydro:		InfoTech:		Air/Shipping Transportation:	
						Fuel Cells:		Specialty Services:	Y		

TYPES OF BUSINESS:

Electric Utility Development & Operation
Construction, Heavy & Civil Engineering
Cement, Stone & Asphalt Production
Road & Bridge Holdings
Water Utility
Electricity Distribution

BRANDS/DIVISIONS/AFFILIATES:

Green Island Cement
Alliance Construction Materials Limited
Hongkong Electric
Spark Infrastructure Group
Stanley Power, Inc.
AquaTower Pty Limited
Northern Gas Network Limited
Cambridge Water plc

CONTACTS: *Note: Officers with more than one job title may be intentionally listed here more than once.*

Kam Hing Lam, Managing Dir.
Dominic Chan Loi Shun, CFO
Victor Luk Sai Hong, General Counsel
Ivan Chan Kee Ham, Chief Planning & Investment Officer
Wendy Tong Barnes Wai Che, Chief Corp. Affairs Officer
Edmond Ip Tak Chuen, Deputy Chmn./Exec. Dir.
Canning Fok Kin Ning, Deputy Chmn./Exec. Dir.
Andrew John Hunter, Deputy Managing Dir./Exec. Dir.
Joanna Chen Tsien Hua, Head-Bus. Dev.
Victor Li Tzar Kuoi, Chmn.

Phone: 852-2122-3133 **Fax:** 852-2501-4550
Toll-Free:
Address: 2 Queen's Rd. Central, Cheung Kong Ctr., 12th Fl., Hong Kong, China

GROWTH PLANS/SPECIAL FEATURES:

Cheung Kong Infrastructure Holdings, Ltd. (CKI) is an investment holding company with interests in energy, transportation and water infrastructure and other infrastructure-related businesses. CKI is one of the largest publicly listed infrastructure companies in Hong Kong, with operations in Hong Kong, China, Australia, the U.K., Canada and New Zealand. In Hong Kong, the firm owns: Green Island Cement; 50% of concrete company Alliance Construction Materials Limited; and a 38.9% stake in Hongkong Electric (HK Electric), distributing electricity to 560,000 customers. In China, CKI has interests in several toll road projects and bridges totaling nearly 250 miles, including a 30% stake in the Shantou Bay Bridge, a 33.5% interest in the Shen-Shan Highway and a 51% stake in Tangshan Tangle Road. In Australia, the company and HK Electric jointly own a 51% interest in each of three power companies, ETSA Utilities, Powercor and CitiPower; as well as 8.5% of Spark Infrastructure Group, which owns 49% of ETSA, Powercor and CitiPower. In total, these power companies serve over 1.8 million customers. CKI also holds 49% of AquaTower Pty Limited, which provides potable water to four towns in Australia; and an 18% stake in Envestra Limited, a natural gas distribution company. In New Zealand, CKI and HK Electricity each own 50% of Wellington Electricity, which serves 163,000 residential and businesses customers. In the U.K., CKI owns: Cambridge Water plc, supplying water to a 450-square-mile area; and a 47.1% interest in Northern Gas Network Limited, serving 2.6 million customers. In Canada, CKI and HK Electric each own 50% of Stanley Power, Inc., which in turn owns 49.9% of TransAlta Cogeneration L.P., with interests in six electricity generation plants. In April 2010, the company acquired 50% of U.K.-based Seabank Power Limited, which it agreed to sell to Hongkong Electric Holdings Ltd. in June 2010.

FINANCIALS: **Sales and profits are in thousands of dollars—add 000 to get the full amount. 2010 Note: Financial information for 2010 was not available for all companies at press time.**

2010 Sales: $	2010 Profits: $	**U.S. Stock Ticker: CKISF**
2009 Sales: $295,530	2009 Profits: $718,250	**Int'l Ticker: 1038** Int'l Exchange: Hong Kong-HKEX
2008 Sales: $315,470	2008 Profits: $571,590	Employees: 1,032
2007 Sales: $240,640	2007 Profits: $616,620	Fiscal Year Ends: 12/31
2006 Sales: $341,100	2006 Profits: $477,100	Parent Company:

SALARIES/BENEFITS:

Pension Plan:	ESOP Stock Plan:	Profit Sharing:	Top Exec. Salary: $	Bonus: $
Savings Plan:	Stock Purch. Plan:		Second Exec. Salary: $	Bonus: $

OTHER THOUGHTS:

Apparent Women Officers or Directors: 7
Hot Spot for Advancement for Women/Minorities: Y

LOCATIONS: ("Y" = Yes)

West:	Southwest:	Midwest:	Southeast:	Northeast:	International:
					Y

CHEVRON CORPORATION

www.chevron.com

Industry Group Code: 211111 **Ranks within this company's industry group:** Sales: 7 Profits: 10

Exploration/Production:		Refining/Retailing:		Utilities:		Alternative Energy:		Specialty Services:		Energy Mktg./Other Svcs.	
Exploration:	Y	Refining:	Y	Electric Utility:		Waste/Solar/Other:		Consulting/Eng.:		Energy Marketing:	
Production:	Y	Retailing:	Y	Gas Utility:		Thermal/Steam:		Seismic:		Equipment/Machinery:	
Coal Production:	Y	Convenience Stores:	Y	Pipelines:	Y	Wind:		Drilling:		Oil Field Services:	
		Chemicals:	Y	Water:		Hydro:		InfoTech:		Air/Shipping Transportation:	
						Fuel Cells:		Specialty Services:			

TYPES OF BUSINESS:

Oil & Gas Exploration & Production
Power Generation
Petrochemicals
Gasoline Retailing
Coal Mining
Fuel & Oil Additives
Convenience Stores
Pipelines

BRANDS/DIVISIONS/AFFILIATES:

Texaco
Youngs Creek Mining Company LLC
Chevron Phillips Chemical Company
Caltex
Chevron Technology Ventures

CONTACTS:

Note: Officers with more than one job title may be intentionally listed here more than once.

John S. Watson, CEO
Patricia E. Yarrington, CFO/VP
Joe W. Laymon, VP-Human Resources
John W. McDonald, CTO/VP
R. Hewitt Pate, General Counsel/VP
Jay R. Pryor, VP-Corp. Bus. Dev.
Rhonda I. Zygocki, VP-Policy, Gov't & Public Affairs
Pierre R. Breber, Treas./VP
Michael (Mike) K. Wirth, Exec. VP-Global Downstream
George L. Kirkland, Exec. VP-Global Upstream & Gas/Vice Chmn.
John D. Gass, VP/Pres., Global Gas
Charles A. Taylor, VP-Health, Environment & Safety
John S. Watson, Chmn.

Phone: 925-842-1000	**Fax:** 925-842-3530
Toll-Free:	
Address: 6001 Bollinger Canyon Rd., San Ramon, CA 94583 US	

GROWTH PLANS/SPECIAL FEATURES:

Chevron Corporation is an integrated energy company that conducts refining, marketing and transportation operations and, to a lesser degree, chemical operations, mining operations and power generation. Refining operations maintains a refining network capable of processing more than 2 million barrels of crude oil per day. Marketing operations operates primarily under the brands Chevron, Texaco and Caltex. In the U.S., the company markets under the Chevron and Texaco brands. The company supplies directly or through retailers and marketers approximately 9,600 Chevron- and Texaco-branded motor vehicle retail outlets. Outside the U.S., the firm supplies approximately 12,400 branded service stations, including affiliates. Transportation operations maintains the Chevron owned and operated system of crude oil, refined products, chemicals, natural gas liquids and natural gas pipelines in the U.S. The company also has direct or indirect interests in other U.S. and international pipelines. Chemical operations include the manufacturing and marketing of fuel and lubricating oil additives and commodity petrochemicals through Chevron Phillips Chemical Company (CPChem), a joint venture company. CPChem operates manufacturing and research facilities in five countries. Mining operations produces and markets coal and molybdenum. The firm owns three coal mines and controls a 50% interest in Youngs Creek Mining Company LLC. The power generation business develops and operates commercial power projects and has interests in 13 power assets through joint ventures in the U.S. and Asia. The company manages the production of more than 3,100 megawatts (MW) of electricity at 13 facilities it owns through joint ventures. Additionally, Chevron operates gas-fired cogeneration facilities that use waste heat recovery to produce additional electricity or to support industrial thermal hosts. In November 2010, the company announced plans to acquire Atlas Energy, Inc. for $3.2 billion.

Chevron offers employees medical and dental insurance; domestic partner benefits; a retirement plan; tuition reimbursement; flexible work schedules; and fitness centers and/or memberships.

FINANCIALS:

Sales and profits are in thousands of dollars—add 000 to get the full amount. 2010 Note: Financial information for 2010 was not available for all companies at press time.

2010 Sales: $	2010 Profits: $	**U.S. Stock Ticker: CVX**
2009 Sales: $171,636,000	2009 Profits: $10,483,000	**Int'l Ticker:** Int'l Exchange:
2008 Sales: $273,005,000	2008 Profits: $23,931,000	Employees: 64,000
2007 Sales: $220,904,000	2007 Profits: $18,688,000	Fiscal Year Ends: 12/31
2006 Sales: $210,118,000	2006 Profits: $17,138,000	Parent Company:

SALARIES/BENEFITS:

Pension Plan: Y	ESOP Stock Plan:	Profit Sharing:	Top Exec. Salary: $1,650,000	Bonus: $3,220,000
Savings Plan: Y	Stock Purch. Plan:		Second Exec. Salary: $1,035,417	Bonus: $1,350,000

OTHER THOUGHTS:

Apparent Women Officers or Directors: 3
Hot Spot for Advancement for Women/Minorities: Y

LOCATIONS: ("Y" = Yes)

West:	Southwest:	Midwest:	Southeast:	Northeast:	International:
Y	Y	Y	Y	Y	Y

CHICAGO BRIDGE & IRON COMPANY NV

www.cbi.com

Industry Group Code: 237 **Ranks within this company's industry group:** Sales: 6 Profits: 4

Exploration/Production:		Refining/Retailing:		Utilities:		Alternative Energy:		Specialty Services:		Energy Mktg./Other Svcs.	
Exploration:		Refining:		Electric Utility:		Waste/Solar/Other:		Consulting/Eng.:	Y	Energy Marketing:	
Production:		Retailing:		Gas Utility:		Thermal/Steam:		Seismic:		Equipment/Machinery:	Y
Coal Production:		Convenience Stores:		Pipelines:		Wind:		Drilling:		Oil Field Services:	Y
		Chemicals:		Water:		Hydro:		InfoTech:		Air/Shipping Transportation:	
						Fuel Cells:		Specialty Services:	Y		

TYPES OF BUSINESS:

Heavy Construction & Civil Engineering
Specialty Engineering & Procurement Services
Liquid & Gas Storage Facilities
Maintenance & Support Services

BRANDS/DIVISIONS/AFFILIATES:

CB&I Steel Plate Structures
CB&I Lummus
Lummus Technology

CONTACTS:

Note: Officers with more than one job title may be intentionally listed here more than once.

Phillip K. Asheman, CEO
Lasse Petterson, COO
Phillip K. Asheman, Pres.
Ronald A. Ballschmiede, CFO/Exec. VP
Jan Sieving, VP-Mktg.
Beth A. Bailey, Chief Admin. Officer/Exec. VP
David A. Delman, Chief Legal Officer/Sec./Exec. VP
E. Chip Ray, Exec. VP-Corp. Planning
Jan Sieving, VP-Corp. Comm.
Luciano Reyes, Treas./VP
Ronald E. Blum, Pres., Steel Plate Structures
Daniel M. McCarthy, Pres., Lummus Technology
Mark Coscio, VP-Corp. Planning
L. Richard Flury, Chmn.
Ronald E. Blum, Exec. VP-Global Bus. Dev.

Phone: 31-70-373-2722 **Fax:**
Toll-Free:
Address: Oostduinlaan 75, Hoofddorp, The Hague, 2596JJ The Netherlands

GROWTH PLANS/SPECIAL FEATURES:

Chicago Bridge & Iron Company N.V. (CB&I), a global engineering, procurement and construction (EPC) company, provides specialty construction for liquid and gas storage facilities. Company operations include over 80 offices, warehouses and other facilities on six continents. CB&I maintains three business units, operating both independently and on an integrated basis. CB&I Steel Plate Structures provides engineering, procurement, fabrication and construction services for the petroleum, water and nuclear industries. CB&I Lummus provides infrastructure engineering, fabrication and construction services to the upstream and downstream energy industry. Lummus Technology provides proprietary technologies used to process natural gas, manufacture petrochemicals and convert crude oil into consumer products. Some of the many projects CB&I works on include hydrocarbon processing plants, liquid natural gas (LNG) terminals and peak shaving plants, offshore structures, pipelines, bulk liquid terminals and water storage and treatment facilities. The company provides complete services, from the initial design and engineering through procurement and construction and maintenance. Additionally, it offers numerous complementary products and services including low temperature or cryogenic tanks and systems, primarily used by petroleum, chemical, petrochemical and other companies to store, transport and handle liquefied gases and specialty structures including iron and aluminum processing facilities and hydroelectric structures. In May 2010, the firm was awarded a contract to design and construct a new gas processing plant at the Elk Hills oil and gas field in Central California. In October 2010, Lummus Technology signed an agreement with BP for the exclusive right to license and market BP's paraxylene recovery and isomerization technology and catalyst.

The firm offers its U.S. employees medical, dental and vision plans; employee and dependent life insurance options; a 401(k) plan; profit sharing; a stock purchase program; and an education assistance plan.

FINANCIALS:

Sales and profits are in thousands of dollars—add 000 to get the full amount. 2010 Note: Financial information for 2010 was not available for all companies at press time.

2010 Sales: $	2010 Profits: $	**U.S. Stock Ticker: CBI**
2009 Sales: $4,556,503	2009 Profits: $174,289	**Int'l Ticker: BDZ** Int'l Exchange: Frankfurt-Euronext
2008 Sales: $5,944,981	2008 Profits: $-21,146	Employees: 15,755
2007 Sales: $4,363,492	2007 Profits: $165,640	Fiscal Year Ends: 12/31
2006 Sales: $3,125,307	2006 Profits: $116,968	Parent Company:

SALARIES/BENEFITS:

Pension Plan:	ESOP Stock Plan:	Profit Sharing: Y	Top Exec. Salary: $955,000	Bonus: $1,806,860
Savings Plan: Y	Stock Purch. Plan: Y		Second Exec. Salary: $546,000	Bonus: $567,840

OTHER THOUGHTS:

Apparent Women Officers or Directors: 3
Hot Spot for Advancement for Women/Minorities: Y

LOCATIONS: ("Y" = Yes)

West:	Southwest:	Midwest:	Southeast:	Northeast:	International:
Y	Y	Y	Y	Y	Y

CHINA NATIONAL PETROLEUM CORP (CNPC)

www.cnpc.com.cn

Industry Group Code: 211111 **Ranks within this company's industry group:** Sales: 6 Profits: 3

Exploration/Production:		Refining/Retailing:		Utilities:		Alternative Energy:		Specialty Services:		Energy Mktg./Other Svcs.	
Exploration:	Y	Refining:	Y	Electric Utility:		Waste/Solar/Other:		Consulting/Eng.:	Y	Energy Marketing:	Y
Production:	Y	Retailing:	Y	Gas Utility:		Thermal/Steam:		Seismic:		Equipment/Machinery:	Y
Coal Production:		Convenience Stores:	Y	Pipelines:	Y	Wind:		Drilling:	Y	Oil Field Services:	Y
		Chemicals:	Y	Water:		Hydro:		InfoTech:		Air/Shipping Transportation:	
						Fuel Cells:		Specialty Services:	Y		

TYPES OF BUSINESS:

Oil & Gas Exploration & Production
Refining
Petrochemicals
Pipelines
Engineering & Construction
Equipment Manufacturing
Oil Field Services
Service Stations

BRANDS/DIVISIONS/AFFILIATES:

PetroChina Co., Ltd.
Jilin Chemical Industries
Shell Energy Australia
Arrow Energy Ltd.
Athabasca Oil Sands Corp.
Syria Shell Petroleum Development
Kunlun Gas Company
Kunlun Gas Utilization Company

CONTACTS:

Note: Officers with more than one job title may be intentionally listed here more than once.

Jiang Jiemin, Pres.
Wang Guoliang, CFO
Chen Ming, Chief-Discipline & Inspection Group
Zhou Jiping, VP
Zeng Yukang, VP
Wang Yilin, VP
Xu Zhiqiang, VP-PetroKazakhstan, Inc.

Phone: 86-10-6209-4114 **Fax:** 86-10-6209-5148
Toll-Free:
Address: 6, Liupukang Jie, Xicheng District, Beijing, 100724 China

GROWTH PLANS/SPECIAL FEATURES:

China National Petroleum Corp. (CNPC) is one of the world's leading integrated energy companies. Operating domestically and internationally, CNPC's businesses fall into six categories: exploration and production; natural gas and pipelines; oilfield services; refining and chemicals; marketing and trading; and engineering and construction. CNPC's oil production for 2009 totaled roughly 137.45 million tons of crude oil and 242.2 billion cubic feet of natural gas, including 34.32 million tons and 18.1 billion cubic feet from overseas projects in some 30 countries. The natural gas and pipelines division owns and operates a network of pipelines covering 26 provinces, municipalities and autonomous regions in China. It also manages the distribution of natural gas and compressed natural gas through subsidiaries Kunlun Gas Company and Kunlun Gas Utilization Company. The oilfield services division entails the firm's geophysical prospecting, drilling, well logging, mud logging and downhole operations, which it conducts with a fleet of 1,009 drilling rigs, 175 seismic crews and 644 professional logging crews in 49 countries. The refining and chemicals division, which operates 26 refining and petrochemical facilities, produces 40% of China's oil products. Marketing and trading activities include retail gas and service stations, as well as trading activities on the global oil market. In 2009, CNPC had 17,262 service stations and 2,100 self-service stations across China. The engineering and construction segment is responsible for all the construction needs of the firm's oil and gas field and petrochemical refining endeavors. Although the firm operates through various subsidiaries, its largest is 86.3%-owned PetroChina Co. Ltd. In February 2010, CNPC acquired assets in Canada's oil sands area from Athabasca Oil Sands Corp. In May 2010, the company acquired a 35% stake in Shell's Syria Shell Petroleum Development project. In August 2010, CNPC, in cooperation with Shell Energy Australia, acquired Arrow Energy Ltd. In September 2010, the firm completed construction on a nearly 650-mile crude oil pipeline from Russia to northern China.

FINANCIALS:

Sales and profits are in thousands of dollars—add 000 to get the full amount. 2010 Note: Financial information for 2010 was not available for all companies at press time.

2010 Sales: $	2010 Profits: $	**U.S. Stock Ticker: Government-Owned**
2009 Sales: $179,545,000	2009 Profits: $18,952,200	**Int'l Ticker:** Int'l Exchange:
2008 Sales: $181,123,000	2008 Profits: $10,271,000	Employees:
2007 Sales: $129,798,300	2007 Profits: $14,925,300	Fiscal Year Ends: 12/31
2006 Sales: $110,820,200	2006 Profits: $13,265,600	Parent Company:

SALARIES/BENEFITS:

Pension Plan:	ESOP Stock Plan:	Profit Sharing:	Top Exec. Salary: $	Bonus: $
Savings Plan:	Stock Purch. Plan:		Second Exec. Salary: $	Bonus: $

OTHER THOUGHTS:

Apparent Women Officers or Directors:
Hot Spot for Advancement for Women/Minorities:

LOCATIONS: ("Y" = Yes)

West:	Southwest:	Midwest:	Southeast:	Northeast:	International:
					Y

CHINA OILFIELD SERVICES LIMITED (COSL)

www.cosl.com.cn

Industry Group Code: 213112 **Ranks within this company's industry group:** Sales: 8 Profits: 5

Exploration/Production:		**Refining/Retailing:**		**Utilities:**		**Alternative Energy:**		**Specialty Services:**		**Energy Mktg./Other Svcs.**	
Exploration:		Refining:		Electric Utility:		Waste/Solar/Other:		Consulting/Eng.:		Energy Marketing:	
Production:	Y	Retailing:		Gas Utility:		Thermal/Steam:		Seismic:	Y	Equipment/Machinery:	
Coal Production:		Convenience Stores:		Pipelines:		Wind:		Drilling:	Y	Oil Field Services:	Y
		Chemicals:		Water:		Hydro:		InfoTech:	Y	Air/Shipping Transportation:	Y
						Fuel Cells:		Specialty Services:	Y		

TYPES OF BUSINESS:

Oil Well Drilling, Marine Support & Transportation Services
Seismic & Survey Services
Well Services
Oilfield Chemicals

BRANDS/DIVISIONS/AFFILIATES:

COSL Chemicals Tianjin Co. Ltd.

CONTACTS:

Note: Officers with more than one job title may be intentionally listed here more than once.

Li Yong, CEO
Li Yong, Pres.
Li Feilong, CFO/Exec. VP
Dong Weiliang, CTO/Exec. VP
Yang Haijiang, Corp. Sec.
Xu Xiongfei, VP/Chmn.-Labor Committee
Yu Zhanhai, VP
Cao Shujie, VP
Liu Jian, Chmn.

Phone: 86-10-8452-1687 **Fax:** 86-10-8452-1325

Toll-Free:

Address: 25 North Chaoyangmen, North Ave., Rm. 610, Beijing, BEJ 300451 China

GROWTH PLANS/SPECIAL FEATURES:

China Oilfield Services Limited (COSL) is a leader in the Chinese offshore oil services market. The firm's segments consist of drilling services; well services; marine services; and geophysical services. The drilling segment owns 39 rigs, including 27 drilling rigs (some of which are under construction), including semi-submersible rigs and jack-ups; and 12 other rigs, including two accommodation rigs, four module rigs and six land drilling rigs. Most of the firm's drilling rigs function in water depths from 20–1,500 feet. The COSL 941, the only jack-up rig constructed by the company, has a maximum operating depth of 400 feet. This segment also provides rig management services, including operator training and pre- and post-installation supervision; casing and tubing running services; and tools services, such as well tools assembling and oil tools renting. The well services segment offers directional engineering services; downhole seismic services; ceased hole services; open hole log-taking services and log data analysis, as well as log-taking equipment; data management; oilfield chemicals, including drilling and completion fluids, through COSL Chemicals Tianjin Co. Ltd.; cementing services; drilling and well workover services; and technical support solutions. The marine services segment owns and operates five chemical carriers, three oil tankers, one barge and 35 other vessels. The geophysical segment operates four survey vessels and eight seismic vessels. This segment also provides seismic data processing and interpretation, and underwater and land-based engineering services. In June 2009, the company announced that it had signed a service contract with the U.A.E. company Global Petro Tech to install a jack-up drilling rig in the Gulf region. This will allow COSL to penetrate the heavily competitive Gulf region oil markets. In August 2009, COSL shut down its only U.S.-based office in Houston, Texas. In December 2009 and January 2010, the company took delivery of two jack-up drilling rigs.

FINANCIALS:

Sales and profits are in thousands of dollars—add 000 to get the full amount. 2010 Note: Financial information for 2010 was not available for all companies at press time.

2010 Sales: $	2010 Profits: $	**U.S. Stock Ticker: CHOLY**
2009 Sales: $2,752,080	2009 Profits: $470,340	**Int'l Ticker: 2883** Int'l Exchange: Hong Kong-HKEX
2008 Sales: $1,820,250	2008 Profits: $454,280	Employees:
2007 Sales: $820,000	2007 Profits: $140,000	Fiscal Year Ends: 12/31
2006 Sales: $	2006 Profits: $	Parent Company:

SALARIES/BENEFITS:

Pension Plan:	ESOP Stock Plan:	Profit Sharing:	Top Exec. Salary: $	Bonus: $
Savings Plan:	Stock Purch. Plan:		Second Exec. Salary: $	Bonus: $

OTHER THOUGHTS:

Apparent Women Officers or Directors:
Hot Spot for Advancement for Women/Minorities:

LOCATIONS: ("Y" = Yes)

West:	Southwest:	Midwest:	Southeast:	Northeast:	International:
					Y

CHINA PETROLEUM & CHEMICAL (SINOPEC) english.sinopec.com.

Industry Group Code: 211111 **Ranks within this company's industry group:** Sales: 4 Profits: 11

Exploration/Production:		Refining/Retailing:		Utilities:		Alternative Energy:		Specialty Services:		Energy Mktg./Other Svcs.	
Exploration:	Y	Refining:	Y	Electric Utility:		Waste/Solar/Other:		Consulting/Eng.:		Energy Marketing:	
Production:	Y	Retailing:	Y	Gas Utility:		Thermal/Steam:		Seismic:		Equipment/Machinery:	
Coal Production:		Convenience Stores:		Pipelines:	Y	Wind:		Drilling:		Oil Field Services:	
		Chemicals:	Y	Water:		Hydro:		InfoTech:		Air/Shipping Transportation:	
						Fuel Cells:		Specialty Services:			

TYPES OF BUSINESS:

Petroleum Refining
Oil & Gas Exploration & Production
Oil & Gas Marketing & Distribution
Chemicals & Petrochemicals
Pipelines
Gas Stations

BRANDS/DIVISIONS/AFFILIATES:

Sinopec Corp.
China Petrochemical Company (Sinopec Group)
Addax Petroleum Corporation
SINOPEC Catalyst Company
Fujian Pretrochemical Company Ltd.
China Petrochemical Technology Company Ltd.
BASF-YPC Company Limited
Sinopec Geophysical Research Institute

CONTACTS: *Note: Officers with more than one job title may be intentionally listed here more than once.*

Wang Tianpu, Pres.
Wang Xinhua, CFO
Zhang Haichao, VP-Sales
Zhang Kehua, VP/Dir. Gen.-Eng.
Chen Ge, Sec.
Zhang Jianhua, Sr. VP-Oper.
Liu Yun, Chief Accountant
Wang Zhigang, Sr. VP
Dai Houliang, Sr. VP
Cai Xiyou, Sr. VP
Lei Dianwu, VP
Su Shulin, Chmn./Pres., Sinopec Corp.

Phone: 86-10-5996-0028 **Fax:** 86-10-5996-0386
Toll-Free:
Address: 22 Chaoyangmen N. St., Chaoyang District, Beijing, 100728 China

GROWTH PLANS/SPECIAL FEATURES:

China Petroleum & Chemical Corporation (Sinopec Corp.) is a leading Chinese petroleum company. It explores for, develops, produces and markets oil and natural gas, and refines, stores and transports refined petroleum products, petrochemicals, chemicals and other commodities. Sinopec is controlled by government-owned China Petrochemical Company (Sinopec Group). The firm operates its business through four segments: exploration and production; refining; marketing and distribution; and chemicals. The exploration and production segment consists of the company's activities relates to developing, producing and selling crude oil and natural gas. Sinopec's proved reserves total about 2.8 billion barrels of oil and about 6.95 trillion cubic feet (tcf) of natural gas. The firm annually produces around 296 million barrels of oil and 291 billion cubic feet of natural gas. In its refining segment, the company purchases crude oil from its exploration and production segment and from third parties; processes crude oil into refined petroleum products; and sells refined petroleum products principally to its marketing and distribution segment. The segment annually sells approximately 29 million tons of gasoline, 67 million tons of diesel and 24 million tons of light chemical feedstock. The marketing and distribution segment purchases refined oil products from the firm's refining segment and third parties; makes wholesale and direct sales to domestic customers; and retails the refined oil products through its retail distribution network. The segment annually sells approximately 38 million tons of gasoline, 30 million of which are retailed; 81 million tons of diesel, 45 million of which are retailed; 10 million tons of kerosene; and 14 million tons of fuel oil. Sinopec's chemicals segment purchases chemical feedstock from its refining segment and third parties and produces, markets and distributes petrochemicals and inorganic chemical products. In October 2009, Sinopec acquired Canada-based Addax Petroleum Corporation, in a transaction valued at $8 billion.

FINANCIALS: **Sales and profits are in thousands of dollars—add 000 to get the full amount. 2010 Note: Financial information for 2010 was not available for all companies at press time.**

2010 Sales: $	2010 Profits: $	**U.S. Stock Ticker: SNP**
2009 Sales: $196,769,000	2009 Profits: $9,433,420	**Int'l Ticker: 0386** Int'l Exchange: Hong Kong-HKEX
2008 Sales: $212,093,000	2008 Profits: $4,349,520	Employees: 371,333
2007 Sales: $167,686,000	2007 Profits: $8,391,380	Fiscal Year Ends: 12/31
2006 Sales: $140,434,000	2006 Profits: $7,262,620	Parent Company:

SALARIES/BENEFITS:

Pension Plan: Y	ESOP Stock Plan:	Profit Sharing:	Top Exec. Salary: $	Bonus: $
Savings Plan:	Stock Purch. Plan:		Second Exec. Salary: $	Bonus: $

OTHER THOUGHTS:

Apparent Women Officers or Directors:
Hot Spot for Advancement for Women/Minorities:

LOCATIONS: ("Y" = Yes)

West:	Southwest:	Midwest:	Southeast:	Northeast:	International:
				Y	Y

Note: Financial information, benefits and other data can change quickly and may vary from those stated here.

CHINA SHENHUA ENERGY COMPANY LIMITED

www.shenhuachina.com

Industry Group Code: 21211 **Ranks within this company's industry group:** Sales: 3 Profits: 1

Exploration/Production:		Refining/Retailing:		Utilities:		Alternative Energy:		Specialty Services:		Energy Mktg./Other Svcs.	
Exploration:	Y	Refining:		Electric Utility:	Y	Waste/Solar/Other:		Consulting/Eng.:		Energy Marketing:	
Production:		Retailing:		Gas Utility:		Thermal/Steam:		Seismic:		Equipment/Machinery:	
Coal Production:	Y	Convenience Stores:		Pipelines:		Wind:	Y	Drilling:		Oil Field Services:	
		Chemicals:		Water:		Hydro:		InfoTech:		Air/Shipping Transportation:	Y
						Fuel Cells:		Specialty Services:			

TYPES OF BUSINESS:

Coal Mining
Coal Transportation & Export
Power Generation

BRANDS/DIVISIONS/AFFILIATES:

Huanghua Port
Shenhua Tianjin Coal Dock

CONTACTS:

Note: Officers with more than one job title may be intentionally listed here more than once.

Ling Wen, Pres.
Zhang Kehui, CFO
Hua Zeqiao, VP-Coal Sales & Mktg.
Huang Qing, Sec.
Wang Pingang, VP-Power Oper.
Hao Gui, VP-Safety, Health & Environmental Mgmt.
Wang Jinli, VP-Coal Prod.
Xue Jilian, VP-Transportation Oper.
Zhang Xiwu, Chmn.

Phone: 86-10-58133376 **Fax:** 86-10-84882107
Toll-Free:
Address: 4th Fl., Zhouji Tower, 16 Ande Rd., Dongcheng, Beijing, 100011 China

GROWTH PLANS/SPECIAL FEATURES:

China Shenhua Energy Company Limited is one of the largest coal mining companies in China, and a leading coal seller worldwide. The firm produced 231.8 million tons of coal and sold over 280.3 million tons in 2009, of which nearly 15 million tons were exported internationally. The firm has two main segments: coal operations and power operations. The coal segment produces coal from both surface and underground mines as well as engaging in the sale and transportation of coal to the power segment and external customers, typically under long-term contracts. Total marketable coal reserves at its three primary mining sites, Shendong, Zhungr'er and Shengli, exceed 7.63 billion tons. Its transportation system, which consists of the Baoshen, Shenshuo, Shuohuang, Dazhun and Huangwan railways, hauls a total of 328.8 million tons yearly across 850 miles of rail lines. Additionally, Shenhua Energy manages the Huanghua Port and Shenhua Tianjin Coal Dock, which are connected to its railway lines. The power segment, which sources coal internally and from external suppliers, sells its electricity to external power grid companies, as well as to the coal segment. The firm has 13 power plants with a total capacity greater than 23,500 megawatts, which generated a gross power sum of 105.1 billion kilowatt hours in 2009. Subsidiaries of Shenhua Energy include two port, four railway, 14 power, five coal sales and five coal production companies. The firm currently has international projects that include coal exploration in Australia's New South Wales region and construction of an integrated coal and power project in the South Sumatra Province of Indonesia.

FINANCIALS:

Sales and profits are in thousands of dollars—add 000 to get the full amount. 2010 Note: Financial information for 2010 was not available for all companies at press time.

2010 Sales: $	2010 Profits: $
2009 Sales: $18,198,600	2009 Profits: $4,756,360
2008 Sales: $15,688,180	2008 Profits: $3,893,450
2007 Sales: $8,230,000	2007 Profits: $2,240,000
2006 Sales: $6,470,000	2006 Profits: $1,940,000

U.S. Stock Ticker:
Int'l Ticker: 1088 Int'l Exchange: Hong Kong-HKE
Employees: 62,286
Fiscal Year Ends: 12/31
Parent Company:

SALARIES/BENEFITS:

Pension Plan:	ESOP Stock Plan:	Profit Sharing:	Top Exec. Salary: $	Bonus: $
Savings Plan:	Stock Purch. Plan:		Second Exec. Salary: $	Bonus: $

OTHER THOUGHTS:

Apparent Women Officers or Directors: 1
Hot Spot for Advancement for Women/Minorities:

LOCATIONS: ("Y" = Yes)

West:	Southwest:	Midwest:	Southeast:	Northeast:	International:
					Y

CHUBU ELECTRIC POWER CO INC

www.chuden.co.jp

Industry Group Code: 2211 **Ranks within this company's industry group:** Sales: 6 Profits: 46

Exploration/Production:		Refining/Retailing:		Utilities:		Alternative Energy:		Specialty Services:		Energy Mktg./Other Svcs.	
Exploration:		Refining:		Electric Utility:	Y	Waste/Solar/Other:	Y	Consulting/Eng.:	Y	Energy Marketing:	Y
Production:		Retailing:		Gas Utility:		Thermal/Steam:	Y	Seismic:		Equipment/Machinery:	
Coal Production:		Convenience Stores:		Pipelines:		Wind:	Y	Drilling:		Oil Field Services:	
		Chemicals:		Water:		Hydro:	Y	InfoTech:		Air/Shipping Transportation:	
						Fuel Cells:		Specialty Services:	Y		

TYPES OF BUSINESS:

Utilities-Electricity
Hydroelectric Generation
Nuclear Generation
Wind Generation
Biofuel Manufacturing
Telecommunications Services
Biomass Power
Home Building Support

BRANDS/DIVISIONS/AFFILIATES:

Chubu Telecommunications Co., Inc.
Transformer Recycling Center
Shin-Nagoya Thermal Power Station
Int'l Nuclear Energy Development of Japan Co. Ltd.
ITOCHU Corp.
Tenaska, Inc.

CONTACTS: *Note: Officers with more than one job title may be intentionally listed here more than once.*

Akihisa Mizuno, Pres.
Tomohiko Ohno, Sr. Managing Exec. Officer/Dir.-Mktg.
Masakazu Aida, Sr. Managing Exec.-R&D
Yoshihito Miyaike, Exec. VP/Gen. Mgr.-Info. Systems
Takaaki Tanaka, Sr. Managing Exec. Officer/Dir.-Tech. Dev.
Norihisa Ito, Exec. VP/Gen. Mgr.-Legal Affairs Dept.
Satoru Katsuno, Gen. Mgr.-Corp. Planning & Strategy
Norihisa Ito, Exec. VP/Gen. Mgr.-Corp. Comm. Dept.
Kazuhiro Matsubara, Exec. VP/Gen. Mgr.-Finance & Acct.
Masatoshi Sakaguchi, Exec. VP/Gen. Mgr.-Power Generation Div.
Yoshihito Miyaike, Exec. VP/Gen. Mgr.-Environmental Affairs
Akira Matsuyama, Gen. Mgr.-Land Affairs & Power Sys.
Katsuji Noda, Gen. Mgr.-Fuels & Gas Sales & Svcs. Dept.
Toshio Mita, Chmn.
Toshiyuki Nosaka, Sr. Managing Exec. Officer/Dir.-Dist.

Phone: 052-951-8211 **Fax:** 052-962-4624
Toll-Free:
Address: 1, Higashi-shincho, Higashi-ku, Nagoya, 461-8680 Japan

GROWTH PLANS/SPECIAL FEATURES:

Chubu Electric Power Co., Inc., the third-largest power company in Japan, supplies electricity to the Chubu region, covering a service area of 24,233 square miles and containing over 16 million people. The company has a total power generating capacity of 32.62 gigawatts (GW), including 5.22 GW from its 182 hydroelectric plants; 23.9 GW from its 11 coal-, oil- and liquid natural gas (LNG)-fired plants; and 3.5 GW from its single nuclear power plant. In addition, it operates nearly 12,212 miles of transmission lines and 176,200 miles of distribution lines. Chubu is currently developing wind energy projects, as well as a 7.5 megawatt mega solar power station in Taketoyo. Internationally, the company aided in the development of biomass generation facilities in Malaysia and Thailand. The company maintains nearly 60 subsidiaries and affiliate companies, through which the company is active in the energy, transportation, manufacturing, construction, IT and telecommunications, electric power, real estate management and other market segments. In February 2010, the firm commenced operating three wind turbines as part of a phase I development of the Omaezaki Wind Power Station. In July 2010, the company was commissioned to aide in a rural electrification project in Zambia. In October 2010, Chubu and 12 other Japanese companies formed the International Nuclear Energy Development of Japan Co., Ltd., with the purpose of supporting nuclear power projects in emerging countries. Also in October 2010, the firm agreed, in cooperation with ITOCHU Corp., to acquire interests in five gas-fired generation plants in the U.S. from Tenaska, Inc.

FINANCIALS: **Sales and profits are in thousands of dollars—add 000 to get the full amount. 2010 Note: Financial information for 2010 was not available for all companies at press time.**

2010 Sales: $	2010 Profits: $	**U.S. Stock Ticker:**
2009 Sales: $27,850,780	2009 Profits: $-210,470	**Int'l Ticker: 9502** Int'l Exchange: Tokyo-TSE
2008 Sales: $24,984,000	2008 Profits: $-189,000	Employees:
2007 Sales: $18,840,000	2007 Profits: $770,000	Fiscal Year Ends: 3/31
2006 Sales: $18,753,011	2006 Profits: $767,053	Parent Company:

SALARIES/BENEFITS:

Pension Plan:	ESOP Stock Plan:	Profit Sharing:	Top Exec. Salary: $	Bonus: $
Savings Plan:	Stock Purch. Plan:		Second Exec. Salary: $	Bonus: $

OTHER THOUGHTS:

Apparent Women Officers or Directors:
Hot Spot for Advancement for Women/Minorities:

LOCATIONS: ("Y" = Yes)

West:	Southwest:	Midwest:	Southeast:	Northeast:	International:
				Y	Y

CIMAREX ENERGY CO

www.cimarex.com

Industry Group Code: 211111 **Ranks within this company's industry group:** Sales: 78 Profits: 101

Exploration/Production:		Refining/Retailing:		Utilities:		Alternative Energy:		Specialty Services:		Energy Mktg./Other Svcs.	
Exploration:	Y	Refining:		Electric Utility:		Waste/Solar/Other:		Consulting/Eng.:		Energy Marketing:	Y
Production:	Y	Retailing:		Gas Utility:		Thermal/Steam:		Seismic:		Equipment/Machinery:	
Coal Production:		Convenience Stores:		Pipelines:		Wind:		Drilling:		Oil Field Services:	
		Chemicals:		Water:		Hydro:		InfoTech:		Air/Shipping Transportation:	
						Fuel Cells:		Specialty Services:			

TYPES OF BUSINESS:

Oil & Gas Exploration & Production
Natural Gas Marketing

BRANDS/DIVISIONS/AFFILIATES:

CONTACTS:
Note: Officers with more than one job title may be intentionally listed here more than once.

F. H. Merelli, CEO
F. H. Merelli, Pres.
Paul Korus, CFO/VP/Treas.
Richard S. Dinkins, VP-Human Resources
Thomas E. Jorden, Exec. VP-Exploration
Gary R. Abbott, VP-Eng.
Thomas A. Richardson, General Counsel/VP
Joseph R. Albi, Exec. VP-Oper.
Stephen P. Bell, Sr. VP-Bus. Dev. & Land
James H. Shonsey, Chief Acct. Officer/Controller
F. H. Merelli, Chmn.

Phone: 303-295-3995	**Fax:** 303-295-3494
Toll-Free:	
Address: 1700 Lincoln St., Ste. 1800, Denver, CO 80203 US	

GROWTH PLANS/SPECIAL FEATURES:

Cimarex Energy Co. is an independent oil and gas exploration and production company. The company controls proved reserves of 1.2 trillion cubic feet of gas and 58 million barrels of oil and natural gas liquid, with large reserves in the Anadarko basin of Oklahoma. The company has significant operations in the mid-continent region, which consists of Oklahoma, the Texas Panhandle and southwest Kansas; the Permian Basin region of west Texas and southeast New Mexico; and the Gulf Coast areas of Texas, south Louisiana and offshore Louisiana. The firm also has operations in Michigan and Wyoming. Cimarex participated in drilling 110 gross wells in 2009 with a 93% overall completion rate. The company's production for 2009 averaged 462.9 million cubic feet of equivalent (MMcfe) per day, comprised of 323.2 MMcf of gas per day and 23,283 barrels of oil per day (BOPD). For each of the firm's core exploration areas, it assembles teams of landmen, geoscientists and petroleum engineers, who base drilling decisions on detailed analysis of potential reserve size, geologic and mechanical risks, expected costs and future production profiles. Cimarex's centralized exploration management system measures actual drilling results and provides feedback to the originating exploration teams in order to help them improve future investment decisions. The company sells its oil and gas to a broad portfolio of customers that tend to be located near its Kansas, Oklahoma, Texas and Louisiana wells.

FINANCIALS:
Sales and profits are in thousands of dollars—add 000 to get the full amount. 2010 Note: Financial information for 2010 was not available for all companies at press time.

2010 Sales: $	2010 Profits: $	**U.S. Stock Ticker: XEC**
2009 Sales: $1,009,794	2009 Profits: $-311,943	**Int'l Ticker:** Int'l Exchange:
2008 Sales: $1,970,347	2008 Profits: $-915,245	Employees: 756
2007 Sales: $1,430,513	2007 Profits: $345,262	Fiscal Year Ends: 12/31
2006 Sales: $1,265,400	2006 Profits: $345,719	Parent Company:

SALARIES/BENEFITS:

Pension Plan:	ESOP Stock Plan:	Profit Sharing:	Top Exec. Salary: $850,000	Bonus: $1,700,000
Savings Plan: Y	Stock Purch. Plan:		Second Exec. Salary: $468,000	Bonus: $936,000

OTHER THOUGHTS:

Apparent Women Officers or Directors:
Hot Spot for Advancement for Women/Minorities:

LOCATIONS: ("Y" = Yes)

West:	Southwest:	Midwest:	Southeast:	Northeast:	International:
Y	Y	Y	Y		

CITGO PETROLEUM CORPORATION

www.citgo.com

Industry Group Code: 324110 **Ranks within this company's industry group:** Sales: Profits:

Exploration/Production:		**Refining/Retailing:**		**Utilities:**		**Alternative Energy:**		**Specialty Services:**		**Energy Mktg./Other Svcs.**	
Exploration:		Refining:	Y	Electric Utility:		Waste/Solar/Other:		Consulting/Eng.:		Energy Marketing:	
Production:		Retailing:	Y	Gas Utility:		Thermal/Steam:		Seismic:		Equipment/Machinery:	
Coal Production:		Convenience Stores:	Y	Pipelines:		Wind:		Drilling:		Oil Field Services:	
		Chemicals:	Y	Water:		Hydro:		InfoTech:		Air/Shipping Transportation:	
						Fuel Cells:		Specialty Services:			

TYPES OF BUSINESS:

Petroleum Refining
Petroleum Marketing & Transportation
Petrochemicals, Feedstocks & Lubricants
Asphalt
Convenience Store Brand

BRANDS/DIVISIONS/AFFILIATES:

PDV America, Inc.
Petroleos de Venezuela S.A.

CONTACTS: *Note: Officers with more than one job title may be intentionally listed here more than once.*

Alejandro Granado, CEO
Alejandro Granado, Pres.
Gustavo Velasquez, VP-Mktg.
Dean M. Hasseman, General Counsel
Daniel Cortez, VP-Gov't & Public Affairs
Brian O'Kelly, VP-Finance
John Butts, Corp. Controller
Maritza Villanueva, Treas.
Bob Kent, VP-Refining
Kevin Ferrall, VP/Gen. Mgr.-Corpus Christi Refinery
Alejandro Granado, Chmn.
Gustavo Velasquez, VP-Supply

Phone: 832-486-4000	**Fax:** 832-486-1814
Toll-Free:	
Address: 1293 Eldridge Pkwy., Houston, TX 77077-1670 US	

GROWTH PLANS/SPECIAL FEATURES:

CITGO Petroleum Corporation is a wholly-owned subsidiary of PDV America, Inc., an indirect wholly-owned subsidiary of Petroleos de Venezuela S.A., the national oil company of the Bolivarian Republic of Venezuela. The company and its subsidiaries refine, market and transport petroleum products including gasoline, diesel fuel, jet fuel, petrochemicals, lubricants, asphalt and refined waxes, mainly within the continental U.S. east of the Rocky Mountains. The firm has a direct refining capacity of 749,000 barrels of oil per day (bo/d) and more than 8,000 independent retail stores throughout the U.S. The firm's transportation fuel customers include CITGO-branded wholesale marketers, convenience stores and airlines. Asphalt is generally marketed to independent paving contractors on the East and Gulf Coasts and in the Midwest. Lubricants are sold primarily in the U.S. to independent marketers, mass marketers and industrial customers. Petrochemical feedstocks and industrial products are sold to various manufacturers and industrial companies throughout the U.S. Petroleum coke is sold primarily in international markets. The company also sells lubricants, gasoline and distillates in various Latin American markets. CITGO owns refinery operations in Lake Charles, Louisiana; Corpus Christi, Texas; and Lemont, Illinois, as well as a 41% interest in the Lyondell-CITGO refinery in Houston, Texas.

The company offers its employees medical, dental and vision; a 401(k) plan; a pension plan; life insurance; a tuition assistance plan; and a host of professional development programs.

FINANCIALS: **Sales and profits are in thousands of dollars—add 000 to get the full amount. 2010 Note: Financial information for 2010 was not available for all companies at press time.**

2010 Sales: $	2010 Profits: $	**U.S. Stock Ticker: Subsidiary**
2009 Sales: $	2009 Profits: $	**Int'l Ticker:** Int'l Exchange:
2008 Sales: $	2008 Profits: $	Employees:
2007 Sales: $	2007 Profits: $	Fiscal Year Ends: 12/31
2006 Sales: $	2006 Profits: $	Parent Company: PDV AMERICA INC

SALARIES/BENEFITS:

Pension Plan: Y	ESOP Stock Plan:	Profit Sharing:	Top Exec. Salary: $	Bonus: $
Savings Plan: Y	Stock Purch. Plan:		Second Exec. Salary: $	Bonus: $

OTHER THOUGHTS:

Apparent Women Officers or Directors: 1
Hot Spot for Advancement for Women/Minorities:

LOCATIONS: ("Y" = Yes)

West:	Southwest:	Midwest:	Southeast:	Northeast:	International:
Y	Y	Y	Y	Y	

CLAYTON WILLIAMS ENERGY INC

www.claytonwilliams.com

Industry Group Code: 211111 **Ranks within this company's industry group:** Sales: 98 Profits: 90

Exploration/Production:		Refining/Retailing:		Utilities:		Alternative Energy:		Specialty Services:		Energy Mktg./Other Svcs.	
Exploration:	Y	Refining:		Electric Utility:		Waste/Solar/Other:		Consulting/Eng.:		Energy Marketing:	
Production:	Y	Retailing:		Gas Utility:		Thermal/Steam:		Seismic:		Equipment/Machinery:	
Coal Production:		Convenience Stores:		Pipelines:	Y	Wind:		Drilling:		Oil Field Services:	
		Chemicals:		Water:		Hydro:		InfoTech:		Air/Shipping Transportation:	
						Fuel Cells:		Specialty Services:			

TYPES OF BUSINESS:

Oil & Gas Exploration & Production
Pipelines

BRANDS/DIVISIONS/AFFILIATES:

Clayton Williams Pipeline, Inc.
Desta Drilling

CONTACTS:

Note: Officers with more than one job title may be intentionally listed here more than once.

Clayton W. Williams, CEO
L. Paul Latham, COO/Exec. VP
Clayton W. Williams, Pres.
Mel G. Riggs, CFO/Corp. Sec./Sr. VP-Finance/Treas.
Robert C. Lyon, VP-Gas Gathering & Mktg.
T. Mark Tisdale, General Counsel/VP
Patrick C. Reesby, VP-Acquisitions & New Ventures
Patti Hollums, Dir.-Investor Rel.
Michael L. Pollard, VP-Acct.
Greg S. Welborn, VP-Land
Clayton W. Williams, Chmn.

Phone: 432-682-6324	**Fax:** 432-688-3247
Toll-Free:	
Address: 6 Desta Dr., Ste. 6500, Midland, TX 79705 US	

GROWTH PLANS/SPECIAL FEATURES:

Clayton Williams Energy, Inc. is an independent oil and gas company engaged in the exploration and production of oil and natural gas. The company operates primarily in Texas, Louisiana, Mississippi and New Mexico. Clayton also has minor operations in Colorado and an interest in a joint exploration program in the Overthrust play in central Utah. Before drilling an exploratory well, the company uses geophysical technology to attempt to make a picture of the underlying geography of an area. The factors considered include the field recording parameters of the data, type of processing, extent of attribute analyses, availability of subsurface geological data and the depth and complexity of the subsurface. The company will only attempt an exploratory well if the reserve potential is higher than an ordinary development prospect. The company has proved reserves of 33.63 million barrels of oil equivalent (MMBOE), of which 85% are proved developed, as well as 94 miles of gas pipeline, three treating plants, one dehydration facility, three compressor stations and four wellhead-type treating and compression facilities. Clayton Williams Energy owns the drilling company Desta Drilling, which possesses a rig fleet of 10 mid-sized rigs and two large rigs. In 2009, the firm's production totaled 2.87 million barrels of oil, 15.95 billion cubic feet of natural gas and 240,000 barrels of natural gas liquids, for a combined total of 5.76 MMBOE.

FINANCIALS:

Sales and profits are in thousands of dollars—add 000 to get the full amount. 2010 Note: Financial information for 2010 was not available for all companies at press time.

2010 Sales: $	2010 Profits: $	**U.S. Stock Ticker: CWEI**
2009 Sales: $255,961	2009 Profits: $-117,415	**Int'l Ticker:** Int'l Exchange:
2008 Sales: $565,517	2008 Profits: $140,534	Employees: 312
2007 Sales: $393,895	2007 Profits: $5,900	Fiscal Year Ends: 12/31
2006 Sales: $265,998	2006 Profits: $17,799	Parent Company:

SALARIES/BENEFITS:

Pension Plan:	ESOP Stock Plan:	Profit Sharing:	Top Exec. Salary: $544,500	Bonus: $42,688
Savings Plan:	Stock Purch. Plan:		Second Exec. Salary: $308,000	Bonus: $164,679

OTHER THOUGHTS:

Apparent Women Officers or Directors: 1
Hot Spot for Advancement for Women/Minorities:

LOCATIONS: ("Y" = Yes)

West:	Southwest:	Midwest:	Southeast:	Northeast:	International:
Y	Y		Y		

CLOUD PEAK ENERGY INC

www.cloudpeakenergy.com

Industry Group Code: 21211 **Ranks within this company's industry group:** Sales: 11 Profits: 7

Exploration/Production:		Refining/Retailing:		Utilities:		Alternative Energy:		Specialty Services:		Energy Mktg./Other Svcs.	
Exploration:		Refining:		Electric Utility:		Waste/Solar/Other:		Consulting/Eng.:		Energy Marketing:	
Production:		Retailing:		Gas Utility:		Thermal/Steam:		Seismic:		Equipment/Machinery:	
Coal Production:	Y	Convenience Stores:		Pipelines:		Wind:		Drilling:		Oil Field Services:	
		Chemicals:		Water:		Hydro:		InfoTech:		Air/Shipping Transportation:	
						Fuel Cells:		Specialty Services:			

TYPES OF BUSINESS:

Coal Production

BRANDS/DIVISIONS/AFFILIATES:

CPE Resources LLC
Rio Tinto America

CONTACTS:

Note: Officers with more than one job title may be intentionally listed here more than once.

Colin Marshall, CEO
Gary Rivenes, COO
Colin Marshall, Pres.
Michael Barrett, CFO/Exec. VP
Jim Orchard, VP-Mktg. & Gov't Affairs
Cary W. Martin, Exec. VP-Human Resources
Nick Taylor, Exec. VP-Tech. Svcs.
Bryan Pechersky, General Counsel/Exec. VP
Todd A. Myers, Sr. VP-Bus. Dev.
Karla Kimrey, VP-Investor Rel.
Terri Eggert, Chief Acct. Officer/VP-Finance
Keith Bailey, Chmn.

Phone: 307-687-6000 | **Fax:** 307-687-6015
Toll-Free:
Address: 505 S. Gillette Ave., Gillette, WY 82718 US

GROWTH PLANS/SPECIAL FEATURES:

Cloud Peak Energy, Inc. is a leading U.S. coal producer based in Wyoming, with total reserves of more than 1 billion tons of coal. Cloud Peak is a holding company for CPE Resources LLC, which is owned in conjunction with Rio Tinto America. The firm operates solely in the Powder River Basin (PRB), one of the lowest-cost coal producing regions in the U.S., managing several of the five largest coal mines in the U.S. Cloud Peak Energy's operations include three wholly-owned surface coal mines, two of which are in Wyoming (Antelope and Cordero Rojo) and one in Montana (Spring Creek), and a 50% interest in another surface coal mine in Montana. The Antelope and Cordero Rojo mines in Wyoming have an annual production capacity of 42 and 65 million tons, respectively. The Spring Creek mine has an annual production capacity of 20 million tons. The firm produces sub-bituminous steam coal with low sulfur content, using dragline and truck-and-shovel mining methods, and sells primarily to electric utilities and industrial customers for electricity generation. In 2009, the firm produced approximately 93.3 million tons of coal. The company went public in November 2009.

FINANCIALS:

Sales and profits are in thousands of dollars—add 000 to get the full amount. 2010 Note: Financial information for 2010 was not available for all companies at press time.

2010 Sales: $	2010 Profits: $	**U.S. Stock Ticker: CLD**
2009 Sales: $1,398,200	2009 Profits: $381,701	**Int'l Ticker:** Int'l Exchange:
2008 Sales: $1,239,711	2008 Profits: $63,125	Employees: 1,529
2007 Sales: $	2007 Profits: $	Fiscal Year Ends: 12/31
2006 Sales: $	2006 Profits: $	Parent Company:

SALARIES/BENEFITS:

Pension Plan: Y	ESOP Stock Plan:	Profit Sharing: Y	Top Exec. Salary: $412,273	Bonus: $686,037
Savings Plan: Y	Stock Purch. Plan:		Second Exec. Salary: $240,897	Bonus: $313,462

OTHER THOUGHTS:

Apparent Women Officers or Directors: 2
Hot Spot for Advancement for Women/Minorities:

LOCATIONS: ("Y" = Yes)

West:	Southwest:	Midwest:	Southeast:	Northeast:	International:
Y					

CLP HOLDINGS LIMITED

www.clpgroup.com

Industry Group Code: 2211 **Ranks within this company's industry group:** Sales: 26 Profits: 13

Exploration/Production:		Refining/Retailing:		Utilities:		Alternative Energy:		Specialty Services:		Energy Mktg./Other Svcs.	
Exploration:		Refining:		Electric Utility:	Y	Waste/Solar/Other:	Y	Consulting/Eng.:	Y	Energy Marketing:	
Production:		Retailing:		Gas Utility:		Thermal/Steam:	Y	Seismic:		Equipment/Machinery:	
Coal Production:		Convenience Stores:		Pipelines:		Wind:	Y	Drilling:		Oil Field Services:	
		Chemicals:		Water:		Hydro:		InfoTech:		Air/Shipping Transportation:	
						Fuel Cells:		Specialty Services:	Y		

TYPES OF BUSINESS:

Electric Utility
Engineering Services

BRANDS/DIVISIONS/AFFILIATES:

CLP Power Hong Kong Limited
Castle Peak Power
TRUenergy
Gujarat Paguthan Energy Corporation Pvt. Ltd.
OneEnergy Limited
Mitsubishi Corporation

CONTACTS: *Note: Officers with more than one job title may be intentionally listed here more than once.*

Andrew C. W. Brandler, CEO
Mark Takahashi, CFO/Group Dir.
Giuseppe Jacobelli, Dir.-Carbon Ventures
Peter Albert Littlewood, Group Dir.-Oper.
Peter William Greenwood, Exec. Dir.-Strategy
John S. Robertsson, Dir.-Group Corp. Finance & Dev.
Mark C. Jobling, Managing Dir.-Southeast Asia/CEO-OneEnergy Ltd.
Richard Kendall Lancaster, Managing Dir.-Hong Kong
Richard I. J. McIndoe, Managing Dir.-Australia
Ko Yu Ming, Managing Dir.-China
Michael D. Kadoorie, Chmn.
Rajiv Ranjan Mishra, Managing Dir.-India

Phone: 852-2678-8111	**Fax:** 852-2760-4448
Toll-Free:	
Address: 147 Argyle St., Kowloon, Hong Kong, China	

GROWTH PLANS/SPECIAL FEATURES:

CLP Holdings Limited (CLP) is an electric utility operating primarily in Southeast Asia, India and Australia. The company operates in six segments: Hong Kong; Australia; Chinese mainland; India; Southeast Asia and Taiwan. CLP Power Hong Kong Limited (CLP Power), one of the largest electric utility businesses in Hong Kong, serves approximately 2.3 million customers in a service area that covers 80% of Hong Kong's total population. The firm is responsible for the operation of 6,908 megawatts (MW) of installed generating capacity owned by Castle Peak Power Co. Ltd. In Australia, the firm operates as TRUenergy, a vertically integrated energy business serving 1.28 million electricity customers with an installed capacity of 2,080 MW. The firm's Chinese mainland operations include management and investment in a diversified mix of generation sources, from nuclear and coal-fired facilities to wind and biomass plants. Its total equity interests in China amount to 5,578 MW of capacity. India operations currently include the management of Gujarat Paguthan Energy Corporation Private Limited, investment in 446 MW of wind energy and the construction of a 1,320 MW coal-fired plant in Jhajjar, Haryana. In Southeast Asia and Taiwan, CLP develops, invests and operates power projects through OneEnergy Limited, a joint venture with Mitsubishi Corporation. It currently has a presence in Taiwan, Thailand, the Philippines, Laos and Vietnam. In July 2010, CLP agreed to invest in a 73 MW solar farm in Thailand. Also in July 2010, the company agreed to a 17% investment in the Yangjiang Nuclear Power Station in Guangdong, China. In October 2010, the firm commenced phase I operations at its first wholly-owned wind farm in mainland China.

FINANCIALS: **Sales and profits are in thousands of dollars—add 000 to get the full amount. 2010 Note: Financial information for 2010 was not available for all companies at press time.**

2010 Sales: $	2010 Profits: $	**U.S. Stock Ticker: CLPHY**
2009 Sales: $6,536,590	2009 Profits: $1,057,350	**Int'l Ticker: 0002** Int'l Exchange: Hong Kong-HKEX
2008 Sales: $7,005,770	2008 Profits: $1,346,270	Employees: 5,777
2007 Sales: $6,553,140	2007 Profits: $1,369,100	Fiscal Year Ends: 12/31
2006 Sales: $2,876,000	2006 Profits: $1,256,000	Parent Company:

SALARIES/BENEFITS:

Pension Plan:	ESOP Stock Plan:	Profit Sharing:	Top Exec. Salary: $876,335	Bonus: $747,462
Savings Plan:	Stock Purch. Plan:		Second Exec. Salary: $657,247	Bonus: $489,713

OTHER THOUGHTS:

Apparent Women Officers or Directors: 1
Hot Spot for Advancement for Women/Minorities:

LOCATIONS: ("Y" = Yes)

West:	Southwest:	Midwest:	Southeast:	Northeast:	International:
					Y

CMS ENERGY CORP

www.cmsenergy.com

Industry Group Code: 221 **Ranks within this company's industry group:** Sales: 28 Profits: 35

Exploration/Production:		Refining/Retailing:		Utilities:		Alternative Energy:		Specialty Services:		Energy Mktg./Other Svcs.	
Exploration:		Refining:		Electric Utility:	Y	Waste/Solar/Other:	Y	Consulting/Eng.:		Energy Marketing:	Y
Production:	Y	Retailing:		Gas Utility:	Y	Thermal/Steam:		Seismic:		Equipment/Machinery:	
Coal Production:		Convenience Stores:		Pipelines:	Y	Wind:		Drilling:		Oil Field Services:	
		Chemicals:		Water:		Hydro:	Y	InfoTech:		Air/Shipping Transportation:	
						Fuel Cells:		Specialty Services:			

TYPES OF BUSINESS:

Utilities-Electricity & Natural Gas
Power Plant Operation
Natural Gas Pipelines
Oil & Gas Exploration & Production
Energy Marketing

BRANDS/DIVISIONS/AFFILIATES:

Consumers Energy Company
CMS Enterprises Company

CONTACTS: *Note: Officers with more than one job title may be intentionally listed here more than once.*

John G. Russell, CEO
John G. Russell, Pres.
Thomas J. Webb, CFO/Exec. VP
John M. Butler, Sr. VP-Human Resources & Shared Svcs.
Mamatha Chamarthi, CIO/VP
John M. Butler, Sr. VP-Admin. Svcs.
James E. Brunner, General Counsel/Sr. VP
Laura L. Mountcastle, VP-Investor Rel./Treas.
Glenn P. Barba, Chief Acct. Officer/Controller/VP
David G. Mengebier, Chief Compliance Officer/Sr. VP
Laura L. Mountcastle, Treas./VP
Catherine M. Reynolds, Corp. Sec/VP
Theodore J. Vogel, Chief Tax Counsel/VP
David W. Joos, Chmn.

Phone: 517-788-0550	**Fax:** 517-788-1859
Toll-Free:	
Address: 1 Energy Plz., Jackson, MI 49201 US	

GROWTH PLANS/SPECIAL FEATURES:

CMS Energy Corporation is an energy company that operates electric utilities and natural gas utilities; owns natural gas and biomass-fueled power generation facilities; and markets energy. It has three principle divisions and two primary subsidiaries. The electric utility and gas utility business segments' operations are carried out by the subsidiary Consumers Energy Company, while subsidiary CMS Enterprises Company is responsible for the enterprises segment. Consumers Energy is a public utility that provides natural gas and electricity to 65% of Michigan's residents, providing electric service to 1.8 million customers in 275 cities; and natural gas service to 1.7 million customers in 215 cities. It has 4,244 miles of high-voltage distribution overhead lines operating at 23 kilovolts (KV) and 46 KV; and 409 miles of high-voltage distribution radial lines operating at 120 KV or higher. Its natural gas distribution network includes approximately 26,526 miles of pipelines, seven compressor stations and 15 gas storage fields with an aggregate capacity of 307 billion cubic feet. The subsidiary has ownership interests in seven mixed oil and gas combustion turbines, and 13 hydroelectric power plants. Consumers Energy primarily serves the alternative energy, automotive, chemical, metal and food products industries. The enterprises segment focuses on the production and marketing of domestic independent power. It has an ownership interest in eight generating plants in the U.S. with a generation capacity of 1,202 megawatts.

FINANCIALS: **Sales and profits are in thousands of dollars—add 000 to get the full amount. 2010 Note: Financial information for 2010 was not available for all companies at press time.**

2010 Sales: $	2010 Profits: $	**U.S. Stock Ticker: CMS**
2009 Sales: $6,205,000	2009 Profits: $220,000	**Int'l Ticker:** Int'l Exchange:
2008 Sales: $6,807,000	2008 Profits: $301,000	Employees: 7,755
2007 Sales: $6,464,000	2007 Profits: $-215,000	Fiscal Year Ends: 12/31
2006 Sales: $6,126,000	2006 Profits: $-79,000	Parent Company:

SALARIES/BENEFITS:

Pension Plan:	ESOP Stock Plan:	Profit Sharing:	Top Exec. Salary: $1,085,000	Bonus: $1,605,800
Savings Plan:	Stock Purch. Plan:		Second Exec. Salary: $665,000	Bonus: $541,310

OTHER THOUGHTS:

Apparent Women Officers or Directors: 5
Hot Spot for Advancement for Women/Minorities: Y

LOCATIONS: ("Y" = Yes)

West:	Southwest:	Midwest:	Southeast:	Northeast:	International:
		Y		Y	Y

CNOOC LIMITED

www.cnoocltd.com

Industry Group Code: 211111 **Ranks within this company's industry group:** Sales: 39 Profits: 18

Exploration/Production:		Refining/Retailing:		Utilities:		Alternative Energy:		Specialty Services:		Energy Mktg./Other Svcs.	
Exploration:	Y	Refining:		Electric Utility:		Waste/Solar/Other:		Consulting/Eng.:		Energy Marketing:	
Production:	Y	Retailing:		Gas Utility:		Thermal/Steam:		Seismic:		Equipment/Machinery:	
Coal Production:		Convenience Stores:		Pipelines:		Wind:		Drilling:		Oil Field Services:	
		Chemicals:		Water:		Hydro:		InfoTech:		Air/Shipping Transportation:	
						Fuel Cells:		Specialty Services:			

TYPES OF BUSINESS:

Oil & Gas Exploration & Production
Natural Gas Processing
Oil Refining

BRANDS/DIVISIONS/AFFILIATES:

China National Offshore Oil Corp.
Bridas Energy Holdings
CNOOC International Ltd.
Chesapeake Energy Corporation

CONTACTS: *Note: Officers with more than one job title may be intentionally listed here more than once.*

Yang Hua, CEO
Li Fanrong, Pres.
Zhong Hua, CFO
Chen Wei, Sr. VP/Gen. Dir.-CNOOC Research Institute
Yuan Guangyu, Exec. VP-Eng. & Construction
Zhao Liguo, General Counsel
Yuan Guangyu, Exec. VP-Oper.
Jiang Yongzhi, Gen. Mgr.-Investor Rel./Joint Company Sec.
Wu Guangqi, Chief Compliance Officer/Exec. Dir.
Zhu Weilin, Exec. VP/Gen. Mgr.-Exploration Dept.
Tsue Sik Yu, May, Joint Company Sec.
Fu Chengyu, Chmn.
Fang Zhi, VP/Gen. Mgr.-Int'l Affairs

Phone: 852-2213-2500	**Fax:** 852-2525-9322
Toll-Free:	
Address: 1 Garden Rd., Bank of China Tower, 65th Fl., Hong Kong, K3 00000 China	

GROWTH PLANS/SPECIAL FEATURES:

CNOOC Limited (China National Offshore Oil Corp.) explores for and produces crude oil and natural gas offshore in China and Indonesia. The company conducts its production activities through production sharing contracts (PSCs) with international oil and gas companies and is presently the only energy company in China allowed to collaborate with foreign companies. PSCs help CNOOC minimize its finding costs, exploration risks and capital requirements because foreign partners take on all of the costs associated with exploration. Bohai Bay is the firm's most important and largest oil and gas production base offshore China. Other offshore oil production areas of significance are the Western South China Sea, the Eastern South China Sea and the East China Sea. The proximity of CNOOC's natural gas reserves to the major demand areas in the coastal regions of China results in a competitive advantage over many Chinese energy providers whose reserves are located primarily in northwest and southwest China. CNOOC proved reserves total 2.6 billion BOE (barrels of oil equivalent). In 2009, the company produced an average of 623,896 BOE per day, with operations at Bohai Bay representing 43% of total production. In May 2010, CNOOC entered a joint venture agreement with Bridas Energy Holdings, expanding its presence into Latin America. In October 2010, the company's subsidiary CNOOC International Ltd. agreed to purchase a 33% interest in Chesapeake Energy Corporation's leasehold acres in the Eagle Ford Shale project in Texas.

Employees of CNOOC receive comprehensive training programs, opportunities for further development, as well as competitive compensation packages.

FINANCIALS: **Sales and profits are in thousands of dollars—add 000 to get the full amount. 2010 Note: Financial information for 2010 was not available for all companies at press time.**

2010 Sales: $	2010 Profits: $	**U.S. Stock Ticker: CEO**
2009 Sales: $15,384,400	2009 Profits: $4,312,160	**Int'l Ticker: 0883** Int'l Exchange: Hong Kong-HKEX
2008 Sales: $18,464,000	2008 Profits: $6,504,000	Employees: 4,019
2007 Sales: $11,160,000	2007 Profits: $3,880,000	Fiscal Year Ends: 12/31
2006 Sales: $11,397,000	2006 Profits: $3,963,000	Parent Company:

SALARIES/BENEFITS:

Pension Plan:	ESOP Stock Plan:	Profit Sharing:	Top Exec. Salary: $	Bonus: $
Savings Plan:	Stock Purch. Plan:		Second Exec. Salary: $	Bonus: $

OTHER THOUGHTS:

Apparent Women Officers or Directors: 1
Hot Spot for Advancement for Women/Minorities:

LOCATIONS: ("Y" = Yes)

West:	Southwest:	Midwest:	Southeast:	Northeast:	International:
					Y

CNX GAS CORPORATION

www.cnxgas.com

Industry Group Code: 211111 **Ranks within this company's industry group:** Sales: 87 Profits: 58

Exploration/Production:		**Refining/Retailing:**		**Utilities:**		**Alternative Energy:**		**Specialty Services:**		**Energy Mktg./Other Svcs.**	
Exploration:	Y	Refining:		Electric Utility:		Waste/Solar/Other:		Consulting/Eng.:		Energy Marketing:	Y
Production:	Y	Retailing:		Gas Utility:		Thermal/Steam:		Seismic:		Equipment/Machinery:	
Coal Production:		Convenience Stores:		Pipelines:		Wind:		Drilling:		Oil Field Services:	
		Chemicals:		Water:		Hydro:		InfoTech:		Air/Shipping Transportation:	
						Fuel Cells:		Specialty Services:			

TYPES OF BUSINESS:

Natural Gas Exploration & Production
Coalbed Methane Development
Power Generation
Gathering & Pipelines

BRANDS/DIVISIONS/AFFILIATES:

CONSOL Energy Inc

CONTACTS:

Note: Officers with more than one job title may be intentionally listed here more than once.

J. Brett Harvey, CEO
Nicholas J. Deluliis, COO
Nicholas J. Deluliis, Pres.
William Lyons, CFO/Exec. VP
Robert F. Pusateri, Exec. VP-Mktg. & Sales
Kurt Salvatori, Dir.-Human Resources
P. Jerome Richey, Chief Legal Officer/Sec.
Robert P. King, Exec. VP-Support Svcs. & Bus. Advancement
Daniel J. Zajdel, VP-Public Rel.
P. Jerome Richey, Exec. VP-Corp. Affairs
Robert F. Pusateri, Exec. VP-Transportation Svcs.
William Gillenwater, VP-Land Resources
J. Brett Harvey, Chmn.

Phone: 724-485-4000	**Fax:**
Toll-Free:	
Address: 1000 Consol Energy Dr., Canonsburg, PA 15317 US	

GROWTH PLANS/SPECIAL FEATURES:

CNX Gas Corporation, a wholly-owned subsidiary of CONSOL Energy, Inc., seeks, develops and produces coalbed methane and other natural gases, mostly in the Appalachian and Illinois Basins. CNX Gas Corp. has 4.5 billion tons of proved coal reserves, roughly 1.9 trillion cubic feet of net proved reserves and development rights to approximately 3.71 million net acres of coalbed. In addition, the firm has over 1 million acres of total net oil and gas property. CNX Gas Corp. maintains conventional and unconventional natural gas operations in several eastern U.S. states, including Pennsylvania, Virginia, West Virginia and Tennessee. The company has 247 development wells, all of which are located either in the central or northern Appalachia region and 3,926 producing wells. In 2009, the firm produced 94.42 billion cubic feet of gas. In June 2010, CONSOL acquired the remaining outstanding shares of CNX it did not already own, converting CNX into its wholly-owned subsidiary.

The company offers employees benefits including life, medical, dental, vision and disability insurance; a 401K; an assistance program; vacation; short- and long-term incentive bonus programs; and tuition reimbursement.

FINANCIALS:

Sales and profits are in thousands of dollars—add 000 to get the full amount. 2010 Note: Financial information for 2010 was not available for all companies at press time.

2010 Sales: $	2010 Profits: $	**U.S. Stock Ticker: Subsidiary**
2009 Sales: $683,400	2009 Profits: $164,500	**Int'l Ticker:** Int'l Exchange:
2008 Sales: $789,421	2008 Profits: $239,073	Employees: 174
2007 Sales: $479,482	2007 Profits: $135,678	Fiscal Year Ends: 12/31
2006 Sales: $514,837	2006 Profits: $159,867	Parent Company: CONSOL ENERGY INC

SALARIES/BENEFITS:

Pension Plan:	ESOP Stock Plan:	Profit Sharing:	Top Exec. Salary: $309,570	Bonus: $326,290
Savings Plan: Y	Stock Purch. Plan:		Second Exec. Salary: $309,570	Bonus: $326,290

OTHER THOUGHTS:

Apparent Women Officers or Directors:
Hot Spot for Advancement for Women/Minorities:

LOCATIONS: ("Y" = Yes)

West:	Southwest:	Midwest:	Southeast:	Northeast:	International:
		Y		Y	

COGENTRIX ENERGY LLC

www.cogentrix.com

Industry Group Code: 221 **Ranks within this company's industry group:** Sales: Profits:

Exploration/Production:		Refining/Retailing:		Utilities:		Alternative Energy:		Specialty Services:		Energy Mktg./Other Svcs.	
Exploration:		Refining:		Electric Utility:		Waste/Solar/Other:	Y	Consulting/Eng.:		Energy Marketing:	Y
Production:		Retailing:		Gas Utility:		Thermal/Steam:	Y	Seismic:		Equipment/Machinery:	
Coal Production:		Convenience Stores:		Pipelines:		Wind:	Y	Drilling:		Oil Field Services:	
		Chemicals:		Water:		Hydro:	Y	InfoTech:		Air/Shipping Transportation:	
						Fuel Cells:		Specialty Services:	Y		

TYPES OF BUSINESS:

Wholesale Power Marketing
Electricity Generation

BRANDS/DIVISIONS/AFFILIATES:

Goldman Sachs Group, Inc.
Eti Elektrik
Cogentrix Solar Services

CONTACTS: *Note: Officers with more than one job title may be intentionally listed here more than once.*

Bob Mancini, CEO
Thomas J. Bonner, Pres.
S. Mark Rudolph, Interim CFO/Sr. VP-Finance
Linda A. Okowita, Sr. VP-Human Resources
Ed MacGuffie, VP-Solar Dev.
Richard W. Gray, Jr., Sr. VP-Eng. & Construction
Gary M. Carraux, Chief Admin. Officer/Sr. VP
Doug Miller, General Counsel/Exec. VP
William L. Felts, Exec. VP-Dev.
Kevin McNamara, VP-Project Finance
John Gasbarro, Sr. VP-Fuels & Asset Mgmt.
Richard Neff, VP-Environmental Affairs
Clifford D. Evans, Jr., Sr. VP-Asset Mgmt.

Phone: 704-525-3800	**Fax:** 704-525-9934
Toll-Free:	
Address: 9405 Arrowpoint Blvd., Charlotte, NC 28273 US	

GROWTH PLANS/SPECIAL FEATURES:

Cogentrix Energy LLC, controlled by Goldman Sachs Group, Inc., is an independent power generating company that sells wholesale power to utilities and power marketers. The company develops, operates and owns or has interests in more than 15 electric generating facilities, with a total generating capacity in excess of 3,300 megawatts (MW). The firm is also focused on the development of renewable and low-emission power resources, primarily solar electricity. The company's facilities include gas-fired combined-cycle, rapid-start peaking, solar thermal, hydro and lower energy cost coal-fired facilities, which are located throughout the U.S. in Virginia, West Virginia, North Carolina, Florida, New Jersey, New York, Pennsylvania, Minnesota, Wisconsin, Colorado, California and Idaho. In February 2010, the company finalized the acquisition of Eti Elektrik, a Turkish joint stock company that owns a portfolio of in-construction, licensed and license-pending power generation assets in Turkey with a capacity of 2,300 MW of hydro, wind, and thermal projects. In August 2010, the firm received a contract from the Public Service Company of Colorado to develop a 30,000 kilowatt solar generating project in southern Colorado.

FINANCIALS: **Sales and profits are in thousands of dollars—add 000 to get the full amount. 2010 Note: Financial information for 2010 was not available for all companies at press time.**

2010 Sales: $	2010 Profits: $	**U.S. Stock Ticker: Subsidiary**
2009 Sales: $	2009 Profits: $	**Int'l Ticker:** Int'l Exchange:
2008 Sales: $	2008 Profits: $	Employees:
2007 Sales: $26,000	2007 Profits: $	Fiscal Year Ends: 12/31
2006 Sales: $	2006 Profits: $	Parent Company: GOLDMAN SACHS GROUP INC

SALARIES/BENEFITS:

Pension Plan:	ESOP Stock Plan:	Profit Sharing:	Top Exec. Salary: $	Bonus: $
Savings Plan:	Stock Purch. Plan:		Second Exec. Salary: $	Bonus: $

OTHER THOUGHTS:

Apparent Women Officers or Directors: 1
Hot Spot for Advancement for Women/Minorities:

LOCATIONS: ("Y" = Yes)

West:	Southwest:	Midwest:	Southeast:	Northeast:	International:
Y		Y	Y	Y	Y

COLONIAL GROUP INC

www.colonialgroupinc.com

Industry Group Code: 424710 **Ranks within this company's industry group:** Sales: 5 Profits:

Exploration/Production:		Refining/Retailing:		Utilities:		Alternative Energy:		Specialty Services:		Energy Mktg./Other Svcs.	
Exploration:		Refining:		Electric Utility:		Waste/Solar/Other:		Consulting/Eng.:		Energy Marketing:	
Production:		Retailing:		Gas Utility:		Thermal/Steam:		Seismic:		Equipment/Machinery:	
Coal Production:		Convenience Stores:	Y	Pipelines:	Y	Wind:		Drilling:		Oil Field Services:	
		Chemicals:	Y	Water:		Hydro:		InfoTech:		Air/Shipping Transportation:	Y
						Fuel Cells:		Specialty Services:	Y		

TYPES OF BUSINESS:

Liquid & Dry Bulk Storage
Oil & Natural Gas Storage & Distribution
Port Terminal Operations
Tugboat & Tanker Services
Shipping & Regulatory Compliance Services
Chemical Products
Gas Stations

BRANDS/DIVISIONS/AFFILIATES:

Colonial Oil Industries Inc
Colonial Terminals Inc
Georgia Kaolin Terminals Inc
Enmark Stations Inc
Chatham Towing Company Inc
Sun State Towing
Colonial Energy Inc
Colonial Marine Industries Inc

CONTACTS:

Note: Officers with more than one job title may be intentionally listed here more than once.

Robert H. Demere, Jr., Pres.

Phone: 912-236-1331	**Fax:** 912-235-3881
Toll-Free: 800-944-3835	
Address: 101 N. Lathrop Ave., Savannah, GA 31415 US	

GROWTH PLANS/SPECIAL FEATURES:

Colonial Group, Inc., founded in 1921, provides storage and distribution services for liquid and dry bulk products through more than a dozen subsidiaries. Colonial Oil Industries, Inc. is one of the largest independent oil distribution companies in the Southeast, with ocean terminals in Savannah, Georgia; Charleston, South Carolina; Jacksonville, Port Everglades and Tampa, Florida; and Wilmington, North Carolina, as well as more than 40 pipeline terminals throughout the Southeast. Colonial Terminals, Inc. operates some of the largest liquid and dry bulk storage facilities in the Southeast, with two locations in Savannah and Wilmington. Georgia Kaolin Terminals, Inc. is one of the group's marine facilities, designed to connect the kaolin industry to the world's larger forest commodity shipping lines. Enmark Stations, Inc. operates more than 70 gas stations in Georgia, North Carolina and South Carolina. Chatham Towing Company, Inc. and Colonial Towing, Inc., which conducts its business as Sun State Towing, own and operate a fleet of tugboats and tank barges based out of Savannah, Jacksonville, Wilmington and Charleston that transport cargo along inland waters from Morehead City, North Carolina to Cape Canaveral, Florida. Colonial Energy, Inc. delivers natural gas to wholesale and retail customers through its main operations in Fairfax, Virginia and its regional offices in Houston, Texas and Pittsburgh, Pennsylvania. Colonial Chemical Solutions, Inc. provides products and services for the food, chemical process and basic chemical industries. Colonial Marine Industries, Inc. provides ship management, chartering, brokerage and port agency services. Its wholly-owned subsidiary, Compliance Systems, Inc., provides regulatory compliance solutions for the shipping industry that are designed to reduce port delays, reduce U.S. Coast Guard and state imposed fines and document a client's good faith efforts in ship safety and environmental compliance. Colonial Caribbean, Inc., based in Puerto Rico, acquires light products supply systems for the independent gasoline market in the Caribbean.

FINANCIALS:

Sales and profits are in thousands of dollars—add 000 to get the full amount. 2010 Note: Financial information for 2010 was not available for all companies at press time.

2010 Sales: $	2010 Profits: $	**U.S. Stock Ticker: Private**
2009 Sales: $3,800,000	2009 Profits: $	**Int'l Ticker:** Int'l Exchange:
2008 Sales: $3,400,000	2008 Profits: $	Employees: 900
2007 Sales: $	2007 Profits: $	Fiscal Year Ends: 12/31
2006 Sales: $5,000,000	2006 Profits: $	Parent Company:

SALARIES/BENEFITS:

Pension Plan:	ESOP Stock Plan:	Profit Sharing:	Top Exec. Salary: $	Bonus: $
Savings Plan:	Stock Purch. Plan:		Second Exec. Salary: $	Bonus: $

OTHER THOUGHTS:

Apparent Women Officers or Directors:
Hot Spot for Advancement for Women/Minorities:

LOCATIONS: ("Y" = Yes)

West:	Southwest:	Midwest:	Southeast:	Northeast:	International:
	Y		Y	Y	Y

COMMONWEALTH EDISON COMPANY

www.comed.com

Industry Group Code: 2211 **Ranks within this company's industry group:** Sales: Profits:

Exploration/Production:		Refining/Retailing:		Utilities:		Alternative Energy:		Specialty Services:		Energy Mktg./Other Svcs.	
Exploration:		Refining:		Electric Utility:	Y	Waste/Solar/Other:		Consulting/Eng.:		Energy Marketing:	
Production:		Retailing:		Gas Utility:		Thermal/Steam:		Seismic:		Equipment/Machinery:	
Coal Production:		Convenience Stores:		Pipelines:		Wind:		Drilling:		Oil Field Services:	
		Chemicals:		Water:		Hydro:		InfoTech:		Air/Shipping Transportation:	
						Fuel Cells:		Specialty Services:			

TYPES OF BUSINESS:

Electric Utilities
Electric Power Distribution

BRANDS/DIVISIONS/AFFILIATES:

Exelon Corporation

CONTACTS: *Note: Officers with more than one job title may be intentionally listed here more than once.*

Frank M. Clark, CEO
Anne Pramaggiore, COO
Anne Pramaggiore, Pres.
Joseph Trpik, Jr., CFO/Sr. VP/Treas.
Val Jensen, VP-Mktg. & Environmental Programs
Michael Latino, VP-Human Resources
Ron Donovan, VP-Tech. & Customer Bus. Transformation
Michelle Blaise, VP-Eng. & Project Mgmt.
Thomas O'Neill, General Counsel/Sr. VP-Regulatory Policy & Rates
Terence Donnelly, Exec. VP-Oper.
Rita Stols, VP-Strategic & Support Svcs.
Tabrina Davis, VP-Comm.
Kevin Waden, VP/Controller
John Hooker, Exec. VP-Legislative & External Affairs
William McNeil, VP-Energy Acquisition
Fidel Marquez, Jr., Sr. VP-Customer Oper.
Frank M. Clark, Chmn.
Tyler Anthony, Sr. VP-Dist. Oper.

Phone: 312-394-4321	**Fax:** 312-394-2231
Toll-Free: 800-334-7661	
Address: 440 S. LaSalle St., Chicago, IL 60605 US	

GROWTH PLANS/SPECIAL FEATURES:

Commonwealth Edison Company (ComEd) is an electricity delivery firm. The company, which is a subsidiary of Exelon Corp., provides electricity to approximately 3.8 million people in Northern Illinois and the greater Chicago area (70% of the region's population). The company's service territory includes the Wisconsin border in the north, Iroquois County in the south, the Iowa border to the west and the Indiana border to the east. ComEd owns and operates roughly 90,000 miles of power lines in a service territory of roughly 11,400 square miles. The firm receives most of its power from Exelon Generation. Exelon owns generation assets with a net capacity of nearly 25,000 megawatts. ComEd offers its residential and commercial customers online account management and bill payment services.

FINANCIALS: **Sales and profits are in thousands of dollars—add 000 to get the full amount. 2010 Note: Financial information for 2010 was not available for all companies at press time.**

2010 Sales: $	2010 Profits: $	**U.S. Stock Ticker: Subsidiary**
2009 Sales: $	2009 Profits: $	**Int'l Ticker:** Int'l Exchange:
2008 Sales: $	2008 Profits: $	Employees:
2007 Sales: $6,104,000	2007 Profits: $165,000	Fiscal Year Ends: 12/31
2006 Sales: $6,101,000	2006 Profits: $-112,000	Parent Company: EXELON CORPORATION

SALARIES/BENEFITS:

Pension Plan:	ESOP Stock Plan:	Profit Sharing:	Top Exec. Salary: $	Bonus: $341,591
Savings Plan:	Stock Purch. Plan:		Second Exec. Salary: $	Bonus: $

OTHER THOUGHTS:

Apparent Women Officers or Directors: 7
Hot Spot for Advancement for Women/Minorities: Y

LOCATIONS: ("Y" = Yes)

West:	Southwest:	Midwest:	Southeast:	Northeast:	International:
		Y			

COMPANHIA DE TRANSMISSAO DE ENERGIA ELETRICA PAULISTA (CTEEP)

www.cteep.com.br

Industry Group Code: 2211 **Ranks within this company's industry group:** Sales: 44 Profits: 23

Exploration/Production:		Refining/Retailing:		Utilities:		Alternative Energy:		Specialty Services:		Energy Mktg./Other Svcs.	
Exploration:		Refining:		Electric Utility:	Y	Waste/Solar/Other:		Consulting/Eng.:		Energy Marketing:	
Production:		Retailing:		Gas Utility:		Thermal/Steam:		Seismic:		Equipment/Machinery:	
Coal Production:		Convenience Stores:		Pipelines:		Wind:		Drilling:		Oil Field Services:	
		Chemicals:		Water:		Hydro:		InfoTech:		Air/Shipping Transportation:	
						Fuel Cells:		Specialty Services:			

TYPES OF BUSINESS:

Electricity Transmission

BRANDS/DIVISIONS/AFFILIATES:

Interconexion Electrica SA
Centrais Eletricas Brasileiras SA (Eletrobras)
ISA

CONTACTS:

Note: Officers with more than one job title may be intentionally listed here more than once.

Cesar Augusto Ramirez Rojas, CEO
Celso Sebastiao Cerchiari, COO
Marcio Lopes Almeida, CFO
Pio Adolfo Barcena Villarreal, Chief Admin. Officer
Mirana Bertolini, Contact-Corp. Comm.
Marcio Lopes Almeida, Dir.-Investor Rel.
Jorge Rodriguez Ortiz, Chief Enterprise Officer
Luis Fernando Alarcon Mantilla, Chmn.

Phone: 55-11-3138-7000 **Fax:** 55-11-3138-7161
Toll-Free:
Address: Rua Casa do Ator, 1155 Vila Olimpia, Sao Paulo, 04546 Brazil

GROWTH PLANS/SPECIAL FEATURES:

Companhia De Transmissao De Energia Eletrica Paulista (CTEEP) is one of the largest private electric energy companies in Brazil. CTEEP transmits 30% of Brazil's produced electricity and is essentially the sole provider of electric energy to the state of Sao Paulo. The company's grid has a 43,223 MW capacity over 7,000 miles of transmission lines, 1,215 miles of fiber optic cables and 105 substations. CTEEP serves 12 states within Brazil, including Rio Grade do Sul, Santa Catarina, Parana, Sao Paulo, Minas Gerais, Rondonia, Mato Grosso, Mato Grosso do Sul, Goias, Tocantins, Maranhao and Piaui. As part of that service, the company operates through five regional offices, all of which are located in the state of Sao Paulo. The company also leases its transmission grid out to other electricity companies, sector traders as well as individual consumers. CTEEP is a subsidiary company of ISA, Latin America's highest volume electric energy transmission service group.

FINANCIALS:

Sales and profits are in thousands of dollars—add 000 to get the full amount. 2010 Note: Financial information for 2010 was not available for all companies at press time.

2010 Sales: $	2010 Profits: $	**U.S. Stock Ticker: CTPZY**
2009 Sales: $967,080	2009 Profits: $487,040	**Int'l Ticker: TRPL4** Int'l Exchange: Sao Paulo-SAO
2008 Sales: $914,370	2008 Profits: $486,510	Employees:
2007 Sales: $	2007 Profits: $	Fiscal Year Ends:
2006 Sales: $	2006 Profits: $	Parent Company:

SALARIES/BENEFITS:

Pension Plan:	ESOP Stock Plan:	Profit Sharing:	Top Exec. Salary: $	Bonus: $
Savings Plan:	Stock Purch. Plan:		Second Exec. Salary: $	Bonus: $

OTHER THOUGHTS:

Apparent Women Officers or Directors:
Hot Spot for Advancement for Women/Minorities:

LOCATIONS: ("Y" = Yes)

West:	Southwest:	Midwest:	Southeast:	Northeast:	International:
					Y

COMPANHIA PARANAENSE DE ENERGIA - COPEL www.copel.com

Industry Group Code: 221 **Ranks within this company's industry group:** Sales: 37 Profits: 20

Exploration/Production:		Refining/Retailing:		Utilities:		Alternative Energy:		Specialty Services:		Energy Mktg./Other Svcs.	
Exploration:		Refining:		Electric Utility:	Y	Waste/Solar/Other:		Consulting/Eng.:	Y	Energy Marketing:	Y
Production:		Retailing:		Gas Utility:	Y	Thermal/Steam:	Y	Seismic:		Equipment/Machinery:	
Coal Production:	Y	Convenience Stores:		Pipelines:		Wind:		Drilling:		Oil Field Services:	
		Chemicals:		Water:		Hydro:	Y	InfoTech:	Y	Air/Shipping Transportation:	
						Fuel Cells:		Specialty Services:	Y		

TYPES OF BUSINESS:

Utilities-Electricity
Hydroelectric & Thermoelectric Generation
Telecommunications Services
Information Technology
Utilities-Gas

BRANDS/DIVISIONS/AFFILIATES:

Copel Geracao Y Transmissao S.A.
COPEL Distribuicao S.A.
COPEL Telecomunicacoes S.A.
COPEL Participacoes S.A.

CONTACTS:

Note: Officers with more than one job title may be intentionally listed here more than once.

Ronaldo T. Ravedutti, CEO
Rafael Iatauro, CFO
Edson Sardeto, Chief Eng. Officer
Regina Maria Bueno Bacellar, Chief Legal Officer
Luiz Antonio Rossafa, Chief Bus. Mgmt. Officer
Rafael Iatauro, Chief Investor Rel. Officer
Marlene Zannin, Chief Environment & Corp. Citizenship Officer
Raul M. Neto, Chief Generation & Transmission Officer
Raul M. Neto, Chief Telecomm. Officer
Leo de Almeida Neves, Chmn.
Vlademir Santo Daleffe, Chief Dist. Officer

Phone: 55-41-322-3535	**Fax:** 55-41-331-4145
Toll-Free:	
Address: Rua Coronel Dulcidio, 800, Curitiba, 80420-170 Brazil	

GROWTH PLANS/SPECIAL FEATURES:

Companhia Paranaense de Energia - Copel (Copel) is a power utility company that generates, transmits and distributes electricity, as well as providing telecommunications services to its customers in the state of Parana, Brazil. The state government of Parana owns 58.63% of the voting rights for Copel. The company is organized into four wholly-owned subsidiaries: Copel Geracao Y Transmissao S.A.; Copel Distribuicao S.A.; Copel Telecomunicacoes S.A.; and Copel Participacoes S.A. Copel Geracao Y Transmissao operates the power generation assets of the firm, consisting of 17 hydroelectric plants and one thermoelectric plant, with a total capacity of 4,550 megawatts (MW). Roughly 7% of the electricity consumed in Brazil is generated by Copel, which it transmits through 30 substations and over approximately 1,188 miles of transmission lines. Copel Distribuicao, the firm's distribution subsidiary, then supplies the power to over 2.8 million customers within Parana. Copel Telecomunicacoes supplies Copel's own telecommunications needs and also provides carrier services to such operators as Embratel, Global Telecom GVT, Brasil Telecom, Impsat and Sercomtel, as well as data, voice and video transmission services to other corporate customers such as supermarkets, schools, banks and industries. In sum, it serves 226 cities and operates over 3,500 miles of optical cable. Copel Participacoes implements the firm's investment strategies through partnerships, with business interests in sanitation, gas supply, telecommunications and coal mining; and interests in companies adding 1,790 MW of power generation to its capacity.

FINANCIALS:

Sales and profits are in thousands of dollars—add 000 to get the full amount. 2010 Note: Financial information for 2010 was not available for all companies at press time.

2010 Sales: $	2010 Profits: $	**U.S. Stock Ticker: ELP**
2009 Sales: $3,304,160	2009 Profits: $603,740	**Int'l Ticker:** Int'l Exchange:
2008 Sales: $3,093,680	2008 Profits: $611,340	Employees: 8,682
2007 Sales: $3,059,200	2007 Profits: $686,100	Fiscal Year Ends: 12/31
2006 Sales: $3,030,900	2006 Profits: $770,500	Parent Company:

SALARIES/BENEFITS:

Pension Plan: Y	ESOP Stock Plan:	Profit Sharing: Y	Top Exec. Salary: $	Bonus: $
Savings Plan:	Stock Purch. Plan:		Second Exec. Salary: $	Bonus: $

OTHER THOUGHTS:

Apparent Women Officers or Directors: 2
Hot Spot for Advancement for Women/Minorities:

LOCATIONS: ("Y" = Yes)

West:	Southwest:	Midwest:	Southeast:	Northeast:	International:
					Y

COMPANIA ESPANOLA DE PETROLEOS SA (CEPSA)

www.cepsa.com

Industry Group Code: 324110 **Ranks within this company's industry group:** Sales: 10 Profits: 4

Exploration/Production:		Refining/Retailing:		Utilities:		Alternative Energy:		Specialty Services:		Energy Mktg./Other Svcs.	
Exploration:	Y	Refining:	Y	Electric Utility:		Waste/Solar/Other:		Consulting/Eng.:		Energy Marketing:	
Production:	Y	Retailing:	Y	Gas Utility:		Thermal/Steam:		Seismic:		Equipment/Machinery:	
Coal Production:		Convenience Stores:	Y	Pipelines:		Wind:		Drilling:		Oil Field Services:	
		Chemicals:	Y	Water:		Hydro:		InfoTech:		Air/Shipping Transportation:	
						Fuel Cells:		Specialty Services:	Y		

TYPES OF BUSINESS:

Petroleum Refineries & Retail Marketing
Oil & Gas Exploration & Production
Petrochemicals
Propane & Butane
Bunker Services
Aviation Fuels
Marine Lubricant Supply
Gas Stations

BRANDS/DIVISIONS/AFFILIATES:

CEPSA
CEPSA STAR
PETROCAN
ATLAS

CONTACTS:

Note: Officers with more than one job title may be intentionally listed here more than once.

Dominique de Riberolles, CEO
Miguel del Marmol, Sr. VP-Oil Mktg.
Juan Rodriguez, Dir.-Human Resources
Jaime Berbes, VP-Tech.
Juan Rodriguez, Dir.-Legal Affairs
Jose Eulogio Aranguren, Sr. VP-Strategy & Control
Luis Calderon, VP-Comm. & Institutional Rel.
Fernando Maravall Herrero, Sr. VP-Exploration, Prod. & Natural Gas
Fernando Iturrieta, VP-Petrochemicals
Pedro Miro, Sr. VP-Corp. Tech. Area
Jose Maria Garcia, VP-Refining
Santiago Bergareche Busquet, Chmn.
Inigo Diaz de Espada, VP-Supply, Trading, Marine & Aviation

Phone: 91-337-60-00	**Fax:** 91-721-16-13
Toll-Free:	
Address: Campo de las Naciones-Avda. del Partenon 12, Madrid, MAD 28024 Spain	

GROWTH PLANS/SPECIAL FEATURES:

Compania Espanola de Petroleos SA (CEPSA), based in Madrid, Spain, is an international petroleum and petrochemical company with operations in Spain, Portugal, Italy, the U.K., the Netherlands, Belgium, Colombia, Brazil, Portugal, Panama, Peru Morocco, Algeria, Egypt and Canada. CEPSA Group operates through dozens of subsidiary and affiliate companies in the trading, refining, exploration, production, gas, electricity and petrochemical fields with services offered to private, agricultural, industrial, marine, aviation and energy customers. Its operations include the exploration and production of crude oil and natural gas, refining, transport and marketing of petroleum derivatives and the production of value-added petrochemical products such as plastics, synthetic fibers and detergents. The firm also provides home delivery of diesel and fuel oil and supplies propane through bulk delivery and pipelines. The company owns and operates 1,762 service stations throughout Spain and Portugal under the CEPSA brand, with over 850 shops that are located inside. The firm's retail division offers payment cards under the CEPSA STAR brand. Bunker activities relate to fueling ships with coal or oil, supplying marine lubricant or transferring cargo from ships to warehouses. The company's PETROCAN and ATLAS subsidiaries provide bunker services in the ports of Las Palmas, Tenerife, Algeciras, Huelva, Ceuta, Gibraltar, Balboa and Cristobal. In addition, CEPSA supplies airplane fuels for civil, military and general aviation. The International Petroleum Investment Company owns 47.02% of CEPSA.

FINANCIALS:

Sales and profits are in thousands of dollars—add 000 to get the full amount. 2010 Note: Financial information for 2010 was not available for all companies at press time.

2010 Sales: $	2010 Profits: $	**U.S. Stock Ticker:**
2009 Sales: $22,762,500	2009 Profits: $462,730	**Int'l Ticker: CPS** Int'l Exchange: Frankfurt-Euronext
2008 Sales: $35,481,700	2008 Profits: $387,400	Employees:
2007 Sales: $28,448,600	2007 Profits: $1,002,600	Fiscal Year Ends: 12/31
2006 Sales: $27,747,600	2006 Profits: $1,087,600	Parent Company:

SALARIES/BENEFITS:

Pension Plan:	ESOP Stock Plan:	Profit Sharing:	Top Exec. Salary: $	Bonus: $
Savings Plan:	Stock Purch. Plan:		Second Exec. Salary: $	Bonus: $

OTHER THOUGHTS:

Apparent Women Officers or Directors: 1
Hot Spot for Advancement for Women/Minorities:

LOCATIONS: ("Y" = Yes)

West:	Southwest:	Midwest:	Southeast:	Northeast:	International:
					Y

Note: Financial information, benefits and other data can change quickly and may vary from those stated here.

CONOCOPHILLIPS COMPANY

www.conocophillips.com

Industry Group Code: 211111 **Ranks within this company's industry group:** Sales: 9 Profits: 17

Exploration/Production:		Refining/Retailing:		Utilities:		Alternative Energy:		Specialty Services:		Energy Mktg./Other Svcs.	
Exploration:	Y	Refining:	Y	Electric Utility:		Waste/Solar/Other:		Consulting/Eng.:		Energy Marketing:	Y
Production:	Y	Retailing:	Y	Gas Utility:		Thermal/Steam:		Seismic:		Equipment/Machinery:	
Coal Production:		Convenience Stores:		Pipelines:	Y	Wind:		Drilling:		Oil Field Services:	
		Chemicals:		Water:		Hydro:		InfoTech:		Air/Shipping Transportation:	
						Fuel Cells:		Specialty Services:			

TYPES OF BUSINESS:

Oil & Gas Exploration & Production
Natural Gas Distribution
Refining
Pipelines
Oil Sands Operations
Chemical Production
Technology Investment
Gasoline Retail

BRANDS/DIVISIONS/AFFILIATES:

JET
Conoco
Phillips 66
DCP Midstream LLC
Chevron Phillips Chemical Company LLC
Alaska Gas Pipe
Origin Energy

CONTACTS:

Note: Officers with more than one job title may be intentionally listed here more than once.

James J. Mulva, CEO
John A. Carrig, COO
John A. Carrig, Pres.
Sigmund L. Cornelius, CFO/Sr. VP
W.C.W. Chiang, Sr. VP-Mktg.
Carin S. Knickel, VP-Human Resources
Kevin Meyers, Sr. VP-Exploration & Prod., Americas
Stephen R. Brand, Sr. VP-Tech.
Luc J. Messier, Sr. VP-Project Dev.
Gene L. Batchelder, Chief Admin. Officer/Sr. VP
Janet Langford Kelly, General Counsel/Corp. Sec./Sr. VP-Legal
Jeff Sheets, Sr. VP-Planning & Strategy
Red Cavaney, Sr. VP-Public Affairs
Sigmund L. Cornelius, Sr. VP-Finance
Robert A. Herman, VP-Health, Safety & Environment
W.C.W Chiang, Sr. VP-Refining & Transportation
Gregory Goff, Sr. VP-Commercial
James J. Mulva, Chmn.
Ryan M. Lance, Sr. VP-Exploration & Prod., Int'l

Phone: 281-293-1000	**Fax:**
Toll-Free:	
Address: 600 N. Dairy Ashford Rd., Houston, TX 77079-1175 US	

GROWTH PLANS/SPECIAL FEATURES:

ConocoPhillips Company is an integrated global energy company. Its business segments include exploration and production, midstream, refining and marketing, chemicals and emerging businesses. The exploration and production segment explores for, produces, transports and markets crude oil, natural gas and natural gas liquids worldwide. It also mines oil sands to extract bitumen, which it upgrades into synthetic crude oil. The midstream division gathers, processes and markets natural gas produced by the company and others, and also fractionates and markets natural gas liquids. This segment includes the firm's 50% equity investment in DCP Midstream, LLC. The refining and marketing segment purchases, refines, markets and transports crude oil and petroleum products, mainly in the U.S., Europe and Asia. The chemicals group, including the company's 50% equity investment in Chevron Phillips Chemical Company LLC, manufactures and markets petrochemicals and plastics worldwide. The emerging businesses segment oversees businesses such as technologies related to hydrocarbon recovery (including heavy oil), refining, alternative energy, biofuels and the environment. In June 2009, ConocoPhillips, KazMunayGas and Mubadala announced the signing of project agreements for the joint exploration and development of the Nursultan Block, which is located in offshore Kazakhstan. In July 2009, ConocoPhillips and Abu Dhabi National Oil Company (ADNOC) signed the Shah Gas Field Joint Venture and Field Entry agreements. The two companies are working together to develop the Shah Gas field in Abu Dhabi. ConocoPhillips owns 40% interest in the project, and ADNOC owns the remaining 60 %. In July 2010, the firm announced plans to sell its 20% stake in Lukoil (OAO).

ConocoPhillips' employees receive medical and dental insurance; a retirement plan; a savings plan; short-term and long-term disability; life insurance; a health savings account; spending accounts; a Healthy Lifestyle Coach; and scholarships and tuition reimbursement.

FINANCIALS:

Sales and profits are in thousands of dollars—add 000 to get the full amount. 2010 Note: Financial information for 2010 was not available for all companies at press time.

2010 Sales: $	2010 Profits: $	**U.S. Stock Ticker: COP**
2009 Sales: $149,341,000	2009 Profits: $4,858,000	**Int'l Ticker:** Int'l Exchange:
2008 Sales: $240,842,000	2008 Profits: $-16,998,000	Employees: 30,000
2007 Sales: $187,437,000	2007 Profits: $11,891,000	Fiscal Year Ends: 12/31
2006 Sales: $183,650,000	2006 Profits: $15,550,000	Parent Company:

SALARIES/BENEFITS:

Pension Plan: Y	ESOP Stock Plan: Y	Profit Sharing:	Top Exec. Salary: $1,500,000	Bonus: $1,278,788
Savings Plan: Y	Stock Purch. Plan:		Second Exec. Salary: $1,145,000	Bonus: $1,474,560

OTHER THOUGHTS:

Apparent Women Officers or Directors: 5
Hot Spot for Advancement for Women/Minorities: Y

LOCATIONS: ("Y" = Yes)

West:	Southwest:	Midwest:	Southeast:	Northeast:	International:
Y	Y	Y	Y	Y	Y

CONSOL ENERGY INC

www.consolenergy.com

Industry Group Code: 21211 **Ranks within this company's industry group:** Sales: 5 Profits: 5

Exploration/Production:		Refining/Retailing:		Utilities:		Alternative Energy:		Specialty Services:		Energy Mktg./Other Svcs.	
Exploration:	Y	Refining:		Electric Utility:		Waste/Solar/Other:		Consulting/Eng.:		Energy Marketing:	
Production:	Y	Retailing:		Gas Utility:		Thermal/Steam:		Seismic:		Equipment/Machinery:	
Coal Production:	Y	Convenience Stores:		Pipelines:		Wind:		Drilling:		Oil Field Services:	
		Chemicals:		Water:		Hydro:		InfoTech:		Air/Shipping Transportation:	
						Fuel Cells:		Specialty Services:			

TYPES OF BUSINESS:

Coal Mining
Energy Services
Gas Exploration & Production

BRANDS/DIVISIONS/AFFILIATES:

CNX Gas Corporation
CNX Land Resources Inc

CONTACTS:

Note: Officers with more than one job title may be intentionally listed here more than once.

J. Brett Harvey, CEO
Nicholas J. Deluliis, COO/Exec. VP
J. Brett Harvey, Pres.
William J. Lyons, CFO/Exec. VP
Robert Pusateri, Exec. VP-Energy Sales
P. Jerome Richey, Chief Legal Officer/Sec./Exec. VP-Corp. Affairs
Robert P. King, Exec. VP-Bus. Advancement & Support Svcs.
Robert Pusateri, Exec. VP-Transportation Svcs.
J. Brett Harvey, Chmn.

Phone: 724-485-4000 **Fax:** 724-485-4833
Toll-Free:
Address: 1000 Consol Energy Dr., CNX Center, Canonsburg, PA 15317-6506 US

GROWTH PLANS/SPECIAL FEATURES:

CONSOL Energy, Inc. is a multi-fuel energy producer and energy services provider, primarily serving the U.S. electric power generation industry. It produces high-BTU bituminous coal from 16 mining complexes in the U.S., as well as pipeline-quality coalbed methane gas from coal properties in Pennsylvania, Virginia and West Virginia, and conventional gas from Tennessee and Virginia. The company's mining complexes contain an approximate reserve base of 4.5 billion tons of coal. CONSOL is one of the largest producers of bituminous coal in the U.S., as well as one of the largest coal producers from underground mines, one of the largest coal producers east of the Mississippi River and one of the largest coal exporters. The company operates 26 towboats and a fleet of more than 700 barges. It employs transportation specialists who negotiate freight and equipment agreements with railroads, barge lines, terminal operators, ocean vessel brokers and trucking companies. CONSOL's gas operations involve producing coalbed methane and natural gas. The company owns over 2,600 wells and has estimated proved reserves of approximately 1.4 trillion cubic feet of oil equivalent. Through its subsidiary, CNX Land Resources, Inc., the firm has timber and farming operations, as well as commercial development ventures. CNX Gas Corp., an 83.3% owned subsidiary, produces pipeline-quality coalbed methane gas from coal properties in the Northern and Central Appalachian basin. In addition, the firm provides industrial supply services, terminal services, river and dock services and coal waste disposal services. In April 2010, the company acquired the natural gas business of Virginia-based Dominion Resources, Inc. for $3.48 billion, which includes 1.46 million acres and over 9,000 wells.

CONSOL offers its employees medical, dental, vision and prescription drug coverage; life and AD&D insurance; short- and long-term disability; a 401(k) plan; pension plans; an employee assistance program; relocation assistance; and access to a credit union.

FINANCIALS:

Sales and profits are in thousands of dollars—add 000 to get the full amount. 2010 Note: Financial information for 2010 was not available for all companies at press time.

2010 Sales: $	2010 Profits: $
2009 Sales: $4,621,875	2009 Profits: $539,717
2008 Sales: $4,652,445	2008 Profits: $442,470
2007 Sales: $3,762,197	2007 Profits: $267,782
2006 Sales: $3,715,171	2006 Profits: $408,882

U.S. Stock Ticker: CNX
Int'l Ticker: Int'l Exchange:
Employees: 8,012
Fiscal Year Ends: 12/31
Parent Company:

SALARIES/BENEFITS:

Pension Plan: Y	ESOP Stock Plan:	Profit Sharing:	Top Exec. Salary: $1,038,462	Bonus: $2,262,000
Savings Plan: Y	Stock Purch. Plan:		Second Exec. Salary: $621,077	Bonus: $1,050,000

OTHER THOUGHTS:

Apparent Women Officers or Directors: 1
Hot Spot for Advancement for Women/Minorities:

LOCATIONS: ("Y" = Yes)

West:	Southwest:	Midwest:	Southeast:	Northeast:	International:
Y				Y	Y

CONSOLIDATED EDISON INC

www.conedison.com

Industry Group Code: 221 **Ranks within this company's industry group:** Sales: 12 Profits: 16

Exploration/Production:		**Refining/Retailing:**		**Utilities:**		**Alternative Energy:**		**Specialty Services:**		**Energy Mktg./Other Svcs.**	
Exploration:		Refining:		Electric Utility:	Y	Waste/Solar/Other:		Consulting/Eng.:	Y	Energy Marketing:	Y
Production:		Retailing:		Gas Utility:	Y	Thermal/Steam:		Seismic:		Equipment/Machinery:	
Coal Production:		Convenience Stores:		Pipelines:		Wind:		Drilling:		Oil Field Services:	
		Chemicals:		Water:		Hydro:		InfoTech:		Air/Shipping Transportation:	
						Fuel Cells:		Specialty Services:	Y		

TYPES OF BUSINESS:

Utilities-Electricity & Natural Gas
Steam Utility
Electric Generation
Electricity Marketing

BRANDS/DIVISIONS/AFFILIATES:

Orange and Rockland Utilities, Inc.
Consolidated Edison Company of New York, Inc.
Consolidated Edison Development
Consolidated Edison Solutions
Consolidated Edison Energy
Smart Grid Pilot Program
Panda Solar Ventures LLC

CONTACTS:

Note: Officers with more than one job title may be intentionally listed here more than once.

Kevin Burke, CEO
Kevin Burke, Pres.
Robert N. Hoglund, CFO/Sr. VP
Elizabeth D. Moore, General Counsel
Gurudatta Nadkarni, VP-Strategic Planning
Jan C. Childress, Dir.-Investor Rel.
Robert Muccilo, Chief Acct. Officer/Controller/VP
Scott L. Sanders, Treas./VP
Carole Sobin, Sec.
Craig S. Ivey, Pres., Consolidated Energy Co. of NY, Inc.
William G. Longhi, CEO/Pres., Orange & Rockland Utilities, Inc.
Kevin Burke, Chmn.

Phone: 212-460-4600	**Fax:** 212-475-0734
Toll-Free:	
Address: 4 Irving Pl., New York, NY 10003 US	

GROWTH PLANS/SPECIAL FEATURES:

Consolidated Edison, Inc. (Con Edison) principally operates through the regulated electric, gas and steam utility segments of its two main subsidiaries, Consolidated Edison Company of New York, Inc. (CECONY) and Orange and Rockland Utilities, Inc. (O&R). CECONY provides electric services to 3.3 million customers in New York City and most of Westchester County, a service area covering approximately 660 square miles with a population of more than 9 million. The company provides gas services to 1.1 million customers in Manhattan, the Bronx and parts of Queens and Westchester, and steam services to 1,760 customers in parts of Manhattan. O&R and its subsidiaries, Rockland Electric Company and Pike County Power & Light Company, provide electricity and natural gas to southeastern New York, northern New Jersey and northeastern Pennsylvania, an approximately 1,350-square-mile service area. The firm's non-utilities subsidiaries include Consolidated Edison Energy, Inc.; Consolidated Edison Development; and Consolidated Edison Solutions. Consolidated Edison Energy manages the output and fuel requirements for over 8,000 megawatts (MW) of third-party generating plants and sells electricity to utilities customers in the northeastern U.S. Consolidated Edison Development owns or operates energy infrastructure projects, principally internationally. Consolidated Edison Solutions sells electricity to approximately 75,000 industrial and large commercial customers, principally in the northeastern U.S. In May 2009, the firm announced plans to invest $1.5 billion, over a five year period, to upgrade its electric delivery system. In August 2009, the firm launched its Smart Grid Pilot Program, conducted in Queens, New York, which will test how various technologies support electronic grid modernization efforts. In April 2010, Consolidated Edison Development and Panda Solar Ventures LLC announced an agreement to develop, construct and operate solar electric power projects for utilities power in the northeastern U.S., including two 15-20 MW solar photovoltaic farms.

FINANCIALS:

Sales and profits are in thousands of dollars—add 000 to get the full amount. 2010 Note: Financial information for 2010 was not available for all companies at press time.

2010 Sales: $	2010 Profits: $	**U.S. Stock Ticker: ED**
2009 Sales: $13,032,000	2009 Profits: $868,000	**Int'l Ticker:** Int'l Exchange:
2008 Sales: $13,583,000	2008 Profits: $1,196,000	Employees: 15,541
2007 Sales: $13,120,000	2007 Profits: $929,000	Fiscal Year Ends: 12/31
2006 Sales: $11,962,000	2006 Profits: $737,000	Parent Company:

SALARIES/BENEFITS:

Pension Plan:	ESOP Stock Plan:	Profit Sharing:	Top Exec. Salary: $1,107,200	Bonus: $1,179,100
Savings Plan:	Stock Purch. Plan:		Second Exec. Salary: $727,850	Bonus: $620,100

OTHER THOUGHTS:

Apparent Women Officers or Directors: 6
Hot Spot for Advancement for Women/Minorities: Y

LOCATIONS: ("Y" = Yes)

West:	Southwest:	Midwest:	Southeast:	Northeast:	International:
				Y	

CONSTELLATION ENERGY GROUP

www.constellation.com

Industry Group Code: 221 **Ranks within this company's industry group:** Sales: 8 Profits: 3

Exploration/Production:		Refining/Retailing:		Utilities:		Alternative Energy:		Specialty Services:		Energy Mktg./Other Svcs.	
Exploration:		Refining:		Electric Utility:	Y	Waste/Solar/Other:	Y	Consulting/Eng.:	Y	Energy Marketing:	Y
Production:		Retailing:		Gas Utility:	Y	Thermal/Steam:	Y	Seismic:		Equipment/Machinery:	
Coal Production:		Convenience Stores:		Pipelines:		Wind:	Y	Drilling:		Oil Field Services:	
		Chemicals:		Water:		Hydro:	Y	InfoTech:		Air/Shipping Transportation:	
						Fuel Cells:		Specialty Services:	Y		

TYPES OF BUSINESS:

Utilities
Wholesale Power Sales
Fuel & Energy Services
Consulting Services
Nuclear Energy Production
Energy Trading
Natural Gas Distribution
Wind and other Renewable Energy

BRANDS/DIVISIONS/AFFILIATES:

Baltimore Gas & Electric Company
Constellation Energy Commodities Group
Constellation Generation Group
Constellation NewEnergy
Cornerstone Energy
Fell McCord & Associates
Cpower

CONTACTS:

Note: Officers with more than one job title may be intentionally listed here more than once.

Mayo A. Shattuck, III, CEO
Michael J. Wallace, COO
Mayo A. Shattuck, III, Pres.
Jonathan W. Thayer, CFO/Sr. VP
Bruce J. Stewart, Chief Mktg. Officer
Shon J. Manasco, Chief Human Resources Officer/Sr. VP
Paul J. Allen, Chief Environmental Officer
Charles A. Berardesco, General Counsel/Chief Compliance Officer/Sr. VP
Andrew L. Good, Sr. VP-Corp. Strategy & Dev.
Paul J. Allen, Sr. VP-Corp. Affairs
Carim V. Khouzami, Exec. Dir.-Investor Rel.
James L. Connaughton, Exec. VP-Corp. Affairs, Public & Environmental
Kathleen W. Hyle, Sr. VP/COO-Constellation Energy Resources
Henry B. Barron, Pres./CEO-Constellation Energy Nuclear Group LLC
Brenda L. Boultwood, Chief Risk Officer/Sr. VP
Mayo A. Shattuck, III, Chmn.

Phone: 410-470-2800 **Fax:** 410-234-5220
Toll-Free:
Address: 100 Constellation Way, Baltimore, MD 21202 US

GROWTH PLANS/SPECIAL FEATURES:

Constellation Energy Group (CE) supplies electricity to commercial, wholesale and industrial customers. The company also manages fuels and energy services for energy-intensive industries and utilities. The firm owns approximately 7,118 megawatts of generating capacity across the U.S. Overall, nuclear generation accounts for roughly 65% of the company's capacity; coal, gas and oil account for approximately 31%; and renewable fuels such as biomass, geothermal, hydro or solar account for approximately 4%. Baltimore Gas and Electric Company, CE's main subsidiary, is a regulated utility company that serves central Maryland with electricity and natural gas. The firm's other business units include Constellation Energy Commodities Group (CECG), which provides wholesale energy to utilities, co-ops, municipalities and power markets nationwide; Constellation Generation Group, which oversees the ownership, operation, and maintenance of CE's nuclear, coal, natural gas, oil and renewable power generation facilities; Cornerstone Energy, which provides natural gas supply and related services to commercial, industrial and institutional customers in the U.S.; and Constellation NewEnergy, which supplies commercial and industrial customers with energy services and products. CE also offers consulting services through Fellon-McCord & Associates. In November 2009, the firm completed the sale of a 49.99% interest in Constellation Energy Nuclear Group LLC, its nuclear generation and operation business, to Electricite de France (EDF Group) for total considerations of approximately $4.7 billion. In April 2010, CE acquired the Criterion wind project, a 70-megawatt generating facility in Maryland. In May 2010, the firm acquired two natural gas generation facilities in Texas from Navasota Holdings. In August 2010, the company agreed to acquire Boston Generating's 2,950-megawatt fleet, which includes four natural gas-fired plants and a fuel oil plant. In October 2010, CE acquired CPower, an energy management and demand response provider.

FINANCIALS:

Sales and profits are in thousands of dollars—add 000 to get the full amount. 2010 Note: Financial information for 2010 was not available for all companies at press time.

2010 Sales: $	2010 Profits: $	**U.S. Stock Ticker: CEG**
2009 Sales: $15,598,800	2009 Profits: $4,443,400	**Int'l Ticker:** Int'l Exchange:
2008 Sales: $19,741,900	2008 Profits: $-1,314,400	Employees: 10,200
2007 Sales: $21,185,100	2007 Profits: $821,500	Fiscal Year Ends: 12/31
2006 Sales: $19,284,900	2006 Profits: $936,400	Parent Company:

SALARIES/BENEFITS:

Pension Plan:	ESOP Stock Plan:	Profit Sharing:	Top Exec. Salary: $1,300,000	Bonus: $3,000,000
Savings Plan: Y	Stock Purch. Plan:		Second Exec. Salary: $575,000	Bonus: $1,060,000

OTHER THOUGHTS:

Apparent Women Officers or Directors: 4
Hot Spot for Advancement for Women/Minorities: Y

LOCATIONS: ("Y" = Yes)

West:	Southwest:	Midwest:	Southeast:	Northeast:	International:
Y	Y	Y	Y	Y	Y

CONSUMERS ENERGY COMPANY

www.consumersenergy.com

Industry Group Code: 221 **Ranks within this company's industry group:** Sales: Profits:

Exploration/Production:		Refining/Retailing:		Utilities:		Alternative Energy:		Specialty Services:		Energy Mktg./Other Svcs.	
Exploration:		Refining:		Electric Utility:	Y	Waste/Solar/Other:		Consulting/Eng.:		Energy Marketing:	
Production:		Retailing:		Gas Utility:	Y	Thermal/Steam:		Seismic:		Equipment/Machinery:	
Coal Production:		Convenience Stores:		Pipelines:	Y	Wind:		Drilling:		Oil Field Services:	
		Chemicals:		Water:		Hydro:	Y	InfoTech:		Air/Shipping Transportation:	
						Fuel Cells:		Specialty Services:			

TYPES OF BUSINESS:

Utilities-Electricity & Natural Gas
Pipelines
Power Generation
Hydroelectric Generation

BRANDS/DIVISIONS/AFFILIATES:

CMS Energy Corp
C&C Landfill
Palisades Nuclear Plant
Karn/Weadock Generating Complex
Marshall Training Center

CONTACTS:

Note: Officers with more than one job title may be intentionally listed here more than once.

John G. Russell, CEO
Thomas J. Webb, CFO/Exec. VP
Mamatha Chamarthi, CIO/VP
James E. Brunner, General Counsel/Sr. VP
Jeff Holyfield, Dir.-News & Info.
Glenn P. Barba, Chief Acct. Officer/Controller/VP
John M. Butler, Sr. VP
David G.Mengebier, Chief Compliance Officer/Sr. VP
Richard J. Ford, VP
Laura L.Mountcastle, VP/Treas.
Kenneth Whipple, Chmn.

Phone: 517-788-0550	**Fax:**
Toll-Free:	
Address: 1 Energy Plz., Jackson, MI 49201 US	

GROWTH PLANS/SPECIAL FEATURES:

Consumers Energy Company is the principal subsidiary of CMS Energy. The firm is an electric and natural gas utility providing electric and natural gas service to 6 million of Michigan's 10 million residents, in all 68 counties of Michigan's Lower Peninsula. The firm provides electricity to more than 1.8 million customers in 61 counties (275 cities and villages) and natural gas to more than 1.7 million customers in 44 counties (215 cities and villages). Consumers Energy's electricity comes from its 12 coal-fired generating plants; 13 hydroelectric plants; several combustion-turbine facilities; two oil-fired generating facilities; and a pumped storage generating plant. The firm also purchases power from outside sources when necessary. The company has a total system generating capacity of more than 6,000 megawatts, more than 65,792 miles of electric lines and over 27,000 miles of natural gas transmission, distribution pipelines and storage fields with an aggregate capacity of 130 billion cubic feet. Consumer Energy purchases all of the natural gas it sells. The company's main cities served include Detroit, Bay City, Flint, Jackson, Kalamazoo, Lansing, Macomb, Midland, Royal Oak, Warren, Battle Creek, Cadillac, Grand Rapids, Muskegon and Saginaw. In April 2010, the firm opened a new service facility in Howell, Michigan.

Consumer Energy offers its employees an employee assistance program, an educational assistance program and health and wellness programs.

FINANCIALS:

Sales and profits are in thousands of dollars—add 000 to get the full amount. 2010 Note: Financial information for 2010 was not available for all companies at press time.

2010 Sales: $	2010 Profits: $	**U.S. Stock Ticker: Subsidiary**
2009 Sales: $	2009 Profits: $	**Int'l Ticker:** Int'l Exchange:
2008 Sales: $	2008 Profits: $	Employees:
2007 Sales: $6,064,000	2007 Profits: $312,000	Fiscal Year Ends: 12/31
2006 Sales: $5,721,000	2006 Profits: $186,000	Parent Company: CMS ENERGY CORP

SALARIES/BENEFITS:

Pension Plan:	ESOP Stock Plan:	Profit Sharing:	Top Exec. Salary: $	Bonus: $822,125
Savings Plan:	Stock Purch. Plan:		Second Exec. Salary: $	Bonus: $

OTHER THOUGHTS:

Apparent Women Officers or Directors: 4
Hot Spot for Advancement for Women/Minorities: Y

LOCATIONS: ("Y" = Yes)

West:	Southwest:	Midwest:	Southeast:	Northeast:	International:
		Y			

CONTINENTAL RESOURCES INC

www.contres.com

Industry Group Code: 211111 **Ranks within this company's industry group:** Sales: 89 Profits: 64

Exploration/Production:		Refining/Retailing:		Utilities:		Alternative Energy:		Specialty Services:		Energy Mktg./Other Svcs.	
Exploration:	Y	Refining:		Electric Utility:		Waste/Solar/Other:		Consulting/Eng.:		Energy Marketing:	
Production:	Y	Retailing:		Gas Utility:		Thermal/Steam:		Seismic:		Equipment/Machinery:	
Coal Production:		Convenience Stores:		Pipelines:		Wind:		Drilling:		Oil Field Services:	
		Chemicals:		Water:		Hydro:		InfoTech:		Air/Shipping Transportation:	
						Fuel Cells:		Specialty Services:			

TYPES OF BUSINESS:

Oil & Gas Exploration
Oil & Gas Production

BRANDS/DIVISIONS/AFFILIATES:

GROWTH PLANS/SPECIAL FEATURES:

Continental Resources, Inc. is an independent oil and natural gas exploration and production company with primary operations in the Rocky Mountain and Mid-Continent regions of the United States. Continental has estimated proved reserves of 257.3 million barrels of oil equivalent (MMBoe), with estimated proved developed reserves of 113.6 MMBoe, or 44% of its total proved reserves. Approximately 67% of the company's proved reserves consist of crude oil. The company targets large repeatable resource plays where it uses horizontal drilling, advanced fracture stimulation and enhanced recovery technologies to develop and produce oil and natural gas reserves with unconventional formations. The company's Rocky Mountain operations produced approximately 29,132 barrels (Bbls) equivalent per day in 2009, with the principal producing properties in the Red River units, representing approximately 38% of total production; the Bakken fields in Montana and North Dakota, representing roughly 34%; and the Big Horn Basin, representing approximately 5.3%. Continental's average production from its Mid-Continent Region operations was 7,144 Bbls equivalent per day, with the principal producing properties located in the Anadarko Shelf of western Oklahoma and the Arkoma Shale in southeastern Oklahoma. Other minor operations are located in the Haynesville Shale in the East Texas and North Louisiana Salt Basin, the Illinois Basin and the Trenton-Black River properties in Michigan. In 2009, the company's total production reached 13.6 MMBoe.

Employees are offered health, dental and vision insurance; life insurance; disability coverage; flexible spending accounts; a 401(k) plan; an incentive bonus plan; an employee assistance program; and an education assistance program.

CONTACTS: *Note: Officers with more than one job title may be intentionally listed here more than once.*

Harold G. Hamm, CEO
Jeff Hume, COO
Jeff Hume, Pres.
John D. Hart, CFO/Sr. VP
Jack Stark, Sr. VP-Exploration
Richard E. Muncrief, Sr. VP-Oper.
Brian Engel, VP-Public Affairs
Warren Henry, VP-Investor Rel.
John D. Hart, Treas.
Steven K. Owen, Sr. VP-Land
Richard H. Straeter, Pres., Eastern Div.
Gene R. Carlson, Sr. VP-Resource Dev.

Phone: 580-233-8955 **Fax:** 580-548-5253
Toll-Free: 800-256-8955
Address: 302 N. Independence, Enid, OK 73702 US

FINANCIALS: **Sales and profits are in thousands of dollars—add 000 to get the full amount. 2010 Note: Financial information for 2010 was not available for all companies at press time.**

2010 Sales: $	2010 Profits: $	**U.S. Stock Ticker: CLR**
2009 Sales: $626,211	2009 Profits: $71,338	**Int'l Ticker:** Int'l Exchange:
2008 Sales: $960,490	2008 Profits: $320,950	Employees: 408
2007 Sales: $582,215	2007 Profits: $28,580	Fiscal Year Ends: 12/31
2006 Sales: $483,652	2006 Profits: $253,088	Parent Company:

SALARIES/BENEFITS:

Pension Plan:	ESOP Stock Plan:	Profit Sharing:	Top Exec. Salary: $745,000	Bonus: $550,000
Savings Plan: Y	Stock Purch. Plan:		Second Exec. Salary: $299,231	Bonus: $220,000

OTHER THOUGHTS:

Apparent Women Officers or Directors:
Hot Spot for Advancement for Women/Minorities:

LOCATIONS: ("Y" = Yes)

West:	Southwest:	Midwest:	Southeast:	Northeast:	International:
Y	Y	Y	Y		

COOPER INDUSTRIES PLC

www.cooperindustries.com

Industry Group Code: 335 **Ranks within this company's industry group:** Sales: 7 Profits: 7

Exploration/Production:		**Refining/Retailing:**		**Utilities:**		**Alternative Energy:**		**Specialty Services:**		**Energy Mktg./Other Svcs.**	
Exploration:		Refining:		Electric Utility:		Waste/Solar/Other:		Consulting/Eng.:		Energy Marketing:	
Production:		Retailing:		Gas Utility:		Thermal/Steam:		Seismic:		Equipment/Machinery:	Y
Coal Production:		Convenience Stores:		Pipelines:		Wind:		Drilling:		Oil Field Services:	
		Chemicals:		Water:		Hydro:		InfoTech:		Air/Shipping Transportation:	
						Fuel Cells:		Specialty Services:			

TYPES OF BUSINESS:

Manufacturing-Electrical Products
Tool & Hardware Manufacturing
Electrical Transmission & Distribution Products

BRANDS/DIVISIONS/AFFILIATES:

CI Finance, Inc.
Cooper US, Inc.
Cooper Power Systems Finance, Inc.
Cooper Securities, Inc.
Cooper Global LLC
Cooper Industries, Inc.
Pauluhn Electric
Eka Systems, Inc.

CONTACTS:

Note: Officers with more than one job title may be intentionally listed here more than once.

Kirk S. Hachigian, CEO
Kirk S. Hachigian, Pres.
David A. Barta, CFO/Sr. VP
Robert Taylor, Chief Mktg. Officer
James Williams, Sr. VP-Human Resources
Bruce Taten, General Counsel/Chief Compliance Officer/Sr. VP
C. Thomas O'Grady, Sr. VP-Bus. Dev.
Rick L. Johnson, Chief Acct. Officer/VP/Controller
Laura K. Ulz, Pres., Cooper Tools
Michael A. Stoessl, Pres., Cooper Power Systems
Tyler Johnson, VP/Treas.
Neil Schrimsher, Exec. VP-Cooper Connection/Pres., Cooper Lighting
Kirk S. Hachigian, Chmn.

Phone: 713-209-8400	**Fax:**
Toll-Free:	
Address: 5 Fitzwilliam Square, Dublin, Ireland	

GROWTH PLANS/SPECIAL FEATURES:

Cooper Industries plc, based in Dublin, manufactures, markets and sells electrical products, tools and hardware to the industrial, commercial construction, residential and utility markets. The firm owns and operates more than 100 manufacturing facilities in 23 countries, including China, Mexico, India and Eastern European countries. The company is organized into two segments: electrical products and tools. Roughly 90% of revenues are derived from electrical products and 10% from the tools segment. The electrical products segment manufactures and sells electrical and circuit protection products, as well as fire detection systems and security products for use in residential, commercial and industrial construction, maintenance and repair applications. The segment also manufactures products used by utilities for electrical power transmission and distribution, including distribution switchgear; transformers; transformer terminations and accessories; capacitors; voltage regulators; surge arresters; and other related power systems components. The tools segment manufactures hand tools for industrial, construction and consumer markets; automated assembly systems for industrial markets; and electric and pneumatic industrial power tools for general industry, primarily automotive and aerospace manufacturers. Brands manufactured by the firm include Bussmann; Crouse-Hinds; Halo; Metalux; and McGraw-Edison. Subsidiaries of the firm include CI Finance, Inc.; Cooper US, Inc.; Cooper Power Systems Finance, Inc.; Cooper Securities, Inc.; Cooper Global LLC; Cooper Industries, Inc.; and Cooper International Finance, Inc. In November 2009, the firm acquired Texas-based Pauluhn Electric. In December 2009, it opened a new manufacturing facility located in Dammam, Saudi Arabia. In April 2010, Cooper acquired wireless networking technology firm Eka Systems, Inc. In July 2010, the firm entered a joint venture combining its tools segment with certain tools businesses of Danaher Corporation.

The company offers its employees medical and life insurance; a savings plan; a pension plan; an employee stock ownership plan; disability benefits; tuition reimbursement; and an employee assistance program.

FINANCIALS:

Sales and profits are in thousands of dollars—add 000 to get the full amount. 2010 Note: Financial information for 2010 was not available for all companies at press time.

2010 Sales: $	2010 Profits: $	**U.S. Stock Ticker: CBE**
2009 Sales: $5,069,600	2009 Profits: $439,100	**Int'l Ticker:** Int'l Exchange:
2008 Sales: $6,521,300	2008 Profits: $632,200	Employees: 28,255
2007 Sales: $5,903,100	2007 Profits: $692,300	Fiscal Year Ends: 12/31
2006 Sales: $5,184,600	2006 Profits: $464,000	Parent Company:

SALARIES/BENEFITS:

Pension Plan: Y	ESOP Stock Plan: Y	Profit Sharing:	Top Exec. Salary: $1,200,000	Bonus: $2,550,000
Savings Plan: Y	Stock Purch. Plan:		Second Exec. Salary: $565,000	Bonus: $750,000

OTHER THOUGHTS:

Apparent Women Officers or Directors: 1
Hot Spot for Advancement for Women/Minorities:

LOCATIONS: ("Y" = Yes)

West:	Southwest:	Midwest:	Southeast:	Northeast:	International:
Y	Y	Y	Y	Y	Y

COSMO OIL CO LTD

www.cosmo-oil.co.jp

Industry Group Code: 486 **Ranks within this company's industry group:** Sales: 2 Profits: 21

Exploration/Production:		Refining/Retailing:		Utilities:		Alternative Energy:		Specialty Services:		Energy Mktg./Other Svcs.	
Exploration:	Y	Refining:	Y	Electric Utility:		Waste/Solar/Other:		Consulting/Eng.:		Energy Marketing:	
Production:	Y	Retailing:	Y	Gas Utility:		Thermal/Steam:		Seismic:		Equipment/Machinery:	Y
Coal Production:		Convenience Stores:		Pipelines:		Wind:	Y	Drilling:		Oil Field Services:	
		Chemicals:		Water:		Hydro:		InfoTech:		Air/Shipping Transportation:	
						Fuel Cells:		Specialty Services:			

TYPES OF BUSINESS:

Oil Refining & Distribution
Petrochemical Sales
Wind Energy Generation
Photovoltaic Cell Manufacture
5-Amino Levulinic Acid (ALA) Production

BRANDS/DIVISIONS/AFFILIATES:

Abu Dhabi Oil Co.
United Petroleum Development Co., Ltd.
Qatar Petroleum Development Co., Ltd.
Cosmo Oil Ashmore Ltd.
Cosmo Exploration and Development Co. Ltd.,
Laffan Refinery Co., Ltd
Cosmo Oil Group
Eco Power Co. Ltd.

CONTACTS: *Note: Officers with more than one job title may be intentionally listed here more than once.*

Yaichi Kimura, Pres.
Hisashi Kobayashi, Sr. Exec. Officer-Sales & Wholesale Mktg.
Keizo Morikawa, Exec. VP-Personnel Dept.
Hideto Matsumura, Sr. Exec. Officer-R&D
Yoshimitsu Watanabe, Exec. Officer-Info. Systems Planning
Katsuyuki Ihara, Exec. Officer/Gen. Mgr.-Tech. & Refining
Teruyuki Takisshima, Exec. Officer/Dir.-Eng. Works
Hiroshi Kiriyama, Exec. Officer/Gen. Mgr.-Corp. Planning
Hideto Matsumura, Sr. Exec. Officer-Corp. Comm.
Satoshi Nishi, Sr. Exec. Officer/Gen. Mgr.-Acct.
Hirohiko Ogiwara, Sr. Exec. Officer/Gen. Mgr.-Tokyo
Hideo Matsushita, Sr. Exec. Officer/Gen. Mgr.-Petroleum Exploration
Muneyuki Sano, Gen. Mgr.-Industrial Fuel Mktg.
Kanesada Sufu, Sr. Exec. Officer/Gen. Mgr.-Project Dev.
Keiichiro Okabe, Chmn.
Isao Kusakabe, Exec. Officer/Dir.-Overseas Bus.
Hisashi Kobayashi, Sr. Exec. Officer-Demand & Supply Coordination

Phone: 81-3-3798-3241 **Fax:** 81-3-3798-3841
Toll-Free:
Address: 1-1-1 Shibaura, Minato-Ku, Tokyo, 105-8528 Japan

GROWTH PLANS/SPECIAL FEATURES:

Cosmo Oil Co. Ltd. is one of Japan's top oil refiners and petroleum distributors. The Cosmo Oil Group produces crude oil in the United Arab Emirates (U.A.E.) through Abu Dhabi Oil Co.; United Petroleum Development Co., Ltd; and Qatar Petroleum Development Co., Ltd. Abu Dhabi and Qatar are the firm's core production areas. The Abu Dhabi Oil Co. and United Petroleum Development Co., Ltd. produced an average total of 38,123 barrels a day of crude oil in 2009. The Qatar Petroleum Development had a crude oil production average of 6,191 barrels per day. The firm has additional exploration assets off the coast of Australia in the Northwest Shelf, where it operates as Cosmo Oil Ashmore Ltd. and Cosmo Exploration and Development Co. Ltd. Cosmo Oil has four refineries in Japan: the Chiba plant; the Yokkaichi plant; the Sakai plant; and the Sakaide plant. In the domestic market, the company sells petrochemicals through Cosmo Matsuyama Oil Co., Ltd.; CM Aromatics Co., Ltd.; and Maruzen Petrochemical Co., Ltd. The company also sells gasoline directly to consumers in Japan via 3,913 service stations. The firm has partnerships with companies in Singapore, the U.K. and the U.S. for crude oil and gas transportation, storage, development and refining, distribution and marketing services. Other business engagements include renewable energy investments and the manufacture of polysilicon for photovoltaic cells. Cosmo also developed a patented process for the mass production of 5-Amino Levulinic Acid (ALA), with applications for fertilizers, food and cosmetics. In October 2009, the company established a joint venture in Korea with Hyundai Oilbank Co. that will produce and sell paraxylene and other related products. In March 2010, Cosmo acquired Eco Power Co. Ltd., a wind energy generating company in Japan.

FINANCIALS: **Sales and profits are in thousands of dollars—add 000 to get the full amount. 2010 Note: Financial information for 2010 was not available for all companies at press time.**

2010 Sales: $	2010 Profits: $	**U.S. Stock Ticker: CMOOF**
2009 Sales: $37,547,400	2009 Profits: $-1,012,330	**Int'l Ticker:** Int'l Exchange:
2008 Sales: $34,282,000	2008 Profits: $-924,000	Employees:
2007 Sales: $25,944,464	2007 Profits: $224,786	Fiscal Year Ends: 3/31
2006 Sales: $22,734,554	2006 Profits: $526,049	Parent Company:

SALARIES/BENEFITS:

Pension Plan:	ESOP Stock Plan:	Profit Sharing:	Top Exec. Salary: $	Bonus: $
Savings Plan:	Stock Purch. Plan:		Second Exec. Salary: $	Bonus: $

OTHER THOUGHTS:

Apparent Women Officers or Directors:
Hot Spot for Advancement for Women/Minorities:

LOCATIONS: ("Y" = Yes)

West:	Southwest:	Midwest:	Southeast:	Northeast:	International:
Y					Y

CPFL ENERGIA SA

www.cpfl.com.br

Industry Group Code: 221121 **Ranks within this company's industry group:** Sales: 1 Profits: 1

Exploration/Production:		Refining/Retailing:		Utilities:		Alternative Energy:		Specialty Services:		Energy Mktg./Other Svcs.	
Exploration:		Refining:		Electric Utility:	Y	Waste/Solar/Other:		Consulting/Eng.:	Y	Energy Marketing:	Y
Production:		Retailing:		Gas Utility:		Thermal/Steam:		Seismic:		Equipment/Machinery:	
Coal Production:		Convenience Stores:		Pipelines:		Wind:		Drilling:		Oil Field Services:	
		Chemicals:		Water:		Hydro:		InfoTech:		Air/Shipping Transportation:	
						Fuel Cells:		Specialty Services:			

TYPES OF BUSINESS:

Electricity Distribution
Electricity Commercialization
Electricity Generation

BRANDS/DIVISIONS/AFFILIATES:

CPFL Paulista
CPFL Piratininga
Rio Grande Energia
CPFL Geracao de Energia SA
CPFL Comercializacao Brasil SA
CPFL Meridional
CPFL Jaquari
CPFL Santa Cruz

CONTACTS:

Note: Officers with more than one job title may be intentionally listed here more than once.

Wilson F. Junior, CEO
Jose M.C. de Melo, VP-Admin.
Jose A. de Almeida Filippo, Head-Investor Rel.
Jose A. de Almeida Filippo, VP-Finance
Paulo C.C. Tavares, VP-Energy Mgmt.
Miguel N.A. Saad, VP-Generation
Pedro P. Parente, Chmn.
Helio V. Pereira, VP-Dist.

Phone: 55-19-3756-6083 **Fax:** 55-11-3756-6089
Toll-Free:
Address: 1510 Gomes de Carvalho Rd., 14th Fl., Sao Paulo, SP 04547-005 Brazil

GROWTH PLANS/SPECIAL FEATURES:

CPFL Energia S.A. is a Brazilian holding company in the energy industry. Through its subsidiaries, the firm distributes, generates and commercializes electricity. The company has eight electrical distribution subsidiaries: CPFL Paulista; CPFL Piratininga; CPFL Santa Cruz; CPFL Leste Paulista; Rio Grande Energia; CPFL Sul Paulista; CPFL Mococa; and CPFL Jaquari. Combined, these companies serve 568 municipalities and distribute approximately 37,323 gigawatt hours (GWh) of energy to 6.4 million customers in the states of Sao Paulo, Minas Gerais and Rio Grande do Sul, Parana. With regard to generation, CPFL Energia owns holding company CPFL Geracao de Energia S.A. (CPFL Geracao). CPFL Geracao owns stake in five generation subsidiaries: BAESA - Energetica Barra Grande S.A.; CPFL Sul Centrais Eletricas Ltda.; Campos Novos Energia S.A.; Foz do Chapeco Energia S.A.; and Companhia Energetica Rio das Antas S.A. These companies have a total combined installed capacity of over 1,704 megawatts (MW) of electricity. In addition, subsidiary CPFL Jaguariuna holds stake in nine small hydroelectric power plants. Through wholly-owned subsidiary CPFL Comercializacao Brasil S.A. (CPFL Brasil), CPFL Energia commercializes electricity nationwide and provides value added services such as energy maintenance/management consultancy and project management. CPFL Brasil holds approximately 22% of the electricity commercial market share in Brazil. CPFL Brasil also owns stake in three subsidiaries: energy marketers CPFL Meridional and Cone Sul, and private equity firm Sul Geradora. CPFL Energia also owns electricity commercialization firm CPFL Planalto and electrical services/equipment provider CPFL Servicos. In September 2009, CPFL Geracao agreed to acquire Santa Clara Energias Renovaveis Ltda. and Eurus VI Energias Renovaveis Ltda. for roughly $17 million.

FINANCIALS:

Sales and profits are in thousands of dollars—add 000 to get the full amount. 2010 Note: Financial information for 2010 was not available for all companies at press time.

2010 Sales: $
2009 Sales: $6,215,040
2008 Sales: $5,630,300
2007 Sales: $
2006 Sales: $

2010 Profits: $
2009 Profits: $756,730
2008 Profits: $750,380
2007 Profits: $
2006 Profits: $

U.S. Stock Ticker: CPL
Int'l Ticker: CPFE3 Int'l Exchange: Sao Paulo-SAO
Employees: 7,450
Fiscal Year Ends: 12/31
Parent Company:

SALARIES/BENEFITS:

Pension Plan: ESOP Stock Plan: Profit Sharing: Top Exec. Salary: $ Bonus: $
Savings Plan: Stock Purch. Plan: Second Exec. Salary: $ Bonus: $

OTHER THOUGHTS:

Apparent Women Officers or Directors: 4
Hot Spot for Advancement for Women/Minorities: Y

LOCATIONS: ("Y" = Yes)

West:	Southwest:	Midwest:	Southeast:	Northeast:	International:
					Y

CROSSTEX ENERGY LP

www.crosstexenergy.com

Industry Group Code: 486 **Ranks within this company's industry group:** Sales: 16 Profits: 12

Exploration/Production:		Refining/Retailing:		Utilities:		Alternative Energy:		Specialty Services:		Energy Mktg./Other Svcs.	
Exploration:		Refining:	Y	Electric Utility:		Waste/Solar/Other:		Consulting/Eng.:		Energy Marketing:	Y
Production:		Retailing:		Gas Utility:		Thermal/Steam:		Seismic:		Equipment/Machinery:	
Coal Production:		Convenience Stores:		Pipelines:	Y	Wind:		Drilling:		Oil Field Services:	
		Chemicals:		Water:		Hydro:		InfoTech:		Air/Shipping Transportation:	
						Fuel Cells:		Specialty Services:	Y		

TYPES OF BUSINESS:

Midstream Energy Services
Natural Gas Pipelines
Natural Gas Processing
Natural Gas Purchase & Resale

BRANDS/DIVISIONS/AFFILIATES:

Crosstex Energy Services, L.P
Crosstex Energy, Inc.

GROWTH PLANS/SPECIAL FEATURES:

Crosstex Energy, LP is an independent midstream energy company engaged in the gathering, transmission, processing and marketing of natural gas and natural gas liquids (NGLs). The company's business activities are conducted through its subsidiary, Crosstex Energy Services, L.P. The firm connects the wells of natural gas producers in its market area to its gathering systems; transports natural gas; and provides natural gas to a variety of markets. It currently provides 3 bcf per day of natural gas. The firm's primary midstream assets include roughly 3,700 miles of natural gas gathering and transmission pipelines; nine natural gas processing plants; and three fractionators. Crosstex purchases natural gas from natural gas producers and other supply points; and sells that natural gas to utilities, industrial customers, other marketers and pipelines. The company operates processing plants that process gas transported to the plants by major interstate pipelines or from its own gathering lines under a variety of fee arrangements. In addition, it purchases natural gas from producers not connected to its gathering systems for resale; and sells natural gas on behalf of producers for a fee. In January 2010, the company, along with its partner Crosstex Energy, Inc., acquired the 60 mile NGL Intracoastal Pipeline from Chevron Midstream Pipelines. Also in January 2010, the partnership sold its East Texas gathering and treating assets to Waskom Gas Processing Company for $40 million.

CONTACTS: *Note: Officers with more than one job title may be intentionally listed here more than once.*

Barry E. Davis, CEO
Barry E. Davis, Pres.
William W. Davis, CFO/Exec. VP
Jennifer K. Johnson, Sr. VP-Human Resources & Organizational Dev.
Stan Golemon, Sr. VP-Eng.
Joe A. Davis, General Counsel/Exec. VP
Stan Golemon, Sr. VP-Oper.
Jill McMilllian, Dir.-Public Affairs
Michael J. Garberding, Sr. VP-Finance
Steve Spaulding, Sr. VP-Processing & NGLs
Scott D. Williams, Sr. VP-Commercial
Barry E. Davis, Chmn.

Phone: 214-953-9500 **Fax:** 214-953-9501
Toll-Free: 866-427-8732
Address: 2501 Cedar Springs, Ste. 100, Dallas, TX 75201 US

FINANCIALS:

Sales and profits are in thousands of dollars—add 000 to get the full amount. 2010 Note: Financial information for 2010 was not available for all companies at press time.

2010 Sales: $	2010 Profits: $	**U.S. Stock Ticker: XTEX**
2009 Sales: $1,459,090	2009 Profits: $104,406	**Int'l Ticker:** Int'l Exchange:
2008 Sales: $3,076,011	2008 Profits: $10,771	Employees: 456
2007 Sales: $3,849,088	2007 Profits: $13,889	Fiscal Year Ends: 12/31
2006 Sales: $3,130,086	2006 Profits: $-4,191	Parent Company:

SALARIES/BENEFITS:

Pension Plan:	ESOP Stock Plan:	Profit Sharing:	Top Exec. Salary: $435,000	Bonus: $435,000
Savings Plan:	Stock Purch. Plan:		Second Exec. Salary: $315,000	Bonus: $315,000

OTHER THOUGHTS:

Apparent Women Officers or Directors: 2
Hot Spot for Advancement for Women/Minorities:

LOCATIONS: ("Y" = Yes)

West:	Southwest:	Midwest:	Southeast:	Northeast:	International:
	Y				

CROWN CENTRAL PETROLEUM LLC

www.crowncentral.com

Industry Group Code: 324110 **Ranks within this company's industry group:** Sales: Profits:

Exploration/Production:		Refining/Retailing:		Utilities:		Alternative Energy:		Specialty Services:		Energy Mktg./Other Svcs.	
Exploration:		Refining:		Electric Utility:		Waste/Solar/Other:		Consulting/Eng.:		Energy Marketing:	
Production:		Retailing:	Y	Gas Utility:		Thermal/Steam:		Seismic:		Equipment/Machinery:	
Coal Production:		Convenience Stores:	Y	Pipelines:		Wind:		Drilling:		Oil Field Services:	
		Chemicals:		Water:		Hydro:		InfoTech:		Air/Shipping Transportation:	
						Fuel Cells:		Specialty Services:	Y		

TYPES OF BUSINESS:

Gas Stations
Fleet Purchase Program

BRANDS/DIVISIONS/AFFILIATES:

Rosemore, Inc.
Crown
Fast Fare
Crown Fleet Services Program
ExpressMart
Zippy Mart
First National Bank of Omaha

CONTACTS: *Note: Officers with more than one job title may be intentionally listed here more than once.*

Robert A. (Bob) Fritz, Gen. Mgr.
Thomas L. Owlsey, Pres.
John E. Wheeler, CFO
J. Michael Mims, Sr. VP-Human Resources
Philip A. Millington, Treas./VP
Andrew Lapayowker, VP
Henry A. Rosenberg, Jr., Chmn.

Phone: 410-539-7400 **Fax:** 410-659-4747
Toll-Free:
Address: 1 N. Charles St., Ste. 2100, Baltimore, MD 21201 US

GROWTH PLANS/SPECIAL FEATURES:

Crown Central Petroleum LLC, founded in 1917, is a refiner and convenience store and gas station franchiser operating in the east coast region of the U.S. The company is a subsidiary of Rosemore, Inc., a holding company for the Rosenberg family. Independent licensors in Maryland, Pennsylvania, Virginia, North and South Carolina, Georgia and Alabama operate the firm's gas stations. Crown's approximately 88 stores are formatted in three basic types: convenience stores; mini-marts; and gasoline filling stations. Some facilities include additional services such as car wash or auto repair capabilities. Store brands offered by Crown to licensees include Fast Fare, ExpressMart and Zippy Mart, either as standalone brands or in conjunction with the Crown brand. Crown licensees are allowed to select their own gasoline suppliers from a pre-approved list of refiners and resellers. The company maintains partnerships with a variety of bulk fuel supply and site development partners, such as Mansfield Oil Company, TAC Energy, Sun Coast Resources, Inc. and TelaPoint, Inc.; credit card communication partners, such as the EchoSat Communications Group; and graphics and signage companies, such as LSI Graphics Solutions Plus, Sawyers Sign Service, Complete Service Imaging, Inc., Everbrite LLC and the Sherwin-Williams Company. In addition, the firm offers a Crown Fleet Services Program, which allows trucking companies to track individual drivers' purchases at any of Crown Central's stores. The company is currently looking to expand in the U.S., seeking to license the store brands Fast Fare, ExpressMart and Zippy Mart. In November 2009, the firm began offering a co-branded credit card with Clark Brands, LLC, issued by First National Bank of Omaha. The card offers consumers cash back rewards for purchases made at Clark and Crown locations, as well as other perks.

FINANCIALS: **Sales and profits are in thousands of dollars—add 000 to get the full amount. 2010 Note: Financial information for 2010 was not available for all companies at press time.**

2010 Sales: $	2010 Profits: $	**U.S. Stock Ticker: Subsidiary**
2009 Sales: $	2009 Profits: $	**Int'l Ticker:** Int'l Exchange:
2008 Sales: $	2008 Profits: $	Employees:
2007 Sales: $1,566,400	2007 Profits: $	Fiscal Year Ends: 12/31
2006 Sales: $	2006 Profits: $	Parent Company: ROSEMORE INC

SALARIES/BENEFITS:

Pension Plan:	ESOP Stock Plan:	Profit Sharing:	Top Exec. Salary: $	Bonus: $
Savings Plan:	Stock Purch. Plan:		Second Exec. Salary: $	Bonus: $

OTHER THOUGHTS:

Apparent Women Officers or Directors:
Hot Spot for Advancement for Women/Minorities:

LOCATIONS: ("Y" = Yes)

West:	Southwest:	Midwest:	Southeast:	Northeast:	International:
			Y	Y	

DAKOTA GASIFICATION COMPANY

www.dakotagas.com

Industry Group Code: 324199 **Ranks within this company's industry group:** Sales: Profits:

Exploration/Production:		Refining/Retailing:		Utilities:		Alternative Energy:		Specialty Services:		Energy Mktg./Other Svcs.	
Exploration:		Refining:	Y	Electric Utility:		Waste/Solar/Other:		Consulting/Eng.:		Energy Marketing:	
Production:		Retailing:		Gas Utility:		Thermal/Steam:		Seismic:		Equipment/Machinery:	
Coal Production:		Convenience Stores:		Pipelines:		Wind:		Drilling:		Oil Field Services:	
		Chemicals:	Y	Water:		Hydro:		InfoTech:		Air/Shipping Transportation:	
						Fuel Cells:		Specialty Services:			

TYPES OF BUSINESS:

Coal Gasification
Byproduct Production & Marketing

BRANDS/DIVISIONS/AFFILIATES:

Basin Electric Power Cooperative
Great Plains Synfuels Plant
Souris Valley Pipeline Ltd
Deer Creek Station

CONTACTS:

Note: Officers with more than one job title may be intentionally listed here more than once.

Ronald R. Harper, CEO
Gary G. Loop, COO/Sr. VP
Ronald R.Harper, Pres.
Steven Liebelt, Mgr.-Mktg
Deb Haga, Human Resources
Mark Foss, General Counsel
Floyd Robb, VP-Comm.
Cliff Gjellstad, Treas.
A.T. Funkhouser, Mgr.-Health, Safety & Environment
Bob Fagerstrom, Mgr.-Plant
Don Applegate, Chmn.

Phone: 701-221-4400	**Fax:** 701-221-4450
Toll-Free:	
Address: 1600 E. Interstate Ave., Bismarck, ND 58506-5540 US	

GROWTH PLANS/SPECIAL FEATURES:

Dakota Gasification Company (Dakota Gas), a subsidiary of Basin Electric Power Cooperative, is the owner and operator of a gas field plant near Beulah, North Dakota (Great Plains Synfuels Plant). Through this plant, the company is engaged in the gasification of lignite coal for the purposes of producing pipeline-quality natural gas. The plant consumes more than 6 billion tons of coal annually for an annual production of 54 billion cubic feet of synthetic natural gas. Of this, the majority is shipped to Ventura, Iowa and then distributed all over the eastern U.S. In addition to producing synthetic natural gas, the plant produces and markets byproducts and co-byproducts that occur during the gasification process, including ammonium sulfate and anhydrous ammonia for fertilizers; methanol for solvents; phenol for the production of resins in the plywood industry; liquid nitrogen for refrigeration and oil field services; naphtha for gasoline blend stocks; krypton and xenon gases for the lighting industry; carbon dioxide, which can be used for enhanced oil recovery; and cresylic acid for the chemical industry. Dakota Gas also owns and maintains a carbon dioxide (CO2) pipeline that runs 205miles to the GoodWater Unit (a part of EnCana's Weyburn oil field in Canada). The pipeline is capable of transporting up to 152 million standard cubic feet per day (mmscfd) of CO2 gas to the Tioga Station (a booster pump station) and then continues with 150mmmscfd to its destination at GoodWater. The portion of the pipeline that runs in Canada operates under the name Souris Valley Pipeline, Ltd., which is Dakota Gas's only wholly-owned subsidiary. In July 2010, the firm began construction on the Deer Creek Station, a new 300-megawatt natural gas-fired power plant near White, South Dakota.

Dakota Gas offers its employees benefits including medical, vision, dental, life and long-term disability insurance; educational assistance; and an employee assistance program.

FINANCIALS:

Sales and profits are in thousands of dollars—add 000 to get the full amount. 2010 Note: Financial information for 2010 was not available for all companies at press time.

2010 Sales: $	2010 Profits: $	**U.S. Stock Ticker: Subsidiary**
2009 Sales: $	2009 Profits: $	**Int'l Ticker:** Int'l Exchange:
2008 Sales: $	2008 Profits: $	Employees:
2007 Sales: $500,000	2007 Profits: $	Fiscal Year Ends: 12/31
2006 Sales: $452,200	2006 Profits: $	Parent Company: BASIN ELECTRIC POWER COOPERATIVE

SALARIES/BENEFITS:

Pension Plan: Y	ESOP Stock Plan:	Profit Sharing:	Top Exec. Salary: $	Bonus: $
Savings Plan: Y	Stock Purch. Plan:		Second Exec. Salary: $	Bonus: $

OTHER THOUGHTS:

Apparent Women Officers or Directors: 3
Hot Spot for Advancement for Women/Minorities: Y

LOCATIONS: ("Y" = Yes)

West:	Southwest:	Midwest:	Southeast:	Northeast:	International:
		Y			

DAWSON GEOPHYSICAL COMPANY

www.dawson3d.com

Industry Group Code: 541360 **Ranks within this company's industry group:** Sales: 3 Profits: 1

Exploration/Production:		Refining/Retailing:		Utilities:		Alternative Energy:		Specialty Services:		Energy Mktg./Other Svcs.	
Exploration:		Refining:		Electric Utility:		Waste/Solar/Other:		Consulting/Eng.:	Y	Energy Marketing:	
Production:		Retailing:		Gas Utility:		Thermal/Steam:		Seismic:	Y	Equipment/Machinery:	
Coal Production:		Convenience Stores:		Pipelines:		Wind:		Drilling:		Oil Field Services:	
		Chemicals:		Water:		Hydro:		InfoTech:		Air/Shipping Transportation:	
						Fuel Cells:		Specialty Services:	Y		

TYPES OF BUSINESS:

Seismic Data Acquisition
Geophysical Services
3-D Seismic Interpretation

BRANDS/DIVISIONS/AFFILIATES:

ARAM ARIES
IO System II RSR Radio Telemetry
IO System II Cable Based Recording Systems
OYO Geospace Seismic Recorder
OYO Geospace Company

CONTACTS: *Note: Officers with more than one job title may be intentionally listed here more than once.*

Stephen C. Jumper, CEO
C. Ray Tobias, COO/Exec. VP
Stephen C. Jumper, Pres.
Christina W. Hagan, CFO/Exec. VP
Mark Pruitt, VP-Mktg.
Olga Smoot, Mgr.-Human Resources
Stuart A. Wright, VP-Applied Geophysics
Howell (Hal) W. Pardue, Exec. VP-Data Processing
Robert C. Chandler, Dir.-Eng. & Tech. Support
Christina W. Hagan, Corp. Sec.
George E. McDonald, VP-Oper.
Sam Dobbs, VP-Data Processing
K.S. Forsdick, VP
Dave Wisniewski, VP
L. Decker Dawson, Chmn.

Phone: 915-684-3000	**Fax:** 915-684-3030
Toll-Free: 800-332-9766	
Address: 508 W. Wall St., Ste. 800, Midland, TX 79701-5010 US	

GROWTH PLANS/SPECIAL FEATURES:

Dawson Geophysical Company, headquartered in Midland, Texas, is one of the leading providers of onshore seismic data acquisition services in the U.S. The company acquires and processes 2-D, 3-D and multi-component seismic data used to analyze subsurface geologic conditions to identify favorable areas for potential oil and natural gas accumulation. In-house services include seismic survey design, permitting, surveying, data acquisition and processing functions for each seismic program. Dawson, with nine 3-D seismic data acquisition crews operating in the continental 48 states and a seismic data processing center, serves major and intermediate-sized oil and gas companies, independent oil operators and providers of multi-client data libraries. The firm has six crews that are equipped with the ARAM ARIES precise data, six with IO System II RSR Radio Telemetry and three with IO System II cable based recording systems. The survey personnel uses dynamite charges or vibrator energy sources mounted on vehicles, the majority of which weigh over 62,000 pounds, to generate seismic energy. The crew utilizes its seismic recording devices, or geophones, to detect and record shear wave data, before rendering the information visually. The company's data processing center is operated in Midland, Texas and includes processes such as the enhancement of seismic data by improving signal resolution, removing ambient noise and applying proper spatial relationships of geologic features. To avoid potential conflicts, Dawson does not acquire data for its own account or participate in oil and gas ventures. In October 2010, the company placed an order for 2,000 OYO Geospace Seismic Recorder (GSR) four channel boxes with three component geophones from OYO Geospace for $6.1 million. The new equipment will allow the firm to record 12,000 channels of multi-component data or 16,000 channels of conventional seismic data.

FINANCIALS: **Sales and profits are in thousands of dollars—add 000 to get the full amount. 2010 Note: Financial information for 2010 was not available for all companies at press time.**

2010 Sales: $	2010 Profits: $	**U.S. Stock Ticker: DWSN**
2009 Sales: $243,995	2009 Profits: $10,222	**Int'l Ticker:** Int'l Exchange:
2008 Sales: $324,926	2008 Profits: $35,007	Employees: 942
2007 Sales: $257,763	2007 Profits: $27,158	Fiscal Year Ends: 9/30
2006 Sales: $168,550	2006 Profits: $15,855	Parent Company:

SALARIES/BENEFITS:

Pension Plan:	ESOP Stock Plan:	Profit Sharing:	Top Exec. Salary: $350,000	Bonus: $
Savings Plan: Y	Stock Purch. Plan:		Second Exec. Salary: $210,000	Bonus: $

OTHER THOUGHTS:

Apparent Women Officers or Directors: 3
Hot Spot for Advancement for Women/Minorities: Y

LOCATIONS: ("Y" = Yes)

West:	Southwest:	Midwest:	Southeast:	Northeast:	International:
Y	Y	Y		Y	

DCP MIDSTREAM LLC

www.dcpmidstream.com

Industry Group Code: 486 **Ranks within this company's industry group:** Sales: Profits:

Exploration/Production:		Refining/Retailing:		Utilities:		Alternative Energy:		Specialty Services:		Energy Mktg./Other Svcs.	
Exploration:		Refining:	Y	Electric Utility:		Waste/Solar/Other:		Consulting/Eng.:		Energy Marketing:	Y
Production:		Retailing:		Gas Utility:		Thermal/Steam:		Seismic:		Equipment/Machinery:	
Coal Production:		Convenience Stores:		Pipelines:	Y	Wind:		Drilling:		Oil Field Services:	
		Chemicals:		Water:		Hydro:		InfoTech:		Air/Shipping Transportation:	
						Fuel Cells:		Specialty Services:	Y		

TYPES OF BUSINESS:

Natural Gas-Gathering & Processing
Midstream Services
Natural Gas Liquids Processing & Marketing

BRANDS/DIVISIONS/AFFILIATES:

DCP Midstream Partners LP
ConocoPhillips
Spectra Energy Corp
Centana Intrastate Pipeline
Buckeye Partners LP
EQT Corporation

CONTACTS:

Note: Officers with more than one job title may be intentionally listed here more than once.

Thomas C. O'Connor, CEO
Thomas C. O'Connor, Pres.
Rose M. Robeson, CFO/VP
Robert P. Reed, VP-Natural Gas & Natural Gas Liquids Mktg.
Chris Lewis, Chief Admin. Officer/VP
Brent L. Backes, General Counsel/VP/Corp. Sec.
Richard Rehm, VP-Oper., East Southern Bus. Unit
Rosslyn Elliott, Dir.-Public Rel.
D. Robert Sadler, Treas./VP
William Waldheim, Pres., Northern Bus. Unit
Richard A. Cargile, Pres., Southern Bus. Unit
Bill Gifford, VP-Mid Continent Northern Bus. Unit
Ronnie Trammell, VP-Area Oper., West Southern Bus. Unit
Thomas C. O'Connor, Chmn.

Phone: 303-595-3331	Fax:
Toll-Free:	
Address: 370 17th St., Ste. 2500, Denver, CO 80202 US	

GROWTH PLANS/SPECIAL FEATURES:

DCP Midstream, LLC, is a 50-50 joint venture between Spectra Energy Corp. and ConocoPhillips. The company, which operates in 17 states, is one of the U.S.'s largest producers and marketers of natural gas liquids (NGLs). The company owns and operates gathering systems for NGLs in areas including Texas, Oklahoma, Louisiana and Colorado. DCP Midstream owns or operates 59 plants, 10 fractioning facilities and about 60,000 miles of gathering and transmission pipeline with connections to roughly 38,000 active receipt points. With regard to NGL logistics, the firm provides gathering systems and processing plants which are connected to multiple interstate and intrastate natural gas pipelines. DCP Midstream produces an average of 360,000 barrels per day of NGLs; markets and trades an average of over 480,000 barrels per day of NGLs; and gathers and/or transports an average of about 7.1 trillion British thermal units per day (Tbtu/d) of natural gas. The company primarily serves these customer groups: natural gas marketers; natural gas producers; large industrial customers and natural gas and electric utilities serving individual customers; large multinational petrochemical and refining companies; and small regional retail propane distributors. DCP Midstream owns and operates the DCP Midstream Partners, LP, which offers wholesale propane logistics, natural gas services and NGL logistics. In May 2009, the company began operating new high- pressure booster facilities in central Oklahoma. In January 2010, subsidiary, DCP Midstream Partners, LP acquired an interstate NGL pipeline system from Buckeye Partners, L.P., for $22 million. The 350 mile pipeline originates in the Denver-Julesburg Basin in Colorado and ends near the Conway hub in Bushton, Kansas. In May 2010, the company and EQT Corporation signed a letter of intent to create a joint venture to build a natural gas processing and related NGL infrastructure to serve EQT and third-party producers in the shale areas of the Appalachian basin.

FINANCIALS:

Sales and profits are in thousands of dollars—add 000 to get the full amount. 2010 Note: Financial information for 2010 was not available for all companies at press time.

2010 Sales: $	2010 Profits: $	**U.S. Stock Ticker: Joint Venture**
2009 Sales: $	2009 Profits: $	**Int'l Ticker:** Int'l Exchange:
2008 Sales: $	2008 Profits: $	Employees:
2007 Sales: $	2007 Profits: $	Fiscal Year Ends: 12/31
2006 Sales: $	2006 Profits: $	Parent Company:

SALARIES/BENEFITS:

Pension Plan:	ESOP Stock Plan:	Profit Sharing:	Top Exec. Salary: $	Bonus: $
Savings Plan:	Stock Purch. Plan:		Second Exec. Salary: $	Bonus: $

OTHER THOUGHTS:

Apparent Women Officers or Directors: 1
Hot Spot for Advancement for Women/Minorities:

LOCATIONS: ("Y" = Yes)

West:	Southwest:	Midwest:	Southeast:	Northeast:	International:
Y	Y	Y	Y	Y	Y

DELMARVA POWER AND LIGHT COMPANY

www.delmarva.com

Industry Group Code: 221 **Ranks within this company's industry group:** Sales: Profits:

Exploration/Production:		Refining/Retailing:		Utilities:		Alternative Energy:		Specialty Services:		Energy Mktg./Other Svcs.	
Exploration:		Refining:		Electric Utility:	Y	Waste/Solar/Other:		Consulting/Eng.:		Energy Marketing:	
Production:		Retailing:		Gas Utility:	Y	Thermal/Steam:		Seismic:		Equipment/Machinery:	
Coal Production:		Convenience Stores:		Pipelines:		Wind:	Y	Drilling:		Oil Field Services:	
		Chemicals:		Water:		Hydro:		InfoTech:		Air/Shipping Transportation:	
						Fuel Cells:		Specialty Services:			

TYPES OF BUSINESS:

Utilities-Electricity & Natural Gas

BRANDS/DIVISIONS/AFFILIATES:

Pepco Holdings Inc
Atlantic City Electric Company
Potomac Electric Power Company

CONTACTS:

Note: Officers with more than one job title may be intentionally listed here more than once.

Anthony J. Kamerick, CFO/Sr. VP
Kirk J. Emge, General Counsel/Sr. VP
Ronald K. Clark, Controller/VP
Joseph M. Rigby, Pres., Pepco Holdings, Inc.
Joseph M. Rigby, Chmn.

Phone: 202-872-2000	**Fax:**
Toll-Free: 800-375-7117	
Address: 800 King St., Wilmington, DE 19899 US	

GROWTH PLANS/SPECIAL FEATURES:

Delmarva Power and Light Company (DPL) is a provider of electricity and natural gas. The firm is a subsidiary of Pepco Holdings, Inc.; it operates as one of three Pepco delivery companies, along with Potomac Electric Power Company and Atlantic City Electric Company. For residential customers, the company provides an online resource for users to pay bills, report outages and turn services on or off. The firm has specialized services for large commercial clients, small business and new construction projects. DPL's electricity distribution service territory has a population of 1.3 million and covers roughly 5,000 square miles. DPL transmits and distributes electricity to roughly 498,000 businesses and households in Delaware and Maryland. The firm's natural gas distribution service territory has a population of 500,000 and covers approximately 275 square miles. The company maintains approximately 123,000 natural gas customers in northern Delaware. In addition, the firm supplies and distributes natural gas to retail customers and provides transportation-only services to retail customers in the state of Delaware. DPL maintains several partnerships which aim to create and implement more energy efficient alternatives to standard energy sources. Its partners include Edison Electric Institute, Energy Star and IBM. The firm's web site offers customers several downloadable brochures regarding energy conservation, environmental issues, utility safety, money/energy saving tips and more.

Delmarva offers its employees a range of benefits including medical, dental and vision coverage; life insurance; healthcare and dependent care reimbursement accounts; a 401(k) retirement savings plan; and educational assistance.

FINANCIALS:

Sales and profits are in thousands of dollars—add 000 to get the full amount. 2010 Note: Financial information for 2010 was not available for all companies at press time.

2010 Sales: $	2010 Profits: $	**U.S. Stock Ticker: Subsidiary**
2009 Sales: $	2009 Profits: $	**Int'l Ticker:** Int'l Exchange:
2008 Sales: $	2008 Profits: $	Employees:
2007 Sales: $1,496,000	2007 Profits: $44,900	Fiscal Year Ends: 12/31
2006 Sales: $1,423,400	2006 Profits: $42,500	Parent Company: PEPCO HOLDINGS INC

SALARIES/BENEFITS:

Pension Plan: Y	ESOP Stock Plan:	Profit Sharing:	Top Exec. Salary: $	Bonus: $
Savings Plan: Y	Stock Purch. Plan:		Second Exec. Salary: $	Bonus: $

OTHER THOUGHTS:

Apparent Women Officers or Directors:
Hot Spot for Advancement for Women/Minorities:

LOCATIONS: ("Y" = Yes)

West:	Southwest:	Midwest:	Southeast:	Northeast:	International:
				Y	

DENBURY RESOURCES INC

www.denbury.com

Industry Group Code: 211111 **Ranks within this company's industry group:** Sales: 80 Profits: 83

Exploration/Production:		Refining/Retailing:		Utilities:		Alternative Energy:		Specialty Services:		Energy Mktg./Other Svcs.	
Exploration:	Y	Refining:		Electric Utility:		Waste/Solar/Other:		Consulting/Eng.:		Energy Marketing:	
Production:	Y	Retailing:		Gas Utility:		Thermal/Steam:		Seismic:		Equipment/Machinery:	
Coal Production:		Convenience Stores:		Pipelines:	Y	Wind:		Drilling:		Oil Field Services:	
		Chemicals:		Water:		Hydro:		InfoTech:		Air/Shipping Transportation:	
						Fuel Cells:		Specialty Services:	Y		

TYPES OF BUSINESS:

Oil & Gas Exploration & Production
CO2 Reserves
CO2 Pipeline

BRANDS/DIVISIONS/AFFILIATES:

Encore Acquisition Company

CONTACTS:

Note: Officers with more than one job title may be intentionally listed here more than once.

Phil Rykhoek, CEO
Ronald T. Evans, COO
Ronald T. Evans, Pres.
Mark C. Allen, CFO/Sr. VP
Dan E. Cole, VP-Mktg.
Whitney Shelley, VP-Human Resources
Ray Dubuisson, VP-Legal
Robert Cornelius, Sr. VP-Oper.
Bradley A. Cox, VP-Bus. Dev.
Laurie Burkes, Mgr.-Investor Rel.
Alan Rhoades, VP-Acct.
Wieland F. Wettstein, Co-Chmn.
Charlie Gibson, VP-West Region
Barry Schneider, VP-East Region
Greg Dover, VP-North Region
Gareth Roberts, Co-Chmn.

Phone: 972-673-2000	**Fax:** 972-673-2150
Toll-Free:	
Address: 5100 Tennyson Pkwy., Ste. 1200, Plano, TX 75024 US	

GROWTH PLANS/SPECIAL FEATURES:

Denbury Resources, Inc., headquartered in Plano, Texas, is an oil and gas acquisition, development, operation and exploration company with operations primarily in Louisiana, Mississippi, Alabama and Texas. The company is one of the largest oil and natural gas operators in Mississippi, and owns some of the leading reserves of sequestered carbon dioxide (CO2), used for tertiary oil recovery east of the Mississippi. CO2 injection is one of the most efficient ways of extraction crude oil, although it is not often practiced due to limited supplies of CO2, which is a resource that is typically centralized in West Texas and Mississippi. The firm utilizes its reserves at the Jackson Dome field to supply CO2 to its planned projects through a network of pipelines, and seeks to achieve its returns on capital through further development of its carbon dioxide and tertiary flooding operations. The company divides its operations into eight phases. Phase 1 includes several fields along its 183-mile CO2 pipeline, running through southwest Mississippi and into Louisiana. Its fields are in Little Creek, Mallalieu, McComb and Brookhaven. Phase 2 includes Eucutta, Soso, Martinville and Heidelberg Fields in Eastern Mississippi. The company runs its Phase 3 operations in Tinsley Field, Northwest of Jackson Dome in Mississippi. Phase 4 includes the Cranfield and Lake St. John Fields, located, respectively, in Mississippi and Louisiana. Phase 5 is Delhi Field, located in Louisiana. Phase 6 consists of the Citronelle Field in Southwest Alabama. Phase 7 includes Hastings Field in Houston, Texas. Phase 8 is made up of the Seabreeze Complex, also in Houston. Finally, Phase 9 consists of the recently acquired Conroe Field located north of Houston. In March 2010, the firm acquired Encore Acquisition Company and absorbed its operations.

The company offers employees medical, dental and vision insurance; life insurance; educational assistance; an employee assistance program; and flexible spending accounts.

FINANCIALS:

Sales and profits are in thousands of dollars—add 000 to get the full amount. 2010 Note: Financial information for 2010 was not available for all companies at press time.

2010 Sales: $	2010 Profits: $	**U.S. Stock Ticker: DNR**
2009 Sales: $889,150	2009 Profits: $-75,156	**Int'l Ticker:** Int'l Exchange:
2008 Sales: $1,371,056	2008 Profits: $388,396	Employees: 797
2007 Sales: $971,950	2007 Profits: $253,147	Fiscal Year Ends: 12/31
2006 Sales: $732,312	2006 Profits: $202,457	Parent Company:

SALARIES/BENEFITS:

Pension Plan:	ESOP Stock Plan:	Profit Sharing:	Top Exec. Salary: $425,000	Bonus: $9,615
Savings Plan: Y	Stock Purch. Plan: Y		Second Exec. Salary: $415,000	Bonus: $436,635

OTHER THOUGHTS:

Apparent Women Officers or Directors: 2
Hot Spot for Advancement for Women/Minorities:

LOCATIONS: ("Y" = Yes)

West:	Southwest:	Midwest:	Southeast:	Northeast:	International:
	Y		Y		

Note: Financial information, benefits and other data can change quickly and may vary from those stated here.

DETROIT EDISON COMPANY (THE)

www.dteenergy.com

Industry Group Code: 2211 **Ranks within this company's industry group:** Sales: Profits:

Exploration/Production:		Refining/Retailing:		Utilities:		Alternative Energy:		Specialty Services:		Energy Mktg./Other Svcs.	
Exploration:		Refining:		Electric Utility:	Y	Waste/Solar/Other:	Y	Consulting/Eng.:		Energy Marketing:	
Production:		Retailing:		Gas Utility:		Thermal/Steam:		Seismic:		Equipment/Machinery:	
Coal Production:		Convenience Stores:		Pipelines:		Wind:	Y	Drilling:		Oil Field Services:	
		Chemicals:		Water:		Hydro:	Y	InfoTech:		Air/Shipping Transportation:	Y
						Fuel Cells:		Specialty Services:	Y		

TYPES OF BUSINESS:

Electric Utility
Fuel Supply Services
Hydroelectric Power
Nuclear Power
Coal Terminal Facility

BRANDS/DIVISIONS/AFFILIATES:

DTE Energy Company
Fermi 2 Nuclear Power Plant
Midwest Energy Resources Co.
Superior Midwest Energy Terminal
Consumers Energy Co.
Invenergy Wind

CONTACTS:

Note: Officers with more than one job title may be intentionally listed here more than once.

Steven E. Kurmas, COO
Steven E. Kurmas, Pres.
Vince Dow, VP-Dist. Oper.
Paul Fessler, VP-Fossil Generation

Phone: 313-235-4000	**Fax:**
Toll-Free:	
Address: 2000 2nd Ave., Detroit, MI 48226 US	

GROWTH PLANS/SPECIAL FEATURES:

The Detroit Edison Company is one of the main operating subsidiaries of DTE Energy Company, one of the largest electric utilities in the U.S. Detroit Edison generates, transmits and distributes electricity; serving its 2.1 million business and residential customers in a 7,600-square-mile area of southeastern Michigan through approximately 1 million utility poles and 44,000 miles of overhead and underground power lines, as well as 677 distribution stations. The firm has a total system generating capacity of more than 11 gigawatts (GW), with coal being the primary fuel source and the remainder produced by nuclear fuel, natural gas and hydroelectricity. Detroit Edison operates 10 base-load generating plants, including its Fermi 2 Nuclear Power Plant in Monroe County with 1.1 GW of power. The Fermi 2 Nuclear Power Plant represents roughly 30% of Michigan's nuclear capacity. With Consumers Energy Co., the firm is a co-owner of a hydroelectric pumped storage facility in Ludington, Michigan. Midwest Energy Resources Co., a wholly-owned subsidiary of the company, owns and operates the Superior Midwest Energy Terminal, a coal blending and trans-shipment terminal facility on Lake Superior. It also functions as a full-service fuel supply organization, providing U.S. Western with such services as coal sourcing, coal blending, rail, vessel and truck transportation, combustion engineering and material handling for other electric utilities and industrial consumers, including Detroit Edison's power plants. The firm plans to install photovoltaic solar systems at locations throughout the company's service area during 2010 in an effort to generate 10% of its electricity from renewable resources by 2015. In September 2010, Detroit Edison signed a 20-year energy purchase agreement with Invenergy Wind, which will add 200 megawatts (MW) of wind energy to the company's portfolio.

FINANCIALS:

Sales and profits are in thousands of dollars—add 000 to get the full amount. 2010 Note: Financial information for 2010 was not available for all companies at press time.

2010 Sales: $	2010 Profits: $	**U.S. Stock Ticker: Subsidiary**
2009 Sales: $	2009 Profits: $	**Int'l Ticker:** Int'l Exchange:
2008 Sales: $	2008 Profits: $	Employees:
2007 Sales: $	2007 Profits: $	Fiscal Year Ends: 12/31
2006 Sales: $4,737,000	2006 Profits: $321,000	Parent Company: DTE ENERGY COMPANY

SALARIES/BENEFITS:

Pension Plan:	ESOP Stock Plan:	Profit Sharing:	Top Exec. Salary: $	Bonus: $
Savings Plan:	Stock Purch. Plan:		Second Exec. Salary: $	Bonus: $

OTHER THOUGHTS:

Apparent Women Officers or Directors:
Hot Spot for Advancement for Women/Minorities:

LOCATIONS: ("Y" = Yes)

West:	Southwest:	Midwest:	Southeast:	Northeast:	International:
		Y			

DEVON ENERGY CORPORATION

www.devonenergy.com

Industry Group Code: 211111 **Ranks within this company's industry group:** Sales: 54 Profits: 108

Exploration/Production:		Refining/Retailing:		Utilities:		Alternative Energy:		Specialty Services:		Energy Mktg./Other Svcs.	
Exploration:	Y	Refining:		Electric Utility:		Waste/Solar/Other:		Consulting/Eng.:		Energy Marketing:	
Production:	Y	Retailing:		Gas Utility:		Thermal/Steam:		Seismic:		Equipment/Machinery:	
Coal Production:		Convenience Stores:		Pipelines:	Y	Wind:		Drilling:		Oil Field Services:	
		Chemicals:		Water:		Hydro:		InfoTech:		Air/Shipping Transportation:	
						Fuel Cells:		Specialty Services:	Y		

TYPES OF BUSINESS:

Oil & Gas Exploration & Production
Pipelines
Gas Storage & Processing

BRANDS/DIVISIONS/AFFILIATES:

CONTACTS:

Note: Officers with more than one job title may be intentionally listed here more than once.

John Richels, CEO
John Richels, Pres.
Jeff A. Agosta, CFO/Exec. VP
Darryl G. Smette, Exec. VP-Mktg. & Midstream
Frank W. Rudolph, Exec. VP-Human Resources
David A. Hager, Exec. VP-Exploration & Prod.
R. Alan Marcum, Exec. VP-Admin.
Lyndon C. Taylor, General Counsel/Exec. VP
J. Larry Nichols, Chmn.

Phone: 405-235-3611	**Fax:** 405-552-4550
Toll-Free:	
Address: 20 N. Broadway, Oklahoma City, OK 73102-8260 US	

GROWTH PLANS/SPECIAL FEATURES:

Devon Energy Corporation is an independent energy company engaged primarily in oil and gas exploration, development and production; the transportation of oil, gas and natural gas liquids (NGL); and the processing of natural gas. In addition to its oil and gas operations, the company has marketing and midstream operations primarily in North America. Devon's U.S. operations include the Barnett Shale in north Texas; the Cana-Woodford Shale in western Oklahoma; the Haynesville Shale in the Carthage area of east Texas; and other areas in the Rocky Mountains, Mid-Continent, and Gulf Coast regions. Devon's Canadian operations are involved in natural gas and liquids at a near equitable level. The company's operations include the Foothill region of British Columbia, the Horn River in British Columbia, the Deep Basin in British Columbia and Alberta, the Northwest region in British Columbia and Alberta, the Central region in Alberta and Saskatchewan, the Lloydminster region in Alberta and Saskatchewan and the Thermal territory in Alberta. In November 2009, the company announced a new strategic plan to transition itself to an on-shore, North American exploration and production company. To accomplish this, Devon will divest itself from offshore and foreign assets. In June 2010, the company announced it sold its Gulf of Mexico shelf asset to Apache Corp. for $1.05 billion. With this sale, the company completely exited from the Gulf of Mexico. Also in June 2010, the firm sold its Panyu Field in China to the China National Offshore Oil Corporation for $515 million. In August 2010, Devon sold its ACG field asset in the Caspian Sea, near Azerbaijan, to BP for $2 billion.

Devon offers its employees medical, dental and vision coverage; short- and long-term disability; life and AD&D insurance; business travel insurance; an employee assistance program; a 401(k) plan; retirement contributions; flexible spending accounts; and tuition reimbursement.

FINANCIALS:

Sales and profits are in thousands of dollars—add 000 to get the full amount. 2010 Note: Financial information for 2010 was not available for all companies at press time.

2010 Sales: $	2010 Profits: $	**U.S. Stock Ticker: DVN**
2009 Sales: $8,015,000	2009 Profits: $-2,479,000	**Int'l Ticker:** Int'l Exchange:
2008 Sales: $13,858,000	2008 Profits: $-2,148,000	Employees: 5,400
2007 Sales: $9,975,000	2007 Profits: $3,606,000	Fiscal Year Ends: 12/31
2006 Sales: $9,767,000	2006 Profits: $2,846,000	Parent Company:

SALARIES/BENEFITS:

Pension Plan: Y	ESOP Stock Plan:	Profit Sharing:	Top Exec. Salary: $1,400,000	Bonus: $2,100,600
Savings Plan: Y	Stock Purch. Plan:		Second Exec. Salary: $1,150,000	Bonus: $1,400,600

OTHER THOUGHTS:

Apparent Women Officers or Directors: 1
Hot Spot for Advancement for Women/Minorities:

LOCATIONS: ("Y" = Yes)

West:	Southwest:	Midwest:	Southeast:	Northeast:	International:
	Y				Y

DIAMOND OFFSHORE DRILLING INC

www.diamondoffshore.com

Industry Group Code: 213111 **Ranks within this company's industry group:** Sales: 4 Profits: 2

Exploration/Production:		**Refining/Retailing:**		**Utilities:**		**Alternative Energy:**		**Specialty Services:**		**Energy Mktg./Other Svcs.**	
Exploration:		Refining:		Electric Utility:		Waste/Solar/Other:		Consulting/Eng.:		Energy Marketing:	
Production:		Retailing:		Gas Utility:		Thermal/Steam:		Seismic:		Equipment/Machinery:	
Coal Production:		Convenience Stores:		Pipelines:		Wind:		Drilling:	Y	Oil Field Services:	
		Chemicals:		Water:		Hydro:		InfoTech:		Air/Shipping Transportation:	
						Fuel Cells:		Specialty Services:			

TYPES OF BUSINESS:

Oil & Gas Drilling
Contract Drilling

BRANDS/DIVISIONS/AFFILIATES:

Diamond Offshore Drilling Limited

CONTACTS:

Note: Officers with more than one job title may be intentionally listed here more than once.

Lawrence Dickerson, CEO
Lawrence Dickerson, Pres.
Gary Krenek, CFO/Sr. VP
Bodley Thornton, VP-Mktg.
R. Lynn Charles, VP-Human Resources
Karl S. Sellers, VP-Eng.
Mark Baudoin, Sr. VP-Admin.
William Long, General Counsel/Sr. VP/Sec.
Lyndol Dew, Sr. VP-Worldwide Oper.
Beth Gordon, Controller
John M. Vecchio, Exec. VP
Steven Nelson, VP-Domestic Oper.
Stephen Elwood, VP-Tax
James S. Tisch, Chmn.
Mark Baudoin, Sr. VP-South America

Phone: 281-492-5300 **Fax:** 281-492-5316
Toll-Free: 800-848-1980
Address: 15415 Katy Fwy., Ste. 100, Houston, TX 77094-1810 US

GROWTH PLANS/SPECIAL FEATURES:

Diamond Offshore Drilling, Inc. is a leading deepwater drilling contractor. Diamond operates one of the world's largest fleets of offshore drilling units, consisting of 32 semi-submersibles, 13 jack-ups and one drill ship. Its semi-submersible rigs float with their lower hulls between 55 and 90 feet below the water line and are held in position partly with anchors and partly through a special hull characteristic known as wave transparency; five of the rigs also have a special computer-controlled thruster system known as dynamic-positioning. Thirteen of Diamond's 32 semi-submersibles are high-specification, which means that they are capable of drilling in harsh environments and water depths greater than 4,000 feet; and the other 19 rigs may only work in depths up to 4,000 feet. The company operates in many geographic areas, including the Gulf of Mexico, including the U.S. and Mexico; Europe, principally in the U.K. and Norway; the Mediterranean Basin, including Egypt, Libya, Tunisia and other parts of Africa; South America, principally in Brazil; Australia and Asia, including Malaysia, Indonesia and Vietnam; Angola; and the Middle East, including Kuwait, Qatar and Saudi Arabia. In September 2009, the company's subsidiary, Diamond Offshore Drilling Limited, acquired a semi-submersible drilling rig from Jurong Shipyard Pte Ltd. for about $490 million.

Employees are offered medical, vision, dental and prescription drug coverage; life and AD&D insurance; disability coverage; an employee assistance plan; flexible spending accounts; a 401(k) plan; and profit sharing.

FINANCIALS:

Sales and profits are in thousands of dollars—add 000 to get the full amount. 2010 Note: Financial information for 2010 was not available for all companies at press time.

2010 Sales: $	2010 Profits: $	**U.S. Stock Ticker: DO**
2009 Sales: $3,631,284	2009 Profits: $1,376,219	**Int'l Ticker:** Int'l Exchange:
2008 Sales: $3,544,057	2008 Profits: $1,310,547	Employees: 5,500
2007 Sales: $2,567,723	2007 Profits: $844,464	Fiscal Year Ends: 12/31
2006 Sales: $2,052,572	2006 Profits: $706,847	Parent Company:

SALARIES/BENEFITS:

Pension Plan:	ESOP Stock Plan:	Profit Sharing: Y	Top Exec. Salary: $782,500	Bonus: $555,000
Savings Plan: Y	Stock Purch. Plan:		Second Exec. Salary: $442,500	Bonus: $305,000

OTHER THOUGHTS:

Apparent Women Officers or Directors: 1
Hot Spot for Advancement for Women/Minorities:

LOCATIONS: ("Y" = Yes)

West:	Southwest:	Midwest:	Southeast:	Northeast:	International:
	Y		Y		Y

DIRECT ENERGY

www.directenergy.com

Industry Group Code: 221 **Ranks within this company's industry group:** Sales: Profits:

Exploration/Production:		Refining/Retailing:		Utilities:		Alternative Energy:		Specialty Services:		Energy Mktg./Other Svcs.	
Exploration:		Refining:		Electric Utility:	Y	Waste/Solar/Other:		Consulting/Eng.:		Energy Marketing:	Y
Production:	Y	Retailing:	Y	Gas Utility:	Y	Thermal/Steam:		Seismic:		Equipment/Machinery:	
Coal Production:		Convenience Stores:		Pipelines:		Wind:	Y	Drilling:		Oil Field Services:	
		Chemicals:		Water:		Hydro:		InfoTech:		Air/Shipping Transportation:	
						Fuel Cells:		Specialty Services:	Y		

TYPES OF BUSINESS:

Gas & Electric Utility
Heating and Air Conditioning Equipment
Energy Advisory Services

BRANDS/DIVISIONS/AFFILIATES:

DE Business
DE Residential
DE Services
CPL Retail Energy
WTU Retail Energy
DE Upstream and Trading
PowerPortfolio
Make Me Green

CONTACTS: *Note: Officers with more than one job title may be intentionally listed here more than once.*

Mike Senff, VP-Mktg. & Sales, North America
Emma Canter, Dir.-Human Resources
Paul Dobson, Sr. VP-Info. Svcs.
Lisa Delsante, Principal Legal Counsel
Paul Dobson, Sr. VP-Oper.
Stephane Kirkland, VP-Strategy & Solutions
Hillary Marshall, VP-Corp. Comm.
Paul Dobson, Sr. VP-Finance
Geoffrey Duda, VP-Oper., Canada

Phone:	**Fax:** 416-758-4553
Toll-Free: 866-8678167	
Address: 2225 Sheppard Ave. E., Toronto, PA M2J 5C2 Canada	

GROWTH PLANS/SPECIAL FEATURES:

Direct Energy, a subsidiary of Centrica plc, is a leading energy retailer in North America. The firm provides gas, electricity and related services to roughly 6 million businesses and residential customers in 10 Canadian Provinces and 46 U.S. states. The company operates through four divisions: DE Business; DE Residential; DE Services; and DE Upstream and Trading. DE Business offers electricity, natural gas and energy efficiency management services to small, medium and large-sized corporations; public institutions; government sectors; and national accounts. The division's products include fixed-rate energy service; market-based energy service; PowerPortfolio, an electricity plan which includes fixed and market-based terms; and Make Me Green, which offers renewable energy certificates in both regulated and deregulated electricity markets. DE Residential provides natural gas, electricity, carbon-neutral, and variable/flexible pricing plans to residential customers. In Texas, the firm operates under the brands CPL Retail Energy and WTU Retail Energy. Direct Energy's DE Services segment offers building automation; heating, ventilation, and air conditioning installation and service; protection plans; plumbing; water heater and electrical services; facility maintenance; energy audits; and management consulting; and operational/business management counseling to independent home services contractors. DE Upstream & Trading provides services such as natural gas production; gas-fired power generation; carbon credits; wind power purchase agreements; proprietary trading; the storage and transportation of gas; open market energy procurement; energy auctions; and renewable energy credits. Direct Energy owns/operates three gas-fired power plants and 813 megawatts of wind power in Texas; and 4,550 natural gas wells in Alberta. In July 2010, the firm acquired the assets of Clockwork Home Services, Inc. In October 2010, the company acquired the Wildcat Hills natural gas assets of Suncor Energy.

Direct Energy offers its employees a pension plan, an employee assistance program, an annual incentive bonus plan, an annual employee engagement survey, discounts on energy and health, prescription, dental and vision insurance.

FINANCIALS: **Sales and profits are in thousands of dollars—add 000 to get the full amount. 2010 Note: Financial information for 2010 was not available for all companies at press time.**

2010 Sales: $	2010 Profits: $	**U.S. Stock Ticker: Subsidiary**
2009 Sales: $	2009 Profits: $	**Int'l Ticker:** Int'l Exchange:
2008 Sales: $	2008 Profits: $	Employees:
2007 Sales: $	2007 Profits: $	Fiscal Year Ends:
2006 Sales: $7,600,000	2006 Profits: $	Parent Company: CENTRICA PLC

SALARIES/BENEFITS:

Pension Plan: Y	ESOP Stock Plan: Y	Profit Sharing:	Top Exec. Salary: $	Bonus: $
Savings Plan:	Stock Purch. Plan:		Second Exec. Salary: $	Bonus: $

OTHER THOUGHTS:

Apparent Women Officers or Directors: 1
Hot Spot for Advancement for Women/Minorities:

LOCATIONS: ("Y" = Yes)

West:	Southwest:	Midwest:	Southeast:	Northeast:	International:
	Y	Y	Y	Y	Y

DOMINION RESOURCES INC

www.dom.com

Industry Group Code: 221 **Ranks within this company's industry group:** Sales: 9 Profits: 11

Exploration/Production:		**Refining/Retailing:**		**Utilities:**		**Alternative Energy:**		**Specialty Services:**		**Energy Mktg./Other Svcs.**	
Exploration:	Y	Refining:		Electric Utility:	Y	Waste/Solar/Other:		Consulting/Eng.:		Energy Marketing:	Y
Production:	Y	Retailing:		Gas Utility:	Y	Thermal/Steam:		Seismic:		Equipment/Machinery:	
Coal Production:		Convenience Stores:		Pipelines:	Y	Wind:		Drilling:	Y	Oil Field Services:	
		Chemicals:		Water:		Hydro:	Y	InfoTech:		Air/Shipping Transportation:	
						Fuel Cells:		Specialty Services:	Y		

TYPES OF BUSINESS:

Utilities-Electricity & Natural Gas
Oil & Natural Gas Exploration & Production
Natural Gas Transportation & Storage
Energy Marketing
Price Risk Management Services
Merchant Generation

BRANDS/DIVISIONS/AFFILIATES:

Virginia Electric and Power Company
Dominion Transmission, Inc.
Dominion Resources Services, Inc.
Virginia Power Energy Marketing, Inc.

CONTACTS:

Note: Officers with more than one job title may be intentionally listed here more than once.

Thomas F. Farrell, II, CEO
Thomas F. Farrell, II, Pres.
Mark F. McGettrick, CFO/Exec. VP
James F. Stutts, General Counsel/Sr. VP
Ashwini Sawhney, Controller/VP
Carter M. Reid, VP-Governance & Corp. Sec.
Gary L. Sypolt, CEO-Dominion Energy
Paul D. Koonce, CEO-Dominion Virginia Power
David A. Christian, CEO-Dominion Generation
Thomas F. Farrell, II, Chmn.

Phone: 804-819-2000 **Fax:** 804-819-2233
Toll-Free:
Address: 120 Tredegar St., Richmond, VA 23219 US

GROWTH PLANS/SPECIAL FEATURES:

Dominion Resources, Inc. is a gas and electric holding company that concentrates largely in the eastern region of the U.S. The firm's asset portfolio includes 27,500 megawatts (MW) of power generation; 1.3 trillion cubic feet equivalent of proved natural gas reserves; and 6,000 miles of electric transmission lines. Dominion serves retail energy customers in 12 states. The firm manages its operations through three operating segments: Dominion Virginia Power (DVP), Dominion Generation and Dominion Energy. DVP includes the firm's regulated electric transmission, distribution and customer service operations, as well as its non-regulated retail energy marketing operations. Dominion Generation includes the generation operations of the company's merchant fleet and regulated electric utility, as well as energy marketing and price risk management activities for its generation assets. The company's generation mix includes coal, nuclear, gas, oil and renewables. Dominion Energy includes the firm's Ohio and West Virginia regulated natural gas distribution companies; regulated gas transmission pipeline and storage operations; regulated LNG operations; and its Appalachian natural gas exploration and production business. Dominion Energy also includes its producer services business. Subsidiaries include Virginia Electric and Power Company; Dominion Transmission, Inc.; Dominion Resources Services, Inc.; and Virginia Power Energy Marketing, Inc. In February 2010, the firm sold its natural gas distribution company in Pennsylvania, Dominion Peoples, to PNG Companies LLC for $780 million.

The company offers employees medical, dental and vision insurance; life insurance; pension plans; a 401(k) plan; tuition reimbursement; adoption assistance; an employee assistance program; and group auto and home insurance.

FINANCIALS:

Sales and profits are in thousands of dollars—add 000 to get the full amount. 2010 Note: Financial information for 2010 was not available for all companies at press time.

2010 Sales: $	2010 Profits: $	**U.S. Stock Ticker: D**
2009 Sales: $15,131,000	2009 Profits: $1,287,000	**Int'l Ticker:** Int'l Exchange:
2008 Sales: $16,290,000	2008 Profits: $1,834,000	Employees: 17,900
2007 Sales: $15,674,000	2007 Profits: $2,539,000	Fiscal Year Ends: 12/31
2006 Sales: $16,297,000	2006 Profits: $1,380,000	Parent Company:

SALARIES/BENEFITS:

Pension Plan: Y	ESOP Stock Plan:	Profit Sharing:	Top Exec. Salary: $1,200,000	Bonus: $5,532,000
Savings Plan: Y	Stock Purch. Plan:		Second Exec. Salary: $648,250	Bonus: $1,665,292

OTHER THOUGHTS:

Apparent Women Officers or Directors: 3
Hot Spot for Advancement for Women/Minorities: Y

LOCATIONS: ("Y" = Yes)

West:	Southwest:	Midwest:	Southeast:	Northeast:	International:
	Y	Y	Y	Y	Y

DORCHESTER MINERALS LP

www.dmlp.net

Industry Group Code: 211111 **Ranks within this company's industry group:** Sales: 112 Profits: 69

Exploration/Production:		Refining/Retailing:		Utilities:		Alternative Energy:		Specialty Services:		Energy Mktg./Other Svcs.	
Exploration:	Y	Refining:		Electric Utility:		Waste/Solar/Other:		Consulting/Eng.:		Energy Marketing:	
Production:	Y	Retailing:		Gas Utility:		Thermal/Steam:		Seismic:		Equipment/Machinery:	
Coal Production:		Convenience Stores:		Pipelines:		Wind:		Drilling:		Oil Field Services:	
		Chemicals:		Water:		Hydro:		InfoTech:		Air/Shipping Transportation:	
						Fuel Cells:		Specialty Services:	Y		

TYPES OF BUSINESS:

Oil & Gas Exploration & Production
Property Investment & Acquisitions

BRANDS/DIVISIONS/AFFILIATES:

Republic Royalty Co., LP
Spinnaker Royalty Co., LP
Dorchester Hugoton, Ltd.
Dorchester Minerals Management LP
Dorchester Minerals Operating LP

CONTACTS: *Note: Officers with more than one job title may be intentionally listed here more than once.*

William C. McManemin, CEO
James E. Raley, COO
H. C. Allen, Jr., CFO

Phone: 214-559-0300	**Fax:** 214-559-0301
Toll-Free:	
Address: 3838 Oak Lawn Ave., Ste. 300, Dallas, TX 75219 US	

GROWTH PLANS/SPECIAL FEATURES:

Dorchester Minerals, LP is a limited partnership whose primary business is the acquisition, ownership and administration of Net Profits Interests and Royalty Properties. The Net Profits Interests represent net profits overriding royalty interests in various properties owned by the company's operating partnership, Dorchester Minerals Operating LP. The Royalty Properties consist of producing and nonproducing mineral, royalty, overriding royalty, net profits and leasehold interests located in 573 counties and parishes in 25 U.S. states. The company was formed in connection with the combination of Dorchester Hugoton, Ltd.; Republic Royalty Company, LP; and Spinnaker Royalty Company, LP. The firm's general partner, Dorchester Minerals Management, LP, holds the working interests in properties previously owned by Dorchester Hugoton and a minor portion of mineral interest properties previously owned by Republic and Spinnaker. Dorchester Minerals holds approximately 60.3 billion cubic feet of proved natural gas reserves and 3.2 billion barrels of oil reserves. The firm also holds a total of 355,692 net acres. In 2009, the company identified 353 new wells on Royalty Properties in 11 states and identified 48 new wells located on Net Profits Interests properties in four states, as well as consummating 47 leases of its mineral interest in undeveloped properties.

FINANCIALS: **Sales and profits are in thousands of dollars—add 000 to get the full amount. 2010 Note: Financial information for 2010 was not available for all companies at press time.**

2010 Sales: $	2010 Profits: $	**U.S. Stock Ticker: DMLP**
2009 Sales: $43,631	2009 Profits: $21,681	**Int'l Ticker:** Int'l Exchange:
2008 Sales: $89,925	2008 Profits: $66,783	Employees: 27
2007 Sales: $65,365	2007 Profits: $42,340	Fiscal Year Ends: 12/31
2006 Sales: $74,927	2006 Profits: $50,210	Parent Company:

SALARIES/BENEFITS:

Pension Plan:	ESOP Stock Plan:	Profit Sharing:	Top Exec. Salary: $96,000	Bonus: $
Savings Plan:	Stock Purch. Plan:		Second Exec. Salary: $96,000	Bonus: $

OTHER THOUGHTS:

Apparent Women Officers or Directors:
Hot Spot for Advancement for Women/Minorities:

LOCATIONS: ("Y" = Yes)

West:	Southwest:	Midwest:	Southeast:	Northeast:	International:
	Y				

DOW CHEMICAL COMPANY (THE)

www.dow.com

Industry Group Code: 325 **Ranks within this company's industry group:** Sales: 2 Profits: 2

Exploration/Production:		Refining/Retailing:		Utilities:		Alternative Energy:		Specialty Services:		Energy Mktg./Other Svcs.	
Exploration:		Refining:		Electric Utility:		Waste/Solar/Other:		Consulting/Eng.:		Energy Marketing:	
Production:		Retailing:		Gas Utility:		Thermal/Steam:		Seismic:		Equipment/Machinery:	
Coal Production:		Convenience Stores:		Pipelines:		Wind:		Drilling:		Oil Field Services:	
		Chemicals:	Y	Water:		Hydro:		InfoTech:		Air/Shipping Transportation:	
						Fuel Cells:		Specialty Services:	Y		

TYPES OF BUSINESS:

Chemicals Manufacturer
Basic Chemicals
Plastics
Performance Chemicals
Agrochemicals
Hydrocarbons & Fuels

BRANDS/DIVISIONS/AFFILIATES:

Dow Agrosciences LLC
Union Carbide Corporation
Rohm & Haas Company
Pfenex, Inc.
Clean Filtration Technologies, Inc.

CONTACTS:

Note: Officers with more than one job title may be intentionally listed here more than once.

Andrew N. Liveris, CEO
William H. Weidemann, CFO/Exec. VP
Heinz Haller, Chief Commercial Officer/Exec. VP
Gregory M. Freiwald, Exec. VP-Human Resources & Aviation
Jerome A. Peribere, Exec. VP/CEO-Dow Advanced Materials
David E. Kepler, CIO/Exec. VP-Bus. Svcs.
William F. Banholzer, CTO/Exec. VP
Michael R. Gambrell, Exec. VP-Eng. Oper.
Michael R. Gambrell, Exec. VP-Mfg. Oper.
Charles J. Kalil, General Counsel/Sec./Exec. VP-Law & Gov't Affairs
William F. Banholzer, Exec. VP-Ventures, New Bus. Dev. & Licensing
Gregory M. Freiwald, Exec. VP-Corp. Affairs
Ron Edmonds, Controller/VP
James D. McIlvenny, Sr. VP-Mega Projects
James R. Fitterling, Exec. VP/Pres., Plastics & Hydrocarbons
Carol Williams, Sr. VP/Pres., Chemicals & Energy
Andrew N. Liveris, Chmn.
Geoffery E. Merszei, Exec. VP/Pres., EMEA/Chmn.-DOW Europe

Phone: 989-636-1463 **Fax:** 989-636-1830
Toll-Free: 800-422-8193
Address: 2030 Dow Ctr., Midland, MI 48674 US

GROWTH PLANS/SPECIAL FEATURES:

The Dow Chemical Company is a global chemical and plastics company. It delivers a broad range of products and services to customers in about 160 countries, has 214 manufacturing sites in 37 countries and produces roughly 5,000 products. The company operates in eight segments. The electronic and specialty materials segment manufactures semiconductor, display and filtration technology materials. The coatings and infrastructure segment manufactures architectural and industrial coatings, construction chemicals, adhesives and textiles. The health and agricultural sciences segment produces biotechnology products and pest management solutions. The performance systems segment manufactures automotive, polyurethane and epoxy systems, elastomers and oil and gas exploration products. The performance products segment manufactures polyurethanes, epoxy, amines, oxygenated solvents and emulsion polymers. The basic plastics segment manufactures polyethylene, polypropylene and polystyrene. The basic chemicals segment produces ethylene oxide, chlor-alkali and chlorinated organics. Finally, the hydrocarbons and energy segment procures fuels, natural gas liquids and crude oil-based raw materials, and also supplies monomers, power and steam to Dow's operations. The firm's long-term strategy is to move away from commodity chemicals, which do not earn large profit margins, and focus on specialty chemicals. During 2009, in line with this strategy, it announced the shutdown of styrene monomer and ethylbenzene production units in Freeport, Texas. In April 2009, the firm acquired chemicals giant Rohm & Haas for $15 billion. Following this acquisition, the company announced a restructuring plan that includes the elimination of 2,500 employees. Other activities during 2009 included the divestiture of Morton International, Inc.; the divestiture of its stake in the OPTIMAL Group of Companies; and the formation of biotechnology company Pfenex, Inc. In early 2010, Dow sold its acrylic acid and esters business; and announced its investment in Clean Filtration Technologies, Inc. In June 2010, the company sold Dow Haltermann Custom Processing, and divested its Styron division.

FINANCIALS:

Sales and profits are in thousands of dollars—add 000 to get the full amount. 2010 Note: Financial information for 2010 was not available for all companies at press time.

2010 Sales: $	2010 Profits: $	**U.S. Stock Ticker: DOW**
2009 Sales: $44,875,000	2009 Profits: $336,000	**Int'l Ticker:** Int'l Exchange:
2008 Sales: $57,361,000	2008 Profits: $579,000	Employees: 52,195
2007 Sales: $53,375,000	2007 Profits: $2,887,000	Fiscal Year Ends: 12/31
2006 Sales: $49,124,000	2006 Profits: $3,724,000	Parent Company:

SALARIES/BENEFITS:

Pension Plan:	ESOP Stock Plan:	Profit Sharing:	Top Exec. Salary: $1,650,000	Bonus: $4,485,937
Savings Plan:	Stock Purch. Plan:		Second Exec. Salary: $861,396	Bonus: $1,187,111

OTHER THOUGHTS:

Apparent Women Officers or Directors: 5
Hot Spot for Advancement for Women/Minorities: Y

LOCATIONS: ("Y" = Yes)

West:	Southwest:	Midwest:	Southeast:	Northeast:	International:
Y	Y	Y	Y	Y	Y

DPL INC

www.dplinc.com

Industry Group Code: 2211 **Ranks within this company's industry group:** Sales: 38 Profits: 31

Exploration/Production:		Refining/Retailing:		Utilities:		Alternative Energy:		Specialty Services:		Energy Mktg./Other Svcs.	
Exploration:		Refining:		Electric Utility:	Y	Waste/Solar/Other:		Consulting/Eng.:		Energy Marketing:	Y
Production:		Retailing:		Gas Utility:	Y	Thermal/Steam:		Seismic:		Equipment/Machinery:	Y
Coal Production:		Convenience Stores:		Pipelines:		Wind:		Drilling:		Oil Field Services:	
		Chemicals:		Water:		Hydro:		InfoTech:		Air/Shipping Transportation:	
						Fuel Cells:		Specialty Services:	Y		

TYPES OF BUSINESS:

Utilities-Electricity & Natural Gas
Power Generation
Real Estate
Equipment Leasing
Financial Services

BRANDS/DIVISIONS/AFFILIATES:

Dayton Power and Light Company
DPL Energy, LLC
DPL Energy Resources, Inc.
MVE, Inc.
Miami Valley Insurance Company

CONTACTS:
Note: Officers with more than one job title may be intentionally listed here more than once.

Paul M. Barbas, CEO
Paul M. Barbas, Pres.
Frederick J. Boyle, CFO/Sr. VP/Controller/Treas.
Daniel J. McCabe, Sr. VP-Human Resources
Daniel J. McCabe, Chief Admin. Officer/Sr. VP
Arthur G. Meyer, General Counsel
Gary G. Stephenson, Exec. VP-Oper.
Arthur G. Meyer, Sr. VP-Corp. & Regulatory Affairs
Joseph Mulpas, Chief Acct. Officer/VP/Controller
Kevin W. Crawford, VP-Plant Oper.
Bryce Nickel, VP-Service Oper.
Teresa Marrinan, Sr. VP-Commercial Oper.
Scott J. Kelly, Sr. VP-Commercial Oper.
Glenn E. Harder, Chmn.

Phone: 937-224-6000	Fax: 937-259-7147
Toll-Free:	
Address: 1065 Woodman Dr., Dayton, OH 45432 US	

GROWTH PLANS/SPECIAL FEATURES:

DPL, Inc. is a diversified regional energy company operating primarily through its subsidiary Dayton Power and Light Company (DP&L). Providing approximately 98% of DPL's total consolidated revenue and approximately 95% of DPL's total consolidated asset base, DP&L is a public utility selling electricity to residential, commercial, industrial and governmental customers in a 6,000-square-mile area of west central Ohio. Electricity for DP&L's 24 county service area is generated at eight coal-fired power plants and is distributed to more than 500,000 retail customers. DP&L also purchases retail peak load requirements from another of DPL's subsidiaries, DPL Energy, LLC (DPLE). Principal industries served by DP&L include automotive, food processing, paper, plastic manufacturing and defense. DP&L sells any excess energy and capacity into the wholesale market. Other significant subsidiaries of DPL include DPL Energy Resources, Inc. (DPLER), which sells retail electric energy under contract to major industrial and commercial customers in west central Ohio; MVE, Inc., which is primarily responsible for the management of its financial asset portfolio; and Miami Valley Insurance Company (MVIC), which is DPL's captive insurance company, providing DPL and its subsidiaries with insurance sources. DPL has more than $4 billion in assets. The company's generation capacity at its 10 power plants is 3,700 megawatts, 2,800 of which are low priced coal-fired units and 900 of which are natural gas and diesel peaking units. In June 2010, DP&L opened a 1.1. Megawatt solar power facility in Washington Township, Montgomery County, Ohio.

The company offers employees medical benefits, flexible spending accounts, a bonus incentive program, educational assistance, a 401(k) savings plan and life insurance.

FINANCIALS:
Sales and profits are in thousands of dollars—add 000 to get the full amount. 2010 Note: Financial information for 2010 was not available for all companies at press time.

2010 Sales: $	2010 Profits: $	**U.S. Stock Ticker: DPL**
2009 Sales: $1,588,900	2009 Profits: $229,100	**Int'l Ticker:** Int'l Exchange:
2008 Sales: $1,601,600	2008 Profits: $244,500	Employees: 1,588
2007 Sales: $1,515,700	2007 Profits: $221,800	Fiscal Year Ends: 12/31
2006 Sales: $1,393,519	2006 Profits: $139,600	Parent Company:

SALARIES/BENEFITS:

Pension Plan:	ESOP Stock Plan:	Profit Sharing:	Top Exec. Salary: $683,654	Bonus: $447,633
Savings Plan: Y	Stock Purch. Plan:		Second Exec. Salary: $330,192	Bonus: $154,252

OTHER THOUGHTS:

Apparent Women Officers or Directors: 3
Hot Spot for Advancement for Women/Minorities: Y

LOCATIONS: ("Y" = Yes)

West:	Southwest:	Midwest:	Southeast:	Northeast:	International:
		Y		Y	

DRIL-QUIP INC

www.dril-quip.com

Industry Group Code: 33313 **Ranks within this company's industry group:** Sales: 6 Profits: 3

Exploration/Production:		Refining/Retailing:		Utilities:		Alternative Energy:		Specialty Services:		Energy Mktg./Other Svcs.	
Exploration:		Refining:		Electric Utility:		Waste/Solar/Other:		Consulting/Eng.:	Y	Energy Marketing:	
Production:		Retailing:		Gas Utility:		Thermal/Steam:		Seismic:		Equipment/Machinery:	Y
Coal Production:		Convenience Stores:		Pipelines:		Wind:		Drilling:		Oil Field Services:	Y
		Chemicals:		Water:		Hydro:		InfoTech:		Air/Shipping Transportation:	
						Fuel Cells:		Specialty Services:	Y		

TYPES OF BUSINESS:

Drilling & Production Equipment
Specialty Connectors
Subsea Equipment
Surface Equipment
Gate Valves
Equipment Installation & Reconditioning
Equipment Rental

BRANDS/DIVISIONS/AFFILIATES:

Dril-Quip Europe Limited
Dril-Quip Asia Pacific PTE Ltd.
Dril-Quip Nigeria Ltd.
Dril-Quip do Brasil LTDA
Dril-Quip Egypt for Petroleum Services S.A.E,
Dril-Quip Holdings Pty Ltd

CONTACTS:

Note: Officers with more than one job title may be intentionally listed here more than once.

Larry E. Reimert, Co-CEO/Co-Chmn.
Jerry M. Brooks, CFO
Jerry M. Brooks, VP-Finance
J. Mike Walker, Co-Chmn./Co-CEO

Phone: 713-939-7711	**Fax:** 713-939-8063
Toll-Free:	
Address: 13550 Hempstead Hwy., Houston, TX 77040 US	

GROWTH PLANS/SPECIAL FEATURES:

Dril-Quip, Inc. is a producer of offshore drilling and production equipment, specializing in deepwater, harsh environment and severe service applications in the oil and gas industry. The company's products are used to explore for oil and gas from offshore drilling rigs as well as for drilling and production of oil and gas wells from offshore platforms, tension leg platforms, spars and moored vessels. Its main products consist of subsea and surface wellheads; subsea and surface production trees; subsea and platform valves; mudline hanger systems; specialty connectors and associated pipe; drilling and production riser systems; and wellhead connectors and diverters. In 2009, 84% of the company's revenue was derived from product sales, 66% of which were to foreign customers. Six subsidiaries market and manufacture Dril-Quip products: Dril-Quip Europe Limited, with offices in Scotland, Norway, Holland and Denmark; Dril-Quip Asia Pacific PTE Ltd., located in Singapore; Dril-Quip Nigeria Ltd., located in Port Harcourt, Nigeria; Dril-Quip Egypt for Petroleum Services S.A.E, in Alexandria, Egypt; Dril-Quip Holdings Pty Ltd. in Perth, Australia; and Dril-Quip do Brasil LTDA., in Macae, Brazil. The firm's manufacturing operations are vertically integrated, and it performs all of its forging, heat-treating, machining, fabrication, inspection, assembly and testing at its own facilities. Dril-Quip also provides installation and reconditioning services and rents running tools for use in connection with the installation and retrieval of its products. Dril-Quip develops its line of subsea equipment, surface equipment and offshore rig equipment primarily through internal product development.

FINANCIALS:

Sales and profits are in thousands of dollars—add 000 to get the full amount. 2010 Note: Financial information for 2010 was not available for all companies at press time.

2010 Sales: $	2010 Profits: $	**U.S. Stock Ticker: DRQ**
2009 Sales: $240,204	2009 Profits: $105,141	**Int'l Ticker:** Int'l Exchange:
2008 Sales: $542,771	2008 Profits: $105,585	Employees: 2,130
2007 Sales: $495,557	2007 Profits: $107,941	Fiscal Year Ends: 12/31
2006 Sales: $442,742	2006 Profits: $86,891	Parent Company:

SALARIES/BENEFITS:

Pension Plan: Y	ESOP Stock Plan:	Profit Sharing:	Top Exec. Salary: $569,615	Bonus: $477,000
Savings Plan: Y	Stock Purch. Plan:		Second Exec. Salary: $569,615	Bonus: $477,000

OTHER THOUGHTS:

Apparent Women Officers or Directors:
Hot Spot for Advancement for Women/Minorities:

LOCATIONS: ("Y" = Yes)

West:	Southwest:	Midwest:	Southeast:	Northeast:	International:
	Y		Y		Y

DRUMMOND COMPANY INC

www.drummondco.com

Industry Group Code: 21211 **Ranks within this company's industry group:** Sales: 8 Profits:

Exploration/Production:		**Refining/Retailing:**		**Utilities:**		**Alternative Energy:**		**Specialty Services:**		**Energy Mktg./Other Svcs.**	
Exploration:		Refining:		Electric Utility:		Waste/Solar/Other:		Consulting/Eng.:		Energy Marketing:	
Production:		Retailing:		Gas Utility:		Thermal/Steam:		Seismic:		Equipment/Machinery:	Y
Coal Production:	Y	Convenience Stores:		Pipelines:		Wind:		Drilling:		Oil Field Services:	
		Chemicals:		Water:		Hydro:		InfoTech:		Air/Shipping Transportation:	
						Fuel Cells:		Specialty Services:	Y		

TYPES OF BUSINESS:

Coal Production & Sales
Coke Production & Sales
Equipment Supply
Real Estate Development

BRANDS/DIVISIONS/AFFILIATES:

Shoal Creek
Mina Pribbenow
Aire Amigo
ABC Coke
Perry Supply
Induserve Supply Cooperative
Oakbridge
Liberty Park

CONTACTS:

Note: Officers with more than one job title may be intentionally listed here more than once.

Garry N. Drummond, Sr., CEO
Jack Stilwell, CFO/Exec. VP
Bruce C. Webster, General Counsel/Exec. VP
Matt Brown, Contact-Investor Rel.
Matt Brown, Treas.
Larry Drummond, Vice Chmn.
George Wilbanks, Pres., Drummond Coal Sales, Inc.
John Pearson, Pres., ABC Coke Div.
Richard Mullen, Exec. VP-Mining
Garry N. Drummond, Sr., Chmn.
Augusto Jimenez, Pres., Drummond Ltd. Colombia

Phone: 205-945-6300	**Fax:** 205-945-6440
Toll-Free:	
Address: P.O. Box 10246, Birmingham, AL 35242 US	

GROWTH PLANS/SPECIAL FEATURES:

Drummond Company, Inc., founded in 1935, is principally in the business of mining, purchasing, processing and selling coal and coal derivatives. Through its Coal division, the company produces metallurgical coal and steam coal. Metallurgical coal is produced from Shoal Creek in the Warrior Coal Basin, which stretches across Jefferson, Tuscaloosa and Walker Counties in Alabama. Shoal Creek, one of the largest underground facilities nationwide, produces medium-volatility, low sulfur compliance coal. Steam coal is produced from Mina Pribbenow, an open-pit coal mine in La Loma, near Colombia, and marketed under the trade name Aire Amigo internationally to 13 countries. The firm ships approximately 22.9 million tons of steam coal annually. Drummond's coke operation, ABC Coke, is a leading merchant foundry coke producer in the U.S., with over 132 ovens and an annual capacity of approximately 730,000 tons of saleable coke. ABC Coke's typical product characteristic consists of 92.5% fixed carbon, 7% ash, 0.5% volatile matter and 0.6% sulfer. Drummond's mining and foundry supply business, Perry Supply, was started in 1913, is a distributor for over 20 different manufacturers and is a preferred member of the Induserve Supply Cooperative, which provides the company access to 500,000 different products. Over half of Perry Supply's products are sold outside of the U.S., and all of the company's products are available through its online catalog. Through its real estate division, Drummond directly owns or has interests in four golf-oriented residential real estate developments: Oakbridge, located in Lakeland, Florida, with 1,500 acres; Liberty Park, located near Birmingham in Vestavia Hills, Alabama, with nearly 4,000 acres; Rancho La Quinta, located near Palm Springs in La Quinta, California, with 1,000 acres; and Andalusa at Coral Mountain, also located in La Quinta, with 1,000 acres.

FINANCIALS:

Sales and profits are in thousands of dollars—add 000 to get the full amount. 2010 Note: Financial information for 2010 was not available for all companies at press time.

2010 Sales: $	2010 Profits: $	**U.S. Stock Ticker: Private**
2009 Sales: $2,850,000	2009 Profits: $	**Int'l Ticker:** Int'l Exchange:
2008 Sales: $2,870,000	2008 Profits: $	Employees: 6,300
2007 Sales: $	2007 Profits: $	Fiscal Year Ends: 12/31
2006 Sales: $1,770,000	2006 Profits: $	Parent Company:

SALARIES/BENEFITS:

Pension Plan:	ESOP Stock Plan:	Profit Sharing:	Top Exec. Salary: $	Bonus: $
Savings Plan:	Stock Purch. Plan:		Second Exec. Salary: $	Bonus: $

OTHER THOUGHTS:

Apparent Women Officers or Directors:
Hot Spot for Advancement for Women/Minorities:

LOCATIONS: ("Y" = Yes)

West:	Southwest:	Midwest:	Southeast:	Northeast:	International:
Y			Y		Y

DTE ENERGY COMPANY

www.dteenergy.com

Industry Group Code: 221 **Ranks within this company's industry group:** Sales: 23 Profits: 21

Exploration/Production:		Refining/Retailing:		Utilities:		Alternative Energy:		Specialty Services:		Energy Mktg./Other Svcs.	
Exploration:		Refining:		Electric Utility:	Y	Waste/Solar/Other:		Consulting/Eng.:	Y	Energy Marketing:	Y
Production:		Retailing:		Gas Utility:	Y	Thermal/Steam:		Seismic:		Equipment/Machinery:	
Coal Production:		Convenience Stores:		Pipelines:	Y	Wind:		Drilling:		Oil Field Services:	
		Chemicals:		Water:		Hydro:	Y	InfoTech:		Air/Shipping Transportation:	Y
						Fuel Cells:		Specialty Services:	Y		

TYPES OF BUSINESS:

Utilities-Electricity & Natural Gas
Energy Management
Wholesale Energy Trading
Fuel Supply Services
Hydroelectric Power
Nuclear Power
Coal Shipping-Rail & Boat
Consulting Services

BRANDS/DIVISIONS/AFFILIATES:

Detroit Edison Company (The)
Michigan Consolidated Gas Company
Citizen's Gas Fuel Corp.
DTE Biomass Energy
DTE Coal Services
DTE Energy Services

CONTACTS: *Note: Officers with more than one job title may be intentionally listed here more than once.*

Anthony F. Earley, Jr., CEO
Gerard M. Anderson, COO
Gerard M. Anderson, Pres.
David E. Meador, CFO/Exec. VP
Trevor F. Lauer, VP-Retail Mktg.
Larry Steward, VP-Human Resources
Lynne Ellyn, CIO/Sr. VP
Lisa Muschong, Chief of Staff/Corp. Sec.
Bruce Peterson, General Counsel/Sr. VP
Paul Hillegonds, Sr. VP-Corp. Affairs
Peter Oleksiak, VP-Investor Rel.
Peter Oleksiak, Controller/VP
Steven E. Kurmas, Pres./COO-Detroit Edison
Jerry Norcia, Pres./COO-MichCon
Fred Shusterich, Pres., Midwest Energy Resources
Knut Simonsen, Pres., DTE Energy Ventures
Anthony F. Earley, Jr., Chmn.

Phone: 313-235-4000 **Fax:** 313-235-6743
Toll-Free: 866-966-5555
Address: 1 Energy Plz., Detroit, MI 48226 US

GROWTH PLANS/SPECIAL FEATURES:

DTE Energy Company is a diversified energy and energy technology company that develops merchant power and industrial energy projects and works in energy trading, selling electricity, natural gas, coal, chilled water, landfill gas and steam. DTE is one of the nation's largest purchasers, transporters and marketers of coal. The company's principal operating segments include its Electric Utility division, which consists of The Detroit Edison Company, an electric utility in southeastern Michigan that has a generating capacity of 11,000 megawatts (MW) and serves 2.1 million customers, and its Gas Utilities division, represented by Michigan Consolidated Gas (MichCon), which distributes natural gas to 1.2 million customers. The firm's Non-Utility Operations segments include Coal-Related Services, which procures and transports coal; Gas Storage and Pipelines, encompassing DTE's two interstate gas transmission pipelines and storage facilities; Power and Industrial Projects, primarily consisting of energy product delivery, coal transportation and marketing and electricity provided by biomass-fueled energy projects; Unconventional Gas Production, primarily consisting of unconventional gas project development and production; and DTE Energy Trading, which buys, sells and trades electricity, coal and natural gas and provides risk management services consisting of energy marketing and trading operations. In January 2010, the company launched a 2,000 acre wind farm operation with Heritage Sustainable Energy. In August 2010, DTE Energy announced plans to obtain 20 megawatts of annual electricity from two biomass facilities in Michigan. Also in August 2010, the firm unveiled plans to build a solar power generation and storage facility at Ford's Michigan Assembly Plant.

DTE Energy offers its employees medical, dental and vision coverage; comprehensive wellness programs; a 401(k) plan; flexible spending accounts; an employee assistance program; long-term care insurance; life, disability and AD&D insurance; and a cash balance pension.

FINANCIALS: **Sales and profits are in thousands of dollars—add 000 to get the full amount. 2010 Note: Financial information for 2010 was not available for all companies at press time.**

2010 Sales: $	2010 Profits: $	**U.S. Stock Ticker: DTE**
2009 Sales: $8,014,000	2009 Profits: $532,000	**Int'l Ticker:** Int'l Exchange:
2008 Sales: $9,329,000	2008 Profits: $546,000	Employees: 10,244
2007 Sales: $8,506,000	2007 Profits: $971,000	Fiscal Year Ends: 12/31
2006 Sales: $8,159,000	2006 Profits: $433,000	Parent Company:

SALARIES/BENEFITS:

Pension Plan: Y	ESOP Stock Plan:	Profit Sharing:	Top Exec. Salary: $1,200,000	Bonus: $2,275,000
Savings Plan: Y	Stock Purch. Plan:		Second Exec. Salary: $820,000	Bonus: $1,170,000

OTHER THOUGHTS:

Apparent Women Officers or Directors: 7
Hot Spot for Advancement for Women/Minorities: Y

LOCATIONS: ("Y" = Yes)

West:	Southwest:	Midwest:	Southeast:	Northeast:	International:
		Y			

DUKE ENERGY CORP

www.duke-energy.com

Industry Group Code: 221 **Ranks within this company's industry group:** Sales: 13 Profits: 14

Exploration/Production:		**Refining/Retailing:**		**Utilities:**		**Alternative Energy:**		**Specialty Services:**		**Energy Mktg./Other Svcs.**	
Exploration:		Refining:		Electric Utility:	Y	Waste/Solar/Other:		Consulting/Eng.:	Y	Energy Marketing:	Y
Production:		Retailing:		Gas Utility:	Y	Thermal/Steam:		Seismic:		Equipment/Machinery:	
Coal Production:		Convenience Stores:		Pipelines:	Y	Wind:		Drilling:		Oil Field Services:	
		Chemicals:		Water:		Hydro:		InfoTech:		Air/Shipping Transportation:	
						Fuel Cells:		Specialty Services:	Y		

TYPES OF BUSINESS:

Utilities-Electricity & Natural Gas
Merchant Power Generation
Natural Gas Transportation & Storage
Electricity Transmission
Energy Marketing
Real Estate
Telecommunications
Facility & Plant Services

BRANDS/DIVISIONS/AFFILIATES:

Franchised Electric & Gas Service
Duke Energy Generation Services, Inc.
Duke Energy International, LLC
DukeNet Communications, LLC

CONTACTS: *Note: Officers with more than one job title may be intentionally listed here more than once.*

James E. Rogers, CEO
James E. Rogers, Pres.
Lynn J. Good, CFO/Group Exec.
Jennifer L. Weber, Chief Human Resources/Sr. VP
David W. Mohler, CTO/VP
Marc E. Manly, Chief Legal Officer/Corp. Sec./Group Exec.
Virginia S. Mackin, Chief Comm. Officer/Sr. VP
Stephen G. De May, Sr. VP-Investor Rel./Treas.
Steven K. Young, Controller/Sr. VP
Swati V. Daji, Chief Risk Officer/VP-Global Risk Mgmt.
Roberta B. Bowman, Chief Sustainability Officer/Sr. VP
Dhiaa M. Jamil, Chief Nuclear & Generation Officer/Group Exec.
Jeffrey G. Browning, Chief Ethics & Compliance Officer
James E. Rogers, Chmn.
Ronald R. Reising, Chief Procurement Officer/Sr. VP

Phone: 704-594-6200 **Fax:** 704-382-3814
Toll-Free: 800-873-3853
Address: 526 S. Church St., Charlotte, NC 28202 US

GROWTH PLANS/SPECIAL FEATURES:

Duke Energy Corp. is an integrated energy and energy services provider that offers delivery and management of electricity and natural gas throughout the U.S. The company's operations can be divided into five segments: franchised electric & gas service; commercial power, generation services, international energy and telecommunications. The franchised electric & gas service segment can generate 27,000 megawatts (MW) of electricity, has 4 million customers, including approximately 500,000 retail gas customers, and has locations in Ohio, Indiana, Kentucky and the Carolinas, covering approximately 50,000 square miles. This segment operates three nuclear power plants; 15 coal-fire plants; 31 hydroelectric stations; 15 combustion turbines that burn natural gas, oil or other fuels; and one combined cycle station that burns natural gas. The commercial power segment owns, operates and manages non-regulated power plants and engages in the marketing and procurement of electric power, fuel and emissions allowances related to the plants. Its plants utilize a variety of fuels such as natural gas, waste coal and wood, and can generate approximately 7,550 MW of power primarily in the Midwestern U.S. The generation services segment, operated by Duke Energy Generation Services, Inc., provides electric generation for municipalities, industrial facilities and other large energy consumers. The subsidiary maintains around 5,000 MW of electric generation at 32 locations in the U.S. The international energy segment owns, operates and manages power generation facilities and sells and markets electric power and natural gas outside the U.S. Subsidiary, Duke Energy International, LLC, operates power generation plants primarily in Latin America. The telecommunications segment consists of the company's 50% stake in DukeNet Communications, LLC, a fiber optic communications developer.

Employees are offered medical, dental and vision insurance; a 401(k) plan; adoption assistance; flexible spending accounts; a pension plan; life insurance; disability coverage; and employee discounts.

FINANCIALS: **Sales and profits are in thousands of dollars—add 000 to get the full amount. 2010 Note: Financial information for 2010 was not available for all companies at press time.**

2010 Sales: $	2010 Profits: $	**U.S. Stock Ticker: DUK**
2009 Sales: $12,731,000	2009 Profits: $1,075,000	**Int'l Ticker:** Int'l Exchange:
2008 Sales: $13,207,000	2008 Profits: $1,362,000	Employees: 18,680
2007 Sales: $12,720,000	2007 Profits: $1,500,000	Fiscal Year Ends: 12/31
2006 Sales: $10,607,000	2006 Profits: $1,863,000	Parent Company:

SALARIES/BENEFITS:

Pension Plan: Y	ESOP Stock Plan:	Profit Sharing:	Top Exec. Salary: $650,004	Bonus: $744,970
Savings Plan: Y	Stock Purch. Plan:		Second Exec. Salary: $600,000	Bonus: $691,620

OTHER THOUGHTS:

Apparent Women Officers or Directors: 9
Hot Spot for Advancement for Women/Minorities: Y

LOCATIONS: ("Y" = Yes)

West:	Southwest:	Midwest:	Southeast:	Northeast:	International:
		Y	Y		Y

Note: Financial information, benefits and other data can change quickly and may vary from those stated here.

DUNCAN ENERGY PARTNERS LP

www.deplp.com

Industry Group Code: 424710 **Ranks within this company's industry group:** Sales: 7 Profits: 4

Exploration/Production:		Refining/Retailing:		Utilities:		Alternative Energy:		Specialty Services:		Energy Mktg./Other Svcs.	
Exploration:		Refining:		Electric Utility:		Waste/Solar/Other:		Consulting/Eng.:		Energy Marketing:	
Production:		Retailing:	Y	Gas Utility:		Thermal/Steam:		Seismic:		Equipment/Machinery:	
Coal Production:		Convenience Stores:		Pipelines:	Y	Wind:		Drilling:		Oil Field Services:	
		Chemicals:		Water:		Hydro:		InfoTech:		Air/Shipping Transportation:	
						Fuel Cells:		Specialty Services:			

TYPES OF BUSINESS:

Natural Gas Pipelines
Petrochemical Pipelines
NGL & Petrochemical Storage
NGL Gathering

BRANDS/DIVISIONS/AFFILIATES:

Enterprise Products Partners LP
Mont Belvieu Caverns
Acadian Gas
Lou-Tex Propylene
Sabine Propylene
South Texas NGL
Acadian Gas System
Enterprise GC

CONTACTS: *Note: Officers with more than one job title may be intentionally listed here more than once.*

W. Randall Fowler, CEO
William Ordemann, COO/Exec. VP
W. Randall Fowler, Pres.
Bryan F. Bulawa, CFO/Sr. VP/Treas.
Stephanie C. Hildebrandt, Chief Legal Officer/Sr. VP/Sec.
Michael J. Knesek, Principal Acct. Officer/Sr. VP/Controller
A. James Teague, Chief Commercial Officer/Exec. VP
Dan L. Duncan, Chmn.

Phone: 713-381-6500	**Fax:**
Toll-Free:	
Address: 1100 Louisiana St., 10th Fl., Houston, TX 77002 US	

GROWTH PLANS/SPECIAL FEATURES:

Duncan Energy Partners L.P., formed by Enterprise Products Partners to acquire, own and operate midstream energy assets, is engaged in the business of gathering, transporting, marketing and storing natural gas in addition to transporting and storing natural gas liquids (NGLs) and petrochemicals. In total, the company has over 11,000 miles of natural gas, NGL and petrochemical pipelines and 34 underground salt dome caverns with about 100 million barrels of NGL storage capacity. The company has controlling equity interests in the following firms, acquired in a drop-down transaction from Enterprise: Mont Belvieu Caverns, which owns and operates 34 salt dome caverns and a brine system located in Mont Belvieu, Texas; Acadian Gas, which gathers, transports, stores and markets natural gas in Louisiana through the 1,000 mile Acadian Gas System; Lou-Tex Propylene, which owns a 263-mile pipeline used to transport chemical-grade propylene from Sorrento, Louisiana to Mont Belvieu; Sabine Propylene, which owns a 21-mile pipeline used to transport polymer-grade propylene from port Arthur, Texas to a pipeline interconnect in Cameron Parish, Louisiana on a transport-or-pay basis; and South Texas NGL, which owns a 286-mile pipeline extending from Corpus Christi, Texas to Pasadena, Texas. In a second drop-down transaction Duncan received interests in Enterprise GC, a firm that owns and operates two NGL fractionation facilities, a 1,020-mile NGL pipeline system located in south Texas and 1,112 miles of natural gas gathering pipelines; Enterprise Intrastate, which operates the 641-mile Channel natural gas pipeline; and Enterprise Texas, which owns a 6,560-mile natural gas pipeline system. In October 2009, Duncan announced plans to extend the Acadian Gas pipeline system into the Haynesville Shale play in northwest Louisiana.

FINANCIALS: **Sales and profits are in thousands of dollars—add 000 to get the full amount. 2010 Note: Financial information for 2010 was not available for all companies at press time.**

2010 Sales: $	2010 Profits: $	**U.S. Stock Ticker: DEP**
2009 Sales: $979,300	2009 Profits: $45,800	**Int'l Ticker:** Int'l Exchange:
2008 Sales: $1,598,068	2008 Profits: $47,946	Employees:
2007 Sales: $1,220,292	2007 Profits: $3,626	Fiscal Year Ends: 12/31
2006 Sales: $924,478	2006 Profits: $55,337	Parent Company:

SALARIES/BENEFITS:

Pension Plan:	ESOP Stock Plan:	Profit Sharing:	Top Exec. Salary: $162,500	Bonus: $
Savings Plan:	Stock Purch. Plan:		Second Exec. Salary: $129,000	Bonus: $

OTHER THOUGHTS:

Apparent Women Officers or Directors: 1
Hot Spot for Advancement for Women/Minorities:

LOCATIONS: ("Y" = Yes)

West:	Southwest:	Midwest:	Southeast:	Northeast:	International:
	Y		Y		

DYNEGY INC

www.dynegy.com

Industry Group Code: 221 **Ranks within this company's industry group:** Sales: 42 Profits: 50

Exploration/Production:		Refining/Retailing:		Utilities:		Alternative Energy:		Specialty Services:		Energy Mktg./Other Svcs.	
Exploration:		Refining:		Electric Utility:	Y	Waste/Solar/Other:		Consulting/Eng.:		Energy Marketing:	Y
Production:		Retailing:		Gas Utility:	Y	Thermal/Steam:		Seismic:		Equipment/Machinery:	
Coal Production:		Convenience Stores:		Pipelines:	Y	Wind:		Drilling:		Oil Field Services:	
		Chemicals:		Water:		Hydro:	Y	InfoTech:		Air/Shipping Transportation:	
						Fuel Cells:		Specialty Services:			

TYPES OF BUSINESS:

Utilities-Electricity
Natural Gas Distribution & Marketing
Hydroelectric Generation

BRANDS/DIVISIONS/AFFILIATES:

CONTACTS:

Note: Officers with more than one job title may be intentionally listed here more than once.

Bruce A. Williamson, CEO
Bruce A. Williamson, Pres.
Holli C. Nichols, CFO/Exec. VP
J. Kevin Blodgett, Exec. VP-Admin.
J. Kevin Blodgett, General Counsel
Lynn Lednicky, Exec. VP-Oper.
Norelle Lundy, VP-Public Rel.
Norelle Lundy, VP-Investor Rel.
Kimberly M. O'Brien, Corp. Sec.
Bruce A. Williamson, Chmn.

Phone: 713-507-6400	**Fax:** 713-507-6808
Toll-Free: 800-633-4704	
Address: 1000 Louisiana St., Ste. 5800, Houston, TX 77002 US	

GROWTH PLANS/SPECIAL FEATURES:

Dynegy, Inc., through its subsidiaries, provides electric energy, capacity and ancillary services. The company's power generation operations, which are divided into the Midwest, West and Northeast segments, sell power and related products and services, including capacity, into real-time and day-ahead markets, as well as on a forward basis. Customers include independent system operators (ISOs), municipalities, electric cooperatives, integrated utilities, transmission and distribution utilities, industrial customers, power marketers, other power generators and commercial end-users. The division operates about 18 electric power generation facilities in seven states, the majority of which are gas-fired. These plants produce over 12,200 megawatts and are fueled by a combination of natural gas, coal and fuel oil. In August 2010, the company agreed to be acquired by The Blackstone Group, LP, a private equity firm, for $4.7 billion.

The firm offers employees medical and dental insurance; a 401(k) plan; a pension plan; and flexible work schedules.

FINANCIALS:

Sales and profits are in thousands of dollars—add 000 to get the full amount. 2010 Note: Financial information for 2010 was not available for all companies at press time.

2010 Sales: $	2010 Profits: $	**U.S. Stock Ticker: DYN**
2009 Sales: $2,468,000	2009 Profits: $-1,247,000	**Int'l Ticker:** Int'l Exchange:
2008 Sales: $3,324,000	2008 Profits: $174,000	Employees: 1,735
2007 Sales: $2,918,000	2007 Profits: $264,000	Fiscal Year Ends: 12/31
2006 Sales: $1,770,000	2006 Profits: $-333,000	Parent Company:

SALARIES/BENEFITS:

Pension Plan: Y	ESOP Stock Plan:	Profit Sharing:	Top Exec. Salary: $1,038,462	Bonus: $850,000
Savings Plan: Y	Stock Purch. Plan:		Second Exec. Salary: $519,231	Bonus: $425,000

OTHER THOUGHTS:

Apparent Women Officers or Directors: 4
Hot Spot for Advancement for Women/Minorities: Y

LOCATIONS: ("Y" = Yes)

West:	Southwest:	Midwest:	Southeast:	Northeast:	International:
Y	Y	Y	Y	Y	Y

E.ON AG

www.eon.com

Industry Group Code: 221 **Ranks within this company's industry group:** Sales: 1 Profits: 1

Exploration/Production:		Refining/Retailing:		Utilities:		Alternative Energy:		Specialty Services:		Energy Mktg./Other Svcs.	
Exploration:	Y	Refining:		Electric Utility:	Y	Waste/Solar/Other:	Y	Consulting/Eng.:		Energy Marketing:	Y
Production:	Y	Retailing:		Gas Utility:	Y	Thermal/Steam:		Seismic:		Equipment/Machinery:	
Coal Production:		Convenience Stores:		Pipelines:	Y	Wind:	Y	Drilling:		Oil Field Services:	
		Chemicals:	Y	Water:		Hydro:	Y	InfoTech:		Air/Shipping Transportation:	
						Fuel Cells:		Specialty Services:			

TYPES OF BUSINESS:

Utilities-Electricity, Natural Gas & Water
Pipelines
Chemicals
Real Estate
Telecommunications
Electric Generation

BRANDS/DIVISIONS/AFFILIATES:

E.ON Energie
Ruhrgas
E.ON U.K.
E.ON U.S.
Powergen
E.ON Sverige
Louisville Gas & Electric Company
Kentucky Utilities Company

CONTACTS: *Note: Officers with more than one job title may be intentionally listed here more than once.*

Johannes Teyssen, CEO
Regine Stachelhaus, Dir.-Group Human Resources
Klaus-Dieter Maubach, Dir.-R&D
Regine Stachelhaus, Dir.-IT
Klaus-Dieter Maubach, Dir.-Tech. & New Build
Regine Stachelhaus, Dir.-Legal & Compliance
Marcus Schenck, Dir.-Corp. Planning, Mergers & Acquisitions
Carsten Thomsen-Bendixen, Head-Corp. Comm.
Marcus Schenck, Dir.-Finance & Acct.
Klaus-Dieter Maubach, Dir.-Health, Safety & Environment
Jorgen Kildahl, Dir.-Upstream/Generation, Trading & Optimization
Regine Stachelhaus, Dir.-Real Estate, Mining & Facility Mgmt.
Ulrich Hartmann, Chmn.
Bernhard Reutersberg, Dir.-Dist. & Retail

Phone: 49-211-4579-0	**Fax:** 49-211-4579-501
Toll-Free:	
Address: E.ON Platz 1, Dusseldorf, 40479 Germany	

GROWTH PLANS/SPECIAL FEATURES:

E.ON AG is one of Europe's largest utility providers and one of the largest investor-owned utilities in the world. The company has operations throughout central Europe, the U.K. and the U.S., operating through two major divisions, power and gas. The power generation operations of E.ON maintain a portfolio of generation capacity exceeding 73 gigawatts (GW). The firm operates through several geographic centered subsidiaries: E.ON Energie; E.ON U.K.; E.ON Sverige; and E.ON U.S. E.ON Energie is a multi-utility provider in central Europe, with approximately 17 million customers. E.ON Energie also provides gas utilities. E.ON U.K., operating with the brand Powergen, distributes electricity to approximately eight million customers. E.ON Sverige, operating in the Nordic market, provides about 1 million customers in northern Europe with gas, electricity and heating. E.ON U.S., which functions through subsidiaries Louisville Gas & Electric Company and Kentucky Utilities Company, manages about 7.6 GW of generating capacity. Ruhrgas AG, the primary gas division subsidiary, is one of Europe's largest gas merchants, with a network of about 6,835 miles of pipeline and 28 compressor stations. Ruhrgas sells primarily to distribution companies, industrial consumers and power stations. The firm also has natural gas exploration and production operations in the North Sea and Russia. E.ON has other operations or interests in a number of areas, including real estate, chemicals and telecommunications. In January 2010, the company divested interests in approximately 5 GW of generation assets in the German market. In April 2010, the firm agreed to sell its U.S. business to utility company, PPL Corp. for $6.7 billion. In October 2010, E.ON received UN approval for a joint implementation project in Russia to complete the construction of a 400 MW combined cycle gas turbine plant.

Employees receive medical, dental and vision; a 401(k) matching plan; a pension plan; flexible spending account; and tuition assistance.

FINANCIALS: **Sales and profits are in thousands of dollars—add 000 to get the full amount. 2010 Note: Financial information for 2010 was not available for all companies at press time.**

2010 Sales: $	2010 Profits: $	**U.S. Stock Ticker: EON**
2009 Sales: $105,614,000	2009 Profits: $11,159,500	**Int'l Ticker: EOA** Int'l Exchange: Frankfurt-Euronext
2008 Sales: $127,278,000	2008 Profits: $1,853,000	Employees:
2007 Sales: $94,040,000	2007 Profits: $9,860,000	Fiscal Year Ends: 12/31
2006 Sales: $89,422,000	2006 Profits: $6,674,000	Parent Company:

SALARIES/BENEFITS:

Pension Plan: Y	ESOP Stock Plan: Y	Profit Sharing: Y	Top Exec. Salary: $1,708,224	Bonus: $2,934,288
Savings Plan:	Stock Purch. Plan:		Second Exec. Salary: $1,377,600	Bonus: $2,355,696

OTHER THOUGHTS:

Apparent Women Officers or Directors: 1
Hot Spot for Advancement for Women/Minorities:

LOCATIONS: ("Y" = Yes)

West:	Southwest:	Midwest:	Southeast:	Northeast:	International:
		Y			Y

E.ON UK PLC

www.eon-uk.com

Industry Group Code: 221 **Ranks within this company's industry group:** Sales: Profits:

Exploration/Production:		**Refining/Retailing:**		**Utilities:**		**Alternative Energy:**		**Specialty Services:**		**Energy Mktg./Other Svcs.**	
Exploration:		Refining:		Electric Utility:	Y	Waste/Solar/Other:	Y	Consulting/Eng.:		Energy Marketing:	Y
Production:		Retailing:		Gas Utility:	Y	Thermal/Steam:	Y	Seismic:		Equipment/Machinery:	
Coal Production:		Convenience Stores:		Pipelines:		Wind:	Y	Drilling:		Oil Field Services:	
		Chemicals:		Water:		Hydro:		InfoTech:		Air/Shipping Transportation:	
						Fuel Cells:		Specialty Services:			

TYPES OF BUSINESS:

Utilities-Electricity & Natural Gas

BRANDS/DIVISIONS/AFFILIATES:

E.ON AG
Powergen
Central Networks

CONTACTS:

Note: Officers with more than one job title may be intentionally listed here more than once.

Paul Golby, CEO
Brian Tear, CFO
Maria Antoniou, Dir.-Human Resources
Fiona Stark, General Counsel/Corp. Sec.
Fiona Stark, Dir.-Corp. Affairs
John Crackett, Managing Dir.-Central Networks
Klaus Hammer, Managing Dir.-Generation
Graham Bartlett, Managing Dir.-Retail
Paul Golby, Chmn.

Phone: 44-24-7642-4000 **Fax:** 44-24-7642-5432
Toll-Free:
Address: Westwood Way, Westwood Business Park, Coventry, West Midlands CV4 8LG UK

GROWTH PLANS/SPECIAL FEATURES:

E.ON UK plc, formerly Powergen, is the U.K. utility subsidiary of German energy company E.ON AG. It produces and sells electricity, gas and related services to residential, business and government customers, with a generation capacity of 10,330 megawatts (MW). In 2009, approximately 38.8% of E.ON's electricity output was fuelled by coal and approximately 60.5% by gas, with the remaining 0.7% being generated from wind and oil-fired plants. The company provides nearly 8 million retail customers with electricity and natural gas and distributes power over an area of 11,312 square miles, containing roughly 10 million residents, via its distribution division, Central Networks. In addition, the company is one of the U.K.'s leading providers of combined heat and power, with 12 sites across England, as well as an extensive green generation portfolio, which includes one biomass co-firing program and over 20 operational wind farms. In September 2010, the firm commenced operations of its third offshore wind farm, a 180 MW, 60-turbine project in Cumbria. In the following month, it finished construction and connection of an additional 10 MW wind farm onshore, in Durham County.

The company offers its employees medical, dental and vision; a 401 (k); a pension plan; tuition assistance; a scholarship program for the children of employees; life insurance; and a stock ownership program.

FINANCIALS:

Sales and profits are in thousands of dollars—add 000 to get the full amount. 2010 Note: Financial information for 2010 was not available for all companies at press time.

2010 Sales: $	2010 Profits: $	**U.S. Stock Ticker: Subsidiary**
2009 Sales: $	2009 Profits: $	**Int'l Ticker:** Int'l Exchange:
2008 Sales: $	2008 Profits: $	Employees:
2007 Sales: $	2007 Profits: $	Fiscal Year Ends: 12/31
2006 Sales: $	2006 Profits: $	Parent Company: E.ON AG

SALARIES/BENEFITS:

Pension Plan: Y	ESOP Stock Plan: Y	Profit Sharing:	Top Exec. Salary: $	Bonus: $
Savings Plan: Y	Stock Purch. Plan:		Second Exec. Salary: $	Bonus: $

OTHER THOUGHTS:

Apparent Women Officers or Directors: 2
Hot Spot for Advancement for Women/Minorities:

LOCATIONS: ("Y" = Yes)

West:	Southwest:	Midwest:	Southeast:	Northeast:	International:
					Y

E.ON US LLC

www.eon-us.com

Industry Group Code: 221 **Ranks within this company's industry group:** Sales: Profits:

Exploration/Production:		Refining/Retailing:		Utilities:		Alternative Energy:		Specialty Services:		Energy Mktg./Other Svcs.	
Exploration:		Refining:		Electric Utility:	Y	Waste/Solar/Other:		Consulting/Eng.:		Energy Marketing:	
Production:		Retailing:		Gas Utility:	Y	Thermal/Steam:	Y	Seismic:		Equipment/Machinery:	
Coal Production:		Convenience Stores:		Pipelines:		Wind:		Drilling:		Oil Field Services:	
		Chemicals:		Water:		Hydro:		InfoTech:		Air/Shipping Transportation:	
						Fuel Cells:		Specialty Services:	Y		

TYPES OF BUSINESS:

Utilities-Electricity & Natural Gas

BRANDS/DIVISIONS/AFFILIATES:

E.ON AG
LG&E Energy, LLC
Louisville Gas and Electric Company
Old Dominion Power
Kentucky Utilities Company
PPL Corporation

CONTACTS: *Note: Officers with more than one job title may be intentionally listed here more than once.*

Vic Staffieri, CEO
Vic Staffieri, Pres.
Brad Rives, CFO
David Sinclair, VP-Energy Mktg.
Paula Pottinger, Sr. VP-Human Resources
John McCall, General Counsel/Exec. VP/Corp. Sec.
Kent Blake, VP-Corp. Planning & Dev.
Chip Keeling, VP-Comm.
Valerie Scott, Controller
Mike Beer, VP-Federal Regulation & Policy
Ralph Bowling, VP-Power Production
Chris Hermann, Sr. VP-Energy Delivery
Paul Thompson, Sr. VP-Energy Svcs.
Vic Staffieri, Chmn.

Phone: 502-627-2000	**Fax:** 502-627-3609
Toll-Free:	
Address: 220 W. Main St., Louisville, KY 40232 US	

GROWTH PLANS/SPECIAL FEATURES:

E.ON U.S. LLC, formerly LG&E Energy, LLC, is a subsidiary of the German energy conglomerate E.ON AG. The company's regulated U.S. operations include two utilities: Louisville Gas and Electric Company, which provides electricity to 396,000 customers and natural gas to 321,000 customers in the Louisville, Kentucky area, and Kentucky Utilities Company, an electric utility that provides electricity to 545,000 customers in 77 Kentucky counties and five counties in Virginia under the name Old Dominion Power. Combined, the two utilities have a total generating capacity greater than 7,500 megawatts (MW), with a fuel mix of 5,300 MW from coal and 2,200 MW from natural gas. Its service territory covers approximately 7,300 square miles. In April 2010, the firm's parent company, E.ON AG, agreed to sell E.ON U.S. to PPL Corporation for $7.625 billion.

Employees are offered medical, dental and vision insurance; a 401(k) plan; health and dependent care reimbursement accounts; life insurance; business travel accident insurance; disability coverage; a family assistance plan; adoption assistance; tuition reimbursement; a scholarship program for employees' children; a home computer purchase program; fitness, weight-loss and smoking cessation reimbursements; free mammograms and flu shots; special needs rooms; and credit union membership.

FINANCIALS: **Sales and profits are in thousands of dollars—add 000 to get the full amount. 2010 Note: Financial information for 2010 was not available for all companies at press time.**

2010 Sales: $	2010 Profits: $	**U.S. Stock Ticker: Subsidiary**
2009 Sales: $	2009 Profits: $	**Int'l Ticker:** Int'l Exchange:
2008 Sales: $	2008 Profits: $	Employees:
2007 Sales: $	2007 Profits: $	Fiscal Year Ends: 12/31
2006 Sales: $	2006 Profits: $	Parent Company: E.ON AG

SALARIES/BENEFITS:

Pension Plan:	ESOP Stock Plan:	Profit Sharing:	Top Exec. Salary: $	Bonus: $
Savings Plan: Y	Stock Purch. Plan:		Second Exec. Salary: $	Bonus: $

OTHER THOUGHTS:

Apparent Women Officers or Directors: 5
Hot Spot for Advancement for Women/Minorities: Y

LOCATIONS: ("Y" = Yes)

West:	Southwest:	Midwest:	Southeast:	Northeast:	International:
				Y	

ECOPETROL SA

www.ecopetrol.com.co

Industry Group Code: 211111 **Ranks within this company's industry group:** Sales: 37 Profits: 26

Exploration/Production:		Refining/Retailing:		Utilities:		Alternative Energy:		Specialty Services:		Energy Mktg./Other Svcs.	
Exploration:	Y	Refining:	Y	Electric Utility:		Waste/Solar/Other:		Consulting/Eng.:		Energy Marketing:	
Production:	Y	Retailing:	Y	Gas Utility:		Thermal/Steam:		Seismic:		Equipment/Machinery:	
Coal Production:		Convenience Stores:		Pipelines:		Wind:		Drilling:		Oil Field Services:	
		Chemicals:	Y	Water:		Hydro:		InfoTech:		Air/Shipping Transportation:	Y
						Fuel Cells:		Specialty Services:	Y		

TYPES OF BUSINESS:

Oil & Gas Exploration & Production
Oil Refining
Petroleum Transport
Research & Technical Services
Petrochemicals
Fuel Marketing

BRANDS/DIVISIONS/AFFILIATES:

Colombian Petroleum Institute

CONTACTS:

Note: Officers with more than one job title may be intentionally listed here more than once.

Javier Genaro Gutierrez Pemberty, Pres.
Claudia Castellanos, VP-Mktg.
Martha Cecilia Castano, VP-Human Talent
Nelson Navarrete Hurtado, Exec. VP-Exploration & Prod.
Oscar Alfredo Villadiego, VP-Tech. & Svcs.
Hector Manosalva, VP-Prod.
Margarita Obregon, Gen. Sec.
Camilo Marulanda Lopez, VP-Strategy & Growth
Adriana Marcela Echeverri, VP-Finance
Diego Alfonso Carvajal Pabon, VP-Exploration
Pedro Rosales, Exec. VP-Downstream
Federico Maya Molina, VP-Refining
Claudia Castellanos, VP-Supply Chain

Phone: 57-1-234-4000	**Fax:** 57-1-234-4099
Toll-Free:	
Address: Carrera 7, No. 37-65, Bogota, Colombia	

GROWTH PLANS/SPECIAL FEATURES:

Ecopetrol SA is a Colombian petroleum company. The company has an operational framework consisting of five segments: exploration; production; refining/petrochemical; transportation; and supply/marketing. The firm has exploration operations in Colombia, Brazil, Peru and the Gulf of Mexico. Production operations include extraction, treatment and storage of hydrocarbons. The firm produces crude oil and gas though its 163 production fields. Ecopetrol's refining and petrochemicals operations are concentrated in two refineries in Colombia and Cartagena, which produce products such as virgin naphtha, cracked naphtha, aviation gasoline and Fuel Oil N 6. With regard to transportation, the firm owns several thousand miles of pipelines and polyducts that transport hydrocarbons from production centers to refineries and ports in the Atlantic and Pacific oceans. It also has 53 stations that pump crude oil and products throughout Colombia. The supply/marketing segment sells oil surplus on the domestic market and exports fuels and petrochemicals to the international market. Ecopetrol runs the Colombian Petroleum Institute (its Spanish initials are ICP), which conducts research for the petroleum industry. It provides specialized technical services for the oil and gas industry through 29 pilot plants and 24 laboratories. The firm recently announced plans to participate in the commercial development of the Quifa and Rubiales fields, in which it owns 40% and 60% of the fields' hydrocarbon production, respectively. In December 2009, the firm acquired 20% participation in the in the Borojo North and Borojo South blocks in the Colombian Pacific. In April 2010, the firm was granted two invention patents from the Nigerian government, increasing the firm's total number of patents to 25. These patents are for the development of tools and equipment to reduce oil theft in hydrocarbon transportation lines.

FINANCIALS:

Sales and profits are in thousands of dollars—add 000 to get the full amount. 2010 Note: Financial information for 2010 was not available for all companies at press time.

2010 Sales: $	2010 Profits: $	**U.S. Stock Ticker: ECOPETROL**
2009 Sales: $15,769,900	2009 Profits: $2,661,850	**Int'l Ticker:** Int'l Exchange:
2008 Sales: $15,553,800	2008 Profits: $5,336,400	Employees:
2007 Sales: $11,084,359	2007 Profits: $2,570,923	Fiscal Year Ends: 12/31
2006 Sales: $9,127,621	2006 Profits: $1,683,265	Parent Company:

SALARIES/BENEFITS:

Pension Plan:	ESOP Stock Plan:	Profit Sharing:	Top Exec. Salary: $	Bonus: $
Savings Plan:	Stock Purch. Plan:		Second Exec. Salary: $	Bonus: $

OTHER THOUGHTS:

Apparent Women Officers or Directors: 5
Hot Spot for Advancement for Women/Minorities: Y

LOCATIONS: ("Y" = Yes)

West:	Southwest:	Midwest:	Southeast:	Northeast:	International:
					Y

EDISON INTERNATIONAL

www.edison.com

Industry Group Code: 2211 **Ranks within this company's industry group:** Sales: 17 Profits: 16

Exploration/Production:		Refining/Retailing:		Utilities:		Alternative Energy:		Specialty Services:		Energy Mktg./Other Svcs.	
Exploration:		Refining:		Electric Utility:	Y	Waste/Solar/Other:	Y	Consulting/Eng.:		Energy Marketing:	Y
Production:		Retailing:		Gas Utility:		Thermal/Steam:		Seismic:		Equipment/Machinery:	
Coal Production:		Convenience Stores:		Pipelines:		Wind:	Y	Drilling:		Oil Field Services:	
		Chemicals:		Water:		Hydro:	Y	InfoTech:		Air/Shipping Transportation:	
						Fuel Cells:		Specialty Services:	Y		

TYPES OF BUSINESS:

Utilities-Electricity & Natural Gas
Financial Services
Operations Services
Energy Trading

BRANDS/DIVISIONS/AFFILIATES:

Southern California Edison Company
Edison Mission Energy
Edison Capital

CONTACTS: *Note: Officers with more than one job title may be intentionally listed here more than once.*

Theodore F. Craver Jr., CEO
Theodore F. Craver Jr., Pres.
Jim Scilacci, CFO/Exec. VP/Treas.
Daryl David, Sr. VP-Human Resources
Robert L. Adler, General Counsel/Exec. VP
Andrew J. Hertneky, VP-Strategy
Barbara J. Parsky, Sr. VP-Corp. Comm.
Scott Cunningham, VP-Investor Rel.
Mark Clarke, Controller/VP
Polly Gault, Exec. VP-Public Affairs
Jeff Barnett, VP-Tax
Barbara E. Matthews, Chief Governance Officer/VP/Corp. Sec.
David Heller, Chief Ethics & Compliance Officer/VP
Theodore F. Craver Jr., Chmn.

Phone: 626-302-2222	**Fax:** 626-302-2517
Toll-Free: 800-655-4555	
Address: 2244 Walnut Grove Ave., Rosemead, CA 91770 US	

GROWTH PLANS/SPECIAL FEATURES:

Edison International is a California-based holding company with subsidiaries operating primarily in the U.S., with some investments abroad. Major subsidiaries include Southern California Edison Company (SCE), a utility corporation, and non-utility companies Edison Mission Energy (EME) and Edison Capital. SCE is one of the nation's largest electric utilities, providing electric service to a 50,000-square-mile area of California, including over 400 cities and communities, serving over 13 million customers. The energy provided is developed from a range of different kinds of power plants including coal-burning, nuclear, hydroelectric and diesel-burning facilities. SCE also owns over 70,000 circuit miles of overhead lines and about 43,500 circuit miles of underground lines. SCE also owns and operates a solar photovoltaic installation on a 600,000 square-foot warehouse roof. Composed of 33,700 advanced thin-film solar panels, the installation has the ability to power 1,300 homes. EME is an independent power producer engaged in the business of developing, acquiring, owning or leasing, operating and selling energy and capacity from independent power production facilities. These operations consist in owning or leasing interests in 39 domestic operating power plants with a capacity of 11,269 megawatts. EME also conducts price risk management and energy trading activities in power markets open to competition. Edison Capital invests in energy and infrastructure projects, including power generation; electric transmission and distribution; transportation; affordable housing; and telecommunications.

Employees are offered medical, dental and vision insurance; disability benefits; an employee assistance program; life insurance; educational reimbursement; credit union membership; and business travel accident insurance.

FINANCIALS: **Sales and profits are in thousands of dollars—add 000 to get the full amount. 2010 Note: Financial information for 2010 was not available for all companies at press time.**

2010 Sales: $	2010 Profits: $	**U.S. Stock Ticker: EIX**
2009 Sales: $12,361,000	2009 Profits: $945,000	**Int'l Ticker:** Int'l Exchange:
2008 Sales: $14,112,000	2008 Profits: $1,348,000	Employees: 19,244
2007 Sales: $12,868,000	2007 Profits: $1,307,000	Fiscal Year Ends: 12/31
2006 Sales: $12,622,000	2006 Profits: $1,181,000	Parent Company:

SALARIES/BENEFITS:

Pension Plan: Y	ESOP Stock Plan:	Profit Sharing:	Top Exec. Salary: $1,054,038	Bonus: $1,365,000
Savings Plan: Y	Stock Purch. Plan:		Second Exec. Salary: $719,758	Bonus: $609,000

OTHER THOUGHTS:

Apparent Women Officers or Directors: 6
Hot Spot for Advancement for Women/Minorities: Y

LOCATIONS: ("Y" = Yes)

West:	Southwest:	Midwest:	Southeast:	Northeast:	International:
Y	Y	Y	Y	Y	Y

EDISON MISSION GROUP

www.edison.com/ourcompany/emg.asp

Industry Group Code: 221 **Ranks within this company's industry group:** Sales: Profits:

Exploration/Production:		Refining/Retailing:		Utilities:		Alternative Energy:		Specialty Services:		Energy Mktg./Other Svcs.	
Exploration:		Refining:		Electric Utility:	Y	Waste/Solar/Other:	Y	Consulting/Eng.:		Energy Marketing:	Y
Production:		Retailing:		Gas Utility:		Thermal/Steam:	Y	Seismic:		Equipment/Machinery:	
Coal Production:		Convenience Stores:		Pipelines:		Wind:	Y	Drilling:		Oil Field Services:	
		Chemicals:		Water:		Hydro:		InfoTech:		Air/Shipping Transportation:	
						Fuel Cells:		Specialty Services:			

TYPES OF BUSINESS:

Electric Generation
Energy Trading

BRANDS/DIVISIONS/AFFILIATES:

Edison International
Edison Mission Energy
Edison Mission Marketing and Trading
Midwest Generation
Edison Mission Operation & Maintenance, Inc.
Edison Capital

CONTACTS: *Note: Officers with more than one job title may be intentionally listed here more than once.*

Ronald L. Litzinger, CEO
Ronald L. Litzinger, Pres.
John P. Finneran, CFO/Sr. VP
Paul Jacob, Sr. VP-Mktg. & Trading
Jenene J. Wilson, VP-Human Resources
Randolph P. Mann, VP-Wind Dev.
Steven D. Eisenberg, General Counsel/Sr. VP
John C. Kennedy, VP-Oper.
Gerald P. Loughman, Sr. VP-Dev.
Douglas McFarlan, Sr. VP-Comm. & Public Affairs
Guy F. Gorney, Sr. VP-Generation/Pres., Midwest Generation EME
Letitia Davis, Chief Ethics & Compliance Officer/VP
Philip Herrington, VP-Commercial Mgmt. & Oper.
Ronald L. Litzinger, Chmn.

Phone: 949-752-5588	**Fax:** 949-263-9162
Toll-Free:	
Address: 18101 Von Karman Ave., Ste. 1700, Irvine, CA 92612 US	

GROWTH PLANS/SPECIAL FEATURES:

Edison Mission Group (EMG), a subsidiary of Edison International, is an independent power producer engaged in the business of owning, leasing, operating and selling energy and capacity from electric power generation facilities. The company operates through four subsidiaries: Edison Mission Energy (EME); Midwest Generation (MWG); Edison Mission Operations & Maintenance, Inc. (EMOMI); and Edison Capital. EME has interests in 44 power plants in the U.S., as well as one in Turkey. These plants have a total generating capacity of approximately 11,274 megawatts (MW), of which EME's ownership share is 10,174 MW. In addition to fossil fuel-based plants, EME has 28 wind projects currently in operation or under construction and is developing solar and thermal projects as well. EME's subsidiary, Edison Mission Marketing and Trading (EMMT) based in Boston, conducts its price risk management and energy trading activities. MWG operates six coal-fired electric power-generating facilities, including the Powerton, Joliet, Will County, Waukegan, Crawford and Fisk Stations, and the Fisk and Waukegan on-site generating peakers. Together, these facilities have a generation capacity of 5,776 MW. MWG also supervises operation of the EME Homer City Generation plant in Homer City, Pennsylvania. EMOMI operates nine natural gas power plants in California; a waste coal plant in West Virginia; and wind farms located in Iowa, New Mexico, Oklahoma and Texas. Edison Capital provides financial services and has investments worldwide in energy and infrastructure projects, including power generation, electric transmission and distribution, transportation and telecommunications. It also has investments in affordable housing projects located throughout the U.S.

Employees are offered medical, dental and vision insurance; a 401(k) plan; disability benefits; an employee assistance program; and life insurance.

FINANCIALS: **Sales and profits are in thousands of dollars—add 000 to get the full amount. 2010 Note: Financial information for 2010 was not available for all companies at press time.**

2010 Sales: $	2010 Profits: $	**U.S. Stock Ticker: Subsidiary**
2009 Sales: $	2009 Profits: $	**Int'l Ticker:** Int'l Exchange:
2008 Sales: $	2008 Profits: $	Employees:
2007 Sales: $	2007 Profits: $	Fiscal Year Ends: 12/31
2006 Sales: $2,239,000	2006 Profits: $414,000	Parent Company: EDISON INTERNATIONAL

SALARIES/BENEFITS:

Pension Plan:	ESOP Stock Plan:	Profit Sharing:	Top Exec. Salary: $	Bonus: $
Savings Plan: Y	Stock Purch. Plan:		Second Exec. Salary: $	Bonus: $

OTHER THOUGHTS:

Apparent Women Officers or Directors: 2
Hot Spot for Advancement for Women/Minorities:

LOCATIONS: ("Y" = Yes)

West:	Southwest:	Midwest:	Southeast:	Northeast:	International:
Y	Y	Y		Y	Y

EDP - ENERGIAS DE PORTUGAL SA

www.edp.pt

Industry Group Code: 2211 **Ranks within this company's industry group:** Sales: 13 Profits: 10

Exploration/Production:		Refining/Retailing:		Utilities:		Alternative Energy:		Specialty Services:		Energy Mktg./Other Svcs.	
Exploration:		Refining:		Electric Utility:	Y	Waste/Solar/Other:	Y	Consulting/Eng.:	Y	Energy Marketing:	
Production:		Retailing:		Gas Utility:	Y	Thermal/Steam:	Y	Seismic:		Equipment/Machinery:	
Coal Production:		Convenience Stores:		Pipelines:		Wind:	Y	Drilling:		Oil Field Services:	
		Chemicals:		Water:	Y	Hydro:	Y	InfoTech:		Air/Shipping Transportation:	
						Fuel Cells:		Specialty Services:			

TYPES OF BUSINESS:

Utilities-Electricity, Natural Gas & Water
Electricity Generation & Distribution
Wind Generation
Solid Waste & Biomass Generation
Hydroelectric Generation

BRANDS/DIVISIONS/AFFILIATES:

EDP Renewables
EDP Comercial-Comercializacao de Energia, S.A.
EDP Distribuicao-Energia, S.A.
Naturgas Energia
Energias do Brasil
HC Energia
EDP Gas
Horizon Wind Energy

CONTACTS:

Note: Officers with more than one job title may be intentionally listed here more than once.

Antonio Mexia, CEO
Nuno Alves, CFO
Ana Fernandes, Exec. Dir.
Antonio M. da Costa, Exec. Dir.
Antonio P. de Abreu, Exec. Dir.
Jorge C. Morais, Exec. Dir.
Antonio de Almeida, Chmn.

Phone: 351-21-001-2500	**Fax:** 351-21-002-1403
Toll-Free:	
Address: Praca Marques de Pombal, 12, Lisbon, 1250-162 Portugal	

GROWTH PLANS/SPECIAL FEATURES:

EDP - Energias de Portugal S.A. (EDP) serves as the principal operator in the public service electricity sector in Portugal, with the Portuguese government controlling approximately 20% of EDP. With over 9.9 million customers, it is one of Europe's major electricity providers; and is one of the only companies in the Iberian Peninsula with generation, distribution and supply activities in Portugal and Spain. The firm's operations are divided into six business units: Electricity Generation, Renewable Energies, Electricity Distribution, Electricity Supply, Gas and Brazil Operations. The Electricity Division has a generation installed capacity of 9,675 megawatts (MW) in Portugal. Hydroelectric power stations represent 4,578 MW and thermal power stations represent 5,097 MW. This segment also operates in Spain through HC Energia, and maintains 3,271 MW of installed generation capacity. The Renewable Energies unit carries out its operations through 77.5%-owned EDP Renewables. This unit focuses on renewable energy, particularly wind energy, and carries out its activities in Europe, Brazil and the U.S. (through independent power company Horizon Wind Energy). The Electricity Distribution unit distributes electricity in both Portugal (through EDP Distribuicao -Energia S.A.) and Spain (through HC Energia). The Electricity Supply unit also operates in both Portugal (through EDP Commercial) and Spain (though either HC Energia or Naturgas Energia) and provides maintenance and assistance service; technical services; and electricity quality and efficiency services. The Gas unit services Portugal through 72% owned EDP Gas and Spain through Naturagas Energia. The firm's Brazilian operations, run by Energias do Brasil, consist of electricity generation, distribution and supply businesses, with a total installed capacity of over 1.7 MW.

FINANCIALS:

Sales and profits are in thousands of dollars—add 000 to get the full amount. 2010 Note: Financial information for 2010 was not available for all companies at press time.

2010 Sales: $	2010 Profits: $	**U.S. Stock Ticker: EDPFY**
2009 Sales: $14,963,400	2009 Profits: $1,256,130	**Int'l Ticker: EDP** Int'l Exchange: Lisbon-Euronext
2008 Sales: $20,337,000	2008 Profits: $1,598,000	Employees:
2007 Sales: $13,650,000	2007 Profits: $1,240,000	Fiscal Year Ends: 12/31
2006 Sales: $12,980,000	2006 Profits: $1,180,000	Parent Company:

SALARIES/BENEFITS:

Pension Plan:	ESOP Stock Plan:	Profit Sharing:	Top Exec. Salary: $	Bonus: $
Savings Plan:	Stock Purch. Plan:		Second Exec. Salary: $	Bonus: $

OTHER THOUGHTS:

Apparent Women Officers or Directors: 1
Hot Spot for Advancement for Women/Minorities:

LOCATIONS: ("Y" = Yes)

West:	Southwest:	Midwest:	Southeast:	Northeast:	International:
		Y			Y

EL PASO CORP

www.elpaso.com

Industry Group Code: 486 **Ranks within this company's industry group:** Sales: 12 Profits: 20

Exploration/Production:		Refining/Retailing:		Utilities:		Alternative Energy:		Specialty Services:		Energy Mktg./Other Svcs.	
Exploration:	Y	Refining:		Electric Utility:		Waste/Solar/Other:		Consulting/Eng.:		Energy Marketing:	Y
Production:	Y	Retailing:		Gas Utility:		Thermal/Steam:		Seismic:		Equipment/Machinery:	
Coal Production:		Convenience Stores:		Pipelines:	Y	Wind:		Drilling:		Oil Field Services:	
		Chemicals:		Water:		Hydro:		InfoTech:		Air/Shipping Transportation:	
						Fuel Cells:		Specialty Services:			

TYPES OF BUSINESS:

Gas Pipelines & Storage
Oil & Natural Gas Exploration & Production
Crude Oil & Refined Products
Power Generation
Energy Infrastructure Development
Commodities & Product Marketing

BRANDS/DIVISIONS/AFFILIATES:

Southern Natural Gas
El Paso E&P Company, L.P.
Southern LNG, Inc.
Elba Express Company, LLC
Colorado Interstate Gas Company
El Paso Midstream Group, Inc.
AGL Resources, Inc.
Sempra Pipelines & Storage

CONTACTS: *Note: Officers with more than one job title may be intentionally listed here more than once.*

Douglas Foshee, CEO
Douglas Foshee, Pres.
John R. Sult, CFO/Exec. VP
Susan Ortenstone, Chief Admin. Officer/Exec. VP
Robert W. Baker, General Counsel/Exec. VP
Bryan W. Neskora, Sr. VP-Oper.
Dane E. Whitehead, Sr. VP-Strategy & Enterprise Bus. Dev.
Bruce Connery, VP-Investor Rel.
James J. Cleary, Pres., Western Pipeline Group
Brent J. Smolik, Exec. VP/Pres., El Paso Exploration & Prod. Co.
James Yardley, Exec. VP-Pipeline Group
D. Mark Leland, Exec. VP/Pres., Midstream
Doug Foshee, Chmn.

Phone: 713-420-2600	**Fax:** 713-420-4417
Toll-Free:	
Address: 1001 Louisiana St., Houston, TX 77002 US	

GROWTH PLANS/SPECIAL FEATURES:

El Paso Corp., headquarter in Houston, Texas, is involved in the exploration, production and transmission of natural gas. The natural gas transmission segment of the firm has approximately 42,000 miles of natural gas pipelines in North America, supplying gas to its six largest consuming areas. The company's wholly-owned pipelines include the Tennessee Gas Pipeline, which extends from east Texas and Louisiana to the northeast; the El Paso Natural Gas, connecting Northern Mexico to markets in the Southwest U.S.; the Mojave Pipeline, which connects different regions of California; and Cheyenne Plains Gas Pipeline, extending from Kansas to Wyoming. El Paso Corp. maintains equity interests in additional pipeline systems in the U.S. It also has over 230 billion cubic feet of storage capacity and maintains a liquefied natural gas receiving terminal in Georgia. The exploration and production segment retrieves natural gas, oil and natural gas liquids in the U.S., Brazil and Egypt. The firm's central U.S. operations are primary focused on tight gas sands and unconventional shale gas plays, controlling roughly 3.9 million net leasehold acres. In 2009, the firm produced approximately 763 million cubic feet of gas equivalent per day. Its gas and oil reserves are about 2.7 trillion cubic feet equivalent. The firm also has a power unit that holds a 50% interest in a power plant in Pakistan. In May 2010, El Paso Corp. sold its interests in several pipeline assets within Mexico to Sempra Pipelines & Storage. In July 2010, the firm entered a joint venture agreement with AGL Resources, Inc. to distribute LNG within the southeastern U.S. In October 2010, subsidiary El Paso Midstream Group, Inc. executed a memorandum of understanding with Spectra Energy to jointly develop the Marcellus Ethane Pipeline system.

The company offers employees medical insurance, long-term disability and accidental death and dismemberment insurance.

FINANCIALS: **Sales and profits are in thousands of dollars—add 000 to get the full amount. 2010 Note: Financial information for 2010 was not available for all companies at press time.**

2010 Sales: $	2010 Profits: $	**U.S. Stock Ticker: EP**
2009 Sales: $4,631,000	2009 Profits: $-474,000	**Int'l Ticker:** Int'l Exchange:
2008 Sales: $5,363,000	2008 Profits: $-789,000	Employees: 4,991
2007 Sales: $4,648,000	2007 Profits: $1,073,000	Fiscal Year Ends: 12/31
2006 Sales: $4,281,000	2006 Profits: $438,000	Parent Company:

SALARIES/BENEFITS:

Pension Plan: Y	ESOP Stock Plan:	Profit Sharing:	Top Exec. Salary: $1,050,000	Bonus: $1,800,000
Savings Plan: Y	Stock Purch. Plan: Y		Second Exec. Salary: $566,520	Bonus: $1,000,000

OTHER THOUGHTS:

Apparent Women Officers or Directors: 1
Hot Spot for Advancement for Women/Minorities:

LOCATIONS: ("Y" = Yes)

West:	Southwest:	Midwest:	Southeast:	Northeast:	International:
Y	Y	Y	Y	Y	Y

ELECTRABEL SA

www.electrabel.com

Industry Group Code: 221 **Ranks within this company's industry group:** Sales: Profits:

Exploration/Production:		Refining/Retailing:		Utilities:		Alternative Energy:		Specialty Services:		Energy Mktg./Other Svcs.	
Exploration:		Refining:		Electric Utility:	Y	Waste/Solar/Other:	Y	Consulting/Eng.:		Energy Marketing:	Y
Production:		Retailing:		Gas Utility:	Y	Thermal/Steam:	Y	Seismic:		Equipment/Machinery:	
Coal Production:		Convenience Stores:		Pipelines:		Wind:	Y	Drilling:		Oil Field Services:	
		Chemicals:		Water:		Hydro:	Y	InfoTech:		Air/Shipping Transportation:	
						Fuel Cells:		Specialty Services:			

TYPES OF BUSINESS:

Electric Utility
Electric Power Distribution & Transmission
Energy Marketing
Nuclear Generation
Wind & Hydroelectric Generation

BRANDS/DIVISIONS/AFFILIATES:

GDF Suez SA
NV Bekaert S.A.
Fluxys
Elia System Operator S.A.

CONTACTS:

Note: Officers with more than one job title may be intentionally listed here more than once.

Dirk Beeuwsaert, CEO
Marc Josz, Mgr.-Mktg. & Sales
Sophie Dutordoir, Gen. Mgr.
Jean Van Vyve, Mgr.-Nuclear Generation
Bruno Defrasnes, Mgr.-Sustainable Dev.
Philippe Van Troeye, Mgr.-Generation

Phone: 32-2-518-6111	**Fax:** 32-2-518-64-00
Toll-Free:	
Address: Blvd. du Regent 8, Brussels, 1000 Belgium	

GROWTH PLANS/SPECIAL FEATURES:

Electrabel S.A., a subsidiary of the utility group GDF Suez S.A., is one of the largest power companies in the Benelux region (a region that includes Belgium, the Netherlands and Luxembourg). The firm's business consists of three core activities: sales of electricity, natural gas and energy products; electricity generation; and electricity and natural gas trading. The company distributes electricity to about 4.08 million customers and distributes natural gas to more than 2.23 million customers. The firm has a generating capacity of around 16,265 megawatts (MW). In 2009, it sold roughly 118.6 terawatt hours (TWh) of electricity and 75.8 TWh of natural gas to customers across the Benelux region. Electrabel's power is generated from various sources including conventional, representing 31% of capacity; combined cycle gas turbine plants, 24.7%; nuclear stations, 26%; hydroelectric, .1%; combined heat and power, 5.5%; pumped storage, 8%; wind turbine, .8%; turbojet, 1.3%; gas turbine, 1.5%; and energy recovery, .5%. It is one of the largest producers and biggest suppliers of green power in Belgium, supplying reduced CO2 electricity under its GreenPlus label to over 350,000 customers. In December 2009, the firm established a cooperation agreement with NV Bekaert SA for the construction of a wind farm in Zwevegem, located in the Belgian province of West Flanders. In March 2010, Electrabel agreed to sell its 38.5% interest in Fluxys, Belgian operator of natural gas transmission pipelines and storage infrastructure. In the same month, it also agreed to sell its interests in Elia System Operator S.A., which operates electricity transmission systems in Belgium.

FINANCIALS:

Sales and profits are in thousands of dollars—add 000 to get the full amount. 2010 Note: Financial information for 2010 was not available for all companies at press time.

2010 Sales: $	2010 Profits: $	**U.S. Stock Ticker: Subsidiary**
2009 Sales: $	2009 Profits: $	**Int'l Ticker:** Int'l Exchange:
2008 Sales: $	2008 Profits: $	Employees:
2007 Sales: $20,673,500	2007 Profits: $4,070,040	Fiscal Year Ends: 12/31
2006 Sales: $19,602,700	2006 Profits: $3,343,800	Parent Company: GDF SUEZ SA

SALARIES/BENEFITS:

Pension Plan:	ESOP Stock Plan:	Profit Sharing:	Top Exec. Salary: $	Bonus: $
Savings Plan:	Stock Purch. Plan:		Second Exec. Salary: $	Bonus: $

OTHER THOUGHTS:

Apparent Women Officers or Directors: 1
Hot Spot for Advancement for Women/Minorities:

LOCATIONS: ("Y" = Yes)

West:	Southwest:	Midwest:	Southeast:	Northeast:	International:
					Y

ELECTRICITE DE FRANCE SA (EDF)

www.edf.fr

Industry Group Code: 221113 **Ranks within this company's industry group:** Sales: 1 Profits: 1

Exploration/Production:		Refining/Retailing:		Utilities:		Alternative Energy:		Specialty Services:		Energy Mktg./Other Svcs.	
Exploration:		Refining:		Electric Utility:	Y	Waste/Solar/Other:	Y	Consulting/Eng.:		Energy Marketing:	
Production:		Retailing:		Gas Utility:		Thermal/Steam:	Y	Seismic:		Equipment/Machinery:	
Coal Production:		Convenience Stores:		Pipelines:		Wind:	Y	Drilling:		Oil Field Services:	
		Chemicals:		Water:		Hydro:	Y	InfoTech:		Air/Shipping Transportation:	
						Fuel Cells:		Specialty Services:	Y		

TYPES OF BUSINESS:

Electric Utility
Nuclear Generation
Hydroelectric Generation
Wind Generation
Thermal Generation
Boiler Maintenance
Photovoltaic Cells
Renewable Energy

BRANDS/DIVISIONS/AFFILIATES:

British Energy Group plc
Electricite Reseau Distribution France
EDF Energies Nouvelles
Unistar
EnBW
Edison
Constellation Energy Nuclear Group, LLC
RTE-EDF Transport

CONTACTS:

Note: Officers with more than one job title may be intentionally listed here more than once.

Henri Proglio, CEO
Jean-Louis Mathias, Sr. Exec. VP-Human Resources
Alain Tchernonog, Gen. Sec.
Daniel Camus, Sr. Exec. VP-Strategy
Bernard Sananes, Sr. Exec. VP-Corp. Comm.
Thomas Piquemal, Sr. Exec. VP-Corp. Finance
Vincent de Rivas, CEO-EDF Energy
Pierre Lederer, Sr. Exec. VP-Customers, Optimization & Trading
Herve Machenaud, Sr. Exec. VP-Generation
Henri Proglio, Chmn.
Daniel Camus, Sr. Exec. VP-Int'l Activities

Phone: 33-1-40-42-22-22	**Fax:** 33-1-40-42-79-40
Toll-Free:	
Address: 22-30, Ave. de Wagram, Paris, 75008 France	

GROWTH PLANS/SPECIAL FEATURES:

Electricite de France S.A. (EDF) is an integrated energy group operating a range of electricity generating facilities. The firm's primary generating source is nuclear power. Its fleet of nuclear power plants, which generate roughly 65% of EDF's electricity, comprises 58 PWRs (pressurized water reactors) facilities and two EPR (European Pressurized Reactor) plants. The EPR plants are currently under construction. EDF's renewable energy operations, accounting for 21% of generation, are conducted through 50%-owned subsidiary EDF Energies Nouvelles and consist primarily of hydroelectric generating resources, including 640 dams and 447 power stations. EDF also utilizes wind, solar and geothermal power to a lesser extent. EDF's fossil fuel generating plants, accounting for 14% of the firm's electricity, comprise 36 active generation units and four inactive production units. EDF has a total generating capacity of almost 96.6 gigawatts (GW). EDF controls two distribution and transportation subsidiaries in France, RTE-EDF Transport and Electricite Reseau Distribution France. Together, these companies control roughly 62,137 miles of high and very high voltage transmission lines and 774,228 miles of medium and low voltage power distribution lines. EDF operates via numerous regional subsidiaries and joint ventures, including wholly-owned subsidiary EDF Energy in the U.K., which operates the majority of Britain's nuclear plants; 45%-owned joint venture EnBW in Germany; and joint venture Edison in Italy. The firm supplies energy and services to 38 million customers worldwide, of which 26.5 million are in France. France generates the majority of the firm's sales, followed by the U.K., Germany and Italy. The French government maintains an approximate 84.66% stake in the company. EDF hopes to use its expertise to construct four new nuclear reactors in the UK, four in America and two in China. In October 2010, the firm completed the sale of its British electricity distribution networks to the Hong-Kong based Cheung Kong Group for $5.1 million. EDF hopes to use its considerable nuclear expertise to construct new nuclear generation plants in other nations, including the U.S. and China. It owns a 49.5% interest in Constellation Energy Nuclear Group, LLC, an operator of several nuclear plants in the Untied States.

FINANCIALS:

Sales and profits are in thousands of dollars—add 000 to get the full amount. 2010 Note: Financial information for 2010 was not available for all companies at press time.

2010 Sales: $	2010 Profits: $	**U.S. Stock Ticker: Government-Owned**
2009 Sales: $85,630,500	2009 Profits: $5,040,810	**Int'l Ticker:** Int'l Exchange:
2008 Sales: $82,417,500	2008 Profits: $4,497,360	Employees: 160,000
2007 Sales: $81,629,000	2007 Profits: $7,689,700	Fiscal Year Ends: 12/31
2006 Sales: $77,706,800	2006 Profits: $7,394,700	Parent Company:

SALARIES/BENEFITS:

Pension Plan:	ESOP Stock Plan:	Profit Sharing:	Top Exec. Salary: $	Bonus: $
Savings Plan:	Stock Purch. Plan:		Second Exec. Salary: $	Bonus: $

OTHER THOUGHTS:

Apparent Women Officers or Directors: 2
Hot Spot for Advancement for Women/Minorities: Y

LOCATIONS: ("Y" = Yes)

West:	Southwest:	Midwest:	Southeast:	Northeast:	International:
				Y	Y

ELECTRICITY GENERATING AUTHORITY OF THAILAND

www.egat.co.th

Industry Group Code: 2211 **Ranks within this company's industry group:** Sales: 16 Profits: 11

Exploration/Production:		Refining/Retailing:		Utilities:		Alternative Energy:		Specialty Services:		Energy Mktg./Other Svcs.	
Exploration:		Refining:		Electric Utility:	Y	Waste/Solar/Other:		Consulting/Eng.:		Energy Marketing:	
Production:		Retailing:		Gas Utility:		Thermal/Steam:		Seismic:		Equipment/Machinery:	
Coal Production:		Convenience Stores:		Pipelines:		Wind:		Drilling:		Oil Field Services:	
		Chemicals:		Water:		Hydro:		InfoTech:		Air/Shipping Transportation:	
						Fuel Cells:		Specialty Services:			

TYPES OF BUSINESS:

Electricity Generation
Electricity Transmission
Energy-Related Construction, Maintenance & Supply Services

BRANDS/DIVISIONS/AFFILIATES:

CONTACTS:

Note: Officers with more than one job title may be intentionally listed here more than once.

Sombat Sarntijareee, Governor
Sineenat Sittiratanarangsee, CFO
Sahust Pratuknukul, Deputy Governor-Planning & Policy
Sineenat Sittiratanarangsee, Deputy Governor-Finance & Acct.
Sutat Patmasiriwat, Deputy Governor-Generation
Ratanapong Jongdamgerng, Deputy Governor-Transmission System
Wirash Kanchanapibul, Deputy Governor-Corp. Social Responsibility
Pornchai Rujiprapa, Chmn.

Phone: 66-2436-0000	**Fax:**
Toll-Free:	
Address: 53 Moo 2 Charunsanitwong Rd., Bang Kruai, 11130 Thailand	

GROWTH PLANS/SPECIAL FEATURES:

Electricity Generating Authority of Thailand (EGAT) is the national power company of Thailand, with roughly 15 megawatts (MW) of installed capacity. The company has 38 company-run facilities, consisting of 21 hydroelectric plants, eight renewable energy power plants, five combined cycle power plants, three thermal power plants, and one diesel power plant. The firm also purchases electricity produced by domestic independent power producers (IPPs) and small power producers (SPPs) as well as from power companies in other countries, primarily Laos and Malaysia. The firm's natural gas facilities account for 27.7% of the country's total electricity, with lignite accounting for 11.6%, hydropower accounting for 4.8% and fuel and diesel oil accounting for 0.32%. Besides generating electricity, the company operates Thailand's electricity transmission system. It operates over 19,000 circuit-miles of transmission lines, ranging in transmission capacity from 69-500 kilovolts (kV), as well as 209 substations. In terms of energy sales, the Provincial Electricity Authority buys the largest share (typically 67%) of the firm's electricity, followed by the Metropolitan Electricity Authority (31%), direct customers (1%) and minor customers and neighboring countries (1%). While power generation and transmission constitute its core businesses, EGAT also offers energy-related services, including operating power plants, maintaining transmission and distribution systems, offering engineering and construction services, supplying energy-related chemicals and supplying power plant related parts.

FINANCIALS:

Sales and profits are in thousands of dollars—add 000 to get the full amount. 2010 Note: Financial information for 2010 was not available for all companies at press time.

2010 Sales: $	2010 Profits: $	**U.S. Stock Ticker: Government-Owned**
2009 Sales: $12,569,300	2009 Profits: $1,174,990	**Int'l Ticker:** Int'l Exchange:
2008 Sales: $10,966,690	2008 Profits: $821,950	Employees:
2007 Sales: $10,379,730	2007 Profits: $942,330	Fiscal Year Ends:
2006 Sales: $	2006 Profits: $	Parent Company:

SALARIES/BENEFITS:

Pension Plan:	ESOP Stock Plan:	Profit Sharing:	Top Exec. Salary: $	Bonus: $
Savings Plan:	Stock Purch. Plan:		Second Exec. Salary: $	Bonus: $

OTHER THOUGHTS:

Apparent Women Officers or Directors: 1
Hot Spot for Advancement for Women/Minorities:

LOCATIONS: ("Y" = Yes)

West:	Southwest:	Midwest:	Southeast:	Northeast:	International:
					Y

ELETROBRAS PARTICIPACOES SA

www.lightpar.com.br

Industry Group Code: 2211 **Ranks within this company's industry group:** Sales: Profits:

Exploration/Production:		Refining/Retailing:		Utilities:		Alternative Energy:		Specialty Services:		Energy Mktg./Other Svcs.	
Exploration:		Refining:		Electric Utility:	Y	Waste/Solar/Other:		Consulting/Eng.:		Energy Marketing:	
Production:		Retailing:		Gas Utility:		Thermal/Steam:		Seismic:		Equipment/Machinery:	
Coal Production:		Convenience Stores:		Pipelines:		Wind:		Drilling:		Oil Field Services:	
		Chemicals:		Water:		Hydro:		InfoTech:		Air/Shipping Transportation:	
						Fuel Cells:		Specialty Services:			

TYPES OF BUSINESS:

Electricity Transmission
Electricity Generation & Distribution

BRANDS/DIVISIONS/AFFILIATES:

Cia. Hidroeletrica do S.Francisco (Chesf)
Furnas Centrais Eletricas S.A. (Furnas)
Centrais Eletricas do Norte do Brasil
Eletrobras Termonuclear S.A. (Eletronuclear)
Eletrosul Centrais Eletricas (Eletrosul)
Companhia de Geracao Termica de Energia Eletrica
Itaipu Binacional
Cepel

CONTACTS: *Note: Officers with more than one job title may be intentionally listed here more than once.*

Marcelo Lobo de Oliveira Figueiredo, CEO
Jose Antonio Muniz Lopes, Pres.
Astrogildo Fraguglia Quental, CFO
Ubirajara Rocha Meira, CTO
Valter Luiz Cardeal de Souza, Chief Eng. Officer
Miguel Colasuonno, Chief Admin. Officer
Jorge Jose Teles Rodrigues, Dir.-Investor Rel.
Marcelo Lobo de Oliveira Figueiredo, Chmn.
Flavio Decat de Moura, Chief Dist. Officer

Phone: 55-21-25145418 **Fax:** 55-21-25145562
Toll-Free:
Address: Ave. Marechal Floriano 19-15, Rio De Janeiro, 20080-003 Brazil

GROWTH PLANS/SPECIAL FEATURES:

Eletrobras Participacoes S.A., controlled by the Brazilian government, is a publicly traded mixed-capital company active in the Brazilian energy sector. Created in 1962, the firm's original intention was to conduct and promote studies, projects of construction and operation of generator plants, transmission lines and substations in order to supply Brazil's electricity. It is now the principal agent and investor for the government in the domestic electric energy sector. Eletrobras is one of the largest holding companies in Latin America's energy sector, responsible for nearly 60% of the transmission lines and 40% of Brazil's installed generation capacity. The companies of the Eletrobras system have an installed capacity of 39,753 MW, provided by 30 hydroelectric power plants, 15 thermal electric plants and two thermo-nuclear plants. Eletrobras comprises six companies responsible for the transmission and generation of electric energy: Cia. Hidroeletrica do S.Francisco (Chesf); Furnas Centrais Eletricas S.A. (Furnas); Centrais Eletricas do Norte do Brasil (Eletronorte); Eletrobras Termonuclear S.A. (Eletronuclear); Eletrosul Centrais Eletricas (Eletrosul); and Companhia de Geracao Termica de Energia Eletrica (CGTEE). Additioanlly, the firm holds a 50% interest in Itaipu Binacional and has six electric power distribution companies (Ceal, Ceron, Cepisa, Manaus Energia, Boa Vista Energia, Eletroacre). The company also controls Cepel, one of the largest electric power research centers in Latin America. In addition to financing energy development and distribution projects, Eletrobras manages government programs such as Luz para Todos (Light for Everyone), which seeks to extend electric service to rural and underdeveloped areas. The common shares of Eletrobras, of which the Brazilian government owns 53.99%, are traded on the New York, Sao Paulo and Madrid Stock Exchanges.

FINANCIALS: **Sales and profits are in thousands of dollars—add 000 to get the full amount. 2010 Note: Financial information for 2010 was not available for all companies at press time.**

2010 Sales: $ | 2010 Profits: $
2009 Sales: $ | 2009 Profits: $
2008 Sales: $ | 2008 Profits: $
2007 Sales: $ | 2007 Profits: $
2006 Sales: $ | 2006 Profits: $

U.S. Stock Ticker: Subsidiary
Int'l Ticker: LIPR3 Int'l Exchange: Sao Paulo-SAO
Employees:
Fiscal Year Ends: 12/31
Parent Company: CENTRAIS ELETRICAS BRASILEIRAS SA

SALARIES/BENEFITS:

Pension Plan: | ESOP Stock Plan: | Profit Sharing: | Top Exec. Salary: $ | Bonus: $
Savings Plan: | Stock Purch. Plan: | | Second Exec. Salary: $ | Bonus: $

OTHER THOUGHTS:

Apparent Women Officers or Directors:
Hot Spot for Advancement for Women/Minorities:

LOCATIONS: ("Y" = Yes)

West:	Southwest:	Midwest:	Southeast:	Northeast:	International:
					Y

ELETROPAULO METROPOLITANA ELECTRICIDADE DE SAO PAULO SA

www.eletropaulo.com.br

Industry Group Code: 2211 **Ranks within this company's industry group:** Sales: Profits:

Exploration/Production:		**Refining/Retailing:**		**Utilities:**		**Alternative Energy:**		**Specialty Services:**		**Energy Mktg./Other Svcs.**	
Exploration:		Refining:		Electric Utility:	Y	Waste/Solar/Other:		Consulting/Eng.:		Energy Marketing:	
Production:		Retailing:		Gas Utility:		Thermal/Steam:		Seismic:		Equipment/Machinery:	
Coal Production:		Convenience Stores:		Pipelines:		Wind:		Drilling:		Oil Field Services:	
		Chemicals:		Water:		Hydro:		InfoTech:		Air/Shipping Transportation:	
						Fuel Cells:		Specialty Services:			

TYPES OF BUSINESS:

Energy Distribution

BRANDS/DIVISIONS/AFFILIATES:

AES Corp.

GROWTH PLANS/SPECIAL FEATURES:

Eletropaulo Metropolitana Electricidade de Sao Paulo SA (AES Eletropaulo) is an energy distributor to the Brazilian state of Sao Paulo, as well as to 24 municipalities in the metropolitan area of the city of Sao Paulo, as well as the city itself. AES Eletropaulo's concession area spans 1,747 square miles. The company serves approximately 16.3 million people in 5.9 million homes and businesses. The firm maintains 135 distribution transformer stations, with sub-station capacity of 13.2 megavolt ampere (MVA), 26,720 miles of distribution network, and 1.1 miles of subtransmission lines and a total of 1.1 million electricity poles. The company sells approximately 33,860 gigawatt hours (GWh). It is controlled by AES Corp., an international power company that supplies renewable and sustainable energy in 29 countries.

CONTACTS:

Note: Officers with more than one job title may be intentionally listed here more than once.

Cibele Castro, Co-CEO/Managing Dir.
Rinaldo Pecchio, Jr., Dir.-Investor Rel.
Roberto Mario Di Nardo, Co-CEO
Jorge Luiz Busato, Co-CEO/Managing Dir.
Sheilly Caden Contente, Co-CEO/Managing Dir.
Britaldo Pedrosa Soares, Chmn./Co-CEO

Phone: 55-11-21952306 **Fax:** 55-11-21952291

Toll-Free:

Address: Rua Lorenco Marques, 158 14 andar Vila Olimpia, Sao Paulo, 04547-100 Brazil

FINANCIALS:

Sales and profits are in thousands of dollars—add 000 to get the full amount. 2010 Note: Financial information for 2010 was not available for all companies at press time.

2010 Sales: $	2010 Profits: $	**U.S. Stock Ticker:**
2009 Sales: $	2009 Profits: $	**Int'l Ticker: ELPL6** Int'l Exchange: Sao Paulo-SAO
2008 Sales: $	2008 Profits: $	Employees:
2007 Sales: $	2007 Profits: $	Fiscal Year Ends: 12/31
2006 Sales: $	2006 Profits: $	Parent Company:

SALARIES/BENEFITS:

Pension Plan:	ESOP Stock Plan:	Profit Sharing:	Top Exec. Salary: $	Bonus: $
Savings Plan:	Stock Purch. Plan:		Second Exec. Salary: $	Bonus: $

OTHER THOUGHTS:

Apparent Women Officers or Directors: 1
Hot Spot for Advancement for Women/Minorities:

LOCATIONS: ("Y" = Yes)

West:	Southwest:	Midwest:	Southeast:	Northeast:	International:
					Y

ELSTER GROUP SE

www.elster.com

Industry Group Code: 3345 **Ranks within this company's industry group:** Sales: Profits:

Exploration/Production:		Refining/Retailing:		Utilities:		Alternative Energy:		Specialty Services:		Energy Mktg./Other Svcs.	
Exploration:		Refining:		Electric Utility:	Y	Waste/Solar/Other:		Consulting/Eng.:		Energy Marketing:	
Production:		Retailing:		Gas Utility:	Y	Thermal/Steam:		Seismic:		Equipment/Machinery:	Y
Coal Production:		Convenience Stores:		Pipelines:		Wind:		Drilling:		Oil Field Services:	
		Chemicals:		Water:	Y	Hydro:		InfoTech:	Y	Air/Shipping Transportation:	
						Fuel Cells:		Specialty Services:			

TYPES OF BUSINESS:

Gas, Water & Electric Meters
Advanced Metering Infrastructure

BRANDS/DIVISIONS/AFFILIATES:

EnergyAxis
EnergyICT
evolution
TRACE
Coronis

CONTACTS:

Note: Officers with more than one job title may be intentionally listed here more than once.

Simon Beresford-Wylie, CEO
Christoph Schmidt-Wolf, CFO
Ronald Botoff, Dir.-Investor Rel.
Thomas Preute, Chief Compliance Officer
Theo Bettray, Exec. VP-Special Projects
Frank Hyldmar, Exec. VP-Electricity RoW
Jerry Lauzze, Exec. VP-Water Global
Lars Beumer, Chief Procurement Officer

Phone: 49-201-54-58-0 **Fax:** 49-201-54-58-362
Toll-Free:
Address: Frankenstrasse 362, Essen, 45133 Germany

GROWTH PLANS/SPECIAL FEATURES:

Elster Group SE is a German utilities metering and delivery company that has operations in 36 countries on six continents. Elster functions in three business segments: gas, water and electricity. In the gas segment, the company produces technologies used for measuring, regulating and safely controlling natural gas and its usage. The product range includes valves, filter, pressure switches, rotary meters, volume correctors, diaphragm meters, couplings and other tools and accessories utilized in the installation of gas distribution products. The water segment is composed of advanced water usage meters that integrate software and wireless connectivity to improve accuracy and efficiency of measurements. The company's electricity segment offers meters, transmitters, receivers, and control systems that also utilize advanced technology so meter readings can be done remotely. As part of Elster's high technology approach to utilities metering, the company has developed a number of solutions that connect utility companies over a significant area, including EnergyAxis, a two-way communications network; evolution, a water-metering technology that accurately measures consumption and helps to reduce waste; and TRACE, a system that utilizes two-way radio frequencies to collect billing information and detailed readings. The company's two subsidiary companies, EnergyICT and Coronis, develop utility management software platforms, and wireless products for the utilities market, respectively.

FINANCIALS:

Sales and profits are in thousands of dollars—add 000 to get the full amount. 2010 Note: Financial information for 2010 was not available for all companies at press time.

2010 Sales: $	2010 Profits: $	**U.S. Stock Ticker: ELT**
2009 Sales: $	2009 Profits: $	**Int'l Ticker:** Int'l Exchange:
2008 Sales: $	2008 Profits: $	Employees:
2007 Sales: $	2007 Profits: $	Fiscal Year Ends:
2006 Sales: $	2006 Profits: $	Parent Company:

SALARIES/BENEFITS:

Pension Plan:	ESOP Stock Plan:	Profit Sharing:	Top Exec. Salary: $	Bonus: $
Savings Plan:	Stock Purch. Plan:		Second Exec. Salary: $	Bonus: $

OTHER THOUGHTS:

Apparent Women Officers or Directors:
Hot Spot for Advancement for Women/Minorities:

LOCATIONS: ("Y" = Yes)

West:	Southwest:	Midwest:	Southeast:	Northeast:	International:
	Y	Y	Y	Y	Y

EMERA INC

www.emera.com

Industry Group Code: 221 **Ranks within this company's industry group:** Sales: 49 Profits: 39

Exploration/Production:		Refining/Retailing:		Utilities:		Alternative Energy:		Specialty Services:		Energy Mktg./Other Svcs.	
Exploration:		Refining:		Electric Utility:	Y	Waste/Solar/Other:	Y	Consulting/Eng.:		Energy Marketing:	Y
Production:		Retailing:		Gas Utility:	Y	Thermal/Steam:	Y	Seismic:		Equipment/Machinery:	
Coal Production:		Convenience Stores:		Pipelines:	Y	Wind:	Y	Drilling:		Oil Field Services:	
		Chemicals:		Water:		Hydro:	Y	InfoTech:		Air/Shipping Transportation:	
						Fuel Cells:		Specialty Services:	Y		

TYPES OF BUSINESS:

Utilities-Electricity & Natural Gas
Pipelines
Thermal & Hydroelectric Generation
Tidal Power Generation
Wind Generation
Utility Servicing

BRANDS/DIVISIONS/AFFILIATES:

Nova Scotia Power Inc
Bangor Hydro-Electric Company
Brunswick Pipeline
Emera Utility Services, Inc.
Cablecom
Maritimes and Northeast Pipeline
OpenHydro Group Limited
Maine & Maritimes Corporation

CONTACTS: *Note: Officers with more than one job title may be intentionally listed here more than once.*

Christopher Huskilson, CEO
Wayne O'Connor, COO
Christopher Huskilson, Pres.
Nancy Tower, CFO
Sarah MacDonald, Exec. VP-Human Resources
James Spurr, General Counsel/VP-Gov't Rel.
Ray Robinson, VP-Integrated Oper.
Sasha Irving, Dir.-Corp. Comm.
Rob Bennett, CEO/Pres., Nova Scotia Power, Inc.
Robert Hanf, CEO/Pres., Bangor Hydro Electric Company
Stephen Aftanas, Corp. Sec.
Rick Smith, VP-Corp. Insurance & Asset Protection
John T. McLennan, Chmn.

Phone: 902-450-0507 **Fax:** 902-428-6112
Toll-Free: 888-450-0507
Address: 1894 Barrington St., Barrington Tower, Halifax, NS B3J 2A8 Canada

GROWTH PLANS/SPECIAL FEATURES:

Emera, Inc. is an electricity and gas utilities holding company operating primarily in Nova Scotia, Canada, Maine and the Bahamas. Nova Scotia Power, Inc. (NSPI) and Bangor Hydro-Electric (BHE), Emera's two principal subsidiaries, accounted for 62% and 16% of the company's consolidated revenue in 2009, respectively. NSPI is one of the largest electricity providers in the Nova Scotia area, supplying 97% of the generation, transmission and distribution demand to 486,000 customers in the area. A supplier of electricity to Nova Scotians for over 80 years, NSPI is a Canadian leader in the use of renewable energy. It owns and operates one of only three tidal power plants in the world, as well as five thermal plants, 33 hydroelectric plants, two wind turbine sites and four combustion turbine plants. It produces over 13,000 gigawatt hours (GWh) of electricity per year, with a generating capacity of 2,293 megawatts (MW). BHE, a transmission and distribution company operating in east Maine, serves 110,000 customers and manages about 800 miles of transmission lines and around 4,225 miles of distribution lines. Additionally, Emera operates a pipeline division composed of a wholly-owned subsidiary, Brunswick Pipeline, along with its 12.9% interest in Maritimes & Northeast Pipeline. Other subsidiaries include Emera Utility Services, Inc., the parent company of Cablecom, one of the largest telecommunications and power utility servicing contractors in Atlantic Canada; and Emera Energy, which invests in various energy industry opportunities, handles Emera's assets in the Caribbean and manages the firm's 8.2% equity interest in OpenHydro, a tidal energy company in Ireland that designs and manufactures marine turbines. In March 2010, the firm agreed to acquire Maine & Maritimes Corporation, the parent of Maine Public Service Company and MAM Utility Services Group. In May 2010, Emera agreed to purchase a 38% interest in Light & Power Holdings Ltd., which owns The Barbados Light & Power Company Ltd.

FINANCIALS: **Sales and profits are in thousands of dollars—add 000 to get the full amount. 2010 Note: Financial information for 2010 was not available for all companies at press time.**

2010 Sales: $	2010 Profits: $	**U.S. Stock Ticker:**
2009 Sales: $1,408,350	2009 Profits: $168,850	**Int'l Ticker: EMA** Int'l Exchange: Toronto-TSX
2008 Sales: $1,227,780	2008 Profits: $132,840	Employees: 2,350
2007 Sales: $1,244,100	2007 Profits: $148,300	Fiscal Year Ends: 12/31
2006 Sales: $1,142,700	2006 Profits: $123,300	Parent Company:

SALARIES/BENEFITS:

Pension Plan:	ESOP Stock Plan:	Profit Sharing:	Top Exec. Salary: $636,576	Bonus: $680,430
Savings Plan:	Stock Purch. Plan:		Second Exec. Salary: $330,227	Bonus: $191,491

OTHER THOUGHTS:

Apparent Women Officers or Directors: 6
Hot Spot for Advancement for Women/Minorities: Y

LOCATIONS: ("Y" = Yes)

West:	Southwest:	Midwest:	Southeast:	Northeast:	International:
				Y	Y

ENBRIDGE ENERGY PARTNERS LP

www.enbridgepartners.com

Industry Group Code: 486 **Ranks within this company's industry group:** Sales: 9 Profits: 9

Exploration/Production:		**Refining/Retailing:**		**Utilities:**		**Alternative Energy:**		**Specialty Services:**		**Energy Mktg./Other Svcs.**	
Exploration:		Refining:		Electric Utility:		Waste/Solar/Other:		Consulting/Eng.:		Energy Marketing:	Y
Production:		Retailing:		Gas Utility:		Thermal/Steam:		Seismic:		Equipment/Machinery:	
Coal Production:		Convenience Stores:		Pipelines:	Y	Wind:		Drilling:		Oil Field Services:	
		Chemicals:		Water:		Hydro:		InfoTech:		Air/Shipping Transportation:	
						Fuel Cells:		Specialty Services:			

TYPES OF BUSINESS:

Pipelines
Gas Marketing Services

BRANDS/DIVISIONS/AFFILIATES:

Lakehead System
North Dakota System
Mid-Continent System
Ozark Pipeline
West Tulsa Pipeline

CONTACTS:

Note: Officers with more than one job title may be intentionally listed here more than once.

Stephen J. J. Letwin, Principal Exec. Officer/Managing Dir.
Terrence L. McGill, Pres.
Mark A. Maki, VP-Finance
Stephen Wuori, Exec. VP-Liquids Pipelines
Al Monaco, Exec. VP-Major Projects
Martha O. Hesse, Chmn.

Phone: 713-821-2000 **Fax:**
Toll-Free:
Address: 1100 Louisiana, Ste. 3300, Houston, TX 77002 US

GROWTH PLANS/SPECIAL FEATURES:

Enbridge Energy Partners, L.P., (EEP) owns and operates the Lakehead System, which is the U.S. portion of a crude oil and liquid petroleum pipeline system extending from western Canada through the upper and lower Great Lakes region of the U.S. to eastern Canada. A subsidiary of EEP owns the Canadian portion of this System. The company conducts its business through three business segments: liquids transportation, natural gas transportation and marketing. The liquids transportation pipeline network, also known as the Lakehead System, is one of the world's largest pipelines, spanning a distance of approximately 1,900 miles. The Lakehead system consists of approximately 4,700 miles of pipe, 60 pump station locations and 66 crude oil storage tanks. EEP's Lakehead System serves each of the major refining centers in the Midwestern U.S., the Great Lakes area and Ontario, Canada. The North Dakota System is 240 mile crude oil gathering and 730 mile interstate transportation system servicing 22 oil fields in North Dakota and Montana. It provides connections with the Lakehead System and is currently expanding to a capacity of 161,000 barrels per day. The Mid-Continent System has 480 miles of pipeline with 96 storage tanks and includes the Ozark and West Tulsa pipeline and storage terminals in Oklahoma and Kansas. The natural gas segment owns and operates natural gas gathering, treating, processing and transporting systems as well as trucking operations. The company's natural gas assets are primarily located in the U.S. Gulf Coast region. The marketing segment's primary objectives are to mitigate financial risk and maximize the value of the natural gas purchased by EEP's gathering systems and the throughput on its gathering and intrastate wholesale customer pipelines. The marketing segment conducts the majority of its activities in Texas and Oklahoma.

FINANCIALS:

Sales and profits are in thousands of dollars—add 000 to get the full amount. 2010 Note: Financial information for 2010 was not available for all companies at press time.

2010 Sales: $	2010 Profits: $	**U.S. Stock Ticker: EEP**
2009 Sales: $5,731,800	2009 Profits: $316,600	**Int'l Ticker:** Int'l Exchange:
2008 Sales: $10,060,000	2008 Profits: $587,900	Employees:
2007 Sales: $7,282,600	2007 Profits: $216,900	Fiscal Year Ends: 12/31
2006 Sales: $6,509,000	2006 Profits: $284,900	Parent Company:

SALARIES/BENEFITS:

Pension Plan:	ESOP Stock Plan:	Profit Sharing:	Top Exec. Salary: $540,000	Bonus: $530,000
Savings Plan:	Stock Purch. Plan:		Second Exec. Salary: $496,497	Bonus: $472,855

OTHER THOUGHTS:

Apparent Women Officers or Directors: 1
Hot Spot for Advancement for Women/Minorities:

LOCATIONS: ("Y" = Yes)

West:	Southwest:	Midwest:	Southeast:	Northeast:	International:
Y	Y	Y	Y	Y	Y

ENBRIDGE INC

www.enbridge.com

Industry Group Code: 486 **Ranks within this company's industry group:** Sales: 6 Profits: 1

Exploration/Production:		**Refining/Retailing:**		**Utilities:**		**Alternative Energy:**		**Specialty Services:**		**Energy Mktg./Other Svcs.**	
Exploration:		Refining:		Electric Utility:		Waste/Solar/Other:	Y	Consulting/Eng.:		Energy Marketing:	Y
Production:		Retailing:	Y	Gas Utility:	Y	Thermal/Steam:		Seismic:		Equipment/Machinery:	
Coal Production:		Convenience Stores:		Pipelines:	Y	Wind:	Y	Drilling:		Oil Field Services:	
		Chemicals:		Water:		Hydro:		InfoTech:		Air/Shipping Transportation:	
						Fuel Cells:	Y	Specialty Services:	Y		

TYPES OF BUSINESS:

Pipeline Transportation
Energy Transportation & Distribution
Liquids Marketing
Crude Oil & Liquids Pipeline System
International Energy Projects

BRANDS/DIVISIONS/AFFILIATES:

Enbridge Energy Partners, LP
Enbridge Pipelines, Inc.
Enbridge Gas Distribution Inc.
Renewable Energy Systems Canada, Inc.
U.S. Geothermal, Inc.
First Solar, Inc.
Sania Solar Project

CONTACTS: *Note: Officers with more than one job title may be intentionally listed here more than once.*

Patrick D. Daniel, CEO
Patrick D. Daniel, Pres.
J. Richard Bird, CFO/Exec. VP-Corp. Dev.
J. L. Balko, VP-Human Resources
B.D. Poohkay, CIO/VP
C.J. Szmurlo, VP-Emerging & Alternative Tech.
J. L. Balko, VP-Admin.
David T. Robottom, Chief Legal Officer/Exec. VP-IT & Public Affairs
J.K. Whelen, Sr. VP-Corp. Dev.
D. L. Levesque, VP-Public & Gov't Affairs
D.G. Jarvis, Sr. VP-Investor Rel. & Enterprise Risk
C.K. Gruending, Controller/VP
Stephen J. Wuori, Pres., Liquids Pipelines
Janet Holder, Pres., Enbridge Gas Dist.
S. R. Bloxom, VP-Acquisitions
A. T. Love, VP/Corp. Sec./Chief Compliance Officer
David A. Arledge, Chmn.
Al Monaco, Pres., Int'l, Gas Pipelines & Green Energy

Phone: 403-231-3900 **Fax:** 403-231-3920
Toll-Free: 800-481-2804
Address: 3000 Fifth Ave. Pl., 425 1st St. SW, Calgary, AB T2P 3L8 Canada

GROWTH PLANS/SPECIAL FEATURES:

Enbridge, Inc. is a Canadian natural gas distributor that also operates one of the world's longest crude oil and liquids pipeline systems. The company operates in four segments: liquids pipelines, which accounted for 29% of 2009 revenue; natural gas delivery and services, 41%; sponsored investments, 9%; and corporate, 21%. The liquids pipelines segment operates a network of pipelines transporting crude oil, natural gas liquids (NGLs) and refined products through Canada and the U.S. Subsidiary Enbridge Pipelines, Inc. owns the Canadian portion of the Edmonton to Chicago liquids pipeline. Extending over 8,500 miles, this network delivers over 2 million barrels per day of crude oil and liquids. The natural gas delivery and services segment combines the operations of natural gas utilities (primarily the business of Enbridge Gas Distribution, Inc.), pipeline investments, commodity marketing and various international activities. Subsidiary Enbridge Gas Distribution, a natural gas distribution company, serves over 1.9 million customers in Quebec, Ontario and New York and is developing a distribution network in New Brunswick. This segment also includes the company's investment in Aux Sable, a natural gas fractionation and extraction business. The sponsored investments segment entails the firm's 27% interest in Enbridge Energy Partners, LP (EEP), owner of the Lakehead Pipeline System in the U.S., among other interests. The corporate unit consists of new business development and financing activities, as well as investments in green energy projects. In March 2010, the firm singed a partnership with Renewable Energy Systems Canada, Inc. to construct a 99-megawatt (MW) wind project. In September 2010, Enbridge partnered with U.S. Geothermal, Inc. on the construction of a 35 MW hot springs geothermal facility in which the firm will hold 20% interest. In October 2010, commercial operation began at the 80 MW Sania Solar Project built in concert with First Solar, Inc.

FINANCIALS: **Sales and profits are in thousands of dollars—add 000 to get the full amount. 2010 Note: Financial information for 2010 was not available for all companies at press time.**

2010 Sales: $	2010 Profits: $	**U.S. Stock Ticker: ENB**
2009 Sales: $11,920,400	2009 Profits: $1,493,640	**Int'l Ticker: ENB** Int'l Exchange: Toronto-TSX
2008 Sales: $14,870,230	2008 Profits: $1,223,910	Employees: 6,065
2007 Sales: $12,020,000	2007 Profits: $710,000	Fiscal Year Ends: 12/31
2006 Sales: $9,134,000	2006 Profits: $534,000	Parent Company:

SALARIES/BENEFITS:

Pension Plan: Y	ESOP Stock Plan:	Profit Sharing:	Top Exec. Salary: $1,172,880	Bonus: $2,084,794
Savings Plan:	Stock Purch. Plan:		Second Exec. Salary: $580,419	Bonus: $591,581

OTHER THOUGHTS:

Apparent Women Officers or Directors: 3
Hot Spot for Advancement for Women/Minorities: Y

LOCATIONS: ("Y" = Yes)

West:	Southwest:	Midwest:	Southeast:	Northeast:	International:
Y	Y	Y	Y	Y	Y

ENCANA CORP

www.encana.com

Industry Group Code: 211111 **Ranks within this company's industry group:** Sales: 46 Profits: 28

Exploration/Production:		Refining/Retailing:		Utilities:		Alternative Energy:		Specialty Services:		Energy Mktg./Other Svcs.	
Exploration:	Y	Refining:		Electric Utility:		Waste/Solar/Other:		Consulting/Eng.:		Energy Marketing:	Y
Production:	Y	Retailing:		Gas Utility:		Thermal/Steam:		Seismic:		Equipment/Machinery:	
Coal Production:		Convenience Stores:		Pipelines:	Y	Wind:		Drilling:		Oil Field Services:	
		Chemicals:		Water:		Hydro:		InfoTech:		Air/Shipping Transportation:	
						Fuel Cells:		Specialty Services:			

TYPES OF BUSINESS:

Natural Gas Production
Natural Gas Exploration

BRANDS/DIVISIONS/AFFILIATES:

Cenovus Energy, Inc.

CONTACTS:

Note: Officers with more than one job title may be intentionally listed here more than once.

Randy Eresman, CEO
Randy Eresman, Pres.
Sherri Brillon, CFO/Exec. VP
Renee Zemljak, Exec. VP-Mktg., Midstream & Fundamentals
Bob Grant, Exec. VP-Corp. Dev.
Alan Boras, VP-Media Rel.
Ryder McRitchie, VP-Investor Rel.
Bill Stevenson, Chief Acct. Officer/Exec. VP
Mike Graham, Exec. VP/Pres., Canadian Oper.
Eric Marsh, Exec. VP-Natural Gas Economy
Bill Oliver, Chief Corp. Officer/Exec. VP
David P. O'Brien, Chmn.
Jeff Wojahn, Exec. VP/Pres., U.S. Oper.

Phone: 403-645-2000 **Fax:** 403-645-3400
Toll-Free:
Address: 1800, 855 2nd St. SW, Calgary, AB T2P 2S5 Canada

GROWTH PLANS/SPECIAL FEATURES:

EnCana Corp. is an independent gas exploration and production company that markets natural gas and natural gas liquids (NGLs) for consumption throughout Canada and the U.S. EnCana owns proved reserves of 11 trillion cubic feet of natural gas. It is one of North America's chief natural gas producers with 47,000 possible well locations in nine natural gas resource plays. EnCana operates in two divisions; the Canadian Division and the USA Division. The Canadian Division, which holds approximately 11 million gross acres, includes natural gas development and production assets located in British Columbia and Alberta and the Deep Panuke natural gas project offshore Nova Scotia. Activity is focused in four key resource plays: the Greater Sierra in northeast British Columbia (BC), the Cutback Ridge on the border of BC and Alberta, the Bighorn area in west-central Alberta and coalbed methane in southern Alberta. The USA Division, which holds 4.3 million gross acres, focuses its natural gas production activities in four key areas also: Jonah in southwest Wyoming, Piceance in northwest Colorado, east Texas assets and assets in Fort Worth, Texas. The firm also has development interests in the Haynesville shale play in Louisiana, the Collingwood shale in Michigan and the Marcellus shale in Pennsylvania. In 2009, the firm's total daily production averaged 3 billion cubic feet of gas equivalent per day (bcfe/d), of which 56% was produced in the U.S. In November 2009, the company underwent a reorganization whereby it was split into two separate entities: EnCana Corp., which now solely operates in the gas industry, and Cenovus Energy, Inc., operating in the oil industry. In June 2010, EnCana signed a memorandum of understanding with China National Petroleum Corp. to negotiate a possible development joint venture in certain of EnCana's natural gas plays.

FINANCIALS:

Sales and profits are in thousands of dollars—add 000 to get the full amount. 2010 Note: Financial information for 2010 was not available for all companies at press time.

2010 Sales: $	2010 Profits: $	**U.S. Stock Ticker: ECA**
2009 Sales: $11,114,000	2009 Profits: $1,862,000	**Int'l Ticker: ECA** Int'l Exchange: Toronto-TSX
2008 Sales: $21,053,000	2008 Profits: $5,944,000	Employees: 3,797
2007 Sales: $14,385,000	2007 Profits: $3,959,000	Fiscal Year Ends: 12/31
2006 Sales: $16,399,000	2006 Profits: $5,652,000	Parent Company:

SALARIES/BENEFITS:

Pension Plan:	ESOP Stock Plan:	Profit Sharing:	Top Exec. Salary: $1,176,756	Bonus: $2,615,015
Savings Plan:	Stock Purch. Plan:		Second Exec. Salary: $570,945	Bonus: $894,956

OTHER THOUGHTS:

Apparent Women Officers or Directors: 2
Hot Spot for Advancement for Women/Minorities: Y

LOCATIONS: ("Y" = Yes)

West:	Southwest:	Midwest:	Southeast:	Northeast:	International:
Y	Y	Y	Y	Y	Y

ENDESA SA

www.endesa.es

Industry Group Code: 2211 **Ranks within this company's industry group:** Sales: 4 Profits: 2

Exploration/Production:		Refining/Retailing:		Utilities:		Alternative Energy:		Specialty Services:		Energy Mktg./Other Svcs.	
Exploration:		Refining:		Electric Utility:	Y	Waste/Solar/Other:	Y	Consulting/Eng.:		Energy Marketing:	Y
Production:		Retailing:		Gas Utility:	Y	Thermal/Steam:	Y	Seismic:		Equipment/Machinery:	
Coal Production:	Y	Convenience Stores:		Pipelines:	Y	Wind:	Y	Drilling:		Oil Field Services:	
		Chemicals:		Water:		Hydro:	Y	InfoTech:		Air/Shipping Transportation:	
						Fuel Cells:		Specialty Services:	Y		

TYPES OF BUSINESS:

Electricity Generation & Distribution
Renewable Energy
Telecommunications
Mining Assets
Nuclear Power Generation
Hydroelectric Power
Wind Energy Generation

BRANDS/DIVISIONS/AFFILIATES:

Enel SpA
Endesa Portugal
Tejo Energia
Finerge
Enersis Group
Telefonica Espana
Mitsubishi Corp.

CONTACTS: *Note: Officers with more than one job title may be intentionally listed here more than once.*

Andrea Brentan, CEO
Paolo Bondi, CFO/Sr. VP
Jose Luis Puche Castillejo, Sr. VP-Human Resources & Organization
Francisco de Borja Acha Besga, Sr. VP-Legal Affairs
Hector Lopez Vilaseco, Sr. VP-Strategy & Dev.
Alfonso Lopez Sanchez, Sr. VP-Comm.
Jose Damian Bogas Galvez, Sr. VP-Spain & Portugal
Salvador Montejo Velilla, Gen. Sec.
Rafael Lopez Rueda, Sr. VP-Systems & Telecomm.
Borja Prado Eulate, Chmn.
Ignacio Antonanzas Alvear, Sr. VP-Latin America
Francesco Buresti, Sr. VP/Gen. Mgr.-Purchasing

Phone: 34-91-213-10-00	**Fax:** 34-91-563-81-81
Toll-Free:	
Address: Ribera del Loira, 60, Madrid, 28042 Spain	

GROWTH PLANS/SPECIAL FEATURES:

Endesa S.A., subsidiary of Italian utility firm Enel SpA, is a leading supplier of electricity and gas in Spain, Portugal and Latin America, with interests in renewable energy and telecommunications. Endesa's electricity business is conducted in Spain, Portugal and Latin America, while its gas business is conducted in Spain only. The firm's total generation capacity in Spain and Portugal is approximately 22.93 gigawatts (GW). In Portugal the company does business under the Endesa Portugal brand and owns 38.9% of Tejo Energia, which operates a 600 megawatt coal-fired power station. It also wholly owns Finerge, winch operates wind farm and cogeneration facilities. Endesa, through Enersis Group and other equity holdings, is involved in the generation, transmission, distribution and supply of electricity in five countries in Latin America, with a total installed capacity of 15.85 GW. The company operates a network of 185,510 miles transmission and distribution lines. The firm also maintains a presence in the coal mining industry, operating three coal mines in Spain. Total output at its mines in 2009 was nearly 2 million tons. In June 2009, Italian electric and gas utility Enel SpA bought the stake in Endesa held by Acciona S.A., increasing its stake to 92% and giving Enel control of the company. In February 2010, the firm started construction on a plant for the cultivation of microalgae which capture CO_2 and transform it into biomass. In April 2010, Endesa commenced operating a CO_2 capture plant using chemical absorption installed at its Compostilla thermal plant. In June 2010, the company, in partnership with Telefonica Espana, introduced electric vehicle recharging stations at telephone booths in Valencia, Spain. In September 2010, Endesa signed a memorandum of understanding with Mitsubishi Corp. to collaborate on the development of electric vehicle infrastructure and vehicle to grid (V2G) technology.

FINANCIALS: **Sales and profits are in thousands of dollars—add 000 to get the full amount. 2010 Note: Financial information for 2010 was not available for all companies at press time.**

2010 Sales: $	2010 Profits: $	**U.S. Stock Ticker: Subsidiary**
2009 Sales: $30,574,100	2009 Profits: $4,235,780	**Int'l Ticker:** Int'l Exchange:
2008 Sales: $27,373,200	2008 Profits: $8,853,140	Employees: 26,587
2007 Sales: $27,133,000	2007 Profits: $3,303,410	Fiscal Year Ends: 12/31
2006 Sales: $24,740,100	2006 Profits: $4,542,600	Parent Company: ENEL SPA

SALARIES/BENEFITS:

Pension Plan:	ESOP Stock Plan:	Profit Sharing:	Top Exec. Salary: $	Bonus: $
Savings Plan:	Stock Purch. Plan:		Second Exec. Salary: $	Bonus: $

OTHER THOUGHTS:

Apparent Women Officers or Directors:
Hot Spot for Advancement for Women/Minorities:

LOCATIONS: ("Y" = Yes)

West:	Southwest:	Midwest:	Southeast:	Northeast:	International:
					Y

ENEL SPA

www.enel.it

Industry Group Code: 2211 **Ranks within this company's industry group:** Sales: 1 Profits: 1

Exploration/Production:		**Refining/Retailing:**		**Utilities:**		**Alternative Energy:**		**Specialty Services:**		**Energy Mktg./Other Svcs.**	
Exploration:		Refining:		Electric Utility:	Y	Waste/Solar/Other:	Y	Consulting/Eng.:		Energy Marketing:	
Production:		Retailing:		Gas Utility:	Y	Thermal/Steam:	Y	Seismic:		Equipment/Machinery:	
Coal Production:		Convenience Stores:		Pipelines:		Wind:	Y	Drilling:		Oil Field Services:	
		Chemicals:		Water:		Hydro:	Y	InfoTech:		Air/Shipping Transportation:	
						Fuel Cells:		Specialty Services:	Y		

TYPES OF BUSINESS:

Electric Utility
Mini-Hydroelectric Generation
Solar Generation
Wind Power Generation
Geothermal Generation

BRANDS/DIVISIONS/AFFILIATES:

Neftegaztechnologiya
RusEnergoSbyt LLC
Sviluppo Nucleare Italia Srl
Enel Green Power

CONTACTS:

Note: Officers with more than one job title may be intentionally listed here more than once.

Fulvio Conti, CEO
Claudio Machetti, CFO
S. Cardillo, Dir.-Legal Affairs
Piero Gnudi, Chmn.

Phone: 39-06-8305-2783	**Fax:** 3906-8305-3659
Toll-Free:	
Address: Viale Regina Margherita 137, Rome, 00198 Italy	

GROWTH PLANS/SPECIAL FEATURES:

Enel S.p.A. is one of Italy's largest power companies, as well as one of the largest in Europe. The company produces, distributes and sells electricity and gas. Due to its recent multiple international acquisitions the company now operates in 23 countries and provides power and gas to approximately 60.5 million customers. The company is also one of the largest in Italy in terms of shareholders and product market share; Enel provides natural gas to more than 2.7 million customers within Italy. The company has a total generating capacity of 95,400 MW. The company is also among the largest in terms of generating renewable energy. In North America Enel operates through Enel Green Power and has hydroelectric and wind power plants that generate more than 788 MW. The company also has a sizeable renewable and traditional energy presence throughout Latin America, with approximately 16 GW of installed capacity. In Russia Enel operates through several companies; RusEnergoSbyt and Neftegaztechnologiya are among the most substantial and generate over 8,200 MW of electricity. In order to better focus its efforts strictly in the energy sector the company has in recent years divested its non-core assets, including its telecommunications, property management and water supply businesses. In February 2009, Italian electric and gas utility Enel SpA reached an agreement whereby it will acquire enough stock in Spanish utility firm Endesa to give Enel control of the company, increasing its stake to 92%.

FINANCIALS:

Sales and profits are in thousands of dollars—add 000 to get the full amount. 2010 Note: Financial information for 2010 was not available for all companies at press time.

2010 Sales: $	2010 Profits: $	**U.S. Stock Ticker: EN**
2009 Sales: $82,128,400	2009 Profits: $6,964,190	**Int'l Ticker: ENEL** Int'l Exchange: Milan-BI
2008 Sales: $78,495,900	2008 Profits: $6,832,520	Employees: 81,208
2007 Sales: $56,395,100	2007 Profits: $5,055,010	Fiscal Year Ends: 12/31
2006 Sales: $50,826,000	2006 Profits: $4,092,000	Parent Company:

SALARIES/BENEFITS:

Pension Plan:	ESOP Stock Plan:	Profit Sharing:	Top Exec. Salary: $970,693	Bonus: $
Savings Plan:	Stock Purch. Plan:		Second Exec. Salary: $791,580	Bonus: $

OTHER THOUGHTS:

Apparent Women Officers or Directors:
Hot Spot for Advancement for Women/Minorities:

LOCATIONS: ("Y" = Yes)

West:	Southwest:	Midwest:	Southeast:	Northeast:	International:
					Y

ENERCON GMBH

www.enercon.de

Industry Group Code: 33361 **Ranks within this company's industry group:** Sales: Profits:

Exploration/Production:		**Refining/Retailing:**		**Utilities:**		**Alternative Energy:**		**Specialty Services:**		**Energy Mktg./Other Svcs.**	
Exploration:		Refining:		Electric Utility:		Waste/Solar/Other:		Consulting/Eng.:		Energy Marketing:	
Production:		Retailing:		Gas Utility:		Thermal/Steam:		Seismic:		Equipment/Machinery:	Y
Coal Production:		Convenience Stores:		Pipelines:		Wind:	Y	Drilling:		Oil Field Services:	
		Chemicals:		Water:		Hydro:		InfoTech:		Air/Shipping Transportation:	
						Fuel Cells:		Specialty Services:			

TYPES OF BUSINESS:

Wind Turbine Manufacturing
Desalination Systems

BRANDS/DIVISIONS/AFFILIATES:

CONTACTS:

Note: Officers with more than one job title may be intentionally listed here more than once.

Aloys Wobben, Co-Managing Dir.
Andreas Duser, Mgr.-Sales
Petra Engelhardt, Dir.-Human Resources
Stefan Hartge, Head-Electrical Eng., Development Div.
Volker Uphoff, Public Rel.
Volker Uphoff, Head-Mktg.
Hans-Dieter Kettewig, Co-Managing Dir.
Aloys Wobben, Chmn./Managing Dir.

Phone: 49-49-41-927-0 **Fax:** 49-49-41-927-109
Toll-Free:
Address: Dreekamp 5, Aurich, D-26605 Germany

GROWTH PLANS/SPECIAL FEATURES:

ENERCON GmbH, founded in 1984, manufactures and designs wind turbines. To support turbine installation, the firm operates mobile cranes of up to 800 tons; special transporters for blades and towers; and hundreds of service vehicles. The firm's turbines have featured gearless systems since 1992, allowing the turbines to operate with fewer rotating parts, resulting in almost frictionless performance. ENERCON currently offers turbine configurations rated from 330 kilowatts to 6,000 kilowatts. Generally, all of ENERCON's turbine systems feature independent pitch control for each of the three rotor blades, as well as integrated lighting protection and typically operate at speeds around 12-20 revolutions per minute (rpm), with some capable of operating as slow as six rpm and some as fast as 34 rpm. In order to prevent the shut-downs caused by high winds that other turbines systems may suffer from, the firm has developed ENERCON Storm Control software, which causes the rotor blades to rotate slightly out of sync with the wind, thus preventing damage by reducing the rotation speed rather than ceasing rotation altogether. In order to connect the turbines to a power grid, the firm offers ENERCON SCADA, an upgradable and adaptable monitoring and control interface. Each turbine also comes equipped with a modem to signal a central data transmission facility of any malfunction. The firm's service and support division operates over 160 stations worldwide. ENERCON has three production facilities in Germany, as well as facilities in Turkey, India, Brazil, Sweden and Portugal. It has installed more than 13,000 turbines in over 30 countries to date. The firm also offers eight low energy reverse osmosis desalination systems.

FINANCIALS:

Sales and profits are in thousands of dollars—add 000 to get the full amount. 2010 Note: Financial information for 2010 was not available for all companies at press time.

2010 Sales: $	2010 Profits: $	**U.S. Stock Ticker:**
2009 Sales: $	2009 Profits: $	**Int'l Ticker: EWEC** Int'l Exchange: Brussels-Euronext
2008 Sales: $	2008 Profits: $	Employees:
2007 Sales: $	2007 Profits: $	Fiscal Year Ends: 12/31
2006 Sales: $	2006 Profits: $	Parent Company:

SALARIES/BENEFITS:

Pension Plan:	ESOP Stock Plan:	Profit Sharing:	Top Exec. Salary: $	Bonus: $
Savings Plan:	Stock Purch. Plan:		Second Exec. Salary: $	Bonus: $

OTHER THOUGHTS:

Apparent Women Officers or Directors:
Hot Spot for Advancement for Women/Minorities:

LOCATIONS: ("Y" = Yes)

West:	Southwest:	Midwest:	Southeast:	Northeast:	International:
					Y

ENERGY FUTUREHOLDINGS CORP (TXU)

www.energyfutureholdings.com

Industry Group Code: 221 **Ranks within this company's industry group:** Sales: 17 Profits:

Exploration/Production:		Refining/Retailing:		Utilities:		Alternative Energy:		Specialty Services:		Energy Mktg./Other Svcs.	
Exploration:		Refining:		Electric Utility:	Y	Waste/Solar/Other:	Y	Consulting/Eng.:		Energy Marketing:	Y
Production:		Retailing:		Gas Utility:	Y	Thermal/Steam:		Seismic:		Equipment/Machinery:	
Coal Production:		Convenience Stores:		Pipelines:		Wind:	Y	Drilling:		Oil Field Services:	
		Chemicals:		Water:		Hydro:		InfoTech:		Air/Shipping Transportation:	
						Fuel Cells:		Specialty Services:			

TYPES OF BUSINESS:

Utilities-Electricity & Natural Gas
Energy Trading & Marketing
Electric Power Generation
Nuclear Generation
Pipelines
Wind Energy Trading

BRANDS/DIVISIONS/AFFILIATES:

TXU Corporation
TPG (Texas Pacific Group)
KKR & Co LP (Kohlberg Kravis Roberts & Co)
Goldman Sachs Group Inc
Luminant
Oncor Electric Delivery Company
TXU Energy
TXU Energy Access

CONTACTS:

Note: Officers with more than one job title may be intentionally listed here more than once.

John F. Young, CEO
John F. Young, Pres.
Paul Keglevic, CFO/Exec. VP
Richard Landy, Exec. VP-Human Resources
Robert Walters, General Counsel/Exec. VP
Mac McFarland, Exec. VP-Strategy, Mergers & Acquisitions
Lisa Singleton, Contact-Media
Rima Hyder, Dir.-Investor Rel.
Chuck Enze, CEO-Luminant Construction
Jim Burke, CEO-TXU Energy
David Campbell, CEO-Luminant
James A. Baker, III, Advisory Chmn.
Donald L. Evans, Chmn.

Phone: 214-812-4600	**Fax:**
Toll-Free:	
Address: 1601 Bryan St., Energy Plz., Dallas, TX 75201 US	

GROWTH PLANS/SPECIAL FEATURES:

Energy Future Holdings Corp. (EFH), formerly TXU Corporation, is a domestic private energy services company. EFH operates through three independently managed businesses: Luminant; Oncor; and TXU Energy. Luminant encompasses the firm's power, wholesale marketing, development and construction businesses; it has more than 18,300 megawatts of generation capacity in Texas, including 8,000 megawatts of coal-fueled and over 2,300 megawatts of nuclear generation capacity. It is also a leading purchaser of domestic wind-generated electricity. Oncor with more than 117,000 miles of transmission and distribution lines in Texas delivers power to more than 3 million homes and businesses. TXU Energy operates EFH's retail business, providing electricity and related services to over 2 million electricity customers in Texas. The subsidiary provides over $150 million in annual support to low-income consumers through its TXU Energy Access programs. It offers renewable energy products through the TXU Energy EarthWise brand. EFH changed its name from TXU following its recent acquisition for $32 billion by a group of investors led by Kohlberg Kravis Roberts & Co., TPG (Texas Pacific Group) and Goldman Sachs Capital Partners. In February 2009, Oncor released Take A Load Off, Texas Solar Photovoltaic Incentive Program, its first solar power plan, which will offer cash incentives to businesses and individuals who agree to install new solar systems for their energy needs. Also in February 2009, Luminant and Mitsubishi Heavy Industries, Ltd. formed a joint venture, Comanche Peak Nuclear Power Company, to further develop Luminant's Comanche Peak Nuclear Power Plant. In September 2010, TXU Energy to install electric vehicle charging stations in Dallas and Fort Worth and will fund the cost of the charging station equipment and installation.

Employees are offered benefits such as medical, dental, life and AD&D insurance; education expense reimbursement plan; a 401(k); paid holidays; a relocation expense reimbursement plan; an employee assistance plan; and flexible spending accounts.

FINANCIALS:

Sales and profits are in thousands of dollars—add 000 to get the full amount. 2010 Note: Financial information for 2010 was not available for all companies at press time.

2010 Sales: $	2010 Profits: $	**U.S. Stock Ticker: Private**
2009 Sales: $9,550,000	2009 Profits: $	**Int'l Ticker:** Int'l Exchange:
2008 Sales: $11,360,000	2008 Profits: $	Employees: 9,030
2007 Sales: $7,992,000	2007 Profits: $-637,000	Fiscal Year Ends: 12/31
2006 Sales: $10,856,000	2006 Profits: $2,552,000	Parent Company: TPG (TEXAS PACIFIC GROUP)

SALARIES/BENEFITS:

Pension Plan:	ESOP Stock Plan:	Profit Sharing:	Top Exec. Salary: $	Bonus: $3,325,000
Savings Plan: Y	Stock Purch. Plan:		Second Exec. Salary: $	Bonus: $

OTHER THOUGHTS:

Apparent Women Officers or Directors: 2
Hot Spot for Advancement for Women/Minorities:

LOCATIONS: ("Y" = Yes)

West:	Southwest:	Midwest:	Southeast:	Northeast:	International:
	Y				

ENERGY PARTNERS LTD

www.eplweb.com

Industry Group Code: 211111 **Ranks within this company's industry group:** Sales: 102 Profits: 82

Exploration/Production:		Refining/Retailing:		Utilities:		Alternative Energy:		Specialty Services:		Energy Mktg./Other Svcs.	
Exploration:	Y	Refining:		Electric Utility:		Waste/Solar/Other:		Consulting/Eng.:		Energy Marketing:	
Production:	Y	Retailing:		Gas Utility:		Thermal/Steam:		Seismic:		Equipment/Machinery:	
Coal Production:		Convenience Stores:		Pipelines:	Y	Wind:		Drilling:		Oil Field Services:	
		Chemicals:		Water:		Hydro:		InfoTech:		Air/Shipping Transportation:	
						Fuel Cells:		Specialty Services:			

TYPES OF BUSINESS:

Oil & Gas Exploration & Production
Pipelines

BRANDS/DIVISIONS/AFFILIATES:

EPL Pipeline LLC

CONTACTS:

Note: Officers with more than one job title may be intentionally listed here more than once.

Gary C. Hanna, CEO
T.J. Thom, CFO/Sr. VP/Treas.
Jonathan S. Gross, Sr. VP-Geosciences
Chad E. Williams, Sr. VP-Prod.
John H. Peper, General Counsel/Exec. VP/Corp. Sec.
T.J. Thom, Sr. VP-Investor Rel.
David P. Cedro, Chief Acct. Officer/Controller/Sr. VP
Paul B. Jones, VP-Geosciences
Marc McCarthy, Chmn.

Phone: 504-569-1875	**Fax:** 504-569-1874
Toll-Free:	
Address: 201 St. Charles Ave., Ste. 3400, New Orleans, LA 70170 US	

GROWTH PLANS/SPECIAL FEATURES:

Energy Partners, Ltd. is an independent oil and natural gas exploration and production company. The firm's operations are concentrated in the shallow to moderate-depth waters in the Gulf of Mexico focusing on the areas offshore Louisiana as well as the deepwater Gulf of Mexico at depths of less than 5,000 feet. The company employs a team of geoscientists and management professionals with region-specific geological, geophysical, technical and operational experience. It has grown through a combination of exploration, exploitation and development drilling and multi-year, multi-well drill-to-earn programs, as well as strategic acquisitions of mature oil and natural gas fields in the Gulf of Mexico Shelf area. The company has proved reserves of approximately 67.4 billion cubic feet of natural gas and 19.9 million barrels of oil. It holds interests in 20 producing fields. Energy Partners' subsidiary EPL Pipeline, L.L.C. owns a 12-mile pipeline that transports oil from two fields in the Gulf of Mexico into Louisiana. Major oil customers include Shell Trading (US) Company, which accounts for approximately 30% of the firm's revenue; Chevron Texaco Exploration & Production Company, from which Energy Partners derives 27%; and Louis Dreyfus Energy Services, L.P., which accounts for 19%. EPL has a 15-33% working interest in 22 undeveloped deepwater wells in the Gulf of Mexico. In September 2009, the firm successfully emerged from bankruptcy after filing for it earlier in the year.

FINANCIALS:

Sales and profits are in thousands of dollars—add 000 to get the full amount. 2010 Note: Financial information for 2010 was not available for all companies at press time.

2010 Sales: $	2010 Profits: $	**U.S. Stock Ticker: EPL**
2009 Sales: $191,600	2009 Profits: $-57,100	**Int'l Ticker:** Int'l Exchange:
2008 Sales: $356,252	2008 Profits: $-52,212	Employees: 101
2007 Sales: $454,649	2007 Profits: $-79,955	Fiscal Year Ends: 12/31
2006 Sales: $449,550	2006 Profits: $-50,400	Parent Company:

SALARIES/BENEFITS:

Pension Plan:	ESOP Stock Plan:	Profit Sharing:	Top Exec. Salary: $275,000	Bonus: $27,000
Savings Plan:	Stock Purch. Plan:		Second Exec. Salary: $270,000	Bonus: $

OTHER THOUGHTS:

Apparent Women Officers or Directors: 1
Hot Spot for Advancement for Women/Minorities:

LOCATIONS: ("Y" = Yes)

West:	Southwest:	Midwest:	Southeast:	Northeast:	International:
	Y		Y		

Note: Financial information, benefits and other data can change quickly and may vary from those stated here.

ENERGY TRANSFER PARTNERS LP

www.energytransfer.com

Industry Group Code: 486 **Ranks within this company's industry group:** Sales: 11 Profits: 5

Exploration/Production:		**Refining/Retailing:**		**Utilities:**		**Alternative Energy:**		**Specialty Services:**		**Energy Mktg./Other Svcs.**	
Exploration:		Refining:	Y	Electric Utility:		Waste/Solar/Other:		Consulting/Eng.:		Energy Marketing:	Y
Production:		Retailing:	Y	Gas Utility:		Thermal/Steam:		Seismic:		Equipment/Machinery:	
Coal Production:		Convenience Stores:		Pipelines:	Y	Wind:		Drilling:		Oil Field Services:	
		Chemicals:		Water:		Hydro:		InfoTech:		Air/Shipping Transportation:	
						Fuel Cells:		Specialty Services:			

TYPES OF BUSINESS:

Pipelines
Natural Gas Midstream Services
Propane, Retail
Natural Gas Treatment & Processing

BRANDS/DIVISIONS/AFFILIATES:

La Grange Acquisition LP
Energy Transfer Company
Transwestern Pipeline Company
Midcontinent Express Pipeline LLC
Energy Transfer Interstate Holdings LLC
Heritage Operating LP
Titan Energy Partners LP

CONTACTS:

Note: Officers with more than one job title may be intentionally listed here more than once.

Kelcy L. Warren, CEO
Mackie McCrea, COO
Mackie McCrea, Pres.
Martin Salinas, Jr., CFO
Jerry J. Langdon, Chief Admin. & Compliance Officer
Thomas P. Mason, General Counsel/VP/Sec.
Mike Howard, Pres., Midstream Oper.
Brent Ratliff, Contact-Investor Rel.
John W. McReynolds, Pres./CFO-Energy Transfer Equity, L.P.
Bill Powers, Pres., Heritage Propane
Kelcy L. Warren, Chmn.

Phone: 214-981-0700 **Fax:** 214-981-0703
Toll-Free:
Address: 3738 Oak Lawn Ave., Dallas, TX 75219 US

GROWTH PLANS/SPECIAL FEATURES:

Energy Transfer Partners, LP (ETP) is a company mainly engaged in the natural gas transportation business and the U.S. propane retail marketing. The company's natural gas operations consist of intrastate/interstate transportation and storage services provided by La Grange Acquisition LP, which does business as Energy Transfer Company; and interstate transportation services provided by Transwestern Pipeline Company and ETC Midcontinent Express Pipeline LLC, subsidiaries of Energy Transfer Interstate Holdings, LLC. In total, ETP operates roughly 7,800 miles of intrastate and 2,700 miles of interstate pipelines. Through joint ventures, the firm has an additional 500 miles of interstate natural gas pipeline and 185 miles under construction. Its intrastate transportation/storage operations include the ET Fuel System, with 2,570 miles of pipeline and two storage facilities with a capacity of 12.4 billion cubic feet (Bcf) of gas; and the HPL System, with 4,300 miles of pipeline and a storage facility with capacity of 62 Bcf. The firm's midstream operations are concentrated in the Austin Chalk trend of southeast Texas; the Permian Basin of New Mexico and west Texas; the Bossier Sands in east Texas; the Barnett Shale in north Texas; the Uinta Basin in Utah; and the Piceance Basin in Colorado. Besides 7,000 miles of pipelines, the segment operates three natural gas processing plants; 11 treating facilities, which remove carbon dioxide and hydrogen sulfide before the gas is introduced into the pipelines; and 11 conditioning facilities, which remove heavy hydrocarbons. Intrastate operations account for roughly 56% of ETP's operating income; interstate, 12%; midstream, 12%; and retail, 20%. The retail propane division markets propane through subsidiaries Heritage Operating, LP and Titan Energy Partners, LP to over 1 million customers through roughly 440 locations in 40 states.

Employees are offered life, AD&D, medical, dental, and vision insurance; paid time off; flexible spending accounts; and a 401(k) plan.

FINANCIALS:

Sales and profits are in thousands of dollars—add 000 to get the full amount. 2010 Note: Financial information for 2010 was not available for all companies at press time.

2010 Sales: $	2010 Profits: $	**U.S. Stock Ticker: ETP**
2009 Sales: $5,417,295	2009 Profits: $791,542	**Int'l Ticker:** Int'l Exchange:
2008 Sales: $9,293,868	2008 Profits: $866,023	Employees: 1,334
2007 Sales: $6,792,037	2007 Profits: $676,139	Fiscal Year Ends: 12/31
2006 Sales: $7,859,096	2006 Profits: $515,852	Parent Company:

SALARIES/BENEFITS:

Pension Plan:	ESOP Stock Plan:	Profit Sharing:	Top Exec. Salary: $500,000	Bonus: $
Savings Plan: Y	Stock Purch. Plan:		Second Exec. Salary: $420,240	Bonus: $

OTHER THOUGHTS:

Apparent Women Officers or Directors:
Hot Spot for Advancement for Women/Minorities:

LOCATIONS: ("Y" = Yes)

West:	Southwest:	Midwest:	Southeast:	Northeast:	International:
Y	Y	Y		Y	

ENGLOBAL CORP

www.englobal.com

Industry Group Code: 541330 **Ranks within this company's industry group:** Sales: 5 Profits: 4

Exploration/Production:		Refining/Retailing:		Utilities:		Alternative Energy:		Specialty Services:		Energy Mktg./Other Svcs.	
Exploration:		Refining:		Electric Utility:		Waste/Solar/Other:		Consulting/Eng.:	Y	Energy Marketing:	
Production:		Retailing:		Gas Utility:		Thermal/Steam:		Seismic:		Equipment/Machinery:	Y
Coal Production:		Convenience Stores:		Pipelines:		Wind:		Drilling:		Oil Field Services:	
		Chemicals:		Water:		Hydro:		InfoTech:	Y	Air/Shipping Transportation:	
						Fuel Cells:		Specialty Services:			

TYPES OF BUSINESS:

Engineering Services
Petrochemicals Industry Support Services
Control & Instrumentation Systems
Consulting & Inspection Services
Project Management

BRANDS/DIVISIONS/AFFILIATES:

CONTACTS:

Note: Officers with more than one job title may be intentionally listed here more than once.

Edward L. Pagano, CEO
Edward L. Pagano, Pres.
Robert W. Raiford, CFO
Fred Bridgewater, VP-Human Resources
Alex Schroeder, Mgr.-Corp. IT
David W. Smith, Pres., ENGlobal Engineering, Inc.
Natalie S. Hairston, Corp. Sec./Chief Governance Officer
Rochelle D. Leedy, Sr. VP-Bus. Dev.
Natalie S. Hairston, VP-Investor Rel.
Robert W. Raiford, Treas.
R. David Kelley, VP-Governmental Svcs.
William Wells, VP-Health, Safety & Environmental
Katrina Hamrick, VP-Legal Affairs
William A. Coskey, Chmn.

Phone: 281-878-1000 **Fax:** 281-878-1010
Toll-Free: 800-411-6040
Address: 654 N. Sam Houston Pkwy E., Ste. 400, Houston, TX 77060-5914 US

GROWTH PLANS/SPECIAL FEATURES:

ENGlobal Corp. is an international provider of engineering services and systems to the petroleum refining, petrochemical, pipeline, production and processing industries. The firm operates in five primary segments: Engineering; Construction; Automation; Land; and Government and Infrastructure. The engineering segment provides consulting services including feasibility studies, engineering, design, procurement and construction management. The segment provides these services to the upstream, midstream and downstream energy industries and branches of the U.S. military, and in some instances it delivers its services via in-plant personnel assigned throughout the U.S. and internationally. ENGlobal's construction segment provides construction management personnel and services in the areas of inspection, mechanical integrity, vendor and turnaround surveillance, field support, construction, quality assurance and plant asset management. Its customers include pipeline, refining, utility, chemical, petroleum, petrochemical, oil and gas, and power industries throughout the U.S. Construction segment personnel are typically assigned to client facilities throughout the U.S. The automation segment provides services related to the design, fabrication, and implementation of process distributed control and analyzer systems, advanced automation and information technology projects. This segment's customers include members of the domestic and foreign energy related industries. Automation segment personnel assist in on-site commissioning, start-up and training for the company's specialized systems. The land segment provides land management, right-of-way, environmental compliance and governmental regulatory compliance services primarily to the pipeline, utility and telecom companies and other owner/operators of infrastructure facilities throughout the U.S. and Canada. ENGlobal's Government and Infrastructure unit, formed in October 2009, was created to discover potential new operating markets for the firm and offer the company's technical services. In April 2010, the firm acquired certain assets of industrial automation control system provider CDI.

Employees are offered life, disability, medical, dental and vision insurance; flexible spending accounts; educational reimbursement; a 401(k); paid time off; direct deposit services; and employee referral bonuses.

FINANCIALS:

Sales and profits are in thousands of dollars—add 000 to get the full amount. 2010 Note: Financial information for 2010 was not available for all companies at press time.

2010 Sales: $	2010 Profits: $	**U.S. Stock Ticker: ENG**
2009 Sales: $343,462	2009 Profits: $1,233	**Int'l Ticker:** Int'l Exchange:
2008 Sales: $493,332	2008 Profits: $18,258	Employees: 2,000
2007 Sales: $363,227	2007 Profits: $12,464	Fiscal Year Ends: 12/31
2006 Sales: $303,090	2006 Profits: $-3,486	Parent Company:

SALARIES/BENEFITS:

Pension Plan:	ESOP Stock Plan:	Profit Sharing:	Top Exec. Salary: $260,000	Bonus: $
Savings Plan: Y	Stock Purch. Plan:		Second Exec. Salary: $245,000	Bonus: $

OTHER THOUGHTS:

Apparent Women Officers or Directors: 2
Hot Spot for Advancement for Women/Minorities: Y

LOCATIONS: ("Y" = Yes)

West:	Southwest:	Midwest:	Southeast:	Northeast:	International:
Y	Y	Y	Y	Y	Y

ENI SPA

www.eni.com

Industry Group Code: 211111 **Ranks within this company's industry group:** Sales: 11 Profits: 15

Exploration/Production:		Refining/Retailing:		Utilities:		Alternative Energy:		Specialty Services:		Energy Mktg./Other Svcs.	
Exploration:	Y	Refining:	Y	Electric Utility:	Y	Waste/Solar/Other:		Consulting/Eng.:	Y	Energy Marketing:	Y
Production:	Y	Retailing:		Gas Utility:		Thermal/Steam:		Seismic:		Equipment/Machinery:	
Coal Production:		Convenience Stores:		Pipelines:		Wind:		Drilling:		Oil Field Services:	Y
		Chemicals:	Y	Water:		Hydro:		InfoTech:		Air/Shipping Transportation:	Y
						Fuel Cells:		Specialty Services:	Y		

TYPES OF BUSINESS:

Oil & Gas-Exploration & Production
Engineering & Construction Services
Oilfield Services
Refining & Transportation
Petrochemicals
Petroleum & Energy Research
Electricity Generation
Gas Stations

BRANDS/DIVISIONS/AFFILIATES:

Snam Rete Gas SpA
Italgas
EniPower SpA
Saipem SpA
Snamprogetti SpA
Agip
Polimeri Europa SpA
First Calgary Petroleums Ltd.

CONTACTS: *Note: Officers with more than one job title may be intentionally listed here more than once.*

Paolo Scaroni, CEO
Salvatore Sardo, Chief Corp. Oper. Officer
Alessandro Bernini, CFO/Sr. VP
Angelo Caridi, COO-Refining & Mktg. Div.
Claudio Descalzi, COO-Exploration & Prod. Div.
Massimo Mantovani, Sr. VP-Legal Affairs
Stefano Lucchini, Sr. VP-Public Affairs & Comm. Group
Claudia Carloni, Head-Investor Rel.
Roberto Ulissi, Sr. VP-Corp. Affairs & Governance
Domenico Dispenza, COO-Gas & Power Div.
Roberto Poli, Chmn.

Phone: 39-065-982-1	**Fax:** 39-065-982-2141
Toll-Free:	
Address: Piazzale Enrico Mattei, 1, Rome, 00144 Italy	

GROWTH PLANS/SPECIAL FEATURES:

Eni SpA is a diversified energy company that is approximately 30% owned by the Italian government. It conducts business in more than 70 countries and produces almost 1.8 million Barrels of Oil Equivalent (BOE) daily. The firm has four major divisions. The Exploration & Production Division has oil and natural gas projects in Italy, North Africa, West Africa, the North Sea, the Gulf of Mexico, Australia, South America, the Caspian Sea, the Middle East, Asia, India and Alaska. The firm estimates its reserves at approximately 6.4 billion BOE. The Gas & Power division sells approximately 2.785 trillion cubic feet of gas annually. It holds transmission rights on over 3,800 miles of high pressure gas pipelines outside Italy. The division also owns 50% of Snam Rete Gas SpA, which owns and manages almost 30,000 miles of pipeline. Italgas SpA and other subsidiaries distribute low pressure natural gas to over 1,310 municipalities, while EniPower Spa owns and manages power stations in seven Italian cities, with an installed capacity around of 5 gigawatts and an average annual output of 24.8 terawatts. The Refining & Marketing Division, mainly active in Europe, has an average processing rate of 710,000 barrels a day. The division's Agip brand gasoline stations dominate the Italian market while branching out into neighboring European countries. Polimeri Europa SpA produces and markets petrochemical products. The Engineering & Construction division operates through 43%-owned subsidiary Saipem SpA and Saipem's subsidiary Snamprogetti SpA. This segment offers oilfield services, engineering and contracting, developing everything from pipelines to offshore rigs. Eni also maintains a financing division, Sofid SpA.

FINANCIALS: **Sales and profits are in thousands of dollars—add 000 to get the full amount. 2010 Note: Financial information for 2010 was not available for all companies at press time.**

2010 Sales: $	2010 Profits: $	**U.S. Stock Ticker: E**
2009 Sales: $106,284,000	2009 Profits: $5,576,830	**Int'l Ticker: ENI** Int'l Exchange: Milan-BI
2008 Sales: $145,792,000	2008 Profits: $12,884,900	Employees: 78,417
2007 Sales: $137,027,000	2007 Profits: $15,721,300	Fiscal Year Ends: 12/31
2006 Sales: $114,743,000	2006 Profits: $13,090,000	Parent Company:

SALARIES/BENEFITS:

Pension Plan:	ESOP Stock Plan:	Profit Sharing:	Top Exec. Salary: $	Bonus: $53,278
Savings Plan:	Stock Purch. Plan:		Second Exec. Salary: $	Bonus: $

OTHER THOUGHTS:

Apparent Women Officers or Directors: 1
Hot Spot for Advancement for Women/Minorities:

LOCATIONS: ("Y" = Yes)

West:	Southwest:	Midwest:	Southeast:	Northeast:	International:
Y	Y			Y	Y

ENOGEX LLC

www.enogex.com

Industry Group Code: 486 **Ranks within this company's industry group:** Sales: 20 Profits: 13

Exploration/Production:		Refining/Retailing:		Utilities:		Alternative Energy:		Specialty Services:		Energy Mktg./Other Svcs.	
Exploration:		Refining:	Y	Electric Utility:		Waste/Solar/Other:		Consulting/Eng.:		Energy Marketing:	
Production:		Retailing:		Gas Utility:		Thermal/Steam:		Seismic:		Equipment/Machinery:	
Coal Production:		Convenience Stores:		Pipelines:	Y	Wind:		Drilling:		Oil Field Services:	
		Chemicals:		Water:		Hydro:		InfoTech:		Air/Shipping Transportation:	
						Fuel Cells:		Specialty Services:	Y		

TYPES OF BUSINESS:

Midstream Energy Services
Natural Gas Processing
Pipelines & Storage
Natural Gas Gathering

BRANDS/DIVISIONS/AFFILIATES:

OGE Energy Corp
OG&E
Enogex Gas Gathering LLC
Enogex Products LLC

CONTACTS: *Note: Officers with more than one job title may be intentionally listed here more than once.*

Peter B. Delaney, CEO
E. Keith Mitchell, COO/Sr. VP
Danny P. Harris, Pres.
Paul Brewer, VP-Oper.
Dwaine Shroyer, VP-Bus. Dev.
Thomas Levescy, Chief Acct. Officer
Ramiro Rangel, VP-Commercial Oper.
Peter B. Delaney, Chmn.-OGE Energy Corp.
Danny P. Harris, COO-OGE Energy Corp.
Peter B. Delaney, Chmn.

Phone: 405-525-7788 **Fax:** 405-558-4640
Toll-Free: 800-736-8492
Address: 515 Central Park Dr., Ste. 110, Oklahoma City, OK 73105 US

GROWTH PLANS/SPECIAL FEATURES:

Enogex LLC, a subsidiary of OGE Energy Corp., is a midstream services company providing natural gas gathering, processing, transportation and storage services primarily in the major natural gas producing basins of Oklahoma. Enogex manages its operations through three related businesses: pipeline services, gathering services and processing services. The pipeline services business provides natural gas transportation and storage within Oklahoma through approximately 8,000 miles of intrastate pipelines and storage facilities capable of holding 24 billion cubic feet of natural gas. Enogex is also connected to 15 other major pipelines at 65 pipeline interconnect points which provide access to markets in the western U.S., Midwest, Northeast and Gulf Coast regions, as well as Oklahoma and adjoining states. The gathering services business, operating through Enogex Gas Gathering LLC, provides gas gathering services in Oklahoma through its 500,000-horsepower compression fleet. The company pursues new supplies from wells drilled by producers primarily in the Anadarko and Arkoma basins. The processing services business, operating as Enogex Products LLC, provides natural gas processing services through a treatment facility and seven processing plants, with an additional plant under construction. Enogex extracts impurities, including hydrocarbons such as ethane and propane, during the processing of natural gas and sells these byproducts to large manufacturers and industrial users. This business also operates three depropanizers, providing wholesale propane fuel to local retail markets for distribution and home heating. OG&E, another subsidiary of OGE Energy, generates electricity from natural gas, western coal, and wind and serves about 780,000 retail customers in Oklahoma and Arkansas.

FINANCIALS: **Sales and profits are in thousands of dollars—add 000 to get the full amount. 2010 Note: Financial information for 2010 was not available for all companies at press time.**

2010 Sales: $	2010 Profits: $	**U.S. Stock Ticker: Subsidiary**
2009 Sales: $851,000	2009 Profits: $66,000	**Int'l Ticker:** Int'l Exchange:
2008 Sales: $1,103,000	2008 Profits: $91,000	Employees:
2007 Sales: $2,065,200	2007 Profits: $86,000	Fiscal Year Ends: 12/31
2006 Sales: $2,367,800	2006 Profits: $138,800	Parent Company: OGE ENERGY CORP

SALARIES/BENEFITS:

Pension Plan: Y	ESOP Stock Plan:	Profit Sharing:	Top Exec. Salary: $	Bonus: $91,241
Savings Plan:	Stock Purch. Plan:		Second Exec. Salary: $	Bonus: $

OTHER THOUGHTS:

Apparent Women Officers or Directors:
Hot Spot for Advancement for Women/Minorities:

LOCATIONS: ("Y" = Yes)

West:	Southwest:	Midwest:	Southeast:	Northeast:	International:
	Y				

ENSCO PLC

www.enscous.com

Industry Group Code: 213111 **Ranks within this company's industry group:** Sales: 7 Profits: 4

Exploration/Production:		**Refining/Retailing:**		**Utilities:**		**Alternative Energy:**		**Specialty Services:**		**Energy Mktg./Other Svcs.**	
Exploration:		Refining:		Electric Utility:		Waste/Solar/Other:		Consulting/Eng.:		Energy Marketing:	
Production:		Retailing:		Gas Utility:		Thermal/Steam:		Seismic:		Equipment/Machinery:	
Coal Production:		Convenience Stores:		Pipelines:		Wind:		Drilling:	Y	Oil Field Services:	Y
		Chemicals:		Water:		Hydro:		InfoTech:		Air/Shipping Transportation:	
						Fuel Cells:		Specialty Services:			

TYPES OF BUSINESS:

Contract Drilling Services

BRANDS/DIVISIONS/AFFILIATES:

Ensco International, Inc.

CONTACTS:

Note: Officers with more than one job title may be intentionally listed here more than once.

Daniel W. Rabun, CEO
William S. Chadwick, Jr., COO/Exec. VP
Daniel W. Rabun, Pres.
Jay W. Swent, CFO/Sr. VP
Michael K. Wiley, VP-Human Resources & Security
John Knowlton, VP-Eng. & Capital Projects
Cary A. Moomjian, Jr., General Counsel/VP/Sec.
Sean P. O'Neill, VP-Investor Rel.
David A. Armour, VP-Finance
Douglas Manko, Controller
Michael B. Howe, Treas.
Carey Lowe, Sr. VP-Deepwater Bus. Unit
Mark Burns, Sr. VP
Daniel W. Rabun, Chmn.

Phone: 44-207-659-4660	**Fax:**
Toll-Free: 800-423-8006	
Address: 6 Chesterfield Gardens, London, W1J 5BQ UK	

GROWTH PLANS/SPECIAL FEATURES:

Ensco plc, formerly Ensco International, Inc., is an international offshore contract drilling company. The company operates an offshore fleet of 41 jackup rigs and five ultra-deepwater semisubmersible rigs. In addition, the firm has three ultra-deepwater semisubmersible rigs under construction. The firm conducts its operations through four major business units: North and South America; Europe and Africa; Asia and the Pacific Rim; and Deepwater. Ensco provides drilling services on a day rate contract basis. Under day rate contracts, it provides the drilling rig and rig crews and receives a fixed amount per day for drilling the well, while customers bear substantially all of the ancillary costs of constructing the well and supporting drilling operations, as well as the economic risk relative to the success of the well. In addition, customers may pay all or a portion of the cost of moving the company's equipment and personnel to the well site. The firm does not provide turnkey or other risk-based drilling services. In December 2009, the company transferred its headquarters to London, and in March 2010, it changed its name to Ensco plc.

Ensco provides its employees with benefits that include medical, dental and vision insurance; life and AD&D insurance; an employee assistance plan; flexible spending accounts; an employer matched retirement savings plan; and a discretionary profit sharing scheme.

FINANCIALS:

Sales and profits are in thousands of dollars—add 000 to get the full amount. 2010 Note: Financial information for 2010 was not available for all companies at press time.

2010 Sales: $	2010 Profits: $	**U.S. Stock Ticker: ESV**
2009 Sales: $1,945,900	2009 Profits: $779,400	**Int'l Ticker:** Int'l Exchange:
2008 Sales: $2,393,600	2008 Profits: $1,150,800	Employees: 3,585
2007 Sales: $2,143,800	2007 Profits: $992,000	Fiscal Year Ends: 12/31
2006 Sales: $1,813,500	2006 Profits: $769,700	Parent Company:

SALARIES/BENEFITS:

Pension Plan:	ESOP Stock Plan:	Profit Sharing: Y	Top Exec. Salary: $878,625	Bonus: $1,165,446
Savings Plan: Y	Stock Purch. Plan:		Second Exec. Salary: $550,605	Bonus: $547,757

OTHER THOUGHTS:

Apparent Women Officers or Directors: 1
Hot Spot for Advancement for Women/Minorities:

LOCATIONS: ("Y" = Yes)

West:	Southwest:	Midwest:	Southeast:	Northeast:	International:
	Y		Y		Y

Note: Financial information, benefits and other data can change quickly and may vary from those stated here.

ENSIGN ENERGY SERVICES INC

www.ensignenergy.com

Industry Group Code: 213111 **Ranks within this company's industry group:** Sales: 11 Profits: 11

Exploration/Production:		Refining/Retailing:		Utilities:		Alternative Energy:		Specialty Services:		Energy Mktg./Other Svcs.	
Exploration:		Refining:		Electric Utility:		Waste/Solar/Other:		Consulting/Eng.:		Energy Marketing:	
Production:		Retailing:		Gas Utility:		Thermal/Steam:		Seismic:		Equipment/Machinery:	Y
Coal Production:		Convenience Stores:		Pipelines:		Wind:		Drilling:	Y	Oil Field Services:	Y
		Chemicals:		Water:		Hydro:		InfoTech:		Air/Shipping Transportation:	
						Fuel Cells:		Specialty Services:	Y		

TYPES OF BUSINESS:

Oilfield Services-Drilling & Workovers
Manufacturing-Oilfield Equipment
Equipment Rental
Oil Sands & Coal-Bed Methane Services

BRANDS/DIVISIONS/AFFILIATES:

Automated Drill Rigs (ADR)
Chandel Equipment Rentals
Ensign Well Services, Inc.
Ensign de Venezuela C.A.
Ensign Drilling Partnership
Tri-City Drilling
Foxxe Energy Services
FE Services Holdings, Inc.

CONTACTS:

Note: Officers with more than one job title may be intentionally listed here more than once.

Robert H. Geddes, COO
Robert H. Geddes, Pres.
Glenn Dagenais, CFO
Suzanne Davies, General Counsel/Sec.
Glenn Dagenais, Exec. VP-Finance
Selby Porter, Vice Chmn.
Rob Williams, VP-Health Safety & Environment
N. Murray Edwards, Chmn.
Ed Kautz, Exec. VP-U.S. & Int'l Oper.

Phone: 403-262-1361	**Fax:** 403-266-3596
Toll-Free:	
Address: 1000, 400 5th Ave. SW, Calgary, AB T2P 0L6 Canada	

GROWTH PLANS/SPECIAL FEATURES:

Ensign Energy Services Inc. is one of the largest land-based drilling contractors and well-servicing contractors in Canada. The company provides drilling services in Canada, the U.S., Australia, New Zealand, Southeast Asia, the Middle East, Africa, and South America. Ensign divides its oilfield services into three regions: Canada, the U.S. and International. Ensign maintains a fleet of approximately 322 drilling rigs, including 79 of its in-house developed Automated Drill Rigs (ADR), and 137 well-servicing rigs, workover units and coiled tubing units worldwide. The company operates through five business segments: Contact Drilling; Underbalanced Drilling, Rental Equipment, Well Servicing; and Manufacturing and Production Services. Contract Drilling's services include oil and natural gas exploration, slant drilling and well drilling services. The Underbalanced Drilling segment supplies integrated packages that include on-site nitrogen generation with closed surface controlled pressure equipment and real time data acquisition. The Rental Equipment division, operating as Chandel Equipment Rentals in Canada, supplies self-contained drilling systems; rents drill strings, tanks, pumps, loaders and other drill rig equipment. The Well Servicing division offerings include completion, abandonment, bottom-hole pump changes and production workovers. Through its Opsco Energy Industries Ltd. subsidiary, the Manufacturing and Production Services division provides telecommunication, production testing services, reporting and technical services. Additionally, it manufactures customized equipment for oil and natural gas production. Some of the firm's subsidiaries include Tri-City Drilling; West Coast Oilfield Rentals; Ensign Well Services, Inc.; Ensign Energy Services International Limited (Australia); and Champion Drilling Inc. In December 2009, Ensign acquired FE Services Holdings, Inc., doing business as Foxxe Energy Services, an oil exploration company operating six drilling rigs in Mexico.

FINANCIALS:

Sales and profits are in thousands of dollars—add 000 to get the full amount. 2010 Note: Financial information for 2010 was not available for all companies at press time.

2010 Sales: $	2010 Profits: $	**U.S. Stock Ticker: ESVIF**
2009 Sales: $1,087,810	2009 Profits: $119,910	**Int'l Ticker: ESI** Int'l Exchange: Toronto-TSX
2008 Sales: $1,572,250	2008 Profits: $239,640	Employees: 6,790
2007 Sales: $1,514,500	2007 Profits: $239,800	Fiscal Year Ends: 12/31
2006 Sales: $1,734,900	2006 Profits: $327,600	Parent Company:

SALARIES/BENEFITS:

Pension Plan:	ESOP Stock Plan:	Profit Sharing:	Top Exec. Salary: $424,240	Bonus: $173,195
Savings Plan:	Stock Purch. Plan:		Second Exec. Salary: $333,130	Bonus: $122,300

OTHER THOUGHTS:

Apparent Women Officers or Directors: 2
Hot Spot for Advancement for Women/Minorities:

LOCATIONS: ("Y" = Yes)

West:	Southwest:	Midwest:	Southeast:	Northeast:	International:
Y	Y				Y

ENTERGY CORP

www.entergy.com

Industry Group Code: 221113 **Ranks within this company's industry group:** Sales: 2 Profits: 2

Exploration/Production:		Refining/Retailing:		Utilities:		Alternative Energy:		Specialty Services:		Energy Mktg./Other Svcs.	
Exploration:		Refining:		Electric Utility:	Y	Waste/Solar/Other:	Y	Consulting/Eng.:		Energy Marketing:	Y
Production:		Retailing:		Gas Utility:	Y	Thermal/Steam:	Y	Seismic:		Equipment/Machinery:	
Coal Production:		Convenience Stores:		Pipelines:	Y	Wind:	Y	Drilling:		Oil Field Services:	
		Chemicals:		Water:		Hydro:	Y	InfoTech:		Air/Shipping Transportation:	
						Fuel Cells:		Specialty Services:	Y		

TYPES OF BUSINESS:

Utilities-Electric
Energy Management
Energy Trading
Nuclear Generation
Hydroelectric Generation
Wind Generation

BRANDS/DIVISIONS/AFFILIATES:

Entergy Arkansas, Inc.
Entergy Louisiana LLC
Entergy Mississippi, Inc.
Entergy Texas, Inc.
Entergy New Orleans, Inc.
Entergy Gulf States Louisiana, LLC
Entergy Nuclear, Inc.

CONTACTS: *Note: Officers with more than one job title may be intentionally listed here more than once.*

J. Wayne Leonard, CEO
Mark T. Savoff, COO
Richard Smith, Pres.
Leo Denault, CFO/Exec. VP
Terry Seamons, Sr. VP-Human Resources
Rod West, Chief Admin. Officer
Robert Sloan, General Counsel/Exec. VP
Gary Taylor, Pres., Utility Oper.
Richard Smith, Pres., Entergy Wholesale Commodity Bus.
Joe Domino, Pres./CEO-Entergy Texas, Inc.
John Herron, Pres./Chief Nuclear Officer-Entergy Nuclear
J. Wayne Leonard, Chmn.

Phone: 504-576-4000 **Fax:** 504-576-4428
Toll-Free: 800-368-3749
Address: 639 Loyola Ave., New Orleans, LA 70113 US

GROWTH PLANS/SPECIAL FEATURES:

Entergy Corp. is an integrated energy company engaged primarily in the electric power production and retail electric distribution operations. The company owns and operates power plants with roughly 30,000 megawatts (MW) of electric general capacity, making it one of the largest nuclear power generators in the U.S. The firm operates in two primary segments, utility and non-utility nuclear. The utility segment, which generated 75% of revenue in 2009, generates, transmits, distributes and sells electric power to 2.7 million customers in a four-state service territory that includes portions of Arkansas, Mississippi, Texas and Louisiana, including New Orleans. The division also operates a small natural gas distribution system. The non-utility nuclear segment, responsible for 24% of revenue in 2009, owns and operates six nuclear power plants located in the northeastern U.S. and sells the electric power produced by those plants primarily to wholesale customers. The division also provides services to other nuclear power plant owners. Nuclear operations are carried out by subsidiary, Entergy Nuclear, Inc. In addition to these two segments, Entergy also operates a non-nuclear wholesale assets business, which sells to wholesale customers the electric power produced by power plants that it owns while it focuses on improving performance and exploring sales or restructuring opportunities for its power plants. The remaining 1% of 2009 revenue was contributed by other miscellaneous business segments. The firm has six main regional subsidiaries, all falling under the U.S. utility segment: Entergy Arkansas; Entergy Gulf States of Louisiana; Entergy Louisiana; Entergy Mississippi; Entergy New Orleans; and Entergy Texas.

Employees are offered medical, dental and vision insurance; life insurance; flexible spending accounts; disability coverage; a 401(k) plan; a retirement plan; an employee assistance program; a relocation assistance program; and education reimbursement.

FINANCIALS: **Sales and profits are in thousands of dollars—add 000 to get the full amount. 2010 Note: Financial information for 2010 was not available for all companies at press time.**

2010 Sales: $
2009 Sales: $10,745,650
2008 Sales: $13,093,756
2007 Sales: $11,484,398
2006 Sales: $10,932,158

2010 Profits: $
2009 Profits: $1,251,050
2008 Profits: $1,220,566
2007 Profits: $1,134,849
2006 Profits: $1,132,602

U.S. Stock Ticker: ETR
Int'l Ticker: Int'l Exchange:
Employees: 15,181
Fiscal Year Ends: 12/31
Parent Company:

SALARIES/BENEFITS:

Pension Plan: Y ESOP Stock Plan: Profit Sharing: Top Exec. Salary: $1,341,174 Bonus: $1,782,270
Savings Plan: Y Stock Purch. Plan: Second Exec. Salary: $669,807 Bonus: $755,900

OTHER THOUGHTS:

Apparent Women Officers or Directors: 3
Hot Spot for Advancement for Women/Minorities: Y

LOCATIONS: ("Y" = Yes)

West:	Southwest:	Midwest:	Southeast:	Northeast:	International:
	Y		Y		

ENTERPRISE PRODUCTS PARTNERS LP

www.epplp.com

Industry Group Code: 486 **Ranks within this company's industry group:** Sales: 3 Profits: 3

Exploration/Production:		Refining/Retailing:		Utilities:		Alternative Energy:		Specialty Services:		Energy Mktg./Other Svcs.	
Exploration:		Refining:	Y	Electric Utility:		Waste/Solar/Other:		Consulting/Eng.:		Energy Marketing:	
Production:		Retailing:		Gas Utility:		Thermal/Steam:		Seismic:		Equipment/Machinery:	
Coal Production:		Convenience Stores:		Pipelines:	Y	Wind:		Drilling:		Oil Field Services:	
		Chemicals:	Y	Water:		Hydro:		InfoTech:		Air/Shipping Transportation:	
						Fuel Cells:		Specialty Services:	Y		

TYPES OF BUSINESS:

Pipelines-Natural Gas
Natural Gas Transportation, Processing & Storage
Natural Gas Liquid Fractionation & Processing
Import/Export Terminals

BRANDS/DIVISIONS/AFFILIATES:

TEPPCO Partners LP
Jonah Gas Gathering Company
Rio Grande Pipeline

CONTACTS:

Note: Officers with more than one job title may be intentionally listed here more than once.

Michael A. Creel, CEO
A.J. Teague, COO/Exec. VP
Michael A. Creel, Pres.
W. Randall Fowler, CFO/Exec. VP
Richard H. Bachmann, Chief Legal Officer/Sec./Exec. VP
Michael J. Knesek, Principal Acct. Officer/Controller/Sr. VP
Stephanie C. Hildebrandt, Sr. VP/General Counsel
Thomas M. Zulim, Sr. VP
Rudy Nix, Sr. VP
Leonard Mallett, Sr. VP
Dan L. Duncan, Chmn.

Phone: 713-381-6500	**Fax:** 713-880-6668
Toll-Free:	
Address: 1100 Louisiana St., 10th Fl., Houston, TX 77002 US	

GROWTH PLANS/SPECIAL FEATURES:

Enterprise Products Partners, LP (EPP) provides natural gas processing, natural gas liquids (NGL) fractionation and transportation and storage services to producers and consumers of NGL products. The company is divided into five business segments the offshore pipelines and services; onshore natural gas pipelines and services; natural gas liquids (NGL) pipelines and services; petrochemical and refined products services; and onshore crude oil pipelines and services. The offshore pipelines and services segment manages assets that the company has interest in or owns in the Gulf of Mexico. The onshore natural gas pipelines and services segment oversees approximately 19,200 miles of pipeline systems, transporting gas in Alabama, Louisiana, Mississippi, Texas, New Mexico, Colorado and Wyoming. Enterprise works in the Greater Green River Basin of southwestern Wyoming through a joint venture with TEPPCO Partners L.P. called the Jonah Gas Gathering Company. This segment also owns or leases three salt domes and other natural gas storage facilities. The NGL pipelines and services segment includes about 16,300 miles of pipelines, 25 natural gas processing plants, 11 fractionation plants and storage facilities with a capacity of 163.4 million barrels. The petrochemical services segment includes four propylene fractionation facilities, an isometrization complex and an octane additive production facility, and 738 miles of petrochemical pipeline systems. The onshore crude oil pipelines and services segment includes approximately 4,400 miles of onshore crude oil pipelines and 10.5 million barrels of above ground storage tank capacity. In October 2009, the firm merged with TEPPCO Partners L.P.; the new company has retained the name Enterprise Products Partners LP. In December 2009, the firm acquired three Louisiana intrastate NGL pipeline systems totaling 212 miles from Chevron Midstream Pipelines LLC; and wholly-owned subsidiary Enterprise Products Operation LLC acquired a 70% interest in the Rio Grande Pipeline from HEP Navajo Southern, L.P.

FINANCIALS:

Sales and profits are in thousands of dollars—add 000 to get the full amount. 2010 Note: Financial information for 2010 was not available for all companies at press time.

2010 Sales: $	2010 Profits: $	**U.S. Stock Ticker: EPD**
2009 Sales: $25,510,900	2009 Profits: $1,155,100	**Int'l Ticker:** Int'l Exchange:
2008 Sales: $35,469,600	2008 Profits: $954,021	Employees: 4,800
2007 Sales: $26,713,800	2007 Profits: $533,674	Fiscal Year Ends: 12/31
2006 Sales: $13,990,969	2006 Profits: $601,155	Parent Company:

SALARIES/BENEFITS:

Pension Plan: Y	ESOP Stock Plan:	Profit Sharing:	Top Exec. Salary: $650,000	Bonus: $950,000
Savings Plan: Y	Stock Purch. Plan:		Second Exec. Salary: $580,000	Bonus: $1,280,000

OTHER THOUGHTS:

Apparent Women Officers or Directors: 2
Hot Spot for Advancement for Women/Minorities:

LOCATIONS: ("Y" = Yes)

West:	Southwest:	Midwest:	Southeast:	Northeast:	International:
Y	Y	Y	Y		

EOG RESOURCES INC

www.eogresources.com

Industry Group Code: 211111 **Ranks within this company's industry group:** Sales: 59 Profits: 46

Exploration/Production:		Refining/Retailing:		Utilities:		Alternative Energy:		Specialty Services:		Energy Mktg./Other Svcs.	
Exploration:	Y	Refining:		Electric Utility:		Waste/Solar/Other:		Consulting/Eng.:		Energy Marketing:	Y
Production:	Y	Retailing:		Gas Utility:		Thermal/Steam:		Seismic:	Y	Equipment/Machinery:	
Coal Production:		Convenience Stores:		Pipelines:		Wind:		Drilling:		Oil Field Services:	
		Chemicals:		Water:		Hydro:		InfoTech:		Air/Shipping Transportation:	
						Fuel Cells:	--	Specialty Services:			

TYPES OF BUSINESS:

Oil & Gas Exploration & Production
Energy Marketing

BRANDS/DIVISIONS/AFFILIATES:

Enron Oil & Gas Company
EOG Resources Canada, Inc.
Galveston LNG, Inc.

CONTACTS:

Note: Officers with more than one job title may be intentionally listed here more than once.

Mark G. Papa, CEO
Timothy K. Driggers, CFO/VP
Marc R. Eschenburg, VP-Mktg. & Regulatory Affairs
Patricia L. Edwards, VP-Human Resources
Sandeep Bhakhri, CIO/VP
Patricia L. Edwards, VP-Admin.
Frederick J. Plaeger, II, General Counsel/Sr. VP
Gary L. Thomas, Sr. Exec. VP-Oper.
Maire A. Baldwin, VP-Investor Rel.
Ann D. Jansen, VP-Acct.
Loren M. Leiker, Sr. Exec. VP-Exploration
Kurt D. Doerr, Exec. VP/Gen. Mgr.-Denver
Micheal P. Donaldson, Corp. Sec.
Robert C. Smith, VP-Drilling
Mark G. Papa, Chmn.
Lindell L. Looger, VP/Gen. Mgr.-Int'l/Pres., EOG Resources Int'l Inc.

Phone: 713-651-7000 **Fax:** 713-651-6995
Toll-Free: 877-363-3647
Address: 1111 Bagby, Sky Lobby 2, Houston, TX 77002-7361 US

GROWTH PLANS/SPECIAL FEATURES:

EOG Resources, Inc. (EOG), formerly Enron Oil and Gas Company, is one of the largest independent oil and gas companies in the U.S. Together with its subsidiaries, EOG explores for, develops, produces and markets natural gas and crude oil in the U.S., Canada, Trinidad, the U.K. and other international areas. EOG's total estimated net proved reserves are 10,776 billion cubic feet, of which 8,898 billion cubic feet are natural gas reserves and 220 million barrels are crude oil, condensate and natural gas liquids (NGL) reserves. Approximately 75% of these reserves are located in the U.S., 16% in Canada and 9% in Trinidad. In the U.S., EOG produced an average of 400 million cubic feet per day (MMcfd) of natural gas and 13.1 thousand barrels per day of crude oil, condensate and NGL at its Fort Worth Basin Barnett Shale play. Additional key producing areas in the U.S. include the Upper Gulf Coast, the Permian Basin, the Rocky Mountains area, the Mid-Continent area, South Texas, the Gulf of Mexico and the Appalachian Basin. In Canada, EOG conducts business through its subsidiary, EOG Resources Canada, Inc. Key producing areas in Canada are the Southeast Alberta/Southwest Saskatchewan shallow natural gas trends including the Drumheller, Twining and Halkirk areas, the Pembina/Highvale area of Central Alberta, the grand Prairie/Wapiti area of Northwest Alberta and the Waskada area in Southwest Manitoba. In May 2010, the firm's subsidiary EOG Resources Canada, Inc. acquired Galveston LNG, Inc.

EOG offers employees comprehensive benefits including retirement plans; flex dollars; flexible work schedules; life, medical, dental and vision insurance; long-term disability, accidental death and dismemberment insurance; healthcare and dependent daycare spending accounts; and retirement health plans.

FINANCIALS:

Sales and profits are in thousands of dollars—add 000 to get the full amount. 2010 Note: Financial information for 2010 was not available for all companies at press time.

2010 Sales: $	2010 Profits: $	**U.S. Stock Ticker: EOG**
2009 Sales: $4,786,959	2009 Profits: $546,627	**Int'l Ticker:** Int'l Exchange:
2008 Sales: $7,127,143	2008 Profits: $2,436,476	Employees: 2,100
2007 Sales: $4,239,303	2007 Profits: $1,083,255	Fiscal Year Ends: 12/31
2006 Sales: $3,912,542	2006 Profits: $1,299,885	Parent Company:

SALARIES/BENEFITS:

Pension Plan: Y	ESOP Stock Plan:	Profit Sharing:	Top Exec. Salary: $976,154	Bonus: $825,000
Savings Plan: Y	Stock Purch. Plan: Y		Second Exec. Salary: $602,481	Bonus: $540,000

OTHER THOUGHTS:

Apparent Women Officers or Directors: 6
Hot Spot for Advancement for Women/Minorities: Y

LOCATIONS: ("Y" = Yes)

West:	Southwest:	Midwest:	Southeast:	Northeast:	International:
Y	Y	Y	Y	Y	Y

EPCOR UTILITIES INC

www.epcor.ca

Industry Group Code: 221 **Ranks within this company's industry group:** Sales: Profits:

Exploration/Production:		**Refining/Retailing:**		**Utilities:**		**Alternative Energy:**		**Specialty Services:**		**Energy Mktg./Other Svcs.**	
Exploration:		Refining:		Electric Utility:	Y	Waste/Solar/Other:		Consulting/Eng.:	Y	Energy Marketing:	Y
Production:		Retailing:		Gas Utility:		Thermal/Steam:		Seismic:		Equipment/Machinery:	
Coal Production:		Convenience Stores:		Pipelines:		Wind:		Drilling:		Oil Field Services:	
		Chemicals:		Water:	Y	Hydro:		InfoTech:		Air/Shipping Transportation:	
						Fuel Cells:		Specialty Services:	Y		

TYPES OF BUSINESS:

Electric Utility
Power Plants
Energy Marketing
Water Utility
Financial Services
Construction Services

BRANDS/DIVISIONS/AFFILIATES:

EPCOR Water Services, Inc.
EPCOR Distribution & Transmissions, Inc.
EPCOR Energy Alberta, Inc.
EPCOR Power Development Corporation
EPCOR Power L.P.

CONTACTS:

Note: Officers with more than one job title may be intentionally listed here more than once.

Don Lowry, CEO
Don Lowry, Pres.
Mark Wiltzen, CFO/Sr. VP
Robert Petryk, Sr. VP-Human Resources
Joe Gysel, Sr. VP-Water Dev.
Wray Steedsman, CIO/Sr. VP-Info. Svcs.
Guy Bridgeman, Sr. VP-Strategic Planning & Dev.
Stephen Stanley, Sr. VP-Water Svcs.
Doreen Cole, Sr. VP-Electricity Svcs.
Hugh J. Bolton, Chmn.

Phone: 780-412-3414	**Fax:** 780-412-3096
Toll-Free: 800-324-1725	
Address: 10065 Jasper Ave., Edmonton, AB T5J 3B1 Canada	

GROWTH PLANS/SPECIAL FEATURES:

EPCOR Utilities, Inc. is a government-owned integrated energy provider, offering power and water solutions to customers in Canada and the U.S. These facilities generate power from renewable resources, wind, small hydro, biomass, landfill gas and waste heat recovery (wood chips, discarded tires). The company's operations are divided among EPCOR Water Services, Inc. (EWSI); EPCOR Distribution & Transmissions, Inc. (EDTI); EPCOR Energy Alberta, Inc.(EEAI); and EPCOR Power Development Corporation (EPDC). EWSI provides water, wastewater and distribution services to over 1 million people in more than 60 communities across Western Canada. EDTI operates electric and power transmission systems, controls the transmission of electricity (i.e., regulating voltages) and distributes it to customers. EEAI provides regulated rate electricity service to residential, farm and small commercial business consumers, as well as providing customer care (including call center and billing services) for EPCOR companies (including water, natural gas and electricity). EPDC is a developer, builder and operator of non-regulated power plants in North America. EPCOR Utilities is owned by the city of Edmonton, in which the company is headquartered. In October 2009, the firm acquired the potable water and wastewater facilities, as well as certain wastewater operations, at three Suncor Energy oil sands sites for approximately $100 million through a sale lease-back agreement. In June 2010, the company agreed to acquire Arizona-based utility Chaparral City Water Company from American States Water Company for roughly $35 million.

FINANCIALS:

Sales and profits are in thousands of dollars—add 000 to get the full amount. 2010 Note: Financial information for 2010 was not available for all companies at press time.

2010 Sales: $	2010 Profits: $	**U.S. Stock Ticker: Government-Owned**
2009 Sales: $	2009 Profits: $	**Int'l Ticker:** Int'l Exchange:
2008 Sales: $	2008 Profits: $	Employees:
2007 Sales: $3,031,250	2007 Profits: $226,907	Fiscal Year Ends: 12/31
2006 Sales: $3,153,190	2006 Profits: $690,820	Parent Company:

SALARIES/BENEFITS:

Pension Plan:	ESOP Stock Plan:	Profit Sharing:	Top Exec. Salary: $	Bonus: $
Savings Plan:	Stock Purch. Plan:		Second Exec. Salary: $	Bonus: $

OTHER THOUGHTS:

Apparent Women Officers or Directors: 3
Hot Spot for Advancement for Women/Minorities: Y

LOCATIONS: ("Y" = Yes)

West:	Southwest:	Midwest:	Southeast:	Northeast:	International:
Y				Y	Y

EQT CORPORATION

www.eqt.com

Industry Group Code: 221210 **Ranks within this company's industry group:** Sales: 17 Profits: 10

Exploration/Production:		**Refining/Retailing:**		**Utilities:**		**Alternative Energy:**		**Specialty Services:**		**Energy Mktg./Other Svcs.**	
Exploration:	Y	Refining:		Electric Utility:		Waste/Solar/Other:		Consulting/Eng.:	Y	Energy Marketing:	Y
Production:	Y	Retailing:		Gas Utility:	Y	Thermal/Steam:		Seismic:		Equipment/Machinery:	
Coal Production:		Convenience Stores:		Pipelines:	Y	Wind:		Drilling:		Oil Field Services:	
		Chemicals:		Water:		Hydro:		InfoTech:		Air/Shipping Transportation:	
						Fuel Cells:		Specialty Services:	Y		

TYPES OF BUSINESS:

Utilities-Natural Gas
Pipelines
Well Operations
Gas Production
Plant Design, Construction & Management
Energy Marketing

BRANDS/DIVISIONS/AFFILIATES:

Equitable Resources Inc
EQT Production
EQT Midstream
EQT Distribution
DCP Midstream Partners
DCP Midstream LLC

CONTACTS:

Note: Officers with more than one job title may be intentionally listed here more than once.

David L. Porges, CEO
David L. Porges, Pres.
Philip P. Conti, CFO/Sr. VP
Charlene G. Petrelli, Chief Human Resources Officer/VP
Steven T. Schlotterbeck, Sr. VP/Pres., Prod. & Exploration
Lewis B. Gardner, General Counsel/VP
Randall L. Crawford, Sr. VP/Pres., Midstream & Commercial
M. Elise Hyland, VP/Pres., Commercial Oper.
Martin A. Fritz, VP/Pres., Midstream
Murry S. Gerber, Chmn.
Randall L. Crawford, Sr. VP-Dist.

Phone: 412-553-5700 **Fax:** 412-553-5757
Toll-Free:
Address: 625 Liberty Ave., Ste. 1700, Pittsburgh, PA 15222 US

GROWTH PLANS/SPECIAL FEATURES:

EQT Corporation, formerly Equitable Resources, Inc., is a fully integrated energy exploration, production, transmission, distribution and marketing company, focusing on Appalachian-area natural gas supply activities. EQT offers energy products, including natural gas, natural gas liquids, crude oil, and services to wholesale and retail customers. It currently operates in three divisions: EQT Production, EQT Midstream and EQT Distribution. The EQT Production segment includes the company's exploration for, and development and production of, natural gas, and a limited amount of crude oil, in the Appalachian Basin which has 4.1 trillion cubic feet of proved reserves across approximately 3.4 million acres. EQT Midstream's operations include the natural gas gathering, processing, transportation and storage activities of the firm; sales of natural gas liquids from 10,650 miles of gathering lines; and 970 miles of transmission lines. EQT Distribution's operations included the distribution and sale of natural gas to commercial, industrial and residential costumers in southwestern Pennsylvania, eastern Kentucky and West Virginia. In early 2009, the company launched the Big Sandy line, a pipe line in Prestonburg, Kentucky, that transports gas approximately 70 miles from the firm's Langley processing plant in Floyd County, Kentucky. In May 2010, the firm agreed to partner with DCP Midstream Partners and DCP Midstream LLC to form a NGL joint venture in the Huron and Marcellus shale areas of the Appalachian basin.

EQT Corporation offers employees benefits including spouse, child medical, dental, vision, life and accident death and dismemberment insurance, a wellness program; short and long-term disability insurance; computer purchase, employee assistance and education assistance programs; and credit union, saving bonds and commuter reimbursement accounts.

FINANCIALS:

Sales and profits are in thousands of dollars—add 000 to get the full amount. 2010 Note: Financial information for 2010 was not available for all companies at press time.

2010 Sales: $	2010 Profits: $	**U.S. Stock Ticker: EQT**
2009 Sales: $1,269,827	2009 Profits: $156,929	**Int'l Ticker:** Int'l Exchange:
2008 Sales: $1,576,488	2008 Profits: $255,604	Employees: 1,800
2007 Sales: $1,361,406	2007 Profits: $257,483	Fiscal Year Ends: 12/31
2006 Sales: $1,267,910	2006 Profits: $220,286	Parent Company:

SALARIES/BENEFITS:

Pension Plan: Y	ESOP Stock Plan:	Profit Sharing:	Top Exec. Salary: $750,000	Bonus: $2,240,000
Savings Plan: Y	Stock Purch. Plan: Y		Second Exec. Salary: $520,000	Bonus: $1,123,200

OTHER THOUGHTS:

Apparent Women Officers or Directors: 2
Hot Spot for Advancement for Women/Minorities: Y

LOCATIONS: ("Y" = Yes)

West:	Southwest:	Midwest:	Southeast:	Northeast:	International:
		Y	Y	Y	

Note: Financial information, benefits and other data can change quickly and may vary from those stated here.

ERGON INC

www.ergon.com

Industry Group Code: 324110 **Ranks within this company's industry group:** Sales: 27 Profits:

Exploration/Production:		Refining/Retailing:		Utilities:		Alternative Energy:		Specialty Services:		Energy Mktg./Other Svcs.	
Exploration:	Y	Refining:	Y	Electric Utility:		Waste/Solar/Other:		Consulting/Eng.:		Energy Marketing:	
Production:		Retailing:	Y	Gas Utility:		Thermal/Steam:		Seismic:		Equipment/Machinery:	Y
Coal Production:		Convenience Stores:		Pipelines:		Wind:		Drilling:		Oil Field Services:	
		Chemicals:	Y	Water:		Hydro:		InfoTech:		Air/Shipping Transportation:	Y
						Fuel Cells:		Specialty Services:	Y		

TYPES OF BUSINESS:

Petroleum Refining
Transportation-River, Rail & Road
Gas Retail
Gas Exploration
Technology Development
Real Estate
Asphalt & Emulsions
Petrochemicals

BRANDS/DIVISIONS/AFFILIATES:

Crafo Inc
Ergon Trucking
Magnolia Marine Transport Company
Ergon Exploration Inc
Lampton-Love Inc
Ergon Marine & Industrial Supply Inc
Diversified Technology Inc
Ergon Properties Inc

CONTACTS:

Note: Officers with more than one job title may be intentionally listed here more than once.

Leslie Lampton III, Pres., Petroleum Specialties Mktg. Div.
Jimmy Rasco, VP-Global Oil Tech.
Jim Temple, Dir.-Comm.
Craig Busbea, VP-Petroleum Specialties Mktg. Div.
Ed Hudgins, Sr. VP-Petroleum Specialties Mktg. Div.
Leslie B. Lampton, Sr., Chmn.
Craig Busbea, VP-North & South America

Phone: 601-933-3000 **Fax:** 601-933-3350
Toll-Free:
Address: P.O. Box 1639, Jackson, MS 39215-1639 US

GROWTH PLANS/SPECIAL FEATURES:

Ergon, Inc. is a diversified company operating in the refining, marketing, asphalt, emulsions, transportation, terminaling, embedded computing, oil and gas and real estate industries. The company operates three crude oil refineries: the Ergon Refining facility in Mississippi, which produces petroleum and asphalt products including naphthenic oils; Ergon-West Virginia, which employs very high-pressure catalytic hydrotreating technology to process selected Appalachian paraffinic lube crudes; and the Lion Oil refinery in El Dorado, Arkansas, which processes sour crude into products such as gasoline, distillates, propane, solvents, asphalts and protective coatings, and operates its own fuel terminals in El Dorado, Arkansas and Memphis, Tennessee. Ergon also has an asphalt and emulsions plant in Memphis under the name Ertech and a subsidiary, Crafo, Inc., which manufactures more than 50 types of asphalt crack sealants in Arizona, Tennessee and Pennsylvania and has supply centers in California and Oregon that distribute products internationally. The firm offers transportation services through subsidiaries Ergon Trucking, Ergon Terminaling, Inc., and Magnolia Marine Transport Company, with a national network of storage terminals and a fleet of 250 trucks and trailers, 17 towboats and 60 barges. Subsidiary Ergon Exploration, Inc. develops natural gas wells and Lampton-Love, Inc. distributes liquefied petroleum gas to 80,000 retail and wholesale customers in the mid-South. Ergon Marine & Industrial Supply, Inc. markets and distributes diesel fuel daily on the Mississippi River through a fleet of towboats and barges operating from terminals in Vicksburg, Mississippi and Memphis, Tennessee. Subsidiary Diversified Technology, Inc. designs and manufactures processor boards, fabric switching products and embedded systems for modular computing. Ergon Properties, Inc. provides mixed-use retail developments, residential developments, commercial and industrial facilities, land management and property management. In May 2009, subsidiary Ergon Asphalt & Emulsions, Inc. added 20 new facilities to its existing network of terminal facilities and will more than double the production capacity of products.

FINANCIALS:

Sales and profits are in thousands of dollars—add 000 to get the full amount. 2010 Note: Financial information for 2010 was not available for all companies at press time.

2010 Sales: $	2010 Profits: $	**U.S. Stock Ticker: Private**
2009 Sales: $3,830,000	2009 Profits: $	**Int'l Ticker:** Int'l Exchange:
2008 Sales: $5,430,000	2008 Profits: $	Employees: 3,000
2007 Sales: $	2007 Profits: $	Fiscal Year Ends: 12/31
2006 Sales: $4,110,000	2006 Profits: $	Parent Company:

SALARIES/BENEFITS:

Pension Plan:	ESOP Stock Plan:	Profit Sharing:	Top Exec. Salary: $	Bonus: $
Savings Plan:	Stock Purch. Plan:		Second Exec. Salary: $	Bonus: $

OTHER THOUGHTS:

Apparent Women Officers or Directors:
Hot Spot for Advancement for Women/Minorities:

LOCATIONS: ("Y" = Yes)

West:	Southwest:	Midwest:	Southeast:	Northeast:	International:
Y	Y	Y	Y	Y	Y

ESSAR GROUP LTD

www.essar.com

Industry Group Code: 523910 **Ranks within this company's industry group:** Sales: Profits:

Exploration/Production:		Refining/Retailing:		Utilities:		Alternative Energy:		Specialty Services:		Energy Mktg./Other Svcs.	
Exploration:	Y	Refining:	Y	Electric Utility:	Y	Waste/Solar/Other:		Consulting/Eng.:	Y	Energy Marketing:	Y
Production:	Y	Retailing:	Y	Gas Utility:		Thermal/Steam:		Seismic:		Equipment/Machinery:	Y
Coal Production:		Convenience Stores:		Pipelines:		Wind:		Drilling:	Y	Oil Field Services:	Y
		Chemicals:		Water:		Hydro:		InfoTech:		Air/Shipping Transportation:	Y
						Fuel Cells:		Specialty Services:	Y		

TYPES OF BUSINESS:

Private Equity Investments
Oil & Gas
Electric Generation
Logistics & Shipping
Steel
Construction
Communications Investments
Trucking

BRANDS/DIVISIONS/AFFILIATES:

Essar Steel
Hypermart
Essar Oil
Essar Energy
Essar Power
Essar Communications Holdings Ltd.
Vodaphone
MobileStore Ltd. (The)

CONTACTS:

Note: Officers with more than one job title may be intentionally listed here more than once.

Prashant Ruia, CEO
V. Ashok, CFO
Adil Malia, Pres., Human Resources
Shishir Agarwal, CEO-Exploration & Prod. Bus. Group
Vikash Saraf, Dir.-Strategy, Planning, Mergers & Acquisitions
Ganesh Pai, Gen. Mgr.-Corp. Comm.
Malay Mukherjee, CEO-Steel Bus. Group
Pradeep Mittal, CEO-Minerals & Mining Bus. Group
Naresh Nayyar, CEO-Energy Bus. Group
Shashi Ruia, Chmn.

Phone: 91-22-5001-1100	**Fax:** 91-22-6660-1809
Toll-Free:	
Address: Essar House, 11 Kesharao Khadye Marg, Mumbai, 400 034 India	

GROWTH PLANS/SPECIAL FEATURES:

The Essar Group, Ltd., based in Mumbai, is a multinational conglomerate active in the steel, energy, oil & gas, communications, construction and shipping industries, as well as other various activities. Essar Steel is an integrated flat carbon steel manufacturer with a production capacity of nearly 9.5 million tons per year. The division is involved in all aspects of production and distribution; from mining iron ore to 474 end user distribution outlets known as Essar Hypermarts. The Essar Energy Group comprises Essar Oil & Gas and Essar Power. Essar Oil operations include exploration and production of oil and gas, as well as refining and retail distribution through more than 1,300 Essar-branded service stations across India. Essar Power operates four power plants with a combined capacity of 1,220 megawatts (MW). It is currently constructing additional plants to add another 5,370 MW to its portfolio. The communications division, under Essar Communications Holdings Ltd, is partner to a joint venture with U.K. firm Vodaphone that offers GSM-based mobile telephony; has a 14% stake in Indus Towers; operates a chain of 1,300 telecom retail outlets, The MobileStore Ltd.; and through Aegis Ltd., offers integrated IT services and business process outsourcing. Essar Projects Limited is a global engineering, procurement and construction company headquartered in Dubai. Essar Shipping ports & logistics operates ports and terminals for crude oil, petroleum and coal; owns 27 sea transportation vessels; and manages an oilfield drilling business that offers on- and offshore contract drilling, with a fleet of 12 onshore rigs and one semi-submersible offshore rig. Other business areas the group is involved in include realty, minerals & mining, financial services (Essar Capital), publishing (Paprika Media) and agribusiness. In 2010, the group made several acquisitions: in May, Sallie Mae's customer service center in Texas; in June, Servosteel, a leading steel processor in the U.K.; in September, a controlling stake in AGC Networks Ltd.; and in October, the outsourcing firm Actionline based in Argentina.

FINANCIALS:

Sales and profits are in thousands of dollars—add 000 to get the full amount. 2010 Note: Financial information for 2010 was not available for all companies at press time.

2010 Sales: $	2010 Profits: $	**U.S. Stock Ticker: Private**
2009 Sales: $	2009 Profits: $	**Int'l Ticker:** Int'l Exchange:
2008 Sales: $	2008 Profits: $	Employees:
2007 Sales: $	2007 Profits: $	Fiscal Year Ends:
2006 Sales: $	2006 Profits: $	Parent Company:

SALARIES/BENEFITS:

Pension Plan:	ESOP Stock Plan:	Profit Sharing:	Top Exec. Salary: $	Bonus: $
Savings Plan:	Stock Purch. Plan:		Second Exec. Salary: $	Bonus: $

OTHER THOUGHTS:

Apparent Women Officers or Directors: 1
Hot Spot for Advancement for Women/Minorities:

LOCATIONS: ("Y" = Yes)

West:	Southwest:	Midwest:	Southeast:	Northeast:	International:
	Y			Y	Y

EVONIK INDUSTRIES AG

www.evonik.com

Industry Group Code: 325 **Ranks within this company's industry group:** Sales: 4 Profits: 3

Exploration/Production:		**Refining/Retailing:**		**Utilities:**		**Alternative Energy:**		**Specialty Services:**		**Energy Mktg./Other Svcs.**	
Exploration:		Refining:		Electric Utility:	Y	Waste/Solar/Other:	Y	Consulting/Eng.:		Energy Marketing:	
Production:		Retailing:		Gas Utility:		Thermal/Steam:		Seismic:		Equipment/Machinery:	
Coal Production:		Convenience Stores:		Pipelines:		Wind:		Drilling:		Oil Field Services:	
		Chemicals:		Water:		Hydro:		InfoTech:		Air/Shipping Transportation:	
						Fuel Cells:		Specialty Services:			

TYPES OF BUSINESS:

Chemicals, Manufacturing
Industrial Engineering
Electricity Generation
Real Estate
Renewable Energy-Biomass

BRANDS/DIVISIONS/AFFILIATES:

Evonik Degussa
STEAG
RAG Immobilien
MADAME
2-EHMA
n-BUMA
i-BUMA

CONTACTS: *Note: Officers with more than one job title may be intentionally listed here more than once.*

Klaus Engel, CEO
Wolfgang Colberg, CFO
Ralf Blauth, Chief Human Resources Officer
Wilhelm Bonse-Geuking, Chmn.

Phone: 49-201-177-01	**Fax:** 49-201-177-3475
Toll-Free:	
Address: Rellinghauser Strasse 1-11, Essen, 45128 Germany	

GROWTH PLANS/SPECIAL FEATURES:

Evonik Industries AG is an international industrial group with activities in more than 100 countries worldwide. The firm operates through three primary business areas: chemicals, energy and real estate. The chemicals segment, operating under subsidiary Evonik Degussa GmbH serves the automobile, plastics and rubbers, pharmaceutical, biotechnology, cosmetics, paint and sealants and adhesives industries. This segment has a strong focus on research and development. The energy segment, operating under subsidiary STEAG GmbH, focuses on coal-fired power generation, with capabilities spanning project development, financing, plant construction and operation. Internationally, this segment has power stations in Turkey, Columbia and the Philippines. This segment also offers Clean Competitive Electricity from Coal (CCEC) technology with 45% increased efficiency that is safer and more environment-friendly than conventional power stations. The energy segment is also engaged in renewable energy sources, including biomass, biogas, geothermal and mine gas, maintaining 10 biomass power plants. The real estate segment, operating under subsidiary RAG Immobilien, maintains housing units in Germany, focusing on the Ruhr region, Aachen and the northern Rhine cities of Düsseldorf, Cologne and Bonn. In March 2010, the firm acquired the Methacrylate Specialty Esters operations of Arkema, including the following monomer products: Dimethylaminoethyl Methacrylate (MADAME), 2-Ethylhexyl Methacrylate (2-EHMA) and n-/i-Butyl Methacrylate (n-BUMA and i-BUMA).

FINANCIALS: **Sales and profits are in thousands of dollars—add 000 to get the full amount. 2010 Note: Financial information for 2010 was not available for all companies at press time.**

2010 Sales: $	2010 Profits: $	**U.S. Stock Ticker: Private**
2009 Sales: $16,030,300	2009 Profits: $294,220	**Int'l Ticker:** Int'l Exchange:
2008 Sales: $21,002,200	2008 Profits: $377,100	Employees:
2007 Sales: $19,603,000	2007 Profits: $1,190,040	Fiscal Year Ends: 12/31
2006 Sales: $19,188,700	2006 Profits: $1,420,980	Parent Company:

SALARIES/BENEFITS:

Pension Plan:	ESOP Stock Plan:	Profit Sharing:	Top Exec. Salary: $	Bonus: $
Savings Plan:	Stock Purch. Plan:		Second Exec. Salary: $	Bonus: $

OTHER THOUGHTS:

Apparent Women Officers or Directors:
Hot Spot for Advancement for Women/Minorities:

LOCATIONS: ("Y" = Yes)

West:	Southwest:	Midwest:	Southeast:	Northeast:	International:
					Y

EXCO RESOURCES INC

www.excoresources.com

Industry Group Code: 211111 **Ranks within this company's industry group:** Sales: 93 Profits: 103

Exploration/Production:		Refining/Retailing:		Utilities:		Alternative Energy:		Specialty Services:		Energy Mktg./Other Svcs.	
Exploration:	Y	Refining:		Electric Utility:		Waste/Solar/Other:		Consulting/Eng.:		Energy Marketing:	
Production:	Y	Retailing:		Gas Utility:		Thermal/Steam:		Seismic:		Equipment/Machinery:	
Coal Production:		Convenience Stores:		Pipelines:		Wind:		Drilling:		Oil Field Services:	
		Chemicals:		Water:		Hydro:		InfoTech:		Air/Shipping Transportation:	
						Fuel Cells:		Specialty Services:			

TYPES OF BUSINESS:

Oil & Gas Exploration & Production

BRANDS/DIVISIONS/AFFILIATES:

BG Group plc
Common Resources LLC

CONTACTS:

Note: Officers with more than one job title may be intentionally listed here more than once.

Douglas H. Miller, CEO
Harold L. Hickey, COO/VP
Stephen F. Smith, Pres./Vice Chmn.
Stephen F. Smith, CFO
Steve Estes, VP-Mktg.
Joe D. Ford, VP-Human Resources
Robert L. Thomas, CIO
Marcia R. Simpson, VP-Eng.
William L. Boeing, General Counsel/VP/Corp. Sec.
Michael R. Chambers, VP-Oper.
John D. Jacobi, Exec. VP-Bus. Dev. & Mktg.
Mark E. Wilson, Chief Acct. Officer/Controller/VP
Michael R. Chambers, Gen. Mgr.-East Texas & North Louisiana Div.
Stephen E. Puckett, VP-Reservoir Eng.
J. Douglas Ramsey, VP-Finance/Treas.
Tommy Knowles, VP/Gen. Mgr.-Permian Div.
Douglas H. Miller, Chmn.

Phone: 214-368-2084	**Fax:** 214-368-2087
Toll-Free:	
Address: 12377 Merit Dr., Ste. 1700, Dallas, TX 75251 US	

GROWTH PLANS/SPECIAL FEATURES:

EXCO Resources, Inc. is an independent oil and natural gas company engaged in the exploration, exploitation, development and production of onshore North American oil and natural gas properties. The company's operations are focused in key oil and natural gas areas, including East Texas, North Louisiana, Appalachia and the Permian Basin in West Texas. In addition, the firm has midstream operations in East Texas, North Louisiana and Appalachia. The firm has proved reserves of about 1 trillion cubic feet equivalent, of which 96.5% is natural gas and 67.1% is proved developed reserves. In its East Texas and North Louisiana areas, it has significant holdings in the Haynesville, Bossier and Marcellus shale resource play. The firm's growth strategy centers on furthering development and exploitation of these resources plays, primarily through horizontal drilling. In June 2009, the firm opened a new Haynesville Shale Field Office and broke ground on a new, state-of-the-art Haynesville Shale Gas Gathering and Treating Facility in Grand Cane, Louisiana. During 2009, EXCO divested certain producing assets in Oklahoma, Kansas, Ohio, Northwestern Pennsylvania and the Texas Panhandle, including all of its mid-continent assets. In April 2010, the company agreed to acquire Common Resources LLC jointly with BG Group plc. Each company will retain a 50% stake in Common Resources. In June 2010, the firm sold its 50% stake in its Appalachian midstream joint venture to BG Group. Also in June 2010, EXCO and BG Group jointly acquired Haynesville and Bossier shale properties in Shelby, San Augustine and Nacogdoches Counties, Texas.

The company offers its employees medical, dental and vision coverage; life and disability insurance; reimbursement accounts; education assistance; emergency travel assistance; employee assistance programs; a 401(k) plan; and Sam's Club memberships.

FINANCIALS:

Sales and profits are in thousands of dollars—add 000 to get the full amount. 2010 Note: Financial information for 2010 was not available for all companies at press time.

2010 Sales: $	2010 Profits: $	**U.S. Stock Ticker: XCO**
2009 Sales: $585,835	2009 Profits: $-496,804	**Int'l Ticker:** Int'l Exchange:
2008 Sales: $1,490,258	2008 Profits: $-1,733,471	Employees: 802
2007 Sales: $894,604	2007 Profits: $49,656	Fiscal Year Ends: 12/31
2006 Sales: $559,449	2006 Profits: $138,954	Parent Company:

SALARIES/BENEFITS:

Pension Plan:	ESOP Stock Plan:	Profit Sharing:	Top Exec. Salary: $800,000	Bonus: $320,000
Savings Plan: Y	Stock Purch. Plan:		Second Exec. Salary: $600,000	Bonus: $240,000

OTHER THOUGHTS:

Apparent Women Officers or Directors: 1
Hot Spot for Advancement for Women/Minorities:

LOCATIONS: ("Y" = Yes)

West:	Southwest:	Midwest:	Southeast:	Northeast:	International:
	Y	Y	Y	Y	

Note: Financial information, benefits and other data can change quickly and may vary from those stated here.

EXELON CORPORATION

www.exeloncorp.com

Industry Group Code: 221 **Ranks within this company's industry group:** Sales: 7 Profits: 4

Exploration/Production:		Refining/Retailing:		Utilities:		Alternative Energy:		Specialty Services:		Energy Mktg./Other Svcs.	
Exploration:		Refining:		Electric Utility:	Y	Waste/Solar/Other:	Y	Consulting/Eng.:		Energy Marketing:	Y
Production:		Retailing:		Gas Utility:	Y	Thermal/Steam:		Seismic:		Equipment/Machinery:	
Coal Production:		Convenience Stores:		Pipelines:		Wind:		Drilling:		Oil Field Services:	
		Chemicals:		Water:		Hydro:	Y	InfoTech:		Air/Shipping Transportation:	
						Fuel Cells:		Specialty Services:	Y		

TYPES OF BUSINESS:

Utilities-Electricity & Natural Gas
Nuclear Generation
Energy Marketing

BRANDS/DIVISIONS/AFFILIATES:

Commonwealth Edison Company
PECO Energy Company
Exelon Generation Company LLC
Exelon Business Services Company
SunPower Corporation
Exelon Transmission Company

CONTACTS:

Note: Officers with more than one job title may be intentionally listed here more than once.

John W. Rowe, CEO
Christopher M. Crane, COO
Christopher M. Crane, Pres.
Matthew F. Helzinger, CFO/Sr. VP
Ruth Ann M. Gillis, Chief Diversity Officer
Ruth Ann M. Gillis, Exec. VP-Admin.
Ian P. McLean, Exec. VP-Dev.
Stacy Frank, VP-Investor Rel.
William A. Von Hoene, Jr., Exec. VP-Finance & Legal
Frank Clark, CEO/Chmn.-ComEd
Denis P. O'Brien, Pres./CEO-PECO Energy
Sonny Garg, Pres., Exelon Power
Ruth Ann M. Gillis, Pres., Exelon Bus. Services Co.
John W. Rowe, Chmn.

Phone: 312-394-7398 **Fax:**
Toll-Free: 800-483-3220
Address: 10 S. Dearborn St., 48th Fl., Chicago, IL 60680-5398 US

GROWTH PLANS/SPECIAL FEATURES:

Exelon Corporation is a utility services company that operates through subsidiaries Exelon Generation Company LLC; Exelon Transmission Company; Commonwealth Edison Company (ComEd); and PECO Energy Company. Exelon Generation's operates in three business units: Exelon Power, Exelon Generation and Power Team. The business consists of its owned and contracted electric generating facilities; its wholesale energy marketing operations; and its competitive retail supply operations. The subsidiary owns generation assets, which include nuclear, fossil, renewable and hydropower, with an aggregate net capacity of nearly 33 gigawatts (GW). ComEd's energy delivery business consists of the purchase and regulated retail sale of electricity and the provision of distribution and transmission services to over 3.8 million retail, commercial and industrial customers in northern Illinois. The subsidiary's retail service territory has an area of roughly 11,400 square miles and an estimated population of 8 million. PECO's energy delivery business consists of the purchase and regulated retail sale of electricity; and the provision of distribution and transmission services to retail customers in southeastern Pennsylvania, including Philadelphia, as well as surrounding counties. The subsidiary's retail service territory has an area of about 2,100 square miles. PECO delivers electricity to roughly 1.6 million customers and natural gas to approximately 486,000 customers. In addition to its primary segments, Exelon Business Services Company provides financial, human resource, legal, IT, supply management and corporate governance services to Exelon and its subsidiaries. In April 2009, the firm signed an agreement with SunPower Corp. for the development of a 10 MW solar photovoltaic (PV) facility in Chicago, Illinois, the largest urban solar power plant in the U.S. In October 2009, the firm created Exelon Transmission Company, dedicated to building transmission lines that facilitate movement of renewable energy. In June 2010, the company's $60 million solar PV facility was completed.

FINANCIALS:

Sales and profits are in thousands of dollars—add 000 to get the full amount. 2010 Note: Financial information for 2010 was not available for all companies at press time.

2010 Sales: $	2010 Profits: $	**U.S. Stock Ticker: EXC**
2009 Sales: $17,318,000	2009 Profits: $2,707,000	**Int'l Ticker:** Int'l Exchange:
2008 Sales: $18,859,000	2008 Profits: $2,737,000	Employees: 19,329
2007 Sales: $18,916,000	2007 Profits: $2,736,000	Fiscal Year Ends: 12/31
2006 Sales: $15,655,000	2006 Profits: $1,592,000	Parent Company:

SALARIES/BENEFITS:

Pension Plan:	ESOP Stock Plan:	Profit Sharing:	Top Exec. Salary: $1,468,077	Bonus: $1,573,825
Savings Plan: Y	Stock Purch. Plan: Y		Second Exec. Salary: $821,154	Bonus: $680,213

OTHER THOUGHTS:

Apparent Women Officers or Directors: 8
Hot Spot for Advancement for Women/Minorities: Y

LOCATIONS: ("Y" = Yes)

West:	Southwest:	Midwest:	Southeast:	Northeast:	International:
	Y	Y		Y	

EXTERRAN HOLDINGS INC

www.exterran.com

Industry Group Code: 213112 **Ranks within this company's industry group:** Sales: 9 Profits: 27

Exploration/Production:		Refining/Retailing:		Utilities:		Alternative Energy:		Specialty Services:		Energy Mktg./Other Svcs.	
Exploration:		Refining:		Electric Utility:		Waste/Solar/Other:		Consulting/Eng.:		Energy Marketing:	
Production:		Retailing:		Gas Utility:		Thermal/Steam:		Seismic:		Equipment/Machinery:	Y
Coal Production:		Convenience Stores:		Pipelines:		Wind:		Drilling:		Oil Field Services:	
		Chemicals:		Water:		Hydro:		InfoTech:		Air/Shipping Transportation:	
						Fuel Cells:		Specialty Services:	Y		

TYPES OF BUSINESS:

Manufacturing-Natural Gas Compression Equipment
Oil & Gas Treatment Facilities
Compressed Natural Gas Fueling Stations
Power Generation Facilities

BRANDS/DIVISIONS/AFFILIATES:

Hanover Compressor Company
Exterran Partners LP
Universal Compression Holdings Inc

CONTACTS:

Note: Officers with more than one job title may be intentionally listed here more than once.

Ernie L. Danner, CEO
Ernie L. Danner, Pres.
J. Michael Anderson, CFO/Sr. VP
J. Michael Anderson, Chief of Staff
Donald C. Wayne, General Counsel/Sr. VP/Sec.
Daniel K. Schlanger, VP-Oper. Svcs.
Kenneth R. Bickett, VP-Finance & Acct.
David Miller, VP
D. Bradley Childers, Pres., North America Oper.
Gordon T. Hall, Chmn.
Joe Kishkill, Pres., Eastern Hemisphere Oper.

Phone: 281-836-7000	**Fax:**
Toll-Free:	
Address: 16666 Northchase Dr., Houston, TX 77060 US	

GROWTH PLANS/SPECIAL FEATURES:

Exterran Holdings, Inc. is a provider of full-service natural gas compression. The firm was formed from the merger of Universal Compression Holdings, Inc., and Hanover Compressor Company. The company's products and services consist of natural gas compression equipment and facilities, such as compression stations; oil and gas production facilities; compressed natural gas (CNG) fueling stations; power generation facilities; and gas plants that can perform fractionation, gas liquids recovery, dewpoint control, treating and dehydration. Exterran Holdings operates in three segments: fabrication, contract operations and aftermarket services. The firm's fabrication operations, which account for roughly 43.1% of revenues, include the fabrication and sale of equipment, as well as engineering, procurement and construction services for refinery/petrochemical facilities, tank farms and desalination plants. Exterran Holdings' contract operations unit (44% of revenues) provides services through approximately 10,433 U.S. and 1,164 international natural gas compression units with a combined aggregate capacity of roughly 5.55 million horsepower. The company's aftermarket unit (12.9% of revenues) sells parts and components; and provides operations, maintenance, overhaul and reconfiguration services. Primary aftermarket clients are owners of production, gas treating, compression and oilfield power generation equipment. The firm's 34%-owned indirect subsidiary Exterran Partners, L.P. operates a fleet of approximately 3,574 compressor units comprising approximately 1.366 million horsepower. Exterran Holdings operates in over 30 countries throughout the Americas, the Middle East, Africa, Australia and Europe. In November 2009, the firm sold 900 compressor units and certain contracts to Exterran Partners. In August 2010, the company sold another 580 compressor units and related contracts to Exterran Partners.

Exterran Holdings offer employees benefits such as life, AD&D, medical, dental and vision insurance; education assistance; paid time off; employee assistance plans; a 401(k); and flexible spending accounts.

FINANCIALS:

Sales and profits are in thousands of dollars—add 000 to get the full amount. 2010 Note: Financial information for 2010 was not available for all companies at press time.

2010 Sales: $	2010 Profits: $	**U.S. Stock Ticker: EXH**
2009 Sales: $2,715,601	2009 Profits: $-545,407	**Int'l Ticker:** Int'l Exchange:
2008 Sales: $3,024,119	2008 Profits: $-947,349	Employees: 11,100
2007 Sales: $2,540,485	2007 Profits: $34,569	Fiscal Year Ends: 12/31
2006 Sales: $1,593,321	2006 Profits: $86,523	Parent Company:

SALARIES/BENEFITS:

Pension Plan:	ESOP Stock Plan:	Profit Sharing:	Top Exec. Salary: $450,000	Bonus: $303,750
Savings Plan: Y	Stock Purch. Plan:		Second Exec. Salary: $355,000	Bonus: $175,000

OTHER THOUGHTS:

Apparent Women Officers or Directors: 1
Hot Spot for Advancement for Women/Minorities:

LOCATIONS: ("Y" = Yes)

West:	Southwest:	Midwest:	Southeast:	Northeast:	International:
Y	Y	Y	Y	Y	Y

EXXON MOBIL CORPORATION (EXXONMOBIL) www.exxonmobil.com

Industry Group Code: 211111 **Ranks within this company's industry group:** Sales: 1 Profits: 2

Exploration/Production:		Refining/Retailing:		Utilities:		Alternative Energy:		Specialty Services:		Energy Mktg./Other Svcs.	
Exploration:	Y	Refining:	Y	Electric Utility:	Y	Waste/Solar/Other:		Consulting/Eng.:		Energy Marketing:	Y
Production:	Y	Retailing:	Y	Gas Utility:	Y	Thermal/Steam:		Seismic:		Equipment/Machinery:	
Coal Production:	Y	Convenience Stores:	Y	Pipelines:		Wind:		Drilling:		Oil Field Services:	
		Chemicals:	Y	Water:		Hydro:		InfoTech:		Air/Shipping Transportation:	
						Fuel Cells:		Specialty Services:			

TYPES OF BUSINESS:

Oil & Gas Exploration & Production
Gas Refining & Supply
Fuel Marketing
Power Generation
Chemicals
Petroleum Products
Convenience Stores

BRANDS/DIVISIONS/AFFILIATES:

ExxonMobil Chemical
XTO Energy Inc
Qatargas 2 Train 5
TonenGeneral
ExxonMobil
Esso
Exxon
Mobil

CONTACTS: *Note: Officers with more than one job title may be intentionally listed here more than once.*

Rex W. Tillerson, CEO
L.J. Cavanaugh, VP-Human Resources
C. W. Matthews, General Counsel/VP
W.M. Colton, VP-Corp. Strategic Planning
K.P. Cohen, VP-Public & Gov't Affairs
D. S. Rosenthal, VP-Investor Rel./Sec.
Donald D. Humphreys, Treas./Sr. VP
Andrew P. Swiger, Sr. VP
P.T. Mulva, Controller/VP
Mark W. Albers, Sr. VP
Suzanne M/ McCarron, Pres., ExxonMobil Foundation
Rex W. Tillerson, Chmn.

Phone: 972-444-1000 **Fax:** 972-444-1505
Toll-Free: 800-252-1800
Address: 5959 Las Colinas Blvd., Irving, TX 75039-2298 US

GROWTH PLANS/SPECIAL FEATURES:

Exxon Mobil Corporation (ExxonMobil) is one of the largest international petroleum and natural gas exploration and production companies in the world. Its principal business is energy, involving exploration for and production of crude oil and natural gas; manufacture of petroleum products; and transportation and sale of crude oil, natural gas and petroleum products. Overall, the firm has eight global business units. The exploration unit manages 72 million exploration acres in 33 countries. The development unit includes a portfolio of 130 major projects expected to develop over 24 billion barrels of oil equivalent (BBOE). The production unit focuses on the recovery of hydrocarbons from oil and gas assets. The natural gas and power marketing unit sells approximately 11 billion cubic feet of natural gas daily and controls 16,000 megawatts (MW) of power generation capacity. The refining and supply unit operates refineries, marine vessels, pipelines and distribution centers with a distillation capacity of 6.3 million barrels per day. The lubricants and specialties unit supplies synthetic lubricants, lube basestocks and asphalt and specialty oil products. The fuels marketing unit serves about 1 million commercial customers through 28,000 service stations. Finally, the chemical unit manufactures olefins, aromatics, polyethylene and polypropylene, as well as specialty hydrocarbon fluids. The company has hundreds of affiliates, many with names that include ExxonMobil, Esso, Exxon or Mobil. During 2009, the firm entered a joint development agreement with Weatherford International, Ltd.; formed an alliance with Synthetic Genomics, Inc. to develop algae-based biofuels; began production at Qatargas 2 Train 5 in Qatar, one of the largest liquefied natural gas (LNG) production facilities worldwide. Also in 2009, affiliate TonenGeneral agreed to establish a joint venture with Toray Industries to develop, manufacture and sell lithium ion battery separator film. In June 2010, ExxonMobil acquired XTO Energy, Inc., a U.S.-based oil and gas producer.

FINANCIALS: **Sales and profits are in thousands of dollars—add 000 to get the full amount. 2010 Note: Financial information for 2010 was not available for all companies at press time.**

2010 Sales: $	2010 Profits: $	**U.S. Stock Ticker: XOM**
2009 Sales: $301,500,000	2009 Profits: $19,280,000	**Int'l Ticker:** Int'l Exchange:
2008 Sales: $459,579,000	2008 Profits: $45,220,000	Employees: 80,700
2007 Sales: $390,328,000	2007 Profits: $40,610,000	Fiscal Year Ends: 12/31
2006 Sales: $365,467,000	2006 Profits: $39,500,000	Parent Company:

SALARIES/BENEFITS:

Pension Plan:	ESOP Stock Plan:	Profit Sharing:	Top Exec. Salary: $2,057,000	Bonus: $2,400,000
Savings Plan:	Stock Purch. Plan:		Second Exec. Salary: $1,010,000	Bonus: $1,418,000

OTHER THOUGHTS:

Apparent Women Officers or Directors: 2
Hot Spot for Advancement for Women/Minorities: Y

LOCATIONS: ("Y" = Yes)

West:	Southwest:	Midwest:	Southeast:	Northeast:	International:
Y	Y	Y	Y	Y	Y

FERRELLGAS PARTNERS LP

www.ferrellgas.com

Industry Group Code: 454312 **Ranks within this company's industry group:** Sales: 3 Profits: 4

Exploration/Production:		Refining/Retailing:		Utilities:		Alternative Energy:		Specialty Services:		Energy Mktg./Other Svcs.	
Exploration:		Refining:		Electric Utility:		Waste/Solar/Other:		Consulting/Eng.:		Energy Marketing:	Y
Production:		Retailing:	Y	Gas Utility:		Thermal/Steam:		Seismic:		Equipment/Machinery:	
Coal Production:		Convenience Stores:		Pipelines:		Wind:		Drilling:		Oil Field Services:	
		Chemicals:	Y	Water:		Hydro:		InfoTech:		Air/Shipping Transportation:	
						Fuel Cells:		Specialty Services:	Y		

TYPES OF BUSINESS:

Propane Sales, Retail
Propane & Natural Gas Trading
Wholesale Propane
Chemical Feedstock
Propane Equipment & Supplies
Transport Hauling

BRANDS/DIVISIONS/AFFILIATES:

Blue Rhino LLC
Ferrellgas Finance Corp.
Ferrellgas, L.P.
Ferrellgas Partners Finance Corp.
Ferrellgas Receivables LLC

CONTACTS: *Note: Officers with more than one job title may be intentionally listed here more than once.*

Stephen L. Wambold, CEO
Stephen L. Wambold, Pres.
J. Ryan VanWinkle, CFO/Sr. VP
Gene D. Caresia, VP-Human Resources
Tod D. Brown, Sr. VP/Pres., Blue Rhino
George Koloroutis, Sr. VP/Pres., Ferrell North America
James E. Ferrell, Chmn.

Phone: 913-661-1500 **Fax:** 816-792-7985
Toll-Free:
Address: 7500 College Blvd., Ste. 1000, Overland Park, KS 66210 US

GROWTH PLANS/SPECIAL FEATURES:

Ferrellgas Partners, L.P., founded in 1939, is a leading distributor of propane and related equipment and supplies to customers primarily in the United States, with over 1 million residential, industrial/commercial, portable tank exchange, agricultural, wholesale and other customers in all 50 states, Washington D.C. and Puerto Rico. The company conducts business through its operating partnership, Ferrellgas, L.P., and subsidiaries Ferrellgas Partners Finance Corp., Ferrellgas Receivables LLC and Ferrellgas Finance Corp. Ferrellgas's operations primarily include the distribution and sale of propane and related equipment and supplies with concentrations in the Midwest, Southeast, Southwest and Northwest regions of the U.S. Ferrellgas' propane distribution business consists principally of transporting propane purchased from third parties to its 884 propane distribution locations in the U.S., and then to tanks on customers' premises or to portable propane tanks delivered to nationwide and local retailers. Delivery trucks are generally fitted with 3,000 gallon tanks. The company's portable tank exchange operations, nationally branded under the name Blue Rhino, are conducted through a network of independent and partnership-owned distribution outlets. About 64% of residential customers rent tanks from Ferrellgas. The company also leases tanks to independent distributors. In the residential and commercial markets, propane is primarily used for space heating, water heating, cooking and other propane fueled appliances, while the agricultural market uses propane for crop drying, space heating, irrigation and weed control. The company also sells gas grills; patio heaters; fireplace and garden accessories; mosquito traps; and other outdoor products through Blue Rhino Global Sourcing.

Employees are offered medical, dental and vision insurance; life insurance; disability coverage; flexible spending accounts; a 401(k) plan; discounts on propane; and an employee stock ownership plan.

FINANCIALS: **Sales and profits are in thousands of dollars—add 000 to get the full amount. 2010 Note: Financial information for 2010 was not available for all companies at press time.**

2010 Sales: $	2010 Profits: $
2009 Sales: $2,069,522	2009 Profits: $52,046
2008 Sales: $2,290,689	2008 Profits: $24,442
2007 Sales: $1,992,440	2007 Profits: $24,452
2006 Sales: $1,895,470	2006 Profits: $25,009

U.S. Stock Ticker: FGP
Int'l Ticker: Int'l Exchange:
Employees: 3,637
Fiscal Year Ends: 7/31
Parent Company:

SALARIES/BENEFITS:

Pension Plan:	ESOP Stock Plan: Y	Profit Sharing:	Top Exec. Salary: $825,032	Bonus: $
Savings Plan: Y	Stock Purch. Plan:		Second Exec. Salary: $500,019	Bonus: $600,000

OTHER THOUGHTS:

Apparent Women Officers or Directors: 2
Hot Spot for Advancement for Women/Minorities:

LOCATIONS: ("Y" = Yes)

West:	Southwest:	Midwest:	Southeast:	Northeast:	International:
Y	Y	Y	Y	Y	Y

FIRSTENERGY CORP

www.firstenergycorp.com

Industry Group Code: 2211 **Ranks within this company's industry group:** Sales: 15 Profits: 14

Exploration/Production:		Refining/Retailing:		Utilities:		Alternative Energy:		Specialty Services:		Energy Mktg./Other Svcs.	
Exploration:		Refining:		Electric Utility:	Y	Waste/Solar/Other:		Consulting/Eng.:		Energy Marketing:	Y
Production:		Retailing:		Gas Utility:	Y	Thermal/Steam:		Seismic:		Equipment/Machinery:	
Coal Production:		Convenience Stores:		Pipelines:		Wind:		Drilling:		Oil Field Services:	
		Chemicals:		Water:		Hydro:		InfoTech:		Air/Shipping Transportation:	
						Fuel Cells:		Specialty Services:	Y		

TYPES OF BUSINESS:

Utilities-Electricity & Natural Gas
Power Generation
Energy Management
Telecommunications

BRANDS/DIVISIONS/AFFILIATES:

Ohio Edison Co.
Cleveland Electric Illuminating Co. (The)
Toledo Edison Co. (The)
Pennsylvania Electric Co.
Jersey Central Power & Light Co.
Metropolitan Edison Co.
Pennsylvania Power Co.
FirstEnergy Service Company

CONTACTS: *Note: Officers with more than one job title may be intentionally listed here more than once.*

Anthony J. Alexander, CEO
R. R. Grigg, COO/Exec. VP
Anthony J. Alexander, Pres.
Mark T. Clark, CFO/Exec. VP
Leila L. Vespoli, General Counsel/Exec. VP
Harvey L. Wagner, Chief Acct. Officer/VP/Controller
James F. Pearson, VP/Treas.
Gary R. Leidich, Exec. VP/Pres., FirstEnergy Generation
Charles E. Jones, Jr., Sr. VP/Pres., First Energy Utilities
Rhonda S. Ferguson, VP/Corp. Sec.
George M. Smart, Chmn.

Phone:	**Fax:** 330-384-3545
Toll-Free: 800-736-3402	
Address: 76 S. Main St., Akron, OH 44308 US	

GROWTH PLANS/SPECIAL FEATURES:

FirstEnergy Corp. is a diversified energy services holding company involved in the generation, transmission and distribution of electricity, energy management and other energy-related services. The firm operates eight principal electric utility subsidiaries: Ohio Edison Co.; The Cleveland Electric Illuminating Co.; The Toledo Edison Co.; Pennsylvania Electric Co.; Jersey Central Power & Light Co.; Metropolitan Edison Co.; and Pennsylvania Power Co. FirstEnergy is one of the largest investor-owned electric systems, serving 4.5 million customers in a service area that ranges over 36,100 square miles of Ohio, Pennsylvania and New Jersey. It has more than 14,000 megawatts (MW) of generating capacity. Generation is conducted through a variety of methods including coal, nuclear power, gas and oil and hydroelectric generation. Other FirstEnergy subsidiaries including FirstEnergy Ventures Corp.; FirstEnergy Properties, Inc.; GPU Power, Inc.; GPU Nuclear, Inc.; FirstEnergy Solutions Corp., FirstEnergy Service Company, FirstEnergy Generation Corp. and FirstEnergy Utilities. In February 2010, the company agreed to acquire Allegheny Energy, Inc. for $4.7 billion.

The firm offers employees medical, dental and vision benefits; a 401(k) savings plan; a pension plan; life insurance; flexible spending accounts; adoption assistance; and disability coverage.

FINANCIALS: **Sales and profits are in thousands of dollars—add 000 to get the full amount. 2010 Note: Financial information for 2010 was not available for all companies at press time.**

2010 Sales: $	2010 Profits: $	**U.S. Stock Ticker: FE**
2009 Sales: $12,967,000	2009 Profits: $990,000	**Int'l Ticker:** Int'l Exchange:
2008 Sales: $13,627,000	2008 Profits: $1,342,000	Employees: 13,379
2007 Sales: $12,802,000	2007 Profits: $1,309,000	Fiscal Year Ends: 12/31
2006 Sales: $11,501,000	2006 Profits: $1,254,000	Parent Company:

SALARIES/BENEFITS:

Pension Plan: Y	ESOP Stock Plan:	Profit Sharing:	Top Exec. Salary: $1,159,615	Bonus: $1,206,000
Savings Plan: Y	Stock Purch. Plan:		Second Exec. Salary: $715,385	Bonus: $507,115

OTHER THOUGHTS:

Apparent Women Officers or Directors: 7
Hot Spot for Advancement for Women/Minorities: Y

LOCATIONS: ("Y" = Yes)

West:	Southwest:	Midwest:	Southeast:	Northeast:	International:
		Y		Y	

FLINT ENERGY SERVICES LTD

www.flintenergy.com

Industry Group Code: 213112 **Ranks within this company's industry group:** Sales: 13 Profits: 18

Exploration/Production:		**Refining/Retailing:**		**Utilities:**		**Alternative Energy:**		**Specialty Services:**		**Energy Mktg./Other Svcs.**	
Exploration:		Refining:		Electric Utility:		Waste/Solar/Other:		Consulting/Eng.:	Y	Energy Marketing:	
Production:		Retailing:		Gas Utility:		Thermal/Steam:		Seismic:		Equipment/Machinery:	Y
Coal Production:		Convenience Stores:		Pipelines:		Wind:		Drilling:		Oil Field Services:	Y
		Chemicals:		Water:		Hydro:		InfoTech:		Air/Shipping Transportation:	
						Fuel Cells:		Specialty Services:	Y		

TYPES OF BUSINESS:

Midstream Services
Equipment Rental
Electrical Instrumentation Products
Facility Construction & Maintenance
Safety & Environmental Services

BRANDS/DIVISIONS/AFFILIATES:

PES Surface, Inc.

CONTACTS:

Note: Officers with more than one job title may be intentionally listed here more than once.

W. J. Lingard, CEO
W. J. Lingard, Pres.
Paul M. Boechler, CFO/Exec. VP
Bob Henderson, VP-Human Resources
Keith Lambert, Sr. VP-Prod.
Glen Greenshields, Corp. VP
Wayne Shaw, Sr. VP-Infrastructure Svcs.
Shawn Carry, Sr. VP-Flint Oilfield Svcs.
Glen Greenshields, Corp. VP
Stuart O'Connor, Chmn.

Phone: 403-218-7100 **Fax:** 403-215-5445
Toll-Free: 877-215-5499
Address: 300 Fifth Ave. SW, Ste. 700, Calgary, AB T2P 3C4 Canada

GROWTH PLANS/SPECIAL FEATURES:

Flint Energy Services, Ltd. is a Canadian midstream services company. It provides a full range of services through over 60 operating locations in North America. The company primarily serves the oil and gas industry. However, it also serves petrochemical, manufacturing, pulp and paper, power generation, agriculture and mining companies. Flint does business in four service areas: production services; facility infrastructure; oilfield services; and plant maintenance. The production services segment consists of pipeline work and other midstream construction services. Services in this segment span from the provision of site-specific personal safety equipment to managing and operating multi-million dollar multi-site field programs. Facility infrastructure, which includes Flint's modular fabrication operations, constructs major projects such as oil sands facilities, and also offers project management. Oilfield services include drilling and service rig relocation and specialty hauling services. This segment also offers fluid hauling, pressure and vacuum services and well cleaning. The maintenance services segment offers plant-wide maintenance, shutdown and turnaround services, management of third party contractors and field and road maintenance. In addition, the segment also offers asset management services to plant maintenance and turnaround services for oil sands production facilities in Alberta and other oil refineries and related facilities. In April 2010, the firm acquired PES Surface, Inc. from Paintearth Energy Services, Inc. for $7.3 million.

FINANCIALS:

Sales and profits are in thousands of dollars—add 000 to get the full amount. 2010 Note: Financial information for 2010 was not available for all companies at press time.

2010 Sales: $	2010 Profits: $	**U.S. Stock Ticker:**
2009 Sales: $1,794,370	2009 Profits: $44,460	**Int'l Ticker: FES** Int'l Exchange: Toronto-TSX
2008 Sales: $2,130,530	2008 Profits: $-329,370	Employees: 10,280
2007 Sales: $1,777,500	2007 Profits: $49,300	Fiscal Year Ends: 12/31
2006 Sales: $1,426,500	2006 Profits: $53,500	Parent Company:

SALARIES/BENEFITS:

Pension Plan:	ESOP Stock Plan:	Profit Sharing:	Top Exec. Salary: $470,897	Bonus: $115,760
Savings Plan:	Stock Purch. Plan:		Second Exec. Salary: $307,387	Bonus: $70,143

OTHER THOUGHTS:

Apparent Women Officers or Directors:
Hot Spot for Advancement for Women/Minorities:

LOCATIONS: ("Y" = Yes)

West:	Southwest:	Midwest:	Southeast:	Northeast:	International:
Y	Y	Y			Y

FLUOR CORP

www.fluor.com

Industry Group Code: 237 **Ranks within this company's industry group:** Sales: 2 Profits: 1

Exploration/Production:		Refining/Retailing:		Utilities:		Alternative Energy:		Specialty Services:		Energy Mktg./Other Svcs.	
Exploration:		Refining:		Electric Utility:		Waste/Solar/Other:		Consulting/Eng.:	Y	Energy Marketing:	
Production:		Retailing:		Gas Utility:		Thermal/Steam:		Seismic:		Equipment/Machinery:	
Coal Production:		Convenience Stores:		Pipelines:		Wind:		Drilling:		Oil Field Services:	
		Chemicals:		Water:		Hydro:		InfoTech:		Air/Shipping Transportation:	
						Fuel Cells:		Specialty Services:	Y		

TYPES OF BUSINESS:

Construction, Heavy & Civil Engineering
Power Plant Construction and Management
Facilities Management
Procurement Services
Consulting Services
Project Management
Asset Management
Staffing Services

BRANDS/DIVISIONS/AFFILIATES:

Fluor Constructors International, Inc.
Fluor Canada

CONTACTS:

Note: Officers with more than one job title may be intentionally listed here more than once.

Alan L. Boeckmann, CEO
David T. Seaton, COO
D. Michael Steuert, CFO/Sr. VP
Glenn Gilkey, Sr. VP-Human Resources
Ray F. Barnard, CIO/VP
Glenn Gilkey, Sr. VP-Admin.
Carlos M. Hernandez, Chief Legal Officer/Corp. Sec.
David E. Constable, Group Pres., Oper.
John L. Hopkins, Group Exec.-Bus. Dev.
Lee Tashjian, VP-Corp. Affairs
Kenneth H. Lockwood, VP-Investor Rel.
Kenneth H. Lockwood, VP-Corp. Finance
Wendy Hallgren, VP-Corp. Compliance
David Marventano, Sr. VP-Gov't Rel.
Joanna M. Oliva, Treas./VP
Richard P. Carter, Pres., Fluor Constructors International, Inc.
Alan L. Boeckmann, Chmn.
Kirk D. Grimes, Pres., Global Svcs.

Phone: 469-398-7000 **Fax:** 469-398-7255
Toll-Free:
Address: 6700 Las Colinas Blvd., Irving, TX 75039 US

GROWTH PLANS/SPECIAL FEATURES:

Fluor Corp. is a global provider of engineering, procurement, construction and maintenance services, with offices in over 25 countries spanning across six continents. As well as being a primary service provider to the U.S. federal government, Fluor serves a diverse set of industries including oil and gas; chemical and petrochemicals; transportation; mining and metals; power; life sciences; and manufacturing. Fluor operates in five business segments: oil and gas; industrial and infrastructure; government; global services; and power. The oil and gas segment offers design, engineering, procurement, construction and project management services to energy-related industries. The industrial and infrastructure segment provides design, engineering and construction services to the transportation, mining, life sciences, telecommunications, manufacturing, microelectronics and healthcare sectors. The government segment provides project management services, including environmental restoration, engineering, construction, site operations and maintenance, to the U.S. government, particularly to the Department of Energy, the Department of Homeland Security and the Department of Defense. The global services segment provides operations, maintenance and construction services, as well as industrial fleet outsourcing, plant turnaround services, temporary staffing, procurement services and construction-related support. The power segment provides such services as engineering, procurement, construction, program management, start-up, commissioning and maintenance to the gas fueled, solid fueled, renewable and nuclear marketplaces. Fluor Constructors International, Inc., which operates separately from the rest of the businesses, provides unionized management and construction services in the U.S. and Canada, both independently.

Employees are offered medical, dental and vision insurance; life insurance; disability coverage; a retirement plan; a 401(k) savings plan; an employee assistance program; a tax savings account; and education assistance; automobile and home insurance; and legal services.

FINANCIALS:

Sales and profits are in thousands of dollars—add 000 to get the full amount. 2010 Note: Financial information for 2010 was not available for all companies at press time.

2010 Sales: $	2010 Profits: $	**U.S. Stock Ticker: FLR**
2009 Sales: $21,990,300	2009 Profits: $732,875	**Int'l Ticker:** Int'l Exchange:
2008 Sales: $22,325,900	2008 Profits: $748,903	Employees: 36,152
2007 Sales: $16,691,000	2007 Profits: $527,961	Fiscal Year Ends: 12/31
2006 Sales: $14,078,500	2006 Profits: $263,500	Parent Company:

SALARIES/BENEFITS:

Pension Plan: Y	ESOP Stock Plan:	Profit Sharing:	Top Exec. Salary: $1,232,270	Bonus: $6,873,200
Savings Plan: Y	Stock Purch. Plan:		Second Exec. Salary: $781,871	Bonus: $2,563,000

OTHER THOUGHTS:

Apparent Women Officers or Directors: 3
Hot Spot for Advancement for Women/Minorities: Y

LOCATIONS: ("Y" = Yes)

West:	Southwest:	Midwest:	Southeast:	Northeast:	International:
Y	Y	Y	Y	Y	Y

FOREST OIL CORPORATION

www.forestoil.com

Industry Group Code: 211111 **Ranks within this company's industry group:** Sales: 85 Profits: 106

Exploration/Production:		Refining/Retailing:		Utilities:		Alternative Energy:		Specialty Services:		Energy Mktg./Other Svcs.	
Exploration:	Y	Refining:		Electric Utility:		Waste/Solar/Other:		Consulting/Eng.:		Energy Marketing:	Y
Production:	Y	Retailing:		Gas Utility:		Thermal/Steam:		Seismic:		Equipment/Machinery:	
Coal Production:		Convenience Stores:		Pipelines:		Wind:		Drilling:	Y	Oil Field Services:	
		Chemicals:		Water:		Hydro:		InfoTech:		Air/Shipping Transportation:	
						Fuel Cells:		Specialty Services:			

TYPES OF BUSINESS:

Oil & Gas Exploration & Production
Oil & Gas Marketing

BRANDS/DIVISIONS/AFFILIATES:

Forest Oil Western Region
Forest Oil Southern Region
Forest Oil Canada
Forest Oil International
Forest Oil Eastern Region

CONTACTS:

Note: Officers with more than one job title may be intentionally listed here more than once.

H. Craig Clark, CEO
J.C. Ridens, COO/Exec. VP
H. Craig Clark, Pres.
Michael N. Kennedy, CFO/Exec. VP
Robert Wofford, VP-Oil & Gas Mktg.
Paul J. Dusha, VP-Human Resources
Rick Hatcher, CTO/VP
Glen J. Mizenko, Sr. VP-Eng.
Cyrus D. Marter, IV, General Counsel/Sec./Sr. VP
Timothy F. Savoy, VP-Oper. Support
Glen J. Mizenko, Sr. VP-Bus. Dev.
Patrick. J. Redmond, VP-Investor Rel. & Corp. Planning
Victor A. Wind, Chief Acct. Officer/Sr. VP
David Anderson, Pres., Canadian Forest Oil
Ronald Nutt, VP-Southern Region
Stephen Harpham, VP-Corp. Eng.
Mark E. Bush, VP-Eastern Region
James Lightner, Chmn.
Cecil N. Colwell, Sr. VP-Worldwide Drilling

Phone: 303-812-1400	Fax:
Toll-Free:	
Address: 707 17th St., Ste. 3600, Denver, CO 80202 US	

GROWTH PLANS/SPECIAL FEATURES:

Forest Oil Corporation is an oil and gas company engaged in the acquisition, exploration, development and production of oil, natural gas and natural gas liquids. The majority of the firm's proved reserves are located in the U.S., with the remainder in Canada and in Italy. The company is organized into five distinct business segments: Southern, Western, Eastern, Canada and International. Forest Oil's Southern segment has production and proved reserves located in South Texas and the upper Texas Gulf Coast, primarily the Charco and Rincon fields; the Katy and McAllen Ranch fields; and the Wilcox and Vicksburg trends. The Western business unit's operations are located primarily in the Texas Panhandle, West Texas and Western Oklahoma as well as in the Uintah field in Utah. Its area of focus is in the Greater Buffalo Wallow area located in Hemphill, Roberts and Wheeler Counties in the Texas Panhandle, which targets the Granite Wash, Atoka, and Morrow formations. The Eastern unit's operations are located in East Texas, Arkansas and Louisiana, and focus on the Cotton Valley/Haynesville trends in East Texas and North Louisiana; the Arkoma Basin in western Arkansas; and the tight-gas sands in the Cotton Valley trend. The Canada business unit operates in the Deep Basin, multi-zone Cretaceous reservoirs in central Alberta. The firm has drilled and completed three horizontal wells in the Utica Shale in Eastern Canada and plans additional evaluation and testing in 2009. The International segment operates primarily in South Africa and Italy and owns three wells, all located in Italy. During 2009, the company drilled a total of 117 gross wells. During 2009, the firm sold its oil and gas properties located in Permian Basin in West Texas and New Mexico as well as other non-core oil and gas properties in the U.S. and Canada for approximately $1.1 billion.

FINANCIALS:

Sales and profits are in thousands of dollars—add 000 to get the full amount. 2010 Note: Financial information for 2010 was not available for all companies at press time.

2010 Sales: $	2010 Profits: $	**U.S. Stock Ticker: FST**
2009 Sales: $767,830	2009 Profits: $-923,133	**Int'l Ticker:** Int'l Exchange:
2008 Sales: $1,647,163	2008 Profits: $-1,026,323	Employees: 705
2007 Sales: $1,083,892	2007 Profits: $169,306	Fiscal Year Ends: 12/31
2006 Sales: $819,992	2006 Profits: $168,502	Parent Company:

SALARIES/BENEFITS:

Pension Plan:	ESOP Stock Plan:	Profit Sharing:	Top Exec. Salary: $650,000	Bonus: $900,000
Savings Plan:	Stock Purch. Plan:		Second Exec. Salary: $419,583	Bonus: $

OTHER THOUGHTS:

Apparent Women Officers or Directors:
Hot Spot for Advancement for Women/Minorities:

LOCATIONS: ("Y" = Yes)

West:	Southwest:	Midwest:	Southeast:	Northeast:	International:
Y	Y		Y		Y

FORMOSA PETROCHEMICAL CORP (FPCC)

www.fpcc.com.tw

Industry Group Code: 211111 **Ranks within this company's industry group:** Sales: 33 Profits: 37

Exploration/Production:		Refining/Retailing:		Utilities:		Alternative Energy:		Specialty Services:		Energy Mktg./Other Svcs.	
Exploration:		Refining:	Y	Electric Utility:	Y	Waste/Solar/Other:		Consulting/Eng.:		Energy Marketing:	
Production:		Retailing:		Gas Utility:		Thermal/Steam:		Seismic:		Equipment/Machinery:	
Coal Production:		Convenience Stores:		Pipelines:		Wind:		Drilling:		Oil Field Services:	
		Chemicals:	Y	Water:		Hydro:		InfoTech:		Air/Shipping Transportation:	
						Fuel Cells:		Specialty Services:	Y		

TYPES OF BUSINESS:

Oil Refining & Marketing
Petrochemicals
Harbor Administration
Storage Facilities

BRANDS/DIVISIONS/AFFILIATES:

Formosa Plastics Group
Taiwan Synthetic Rubber Corp
No.6 Naphtha Cracker Complex
Formosa Oil (Asia Pacific) Corp.
Formosa Petrochemical Transportation Corp.
Formosa Development Corp.
Mailiao Power Corp.
Formosa Plastic Marine Corp.

CONTACTS:

Note: Officers with more than one job title may be intentionally listed here more than once.

C.Y. Su, Pres.
Ming-Hsing Shin, CFO
Ja-Tao Huang, VP-Eng. Div.
Yeong-Fa Wang, VP-Oil Products Div.
Tsai-Shan Kao, VP-Maintenance
Tony Meng-Shiung Wu, VP-Refinery Div.
Jui-Shih Chen, VP-Olefins Div.
Wilfred Wang, Chmn.

Phone: 886-2-2712-2211	**Fax:** 886-2-2712-9211
Toll-Free:	
Address: 201 Tun Hwa North Rd., Taipei, Taiwan	

GROWTH PLANS/SPECIAL FEATURES:

Formosa Petrochemical Corporation (FPCC) is a Taiwanese company primarily engaged in the refining and marketing of oil and petrochemical products for sale in its domestic market as well as international markets. The company conducts its various operations through four divisions: refinery and oil products; petrochemical-olefins; utilities; and other products and services. The refinery and oil products division refines crude oil and sells various resulting products, including naphtha, gasoline, fuel oil, jet fuel, kerosene and liquefied petroleum gas (LPG). The petrochemical-olefins division manufactures and sells olefins, including ethylene, propylene, benzene, toluene, xylene (BTX) and butadiene. The utilities division comprises Formosa's electricity and steam production and sales. The other products and services division consolidates the company's maintenance and administration services for its naphtha cracker complex and harbor activities. These operations include repair and maintenance services at the No.6 Naphtha Cracker Complex and operation of the jetty and storage facilities at this facility, such as loading and unloading services and storage space rental. This division also sells certain other products, including C4, carbon monoxide and industrial water. The company was established by members of the Formosa Plastics Group, and carries out its operations through various subsidiaries. The company's subsidies include: Formosa Oil (Asia Pacific) Corp., an oil product retailer; Formosa Petrochemical Transportation Corp., a transportation services provider; Formosa Development Corp., an industrial site development company; Mailiao Power Corp., providing power generation; Yi-Chi Construction Company, a construction services provider; Formosa Environmental Technology Corp., a developer of environment protection technology; Simosa Oil Corporation, a producer and retailer of asphalt; Formosa Plastic Marine Corp., providing maritime transport services; Formosa Group Ocean Marine Investment Corp., which invests in maritime transportation; and Mailiao Harbor Administration Corp., providing harbor management services. In April 2009, the company announced its intention to purchase a 33% stake in Taiwan Synthetic Rubber Corp.

FINANCIALS:

Sales and profits are in thousands of dollars—add 000 to get the full amount. 2010 Note: Financial information for 2010 was not available for all companies at press time.

2010 Sales: $	2010 Profits: $	**U.S. Stock Ticker:**
2009 Sales: $19,968,500	2009 Profits: $1,231,300	**Int'l Ticker: 6505** Int'l Exchange: Taipei-TPE
2008 Sales: $26,314,500	2008 Profits: $455,800	Employees:
2007 Sales: $21,035,800	2007 Profits: $2,088,300	Fiscal Year Ends:
2006 Sales: $15,945,700	2006 Profits: $1,334,300	Parent Company:

SALARIES/BENEFITS:

Pension Plan:	ESOP Stock Plan:	Profit Sharing:	Top Exec. Salary: $	Bonus: $
Savings Plan:	Stock Purch. Plan:		Second Exec. Salary: $	Bonus: $

OTHER THOUGHTS:

Apparent Women Officers or Directors: 1
Hot Spot for Advancement for Women/Minorities:

LOCATIONS: ("Y" = Yes)

West:	Southwest:	Midwest:	Southeast:	Northeast:	International:
					Y

FORTUM COMPANY

www.fortum.com

Industry Group Code: 324110 **Ranks within this company's industry group:** Sales: 19 Profits: 1

Exploration/Production:		Refining/Retailing:		Utilities:		Alternative Energy:		Specialty Services:		Energy Mktg./Other Svcs.	
Exploration:		Refining:		Electric Utility:	Y	Waste/Solar/Other:	Y	Consulting/Eng.:		Energy Marketing:	Y
Production:		Retailing:		Gas Utility:		Thermal/Steam:	Y	Seismic:		Equipment/Machinery:	
Coal Production:		Convenience Stores:		Pipelines:		Wind:	Y	Drilling:		Oil Field Services:	
		Chemicals:		Water:		Hydro:	Y	InfoTech:		Air/Shipping Transportation:	
						Fuel Cells:		Specialty Services:	Y		

TYPES OF BUSINESS:

Electricity Generation
Hydro, Nuclear, Biomass & Wind Generation
Heat & Steam Service

BRANDS/DIVISIONS/AFFILIATES:

Loviisa Nuclear Power Plant
Fortum Varme samagt med Stockholms stad
OAO Fortum
Seabased Industry AB
Skelleftea Kraft

CONTACTS: *Note: Officers with more than one job title may be intentionally listed here more than once.*

Tapio Kuula, CEO
Tapio Kuula, Pres.
Juha Laaksonen, CFO/Exec. VP
Mikael Frisk, Sr. VP-Corp. Human Resources
Maria Paatero-Kaarnakari, Sr. VP-R&D
Anni Nurmela, Mgr.-Nuclear Eng.
Maria Paatero-Kaarnakari, Sr. VP-Corp. Strategy
Anne Brunila, Exec. VP-Corporate Rel. & Sustainability
Per Langer, Exec. VP-Heat Div.
Timo Karttinen, Exec. VP-Electricity Solutions & Dist.
Matti Ruotsala, Exec. VP-Power Div.
Kari Kautinen, VP-Mergers & Acquisitions
Matti Lehti, Chmn.
Alexander Chuvaev, Exec. VP-Russian Div.
Hakan Grefberg, Dir.-Dist.

Phone: 358-10-45-11	**Fax:** 358-10-45-24447
Toll-Free:	
Address: Keilaniementie 1, Espoo, FI-00048 Finland	

GROWTH PLANS/SPECIAL FEATURES:

Fortum Company is a leading energy company based in Finland. Its activities include generation, distribution and sale of electricity and heat; operation and maintenance of power plants; and other energy-related services. Its main products are electricity, heat and steam, traffic fuels and heating oils. The company operates in 10 countries, primarily in the Nordic region, the Baltic States, Poland and Russia. Fortum's power plants have a total production capacity of 13,940 megawatts (MW) and heat production capacity of 24,300 MW. Approximately 91% of the company's power generation in the EU is carbon-dioxide-free. One third of Fortum's energy production is generated by hydropower, with ownership in 260 hydropower plants in Sweden and Finland. Another roughly 23% comes from nuclear power. The firm owns the Loviisa Nuclear Power Plant located on the island of Hastholmen in Finland. The plant consists of two nuclear units, Loviisa 1 and Loviisa 2. The electricity distribution division serves over 1.6 million customers in the Nordic region and Estonia. Fortum's heat business operates from 22 combined heat and power (CHP) plants and several hundred heat plants and stations in the Nordic countries, the Baltic countries and Poland. In Sweden, the firm's heat production business is operated by Fortum Varme samagt med Stockholms stad, which is 50% owned by the city of Stockholm. In Russia, the firm's operations are conducted through OAO Fortum. In November 2009, the firm received a grant from the Swedish Energy Agency to develop a full-scale wave power project with Seabased Industry AB. In August 2010, Fortum acquired a 40% stake in the Blaiken wind power project being developed by the Swedish energy company Skelleftea Kraft, with a proposed 100 wind turbines and 250 MW capacity. In September 2010, the firm commenced operations at a CHP plant fuelled by biomass and coal in Poland.

FINANCIALS: **Sales and profits are in thousands of dollars—add 000 to get the full amount. 2010 Note: Financial information for 2010 was not available for all companies at press time.**

2010 Sales: $	2010 Profits: $	**U.S. Stock Ticker:**
2009 Sales: $7,628,840	2009 Profits: $1,841,590	**Int'l Ticker: FUM1V** Int'l Exchange: Helsinki-Euronext
2008 Sales: $8,291,230	2008 Profits: $2,268,470	Employees: 11,094
2007 Sales: $6,540,000	2007 Profits: $2,270,000	Fiscal Year Ends: 12/31
2006 Sales: $5,920,000	2006 Profits: $1,410,000	Parent Company:

SALARIES/BENEFITS:

Pension Plan:	ESOP Stock Plan:	Profit Sharing:	Top Exec. Salary: $1,203,384	Bonus: $482,488
Savings Plan:	Stock Purch. Plan:		Second Exec. Salary: $1,036,700	Bonus: $186,477

OTHER THOUGHTS:

Apparent Women Officers or Directors: 2
Hot Spot for Advancement for Women/Minorities: Y

LOCATIONS: ("Y" = Yes)

West:	Southwest:	Midwest:	Southeast:	Northeast:	International:
					Y

FOSTER WHEELER AG

www.fwc.com

Industry Group Code: 237 **Ranks within this company's industry group:** Sales: 5 Profits: 3

Exploration/Production:		Refining/Retailing:		Utilities:		Alternative Energy:		Specialty Services:		Energy Mktg./Other Svcs.	
Exploration:		Refining:		Electric Utility:		Waste/Solar/Other:	Y	Consulting/Eng.:		Energy Marketing:	
Production:		Retailing:		Gas Utility:		Thermal/Steam:	Y	Seismic:		Equipment/Machinery:	Y
Coal Production:		Convenience Stores:		Pipelines:		Wind:		Drilling:		Oil Field Services:	
		Chemicals:		Water:		Hydro:		InfoTech:		Air/Shipping Transportation:	
						Fuel Cells:		Specialty Services:			

TYPES OF BUSINESS:

Engineering & Construction
Industrial Plant Design & Development
Energy Equipment
Power Systems Manufacturer
Steam Generation Equipment
Renewable Energy Technology

BRANDS/DIVISIONS/AFFILIATES:

Foster Wheeler, Ltd.
Foster Wheeler International Corp.
Foster Wheeler Power Systems, Inc.
Foster Wheeler USA Corp.
Foster Wheeler Power Machinery Co., Ltd.
Foster Wheeler SOFCON Consulting Energy Company
Atlas Engineering, Inc.

CONTACTS: *Note: Officers with more than one job title may be intentionally listed here more than once.*

Raymond J. Milchovich, CEO
Umberto della Sala, COO
Umberto della Sala, Pres.
Franco Baseotto, CFO/Exec. VP/Treas.
Michelle Davies, General Counsel
Maureen Bingert, Contact-Media Rel.
Scott Lamb, Contact-Investor Rel.
Lisa Z. Wood, VP/Controller
Robert C. Flexon, Pres./CEO-Foster Wheeler USA Corp.
Gary Nedelka, Acting CEO-Global Power Group
Eric Sherbet, Corp. Sec.
Raymond J. Milchovich, Chmn.
Troy Roder, CEO-Foster Wheeler Energy Ltd. (UK)

Phone: 41-22-741-8000	**Fax:**
Toll-Free:	
Address: 80 Rue de Lausanne, Geneva, 1202 Switzerland	

GROWTH PLANS/SPECIAL FEATURES:

Foster Wheeler AG is an international engineering, construction and project management firm providing services in the oil and gas, oil refining, chemical/petrochemical, pharmaceutical, biotechnology, healthcare, environmental and power industries through offices in more than 28 countries. Foster Wheeler operates under two business groups: the Global Engineering and Construction (E&C) Group and the Global Power Group. The E&C Group provides engineering, project management, and construction management services and purchases equipment, materials and services from third party suppliers and contractors. It operates in the upstream oil and gas; LNG liquefaction, gas-to-liquids, coal-to-gas, coal-to-liquids and carbon capture; oil refining, including delayed coking, chemicals and petrochemicals; and pharmaceuticals, biotechnology and healthcare markets. Additionally the group provides environmental remediation services. The E&C Group generated approximately 66% of revenues in 2009. The Global Power Group designs, manufactures and erects steam generating and auxiliary equipment for electric power generating stations and industrial facilities worldwide. Other services include the design, manufacture and installation of auxiliary equipment, which includes steam generators for solar thermal power plants, feedwater heaters, steam condensers and heat-recovery equipment. The company has engineered and built process, power and industrial facilities in over 125 countries. The company operates through its numerous subsidiaries, including Foster Wheeler Power Machinery Co., Ltd.; Foster Wheeler International Corp.; Foster Wheeler Power Systems, Inc.; and Foster Wheeler USA Corporation. In October 2009, the company acquired a majority of the assets of Atlas Engineering, Inc., a Houston-based engineering firm focused on oil and natural gas. In February 2010, a subsidiary of Foster Wheeler AG and a Saudi Arabian consulting and engineering company agreed to establish a Saudi Arabian Joint-Venture, Foster Wheeler SOFCON Consulting Energy Company.

FINANCIALS: **Sales and profits are in thousands of dollars—add 000 to get the full amount. 2010 Note: Financial information for 2010 was not available for all companies at press time.**

2010 Sales: $	2010 Profits: $	**U.S. Stock Ticker: FWLT**
2009 Sales: $5,056,334	2009 Profits: $361,358	**Int'l Ticker:** Int'l Exchange:
2008 Sales: $6,854,290	2008 Profits: $526,620	Employees: 13,446
2007 Sales: $5,107,243	2007 Profits: $393,874	Fiscal Year Ends: 12/31
2006 Sales: $3,495,048	2006 Profits: $261,984	Parent Company:

SALARIES/BENEFITS:

Pension Plan:	ESOP Stock Plan:	Profit Sharing:	Top Exec. Salary: $1,250,000	Bonus: $1,625,000
Savings Plan:	Stock Purch. Plan:		Second Exec. Salary: $817,111	Bonus: $1,274,700

OTHER THOUGHTS:

Apparent Women Officers or Directors: 3
Hot Spot for Advancement for Women/Minorities: Y

LOCATIONS: ("Y" = Yes)

West:	Southwest:	Midwest:	Southeast:	Northeast:	International:
Y	Y	Y	Y	Y	Y

FRONTIER OIL CORPORATION

www.frontieroil.com

Industry Group Code: 324110 **Ranks within this company's industry group:** Sales: 23 Profits: 20

Exploration/Production:		Refining/Retailing:		Utilities:		Alternative Energy:		Specialty Services:		Energy Mktg./Other Svcs.	
Exploration:		Refining:	Y	Electric Utility:		Waste/Solar/Other:		Consulting/Eng.:		Energy Marketing:	
Production:		Retailing:		Gas Utility:		Thermal/Steam:		Seismic:		Equipment/Machinery:	
Coal Production:		Convenience Stores:		Pipelines:		Wind:		Drilling:		Oil Field Services:	
		Chemicals:		Water:		Hydro:		InfoTech:		Air/Shipping Transportation:	
						Fuel Cells:		Specialty Services:			

TYPES OF BUSINESS:

Petroleum Refining

BRANDS/DIVISIONS/AFFILIATES:

Frontier Oil and Refining Company
Ethanol Management Company
Cheyenne Refinery
El Dorado Refinery
NuStar Pipeline Operating Partnership LP
Magellan Pipeline Company LP
Plains All American Pipeline
ConocoPhillips Pipeline

CONTACTS:

Note: Officers with more than one job title may be intentionally listed here more than once.

Michael C. Jennings, CEO
Michael C. Jennings, Pres.
Doug S. Aron, CFO
J. Currie Bechtol, General Counsel/VP
Paul Eisman, Exec. VP-Refining Oper.
Kristine Boyd, Contact-Media
Nancy J. Zupan, Chief Acct. Officer/VP
Jon D. Galvin, VP
Gerald B. Faudel, VP-Gov't & Environmental Rel.
Leo J. Hoonakker, Treas./VP
Michael C. Jennings, Chmn.

Phone: 713-688-9600 **Fax:** 713-688-0616
Toll-Free:
Address: 10000 Memorial Dr., Ste. 600, Houston, TX 77024-3411 US

GROWTH PLANS/SPECIAL FEATURES:

Frontier Oil Corporation is an independent oil refining and marketing company with refineries located in Wyoming and Kansas and a total crude oil processing capacity of approximately 187,000 barrels per day (bpd). The firm's complex refineries can process heavier, less expensive types of crude oil while producing a high percentage of gasoline, diesel fuel and other high-margin refined products. The company's Cheyenne, Wyoming refinery has a permitted crude processing capacity of 52,000 bpd. The Cheyenne refinery has a coking unit that allows it to process heavy crude oil for use as a feedstock, which is less expensive. Pipeline shipments from the Cheyenne Refinery are handled by the Plains All American Pipeline and the ConocoPhillips Pipeline. In 2009, the Cheyenne Refinery's product yield included gasoline (48%), diesel fuel (37%) and asphalt and other refined petroleum products (15%). El Dorado refinery is one of the largest refineries in the Rocky Mountain region, with a permitted crude processing capacity of 135,000 bpd. The El Dorado refinery's product mix includes gasoline, diesel and jet fuel, chemicals and other refined petroleum products. The refinery's products are primarily shipped via pipeline to terminals for distribution by truck or rail. The NuStar Pipeline Operating Partnership L.P. Pipeline, the Magellan Pipeline Company, L.P. mountain pipeline and the Magellan mid-continent pipeline handle shipments from its El Dorado Refinery. The firm markets its refined products primarily in the eastern slope of the Rocky Mountain region, which encompasses eastern Colorado, which includes the Denver metropolitan area, eastern Wyoming and western Nebraska. In 2009, the El Dorado Refinery's product yield included gasoline (49%), diesel and jet fuel (41%) and chemicals and other refined petroleum products (10%). Subsidiary, Ethanol Management Company, is a 25,000 bpd products terminal and blending facility located near Denver, Colorado.

FINANCIALS:

Sales and profits are in thousands of dollars—add 000 to get the full amount. 2010 Note: Financial information for 2010 was not available for all companies at press time.

2010 Sales: $	2010 Profits: $	**U.S. Stock Ticker: FTO**
2009 Sales: $4,237,213	2009 Profits: $-83,760	**Int'l Ticker:** Int'l Exchange:
2008 Sales: $6,498,780	2008 Profits: $226,053	Employees: 843
2007 Sales: $5,188,740	2007 Profits: $499,125	Fiscal Year Ends: 12/31
2006 Sales: $4,795,953	2006 Profits: $379,277	Parent Company:

SALARIES/BENEFITS:

Pension Plan:	ESOP Stock Plan:	Profit Sharing:	Top Exec. Salary: $975,000	Bonus: $1,889,063
Savings Plan:	Stock Purch. Plan:		Second Exec. Salary: $775,000	Bonus: $1,501,563

OTHER THOUGHTS:

Apparent Women Officers or Directors: 1
Hot Spot for Advancement for Women/Minorities:

LOCATIONS: ("Y" = Yes)

West:	Southwest:	Midwest:	Southeast:	Northeast:	International:
Y	Y	Y			

FRONTLINE LTD

www.frontline.bm

Industry Group Code: 483111 **Ranks within this company's industry group:** Sales: 4 Profits: 3

Exploration/Production:		Refining/Retailing:		Utilities:		Alternative Energy:		Specialty Services:		Energy Mktg./Other Svcs.	
Exploration:		Refining:		Electric Utility:		Waste/Solar/Other:		Consulting/Eng.:		Energy Marketing:	
Production:		Retailing:		Gas Utility:		Thermal/Steam:		Seismic:		Equipment/Machinery:	
Coal Production:		Convenience Stores:		Pipelines:		Wind:		Drilling:		Oil Field Services:	
		Chemicals:		Water:		Hydro:		InfoTech:		Air/Shipping Transportation:	Y
						Fuel Cells:		Specialty Services:			

TYPES OF BUSINESS:

Deep Sea Shipping
Oil Tankers

BRANDS/DIVISIONS/AFFILIATES:

Frontline Management (Bermuda), Ltd.
Frontline Management AS

CONTACTS:

Note: Officers with more than one job title may be intentionally listed here more than once.

John Fredriksen, CEO
John Fredriksen, Pres.
Jens Martin Jensen, CEO-Frontline Mgmt. AS
Inger M. Klemp, CFO-Frontline Mgmt.
John Fredriksen, Chmn.

Phone: 441-295-6935 **Fax:** 441-295-3494
Toll-Free:
Address: 14 Par-la-Ville Rd., Par-la-Ville Pl., Hamilton, HM 08 Bermuda

GROWTH PLANS/SPECIAL FEATURES:

Frontline, Ltd. is a Bermuda-based tanker company. Its fleet totals 84 vessels, including approximately 29 Suezmax tankers, eight OBO (Oil/Bulk/Ore) tankers and 47 VLCC tankers, totaling more than 19 million deadweight tons. The firm's operations consist primarily of short-term contracts for the transportation of oil from the Arabian Gulf, the eastern Mediterranean, the North Sea and West Africa to the Far East, the Gulf of Mexico, the U.S. Atlantic Coast and Western Europe. Frontline's customers include oil companies and government agencies. The firm operates through two management subsidiaries: Frontline Management (Bermuda), Ltd. and Frontline Management AS (Norway). These companies are responsible for the commercial management of the firm's ship-owning subsidiaries, including chartering and insurance. However, the firm seeks independent organizations for crewing, ship management and accounting services. All vessels owned by Frontline and its subsidiaries are registered under Bahamas, Liberian, Singaporean, Norwegian or Panamanian flags. In April 2010, Frontline acquired two additional double hull VLCC tankers built in 2009.

FINANCIALS:

Sales and profits are in thousands of dollars—add 000 to get the full amount. 2010 Note: Financial information for 2010 was not available for all companies at press time.

2010 Sales: $	2010 Profits: $
2009 Sales: $1,133,286	2009 Profits: $102,701
2008 Sales: $2,104,018	2008 Profits: $698,770
2007 Sales: $1,299,927	2007 Profits: $570,418
2006 Sales: $1,583,863	2006 Profits: $516,000

U.S. Stock Ticker: FRO
Int'l Ticker: FRO Int'l Exchange: Oslo-OBX
Employees: 51
Fiscal Year Ends: 12/31
Parent Company:

SALARIES/BENEFITS:

Pension Plan:	ESOP Stock Plan:	Profit Sharing:	Top Exec. Salary: $	Bonus: $
Savings Plan:	Stock Purch. Plan:		Second Exec. Salary: $	Bonus: $

OTHER THOUGHTS:

Apparent Women Officers or Directors: 1
Hot Spot for Advancement for Women/Minorities:

LOCATIONS: ("Y" = Yes)

West:	Southwest:	Midwest:	Southeast:	Northeast:	International:
					Y

FUEL TECH INC

www.fuel-tech.com

Industry Group Code: 541712 **Ranks within this company's industry group:** Sales: 1 Profits: 1

Exploration/Production:		Refining/Retailing:		Utilities:		Alternative Energy:		Specialty Services:		Energy Mktg./Other Svcs.	
Exploration:		Refining:		Electric Utility:		Waste/Solar/Other:		Consulting/Eng.:		Energy Marketing:	
Production:		Retailing:		Gas Utility:		Thermal/Steam:		Seismic:		Equipment/Machinery:	Y
Coal Production:		Convenience Stores:		Pipelines:		Wind:		Drilling:		Oil Field Services:	
		Chemicals:	Y	Water:		Hydro:		InfoTech:		Air/Shipping Transportation:	
						Fuel Cells:		Specialty Services:	Y		

TYPES OF BUSINESS:

Nitrogen Oxide Reduction Technology
Combustion Unit Efficiency Technology
Air Pollution Reduction Technology
Boiler Optimization Technology
Efficiency Improvement Technology
Carbon Emission Reduction Technologies

BRANDS/DIVISIONS/AFFILIATES:

FUEL CHEM
NOxOUT
NOxOUT ULTRA
NOxOUT-SCR
TIFI Targeted In-Furnace Injection
NOxOUT CASCADE
Beijing Fuel Tech Environmental Technologies Co

CONTACTS: *Note: Officers with more than one job title may be intentionally listed here more than once.*

Douglas G. Bailey, CEO
Douglas G. Bailey, Pres.
David S. Collins, CFO/Sr. VP
Robert E. Puissant, Exec. VP-Mktg. & Sales
Paul G. Carmignani, VP-New Prod. Dev.
Albert G. Grigonis, General Counsel/Corp. Sec./VP
Vincent J. Arnone, Exec. VP-Worldwide Oper.
Tracy H. Krumme, VP-Investor Rel.
David S. Collins, Treas.
Vincent M. Albanese, Sr. VP-Regulatory Affairs
Willliam E. Cummings Jr., Sr. VP-Air Pollution Control Sales
Timothy J. Eibes, VP-Project Execution
Stephen P. Brady, Sr. VP-FUEL CHEM Sales
Douglas G. Bailey, Chmn.
M. Linda Lin, VP-China & Pacific Rim

Phone: 630-845-4500 **Fax:** 630-845-4502
Toll-Free: 800-666-9688
Address: 27601 Bella Vista Parkway, Warrenville, IL 60555-1617 US

GROWTH PLANS/SPECIAL FEATURES:

Fuel Tech, Inc. is a fully integrated company that uses a suite of technologies to provide boiler optimization, efficiency improvement and air pollution reduction and control solutions to utility and industrial customers worldwide. It owns exceptional technologies that aid coal-fired electric generating plants in reducing carbon emissions. Fuel Tech's special focus is the worldwide marketing of its nitrogen oxide (NOx) reduction and FUEL CHEM processes. NOx reduction technology includes the NOxOUT, NOxOUT ULTRA and NOxOUT-SCR processes, which can reduce NOx emissions from 30-85% in flue gas from boilers, incinerators, furnaces and other stationary combustion sources. The NOx reduction business is primarily driven by the U.S. air pollution control market, which depends on air pollution regulations and regulation enforcement. Outside the U.S., Fuel Tech sells NOx control systems in Europe, providing technology that enables certain waste incinerators and cement plants to comply with specified NOx reduction targets and certain power plants to meet other regulations by 2010. Fuel Tech is also seeking to expand its NOx control operations in China, where it recently formed Beijing Fuel Tech Environmental Technologies Co., Ltd. FUEL CHEM improves the efficiency, reliability and environmental status of plants in the electric utility, pulp and paper, industrial and waste-to-energy markets. It controls slagging, fouling, corrosion, loss on ignition, opacity and acid plume; and controls sulfur trioxide, ammonium bisulfate, particulate matter, carbon dioxide and NOx formation by adding chemicals into the fuel or via TIFI Targeted In-Furnace Injection programs. FUEL CHEM programs currently operate in over 95 combustion units, treating various solid and liquid fuels, including coal, heavy oil, biomass and municipal waste.

FINANCIALS: **Sales and profits are in thousands of dollars—add 000 to get the full amount. 2010 Note: Financial information for 2010 was not available for all companies at press time.**

2010 Sales: $	2010 Profits: $	**U.S. Stock Ticker: FTEK**
2009 Sales: $71,397	2009 Profits: $-2,306	**Int'l Ticker:** Int'l Exchange:
2008 Sales: $81,074	2008 Profits: $3,602	Employees: 168
2007 Sales: $80,297	2007 Profits: $7,243	Fiscal Year Ends: 12/31
2006 Sales: $75,115	2006 Profits: $6,826	Parent Company:

SALARIES/BENEFITS:

Pension Plan:	ESOP Stock Plan:	Profit Sharing:	Top Exec. Salary: $500,000	Bonus: $
Savings Plan:	Stock Purch. Plan:		Second Exec. Salary: $300,000	Bonus: $

OTHER THOUGHTS:

Apparent Women Officers or Directors: 1
Hot Spot for Advancement for Women/Minorities:

LOCATIONS: ("Y" = Yes)

West:	Southwest:	Midwest:	Southeast:	Northeast:	International:
		Y		Y	Y

FURMANITE CORP

www.furmanite.com

Industry Group Code: 213112 **Ranks within this company's industry group:** Sales: 27 Profits: 20

Exploration/Production:		**Refining/Retailing:**		**Utilities:**		**Alternative Energy:**		**Specialty Services:**		**Energy Mktg./Other Svcs.**	
Exploration:		Refining:		Electric Utility:		Waste/Solar/Other:		Consulting/Eng.:	Y	Energy Marketing:	
Production:		Retailing:		Gas Utility:		Thermal/Steam:		Seismic:		Equipment/Machinery:	
Coal Production:		Convenience Stores:		Pipelines:	Y	Wind:		Drilling:	Y	Oil Field Services:	
		Chemicals:		Water:		Hydro:		InfoTech:	Y	Air/Shipping Transportation:	
						Fuel Cells:		Specialty Services:	Y		

TYPES OF BUSINESS:

Oil & Gas Drilling Support Services
Services for Pipeline Operators
Services for Refineries
Information Management Services
Services for Utility Companies
Web-Based Monitoring Systems
PACS Consulting Services

BRANDS/DIVISIONS/AFFILIATES:

Xtria LLC
Furmanite Worldwide, Inc.
Trevitest

CONTACTS:

Note: Officers with more than one job title may be intentionally listed here more than once.

Charles R. Cox, CEO
Joseph E. Millron, COO/Exec. VP
Joseph E. Millron, Pres.
Robert S. Muff, CFO
Robert S. Muff, Controller/Principal Acct. Officer
Charles R. Cox, Chmn.

Phone: 972-699-4000	**Fax:** 281-842-5100
Toll-Free: 877-777-0800	
Address: 2435 N. Central Expressway, Ste. 700, Richardson, TX 75080 US	

GROWTH PLANS/SPECIAL FEATURES:

Furmanite Corp., formerly Xanser Corporation, provides specialized technical services worldwide through subsidiary Furmanite Worldwide, Inc. and its affiliates, and information technology services through its subsidiary Xtria LLC. Furmanite and its domestic and international subsidiaries and affiliates provide specialized technical engineering services to petroleum refineries, chemical plants, mining, offshore energy production platforms, steel mills, nuclear power stations, conventional power stations, pulp and paper mills, food and beverage processing plants and other flow-process facilities in more than 50 countries. Furmanite provides in-line leak repair (leak sealing) in valves, pipes and other components of piping systems and related equipment typically used in flow-process industries. Other services include on-site machining, bolting, valve testing, valve repair, product distribution, heat treating and repair on such systems and equipment. The company also performs diagnostic services on valves and motors, primarily utilizing its patented Trevitest system. Some of the techniques and materials used in Furmanite's leak sealing under pressure services are proprietary; the company holds approximately 125 patents and trademarks for its techniques, products and materials. All customers are served from the worldwide headquarters in Richardson, Texas with a substantial presence in the U.K., Europe and Asia-Pacific. Sales by major geographic region for 2009 were 44% for the U.S., 43% for Europe and 13% for Asia-Pacific. Xtria offers products and services that include web hosted data processing, consulting, research, program and policy analysis, program implementation and program evaluation to agencies of state and federal government.

FINANCIALS:

Sales and profits are in thousands of dollars—add 000 to get the full amount. 2010 Note: Financial information for 2010 was not available for all companies at press time.

2010 Sales: $	2010 Profits: $	**U.S. Stock Ticker: FRM**
2009 Sales: $275,940	2009 Profits: $-2,830	**Int'l Ticker:** Int'l Exchange:
2008 Sales: $320,942	2008 Profits: $21,868	Employees: 1,737
2007 Sales: $290,287	2007 Profits: $12,495	Fiscal Year Ends: 12/31
2006 Sales: $246,388	2006 Profits: $-3,432	Parent Company:

SALARIES/BENEFITS:

Pension Plan:	ESOP Stock Plan:	Profit Sharing:	Top Exec. Salary: $400,000	Bonus: $
Savings Plan:	Stock Purch. Plan:		Second Exec. Salary: $350,000	Bonus: $

OTHER THOUGHTS:

Apparent Women Officers or Directors:
Hot Spot for Advancement for Women/Minorities:

LOCATIONS: ("Y" = Yes)

West:	Southwest:	Midwest:	Southeast:	Northeast:	International:
Y	Y	Y	Y	Y	Y

GAIL (INDIA) LIMITED

www.gailonline.com

Industry Group Code: 211111 **Ranks within this company's industry group:** Sales: 57 Profits: 45

Exploration/Production:		Refining/Retailing:		Utilities:		Alternative Energy:		Specialty Services:		Energy Mktg./Other Svcs.	
Exploration:		Refining:		Electric Utility:		Waste/Solar/Other:		Consulting/Eng.:		Energy Marketing:	
Production:		Retailing:		Gas Utility:	Y	Thermal/Steam:		Seismic:		Equipment/Machinery:	
Coal Production:		Convenience Stores:		Pipelines:		Wind:		Drilling:		Oil Field Services:	
		Chemicals:		Water:		Hydro:		InfoTech:		Air/Shipping Transportation:	
						Fuel Cells:		Specialty Services:			

TYPES OF BUSINESS:

Natural Gas Exploration, Production & Distribution
Fiber Optic Network

BRANDS/DIVISIONS/AFFILIATES:

GAILTEL
China Gas Holdings
GAIL Gas Limited
Gujarat State Energy Generation Ltd.
GAIL Global (Singapore) Ltd

CONTACTS:

Note: Officers with more than one job title may be intentionally listed here more than once.

B.C. Tripathi, Managing Dir.
Prabhat Singh, Dir.-Mktg.
S.L. Raina, Dir.-Human Resources
N.K. Nagpal, Corp. Sec.
S. Venkatraman, Dir.-Bus. Dev.
R.K. Goel, Dir.-Finance
R.D. Goyal, Dir.-Projects
Arun Singhal, Chief Vigilance Officer
B.C. Tripathi, Chmn.

Phone: 91-11-2617-2580	Fax: 91-11-2618-5941
Toll-Free:	
Address: 16, Bhikaiji Cama Place, R.K. Puram, New Delhi, 110 066 India	

GROWTH PLANS/SPECIAL FEATURES:

GAIL (India) Limited, formerly Gas Authority of India, Ltd., is a natural gas company whose operations encompass exploration, production, processing, transmission, marketing and distribution. The company maintains and operates a 4,847 mile high-pressure natural gas pipeline; seven liquefied petroleum gas (LPG) processing units, which collectively produce 1.2 million tons per annum (MMTPA) of LPG and other liquid hydrocarbons; an LPG pipeline network of approximately 1,194 miles, which can transport 3.8 MMTPA of LPG; a gas-based integrated petrochemical complex which produces over 4 million tons of polymers annually; 27 oil and gas exploration blocks; and one coal bed methane (CBM) block. Through its telecom business, GAILTEL, the company provides broadband and telemetry services to the Indian telecommunications industry through an 8,077 mile fiber optic cable network it owns and maintains. The firm maintains zonal offices in Delhi, Chandigarh, Jaipur, Ahmedabad, Mumbai, Bhopal, Hyderabad, Bangalore, Chennai, Kolkata and Lucknow. Subsidiaries of the company include GAIL Global (Singapore) Ltd., operating in Singapore; Gujarat State Energy Generation Ltd., a joint venture which operates a natural gas-fired power plant; and GAIL Gas Limited, which handles the marketing and distribution of compressed natural gas (CNG), piped natural gas and LPG in urban centers domestically and abroad. The company also has a stake in China Gas Holdings for natural gas exploration in mainland China. GAIL was established by the Government of India in 1984 to provide infrastructure in support of the nation's growing natural gas industry. The Indian Central Government and various Indian state governments collectively own about 57% of the company. In August 2010, GAIL and Tata Institute of Social Sciences formed a CSR (corporate social responsibility) collaboration agreement. In October 2010, the company began construction of the Karanpur-Moradabad-Kashipur-Rudrapur-Pant Nagar natural gas pipeline, which will be 113 miles long when completed.

FINANCIALS:

Sales and profits are in thousands of dollars—add 000 to get the full amount. 2010 Note: Financial information for 2010 was not available for all companies at press time.

2010 Sales: $	2010 Profits: $	**U.S. Stock Ticker:**
2009 Sales: $5,334,870	2009 Profits: $611,460	**Int'l Ticker: 532155** Int'l Exchange: Bombay-BSE
2008 Sales: $5,064,640	2008 Profits: $580,490	Employees: 3,544
2007 Sales: $3,367,990	2007 Profits: $518,220	Fiscal Year Ends: 3/31
2006 Sales: $3,029,300	2006 Profits: $496,590	Parent Company:

SALARIES/BENEFITS:

Pension Plan:	ESOP Stock Plan:	Profit Sharing:	Top Exec. Salary: $	Bonus: $
Savings Plan:	Stock Purch. Plan:		Second Exec. Salary: $	Bonus: $

OTHER THOUGHTS:

Apparent Women Officers or Directors:
Hot Spot for Advancement for Women/Minorities:

LOCATIONS: ("Y" = Yes)

West:	Southwest:	Midwest:	Southeast:	Northeast:	International:
					Y

Note: Financial information, benefits and other data can change quickly and may vary from those stated here.

GALP ENERGIA SGPS SA

www.galpenergia.com

Industry Group Code: 211111 **Ranks within this company's industry group:** Sales: 40 Profits: 49

Exploration/Production:		Refining/Retailing:		Utilities:		Alternative Energy:		Specialty Services:		Energy Mktg./Other Svcs.	
Exploration:	Y	Refining:	Y	Electric Utility:	Y	Waste/Solar/Other:		Consulting/Eng.:		Energy Marketing:	Y
Production:	Y	Retailing:	Y	Gas Utility:	Y	Thermal/Steam:		Seismic:		Equipment/Machinery:	
Coal Production:		Convenience Stores:	Y	Pipelines:		Wind:		Drilling:		Oil Field Services:	
		Chemicals:		Water:		Hydro:		InfoTech:		Air/Shipping Transportation:	
						Fuel Cells:		Specialty Services:			

TYPES OF BUSINESS:

Oil Exploration & Production
Oil Refining
Oil Marketing
Natural Gas Supply & Distribution
Power Generation

BRANDS/DIVISIONS/AFFILIATES:

Petrogal, S.A.
Gas de Portugal, SGPS, S.A.
Transgas, SGPS
GDPd, SGPS
Driftal
PTL
Sacor Maritima
Eival

CONTACTS:

Note: Officers with more than one job title may be intentionally listed here more than once.

Manuel Ferreira De Oliveira, CEO
Claudio De Marco, CFO
Carlos Nuno Gomes da Silver, Head-Oil Prod. Mktg.
Carlos Nuno Gomes da Silver, Head-Human Resources
Fernando Manuel dos Santos Gomes, Head-Exploration & Prod.
Rui Maria Diniz Mayer, Sec.
Tiago Villas-Boas, Dir.-Media Rel.
Tiago Villas-Boas, Dir.-Investor Rel.
Fabrizio Dassogno, Head-Natural Gas & Power
Francisco Luis Murteira Nabo, Chmn.
Andre Freire de Almeida Palmeiro Ribeiro, Head-Supply, Logistics & Refining

Phone: 351-21-724-25-00 **Fax:** 351-21-724-29-65
Toll-Free:
Address: Edificio Galp Energia, Rua Tomas de Fonseca, Lisbon, 1600-209 Portugal

GROWTH PLANS/SPECIAL FEATURES:

Galp Energia SGPS, S.A. is a leading Portuguese integrated oil and natural gas company. Galp controls two pre-existing, formerly government-owned companies: Petrogal, S.A., a leading refiner and distributor of oil products in Portugal; and Gas de Portugal, SGPS, S.A. (GDP), which is responsible for the import, transportation and distribution of natural gas in Portugal. Through these two companies, Galp operates in three business areas: exploration and production; refining and marketing; and natural gas and power. The exploration and production business holds the company's upstream hydrocarbon assets. It is currently active in 46 exploration and production blocks across four continents, with Brazil and Angola being the most significant producers. The firm has contingent resources in these two areas totaling more than 3 billion barrels of oil equivalent. The refining and marketing business area controls two refineries in Portugal and oil transportation and storage facilities. Additionally, the segment manages a network of more than 210 convenience stores and 1,500 services stations, including those acquired and converted from ExxonMobil and Agip. The natural gas and power unit supplies and distributes natural gas to residential, commercial and industrial customers as well as power companies. It also owns interests in four cogeneration plants with an installed capacity of 160 megawatts (MW). Galp has plans to expand its current capacity by building two combined cycle gas turbine (CCGT) power plants and entering the wind energy industry. GDP and Petrogal themselves operate through many subsidiaries, including Transgas, SGPS; GDPd, SGPS; Driftal; PTL; Sacor Maritima; Eival; ASA; and Galpgeste. In April 2010, the firm, in conjunction with Morgan Stanley Infrastructure, jointly acquired the gas supply and distribution businesses in the Madrid region from Gas Natural Fenosa. In June 2010, Galp established a partnership with a subsidiary of International Power plc to aid in the development of a CCGT plant in Sines.

FINANCIALS:

Sales and profits are in thousands of dollars—add 000 to get the full amount. 2010 Note: Financial information for 2010 was not available for all companies at press time.

2010 Sales: $	2010 Profits: $	**U.S. Stock Ticker:**
2009 Sales: $14,909,100	2009 Profits: $428,970	**Int'l Ticker: GALP** Int'l Exchange: Lisbon-Euronext
2008 Sales: $22,230,000	2008 Profits: $171,000	Employees:
2007 Sales: $18,804,300	2007 Profits: $1,157,200	Fiscal Year Ends: 12/31
2006 Sales: $18,246,300	2006 Profits: $1,124,600	Parent Company:

SALARIES/BENEFITS:

Pension Plan:	ESOP Stock Plan:	Profit Sharing:	Top Exec. Salary: $1,499,579	Bonus: $332,049
Savings Plan:	Stock Purch. Plan:		Second Exec. Salary: $595,850	Bonus: $132,124

OTHER THOUGHTS:

Apparent Women Officers or Directors:
Hot Spot for Advancement for Women/Minorities:

LOCATIONS: ("Y" = Yes)

West:	Southwest:	Midwest:	Southeast:	Northeast:	International:
					Y

GAS NATURAL SDG SA

www.gasnatural.com

Industry Group Code: 221 **Ranks within this company's industry group:** Sales: 6 Profits: 9

Exploration/Production:		Refining/Retailing:		Utilities:		Alternative Energy:		Specialty Services:		Energy Mktg./Other Svcs.	
Exploration:	Y	Refining:	Y	Electric Utility:	Y	Waste/Solar/Other:		Consulting/Eng.:		Energy Marketing:	
Production:	Y	Retailing:	Y	Gas Utility:	Y	Thermal/Steam:		Seismic:		Equipment/Machinery:	
Coal Production:		Convenience Stores:		Pipelines:		Wind:		Drilling:		Oil Field Services:	
		Chemicals:		Water:		Hydro:		InfoTech:		Air/Shipping Transportation:	
						Fuel Cells:		Specialty Services:			

TYPES OF BUSINESS:

Natural Gas Utility
Electricity Generation
LNG Production & Distribution

BRANDS/DIVISIONS/AFFILIATES:

Union Fenosa SA
Galp Energia
Morgan Stanley Infrastructure
Red Electrica
Alpiq
Gas Natural Fenosa

CONTACTS:

Note: Officers with more than one job title may be intentionally listed here more than once.

Rafael Villaseca Marco, CEO
Antonio Gallart Gabas, COO
Carlos J. Alvarez Fernandez, CFO
Manuel Garcia Cobaleda, General Counsel/Managing Dir.-Legal Svcs.
Antonio Basolas Tena, Head-Strategy & Dev.
Jordi Garcia Tabernero, Managing Dir.-Comm.
Jose Javier Fernandez Martinez, Managing Dir.-Power Generation
Manuel Fernandez Alvarez, Managing Dir.-Wholesale Energy
Josep Moragas Freixa, Managing Dir.-Retail Energy
Antoni Peris Mingot, Managing Dir.-Regulated Gas
Salvador Gabarro Serra, Chmn.
Sergio Aranda Moreno, Managing Dir.-Latin America

Phone: 34-902-199-199	**Fax:** 34-934-025-896
Toll-Free:	
Address: Placa del Gas 1, Barcelona, 08003 Spain	

GROWTH PLANS/SPECIAL FEATURES:

Gas Natural SDG S.A. is a Spanish electricity generating firm and natural gas utility that serves roughly 20 million customers in 23 countries primarily in Europe and Central and South America. The company operates in four segments: gas distribution; electricity; upstream and midstream; and wholesale and retail. The gas distribution division operates through 10 distribution companies and two sales companies, supplying natural gas products to customers across Spain through a distribution network of 31,500 miles. It is also present in eight regions of Italy and four Latin American countries. The electricity division has an installed capacity of 17.86 gigawatts (GW), with roughly 4.45 GW of installed capacity outside of Spain, and uses a mix of combined cycle gas turbines (CCGT), hydro, nuclear, coal-fired and renewable energies. The firm's upstream and midstream activities include liquid natural gas (LNG) exploration and production, distribution and liquefaction, as well as LNG value-added activities and transport from liquefaction plants to regasification plants. The wholesale and retail division's activities consist of the resale of LNG to wholesale and retail customers in Spain and wholesale customers outside of Spain. Additionally, the firm has setup infrastructure for the distribution of compressed natural gas for use in automobiles. In September 2009, Gas Natural merged with Union Fenosa SA, a Spanish gas and electric company, and created the new brand Gas Natural Fenosa. The total value of the transaction was roughly $26.1 billion. In 2010, following this transaction Gas Natural divested a number of assets in accordance with Spain's National Competition Commission, including gas commercialization and distribution assets in Madrid to Galp Energia and Morgan Stanley Infrastructure; distribution assets in Cantabria and Murcia to EDP Group; and a CCGT plant in Spain to Swiss energy group Alpiq. In July 2010, the company sold its electricity transmission assets to Red Electrica in compliance with a Spanish provision designating it as the sole operator of transmission infrastructure in the country.

FINANCIALS:

Sales and profits are in thousands of dollars—add 000 to get the full amount. 2010 Note: Financial information for 2010 was not available for all companies at press time.

2010 Sales: $	2010 Profits: $	**U.S. Stock Ticker:**
2009 Sales: $18,251,900	2009 Profits: $1,465,890	**Int'l Ticker: GAS** Int'l Exchange: Madrid-MCE
2008 Sales: $20,109,320	2008 Profits: $1,569,370	Employees: 6,842
2007 Sales: $14,985,480	2007 Profits: $1,423,870	Fiscal Year Ends:
2006 Sales: $	2006 Profits: $	Parent Company:

SALARIES/BENEFITS:

Pension Plan:	ESOP Stock Plan:	Profit Sharing:	Top Exec. Salary: $	Bonus: $
Savings Plan:	Stock Purch. Plan:		Second Exec. Salary: $	Bonus: $

OTHER THOUGHTS:

Apparent Women Officers or Directors:
Hot Spot for Advancement for Women/Minorities:

LOCATIONS: ("Y" = Yes)

West:	Southwest:	Midwest:	Southeast:	Northeast:	International:
					Y

GAZ METRO

www.gazmetro.com

Industry Group Code: 221210 **Ranks within this company's industry group:** Sales: 11 Profits: 11

Exploration/Production:		Refining/Retailing:		Utilities:		Alternative Energy:		Specialty Services:		Energy Mktg./Other Svcs.	
Exploration:		Refining:		Electric Utility:	Y	Waste/Solar/Other:		Consulting/Eng.:		Energy Marketing:	
Production:		Retailing:		Gas Utility:	Y	Thermal/Steam:		Seismic:		Equipment/Machinery:	Y
Coal Production:		Convenience Stores:		Pipelines:	Y	Wind:		Drilling:		Oil Field Services:	
		Chemicals:		Water:		Hydro:		InfoTech:		Air/Shipping Transportation:	
						Fuel Cells:		Specialty Services:	Y		

TYPES OF BUSINESS:

Gas Pipelines
Equipment Rental & Maintenance Services
Water Services
Fiber Optics Services

BRANDS/DIVISIONS/AFFILIATES:

Valener, Inc.
Vermont Gas Systems, Inc.
TransQuebec & Maritimes Pipeline, Inc.
Green Mountain Power Corporation
Champion Pipe Line Ltd.
Intragaz

CONTACTS: *Note: Officers with more than one job title may be intentionally listed here more than once.*

Sophie Brochu, CEO
Sophie Brochu, Pres.
Pierre Despars, CFO
Serge Regnier, VP-Employees & Culture
Martin Imbleau, VP-Oper. & Major Projects
Pierre Despars, Exec. VP-Corp. Affairs
Guylaine Lehoux, VP-Growth
Louis P. Gignac, Chmn.
Patrick Cabana, VP-Procurement, Gas Supply and Regulatory Affairs

Phone: 514-598-3444 **Fax:** 514-598-3144
Toll-Free: 800-361-4005
Address: 1717 du Havre, Montreal, QC H2K 2X3 Canada

GROWTH PLANS/SPECIAL FEATURES:

Gaz Metro, formerly Gaz Metro Limited Partnership, with assets of over $3.6 billion, is one of the largest natural gas distributors in Quebec and Vermont, with more than 6,200 miles of gas distribution pipeline. The company serves over 180,000 customers in Quebec and over 136,500 in Vermont through Vermont Gas Systems, Inc. Gaz Metro holds 50% of Trans Quebec and Maritimes Pipeline, Inc., a large network of gas pipelines in Quebec. In addition, the firm owns Champion Pipe Line Ltd., which operates two gas pipelines in Abitibi, and a 50% interest in the Intragaz Limited Partnership, which operates underground natural gas storage facilities. Along with providing natural gas, the company offers rental, financing and maintenance services for natural gas equipment, provides natural gas transportation and storage for distributors, carriers and customers, sells goods and services through companies in the energy and fiber optics fields, and rehabilitates drinking water and wastewater infrastructures. Additionally, Gaz Metro owns a 49.8% interest in fiber optic network, MTO Telecom, Inc., which services Ottawa, Montreal and Toronto. The company distributes electricity in Vermont via subsidiary Green Mountain Power. The firm maintains an interactive, educational web site geared toward young visitors, AllAboutNaturalGas.com. In October 2010, the company abandoned its Limited Partnership format in favor of merging with newly created dividend-paying corporation, Valener, Inc., with Valener owning 29% of the Gaz Metro entity.

FINANCIALS: **Sales and profits are in thousands of dollars—add 000 to get the full amount. 2010 Note: Financial information for 2010 was not available for all companies at press time.**

2010 Sales: $	2010 Profits: $	**U.S. Stock Ticker: Subsidiary**
2009 Sales: $2,121,980	2009 Profits: $149,460	**Int'l Ticker:** Int'l Exchange:
2008 Sales: $2,002,120	2008 Profits: $142,330	Employees:
2007 Sales: $1,840,000	2007 Profits: $115,500	Fiscal Year Ends: 9/30
2006 Sales: $1,883,500	2006 Profits: $138,400	Parent Company: VALENER INC

SALARIES/BENEFITS:

Pension Plan:	ESOP Stock Plan:	Profit Sharing:	Top Exec. Salary: $	Bonus: $
Savings Plan:	Stock Purch. Plan:		Second Exec. Salary: $	Bonus: $

OTHER THOUGHTS:

Apparent Women Officers or Directors: 2
Hot Spot for Advancement for Women/Minorities:

LOCATIONS: ("Y" = Yes)

West:	Southwest:	Midwest:	Southeast:	Northeast:	International:
				Y	Y

GAZPROM (OAO)

www.gazprom.ru

Industry Group Code: 211111 **Ranks within this company's industry group:** Sales: 14 Profits: 1

Exploration/Production:		Refining/Retailing:		Utilities:		Alternative Energy:		Specialty Services:		Energy Mktg./Other Svcs.	
Exploration:	Y	Refining:	Y	Electric Utility:		Waste/Solar/Other:		Consulting/Eng.:		Energy Marketing:	
Production:	Y	Retailing:		Gas Utility:		Thermal/Steam:		Seismic:		Equipment/Machinery:	
Coal Production:		Convenience Stores:		Pipelines:	Y	Wind:		Drilling:		Oil Field Services:	
		Chemicals:	Y	Water:		Hydro:		InfoTech:		Air/Shipping Transportation:	
						Fuel Cells:		Specialty Services:			

TYPES OF BUSINESS:

Natural Gas Exploration & Production
Oil Exploration & Production
Oil & Gas Refining
Pipelines
Telecommunications
Electronics
Financial Services
Construction & Real Estate Development

BRANDS/DIVISIONS/AFFILIATES:

Yamal Peninsula fields
Unified Gas Supply System
Sakhalin Project

CONTACTS: *Note: Officers with more than one job title may be intentionally listed here more than once.*

Alexey Borisovich Miller, Chmn.-Mgmt. Committee
Elena Alexandrovna Vasilieva, CFO/Chief Accountant
Kirill Gennadievich Seleznev, Head-Mktg., Gas & Liquid Hydrocarbons
Nikolai Nikolaevich Dubik, Head-Legal Dept.
Vlada Vilorikovna Rusakova, Head-Strategic Dev.
Olga Petrovna Pavlova, Head-Asset Mgmt. & Corp. Rel. Dept.
Andrey Vyacheslavovich Kruglov, Head-Finance & Economics
Kirill Gennadievich Seleznev, Head-Processing Gas & Liquid Hydrocarbons Dept.
Viktor Alexeevich Zubkov, Chmn.
Alexander Medvedev, Dir.-Gazprom Export
Oleg Evgenievich Aksyutin, Head-Gas Transportation

Phone: 7-495-719-30-01 **Fax:** 7-495-719-83-33
Toll-Free:
Address: 16 Nametkina St., Moscow, Russia

GROWTH PLANS/SPECIAL FEATURES:

Gazprom (OAO) is one of the world's largest natural gas exploration and production companies. The Russian Government owns just over 50% of the company, which produces around 83% of Russia's natural gas. The company also accounts for 25% of Russia's tax revenues. The company has over 33 trillion cubic meters of natural gas reserves and approximately 4.5 billion barrels of oil. Gazprom operates 21 major oil and gas fields across Russia, 96,000 miles of pipelines, 25 storage facilities and six refineries which can process 33 billion cubic meters of natural gas. Additionally, the firm has stakes in financial institutions, real estate ventures, construction, telecommunications and chemical plants. Gazprom owns one of the world's largest transmission systems, the Unified Gas Supply System (UGSS) of Russia, which extends over 96,000 miles. The firm currently exports gas to 32 countries. The company has several major projects underway including the Yamal Peninsula fields, in which there have been 26 field discoveries with recoverable gas; the construction of an integrated gas production, transmission and supply system in the Far East and Eastern Siberia and the exploitation of Russian Arctic shelf resources. In September 2010, the company expanded its natural gas service to the region of Kamchatka Krai, providing the region with natural for the first time ever. In October 2010, Gazprom announced its involvement in the Bolivian Ipati and Aquio gas exploration projects, in cooperation with French oil company Total.

FINANCIALS: **Sales and profits are in thousands of dollars—add 000 to get the full amount. 2010 Note: Financial information for 2010 was not available for all companies at press time.**

2010 Sales: $	2010 Profits: $	**U.S. Stock Ticker: OGZPY**
2009 Sales: $95,472,800	2009 Profits: $24,884,600	**Int'l Ticker: GAZP** Int'l Exchange: Moscow-MICEX
2008 Sales: $141,455,000	2008 Profits: $29,864,000	Employees:
2007 Sales: $98,641,500	2007 Profits: $19,269,200	Fiscal Year Ends: 12/31
2006 Sales: $69,853,500	2006 Profits: $14,704,400	Parent Company:

SALARIES/BENEFITS:

Pension Plan:	ESOP Stock Plan:	Profit Sharing:	Top Exec. Salary: $	Bonus: $
Savings Plan:	Stock Purch. Plan:		Second Exec. Salary: $	Bonus: $

OTHER THOUGHTS:

Apparent Women Officers or Directors: 3
Hot Spot for Advancement for Women/Minorities: Y

LOCATIONS: ("Y" = Yes)

West:	Southwest:	Midwest:	Southeast:	Northeast:	International:
					Y

GDF SUEZ SA

www.gdfsuez.com

Industry Group Code: 221210 **Ranks within this company's industry group:** Sales: 1 Profits: 1

Exploration/Production:		Refining/Retailing:		Utilities:		Alternative Energy:		Specialty Services:		Energy Mktg./Other Svcs.	
Exploration:	Y	Refining:		Electric Utility:	Y	Waste/Solar/Other:		Consulting/Eng.:		Energy Marketing:	Y
Production:	Y	Retailing:		Gas Utility:	Y	Thermal/Steam:		Seismic:		Equipment/Machinery:	
Coal Production:		Convenience Stores:		Pipelines:	Y	Wind:	Y	Drilling:		Oil Field Services:	
		Chemicals:		Water:		Hydro:		InfoTech:		Air/Shipping Transportation:	
						Fuel Cells:		Specialty Services:	Y		

TYPES OF BUSINESS:

Natural Gas Utility
Natural Gas Exploration & Production
Energy Marketing
Pipelines & Storage

BRANDS/DIVISIONS/AFFILIATES:

Maia Eolis
Deutschland Transport

CONTACTS:

Note: Officers with more than one job title may be intentionally listed here more than once.

Gerard Mestrallet, CEO
Jean-Francois Cirelli, COO
Jean-Francois Cirelli, Pres.
Garard Lamarche, CFO
Phillip Saimpert, Dir.-Human Resources
Yves de Gaulle, Sec.
Alain Chiagneneau, Dir.-Bus. Strategy
Valerie Bernis, Dir.-Corp. Comm.
Jean-Marie Dauger, Exec. VP-Global Gas & LNG
Jean-Louis Chaussade, Exec. VP-SUEZ Environment
Jerome Tolot, Dir.-Energy Svcs. Bus.
Pierre Clavel, VP-Energy Europe
Gerard Mestrallet, Chmn.
Dirk Beeuwsart, VP-Int'l Bus.

Phone: 33-1-47-54-2020	**Fax:** 33-1-47-54-3858
Toll-Free:	
Address: 22, rue du docteur Lancereaux, Paris, Cedex 08 75392 France	

GROWTH PLANS/SPECIAL FEATURES:

GDF Suez S.A., formerly Gaz de France, is integrated gas and energy utility that produces, purchases, transports, distributes and sells electricity, natural gas and related services for corporate, residential and local government customers. The firm operates in six business segments: Energy France; Energy Europe and International; Global Gas & LNG; Infrastructures; Energy Services; and Environment. The Energy France segment supplies gas, electricity and services and produces electricity in France. Approximately 64% of its energy comes from renewable resources, including hydroelectric and wind. The segment also offers private customers heating systems. The Energy Europe and International segment is engaged in electricity production, as well as gas and electricity distribution and supply, across Europe and in North America, Latin America, Asia and the Middle East. The Global Gas & LNG segment's activities include liquefied natural gas (LNG) exploration and production; supply; and trading. The segment controls of reserves of roughly 667 million BOE. The Infrastructures segment operates gas transmission in Europe; LNG Terminals; European storage facilities; gas distribution in France; and electricity transportation in Belgium. The Energy Services division is engaged in engineering consultancy services and design; the design, production, operation and management of electrical engineering, mechanical engineering and climate-control facilities; and the operation and maintenance of facilities. The Environment business line is divided into two segments: the water sector and the waste sector. The water sector's operations include the collection, treatment and purification of drinking water, domestic and industrial wastewater and sewage. The waste sector collects and treats a variety of trash and waste. In May 2010, GDF Suez Energy Services acquired the UK-based Utilicom Group from the IDEX Group. In September 2010, the company sold its 5% stake in Gas Natural Fenosa for $758 million.

FINANCIALS:

Sales and profits are in thousands of dollars—add 000 to get the full amount. 2010 Note: Financial information for 2010 was not available for all companies at press time.

2010 Sales: $	2010 Profits: $	**U.S. Stock Ticker:**
2009 Sales: $103,150,000	2009 Profits: $5,779,180	**Int'l Ticker: GSZ** Int'l Exchange: Paris-Euronext
2008 Sales: $99,419,000	2008 Profits: $7,109,000	Employees:
2007 Sales: $43,253,100	2007 Profits: $3,946,450	Fiscal Year Ends: 12/31
2006 Sales: $43,568,800	2006 Profits: $3,630,730	Parent Company:

SALARIES/BENEFITS:

Pension Plan:	ESOP Stock Plan:	Profit Sharing:	Top Exec. Salary: $	Bonus: $
Savings Plan:	Stock Purch. Plan:		Second Exec. Salary: $	Bonus: $

OTHER THOUGHTS:

Apparent Women Officers or Directors: 2
Hot Spot for Advancement for Women/Minorities:

LOCATIONS: ("Y" = Yes)

West:	Southwest:	Midwest:	Southeast:	Northeast:	International:
	Y			Y	Y

GE ENERGY INFRASTRUCTURE

www.gepower.com

Industry Group Code: 335 **Ranks within this company's industry group:** Sales: 2 Profits: 1

Exploration/Production:		Refining/Retailing:		Utilities:		Alternative Energy:		Specialty Services:		Energy Mktg./Other Svcs.	
Exploration:	Y	Refining:		Electric Utility:	Y	Waste/Solar/Other:	Y	Consulting/Eng.:	Y	Energy Marketing:	
Production:	Y	Retailing:		Gas Utility:	Y	Thermal/Steam:	Y	Seismic:		Equipment/Machinery:	Y
Coal Production:	Y	Convenience Stores:		Pipelines:	Y	Wind:	Y	Drilling:	Y	Oil Field Services:	Y
		Chemicals:		Water:	Y	Hydro:	Y	InfoTech:		Air/Shipping Transportation:	
						Fuel Cells:		Specialty Services:	Y		

TYPES OF BUSINESS:

Generation Equipment-Turbines & Generators
Water Processing Technologies and Products
Generators-Wind, Hydro, Geothermal & Turbo
Nuclear Fuel Systems
Pumps & Pipelines
Metering & Control Systems
Energy Management Systems
Consulting-Energy

BRANDS/DIVISIONS/AFFILIATES:

General Electric Co (GE)

CONTACTS:

Note: Officers with more than one job title may be intentionally listed here more than once.

John Krenicki, Jr., CEO
John Krenicki, Jr., Pres.
Daniel Janki, CFO
James Suciu, Pres., Global Sales & Mktg.
Daniel C. Heintzelman, Pres./CEO-Energy Svcs.
Claudi Santiago, Pres./CEO-Oil & Gas
Steve Boze, Pres./CEO-Power & Water
Kishore Hayaraman, Pres./CEO-India

Phone: 678-844-6000 **Fax:** 678-844-6690
Toll-Free:
Address: 4200 Wildwood Pkwy., Atlanta, GA 30339 US

GROWTH PLANS/SPECIAL FEATURES:

GE Energy Infrastructure, a subsidiary of the General Electric Co. (GE), designs and supplies energy technology. The division, which accounts for roughly 23.7% of GE's total revenues, operates in three segments: Energy, Oil & Gas and Water & Process Technologies. The Energy segment serves power generation, industrial, government and other customers worldwide with products and services related to energy production, distribution and management. The firm is a leading provider of Integrated Gasification Combined Cycle (IGCC) technology design and development. IGCC systems convert coal and other hydrocarbons into synthetic gas that is used as the primary fuel for gas turbines in combined-cycle systems. The segment sells steam turbines and generators to the electric utility industry and to private industrial customers for cogeneration applications. Nuclear reactors, fuel and support services for both new and installed boiling water reactors are offered through joint ventures with Hitachi and Toshiba. The energy division designs and manufactures motors and control systems used in industrial applications primarily for oil and gas extraction and mining. Its renewable energy portfolio offers wind turbines solar technology. In addition, it offers water treatment solutions for industrial and municipal water systems including the supply and related services of specialty chemicals, water purification systems, pumps, valves, filters and fluid handling equipment for improving the performance of water, wastewater and process systems, including mobile treatment systems and desalination processes. The segment also sells aircraft engine derivatives for use as industrial power sources. The Oil & Gas segment designs and manufactures surface and subsea drilling and production systems; equipment for floating production platforms; compressors; turbines; turboexpanders; high pressure reactors; industrial power generation; and a broad portfolio of ancillary equipment. The segment also provides services relating to installing and maintaining this equipment. In June 2009, GE Energy opened a new facility in France.

FINANCIALS:

Sales and profits are in thousands of dollars—add 000 to get the full amount. 2010 Note: Financial information for 2010 was not available for all companies at press time.

2010 Sales: $	2010 Profits: $	**U.S. Stock Ticker: Subsidiary**
2009 Sales: $37,134,000	2009 Profits: $6,842,000	**Int'l Ticker:** Int'l Exchange:
2008 Sales: $38,570,000	2008 Profits: $6,080,000	Employees: 67,000
2007 Sales: $30,698,000	2007 Profits: $4,817,000	Fiscal Year Ends: 12/31
2006 Sales: $25,221,000	2006 Profits: $3,518,000	Parent Company: GENERAL ELECTRIC CO (GE)

SALARIES/BENEFITS:

Pension Plan:	ESOP Stock Plan:	Profit Sharing:	Top Exec. Salary: $	Bonus: $
Savings Plan: Y	Stock Purch. Plan:		Second Exec. Salary: $	Bonus: $

OTHER THOUGHTS:

Apparent Women Officers or Directors:
Hot Spot for Advancement for Women/Minorities:

LOCATIONS: ("Y" = Yes)

West:	Southwest:	Midwest:	Southeast:	Northeast:	International:
Y	Y	Y	Y	Y	Y

GENESIS ENERGY LP

www.genesisenergylp.com

Industry Group Code: 486 **Ranks within this company's industry group:** Sales: 17 Profits: 18

Exploration/Production:		Refining/Retailing:		Utilities:		Alternative Energy:		Specialty Services:		Energy Mktg./Other Svcs.	
Exploration:		Refining:	Y	Electric Utility:		Waste/Solar/Other:		Consulting/Eng.:		Energy Marketing:	Y
Production:		Retailing:	Y	Gas Utility:		Thermal/Steam:		Seismic:		Equipment/Machinery:	
Coal Production:		Convenience Stores:		Pipelines:	Y	Wind:		Drilling:		Oil Field Services:	
		Chemicals:		Water:		Hydro:		InfoTech:		Air/Shipping Transportation:	Y
						Fuel Cells:		Specialty Services:	Y		

TYPES OF BUSINESS:

Crude Oil Distribution
Crude Oil Gathering & Marketing
Carbon Dioxide Marketing
Pipelines
Synthetic Fuel
Road Transportation
Carbon Dioxide Processing

BRANDS/DIVISIONS/AFFILIATES:

Denbury Resources Inc
T&P Syngas
Praxair Inc
Sandhill Group LLC
DG Marine Transportation LLC
Quintana Capital Group

CONTACTS:

Note: Officers with more than one job title may be intentionally listed here more than once.

Grant E. Sims, CEO
Robert V. Deere, CFO
Ross A. Benavides, General Counsel/Corp. Sec.
Karen N. Pape, Controller/Sr. VP
Gareth Roberts, Chmn.

Phone: 713-860-2500	**Fax:** 713-860-2640
Toll-Free:	
Address: 919 Milam, Ste. 2100, Houston, TX 77002 US	

GROWTH PLANS/SPECIAL FEATURES:

Genesis Energy, LP is a limited partnership energy firm. The company offers midstream services to oil and gas firms, including crude oil gathering and marketing; crude oil and carbon dioxide pipeline transportation; high sulfur natural gas stream processing; and the supplying of industrial gases. It is an independent gatherer and marketer of crude oil, with operations concentrated in Texas, Arkansas, Louisiana, Alabama, Florida and Mississippi. Genesis Energy is engaged in the purchase and aggregation of crude oil at the wellhead and the bulk purchase of oil at pipeline and terminal facilities for resale at various points along the crude oil distribution chain. The company generates revenues by transporting the relatively inexpensive crude oil along the distribution chain and marketing the oil to refineries at increased prices. The firm operates a 235-mile pipeline system in Mississippi, a 90-mile system in Texas and a 100-mile system extending from northern Florida into southern Alabama. The company also supplies carbon dioxide to industrial customers. Genesis Energy has a 50% interest in T&P Syngas, a joint venture with Praxair that runs a facility producing synthetic gas and high-pressure steam. Genesis also has a 50% interest in Sandhill Group LLC, through which it participates in the production and distribution of liquid carbon dioxide for use in the food, chemical and oil industries; and 100% interest in DG Marine Transportation, Ltd. (which does business as Grifco), an owner of 30 marine vessels that serve refineries and storage terminals in the Gulf Coast, Intracoastal Canal and western U.S. river systems. Originally a joint venture with TD Marine, Genesis Energy acquired TD Marine's 51% ownership in the venture in July 2010. In February 2010, Quintana Capital Group acquired a general partner interest in the firm from Denbury Resources, Inc.

Genesis Energy offers employees a 401(k) and medical, dental, life and disability insurance.

FINANCIALS:

Sales and profits are in thousands of dollars—add 000 to get the full amount. 2010 Note: Financial information for 2010 was not available for all companies at press time.

2010 Sales: $	2010 Profits: $	**U.S. Stock Ticker: GEL**
2009 Sales: $1,435,360	2009 Profits: $8,063	**Int'l Ticker:** Int'l Exchange:
2008 Sales: $2,141,684	2008 Profits: $26,089	Employees: 525
2007 Sales: $1,199,653	2007 Profits: $-13,550	Fiscal Year Ends: 12/31
2006 Sales: $918,369	2006 Profits: $8,381	Parent Company:

SALARIES/BENEFITS:

Pension Plan:	ESOP Stock Plan:	Profit Sharing: Y	Top Exec. Salary: $369,600	Bonus: $
Savings Plan: Y	Stock Purch. Plan:		Second Exec. Salary: $340,000	Bonus: $

OTHER THOUGHTS:

Apparent Women Officers or Directors: 2
Hot Spot for Advancement for Women/Minorities:

LOCATIONS: ("Y" = Yes)

West:	Southwest:	Midwest:	Southeast:	Northeast:	International:
	Y		Y		

GEOKINETICS INC

www.geokinetics.com

Industry Group Code: 541360 **Ranks within this company's industry group:** Sales: 2 Profits: 2

Exploration/Production:		**Refining/Retailing:**		**Utilities:**		**Alternative Energy:**		**Specialty Services:**		**Energy Mktg./Other Svcs.**	
Exploration:		Refining:		Electric Utility:		Waste/Solar/Other:		Consulting/Eng.:		Energy Marketing:	
Production:		Retailing:		Gas Utility:		Thermal/Steam:		Seismic:	Y	Equipment/Machinery:	
Coal Production:		Convenience Stores:		Pipelines:		Wind:		Drilling:		Oil Field Services:	
		Chemicals:		Water:		Hydro:		InfoTech:	Y	Air/Shipping Transportation:	
						Fuel Cells:		Specialty Services:			

TYPES OF BUSINESS:

Seismic Data Acquisition & Processing
Seismic Data Software

BRANDS/DIVISIONS/AFFILIATES:

Geokinetics USA, Inc.
Geokinetics Exploration, Inc.
Geokinetics International Holdings, Inc.
Geophysical Development Corporation

CONTACTS: *Note: Officers with more than one job title may be intentionally listed here more than once.*

Richard Miles, CEO
Richard Miles, Pres.
Gary L. Pittman, CFO
Jim White, Exec. VP-Tech.
Lee Parker, Exec. VP-Oper.
Jim White, Exec. VP-Bus. Dev.
William R. Ziegler, Chmn.

Phone: 713-850-7600	**Fax:** 713-850-7330
Toll-Free:	
Address: 1500 City West Blvd., Ste. 800, Houston, TX 77042 US	

GROWTH PLANS/SPECIAL FEATURES:

Geokinetics, Inc. is a global provider of seismic acquisition services, which include high-end seismic data processing and interpretation services, to the oil and gas industry worldwide. The company is organized into three segments: North American seismic data acquisition, International seismic data acquisition and data processing and interpretation. The company's seismic data acquisition operations are conducted primarily by three wholly-owned subsidiaries: Geokinetics USA, Inc.; Geokinetics Exploration, Inc.; and Geokinetics International Holdings, Inc. Geokinetics' seismic acquisition service is engaged in land, transition zone and shallow water environments seismic acquisition services on a contract basis for its customers. Geokinetics' equipment is capable of collecting 2D, 3D and multi-component seismic acquisition data with a combined recording capacity of approximately 206,000 channels and capabilities of operating up to 38 crews worldwide. Most of the company's land and transition zone acquisition services involve 3D surveys. Crew count, configuration and location can change depending upon industry demand and requirements. The firm's data processing and interpretation operations are conducted by its subsidiary Geophysical Development Corporation (GDC). GDC provides geophysical processing, interpretation, software and consultation services to the oil and gas industry. The company has domestic offices in Texas and international offices in the U.K., Canada, Central and South America, Europe, the Middle East, Australia and Asia. The firm's customers include national oil companies, major international oil companies and smaller independent E&P companies. In February 2010, the firm acquired PGS Onshore, Petroleum Geo-Services' multi-client data library and seismic data acquisition business, for $210 million.

The company offers employee benefits including medical insurance, dental insurance, life insurance, disability benefits, tuition assistance and a 401(k) plan with company match.

FINANCIALS: **Sales and profits are in thousands of dollars—add 000 to get the full amount. 2010 Note: Financial information for 2010 was not available for all companies at press time.**

2010 Sales: $	2010 Profits: $	**U.S. Stock Ticker: GOK**
2009 Sales: $510,966	2009 Profits: $-5,011	**Int'l Ticker:** Int'l Exchange:
2008 Sales: $474,598	2008 Profits: $ 986	Employees: 4,400
2007 Sales: $357,677	2007 Profits: $-15,936	Fiscal Year Ends: 7/31
2006 Sales: $225,183	2006 Profits: $-4,176	Parent Company:

SALARIES/BENEFITS:

Pension Plan: Y	ESOP Stock Plan:	Profit Sharing:	Top Exec. Salary: $375,000	Bonus: $220,000
Savings Plan: Y	Stock Purch. Plan:		Second Exec. Salary: $300,000	Bonus: $102,000

OTHER THOUGHTS:

Apparent Women Officers or Directors:
Hot Spot for Advancement for Women/Minorities:

LOCATIONS: ("Y" = Yes)

West:	Southwest:	Midwest:	Southeast:	Northeast:	International:
	Y				Y

GEORGIA POWER COMPANY

www.georgiapower.com

Industry Group Code: 2211 **Ranks within this company's industry group:** Sales: Profits:

Exploration/Production:		Refining/Retailing:		Utilities:		Alternative Energy:		Specialty Services:		Energy Mktg./Other Svcs.	
Exploration:		Refining:		Electric Utility:	Y	Waste/Solar/Other:	Y	Consulting/Eng.:		Energy Marketing:	
Production:		Retailing:		Gas Utility:		Thermal/Steam:		Seismic:		Equipment/Machinery:	
Coal Production:		Convenience Stores:		Pipelines:		Wind:		Drilling:		Oil Field Services:	
		Chemicals:		Water:		Hydro:	Y	InfoTech:		Air/Shipping Transportation:	
						Fuel Cells:		Specialty Services:	Y		

TYPES OF BUSINESS:

Electric Utility
Fossil-Fuel Plants
Hydroelectric Power
Nuclear Power
Recreational Facilities-Reservoirs

BRANDS/DIVISIONS/AFFILIATES:

Southern Company (The)

CONTACTS:

Note: Officers with more than one job title may be intentionally listed here more than once.

Michael D. Garrett, CEO
W. Paul Bowers, COO
Michael D. Garrett, Pres.
Ronnie R. Labrato, CFO/Exec. VP
Lamont Houston, Sr. VP-Customer Service & Sales
Joseph A. Miller, Exec. VP-Nuclear Dev.
Stan Connally, Sr. Prod. Officer/Sr. VP
James H. Miller, III, General Counsel/Sr. VP
Chris Bell, VP-Energy Planning & Nuclear Dev.
Ronnie R. Labrato, Treas.
Doug Jones, Sr. VP-Fossil & Hydro Power
Anthony Wilson, VP-Transmission
Leslie R. Sibert, VP-Dist.

Phone: 404-506-6526	**Fax:**
Toll-Free:	
Address: 241 Ralph McGill Blvd. NE, Atlanta, GA 30308 US	

GROWTH PLANS/SPECIAL FEATURES:

Georgia Power Company (GPC) is the largest of the five subsidiaries of The Southern Company, a major U.S. utility holding company. GPC is a regulated utility that provides electricity to 2.35 million residential, commercial and industrial customers throughout the state of Georgia. Its service area covers more than 600 communities in 155 of Georgia's 159 counties. The company also sells wholesale electricity to several cooperatives and municipalities in the region. GPC has a generating capacity of roughly 9,600 megawatts (MW) provided by its network of 14 fossil fuel generating plants, two nuclear plants and 20 hydroelectric dams. Coal accounts for 67% of the firm's generating capacity; nuclear, 21%; oil and gas, 10%; and hydro, 2%. GPC offers a Green Energy program, wherein customers can purchase 100-kilowatt-hour blocks of energy (generated by sun, wind, water and biomass) over a one-year period. The company also offers surge protection with a $50,000 per incident warranty, as well as energy related products like water heaters and heat pumps. GPC is the largest non-government provider of recreation facilities in the state, responsible for 18 reservoirs throughout Georgia, including approximately 1,391 miles of shoreline, 58,850 acres of lakes and dozens of parks. GPC is investing $2 billion to reduce the environmental impact of its power plants over the next five years. In October 2010, the firm received permission from the Georgia Public Service Commission to nearly double its solar energy offerings.

GPC's employee benefits include an employee assistance program and business travel insurance.

FINANCIALS:

Sales and profits are in thousands of dollars—add 000 to get the full amount. 2010 Note: Financial information for 2010 was not available for all companies at press time.

2010 Sales: $	2010 Profits: $	**U.S. Stock Ticker: Subsidiary**
2009 Sales: $	2009 Profits: $	**Int'l Ticker:** Int'l Exchange:
2008 Sales: $	2008 Profits: $	Employees:
2007 Sales: $7,571,652	2007 Profits: $842,142	Fiscal Year Ends: 12/31
2006 Sales: $7,245,644	2006 Profits: $792,064	Parent Company: SOUTHERN COMPANY (THE)

SALARIES/BENEFITS:

Pension Plan: Y	ESOP Stock Plan:	Profit Sharing:	Top Exec. Salary: $	Bonus: $850,669
Savings Plan: Y	Stock Purch. Plan:		Second Exec. Salary: $	Bonus: $

OTHER THOUGHTS:

Apparent Women Officers or Directors: 3
Hot Spot for Advancement for Women/Minorities: Y

LOCATIONS: ("Y" = Yes)

West:	Southwest:	Midwest:	Southeast:	Northeast:	International:
			Y		

GETTY PETROLEUM MARKETING

www.getty.com

Industry Group Code: 486 **Ranks within this company's industry group:** Sales: Profits:

Exploration/Production:		Refining/Retailing:		Utilities:		Alternative Energy:		Specialty Services:		Energy Mktg./Other Svcs.	
Exploration:		Refining:		Electric Utility:		Waste/Solar/Other:		Consulting/Eng.:		Energy Marketing:	
Production:		Retailing:	Y	Gas Utility:		Thermal/Steam:		Seismic:		Equipment/Machinery:	
Coal Production:		Convenience Stores:	Y	Pipelines:		Wind:		Drilling:		Oil Field Services:	
		Chemicals:		Water:		Hydro:		InfoTech:		Air/Shipping Transportation:	
						Fuel Cells:		Specialty Services:	Y		

TYPES OF BUSINESS:

Petroleum Distribution
Service Stations
Convenience Stores
Fleet Card Program
Motor Oil

BRANDS/DIVISIONS/AFFILIATES:

LUKOIL (OAO)
KOSCO

CONTACTS:

Note: Officers with more than one job title may be intentionally listed here more than once.

Vadim Gluzman, CEO
Vincent J. DeLaurentis, COO
Vincent J. DeLaurentis, Pres.
Michael K. Hantman, CFO/Sr. VP
Michael G. Lewis, General Counsel/Corp. Sec./VP
VP-Wholesale & Bus. Dev., VP-Bus. Dev. & Wholesale
George Wilkins, Contact-Press
Yelena Bitman, Chief Accountant

Phone: 516-542-4900 **Fax:** 516-832-8272
Toll-Free:
Address: 1500 Hempstead Turnpike, East Meadow, NY 11554 US

GROWTH PLANS/SPECIAL FEATURES:

Getty Petroleum Marketing, Inc., a subsidiary of Russian oil giant LUKOIL, is one of the largest marketers of petroleum products in the U.S. The company operates over 2,000 retail outlets in a 13-state area in the northeastern and mid-Atlantic regions of the U.S., distributing roughly 2 billion gallons of gasoline each year. Many of the firm's current stations were bought from either ConocoPhillips or Mobil over the past few years. Getty Petroleum operates through three marketing regions and maintains offices in New York, Rhode Island and Pennsylvania. The firm has historically emphasized retail gasoline distribution, though many outlets also offer convenience stores, repair centers, car washes and other ancillary services. Through its KOSCO subsidiary, the company also provides passenger car motor oils, industrial hydraulic, transfer and drill oils and transmission fluid under the Getty brand. Getty Petroleum operates a proprietary distribution network consisting of eight petroleum terminals and 17 throughput and exchange terminals, as well as offering clients a fleet program. The distribution network allows the firm to purchase, store and process petroleum products cost-effectively. Getty Petroleum sells petroleum through both the LUKOIL and GETTY brands, and many of the firm's stations have been rebranded to LUKOIL in order to improve brand name recognition in the U.S. The company also offers LUKOIL charge cards for businesses and automotive fleets.

FINANCIALS:

Sales and profits are in thousands of dollars—add 000 to get the full amount. 2010 Note: Financial information for 2010 was not available for all companies at press time.

2010 Sales: $	2010 Profits: $	**U.S. Stock Ticker: Subsidiary**
2009 Sales: $	2009 Profits: $	**Int'l Ticker:** Int'l Exchange:
2008 Sales: $	2008 Profits: $	Employees:
2007 Sales: $	2007 Profits: $	Fiscal Year Ends: 1/31
2006 Sales: $	2006 Profits: $	Parent Company: LUKOIL (OAO)

SALARIES/BENEFITS:

Pension Plan:	ESOP Stock Plan:	Profit Sharing:	Top Exec. Salary: $	Bonus: $412,000
Savings Plan:	Stock Purch. Plan:		Second Exec. Salary: $	Bonus: $

OTHER THOUGHTS:

Apparent Women Officers or Directors: 1
Hot Spot for Advancement for Women/Minorities:

LOCATIONS: ("Y" = Yes)

West:	Southwest:	Midwest:	Southeast:	Northeast:	International:
				Y	

GLOBAL INDUSTRIES LTD

www.globalind.com

Industry Group Code: 213112 **Ranks within this company's industry group:** Sales: 19 Profits: 14

Exploration/Production:		**Refining/Retailing:**		**Utilities:**		**Alternative Energy:**		**Specialty Services:**		**Energy Mktg./Other Svcs.**	
Exploration:		Refining:		Electric Utility:		Waste/Solar/Other:		Consulting/Eng.:	Y	Energy Marketing:	
Production:		Retailing:		Gas Utility:		Thermal/Steam:		Seismic:		Equipment/Machinery:	
Coal Production:		Convenience Stores:		Pipelines:		Wind:		Drilling:		Oil Field Services:	Y
		Chemicals:		Water:		Hydro:		InfoTech:		Air/Shipping Transportation:	Y
						Fuel Cells:		Specialty Services:	Y		

TYPES OF BUSINESS:

Marine Construction & Support Services
Oil Field Support
Marine Transportation
Underwater Services
Diving Services

BRANDS/DIVISIONS/AFFILIATES:

CONTACTS:

Note: Officers with more than one job title may be intentionally listed here more than once.

John B. Reed, CEO
Ashit Jain, COO
Peter S. Atkinson, Pres.
C. Andrew Smith, CFO/Sr. VP
James G. Osborn, Chief Mktg. Officer
David R. Sheil, Sr. VP-Human Resources
Eric van Baars, VP-Eng.
Russell J. Robicheaux, Chief Admin. Officer/Sr. VP
Russell J. Robicheaux, General Counsel
Byron W. Baker, Sr. VP-Oper. & Fleet Mgmt.
Trudy McConnaughhay, Controller/VP
John T. Sprot, VP-Project Mgmt.
James J. Dore, Sr. VP-North America
John A. Clerico, Chmn.
Eduardo Borja, Sr. VP-Latin America
Aaron V. Cooley, VP-Supply Chain Mgmt.

Phone: 337-583-5000	**Fax:** 337-583-5100
Toll-Free:	
Address: 8000 Global Dr., Carlyss, LA 70665 US	

GROWTH PLANS/SPECIAL FEATURES:

Global Industries, Ltd. (GIL) a leading offshore construction company, offers a comprehensive and integrated range of marine construction and support services in the U.S. Gulf of Mexico, Latin America, West Africa, the Middle East, Mediterranean, Asia Pacific and India. These services include pipeline construction, platform installation/removal, subsea construction and diving services. GIL maintains a fleet of 9 major construction vessels, one cargo launch barges, two dive support vessels; four multi-service vessels and one offshore support vessel. Global Industries is equipped to provide services from shallow water to depths of up to 10,000 feet. The company's business consists of two principal activities: offshore construction services and subsea services. Offshore construction services include pipelay, derrick and related services. GIL is capable of installing steel pipe by either the conventional or reel method of pipelaying using either manual or automatic welding processes. The company's subsea services include diving, diverless intervention and marine support services. In 2010, the company was awarded a $70 million project in Malaysia, a $125 million project from Petroleos Mexicanos (Pemex) for pipeline construction in the Gulf of Mexico and a $90 million project in Northeast Brazil.

The company offers employees medical, dental and vision insurance; life insurance; disability coverage; an employee assistance plan; a 401(k) plan; and credit union membership.

FINANCIALS:

Sales and profits are in thousands of dollars—add 000 to get the full amount. 2010 Note: Financial information for 2010 was not available for all companies at press time.

2010 Sales: $	2010 Profits: $	**U.S. Stock Ticker: GLBL**
2009 Sales: $914,348	2009 Profits: $73,731	**Int'l Ticker:** Int'l Exchange:
2008 Sales: $1,070,988	2008 Profits: $-119,191	Employees: 2,793
2007 Sales: $992,513	2007 Profits: $159,960	Fiscal Year Ends: 12/31
2006 Sales: $1,234,849	2006 Profits: $199,745	Parent Company:

SALARIES/BENEFITS:

Pension Plan:	ESOP Stock Plan:	Profit Sharing:	Top Exec. Salary: $410,000	Bonus: $
Savings Plan: Y	Stock Purch. Plan:		Second Exec. Salary: $327,000	Bonus: $

OTHER THOUGHTS:

Apparent Women Officers or Directors: 1
Hot Spot for Advancement for Women/Minorities:

LOCATIONS: ("Y" = Yes)

West:	Southwest:	Midwest:	Southeast:	Northeast:	International:
	Y		Y		Y

GLOBAL PARTNERS LP

www.globalp.com

Industry Group Code: 424710 **Ranks within this company's industry group:** Sales: 2 Profits: 5

Exploration/Production:		Refining/Retailing:		Utilities:		Alternative Energy:		Specialty Services:		Energy Mktg./Other Svcs.	
Exploration:		Refining:		Electric Utility:		Waste/Solar/Other:		Consulting/Eng.:		Energy Marketing:	Y
Production:		Retailing:		Gas Utility:		Thermal/Steam:		Seismic:		Equipment/Machinery:	
Coal Production:		Convenience Stores:		Pipelines:		Wind:		Drilling:		Oil Field Services:	
		Chemicals:		Water:		Hydro:		InfoTech:		Air/Shipping Transportation:	
						Fuel Cells:		Specialty Services:	Y		

TYPES OF BUSINESS:

Energy Marketing
Wholesale Distillates & Gasoline
Fuel Distribution

BRANDS/DIVISIONS/AFFILIATES:

Global Companies LLC
Glen Hes Corp
SubZero
Chelsea Sandwich LLC
Global Operating LLC
Heating Oil Plus
DieselOne
Global Energy Marketing LLC

CONTACTS: *Note: Officers with more than one job title may be intentionally listed here more than once.*

Eric Slifka, CEO
Thomas J. Hollister, COO
Eric Slifka, Pres.
Thomas J. Hollister, CFO
Edward J. Faneuil, General Counsel/Exec. VP/Corp. Sec.
Charles A. Rudinsky, Chief Acct. Officer/Treas./Exec. VP
Alfred A. Slifka, Chmn.

Phone: 781-894-8800 **Fax:**
Toll-Free:
Address: 800 South St., Ste. 200, Waltham, MA 02454-9161 US

GROWTH PLANS/SPECIAL FEATURES:

Global Partners, LP is an energy limited partnership. The firm is a wholesale and commercial distributor of gasoline, distillates (such as home heating oil, diesel and kerosene) and residual oil to wholesalers, retailers and commercial customers. The company is organized within two operating segments: wholesale and commercial. Within these segments, the company divides its products into three categories: distillates, gasoline and residual oil. Gasoline accounts for 51% of the company's total volume sold, with distillates accounting for 44% and residual oil accounting for the remaining 5%. The company is one of the leading wholesalers of distillates and gasoline throughout the northeastern U.S. Global Partners, through wholly-owned subsidiary Global Operating LLC, owns five operating subsidiaries: Global Companies LLC; Global Energy Marketing, LLC; Glen Hes Corp.; Global Montello Group Corp.; and Chelsea Sandwich LLC. Through a network of deepwater and inland terminals, the firm wholesales premium heating oil under the name Heating Oil Plus; generic diesel under the name Diesel One; and kerosene and pour point depressant under the name SubZero to unbranded retail gasoline stations and other resellers. Global Partners also wholesales distillates and gasoline through 22 bulk terminals each with a storage capacity of more than 50,000 barrels. The company also has throughput or exchange agreements at over 50 bulk terminals and inland storage facilities. The commercial segment sells unbranded gasoline, home heating oil, diesel, kerosene and residual oil to customers in the public sector and to large commercial and industrial customers, such as federal and state agencies; municipalities; large industrial companies; transportation and water resource authorities; colleges and universities; and small utilities. In June 2010, Global Partners acquired three New York gasoline and distillate terminals from Warex Terminals Corporation. In September 2010, the firm acquired 148 dealer-operated and 42 Exxon Mobil-operated Mobil stations from Exxon Mobil Corporation.

FINANCIALS: **Sales and profits are in thousands of dollars—add 000 to get the full amount. 2010 Note: Financial information for 2010 was not available for all companies at press time.**

2010 Sales: $	2010 Profits: $	**U.S. Stock Ticker: GLP**
2009 Sales: $5,818,411	2009 Profits: $34,134	**Int'l Ticker:** Int'l Exchange:
2008 Sales: $9,019,123	2008 Profits: $21,055	Employees: 250
2007 Sales: $6,757,834	2007 Profits: $47,013	Fiscal Year Ends: 12/31
2006 Sales: $4,472,418	2006 Profits: $33,416	Parent Company:

SALARIES/BENEFITS:

Pension Plan:	ESOP Stock Plan:	Profit Sharing:	Top Exec. Salary: $800,000	Bonus: $1,032,968
Savings Plan:	Stock Purch. Plan:		Second Exec. Salary: $578,000	Bonus: $550,784

OTHER THOUGHTS:

Apparent Women Officers or Directors:
Hot Spot for Advancement for Women/Minorities:

LOCATIONS: ("Y" = Yes)

West:	Southwest:	Midwest:	Southeast:	Northeast:	International:
				Y	

GLOW ENERGY PCL

www.glow.co.th

Industry Group Code: 2211 **Ranks within this company's industry group:** Sales: 43 Profits: 37

Exploration/Production:		Refining/Retailing:		Utilities:		Alternative Energy:		Specialty Services:		Energy Mktg./Other Svcs.	
Exploration:		Refining:		Electric Utility:	Y	Waste/Solar/Other:		Consulting/Eng.:		Energy Marketing:	
Production:		Retailing:		Gas Utility:		Thermal/Steam:		Seismic:		Equipment/Machinery:	
Coal Production:		Convenience Stores:		Pipelines:		Wind:		Drilling:		Oil Field Services:	
		Chemicals:		Water:		Hydro:	Y	InfoTech:		Air/Shipping Transportation:	
						Fuel Cells:		Specialty Services:			

TYPES OF BUSINESS:

Electricity Generation
Steam Production
Clarified & Demineralized Water Production

BRANDS/DIVISIONS/AFFILIATES:

CONTACTS:

Note: Officers with more than one job title may be intentionally listed here more than once.

Esa Pauli Heiskanen, CEO
Pajongwit Pongsivapai, COO/Exec. VP
Suthiwong Kongsiri, CFO/Exec. VP
Heikki Pudas, Exec. VP-Project Dev. & Bus.
Sriprapha Sumruatruamphol, Chief Commercial Officer/Exec. VP
Guy Richelle, Chmn.

Phone: 66-2-670-1500 **Fax:** 66-2-670-1548
Toll-Free:
Address: 195 Empire Tower, 38th Fl, Park Wing, S Sathorn Rd, Bangkok, 10120 Thailand

GROWTH PLANS/SPECIAL FEATURES:

Glow Energy PCL is one of Thailand's leading electricity generating companies. It is 69.11%-owned by GDF Suez Energy International, a division of French energy company GDF Suez. Glow divides its business into two lines: IPP (Independent Power Producer) and Cogeneration. The IPP business produces electricity under the IPP program of the Electricity Generating Authority of Thailand (EGAT). Its primary customers are EGAT and Electricite du Laos. This business maintains two generating stations, consisting of a 713 megawatt (MW) gas-fired plant in Hemaraj Chonburi Industrial Estate, in Chonburi province, and a 660 MW coal-fired plant in Hemaraj Eastern Industrial Estate, in Rayong province. Additionally, it operates a 152 MW hydroelectric facility in Laos. The Cogeneration business maintains over 20 small, interconnected power generation facilities operating under EGAT's Small Power Producer (SPP) program. Besides electricity, these plants produce steam and clarified and de-mineralized water, all of which it sells to industrial customers in the Hemaraj Eastern Industrial Estate and customers in the surrounding areas of Rayong province. EGAT also buys a portion of its electricity. The facilities have a total capacity of 1,110 MW of electricity, 967 tons per hour of steam and almost 967,000 gallons per hour of clarified and de-mineralized water. Additionally, this business has two more generating facilities under construction, which should increase its electricity capacity by around 400 MW. During 2009, IPP generated 33% of the firm's operating revenue, with the Cogeneration business generating the remaining 67%. Glow operates its plants through eight subsidiaries, all of which are wholly-owned except for three, which are minority-owned by Thai real-estate firm Hemaraj Land & Development PCL, owner of the two industrial estates mentioned above.

FINANCIALS:

Sales and profits are in thousands of dollars—add 000 to get the full amount. 2010 Note: Financial information for 2010 was not available for all companies at press time.

2010 Sales: $	2010 Profits: $	**U.S. Stock Ticker:**
2009 Sales: $1,157,380	2009 Profits: $140,450	**Int'l Ticker: GLOW** Int'l Exchange: Bangkok-BAK
2008 Sales: $1,004,700	2008 Profits: $105,450	Employees: 78
2007 Sales: $961,260	2007 Profits: $142,490	Fiscal Year Ends:
2006 Sales: $	2006 Profits: $	Parent Company:

SALARIES/BENEFITS:

Pension Plan:	ESOP Stock Plan:	Profit Sharing:	Top Exec. Salary: $	Bonus: $
Savings Plan:	Stock Purch. Plan:		Second Exec. Salary: $	Bonus: $

OTHER THOUGHTS:

Apparent Women Officers or Directors: 3
Hot Spot for Advancement for Women/Minorities: Y

LOCATIONS: ("Y" = Yes)

West:	Southwest:	Midwest:	Southeast:	Northeast:	International:
					Y

GOODRICH PETROLEUM CORP

www.goodrichpetroleum.com

Industry Group Code: 211111 **Ranks within this company's industry group:** Sales: 107 Profits: 99

Exploration/Production:		Refining/Retailing:		Utilities:		Alternative Energy:		Specialty Services:		Energy Mktg./Other Svcs.	
Exploration:	Y	Refining:		Electric Utility:		Waste/Solar/Other:		Consulting/Eng.:		Energy Marketing:	
Production:	Y	Retailing:		Gas Utility:		Thermal/Steam:		Seismic:		Equipment/Machinery:	
Coal Production:		Convenience Stores:		Pipelines:		Wind:		Drilling:		Oil Field Services:	
		Chemicals:		Water:		Hydro:		InfoTech:		Air/Shipping Transportation:	
						Fuel Cells:		Specialty Services:			

TYPES OF BUSINESS:

Oil & Gas Exploration & Production

BRANDS/DIVISIONS/AFFILIATES:

CONTACTS:

Note: Officers with more than one job title may be intentionally listed here more than once.

Walter (Gil) Goodrich, CEO
Robert C. Turnham, Jr., COO
Robert C. Turnham, Jr., Pres.
Jan L. Schott, CFO/Sr. VP
Leslee M. Ranly, VP-Human Resources
Bret Hammett, Sr. VP-Exploration
Rusty Mondelli, VP-IT
Leslee M. Ranly, VP-Admin.
Michael J. Killelea, General Counsel/Sr. VP/Corp. Sec.
Tom S. Nemec, Sr. VP-Oper.
James G. Marston, III, VP-Land
Mark E. Ferchau, Exec. VP
Patrick E. Malloy, III, Chmn.

Phone: 713-780-9494	**Fax:** 713-780-9254
Toll-Free:	
Address: 801 Louisiana, Ste. 700, Houston, TX 77002 US	

GROWTH PLANS/SPECIAL FEATURES:

Goodrich Petroleum Corp. is engaged in the exploration, development and production of oil and natural gas in the Cotton Valley trend of East Texas and Northwest Louisiana and the Haynesville Shale play in the same region. The firm's Cotton Valley Trend property is estimated to have approximately 2,300 probable and possible drilling locations. In addition, the firm maintains ownership interests in acreage and/or wells in several additional fields, which include the Midway field in San Patricio County, Texas; the Mott Slough field in Wharton County, Texas and the Garfield Unit in Kalkaska County, Michigan. Currently, the firm owns working interests in 466 active oil and gas wells located in 24 fields in six states. The company has proved reserves of approximately 877,000 barrels of oil and 415.3 billion cubic feet of natural gas. It produces an average of 81.63 million cubic feet equivalent per day. Goodrich sells its natural gas and oil under short-term contracts to a limited pool of customers, including Shell Energy, which accounts for 19% of the firm's revenues; Louis Dreyfus Corporation, which accounts for 32%; and Crosstex Energy, which accounts for 10%. In mid-2009, the company completed a third well in its Haynesvillle Shale.

The company offers its employees medical, dental, vision, AD&D, disability and life insurance; an incentive bonus program; stock awards, a 401(k) plan; transportation benefits; vacation time; a cafeteria plan; a matching gift program and educational assistance.

FINANCIALS:

Sales and profits are in thousands of dollars—add 000 to get the full amount. 2010 Note: Financial information for 2010 was not available for all companies at press time.

2010 Sales: $	2010 Profits: $	**U.S. Stock Ticker: GDP**
2009 Sales: $110,426	2009 Profits: $-257,033	**Int'l Ticker:** Int'l Exchange:
2008 Sales: $216,051	2008 Profits: $115,727	Employees: 125
2007 Sales: $111,305	2007 Profits: $-45,033	Fiscal Year Ends: 12/31
2006 Sales: $74,771	2006 Profits: $1,639	Parent Company:

SALARIES/BENEFITS:

Pension Plan:	ESOP Stock Plan:	Profit Sharing:	Top Exec. Salary: $409,500	Bonus: $358,313
Savings Plan:	Stock Purch. Plan:		Second Exec. Salary: $367,500	Bonus: $321,563

OTHER THOUGHTS:

Apparent Women Officers or Directors: 3
Hot Spot for Advancement for Women/Minorities: Y

LOCATIONS: ("Y" = Yes)

West:	Southwest:	Midwest:	Southeast:	Northeast:	International:
	Y		Y		

GREAT LAKES GAS TRANSMISSION COMPANY

www.glgt.com

Industry Group Code: 486 **Ranks within this company's industry group:** Sales: Profits:

Exploration/Production:		Refining/Retailing:		Utilities:		Alternative Energy:		Specialty Services:		Energy Mktg./Other Svcs.	
Exploration:		Refining:		Electric Utility:		Waste/Solar/Other:		Consulting/Eng.:		Energy Marketing:	Y
Production:		Retailing:		Gas Utility:		Thermal/Steam:		Seismic:		Equipment/Machinery:	
Coal Production:		Convenience Stores:		Pipelines:	Y	Wind:		Drilling:		Oil Field Services:	
		Chemicals:		Water:		Hydro:		InfoTech:		Air/Shipping Transportation:	
						Fuel Cells:		Specialty Services:			

TYPES OF BUSINESS:

Pipelines-Natural Gas

BRANDS/DIVISIONS/AFFILIATES:

TransCanada Corp
ANR Pipeline Company
ANR Storage Company
TransCanada PipeLines Limited
El Paso Corp

CONTACTS:

Note: Officers with more than one job title may be intentionally listed here more than once.

Dean Ferguson, VP-Mktg.
David Montemurro, VP-Eng. & Oper. Svcs.
Catharine Davis, Associate General Counsel
Vern Meier, VP-Field Oper.
Dean Ferguson, VP-Bus. Dev.
Julie Willett, VP-Finance
Lee G. Hobbs, Sr. VP/Gen. Mgr.-U.S. Pipelines Central
Julie Willett, Integration Leader
Tom Janish, Controller

Phone: 832-320-5000 **Fax:**
Toll-Free: 800-573-0640
Address: 717 Texas St., Houston, TX 77002 US

GROWTH PLANS/SPECIAL FEATURES:

Great Lakes Gas Transmission Company (GLGT) is a mid-sized natural gas transportation company operated by TransCanada. It transports approximately 2.2 billion cubic feet of natural gas per day through 2,115 miles of dual, high-pressure pipelines that connect western Canada's natural gas basins to major industrial and market centers in Minnesota, Wisconsin, Michigan and eastern Canada. The company has regional offices in Detroit, Michigan and Duluth, Minnesota. Company affiliates include El Paso Energy and TransCanada Energy. Services offered by GLGT include firm forwardhaul transportation, which provides transportation every day of the year without interruption; limited firm forwardhaul transportation, a less expensive option, providing transportation for a certain number of days over a longer term of service; interruptible forwardhaul transportation, providing transportation on a best effort basis when operational conditions permit; backhaul transportation, which is available to customers every day of the year in the form of firm discounted service and interruptible service; market center services, which allow the company's shippers to park or borrow gas; and storage-related transportation services, which are provided through use of storage fields owned by others close to the company's system. GLGT's customers include regional natural gas transporters, local gas distributors and energy trading firms. GLGT is currently investigating opportunities in system expansion, electricity generation, high-deliverability storage, lateral line development and processing and gathering.

GLGT offers its employees medical, dental, prescription and vision insurance.

FINANCIALS:

Sales and profits are in thousands of dollars—add 000 to get the full amount. 2010 Note: Financial information for 2010 was not available for all companies at press time.

2010 Sales: $	2010 Profits: $	**U.S. Stock Ticker: Private**
2009 Sales: $	2009 Profits: $	**Int'l Ticker:** Int'l Exchange:
2008 Sales: $	2008 Profits: $	Employees:
2007 Sales: $	2007 Profits: $	Fiscal Year Ends: 12/31
2006 Sales: $	2006 Profits: $	Parent Company:

SALARIES/BENEFITS:

Pension Plan:	ESOP Stock Plan:	Profit Sharing:	Top Exec. Salary: $	Bonus: $
Savings Plan:	Stock Purch. Plan:		Second Exec. Salary: $	Bonus: $

OTHER THOUGHTS:

Apparent Women Officers or Directors: 2
Hot Spot for Advancement for Women/Minorities:

LOCATIONS: ("Y" = Yes)

West:	Southwest:	Midwest:	Southeast:	Northeast:	International:
		Y			Y

GREAT PLAINS ENERGY INC

www.greatplainsenergy.com

Industry Group Code: 2211 **Ranks within this company's industry group:** Sales: 36 Profits: 35

Exploration/Production:		Refining/Retailing:		Utilities:		Alternative Energy:		Specialty Services:		Energy Mktg./Other Svcs.	
Exploration:	Y	Refining:		Electric Utility:	Y	Waste/Solar/Other:	Y	Consulting/Eng.:		Energy Marketing:	Y
Production:	Y	Retailing:		Gas Utility:	Y	Thermal/Steam:		Seismic:		Equipment/Machinery:	
Coal Production:		Convenience Stores:		Pipelines:		Wind:	Y	Drilling:		Oil Field Services:	
		Chemicals:		Water:		Hydro:		InfoTech:		Air/Shipping Transportation:	
						Fuel Cells:		Specialty Services:			

TYPES OF BUSINESS:

Utilities-Electricity & Natural Gas
Energy Management Services
Coalbed Methane Properties
Power Generation
Nuclear Plant
Wind Generation

BRANDS/DIVISIONS/AFFILIATES:

Kansas City Power & Light Company
KLT, Inc
Great Plains Energy Services Inc
KLT Gas Inc
MPS Merchant Services Inc
Aquila Inc

CONTACTS: *Note: Officers with more than one job title may be intentionally listed here more than once.*

Michael J. Chesser, CEO
William H. Downey, COO
William H. Downey, Pres.
Jim Shay, CFO
Barbara B. Curry, Sr. VP-Human Resources
Michael Cline, Corp. Sec.
Jim Shay, Sr. VP-Strategic Planning
Michael Cline, VP-Investor Rel./Treas.
Terry Bassham, Exec. VP-Finance
Terry Bassham, Exec. VP-Utility Oper., KCP&L
William Herdegen, III, VP-T&D Oper., KCP&L
Lori Wright, VP/Controller
Jim Alberts, VP-Customer Svc., KCP&L
Michael J. Chesser, Chmn.
Scott Heidtbrink, Sr. VP-Supply, Kansas City Power & Light

Phone: 816-556-2200	**Fax:** 816-556-2992
Toll-Free:	
Address: 1200 Main St., Kansas City, MO 64106 US	

GROWTH PLANS/SPECIAL FEATURES:

Great Plains Energy, Inc. (GPE) is a public utility holding company. The company and its subsidiaries serve over 820,000 customers located in western Missouri and eastern Kansas. Its subsidiaries are Kansas City Power and Light Company (KCP&L); KCP&L Greater Missouri Operations Company (GMO); Great Plains Energy Services, Inc.; and KLT, Inc. KCP&L is an integrated, regulated electric utility that provides electricity to customers primarily in Missouri and Kansas. GMO is also an integrated, regulated electric utility that primarily provides electricity to customers in Missouri. GMO also provides regulated steam service to customers in the St. Joseph, Missouri area. Additionally, GMO owns MPS Merchant Services, Inc., which holds several long-term natural gas contracts. Great Plains Energy Services, Inc. provides services at cost to Great Plains Energy and its subsidiaries. KLT Inc. also owns KLT Gas, Inc. and Home Service Solutions, Inc., which have no active operations. GPE's fuel sources for generation of electricity are coal at 80%, nuclear fuel at 17%, natural gas and oil at 2% and wind power at 1%. KCP&L owns 47% of the Wolf Creek nuclear plant in Burlington, Kansas. KLT Gas specializes in the acquisition, exploration, development and production of unconventional natural gas resources, primarily coal bed methane properties. GPES provides services at cost to the company and its subsidiaries. GPE provides wind power for KCP&L with a wind farm capable of producing 100.5 megawatts (MW) of electricity.

The company offers its employees medical, dental and vision insurance; employee assistance program; a 401(k) and pension plan; and tuition reimbursement.

FINANCIALS: **Sales and profits are in thousands of dollars—add 000 to get the full amount. 2010 Note: Financial information for 2010 was not available for all companies at press time.**

2010 Sales: $	2010 Profits: $	**U.S. Stock Ticker: GXP**
2009 Sales: $1,965,000	2009 Profits: $150,000	**Int'l Ticker:** Int'l Exchange:
2008 Sales: $1,670,000	2008 Profits: $154,500	Employees: 3,197
2007 Sales: $3,267,100	2007 Profits: $159,200	Fiscal Year Ends: 12/31
2006 Sales: $2,675,300	2006 Profits: $127,600	Parent Company:

SALARIES/BENEFITS:

Pension Plan:	ESOP Stock Plan:	Profit Sharing:	Top Exec. Salary: $800,000	Bonus: $1,054,400
Savings Plan: Y	Stock Purch. Plan:		Second Exec. Salary: $510,000	Bonus: $470,526

OTHER THOUGHTS:

Apparent Women Officers or Directors: 3
Hot Spot for Advancement for Women/Minorities: Y

LOCATIONS: ("Y" = Yes)

West:	Southwest:	Midwest:	Southeast:	Northeast:	International:
		Y			

GS CALTEX CORP

www.gscaltex.com

Industry Group Code: 324110 **Ranks within this company's industry group:** Sales: 12 Profits: 2

Exploration/Production:		Refining/Retailing:		Utilities:		Alternative Energy:		Specialty Services:		Energy Mktg./Other Svcs.	
Exploration:		Refining:	Y	Electric Utility:	Y	Waste/Solar/Other:		Consulting/Eng.:		Energy Marketing:	
Production:		Retailing:	Y	Gas Utility:	Y	Thermal/Steam:		Seismic:		Equipment/Machinery:	
Coal Production:		Convenience Stores:	Y	Pipelines:	Y	Wind:		Drilling:		Oil Field Services:	
		Chemicals:	Y	Water:		Hydro:		InfoTech:		Air/Shipping Transportation:	
						Fuel Cells:		Specialty Services:			

TYPES OF BUSINESS:

Petroleum Refining & Marketing
Petrochemicals
Lubricants
Gas Stations
Electrical & Heating Utilities

BRANDS/DIVISIONS/AFFILIATES:

GS Holdings Corp
Chevron Corporation
Kixx
Rando
JoyMart
AutoOasis

CONTACTS: *Note: Officers with more than one job title may be intentionally listed here more than once.*

Dong-Soo Hur, CEO
Dong-Soo Hur, Chmn.

Phone: 82-2-2005-1114	**Fax:** 82-2-567-5174
Toll-Free:	
Address: 135-985, 679 Yoksam-dong, Gangnam-gu, Seoul, Korea	

GROWTH PLANS/SPECIAL FEATURES:

GS Caltex Corp., one of the largest petroleum refining companies in Asia, is a leading producer of petrochemical products. Formerly LG-Caltex Oil, the company is a joint venture between GS Holdings Corp. and Chevron Corporation. The company's business activities consist of petroleum refining and marketing; the production of petrochemicals; and the blending of lubricant oils. The company's crude oil operations have a daily refining capacity of 840,000 barrels; a daily cracking capacity of 155,000 barrels, producing gasoline, kerosene and diesel from bunker C oil; and a daily kerosene and diesel desulfurizing capacity of 272,000 barrels. The firm's petroleum products include gasoline, kerosene, diesel, automotive and marine fuel oils, liquefied petroleum gas (LPG), jet fuel and asphalt. It offers the Kixx line of gasoline and lubricants and the Rando brand hydraulic fluid. The firm's petrochemicals business produces 2.8 million tons of aromatics annually, including 1.2 million tons of paraxylene and 800,000 tons of benzene. The company also annually manufactures 180,000 tons of polypropylene in various grades for use by other industries. GS Caltex's aromatic petroleum products, including solvents and toluene, are used in paints and rubber and to make components of other products. GS Caltex is engaged in the purchase and distribution of LNG (liquefied natural gas) throughout Korea, including maintaining an extensive LNG storage, transportation and sales network, and operating LNG-fueled combine-cycle power plants through subsidiaries running electrical and heating utilities in several major cities. In Korea, it runs a network of about 3,500 gas stations and 400 gas filling stations; the JoyMart chain of combined gas stations and convenience stores; and the AutoOasis light maintenance franchise chain. The firm has some oil exploration and production activities through its 15% interest in an oilfield located on Cambodia's west coast. In June 2010, the firm built a production plant that converts heavy oil into transportation fuels.

FINANCIALS: **Sales and profits are in thousands of dollars—add 000 to get the full amount. 2010 Note: Financial information for 2010 was not available for all companies at press time.**

2010 Sales: $	2010 Profits: $	**U.S. Stock Ticker: Joint Venture**
2009 Sales: $22,629,600	2009 Profits: $566,240	**Int'l Ticker:** Int'l Exchange:
2008 Sales: $26,795,800	2008 Profits: $-64,750	Employees:
2007 Sales: $17,329,200	2007 Profits: $510,170	Fiscal Year Ends: 12/31
2006 Sales: $15,441,800	2006 Profits: $500,530	Parent Company:

SALARIES/BENEFITS:

Pension Plan:	ESOP Stock Plan:	Profit Sharing:	Top Exec. Salary: $	Bonus: $
Savings Plan:	Stock Purch. Plan:		Second Exec. Salary: $	Bonus: $

OTHER THOUGHTS:

Apparent Women Officers or Directors:
Hot Spot for Advancement for Women/Minorities:

LOCATIONS: ("Y" = Yes)

West:	Southwest:	Midwest:	Southeast:	Northeast:	International:
					Y

GS HOLDINGS CORP

www.gsholdings.com

Industry Group Code: 324110 **Ranks within this company's industry group:** Sales: 7 Profits: 5

Exploration/Production:		Refining/Retailing:		Utilities:		Alternative Energy:		Specialty Services:		Energy Mktg./Other Svcs.	
Exploration:	Y	Refining:	Y	Electric Utility:	Y	Waste/Solar/Other:		Consulting/Eng.:		Energy Marketing:	
Production:		Retailing:	Y	Gas Utility:	Y	Thermal/Steam:		Seismic:		Equipment/Machinery:	
Coal Production:		Convenience Stores:	Y	Pipelines:		Wind:		Drilling:		Oil Field Services:	
		Chemicals:	Y	Water:		Hydro:		InfoTech:		Air/Shipping Transportation:	
						Fuel Cells:	Y	Specialty Services:	Y		

TYPES OF BUSINESS:

Oil Refining
Petrochemicals
Convenience Stores
Home Shopping Networks
Telecommunications
Power Generation
Gasoline Sales
Sports Teams

BRANDS/DIVISIONS/AFFILIATES:

GS Caltex
Chevron Corporation
joyMart
GS EPS
GS Retail
GS Sports
Ssangyong Corporation
Lotte Shopping Company Ltd.

CONTACTS:

Note: Officers with more than one job title may be intentionally listed here more than once.

Chang Soo Huh, Co-CEO
Gyeong Seok Seo, Pres./Co-CEO
Sun Gi Hong, CFO
Byung Yong Lim, Exec. VP
Soon Ky Hong, Sr. VP
Eun Joo Yeo, VP
Chang Soo Huh, Chmn.

Phone: 82-2-2005-1114 **Fax:** 82-2-2005-8181
Toll-Free:
Address: 23F, GS Tower, 679 Yoksam Dong, Gangnam Gu, Seoul, Korea

GROWTH PLANS/SPECIAL FEATURES:

GS Holdings Corp. is a holding company comprising several subsidiaries engaged in industries such as energy, television home shopping, petrochemical products and retail establishments. The firm's main subsidiaries include GS Caltex, GS EPS, GS Retail, GS Homeshopping, GS Global, GS Sports and GS Engineering & Construction (GS E&C). GS Caltex, a joint venture with Chevron Corporation, is an energy service business that focuses on the petroleum and petrochemical, liquefied natural gas (LNG), electric power, exploration and production, convenience retail and fuel cell technology industries. The company maintains refining facilities that produce 750,000 barrels per day. It also operates more than 3,500 gas stations as well as joyMart convenience stores throughout Korea. GS EPS is Korea's first independent power producer in the LNG-fired power generation industry. GS Retail operates retail businesses with four business segments: GS25 (a convenience store); GS Supermarket; GS Mart (a discount store) and GS Square (a department store); and GS Watsons (a health and beauty products store). GS Homeshopping, a home shopping network introduced in 1995 under the name LG Home Shopping, offers 24-hour-a-day home shopping through cable and satellite television. Additionally, the firm operates GSeshop.co.kr, one of the largest online shopping retailers in Korea. GS Global, which became an affiliate in 2009 following the acquisition of Ssangyong Corporation, specializes in steel, metal, cement material, machinery and logistics. GS Sports owns and operates a football club known as FC Seoul (Football Club Seoul). GS E&C concentrates on a variety of engineering and construction projects with emphasis on architecture, civil engineering, housing and plant design and construction. In February 2010, the firm agreed to sell its department and discount store operations to Lotte Shopping Company Ltd.

FINANCIALS:

Sales and profits are in thousands of dollars—add 000 to get the full amount. 2010 Note: Financial information for 2010 was not available for all companies at press time.

2010 Sales: $
2009 Sales: $30,955,300
2008 Sales: $35,962,200
2007 Sales: $339,156
2006 Sales: $317,360

2010 Profits: $
2009 Profits: $438,250
2008 Profits: $14,020
2007 Profits: $300,601
2006 Profits: $325,870

U.S. Stock Ticker: GSHDF.PK
Int'l Ticker: Int'l Exchange:
Employees:
Fiscal Year Ends:
Parent Company:

SALARIES/BENEFITS:

Pension Plan: ESOP Stock Plan: Profit Sharing: Top Exec. Salary: $ Bonus: $
Savings Plan: Stock Purch. Plan: Second Exec. Salary: $ Bonus: $

OTHER THOUGHTS:

Apparent Women Officers or Directors:
Hot Spot for Advancement for Women/Minorities:

LOCATIONS: ("Y" = Yes)

West:	Southwest:	Midwest:	Southeast:	Northeast:	International:
					Y

GULF OIL LIMITED PARTNERSHIP

www.gulfoil.com

Industry Group Code: 424710 **Ranks within this company's industry group:** Sales: Profits:

Exploration/Production:		Refining/Retailing:		Utilities:		Alternative Energy:		Specialty Services:		Energy Mktg./Other Svcs.	
Exploration:		Refining:		Electric Utility:		Waste/Solar/Other:		Consulting/Eng.:		Energy Marketing:	
Production:		Retailing:	Y	Gas Utility:		Thermal/Steam:		Seismic:		Equipment/Machinery:	
Coal Production:		Convenience Stores:		Pipelines:		Wind:		Drilling:		Oil Field Services:	
		Chemicals:		Water:		Hydro:		InfoTech:		Air/Shipping Transportation:	
						Fuel Cells:		Specialty Services:	Y		

TYPES OF BUSINESS:

Petroleum Wholesale & Distribution
Gas Stations & Storage Terminals
Gasoline Additives

BRANDS/DIVISIONS/AFFILIATES:

Gulf MasterCard
Cumberland Gulf Group (The)
Great Island Energy
Cumberland Farms Inc

CONTACTS:

Note: Officers with more than one job title may be intentionally listed here more than once.

Ronald R. Sabia, COO
Ronald R. Sabia, Pres.
Jayne Conway, CFO
Rick Dery, Sr. VP-Branded Mktg. & Sales
D. Greggory Scott, Sr. VP-Terminal & Petroleum Oper.
Laura Scott, Sr. VP-Strategy
Lauras Scott, Sr. VP-Finance
Robert Far, Sr. VP/Chief Commercial Officer
Walter Brickowski, VP-Unbranded Mktg.
Jeffrey Sweetman, VP-Branded Sales Oper.
Joseph H. Petrowski, CEO-Cumberland Gulf Group
David Masuret, VP-Supply & Dist.

Phone: 508-270-8300 **Fax:**
Toll-Free: 800-774-4853
Address: 100 Crossing Blvd., Framingham, MA 01702 US

GROWTH PLANS/SPECIAL FEATURES:

Gulf Oil Limited Partnership, headquartered in Massachusetts, is a petroleum wholesaler. The company is a subsidiary of the Cumberland Gulf Group. The firm distributes various grades of gasoline and diesel fuel, through a network of terminals and gas stations. The company operates approximately 1,800 Gulf-branded stations in 11 northeastern states. Gulf Oil's fuel products include gasoline with ethanol; low-sulfur number-one diesel; number-two diesel; unleaded and unleaded plus gasoline; reformulated gasoline; super-unleaded gasoline; kerosene; and number-two heating oil. In addition, the company distributes motor oils, lubricants, dieselect (is a product that prevents wax build-up in fuel during periods of low temperatures) dispersant, detergent additives and heating oil to commercial, industrial and utility customers. The supply and distribution department uses its interconnected network of ocean tankers, barges, truck fleets and pipelines to provide constant supply of petroleum products. Gulf's terminal network consists of 12 storage terminals. The firm has alliances with terminal operators in areas in the Northeast where it does not have proprietary terminals. Gulf operates credit card programs including a commercial fleet fueling card, a prepaid gas card and a Gulf MasterCard. Great Island Energy, (GIE) a division of the firm provides refined petroleum products and bio-fuels to the non-branded wholesaler, retailer, and end-use energy customers in the Northeast U.S. The GIE terminal network consists of twelve owned and operated facilities and has several alliances with other terminal operators. Sister company Cumberland Farms Inc., provides 600 convenience stores in 11 states. In January 2010, the company bought the rights to the Gulf brand name in the U.S. The brand name Gulf has only been available in 11 states in the Northeast through a licensing agreement between the firm's parent company and Chevron U.S.A., Inc. In 2010, Gulf Oil made significant strides in expansion in the Southeast U.S., with distributor agreements in Kentucky, Georgia and Carolina.

FINANCIALS:

Sales and profits are in thousands of dollars—add 000 to get the full amount. 2010 Note: Financial information for 2010 was not available for all companies at press time.

2010 Sales: $	2010 Profits: $	**U.S. Stock Ticker: Private**
2009 Sales: $	2009 Profits: $	**Int'l Ticker:** Int'l Exchange:
2008 Sales: $	2008 Profits: $	Employees:
2007 Sales: $	2007 Profits: $	Fiscal Year Ends: 9/30
2006 Sales: $	2006 Profits: $	Parent Company: CUMBERLAND GULF GROUP (THE)

SALARIES/BENEFITS:

Pension Plan:	ESOP Stock Plan:	Profit Sharing:	Top Exec. Salary: $	Bonus: $
Savings Plan:	Stock Purch. Plan:		Second Exec. Salary: $	Bonus: $

OTHER THOUGHTS:

Apparent Women Officers or Directors: 5
Hot Spot for Advancement for Women/Minorities: Y

LOCATIONS: ("Y" = Yes)

West:	Southwest:	Midwest:	Southeast:	Northeast:	International:
				Y	

GULFMARK OFFSHORE INC

www.gulfmark.com

Industry Group Code: 483111 **Ranks within this company's industry group:** Sales: 6 Profits: 4

Exploration/Production:		Refining/Retailing:		Utilities:		Alternative Energy:		Specialty Services:		Energy Mktg./Other Svcs.	
Exploration:		Refining:		Electric Utility:		Waste/Solar/Other:		Consulting/Eng.:		Energy Marketing:	
Production:		Retailing:		Gas Utility:		Thermal/Steam:		Seismic:		Equipment/Machinery:	
Coal Production:		Convenience Stores:		Pipelines:		Wind:		Drilling:		Oil Field Services:	Y
		Chemicals:		Water:		Hydro:		InfoTech:		Air/Shipping Transportation:	Y
						Fuel Cells:		Specialty Services:	Y		

TYPES OF BUSINESS:

Oil & Gas Drilling Support Services
Offshore Services

BRANDS/DIVISIONS/AFFILIATES:

Gulf Offshore North Sea, Ltd.
Gulf Marine Far East Pte., Ltd.
Gulf Offshore Norge AS
Gulf Marine Do Brasil, Ltda.
GulfMark Servicios de Mexico
GulfMark Americas, Inc.
GM Offshore, Inc.

CONTACTS:

Note: Officers with more than one job title may be intentionally listed here more than once.

Bruce A. Streeter, CEO
Bruce A. Streeter, Pres.
Quintin V. Kneen, CFO/Exec. VP
John E. Leech, Exec. VP-Oper.
Samuel R. Rubio, VP-Acct./Chief Acct. Officer/Controller
David J. Butters, Chmn.

Phone: 713-963-9522 **Fax:** 713-664-5057
Toll-Free:
Address: 10111 Richmond Ave., Ste. 340, Houston, TX 77042 US

GROWTH PLANS/SPECIAL FEATURES:

GulfMark Offshore, Inc. provides offshore marine support and transportation services primarily to companies involved in offshore oil and natural gas exploration and production. Its fleet of 89 vessels is used to transport drilling materials, supplies and personnel to offshore facilities, as well as move and position drilling structures. The firm is organized into three geographically defined operating segments: the North Sea, offshore Southeast Asia and the Americas. The North Sea market includes offshore Norway, Denmark, the Netherlands, Germany and the U.K. The Southeast Asia market includes offshore Brunei, Cambodia, Indonesia, Malaysia, Myanmar, the Philippines, Singapore, Thailand, Australia, New Zealand and Vietnam. The Americas market is comprised of offshore North, Central and South America, including the U.S., Mexico, Trinidad and Brazil. GulfMark also operates in other international markets, including offshore India, the Persian Gulf and the Mediterranean Sea. Presently, the company operates its fleet in the following areas: 38 vessels in the North Sea, 15 vessels offshore Southeast Asia and 36 vessels in the Americas. Its fleet includes anchor handling, towing and support vessels; platform support vessels; fast supply and crew vessels; specialty vessels; standby rescue vessels; construction support vessels; and utility vessels. The firm's customers are major integrated oil companies and large independent oil and natural gas exploration and production companies working in international markets, as well as foreign government-owned oil companies and companies that provide logistic, construction and other services to such organizations. GulfMark subsidiaries include GulfMark North Sea Limited; GulfMark Servicios de Mexico; Gulf Offshore Norge AS; GulfMark Americas, Inc.; GM Offshore, Inc.; Gulf Marine Do Brasil, Ltda.; and Gulf Marine Far East PTE Ltd.

GulfMark offers its employees health, dental, prescription drug and vision coverage, life insurance, short and long-term disability insurance, flexible spending accounts and a 401(k) plan.

FINANCIALS:

Sales and profits are in thousands of dollars—add 000 to get the full amount. 2010 Note: Financial information for 2010 was not available for all companies at press time.

2010 Sales: $	2010 Profits: $	**U.S. Stock Ticker: GLF**
2009 Sales: $388,871	2009 Profits: $50,583	**Int'l Ticker:** Int'l Exchange:
2008 Sales: $411,740	2008 Profits: $183,784	Employees: 1,600
2007 Sales: $306,026	2007 Profits: $98,975	Fiscal Year Ends: 12/31
2006 Sales: $250,921	2006 Profits: $89,729	Parent Company:

SALARIES/BENEFITS:

Pension Plan:	ESOP Stock Plan:	Profit Sharing:	Top Exec. Salary: $592,250	Bonus: $350,000
Savings Plan: Y	Stock Purch. Plan:		Second Exec. Salary: $314,500	Bonus: $200,000

OTHER THOUGHTS:

Apparent Women Officers or Directors:
Hot Spot for Advancement for Women/Minorities:

LOCATIONS: ("Y" = Yes)

West:	Southwest:	Midwest:	Southeast:	Northeast:	International:
	Y		Y	Y	Y

HALLIBURTON COMPANY

www.halliburton.com

Industry Group Code: 213112 **Ranks within this company's industry group:** Sales: 2 Profits: 3

Exploration/Production:		Refining/Retailing:		Utilities:		Alternative Energy:		Specialty Services:		Energy Mktg./Other Svcs.	
Exploration:		Refining:		Electric Utility:		Waste/Solar/Other:		Consulting/Eng.:		Energy Marketing:	
Production:		Retailing:		Gas Utility:		Thermal/Steam:		Seismic:		Equipment/Machinery:	Y
Coal Production:		Convenience Stores:		Pipelines:		Wind:		Drilling:		Oil Field Services:	Y
		Chemicals:		Water:		Hydro:		InfoTech:	Y	Air/Shipping Transportation:	
						Fuel Cells:		Specialty Services:	Y		

TYPES OF BUSINESS:

Oil & Gas Drilling Support Services
Software Information Systems

BRANDS/DIVISIONS/AFFILIATES:

Landmark
Security DBS Drill Bits
Sperry Drilling Services
Easywell
Protech Centerform
Pinnacle Technologies
WellDynamics
GeoTap IDS

CONTACTS:

Note: Officers with more than one job title may be intentionally listed here more than once.

David J. Lesar, CEO
David J. Lesar, Pres.
Mark A. McCollum, CFO/Exec. VP
Lawrence Pope, Chief Human Resources Officer
Lawrence Pope, VP-Admin.
Bert Cornelison, General Counsel/Exec. VP
Tim Probert, Exec. VP-Strategy & Corp. Dev.
Christian Garcia, VP-Investor Rel.
Craig Nunez, Treas./Sr. VP
Sherry Williams, Corp. Sec./VP
Tim Probert, Pres., Global Bus. Lines
Evelyn Angelle, Corp. Controller/Principal Acct. Officer/VP
James S. Brown, Pres., Western Hemisphere
David J. Lesar, Chmn.
Ahmed H.M. Lotfy, Pres., Eastern Hemisphere

Phone: 281-575-3000 **Fax:**
Toll-Free: 888-669-3920
Address: 3000 N. Sam Houston Pkwy. E., Houston, TX 77032 US

GROWTH PLANS/SPECIAL FEATURES:

Halliburton Company provides products and services to the upstream oil and gas industry. The firm serves major, national, and independent oil and gas companies around the world, operating in approximately 70 countries. The company operates through two business segments: Drilling and Evaluation; and Completion and Production. The Drilling and Evaluation segment provides field and reservoir modeling, drilling, evaluation, and precise well-bore placement solutions that enable customers to model, measure, and optimize their well construction activities. This segment consists of Baroid Fluid Services; Sperry Drilling Services; Security DBS Drill Bits; wireline and perforating services; Landmark; and project management. The Completion and Production segment delivers cementing, stimulation, intervention, and completion services. This segment consists of production enhancement services, completion tools and services, and cementing services. Production enhancement services include stimulation services, pipeline process services, sand control services, and well intervention services. Completion tools and services include subsurface safety valves and flow control equipment, surface safety systems, packers and specialty completion equipment, intelligent completion systems, expandable liner hanger systems, sand control systems, well servicing tools and reservoir performance services. Cementing services involve bonding the well and well casing while isolating fluid zones and maximizing wellbore stability. In October 2009, the company acquired Geo-Logic Systems, LLC, a provider of advanced structural interpretation, analysis and restoration software for geologic environments. In April 2010, Halliburton agreed to acquire Boots & Coots, which provides well intervention and pressure control services to oil and gas exploration and drilling companies. In May 2010, the firm successfully completed field tests for the GeoTap IDS fluid identification and sampling sensor, which allows for fluid sampling during short drilling stops. In August 2010, the company obtained a letter of intent from Shell Iraq Petroleum Development B.V. for the development of the Majnoon field in Southern Iraq.

FINANCIALS:

Sales and profits are in thousands of dollars—add 000 to get the full amount. 2010 Note: Financial information for 2010 was not available for all companies at press time.

2010 Sales: $	2010 Profits: $	**U.S. Stock Ticker: HAL**
2009 Sales: $14,675,000	2009 Profits: $1,155,000	**Int'l Ticker:** Int'l Exchange:
2008 Sales: $18,279,000	2008 Profits: $2,215,000	Employees: 51,000
2007 Sales: $15,264,000	2007 Profits: $3,536,000	Fiscal Year Ends: 12/31
2006 Sales: $12,955,000	2006 Profits: $2,348,000	Parent Company:

SALARIES/BENEFITS:

Pension Plan: Y	ESOP Stock Plan:	Profit Sharing:	Top Exec. Salary: $1,328,708	Bonus: $5,000,000
Savings Plan: Y	Stock Purch. Plan: Y		Second Exec. Salary: $577,500	Bonus: $581,000

OTHER THOUGHTS:

Apparent Women Officers or Directors: 5
Hot Spot for Advancement for Women/Minorities: Y

LOCATIONS: ("Y" = Yes)

West:	Southwest:	Midwest:	Southeast:	Northeast:	International:
Y	Y		Y		Y

HARVEST NATURAL RESOURCES INC

www.harvestnr.com

Industry Group Code: 211111 **Ranks within this company's industry group:** Sales: 114 Profits: 74

Exploration/Production:		Refining/Retailing:		Utilities:		Alternative Energy:		Specialty Services:		Energy Mktg./Other Svcs.	
Exploration:	Y	Refining:		Electric Utility:		Waste/Solar/Other:		Consulting/Eng.:		Energy Marketing:	
Production:	Y	Retailing:		Gas Utility:		Thermal/Steam:		Seismic:		Equipment/Machinery:	
Coal Production:		Convenience Stores:		Pipelines:		Wind:		Drilling:		Oil Field Services:	
		Chemicals:		Water:		Hydro:		InfoTech:		Air/Shipping Transportation:	
						Fuel Cells:		Specialty Services:			

TYPES OF BUSINESS:

Oil & Gas Exploration & Production

BRANDS/DIVISIONS/AFFILIATES:

Fusion Geophysical LL
Petrodelta SA
Corporacion Venezolana del Petroleo SA
Newfield Exploration Company

CONTACTS:

Note: Officers with more than one job title may be intentionally listed here more than once.

James A. Edmiston, CEO
James A. Edmiston, Pres.
Steven C. Haynes, CFO/VP/Treas.
Karl L. Nesselrode, VP-Eng. & Bus. Dev.
Keith L. Head, General Counsel/VP/Corp. Sec.
Patrick R. Oenbring, VP-Western Oper.
G. Michael Morgan, VP-Bus. Dev.
Rab Speirs, VP-Eastern Oper.
Stephen D. Chesebro, Chmn.

Phone: 281-899-5700 **Fax:** 281-899-5702
Toll-Free:
Address: 1177 Enclave Pkwy., Ste. 300, Houston, TX 77077 US

GROWTH PLANS/SPECIAL FEATURES:

Harvest Natural Resources, Inc. (HNR) is an independent energy company. The firm specializes in acquiring, exploring, developing, producing and disposing of oil and natural gas properties. The firm's primary assets are in Venezuela, where it operates through joint venture Petrodelta S.A. Petrodelta is 32%-owned by HNR, 60%-owned by Corporacion Venezolana del Petroleo, S.A. and 8%-owned by Oil & Gas Technology Consultants (Netherlands) Cooperatie U.A. Petrodelta has proved reserves of approximately 43.3 million barrels of oil equivalent and a production capacity of roughly 24,000 barrels of oil per day. It controls six fields in Venezuela: Uracoa, Tucupita, Bombal, Isleno, Temblador and El Salto. The Uracoa field has 78 oil and natural gas producing wells and six water injection wells. The Uracoa production facility has a capacity of 60,000 barrels of oil and 130,000 barrels of water per day; and can store up to 75,000 barrels of crude oil. The Tucupita field has 16 oil producing wells and four water injection wells in the field. The Tucupita production facility has capacity to process 30,000 barrels of oil and 125,000 barrels of water per day; and has a storage capacity of 60,000 barrels of crude oil. The oil is transported through a 31-mile, 20,000 barrels of oil per day pipeline from the Tucupita field to the Uracoa plant facilities. The Temblador field has 19 oil-producing wells. The remaining fields do not have productive wells. Petrodelta also controls a 25-mile oil pipeline from its oil processing facilities to Petroleos de Venezuela, S.A.'s storage facility. In addition to Petrodelta, HNR owns interests in fields in Gabon, China, Indonesia, Oman and the U.S. The firm also holds a 49% stake in Fusion Geophysical, LLC, which specializes in geophysics, geosciences and reservoir engineering; and 43%-interest in Newfield Exploration Company, which is currently drilling in Utah.

FINANCIALS:

Sales and profits are in thousands of dollars—add 000 to get the full amount. 2010 Note: Financial information for 2010 was not available for all companies at press time.

2010 Sales: $	2010 Profits: $	**U.S. Stock Ticker: HNR**
2009 Sales: $ 181	2009 Profits: $-3,107	**Int'l Ticker:** Int'l Exchange:
2008 Sales: $	2008 Profits: $-21,464	Employees: 23
2007 Sales: $11,217	2007 Profits: $60,118	Fiscal Year Ends: 12/31
2006 Sales: $59,506	2006 Profits: $58,562	Parent Company:

SALARIES/BENEFITS:

Pension Plan:	ESOP Stock Plan:	Profit Sharing:	Top Exec. Salary: $450,000	Bonus: $452,534
Savings Plan:	Stock Purch. Plan:		Second Exec. Salary: $300,000	Bonus: $167,960

OTHER THOUGHTS:

Apparent Women Officers or Directors:
Hot Spot for Advancement for Women/Minorities:

LOCATIONS: ("Y" = Yes)

West:	Southwest:	Midwest:	Southeast:	Northeast:	International:
	Y				Y

HAWAIIAN ELECTRIC INDUSTRIES INC

www.hei.com

Industry Group Code: 2211 **Ranks within this company's industry group:** Sales: 35 Profits: 40

Exploration/Production:		Refining/Retailing:		Utilities:		Alternative Energy:		Specialty Services:		Energy Mktg./Other Svcs.	
Exploration:		Refining:		Electric Utility:	Y	Waste/Solar/Other:	Y	Consulting/Eng.:		Energy Marketing:	
Production:		Retailing:		Gas Utility:		Thermal/Steam:	Y	Seismic:		Equipment/Machinery:	
Coal Production:		Convenience Stores:		Pipelines:		Wind:	Y	Drilling:		Oil Field Services:	
		Chemicals:		Water:		Hydro:	Y	InfoTech:		Air/Shipping Transportation:	
						Fuel Cells:		Specialty Services:	Y		

TYPES OF BUSINESS:

Utilities-Electricity
Savings Bank
Renewable Energy
Biofuels

BRANDS/DIVISIONS/AFFILIATES:

Hawaiian Electric Company
Hawaiian Electric Light Company
Maui Electric Company, Limited
Renewable Hawaii, Inc.
American Savings Bank, F.S.B.
HEI Diversified
Pacific Energy Conservation Services, Inc.
Uluwehiokama Biofuels Corp.

CONTACTS: *Note: Officers with more than one job title may be intentionally listed here more than once.*

Constance H. Lau, CEO
Constance H. Lau, Pres.
James A. Ajello, CFO/Sr. VP-Financial/Treas.
Chet A. Richardson, Chief Admin. Officer
Chet A. Richardson, General Counsel/Sr. VP/Sec.
Andrew I. T. Chang, VP-External Affairs
Shelee M.T. Kimura, Mgr.-Investor Rel.
David M. Kostecki, VP-Finance/Controller/Chief Acct. Officer
Richard M. Rosenblum, CEO/Pres., Hawaiian Electric Company, Inc.
Jay M. Ignacio, Pres., Hawaii Electric Light Company, Inc.
Timothy K. Schools, Pres., American Savings Bank, F.S.B.
Edward L. Reinhardt, Pres., Maui Electric Company, Ltd.
Jeffrey N. Watanabe, Chmn.

Phone: 808-543-5662	**Fax:** 808-543-7966
Toll-Free:	
Address: 900 Richards St., Honolulu, HI 96813 US	

GROWTH PLANS/SPECIAL FEATURES:

Hawaiian Electric Industries, Inc. (HEI) is a diversified holding company engaged in independent power and utility services and the operation of a savings bank. HEI's Hawaiian Electric Company (HECO) subsidiary, founded in 1891, is a regulated electric public utility company, along with its subsidiaries Hawaiian Electric Light Company (HELCO) and Maui Electric Company, Limited (MECO). HECO's Renewable Hawaii, Inc. subsidiary invests in renewable energy projects, while Uluwehiokama Biofuels Corp. invests in a Maui-based biofuel refining plant. HECO, HELCO and MECO are regulated operating electric public utilities engaged in the production, purchase, transmission, distribution and sale of electricity on the islands of Oahu, Maui, Lanai, Molokai and Hawaii. HEI's electric utility operations generate approximately 88% of its revenues. The islands of Oahu, Maui, Lanai, Molokai and Hawaii have a combined population of approximately 1.2 million, or approximately 95% of the Hawaii population, and comprise a service area of 5,766 square miles. The principle communities served include Honolulu on Oahu; Wailuku and Kahului on Maui; and Hilo and Kona on Hawaii. Each island has its own generation and transmission system that is not connected to any other grid, which results in the company maintaining a larger amount of surplus capacity than most utilities. Additional subsidiaries of HEI include HEI Diversified (HEIDI), a holding company; Pacific Energy Conservation Services, Inc. (PECS), a contract services company; HEI Properties, Inc. (HEIPI); HEI Investments, Inc.; Hawaiian Electric Industries Capital Trusts II and III; and The Old Oahu Tug Service, Inc. (TOOTS). HEIDI's American Savings Bank, F.S.B. subsidiary is a leading financial institution in Hawaii, with more than 60 branch offices offering investment products, financial planning services, insurance, deposit accounts and consumer loans. It manages assets of $4.9 billion and deposits of $4.1 billion.

FINANCIALS: **Sales and profits are in thousands of dollars—add 000 to get the full amount. 2010 Note: Financial information for 2010 was not available for all companies at press time.**

2010 Sales: $	2010 Profits: $	**U.S. Stock Ticker: HE**
2009 Sales: $2,018,623	2009 Profits: $83,011	**Int'l Ticker:** Int'l Exchange:
2008 Sales: $2,844,499	2008 Profits: $90,278	Employees: 3,451
2007 Sales: $2,090,548	2007 Profits: $84,779	Fiscal Year Ends: 12/31
2006 Sales: $2,460,904	2006 Profits: $108,001	Parent Company:

SALARIES/BENEFITS:

Pension Plan: Y	ESOP Stock Plan:	Profit Sharing:	Top Exec. Salary: $771,800	Bonus: $338,106
Savings Plan:	Stock Purch. Plan:		Second Exec. Salary: $580,000	Bonus: $572,289

OTHER THOUGHTS:

Apparent Women Officers or Directors: 8
Hot Spot for Advancement for Women/Minorities: Y

LOCATIONS: ("Y" = Yes)

West:	Southwest:	Midwest:	Southeast:	Northeast:	International:
Y					

HEADWATERS INC

www.headwaters.com

Industry Group Code: 324199 **Ranks within this company's industry group:** Sales: 1 Profits: 1

Exploration/Production:		Refining/Retailing:		Utilities:		Alternative Energy:		Specialty Services:		Energy Mktg./Other Svcs.	
Exploration:		Refining:	Y	Electric Utility:		Waste/Solar/Other:	Y	Consulting/Eng.:	Y	Energy Marketing:	
Production:		Retailing:		Gas Utility:		Thermal/Steam:		Seismic:		Equipment/Machinery:	Y
Coal Production:	Y	Convenience Stores:		Pipelines:		Wind:		Drilling:		Oil Field Services:	
		Chemicals:	Y	Water:		Hydro:		InfoTech:		Air/Shipping Transportation:	
						Fuel Cells:		Specialty Services:	Y		

TYPES OF BUSINESS:

Clean Coal Derivatives Technologies
Synthetic Fuels & Related Technologies
Nanocatalysts
Reagents & Chemicals, Ash
Post-Combustion Coal Products & Services
Architectural Stone & Siding
Technology Licensing
Alternative Energy

BRANDS/DIVISIONS/AFFILIATES:

Headwaters Energy Services
Headwaters Resources
Headwaters Construction Materials
Headwaters Technology Innovation
Tapco Integrated Tool Systems
Eldorado Stone
FlexCrete

CONTACTS: *Note: Officers with more than one job title may be intentionally listed here more than once.*

Kirk A. Benson, CEO
Steven G. Stewart, CFO
Harlan M. Hatfield, General Counsel/VP/Corp. Sec.
Sharon Madden, VP-Investor Rel.
William H. Gehrmann III, Pres., Headwaters Resources, Inc.
John N. Lawless III, Pres., Headwaters Construction Materials, Inc.
Kirk A. Benson, Chmn.

Phone: 801-984-9400 **Fax:** 801-984-9410
Toll-Free:
Address: 10653 S. River Front Pkwy., Ste. 300, South Jordan, UT 84095 US

GROWTH PLANS/SPECIAL FEATURES:

Headwaters, Inc. is a diversified company providing products, technologies and services in three industries: Construction materials, coal combustion products (CCP) and energy. In the construction materials segment, through subsidiary, Headwaters Construction Materials, the company designs, manufactures and sells architectural stone veneer, concrete blocks, siding accessories, and other professional tools used in exterior residential construction under brand names including FlexCrete, Tapco Integrated Tool Systems and Eldorado Stones brands. In the CCP segment, conducted through subsidiary, Headwaters Resources, Inc., the firm manages and markets CCPs, including fly ash used as a substitute for portland cement. In the energy segment, Headwaters is focused on reducing waste and increasing the value of energy feedstocks, primarily in the areas of low-value coal and oil. In coal, the company owns and operates several coal cleaning facilities that remove rock, dirt and other impurities from waste or other low-value coal. The firm also licenses technology and sells reagents to the coal-based solid alternative fuel industry. Subsidiary, Headwaters Energy Services Corp. uses coal cleaning processes that upgrade low value or waste coal by separating ash from the carbon. In oil, its heavy oil upgrading process uses a liquid catalyst precursor to generate a highly active molecular catalyst to convert residual oil feedstocks into higher-value distillates that can be refined into gasoline, diesel and other products. Headwaters' research and development sector, through Headwaters Technology Innovations Group, has the capacity to work at molecular levels in aligning, spacing and adhering nano-sized crystals of precious and transition metals onto substrate materials. This process creates an array of custom-designed nanocatalysts for chemical and refining processes that can achieve better performances with lower precious metal content and higher selectivity during the facilitation of chemical reactions. In August 2010, the firm sold its interest in Evonik Headwaters Korea Co., Ltd. to Evonik Degussa GmbH.

FINANCIALS: **Sales and profits are in thousands of dollars—add 000 to get the full amount. 2010 Note: Financial information for 2010 was not available for all companies at press time.**

2010 Sales: $	2010 Profits: $	**U.S. Stock Ticker: HW**
2009 Sales: $666,676	2009 Profits: $-415,550	**Int'l Ticker:** Int'l Exchange:
2008 Sales: $886,404	2008 Profits: $-169,680	Employees: 2,740
2007 Sales: $1,207,844	2007 Profits: $20,054	Fiscal Year Ends: 9/30
2006 Sales: $1,121,387	2006 Profits: $102,058	Parent Company:

SALARIES/BENEFITS:

Pension Plan:	ESOP Stock Plan:	Profit Sharing:	Top Exec. Salary: $650,000	Bonus: $438,162
Savings Plan:	Stock Purch. Plan:		Second Exec. Salary: $311,640	Bonus: $156,641

OTHER THOUGHTS:

Apparent Women Officers or Directors: 1
Hot Spot for Advancement for Women/Minorities:

LOCATIONS: ("Y" = Yes)

West:	Southwest:	Midwest:	Southeast:	Northeast:	International:
Y	Y	Y	Y	Y	Y

HELIX ENERGY SOLUTIONS GROUP INC

www.helixesg.com

Industry Group Code: 213112 **Ranks within this company's industry group:** Sales: 14 Profits: 11

Exploration/Production:		Refining/Retailing:		Utilities:		Alternative Energy:		Specialty Services:		Energy Mktg./Other Svcs.	
Exploration:	Y	Refining:		Electric Utility:		Waste/Solar/Other:		Consulting/Eng.:	Y	Energy Marketing:	
Production:	Y	Retailing:		Gas Utility:		Thermal/Steam:		Seismic:		Equipment/Machinery:	Y
Coal Production:		Convenience Stores:		Pipelines:		Wind:		Drilling:	Y	Oil Field Services:	Y
		Chemicals:		Water:		Hydro:		InfoTech:		Air/Shipping Transportation:	
						Fuel Cells:		Specialty Services:	Y		

TYPES OF BUSINESS:

Subsea Drilling Support Contractor
Subsea Construction, Maintenance & Salvage Services
Remotely Operated Vehicles & Equipment
Oil & Gas Production
Subsea Cable Burial

BRANDS/DIVISIONS/AFFILIATES:

Remington Oil & Gas Corp.

CONTACTS:

Note: Officers with more than one job title may be intentionally listed here more than once.

Owen Kratz, CEO
Bart H. Heijermans, COO/Exec. VP
Owen Kratz, Pres.
Tony Tripodo, CFO/Exec. VP
Alisa B. Johnson, General Counsel/Corp. Sec./Exec. VP
William E. Morrice, VP-Global Well Oper.
Lloyd A. Hajdik, Chief Acct. Officer/Sr. VP-Finance
Jeremy Woulds, VP-Deepwater Project Execution
Charles McGregor, VP-Tax
Kimberly Seitz, VP-Internal Audit
William L. Transier, Chmn.
Sharon Adams, VP-Global Contracts & Risk
Brent Shinall, VP-Supply Chain Mgmt.

Phone: 281-618-0400	**Fax:** 281-618-0500
Toll-Free:	
Address: 400 N. Sam Houston Pkwy. E., Houston, TX 77060 US	

GROWTH PLANS/SPECIAL FEATURES:

Helix Energy Solutions Group, Inc. is an international offshore energy company providing development services and contracting service operations to the open energy market as well as to its own reservoirs. Helix's contracting services operations contains three divisions: subsea construction, well operations and production facilities. The subsea construction division includes services such as pipelay and robotics in water depths exceeding 1,000 feet. The division also provides construction services for the company's well intervention vessels. The well operations division engineers, manages and conducts well construction, intervention and decommissioning operations in water depths ranging from 200 to 10,000 feet. The production facilities segment focuses on the company's ownership of production facilities in hub locations where there is potential for significant subsea tieback activity, and is in the process of constructing a minimal floating production unit to be utilized on its Phoenix field in the Gulf of Mexico. Helix's oil and gas operations, through the services of its Remington subsidiary, includes 578 billions of cubic feet equivalent (Bcfe) of proved reserves, of which 98% is located in the Gulf of Mexico. In February 2010, the company announced plans to create a joint venture with Australia-based engineering and construction firm, Clough Limited. The joint venture, Clough Helix Pty Ltd, will provide subsea services to the Asia Pacific.

The firm offers employees medical, dental and vision insurance; life insurance; disability coverage; and a 401(k) plan.

FINANCIALS:

Sales and profits are in thousands of dollars—add 000 to get the full amount. 2010 Note: Financial information for 2010 was not available for all companies at press time.

2010 Sales: $	2010 Profits: $	**U.S. Stock Ticker: HLX**
2009 Sales: $1,461,687	2009 Profits: $156,054	**Int'l Ticker:** Int'l Exchange:
2008 Sales: $2,114,074	2008 Profits: $-635,930	Employees: 1,550
2007 Sales: $1,767,445	2007 Profits: $316,762	Fiscal Year Ends: 12/31
2006 Sales: $1,366,924	2006 Profits: $344,036	Parent Company:

SALARIES/BENEFITS:

Pension Plan:	ESOP Stock Plan:	Profit Sharing:	Top Exec. Salary: $700,000	Bonus: $3,476,628
Savings Plan: Y	Stock Purch. Plan:		Second Exec. Salary: $450,000	Bonus: $2,101,083

OTHER THOUGHTS:

Apparent Women Officers or Directors: 4
Hot Spot for Advancement for Women/Minorities: Y

LOCATIONS: ("Y" = Yes)

West:	Southwest:	Midwest:	Southeast:	Northeast:	International:
	Y		Y		Y

HELLENIC PETROLEUM SA

www.hellenic-petroleum.gr

Industry Group Code: 324110 **Ranks within this company's industry group:** Sales: 17 Profits: 10

Exploration/Production:		Refining/Retailing:		Utilities:		Alternative Energy:		Specialty Services:		Energy Mktg./Other Svcs.	
Exploration:	Y	Refining:	Y	Electric Utility:		Waste/Solar/Other:		Consulting/Eng.:	Y	Energy Marketing:	
Production:	Y	Retailing:	Y	Gas Utility:	Y	Thermal/Steam:		Seismic:		Equipment/Machinery:	
Coal Production:		Convenience Stores:	Y	Pipelines:	Y	Wind:		Drilling:		Oil Field Services:	
		Chemicals:	Y	Water:		Hydro:		InfoTech:		Air/Shipping Transportation:	
						Fuel Cells:		Specialty Services:	Y		

TYPES OF BUSINESS:

Petroleum Refining
Petroleum Marketing
Chemicals
Engineering
Pipelines
Exploration & Production
Gas Stations
Natural Gas Distribution

BRANDS/DIVISIONS/AFFILIATES:

EKO
Elda
Hellenic Petroleum Renewable Energy Sources SA
DEPA SA
M
Asprofos SA

CONTACTS:

Note: Officers with more than one job title may be intentionally listed here more than once.

John Costopoulos, CEO
Andreas N. Shiamishis, CFO
Theodoros-Achilleas Vardas, Exec. Dir.
Anastasios Giannitsis, Chmn.

Phone: 30-210-6302-000 **Fax:** 30-210-6302-510
Toll-Free:
Address: 8A Chimarras St., Maroussi, 151 25 Greece

GROWTH PLANS/SPECIAL FEATURES:

Hellenic Petroleum, S.A. is a diversified petroleum company. The firm is engaged in the production, refining and marketing of petroleum; the production of petrochemicals; and engineering. The refining segment constitutes the majority of the company's revenue and serves to provide about 76% of Greece's market requirements. Hellenic operates four refineries in the cities of Aspropyrgos, Elefsina and Thessaloniki in Greece and Skopje in Macedonia. The company's Aspropyrgos refinery is connected through a pipeline with Athens International Airport, and supplies all of its needed fuel. Hellenic Petroleum's marketing segment, with around 2,375 gas stations in Greece, is the country's largest fuel marketing network. It also operates in Georgia, Albania, Macedonia, Cyprus, Bulgaria, Serbia, Montenegro and Albania. These gas stations are branded under the EKO, Elda and M names. The company also owns the only petrochemicals complex in Greece. Vertically integrated with the refineries, the complex produces polypropylene, PVC, hexane, chlorine and caustic soda. The firm's engineering group, through subsidiary Asprofos S.A. provides services ranging from feasibility studies and basic and detailed planning to construction supervision, specializing in refinery, natural gas and infrastructure projects. Hellenic Petroleum is also involved in renewable energy through subsidiary, Hellenic Petroleum Renewable Energy Sources S.A. In addition, the company operates in Egypt through two exploratory concession contracts. The company also has a 35% interest in DEPA S.A., which imports and distributes natural gas in Greece. In late 2009, Hellenic Petroleum acquired BP's Greek ground fuels operations, which included over 6 million cubic feet of storage facilities, 1,200 branded service stations and commercial/industrial supply operations.

Hellenic Petroleum offers its employees a pension plan; a life insurance plan; a health insurance plan; annual check-up; loans; nursery expense coverage; summer camps for dependents; and subscriptions to newspapers, periodicals, professional associations and scientific unions.

FINANCIALS:

Sales and profits are in thousands of dollars—add 000 to get the full amount. 2010 Note: Financial information for 2010 was not available for all companies at press time.

2010 Sales: $	2010 Profits: $	**U.S. Stock Ticker:**
2009 Sales: $9,484,040	2009 Profits: $245,500	**Int'l Ticker: ELPE** Int'l Exchange: Athens-ATHEX
2008 Sales: $15,049,400	2008 Profits: $35,060	Employees:
2007 Sales: $12,683,000	2007 Profits: $521,400	Fiscal Year Ends: 12/31
2006 Sales: $11,880,664	2006 Profits: $381,354	Parent Company:

SALARIES/BENEFITS:

Pension Plan: Y	ESOP Stock Plan:	Profit Sharing:	Top Exec. Salary: $	Bonus: $
Savings Plan:	Stock Purch. Plan:		Second Exec. Salary: $	Bonus: $

OTHER THOUGHTS:

Apparent Women Officers or Directors:
Hot Spot for Advancement for Women/Minorities:

LOCATIONS: ("Y" = Yes)

West:	Southwest:	Midwest:	Southeast:	Northeast:	International:
					Y

HELMERICH & PAYNE INC

www.hpinc.com

Industry Group Code: 211111 **Ranks within this company's industry group:** Sales: 73 Profits: 55

Exploration/Production:		Refining/Retailing:		Utilities:		Alternative Energy:		Specialty Services:		Energy Mktg./Other Svcs.	
Exploration:	Y	Refining:		Electric Utility:		Waste/Solar/Other:		Consulting/Eng.:		Energy Marketing:	Y
Production:	Y	Retailing:		Gas Utility:		Thermal/Steam:		Seismic:		Equipment/Machinery:	
Coal Production:		Convenience Stores:		Pipelines:		Wind:		Drilling:	Y	Oil Field Services:	
		Chemicals:		Water:		Hydro:		InfoTech:		Air/Shipping Transportation:	
						Fuel Cells:		Specialty Services:	Y		

TYPES OF BUSINESS:

Oil & Gas Exploration & Production
Contract Drilling Services
Drilling Technology Development
Commercial Real Estate

BRANDS/DIVISIONS/AFFILIATES:

FlexRigs
FlexRig3
FlexRig4

CONTACTS:

Note: Officers with more than one job title may be intentionally listed here more than once.

Hans Helmerich, CEO
Hans Helmerich, Pres.
Juan Pablo Tardio, CFO/VP
Steven R. Mackey, Chief Admin. Officer
Steven R. Mackey, General Counsel/Exec. VP/Corp. Sec.
John W. Lindsay, Exec. VP-US Oper.
W. H. Helmerich, III, Chmn.
John W. Lindsay, Exec. VP-Int'l Oper., Int'l Drilling Co.

Phone: 918-742-5531 **Fax:** 918-742-0237
Toll-Free:
Address: 1437 S. Boulder Ave., Tulsa, OK 74119 US

GROWTH PLANS/SPECIAL FEATURES:

Helmerich & Payne, Inc. (HP) operates both on and offshore rigs under contract with oil and gas companies. The firm offers clients drilling rigs, equipment, personnel and camps on a contract basis. These drilling rigs include a number of the newest generation of FlexRigs, which allow a greater depth and flexibility of between 8,000 to 18,000 feet, and provide greater operating efficiency. The company has completed design and manufacturing work on the FlexRig3 and FlexRig4, now available to U.S. and international drilling companies. Drilling rigs consist of engines, drawworks, a mast, pumps, blowout preventers, a drillstring and related equipment. HP has 201 land rigs available for work in the U.S., nine offshore platform rigs in the Gulf of Mexico and 44 international rigs. HP's contract drilling business is composed of three reportable business segments: U.S. land drilling, offshore platform drilling and international drilling. The firm's U.S. land drilling is conducted primarily in Oklahoma, California, Texas, Wyoming, Colorado, Louisiana, Mississippi, Pennsylvania, Arkansas, Utah, New Mexico and North Dakota. The company's offshore platform operations are conducted in the Gulf of Mexico, California, Trinidad and Equatorial Guinea. It also operates land rigs in five international locations, including Venezuela, Ecuador, Colombia, Argentina, Mexico and Tunisia. In addition to its oil rig business, HP has real estate operations that are conducted within the metropolitan area of Tulsa, Oklahoma. Its major holdings include a shopping center containing roughly 441,000 leasable square feet, multi-tenant industrial warehouse properties containing 990 leasable square feet and 210 acres of undeveloped real estate. In June 2010, the company had 11 of its rigs nationalized by the Venezuelan government. In July 2010, the firm announced plans to build seven additional FlexRigs.

Employees are offered medical, dental, vision and life insurance; long-term disability coverage; flexible spending accounts; and a 401(k).

FINANCIALS:

Sales and profits are in thousands of dollars—add 000 to get the full amount. 2010 Note: Financial information for 2010 was not available for all companies at press time.

2010 Sales: $	2010 Profits: $	**U.S. Stock Ticker: HP**
2009 Sales: $1,894,038	2009 Profits: $353,545	**Int'l Ticker:** Int'l Exchange:
2008 Sales: $2,036,543	2008 Profits: $461,738	Employees: 5,384
2007 Sales: $1,629,658	2007 Profits: $449,261	Fiscal Year Ends: 9/30
2006 Sales: $1,224,813	2006 Profits: $293,858	Parent Company:

SALARIES/BENEFITS:

Pension Plan:	ESOP Stock Plan:	Profit Sharing:	Top Exec. Salary: $606,442	Bonus: $
Savings Plan: Y	Stock Purch. Plan:		Second Exec. Salary: $385,000	Bonus: $

OTHER THOUGHTS:

Apparent Women Officers or Directors: 1
Hot Spot for Advancement for Women/Minorities:

LOCATIONS: ("Y" = Yes)

West:	Southwest:	Midwest:	Southeast:	Northeast:	International:
Y	Y	Y	Y		Y

HERCULES OFFSHORE INC

www.herculesoffshore.com

Industry Group Code: 213111 **Ranks within this company's industry group:** Sales: 14 Profits: 16

Exploration/Production:		Refining/Retailing:		Utilities:		Alternative Energy:		Specialty Services:		Energy Mktg./Other Svcs.	
Exploration:		Refining:		Electric Utility:		Waste/Solar/Other:		Consulting/Eng.:		Energy Marketing:	
Production:		Retailing:		Gas Utility:		Thermal/Steam:		Seismic:		Equipment/Machinery:	
Coal Production:		Convenience Stores:		Pipelines:		Wind:		Drilling:	Y	Oil Field Services:	
		Chemicals:		Water:		Hydro:		InfoTech:		Air/Shipping Transportation:	
						Fuel Cells:		Specialty Services:	Y		

TYPES OF BUSINESS:

Drilling Services-Oil & Natural Gas

BRANDS/DIVISIONS/AFFILIATES:

Hercules Offshore Drilling
Hercules Offshore Liftboats
Delta Towing

CONTACTS:

Note: Officers with more than one job title may be intentionally listed here more than once.

John T. Rynd, CEO
John T. Rynd, Pres.
Lisa W. Rodriguez, CFO/Sr. VP
James W. Noe, General Counsel/Sr. VP/Chief Compliance Officer
Terrell Carr, VP-Worldwide Oper.
Stephen M. Butz, VP-Finance/Treas.
Todd Pelligrin, VP-Worldwide Liftboat Oper.
Troy L. Carson, VP/Controller/Chief Acct. Officer
Don P. Rodney, Pres., Hercules Oilfield Services Ltd
James W. Noe, Pres., Delta Towing
Thomas R. Bates, Jr., Chmn.
Don P. Rodney, Pres., Hercules International Holdings, Ltd.

Phone: 713-350-5100	**Fax:** 713-350-5105
Toll-Free:	
Address: 9 Greenway Plz., Ste. 2200, Houston, TX 77046 US	

GROWTH PLANS/SPECIAL FEATURES:

Hercules Offshore, Inc. provides shallow-water drilling and marine services to the oil and natural gas exploration and production industry in the U.S. and internationally. The company operates in six segments: domestic offshore, international offshore, inland, domestic liftboats, international liftboats and delta towing. The domestic offshore segment operates 22 jackup rigs and three submersible rigs in the U.S. Gulf of Mexico in water depths ranging from 85-350 feet. The jackup rigs are used primarily for exploration and development drilling in shallow waters. The international offshore segment operates 16 jackup rigs and one platform rig off Mexico, Saudi Arabia, India, Malaysia and Gabon. The inland segment operates a fleet of six conventional and 11 posted barge rigs inland in marshes, rivers, lakes and shallow bay or coastal waterways along the U.S. Gulf Coast. Barge drilling rigs are mobile drilling platforms that are submersible and operate in 7-20 feet of water. The domestic liftboat segment consists of 41 liftboats that operate in the U.S. Gulf of Mexico. The lift boats are self-propelled, self-elevating vessels with a large open deck space that provides a versatile, mobile and stable platform to support a broad range of offshore maintenance and construction services. The international liftboats segment operates 24 liftboats, 21 of which are operating off the West African coast. The delta towing segment mans a fleet of 34 crew boats, 46 deck barges, 29 inland tugs, 12 offshore tugs, 16 shale barges and five spud barges in the U.S. Gulf of Mexico.

FINANCIALS:

Sales and profits are in thousands of dollars—add 000 to get the full amount. 2010 Note: Financial information for 2010 was not available for all companies at press time.

2010 Sales: $	2010 Profits: $	**U.S. Stock Ticker: HERO**
2009 Sales: $742,851	2009 Profits: $-91,734	**Int'l Ticker:** Int'l Exchange:
2008 Sales: $1,111,807	2008 Profits: $-1,083,390	Employees: 2,200
2007 Sales: $726,278	2007 Profits: $136,012	Fiscal Year Ends: 12/31
2006 Sales: $344,312	2006 Profits: $119,050	Parent Company:

SALARIES/BENEFITS:

Pension Plan:	ESOP Stock Plan:	Profit Sharing:	Top Exec. Salary: $653,962	Bonus: $390,600
Savings Plan:	Stock Purch. Plan:		Second Exec. Salary: $373,692	Bonus: $171,360

OTHER THOUGHTS:

Apparent Women Officers or Directors: 2
Hot Spot for Advancement for Women/Minorities: Y

LOCATIONS: ("Y" = Yes)

West:	Southwest:	Midwest:	Southeast:	Northeast:	International:
	Y		Y		Y

HESS CORPORATION

www.hess.com

Industry Group Code: 211111 **Ranks within this company's industry group:** Sales: 26 Profits: 42

Exploration/Production:		Refining/Retailing:		Utilities:		Alternative Energy:		Specialty Services:		Energy Mktg./Other Svcs.	
Exploration:	Y	Refining:	Y	Electric Utility:		Waste/Solar/Other:		Consulting/Eng.:		Energy Marketing:	Y
Production:	Y	Retailing:	Y	Gas Utility:		Thermal/Steam:		Seismic:		Equipment/Machinery:	
Coal Production:		Convenience Stores:	Y	Pipelines:		Wind:		Drilling:		Oil Field Services:	
		Chemicals:		Water:		Hydro:		InfoTech:		Air/Shipping Transportation:	
						Fuel Cells:		Specialty Services:			

TYPES OF BUSINESS:

Oil & Gas Exploration & Production
Natural Gas
Refining
Energy Marketing

BRANDS/DIVISIONS/AFFILIATES:

CONTACTS: *Note: Officers with more than one job title may be intentionally listed here more than once.*

John B. Hess, CEO
John P. Riely, CFO/Sr. VP
F. Borden Walker, Exec. VP-Mktg. & Refining
Mykel Ziolo, Sr. VP-Human Resources
Gregory P. Hill, Exec. VP/Pres., Worldwide Exploration & Prod.
Jeffery L. Steinhorn, CIO/VP
Scott M. Heck, Sr. VP-Tech. & Global Prod.
Timothy B. Goodell, General Counsel/Sr. VP
Howard Paver, Sr. VP-Global New Bus. Dev.
Jon Pepper, VP-Corp. Comm.
Jay R. Wilson, VP-Investor Rel.
Christopher Baldwin, Sr. VP-Retail & Energy Mktg.
William Drennen III, Sr. VP-Global Exploration & New Ventures
R. Gordon Shear, CEO/Sr. VP-Hess LNG
John B. Hess, Chmn.
Gary Doubel, Sr. VP-Global Dev.

Phone: 212-997-8500 **Fax:** 212-536-8590
Toll-Free:
Address: 1185 Ave. of the Americas, 40th Fl., New York, NY 10036 US

GROWTH PLANS/SPECIAL FEATURES:

Hess Corporation is a globally integrated energy company that operates in two segments: exploration and production; and marketing and refining. The exploration and production segment explores for, develops, produces, purchases, transports and sells crude oil and natural gas. These exploration and production activities take place in the U.S., the U.K., Norway, Denmark, Equatorial Guinea, Algeria, Malaysia, Thailand, Russia, Gabon, Azerbaijan, Indonesia, Libya, Egypt and other countries. The manufacturing and refining segment manufactures, purchases, transports, trades and markets refined petroleum products, natural gas and electricity. Other assets of the company include an additional refining facility, as well as various terminals and retail gasoline stations, most of which include convenience stores, located on the east coast of the U.S. In 2009, the company had 967 million barrels of proven reserves of crude oil and natural gas liquids and over 2,800 millions of thousands of cubic feet of natural gas. The company markets refined petroleum products in the U.S. to the motoring public; wholesale distributors; industrial and commercial users; other petroleum companies; governmental agencies; and public utilities. The firm operates approximately 1,357 HESS retail facilities from Massachusetts to Florida. In 2009, 21% of the company's total proved reserves were located in the U.S.; 30% were located in Europe; 23% were in Africa; and 26% were in Asia and other regions. In December 2009, Hess coordinated an asset trade with Shell Oil to gain greater access to Norwegian offshore fields Valhall and Hod in exchange for part of the company's North Sea Clair field and all of the its Gabon assets. In June 2010, the firm gained further access to those Norwegian fields when it purchased BP's interests for $496 million. In July 2010, Hess announced plans to acquire American Oil & Gas, Inc.

FINANCIALS: **Sales and profits are in thousands of dollars—add 000 to get the full amount. 2010 Note: Financial information for 2010 was not available for all companies at press time.**

2010 Sales: $	2010 Profits: $	**U.S. Stock Ticker: HES**
2009 Sales: $29,614,000	2009 Profits: $740,000	**Int'l Ticker:** Int'l Exchange:
2008 Sales: $41,134,000	2008 Profits: $2,360,000	Employees: 13,300
2007 Sales: $31,727,000	2007 Profits: $1,832,000	Fiscal Year Ends: 12/31
2006 Sales: $28,067,000	2006 Profits: $1,916,000	Parent Company:

SALARIES/BENEFITS:

Pension Plan:	ESOP Stock Plan:	Profit Sharing:	Top Exec. Salary: $1,500,000	Bonus: $3,750,000
Savings Plan:	Stock Purch. Plan:		Second Exec. Salary: $900,000	Bonus: $900,000

OTHER THOUGHTS:

Apparent Women Officers or Directors: 3
Hot Spot for Advancement for Women/Minorities: Y

LOCATIONS: ("Y" = Yes)

West:	Southwest:	Midwest:	Southeast:	Northeast:	International:
Y	Y	Y	Y	Y	Y

HINDUSTAN PETROLEUM CORPORATION LTD

www.hindustanpetroleum.com

Industry Group Code: 324110 **Ranks within this company's industry group:** Sales: 9 Profits: 13

Exploration/Production:		Refining/Retailing:		Utilities:		Alternative Energy:		Specialty Services:		Energy Mktg./Other Svcs.	
Exploration:		Refining:	Y	Electric Utility:		Waste/Solar/Other:	Y	Consulting/Eng.:		Energy Marketing:	
Production:		Retailing:	Y	Gas Utility:		Thermal/Steam:		Seismic:		Equipment/Machinery:	
Coal Production:		Convenience Stores:	Y	Pipelines:	Y	Wind:	Y	Drilling:		Oil Field Services:	
		Chemicals:	Y	Water:		Hydro:		InfoTech:		Air/Shipping Transportation:	
						Fuel Cells:		Specialty Services:	Y		

TYPES OF BUSINESS:

Oil Refining & Marketing
Lubricants & Petrochemicals
Oil & Gas Retail Sales
Aviation & Marine Fueling Services
Pipelines
Kerosene
Wind Energy

BRANDS/DIVISIONS/AFFILIATES:

Lubricating Oils Refinery in Mumbai (The)
Turbojet
Mangalore Refinery & Petrochemicals, Ltd.

CONTACTS:

Note: Officers with more than one job title may be intentionally listed here more than once.

S. Roy Chouhury, Managing Dir.
S. Roy Choudhury, Dir.-Mktg.
V. Vizia Saradhi, Dir.-Human Resources
Nishi Vasudeva, Exec. Dir.-Info. Systems
N. R. Narayanan, Company Sec.
O.P. Pradhan, Exec. Dir.-Corp. Planning & Strategy
Bhaswar Mukherjee, Dir.-Finance
K. Murali, Dir.-Refineries
G.A. Shirwaikar, Exec. Dir.-LPG
R. Sudhakara Rao, Exec. Dir.-Direct Sales
S.Roy Choudhury, Chmn.

Phone: 91-22-2286-3900 **Fax:** 91-22-2287-2992

Toll-Free:

Address: Petroleum House, 17, Jamshedji Tata Rd., Mumbai, 400 020 India

GROWTH PLANS/SPECIAL FEATURES:

Hindustan Petroleum Corporation Ltd. (HPCL) is one of the largest oil refining and marketing companies in India. It operates refineries, liquid petroleum gas (LPG) bottling plants, lube blending plants and aviation servicing facilities, in addition to its network of approximately 9,127 retail outlets, terminals and depots. The company currently operates two major refineries, located at Mumbai and Visakhapatnam, with total; refining capacity of nearly 13.8 million metric tons per annum (MTPA). The firm's petroleum products include LPG, gasoline, aviation turbo fuel, carbon black feedstock, industrial fuel oil, bitumen and sulfur for sulfuric acid, and its fuelling network encompasses all major Indian seaports and airports. The Lubricating Oils Refinery in Mumbai is among the largest lube refineries in India and represents 40% of the country's total lube base oil production. Utilizing this refinery, the company sells more than 300 grades of lubricants and greases. HPCL's growing number of branded fuel stations and retail convenience stores in the country offer a wide range of non-fuel services including vehicle servicing and repairs, grocery shopping, bill pay services, fast food and ATMs, in addition to selling Turbojet, the company's branded diesel fuel; Power, the company's branded gasoline; and compressed natural gas (CNG), sold at select stores in Delhi and Mumbai. HPCL also has investments in several alternative energy projects, including wind farms in the Indian states of Maharashtra and Rajasthan. The company owns a 16.95% interest in Mangalore Refinery & Petrochemicals Limited, with a refining capacity of 9 million MTPA. The Indian government is HPCL's majority owner, holding an approximate 51% share.

FINANCIALS:

Sales and profits are in thousands of dollars—add 000 to get the full amount. 2010 Note: Financial information for 2010 was not available for all companies at press time.

2010 Sales: $	2010 Profits: $	**U.S. Stock Ticker:**
2009 Sales: $27,766,000	2009 Profits: $162,950	**Int'l Ticker: 500104** Int'l Exchange: Bombay-BSE
2008 Sales: $28,247,000	2008 Profits: $165,000	Employees: 11,246
2007 Sales: $20,480,000	2007 Profits: $390,000	Fiscal Year Ends: 3/31
2006 Sales: $16,260,000	2006 Profits: $100,000	Parent Company:

SALARIES/BENEFITS:

Pension Plan:	ESOP Stock Plan:	Profit Sharing:	Top Exec. Salary: $	Bonus: $
Savings Plan:	Stock Purch. Plan:		Second Exec. Salary: $	Bonus: $

OTHER THOUGHTS:

Apparent Women Officers or Directors:
Hot Spot for Advancement for Women/Minorities:

LOCATIONS: ("Y" = Yes)

West:	Southwest:	Midwest:	Southeast:	Northeast:	International:
					Y

HOLLY CORP

www.hollycorp.com

Industry Group Code: 324110 **Ranks within this company's industry group:** Sales: 22 Profits: 16

Exploration/Production:		Refining/Retailing:		Utilities:		Alternative Energy:		Specialty Services:		Energy Mktg./Other Svcs.	
Exploration:		Refining:	Y	Electric Utility:		Waste/Solar/Other:		Consulting/Eng.:		Energy Marketing:	
Production:		Retailing:		Gas Utility:		Thermal/Steam:		Seismic:		Equipment/Machinery:	
Coal Production:		Convenience Stores:		Pipelines:	Y	Wind:		Drilling:		Oil Field Services:	
		Chemicals:		Water:		Hydro:		InfoTech:		Air/Shipping Transportation:	
						Fuel Cells:		Specialty Services:	Y		

TYPES OF BUSINESS:

Petroleum Refining
Petroleum Distribution
Pipelines & Terminals
Asphalt

BRANDS/DIVISIONS/AFFILIATES:

Holly Asphalt Co
Holly Energy Partners LP
Rio Grande Pipeline Co
Navajo Refining Co LP
Holly Refining & Marketing Co-Tulsa LLC
Woods Cross Refinery
Holly Refining & Marketing Company-Woods Cross

CONTACTS: *Note: Officers with more than one job title may be intentionally listed here more than once.*

Matthew P. Clifton, CEO
David L. Lamp, Pres.
Bruce R. Shaw, CFO/Sr. VP
George J. Damiris, Sr. VP-Mktg.
Nancy F. Hartmann, VP-Human Resources
Nellson D. Burns, VP-IT
Denise C. McWatters, General Counsel/VP/Sec.
Mark T. Cunningham, VP-Oper.
M. Neale Hickerson, VP-Investor Rel.
Stephen D. Wise, Treas./VP
Scott C. Surplus, Controller/VP
Gary B. Fuller, Sr. VP-Refinery Oper.
James G. Townsend, VP-Special Projects
David G. Blair, Pres., Holly Logistics Svcs. LLC
Matthew P. Clifton, Chmn.
George J. Damiris, Sr. VP-Supply

Phone: 214-871-3555	**Fax:** 214-871-3560
Toll-Free:	
Address: 100 Crescent Ct., Ste. 1600, Dallas, TX 75201-6915 US	

GROWTH PLANS/SPECIAL FEATURES:

Holly Corp. is an independent petroleum refiner. The company produces high-value light products such as diesel fuel, gasoline and jet fuel; specialty lubricant products; and specialty and modified asphalt. The firm operates refineries in New Mexico and Utah and oversees 900 miles of crude oil pipelines located primarily in west Texas and New Mexico. It operates Holly Asphalt Co., which manufactures and markets asphalt products from various terminals in New Mexico, Texas and Arizona. Holly Corp. also owns 34% interest in Holly Energy Partners, L.P. (HEP). HEP has logistics assets including a jet fuel terminal; roughly 2,500 miles of petroleum pipelines in Texas and New Mexico; a 25% interest in the 95-mile, SLC crude oil pipeline; 10 refined product terminals; four refinery truck rack facilities; and a refined products tank farm facility. Holly's wholly-owned subsidiary Navajo Refining Co., L.P. owns the Navajo refinery, which has a crude capacity of 100,000 barrels per stream day (BPSD) of sour and sweet crude oils. The refinery can process up to about 90% sour crude oils and serves markets in the southwestern U.S. and northern Mexico. Subsidiary Holly Refining and Marketing Company-Woods Cross operates the Woods Cross refinery near Salt Lake City, Utah, which specializes in high conversion that processes regional sweet and Canadian sour crude oils (31,000 BPSD). In December 2009, Holly Corp. and HEP (through respective subsidiaries Holly Refining & Marketing-Tulsa LLC and HEP Tulsa LLC) acquired a 75,000 BPSD refinery in Oklahoma from an affiliate of Sinclair Oil Company for $183.3 million. Also in December 2009, the firm sold a 65-mile pipeline to HEP; and HEP sold its interest in Rio Grande Pipeline Company to Enterprise Products Operating, LLC.

FINANCIALS: **Sales and profits are in thousands of dollars—add 000 to get the full amount. 2010 Note: Financial information for 2010 was not available for all companies at press time.**

2010 Sales: $	2010 Profits: $	**U.S. Stock Ticker: HOC**
2009 Sales: $4,834,268	2009 Profits: $53,269	**Int'l Ticker:** Int'l Exchange:
2008 Sales: $5,867,668	2008 Profits: $120,558	Employees:
2007 Sales: $4,791,742	2007 Profits: $334,128	Fiscal Year Ends: 12/31
2006 Sales: $4,023,217	2006 Profits: $266,566	Parent Company:

SALARIES/BENEFITS:

Pension Plan:	ESOP Stock Plan:	Profit Sharing:	Top Exec. Salary: $922,500	Bonus: $1,760,000
Savings Plan:	Stock Purch. Plan:		Second Exec. Salary: $553,500	Bonus: $661,000

OTHER THOUGHTS:

Apparent Women Officers or Directors: 2
Hot Spot for Advancement for Women/Minorities: Y

LOCATIONS: ("Y" = Yes)

West:	Southwest:	Midwest:	Southeast:	Northeast:	International:
Y	Y				

HONG KONG AND CHINA GAS CO LTD (THE)

www.hkcg.com

Industry Group Code: 221210 **Ranks within this company's industry group:** Sales: 16 Profits: 4

Exploration/Production:		Refining/Retailing:		Utilities:		Alternative Energy:		Specialty Services:		Energy Mktg./Other Svcs.	
Exploration:		Refining:		Electric Utility:		Waste/Solar/Other:		Consulting/Eng.:	Y	Energy Marketing:	
Production:		Retailing:	Y	Gas Utility:	Y	Thermal/Steam:		Seismic:		Equipment/Machinery:	Y
Coal Production:		Convenience Stores:		Pipelines:		Wind:		Drilling:		Oil Field Services:	
		Chemicals:		Water:		Hydro:		InfoTech:		Air/Shipping Transportation:	
						Fuel Cells:		Specialty Services:	Y		

TYPES OF BUSINESS:

Natural Gas Utility
Gas Appliances
Telecommunications Services
Consulting, Engineering & Maintenance Services
LPG Filling Stations

BRANDS/DIVISIONS/AFFILIATES:

Towngas
ECO Environmental Investments Ltd
U-Tech Engineering Company Ltd
Towngas Telecommunications Company Ltd
Towngas Avenue
Hong Kong and China Water Limited
GH-Fusion Corporation Limited
Bauhinia

CONTACTS:

Note: Officers with more than one job title may be intentionally listed here more than once.

Alfred Chan Wing Kin, Managing Dir.
James Kwan Yuk Choi, COO/Exec. Dir.
John Ho Hon Ming, CFO
Margaret Cheng Law Wai Fun, Head-Corp. Human Resources
John Ho Hon Ming, Corp. Sec.
Peter Wong Wai Yee, Head-Mainland Utilities
Philip Siu Kam Shing, Head-New Energy
Shau Kee Lee, Chmn.

Phone: 852-2963-3300 **Fax:** 852-2516-7368
Toll-Free:
Address: 363 Java Rd., 23rd Fl., North Point, Hong Kong, China

GROWTH PLANS/SPECIAL FEATURES:

The Hong Kong and China Gas Co., Ltd. (HKCGC), operating under the Towngas name, is an Asian energy firm. The company supplies gas and related utility services through 2,112.7-mile network that covers 85% of Hong Kong's households and serves over 1.7 million customers in Hong Kong. Two plants produce HKCGC's gas; more than 97% comes from the newer Tai Po plant, which can supply a maximum of over 339 million cubic feet of gas per day. The remainder comes from the Ma Tau Kok plant. The firm has actively developed its city piped gas business in mainland China and now has over 110 midstream and joint venture projects throughout the country. HKCGC's wholly-owned subsidiary, ECO Environmental Investments Limited (formerly ECO Energy Company, Ltd.) operates five LPG filling stations that provide 24-hour gas filling services to18, 000 taxis and 2,300 LPG public light buses in Hong Kong. Another subsidiary, U-Tech Engineering Company, Ltd., provides consulting, construction and maintenance services, as well as installation, rehabilitation and replacement of underground pipes for both gas and water. Towngas Telecommunications Company, Ltd. provides customized telecommunications solutions to telecommunications carriers and large corporations. Hong Kong and China Water Limited is involved in supply water and treating wastewater. The subsidiary currently serves more than 700,000 customers. GH-Fusion Corporation Limited, a joint venture between Towngas and U.K.-based The Fusion Group, focuses on the manufacturing and research and development of polyethylene piping systems and equipment. Subsidiary, P-Tech Engineering Company Limited offers gas production facility technical services, as well as engineering services. HKCGC also sells gas appliances and equipment under the Bauhinia brand and offers fine dining through its two Towngas Avenue restaurant/retail locations.

FINANCIALS:

Sales and profits are in thousands of dollars—add 000 to get the full amount. 2010 Note: Financial information for 2010 was not available for all companies at press time.

2010 Sales: $	2010 Profits: $	**U.S. Stock Ticker: HOKCY.PK**
2009 Sales: $1,593,410	2009 Profits: $667,590	**Int'l Ticker: 0003** Int'l Exchange: Hong Kong-HKEX
2008 Sales: $1,593,460	2008 Profits: $555,030	Employees: 1,908
2007 Sales: $1,730,000	2007 Profits: $750,000	Fiscal Year Ends: 12/31
2006 Sales: $1,210,000	2006 Profits: $680,000	Parent Company:

SALARIES/BENEFITS:

Pension Plan: Y	ESOP Stock Plan:	Profit Sharing:	Top Exec. Salary: $	Bonus: $
Savings Plan:	Stock Purch. Plan:		Second Exec. Salary: $	Bonus: $

OTHER THOUGHTS:

Apparent Women Officers or Directors: 1
Hot Spot for Advancement for Women/Minorities:

LOCATIONS: ("Y" = Yes)

West:	Southwest:	Midwest:	Southeast:	Northeast:	International:
					Y

HONGKONG ELECTRIC HOLDINGS LIMITED

www.heh.com

Industry Group Code: 2211 **Ranks within this company's industry group:** Sales: 40 Profits: 17

Exploration/Production:		Refining/Retailing:		Utilities:		Alternative Energy:		Specialty Services:		Energy Mktg./Other Svcs.	
Exploration:		Refining:		Electric Utility:	Y	Waste/Solar/Other:		Consulting/Eng.:		Energy Marketing:	
Production:		Retailing:		Gas Utility:		Thermal/Steam:		Seismic:		Equipment/Machinery:	
Coal Production:		Convenience Stores:		Pipelines:		Wind:	Y	Drilling:		Oil Field Services:	
		Chemicals:		Water:		Hydro:		InfoTech:		Air/Shipping Transportation:	
						Fuel Cells:		Specialty Services:			

TYPES OF BUSINESS:

Electricity Generation & Distribution
Engineering Consultancy

BRANDS/DIVISIONS/AFFILIATES:

Lamma Winds
Hong Kong Electric International Limited
Associated Technical Services Limited
Stanley Power
Powercor Australia
Ratchaburi Power Company Limited
Northern Gas Networks Limited
Seabank Power Limited

CONTACTS:

Note: Officers with more than one job title may be intentionally listed here more than once.

Tso Kai Sum, Managing Dir.
Trini Chan Lai Yee, Gen. Mgr.-Human Resources
Wan Chi Tin, Dir.-Eng.
Lillian Wong Lee Wah, Corp. Sec.
Yuen Sui See, Dir.-Oper.
Wan Chi Tin, Exec. Dir.-Planning & Dev.
Mimi Yeung Yuk Chun, Gen. Mgr.-Public Affairs
Neil Douglas McGee, Dir.-Finance
Francis Cheng Cho Ying, Gen. Mgr.-Generation
Frank Lau Fuk Hoi, Gen. Mgr.-Projects
Chu Wing Kin, Gen. Mgr.-Commercial
Yee Tak Chow, Gen. Mgr.-Corp. Dev.
Canning Fok Kin Ning, Chmn.
Charles Tsai Chao Chung, Gen. Mgr.-Hongkong Electric International Ltd.
Ip Pak Nin, Gen. Mgr.-Transmission & Dist.

Phone: 852-2843-3111 **Fax:** 852-2810-0506
Toll-Free:
Address: 44 Kennedy Rd., Hong Kong Electric Centre, Hong Kong, China

GROWTH PLANS/SPECIAL FEATURES:

Hongkong Electric Holdings Limited, a member of the Cheung Kong Group, is a holding company with interests in electricity generation, distribution and sales. Its primary subsidiary is Hongkong Electric Company Limited (HEC), which serves the island of Hong Kong and nearby Lamma Island, where its main power station is located, producing primarily coal-based electricity. The power station has a total installed capacity of 3,736 megawatts (MW) and serves more than 560,000 customers. Newer additions to the station aim to expand from coal-based generation. The firm's Lamma Winds project is conducting a pilot wind energy program. Subsidiary Hongkong Electric International Limited oversees the firm's holdings outside Hong Kong. These holdings include a 28% share in ETSA Utilities, with more than 765,000 customers in South Australia; a 28% interest in Powercor Australia, serving more than 625,000 customers in Victoria, Australia; a 28% interest in CitiPower, distributing electricity in Victoria, Australia; a 25% interest in Ratchaburi Power Company Limited, an energy development firm in Thailand; a 41% share in Northern Gas Networks Limited, with a large gas distribution infrastructure in the U.K.; a 50% stake in Seabank Power Limited, a U.K.-based electricity generation company; a 50% interest in Stanley Power, active in natural gas-fired electricity generation in Canada; Wellington Electricity Lines Limited, operating an electricity distribution network in New Zealand; and several conventional and renewable energy projects in Mainland China. A third major subsidiary, Associated Technical Services Limited, offers engineering consulting services to energy companies. In 2009, the firm began operation of its first wind project in China, a 48 MW wind farm in Yunnan Province. In June 2010, the company acquired an indirect 50% stake in Seabank Power Limited. In November 2010, Hongkong Electric, as part of a consortium, acquired EDF Energy plc's regulated and non-regulated network activities in the U.K.

FINANCIALS:

Sales and profits are in thousands of dollars—add 000 to get the full amount. 2010 Note: Financial information for 2010 was not available for all companies at press time.

2010 Sales: $	2010 Profits: $	**U.S. Stock Ticker: HGKGY**
2009 Sales: $1,341,090	2009 Profits: $864,000	**Int'l Ticker: 0006** Int'l Exchange: Hong Kong-HKE
2008 Sales: $1,648,010	2008 Profits: $1,035,920	Employees: 1,879
2007 Sales: $1,615,880	2007 Profits: $960,960	Fiscal Year Ends:
2006 Sales: $	2006 Profits: $	Parent Company:

SALARIES/BENEFITS:

Pension Plan:	ESOP Stock Plan:	Profit Sharing:	Top Exec. Salary: $	Bonus: $
Savings Plan:	Stock Purch. Plan:		Second Exec. Salary: $	Bonus: $

OTHER THOUGHTS:

Apparent Women Officers or Directors: 4
Hot Spot for Advancement for Women/Minorities: Y

LOCATIONS: ("Y" = Yes)

West:	Southwest:	Midwest:	Southeast:	Northeast:	International:
					Y

HUNT CONSOLIDATED INC

www.huntoil.com

Industry Group Code: 211111 **Ranks within this company's industry group:** Sales: Profits:

Exploration/Production:		Refining/Retailing:		Utilities:		Alternative Energy:		Specialty Services:		Energy Mktg./Other Svcs.	
Exploration:	Y	Refining:		Electric Utility:		Waste/Solar/Other:		Consulting/Eng.:		Energy Marketing:	
Production:	Y	Retailing:		Gas Utility:		Thermal/Steam:		Seismic:		Equipment/Machinery:	
Coal Production:		Convenience Stores:		Pipelines:		Wind:		Drilling:		Oil Field Services:	
		Chemicals:		Water:		Hydro:		InfoTech:		Air/Shipping Transportation:	
						Fuel Cells:		Specialty Services:	Y		

TYPES OF BUSINESS:

Oil & Gas Exploration & Production
Utility Services
Real Estate
Investments
Venture Capital
Ranching

BRANDS/DIVISIONS/AFFILIATES:

Hunt Oil Company
Hunt Oil Company of Canada
Hunt Refining Company
Hunt Power LP
Hunt Energy Horizons
Hunt Realty Investments
Hunt Private Equity Group
Hoodoo Land and Cattle

CONTACTS: *Note: Officers with more than one job title may be intentionally listed here more than once.*

Ray Hunt, CEO
Steve Hurley, Pres.
Dennis Grindinger, CFO
Dan Ray, VP-Oil & Gas Mktg.
Daniel Carrel, Mgr.-Human Resources & Compensation
Paul Habenicht, Sr. VP-Exploration & Prod., U.S. Onshore
Kevin Campbell, CIO/VP
Russ Darr, Sr. VP-Reservoir Eng.
Jess Nunnelee, VP-Prod.
Mark Gunnin, General Counsel/Sr. VP
Travis Armayor, VP-Corp. Dev.
Jeanne L. Phillips, Sr. VP-Corp. Affairs & Int'l Rel.
Bruce Cope, Chief Acct. Officer/VP
Bill Rex, VP-Land & Negotiations
Mark Griffin, VP-Project Eng.
Mike Pritchard, VP-Global Security
Ray Hunt, Chmn.
Thomas Cwikla, Sr. VP-Int'l Exploration & Prod.
Steve Kuykendall, Mgr.-Strategic Purchasing

Phone: 214-978-8000 **Fax:** 214-978-8888
Toll-Free:
Address: 1445 Ross at Field, Fountain Pl., Ste. 1400, Dallas, TX 75202-2785 US

GROWTH PLANS/SPECIAL FEATURES:

Hunt Consolidated, Inc. is a diversified holding company that engages in oil and gas exploration and production through its subsidiaries. Additionally, the firm is heavily involved in the start up of liquefied natural gas (LNG) projects throughout Yemen and Peru. Hunt Oil Company has operations in the U.S., Canada, Yemen, Peru, Argentina, Chile, Guyana, Morrocoo, Oman, Namibia and Senegal. Canadian activities, directed by the Hunt Oil Company of Canada, are focused primarily on the production of natural gas and associated liquids in the deeper portion of the Western Canadian Sedimentary Basin as well as in the frontier areas of Canada. Hunt Refining Company owns a 52,000 barrel per day refinery in Alabama; operates transportation and storage facilities in Alabama, Mississippi and New Jersey; and markets branded gasoline under the Parade brand in Alabama, Florida and Mississippi. Hunt Power, L.P. is focused on the development of investments in regulated gas and electric assets, as well as alternative energy markets. Hunt Generation Investments provides project development, acquisitions, and partnering with management teams and controls more than 20% of US Power Generating Company. Hunt Transmission Services acquires electric and pipeline transmission and distribution assets. Hunt Energy Enterprises, working in cooperation with Hunt Investment Corporation, invests in early stage energy technology ventures. Hunt Energy Horizons is involved in the development of wind and solar generation, coal gasification and the utilization of nuclear technologies. Hunt Realty Investments is the company's real estate investment firm. The company operates its private equity investments segment through Hunt Investment Corporation, Hunt BioVentures and Hunt Mexico, Inc. In addition, Hunt owns Hoodoo Land and Cattle Company, a management firm that oversees large-scale ranching and farming operations on over 415,000 acres of land in Texas, New Mexico, Montana, Wyoming and Utah.

FINANCIALS: **Sales and profits are in thousands of dollars—add 000 to get the full amount. 2010 Note: Financial information for 2010 was not available for all companies at press time.**

2010 Sales: $	2010 Profits: $	**U.S. Stock Ticker: Private**
2009 Sales: $	2009 Profits: $	**Int'l Ticker:** Int'l Exchange:
2008 Sales: $2,870,000	2008 Profits: $	Employees: 3,000
2007 Sales: $	2007 Profits: $	Fiscal Year Ends: 12/31
2006 Sales: $2,130,000	2006 Profits: $	Parent Company:

SALARIES/BENEFITS:

Pension Plan:	ESOP Stock Plan:	Profit Sharing:	Top Exec. Salary: $	Bonus: $
Savings Plan: Y	Stock Purch. Plan:		Second Exec. Salary: $	Bonus: $

OTHER THOUGHTS:

Apparent Women Officers or Directors: 2
Hot Spot for Advancement for Women/Minorities: Y

LOCATIONS: ("Y" = Yes)

West:	Southwest:	Midwest:	Southeast:	Northeast:	International:
	Y		Y	Y	Y

HUNTING PLC

www.hunting.plc.uk

Industry Group Code: 486 **Ranks within this company's industry group:** Sales: 21 Profits: 15

Exploration/Production:		Refining/Retailing:		Utilities:		Alternative Energy:		Specialty Services:		Energy Mktg./Other Svcs.	
Exploration:	Y	Refining:	Y	Electric Utility:		Waste/Solar/Other:		Consulting/Eng.:	Y	Energy Marketing:	Y
Production:	Y	Retailing:		Gas Utility:		Thermal/Steam:		Seismic:		Equipment/Machinery:	Y
Coal Production:		Convenience Stores:		Pipelines:	Y	Wind:		Drilling:		Oil Field Services:	Y
		Chemicals:		Water:		Hydro:		InfoTech:		Air/Shipping Transportation:	Y
						Fuel Cells:		Specialty Services:	Y		

TYPES OF BUSINESS:

Oil Field Services
Petrochemical Equipment Manufacturing
Energy Marketing & Transport
Propane Distribution
Asphalt & Specialty Distillate Manufacturing
International Shipping
Oil & Gas Exploration & Production
Pipelines

BRANDS/DIVISIONS/AFFILIATES:

Hunting Energy Services
Roforge
Interpec
Larco
Gibson Shipbrokers
Field Aviation Canada
Hunting Specialized Products
Innova-Extel Acquisition Holdings, Inc.

CONTACTS: *Note: Officers with more than one job title may be intentionally listed here more than once.*

Dennis L. Proctor, CEO
Peter Rose, Dir.-Finance
Peter Rose, Corp. Sec.
Stew Hanlon, Exec. VP-Oper.
John Mactaggart, Pres., Field Aviation
Nigel Richardson, Managing Dir.-Gibson Shipbrokers
Richard H. Hunting, Chmn.

Phone: 44-20-7321-0123	**Fax:** 44-20-7839-2072
Toll-Free:	
Address: 3 Cockspur St., London, SW1Y 5BQ UK	

GROWTH PLANS/SPECIAL FEATURES:

Hunting PLC is a global energy company that, through its subsidiaries, offers global oil field services, energy marketing and transport, international shipping, oil and gas exploration and petrochemical equipment manufacturing. Hunting Energy Services provides well construction, well completion and exploration and production products and services. The well construction division provides products and services for the drilling phase of oil and gas wells and associated equipment used by the underground construction for the telecommunication industry. Its products include casing and oil country tubular goods and in house design (Seal-Lock) and threading of premium connections. The well completion division provides products and services for the completion phase of oil and gas wells, including production tubing, accessories, couplings, blast joints, pup joints, as well as wireline and slickline tools. The exploration and production division operates the firm's exploration and production activities in the southern US and offshore Gulf of Mexico. Hunting Energy France provides a wide range of petrochemical equipment through four principal subsidiaries: Interpec, Larco, Setmat and Roforge. The firm's other niche operations include Hunting Specialized Products, providing pipeline services, coatings for industrial applications and waterline equipment for pipe lining; Field Aviation Canada, provides regional aircraft repair services and operates an aircrafts parts manufacturing facility; and Gibson Shipbrokers, which arranges bulk crude oil and product transport, LPG (liquefied petroleum gas) and liquid natural gas (LNG) carriers, as well as providing sale and purchase, offshore, dry cargo and bunker brokering departments. In mid 2009, the firm acquired PT SMB Industri, a threading operation located in Batam, Indonesia, for approximately $10.5 million. In August 2010, the company acquired Innova-Extel Acquisition Holdings Inc. for $125 million.

FINANCIALS: **Sales and profits are in thousands of dollars—add 000 to get the full amount. 2010 Note: Financial information for 2010 was not available for all companies at press time.**

2010 Sales: $	2010 Profits: $	**U.S. Stock Ticker:**
2009 Sales: $582,300	2009 Profits: $46,440	**Int'l Ticker: HTG** Int'l Exchange: London-LSE
2008 Sales: $721,650	2008 Profits: $16,400	Employees: 1,889
2007 Sales: $653,920	2007 Profits: $80,360	Fiscal Year Ends: 12/31
2006 Sales: $3,385,400	2006 Profits: $90,500	Parent Company:

SALARIES/BENEFITS:

Pension Plan:	ESOP Stock Plan:	Profit Sharing:	Top Exec. Salary: $	Bonus: $
Savings Plan:	Stock Purch. Plan:		Second Exec. Salary: $	Bonus: $

OTHER THOUGHTS:

Apparent Women Officers or Directors:
Hot Spot for Advancement for Women/Minorities:

LOCATIONS: ("Y" = Yes)

West:	Southwest:	Midwest:	Southeast:	Northeast:	International:
	Y				Y

HUSKY ENERGY INC

www.huskyenergy.ca

Industry Group Code: 211111 **Ranks within this company's industry group:** Sales: 42 Profits: 36

Exploration/Production:		**Refining/Retailing:**		**Utilities:**		**Alternative Energy:**		**Specialty Services:**		**Energy Mktg./Other Svcs.**	
Exploration:	Y	Refining:	Y	Electric Utility:		Waste/Solar/Other:		Consulting/Eng.:		Energy Marketing:	Y
Production:	Y	Retailing:	Y	Gas Utility:		Thermal/Steam:		Seismic:		Equipment/Machinery:	
Coal Production:		Convenience Stores:	Y	Pipelines:	Y	Wind:		Drilling:		Oil Field Services:	
		Chemicals:	Y	Water:		Hydro:		InfoTech:		Air/Shipping Transportation:	
						Fuel Cells:		Specialty Services:			

TYPES OF BUSINESS:

Oil & Gas Exploration & Production
Wholesale Energy Marketing
Refining & Upgrading
Gas Stations & Convenience Stores
Pipelines
Asphalt
Ethanol

BRANDS/DIVISIONS/AFFILIATES:

Husky Oil Operations Ltd.
Suncor Energy, Inc.
Suncor Energy Products, Inc.

CONTACTS: *Note: Officers with more than one job title may be intentionally listed here more than once.*

Asim Ghosh, CEO
Robert J. Peabody, COO
Asim Ghosh, Pres.
Alister Cowan, CFO/VP
Terry Manning, VP-Eng.
Ron Butler, VP-Corp. Admin.
James D. Girgulis, Corp. Sec./VP-Legal
Ruud B. Zoon, VP-East Coast Oper.
Bill Watson, COO-South East Asia
Paul J. McCloskey, VP-East Coast Oper.
Edward T. Connolly, VP-Heavy Oil
Terrance E. Kutryk, VP-Midstream & Refined Prod.
Canning K. N. Fok, Co-Chmn.
Terry Manning, VP-Procurement Mgmt.

Phone: 403-298-6111	**Fax:** 403-298-7464
Toll-Free:	
Address: 707 8th Ave. SW, Calgary, AB T2P 3G7 Canada	

GROWTH PLANS/SPECIAL FEATURES:

Husky Energy, Inc. is a Canadian oil company that operates through the upstream, midstream and downstream segments of the industry. Husky has roughly 700 million barrels of proved oil reserves and approximately 1.73 trillion cubic feet of natural gas reserves. It operates approximately 1,240 miles of pipeline. Husky Energy, Inc. operates three upstream divisions in the Western Canada Sedimentary Basin through Husky Oil Operations Ltd. These include Northwest Alberta, with over 50 oil and gas pools; Northeast British Columbia and Alberta Foothills, consisting of the Ram River gas plant and its pipeline; and East Central Alberta, with drillable areas from Athabasca in the north to Red Deer and Hussar in the south. Husky has holdings in the Wenchang oil field in the South China Sea and a development opportunity in Indonesia's Madura Straits. In 2009, the company produced 306,500 barrels of oil equivalent per day. The company's midstream operations include a heavy oil upgrader/refinery, which process oil into asphalt; 19 crude oil processing facilities; three facilities capable of extracting natural gas liquids at a capacity of 327,000 cubic feet per day; and 50% interests in two natural gas-fired electricity cogeneration (power and steam) stations generating a total of 305 megawatts. The firm's downstream division produces ethanol; refines light and heavy crude oil; and markets refined petroleum products such as gasoline, diesel, jet fuel, blending stocks, ethanol blended fuels and asphalt. The downstream segment includes the Canadian refined products and U.S. refining/marketing business operations, as well as retail operations through over 570 gas stations and convenience stores across Canada. Husky Energy also operates oil wells in China and Libya. In December 2009, the firm agreed to acquire 98 petroleum retail outlets in the Ontario market from Suncor Energy, Inc. and Suncor Energy Products, Inc.

FINANCIALS: **Sales and profits are in thousands of dollars—add 000 to get the full amount. 2010 Note: Financial information for 2010 was not available for all companies at press time.**

2010 Sales: $	2010 Profits: $	**U.S. Stock Ticker: HUSKF**
2009 Sales: $14,607,700	2009 Profits: $1,372,200	**Int'l Ticker: HSE** Int'l Exchange: Toronto-TSX
2008 Sales: $23,162,000	2008 Profits: $3,520,000	Employees: 4,272
2007 Sales: $15,720,000	2007 Profits: $3,260,000	Fiscal Year Ends: 12/31
2006 Sales: $9,258,900	2006 Profits: $2,382,900	Parent Company:

SALARIES/BENEFITS:

Pension Plan: Y	ESOP Stock Plan:	Profit Sharing:	Top Exec. Salary: $1,472,688	Bonus: $2,950,246
Savings Plan: Y	Stock Purch. Plan:		Second Exec. Salary: $691,540	Bonus: $286,015

OTHER THOUGHTS:

Apparent Women Officers or Directors:
Hot Spot for Advancement for Women/Minorities:

LOCATIONS: ("Y" = Yes)

West:	Southwest:	Midwest:	Southeast:	Northeast:	International:
					Y

HYDRO ONE INC

www.hydroone.com

Industry Group Code: 221111 **Ranks within this company's industry group:** Sales: 2 Profits: 2

Exploration/Production:		Refining/Retailing:		Utilities:		Alternative Energy:		Specialty Services:		Energy Mktg./Other Svcs.	
Exploration:		Refining:		Electric Utility:	Y	Waste/Solar/Other:		Consulting/Eng.:		Energy Marketing:	Y
Production:		Retailing:		Gas Utility:		Thermal/Steam:		Seismic:		Equipment/Machinery:	
Coal Production:		Convenience Stores:		Pipelines:		Wind:		Drilling:		Oil Field Services:	
		Chemicals:		Water:		Hydro:		InfoTech:		Air/Shipping Transportation:	
						Fuel Cells:		Specialty Services:			

TYPES OF BUSINESS:

Electricity Transmission & Distribution
Telecommunications Services

BRANDS/DIVISIONS/AFFILIATES:

Ontario Hydro
Hydro One Remote Communities Inc
Hydro One Networks Inc
Hydro One Brampton Inc
Hydro One Telecom Inc

CONTACTS:

Note: Officers with more than one job title may be intentionally listed here more than once.

Laura Formusa, CEO
Laura Formusa, Pres.
Sandy Struthers, CFO
Nairn McQueen, Dir.-Eng. & Construction Svcs., Hydro One Networks
Joe Agostino, General Counsel
Myles D'Arcey, Dir.-Customer Oper., Hydro One Networks, Inc.
Tom Goldie, Dir.-Corp. Svcs., Hydro One Networks, Inc.
Peter Gregg, Dir.-Corp. & Regulatory Affairs, Hydro One Network
Paul Marchant, Pres./CEO-Hydro One Telecom, Inc.
Remy Fernandes, Pres./CEO-Hydro One Brampton, Inc.
James Arnett, Chmn.

Phone: 416-345-5000	**Fax:** 416-345-6225
Toll-Free: 877-955-1155	
Address: 483 Bay St., N. Tower, 15th Fl., Toronto, ON M5G 2P5 Canada	

GROWTH PLANS/SPECIAL FEATURES:

Hydro One, Inc. (HO) is one of the main power suppliers in Ontario province, Canada. HO acquires almost all of its electricity from Ontario Power Generation. The company's largest subsidiary, Hydro One Networks, is involved in the planning, construction, operation and maintenance of the company's transmission and distribution network, which is one of the 10 largest in North America. The firm operates 280 transmission stations and 1,010 distribution and regulation stations. HO owns 97% of the transmission grid in Ontario. It also operates 26 interconnections with neighboring provinces and states. The firm's distribution systems deliver lower voltages to homes, farms and businesses through the largest network in the province. It has over 76,428.7 miles of distribution lines that serve 1.3 million customers, mostly in rural areas, and also serve 335 municipal utilities. HO has three other smaller subsidiaries: Hydro One Brampton, Inc., which distributes electricity to Brampton, one of the fastest-growing urban centers in Ontario; Hydro One Remote Communities, Inc., which operates and maintains the generation and distribution assets used to supply electricity to 19 communities across northern Ontario that are not connected to the province's electricity grid; and Hydro One Telecom, Inc., which is involved in the marketing of the excess fiber-optic capacity from the company's province-wide telecommunications system. The company actively assesses its properties for potential environmental contamination, and to date has decontaminated over one million gallons of transformer oil and sent over 3,000 tons of PCB contaminated material to be destroyed. In February 2010, HO announced plans to open an office in Orleans.

HO offers its employees life insurance; sick leave; disability coverage; pensions; and health and dental plans.

FINANCIALS:

Sales and profits are in thousands of dollars—add 000 to get the full amount. 2010 Note: Financial information for 2010 was not available for all companies at press time.

2010 Sales: $	2010 Profits: $	**U.S. Stock Ticker: Government-Owned**
2009 Sales: $4,732,220	2009 Profits: $468,830	**Int'l Ticker:** Int'l Exchange:
2008 Sales: $4,338,960	2008 Profits: $469,100	Employees: 5,427
2007 Sales: $4,358,040	2007 Profits: $373,550	Fiscal Year Ends: 12/31
2006 Sales: $4,255,060	2006 Profits: $425,970	Parent Company:

SALARIES/BENEFITS:

Pension Plan: Y	ESOP Stock Plan:	Profit Sharing:	Top Exec. Salary: $	Bonus: $
Savings Plan:	Stock Purch. Plan:		Second Exec. Salary: $	Bonus: $

OTHER THOUGHTS:

Apparent Women Officers or Directors: 8
Hot Spot for Advancement for Women/Minorities: Y

LOCATIONS: ("Y" = Yes)

West:	Southwest:	Midwest:	Southeast:	Northeast:	International:
					Y

HYDRO-QUEBEC

www.hydroquebec.com

Industry Group Code: 221111 **Ranks within this company's industry group:** Sales: 1 Profits: 1

Exploration/Production:		Refining/Retailing:		Utilities:		Alternative Energy:		Specialty Services:		Energy Mktg./Other Svcs.	
Exploration:		Refining:		Electric Utility:	Y	Waste/Solar/Other:		Consulting/Eng.:	Y	Energy Marketing:	Y
Production:		Retailing:		Gas Utility:		Thermal/Steam:		Seismic:		Equipment/Machinery:	Y
Coal Production:		Convenience Stores:		Pipelines:		Wind:	Y	Drilling:		Oil Field Services:	
		Chemicals:		Water:		Hydro:	Y	InfoTech:	Y	Air/Shipping Transportation:	
						Fuel Cells:		Specialty Services:	Y		

TYPES OF BUSINESS:

Electric Utility
Hydroelectric & Wind Power
Hybrid Drive Train Systems
Construction & Engineering
Technical Consulting & Services
Technology & Research

BRANDS/DIVISIONS/AFFILIATES:

Hydro-Quebec Production
Hydro-Quebec Distribution
Hydro-Quebec TransEnergie
Societe d'Energie de la Baie James
Hydro-Quebec Equipement
Technologies M4, Inc.
Hydro-Quebec International

CONTACTS: *Note: Officers with more than one job title may be intentionally listed here more than once.*

Thierry Vandal, CEO
Thierry Vandal, Pres.
Michel Martinez, VP-Human Resources
Elie Saheb, Exec. VP-Tech.
Real Laporte, Pres., Hydro-Quebec Equipment & Shared Svcs.
Marie-Jose Nadeau, Sec. Gen.
Marie-Jose Nadeau, Exec. VP-Corp. Affairs
Lise Croteau, VP-Acct. & Control
Richard Cacchione, Pres., Hydro-Quebec Generation
Isabelle Courville, Pres., Hydro-Quebec TransEnergie
Andre Boulanger, Pres., Hydro-Quebec Dist.
Jean-Hugues Lafleur, VP-Finance, Treasury & Pension Fund
Michael L. Turcotte, Chmn.

Phone: 514-289-2211 **Fax:** 514-289-5440
Toll-Free:
Address: 75 Rene-Levesque Blvd. W., 20th Fl., Montreal, QC H2Z 1A4 Canada

GROWTH PLANS/SPECIAL FEATURES:

Hydro-Quebec (HQ), owned by the government of Quebec, is one of the largest generators and distributors of electric power in Canada, and the largest supplier of electricity to Quebec. Its businesses include distribution, transmission, generation, construction and technological innovation, in partnership with universities, industry and research centers. HQ operates over 571 dams and 26 large reservoirs and holds various oil and gas exploration permits. Although its focus is on the Quebec region, the firm's operations include dozens of subsidiaries in regions including the U.S., Latin America, Asia and Africa. The firm's subsidiaries include the following. Hydro-Quebec Production generates the firm's electricity, operating 59 hydroelectric generating stations, one nuclear facility; four thermal plants and one wind farm, with a combined capacity of 36.8 gigawatts (GW). Hydro-Quebec Distribution, operating almost 70,000 miles of distribution lines, sells the firm's electricity in Quebec and in the U.S. through short- and long-term contracts. Hydro-Quebec TransEnergie operates the firm's transmission system of over 20,600 miles of transmission lines and 515 substations. The firm's engineering and construction services, including building transmission lines and substations, are provided by Societe d'Energie de la Baie James and Hydro-Quebec Equipment. Technologies M4, Inc. is an innovator in developing hybrid drive train systems used by major manufacturers in hybrid cars. Lastly, Hydro-Quebec International offers consultations for dam safety, operations, engineering, nuclear technology, testing and research. In October 2009, the firm agreed to buy most of the assets of New Brunswick Power for $4.4 billion.

FINANCIALS: **Sales and profits are in thousands of dollars—add 000 to get the full amount. 2010 Note: Financial information for 2010 was not available for all companies at press time.**

2010 Sales: $	2010 Profits: $	**U.S. Stock Ticker: Government-Owned**
2009 Sales: $12,303,400	2009 Profits: $3,027,460	**Int'l Ticker:** Int'l Exchange:
2008 Sales: $11,974,600	2008 Profits: $2,957,630	Employees:
2007 Sales: $10,095,200	2007 Profits: $2,379,290	Fiscal Year Ends: 12/31
2006 Sales: $10,589,694	2006 Profits: $3,549,639	Parent Company:

SALARIES/BENEFITS:

Pension Plan: Y	ESOP Stock Plan:	Profit Sharing:	Top Exec. Salary: $408,377	Bonus: $121,508
Savings Plan:	Stock Purch. Plan:		Second Exec. Salary: $358,055	Bonus: $99,034

OTHER THOUGHTS:

Apparent Women Officers or Directors: 8
Hot Spot for Advancement for Women/Minorities: Y

LOCATIONS: ("Y" = Yes)

West:	Southwest:	Midwest:	Southeast:	Northeast:	International:
				Y	Y

IBERDROLA SA

www.iberdrola.es

Industry Group Code: 2211 **Ranks within this company's industry group:** Sales: 5 Profits: 4

Exploration/Production:		Refining/Retailing:		Utilities:		Alternative Energy:		Specialty Services:		Energy Mktg./Other Svcs.	
Exploration:		Refining:		Electric Utility:	Y	Waste/Solar/Other:		Consulting/Eng.:	Y	Energy Marketing:	
Production:		Retailing:		Gas Utility:	Y	Thermal/Steam:		Seismic:		Equipment/Machinery:	
Coal Production:		Convenience Stores:		Pipelines:		Wind:	Y	Drilling:		Oil Field Services:	
		Chemicals:		Water:	Y	Hydro:	Y	InfoTech:		Air/Shipping Transportation:	
						Fuel Cells:		Specialty Services:	Y		

TYPES OF BUSINESS:

Electricity Generation & Distribution
Wind Generation
Hydroelectric Generation
Engineering & Construction
Telecommunications
Real Estate
Gas & Water Distribution

BRANDS/DIVISIONS/AFFILIATES:

ScottishPower UK plc
Energy East Corporation
Rochester Gas and Electric Corp
New York State Electric & Gas Corp
Iberdrola Renovables SAU
Dry Lake

CONTACTS:

Note: Officers with more than one job title may be intentionally listed here more than once.

Jose Ignacio Sanchez Galan, CEO
Jose Sainz Armada, CFO
Federico San Sebastian Flechoso, Counsel
Jose Luis San Pedro Guerenabarrena, Dir.-Oper.
Jose Luis del Valle Doblado, Dir.-Strategy & Studies
Fernando Becker Zuazua, Dir.-Corp. Resources
Julian Martinez-Simancas Sanchez, Sec.
Jose Luis San Pedro, Head-Iberia & Latin America
Jose Ignacio Sanchez Galan, Chmn.
Amparo Moraleda, Head-Int'l Bus.

Phone: 34-944-151-411	Fax: 34-944-663-194
Toll-Free:	
Address: 8 Cardenal Gardoqui, Bilbao, 48008 Spain	

GROWTH PLANS/SPECIAL FEATURES:

Ilberdrola S.A., a Spanish electric utility, serves over 21 million customers on the Iberian Peninsula, with an installed capacity of 43,311 megawatts (MW), with 26,369 MW in Spain, 6701 MW in the U.K., 3,794 MW in the U.S. and 5,554 MW in Mexico and Guatemala. The firm generated 141,268 gigawatts hours of electricity in 2008, Iberdrola is one of the world's leaders in renewable energy and has moved beyond power generation in recent years, due to the deregulation of the Spanish electric industry, and now is involved in engineering and construction, real estate, gas and water distribution and telecommunications. Internationally, Iberdrola recently expanded into the U.S. wind energy market, having installed five wind farms in the U.S. in 2009 through subsidiary, Iberdrola Renovables. The subsidiary currently has 56,000 MW total of renewable energy plants. The company has additional subsidiaries in U.K., Europe, India, South America, Africa, the Middle East and Russia. In August 2010, Iberdrola was awarded a contract to build nine new wind farms in Brazil with a capacity of 258 MW. In October 2010, the company announced plans to build two photovoltaic solar plants, one in Colorado and one in Arizona, through its Renovables subsidiary.

FINANCIALS:

Sales and profits are in thousands of dollars—add 000 to get the full amount. 2010 Note: Financial information for 2010 was not available for all companies at press time.

2010 Sales: $	2010 Profits: $	**U.S. Stock Ticker: IBDRF.PK**
2009 Sales: $30,499,200	2009 Profits: $3,507,440	**Int'l Ticker: IBE** Int'l Exchange: Madrid-MCE
2008 Sales: $36,879,000	2008 Profits: $4,187,000	Employees:
2007 Sales: $25,500,000	2007 Profits: $3,440,000	Fiscal Year Ends: 12/31
2006 Sales: $14,530,000	2006 Profits: $2,190,000	Parent Company:

SALARIES/BENEFITS:

Pension Plan:	ESOP Stock Plan:	Profit Sharing:	Top Exec. Salary: $	Bonus: $
Savings Plan:	Stock Purch. Plan:		Second Exec. Salary: $	Bonus: $

OTHER THOUGHTS:

Apparent Women Officers or Directors:
Hot Spot for Advancement for Women/Minorities:

LOCATIONS: ("Y" = Yes)

West:	Southwest:	Midwest:	Southeast:	Northeast:	International:
	Y			Y	Y

IDEMITSU KOSAN CO LTD

www.idemitsu.co.jp

Industry Group Code: 486 **Ranks within this company's industry group:** Sales: 1 Profits: 17

Exploration/Production:		Refining/Retailing:		Utilities:		Alternative Energy:		Specialty Services:		Energy Mktg./Other Svcs.	
Exploration:	Y	Refining:	Y	Electric Utility:		Waste/Solar/Other:		Consulting/Eng.:	Y	Energy Marketing:	
Production:		Retailing:	Y	Gas Utility:	Y	Thermal/Steam:		Seismic:		Equipment/Machinery:	Y
Coal Production:	Y	Convenience Stores:	Y	Pipelines:		Wind:		Drilling:		Oil Field Services:	
		Chemicals:	Y	Water:		Hydro:		InfoTech:		Air/Shipping Transportation:	Y
						Fuel Cells:		Specialty Services:	Y		

TYPES OF BUSINESS:

Gas & Oil Exploration
Lubricants
Petrochemicals
Oil Transportation
Crude Oil Sales
Uranium & Geothermal Exploration

BRANDS/DIVISIONS/AFFILIATES:

ADAMANTATE
Idemitsu Lube Middle East & Africa FZE
Petro Summit Investment UK Ltd.
Idemitsu Lube South America Ltda.
Idemitsu Apollo Corporation
Global OLED Technology LLC

CONTACTS: *Note: Officers with more than one job title may be intentionally listed here more than once.*

Kazuhisa Nakano, Pres.
Takeshi Yamada, Dir.-R&D
Takashi Tsukioka, Managing Dir.-Bus. Planning
Mitsuru Soneda, Dir.-Acct.
Kenichi Matsui, Exec. VP
Akiro Nishiyori, Exec. VP
Seiji Fukunaga, Managing Dir.
Yoshihisa Matsumoto, Managing Dir.
Akihiko Tembo, Chmn.
Yasunori Maeda, Dir.-Supply & Demand

Phone: 81-3-3213-9307	**Fax:** 81-3-3213-9325
Toll-Free:	
Address: 1-1 Marunouchi, 3-Chome, Chiyoda-ku, Tokyo, 100-8321 Japan	

GROWTH PLANS/SPECIAL FEATURES:

Idemitsu Kosan Co., Ltd., is a Japanese supplier of petroleum and petrochemical products. Founded in 1911, the company divides its operations into five business segments: petroleum products, roughly 79% of total sales; petrochemical products, 14%; oil exploration and production, 2%; coal, 2.5%; and other, 2.5%. The petroleum products business refines crude oil and markets gasoline, kerosene, lubricants and fuel products such as diesel oil and heavy fuel oil. The petrochemical products business manufactures and sells basic chemicals, including ethylene and propylene; engineering plastics, such as polycarbonate; performance chemicals, including ADAMANTATE, a photoresist material used in semiconductor manufacturing; and plastic processed products. The oil exploration and production business operates explores, develops and produces petroleum and natural gas in Norway and Vietnam. The coal business explores for, develops and markets coal, operating four coal mines in Australia. The company's other businesses include the research, exploration and development of uranium and geothermal resources; electronic materials manufacturing; agricultural biotechnology product development; light emitting diode (OLED) material production; and engineering services. In 2009, Idemitsu Kosan established subsidiary Idemitsu Lube Middle East & Africa FZE to market its lubricant products in the Middle East and Africa; expanded its lubricant production capacity in Indonesia; formed a strategic alliance with LG Display Co., Ltd., for the development of OLED displays; commenced production at its Laffan Refinery in Qatar; acquired Petro Summit Investment UK Ltd., an exploration and production company operating in the North Sea; and established subsidiary Idemitsu Lube South America Ltda. in Sao Paulo, Brazil. In April 2010, the company established a limited liability partnership with Mitsui Chemicals, Inc. In May 2010, the firm's affiliate Idemitsu Apollo Corporation acquired the petroleum product wholesale business of U.S.-based New West Petroleum. In June 2010, Idemitsu Kosan acquired a 32.73% stake in Global OLED Technology LLC.

FINANCIALS: **Sales and profits are in thousands of dollars—add 000 to get the full amount. 2010 Note: Financial information for 2010 was not available for all companies at press time.**

2010 Sales: $	2010 Profits: $	**U.S. Stock Ticker:**
2009 Sales: $41,602,900	2009 Profits: $36,400	**Int'l Ticker: 5019** Int'l Exchange: Tokyo-TSE
2008 Sales: $33,522,000	2008 Profits: $33,000	Employees:
2007 Sales: $29,581,200	2007 Profits: $362,410	Fiscal Year Ends: 3/31
2006 Sales: $28,994,400	2006 Profits: $238,680	Parent Company:

SALARIES/BENEFITS:

Pension Plan:	ESOP Stock Plan:	Profit Sharing:	Top Exec. Salary: $	Bonus: $
Savings Plan:	Stock Purch. Plan:		Second Exec. Salary: $	Bonus: $

OTHER THOUGHTS:

Apparent Women Officers or Directors:
Hot Spot for Advancement for Women/Minorities:

LOCATIONS: ("Y" = Yes)

West:	Southwest:	Midwest:	Southeast:	Northeast:	International:
Y		Y		Y	Y

IMPERIAL OIL LIMITED

www.imperialoil.ca

Industry Group Code: 211111 **Ranks within this company's industry group:** Sales: 31 Profits: 33

Exploration/Production:		Refining/Retailing:		Utilities:		Alternative Energy:		Specialty Services:		Energy Mktg./Other Svcs.	
Exploration:	Y	Refining:	Y	Electric Utility:		Waste/Solar/Other:		Consulting/Eng.:		Energy Marketing:	
Production:	Y	Retailing:	Y	Gas Utility:		Thermal/Steam:		Seismic:		Equipment/Machinery:	
Coal Production:		Convenience Stores:		Pipelines:		Wind:		Drilling:		Oil Field Services:	
		Chemicals:	Y	Water:		Hydro:		InfoTech:		Air/Shipping Transportation:	
						Fuel Cells:		Specialty Services:	Y		

TYPES OF BUSINESS:

Crude Oil & Natural Gas Exploration & Production
Petrochemicals Production

BRANDS/DIVISIONS/AFFILIATES:

Exxon Mobil Corp
Esso
Mobil
Syncrude
ExxonMobil Canada Limited

CONTACTS:

Note: Officers with more than one job title may be intentionally listed here more than once.

Bruce March, CEO
Bruce March, Pres.
P.J. (Paul) Masschelin, Sr. VP-Admin.
Brian Livingston, General Counsel/Corp. Sec./VP
P.J. (Paul) Masschelin, Sr. VP-Finance/Treas.
Randy L. Broiles, Sr. VP-Resources Div.
Sean Carleton, Controller
Bruce March, Chmn.

Phone: **Fax:** 800-367-0585
Toll-Free: 800-567-3776
Address: 237 Fourth Ave. S.W., Calgary, AB T2P 3M9 Canada

GROWTH PLANS/SPECIAL FEATURES:

Imperial Oil Ltd. is a Canada-based integrated oil company. It is active in all phases of the petroleum industry in Canada, including the exploration for and production and sale of crude oil and natural gas. The company is a producer of crude oil, natural gas and natural gas liquids; a refiner and marketer of petroleum products; and a supplier of petrochemicals. Imperial Oil operates in three segments: upstream, downstream and chemical. Upstream operations include the exploration for and production of conventional crude oil, natural gas, synthetic oil and bitumen. Downstream operations include the transportation, refining and blending of crude oil and refined products, and the distribution and marketing thereof. Chemical operations consist of the manufacturing and marketing of petrochemicals such as ethylene, benzene, aromatic and aliphatic solvents, plasticizer intermediates and polyethylene resin. The company maintains a distribution system of 24 bulk terminals and nearly 2,000 service stations. Imperial Oil markets more than 650 petroleum products under brands such as Esso and Mobil. The company has major interests in the Normal Wells oil field in the Northwest Territories, which accounts for 56% of net production of conventional crude oil. The firm also has a significant investment in oil sands, including a 25% share in Syncrude and full ownership of the Cold Lake oil sands deposits. The company is also developing operations at the Athabasca oil sands in conjunction with ExxonMobil Canada Limited. Exxon Mobil Corp. owns 69.6% of Imperial Oil.

Employees are offered company training programs; company-paid educational assistance; mentoring programs; health, dental and life insurance during both employment and retirement; short- and long-term disability; a physical fitness refund program; an employee assistance program; a 401(k) plan; a pension plan; relocation assistance; a back-up childcare refund program; and discounts on Esso gasoline and home heating oil.

FINANCIALS:

Sales and profits are in thousands of dollars—add 000 to get the full amount. 2010 Note: Financial information for 2010 was not available for all companies at press time.

2010 Sales: $	2010 Profits: $	**U.S. Stock Ticker: IMO**
2009 Sales: $21,292,000	2009 Profits: $1,579,000	**Int'l Ticker: IMO** Int'l Exchange: Toronto-TSX
2008 Sales: $31,240,000	2008 Profits: $3,878,000	Employees: 5,015
2007 Sales: $25,069,000	2007 Profits: $3,188,000	Fiscal Year Ends: 12/31
2006 Sales: $19,978,700	2006 Profits: $2,617,800	Parent Company:

SALARIES/BENEFITS:

Pension Plan: Y	ESOP Stock Plan:	Profit Sharing:	Top Exec. Salary: $553,870	Bonus: $183,862
Savings Plan: Y	Stock Purch. Plan:		Second Exec. Salary: $462,510	Bonus: $119,910

OTHER THOUGHTS:

Apparent Women Officers or Directors: 2
Hot Spot for Advancement for Women/Minorities:

LOCATIONS: ("Y" = Yes)

West:	Southwest:	Midwest:	Southeast:	Northeast:	International:
					Y

INDIAN OIL CORP LTD

www.iocl.com

Industry Group Code: 324110 **Ranks within this company's industry group:** Sales: 4 Profits: 3

Exploration/Production:		Refining/Retailing:		Utilities:		Alternative Energy:		Specialty Services:		Energy Mktg./Other Svcs.	
Exploration:	Y	Refining:	Y	Electric Utility:		Waste/Solar/Other:		Consulting/Eng.:		Energy Marketing:	Y
Production:	Y	Retailing:	Y	Gas Utility:	Y	Thermal/Steam:		Seismic:		Equipment/Machinery:	
Coal Production:		Convenience Stores:		Pipelines:	Y	Wind:		Drilling:		Oil Field Services:	
		Chemicals:	Y	Water:		Hydro:		InfoTech:		Air/Shipping Transportation:	
						Fuel Cells:		Specialty Services:	Y		

TYPES OF BUSINESS:

Petroleum Refining
Pipelines
Oil & Gas Exploration & Production
Natural Gas Utility
Gas Stations
Storage Terminals & Depots
Aviation Fueling Stations
Lubricants Manufacturing & Retail

BRANDS/DIVISIONS/AFFILIATES:

Chennai Petroleum Corporation Ltd
XtraPremium
SERVO lubricants
LP Gas
Oil India Ltd
Oil & Natural Gas Corporation
Indian Oil Co Ltd
Indian Refineries Ltd

CONTACTS: *Note: Officers with more than one job title may be intentionally listed here more than once.*

Sarthak N. Behuria, Exec. Dir.
Serangulam V. Narasimhan, Dir.-Finance
G. C. Daga, Dir.-Mktg.
Sudhir Bhalla, Dir.-Human Resources
R.K. Malhotra, Dir.-R&D
S Ramasamy, Exec. Dir.-Info. Systems
B V Janakiram, Exec. Dir.-Pipeline Oper.
B. M. Bansal, Dir.-Planning & Bus. Dev.
R. Narayanan, Exec. Dir.-Corp. Affairs
V.K. Sood, Exec. Dir.-Corp. Finance
K.K. Jha, Dir.-Pipelines
B. N. Bankapur, Dir.-Refineries
C. Dasgupta, Exec. Dir.-Gas
V.S. Okhde, Exec. Dir.-Exploration & Prod.
B.M. Bansal, Chmn.
A.S. Ujwal, Exec. Dir.-Int'l Trade

Phone: 011-2626-0000 **Fax:**
Toll-Free:
Address: 3079/3, J B Tito Marg, Sadiq Nagar, New Delhi, 110049 India

GROWTH PLANS/SPECIAL FEATURES:

Indian Oil Corp. Ltd. (IndianOil) was formed by the merger of Indian Oil Co. Ltd. and Indian Refineries Ltd. The company supplies 71% of its downstream pipeline throughput capacity and controls a petroleum market share of 48%. The firm owns and operates 10 of India's 20 refineries with a combined capacity of approximately 1.25 million barrels per day. Two of these refineries are owned by subsidiary Chennai Petroleum Corporation, Ltd. In addition, IndianOil owns and operates one of the country's largest networks of cross-country crude oil and product pipelines, spanning about 6,214 miles. The company also owns a countrywide network of over 35,600 sales points comprised of 140 bulk storage terminals, installations and depots; 98 aviation fueling stations; 88 liquid petroleum gas bottling plants; and a nationwide network of over 18,643 gas and diesel stations. IndianOil's brands include SERVO lubricants, XtraPremium, LPGas, petrol and XtraMile. The firm's aviation service controls more than 63% of the aviation fuel market in India, supplying domestic and international carriers as well as the Indian Defense Services. The company's exploration and production activities consist of exploratory work in 11 coal bed methane blocks, as well as in two blocks awarded to the company and its consortium partners Oil India Ltd. and Oil & Natural Gas Corporation Ltd. IndianOil is also involved in petrochemical production and export, as well as wind, solar, nuclear and biofuel projects. In March 2010, the firm formed a limited liability partnership with edible oils manufacturer M/s. Ruchi Soya Industries Ltd. In May 2010, the company formed a joint venture with five other international oil firms to construct upgrading facilities, heavy oil production facilities and associated infrastructure in Venezuela. In September 2010, IndianOil formed a joint venture with three other petroleum firms and Mumbai International Airport Pvt. Ltd. to construct and operate an integrated fueling facility.

FINANCIALS: **Sales and profits are in thousands of dollars—add 000 to get the full amount. 2010 Note: Financial information for 2010 was not available for all companies at press time.**

2010 Sales: $	2010 Profits: $	**U.S. Stock Ticker:**
2009 Sales: $61,575,500	2009 Profits: $559,260	**Int'l Ticker: 530965** Int'l Exchange: Bombay-BSE
2008 Sales: $62,993,000	2008 Profits: $565,000	Employees: 33,998
2007 Sales: $42,680,000	2007 Profits: $1,820,000	Fiscal Year Ends: 3/31
2006 Sales: $37,158,700	2006 Profits: $1,101,500	Parent Company:

SALARIES/BENEFITS:

Pension Plan:	ESOP Stock Plan:	Profit Sharing:	Top Exec. Salary: $	Bonus: $
Savings Plan:	Stock Purch. Plan:		Second Exec. Salary: $	Bonus: $

OTHER THOUGHTS:

Apparent Women Officers or Directors: 2
Hot Spot for Advancement for Women/Minorities:

LOCATIONS: ("Y" = Yes)

West:	Southwest:	Midwest:	Southeast:	Northeast:	International:
					Y

INERGY LP

www.inergylp.com

Industry Group Code: 454312 **Ranks within this company's industry group:** Sales: 4 Profits: 3

Exploration/Production:		Refining/Retailing:		Utilities:		Alternative Energy:		Specialty Services:		Energy Mktg./Other Svcs.	
Exploration:		Refining:		Electric Utility:		Waste/Solar/Other:		Consulting/Eng.:		Energy Marketing:	Y
Production:		Retailing:	Y	Gas Utility:		Thermal/Steam:		Seismic:		Equipment/Machinery:	
Coal Production:		Convenience Stores:		Pipelines:	Y	Wind:		Drilling:		Oil Field Services:	
		Chemicals:		Water:		Hydro:		InfoTech:		Air/Shipping Transportation:	Y
						Fuel Cells:		Specialty Services:	Y		

TYPES OF BUSINESS:

Retail & Wholesale Propane Sales
Propane Marketing & Distribution
Logistics Services

BRANDS/DIVISIONS/AFFILIATES:

Inergy Propane, LLC
Stueben Gas & Storage
Inergy's West Coast Natural Gas Liquids
Inergy Midstream, LLC
Arlington Storage Company, LLC
Bath Storage Facility
Stagecoach Natural Gas Storage Facility
Liberty Propane LP

CONTACTS: *Note: Officers with more than one job title may be intentionally listed here more than once.*

John J. Sherman, CEO
Phillip L. Elbert, COO
Phillip L. Elbert, Pres.
R. Brooks Sherman, Jr., CFO/Exec. VP
Laura L. Ozenberger, General Counsel/Sr. VP
William R. Moler, Sr. VP-Natural Gas Midstream Oper.
Andrew L. Atterbury, Sr. VP-Corp. Dev.
Carl A. Hughes, Sr. VP-Bus. Dev.

Phone: 816-842-8181 **Fax:** 816-842-1904
Toll-Free: 877-446-3749
Address: 2 Brush Creek Blvd., Ste. 200, Kansas City, MO 64112 US

GROWTH PLANS/SPECIAL FEATURES:

Inergy LP, operating mainly through Inergy Propane, LLC, is a retail and wholesale propane marketing and distribution firm. The firm served approximately 700,000 retail customers in 28 states from 313 customer service centers. The company has an aggregate of approximately 31.1 million gallons of above-ground propane storage. Retail propane falls into four broad categories: residential, industrial, commercial and agricultural. Residential customers use propane primarily for space and water heating. In addition to Inergy's retail propane business, it operates a wholesale supply, marketing and distribution business that provides propane procurement, transportation and supply and price risk management services to its customer service centers, as well as to independent dealers, multistate marketers, petrochemical companies, refinery/gas processors and other natural gas liquids marketing/distribution companies in 40 states. The propane distribution operation consists principally of transporting propane to its customer service centers and other distribution areas and then to tanks located on its customers' premises. Inergy's midstream operations include Stagecoach natural gas storage facility, a liquefied petroleum gas storage facility and a natural gas liquids business; the Bath Storage Facility, a 1.7 million barrel salt cavern liquefied petroleum gas storage facility; Arlington Storage Company, LLC, which owns/operates Steuben Gas Storage Company and has development rights to Thomas Corners natural gas storage project. The company also owns US Salt, an industry-leading solution mining and salt production company. In January 2010, Inergy Propane, LLC acquired Liberty Propane, L.P.; and agreed to acquire the propane business of MGS Corporation. Also in January 2010, subsidiary Inergy Midstream, LLC agreed to acquire a natural gas storage facility and two related pipelines from New York State Electric & Gas Corporation. In August 2010, Inergy and its holding company, Inergy Holding, L.P., agreed to merge under the Inergy, LP name. In October 2010, the firm acquired natural gas storage facility Tres Palacios.

FINANCIALS: **Sales and profits are in thousands of dollars—add 000 to get the full amount. 2010 Note: Financial information for 2010 was not available for all companies at press time.**

2010 Sales: $	2010 Profits: $	**U.S. Stock Ticker: NRGY**
2009 Sales: $1,570,600	2009 Profits: $101,400	**Int'l Ticker:** Int'l Exchange:
2008 Sales: $1,878,900	2008 Profits: $65,100	Employees: 2,910
2007 Sales: $1,483,100	2007 Profits: $67,000	Fiscal Year Ends: 9/30
2006 Sales: $1,387,561	2006 Profits: $9,811	Parent Company:

SALARIES/BENEFITS:

Pension Plan:	ESOP Stock Plan:	Profit Sharing:	Top Exec. Salary: $350,000	Bonus: $350,000
Savings Plan: Y	Stock Purch. Plan:		Second Exec. Salary: $275,000	Bonus: $275,000

OTHER THOUGHTS:

Apparent Women Officers or Directors: 1
Hot Spot for Advancement for Women/Minorities:

LOCATIONS: ("Y" = Yes)

West:	Southwest:	Midwest:	Southeast:	Northeast:	International:
	Y	Y	Y	Y	

INPEX CORPORATION

www.inpex.co.jp

Industry Group Code: 211111 **Ranks within this company's industry group:** Sales: 44 Profits: 32

Exploration/Production:		Refining/Retailing:		Utilities:		Alternative Energy:		Specialty Services:		Energy Mktg./Other Svcs.	
Exploration:	Y	Refining:		Electric Utility:		Waste/Solar/Other:		Consulting/Eng.:		Energy Marketing:	Y
Production:	Y	Retailing:		Gas Utility:		Thermal/Steam:		Seismic:		Equipment/Machinery:	
Coal Production:		Convenience Stores:		Pipelines:	Y	Wind:		Drilling:		Oil Field Services:	
		Chemicals:		Water:		Hydro:		InfoTech:		Air/Shipping Transportation:	
						Fuel Cells:		Specialty Services:			

TYPES OF BUSINESS:

Production-Crude Oil
Production-Natural Gas
Oil & Gas Exploration
Natural Gas Distribution

BRANDS/DIVISIONS/AFFILIATES:

INPEX Holdings, Inc.
Teikoku Oil Co
Minami-Nagaoka Gas Field
Van Gogh Oil Field
Azeri-Chirag-Gunashli
Carabobo Project 3

CONTACTS:

Note: Officers with more than one job title may be intentionally listed here more than once.

Toshiaki Kitamura, Pres.
Sadafumi Tanigawa, Managing Exec. Officer-Sales
Yoshitsugu Takai, Managing Exec. Officer-Info. Systems & Materials
Kunio Kanamori, Sr. Managing Exec. Officer-Tech.
Yoshikazu Kurasawa, Gen. Mgr.-Legal Affairs
Shuhei Miyamoto, Gen. Mgr.-Corp. Strategy & Planning Div.
Kazuhiko Itano, Gen. Mgr.-Public Rel.
Kazuhiko Itano, Gen. Mgr.-Investor Rel.
Masahiro Murayama, Managing Exec. Officer-Finance & Acct.
Masaharu Sano, Sr. Managing Exec. Officer-America & Africa Bus.
Akinori Sakamoto, Managing Exec. Officer/Dir.-Pipeline Construction
Shigeru Usui, Sr. Managing Exec. Officer-Abu Dhabi Bus.
Kasaburo Tamura, Managing Exec. Officer-Sales
Naoki Kuroda, Chmn.
Seiji Yui, Sr. Managing Exec. Officer-Asia & Oceania

Phone: 81-3-5572-0200 **Fax:** 81-3-5572-0205
Toll-Free:
Address: Akasaka Biz Tower 5-3-1 Akasaka, Minato-ku, Tokyo, 107-6332 Japan

GROWTH PLANS/SPECIAL FEATURES:

INPEX Corporation, formerly INPEX Holdings, Inc., is one of Japan's largest oil and gas exploration, distribution, production and retail companies. Through its subsidiaries, the company develops onshore and offshore oil properties in several regions around the world, including Japan, Indonesia, Australia, the Caspian Sea, the Middle East, Africa and the Americas. INPEX is currently engaged in approximately 70 projects spanning 26 countries. The Minami-Nagaoka Gas Field, located in Japan and developed by INPEX, is responsible for approximately half of all Japanese gas production; gas from the field is piped to municipal gas companies and industrial customers in Japan, with annual sales volumes approaching 2 billion cubic meters. The company has net proved reserves of about 1.5 billion barrels of oil equivalent (BBOE), including 495 million BOE of natural gas. The firm produces approximately 405,000 BOE per day, constituting 218,000 barrels of oil and 187,000 BOE of natural gas. INPEX is in the process of developing two of the largest liquid natural gas (LNG) projects worldwide in Australia and Indonesia; when completed, it estimates that these projects will produce the equivalent of about 20% of Japan's currently imported LNG. The Japanese government owns 29.4% of INPEX. Other major shareholders include Japan Petroleum Exploration Co., Ltd.; Mitsui Oil Exploration Co.; and Mitsubishi Corporation. Recently, the firm has acquired interests in areas adjacent to the Van Gogh Oil Field, offshore Western Australia; the Block BM-ES-23, offshore Brazil; and the Azeri-Chirag-Gunashli oilfield development in the Caspian Sea. It also recently sold certain interests offshore Java and Sumatra. In August 2009, INPEX announced a joint venture for the development of an oilfield in the southern Iraqi city of Nassiriyah. In May 2010, INPEX and a consortium including Mitsubishi, Chevron and Suelopetrol signed a joint venture agreement for the development of Carabobo Project 3 in Venezuela.

FINANCIALS:

Sales and profits are in thousands of dollars—add 000 to get the full amount. 2010 Note: Financial information for 2010 was not available for all companies at press time.

2010 Sales: $	2010 Profits: $	**U.S. Stock Ticker:**
2009 Sales: $12,166,800	2009 Profits: $1,640,030	**Int'l Ticker: 1605** Int'l Exchange: Tokyo-TSE
2008 Sales: $13,600,400	2008 Profits: $1,958,660	Employees:
2007 Sales: $8,250,000	2007 Profits: $1,400,000	Fiscal Year Ends: 3/31
2006 Sales: $1,450,600	2006 Profits: $	Parent Company:

SALARIES/BENEFITS:

Pension Plan:	ESOP Stock Plan:	Profit Sharing:	Top Exec. Salary: $	Bonus: $
Savings Plan:	Stock Purch. Plan:		Second Exec. Salary: $	Bonus: $

OTHER THOUGHTS:

Apparent Women Officers or Directors:
Hot Spot for Advancement for Women/Minorities:

LOCATIONS: ("Y" = Yes)

West:	Southwest:	Midwest:	Southeast:	Northeast:	International:
	Y				Y

INTEGRYS ENERGY GROUP INC

www.integrysgroup.com

Industry Group Code: 221 **Ranks within this company's industry group:** Sales: 25 Profits: 49

Exploration/Production:		Refining/Retailing:		Utilities:		Alternative Energy:		Specialty Services:		Energy Mktg./Other Svcs.	
Exploration:		Refining:		Electric Utility:	Y	Waste/Solar/Other:	Y	Consulting/Eng.:		Energy Marketing:	
Production:		Retailing:		Gas Utility:	Y	Thermal/Steam:		Seismic:		Equipment/Machinery:	
Coal Production:		Convenience Stores:		Pipelines:		Wind:	Y	Drilling:		Oil Field Services:	
		Chemicals:		Water:		Hydro:	Y	InfoTech:		Air/Shipping Transportation:	
						Fuel Cells:		Specialty Services:			

TYPES OF BUSINESS:

Utilities-Electricity & Natural Gas
Wind, Hydro & Nuclear Power Generation

BRANDS/DIVISIONS/AFFILIATES:

WPS Resources Corp.
Wisconsin Public Service Corp.
Michigan Gas Utilities Corp.
Minnesota Energy Resources Corp.
Upper Peninsula Power Co.
Integrys Energy Services, Inc.
Peoples Gas Light and Coke Company (The)
WPS Investments, LLC

CONTACTS:

Note: Officers with more than one job title may be intentionally listed here more than once.

Charlie A. Schrock, CEO
Charlie A. Schrock, Pres.
Joseph P. O'Leary, CFO/Sr. VP
William D. Laasko, VP-Human Resources
Barth J. Wolf, Chief Legal Officer/Corp. Sec./VP
Phillip M. Mikulsky, Exec. VP-Corp. Dev. & Shared Svcs.
James Schott, VP-External Affairs
Diane L. Ford, Controller/VP
Bradley A. Johnson, Treas./VP
Mark A. Radtke, Pres./CEO-Integrys Energy Services
Lawrence T. Borgard, Pres./COO-Utilities
Charlie A. Schrock, Chmn.

Phone: 312-228-5400	**Fax:**
Toll-Free: 800-699-1269	
Address: 130 E. Randolph Dr., Chicago, IL 60601 US	

GROWTH PLANS/SPECIAL FEATURES:

Integrys Energy Group, Inc. is a holding company for regulated utility and non-regulated business units. The firm operates in four business segments: Natural Gas Utility, Electric Utility; Integrys Energy Services and Electric Transmission Investment. The Natural Gas Utility segment provides regulated natural gas utility service in the areas around Chicago; northeastern Wisconsin; Michigan's Upper Peninsula; and parts of Minnesota. The company provides natural gas utility service to approximately 1.7 million residential, commercial, industrial and transportation customers. This segment includes the natural gas operations of subsidiaries Wisconsin Public Service Corp. (WPS); Michigan Gas Utilities Corp. (MGU); Minnesota Energy Resources Corp. (MERC); The Peoples Gas Light and Coke Company (PGL); and North Shore Gas Company (NSG). The Electrical Utility segment, which operates through WPS and Upper Peninsula Power Co. (UPPCO), provides wholesale electric service to municipal utilities, electric cooperatives, energy marketers, other investor-owned utilities and municipal joint action agencies. WPS generates and distributes electric energy in northeastern Wisconsin and Michigan's Upper Peninsula; UPPCO provides electric energy in the Upper Peninsula. The Integrys Energy Services segment consists of subsidiary Integrys Energy Services, Inc., a diversified non-regulated natural gas and electric power supply and services company that serves residential, commercial, industrial and wholesale customers in certain markets in the U.S. The Electric Transmission Investment segment consists of WPS Investments, LLC's 34% ownership interest in ATC, a federally regulated electric transmission company with operations in Wisconsin, Michigan, Minnesota and Illinois. WPS Investments is 84.5% owned by Integrys Energy Group, 12.8% by WPS and 2.7% by UPPCO.

Employees are offered medical, dental and vision insurance; a pre-tax spending accounts; disability coverage; a 401(k) plan; an employee stock ownership plan; life insurance; credit union membership; tuition assistance; relocation assistance; and an employee assistance program.

FINANCIALS:

Sales and profits are in thousands of dollars—add 000 to get the full amount. 2010 Note: Financial information for 2010 was not available for all companies at press time.

2010 Sales: $	2010 Profits: $	**U.S. Stock Ticker: TEG**
2009 Sales: $7,499,800	2009 Profits: $-68,800	**Int'l Ticker:** Int'l Exchange:
2008 Sales: $14,047,800	2008 Profits: $129,500	Employees: 5,025
2007 Sales: $10,292,400	2007 Profits: $181,100	Fiscal Year Ends: 12/31
2006 Sales: $6,890,700	2006 Profits: $151,600	Parent Company:

SALARIES/BENEFITS:

Pension Plan:	ESOP Stock Plan: Y	Profit Sharing:	Top Exec. Salary: $1,090,385	Bonus: $1,362,981
Savings Plan: Y	Stock Purch. Plan:		Second Exec. Salary: $806,519	Bonus: $818,796

OTHER THOUGHTS:

Apparent Women Officers or Directors: 3
Hot Spot for Advancement for Women/Minorities: Y

LOCATIONS: ("Y" = Yes)

West:	Southwest:	Midwest:	Southeast:	Northeast:	International:
Y	Y	Y	Y	Y	Y

ITC HOLDINGS CORP

www.itc-holdings.com

Industry Group Code: 2211 **Ranks within this company's industry group:** Sales: 46 Profits: 38

Exploration/Production:		Refining/Retailing:		Utilities:		Alternative Energy:		Specialty Services:		Energy Mktg./Other Svcs.	
Exploration:		Refining:		Electric Utility:	Y	Waste/Solar/Other:		Consulting/Eng.:		Energy Marketing:	
Production:		Retailing:		Gas Utility:		Thermal/Steam:		Seismic:		Equipment/Machinery:	
Coal Production:		Convenience Stores:		Pipelines:		Wind:		Drilling:		Oil Field Services:	
		Chemicals:		Water:		Hydro:		InfoTech:		Air/Shipping Transportation:	
						Fuel Cells:		Specialty Services:			

TYPES OF BUSINESS:

Electric Utility
Electric Transmission
Infrastructure Maintenance

BRANDS/DIVISIONS/AFFILIATES:

ITCTransmission
Michigan Electric Transmission Company LLC (METC)
ITC Midwest
ITC Grid Development LLC
ITC Great Plains
Green Power Express

CONTACTS: *Note: Officers with more than one job title may be intentionally listed here more than once.*

Joseph L. Welch, CEO
Jon E. Jipping, COO/Exec. VP
Joseph L. Welch, Pres.
Cameron M. Bready, CFO
Denis Y. DesRosiers, CIO/VP-IT & Facilities
Daniel J. Oginsky, General Counsel/Sr. VP
Elizabeth A. Howell, VP-Oper.
Gregory Ioanidis, VP-Bus. Strategy
Cameron M. Bready, Treas./Sr. VP
Edward M. Rahill, Sr. VP/Pres., ITC Grid Dev.
Joseph R. Dudak, VP-Major Contracts & Special Projects
Linda H. Blair, Chief Bus. Officer/Exec. VP
Terry S. Harvill, VP-Energy Policy
Joseph L. Welch, Chmn.

Phone: 248-946-3000 | **Fax:**
Toll-Free: 877-482-4829
Address: 27175 Energy Way, Novi, MI 48377 US

GROWTH PLANS/SPECIAL FEATURES:

ITC Holdings Corp. is an electricity holding company. The firm owns ITCTransmission; Michigan Electric Transmission Company LLC (METC); and ITC Midwest, operating subsidiaries engaged in the transmission of electricity over an area of nearly 80,000 square miles in five states in the Midwestern U.S. The firm's subsidiaries operate, maintain and invest in approximately 15,000 circuit miles of overhead and underground transmission lines, allowing power from generating stations to be transmitted to local distribution systems, either entirely through ITC's systems or in conjunction with neighboring transmission systems. The company's infrastructure carries more than 25,000 megawatts (MW) of electric power. Together, ITCTransmission, METC and ITC Midwest serve a population of over 13 million people. These subsidiaries' operations primarily consist of maintaining, improving and expanding transmission systems to meet customers' ongoing needs; scheduling outages to allow for maintenance and construction; balancing electricity generation and demand; maintaining system voltages and monitoring flows over transmission lines and other facilities; and providing engineering, design and construction services for capital, operation and maintenance work. ITC Holdings also maintains subsidiaries ITC Grid Development LLC and ITC Great Plains, the latter of which was established to manage and invest in transmission infrastructure in Kansas. The company's Green Power Express project consists of a network of transmission lines designed to facilitate the movement of 12,000 MW of power from wind-abundant areas in North Dakota, South Dakota, Minnesota and Iowa to Midwest load centers that demand renewable energy.

The firm offers employees medical, dental and vision insurance; flexible spending accounts; life insurance; travel insurance; disability coverage; educational assistance; adoption assistance; and retirement plans.

FINANCIALS: **Sales and profits are in thousands of dollars—add 000 to get the full amount. 2010 Note: Financial information for 2010 was not available for all companies at press time.**

2010 Sales: $	2010 Profits: $	**U.S. Stock Ticker: ITC**
2009 Sales: $621,015	2009 Profits: $130,900	**Int'l Ticker:** Int'l Exchange:
2008 Sales: $617,877	2008 Profits: $109,208	Employees: 413
2007 Sales: $426,249	2007 Profits: $73,296	Fiscal Year Ends: 12/31
2006 Sales: $223,622	2006 Profits: $33,223	Parent Company:

SALARIES/BENEFITS:

Pension Plan: Y	ESOP Stock Plan:	Profit Sharing:	Top Exec. Salary: $737,827	Bonus: $2,652,744
Savings Plan:	Stock Purch. Plan:		Second Exec. Salary: $345,323	Bonus: $ 747

OTHER THOUGHTS:

Apparent Women Officers or Directors: 5
Hot Spot for Advancement for Women/Minorities: Y

LOCATIONS: ("Y" = Yes)

West:	Southwest:	Midwest:	Southeast:	Northeast:	International:
		Y			

ITRON INC

www.itron.com

Industry Group Code: 334220 **Ranks within this company's industry group:** Sales: 1 Profits: 1

Exploration/Production:		Refining/Retailing:		Utilities:		Alternative Energy:		Specialty Services:		Energy Mktg./Other Svcs.	
Exploration:		Refining:		Electric Utility:		Waste/Solar/Other:		Consulting/Eng.:	Y	Energy Marketing:	
Production:		Retailing:		Gas Utility:		Thermal/Steam:		Seismic:		Equipment/Machinery:	
Coal Production:		Convenience Stores:		Pipelines:		Wind:		Drilling:		Oil Field Services:	
		Chemicals:		Water:		Hydro:		InfoTech:	Y	Air/Shipping Transportation:	
						Fuel Cells:		Specialty Services:	Y		

TYPES OF BUSINESS:

Wireless Meter Reading Transmitters
Data Collection Systems & Software
Energy Information Management
Consulting Services

BRANDS/DIVISIONS/AFFILIATES:

OpenWay
Centron
METRIS Remote Disconnect
Flostar
Woltex
Sentinel
Everblu
Pulsadis

CONTACTS:

Note: Officers with more than one job title may be intentionally listed here more than once.

Malcom Unsworth, CEO
Malcom Unsworth, Pres.
Steven M. Helmbrecht, CFO/Sr. VP
Russell E. Vanos, VP-Mktg.
Chuck McAtee, CIO/VP-IT
John Holleran, General Counsel/Sr. VP/Corp. Sec.
Philip Mezey, Sr. VP/COO-North America
Ranny Dwiggins, VP-Investor Rel.
Jared Serff, VP-Competitive Resources
Jon E. Eliassen, Chmn.
Marcel Regnier, Sr. VP/COO-Int'l

Phone: 509-924-9900	**Fax:** 509-891-3355
Toll-Free: 866-635-5461	
Address: 2111 N. Molter Rd., Liberty Lake, WA 99019 US	

GROWTH PLANS/SPECIAL FEATURES:

Itron, Inc. provides products and services to electric, gas and water utilities worldwide to the increase in performance of the delivery and use of energy and water. Itron has two operating segments: Itron North America and Itron International Itron North America generates the majority of its revenue in the U.S. and Canada, offering electric meters, automated meter reading (AMR), advanced metering infrastructure (AMI) systems, software and services. The firm's major AMI, OpenWay, is sold within this segment and is designed for real-time energy communication to thermostats, enabling customers to monitor energy usage. Openway products also provide two-way communication to residential and commercial electricity and gas meters. Other brands in this segment include Itron, Centron, Endpoint-Link, Quantum, Sentinel and Service-Link. Itron International operates primarily in Europe, Africa, South American and Asia/Pacific and offers electric, gas and water meters, AMR and AMI systems, software and services. This segment's trademarks include Actaris, Cyble, Flostar, Woltex, Echo, Everblu, Gallys, Delta, Corus and Pulsadis. In May 2010, the company launched METRIS Remote Disconnect (RD) residential meter, one of North America's first gas meter's containing an integrated remote disconnect valve.

The firm offers its employees medical, dental and vision insurance; disability coverage; business travel and accident insurance; AD&D insurance; an employee assistance program; a 401(k) plan; an employee stock purchase plan; flexible spending accounts; and educational reimbursement.

FINANCIALS:

Sales and profits are in thousands of dollars—add 000 to get the full amount. 2010 Note: Financial information for 2010 was not available for all companies at press time.

2010 Sales: $	2010 Profits: $	**U.S. Stock Ticker: ITRI**
2009 Sales: $1,687,447	2009 Profits: $-2,249	**Int'l Ticker:** Int'l Exchange:
2008 Sales: $1,909,613	2008 Profits: $28,059	Employees: 9,000
2007 Sales: $1,464,048	2007 Profits: $-16,144	Fiscal Year Ends: 12/31
2006 Sales: $644,042	2006 Profits: $33,759	Parent Company:

SALARIES/BENEFITS:

Pension Plan:	ESOP Stock Plan:	Profit Sharing:	Top Exec. Salary: $617,000	Bonus: $
Savings Plan: Y	Stock Purch. Plan: Y		Second Exec. Salary: $526,538	Bonus: $

OTHER THOUGHTS:

Apparent Women Officers or Directors: 2
Hot Spot for Advancement for Women/Minorities: Y

LOCATIONS: ("Y" = Yes)

West:	Southwest:	Midwest:	Southeast:	Northeast:	International:
Y		Y		Y	Y

JOHN WOOD GROUP PLC

www.woodgroup.com

Industry Group Code: 211111 **Ranks within this company's industry group:** Sales: 58 Profits: 59

Exploration/Production:		Refining/Retailing:		Utilities:		Alternative Energy:		Specialty Services:		Energy Mktg./Other Svcs.	
Exploration:		Refining:		Electric Utility:		Waste/Solar/Other:		Consulting/Eng.:	Y	Energy Marketing:	
Production:		Retailing:		Gas Utility:		Thermal/Steam:		Seismic:		Equipment/Machinery:	Y
Coal Production:		Convenience Stores:		Pipelines:		Wind:		Drilling:	Y	Oil Field Services:	Y
		Chemicals:		Water:		Hydro:		InfoTech:		Air/Shipping Transportation:	
						Fuel Cells:		Specialty Services:	Y		

TYPES OF BUSINESS:

Oil Field Services
Engineering & Project Management Services
Submersible Pumps, Pressure Controls & Logging Services
Gas Turbine Maintenance, Repair & Overhaul

BRANDS/DIVISIONS/AFFILIATES:

Shanahan Engineering
SgurrEnergy Ltd.

CONTACTS:

Note: Officers with more than one job title may be intentionally listed here more than once.

Allister G. Langlands, CEO
Alan G. Semple, Group Dir.-Finance
Les Thomas, Group Dir.-Prod. Facilities
Mike Straughen, Group Dir.-Eng.
Mark H. Papworth, Group Dir./CEO-Gas Turbine Svcs. Div.
Jim Renfroe, Group Dir.-Well Support Div.
Ian Wood, Chmn.

Phone: 44-1224-851-000 **Fax:** 44-1224-851-474
Toll-Free:
Address: John Wood House, Greenwell Rd., Aberdeen, AB12 3AX UK

GROWTH PLANS/SPECIAL FEATURES:

John Wood Group PLC is an international energy services company. The firm provides services to oil, gas and power generation customers. Headquartered in Aberdeen, Scotland, with primary U.S. offices in Houston, Texas, the firm operates through dozens of subsidiaries and affiliate companies in 50 countries. The company is active globally in greenfield engineering design, subsea engineering, offshore pipeline design, clean fuel modifications, refinery upgrades, construction management services, commissioning, operations management, maintenance management, production enhancement, abandonment services and brownfield engineering. Wood Group operates through three divisions: engineering and production facilities; well support; and gas turbine services. The engineering and production division, representing approximately 66% of 2009 revenue, provides engineering design and project management services for the development of new offshore and onshore oil and gas fields. This division also offers enhancement, modification, operation and maintenance of existing oil and gas facilities. The well support division, 17% of 2009 revenue, provides products and services designed to enhance production rates and increase economic recovery from oil and gas reservoirs. This division operates through three sub-segments: electric submersible pumps, pressure control and logging services. The gas turbine services division, also representing 17% of 2009 revenue, acts as an aftermarket provider of maintenance, repair and overhaul services for industrial gas and steam turbines; generators and motors; controls; pumps; compressors; power turbines; and industrial and aero gas turbine accessories and components. During 2009, North America represented roughly 40% of revenues and Europe represented 32%, while sales in the rest of the world made up 28%. In December 2009, the firm acquired Dublin, Ireland-based Shanahan Engineering, a provider of services related to power plant installation, commissioning and maintenance. In September 2010, the company acquired a significant stake in Glasgow-based SgurrEnergy Ltd., a renewable energy consulting firm involved in wind farm development in Europe, North America and Asia.

FINANCIALS:

Sales and profits are in thousands of dollars—add 000 to get the full amount. 2010 Note: Financial information for 2010 was not available for all companies at press time.

2010 Sales: $	2010 Profits: $	**U.S. Stock Ticker:**
2009 Sales: $4,927,100	2009 Profits: $163,200	**Int'l Ticker: WG** Int'l Exchange: London-LSE
2008 Sales: $5,243,100	2008 Profits: $441,000	Employees: 28,200
2007 Sales: $4,432,700	2007 Profits: $318,400	Fiscal Year Ends: 12/31
2006 Sales: $3,468,800	2006 Profits: $121,200	Parent Company:

SALARIES/BENEFITS:

Pension Plan:	ESOP Stock Plan:	Profit Sharing:	Top Exec. Salary: $	Bonus: $
Savings Plan:	Stock Purch. Plan:		Second Exec. Salary: $	Bonus: $

OTHER THOUGHTS:

Apparent Women Officers or Directors:
Hot Spot for Advancement for Women/Minorities:

LOCATIONS: ("Y" = Yes)

West:	Southwest:	Midwest:	Southeast:	Northeast:	International:
Y	Y	Y	Y	Y	Y

JOY GLOBAL INC

www.joyglobal.com

Industry Group Code: 33313 **Ranks within this company's industry group:** Sales: 2 Profits: 2

Exploration/Production:		**Refining/Retailing:**		**Utilities:**		**Alternative Energy:**		**Specialty Services:**		**Energy Mktg./Other Svcs.**	
Exploration:		Refining:		Electric Utility:		Waste/Solar/Other:		Consulting/Eng.:		Energy Marketing:	
Production:		Retailing:		Gas Utility:		Thermal/Steam:		Seismic:		Equipment/Machinery:	Y
Coal Production:		Convenience Stores:		Pipelines:		Wind:		Drilling:		Oil Field Services:	
		Chemicals:		Water:		Hydro:		InfoTech:		Air/Shipping Transportation:	
						Fuel Cells:		Specialty Services:			

TYPES OF BUSINESS:

Machinery-Mining & Oil & Gas Field, Manufacturing
Mining Machinery Service & Support

BRANDS/DIVISIONS/AFFILIATES:

Joy Mining Machinery
P&H Mining Equipment
MinePro Services

CONTACTS:

Note: Officers with more than one job title may be intentionally listed here more than once.

Michael W. Sutherlin, CEO
Michael W. Sutherlin, Pres.
Michael S. Olsen, CFO/Exec. VP
Lou Boltik, Dir.-Mktg. Comm.
Dennis R. Winkleman, Exec. VP-Human Resources
Sean D. Major, General Counsel/Sec./Exec. VP
Greg Chaffin, Dir.-Comm.
Michael S. Olsen, Treas.
Randal W. Baker, Exec. VP/COO/Pres., P&H Mining Equipment
Edward L. Doheny, Exec. VP/COO/Pres., Joy Mining Machinery
Steven L. Gerard, Chmn.

Phone: 414-319-8500	**Fax:** 414-319-8520
Toll-Free:	
Address: 100 E. Wisconsin Ave., Ste. 2780, Milwaukee, WI 53202 US	

GROWTH PLANS/SPECIAL FEATURES:

Joy Global, Inc. is a manufacturer and servicer of high-productivity mining equipment. The company's equipment is used to mine coal, copper, iron ore, oil sands and other minerals. Joy Global operates in two business segments: Joy Mining Machinery and P&H Mining Equipment. Joy Mining Machinery is one of the world's largest producers of underground mining machinery for the extraction of coal and other bedded materials. It maintains facilities in Australia, South Africa, the U.K. and the U.S., as well as sales and service facilities in China, India, Poland and Russia. Its products include continuous miners, longwall shearers, powered roof supports, shuttle cars, flexible conveyor trains and complete longwall mining systems. The majority of Joy Mining Machinery's underground mining business relates to coal. P&H Mining Equipment (P&H) is the surface mining equipment arm of the company, producing electric mining shovels, rotary blasthole drills and walking draglines for open-pit mining operations. P&H maintains facilities in Australia, Brazil, Canada, Chile, China, South Africa and the U.S., with sales offices in India, Mexico, Peru, Russia, the U.K. and Venezuela. It provides parts and services to mines through its MinePro Services distribution group. In addition, P&H sells used electric mining shovels in some markets.

FINANCIALS:

Sales and profits are in thousands of dollars—add 000 to get the full amount. 2010 Note: Financial information for 2010 was not available for all companies at press time.

2010 Sales: $	2010 Profits: $	**U.S. Stock Ticker: JOYG**
2009 Sales: $3,598,314	2009 Profits: $454,650	**Int'l Ticker:** Int'l Exchange:
2008 Sales: $3,418,934	2008 Profits: $374,278	Employees: 11,300
2007 Sales: $2,547,322	2007 Profits: $279,784	Fiscal Year Ends: 10/31
2006 Sales: $2,401,710	2006 Profits: $416,421	Parent Company:

SALARIES/BENEFITS:

Pension Plan:	ESOP Stock Plan:	Profit Sharing:	Top Exec. Salary: $828,333	Bonus: $1,574,433
Savings Plan:	Stock Purch. Plan:		Second Exec. Salary: $469,021	Bonus: $588,999

OTHER THOUGHTS:

Apparent Women Officers or Directors:
Hot Spot for Advancement for Women/Minorities:

LOCATIONS: ("Y" = Yes)

West:	Southwest:	Midwest:	Southeast:	Northeast:	International:
		Y			Y

JSC GAZPROM NEFT

www.gazprom-neft.com

Industry Group Code: 211111 **Ranks within this company's industry group:** Sales: 28 Profits: 23

Exploration/Production:		Refining/Retailing:		Utilities:		Alternative Energy:		Specialty Services:		Energy Mktg./Other Svcs.	
Exploration:	Y	Refining:	Y	Electric Utility:		Waste/Solar/Other:		Consulting/Eng.:		Energy Marketing:	Y
Production:	Y	Retailing:	Y	Gas Utility:		Thermal/Steam:		Seismic:	Y	Equipment/Machinery:	
Coal Production:		Convenience Stores:	Y	Pipelines:		Wind:		Drilling:		Oil Field Services:	Y
		Chemicals:		Water:		Hydro:		InfoTech:		Air/Shipping Transportation:	
						Fuel Cells:		Specialty Services:			

TYPES OF BUSINESS:

Oil & Gas Exploration & Production
Oil Refining & Petrochemicals
Oil Marketing & Sales
Geophysical Services, Engineering & Seismic Data
Banking
Media & Sports
Electricity Production & Nuclear Energy
Insurance, Aviation and Agriculture

BRANDS/DIVISIONS/AFFILIATES:

Sibneft
OAO Gazprom
Sibneft-Noyabrskneftgas
Noyabrskneftegas
Omsk Refinery
Sibneft Oil Trade (Siboil)
Chevron Neftegaz
Northern Taiga Neftegas Ltd.

CONTACTS: *Note: Officers with more than one job title may be intentionally listed here more than once.*

Alexander Dyukov, CEO
Vadim Yakovlev, CFO
Anatoly Cherner, Deputy CEO-Sales
Boris Zilbermints, Deputy CEO-Exploration & Prod.
Vitaliy Baranov, Deputy CEO-Admin.
Elena A. Ilyukhina, Deputy CEO-Legal & Corp. Affairs
Vladislav Baryshnikov, Deputy CEO-Int'l Bus. Dev.
Alexander Dybal, Deputy CEO-Corp. Comm.
Alexei B. Miller, Chmn.
Kirill Kravchenko, Deputy CEO-Foreign Asset Mgmt.
Anatoly Cherner, Deputy CEO-Logistics & Processing

Phone: 7-495-777-3152 **Fax:** 7-495-777-3151
Toll-Free:
Address: Kursovoy Pereulok 4, Moscow, 119034 Russia

GROWTH PLANS/SPECIAL FEATURES:

JSC Gazprom Neft, formerly Sibneft, is an integrated oil company that explores for, produces, refines and markets oil in Russia. Gazprom holds approximately 66 oilfield exploration and development licenses in the Yamal-Nenets and Khanti-Mansiisk autonomous regions, as well as in the Omsk and Tomsk regions and in Chukotka. Approximately 80% of the company's total reserves are concentrated in the Noyabrsk area, and four out of five of the company's largest fields are licensed to Sibneft-Noyabrskneftgas, which account for about 46% of the company's reserves. The firm has proven reserves of over 7.4 billion barrels of oil, much of which is culled from its exploration areas in the Noyabrsk area of western Siberia. The company's subsidiary Noyabrskneftegas handles a major portion of its oil exploration, drilling and production operations. Gazprom Neft's major refining operations are conducted at the Omsk Refinery, a facility considered to be one of the most modern in Russia, capable of refining 19.5 million tons of oil per year. It then exports approximately 20% of its refined product and about 40% of its crude oil production, all through subsidiary Sibneft Oil Trade (Siboil). Domestically, the company has a retail network of about 865 outlets. Gazprom supplies roughly 26% of the gas used in Europe through a large system of pipelines. In addition to oil and gas production, the firm is involved in commercial aviation, engineering, the Zenit St. Petersburg football club, electricity production (including nuclear), insurance, banking and agriculture. The firm is 56%-owned by Gazprom OAO. In July 2010, the company announced a joint venture with NOVATEK, OOO Yamal Razvitye, in order to develop potential hydrocarbon assets in the Yamal-Nenets Autonomous Region. In October 2010, Gazprom Neft began construction of a new production complex at its Omsk Lubricants Plant.

FINANCIALS: **Sales and profits are in thousands of dollars—add 000 to get the full amount. 2010 Note: Financial information for 2010 was not available for all companies at press time.**

2010 Sales: $	2010 Profits: $	**U.S. Stock Ticker:**
2009 Sales: $24,166,000	2009 Profits: $3,081,000	**Int'l Ticker: SIBN** Int'l Exchange: Moscow-MICEX
2008 Sales: $33,870,000	2008 Profits: $4,697,000	Employees:
2007 Sales: $22,768,000	2007 Profits: $4,143,000	Fiscal Year Ends: 12/31
2006 Sales: $	2006 Profits: $	Parent Company:

SALARIES/BENEFITS:

Pension Plan:	ESOP Stock Plan:	Profit Sharing:	Top Exec. Salary: $	Bonus: $
Savings Plan:	Stock Purch. Plan:		Second Exec. Salary: $	Bonus: $

OTHER THOUGHTS:

Apparent Women Officers or Directors: 1
Hot Spot for Advancement for Women/Minorities:

LOCATIONS: ("Y" = Yes)

West:	Southwest:	Midwest:	Southeast:	Northeast:	International:
					Y

JX HOLDINGS INC

www.hd.jx-group.co.jp

Industry Group Code: 324110 **Ranks within this company's industry group:** Sales: Profits:

Exploration/Production:		**Refining/Retailing:**		**Utilities:**		**Alternative Energy:**		**Specialty Services:**		**Energy Mktg./Other Svcs.**	
Exploration:	Y	Refining:	Y	Electric Utility:		Waste/Solar/Other:		Consulting/Eng.:		Energy Marketing:	
Production:	Y	Retailing:	Y	Gas Utility:		Thermal/Steam:		Seismic:		Equipment/Machinery:	
Coal Production:		Convenience Stores:	Y	Pipelines:		Wind:		Drilling:		Oil Field Services:	
		Chemicals:		Water:		Hydro:		InfoTech:		Air/Shipping Transportation:	
						Fuel Cells:		Specialty Services:	Y		

TYPES OF BUSINESS:

Petroleum Refining & Marketing
Metals Mining & Processing
Petroleum Products
Power Generation
Industrial Waste Treatment

BRANDS/DIVISIONS/AFFILIATES:

JX Nippon Oil & Energy
JX Nippon Oil & Gas Exploration
JX Nippon Mining & Metals
Nippon Oil Corporation
Nippon Mining Holdings, Inc.

CONTACTS: *Note: Officers with more than one job title may be intentionally listed here more than once.*

Mitsunori Takahagi, Pres.
Shigeo Hirai, Exec. VP
Kiyonobu Sugiuchi, Sr. VP
Yukio Yamagata, Sr. VP
Kazuo Kagami, Sr. VP
Shinji Nishio, Chmn.

Phone: 81-3-6275-5006 **Fax:** 81-3-3276-1245
Toll-Free:
Address: 6-3 Otemachi 2-chome, Chiyoda-ku, Tokyo, 100-8161 Japan

GROWTH PLANS/SPECIAL FEATURES:

JX Holdings, Inc., based in Japan, is a holding company that engages in petroleum processing, refining and retailing, power generation and fuel cell development through its subsidiaries. JX Holdings was created in April 2010 by Nippon Oil Corp. and Nippon Mining Holdings, Inc., after which Nippon Oil and Nippon Mining Holdings, along with other group subsidiaries, were reorganized into three new principal subsidiaries. JX Holdings' primary subsidiaries are: JX Nippon Oil & Energy; JX Nippon Oil & Gas Exploration; and JX Nippon Mining & Metals. JX Nippon Oil & Energy refines and sells petrochemical products, including gasoline, kerosene and lubricants; imports and sells liquefied petroleum gas (LPG) and liquefied natural gas (LNG); and generates and sells electricity. The company is currently pursuing a strategy to consolidate its service stations and credit cards under the ENEOS brand name. JX Nippon Oil & Gas Exploration is an oil and natural gas exploration and production company operating in Japan and internationally in the North Sea, the Middle East, Africa, the Gulf of Mexico, Canada, Southeast Asia and Oceania. Its primary activities include exploration for and development of oil, natural gas and other mineral resources; and the extraction, processing, storage, sale and shipment of petroleum, natural gas, minerals and related products. JX Nippon Mining & Metals' activities include mining, development, smelting, refining and marketing of non-ferrous metals, such as copper, gold and silver; the manufacture of treated rolled copper foils and thin film materials, such as sputtering targets, surface treatment agents and semiconductor materials; the manufacture of precision-rolled copper, copper alloy and special steel products, as well as gold-plated products; and the recycle and treatment of non-ferrous metal materials and industrial waste. In April 2010, JX Holdings was created through a joint-stock transfer between Nippon Oil and Nippon Mining Holdings.

FINANCIALS: **Sales and profits are in thousands of dollars—add 000 to get the full amount. 2010 Note: Financial information for 2010 was not available for all companies at press time.**

2010 Sales: $	2010 Profits: $	**U.S. Stock Ticker:**
2009 Sales: $	2009 Profits: $	**Int'l Ticker: 5020** Int'l Exchange: Tokyo-TSE
2008 Sales: $	2008 Profits: $	Employees:
2007 Sales: $	2007 Profits: $	Fiscal Year Ends: 3/31
2006 Sales: $	2006 Profits: $	Parent Company:

SALARIES/BENEFITS:

Pension Plan:	ESOP Stock Plan:	Profit Sharing:	Top Exec. Salary: $	Bonus: $
Savings Plan:	Stock Purch. Plan:		Second Exec. Salary: $	Bonus: $

OTHER THOUGHTS:

Apparent Women Officers or Directors:
Hot Spot for Advancement for Women/Minorities:

LOCATIONS: ("Y" = Yes)

West:	Southwest:	Midwest:	Southeast:	Northeast:	International:
					Y

JX NIPPON MINING & METALS CORPORATION www.nmm.jx-group.co.jp

Industry Group Code: 324110 **Ranks within this company's industry group:** Sales: 5 Profits: 26

Exploration/Production:		Refining/Retailing:		Utilities:		Alternative Energy:		Specialty Services:		Energy Mktg./Other Svcs.	
Exploration:		Refining:	Y	Electric Utility:		Waste/Solar/Other:		Consulting/Eng.:		Energy Marketing:	
Production:		Retailing:		Gas Utility:		Thermal/Steam:		Seismic:		Equipment/Machinery:	
Coal Production:		Convenience Stores:		Pipelines:		Wind:		Drilling:		Oil Field Services:	
		Chemicals:		Water:		Hydro:		InfoTech:		Air/Shipping Transportation:	
						Fuel Cells:		Specialty Services:	Y		

TYPES OF BUSINESS:

Mining-Copper, Gold & Silver
Electronic Materials
Industrial Waste Treatment Services
Smelting-Copper
Copper Products

BRANDS/DIVISIONS/AFFILIATES:

JX Holdings Inc
Nippon Oil Corporation
Nippon Mining Holdings, Inc.
Nippon Mining & Metals Co., Ltd.
Pan Pacific Copper Co., Ltd.

CONTACTS:

Note: Officers with more than one job title may be intentionally listed here more than once.

Masanori Okada, CEO
Masanori Okada, Pres.
Yoshimasa Adachi, Deputy CEO
Hiroshi Matsui, Deputy CEO
Mitsunori Takahagi, Pres., JX Holdings, Inc.
Shinji Nishio, Chmn.-JX Holdings, Inc.

Phone: 81-3-5299-7000 **Fax:**

Toll-Free:

Address: 6-3, Otemachi 2-chome, Chiyoda-ku, Tokyo, 100-0004 Japan

GROWTH PLANS/SPECIAL FEATURES:

JX Nippon Mining & Metals Corporation, formerly Nippon Mining Holdings, Inc. (NMH), develops, mines and manufactures metal materials and various metal-based products, as well as providing industrial waste treatment services. The firm operates in eight business segments: resources development; smelting and refining; copper foil; thin film materials; precision rolled products; precision fabricated products; recycling and environmental service; and technology development. The resources development segment focuses on developing long-term and high-quality resources, principally copper, through five development projects in Chile and Peru. The smelting and refining segment conducts its operations through subsidiary Pan Pacific Copper Co., Ltd. Its copper smelting production capacity is approximately 450,000 tons annually, with an equivalent annual capacity for refined copper. The copper foil segment produces electro-deposited copper foil and treated rolled copper foil for use in circuit boards, mobile phones and other electronics. The thin film materials segment is a manufacturer of sputtering targets, a type of thin-film forming material used in semiconductors, transparent conductive films for flat panel displays (FPDs), storage media components and magnetic applications. The precision rolled products segment manufactures copper alloy, special steel and foil products for connectors, electronic components, flexible printed circuits, springs and batteries. The precision fabricated products segment manufactures gold-plated products, as well as providing metal molds, precision pressing and injection molding. The recycling and environmental service segment recycles metal materials and provides treatment services for industrial waste. Finally, the technology development segment focuses on advancing the firm's capabilities in the areas of bio-mining, extraction, metal scrap processing and copper alloy enhancement. JX Nippon Mining & Metals is a subsidiary of JX Holdings, Inc., a holding company created by NMH and Nippon Oil Corporation in April 2010. Following this, JX Nippon Mining & Metals was formed through the merger of NMH and former subsidiary Nippon Mining & Metals Co., Ltd.

FINANCIALS:

Sales and profits are in thousands of dollars—add 000 to get the full amount. 2010 Note: Financial information for 2010 was not available for all companies at press time.

2010 Sales: $	2010 Profits: $	**U.S. Stock Ticker: Subsidiary**
2009 Sales: $45,079,100	2009 Profits: $-452,380	**Int'l Ticker:** Int'l Exchange:
2008 Sales: $37,533,000	2008 Profits: $-406,000	Employees:
2007 Sales: $32,360,000	2007 Profits: $910,000	Fiscal Year Ends: 3/31
2006 Sales: $25,735,300	2006 Profits: $824,100	Parent Company: JX HOLDINGS INC

SALARIES/BENEFITS:

Pension Plan:	ESOP Stock Plan:	Profit Sharing:	Top Exec. Salary: $	Bonus: $
Savings Plan:	Stock Purch. Plan:		Second Exec. Salary: $	Bonus: $

OTHER THOUGHTS:

Apparent Women Officers or Directors:
Hot Spot for Advancement for Women/Minorities:

LOCATIONS: ("Y" = Yes)

West:	Southwest:	Midwest:	Southeast:	Northeast:	International:
Y					Y

KANSAI ELECTRIC POWER COMPANY INC

www.kepco.co.jp

Industry Group Code: 2211 **Ranks within this company's industry group:** Sales: 3 Profits: 45

Exploration/Production:		Refining/Retailing:		Utilities:		Alternative Energy:		Specialty Services:		Energy Mktg./Other Svcs.	
Exploration:		Refining:		Electric Utility:	Y	Waste/Solar/Other:		Consulting/Eng.:		Energy Marketing:	Y
Production:		Retailing:		Gas Utility:		Thermal/Steam:		Seismic:		Equipment/Machinery:	
Coal Production:		Convenience Stores:		Pipelines:		Wind:		Drilling:		Oil Field Services:	
		Chemicals:		Water:		Hydro:	Y	InfoTech:		Air/Shipping Transportation:	
						Fuel Cells:		Specialty Services:	Y		

TYPES OF BUSINESS:

Electric Power Generation
Nuclear Generation
Hydroelectric Generation
Telecommunications
Energy Supply
Nursing Care Management Services
Real Estate Leasing

BRANDS/DIVISIONS/AFFILIATES:

Kansai EP
MID Urban Development Co.

CONTACTS: *Note: Officers with more than one job title may be intentionally listed here more than once.*

Makoto Yagi, Pres.
Yoshihiro Doi, Managing Dir.-IT & Bus. Reform
Norihiko Saito, Exec. VP/Chief Dir.-Electric Dist.
Sakae Kanno, Exec. VP/Dir.-Customer
Toshiaki Mukai, Exec. VP
Yasuo Hamada, Exec. VP
Shosuke Mori, Chmn.

Phone: 81-6-6441-8821	**Fax:**
Toll-Free:	
Address: 3-6-16 Nakanoshima, Kita-ku, Osaka, 530-8270 Japan	

GROWTH PLANS/SPECIAL FEATURES:

Kansai Electric Power Company, Inc. (Kansai EP), parent of 60 subsidiaries and numerous associated companies, is one of the largest power companies in Japan, with 13 million customers in the Kansai region, including the entirety of the Osaka, Kyoto, Nara, Shiga and Wakayama prefectures and parts of the Hyogo, Mie, Gifu and Fukui prefectures. Kansai has international operations in several countries, including Bhutan, New Zealand and Australia. The company has three segments: Electric Power, IT and Communications and Other. The Electric Power segment includes three nuclear power plants, accounting for 45% of Kansai EP's total energy generation; its 12 thermal power plants provide approximately 44% of energy generation; and its 148 hydropower plants provide roughly 10%, with the remaining 1% derived from renewable energies. In total, Kansai has a total generation capacity of 34,865 megawatts (MW) and a gross energy sales volume of approximately 141.6 billion kilowatt-hours annually. The company has over 11,430 miles of transmission lines, 799,996 miles of distribution lines and 1,569 substations. This segment also provides utility design, construction, operation, maintenance and operational management services for customers' utility facilities. Currently, Kansai is promoting the adoption of fully electric homes in Japan. The company's IT and Communications segment provides fiber-optic cable to individual and corporate customers throughout the Kansai region, giving them access to phone, television and Internet services. The Other segment includes the company's integrated energy supply business; and its lifecycle-related business, including fully electric home services, home security tools and management tools for nursing care and healthcare. Other business areas include the leasing and administration of real estate, information and telecom consulting services, billing and loan services, heath care business support and building development. In October 2009, Kansai EP announced plans to acquire roughly 80% of MID Urban Development Co., a property development firm.

FINANCIALS: **Sales and profits are in thousands of dollars—add 000 to get the full amount. 2010 Note: Financial information for 2010 was not available for all companies at press time.**

2010 Sales: $	2010 Profits: $	**U.S. Stock Ticker: KAEPF**
2009 Sales: $30,615,400	2009 Profits: $-96,540	**Int'l Ticker: 9503** Int'l Exchange: Tokyo-TSE
2008 Sales: $27,768,000	2008 Profits: $-88,000	Employees:
2007 Sales: $22,100,000	2007 Profits: $1,260,000	Fiscal Year Ends: 3/31
2006 Sales: $21,916,200	2006 Profits: $1,368,550	Parent Company:

SALARIES/BENEFITS:

Pension Plan:	ESOP Stock Plan:	Profit Sharing:	Top Exec. Salary: $	Bonus: $
Savings Plan:	Stock Purch. Plan:		Second Exec. Salary: $	Bonus: $

OTHER THOUGHTS:

Apparent Women Officers or Directors:
Hot Spot for Advancement for Women/Minorities:

LOCATIONS: ("Y" = Yes)

West:	Southwest:	Midwest:	Southeast:	Northeast:	International:
					Y

KBR INC

www.kbr.com

Industry Group Code: 541330 **Ranks within this company's industry group:** Sales: 1 Profits: 2

Exploration/Production:		**Refining/Retailing:**		**Utilities:**		**Alternative Energy:**		**Specialty Services:**		**Energy Mktg./Other Svcs.**	
Exploration:		Refining:		Electric Utility:		Waste/Solar/Other:		Consulting/Eng.:	Y	Energy Marketing:	
Production:		Retailing:		Gas Utility:		Thermal/Steam:		Seismic:		Equipment/Machinery:	
Coal Production:		Convenience Stores:		Pipelines:		Wind:		Drilling:		Oil Field Services:	
		Chemicals:		Water:		Hydro:		InfoTech:		Air/Shipping Transportation:	
						Fuel Cells:		Specialty Services:			

TYPES OF BUSINESS:

Engineering, Construction & Services
Energy & Petrochemical Projects
Program & Project Management
Consulting & Technology Services
Operations & Maintenance Services

BRANDS/DIVISIONS/AFFILIATES:

Energo Engineering
SK-KBR Technologies Pte. Ltd.

CONTACTS: *Note: Officers with more than one job title may be intentionally listed here more than once.*

William P. Utt, CEO
William P. Utt, Pres.
Sue Carter, CFO/Sr. VP
Timothy B. Challand, Pres., Tech.
Klaudia J. Brace, Sr. VP-Admin.
Andrew D. Farley, General Counsel/Sr. VP
Dennis Calton, Exec. VP-Oper.
Rob Kukla, Jr., Dir.-Investor Rel.
Dennis S. Baldwin, Chief Acct. Officer
Roy Oelking, Pres., Oil & Gas
Ted Wright, Pres., North American Gov't & Defense Bus. Unit
Mark S. Williams, Pres., Gov't & Defense/Power & Industrial
John L. Rose, Pres., Hydrocarbons
William P. Utt, Chmn.
Andrew Pringle, Pres., Int'l Gov't & Defense

Phone: 713-753-2000	**Fax:** 713-753-5353
Toll-Free:	
Address: 601 Jefferson St., Houston, TX 77002 US	

GROWTH PLANS/SPECIAL FEATURES:

KBR, Inc. is a global engineering, construction and services company supporting the energy, hydrocarbon, government services, minerals, civil infrastructure, power and industrial sectors. It operates in six segments: government and infrastructure (G&I); upstream; services; downstream; technology; and ventures. The G&I segment provides program and project management, contingency logistics, operations and maintenance, construction management and engineering services to military and civilian branches of governments and private clients in North America, the Middle East, the U.K. and Australia. The upstream business provides services for large, complex upstream projects, including liquefied natural gas; gas-to-liquids; onshore and offshore oil and gas production facilities; and onshore and offshore pipelines. The services division provides engineering, construction, construction management, fabrication, maintenance and turnaround services to the oil and gas, petrochemicals, hydrocarbon processing, alternate energy, pulp and paper, industrial and pharmaceutical industries. This segment also provides commercial building construction services, maintenance, small capital construction and drilling support services. The downstream unit provides front-end engineering design; detailed engineering; procurement and construction; and program management services to petrochemical, refining, coal gasification and syngas clients. The technology segment offers differentiated process technologies, including value-added technologies in the coal monetization, petrochemical, refining and syngas markets. It offers technology licenses, project management and engineering, procurement and construction for integrated solutions. Finally, the ventures business makes equity investments in projects in which one of the firm's business units has a direct role in engineering, construction, management or operations and maintenance. In April 2010, KBR acquired Energo Engineering, a structural engineering services company. In June 2010, the company and Korean firm SK Energy Co., Ltd., announced the creation of a joint venture, SK-KBR Technologies Pte. Ltd., to market SK Energy's petrochemical technologies.

Employees are offered medical, dental, vision, life and disability insurance; flexible spending accounts; disability benefits; a flexible work schedule; and a 401(k) plan.

FINANCIALS: **Sales and profits are in thousands of dollars—add 000 to get the full amount. 2010 Note: Financial information for 2010 was not available for all companies at press time.**

2010 Sales: $	2010 Profits: $	**U.S. Stock Ticker: KBR**
2009 Sales: $12,105,000	2009 Profits: $290,000	**Int'l Ticker:** Int'l Exchange:
2008 Sales: $11,581,000	2008 Profits: $319,000	Employees: 51,000
2007 Sales: $8,745,000	2007 Profits: $302,000	Fiscal Year Ends: 12/31
2006 Sales: $8,805,000	2006 Profits: $168,000	Parent Company:

SALARIES/BENEFITS:

Pension Plan:	ESOP Stock Plan:	Profit Sharing:	Top Exec. Salary: $928,932	Bonus: $3,650,000
Savings Plan: Y	Stock Purch. Plan:		Second Exec. Salary: $448,083	Bonus: $953,690

OTHER THOUGHTS:

Apparent Women Officers or Directors: 2
Hot Spot for Advancement for Women/Minorities: Y

LOCATIONS: ("Y" = Yes)

West:	Southwest:	Midwest:	Southeast:	Northeast:	International:
	Y		Y	Y	Y

KEY ENERGY SERVICES INC

www.keyenergy.com

Industry Group Code: 213112 **Ranks within this company's industry group:** Sales: 18 Profits: 25

Exploration/Production:		Refining/Retailing:		Utilities:		Alternative Energy:		Specialty Services:		Energy Mktg./Other Svcs.	
Exploration:		Refining:		Electric Utility:		Waste/Solar/Other:		Consulting/Eng.:		Energy Marketing:	
Production:		Retailing:		Gas Utility:		Thermal/Steam:		Seismic:		Equipment/Machinery:	Y
Coal Production:		Convenience Stores:		Pipelines:		Wind:		Drilling:	Y	Oil Field Services:	Y
		Chemicals:		Water:		Hydro:		InfoTech:		Air/Shipping Transportation:	Y
						Fuel Cells:		Specialty Services:			

TYPES OF BUSINESS:

Oil & Gas Drilling Support Services
Well Servicing & Workovers
Oilfield Trucking & Fluid Hauling
Drilling Services
Storage & Disposal Services
Equipment Rental

BRANDS/DIVISIONS/AFFILIATES:

GeoStream

CONTACTS:

Note: Officers with more than one job title may be intentionally listed here more than once.

Richard Alario, CEO
Newton W. Wilson III, COO/Exec. VP
Richard Alario, Pres.
T. M. Whichard III, CFO/Sr. VP
Kim B. Clarke, Chief People Officer
Don D. Weinheimer, Sr. VP-Prod. Dev. & Quality
Kim B. Clarke, Sr. VP-Admin.
Kimberly R. Frye, General Counsel/Sr. VP
Don D. Weinheimer, Sr. VP-Strategic Planning
Tommy Pipes, Sr. VP-Industry Rel.
Gary L. Russell, VP-Investor Rel.
Jeff Skelly, Sr. VP-Rig Svcs.
Richard Alario, Chmn.

Phone: 713-651-4300	**Fax:** 713-652-4005
Toll-Free:	
Address: 1301 McKinney St., Ste. 1800, Houston, TX 77010 US	

GROWTH PLANS/SPECIAL FEATURES:

Key Energy Services, Inc. is one of the world's leading onshore, rig-based well servicing contractors. Key operations are located throughout the U.S. and in Canada, Argentina, Mexico and Russia. The company operates in two segments: well servicing and production services. The well services segment is comprised of two subdivisions: rig-based services, which include the maintenance and workover of existing oil and gas wells and well plugging and abandonment solutions; and fluid management services, which include oilfield transportation and produced water disposal services for operators of saltwater and other fluid-producing wells. The production services segment is composed of three subdivisions: pressure pumping services, including fracturing, nitrogen, acidizing, cementing and coiled tubing services, used to enhance oil and natural gas well production; wireline services, including well perforating, completion logging, production logging and casing integrity services; and fishing and rental services. Fishing services involve recovering lost or stuck equipment in the wellbore. The division's rental equipment includes drill pipe, tubulars, handling tools, pressure-control equipment, power swivels and foam air units. In June 2009, the firm opened a new facility in Minden, Louisiana. In September 2009, the firm completed the second tranche of its $31.8 million investment in GeoSream Services Group, a Russian oilfield services company, giving it 50% ownership in GeoStream. In March 2010, Key Energy formed a joint venture with AlMansoori Specialized Engineering to provide well intervention services in the Middle East and North Africa. In June 2010, the company acquired five large diameter coiled tubing units from Express Energy Services CT, LP. In October 2010, the firm acquired certain subsidiaries and assets from OFS Energy Services and sold its pressure pumping and wireline businesses to Patterson-UTI Energy.

The company offers its employees medical, vision and dental coverage; a 401(k) plan; a retirement plan; educational assistance; and life and disability insurance.

FINANCIALS:

Sales and profits are in thousands of dollars—add 000 to get the full amount. 2010 Note: Financial information for 2010 was not available for all companies at press time.

2010 Sales: $	2010 Profits: $	**U.S. Stock Ticker: KEG**
2009 Sales: $1,078,665	2009 Profits: $-156,121	**Int'l Ticker:** Int'l Exchange:
2008 Sales: $1,972,088	2008 Profits: $84,058	Employees: 8,100
2007 Sales: $1,662,012	2007 Profits: $169,289	Fiscal Year Ends: 12/31
2006 Sales: $1,546,177	2006 Profits: $171,033	Parent Company:

SALARIES/BENEFITS:

Pension Plan: Y	ESOP Stock Plan:	Profit Sharing:	Top Exec. Salary: $764,800	Bonus: $
Savings Plan: Y	Stock Purch. Plan:		Second Exec. Salary: $422,740	Bonus: $

OTHER THOUGHTS:

Apparent Women Officers or Directors: 4
Hot Spot for Advancement for Women/Minorities: Y

LOCATIONS: ("Y" = Yes)

West:	Southwest:	Midwest:	Southeast:	Northeast:	International:
Y	Y	Y	Y	Y	

KINDER MORGAN ENERGY PARTNERS LP

www.kindermorgan.com

Industry Group Code: 486 **Ranks within this company's industry group:** Sales: 7 Profits: 2

Exploration/Production:		Refining/Retailing:		Utilities:		Alternative Energy:		Specialty Services:		Energy Mktg./Other Svcs.	
Exploration:		Refining:		Electric Utility:		Waste/Solar/Other:		Consulting/Eng.:		Energy Marketing:	
Production:	Y	Retailing:		Gas Utility:		Thermal/Steam:		Seismic:		Equipment/Machinery:	
Coal Production:		Convenience Stores:		Pipelines:	Y	Wind:		Drilling:		Oil Field Services:	
		Chemicals:		Water:		Hydro:		InfoTech:		Air/Shipping Transportation:	
						Fuel Cells:		Specialty Services:			

TYPES OF BUSINESS:

Gas Pipelines
Natural Gas Storage
Bulk Terminal Facilities
CO2 Transportation

BRANDS/DIVISIONS/AFFILIATES:

Crosstex Energy LP

CONTACTS:

Note: Officers with more than one job title may be intentionally listed here more than once.

Richard D. Kinder, CEO
Steven J. Kean, COO/Exec. VP
C. Park Shaper, Pres.
Kimberly Allen Dang, CFO/VP
James E. Street, VP-Human Resources
Henry W. Neumann, CIO/VP
James E. Street, VP-Admin.
Joseph Listengart, General Counsel/VP
David D. Kinder, VP-Corp. Dev.
Larry S. Pierce, VP-Corp. Comm.
David D. Kinder, VP-Investor Rel.
David D. Kinder, Treas.
James E. Street, VP-IT
Jordan H. Mintz, Chief Tax Officer/VP
Tom Martin, Pres., Natural Gas Pipelines
Jeffrey R. Armstrong, Pres., Terminals
Richard D. Kinder, Chmn.

Phone: 713-369-9000 **Fax:** 713-4952817
Toll-Free:
Address: 500 Dallas St., Ste. 1000, Houston, TX 77002 US

GROWTH PLANS/SPECIAL FEATURES:

Kinder Morgan Energy Partners, L.P. (KMP) owns and operates independent refined petroleum products pipeline systems in the U.S, which consist of more than 37,000 miles of pipelines and 180 terminals in North America. The firm's pipelines transport natural gas, gasoline, crude oil, carbon dioxide and other products, and its terminals store petroleum products and chemicals and handle bulk materials like coal and petroleum coke. The company also provides carbon dioxide (CO2) for enhanced oil recovery projects in North America. The firm operates in five segments. The products pipelines segment consists of roughly 8,400 miles of refined petroleum products pipelines that deliver gasoline, diesel fuel, jet fuel and natural gas liquids, and over 60 associated product terminals and petroleum pipeline transmix processing facilities. The natural gas pipelines segment includes of about 15,000 miles of natural gas transmission pipelines and gathering lines, as well as natural gas storage, treating and processing facilities. The CO2 segment produces, transports and markets CO2 to oil fields and owns interests in and operates eight oil fields and a crude oil pipeline system in west Texas. The terminals segment consists of approximately 121 owned or operated liquids and bulk terminal facilities; and more than 33 rail transloading and materials handling facilities, which transload, store and deliver a wide variety of bulk, petroleum, petrochemical and other liquids products for customers across the U.S. The trans mountain segment includes over 700 miles of common carrier pipelines for the transportation of crude oil and refined petroleum. In October 2009, the company acquired Crosstex Energy LP, a natural gas treatment operation. In 2010, the firm acquired several assets, including 50% interest in Petrohawk Energy Corporation's natural gas gathering/treating operations in the Haynesville Shale; three unit train ethanol handling terminals from U.S. Development Group; and 100 mechanical refrigeration units from Gas-Chill, Inc.

FINANCIALS:

Sales and profits are in thousands of dollars—add 000 to get the full amount. 2010 Note: Financial information for 2010 was not available for all companies at press time.

2010 Sales: $	2010 Profits: $	**U.S. Stock Ticker: KMP**
2009 Sales: $7,003,400	2009 Profits: $1,283,800	**Int'l Ticker:** Int'l Exchange:
2008 Sales: $11,740,300	2008 Profits: $1,304,800	Employees: 7,800
2007 Sales: $9,217,700	2007 Profits: $590,300	Fiscal Year Ends: 12/31
2006 Sales: $9,048,700	2006 Profits: $1,004,100	Parent Company:

SALARIES/BENEFITS:

Pension Plan:	ESOP Stock Plan:	Profit Sharing:	Top Exec. Salary: $257,692	Bonus: $1,300,000
Savings Plan:	Stock Purch. Plan:		Second Exec. Salary: $257,692	Bonus: $1,250,000

OTHER THOUGHTS:

Apparent Women Officers or Directors: 2
Hot Spot for Advancement for Women/Minorities: Y

LOCATIONS: ("Y" = Yes)

West:	Southwest:	Midwest:	Southeast:	Northeast:	International:
Y	Y	Y	Y	Y	

Note: Financial information, benefits and other data can change quickly and may vary from those stated here.

KOCH INDUSTRIES INC

www.kochind.com

Industry Group Code: 324110 **Ranks within this company's industry group:** Sales: 1 Profits:

Exploration/Production:		Refining/Retailing:		Utilities:		Alternative Energy:		Specialty Services:		Energy Mktg./Other Svcs.	
Exploration:	Y	Refining:	Y	Electric Utility:		Waste/Solar/Other:		Consulting/Eng.:	Y	Energy Marketing:	
Production:	Y	Retailing:		Gas Utility:		Thermal/Steam:		Seismic:		Equipment/Machinery:	Y
Coal Production:	Y	Convenience Stores:		Pipelines:	Y	Wind:		Drilling:		Oil Field Services:	
		Chemicals:	Y	Water:		Hydro:		InfoTech:		Air/Shipping Transportation:	
						Fuel Cells:		Specialty Services:	Y		

TYPES OF BUSINESS:

Petroleum Refining
Chemicals
Textiles
Pipelines
Fertilizer Production
Chemical Equipment
Asphalt & Paving Supplies
Beef Production

BRANDS/DIVISIONS/AFFILIATES:

Flint Hills Resources
Koch Mineral Services
Matador Cattle Company
Koch Pipeline Company
Koch Chemical Technologies Group, LLC
Koch Nitrogen Company, LLC
INVISTA
Georgia-Pacific Corp

CONTACTS:

Note: Officers with more than one job title may be intentionally listed here more than once.

Charles G. Koch, CEO
David L. Robertson, COO
David L. Robertson, Pres.
Steve Feilmeier, CFO
Katie Stavinoha, Dir.-Public Affairs
Charles G. Koch, Chmn.

Phone: 316-828-5500	**Fax:** 316-828-5739
Toll-Free:	
Address: 4111 E. 37th St. N., Wichita, KS 67220 US	

GROWTH PLANS/SPECIAL FEATURES:

Koch Industries, Inc. is a diversified group of companies with operations in markets as diverse as refining and chemicals; process and pollution control equipment and technologies; minerals and fertilizers; polymers and fibers; commodity and financial trading and services; and forest and consumer products. It also conducts operations in venture capital investments, municipal finance, capital market investments and business development. Subsidiary Flint Hills Resources operates petroleum refineries in Alaska, Minnesota and Texas, with a combined crude oil processing capacity of more than 800,000 barrels per day. These plants produce aromatics, olefins, polymers and intermediate chemicals. The subsidiary obtains its supply from purchasing offices in Houston, Denver, and Calgary, Canada. Subsidiary Koch Mineral Services supplies coal and petroleum coke as well as cement, pulp and paper, sulfur and related products internationally. Koch Nitrogen Company and its affiliates own or have interests in nitrogen fertilizer plants capable of manufacturing more than 9 million metric tons of nitrogen products annually. Koch's ranching subsidiary, Matador Cattle Company, operates three ranches in Kansas, Montana, and Texas. Subsidiary Koch Pipeline Company, LP and its affiliates operate a 4,000-mile network of pipelines. Subsidiary Koch Chemical Technology Group and its affiliates design, manufacture, sell, install and service process and pollution control equipment. Subsidiary INVISTA is a global producer and marketer of polymers and fibers, primarily for nylon, spandex and polyester applications. Subsidiary Georgia-Pacific manufactures and markets tissue, packaging, paper, building products, related chemicals and fluff, filter and market pulp under such brand names as Quilted Northern, Angel Soft, Brawny and Dixie.

Employees are offered medical and dental insurance; a 401(k) plan; a pension plan; flexible spending accounts; life insurance; business travel accident insurance; disability coverage; and educational assistance.

FINANCIALS:

Sales and profits are in thousands of dollars—add 000 to get the full amount. 2010 Note: Financial information for 2010 was not available for all companies at press time.

2010 Sales: $	2010 Profits: $	**U.S. Stock Ticker: Private**
2009 Sales: $100,000,000	2009 Profits: $	**Int'l Ticker:** Int'l Exchange:
2008 Sales: $100,000,000	2008 Profits: $80,000	Employees: 70,000
2007 Sales: $98,000,000	2007 Profits: $	Fiscal Year Ends: 12/31
2006 Sales: $90,000,000	2006 Profits: $	Parent Company:

SALARIES/BENEFITS:

Pension Plan: Y	ESOP Stock Plan:	Profit Sharing:	Top Exec. Salary: $	Bonus: $
Savings Plan: Y	Stock Purch. Plan:		Second Exec. Salary: $	Bonus: $

OTHER THOUGHTS:

Apparent Women Officers or Directors: 1
Hot Spot for Advancement for Women/Minorities:

LOCATIONS: ("Y" = Yes)

West:	Southwest:	Midwest:	Southeast:	Northeast:	International:
Y	Y	Y	Y	Y	Y

KOCHI REFINERIES LTD

bharatpetroleum.com/EnergisingBusiness/KochiRefinery_Overview.aspx

Industry Group Code: 324110 **Ranks within this company's industry group:** Sales: Profits:

Exploration/Production:		**Refining/Retailing:**		**Utilities:**		**Alternative Energy:**		**Specialty Services:**		**Energy Mktg./Other Svcs.**	
Exploration:		Refining:	Y	Electric Utility:		Waste/Solar/Other:		Consulting/Eng.:		Energy Marketing:	
Production:		Retailing:		Gas Utility:		Thermal/Steam:		Seismic:		Equipment/Machinery:	
Coal Production:		Convenience Stores:		Pipelines:		Wind:		Drilling:		Oil Field Services:	
		Chemicals:	Y	Water:		Hydro:		InfoTech:		Air/Shipping Transportation:	
						Fuel Cells:		Specialty Services:			

TYPES OF BUSINESS:

Petroleum Refining

BRANDS/DIVISIONS/AFFILIATES:

Bharat Petroleum Corporation, Ltd.

CONTACTS:

Note: Officers with more than one job title may be intentionally listed here more than once.

B. K. Menon, Managing Dir.
Cherian N. Punnoose, Dir.-Finance
M.P. Govindarajan, Gen. Mgr.-Human Resources
John M. Mathew, Gen. Mgr.-Tech.
Tomy Mathews, Gen. Mgr.-Oper.
E. Nandakumar, Exec. Dir.
K.N. Ravindran, Gen. Mgr.-Projects
Ashok Sinha, Chmn.

Phone: 91-484-272-2061	**Fax:** 91-484-272-0855
Toll-Free:	
Address: Post Bag 2, Ambalamugal, Kochi, 682 302 India	

GROWTH PLANS/SPECIAL FEATURES:

Kochi Refineries, Ltd., majority-owned by Bharat Petroleum Corporation, Ltd., is one of India's largest petroleum refining companies. It was founded in 1963 as Cochin Refineries, Ltd., and has grown to become one of chief industries in the state of Kerala. The firm has a refining capacity of 7.5 million metric tons per year (MTPA), with plans to expand its capacity to 9.5 million MTPA, and produces liquefied petroleum gas, naphtha, gasoline, diesel, kerosene, aviation turbine fuel, gas oil, fuel oil, asphalt and other petrochemical products. Its various products are used in household and industrial applications, such as automobiles, heavy industry, agriculture (as insecticides or fertilizer), in paints and solvents, textiles, lubricants, sugar, pharmaceuticals and tire production. The company's newest product is rubberized bitumen, which is a critical component used in the surfacing of roads. The firm processes crude oil through two Crude Distillation units (CDU), which together produce 150,000 barrels per day of fuel-based refinery products. In addition, Kochi Refineries runs three captive power plants to generate the energy needed to run its operations.

FINANCIALS:

Sales and profits are in thousands of dollars—add 000 to get the full amount. 2010 Note: Financial information for 2010 was not available for all companies at press time.

2010 Sales: $ | 2010 Profits: $
2009 Sales: $ | 2009 Profits: $
2008 Sales: $ | 2008 Profits: $
2007 Sales: $ | 2007 Profits: $
2006 Sales: $ | 2006 Profits: $

U.S. Stock Ticker: Subsidiary
Int'l Ticker: 500873 Int'l Exchange: Bombay-BSE
Employees:
Fiscal Year Ends: 3/31
Parent Company: BHARAT PETROLEUM CORPORATION LTD

SALARIES/BENEFITS:

Pension Plan: Y	ESOP Stock Plan:	Profit Sharing:	Top Exec. Salary: $	Bonus: $
Savings Plan:	Stock Purch. Plan:		Second Exec. Salary: $	Bonus: $

OTHER THOUGHTS:

Apparent Women Officers or Directors:
Hot Spot for Advancement for Women/Minorities:

LOCATIONS: ("Y" = Yes)

West:	Southwest:	Midwest:	Southeast:	Northeast:	International:
					Y

KOREA ELECTRIC POWER CORPORATION

www.kepco.co.kr

Industry Group Code: 2211 **Ranks within this company's industry group:** Sales: 7 Profits: 44

Exploration/Production:		Refining/Retailing:		Utilities:		Alternative Energy:		Specialty Services:		Energy Mktg./Other Svcs.	
Exploration:		Refining:		Electric Utility:	Y	Waste/Solar/Other:	Y	Consulting/Eng.:	Y	Energy Marketing:	
Production:		Retailing:		Gas Utility:		Thermal/Steam:	Y	Seismic:		Equipment/Machinery:	
Coal Production:		Convenience Stores:		Pipelines:		Wind:	Y	Drilling:		Oil Field Services:	
		Chemicals:		Water:		Hydro:	Y	InfoTech:		Air/Shipping Transportation:	
						Fuel Cells:		Specialty Services:			

TYPES OF BUSINESS:

Electricity Generation, Transmission & Distribution
Consulting

BRANDS/DIVISIONS/AFFILIATES:

Korea Hydro & Nuclear Power Co., Ltd.
Korea South-East Power Co., Ltd.
Korea Midland Power Co., Ltd.
Korea Western Power Co., Ltd.
Korea Southern Power Co., Ltd.
Korea East-West Power Co., Ltd.

CONTACTS: *Note: Officers with more than one job title may be intentionally listed here more than once.*

Ssang-Su Kim, CEO
Ssang-Su Kim, Pres.
Woo-Kyum Kim, Exec. VP-Mktg. & Service
Do-Shik Lee, Exec. VP-Admin.
Chan-Ki Jung, Exec. VP-Planning & Coordination Div.
Seung-Churl Kang, Controller
Young-Jin Chang, Exec. VP-Power Tech. Div.
Chong-Hun Rieh, Chmn.
Jun-Yeon Byun, Exec. VP-Overseas Bus. Div.

Phone: 822-3456-4264 **Fax:** 822-556-3694
Toll-Free:
Address: 411 Youngdong-Daero Gangnam-Gu, Seoul, 135-791 Korea

GROWTH PLANS/SPECIAL FEATURES:

Korea Electric Power Corporation (KEPCO) is an electric utility that, along with its subsidiaries, generates, transmits and distributes substantially all of the electricity in Korea. The Korean government maintains an approximate 51.1% stake in the company. The firm operates in three segments: transmission and distribution; power generation; and all other. The transmission and distribution segment includes operations related to the transmission, distribution and sale to end-users of electricity purchased from independent power producers, as well as the company's six generation subsidiaries. These subsidiaries, sometimes collectively called the GENCOs, are Korea Hydro & Nuclear Power Co., Ltd., which produces around 34% of KEPCO's electricity and handles its 20 nuclear and 27 hydroelectric generating stations; Korea South-East Power Co., Ltd. (KOSEP); Korea Midland Power Co., Ltd. (KOMIPO); Korea Western Power Co., Ltd. (KOWEPO); Korea Southern Power Co., Ltd. (KOSPO); and Korea East-West Power Co., Ltd. (EWP). The power generation segment oversees the generation of electricity sold to the company through the Korea Power Exchange (a government organization that also sets the price of electricity). The remaining segment consists of operations related to the engineering and maintenance of generation plants, information services, sales of nuclear fuel and communication line leasing. The firm's two largest sources of power include nuclear power facilities and thermal plants, including coal-burning, oil and natural gas plants. Other plants include hydroelectric facilities, combined cycle plants, internal combustion plants and wind and solar facilities. In the overseas market, the firm has power projects operating in the Philippines, China and Lebanon. It also has developments in Nigeria, Egypt, Australia and Canada. In December 2009, KEPCO entered into an $18.6 billion contract with a state-owned nuclear energy provider in the U.A.E., to design, build and help operate four civil nuclear power generation units.

FINANCIALS: **Sales and profits are in thousands of dollars—add 000 to get the full amount. 2010 Note: Financial information for 2010 was not available for all companies at press time.**

2010 Sales: $	2010 Profits: $	**U.S. Stock Ticker: KEP**
2009 Sales: $27,171,400	2009 Profits: $-77,310	**Int'l Ticker: 015760** Int'l Exchange: Seoul-KRX
2008 Sales: $25,067,501	2008 Profits: $-2,909,902	Employees:
2007 Sales: $30,893,077	2007 Profits: $1,659,364	Fiscal Year Ends: 12/31
2006 Sales: $29,022,195	2006 Profits: $2,227,349	Parent Company:

SALARIES/BENEFITS:

Pension Plan:	ESOP Stock Plan:	Profit Sharing:	Top Exec. Salary: $	Bonus: $
Savings Plan:	Stock Purch. Plan:		Second Exec. Salary: $	Bonus: $

OTHER THOUGHTS:

Apparent Women Officers or Directors:
Hot Spot for Advancement for Women/Minorities:

LOCATIONS: ("Y" = Yes)

West:	Southwest:	Midwest:	Southeast:	Northeast:	International:
					Y

KOREA GAS CORPORATION

www.kogas.or.kr

Industry Group Code: 211111 **Ranks within this company's industry group:** Sales: 36 Profits: 57

Exploration/Production:		Refining/Retailing:		Utilities:		Alternative Energy:		Specialty Services:		Energy Mktg./Other Svcs.	
Exploration:		Refining:		Electric Utility:		Waste/Solar/Other:		Consulting/Eng.:		Energy Marketing:	
Production:		Retailing:		Gas Utility:	Y	Thermal/Steam:		Seismic:		Equipment/Machinery:	
Coal Production:		Convenience Stores:		Pipelines:		Wind:		Drilling:		Oil Field Services:	
		Chemicals:		Water:		Hydro:		InfoTech:		Air/Shipping Transportation:	
						Fuel Cells:		Specialty Services:			

TYPES OF BUSINESS:

Natural Gas
Research & Development

BRANDS/DIVISIONS/AFFILIATES:

KOGAS
Kogas Vostok Limited Liability Company

CONTACTS:

Note: Officers with more than one job title may be intentionally listed here more than once.

Kangsoo Choo, CEO
Kangsoo Choo, Pres.
Hee Soo Son, Exec. VP-Oper.
Dae-chun Jun, Sr. Exec. VP
Seok-hyo Jang, Exec. VP-Resources Bus. Div.
Berm-young Shon, Exec. VP-LNG Terminal Div.
Sun-jang Yang, Exec. VP-Support Div.

Phone: 82-31-710-0114 **Fax:** 82-31-710-0117
Toll-Free:
Address: 215, Jeongja-dong, Bundang-gu, Seongnam, Gyeonggi-do, 463-754 Korea

GROWTH PLANS/SPECIAL FEATURES:

Korea Gas Corporation (KOGAS) is a government-owned provider of natural gas. It is the sole provider of liquefied natural gas (LNG) in Korea. The company's major lines of business include the production and distribution of natural gas, including the purification and sale of byproducts; exploration and import/export of natural gas and LNG; construction of operation of LNG terminals and a natural gas distribution network; research and technical development for related business areas; and other related businesses. KOGAS operates three LNG terminals and a nationwide pipeline network of about 1,700 miles. The company is one of the largest importers of LNG in the world; it provides LNG to gas utility companies, power generation plants and city gas companies throughout Korea. The firm is also involved in research and development in a variety of fields, such as natural gas cooling/heating systems for households, NOx (nitrogen oxide) reduction technology, natural gas-powered vehicles, fuel cells and cooling energy technology. KOGAS has interests in several foreign projects, including 3% in the Qatar RasGas Investment Project; 10% in the Myanmar A-1 & A-3 Block Development Project; 1.2% in the Oman LNG Investment Project; 25% in the Uzbekistan Uzunkui Block Exploration Project; 8.9% in the Yemen Investment Project; 50% at the Jackpine gas field in Canada; and 10% in each of two blocks in Mozambique and East Timor and 15% in a block in Indonesia, part of the Italy ENI Block Exploration Project. In July 2009, the firm created a subsidiary in Russia, Kogas Vostok Limited Liability Company. This subsidiary focuses on the gas pipeline construction business. In March 2010, the company and an Australian energy exploration company agreed to establish a joint venture to develop a natural gas station project in eastern Australia. In October 2010, KOGAS began commercial production at the Jackpine gas field.

FINANCIALS:

Sales and profits are in thousands of dollars—add 000 to get the full amount. 2010 Note: Financial information for 2010 was not available for all companies at press time.

2010 Sales: $	2010 Profits: $
2009 Sales: $16,655,600	2009 Profits: $204,420
2008 Sales: $21,076,000	2008 Profits: $301,000
2007 Sales: $15,200,208	2007 Profits: $388,788
2006 Sales: $13,744,225	2006 Profits: $256,295

U.S. Stock Ticker: Government-Owned
Int'l Ticker: 036460 Int'l Exchange: Seoul-KRX
Employees:
Fiscal Year Ends: 12/31
Parent Company:

SALARIES/BENEFITS:

Pension Plan:	ESOP Stock Plan:	Profit Sharing:	Top Exec. Salary: $	Bonus: $
Savings Plan:	Stock Purch. Plan:		Second Exec. Salary: $	Bonus: $

OTHER THOUGHTS:

Apparent Women Officers or Directors:
Hot Spot for Advancement for Women/Minorities:

LOCATIONS: ("Y" = Yes)

West:	Southwest:	Midwest:	Southeast:	Northeast:	International:
					Y

KUWAIT PETROLEUM CORPORATION

www.kpc.com.kw

Industry Group Code: 211111 **Ranks within this company's industry group:** Sales: 20 Profits:

Exploration/Production:		Refining/Retailing:		Utilities:		Alternative Energy:		Specialty Services:		Energy Mktg./Other Svcs.	
Exploration:	Y	Refining:	Y	Electric Utility:		Waste/Solar/Other:		Consulting/Eng.:		Energy Marketing:	Y
Production:	Y	Retailing:	Y	Gas Utility:		Thermal/Steam:		Seismic:		Equipment/Machinery:	
Coal Production:		Convenience Stores:		Pipelines:		Wind:		Drilling:		Oil Field Services:	
		Chemicals:	Y	Water:		Hydro:		InfoTech:		Air/Shipping Transportation:	Y
						Fuel Cells:		Specialty Services:			

TYPES OF BUSINESS:

Oil & Gas-Exploration & Production
Oil & Gas Refining, Marketing & Distribution
Gas Stations
Petrochemicals
Oil Tankers
Aviation Fuel Supply

BRANDS/DIVISIONS/AFFILIATES:

Kuwait Oil Company
Kuwait National Petroleum Company
Oil Sector Services Company
Kuwait Oil Tanker Company
Kuwait Aviation Fuel Company
Kuwait Foreign Petroleum Exploration
Kuwait Petroleum International Limited
Kuwait Gulf Oil Company

CONTACTS:

Note: Officers with more than one job title may be intentionally listed here more than once.

Saad Ali Al-Shuwaib, CEO
Abdulatif Al-Houti, Managing Dir.-Int'l. Mktg.
Khaleel Ibraheem, Managing Dir.-IT Div.
Hana Al-Sumeai, Managing Dir.-Admin. Affairs Div.
Sheikh Naw af Al-Sabah, Managing Dir.-General Counsel/Legal Affairs
Jamal Al-Loughani, Managing Dir.-Oper. & Mktg. Div.
Wafaa Al-Zaabi, Managing Dir.-Planning Div.
Sheikh Talal Al-Sabah, Dir.-Public & Media Rel. & Gov't. Parliament
Ali Al-Hajri, Managing Dir.-Finance & Admin Affairs
Sheikha Shatha Al-Sabah, Managing Dir.-Training & Career Dev.
Tareq Al-Roumi, Managing Dir.-Internal Audit Div.
Mona Al-Obaid, Managing Dir.-Admin. Affairs & Mktg. Div.
Mohammad Al-Farhoud, Managing Dir.-Finance Div.
Ahmed Al-Abdullah Al-Ahmed Al-Sabah, Chmn.

Phone: 965-1-85-85-85 **Fax:** 965-2499-4991
Toll-Free:
Address: P.O. Box 26565, Safat, 13126 Kuwait

GROWTH PLANS/SPECIAL FEATURES:

Kuwait Petroleum Corporation (KPC) is Kuwait's national oil company. Its history traces back to 1934 when the Anglo-Persian Oil Company (now BP) and Gulf Oil (now Chevron Corporation) formed the Kuwait Oil Company (KOC). During the 1970s, the Kuwaiti government acquired KOC (Kuwait Oil Company) and the other large oil companies operating in Kuwait, then in 1980 established KPC as the holding company for the following wholly-owned subsidiaries. KOC handles Kuwait's 12 domestic oil fields and oil exports. It produces around 3.0 million barrels of oil and 175 million cubic feet of natural gas per day. Kuwait National Petroleum Company operates four refineries, locally markets petroleum products and manages and supplies Kuwait's gas station network. Petrochemical Industries Company, a leading petrochemical manufacturer, specializes in ammonia products used to produce fertilizers. Kuwait Oil Tanker Company, among the largest tanker companies in the Middle East, owns 38 oil tankers with a total carrying capacity of four tons. Kuwait Aviation Fuelling Company fuels all aircraft using Kuwait International Airport and can service 1,500 aircraft per month. Kuwait Foreign Petroleum Exploration Company handles all of KPC's international upstream oil operations. Kuwait Petroleum International Limited operates two refineries and 4,700 Q8 brand petrol stations in Europe; manufactures and markets over 1,600 lubricant products; and supplies aviation fuel in major and regional airports worldwide. Kuwait Gulf Oil Company manages Kuwait's oil and gas exploration, production, processing and storing activities in the Divided Neutral Zone, shared with Saudi Arabia. Oil Sector Services Company provides construction and security services to KPC; operates and maintains oil service related equipment; and provides residential and medical services to KPC employees. KPC has regional marketing offices located in U.S., Japan, China, U.K., Pakistan, Singapore and India.

FINANCIALS:

Sales and profits are in thousands of dollars—add 000 to get the full amount. 2010 Note: Financial information for 2010 was not available for all companies at press time.

2010 Sales: $	2010 Profits: $
2009 Sales: $65,000,000	2009 Profits: $
2008 Sales: $60,000,000	2008 Profits: $
2007 Sales: $80,000,000	2007 Profits: $
2006 Sales: $59,403,000	2006 Profits: $8,341,270

U.S. Stock Ticker: Government-Owned
Int'l Ticker: Int'l Exchange:
Employees:
Fiscal Year Ends: 12/31
Parent Company:

SALARIES/BENEFITS:

Pension Plan:	ESOP Stock Plan:	Profit Sharing:	Top Exec. Salary: $	Bonus: $
Savings Plan:	Stock Purch. Plan:		Second Exec. Salary: $	Bonus: $

OTHER THOUGHTS:

Apparent Women Officers or Directors: 4
Hot Spot for Advancement for Women/Minorities: Y

LOCATIONS: ("Y" = Yes)

West:	Southwest:	Midwest:	Southeast:	Northeast:	International:
	Y				Y

LACLEDE GROUP INC (THE)

www.thelacledegroup.com

Industry Group Code: 221210 **Ranks within this company's industry group:** Sales: 13 Profits: 16

Exploration/Production:		**Refining/Retailing:**		**Utilities:**		**Alternative Energy:**		**Specialty Services:**		**Energy Mktg./Other Svcs.**	
Exploration:		Refining:		Electric Utility:		Waste/Solar/Other:		Consulting/Eng.:		Energy Marketing:	Y
Production:		Retailing:		Gas Utility:	Y	Thermal/Steam:		Seismic:		Equipment/Machinery:	
Coal Production:		Convenience Stores:		Pipelines:	Y	Wind:		Drilling:		Oil Field Services:	
		Chemicals:		Water:		Hydro:		InfoTech:		Air/Shipping Transportation:	
						Fuel Cells:		Specialty Services:	Y		

TYPES OF BUSINESS:

Utilities-Natural Gas
Underground Natural Gas Storage Fields
Transportation & Storage of Liquid Propane
Underground Locating & Marking Services
Insurance Services
Real Estate Development
Natural Gas Marketing

BRANDS/DIVISIONS/AFFILIATES:

Laclede Gas Company
Laclede Gas Family Services, Inc.
Laclede Development Company
Laclede Venture Corp.
Laclede Investment, LLC
Laclede Pipeline Company
Laclede Energy Resources, Inc.

CONTACTS: *Note: Officers with more than one job title may be intentionally listed here more than once.*

Douglas H. Yaeger, CEO
Douglas H. Yaeger, Pres.
Mark D. Waltermire, CFO
Mark C. Darrell, General Counsel
Michael C. Geiselhart, VP-Strategic Dev. & Planning
Mary C. Kullman, Contact-Investor Rel.
Lynn D. Rawlings, Treas.
Mary C. Kullman, Chief Governance Officer/Corp. Sec.
Michael R. Spotanski, Sr. VP-Oper. & Mktg., Laclede Gas Co.
James A. Fallert, Controller-Laclede Gas Co.
Scott E. Jaskowiak, VP/Gen. Mgr.-Laclede Energy Resources
Douglas H. Yaeger, Chmn.

Phone: 314-342-0500	**Fax:** 314-421-1979
Toll-Free:	
Address: 720 Olive St., St. Louis, MO 63101 US	

GROWTH PLANS/SPECIAL FEATURES:

The Laclede Group, Inc. is a public utility holding company that operates primarily in two divisions, regulated core utility operations and non-regulated activities. It provides natural gas service through its regulated core utility operations. The regulated gas distribution segment includes Laclede Gas Company, Laclede Group's largest subsidiary and core business unit. Laclede Gas is a public utility engaged in the retail distribution and sale of natural gas. It is one of the largest natural gas distribution utility firms in Missouri, serving more than 631,000 residential, commercial, and industrial customers in St. Louis and parts of 10 other counties in eastern Missouri. Laclede Group's non-regulated services segment includes Laclede Energy Resources, Inc. (LER), a subsidiary engaged in the non-regulated marketing of natural gas and related activities. Other non-regulated subsidiaries of the Laclede Group include Laclede Pipeline Company, which operates a propane pipeline to third-party facilities in Illinois; Laclede Investment, LLC, which invests in other enterprises; Laclede Energy Resources, Inc., a natural gas marketing company; Laclede Gas Family Services, Inc., a registered insurance agency in Missouri; Laclede Development Company, which participates in real estate development; and Laclede Venture Corp., which offers services for the compression of natural gas.

FINANCIALS: **Sales and profits are in thousands of dollars—add 000 to get the full amount. 2010 Note: Financial information for 2010 was not available for all companies at press time.**

2010 Sales: $	2010 Profits: $	**U.S. Stock Ticker: LG**
2009 Sales: $1,895,198	2009 Profits: $64,247	**Int'l Ticker:** Int'l Exchange:
2008 Sales: $2,208,973	2008 Profits: $77,922	Employees: 1,762
2007 Sales: $1,855,861	2007 Profits: $49,771	Fiscal Year Ends: 9/30
2006 Sales: $1,835,028	2006 Profits: $48,989	Parent Company:

SALARIES/BENEFITS:

Pension Plan:	ESOP Stock Plan:	Profit Sharing:	Top Exec. Salary: $623,333	Bonus: $702,116
Savings Plan: Y	Stock Purch. Plan:		Second Exec. Salary: $355,000	Bonus: $307,053

OTHER THOUGHTS:

Apparent Women Officers or Directors: 4
Hot Spot for Advancement for Women/Minorities: Y

LOCATIONS: ("Y" = Yes)

West:	Southwest:	Midwest:	Southeast:	Northeast:	International:
	Y	Y			

LAYNE CHRISTENSEN COMPANY

www.laynechristensen.com

Industry Group Code: 237 **Ranks within this company's industry group:** Sales: 8 Profits: 7

Exploration/Production:		**Refining/Retailing:**		**Utilities:**		**Alternative Energy:**		**Specialty Services:**		**Energy Mktg./Other Svcs.**	
Exploration:		Refining:		Electric Utility:		Waste/Solar/Other:		Consulting/Eng.:		Energy Marketing:	
Production:		Retailing:		Gas Utility:		Thermal/Steam:		Seismic:		Equipment/Machinery:	
Coal Production:		Convenience Stores:		Pipelines:		Wind:		Drilling:	Y	Oil Field Services:	Y
		Chemicals:		Water:		Hydro:		InfoTech:		Air/Shipping Transportation:	
						Fuel Cells:		Specialty Services:	Y		

TYPES OF BUSINESS:

Construction & Civil Engineering Services
Water Treatment Plant Development
Drilling Services
Oil & Gas Field Services
Unconventional Natural Gas Production

BRANDS/DIVISIONS/AFFILIATES:

W.L. Hailey & Company, Inc.
Intevras Technologies, LLC
Industrial Water Treatment Processes
Diberil Sociedad Anonima
Costa Fortuna

CONTACTS:

Note: Officers with more than one job title may be intentionally listed here more than once.

Andrew B. Schmitt, CEO
Andrew B. Schmitt, Pres.
Steven F. Crooke, General Counsel/VP/Sec.
Jerry W. Fanska, VP-Finance/Treas.
Gregory F. Aluce, Sr. VP/Pres., Water Resources Div.
Eric Despain, Sr. VP/Pres., Mineral Exploration
Phil Winner, Pres., Layne Energy
Jeffrey J. Reynolds, Exec. VP/Pres., Water Infrastructure Div.
David A. B. Brown, Chmn.

Phone: 913-677-6800	**Fax:** 913-362-0133
Toll-Free:	
Address: 1900 Shawnee Mission Pkwy., Mission Woods, KS 66205 US	

GROWTH PLANS/SPECIAL FEATURES:

Layne Christensen Co. provides drilling and construction services and related products in two principal markets: water infrastructure and mineral exploration. In addition, the company is a producer of unconventional natural gas for the energy market. The firm operates in four segments: Water Infrastructure, Mineral Exploration, Energy Services and Other. Through the Water Infrastructure division, Layne Christensen provides water systems services, such as test hole drilling, well construction, well development and testing, pump selection, equipment installation and pipeline construction; well and pump rehabilitation services; water and wastewater treatment and plant construction services; sewer rehabilitation; and environmental assessment drilling. The Mineral Exploration division conducts aboveground and underground drilling activities for the global mineral exploration industry. The Energy Services segment provides the exploration for, and acquisition, development, and production of, unconventional natural gas. The other segment includes two small specialty energy service companies and any other specialty operations not included in the other divisions. The firm operates throughout North America, as well as Africa, Australia, Europe, Brazil and, through its affiliates, in South America. Layne Christensen's customers include municipalities, investor-owned water utilities, industrial companies, global mining companies, consulting engineering firms, heavy civil construction contractors, oil and gas companies and agribusiness. In November 2009, the company acquired water infrastructure provider, W.L. Hailey & Company, Inc. for $15 million. In July 2010, the firm purchased Intevras Technologies, LLC, the holding company of Austin-based Industrial Water Treatment Processes, for $5.5 million. In August of the same year, the company acquired a 50% stake in Uruguayan firm, Diberil Sociedad Anonima, the parent of geotechnical firm, Costa Fortuna.

FINANCIALS:

Sales and profits are in thousands of dollars—add 000 to get the full amount. 2010 Note: Financial information for 2010 was not available for all companies at press time.

2010 Sales: $	2010 Profits: $	**U.S. Stock Ticker: LAYN**
2009 Sales: $1,008,063	2009 Profits: $26,534	**Int'l Ticker:** Int'l Exchange:
2008 Sales: $868,274	2008 Profits: $37,256	Employees: 3,600
2007 Sales: $722,768	2007 Profits: $26,252	Fiscal Year Ends: 1/31
2006 Sales: $463,015	2006 Profits: $14,681	Parent Company:

SALARIES/BENEFITS:

Pension Plan:	ESOP Stock Plan:	Profit Sharing:	Top Exec. Salary: $618,462	Bonus: $562,437
Savings Plan:	Stock Purch. Plan:		Second Exec. Salary: $363,231	Bonus: $248,334

OTHER THOUGHTS:

Apparent Women Officers or Directors:
Hot Spot for Advancement for Women/Minorities:

LOCATIONS: ("Y" = Yes)

West:	Southwest:	Midwest:	Southeast:	Northeast:	International:
Y	Y	Y	Y	Y	Y

LIGHT SA

www.light.com.br

Industry Group Code: 2211 **Ranks within this company's industry group:** Sales: 31 Profits: 25

Exploration/Production:		Refining/Retailing:		Utilities:		Alternative Energy:		Specialty Services:		Energy Mktg./Other Svcs.	
Exploration:		Refining:		Electric Utility:	Y	Waste/Solar/Other:		Consulting/Eng.:		Energy Marketing:	
Production:		Retailing:		Gas Utility:		Thermal/Steam:		Seismic:		Equipment/Machinery:	
Coal Production:		Convenience Stores:		Pipelines:		Wind:		Drilling:		Oil Field Services:	
		Chemicals:		Water:		Hydro:		InfoTech:		Air/Shipping Transportation:	
						Fuel Cells:		Specialty Services:			

TYPES OF BUSINESS:

Electric Utility

BRANDS/DIVISIONS/AFFILIATES:

Light Electric SA
Light Esco Ltda
Light Energia SA
Rio Minas Energia Participacoes SA
Companhia Energetica de Minas Gerais
Andrade Gutierrez SA Grants
Equatorial Energia SA
Luce Brazil Investment Fund Investments

CONTACTS:

Note: Officers with more than one job title may be intentionally listed here more than once.

Jose Luiz Alqueres, CEO
Ana Silvia Corso Matte, Dir.-Human Resources
Luiz Claudio Salles Cristofaro, Dir.-Legal Constraints
Roberto Manoel Guedes Alcoforado, VP-Oper. & Clients
Carlos Alberto Piazza, Comm. Affairs
Ronnie Vaz Moreira, Dir.-Investor Rel.
Andre Rocha Mahmoud, Superintendent-Internal Audit & Control
Luis Fernando de Almeida Guimaraes, Dir.-Generation
Paulo Roberto Ribeiro Pinto, Dir.-New Bus. & Institutional
Paulo Henrique Siqueira Born, Dir.-Sustainable Development & Concessions
Mozart Vitor Serra, Corp Sec.
Eduardo Borges de Andrade, Chmn.

Phone: 55-21-2211-2559 **Fax:** 55-21-2291-9207
Toll-Free:
Address: 168 Marechal Floriano Centro, P.O. Box 0571, Rio de Janeiro, CEP 20080-002 Brazil

GROWTH PLANS/SPECIAL FEATURES:

Light S.A. is a Brazilian company engaged in the transmission, generation, and exploration of electrical energy. It has 3.9 million customers. In addition, the company offers services related to the electric energy distribution and maintenance. The firm has three integrated companies: Light Electric S.A., which provides distribution for the company; Light Esco Ltda., which provides commercialization; and Light Energia S.A., which engages in generation and transmission for the firm. It operates five generating power plants and two pumping stations. The firm's generating system is composed of hydraulic structures, such as reservoirs, canals, dams and tunnels. RME has 52.1% of the total voting capital of the company and is composed of Companhia Energetica de Minas Gerais (Cemig); Andrade Gutierrez SA Grants (Grants AG); Equatorial Energia SA (Guinea); and Luce Brazil Investment Fund Investments (Luce). The company has 31 offices throughout Rio de Janeiro.

FINANCIALS:

Sales and profits are in thousands of dollars—add 000 to get the full amount. 2010 Note: Financial information for 2010 was not available for all companies at press time.

2010 Sales: $	2010 Profits: $	**U.S. Stock Ticker:**
2009 Sales: $3,168,680	2009 Profits: $355,920	**Int'l Ticker: LIGT3** Int'l Exchange: Sao Paulo-SAO
2008 Sales: $3,152,730	2008 Profits: $573,485	Employees:
2007 Sales: $	2007 Profits: $	Fiscal Year Ends:
2006 Sales: $	2006 Profits: $	Parent Company:

SALARIES/BENEFITS:

Pension Plan:	ESOP Stock Plan:	Profit Sharing:	Top Exec. Salary: $	Bonus: $
Savings Plan:	Stock Purch. Plan:		Second Exec. Salary: $	Bonus: $

OTHER THOUGHTS:

Apparent Women Officers or Directors: 1
Hot Spot for Advancement for Women/Minorities:

LOCATIONS: ("Y" = Yes)

West:	Southwest:	Midwest:	Southeast:	Northeast:	International:
					Y

LOEWS CORPORATION

www.loews.com

Industry Group Code: 524126 **Ranks within this company's industry group:** Sales: 1 Profits: 1

Exploration/Production:		Refining/Retailing:		Utilities:		Alternative Energy:		Specialty Services:		Energy Mktg./Other Svcs.	
Exploration:	Y	Refining:		Electric Utility:		Waste/Solar/Other:		Consulting/Eng.:		Energy Marketing:	
Production:	Y	Retailing:		Gas Utility:		Thermal/Steam:		Seismic:		Equipment/Machinery:	
Coal Production:		Convenience Stores:		Pipelines:	Y	Wind:		Drilling:		Oil Field Services:	
		Chemicals:		Water:		Hydro:		InfoTech:		Air/Shipping Transportation:	
						Fuel Cells:		Specialty Services:			

TYPES OF BUSINESS:

Direct Property & Casualty Insurance
Natural Gas Exploration & Production
Offshore Oil & Gas Drilling
Hotel Operation
Pipelines

BRANDS/DIVISIONS/AFFILIATES:

CNA Financial Corp.
Boardwalk Pipeline Partners, LP
Loews Hotels Holding Corporation
Diamond Offshore Drilling, Inc.
HighMount Exploration & Production, LLC

CONTACTS:

Note: Officers with more than one job title may be intentionally listed here more than once.

James S. Tisch, CEO
James S. Tisch, Pres.
Peter W. Keegan, CFO/Sr. VP
Alan Momeyer, VP-Human Resources
Robert D. Fields, CIO/VP
Gary W. Garson, General Counsel/Sr. VP/Sec.
Jonathan Nathanson, VP-Corp. Dev.
Candace Leeds, VP-Public Rel.
Darren Daugherty, Head-Investor Rel.
John J. Kenny, Treas.
Jonathan M. Tisch, Co-Chmn.
Jonathan M. Tisch, CEO/Chmn.-Loews Hotels
Mark S. Schwartz, Controller
Richard W. Scott, Chief Investment Officer/Sr. VP
Andrew H. Tisch, Co-Chmn.

Phone: 212-521-2000	**Fax:** 212-521-2525
Toll-Free:	
Address: 667 Madison Ave., New York, NY 10065-8087 US	

GROWTH PLANS/SPECIAL FEATURES:

Loews Corporation is a holding firm for companies involved in various industries. The company operates primarily through five subsidiaries: CNA Financial Corp., which accounted for 60% of the firm's 2009 consolidated revenue; Boardwalk Pipeline Partners, LP, 7%; Diamond Offshore Drilling, Inc., 26%; Loews Hotels Holdings Corp., 2%; and HighMount Exploration & Production, LLC, 5%. CNA Financial, a 90%-owned subsidiary, is an insurance holding company; its property and casualty insurance businesses are conducted by Continental Casualty Co. and The Continental Insurance Co. CNA's core business includes two operating segments: CNA Specialty, which provides domestic and international professional liability coverage for clients including, architects, lawyers, accountants, healthcare professionals, financial intermediaries and public and private companies; and CNA Commercial, which markets a broad range of property and casualty insurance products and services to small, middle-market and large businesses and organizations. Boardwalk Pipeline Partners, a 67%-owned subsidiary, specializes in the interstate transportation and storage of natural gas. The subsidiary conducts its operations through three companies: Texas Gas Transmission LLC, Gulf Crossing Pipeline Company LLC and Gulf South Pipeline, LP. Diamond Offshore, a 50.4%-owned subsidiary, owns and operates offshore oil and gas drilling rigs that are used by companies exploring for and producing hydrocarbons. The subsidiary owns 47 offshore rigs, of which 32 are semi-submersible. Loews Hotels, a wholly-owned subsidiary, operates 18 hotels, including Loews Annapolis; Hard Rock Hotel in Orlando, Florida; The Regency in New York; and Loews Hotel Vogue in Montreal, Canada. HighMount Exploration, another wholly-owned subsidiary, explores, produces and markets natural gas, with total proved reserves of 1.96 trillion cubic feet of natural gas equivalents.

FINANCIALS:

Sales and profits are in thousands of dollars—add 000 to get the full amount. 2010 Note: Financial information for 2010 was not available for all companies at press time.

2010 Sales: $	2010 Profits: $	**U.S. Stock Ticker: L**
2009 Sales: $14,117,000	2009 Profits: $564,000	**Int'l Ticker:** Int'l Exchange:
2008 Sales: $13,247,000	2008 Profits: $4,530,000	Employees: 18,500
2007 Sales: $14,302,000	2007 Profits: $2,488,000	Fiscal Year Ends: 12/31
2006 Sales: $17,702,000	2006 Profits: $2,491,300	Parent Company:

SALARIES/BENEFITS:

Pension Plan:	ESOP Stock Plan:	Profit Sharing:	Top Exec. Salary: $990,000	Bonus: $1,570,000
Savings Plan: Y	Stock Purch. Plan:		Second Exec. Salary: $975,000	Bonus: $2,575,000

OTHER THOUGHTS:

Apparent Women Officers or Directors: 5
Hot Spot for Advancement for Women/Minorities: Y

LOCATIONS: ("Y" = Yes)

West:	Southwest:	Midwest:	Southeast:	Northeast:	International:
Y	Y	Y	Y	Y	Y

LS POWER ASSOCIATES LP

www.lspower.com

Industry Group Code: 221121 **Ranks within this company's industry group:** Sales: Profits:

Exploration/Production:		Refining/Retailing:		Utilities:		Alternative Energy:		Specialty Services:		Energy Mktg./Other Svcs.	
Exploration:		Refining:		Electric Utility:	Y	Waste/Solar/Other:	Y	Consulting/Eng.:	Y	Energy Marketing:	Y
Production:		Retailing:		Gas Utility:	Y	Thermal/Steam:	Y	Seismic:		Equipment/Machinery:	
Coal Production:		Convenience Stores:		Pipelines:		Wind:	Y	Drilling:		Oil Field Services:	
		Chemicals:		Water:		Hydro:		InfoTech:		Air/Shipping Transportation:	
						Fuel Cells:		Specialty Services:			

TYPES OF BUSINESS:

Power Generation & Transmission
Infrastructure Development
Alternative Energy

BRANDS/DIVISIONS/AFFILIATES:

Cross Texas Transmission LLC
Wyoming-Colorado Intertie Project
Great Basin Transmission LLC
Dynegy Inc
San Diego Gas & Electric

CONTACTS:

Note: Officers with more than one job title may be intentionally listed here more than once.

Mike Segal, CEO
Eric Crawford, Contact-Media
Paul Thessen, Pres., LS Power Dev. LLC
Lawrence Willick, Sr. VP-LS Power Dev. LLC
Mike Segal, Chmn.

Phone: 212-615-3456	**Fax:**
Toll-Free:	
Address: 1700 Broadway, 35th Fl., New York, NY 10019 US	

GROWTH PLANS/SPECIAL FEATURES:

LS Power Associates, L.P. is a private energy company that engages primarily in the development, management and acquisition of power generation and transmission infrastructure. The company's primary interest is developing power generation products that can be sold to wholesale customers. However, its operations cover all areas of the power sector; these are as diverse as project management; power marketing; construction; regulatory; environmental; financial; legal; and tax. The company has been involved in projects throughout the U.S. that have resulted in 20,000 MW (Mega Watt) of power being generated. The company is involved in power generation through traditional coal-fired plants, but has in recent years invested in alternative energy infrastructure. LS Power currently owns or is developing natural gas, wind and solar power generation facilities. To this effect, the company recently announced the creation of its renewable energy division that will focus its efforts on the development of alternative energy through government incentive financing. The company's subsidiary, Cross Texas Transmission is currently developing $400 million transmission facility that will provide renewable energy state-wide. Subsidiary, Great Basin Transmission, LLC, operates the Southwest Intertie Project. The project is still under construction and will, upon completion, consist of a 180 mile transmission line between Wheatland, Wyoming and Brush, Colorado. This line will eventually supply 850 MW of wind generated electricity from its source in Wyoming to load centers in Colorado. In December 2009, the firm acquired nine coal-fired power stations from Dynegy, Inc. In that same month, the firm sold its West Georgia plant to Southern Power in exchange for the DeSoto plant in Arcadia, Florida. In August 2010, LS Power signed a 20-year power purchase agreement with San Diego Gas & Electric (SDG&E) to procure up to 45 MW of solar energy from the proposed Centinela Solar Energy facility.

FINANCIALS:

Sales and profits are in thousands of dollars—add 000 to get the full amount. 2010 Note: Financial information for 2010 was not available for all companies at press time.

2010 Sales: $	2010 Profits: $	**U.S. Stock Ticker: Private**
2009 Sales: $	2009 Profits: $	**Int'l Ticker:** Int'l Exchange:
2008 Sales: $	2008 Profits: $	Employees:
2007 Sales: $	2007 Profits: $	Fiscal Year Ends:
2006 Sales: $	2006 Profits: $	Parent Company:

SALARIES/BENEFITS:

Pension Plan:	ESOP Stock Plan:	Profit Sharing:	Top Exec. Salary: $	Bonus: $
Savings Plan:	Stock Purch. Plan:		Second Exec. Salary: $	Bonus: $

OTHER THOUGHTS:

Apparent Women Officers or Directors:
Hot Spot for Advancement for Women/Minorities:

LOCATIONS: ("Y" = Yes)

West:	Southwest:	Midwest:	Southeast:	Northeast:	International:
Y	Y	Y	Y	Y	

LUFKIN INDUSTRIES INC

www.lufkin.com

Industry Group Code: 33313 **Ranks within this company's industry group:** Sales: 3 Profits: 4

Exploration/Production:		Refining/Retailing:		Utilities:		Alternative Energy:		Specialty Services:		Energy Mktg./Other Svcs.	
Exploration:		Refining:		Electric Utility:		Waste/Solar/Other:		Consulting/Eng.:		Energy Marketing:	
Production:		Retailing:		Gas Utility:		Thermal/Steam:		Seismic:		Equipment/Machinery:	Y
Coal Production:		Convenience Stores:		Pipelines:		Wind:		Drilling:		Oil Field Services:	
		Chemicals:		Water:		Hydro:		InfoTech:		Air/Shipping Transportation:	
						Fuel Cells:		Specialty Services:			

TYPES OF BUSINESS:

Oil Pump Manufacturing
Gearbox Manufacturing

BRANDS/DIVISIONS/AFFILIATES:

International Lift Systems LLC.
Rotating Machinery Technology, Inc.

CONTACTS:

Note: Officers with more than one job title may be intentionally listed here more than once.

John F. Glick, CEO
John F. Glick, Pres.
Christopher L. Boone, CFO/VP
Brian Gifford, VP-Human Resources
Scott H. Semlinger, VP-Mfg. Tech.
Paul G. Perez, General Counsel/VP/Sec.
Christopher L. Boone, Treas.
Terry L. Orr, VP-Power Transmission Div.
Mark E. Crews, VP-Oilfield Div.
Douglas V. Smith, Chmn.

Phone: 936-634-2211	**Fax:** 936-637-5272
Toll-Free:	
Address: 601 S. Raguet St., Lufkin, TX 75902-0849 US	

GROWTH PLANS/SPECIAL FEATURES:

Lufkin Industries, Inc. is a leading manufacturer of global supplier of oil field and power transmission products. The firm operates through two business segments: oil field and power transmission. The oil field division manufactures, designs, installs and services artificial lift products, including reciprocating rod lift (also called pumping units), gas lift, plunger lift equipment and related products. Pumping units manufactured include air-balanced units; beam-balanced units; crank-balanced units; and a Mark II Unitorque unit. In addition, the company designs, manufactures, installs and services computer control equipment and analytical services for artificial lift equipment; and operates an iron foundry to produce castings for new pumping units. The power transmission segment designs, manufactures and services speed increasing and reducing gearboxes for industrial applications. Speed increasers are those that convert from low-speed and high torque input to high-speed and lower torque output, while the speed reducing gearboxes do the reverse. This segment also manufactures spare parts and parts for aftermarket service; and operates an industrial gear repair facility devoted to the rebuild, repair and overhaul needs of the aftermarket end-user. The company also produces medium to large, low to mid-volume ductile and gray iron castings. These are used in a wide range of applications, including valves, machine tools, pump and compressors, construction equipment and special machinery. In March 2009, the firm acquired International Lift Systems LLC, an artificial lift system manufacturer based in Texas. In July 2009, Lufkin acquired Rotating Machinery Technology, Inc., a designer and manufacturer of precision, custom-engineered tilting-pad bearings for high-speed turbo equipment. In July 2010, the company announced plans for the construction of an oilfield and power transmission manufacturing facility in Romania.

The company offers employees medical, dental and vision insurance; 401(k); a pension plan; a dependant scholarship program; and tuition reimbursement.

FINANCIALS:

Sales and profits are in thousands of dollars—add 000 to get the full amount. 2010 Note: Financial information for 2010 was not available for all companies at press time.

2010 Sales: $	2010 Profits: $	**U.S. Stock Ticker: LUFK**
2009 Sales: $521,359	2009 Profits: $22,026	**Int'l Ticker:** Int'l Exchange:
2008 Sales: $741,194	2008 Profits: $88,239	Employees:
2007 Sales: $555,806	2007 Profits: $74,211	Fiscal Year Ends: 12/31
2006 Sales: $605,492	2006 Profits: $72,994	Parent Company:

SALARIES/BENEFITS:

Pension Plan: Y	ESOP Stock Plan:	Profit Sharing:	Top Exec. Salary: $520,000	Bonus: $
Savings Plan: Y	Stock Purch. Plan:		Second Exec. Salary: $255,000	Bonus: $

OTHER THOUGHTS:

Apparent Women Officers or Directors: 1
Hot Spot for Advancement for Women/Minorities:

LOCATIONS: ("Y" = Yes)

West:	Southwest:	Midwest:	Southeast:	Northeast:	International:
	Y			Y	Y

LUKOIL (OAO)

www.lukoil.com

Industry Group Code: 211111 **Ranks within this company's industry group:** Sales: 17 Profits: 12

Exploration/Production:		**Refining/Retailing:**		**Utilities:**		**Alternative Energy:**		**Specialty Services:**		**Energy Mktg./Other Svcs.**	
Exploration:	Y	Refining:	Y	Electric Utility:		Waste/Solar/Other:		Consulting/Eng.:		Energy Marketing:	
Production:	Y	Retailing:	Y	Gas Utility:		Thermal/Steam:		Seismic:		Equipment/Machinery:	
Coal Production:		Convenience Stores:	Y	Pipelines:	Y	Wind:		Drilling:		Oil Field Services:	
		Chemicals:	Y	Water:		Hydro:		InfoTech:		Air/Shipping Transportation:	Y
						Fuel Cells:		Specialty Services:			

TYPES OF BUSINESS:

Oil & Gas Exploration & Production
Petroleum Refining
Pipeline Operations
Gas Stations
Ocean Terminals & Oil Tankers
Natural Gas & Petrochemical Processing Plants

BRANDS/DIVISIONS/AFFILIATES:

UGK TGK-8

CONTACTS:

Note: Officers with more than one job title may be intentionally listed here more than once.

Vagit Alekperov, Pres.
Vladimir Nekrasov, First VP-Refining & Mktg.
Anatoly Moskalenko, Head-Human Resources
Dzhevan Cheloyants, Head-Tech.
Ivan Masliaev, Head-Legal Support
Leonid Fedun, Head-Strategic Dev. & Investment Analysis
Anatoly Barkov, First VP-Corp. Security & Comm.
Alexander Matytsyn, VP-Treasury & Corp. Financing
Vladimir Mulyak, First VP- Oil & Gas Prod. & Infrastructure
Sergei Petrovich Kukura, First VP-Economics & Finance
Evgueni Havkin, Sec.
Lyubov Khoba, Chief Accountant
Valery Grayfer, Chmn.
Valery Subbotin, VP-Supplies & Sales

Phone: 7-495-627-44-44 **Fax:** 7-495-625-7016
Toll-Free:
Address: 11 Sretensky Blvd., Moscow, 101000 Russia

GROWTH PLANS/SPECIAL FEATURES:

Lukoil OAO, one of Russia's largest oil companies, operates in oil and gas exploration and production and the production and sale of petroleum products. The company owns gas processing and petrochemical refineries in Russia, Eastern and Western Europe. In terms of capacity, the company has roughly 1% of global proven oil reserves and 2.4% of global oil production. It also represents approximately 18% of both Russia's total oil production and its refining capacity. The company controls 13,696 billion barrels of proven oil reserves and 22,850 billion cubic feet of proven natural gas reserves. In Russia, the company owns refineries in Perm, Volgograd, Ukhta and Nizhny Novgorod, with a total capacity of 45.1 million tons of oil per year. The firm has ongoing exploration and production projects in Kazakhstan, Egypt, Azerbaijan, Uzbekistan, Saudi Arabia, Colombia, Venezuela, Cote d'Ivoire, Ghana and Iraq. The company's primary areas of gas production in Russia are the Bolshekhetskaya Depression, the Northern Caspian, the Tsentralno-Astrakhanskoye fields, the Kandym-Khauzak-Shady project in Uzbekistan and the Shakh Deniz project in Azerbaijan. The group recently created a power generation business sector, which consists of the UGK TGK-8 plant in Russia, as well as facilities in Bulgaria, Romania and Ukraine. The firm has a total of 463 small generating units in operation with a total capacity of 336.8 megawatts. The company markets its products in 26 countries, including Russia, Azerbaijan, Belarus, Georgia, Moldova, Ukraine, Bulgaria, Hungary, Finland, Estonia, Latvia, Lithuania, Poland, Serbia, Montenegro, Romania, Macedonia, Cyprus, Turkey, Belgium, Luxemburg, the Czech Republic, Slovakia, Croatia and the U.S. The company also has 199 tank farm facilities and 6,620 filling stations. In March 2010, the company announced the construction of a unique drilling unit at Kaliningrad with a hydraulic mobility system, allowing it to move in all directions and rotate 360 degrees.

FINANCIALS:

Sales and profits are in thousands of dollars—add 000 to get the full amount. 2010 Note: Financial information for 2010 was not available for all companies at press time.

2010 Sales: $	2010 Profits: $	**U.S. Stock Ticker: LUKOY**
2009 Sales: $81,083,000	2009 Profits: $7,011,000	**Int'l Ticker: LKOH** Int'l Exchange: Moscow-MICEX
2008 Sales: $107,680,000	2008 Profits: $9,144,000	Employees:
2007 Sales: $81,891,000	2007 Profits: $9,511,000	Fiscal Year Ends: 12/31
2006 Sales: $67,684,000	2006 Profits: $7,484,000	Parent Company:

SALARIES/BENEFITS:

Pension Plan:	ESOP Stock Plan:	Profit Sharing:	Top Exec. Salary: $	Bonus: $
Savings Plan:	Stock Purch. Plan:		Second Exec. Salary: $	Bonus: $

OTHER THOUGHTS:

Apparent Women Officers or Directors: 1
Hot Spot for Advancement for Women/Minorities:

LOCATIONS: ("Y" = Yes)

West:	Southwest:	Midwest:	Southeast:	Northeast:	International:
				Y	Y

LYONDELLBASELL INDUSTRIES

www.lyondellbasell.com

Industry Group Code: 325110 **Ranks within this company's industry group:** Sales: 3 Profits: 5

Exploration/Production:		Refining/Retailing:		Utilities:		Alternative Energy:		Specialty Services:		Energy Mktg./Other Svcs.	
Exploration:		Refining:	Y	Electric Utility:		Waste/Solar/Other:		Consulting/Eng.:		Energy Marketing:	
Production:		Retailing:		Gas Utility:		Thermal/Steam:		Seismic:		Equipment/Machinery:	
Coal Production:		Convenience Stores:		Pipelines:		Wind:		Drilling:		Oil Field Services:	
		Chemicals:	Y	Water:		Hydro:		InfoTech:		Air/Shipping Transportation:	
						Fuel Cells:		Specialty Services:			

TYPES OF BUSINESS:

Polymers & Petrochemicals
Intermediate & Performance Chemicals
Petroleum Products
Refining
Biofuels
Automotive Parts
Medical Applications
Durable Textiles

BRANDS/DIVISIONS/AFFILIATES:

Lyondell Chemical Co
Basell AF
Access Industries

CONTACTS: *Note: Officers with more than one job title may be intentionally listed here more than once.*

James L. Gallogly, CEO
Kent Potter, CFO/Exec. VP
Paul Davies, Chief Human Resources Officer
Massimo Covezzi, Sr. VP-R&D
Craig Glidden, Chief Legal Officer/Exec. VP
Pat Quarles, Sr. VP-Intermediates & Derivatives
Kevin Brown, Sr. VP-Refining
Sam Smolik, VP-Health, Safety & Environment
Bob Patel, Sr. VP-Olefins & Polyolefins, Americas
Anton de Vries, Pres., Europe, Asia & Int'l

Phone: 31-10-275-5500	**Fax:**
Toll-Free:	
Address: P.O. Box 2416, Rotterdam, 3000 CK The Netherlands	

GROWTH PLANS/SPECIAL FEATURES:

LyondellBasell Industries is one of the world's largest producers and marketers of polymers, petrochemicals and fuels. It is owned by Access Industries, a private equity firm. The firm was formed through the merger of Basell AF S.C.A., a chemical manufacturing company and polypropylene producer, and Lyondell Chemical Co., a leading manufacturer of chemicals and plastics and a refiner of crude oil. It is one of the world's leading providers of propylene oxide, generating sales from more than 100 countries, and has 59 manufacturing sites in 18 countries. The firm operates in five segments: chemicals, polymers, fuels, refining and technology. The chemicals segment offers services and applications including insulation; home furnishings; adhesives and sealants; aircraft deicers; cosmetics; and more. The firm has several polymers joint ventures. This division produces and markets polyolefins and advanced polyolefins. Some of its client services offered include clothing; medical tubing; pharmaceutical packaging; and toys. The fuels segment offers clients automotive and industrial engine lube oils; biofuels; heating oil; and automotive, aviation and diesel fuels. The technology segment is responsible for process licensing, catalyst sales and other services. U.S. sales account for 54% of the firm's sales while Europe and the rest of the world account for 35% and 11% respectively. In April 2010, the firm emerged from bankruptcy, and in October 2010, its shares began trading on the NYSE.

FINANCIALS: **Sales and profits are in thousands of dollars—add 000 to get the full amount. 2010 Note: Financial information for 2010 was not available for all companies at press time.**

2010 Sales: $	2010 Profits: $	**U.S. Stock Ticker: Subsidiary**
2009 Sales: $30,828,000	2009 Profits: $-2,865,000	**Int'l Ticker:** Int'l Exchange:
2008 Sales: $50,706,000	2008 Profits: $-7,321,000	Employees:
2007 Sales: $17,120,000	2007 Profits: $661,000	Fiscal Year Ends: 12/31
2006 Sales: $44,735,000	2006 Profits: $168,000	Parent Company: ACCESS INDUSTRIES

SALARIES/BENEFITS:

Pension Plan:	ESOP Stock Plan:	Profit Sharing:	Top Exec. Salary: $	Bonus: $3,000,000
Savings Plan:	Stock Purch. Plan:		Second Exec. Salary: $	Bonus: $

OTHER THOUGHTS:

Apparent Women Officers or Directors: 1
Hot Spot for Advancement for Women/Minorities:

LOCATIONS: ("Y" = Yes)

West:	Southwest:	Midwest:	Southeast:	Northeast:	International:
	Y	Y	Y	Y	Y

MAGELLAN MIDSTREAM PARTNERS LP

www.magellanlp.com

Industry Group Code: 486 **Ranks within this company's industry group:** Sales: 19 Profits: 11

Exploration/Production:		**Refining/Retailing:**		**Utilities:**		**Alternative Energy:**		**Specialty Services:**		**Energy Mktg./Other Svcs.**	
Exploration:		Refining:		Electric Utility:		Waste/Solar/Other:		Consulting/Eng.:		Energy Marketing:	
Production:		Retailing:		Gas Utility:		Thermal/Steam:		Seismic:		Equipment/Machinery:	
Coal Production:		Convenience Stores:		Pipelines:	Y	Wind:		Drilling:		Oil Field Services:	
		Chemicals:		Water:		Hydro:		InfoTech:		Air/Shipping Transportation:	
						Fuel Cells:		Specialty Services:	Y		

TYPES OF BUSINESS:

Pipelines-Petroleum Storage & Distribution Services
Petroleum Pipelines
Petroleum Products Terminal Facilities
Ammonia Pipelines

BRANDS/DIVISIONS/AFFILIATES:

Longhorn Partners Pipeline LP

CONTACTS:

Note: Officers with more than one job title may be intentionally listed here more than once.

Don R. Wellendorf, CEO
Michael N. Mears, COO
Don R. Wellendorf, Pres.
John D. Chandler, CFO/Sr. VP
Lisa J. Korner, Sr. VP-Human Resources
Richard A. Olson, Sr. VP-Tech. Svcs.
Lisa J. Korner, Sr. VP-Admin.
Lonny E. Townsend, General Counsel/Sr. VP/Compliance & Ethics Officer
Richard A. Olson, Sr. VP-Oper.
Brett C. Riley, Sr. VP-Bus. Dev.
Bruce Heine, Contact-Media Rel.
Paula Farrell, Contact-Investor Rel.
John D. Chandler, Treas.
Suzanne H. Costin, Sec.
Don R. Wellendorf, Chmn.

Phone: 918-574-7000	**Fax:** 918-573-6714
Toll-Free: 800-574-6671	
Address: 1 Williams Ctr., Tulsa, OK 74172 US	

GROWTH PLANS/SPECIAL FEATURES:

Magellan Midstream Partners, LP transports, stores and distributes refined petroleum products. It also has interests in pipelines and terminal facilities. Magellan owns and operates a petroleum products pipeline system of approximately 9,500 miles that covers a 13-state area, extending from the Gulf Coast refining region of Texas through the Midwest to Colorado, North Dakota, Minnesota, Wisconsin and Illinois. Its pipeline system transports petroleum products and liquefied petroleum gas (LPG) and includes 51 terminals. The products transported on its pipeline system are largely transportation fuels, comprised of approximately 57% gasoline, 34% distillates (which include diesel fuels and heating oil) and 9% aviation fuel and LPG. The firm's petroleum products pipeline system segment accounts for approximately 80% of its total revenues. The firm has seven petroleum product marine terminal facilities located along the U.S. East and Gulf Coasts, and 27 inland petroleum product terminals located mainly in the southeastern U.S. The company's ammonia pipeline system provides ammonia, which is used as a nitrogen fertilizer, for ultimate distribution to end-users in Iowa, Kansas, Minnesota, Missouri, Nebraska, Oklahoma and South Dakota. The system extends roughly 1,100 miles from production facilities in Texas and Oklahoma to various points in the Midwest. Magellan's customers include retailers of gasoline and other petroleum products, wholesalers that sell to retailers and large commercial and industrial end users, exchange transaction customers and traders. In mid 2009, the company acquired the assets of Longhorn Partners Pipeline, L.P., including a 700-mile common carrier pipeline system from El Paso to Houston, Texas, for approximately $350 million. In September 2010, Magellan acquired 7.8 million barrels of crude oil storage and over 100 miles of active petroleum pipelines from BP Pipelines (North America), Inc. for $289 million.

The company offer employees benefits including life, AD&D, health and dental insurance; paid time off; and flexible spending accounts.

FINANCIALS:

Sales and profits are in thousands of dollars—add 000 to get the full amount. 2010 Note: Financial information for 2010 was not available for all companies at press time.

2010 Sales: $	2010 Profits: $	**U.S. Stock Ticker: MMP**
2009 Sales: $1,014,171	2009 Profits: $226,205	**Int'l Ticker:** Int'l Exchange:
2008 Sales: $1,212,786	2008 Profits: $346,613	Employees: 1,217
2007 Sales: $1,318,121	2007 Profits: $242,790	Fiscal Year Ends: 12/31
2006 Sales: $1,223,560	2006 Profits: $192,728	Parent Company:

SALARIES/BENEFITS:

Pension Plan:	ESOP Stock Plan:	Profit Sharing:	Top Exec. Salary: $479,769	Bonus: $821,845
Savings Plan: Y	Stock Purch. Plan:		Second Exec. Salary: $351,831	Bonus: $361,612

OTHER THOUGHTS:

Apparent Women Officers or Directors: 3
Hot Spot for Advancement for Women/Minorities: Y

LOCATIONS: ("Y" = Yes)

West:	Southwest:	Midwest:	Southeast:	Northeast:	International:
Y	Y	Y	Y	Y	

MANITOBA HYDRO-ELECTRIC

www.hydro.mb.ca

Industry Group Code: 221 **Ranks within this company's industry group:** Sales: 44 Profits: 30

Exploration/Production:		Refining/Retailing:		Utilities:		Alternative Energy:		Specialty Services:		Energy Mktg./Other Svcs.	
Exploration:		Refining:		Electric Utility:	Y	Waste/Solar/Other:		Consulting/Eng.:	Y	Energy Marketing:	
Production:		Retailing:		Gas Utility:	Y	Thermal/Steam:	Y	Seismic:		Equipment/Machinery:	
Coal Production:		Convenience Stores:		Pipelines:	Y	Wind:	Y	Drilling:		Oil Field Services:	
		Chemicals:		Water:		Hydro:	Y	InfoTech:		Air/Shipping Transportation:	
						Fuel Cells:		Specialty Services:	Y		

TYPES OF BUSINESS:

Utilities-Electricity & Natural Gas
Utility Services
Pipelines
Research & Development
Thermal Rating Services
Hydroelectric Power Generation
Natural Gas Utility

BRANDS/DIVISIONS/AFFILIATES:

Centra Gas
Manitoba Hydro International, Ltd.
Manitoba HVDC Research Centre, Inc.
PSCAD
Manitoba Hydro Utility Services, Ltd.

CONTACTS: *Note: Officers with more than one job title may be intentionally listed here more than once.*

Robert B. Brennan, CEO
Robert B. Brennan, Pres.
Vince A. Warden, CFO
Lloyd Kuczek, VP-Mktg. & Customer Service
Gary Maksymyk, Head-Human Resources
Rhonda Orr, VP-R&D
Glen Reitmeier, Head-IT
Randy Raban, Head-Eng. Svcs.
Vince A. Warden, Sr. VP-Admin.
Ken M. Tennenhouse, General Counsel/Corp. Sec.
Dave Cormie, Head-Power Oper. & Sales
Lyn Wray, VP-Corp. Planning & Strategic Analysis
Ruth Kristjanson, VP-Corp. Rel.
Vince A. Warden, Sr. VP-Finance
Ken R. F. Adams, Sr. VP-Power Supply
Al M. Snyder, VP-Special Projects
Ed Tymofichuk, VP-Transmission
Andy Miles, Head-Aboriginal Rel.
Victor H. (Vic) Schroeder, Chmn.
Brent Reed, VP-Customer Service & Dist.

Phone: 204-474-3311	**Fax:** 204-474-4868
Toll-Free: 888-624-9376	
Address: 360 Portage Ave., Winnipeg, MB R3C 0G8 Canada	

GROWTH PLANS/SPECIAL FEATURES:

Manitoba Hydro-Electric (Manitoba Hydro), one of Manitoba's major energy utilities, serves 532,000 electric customers. It operates 14 hydroelectric generating plants and two thermal generating stations, for a combined generating capacity of 5.49 gigawatts. Approximately 97% of the firm's sold power is hydroelectrically generated, less than 1% is thermally generated, 1% is wind generated and 1% is imported. The firm generates roughly 80% of its electricity on the Nelson River. Through 13 interconnecting transmission lines, Manitoba Hydro connects its transmission network to neighboring utilities in Ontario, Saskatchewan and the Midwestern U.S., which allows it to export surplus power and import power when low water flows hinder its generation capabilities. Subsidiary Centra Gas delivers natural gas to nearly 264,000 residential, commercial and industrial customers through a network of 1,081 miles of transmission pipeline and 4,415 miles of distribution pipeline. Approximately 90% of the firm's total revenue comes from electricity sales, while the remaining 10% from natural gas. The firm's subsidiaries include the following. Manitoba Hydro International, Ltd. provides electric utility expertise in the planning, design, construction, management and operation of generation, transmission and distribution facilities to clients in over 60 countries worldwide. Manitoba HVDC Research Centre, Inc. performs research and development in high-voltage direct current and power electronic technologies, instrumentation and simulation. Its PSCAD family of simulation products, the core of its technologies, is used worldwide. Manitoba Hydro Utility Services, Ltd. provides meter-reading services for the company and other utilities.

Employees of Manitoba Hydro receive dental and prescription drug benefits; life insurance; long-term disability coverage; flex-time and telecommuting options; and employee assistance.

FINANCIALS: **Sales and profits are in thousands of dollars—add 000 to get the full amount. 2010 Note: Financial information for 2010 was not available for all companies at press time.**

2010 Sales: $	2010 Profits: $	**U.S. Stock Ticker: Government-Owned**
2009 Sales: $2,233,770	2009 Profits: $281,580	**Int'l Ticker:** Int'l Exchange:
2008 Sales: $2,126,050	2008 Profits: $326,940	Employees:
2007 Sales: $2,261,340	2007 Profits: $128,910	Fiscal Year Ends: 3/31
2006 Sales: $1,899,666	2006 Profits: $393,718	Parent Company:

SALARIES/BENEFITS:

Pension Plan: Y	ESOP Stock Plan:	Profit Sharing:	Top Exec. Salary: $	Bonus: $
Savings Plan:	Stock Purch. Plan:		Second Exec. Salary: $	Bonus: $

OTHER THOUGHTS:

Apparent Women Officers or Directors: 10
Hot Spot for Advancement for Women/Minorities: Y

LOCATIONS: ("Y" = Yes)

West:	Southwest:	Midwest:	Southeast:	Northeast:	International:
					Y

MARATHON OIL CORP

www.marathon.com

Industry Group Code: 211111 **Ranks within this company's industry group:** Sales: 21 Profits: 35

Exploration/Production:		Refining/Retailing:		Utilities:		Alternative Energy:		Specialty Services:		Energy Mktg./Other Svcs.	
Exploration:	Y	Refining:	Y	Electric Utility:		Waste/Solar/Other:		Consulting/Eng.:		Energy Marketing:	Y
Production:	Y	Retailing:	Y	Gas Utility:	Y	Thermal/Steam:		Seismic:		Equipment/Machinery:	
Coal Production:		Convenience Stores:		Pipelines:	Y	Wind:		Drilling:		Oil Field Services:	Y
		Chemicals:		Water:		Hydro:		InfoTech:		Air/Shipping Transportation:	
						Fuel Cells:		Specialty Services:			

TYPES OF BUSINESS:

Oil & Gas Exploration & Production
Petroleum Marketing, Refining & Transportation
Gas Stations
Energy Marketing

BRANDS/DIVISIONS/AFFILIATES:

Marathon Petroleum Company LLC
Pilot Travel Centers LLC
Speedway SuperAmerica LLC
Marathon Oil Ireland, Ltd.

CONTACTS:

Note: Officers with more than one job title may be intentionally listed here more than once.

Clarence P. Cazalot, Jr., CEO
Clarence P. Cazalot, Jr., Pres.
Janet F. Clark, CFO/Exec. VP
Eileen M. Campbell, VP-Human Resources
Thomas K. Sneed, CIO
Sylvia J. Kerrigan, General Counsel/VP/Sec.
Jerry Howard, Sr. VP-Corp. Affairs
Howard J. Thill, VP-Investor Rel. & Public Affairs
Paul C. Reinbolt, VP-Finance/Treas.
R. Douglas Rogers, VP-Health, Environment & Safety
Michael K. Stewart, VP-Acct./Controller
Daniel J. Sullenbarger, VP-Corp. Compliance & Ethics
Stephen J. Landry, VP-Tax
Thomas J. Usher, Chmn.

Phone: 713-629-6600	**Fax:**
Toll-Free: 866-462-7284	
Address: 5555 San Felipe Rd., Houston, TX 77056-2723 US	

GROWTH PLANS/SPECIAL FEATURES:

Marathon Oil Corp. explores for crude oil and natural gas worldwide, operates refineries and maintains U.S. retail gas outlets. It operates in four segments: Exploration and products (E&P); oil sands mining (OSM); refining, marketing and transportation (RM&T); and integrated gas (IG). The E&P segment explores for, produces and markets liquid hydrocarbons and natural gas on a worldwide basis. It conducts its exploration, development and production activities in eight countries. Principal exploration activities are in the U.S., Angola, Norway and Indonesia. The company plans to begin exploration activities in Poland in 2010. Principal development and production activities are in the U.S., the U.K., Norway, Equatorial Guinea and Libya. In 2009, the division's net sales averaged 400,000 barrels of oil equivalent per day. The OSM segment mines, extracts and transports bitumen from oil sands deposits in Alberta, Canada, and upgrades the bitumen to produce and market synthetic crude oil and by-products. The RM&T segment refines, markets and transports crude oil and petroleum products, primarily in the Midwest, upper Great Plains, Gulf Coast and southeastern regions of the U.S. The IG segments markets and transports products manufactured from natural gas, such as liquefied natural gas and methanol, on a worldwide basis. This segment is also developing other projects to link stranded natural gas resources with key demand areas. Marathon-branded retail gas outlets, operated by third-party entrepreneurs, include more than 4,600 locations across 24 states, as well as 1,603 Speedway locations. In February 2010, the company sold 20% working interest in the Production Sharing Contract and Joint Operating Agreement in Angola Block 32 to Sociedad Nacional de Combustiveis de Angola, E.P.'s wholly-owned subsidiary, Sonangol Pesquisa e Producao, S.A. Marathon will retain a 10% working interest.

The company offers its employees medical and dental coverage; life and disability insurance; flexible spending accounts; tuition reimbursement; and an employee assistance program.

FINANCIALS:

Sales and profits are in thousands of dollars—add 000 to get the full amount. 2010 Note: Financial information for 2010 was not available for all companies at press time.

2010 Sales: $	2010 Profits: $	**U.S. Stock Ticker: MRO**
2009 Sales: $54,139,000	2009 Profits: $1,463,000	**Int'l Ticker:** Int'l Exchange:
2008 Sales: $78,130,000	2008 Profits: $3,528,000	Employees: 28,855
2007 Sales: $64,751,000	2007 Profits: $3,956,000	Fiscal Year Ends: 12/31
2006 Sales: $64,896,000	2006 Profits: $5,234,000	Parent Company:

SALARIES/BENEFITS:

Pension Plan: Y	ESOP Stock Plan:	Profit Sharing:	Top Exec. Salary: $1,400,000	Bonus: $2,100,000
Savings Plan: Y	Stock Purch. Plan:		Second Exec. Salary: $900,000	Bonus: $950,000

OTHER THOUGHTS:

Apparent Women Officers or Directors: 4
Hot Spot for Advancement for Women/Minorities: Y

LOCATIONS: ("Y" = Yes)

West:	Southwest:	Midwest:	Southeast:	Northeast:	International:
Y	Y	Y	Y	Y	Y

MARATHON PETROLEUM COMPANY LLC www.marathonpetroleum.com

Industry Group Code: 324110 **Ranks within this company's industry group:** Sales: Profits:

Exploration/Production:		Refining/Retailing:		Utilities:		Alternative Energy:		Specialty Services:		Energy Mktg./Other Svcs.	
Exploration:		Refining:	Y	Electric Utility:		Waste/Solar/Other:		Consulting/Eng.:		Energy Marketing:	
Production:		Retailing:	Y	Gas Utility:		Thermal/Steam:		Seismic:		Equipment/Machinery:	
Coal Production:		Convenience Stores:	Y	Pipelines:	Y	Wind:		Drilling:		Oil Field Services:	
		Chemicals:	Y	Water:		Hydro:		InfoTech:		Air/Shipping Transportation:	
						Fuel Cells:		Specialty Services:			

TYPES OF BUSINESS:

Petroleum Refining
Gas Stations
Asphalt Production & Retail
Petrochemicals & Lubricants
Pipelines
Ethanol Production

BRANDS/DIVISIONS/AFFILIATES:

Marathon Oil Corp
Marathon Pipe Line LLC
Speedway SuperAmerica
Centennial Pipeline LLC

GROWTH PLANS/SPECIAL FEATURES:

Marathon Petroleum Company, LLC is a subsidiary of Marathon Oil Corporation. The firm is engaged in refining, marketing and transportation operations. The company has operations in the Midwest, Upper Great Plains and Southeast regions of the U.S. as a petroleum products marketer, owning or operating 87 light product and asphalt terminals, including two refinery light products terminals. Marathon Petroleum affiliate Marathon Pipe Line, LLC operates roughly 5,000 miles of pipeline through 15 states, which transport natural gas, crude oil and petroleum products to and from refineries, terminals and other pipelines. The company also operates Centennial Pipeline LLC, a joint venture with Texas Eastern Products Pipeline Company, LLC that operates a 795-mile pipeline from Texas to Illinois. Marathon Petroleum's retail operations include Speedway SuperAmerica, which has more than 1,600 stores in nine Midwestern states; and approximately 4,600 Marathon branded stations in 16 states in the Midwest and Southeast. Through its marketing division, the firm is a major wholesale supplier of gasoline and distillate to resellers and consumer end users. The company also markets special products such as propane, propylene, off-gas, benzene, toluene, aliphatic solvents, base oils, slack wax, aromatic oils, pitch, dilute naphthalene oil, molten sulfur and maleic anhydride.

CONTACTS: *Note: Officers with more than one job title may be intentionally listed here more than once.*

Gary R. Heminger, Pres.
Tom Kelley, Sr. VP-Mktg.
David Heppner, Mgr.-Wholesale Mktg.
Paul Smith, Mgr.-Real Estate
Gary Hewitt, Mgr.-Asphalt Mktg.
Bill McCleave, Mgr.-Brand Mktg.

Phone: 419-422-2121 **Fax:** 419-425-7040
Toll-Free:
Address: 539 S. Main St., Findlay, OH 45840-3295 US

FINANCIALS: **Sales and profits are in thousands of dollars—add 000 to get the full amount. 2010 Note: Financial information for 2010 was not available for all companies at press time.**

2010 Sales: $	2010 Profits: $	**U.S. Stock Ticker: Subsidiary**
2009 Sales: $	2009 Profits: $	**Int'l Ticker:** Int'l Exchange:
2008 Sales: $	2008 Profits: $	Employees:
2007 Sales: $	2007 Profits: $	Fiscal Year Ends: 12/31
2006 Sales: $	2006 Profits: $	Parent Company: MARATHON OIL CORP

SALARIES/BENEFITS:

Pension Plan: Y	ESOP Stock Plan:	Profit Sharing:	Top Exec. Salary: $	Bonus: $950,000
Savings Plan:	Stock Purch. Plan:		Second Exec. Salary: $	Bonus: $

OTHER THOUGHTS:

Apparent Women Officers or Directors:
Hot Spot for Advancement for Women/Minorities:

LOCATIONS: ("Y" = Yes)

West:	Southwest:	Midwest:	Southeast:	Northeast:	International:
	Y	Y	Y	Y	

MASSEY ENERGY COMPANY

www.masseyenergyco.com

Industry Group Code: 21211 **Ranks within this company's industry group:** Sales: 9 Profits: 9

Exploration/Production:		Refining/Retailing:		Utilities:		Alternative Energy:		Specialty Services:		Energy Mktg./Other Svcs.	
Exploration:		Refining:		Electric Utility:		Waste/Solar/Other:		Consulting/Eng.:		Energy Marketing:	
Production:	Y	Retailing:		Gas Utility:		Thermal/Steam:		Seismic:		Equipment/Machinery:	
Coal Production:	Y	Convenience Stores:		Pipelines:		Wind:		Drilling:		Oil Field Services:	
		Chemicals:		Water:		Hydro:		InfoTech:		Air/Shipping Transportation:	
						Fuel Cells:		Specialty Services:			

TYPES OF BUSINESS:

Coal Mining
Natural Gas Gathering
Synthetic Fuel Manufacturing
Rail Cargo Transport

BRANDS/DIVISIONS/AFFILIATES:

CONTACTS:

Note: Officers with more than one job title may be intentionally listed here more than once.

Don L. Blankenship, CEO
J. Christopher Adkins, COO/Sr. VP
Baxter F. Phillips, Jr., Pres.
Eric B. Tolbert, CFO/VP
Steve E. Sears, VP-Sales
Jeff Gillenwater, VP-Human Resources
John M. Poma, Chief Admin. Officer/VP
M. Shane Harvey, General Counsel/VP
Mark A. Clemens, Sr. VP-Group Oper.
Michael D. Bauersachs, VP-Planning
Jeffrey Jarosinski, VP-Finance
Richard R. Grinnan, Corp. Sec./VP
Jeffrey Jarosinski, Chief Compliance Officer
Michael K. Snelling, VP-Surface Oper.
David W. Owings, Corp. Controller
Don L. Blankenship, Chmn.

Phone: 804-788-1800	**Fax:** 804-788-1870
Toll-Free:	
Address: 4 N. 4th St., Richmond, VA 23219 US	

GROWTH PLANS/SPECIAL FEATURES:

Massey Energy Company is a leading coal company in the U.S. and is one of the largest in the Central Appalachian region. The company produces, processes and sells bituminous, low-sulfur coal of steam and metallurgical grades, operating 42 underground and 14 surface mine complexes in West Virginia, Kentucky and Virginia. These complexes blend, process and ship coal that is produced the mines to one of the company's 23 resource groups. Any one of these preparation plants can handle the coal production from as many as 10 distinct underground or surface mines. The mines have been strategically developed in close proximity to the Massey preparation plants and rail shipping facilities in order to cut down transportation costs. Once prepared, the coal is transported to customers by means of railroad cars, trucks or barges. Massey's steam coal is primarily purchased by utilities and industrial clients as fuel for power plants, and its metallurgical coal is used primarily to make coke for use in the manufacture of steel. Massey owns and operates approximately 160 gas wells, 200 miles of gathering line and various small compression facilities, as well as interests in 63 wells operated by others. In 2009, the firm acquired mining assets from bankrupt company, Appalachian Fuels, LLC. The assets include 38 million tons of coal reserves; deep and surface mines, mining equipment and a preparation plant. In April 2010, the company purchased coal mining firm, Cumberland Resources Corporation for $640 million. In July 2010, Massey purchased the assets and permits of the Marmet Dock, a river terminal, from Kanawha River Terminals, LLC.

Employees are offered medical, dental and vision insurance; a 401(k) plan; and a pension plan.

FINANCIALS:

Sales and profits are in thousands of dollars—add 000 to get the full amount. 2010 Note: Financial information for 2010 was not available for all companies at press time.

2010 Sales: $	2010 Profits: $	**U.S. Stock Ticker: MEE**
2009 Sales: $2,691,159	2009 Profits: $104,433	**Int'l Ticker:** Int'l Exchange:
2008 Sales: $2,989,789	2008 Profits: $56,248	Employees: 5,851
2007 Sales: $2,413,523	2007 Profits: $94,098	Fiscal Year Ends: 12/31
2006 Sales: $2,219,854	2006 Profits: $40,977	Parent Company:

SALARIES/BENEFITS:

Pension Plan: Y	ESOP Stock Plan:	Profit Sharing:	Top Exec. Salary: $933,369	Bonus: $11,549,156
Savings Plan: Y	Stock Purch. Plan:		Second Exec. Salary: $606,690	Bonus: $826,193

OTHER THOUGHTS:

Apparent Women Officers or Directors: 1
Hot Spot for Advancement for Women/Minorities:

LOCATIONS: ("Y" = Yes)

West:	Southwest:	Midwest:	Southeast:	Northeast:	International:
				Y	

MATRIX SERVICE COMPANY

www.matrixservice.com

Industry Group Code: 237 **Ranks within this company's industry group:** Sales: 9 Profits: 6

Exploration/Production:		**Refining/Retailing:**		**Utilities:**		**Alternative Energy:**		**Specialty Services:**		**Energy Mktg./Other Svcs.**	
Exploration:		Refining:		Electric Utility:		Waste/Solar/Other:		Consulting/Eng.:	Y	Energy Marketing:	
Production:		Retailing:		Gas Utility:		Thermal/Steam:		Seismic:		Equipment/Machinery:	
Coal Production:		Convenience Stores:		Pipelines:		Wind:		Drilling:		Oil Field Services:	Y
		Chemicals:		Water:		Hydro:		InfoTech:		Air/Shipping Transportation:	
						Fuel Cells:		Specialty Services:	Y		

TYPES OF BUSINESS:

Heavy Construction & Civil Engineering
Plant Maintenance Services
Storage Tank Services
Petrochemical Industry Services

BRANDS/DIVISIONS/AFFILIATES:

Matrix Service Industrial Contractors, Inc.
Matrix Service, Inc.

CONTACTS: *Note: Officers with more than one job title may be intentionally listed here more than once.*

Michael J. Bradley, CEO
Joseph F. Montalbano, COO
Michael J. Bradley, Pres.
Thomas E. Long, CFO/VP
Nancy E. Austin, VP-Human Resources
Lansing G. Smith, VP-Eng. & Fabrication
Robert A. Long, VP-Gulf Coast Oper.
Kevin S. Cavanah, VP-Acct. & Financial Reporting
James P. Ryan, Pres., Matrix Service, Inc.
Matthew J. Petrizzo, Pres., Matrix Service Industrial Contractors, Inc.
Jason W. Turner, Treas./VP
Michael J. Hall, Chmn.
Lansing G. Smith, VP-Procurement

Phone:	**Fax:** 918-838-8810
Toll-Free: 866-367-6879	
Address: 5100 E. Skelly Dr., Ste. 700, Tulsa, OK 74135 US	

GROWTH PLANS/SPECIAL FEATURES:

Matrix Service Company and its subsidiaries provide construction, repair and maintenance services, primarily to the petroleum, pipeline, bulk storage terminal and industrial gas markets. The company operates in two segments: construction services and repair and maintenance services. Construction services include turnkey projects; renovations, upgrades and expansions for large and small projects, electrical and instrumentation; mechanical, piping and equipment installations; tank engineering, design, fabrication and erection; and steel, steel plate, vessel and pipe fabrication. The company's repair and maintenance services include plant maintenance, turnaround services, outages, industrial cleaning, hydroblasting and substation and above ground storage tank repair and maintenance. Matrix's major customers are Public Service Enterprise Group, British Petroleum and Chevron. Subsidiaries of the company include Matrix Service, Inc. and Matrix Service Industrial Contractors, Inc.

Employees are offered medical, dental and vision insurance; life and AD&D insurance; medical and dependant care flexible spending accounts; pre-paid legal services; and an employee assistance program.

FINANCIALS: **Sales and profits are in thousands of dollars—add 000 to get the full amount. 2010 Note: Financial information for 2010 was not available for all companies at press time.**

2010 Sales: $	2010 Profits: $	**U.S. Stock Ticker: MTRX**
2009 Sales: $689,720	2009 Profits: $30,589	**Int'l Ticker:** Int'l Exchange:
2008 Sales: $731,301	2008 Profits: $21,414	Employees: 2,818
2007 Sales: $639,846	2007 Profits: $19,171	Fiscal Year Ends: 5/31
2006 Sales: $493,927	2006 Profits: $7,653	Parent Company:

SALARIES/BENEFITS:

Pension Plan:	ESOP Stock Plan:	Profit Sharing:	Top Exec. Salary: $670,000	Bonus: $335,000
Savings Plan: Y	Stock Purch. Plan:		Second Exec. Salary: $350,000	Bonus: $175,000

OTHER THOUGHTS:

Apparent Women Officers or Directors: 1
Hot Spot for Advancement for Women/Minorities:

LOCATIONS: ("Y" = Yes)

West:	Southwest:	Midwest:	Southeast:	Northeast:	International:
Y	Y	Y		Y	Y

MCDERMOTT INTERNATIONAL INC

www.mcdermott.com

Industry Group Code: 541330 **Ranks within this company's industry group:** Sales: 2 Profits: 1

Exploration/Production:		Refining/Retailing:		Utilities:		Alternative Energy:		Specialty Services:		Energy Mktg./Other Svcs.	
Exploration:		Refining:		Electric Utility:		Waste/Solar/Other:		Consulting/Eng.:	Y	Energy Marketing:	
Production:		Retailing:		Gas Utility:		Thermal/Steam:		Seismic:		Equipment/Machinery:	Y
Coal Production:		Convenience Stores:		Pipelines:		Wind:		Drilling:		Oil Field Services:	
		Chemicals:		Water:		Hydro:		InfoTech:		Air/Shipping Transportation:	
						Fuel Cells:		Specialty Services:	Y		

TYPES OF BUSINESS:

Engineering Services
Power Generation Services
Nuclear Fuel Assemblies
Government Services
Marine Construction
Procurement Services
Project Management
Consulting

BRANDS/DIVISIONS/AFFILIATES:

J. Ray McDermott, S.A.
J. Ray McDermott Holdings, LLC
Babcock & Wilcox Nuclear Operations Group, Inc
Babcock & Wilcox Technical Services Group, Inc
Babcock & Wilcox Power Generation Group, Inc
Babcock & Wilcox Modular Nuclear Energy, LLC

CONTACTS:

Note: Officers with more than one job title may be intentionally listed here more than once.

Stephen M. Johnson, CEO
John T. Nesser, III, COO
Stephen M. Johnson, Pres.
Perry L. Elders, CFO/Sr. VP
Gary L. Carlson, Chief Human Resources Officer/Sr. VP
William L. Soester, VP-Eng.
Liane K. Hinrichs, General Counsel/Sr. VP/Corp. Sec.
John T. McCormack, Sr. VP-Oper.
Peter A. Marler, VP-Bus. Dev.
Jeff J. Hightower, VP-Finance
David P. Roquemore, Sr. VP-Oper.
Daniel M. Houser, VP-Global Marine
Claire P. Hunter, VP-Litigation, Claims & Disputes
Thomas A. Henzler, VP/Corp. Compliance officer
Ronald C. Cambre, Chmn.
Stewart A. Mitchell, VP/Gen. Mgr.-Middle East

Phone: 281-870-5901	**Fax:**
Toll-Free:	
Address: 777 N. Eldridge Pkwy., Houston, TX 77079 US	

GROWTH PLANS/SPECIAL FEATURES:

McDermott International, Inc. is a multinational engineering and construction services company. The firm operates in three main business segments: offshore oil and gas construction services; government operations; and power generation systems. The offshore construction services are provided through subsidiaries J. Ray McDermott, S.A. and J. Ray McDermott Holdings, LLC, as well as their respective subsidiaries. This segment designs, engineers, fabricates and installs offshore drilling and production facilities, marine pipelines and subsea production systems. It operates in most major offshore oil and gas producing regions throughout the world, including the U.S., Mexico, Canada, the Middle East, India, the Caspian Sea and Asia Pacific Presently, this segment also operates fabrication facilities located in Indonesia on Batam Island; in Dubai, U.A.E.; Altamira, Mexico; and near Morgan City, Louisiana. These facilities construct a full range of offshore structures, from conventional jacket-type fixed platforms to intermediate water and deepwater platform configurations. The government operations segment operates through Babcock & Wilcox Nuclear Operations Group, Inc.; Babcock & Wilcox Technical Services Group, Inc.; and their respective subsidiaries. This division supplies nuclear components to the U.S. government, processes uranium, provides environmental site restoration services and manages and operates U.S. government-owned facilities, primarily within the nuclear weapons complex of the U.S. Department of Energy. Facilities served by the segment include the Y-12 National Security Complex, the Pantex Plant and Los Alamos National Laboratory. The power generation systems segment, run by Babcock & Wilcox Power Generation Group, Inc.; Babcock & Wilcox Nuclear Power Generation Group, Inc.; and Babcock & Wilcox Modular Nuclear Energy LLC, provides a variety of services, equipment and systems to generate steam and electric power at energy facilities worldwide. In March 2010, the company signed an agreement to acquire the electrostatic precipitator and emissions monitoring businesses of GE Energy.

FINANCIALS:

Sales and profits are in thousands of dollars—add 000 to get the full amount. 2010 Note: Financial information for 2010 was not available for all companies at press time.

2010 Sales: $	2010 Profits: $	**U.S. Stock Ticker: MDR**
2009 Sales: $6,193,077	2009 Profits: $387,056	**Int'l Ticker:** Int'l Exchange:
2008 Sales: $6,572,423	2008 Profits: $429,302	Employees: 29,000
2007 Sales: $5,631,610	2007 Profits: $607,828	Fiscal Year Ends: 12/31
2006 Sales: $4,120,141	2006 Profits: $330,515	Parent Company:

SALARIES/BENEFITS:

Pension Plan: Y	ESOP Stock Plan:	Profit Sharing:	Top Exec. Salary: $900,000	Bonus: $1,665,000
Savings Plan: Y	Stock Purch. Plan:		Second Exec. Salary: $526,200	Bonus: $663,012

OTHER THOUGHTS:

Apparent Women Officers or Directors: 2
Hot Spot for Advancement for Women/Minorities: Y

LOCATIONS: ("Y" = Yes)

West:	Southwest:	Midwest:	Southeast:	Northeast:	International:
Y	Y	Y	Y	Y	Y

MCMORAN EXPLORATION CO

www.mcmoran.com

Industry Group Code: 211111 **Ranks within this company's industry group:** Sales: 96 Profits: 97

Exploration/Production:		Refining/Retailing:		Utilities:		Alternative Energy:		Specialty Services:		Energy Mktg./Other Svcs.	
Exploration:	Y	Refining:		Electric Utility:		Waste/Solar/Other:		Consulting/Eng.:		Energy Marketing:	
Production:	Y	Retailing:		Gas Utility:		Thermal/Steam:		Seismic:		Equipment/Machinery:	
Coal Production:		Convenience Stores:		Pipelines:	Y	Wind:		Drilling:		Oil Field Services:	
		Chemicals:		Water:		Hydro:		InfoTech:		Air/Shipping Transportation:	
						Fuel Cells:		Specialty Services:			

TYPES OF BUSINESS:

Oil & Gas-Exploration & Production
Liquefied Natural Gas Transportation & Storage
Pipelines

BRANDS/DIVISIONS/AFFILIATES:

Main Pass Energy Hub
McMoRan Oil & Gas LLC
Freeport-McMoRan Energy LLC
K-McVentures I LLC

CONTACTS:

Note: Officers with more than one job title may be intentionally listed here more than once.

James R. Moffet, CEO
James R. Moffet, Pres.
Nancy D. Parmelee, CFO/Sr. VP
Nancy D. Parmelee, Sec.
C. Donald Whitmire, Jr., Controller/VP
Richard C. Adkerson, Co-Chmn.
Richard C. Adkerson, CEO/Pres., Freeport-McMoRan Copper & Gold, Inc.
C. Howard Murrish, Exec. VP
James R. Moffet, Chmn.-Freeport-McMoRan Copper & Gold, Inc.
James R. Moffet, Co-Chmn.

Phone: 504-582-4000 **Fax:** 504-582-4899
Toll-Free:
Address: 1615 Poydras St., New Orleans, LA 70112 US

GROWTH PLANS/SPECIAL FEATURES:

McMoRan Exploration Co. engages in the exploration, development and production of oil and natural gas. The firm operates offshore in the Gulf of Mexico and onshore in the Gulf Coast region, primarily in high-risk, high-potential, deep exploration prospects. The company focuses on exploring for deeper pools of hydrocarbons below existing or previous shallow production operations. The process is advantageous because the drilling infrastructure is already available to the company in most cases, significantly decreasing development costs. Typically these operations occur in depths of 15,000-25,000 feet, though the firm also operates at depths of over 25,000 feet. McMoRan has expertise in various exploration and production technologies, including incorporating 3-D seismic interpretation capabilities with traditional structural geological techniques, offshore drilling to significant total depths and horizontal drilling. The company also owns or has rights to an extensive seismic database, including 3-D seismic data on substantially all of its acreage. McMoRan operates primarily through two wholly-owned subsidiaries. McMoRan Oil & Gas LLC, which is the firm's principal operating subsidiary, conducts the company's oil and gas operations. Its other subsidiary, Freeport-McMoRan Energy LLC, develops the Main Pass Energy Hub (MPEH) project. The MPEH project will include an offshore LNG regasification terminal capable of 1 billion cubic feet per day and onsite cavern storage for natural gas in the large salt dome at the site, as well as a pipeline system to deliver gas to markets in the U.S. Freeport Energy owns all of the oil operations at Main Pass through K-Mc Ventures I LLC. In September 2010, the firm agreed to acquire the shallow water Gulf of Mexico shelf assets of Plains Exploration & Production Company for $75 million and stock.

FINANCIALS:

Sales and profits are in thousands of dollars—add 000 to get the full amount. 2010 Note: Financial information for 2010 was not available for all companies at press time.

2010 Sales: $	2010 Profits: $	**U.S. Stock Ticker: MMR**
2009 Sales: $435,435	2009 Profits: $-204,889	**Int'l Ticker:** Int'l Exchange:
2008 Sales: $1,072,482	2008 Profits: $-211,292	Employees:
2007 Sales: $481,167	2007 Profits: $-59,734	Fiscal Year Ends: 12/31
2006 Sales: $209,738	2006 Profits: $-44,716	Parent Company:

SALARIES/BENEFITS:

Pension Plan:	ESOP Stock Plan:	Profit Sharing:	Top Exec. Salary: $325,000	Bonus: $500,000
Savings Plan:	Stock Purch. Plan:		Second Exec. Salary: $300,000	Bonus: $500,000

OTHER THOUGHTS:

Apparent Women Officers or Directors: 3
Hot Spot for Advancement for Women/Minorities: Y

LOCATIONS: ("Y" = Yes)

West:	Southwest:	Midwest:	Southeast:	Northeast:	International:
	Y		Y		

MDU RESOURCES GROUP INC

www.mdu.com

Industry Group Code: 211111 **Ranks within this company's industry group:** Sales: 61 Profits: 91

Exploration/Production:		Refining/Retailing:		Utilities:		Alternative Energy:		Specialty Services:		Energy Mktg./Other Svcs.	
Exploration:	Y	Refining:		Electric Utility:	Y	Waste/Solar/Other:		Consulting/Eng.:	Y	Energy Marketing:	Y
Production:	Y	Retailing:		Gas Utility:	Y	Thermal/Steam:		Seismic:		Equipment/Machinery:	Y
Coal Production:		Convenience Stores:		Pipelines:	Y	Wind:		Drilling:		Oil Field Services:	
		Chemicals:		Water:		Hydro:		InfoTech:		Air/Shipping Transportation:	
						Fuel Cells:		Specialty Services:	Y		

TYPES OF BUSINESS:

Oil & Gas Exploration & Production
Construction Materials & Mining
Utilities-Electric & Natural Gas
Pipelines & Storage
Energy Products & Services
Equipment & Maintenance-Electric & HVAC
Utility Construction
Energy Management Services

BRANDS/DIVISIONS/AFFILIATES:

Montana-Dakota Utilities Co.
Great Plains Natural Gas Co.
MDU Construction Services Group, Inc.
WBI Holdings, Inc.
Fidelity Exploration and Production Company
Knife River Corporation
Cascade Natural Gas Corporation

CONTACTS: *Note: Officers with more than one job title may be intentionally listed here more than once.*

Terry D. Hildestad, CEO
Terry D. Hildestad, Pres.
Doran N. Schwartz, CFO/VP
Mark Del Vecchio, VP-Human Resources
William E. Connors, VP-Renewable Resources
Cynthia J. Norland, VP-Admin.
Paul K. Sandness, General Counsel/Sec.
John P. Stumpf, VP-Strategic Planning
Phyllis A. Rittenbach, Dir.-Investor Rel.
Nicole A. Kivisto, Chief Acct. Officer/VP/Controller
Douglass A. Mahowald, Treas.
Harry J. Pearce, Chmn.

Phone: 701-530-1000 **Fax:** 701-222-7607
Toll-Free: 866-760-4852
Address: 1200 W. Century Ave., Bismarck, ND 58506 US

GROWTH PLANS/SPECIAL FEATURES:

MDU Resources Group, Inc. is a diversified natural resources company. Through its subsidiaries, the company is primarily engaged in electric and natural gas utilities, natural gas pipelines and energy services, natural gas and oil production, construction materials and mining services and construction services. Subsidiary Montana-Dakota Utilities Co. provides electricity to over 122,000 residential, commercial, industrial and municipal customers in North Dakota, Montana, South Dakota and Wyoming. Great Plains Natural Gas Co. distributes natural gas in western Minnesota and southeastern North Dakota. Subsidiary, Cascade Natural Gas Corp provides natural gas to approximately 250,000 customers in 96 cities in Washington and Oregon. WBI Holdings, Inc. offers natural gas transportation, underground storage and gathering services through regulated and non-regulated pipeline systems in the Rocky Mountain, Midwest and Central regions of the U.S. Fidelity Exploration and Production Company is engaged in natural gas and oil acquisition, exploration and production, primarily in the Rocky Mountain region as well as in the Gulf of Mexico. Knife River Corporation mines and markets stone, sand, gravel and related construction materials in Alaska, California, Hawaii, Idaho, Iowa, Minnesota, Montana, North Dakota, Oregon, Texas, Washington and Wyoming. Subsidiary MDU Construction Services Group, Inc. (MCSG) specializes in electric, natural gas and telecommunications utility construction as well as interior industrial electrical, exterior lighting and traffic signals. MCSG also provides related specialty equipment and rental services. In March 2010, Fidelity Exploration and Production Company agreed to acquire natural gas properties in the Green River Basin in southwest Wyoming.

Employees are offered medical, dental and vision insurance; life and dependent life insurance; AD&D insurance; flexible spending accounts; a 401(k) plan; an employee assistance plan; disability insurance; education assistance; and employee discount programs.

FINANCIALS: **Sales and profits are in thousands of dollars—add 000 to get the full amount. 2010 Note: Financial information for 2010 was not available for all companies at press time.**

2010 Sales: $	2010 Profits: $	**U.S. Stock Ticker: MDU**
2009 Sales: $4,176,501	2009 Profits: $-123,274	**Int'l Ticker:** Int'l Exchange:
2008 Sales: $5,003,278	2008 Profits: $293,673	Employees: 8,081
2007 Sales: $4,247,896	2007 Profits: $432,120	Fiscal Year Ends: 12/31
2006 Sales: $4,004,539	2006 Profits: $315,757	Parent Company:

SALARIES/BENEFITS:

Pension Plan:	ESOP Stock Plan:	Profit Sharing:	Top Exec. Salary: $750,000	Bonus: $1,500,000
Savings Plan: Y	Stock Purch. Plan:		Second Exec. Salary: $450,000	Bonus: $585,000

OTHER THOUGHTS:

Apparent Women Officers or Directors: 5
Hot Spot for Advancement for Women/Minorities: Y

LOCATIONS: ("Y" = Yes)

West:	Southwest:	Midwest:	Southeast:	Northeast:	International:
Y	Y	Y	Y	Y	Y

MESA ENERGY HOLDINGS INC

www.mesaenergy.us

Industry Group Code: 211111 **Ranks within this company's industry group:** Sales: Profits:

Exploration/Production:		Refining/Retailing:		Utilities:		Alternative Energy:		Specialty Services:		Energy Mktg./Other Svcs.	
Exploration:	Y	Refining:		Electric Utility:		Waste/Solar/Other:		Consulting/Eng.:		Energy Marketing:	
Production:	Y	Retailing:		Gas Utility:		Thermal/Steam:		Seismic:		Equipment/Machinery:	
Coal Production:		Convenience Stores:		Pipelines:		Wind:		Drilling:		Oil Field Services:	
		Chemicals:		Water:		Hydro:		InfoTech:		Air/Shipping Transportation:	
						Fuel Cells:		Specialty Services:			

TYPES OF BUSINESS:

Oil & Gas Exploration & Production

BRANDS/DIVISIONS/AFFILIATES:

Mesa Energy Operating LLC
Mesquite Mining, Inc.
Mesa Energy, Inc.
Java Field
Coal Creek Prospect

CONTACTS:

Note: Officers with more than one job title may be intentionally listed here more than once.

Randy M. Griffin, CEO
Ray L. Unruh, Pres.
Ray L. Unruh, Acting CFO
Ray L. Unruh, Sec.
David L. Freeman, Exec. VP-Oil & Gas Oper.

Phone: 972-490-9595	**Fax:** 972-490-9161
Toll-Free:	
Address: 5220 Spring Valley Rd., Ste. 525, Dallas, TX 75254 US	

GROWTH PLANS/SPECIAL FEATURES:

Mesa Energy Holdings, Inc., formerly Mesquite Mining, Inc., is a firm engaged in the acquisition, exploration and rehabilitation of oil and gas properties. The firm operates via subsidiary Mesa Energy, Inc. (Mesa) and its subsidiary, Mesa Energy Operating LLC. The firm focuses on the acquisition of shallow drilling prospects in shale (both oil and gas), tight gas or coal bed methane reservoirs with the opportunity to control large acreage positions that could accommodate the drilling of hundreds of wells and boast significant recoverable reserves. Mesa's primary property is the Coal Creek Prospect, a developmental prospect targeting the Brent Sand shallow gas reservoir in the Arkoma Basin of eastern Oklahoma. Mesa controls interests in 677 acres in the Coal Creek Prospect, as well as a 35% working interest in the Cook #1 well and a 25% working interest in the Gipson #1 well. The firm's other assets are located in the Java Field, a natural gas development project in Wyoming County, New York. Java Field is located at the northern end of the Marcellus Shale trend, which spans approximately 600 miles extending from West Virginia to western New York. Mesa's assets include a 100% working interest in 19 leases covering approximately 3,235 mineral acres with 19 existing wells; two tracts of land totaling approximately 36 acres; and two pipeline systems, including a 12.4 mile pipeline and gathering system that serves the existing field as well as a separate 2.5 mile system located east of the field. Mesa acquired these assets from Hydrocarbon Generation, Inc. in August 2009, closing the acquisition of the pipelines separately in March 2010. Mesa is an exploration stage company and has not yet commenced production. In October 2009, Mesa Energy Holding, Inc. acquired Mesa Energy, Inc. via a reverse merger.

FINANCIALS:

Sales and profits are in thousands of dollars—add 000 to get the full amount. 2010 Note: Financial information for 2010 was not available for all companies at press time.

2010 Sales: $	2010 Profits: $	**U.S. Stock Ticker: MSEH**
2009 Sales: $	2009 Profits: $	**Int'l Ticker:** Int'l Exchange:
2008 Sales: $	2008 Profits: $	Employees:
2007 Sales: $	2007 Profits: $	Fiscal Year Ends: 12/31
2006 Sales: $	2006 Profits: $	Parent Company:

SALARIES/BENEFITS:

Pension Plan:	ESOP Stock Plan:	Profit Sharing:	Top Exec. Salary: $	Bonus: $
Savings Plan:	Stock Purch. Plan:		Second Exec. Salary: $	Bonus: $

OTHER THOUGHTS:

Apparent Women Officers or Directors:
Hot Spot for Advancement for Women/Minorities:

LOCATIONS: ("Y" = Yes)

West:	Southwest:	Midwest:	Southeast:	Northeast:	International:
	Y			Y	

METROGAS SA

www.metrogas.com.ar

Industry Group Code: 221210 **Ranks within this company's industry group:** Sales: 18 Profits: 18

Exploration/Production:		Refining/Retailing:		Utilities:		Alternative Energy:		Specialty Services:		Energy Mktg./Other Svcs.	
Exploration:		Refining:		Electric Utility:		Waste/Solar/Other:		Consulting/Eng.:		Energy Marketing:	
Production:		Retailing:		Gas Utility:	Y	Thermal/Steam:		Seismic:		Equipment/Machinery:	
Coal Production:		Convenience Stores:		Pipelines:		Wind:		Drilling:		Oil Field Services:	
		Chemicals:		Water:		Hydro:		InfoTech:		Air/Shipping Transportation:	
						Fuel Cells:		Specialty Services:			

TYPES OF BUSINESS:

Natural Gas Distribution
Gas and Carbon Monoxide Detectors
Compressed Natural Gas

BRANDS/DIVISIONS/AFFILIATES:

Gas del Estado

CONTACTS:

Note: Officers with more than one job title may be intentionally listed here more than once.

Andres Cordero Gimenez, CEO
Patricia Carcagno, COO
Eduardo Villegas Contte, CFO
Enrique Barruti, Dir.-Human Resources
Eduardo Villegas Contte, Chief Admin. Officer
Magdalena Gonzalez Garano, Dir.-Legal & Regulatory Affairs
Eugenia Gatti, Investor Rel.
Fernando Nardini, Controller
Juan Pablo Mirazon, Dir.-Internal Auditor
Fernando Aceiro, Dir.-Commercial
Juan Carlos Fronza, Chmn.

Phone: 54-11-4309-1000	**Fax:**
Toll-Free:	
Address: Gregorio Araoz de Lamadrid 1360, Buenos Aires, 1267 Argentina	

GROWTH PLANS/SPECIAL FEATURES:

MetroGAS S.A. is one of the largest natural gas distribution companies in Argentina. The company is one of nine natural gas distribution companies formed as a result of the 1992 privatization of the state-run Gas del Estado. MetroGAS has over 1.9 million customers in its service area, which includes the Federal Capital and the southern and eastern regions of greater metropolitan Buenos Aires. The company's service area constitutes densely populated areas with major dual-fuel electric power plants and industrial and commercial users of natural gas. Currently, the firm distributes approximately 22% of the total natural gas among all gas distribution companies in Argentina. MetroGAS' distribution system consists of approximately 9,200 miles of distribution mains and service pipelines. The firm purchases gas primarily from producers in southern and western Argentina. The gas purchased by the company is then transported through Argentina's two trunk pipeline systems, which are operated by third parties. MertroGAS also offers additional products and services including gas and carbon monoxide detectors. The company is currently focused on promoting the use of compressed natural gas (CNG), a cleaner fuel source than diesel. For business and developers, the firm offers consulting services for the application of gas and gas operated equipments such as: air conditioning, cogeneration of electricity and CNG for industrial and service vehicles.

FINANCIALS:

Sales and profits are in thousands of dollars—add 000 to get the full amount. 2010 Note: Financial information for 2010 was not available for all companies at press time.

2010 Sales: $	2010 Profits: $	**U.S. Stock Ticker: MGS**
2009 Sales: $271,110	2009 Profits: $-19,760	**Int'l Ticker: METR** Int'l Exchange: Buenos Aires-BCBA
2008 Sales: $235,270	2008 Profits: $-3,520	Employees: 1,052
2007 Sales: $249,440	2007 Profits: $4,120	Fiscal Year Ends: 12/31
2006 Sales: $	2006 Profits: $	Parent Company:

SALARIES/BENEFITS:

Pension Plan:	ESOP Stock Plan:	Profit Sharing:	Top Exec. Salary: $	Bonus: $
Savings Plan:	Stock Purch. Plan:		Second Exec. Salary: $	Bonus: $

OTHER THOUGHTS:

Apparent Women Officers or Directors: 3
Hot Spot for Advancement for Women/Minorities: Y

LOCATIONS: ("Y" = Yes)

West:	Southwest:	Midwest:	Southeast:	Northeast:	International:
					Y

MICHIGAN CONSOLIDATED GAS COMPANY

my.dteenergy.com

Industry Group Code: 221210 **Ranks within this company's industry group:** Sales: Profits:

Exploration/Production:		Refining/Retailing:		Utilities:		Alternative Energy:		Specialty Services:		Energy Mktg./Other Svcs.	
Exploration:		Refining:		Electric Utility:		Waste/Solar/Other:		Consulting/Eng.:		Energy Marketing:	
Production:		Retailing:		Gas Utility:	Y	Thermal/Steam:		Seismic:		Equipment/Machinery:	
Coal Production:		Convenience Stores:		Pipelines:	Y	Wind:		Drilling:		Oil Field Services:	
		Chemicals:		Water:		Hydro:		InfoTech:		Air/Shipping Transportation:	
						Fuel Cells:		Specialty Services:			

TYPES OF BUSINESS:

Natural Gas Utility
Gas Pipelines & Storage

BRANDS/DIVISIONS/AFFILIATES:

DTE Energy Company

CONTACTS:

Note: Officers with more than one job title may be intentionally listed here more than once.

Anthony F. Earley Jr., CEO
Jerry Norcia, COO
Jerry Norcia, Pres.
Mark Stiers, VP-Gas Sales & Supply
Lynne Ellyn, CIO/Sr. VP
Anthony F. Earley Jr., Chmn.

Phone: 313-235-4000	**Fax:** 313-235-8055
Toll-Free:	
Address: 1 Energy Plz., Detroit, MI 48226 US	

GROWTH PLANS/SPECIAL FEATURES:

Michigan Consolidated Gas Company (MichCon), a subsidiary of DTE Energy, is one of the nation's largest natural gas distributors. The company offers the purchase, storage, transmission, distribution and sale of natural gas to more than 1.2 million residential, commercial and industrial customers in approximately 550 communities throughout Michigan, covering a 14,700 mile service area. Within this service area the firm operates 2,471 miles of transmission and gathering pipelines and over 19,000 miles of distribution main pipelines. The company owns and operates 278 storage wells, representing approximately 34 percent of the underground working capacity in Michigan. In addition to relying on Michigan's abundant supply of natural gas, the firm's pipelines link customers to energy sources in Texas, Oklahoma, the Rockies, Louisiana, the Gulf of Mexico and western Canada. During the summer, MichCon uses Michigan's unique geology to store up to 132 billion cubic feet of gas in naturally occurring, underground rock formations. The company's storage capacity assures its customers a reliable gas supply at competitive prices. In Mid 2009, the company completed an approximately 15-mile pipeline that interconnects with the Panhandle Eastern Pipeline.

DTE Energy offers its employees medical, dental and vision coverage, flexible spending accounts, group auto and homeowners insurance and an employee assistance program.

FINANCIALS:

Sales and profits are in thousands of dollars—add 000 to get the full amount. 2010 Note: Financial information for 2010 was not available for all companies at press time.

2010 Sales: $	2010 Profits: $	**U.S. Stock Ticker: Subsidiary**
2009 Sales: $	2009 Profits: $	**Int'l Ticker:** Int'l Exchange:
2008 Sales: $	2008 Profits: $	Employees:
2007 Sales: $	2007 Profits: $	Fiscal Year Ends: 12/31
2006 Sales: $	2006 Profits: $	Parent Company: DTE ENERGY COMPANY

SALARIES/BENEFITS:

Pension Plan: Y	ESOP Stock Plan:	Profit Sharing:	Top Exec. Salary: $	Bonus: $1,850,000
Savings Plan: Y	Stock Purch. Plan:		Second Exec. Salary: $	Bonus: $

OTHER THOUGHTS:

Apparent Women Officers or Directors: 1
Hot Spot for Advancement for Women/Minorities:

LOCATIONS: ("Y" = Yes)

West:	Southwest:	Midwest:	Southeast:	Northeast:	International:
		Y			

MIDAMERICAN ENERGY HOLDINGS CO

www.midamerican.com

Industry Group Code: 221 **Ranks within this company's industry group:** Sales: 15 Profits:

Exploration/Production:		Refining/Retailing:		Utilities:		Alternative Energy:		Specialty Services:		Energy Mktg./Other Svcs.	
Exploration:		Refining:		Electric Utility:	Y	Waste/Solar/Other:		Consulting/Eng.:		Energy Marketing:	
Production:		Retailing:		Gas Utility:	Y	Thermal/Steam:	Y	Seismic:		Equipment/Machinery:	
Coal Production:		Convenience Stores:		Pipelines:	Y	Wind:	Y	Drilling:		Oil Field Services:	
		Chemicals:		Water:		Hydro:	Y	InfoTech:		Air/Shipping Transportation:	
						Fuel Cells:		Specialty Services:	Y		

TYPES OF BUSINESS:

Utilities-Electricity & Natural Gas
Pipelines
Wind Generation
Hydroelectric Generation
Thermal Generation
Real Estate Brokerage

BRANDS/DIVISIONS/AFFILIATES:

PacifiCorp
BYD COMPANY LIMITED
Northern Natural Gas Company
Kern River Gas Transmission Company
CE Electric U.K.
CalEnergy Generation
HomeServices of America Inc
Berkshire Hathaway Inc

CONTACTS: *Note: Officers with more than one job title may be intentionally listed here more than once.*

Gregory E. Abel, CEO
Gregory E. Abel, Pres.
Patrick J. Goodman, CFO/Sr. VP
Maureen E. Sammon, Chief Admin. Officer/Sr. VP
Douglas L. Anderson, General Counsel/Sr. VP/Sec.
David L. Sokol, Chmn.

Phone: 515-242-4300	**Fax:**
Toll-Free:	
Address: 666 Grand Ave., Ste. 500, Des Moines, IA 50309-2580 US	

GROWTH PLANS/SPECIAL FEATURES:

MidAmerican Energy Holdings Co. (MEHC), with over $45 billion in assets, generates, transmits, stores, distributes and supplies energy through its subsidiaries to over 6.9 million customers. The company has six primary subsidiaries. PacifiCorp serves more than 1.7 million customers, operating in three business units: Pacific Power, delivering electricity in Oregon, Washington and California; Rocky Mountain Power, delivery electricity in Wyoming, Utah and Idaho; and PacifiCorp Energy, which constitutes the company's electric generation, energy trading and coal mining operations. MidAmerican Energy Company generates, transmits and sells electricity to 725,000 customers and supplies natural gas to an additional 707,000 customers. It operates in Iowa, Illinois, Nebraska and South Dakota. Northern Natural Gas Company owns largest 15,000-mile interstate natural gas pipeline system extending from Texas to the upper Midwest. Kern River Gas Transmission Company owns 1,680 miles of interstate pipeline and delivers more than 1.9 billion cubic feet of natural gas per day to Nevada, Utah and California. CE Electric U.K., a holding company for Northern Electric and Yorkshire Electric, distributes electricity to 3.8 million customers in the U.K. Through another subsidiary, Integrated Utility Services, CE Electric provides strategic and technical engineering design services. CalEnergy Generation is an international leader in energy production and development from diversified fuel sources, including geothermal, natural gas and hydroelectric. MEHC also owns Homeservices of America, Inc., a leading U.S. residential real estate brokerage firm. MEHC is one of America's largest operators of wind energy. It has invested billions of dollars in wind farms, particularly in Iowa. The firm also owns about 9.9% of Chinese battery maker BYD Co. MEHC is owned by Berkshire Hathaway, Inc.

The company offers its employees medical, dental, vision and life insurance; a 401 (k) plan; a profit sharing plan; an employee assistance program; flexible spending accounts; tuition reimbursement; and adoption assistance.

FINANCIALS: **Sales and profits are in thousands of dollars—add 000 to get the full amount. 2010 Note: Financial information for 2010 was not available for all companies at press time.**

2010 Sales: $	2010 Profits: $	**U.S. Stock Ticker: Subsidiary**
2009 Sales: $11,200,000	2009 Profits: $	**Int'l Ticker:** Int'l Exchange:
2008 Sales: $12,700,000	2008 Profits: $	Employees: 16,300
2007 Sales: $12,376,000	2007 Profits: $	Fiscal Year Ends: 12/31
2006 Sales: $10,300,700	2006 Profits: $916,100	Parent Company: BERKSHIRE HATHAWAY INC

SALARIES/BENEFITS:

Pension Plan:	ESOP Stock Plan:	Profit Sharing: Y	Top Exec. Salary: $1,000,000	Bonus: $13,000,000
Savings Plan: Y	Stock Purch. Plan:		Second Exec. Salary: $822,917	Bonus: $5,000,000

OTHER THOUGHTS:

Apparent Women Officers or Directors: 1
Hot Spot for Advancement for Women/Minorities:

LOCATIONS: ("Y" = Yes)

West:	Southwest:	Midwest:	Southeast:	Northeast:	International:
Y	Y	Y	Y	Y	Y

MIRANT CORP

www.mirant.com

Industry Group Code: 221 **Ranks within this company's industry group:** Sales: 43 Profits: 22

Exploration/Production:		Refining/Retailing:		Utilities:		Alternative Energy:		Specialty Services:		Energy Mktg./Other Svcs.	
Exploration:		Refining:		Electric Utility:	Y	Waste/Solar/Other:		Consulting/Eng.:		Energy Marketing:	Y
Production:		Retailing:		Gas Utility:		Thermal/Steam:		Seismic:		Equipment/Machinery:	
Coal Production:		Convenience Stores:		Pipelines:		Wind:		Drilling:		Oil Field Services:	
		Chemicals:		Water:		Hydro:		InfoTech:		Air/Shipping Transportation:	
						Fuel Cells:		Specialty Services:	Y		

TYPES OF BUSINESS:

Utilities
Energy Marketing
Risk Management Consulting

BRANDS/DIVISIONS/AFFILIATES:

RRI Energy Inc
Mirant Marsh Landing LLC
GenOn Energy Inc

CONTACTS: *Note: Officers with more than one job title may be intentionally listed here more than once.*

Edward R. Muller, CEO
Edward R. Muller, Pres.
J. William Holden III, CFO/Sr. VP
Julia Houston, General Counsel/Chief Compliance Officer
James Garlick, VP-Oper.
Julia Houston, Sec./Sr. VP
John O'Neal, Chief Commercial Officer/Sr. VP
Anne M. Cleary, Sr. VP-Asset Mgmt.
Edward R. Muller, Chmn.

Phone: 678-579-5000	**Fax:** 678-579-5001
Toll-Free:	
Address: 1155 Perimeter Ctr. W., Atlanta, GA 30338 US	

GROWTH PLANS/SPECIAL FEATURES:

Mirant Corp. is an energy company that produces and sells energy, in addition to providing risk management and asset management consulting. The firm principally develops, constructs, owns and operates power plants and sells wholesale electricity, gas and other energy-related products. Mirant owns and operates 11 power plants, as well as various electricity distribution companies. The firm generates approximately 10,076 megawatts (MW) of energy in the U.S. The company operates in four business segments: Mid-Atlantic, Northeast, California and other. The Mid-Atlantic segment consists of Mirant's generating facilities in Maryland and Virginia. Mirant owns or leases four generating facilities in the Mid-Atlantic region with total net generating capacity of 5,194 MW. The Northeast division is comprised of the company's facilities in New York and New England with total net generating capacity of 2,535 MW. The California segment encompasses gas-generating facilities in the state of California. Mirant owns three generating facilities in California with a total net generating capacity of 2,347 MW. The other segment includes proprietary trading and fuel oil management activities. Mirant uses oil, gas and coal as fuel for generating energy for its plants. The company's commercial operations business consists primarily of risk management; procuring fuel; dispatching electricity; hedging the production and sale of electricity by the firm's generating facilities; fuel oil management; and providing logistical support for the operation of the facilities. In September 2009, subsidiary Mirant Marsh Landing, LLC entered into a purchase agreement with Pacific Gas and Electric Company to construct a 760 MW of natural gas-fired peaking generation facility at the Contra Costa plant in Antioch, California. In April 2010, the firm agreed to merge with RRI Energy, Inc. to form GenOn Energy, Inc.

Mirant offers its employees medical, dental, disability and life insurance, a 401(k), a profit sharing arrangement and an assistance program.

FINANCIALS: **Sales and profits are in thousands of dollars—add 000 to get the full amount. 2010 Note: Financial information for 2010 was not available for all companies at press time.**

2010 Sales: $	2010 Profits: $	**U.S. Stock Ticker: MIR**
2009 Sales: $2,309,000	2009 Profits: $494,000	**Int'l Ticker:** Int'l Exchange:
2008 Sales: $3,188,000	2008 Profits: $1,265,000	Employees: 1,179
2007 Sales: $2,019,000	2007 Profits: $1,995,000	Fiscal Year Ends: 12/31
2006 Sales: $3,087,000	2006 Profits: $1,864,000	Parent Company:

SALARIES/BENEFITS:

Pension Plan:	ESOP Stock Plan:	Profit Sharing: Y	Top Exec. Salary: $1,135,000	Bonus: $1,600,000
Savings Plan: Y	Stock Purch. Plan:		Second Exec. Salary: $404,536	Bonus: $314,525

OTHER THOUGHTS:

Apparent Women Officers or Directors: 2
Hot Spot for Advancement for Women/Minorities:

LOCATIONS: ("Y" = Yes)

West:	Southwest:	Midwest:	Southeast:	Northeast:	International:
Y	Y	Y	Y	Y	

MITSUBISHI CHEMICAL HOLDINGS CORPORATION

www.mitsubishichem-hd.co.jp

Industry Group Code: 325 **Ranks within this company's industry group:** Sales: 3 Profits: 4

Exploration/Production:		**Refining/Retailing:**		**Utilities:**		**Alternative Energy:**		**Specialty Services:**		**Energy Mktg./Other Svcs.**	
Exploration:		Refining:		Electric Utility:		Waste/Solar/Other:		Consulting/Eng.:		Energy Marketing:	
Production:		Retailing:		Gas Utility:		Thermal/Steam:		Seismic:		Equipment/Machinery:	
Coal Production:		Convenience Stores:		Pipelines:		Wind:		Drilling:		Oil Field Services:	
		Chemicals:	Y	Water:		Hydro:		InfoTech:		Air/Shipping Transportation:	
						Fuel Cells:		Specialty Services:			

TYPES OF BUSINESS:

Agricultural Chemicals Manufacturer
Petrochemicals
Optical Recording Media
Polymers
Pharmaceuticals
Clinical Testing Equipment
Logistics
Engineering Services

BRANDS/DIVISIONS/AFFILIATES:

Mitsubishi Tanabe Pharma Corporation
Mitsubishi Plastics Inc
Mitsubishi Chemical Corporation
Mitsubishi Rayon Co Ltd

CONTACTS:

Note: Officers with more than one job title may be intentionally listed here more than once.

Yoshimitsu Kobayashi, CEO
Yoshimitsu Kobayashi, Pres.
Noriyoshi Ohira, Gen. Mgr.-Human Resources
Tomihisa Ikeura, Dir.-R&D
Motoo Kobayashi, Dir.-Info. Systems
Iwao Yamamoto, Dir.-Process & Material Tech.
Tomiaki Ito, Dir.-Prod. Dev.
Hitoshi Ochi, Gen. Mgr.-Corp. Strategy
Shotaro Yoshimura, Dir.-Public Rel.
Shotaro Yoshimura, Dir.-Investor Rel.
Noboru Tsuda, Chief Compliance Officer
Kenichi Uno, Gen. Mgr.-Tech. & Prod. Center
Ryuichi Tomizawa, Chmn.
Masanori Karatsu, Dir.-Purchasing & Supply Chain Innovation

Phone: 81-3-6414-4850	**Fax:** 81-3-6414-3745
Toll-Free:	
Address: 4-14-1 Shiba, Minato-ku, Tokyo, 108-0014 Japan	

GROWTH PLANS/SPECIAL FEATURES:

Mitsubishi Chemical Holdings Corporation (MCHC) is a major petrochemical manufacturer in Japan. The firm operates through four subsidiaries: Mitsubishi Chemical Corporation (MCC); Mitsubishi Plastics, Inc.; Mitsubishi Rayon Co., Ltd.; and Mitsubishi Tanabe Pharma Corporation. These companies offer products in five segments: electronics applications, design materials, health care, chemicals and polymers. The electronics applications segment (operated by MCC) manufactures products such as display materials, organic photo conductors/chemical toners and optical recording media through brands including Verbatim. The design materials division (operated by MCC, Mitsubishi Plastics and Mitsubishi Rayon) utilizes polymer processing, composite technology and carbon chemistry to offer performance products such as polymer films, food packaging materials, li-ion battery materials, engineering plastics, plastic optical fibers, construction materials, carbon fiber and agricultural materials. The healthcare segment (operated by MCC and Mitsubishi Tanabe Pharma) offers pharmaceutical tools such as the Remicade monoclonal antibody, PATHFAST, a compact automated immunoassay analyzer; and IMM-FAST Check, a point-of-care testing reagent. The chemicals division (operated by MCC) produces basic chemicals and carbon materials such as poytetramethylene ether glycol, 1,4-butanediol, purified terephthalic acid and acrylonitrile. The polymers segment (operated by Mitsubishi Rayon) offers chemicals such as polyethylene, polypropylene, MMA acrylic resin and polycarbonate/phenol chain. In April 2010, the firm acquired public firm Mitsubishi Rayon Co., Ltd., making it a wholly-owned subsidiary. In May 2010, MCHC agreed to form a 50-50 joint venture with Asahi Kasei to combine the two firms' naphtha cracker petrochemical operations in the Mizushima industrial area of Okayama, Japan.

FINANCIALS:

Sales and profits are in thousands of dollars—add 000 to get the full amount. 2010 Note: Financial information for 2010 was not available for all companies at press time.

2010 Sales: $	2010 Profits: $	**U.S. Stock Ticker:**
2009 Sales: $31,926,400	2009 Profits: $-737,270	**Int'l Ticker: 4188** Int'l Exchange: Tokyo-TSE
2008 Sales: $30,543,100	2008 Profits: $512,480	Employees:
2007 Sales: $22,320,000	2007 Profits: $850,000	Fiscal Year Ends: 3/31
2006 Sales: $21,254,900	2006 Profits: $812,820	Parent Company:

SALARIES/BENEFITS:

Pension Plan:	ESOP Stock Plan:	Profit Sharing:	Top Exec. Salary: $	Bonus: $
Savings Plan:	Stock Purch. Plan:		Second Exec. Salary: $	Bonus: $

OTHER THOUGHTS:

Apparent Women Officers or Directors:
Hot Spot for Advancement for Women/Minorities:

LOCATIONS: ("Y" = Yes)

West:	Southwest:	Midwest:	Southeast:	Northeast:	International:
				Y	Y

MITSUBISHI CORP

www.mitsubishicorp.com

Industry Group Code: 333 **Ranks within this company's industry group:** Sales: Profits:

Exploration/Production:		Refining/Retailing:		Utilities:		Alternative Energy:		Specialty Services:		Energy Mktg./Other Svcs.	
Exploration:	Y	Refining:		Electric Utility:		Waste/Solar/Other:		Consulting/Eng.:		Energy Marketing:	
Production:	Y	Retailing:		Gas Utility:		Thermal/Steam:		Seismic:		Equipment/Machinery:	
Coal Production:	Y	Convenience Stores:		Pipelines:		Wind:		Drilling:		Oil Field Services:	
		Chemicals:	Y	Water:		Hydro:		InfoTech:		Air/Shipping Transportation:	
						Fuel Cells:		Specialty Services:			

TYPES OF BUSINESS:

Machinery & Automotive Manufacturing
Financial Services
Metals Mining & Production
Chemicals
Food Products & Commodities
Petroleum Exploration & Production
IT Services & Equipment
Solar Cells & Fuel-Cell Systems

BRANDS/DIVISIONS/AFFILIATES:

Mitsubishi Chemical
Mitsubishi Corporation Unimetals, Ltd.
Mitsubishi Motors
Petro-Diamond, Inc.
Jeco Corporation
Nikken Corporation
Mitsubishi Shoji Plastics
San-Esu, Inc.

CONTACTS: *Note: Officers with more than one job title may be intentionally listed here more than once.*

Yorihiko Kojima, CEO
Yorihiko Kojima, Pres.
Ryoichi Ueda, CFO
Tsuneo Iyobe, Exec. VP-Human Resources
Kiyoshi Fujimara, CIO
Hideto Nakahara, Exec. VP-Global Strategy & Regional Dev.
Hideyuki Nabeshima, Sr. Exec. VP-Corp. Comm.
Ichiro Ando, Controller
Jun Kinukawa, Exec. VP/CEO-Metals Group
Koichi Komatsu, Exec. VP/Regional CEO-Americas
Hajime Katsumura, Exec. VP/CEO-Machinery Group
Seiji Kato, Exec. VP/CEO-Energy Bus. Group
Mikio Sasaki, Chmn.
Tetsuo Nishiumi, Exec. VP-Mitsubishi Int'l

Phone: 81-3-3210-2121 **Fax:** 81-3-3210-8583
Toll-Free:
Address: 3-1 Marunouchi 2-chome, Chiyoda-ku, Tokyo, 100-8086 Japan

GROWTH PLANS/SPECIAL FEATURES:

Mitsubishi Corp. is one of Japan's largest general trading companies, with customers around the world in virtually every industry, including energy, metals, machinery, chemicals, food and general merchandise. The company's 562 consolidated subsidiaries and affiliates fall into six business groups: the industrial finance, logistics and development group; the energy business group; the metals group; the machinery group; the chemicals group; and the living essentials group. The industrial finance, logistics and development group consists of three smaller divisions: asset finance and business development; development and construction projects; and logistics. The energy business group includes liquefied natural gas and petroleum exploration and production and carbon and propane businesses. The metals group is involved in the mining of coal and ferrous and non-ferrous metals, as well as the production of automotive components, steel and other metallic components. The machinery group manufactures power and electrical systems, power plants, defense systems, aeronautical and space systems, industrial and agricultural machinery and automotive parts and vehicles. The automotive business also produces parts for Isuzu and Honda cars and trucks. The chemicals group manufactures petrochemicals, methanol, ammonia, fertilizer, plastics and other substances. The living essentials group produces food products, food commodities, textiles and other consumer products including paper products, packaging material, building materials, cement, glass and tires. In March 2010, the company announced the merger of its subsidiaries MC Unimetals and Shoji Light Metal under the name Mitsubishi Corporation Unimetals, Ltd. In April 2010, Mitsubishi established the Global Environment Business Development Group, concerned primarily with the development of alternative forms of energy generation and sustainability, and the Business Service Group, which integrates information technology and aspects of logistics management. In June 2010, the firm acquired a 2.5% ownership interest in Minera Escondida Limitade, a Chilean company which operates the world's largest cooper mine, with an interest in expanding its copper mining sector.

FINANCIALS: **Sales and profits are in thousands of dollars—add 000 to get the full amount. 2010 Note: Financial information for 2010 was not available for all companies at press time.**

2010 Sales: $	2010 Profits: $	**U.S. Stock Ticker: MSBHY.PK**
2009 Sales: $67,854,600	2009 Profits: $4,083,990	**Int'l Ticker: 8058** Int'l Exchange: Tokyo-TSE
2008 Sales: $60,308,100	2008 Profits: $4,627,900	Employees:
2007 Sales: $46,297,333	2007 Profits: $3,784,493	Fiscal Year Ends: 3/31
2006 Sales: $40,430,200	2006 Profits: $2,931,950	Parent Company:

SALARIES/BENEFITS:

Pension Plan:	ESOP Stock Plan:	Profit Sharing:	Top Exec. Salary: $	Bonus: $
Savings Plan:	Stock Purch. Plan:		Second Exec. Salary: $	Bonus: $

OTHER THOUGHTS:

Apparent Women Officers or Directors:
Hot Spot for Advancement for Women/Minorities:

LOCATIONS: ("Y" = Yes)

West:	Southwest:	Midwest:	Southeast:	Northeast:	International:
					Y

MITSUI OSK LINES LTD

www.mol.co.jp

Industry Group Code: 483111 **Ranks within this company's industry group:** Sales: 2 Profits: 1

Exploration/Production:		Refining/Retailing:		Utilities:		Alternative Energy:		Specialty Services:		Energy Mktg./Other Svcs.	
Exploration:		Refining:		Electric Utility:		Waste/Solar/Other:		Consulting/Eng.:		Energy Marketing:	
Production:		Retailing:		Gas Utility:		Thermal/Steam:		Seismic:		Equipment/Machinery:	
Coal Production:		Convenience Stores:		Pipelines:		Wind:		Drilling:		Oil Field Services:	
		Chemicals:		Water:		Hydro:		InfoTech:		Air/Shipping Transportation:	Y
						Fuel Cells:		Specialty Services:	Y		

TYPES OF BUSINESS:

Deep Sea Freight Transportation
Domestic Shipping
Logistics
Trucking
Cruise Ships
Shipping Research
Bulk Shipping
LNG Carriers

BRANDS/DIVISIONS/AFFILIATES:

New World Alliance (The)
APL Ltd
Hyundai Merchant Marine Co Ltd
MOL (America) Inc
MOL (Europe) BV
MOL (Asia) Ltd
Mitsui OSK Bulk Shipping (USA) Inc
Mitsui OSK Bulk Shipping (Europe) Ltd

CONTACTS: *Note: Officers with more than one job title may be intentionally listed here more than once.*

Tetsuya Minato, Managing Exec. Officer-Liner Mktg.
Yoichi Aoki, Sr. Managing Exec.-Human Resources
Yoichi Aoki, Sr. Managing Exec.-Tech. Div.
Shizou Takahashi, Exec. Officer-Corp. Planning
Koichi Muto, Managing Exec.-Public Rel.
Shugo Aoto, Managing Exec. Officer-Investor Rel.
Shugo Aoto, Managing Exec. Officer-Finance & Acct.
Toshitaka Shishido, Managing Exec.-Car Carrier Div.
Kenichi Nagata, Managing Exec.-Coal & Iron Ore Carrier Div.
Akimitsu Ashida, Chmn.
Masahiro Tanabe, Managing Dir.-MOL (Europe), B.V.
Masakazu Yakushiji, Exec. VP-Logistics Bus. Div.

Phone: 81-3-3587-6224	**Fax:** 81-3-3587-7734
Toll-Free:	
Address: 1-1 Toranomon 2-Chome, Minato-ku, Tokyo, 105-8688 Japan	

GROWTH PLANS/SPECIAL FEATURES:

Mitsui O.S.K. Lines, Ltd. (MOL) operates a fleet of approximately 905 vessels consisting of containerships, bulk carriers, car carriers and liquid natural gas carriers, as well as passenger ferries and two cruise ships. The company operates in The New World Alliance (TNWA) with APL, Ltd. of the U.S. and Hyundai Merchant Marine Co., Ltd. (HMM) of South Korea, serving Trans-Pacific, Asia-Europe and trans-Atlantic routes. MOL's advanced logistics network serves about 40 routes and approximately 70 fleets all over the world; and it owns seven container terminals in Japan and overseas. The firm also maintains a shipping research division and makes available on its web site the trend data it has collated and analyzed to assist shipping companies in their endeavors. MOL operates through many subsidiaries worldwide, including MOL (America), Inc.; MOL (Europe), B.V.; MOL (Asia), Ltd.; Mitsui O.S.K. Bulk Shipping (USA), Inc.; Mitsui O.S.K. Bulk Shipping (Europe), Ltd.; and Mitsui O.S.K. Lines (India) Private Ltd. In total, it has approximately 331 subsidiaries and affiliated companies in the MOL group. Bulk ship operations generate roughly 54% of the firm's revenue; operate containerships generate 34%; associated businesses account for 5.7%; logistics services for 3%; and ferries and other domestic transports for 2.9%.

FINANCIALS: **Sales and profits are in thousands of dollars—add 000 to get the full amount. 2010 Note: Financial information for 2010 was not available for all companies at press time.**

2010 Sales: $	2010 Profits: $	**U.S. Stock Ticker: MSLOF**
2009 Sales: $20,745,700	2009 Profits: $1,411,960	**Int'l Ticker: 9104** Int'l Exchange: Tokyo-TSE
2008 Sales: $18,572,000	2008 Profits: $1,264,000	Employees:
2007 Sales: $13,350,000	2007 Profits: $1,030,000	Fiscal Year Ends: 3/31
2006 Sales: $11,634,673	2006 Profits: $968,179	Parent Company:

SALARIES/BENEFITS:

Pension Plan:	ESOP Stock Plan:	Profit Sharing:	Top Exec. Salary: $	Bonus: $
Savings Plan:	Stock Purch. Plan:		Second Exec. Salary: $	Bonus: $

OTHER THOUGHTS:

Apparent Women Officers or Directors:
Hot Spot for Advancement for Women/Minorities:

LOCATIONS: ("Y" = Yes)

West:	Southwest:	Midwest:	Southeast:	Northeast:	International:
Y	Y	Y	Y	Y	Y

MOTIVA ENTERPRISES LLC

www.motivaenterprises.com

Industry Group Code: 324110 **Ranks within this company's industry group:** Sales: Profits:

Exploration/Production:		Refining/Retailing:		Utilities:		Alternative Energy:		Specialty Services:		Energy Mktg./Other Svcs.	
Exploration:		Refining:	Y	Electric Utility:		Waste/Solar/Other:		Consulting/Eng.:		Energy Marketing:	
Production:		Retailing:	Y	Gas Utility:		Thermal/Steam:		Seismic:		Equipment/Machinery:	
Coal Production:		Convenience Stores:	Y	Pipelines:		Wind:		Drilling:		Oil Field Services:	
		Chemicals:	Y	Water:		Hydro:		InfoTech:		Air/Shipping Transportation:	
						Fuel Cells:		Specialty Services:			

TYPES OF BUSINESS:

Oil Refining & Marketing
Gasoline Distribution & Retail

BRANDS/DIVISIONS/AFFILIATES:

Shell Oil Company
Saudi Aramco
Saudi Refining Inc
Port Arthur Refinery

CONTACTS:

Note: Officers with more than one job title may be intentionally listed here more than once.

Robert W. Pease, CEO
Robert W. Pease, Pres.

Phone: 713-277-8000	**Fax:**
Toll-Free:	
Address: 700 Milam St., Houston, TX 77002 US	

GROWTH PLANS/SPECIAL FEATURES:

Motiva Enterprises, LLC, is a joint venture between Shell Oil Company and Saudi Refining Inc., a subsidiary of Saudi Aramco. Based in Houston, Texas, the company operates the refining and marketing businesses of its parent companies in the southeastern and eastern U.S. These operations include three refineries in Louisiana and Texas with a capacity of 740,000 barrels per day; ownership interest in 41 refined product storage terminals with an aggregate storage capacity of approximately 19.8 million barrels; and 320 contracted locations where products are stored on behalf of the firm's customers. Motiva markets its fuel to nearly 7,700 Shell-branded gas stations in 26 states and Washington, D.C. Together, with its sister company Shell Oil Products US, which operates in the Midwest and West, the firm is one of the leading gasoline retailers in the country. Motiva's commercial marketing division provides truckload, bulk products and other services to businesses, fleets and wholesalers. Products include unbranded gasoline; coke; sulfur; and distillates, such as home heating oil, kerosene and diesel fuel. Motiva Enterprises is in the process of expanding its Port Arthur Refinery to augment the production of transportation fuels. Upon construction completion (which is expected to occur in 2012) Port Arthur will be one of the largest refineries in the world, with a production capacity of roughly 600,000 barrels per day.

FINANCIALS:

Sales and profits are in thousands of dollars—add 000 to get the full amount. 2010 Note: Financial information for 2010 was not available for all companies at press time.

2010 Sales: $	2010 Profits: $	**U.S. Stock Ticker: Joint Venture**
2009 Sales: $	2009 Profits: $	**Int'l Ticker:** Int'l Exchange:
2008 Sales: $	2008 Profits: $	Employees:
2007 Sales: $	2007 Profits: $	Fiscal Year Ends: 12/31
2006 Sales: $	2006 Profits: $	Parent Company:

SALARIES/BENEFITS:

Pension Plan:	ESOP Stock Plan:	Profit Sharing:	Top Exec. Salary: $	Bonus: $
Savings Plan:	Stock Purch. Plan:		Second Exec. Salary: $	Bonus: $

OTHER THOUGHTS:

Apparent Women Officers or Directors:
Hot Spot for Advancement for Women/Minorities:

LOCATIONS: ("Y" = Yes)

West:	Southwest:	Midwest:	Southeast:	Northeast:	International:
	Y		Y	Y	

MURPHY OIL CORPORATION

www.murphyoilcorp.com

Industry Group Code: 211111 **Ranks within this company's industry group:** Sales: 34 Profits: 40

Exploration/Production:		Refining/Retailing:		Utilities:		Alternative Energy:		Specialty Services:		Energy Mktg./Other Svcs.	
Exploration:	Y	Refining:	Y	Electric Utility:		Waste/Solar/Other:		Consulting/Eng.:		Energy Marketing:	Y
Production:	Y	Retailing:	Y	Gas Utility:		Thermal/Steam:		Seismic:		Equipment/Machinery:	
Coal Production:		Convenience Stores:	Y	Pipelines:	Y	Wind:		Drilling:		Oil Field Services:	
		Chemicals:		Water:		Hydro:		InfoTech:		Air/Shipping Transportation:	
						Fuel Cells:		Specialty Services:			

TYPES OF BUSINESS:

Oil & Gas Exploration & Production
Refining
Pipelines
Retail Gas Stations
Wholesale Marketing
Synthetic Crude

BRANDS/DIVISIONS/AFFILIATES:

Syncrude Canada, Ltd.
Murco Petroleum, Ltd.
Murphy Oil USA, Inc.
SPUR
Murphy USA
Murphy Canada
Murphy Oil Company, Ltd.

CONTACTS: *Note: Officers with more than one job title may be intentionally listed here more than once.*

David Wood, CEO
David Wood, Pres.
Kevin G. Fitzgerald, CFO/Sr. VP
Henry J. Heithaus, VP-Mktg.
Robert W. Jenkins, Exec. VP-Exploration & Prod.
Thomas McKinlay, VP-Mfg.
Kelli Hammock, VP-Admin.
Steven Cosse, General Counsel/Exec. VP
John Eckart, Controller/VP
Bill H. Stobaugh, Sr. VP
Mindy West, Treas./VP
Walter Compton, VP-Law/Corp. Sec.
William Nolan, Chmn.

Phone: 870-862-6411 **Fax:** 870-864-6371
Toll-Free:
Address: 200 Peach St., El Dorado, AR 71730 US

GROWTH PLANS/SPECIAL FEATURES:

Murphy Oil Corporation, through its subsidiaries, is a global oil and gas exploration and production company with refining and marketing operations in North America and the U.K. The company's U.S. exploration and production activities are located primarily in the Gulf of Mexico, onshore Louisiana and Alaska. Murphy's Canadian assets include interests in the Hibernia and Terra Nova properties offshore Newfoundland and in Syncrude Canada, Ltd., which produces synthetic crude from bitumen oil sands. Western and offshore eastern Canadian operations are carried out by Murphy Oil Company Ltd. The company's crude oil, condensate and natural gas liquids production averages 131,839 barrels per day from its facilities in the U.S., Canada, Malaysia, the Republic of Congo and the North Sea. Murphy conducts its refining and marketing operations through Murphy Oil USA, Inc. and the U.K. subsidiary Murco Petroleum, Ltd. These companies refine crude oil and feedstock into petroleum products such as gasoline and distillates; buy and sell crude oil and refined products; and transport and market petroleum products. Murphy owns interests in three refineries in Louisiana, Wisconsin and Wales. The company's petroleum products are marketed under the brands SPUR, Murphy Express and Murphy USA, with most locations in the parking areas of Wal-Mart stores. The company also has an agreement to market products through Murphy Canada stations at Canadian Wal-Mart stores. Murphy also owns interests in a number of pipelines in North America and the U.K. In October 2009, a subsidiary of the firm acquired an ethanol plan in Hankinson, North Dakota, for $92 million.

Employees are offered medical, dental and vision coverage; a 401(k) plan; life insurance and AD&D insurance; long-term disability coverage; a pension plan; and a stock purchase plan.

FINANCIALS: **Sales and profits are in thousands of dollars—add 000 to get the full amount. 2010 Note: Financial information for 2010 was not available for all companies at press time.**

2010 Sales: $	2010 Profits: $	**U.S. Stock Ticker: MUR**
2009 Sales: $18,918,181	2009 Profits: $837,621	**Int'l Ticker:** Int'l Exchange:
2008 Sales: $27,360,625	2008 Profits: $1,739,986	Employees: 8,369
2007 Sales: $18,297,637	2007 Profits: $766,529	Fiscal Year Ends: 12/31
2006 Sales: $14,279,325	2006 Profits: $638,279	Parent Company:

SALARIES/BENEFITS:

Pension Plan: Y	ESOP Stock Plan:	Profit Sharing:	Top Exec. Salary: $1,150,000	Bonus: $2,050,000
Savings Plan: Y	Stock Purch. Plan: Y		Second Exec. Salary: $625,000	Bonus: $969,531

OTHER THOUGHTS:

Apparent Women Officers or Directors: 2
Hot Spot for Advancement for Women/Minorities: Y

LOCATIONS: ("Y" = Yes)

West:	Southwest:	Midwest:	Southeast:	Northeast:	International:
Y	Y	Y	Y	Y	Y

NABORS INDUSTRIES LTD

www.nabors.com

Industry Group Code: 213111 **Ranks within this company's industry group:** Sales: 5 Profits: 15

Exploration/Production:		Refining/Retailing:		Utilities:		Alternative Energy:		Specialty Services:		Energy Mktg./Other Svcs.	
Exploration:		Refining:		Electric Utility:		Waste/Solar/Other:		Consulting/Eng.:		Energy Marketing:	
Production:		Retailing:		Gas Utility:		Thermal/Steam:		Seismic:		Equipment/Machinery:	Y
Coal Production:		Convenience Stores:		Pipelines:		Wind:		Drilling:	Y	Oil Field Services:	Y
		Chemicals:		Water:		Hydro:		InfoTech:	Y	Air/Shipping Transportation:	Y
						Fuel Cells:		Specialty Services:	Y		

TYPES OF BUSINESS:

Contract Drilling Services
Oil Field Management
Site Construction
Drilling Instrumentation & Software
Marine & Land Transportation Services
Drilling Systems, Manufacturing

BRANDS/DIVISIONS/AFFILIATES:

Nabors International
Canrig Drilling Technologies
Ryan Energy Technologies
Peak Oilfield Services Company
Superior Well Services Inc

CONTACTS:

Note: Officers with more than one job title may be intentionally listed here more than once.

Eugene M. Isenberg, CEO
Anthony G. Petrello, COO
Anthony G. Petrello, Pres.
R. Clark Wood, CFO
Mark D. Andrews, Corp. Sec.
Dennis A. Smith, Dir.-Bus. Dev.
R. Clark Wood, Chief Acct. Officer
Eugene M. Isenberg, Chmn.

Phone: 441-292-1510	**Fax:** 441-292-1334
Toll-Free:	
Address: 8 Par-La-Ville Rd., Mintflower Pl., Hamilton, HM08 Bermuda	

GROWTH PLANS/SPECIAL FEATURES:

Nabors Industries, Ltd. is one of the largest land-drilling contractors in the world. The company's operations include approximately 730 land workover rigs in the U.S. and Canada; 542 actively marketed land-drilling rigs; 40 offshore platform rigs; and three inland barge rigs. The company conducts oil, gas and geothermal land-drilling operations in the continental U.S., Alaska, Canada, South America, Mexico, the Caribbean, Russia, Africa, Asia and the Middle East. In addition, Nabors is one of the largest land-well-servicing and workover contractors in the U.S. and Canada. The company provides a number of services in select domestic and international markets, including oil field management, engineering, transportation, construction, maintenance, well logging, directional drilling, rig instrumentation, data collection and other support services. The firm also operates through several subsidiaries. Canrig Drilling Technology, Ltd., manufacturers, markets and supplies a range of portable and fixed top drive drilling systems for oil and gas exploration. Ryan Energy Technologies, Inc. is a leader in the development and provision of drilling technology and services. Ryan Energy specializes in downhole and surface technologies and equipment. In addition, Nabors Industries owns 50%-interest in Peak Oilfield Services Company, a joint venture with Cook Inlet Region, Inc., which primarily provides rig moving, site construction, custom heavy hauling, crane and rigging services and general freight services. Peak Oilfield Services conducts its business through multiple terminals within Texas. In September 2010, Nabors Industries acquired Superior Well Services, Inc. for roughly $900 million.

FINANCIALS:

Sales and profits are in thousands of dollars—add 000 to get the full amount. 2010 Note: Financial information for 2010 was not available for all companies at press time.

2010 Sales: $	2010 Profits: $	**U.S. Stock Ticker: NBR**
2009 Sales: $3,503,431	2009 Profits: $-85,888	**Int'l Ticker:** Int'l Exchange:
2008 Sales: $5,303,788	2008 Profits: $475,737	Employees: 18,390
2007 Sales: $4,940,681	2007 Profits: $930,691	Fiscal Year Ends: 12/31
2006 Sales: $4,942,714	2006 Profits: $1,020,736	Parent Company:

SALARIES/BENEFITS:

Pension Plan:	ESOP Stock Plan:	Profit Sharing:	Top Exec. Salary: $1,141,750	Bonus: $19,891,275
Savings Plan:	Stock Purch. Plan:		Second Exec. Salary: $965,806	Bonus: $7,886,551

OTHER THOUGHTS:

Apparent Women Officers or Directors:
Hot Spot for Advancement for Women/Minorities:

LOCATIONS: ("Y" = Yes)

West:	Southwest:	Midwest:	Southeast:	Northeast:	International:
Y	Y	Y	Y		Y

NATIONAL FUEL GAS CO

www.natfuel.com

Industry Group Code: 221210 **Ranks within this company's industry group:** Sales: 12 Profits: 14

Exploration/Production:		Refining/Retailing:		Utilities:		Alternative Energy:		Specialty Services:		Energy Mktg./Other Svcs.	
Exploration:	Y	Refining:		Electric Utility:		Waste/Solar/Other:		Consulting/Eng.:		Energy Marketing:	Y
Production:	Y	Retailing:		Gas Utility:	Y	Thermal/Steam:		Seismic:		Equipment/Machinery:	
Coal Production:		Convenience Stores:		Pipelines:	Y	Wind:		Drilling:		Oil Field Services:	
		Chemicals:		Water:		Hydro:		InfoTech:		Air/Shipping Transportation:	
						Fuel Cells:		Specialty Services:	Y		

TYPES OF BUSINESS:

Oil & Gas Exploration & Production
Natural Gas Utility
Pipelines & Storage
Sawmills & Timber Marketing
Energy Marketing
Energy Management Services

BRANDS/DIVISIONS/AFFILIATES:

National Fuel Gas Distribution Corp
National Fuel Gas Supply Corp
Empire State Pipeline
Seneca Resources Corp
Horizon Energy Development Inc
National Fuel Resources Inc
Highland Forest Resources Inc
Horizon LFG Inc

CONTACTS:

Note: Officers with more than one job title may be intentionally listed here more than once.

Ronald J. Tanski, COO
Ronald J. Tanski, Pres.
Paula M. Ciprich, General Counsel/Sec.
Donna L. DeCarolis, VP-Bus. Dev.
Matthew D. Cabell, Pres., Seneca Resources Corporation
Ronald J. Tanski, Pres., Empire State Pipeline
John U. Clarke, Chmn.
Anna Marie Cellino, Pres., National Fuel Gas Distribution Corporation

Phone: 716-857-7000	Fax:
Toll-Free: 800-365-3234	
Address: 6363 Main St., Williamsville, NY 14221 US	

GROWTH PLANS/SPECIAL FEATURES:

National Fuel Gas Co. is a holding company with operations in five business segments: utility; pipeline and storage; exploration and production; energy marketing; and timber. The utility operations are carried out by National Fuel Gas Distribution Corp., which sells or transports natural gas to approximately 727,000 customers in New York and northwestern Pennsylvania. The pipeline and storage operations are carried out by National Fuel Gas Supply Corp. and Empire State Pipeline. It provides interstate natural gas transmission and storage for affiliated and nonaffiliated companies from southwestern Pennsylvania to the New York-Canadian border at the Niagara River. Seneca Resources Corp., Inc. conducts the company's exploration and production activities. They explore for, develop and purchase oil and natural gas reserves in California; the Appalachian region of the U.S.; Wyoming; and the Gulf Coast regions of Texas, Louisiana, and Alabama. The energy marketing operations, carried out by National Fuel Resources, Inc., markets natural gas to industrial, commercial, public authority and residential end users in New York and Pennsylvania. The timber division, through Highland Forest Resources, Inc., operates two sawmills and processes hardwoods residing in about 103,317 acres of timber property in Pennsylvania and New York. In addition, Highland Forest Resources, Inc. manages an additional 3,424 acres of timber rights. Other subsidiaries include Horizon Energy Development, Inc., which engages in foreign and domestic energy projects; Horizon LFG, Inc., is engaged in the purchase, sale and transportation of landfill gas in Ohio, Michigan, Kentucky, Missouri, Maryland and Indiana; Leidy Hub, Inc., provides various natural gas hub services to customers in the eastern U.S.; and Horizon Power, Inc., which develops and operates mid-range independent power production facilities and landfill gas electric generation facilities.

FINANCIALS:

Sales and profits are in thousands of dollars—add 000 to get the full amount. 2010 Note: Financial information for 2010 was not available for all companies at press time.

2010 Sales: $	2010 Profits: $	**U.S. Stock Ticker: NFG**
2009 Sales: $2,057,852	2009 Profits: $100,708	**Int'l Ticker:** Int'l Exchange:
2008 Sales: $2,400,361	2008 Profits: $268,728	Employees: 1,949
2007 Sales: $2,039,566	2007 Profits: $337,455	Fiscal Year Ends: 9/30
2006 Sales: $2,239,675	2006 Profits: $138,091	Parent Company:

SALARIES/BENEFITS:

Pension Plan:	ESOP Stock Plan:	Profit Sharing:	Top Exec. Salary: $707,000	Bonus: $1,889,885
Savings Plan:	Stock Purch. Plan:		Second Exec. Salary: $567,000	Bonus: $1,249,650

OTHER THOUGHTS:

Apparent Women Officers or Directors: 2
Hot Spot for Advancement for Women/Minorities: Y

LOCATIONS: ("Y" = Yes)

West:	Southwest:	Midwest:	Southeast:	Northeast:	International:
Y	Y		Y	Y	Y

NATIONAL GRID PLC

www.nationalgrid.com

Industry Group Code: 221 **Ranks within this company's industry group:** Sales: 5 Profits: 7

Exploration/Production:		Refining/Retailing:		Utilities:		Alternative Energy:		Specialty Services:		Energy Mktg./Other Svcs.	
Exploration:		Refining:		Electric Utility:	Y	Waste/Solar/Other:		Consulting/Eng.:		Energy Marketing:	
Production:		Retailing:		Gas Utility:	Y	Thermal/Steam:		Seismic:		Equipment/Machinery:	
Coal Production:		Convenience Stores:		Pipelines:	Y	Wind:		Drilling:		Oil Field Services:	
		Chemicals:		Water:		Hydro:		InfoTech:		Air/Shipping Transportation:	
						Fuel Cells:		Specialty Services:	Y		

TYPES OF BUSINESS:

Electricity Transmission Systems
Electric & Gas Utilities
Gas Connection Services
Energy Management Software
Pipelines

BRANDS/DIVISIONS/AFFILIATES:

National Grid USA
National Grid Metering
Onstream
National Grid Grain LNG
National Grid Property

CONTACTS:

Note: Officers with more than one job title may be intentionally listed here more than once.

Steve Holiday, CEO
Helen Mahy, General Counsel/Sec.
Steve Lucas, Dir.-Finance
Nick Winser, Exec. Dir.-Transmission
Tom King, Exec. Dir.-Electricity Dist. & Generation
John Parker, Chmn.
Mark Fairbairn, Exec. Dir.-Gas Dist.

Phone: 44-20-7004-3220	**Fax:** 44-20-7004-3004
Toll-Free:	
Address: 1-3 Strand, London XO, WC2N 5EH UK	

GROWTH PLANS/SPECIAL FEATURES:

National Grid PLC is primarily engaged in the building, owning and operating of electricity and gas networks around the world. In the U.K., the company owns and operates a 4,473.87-mile overhead electricity transmission network; a 428.75-mile underground cable system; 337 substations at 241 locations; and two transmission networks. It also operates two transmission systems in Scotland. Additionally, the firm owns and operates the U.K.'s 4,722.42-mile natural gas transportation system that serves roughly 11 million residential buildings and businesses. Through subsidiary National Grid USA, it operates an 8,574.92-mile overhead transmission network, 86.99 miles of underground cables and 524 substations in New England. National Grid also owns a 72,600-mile electricity distribution network supplying power to approximately 3.3 million U.S. customers in New England. Its gas distribution business operates 82,020.99 miles of pipeline in the U.K. that serves 10.8 million customers; and approximately 36,039.53 miles of pipeline that serves 3.5 million customers in upstate New York, New York City, Long Island, Massachusetts, New Hampshire and Rhode Island. Additionally, the company has subsidiaries in various non-regulated businesses. Subsidiaries National Grid Metering and OnStream both provide gas metering and metering-related services in the U.K.; OnStream also meters electricity. National Grid Grain LNG operates the firm's liquefied natural gas import terminal. Finally, National Grid Property manages approximately 1,500 buildings in the U.K. The jointly owned xoserve Limited (with all U.K. gas distributors) is an internal department of National Grid that operates as an interface between the U.K. gas distribution industry, national gas transmission and shipper companies delivering transportation transaction services.

The company provides its employees accident, travel, private medical and dental insurance; childcare vouchers; 25 paid holidays per year; up to 52 weeks maternity/adoption leave and 2 weeks paternity leave; a pension plan; a Sharesave and Share Incentive Plan (SIP); educational incentives; and an employee assistance program.

FINANCIALS:

Sales and profits are in thousands of dollars—add 000 to get the full amount. 2010 Note: Financial information for 2010 was not available for all companies at press time.

2010 Sales: $	2010 Profits: $	**U.S. Stock Ticker: NGG**
2009 Sales: $25,165,100	2009 Profits: $1,525,300	**Int'l Ticker: NG** Int'l Exchange: London-LSE
2008 Sales: $26,606,000	2008 Profits: $1,591,000	Employees: 27,500
2007 Sales: $18,085,900	2007 Profits: $2,903,720	Fiscal Year Ends: 3/31
2006 Sales: $17,563,600	2006 Profits: $2,490,840	Parent Company:

SALARIES/BENEFITS:

Pension Plan: Y	ESOP Stock Plan:	Profit Sharing:	Top Exec. Salary: $	Bonus: $1,378,972
Savings Plan: Y	Stock Purch. Plan: Y		Second Exec. Salary: $	Bonus: $

OTHER THOUGHTS:

Apparent Women Officers or Directors: 3
Hot Spot for Advancement for Women/Minorities: Y

LOCATIONS: ("Y" = Yes)

West:	Southwest:	Midwest:	Southeast:	Northeast:	International:
				Y	Y

NATIONAL GRID USA

www.nationalgridus.com

Industry Group Code: 221 **Ranks within this company's industry group:** Sales: Profits:

Exploration/Production:		Refining/Retailing:		Utilities:		Alternative Energy:		Specialty Services:		Energy Mktg./Other Svcs.	
Exploration:		Refining:		Electric Utility:	Y	Waste/Solar/Other:		Consulting/Eng.:		Energy Marketing:	
Production:		Retailing:		Gas Utility:	Y	Thermal/Steam:		Seismic:		Equipment/Machinery:	
Coal Production:		Convenience Stores:		Pipelines:		Wind:		Drilling:		Oil Field Services:	
		Chemicals:		Water:		Hydro:		InfoTech:		Air/Shipping Transportation:	
						Fuel Cells:		Specialty Services:			

TYPES OF BUSINESS:

Utilities-Electricity & Natural Gas
Telecommunications Services

BRANDS/DIVISIONS/AFFILIATES:

National Grid plc

CONTACTS:

Note: Officers with more than one job title may be intentionally listed here more than once.

Steve Holliday, CEO
Thomas B. King, Pres.
Helen Mahy, General Counsel/Sec.
John Parker, Chmn.

Phone: 508-389-2000	**Fax:** 508-389-2605
Toll-Free:	
Address: 25 Research Dr., Westborough, MA 01582 US	

GROWTH PLANS/SPECIAL FEATURES:

National Grid USA is the U.S. subsidiary of National Grid plc, an international U.K.-based electricity and natural gas company. National Grid USA's energy delivery business serves approximately 3.3 million electricity and 3.4 million natural gas customers. The company serves a 29,000-square-mile service area in New York, Massachusetts, Rhode Island and New Hampshire, with a distribution network of approximately 72,600 miles of lines. Its network also includes approximately 501 substations; 57 generation plants at 13 facilities in Long Island; 850 substations (680 owned); and 36,039 miles of gas pipe. National Grid USA operates in Long Island through an agreement with the Long Island Power Authority. It is one of the largest power producers in the state of New York, with ownership of roughly 6,650 megawatts of electricity. The firm is developing solar installations at four locations in the Greater Boston area. In mid 2009, the company opened a corporate office in Waltham, Massachusetts. In June 2010, National Grid USA opened a new transactions delivery center in Syracuse, New York.

National Grid offers its employees health care flexible spending accounts, coverage for domestic partners, a defined benefit pension plan, a 401(k), credit union membership, tuition reimbursement, scholarships for children of employees, dependent care assistance, an employee assistance program and adoption assistance.

FINANCIALS:

Sales and profits are in thousands of dollars—add 000 to get the full amount. 2010 Note: Financial information for 2010 was not available for all companies at press time.

2010 Sales: $	2010 Profits: $	**U.S. Stock Ticker: Subsidiary**
2009 Sales: $	2009 Profits: $	**Int'l Ticker:** Int'l Exchange:
2008 Sales: $	2008 Profits: $	Employees:
2007 Sales: $	2007 Profits: $	Fiscal Year Ends: 3/31
2006 Sales: $7,866,000	2006 Profits: $	Parent Company: NATIONAL GRID PLC

SALARIES/BENEFITS:

Pension Plan: Y	ESOP Stock Plan:	Profit Sharing:	Top Exec. Salary: $	Bonus: $
Savings Plan: Y	Stock Purch. Plan:		Second Exec. Salary: $	Bonus: $

OTHER THOUGHTS:

Apparent Women Officers or Directors: 3
Hot Spot for Advancement for Women/Minorities: Y

LOCATIONS: ("Y" = Yes)

West:	Southwest:	Midwest:	Southeast:	Northeast:	International:
				Y	

NATIONAL OILWELL VARCO INC

www.nov.com

Industry Group Code: 213112 **Ranks within this company's industry group:** Sales: 4 Profits: 2

Exploration/Production:		Refining/Retailing:		Utilities:		Alternative Energy:		Specialty Services:		Energy Mktg./Other Svcs.	
Exploration:		Refining:		Electric Utility:		Waste/Solar/Other:		Consulting/Eng.:		Energy Marketing:	
Production:		Retailing:		Gas Utility:		Thermal/Steam:		Seismic:		Equipment/Machinery:	Y
Coal Production:		Convenience Stores:		Pipelines:		Wind:		Drilling:		Oil Field Services:	
		Chemicals:		Water:		Hydro:		InfoTech:		Air/Shipping Transportation:	
						Fuel Cells:		Specialty Services:	Y		

TYPES OF BUSINESS:

Oil & Gas Drilling Equipment & Systems
Distribution & Logistics Services
IT Services

BRANDS/DIVISIONS/AFFILIATES:

NOV IntelliServ
Voest-Alpine Tubulars
Hochang Machinery Industries Co., Ltd
South Seas Inspection Pte. Ltd

CONTACTS:

Note: Officers with more than one job title may be intentionally listed here more than once.

Merrill (Pete) Miller, Jr., CEO
Merrill (Pete) Miller, Jr., Pres.
Clay C. Williams, CFO/Sr. VP
Hege Kverneland, CTO/VP
Dwight W. Rettig, General Counsel/VP
Robert Blanchard, Chief Acct. Officer/Corp. Controller/VP
Mark Reese, Pres., Rig Tech.
Haynes B. Smith, III, Pres., Svcs.
Merrill (Pete) Miller, Jr., Chmn.

Phone: 713-375-3700	**Fax:**
Toll-Free: 888-262-8645	
Address: 7909 Parkwood Circle Dr., Houston, TX 77036 US	

GROWTH PLANS/SPECIAL FEATURES:

National Oilwell Varco, Inc. designs, manufactures and sells equipment and components used in oil and gas drilling and production operations, and provides oilfield services and supply chain integration services to the upstream oil and gas industry. The company has operations in over 800 locations on six continents. The firm operates through three business segments: rig technology, which accounted for 62% of the company's total 2009 revenue; petroleum services and supplies, 28%; and distribution services, 10%. The firm's rig technology segment designs, manufactures, sells and services offshore and onshore drilling rigs; derricks; rig instrumentation systems; coiled tubing equipment and pressure pumping units; wireline winches; and cranes. Its operations extend to Canada, Norway, the U.K., India, China and Belarus. The petroleum services and supplies segment manufactures, rents and sells drill pipe, wired drill pipe, transfer pumps, solids control systems, drilling motors, drill bits and mud pump consumables. Its operations extend to Canada, the U.K., China, Kazakhstan, Mexico, Russia, Argentina, India, Bolivia, the Netherlands, Singapore, Malaysia, Vietnam and the United Arab Emirates. The company's distribution services segment provides maintenance, repair and operating supplies and spare parts to drill site and production locations throughout North America, Mexico, the Middle East, Europe, Southeast Asia and South America. Through its information technology platforms and processes, this segment provides complete procurement, inventory management and logistics services to its customers. The firm also maintains interests in several joint ventures including NOV IntelliServ, which provides wellbore data transmission services; and Voest-Alpine Tubulars, a manufacturer of green tubing. In December 2009, the firm acquired Hochang Machinery Industries Co., Ltd, a manufacturing and fabrication company serving the oil and gas industries, and South Seas Inspection Pte. Ltd, which provides inspection, repair and maintenance services to oil and gas companies.

FINANCIALS:

Sales and profits are in thousands of dollars—add 000 to get the full amount. 2010 Note: Financial information for 2010 was not available for all companies at press time.

2010 Sales: $	2010 Profits: $	**U.S. Stock Ticker: NOV**
2009 Sales: $12,712,000	2009 Profits: $1,469,000	**Int'l Ticker:** Int'l Exchange:
2008 Sales: $13,431,400	2008 Profits: $1,952,000	Employees: 36,802
2007 Sales: $9,789,000	2007 Profits: $1,337,100	Fiscal Year Ends: 12/31
2006 Sales: $7,025,800	2006 Profits: $684,000	Parent Company:

SALARIES/BENEFITS:

Pension Plan: Y	ESOP Stock Plan:	Profit Sharing:	Top Exec. Salary: $823,077	Bonus: $1,054,258
Savings Plan: Y	Stock Purch. Plan:		Second Exec. Salary: $550,000	Bonus: $579,842

OTHER THOUGHTS:

Apparent Women Officers or Directors:
Hot Spot for Advancement for Women/Minorities:

LOCATIONS: ("Y" = Yes)

West:	Southwest:	Midwest:	Southeast:	Northeast:	International:
Y	Y	Y	Y	Y	Y

NATIONAL THERMAL POWER CORP LTD

www.ntpc.co.in

Industry Group Code: 2211 **Ranks within this company's industry group:** Sales: Profits:

Exploration/Production:		Refining/Retailing:		Utilities:		Alternative Energy:		Specialty Services:		Energy Mktg./Other Svcs.	
Exploration:	Y	Refining:		Electric Utility:	Y	Waste/Solar/Other:	Y	Consulting/Eng.:	Y	Energy Marketing:	Y
Production:	Y	Retailing:		Gas Utility:		Thermal/Steam:		Seismic:		Equipment/Machinery:	
Coal Production:	Y	Convenience Stores:		Pipelines:		Wind:		Drilling:		Oil Field Services:	
		Chemicals:		Water:		Hydro:	Y	InfoTech:		Air/Shipping Transportation:	
						Fuel Cells:		Specialty Services:	Y		

TYPES OF BUSINESS:

Electric Utility
Power Generation
Engineering & Construction Services
Power Consulting Services
Ash Utilization
Hydroelectric Generation

BRANDS/DIVISIONS/AFFILIATES:

SAIL Power Supply Corporation, Ltd
Ratnagiri Gas and Power Private Ltd
NTPC Electric Supply Company
NTPC Hydro Ltd
NTPC Vidyut Vyapar Nigam Ltd
Utility Powertech Limited
NTPC Tamilnadu Energy Company Limited
Kanti Bijlee Utpadan Nigam Ltd

CONTACTS: *Note: Officers with more than one job title may be intentionally listed here more than once.*

Arup Roy Choudhury, Managing Dir.
P.K.Sengupta, Dir.-Finance
S.P. Singh, Dir.-Human Resources
R. K. Jain, Dir.-Tech.
A. K. Rastogi, Company Sec.
N. N. Misra, Dir.-Oper.
I.J. Kapoor, Dir.-Commercial
B.P. Singh, Dir.-Projects
Arup Roy Choudhury, Chmn.

Phone: 91-11-2436-0100	**Fax:** 91-11-2436-1018
Toll-Free:	
Address: NTPC Bhawan, Institutional Area, Lodi Rd., New Delhi, 110 003 India	

GROWTH PLANS/SPECIAL FEATURES:

National Thermal Power Corp. Ltd. (NTPC), which does business as NTPC Ltd., is one of the world's largest power generation companies and is approximately 89.5% owned by the Indian government. Its subsidiary businesses include NTPC Electric Supply CompanyLtd., an electricity distribution business; NTPC Hydro Ltd., a hydroelectric power business; and NTPC Vidyut Vyapar Nigam Ltd., which sells surplus power. NTPC's core business is the engineering, construction and operation of its 22 power plants, through which it supplies power to government-owned distribution grids throughout India. The firm has a total installed generating capacity of 32,194 megawatts (MW); through its 15 coal-based power plants and its seven gas-fired power plants. The firm has four additional stations that are coal based and another station that uses naphtha/LNG as fuel. Joint venture SAIL Power Supply Corporation, Ltd. operates coal power plants in at Durgapur, Rourkela and Bhilai, with a capacity of 814 MW. Joint venture Ratnagiri Gas and Power Private Ltd. operate a naphtha and liquefied natural gas (LNG) power plant in Maharastra. The company has an additional 16 joint ventures with companies such as Utility Powertech Limited; NTPC Tamilnadu Energy Company Limited; Kanti Bijlee Utpadan Nigam Ltd.; Aravali Power Company Private Ltd.; and Bharatiya Rail Bijlee Company Ltd. NTPC hopes to increase its installed capacity to approximately 53,000 MW comprised of 10,000 MW of gas, 9,000 MW of hydro generation, 2,000 MW of nuclear sources and 1,000 MW of renewable energy sources by 2017.

FINANCIALS: **Sales and profits are in thousands of dollars—add 000 to get the full amount. 2010 Note: Financial information for 2010 was not available for all companies at press time.**

2010 Sales: $	2010 Profits: $	**U.S. Stock Ticker: Government-Owned**
2009 Sales: $	2009 Profits: $	**Int'l Ticker:** Int'l Exchange:
2008 Sales: $	2008 Profits: $	Employees:
2007 Sales: $7,877,490	2007 Profits: $1,523,080	Fiscal Year Ends: 3/31
2006 Sales: $6,899,650	2006 Profits: $1,406,530	Parent Company:

SALARIES/BENEFITS:

Pension Plan:	ESOP Stock Plan:	Profit Sharing:	Top Exec. Salary: $	Bonus: $
Savings Plan:	Stock Purch. Plan:		Second Exec. Salary: $	Bonus: $

OTHER THOUGHTS:

Apparent Women Officers or Directors:
Hot Spot for Advancement for Women/Minorities:

LOCATIONS: ("Y" = Yes)

West:	Southwest:	Midwest:	Southeast:	Northeast:	International:
					Y

NEDERLANDSE GASUNIE NV

www.nvnederlandsegasunie.nl

Industry Group Code: 486 **Ranks within this company's industry group:** Sales: Profits:

Exploration/Production:		Refining/Retailing:		Utilities:		Alternative Energy:		Specialty Services:		Energy Mktg./Other Svcs.	
Exploration:		Refining:		Electric Utility:		Waste/Solar/Other:	Y	Consulting/Eng.:	Y	Energy Marketing:	Y
Production:		Retailing:		Gas Utility:		Thermal/Steam:		Seismic:		Equipment/Machinery:	
Coal Production:		Convenience Stores:		Pipelines:	Y	Wind:		Drilling:		Oil Field Services:	
		Chemicals:		Water:		Hydro:		InfoTech:		Air/Shipping Transportation:	
						Fuel Cells:		Specialty Services:	Y		

TYPES OF BUSINESS:

Natural Gas Transportation & Sales
Research, Engineering & Consulting

BRANDS/DIVISIONS/AFFILIATES:

GasTransport Services B.V.
Gasunie Engineering & Technology
North European Gas Pipeline
Balgzand-Bacton Line Company
Nord Stream AG
BEB Erdgas und Erdol GMbH
Koninklijke Vopak N.V.

CONTACTS:

Note: Officers with more than one job title may be intentionally listed here more than once.

Paul C. van Gelder, CEO
Henk A. T. Chin-Sue, CFO
Pieter E. G. Trienekens, Dir.-Bus. Dev. & Joint Ventures
Eric Dam, Dir.-Construction & Maintenance
Paul C. van Gelder, Chmn.

Phone: 31-50-521-9111	**Fax:** 31-50-521-1999
Toll-Free:	
Address: Concourslaan 17, Groningen, 9727 KC The Netherlands	

GROWTH PLANS/SPECIAL FEATURES:

Nederlandse Gasunie N.V., owned by the State of the Netherlands, purchases, transports and sells natural gas in the Netherlands and Western Europe. The firm is divided into three main groups: gas transport services; Gasunie construction and maintenance; and Gasunie participations and business development. Its gas transport subsidiary, GasTransport Services B.V., is responsible for the Netherlands' national gas grid. This pipeline grid includes approximately 9,320 miles of pipeline, dozens of installations and approximately 1,300 gas receiving stations. Annual gas throughput is over 3.4 trillion cubic feet. Nederlandse Gasunie's construction and maintenance segment focuses on asset management for the gas grid, as well as activities such as maintenance and construction works. The Participations & Business Development segment focuses on involvement in joint national and international gas infrastructure projects and non-regulated services. It participates in several joint ventures that connect the Dutch gas pipeline network with foreign markets. Gasunie Deutschland GmbH & Co. KG, a wholly owned subsidiary of Nederlandse Gasunie based in Hannover, manages the North German pipeline network. In August 2010, the company announced the opening of a supply valve that would biogas created from organic waste to begin to flow into the national natural gas transmission network.

FINANCIALS:

Sales and profits are in thousands of dollars—add 000 to get the full amount. 2010 Note: Financial information for 2010 was not available for all companies at press time.

2010 Sales: $	2010 Profits: $	**U.S. Stock Ticker: Government-Owned**
2009 Sales: $	2009 Profits: $	**Int'l Ticker:** Int'l Exchange:
2008 Sales: $	2008 Profits: $	Employees:
2007 Sales: $1,661,570	2007 Profits: $547,980	Fiscal Year Ends: 12/31
2006 Sales: $1,575,910	2006 Profits: $482,470	Parent Company:

SALARIES/BENEFITS:

Pension Plan: Y	ESOP Stock Plan:	Profit Sharing:	Top Exec. Salary: $490,739	Bonus: $130,065
Savings Plan:	Stock Purch. Plan:		Second Exec. Salary: $332,324	Bonus: $91,392

OTHER THOUGHTS:

Apparent Women Officers or Directors:
Hot Spot for Advancement for Women/Minorities:

LOCATIONS: ("Y" = Yes)

West:	Southwest:	Midwest:	Southeast:	Northeast:	International:
					Y

NEW JERSEY RESOURCES CORPORATION

www.njresources.com

Industry Group Code: 221210 **Ranks within this company's industry group:** Sales: 8 Profits: 17

Exploration/Production:		Refining/Retailing:		Utilities:		Alternative Energy:		Specialty Services:		Energy Mktg./Other Svcs.	
Exploration:		Refining:		Electric Utility:		Waste/Solar/Other:		Consulting/Eng.:		Energy Marketing:	Y
Production:		Retailing:		Gas Utility:	Y	Thermal/Steam:		Seismic:		Equipment/Machinery:	Y
Coal Production:		Convenience Stores:		Pipelines:	Y	Wind:		Drilling:		Oil Field Services:	
		Chemicals:		Water:		Hydro:		InfoTech:		Air/Shipping Transportation:	
						Fuel Cells:		Specialty Services:			

TYPES OF BUSINESS:

Utilities-Natural Gas
Energy-Related Services
Appliance Repair
Storage Management
Pipeline Capacity
Energy Investments

BRANDS/DIVISIONS/AFFILIATES:

New Jersey Natural Gas Company
NJR Home Services Company
NJR Energy Services Company
Iroquois Gas and Transmission System LP
NJR Services Company
NJR Energy Holdings
Commercial Realty & Resources
NJR Investment

CONTACTS: *Note: Officers with more than one job title may be intentionally listed here more than once.*

Laurence M. Downes, CEO
Glenn C. Lockwood, CFO/Sr. VP
Mariellen Dugan, General Counsel/Sr. VP
Michael Kinney, Contact-Comm.
Dennis Puma, Dir.-Investor Rel.
William Foley, Treas.
Rhonda M. Figueroa, Corp. Sec.
Kathleen T. Ellis, Exec. VP/COO-New Jersey Natural Gas
Stephen D. Westhoven, Sr. VP-NJR Energy Svcs.
Stan Kosierowski, Pres., NJR Clean Energy Ventures/NJR Home Svcs.
Laurence M. Downes, Chmn.

Phone: 732-938-1000 **Fax:** 732-938-3154
Toll-Free:
Address: 1415 Wyckoff Rd., Wall, NJ 07719 US

GROWTH PLANS/SPECIAL FEATURES:

New Jersey Resources Corporation (NJR) is an energy services holding company providing retail and wholesale natural gas and energy-related services from the Gulf Coast to New England, the Mid-Continent region, the West Coast and Canada. NJR operates through two segments: natural gas distribution and energy services. The natural gas distribution segment consists of wholly-owned subsidiary New Jersey Natural Gas Company (NJNG), a provider of natural gas energy services to roughly 487,000 residential and commercial customers in New Jersey's Monmouth, Ocean, Middlesex, Morris and Burlington counties, as well as a participant in off-system sales and capacity release markets. NJNG purchases its gas supply in long-term, winter-term and short-term contracts from 95 suppliers. NJNG transports its natural gas by means of agreements for firm transportation with several interstate pipeline companies, including Transcontinental Gas Pipe Line Corp.; Columbia Gas Transmission Corp.; and Tennessee Gas Pipeline Co. The energy services segment consists of subsidiary NJR Energy Services, which provides unregulated wholesale energy services and natural gas storage and transportation asset optimization services. NJR also maintains retail and other subsidiaries, including NJR Home Services Company, a provider of repair services for heating, ventilation and cooling (HVAC) appliances; NJR Service Corporation, which provides NJR companies with shared support services such as communications, financial and planning, legal and human resources services; NJR Energy Holdings, an investor in energy-related ventures through its subsidiary, NJNR Pipeline, which primarily consists of its interest in the Iroquois Gas and Transmission System, LP; NJR Plumbing Services, a plumbing repair and installation service company; Commercial Realty & Resources, a commercial real estate developing company; and NJR Investment, which makes certain energy-related equity investments.

Employee benefits provided by the firm include medical, dental and life insurance; a 401(k) plan; disability protection; long-term care coverage; and flexible spending accounts.

FINANCIALS: **Sales and profits are in thousands of dollars—add 000 to get the full amount. 2010 Note: Financial information for 2010 was not available for all companies at press time.**

2010 Sales: $	2010 Profits: $	**U.S. Stock Ticker: NJR**
2009 Sales: $2,592,460	2009 Profits: $27,242	**Int'l Ticker:** Int'l Exchange:
2008 Sales: $3,816,210	2008 Profits: $113,910	Employees: 900
2007 Sales: $3,021,765	2007 Profits: $65,281	Fiscal Year Ends: 9/30
2006 Sales: $3,299,608	2006 Profits: $78,519	Parent Company:

SALARIES/BENEFITS:

Pension Plan: Y	ESOP Stock Plan:	Profit Sharing:	Top Exec. Salary: $690,577	Bonus: $700,000
Savings Plan: Y	Stock Purch. Plan:		Second Exec. Salary: $324,500	Bonus: $500,000

OTHER THOUGHTS:

Apparent Women Officers or Directors: 9
Hot Spot for Advancement for Women/Minorities: Y

LOCATIONS: ("Y" = Yes)

West:	Southwest:	Midwest:	Southeast:	Northeast:	International:
				Y	

NEW YORK STATE ELECTRIC & GAS CORP

www.nyseg.com

Industry Group Code: 221 **Ranks within this company's industry group:** Sales: Profits:

Exploration/Production:		Refining/Retailing:		Utilities:		Alternative Energy:		Specialty Services:		Energy Mktg./Other Svcs.	
Exploration:		Refining:		Electric Utility:	Y	Waste/Solar/Other:		Consulting/Eng.:		Energy Marketing:	
Production:		Retailing:		Gas Utility:	Y	Thermal/Steam:		Seismic:		Equipment/Machinery:	
Coal Production:		Convenience Stores:		Pipelines:		Wind:	Y	Drilling:		Oil Field Services:	
		Chemicals:		Water:		Hydro:	Y	InfoTech:		Air/Shipping Transportation:	
						Fuel Cells:		Specialty Services:	Y		

TYPES OF BUSINESS:

Electric Utility
Natural Gas Utility
Hydroelectric Generation
Environmental & Efficiency Technologies

BRANDS/DIVISIONS/AFFILIATES:

Iberdrola USA Inc
CA$HBACK
CA$HBACK plus
Iberdrola SA
NYSEG
Corning Valley Transmission Project
Ithaca Transmission Project

CONTACTS:

Note: Officers with more than one job title may be intentionally listed here more than once.

Michael Conroy, COO/Sr. VP
Mark S. Lynch, Pres.
Joseph J. Syta, Treas./Controller/VP
Walt Matyjas, Dir.-Electric Dist.

Phone: 607-762-7200	**Fax:** 607-762-4422
Toll-Free: 800-572-1111	
Address: 18 Link Dr., Kirkwood Industrial Park, Binghamton, NY 13902-5224 US	

GROWTH PLANS/SPECIAL FEATURES:

New York State Electric & Gas Corp. (NYSEG) is a regulated electricity and distribution company. The firm is a wholly-owned subsidiary of Iberdrola USA, Inc. (formerly Energy East Corporation), which in turn is a wholly-owned subsidiary of Iberdrola S.A. NYSEG serves 872,000 electricity customers and 256,000 natural gas customers across a 20,000-square-mile service area, covering over 40% of upstate New York. The company operates more than 40,000 miles of transmission and distribution lines, which are overseen by the New York Independent System Operator. The production division of the company owns and maintains several hydroelectric power generation facilities. The company's CA$HBACK and CA$HBACK plus programs offer incentives to businesses that reduce their electrical usages. The firm's recent construction project activities include the Ithaca Transmission Project, which began in mid 2009. This project included the construction of a 345-kilovolt (kv) to 115-kv substation in Lapeer, New York; a new 15 mile 115-kv electric transmission line from Etna Substation; and the rebuilding of existing lines between the Etna and Lapeer substations. The project was completed in August 2010. Its Corning Valley Transmission Project, for which the company received construction permits in August 2010, includes the construction of a new 9.2-mile overhead 115-kv transmission line and two substations in Corning, New York. The firm expects it to be operational by mid 2011. In addition to its distribution and production businesses, the firm works in emerging efficiency and environmental restoration technologies, such as aquaculture, erosion control, high-efficiency greenhouses and optical methane detectors. Approximately 67.65% of NYSEG's revenues are derived from electric sales, while the remaining 32.35% is derived from the sale of natural gas.

The company offers its employees life, medical, dental and vision insurance; pension plans; a 401(k) plan; and flexible spending accounts.

FINANCIALS:

Sales and profits are in thousands of dollars—add 000 to get the full amount. 2010 Note: Financial information for 2010 was not available for all companies at press time.

2010 Sales: $	2010 Profits: $	**U.S. Stock Ticker: Subsidiary**
2009 Sales: $	2009 Profits: $	**Int'l Ticker:** Int'l Exchange:
2008 Sales: $	2008 Profits: $	Employees:
2007 Sales: $	2007 Profits: $	Fiscal Year Ends: 12/31
2006 Sales: $1,243,334	2006 Profits: $143,018	Parent Company: IBERDROLA SA

SALARIES/BENEFITS:

Pension Plan: Y	ESOP Stock Plan:	Profit Sharing:	Top Exec. Salary: $	Bonus: $
Savings Plan: Y	Stock Purch. Plan:		Second Exec. Salary: $	Bonus: $

OTHER THOUGHTS:

Apparent Women Officers or Directors: 1
Hot Spot for Advancement for Women/Minorities:

LOCATIONS: ("Y" = Yes)

West:	Southwest:	Midwest:	Southeast:	Northeast:	International:
				Y	

NEWFIELD EXPLORATION CO

www.newfld.com

Industry Group Code: 211111 **Ranks within this company's industry group:** Sales: 76 Profits: 104

Exploration/Production:		Refining/Retailing:		Utilities:		Alternative Energy:		Specialty Services:		Energy Mktg./Other Svcs.	
Exploration:	Y	Refining:		Electric Utility:		Waste/Solar/Other:		Consulting/Eng.:		Energy Marketing:	
Production:	Y	Retailing:		Gas Utility:		Thermal/Steam:		Seismic:		Equipment/Machinery:	
Coal Production:		Convenience Stores:		Pipelines:		Wind:		Drilling:		Oil Field Services:	
		Chemicals:		Water:		Hydro:		InfoTech:		Air/Shipping Transportation:	
						Fuel Cells:		Specialty Services:			

TYPES OF BUSINESS:

Oil & Gas Exploration & Production

BRANDS/DIVISIONS/AFFILIATES:

Monument Butte
Woodford Shale
Granite Wash
Maverick Basin

CONTACTS:

Note: Officers with more than one job title may be intentionally listed here more than once.

Lee K. Boothby, CEO
Gary D. Packer, COO/Exec. VP
Lee K. Boothby, Pres.
Terry W. Rathert, CFO/Exec. VP
Deanna L. Jones, VP-Human Resources
Mark Spicer, VP-IT
James T. Zernell, VP-Prod.
John D. Marziotti, General Counsel/Corp. Sec.
Samuel E. Langford, VP-Corp. Dev.
Stephen C. Campbell, VP-Investor Rel.
Susan G. Riggs, Treas.
W. Mark Blumenshine, VP-Land
John H. Jasek, VP-Gulf of Mexico
Michael D. Van Horn, VP-Geoscience
George T. Dunn, VP-Mid-Continent
Lee K. Boothby, Chmn.
William D. Schneider, VP-Onshore Gulf Coast & Int'l

Phone: 281-847-6000 **Fax:** 281-405-4242
Toll-Free:
Address: 363 N. Sam Houston Pkwy. E., Ste. 100, Houston, TX 77060 US

GROWTH PLANS/SPECIAL FEATURES:

Newfield Exploration Co. (NEC) independently explores, develops and acquires crude oil and natural gas properties both domestically and internationally. Approximately 72% of Newfield's 3.6 trillion cubic feet equivalent of proved reserves is natural gas and 53% is proved developed. The firm's main Mid-Continent plays are Woodford Shale and Granite Wash, which represent 55% of its proved resources. NEC's largest asset is the Monument Butte oil field, located in the Uinta Basin of Utah in the Rocky Mountains. The field accounts for approximately 20% proved reserves and encompasses about 180,000 net acres, including 63,000 net acres added through several ventures with Ute Energy LLC. The firm's working interest in the field averages 80%. The company owns roughly 224,000 net acres with 1,000 producing wells in the Maverick Basin of southern Texas; this area produces roughly 1,500 barrels of oil equivalent (boe) per day. Its Gulf of Mexico operations has a production capacity of approximately 90 million cubic feet equivalent a day. NEC's international reserves are mainly offshore China and Malaysia, with production of over 20,000 barrels of oil a day. In September 2009, the company announced a successful drilling test in the Pearl River Mouth basin in China with its LF 7-1 well testing at 6,000 barrels a day. In October 2009, the company entered into a joint agreement with the Hess Corporation in which each company owns 50% interest in the 140,000 acres in the Marcellus Shale natural gas resource plays in Pennsylvania. In February 2010, NEC acquired roughly 300,000 net acres in the Maverick Basin formerly belonging to the bankrupt TXCO Resources, Inc. for approximately $209 million.

The company offers its employees annual bonus plans, company stock options, a 401(k) plan, a wellness program, long-term disability insurance, life insurance and education reimbursement.

FINANCIALS:

Sales and profits are in thousands of dollars—add 000 to get the full amount. 2010 Note: Financial information for 2010 was not available for all companies at press time.

2010 Sales: $	2010 Profits: $	**U.S. Stock Ticker: NFX**
2009 Sales: $1,338,000	2009 Profits: $-542,000	**Int'l Ticker:** Int'l Exchange:
2008 Sales: $2,225,000	2008 Profits: $-373,000	Employees:
2007 Sales: $1,783,000	2007 Profits: $450,000	Fiscal Year Ends: 12/31
2006 Sales: $1,673,000	2006 Profits: $591,000	Parent Company:

SALARIES/BENEFITS:

Pension Plan:	ESOP Stock Plan: Y	Profit Sharing: Y	Top Exec. Salary: $439,018	Bonus: $1,200,000
Savings Plan: Y	Stock Purch. Plan:		Second Exec. Salary: $373,866	Bonus: $750,000

OTHER THOUGHTS:

Apparent Women Officers or Directors: 4
Hot Spot for Advancement for Women/Minorities: Y

LOCATIONS: ("Y" = Yes)

West:	Southwest:	Midwest:	Southeast:	Northeast:	International:
Y	Y				Y

NEWPARK RESOURCES INC

www.newpark.com

Industry Group Code: 213112 **Ranks within this company's industry group:** Sales: 25 Profits: 21

Exploration/Production:		Refining/Retailing:		Utilities:		Alternative Energy:		Specialty Services:		Energy Mktg./Other Svcs.	
Exploration:		Refining:		Electric Utility:		Waste/Solar/Other:		Consulting/Eng.:	Y	Energy Marketing:	
Production:		Retailing:		Gas Utility:		Thermal/Steam:		Seismic:		Equipment/Machinery:	Y
Coal Production:		Convenience Stores:		Pipelines:		Wind:		Drilling:	Y	Oil Field Services:	Y
		Chemicals:		Water:		Hydro:		InfoTech:		Air/Shipping Transportation:	
						Fuel Cells:		Specialty Services:	Y		

TYPES OF BUSINESS:

Oil & Gas Drilling Services-Drilling Fluids
Waste Disposal Services
Engineering & Technical Services
Composite Construction Mats
Environmental & Oil Field Construction Services

BRANDS/DIVISIONS/AFFILIATES:

Newpark Drilling Fluids
Newpark Mats and Integrated Services
Newpark Environmental Services
DeepDrill
FlexDrill
DuraBase

CONTACTS:

Note: Officers with more than one job title may be intentionally listed here more than once.

Paul L. Howes, CEO
Paul L. Howes, Pres.
James E. Braun, CFO/VP
Sammy L. Cooper, VP-Sales
David Bock, CIO
Frank Lyon, VP-Tech. Svcs.
Bruce Smith, VP/Pres., Fluids Systems & Eng.
Mark J. Airola, Chief Admin. Officer
Mark J. Airola, General Counsel/Corp. Sec./VP
William D. Moss, VP-Corp. Strategy & Dev.
Gregg Piontek, Chief Acct. Officer/Controller/VP
Mark J. Airola, Chief Compliance Officer
Frank Lyon, VP-Quality, Health, Safety & Environment
Jeffrey L. Juergens, Pres., Mats & Integrated Svcs./Environmental Svcs.
Jerry W. Box, Chmn.
Bruce C. Smith, VP-Int'l

Phone: 281-362-6800 **Fax:** 281-362-6801
Toll-Free:
Address: 2700 Research Forest Dr., Ste. 100, The Woodlands, TX 77381 US

GROWTH PLANS/SPECIAL FEATURES:

Newpark Resources, Inc. supplies products and services to the oil and gas exploration and production industry (E&P) in the Gulf Coast, West Texas, East Texas, Oklahoma, North Louisiana, the Rocky Mountains and Northeast regions, as well as Canada, Brazil, the U.K., Mexico and parts of Europe and North Africa. The company operates in three segments: fluid systems and engineering; mats and integrated services; and environmental services. The fluids systems and engineering business offers solutions to highly technical drilling projects involving complex subsurface conditions, such as horizontal, directional, geologically deep or deep water drilling. Newpark owns the patent rights to a family of high-performance, water-based products, which it markets as the DeepDrill and FlexDrill systems. These systems can provide improved penetration rates; superior lubricity; torque and drag reduction; shale inhibition; solids management; minimized hole enlargement; and enhanced ability to log results and use measurement tools. The firm also provides completion fluids services and equipment rental services to customers in Oklahoma and Texas. The mat and integrated services segment provides mat rentals, location construction and related well site services to E&P customers in the onshore U.S. Gulf Coast, Western Colorado, and Northeast U.S. regions, and mat rentals to the utility industry in the U.K.. Mats ensure all-weather access to E&P sites in unstable soil conditions common to these areas. The company markets the DuraBase composite mat system, as well as installing access roads and temporary work sites for pipeline, electrical utility and highway construction projects. Newpark's environmental services segment processes and disposes of waste generated by its oil and gas customers, as well as offering disposal services in the West Texas market. Environmental solutions include refuse reclamation, disposal through deep well injection, waste fluid recycling and waste land farming. It operates six receiving and transfer facilities located along the U.S. Gulf Coast.

FINANCIALS:

Sales and profits are in thousands of dollars—add 000 to get the full amount. 2010 Note: Financial information for 2010 was not available for all companies at press time.

2010 Sales: $	2010 Profits: $	**U.S. Stock Ticker: NR**
2009 Sales: $490,275	2009 Profits: $-20,573	**Int'l Ticker:** Int'l Exchange:
2008 Sales: $858,350	2008 Profits: $38,458	Employees: 1,664
2007 Sales: $671,207	2007 Profits: $26,662	Fiscal Year Ends: 12/31
2006 Sales: $581,908	2006 Profits: $-32,281	Parent Company:

SALARIES/BENEFITS:

Pension Plan:	ESOP Stock Plan:	Profit Sharing:	Top Exec. Salary: $453,600	Bonus: $
Savings Plan:	Stock Purch. Plan:		Second Exec. Salary: $314,580	Bonus: $

OTHER THOUGHTS:

Apparent Women Officers or Directors:
Hot Spot for Advancement for Women/Minorities:

LOCATIONS: ("Y" = Yes)

West:	Southwest:	Midwest:	Southeast:	Northeast:	International:
Y	Y		Y		Y

NEXEN INC

www.nexeninc.com

Industry Group Code: 211111 **Ranks within this company's industry group:** Sales: 52 Profits: 47

Exploration/Production:		Refining/Retailing:		Utilities:		Alternative Energy:		Specialty Services:		Energy Mktg./Other Svcs.	
Exploration:	Y	Refining:		Electric Utility:		Waste/Solar/Other:		Consulting/Eng.:		Energy Marketing:	
Production:	Y	Retailing:		Gas Utility:		Thermal/Steam:		Seismic:		Equipment/Machinery:	
Coal Production:		Convenience Stores:		Pipelines:		Wind:		Drilling:		Oil Field Services:	
		Chemicals:	Y	Water:		Hydro:		InfoTech:		Air/Shipping Transportation:	
						Fuel Cells:		Specialty Services:			

TYPES OF BUSINESS:

Oil & Gas Exploration & Production
Chemicals
Oil Sands Production
Energy Marketing

BRANDS/DIVISIONS/AFFILIATES:

Canexus Income Fund
Long Lake Project
OPTI Canada, Inc.

CONTACTS:

Note: Officers with more than one job title may be intentionally listed here more than once.

Marvin F. Romanow, CEO
Marvin F. Romanow, Pres.
Kevin Reinhart, CFO/Exec. VP
Bob Black, VP-Energy Mktg.
Catherine Hughes, VP-Human Resources
Kevin McLachlan, VP-Global Exploration
Kim McKenzie, CIO/VP
Catherine Hughes, VP-Tech.
Eric Miller, General Counsel/Sr. VP/Sec.
Catherine Hughes, VP-Oper. Svcs.
Una Power, VP-Corp. Planning & Bus. Dev.
Mike Mackus, Treas.
Gary Nieuwenburg, Exec. VP-Canada
Brendam Muller, Controller
Brian Reinsborough, Sr. VP-U.S. Oil & Gas
Francis M. Saville, Chmn.
Matt Fox, Exec. VP-Int'l Oil & Gas

Phone: 403-699-4000 **Fax:** 403-699-5800
Toll-Free:
Address: 801 7th Ave. SW, Calgary, AB T2P 3P7 Canada

GROWTH PLANS/SPECIAL FEATURES:

Nexen, Inc. is an independent global energy and chemicals company. It is involved in the exploration, development and production of crude oil, natural gas and natural gas liquids, as well as the manufacturing, distribution and marketing of sodium chlorate, caustic soda, muriatic acid and chlorine through the Canexus Income Fund. The company, headquartered in Calgary, Alberta, reports in three business sectors: oil and gas; energy marketing; and chemicals. Nexen has core oil and gas operations in the U.K. North Sea, the Gulf of Mexico, western Canada, Yemen, offshore West Africa, Colombia and Norway. The firm produces over 240,000 barrels of oil equivalent per day (boe/d) and has approximately 920 million barrels of oil equivalent in proved oil and gas reserves. Nexen also has an investment in the Athabasca oil sands in Alberta, Canada. The energy marketing sector sells natural gas, crude oil, natural gas liquids and power through key offices in Calgary; Houston; Denver; Dubai; London; Uxbridge; and Singapore. It is also a retail provider of electricity and natural gas. Nexen's chemical sector operates through Canexus Income Fund, in which Nexen retains a 65.7% interest. Its major product is sodium chlorate, primarily sold to the North American pulp and paper industry. This sector also produces chlor-alkali products (caustic soda, chlorine and muriatic acid) for use in pulp and paper mills, water purification industries and oil and gas operations. Nexen has a joint venture, Long Lake Project with OPTI Canada, Inc., to produce premium synthetic crude oil. In January 2009, Nexen acquired an additional 15% interest in Long Lake Project from OPTI Canada for $735 million, raising its ownership stake to 65%. In May 2010, the firm agreed to sell its heavy oil properties in western Canada to Northern Blizzard Resources, Inc.

FINANCIALS:

Sales and profits are in thousands of dollars—add 000 to get the full amount. 2010 Note: Financial information for 2010 was not available for all companies at press time.

2010 Sales: $	2010 Profits: $	**U.S. Stock Ticker: NXY**
2009 Sales: $8,268,750	2009 Profits: $476,830	**Int'l Ticker: NXY** Int'l Exchange: Toronto-TSX
2008 Sales: $6,772,500	2008 Profits: $1,474,900	Employees: 4,594
2007 Sales: $5,700,100	2007 Profits: $934,000	Fiscal Year Ends: 12/31
2006 Sales: $4,536,500	2006 Profits: $516,900	Parent Company:

SALARIES/BENEFITS:

Pension Plan: Y	ESOP Stock Plan:	Profit Sharing:	Top Exec. Salary: $1,076,268	Bonus: $419,678
Savings Plan: Y	Stock Purch. Plan:		Second Exec. Salary: $463,701	Bonus: $152,546

OTHER THOUGHTS:

Apparent Women Officers or Directors: 3
Hot Spot for Advancement for Women/Minorities: Y

LOCATIONS: ("Y" = Yes)

West:	Southwest:	Midwest:	Southeast:	Northeast:	International:
	Y				Y

NEXTERA ENERGY INC

www.nexteraenergy.com

Industry Group Code: 2211 **Ranks within this company's industry group:** Sales: 11 Profits: 7

Exploration/Production:		Refining/Retailing:		Utilities:		Alternative Energy:		Specialty Services:		Energy Mktg./Other Svcs.	
Exploration:		Refining:		Electric Utility:	Y	Waste/Solar/Other:	Y	Consulting/Eng.:		Energy Marketing:	Y
Production:		Retailing:		Gas Utility:	Y	Thermal/Steam:		Seismic:		Equipment/Machinery:	
Coal Production:		Convenience Stores:		Pipelines:		Wind:	Y	Drilling:		Oil Field Services:	
		Chemicals:		Water:		Hydro:		InfoTech:		Air/Shipping Transportation:	
						Fuel Cells:		Specialty Services:			

TYPES OF BUSINESS:

Utilities-Electricity & Natural Gas
Fiber-Optic Services
Financial Services
Nuclear Power
Energy Trading & Marketing
Wind Power
Solar Power

BRANDS/DIVISIONS/AFFILIATES:

Florida Power & Light Company
NextEra Energy Resources LLC
FPL FiberNet, LLC
NextEra Energy Power Marketing LLC
FPL Group, Inc.

CONTACTS: *Note: Officers with more than one job title may be intentionally listed here more than once.*

Lewis Hay, III, CEO
James L. Robo, COO
James L. Robo, Pres.
Armando Pimentel, Jr., CFO/Exec. VP-Finance
James W. Poppell, Exec. VP-Human Resources
Robert L. McGrath, Exec. VP-Eng., Construction & Corp. Svcs.
Charles E. Sieving, General Counsel/Exec. VP
Christopher A. Bennett, Chief Strategy, Policy & Bus. Officer/Exec. VP
K. Michael Davis, Chief Acct. Officer/Controller/VP
Carmen Perez, Pres., FPL FiberNet LLC
F. Mitchell Davidson, CEO/Pres., NextEra Energy Resources
Armando J. Olivera, CEO/Pres., Florida Power & Light Company
Alissa E. Ballot, VP/Corp. Sec.
Lewis Hay, III, Chmn.

Phone: 561-694-4000	Fax:
Toll-Free:	
Address: 700 Universe Blvd., Juno Beach, FL 33408 US	

GROWTH PLANS/SPECIAL FEATURES:

NextEra Energy, Inc., formerly FPL Group, Inc., is a public utility holding company. Its primary subsidiaries are Florida Power & Light Company (FPL), which generates, transmits, distributes, buys and sells electricity; and NextEra Energy Resources LLC, a leading renewable energy generator. FPL supplies electric service to over 8.7 million people throughout the east and lower west coasts of Florida and has 4.5 million customer accounts. Approximately 65% of the company's 2009 power was produced by natural gas fueled plants, 24% by nuclear plants, 7% by oil plants and 4% by coal plants. and 14% was purchased from other companies. In all, FPL operates 81 plants that burn natural gas, oil or a combination of both; three coal plants; and four nuclear plants. FPL also has one solar generation facility in operation and two under construction. NextEra Energy Resources has a capacity of over 18,000 megawatts (MW), utilizing 41.6% wind, 36.6% natural gas, 14.1% nuclear, 4.7% oil, 2% hydro and 1% combined solar and coal. NextEra Energy Resources' portfolio includes more than 100 operating projects in 26 states and Canada. NextEra Energy Power Marketing LLC, a subsidiary of NextEra Energy Resources, buys and sells wholesale energy commodities, such as natural gas, oil and electricity, and manages the fuel needs of NextEra Energy Resources' power generation fleet. Additionally, the company operates FPL FiberNet LLC, which leases wholesale fiber-optic network capacity and dark fiber to various clients; and Gexa Energy, a retail power supplier in Texas. In December 2009, NextEra Energy Resources acquired three operating wind power facilities in Texas, Wisconsin and South Dakota from Babcock & Brown.

NextEra Energy offers medical, dental and vision benefits; flexible spending plans; life insurance and dependant life insurance; and education and adoption assistance.

FINANCIALS: **Sales and profits are in thousands of dollars—add 000 to get the full amount. 2010 Note: Financial information for 2010 was not available for all companies at press time.**

2010 Sales: $	2010 Profits: $	**U.S. Stock Ticker: NEE**
2009 Sales: $15,643,000	2009 Profits: $1,615,000	**Int'l Ticker:** Int'l Exchange:
2008 Sales: $16,410,000	2008 Profits: $1,639,000	Employees: 10,500
2007 Sales: $15,263,000	2007 Profits: $1,312,000	Fiscal Year Ends: 12/31
2006 Sales: $15,710,000	2006 Profits: $1,281,000	Parent Company:

SALARIES/BENEFITS:

Pension Plan: Y	ESOP Stock Plan: Y	Profit Sharing:	Top Exec. Salary: $1,293,500	Bonus: $1,746,225
Savings Plan: Y	Stock Purch. Plan:		Second Exec. Salary: $831,600	Bonus: $798,336

OTHER THOUGHTS:

Apparent Women Officers or Directors: 7
Hot Spot for Advancement for Women/Minorities: Y

LOCATIONS: ("Y" = Yes)

West:	Southwest:	Midwest:	Southeast:	Northeast:	International:
Y	Y	Y	Y	Y	Y

NIAGARA MOHAWK POWER CORPORATION

www.nationalgridus.com/niagaramohawk/index.asp

Industry Group Code: 221 **Ranks within this company's industry group:** Sales: Profits:

Exploration/Production:		Refining/Retailing:		Utilities:		Alternative Energy:		Specialty Services:		Energy Mktg./Other Svcs.	
Exploration:		Refining:		Electric Utility:	Y	Waste/Solar/Other:		Consulting/Eng.:	Y	Energy Marketing:	
Production:		Retailing:		Gas Utility:	Y	Thermal/Steam:		Seismic:		Equipment/Machinery:	
Coal Production:		Convenience Stores:		Pipelines:		Wind:		Drilling:		Oil Field Services:	
		Chemicals:		Water:		Hydro:		InfoTech:		Air/Shipping Transportation:	
						Fuel Cells:		Specialty Services:			

TYPES OF BUSINESS:

Utilities-Electricity & Natural Gas
Energy Consulting
Telecommunications Services

BRANDS/DIVISIONS/AFFILIATES:

National Grid USA
National Grid plc
National Grid New York

CONTACTS:

Note: Officers with more than one job title may be intentionally listed here more than once.

Helen Mahy, General Counsel/Sec.
Steve Holliday, CEO-Nat'l Grid USA
John Parker, Chmn.-Nat'l Grid USA

Phone: 315-474-1511 **Fax:** 315-460-1429
Toll-Free: 800-642-4272
Address: 300 Erie Blvd. W., Syracuse, NY 13202 US

GROWTH PLANS/SPECIAL FEATURES:

Niagara Mohawk Power Corporation, which operates as National Grid New York, is a subsidiary of National Grid USA. The company provides electricity to approximately 1.5 million customers and natural gas service to approximately 540,000 customers in upstate New York, and supplies roughly a quarter of New York City's electricity needs. The company has adopted the International Standard for environmental management systems (EMS), ISO 14001 and implements its EMS along the guidelines specified therein. The company's ultimate parent is National Grid plc, a U.K. based distributor of electricity and natural gas, which owns several other subsidiaries in the U.S. grouped under the National Grid USA brand. These companies operate in Massachusetts, Nantucket, New Hampshire and Rhode Island. National Grid New York owns approximately 6,650 megawatts of electricity generation, making it one of the largest power producers in the state of New York. In June 2010, Niagara Mohawk Power opened a new transactions delivery center in Syracuse, New York.

Through National Grid, Niagara Mohawk Power employees receive benefits including health care flexible spending accounts, coverage for domestic partners, a defined benefit pension plan, a 401(k), credit union membership, tuition reimbursement, scholarships for children of employees, dependent care assistance, an employee assistance program and adoption assistance.

FINANCIALS:

Sales and profits are in thousands of dollars—add 000 to get the full amount. 2010 Note: Financial information for 2010 was not available for all companies at press time.

2010 Sales: $	2010 Profits: $	**U.S. Stock Ticker: Subsidiary**
2009 Sales: $	2009 Profits: $	**Int'l Ticker:** Int'l Exchange:
2008 Sales: $	2008 Profits: $	Employees:
2007 Sales: $	2007 Profits: $	Fiscal Year Ends: 12/31
2006 Sales: $	2006 Profits: $	Parent Company: NATIONAL GRID PLC

SALARIES/BENEFITS:

Pension Plan: Y	ESOP Stock Plan:	Profit Sharing:	Top Exec. Salary: $	Bonus: $592,078
Savings Plan: Y	Stock Purch. Plan:		Second Exec. Salary: $	Bonus: $

OTHER THOUGHTS:

Apparent Women Officers or Directors: 1
Hot Spot for Advancement for Women/Minorities:

LOCATIONS: ("Y" = Yes)

West:	Southwest:	Midwest:	Southeast:	Northeast:	International:
				Y	

NICOR INC

www.nicor.com

Industry Group Code: 221210 **Ranks within this company's industry group:** Sales: 7 Profits: 12

Exploration/Production:		Refining/Retailing:		Utilities:		Alternative Energy:		Specialty Services:		Energy Mktg./Other Svcs.	
Exploration:		Refining:		Electric Utility:		Waste/Solar/Other:		Consulting/Eng.:		Energy Marketing:	Y
Production:		Retailing:		Gas Utility:	Y	Thermal/Steam:		Seismic:		Equipment/Machinery:	
Coal Production:		Convenience Stores:		Pipelines:	Y	Wind:		Drilling:		Oil Field Services:	
		Chemicals:		Water:		Hydro:		InfoTech:		Air/Shipping Transportation:	Y
						Fuel Cells:		Specialty Services:			

TYPES OF BUSINESS:

Natural Gas Utility
Shipping Services
Energy Services
Natural Gas Marketing
Natural Gas Storage
Maintenance and Repair Services
Energy Conservation Services
Billing Management

BRANDS/DIVISIONS/AFFILIATES:

Nicor Gas
Tropical Shipping
Horizon Pipeline
Nicor Enerchange LLC
Nicor Advanced Energy
Nicor Solutions
Nicor Services
Nicor National

CONTACTS: *Note: Officers with more than one job title may be intentionally listed here more than once.*

Russ M. Strobel, CEO
Russ M. Strobel, Pres.
Richard L. Hawley, CFO/Exec. VP
Claudia J. Colalillo, Sr. VP-Human Resources
Barbara A. Zeller, VP-IT
Paul C. Gracey, Jr., General Counsel/Sr. VP/Sec.
Rocco D'Alessandro, Exec. VP-Oper.
Gerald P. O'Connor, Sr. VP-Strategic Planning
Claudia J. Colalillo, Sr. VP-Corp. Comm.
Kary D. Brunner, Dir.-Investor Rel.
Gerald P. O'Connor, Sr. VP-Finance
Karen K. Pepping, Controller/VP
Douglas M. Ruschau, Treas./VP
Daniel R. Dodge, Exec. VP-Diversified Ventures
Russ M. Strobel, Chmn.

Phone: 630-305-9500 **Fax:** 630-983-4229
Toll-Free:
Address: 1844 Ferry Rd., Naperville, IL 60563-9600 US

GROWTH PLANS/SPECIAL FEATURES:

Nicor, Inc. is a holding company whose principal business is the distribution of natural gas. The firm operates primarily through subsidiary Nicor Gas, one of the largest natural gas distributors in the U.S. A regulated utility, Nicor Gas serves roughly 2.2 million residential, commercial and industrial customers in most of northern Illinois, excluding the city of Chicago. The distributor is connected to eight interstate pipelines, offering access to the majority of the major natural gas regions in North America. This includes Horizon Pipeline, a 50/50 joint venture Nicor and Natural Gas Pipeline of America. Nicor Gas owns and operates a system of eight natural gas storage facilities with 150 billion cubic feet of annual storage capacity. The firm also owns Tropical Shipping, which transports container freight between Florida and ports in the Caribbean region, with 11 owned vessels and four chartered vessels. In addition to these primary subsidiaries, Nicor owns or holds interests in several unregulated energy-related companies. Nicor Services, which does business as Nicor National, offers maintenance and repair contracts for residential and business space heating, water heating and air conditioning equipment. Nicor Solutions evaluates opportunities for customers to save money on energy consumption and offers energy-related products that provide for natural gas price stability and utility bill management. Nicor Advanced Energy operates as a non-utility marketer of natural gas for residential and small commercial customers in northern Illinois. Nicor Enerchange, LLC engages in wholesale marketing of natural gas supply services, primarily in the Midwest. In February 2010, Nicor opened a new location in Des Plaines, Illinois.

Nicor, Inc. offers employee benefits that include life, disability, health and dental insurance; a 401(k); flexible spending accounts; and paid vacation and holidays. It also offers work/life balance programs, such as wellness programs and personal days, which vary by area and subsidiary.

FINANCIALS: Sales and profits are in thousands of dollars—add 000 to get the full amount. 2010 Note: Financial information for 2010 was not available for all companies at press time.

2010 Sales: $	2010 Profits: $	**U.S. Stock Ticker: GAS**
2009 Sales: $2,652,100	2009 Profits: $135,500	**Int'l Ticker:** Int'l Exchange:
2008 Sales: $3,776,600	2008 Profits: $119,500	Employees: 3,900
2007 Sales: $3,176,300	2007 Profits: $135,200	Fiscal Year Ends: 12/31
2006 Sales: $2,960,000	2006 Profits: $128,300	Parent Company:

SALARIES/BENEFITS:

Pension Plan:	ESOP Stock Plan:	Profit Sharing:	Top Exec. Salary: $750,000	Bonus: $894,848
Savings Plan: Y	Stock Purch. Plan:		Second Exec. Salary: $425,000	Bonus: $309,883

OTHER THOUGHTS:

Apparent Women Officers or Directors: 4
Hot Spot for Advancement for Women/Minorities: Y

LOCATIONS: ("Y" = Yes)

West:	Southwest:	Midwest:	Southeast:	Northeast:	International:
		Y	Y		

NIGERIAN NATIONAL PETROLEUM CORPORATION

www.nnpcgroup.com

Industry Group Code: 211111 **Ranks within this company's industry group:** Sales: Profits:

Exploration/Production:		Refining/Retailing:		Utilities:		Alternative Energy:		Specialty Services:		Energy Mktg./Other Svcs.	
Exploration:	Y	Refining:	Y	Electric Utility:		Waste/Solar/Other:		Consulting/Eng.:	Y	Energy Marketing:	
Production:	Y	Retailing:	Y	Gas Utility:		Thermal/Steam:		Seismic:	Y	Equipment/Machinery:	
Coal Production:		Convenience Stores:		Pipelines:	Y	Wind:		Drilling:		Oil Field Services:	
		Chemicals:	Y	Water:		Hydro:		InfoTech:	Y	Air/Shipping Transportation:	
						Fuel Cells:		Specialty Services:	Y		

TYPES OF BUSINESS:

Oil & Gas Exploration & Production
Petroleum Refining
Oil & Gas, Transportation & Storage
Gasoline Retailing
Pipelines
Petrochemicals

BRANDS/DIVISIONS/AFFILIATES:

National Petroleum Investment Management Services
Nigeria Petroleum Development Co
Pipelines and Products Marketing Co. Ltd.
Warri Refining & Petrochemical Co Ltd
Port Harcourt Refining Co Ltd
Integrated Data Services Ltd
Hyson (Nigeria) Ltd
National Engineering & Technical Co Ltd

CONTACTS: *Note: Officers with more than one job title may be intentionally listed here more than once.*

Augustine O. Oniwan, Group Managing Dir.
Philip O. Chukwu, Gen. Exec. Dir.-Exploration & Prod.
Billy Agha, Gen. Exec. Dir.-Tech.
Billy Agha, Gen. Exec. Dir.-Eng.
Yinka Omorogbe, Sec./Legal Advisor
Michael A. Arokodare, Gen. Exec. Dir.-Finance & Accounts
Attahir B. Yusuf, Gen. Exec. Dir.-Commercial & Investment
Faithful A. AbbiyeSuku, Gen. Exec. Dir.-Corp. Svcs.
V. Mukoro, Gen. Exec. Dir.-Gas & Power
Diezani Alison-Madueke, Chmn.

Phone: 234-9-234-8200 **Fax:** 234-9-234-0029
Toll-Free:
Address: NNPC Towers, Herbert Macaulay Way, PMB 190, Garki Abuja, Nigeria

GROWTH PLANS/SPECIAL FEATURES:

Nigerian National Petroleum Corporation (NNPC) is Nigeria's national oil company. The firm produces approximately 2.1 million barrels of oil per day. NNPC collaborates with companies including Royal Dutch Shell, Chevron, Mobil, Agip, Elf and Texaco, and operates through numerous subsidiaries, including the following. Subsidiary National Petroleum Investment Management Services provides oversight for joint venture and production-sharing companies in which the country has invested. Nigeria Petroleum Development Co. performs exploration, development and production activities onshore and offshore coastal Nigeria. Nigerian Gas Company distributes and markets gas through 12 pipeline systems comprising over 770 miles of pipeline. The Pipelines and Products Marketing Co. Ltd. transports petroleum. Integrated Data Services Ltd. offers seismic data acquisition and processing; data storage and management; and reservoir engineering services. National Engineering & Technical Co. Ltd. provides engineering, procurement, construction management, project management, environmental consulting and training services related to oil and gas facilities. Hyson (Nigeria) Ltd., a joint venture with two other companies, markets the firm's excess petroleum products. Warri Refining & Petrochemical Co. Ltd. manufactures and markets petrochemical products and operates the Warri Refinery, with a processing capacity of 125,000 barrels a day. Port Harcourt Refining Co. Ltd. produces unleaded gasoline, liquefied petroleum gas (LPG), kerosene, automotive gas oil and fuel oil. Kaduna Refining & Petrochemical Co. produces refined petroleum products, including asphalt, diesel, base oils, LPG, kerosene, fuel oil and other products. In June 2009, NNPC and Russia's Gazprom agreed to form a joint venture for the production/transportation of hydrocarbons, geological exploration, the construction of electric power facilities and other activities in Nigeria.

FINANCIALS: **Sales and profits are in thousands of dollars—add 000 to get the full amount. 2010 Note: Financial information for 2010 was not available for all companies at press time.**

2010 Sales: $	2010 Profits: $	**U.S. Stock Ticker: Government-Owned**
2009 Sales: $	2009 Profits: $	**Int'l Ticker:** Int'l Exchange:
2008 Sales: $	2008 Profits: $	Employees:
2007 Sales: $	2007 Profits: $	Fiscal Year Ends: 12/31
2006 Sales: $	2006 Profits: $	Parent Company:

SALARIES/BENEFITS:

Pension Plan:	ESOP Stock Plan:	Profit Sharing:	Top Exec. Salary: $	Bonus: $
Savings Plan:	Stock Purch. Plan:		Second Exec. Salary: $	Bonus: $

OTHER THOUGHTS:

Apparent Women Officers or Directors: 2
Hot Spot for Advancement for Women/Minorities:

LOCATIONS: ("Y" = Yes)

West:	Southwest:	Midwest:	Southeast:	Northeast:	International:
					Y

NISOURCE INC

www.nisource.com

Industry Group Code: 221 **Ranks within this company's industry group:** Sales: 27 Profits: 36

Exploration/Production:		Refining/Retailing:		Utilities:		Alternative Energy:		Specialty Services:		Energy Mktg./Other Svcs.	
Exploration:		Refining:		Electric Utility:	Y	Waste/Solar/Other:		Consulting/Eng.:		Energy Marketing:	Y
Production:		Retailing:		Gas Utility:	Y	Thermal/Steam:		Seismic:		Equipment/Machinery:	
Coal Production:		Convenience Stores:		Pipelines:	Y	Wind:		Drilling:		Oil Field Services:	
		Chemicals:		Water:		Hydro:		InfoTech:		Air/Shipping Transportation:	
						Fuel Cells:		Specialty Services:	Y		

TYPES OF BUSINESS:

Utilities-Electricity & Natural Gas
Energy Marketing
Electricity Generation & Distribution
Gas Transmission & Storage
Gas Distribution

BRANDS/DIVISIONS/AFFILIATES:

Columbia Group
Northern Indiana Public Service Company
Bay State Gas
Kokomo Gas and Fuel Co.
Northern Indiana Fuel and Light Company

CONTACTS:

Note: Officers with more than one job title may be intentionally listed here more than once.

Robert C. Skaggs, Jr., CEO
Robert C. Skaggs, Jr., Pres.
Stephen P. Smith, CFO/Exec. VP
Robert D. Campbell, Sr. VP-Human Resources
Violet G. Sistovaris, CIO/Sr. VP
Carrie J. Hightman, Chief Legal Officer/Exec. VP
Glen L. Kettering, Sr. VP-Corp. Affairs
Jon D. Veurink, Controller/VP/Chief Acct. Officer
Gary W. Pottorff, VP-Ethics & Compliance/Corp. Sec.
David J. Vajda, Chief Risk Officer/VP/Treas.
Christopher A. Helms, Exec. VP/CEO-NiSource Gas Transmission & Storage
Jimmy Staton, Exec. VP/Group CEO-Gas Dist.
Ian M. Rolland, Chmn.

Phone: 219-647-5581	**Fax:**
Toll-Free: 877-647-5990	
Address: 801 E. 86th Ave., Merrillville, IN 46410 US	

GROWTH PLANS/SPECIAL FEATURES:

NiSource, Inc. is an energy holding company with subsidiaries that provide natural gas, electricity and other products and services to approximately 3.8 million customers in the Gulf Coast region, the Midwest and New England. The firm's principal subsidiaries include Columbia, a natural gas distribution, transmission and storage holding company whose subsidiaries serve the Midwestern, Mid-Atlantic and Northeastern regions of the U.S.; Northern Indiana, a gas and electric company serving northern Indiana; and Bay State, a natural gas distribution company serving Massachusetts. NiSource operates in four business segments: gas distribution operates; gas transmission and storage operations; electric operations; and other operations. The gas transmission operations segment serves approximately 3.3 million customers in seven states and operates 58,000 miles of pipeline. Columbia's subsidiaries provide natural gas to approximately 2.2 million residential, commercial and industrial customers in Ohio, Pennsylvania, Virginia, Kentucky and Maryland. NiSource also distributes natural gas to approximately 792,000 customers in northern Indiana through Northern Indiana and two other subsidiaries, Kokomo Gas and Northern Indiana Fuel and Light. Bay State distributes natural gas to approximately 294,000 customers in Massachusetts. Through the gas transmission and storage operations segment, the firm owns and operates nearly 15,000 miles of interstate pipelines and operates one of the largest underground natural gas storage systems in the U.S. The electric operations segment consists of the generation, transmission and distribution activities of Northern Indiana, which serves 457,000 customers in 20 counties in northern Indiana. Northern Indiana owns four and operates three coal-fired electric generating stations. The company's other operations primarily include unregulated natural gas marketing activities, though the firm is scaling back these operations.

Employees are offered a 401(k) plan and profit sharing plan; life insurance; medical, dental, vision, disability and prescription drug coverage; flexible spending accounts; tuition reimbursement; an employee assistance program; work-at-home opportunities; and adoption assistance.

FINANCIALS:

Sales and profits are in thousands of dollars—add 000 to get the full amount. 2010 Note: Financial information for 2010 was not available for all companies at press time.

2010 Sales: $	2010 Profits: $	**U.S. Stock Ticker: NI**
2009 Sales: $6,649,400	2009 Profits: $217,700	**Int'l Ticker:** Int'l Exchange:
2008 Sales: $8,874,200	2008 Profits: $79,000	Employees: 7,616
2007 Sales: $7,939,800	2007 Profits: $321,400	Fiscal Year Ends: 12/31
2006 Sales: $7,490,000	2006 Profits: $282,200	Parent Company:

SALARIES/BENEFITS:

Pension Plan:	ESOP Stock Plan:	Profit Sharing: Y	Top Exec. Salary: $800,000	Bonus: $690,000
Savings Plan: Y	Stock Purch. Plan:		Second Exec. Salary: $520,000	Bonus: $500,000

OTHER THOUGHTS:

Apparent Women Officers or Directors: 4
Hot Spot for Advancement for Women/Minorities: Y

LOCATIONS: ("Y" = Yes)

West:	Southwest:	Midwest:	Southeast:	Northeast:	International:
	Y	Y	Y	Y	

NOBLE CORPORATION

www.noblecorp.com

Industry Group Code: 213111 **Ranks within this company's industry group:** Sales: 3 Profits: 1

Exploration/Production:		Refining/Retailing:		Utilities:		Alternative Energy:		Specialty Services:		Energy Mktg./Other Svcs.	
Exploration:		Refining:		Electric Utility:		Waste/Solar/Other:		Consulting/Eng.:	Y	Energy Marketing:	
Production:		Retailing:		Gas Utility:		Thermal/Steam:		Seismic:		Equipment/Machinery:	Y
Coal Production:		Convenience Stores:		Pipelines:		Wind:		Drilling:	Y	Oil Field Services:	Y
		Chemicals:		Water:		Hydro:		InfoTech:		Air/Shipping Transportation:	
						Fuel Cells:		Specialty Services:			

TYPES OF BUSINESS:

Oil & Gas Services
Drilling Services

BRANDS/DIVISIONS/AFFILIATES:

Noble Drilling Holding LLC

CONTACTS:

Note: Officers with more than one job title may be intentionally listed here more than once.

David W. Williams, CEO
David W. Williams, Pres.
Thomas L. Mitchell, CFO/Sr. VP
Roger B. Hunt, Sr. VP-Mktg. & Contracts
Scott W. Marks, Sr. VP-Eng.
William E. Turcotte, General Counsel/Sr. VP
Donald Jacobsen, Sr. VP-Oper.
John Breed, Dir.-Corp. Comm.
Lee M. Ahlstrom, VP-Investor Rel.
Thomas L. Mitchell, Controller/Treas.
Julie J. Robertson, Exec. VP/Corp. Sec.
David W. Williams, Chmn.

Phone: 41-41-761-6555	**Fax:** 281-596-4486
Toll-Free:	
Address: Dorfstrasse 19a, Baar, CH-6340 Switzerland	

GROWTH PLANS/SPECIAL FEATURES:

Noble Corporation, a Swedish incorporated company, provides contract drilling services for the oil and gas industry through its fleet of 69 mobile offshore drilling units located in key markets worldwide. The fleet includes 43 jackup drilling rigs, 13 semi-submersible rigs, four dynamically positioned drillships and two submersible drilling platforms, with three rigs currently under construction. Noble generally buys only specially contracted rigs, rather than those built on speculation. Approximately 87% of Noble's fleet is deployed in international markets including the Middle East, India, Mexico, the North Sea, Brazil and West Africa. Contracts with Petroleos Mexicanos (PEMEX), a Mexican oil company, accounted for 23% of the firm's 2009 revenue. In July 2010, the company acquired drilling outfit, FDR Holdings Ltd., for $2.16 billion, adding seven additional rigs to Noble's fleet. In August 2010, Noble, through a subsidiary, signed contracts for the construction of an ultra-deepwater globetrotter-class drillship with the South Korean company STX Offshore & Shipbuilding Co., Ltd. and Dutch-based design and construction firm Huisman Equipment B.V.

FINANCIALS:

Sales and profits are in thousands of dollars—add 000 to get the full amount. 2010 Note: Financial information for 2010 was not available for all companies at press time.

2010 Sales: $	2010 Profits: $	**U.S. Stock Ticker: NE**
2009 Sales: $3,640,784	2009 Profits: $1,678,642	**Int'l Ticker:** Int'l Exchange:
2008 Sales: $3,446,501	2008 Profits: $1,560,995	Employees: 5,700
2007 Sales: $2,995,311	2007 Profits: $1,206,011	Fiscal Year Ends: 12/31
2006 Sales: $2,100,239	2006 Profits: $731,866	Parent Company:

SALARIES/BENEFITS:

Pension Plan:	ESOP Stock Plan:	Profit Sharing:	Top Exec. Salary: $765,001	Bonus: $1,223,750
Savings Plan:	Stock Purch. Plan:		Second Exec. Salary: $452,500	Bonus: $540,000

OTHER THOUGHTS:

Apparent Women Officers or Directors: 3
Hot Spot for Advancement for Women/Minorities: Y

LOCATIONS: ("Y" = Yes)

West:	Southwest:	Midwest:	Southeast:	Northeast:	International:
	Y		Y		Y

NOBLE ENERGY INC

www.nobleenergyinc.com

Industry Group Code: 211111 **Ranks within this company's industry group:** Sales: 68 Profits: 92

Exploration/Production:		**Refining/Retailing:**		**Utilities:**		**Alternative Energy:**		**Specialty Services:**		**Energy Mktg./Other Svcs.**	
Exploration:	Y	Refining:		Electric Utility:		Waste/Solar/Other:		Consulting/Eng.:		Energy Marketing:	Y
Production:	Y	Retailing:		Gas Utility:		Thermal/Steam:		Seismic:		Equipment/Machinery:	
Coal Production:		Convenience Stores:		Pipelines:		Wind:		Drilling:		Oil Field Services:	
		Chemicals:		Water:		Hydro:		InfoTech:		Air/Shipping Transportation:	
						Fuel Cells:		Specialty Services:			

TYPES OF BUSINESS:

Oil & Gas Exploration & Production
Oil & Gas Marketing
Methanol Production

BRANDS/DIVISIONS/AFFILIATES:

Noble Energy Marketing, Inc.
Atlantic Methanol Production Company, LLC

CONTACTS:

Note: Officers with more than one job title may be intentionally listed here more than once.

Charles D. Davidson, CEO
David L. Stover, COO
David L. Stover, Pres.
Kenneth M. Fisher, CFO/Sr. VP
Andrea Lee Robison, VP-Human Resources
Susan M. Cunningham, Sr. VP-Exploration
Arnold J. Johnson, General Counsel/Sr. VP/Sec.
Ted D. Brown, Sr. VP-Northern Region
Charles D. Davidson, Chmn.
Rodney D. Cook, Sr. VP-Int'l

Phone: 281-872-3100	**Fax:** 281-872-3111
Toll-Free:	
Address: 100 Glenborough Dr., Ste. 100, Houston, TX 77067 US	

GROWTH PLANS/SPECIAL FEATURES:

Noble Energy, Inc. is an independent energy company whose activities include the exploration, development, production and marketing of crude oil, natural gas and natural gas liquids (NGLs). The firm's areas of operations are divided into three divisions: U.S. onshore, deepwater Gulf of Mexico and international. U.S. onshore operations, accounting for 56% of 2009 sales and 56% of total proved reserves, are conducted on the Gulf Coast; in the mid-continent area of Oklahoma, Texas and New Mexico; and in the Rocky Mountain region of Colorado. The deepwater Gulf of Mexico division includes leases on 103 deepwater Gulf of Mexico blocks, representing approximately 390,000 net acres. The company operates 86% of these leases. International operations, which accounted for 44% of sales and 44% of total proved reserves, are conducted in Ecuador, the North Sea, the Mediterranean Sea, Equatorial Guinea, Israel, China, Cameroon and Suriname. In Ecuador, the company owns the only natural gas fired power plant in the country. The power plant is also one of the lowest cost producers of thermal power in Ecuador. In Equatorial Guinea, the majority of the firm's production is sold to a methanol plant, which is owned by Atlantic Methanol Production Company (AMPCO), in which Noble Energy has a 45% interest. In Israel, the firm has a long-term contract to provide natural gas to Israel Electric Corporation Limited and has recently initiated natural gas sales to a new customer, Israel Chemicals Ltd. The marketing of Noble Energy's domestic resources is conducted by wholly-owned subsidiary Noble Energy Marketing, Inc. (NEMI). NEMI markets the company's oil and natural gas directly to end-users through other natural gas marketers' pipelines. International resources are marketed through short- and long-term contracts. In March 2010, the firm acquired the Rocky Mountain upstream assets of Petro-Canada Resources (USA), Inc. and Suncor Energy (Natural Gas) America, Inc. located in the Denver Basin in eastern Colorado.

FINANCIALS:

Sales and profits are in thousands of dollars—add 000 to get the full amount. 2010 Note: Financial information for 2010 was not available for all companies at press time.

2010 Sales: $	2010 Profits: $	**U.S. Stock Ticker: NBL**
2009 Sales: $2,313,000	2009 Profits: $-131,000	**Int'l Ticker:** Int'l Exchange:
2008 Sales: $3,901,000	2008 Profits: $1,350,000	Employees:
2007 Sales: $3,272,030	2007 Profits: $943,870	Fiscal Year Ends: 12/31
2006 Sales: $2,940,082	2006 Profits: $678,428	Parent Company:

SALARIES/BENEFITS:

Pension Plan:	ESOP Stock Plan:	Profit Sharing: Y	Top Exec. Salary: $1,025,000	Bonus: $1,435,000
Savings Plan: Y	Stock Purch. Plan:		Second Exec. Salary: $600,000	Bonus: $756,000

OTHER THOUGHTS:

Apparent Women Officers or Directors: 2
Hot Spot for Advancement for Women/Minorities:

LOCATIONS: ("Y" = Yes)

West:	Southwest:	Midwest:	Southeast:	Northeast:	International:
Y	Y	Y			Y

NORTHEAST UTILITIES

www.nu.com

Industry Group Code: 221 **Ranks within this company's industry group:** Sales: 29 Profits: 29

Exploration/Production:		Refining/Retailing:		Utilities:		Alternative Energy:		Specialty Services:		Energy Mktg./Other Svcs.	
Exploration:		Refining:		Electric Utility:	Y	Waste/Solar/Other:		Consulting/Eng.:		Energy Marketing:	
Production:		Retailing:		Gas Utility:	Y	Thermal/Steam:		Seismic:		Equipment/Machinery:	
Coal Production:		Convenience Stores:		Pipelines:		Wind:		Drilling:		Oil Field Services:	
		Chemicals:		Water:		Hydro:	Y	InfoTech:		Air/Shipping Transportation:	
						Fuel Cells:		Specialty Services:			

TYPES OF BUSINESS:

Utilities-Electricity & Natural Gas
Nuclear Generation
Hydroelectric Power
Energy-Related Services
Real Estate

BRANDS/DIVISIONS/AFFILIATES:

Connecticut Light & Power Company
Public Service Company of New Hampshire
Western Massachusetts Electric Company
Yankee Gas Services Company

CONTACTS: *Note: Officers with more than one job title may be intentionally listed here more than once.*

Charles W. Shivery, CEO
Leon J. Oliver, COO/Exec. VP
Charles W. Shivery, Pres.
David R. McHale, CFO/Exec. VP
Gregory B. Butler, General Counsel/Sr. VP
Jay S. Buth, VP-Acct./Controller
Samuel K. Lee, Sec.
Randy A. Shoop, Treas./VP
Charles W. Shivery, Chmn.

Phone: 413-785-5871	**Fax:**
Toll-Free: 800-286-5000	
Address: 56 Prospect St., Hartford, CT 06103 US	

GROWTH PLANS/SPECIAL FEATURES:

Northeast Utilities (NU) is a public utilities holding company. The firm provides electricity and natural gas to over 2 million customers in 419 cities and towns in Connecticut, New Hampshire and western Massachusetts. The company operates through three electric subsidiaries and one gas subsidiary: The Connecticut Light and Power Company; Public Service Company of New Hampshire; Western Massachusetts Electric Company; and Yankee Gas Services Company. The Connecticut Light and Power Company is a regulated electric utility company that serves roughly 1.2 million customers in 149 cities in Connecticut. Public Service Company of New Hampshire is a regulated electric utility with approximately 490,000 customers in 211 cities and towns of New Hampshire. The subsidiary owns and operates approximately 1,200 megawatts of electricity generation assets. Western Massachusetts Electric Company is a regulated electric utility that serves about 205,000 customers in 59 cities and towns in western Massachusetts. Approximately 58% of these electric utilities' combined customers are residential customers; 34% are commercial; 7% are industrial; and 1% is other customers. Yankee Gas Services Company is a regulated gas utility which serves 205,000 in a 2,187 square mile service area in Connecticut. Approximately 48% of Yankee Gas Services' customers are residential customers; 31% are commercial; 18% are industrial; and 3% are others. It has a total annual sale and transportation throughput of roughly 52.5 billion cubic feet. In October 2010, the company announced plans to acquire electric utility company, NStar, for $4.3 billion.

Employee benefits offered by NU include group auto, group home, medical, dental, life, AD&D and long-term disability insurance; a 401(k); an employee share purchase plan; education reimbursement and training; child care referral; credit union access; floating vacation days; onsite ATMs; incentive wellness programs; fitness programs; full-service cafeterias; and free parking.

Employee benefits offered by NU include group auto, group home, medical, dental, life, AD&D and long-term disability insurance; a 401(k); an employee share purchase plan; education reimbursement and training; child care referral; credit union access; floating vacation days; onsite ATMs; incentive wellness programs; fitness programs; full-service cafeterias; and free parking.

FINANCIALS: **Sales and profits are in thousands of dollars—add 000 to get the full amount. 2010 Note: Financial information for 2010 was not available for all companies at press time.**

2010 Sales: $	2010 Profits: $	**U.S. Stock Ticker: NU**
2009 Sales: $5,439,430	2009 Profits: $330,033	**Int'l Ticker:** Int'l Exchange:
2008 Sales: $5,800,095	2008 Profits: $260,828	Employees: 6,078
2007 Sales: $5,822,226	2007 Profits: $246,483	Fiscal Year Ends: 12/31
2006 Sales: $6,884,388	2006 Profits: $470,578	Parent Company:

SALARIES/BENEFITS:

Pension Plan:	ESOP Stock Plan:	Profit Sharing:	Top Exec. Salary: $1,035,000	Bonus: $3,280,650
Savings Plan: Y	Stock Purch. Plan: Y		Second Exec. Salary: $550,000	Bonus: $882,009

OTHER THOUGHTS:

Apparent Women Officers or Directors: 9
Hot Spot for Advancement for Women/Minorities: Y

LOCATIONS: ("Y" = Yes)

West:	Southwest:	Midwest:	Southeast:	Northeast:	International:
				Y	

Note: Financial information, benefits and other data can change quickly and may vary from those stated here.

NORTHERN INDIANA PUBLIC SERVICE COMPANY www.nipsco.com

Industry Group Code: 221 **Ranks within this company's industry group:** Sales: Profits:

Exploration/Production:		Refining/Retailing:		Utilities:		Alternative Energy:		Specialty Services:		Energy Mktg./Other Svcs.	
Exploration:		Refining:		Electric Utility:	Y	Waste/Solar/Other:		Consulting/Eng.:		Energy Marketing:	
Production:		Retailing:		Gas Utility:	Y	Thermal/Steam:		Seismic:		Equipment/Machinery:	
Coal Production:		Convenience Stores:		Pipelines:		Wind:		Drilling:		Oil Field Services:	
		Chemicals:		Water:		Hydro:		InfoTech:		Air/Shipping Transportation:	
						Fuel Cells:		Specialty Services:	Y		

TYPES OF BUSINESS:

Natural Gas & Electric Utility
Hydroelectric Generation
Forestry

BRANDS/DIVISIONS/AFFILIATES:

NiSource, Inc.
NIPSTEEL
Energy Access Online
TREE LINE USA

CONTACTS:

Note: Officers with more than one job title may be intentionally listed here more than once.

Jimmy Staton, CEO
Michael J. Finissi, COO/Sr. VP
Timothy A. Dehring, Gen. Mgr.-Oper.
Bradley K. Sweet, VP-Strategic Planning & Oper. Support
Nick Meyer, Mgr.-NIPSCO Comm. & Public Affairs
Keith G.Wooldridge, Sr. VP-Field Oper.
David W. Hadley, Sr. VP-Regulatory Affairs

Phone: 219-647-5990 **Fax:** 219-647-5589
Toll-Free: 877-647-5990
Address: 801 E. 86th Ave., Merrillville, IN 46410 US

GROWTH PLANS/SPECIAL FEATURES:

Northern Indiana Public Service Company (NIPSCO) is a subsidiary of NiSource, Inc., an energy holding company that specializes in utilities. The firm is one of the largest electric distribution companies in Indiana. The company has over 712,000 natural gas customers and 457,000 electric customers across the northern third of Indiana. NIPSCO has a total generating capacity of approximately 2,574 megawatts, largely through coal-fired generating plants. The company also has two small hydroelectric dams on the Tippecanoe River in White and Carroll counties in Indiana. NIPSTEEL is an organization of representatives from NIPSCO and all its customers served at approximately 138,000 volts or greater that discusses areas of mutual concern and establishes guidelines for all who are connected to the high voltage grid. The company's other products include builder/developer, commercial/small business programs and Energy Access Online. Energy Access Online is a service that provides exchange gas transportation information to marketers including daily pricing and operation notices. The firm has a Forestry Operations department that is involved in educating the public about tree placement and regularly funds tree-planting projects in Northern Indiana. NIPSCO is one of the few utilities in the nation consistently honored by the National Arbor Day Foundation as a TREE LINE USA Utility.

FINANCIALS:

Sales and profits are in thousands of dollars—add 000 to get the full amount. 2010 Note: Financial information for 2010 was not available for all companies at press time.

2010 Sales: $	2010 Profits: $	**U.S. Stock Ticker: Subsidiary**
2009 Sales: $	2009 Profits: $	**Int'l Ticker:** Int'l Exchange:
2008 Sales: $	2008 Profits: $	Employees:
2007 Sales: $	2007 Profits: $	Fiscal Year Ends: 12/31
2006 Sales: $	2006 Profits: $	Parent Company: NISOURCE INC

SALARIES/BENEFITS:

Pension Plan:	ESOP Stock Plan:	Profit Sharing:	Top Exec. Salary: $	Bonus: $
Savings Plan:	Stock Purch. Plan:		Second Exec. Salary: $	Bonus: $

OTHER THOUGHTS:

Apparent Women Officers or Directors:
Hot Spot for Advancement for Women/Minorities:

LOCATIONS: ("Y" = Yes)

West:	Southwest:	Midwest:	Southeast:	Northeast:	International:
		Y			

NORTHWESTERN CORPORATION

www.northwesternenergy.com

Industry Group Code: 221 **Ranks within this company's industry group:** Sales: 51 Profits: 47

Exploration/Production:		Refining/Retailing:		Utilities:		Alternative Energy:		Specialty Services:		Energy Mktg./Other Svcs.	
Exploration:		Refining:		Electric Utility:	Y	Waste/Solar/Other:		Consulting/Eng.:		Energy Marketing:	
Production:		Retailing:		Gas Utility:	Y	Thermal/Steam:		Seismic:		Equipment/Machinery:	
Coal Production:		Convenience Stores:		Pipelines:	Y	Wind:		Drilling:		Oil Field Services:	
		Chemicals:		Water:		Hydro:		InfoTech:		Air/Shipping Transportation:	
						Fuel Cells:		Specialty Services:			

TYPES OF BUSINESS:

Utilities-Electricity & Natural Gas
Energy Transmission & Distribution
Natural Gas Transmission & Distribution
Pipelines
Electrical Generation

BRANDS/DIVISIONS/AFFILIATES:

Northwestern Energy
Battle Creek Natural Gas Field

CONTACTS: *Note: Officers with more than one job title may be intentionally listed here more than once.*

Robert C. Rowe, CEO
Robert C. Rowe, Pres.
Brian B. Bird, CFO/VP/Treas.
Bobbi L. Schroeppel, VP-Human Resources
Heather H. Grahame, General Counsel/VP
David G. Gates, VP-Wholesale Oper.
Bobbi L. Schroeppel, VP-Customer Care & Comm.
Kendall G. Kliewer, Controller/VP
Michael R. Cashell, Chief Transmission Officer
Curtis T. Pohl, VP-Retail Oper.
Patrick R. Corcoran, VP-Gov't & Regulatory Affairs
E. Linn Draper, Jr., Chmn.
John D. Hines, Chief Supply Officer

Phone: 605-978-2900	**Fax:** 605-978-2910
Toll-Free:	
Address: 3010 W. 69th St., Sioux Falls, SD 57108 US	

GROWTH PLANS/SPECIAL FEATURES:

NorthWestern Corporation, doing business as NorthWestern Energy, is one of the largest providers of electricity and natural gas in the upper Midwest and Northwest, serving roughly 661,000 customers in Montana, South Dakota and Nebraska. The company operates in three segments: regulated electric operations; regulated natural gas operations; and all other, which primarily consists of an unregulated natural gas contract, the wind down of its captive insurance subsidiary and miscellaneous service activities. Through the regulated electric operations segment, the firm generates, transmits and delivers electricity to about 335,000 customers in 187 communities in Montana; and more than 60,500 customers in 110 communities in South Dakota. Through the regulated natural gas operations segment, the company distributes natural gas to 180,100 customers in 105 Montana communities and 85,100 customers in 60 South Dakota and four Nebraska communities. In August 2009, NorthWestern Energy joined with BP Energy in the groundbreaking of the Titan I Wind Farm, which is owned by BP Wind Energy. NorthWestern Energy will purchase the energy produced by the wind farm for use by customers in South Dakota. The wind farm began operation in December 2009. In September 2010, the company announced that it had entered joint transmission planning agreements with Western Area Power Administration for the coordination of regional transmission projects in the Mountain States region. Also in September 2010, NorthWestern acquired a majority stake in the Battle Creek Natural Gas Field in Blaine County, Montana, with estimated net proven developed producing reserves of 7.6 billion cubic feet.

The company offers its employees medical, dental, vision and prescription drug coverage; flexible spending accounts; life and accident insurance; short and long-term disability coverage; workers' compensation; an employee assistance program; tuition reimbursement; and adoption benefits.

FINANCIALS: **Sales and profits are in thousands of dollars—add 000 to get the full amount. 2010 Note: Financial information for 2010 was not available for all companies at press time.**

2010 Sales: $	2010 Profits: $	**U.S. Stock Ticker: NEW**
2009 Sales: $1,141,910	2009 Profits: $73,420	**Int'l Ticker:** Int'l Exchange:
2008 Sales: $1,260,793	2008 Profits: $67,601	Employees:
2007 Sales: $1,200,060	2007 Profits: $53,191	Fiscal Year Ends: 12/31
2006 Sales: $1,132,653	2006 Profits: $37,900	Parent Company:

SALARIES/BENEFITS:

Pension Plan:	ESOP Stock Plan:	Profit Sharing:	Top Exec. Salary: $519,231	Bonus: $378,000
Savings Plan: Y	Stock Purch. Plan:		Second Exec. Salary: $340,624	Bonus: $177,124

OTHER THOUGHTS:

Apparent Women Officers or Directors: 5
Hot Spot for Advancement for Women/Minorities: Y

LOCATIONS: ("Y" = Yes)

West:	Southwest:	Midwest:	Southeast:	Northeast:	International:
Y		Y			

NOVATEK OAO

www.novatek.ru/eng

Industry Group Code: 211111 **Ranks within this company's industry group:** Sales: 66 Profits: 39

Exploration/Production:		Refining/Retailing:		Utilities:		Alternative Energy:		Specialty Services:		Energy Mktg./Other Svcs.	
Exploration:	Y	Refining:	Y	Electric Utility:		Waste/Solar/Other:		Consulting/Eng.:		Energy Marketing:	Y
Production:	Y	Retailing:		Gas Utility:		Thermal/Steam:		Seismic:	Y	Equipment/Machinery:	
Coal Production:		Convenience Stores:		Pipelines:	Y	Wind:		Drilling:		Oil Field Services:	
		Chemicals:	Y	Water:		Hydro:		InfoTech:		Air/Shipping Transportation:	
						Fuel Cells:		Specialty Services:	Y		

TYPES OF BUSINESS:

Gas Exploration & Production
Natural Gas & Hydrocarbon Processing
Plastic Products
Seismic Surveys

BRANDS/DIVISIONS/AFFILIATES:

Purovsky Gas Condensate Processing Plant
Novatek-Polimer
OAO Yamal LNG
Terneftegas LLC

CONTACTS:

Note: Officers with more than one job title may be intentionally listed here more than once.

Leonid V. Mikhelson, Chmn.-Mgmt. Committee
Mark A. Gyetvay, CFO
Tatyana S. Kuznetsova, Dir.-Legal Dept.
Gregory Madick, Head-Investor Rel.
Sergei V. Protosenya, Chief Acct. Officer
Mikhail V. Popov, First Deputy Chmn.-Mgmt. Committee
Vladimir A. Smirnov, Deputy Chmn.-Mgmt. Committee
Alexander M. Fridman, Deputy Chmn.-Mgmt. Committee
Nikolai N. Titarenko, Dir.-Commercial
Alexander Y. Natalenko, Chmn.

Phone: 7-349-972-4951 **Fax:** 7-349-972-4479
Toll-Free:
Address: 22A Pobedy St., Tarko-Sale, Yamalo-Nenets, 629850 Russia

GROWTH PLANS/SPECIAL FEATURES:

Novatek OAO is one of Russia's largest producers of natural gas. The firm specializes in the exploration, development, production, processing and marketing of natural gas, gas condensate, crude oil and other oil products. The company has roughly 6.86 billion barrels of oil equivalent (BOE) proved in its reserves, with production levels averaging 658,000 BOE per day. The large part of these reserves consists of natural gas and liquids. Novatek's operations are centralized in the Yamal-Nenets Autonomous District of western Siberia, which is one of the largest natural gas producing regions in the world. In its exploration projects, the company develops three-dimensional hydrodynamic models based on the results of seismic surveys. Production of natural gas and other liquids is handled by Novatek's subsidiaries, which are based at its main fields of East Tarkosalinskoye, Yurkharovskoye and Khancheyskoye. The liquids are then transferred to its Purovsky Gas Condensate Stabilization Plant in Purovsky. The raw materials are moved directly from East Tarkosalinskoye and Khancheyskoye via the company's own pipeline and from Yurkharovskoye through pipelines owned by competitor Gazprom. From Purovsky, the refined products are shipped on the Russian railway system. Subsidiary Novatek-Polimer manufactures plastic products for use in the Russian gas and automotive industries. In mid 2009, the company acquired 51% ownership of OAO Yamal LNG; and sold 49% interest in its wholly-owned subsidiary, Terneftegas LLC, to Total SA, making Terneftegas a joint venture. In September 2010, the firm sold wholly-owned subsidiary OOO NOVATEK-Polymer to OAO SIBUR Holding. In October 2010, Novatek completed the final stage of phase II construction on its Yurkharovskoye field, increasing the field's annual production capacity to 1.13 trillion cubic feet of natural gas and 3 million tons of gas condensate.

FINANCIALS:

Sales and profits are in thousands of dollars—add 000 to get the full amount. 2010 Note: Financial information for 2010 was not available for all companies at press time.

2010 Sales: $	2010 Profits: $	**U.S. Stock Ticker:**
2009 Sales: $2,921,040	2009 Profits: $845,680	**Int'l Ticker: RTS.NVTK** Int'l Exchange: Moscow-RTS
2008 Sales: $2,705,280	2008 Profits: $784,760	Employees:
2007 Sales: $1,850,000	2007 Profits: $530,000	Fiscal Year Ends: 12/31
2006 Sales: $1,340,000	2006 Profits: $480,000	Parent Company:

SALARIES/BENEFITS:

Pension Plan:	ESOP Stock Plan:	Profit Sharing:	Top Exec. Salary: $	Bonus: $
Savings Plan:	Stock Purch. Plan:		Second Exec. Salary: $	Bonus: $

OTHER THOUGHTS:

Apparent Women Officers or Directors: 1
Hot Spot for Advancement for Women/Minorities:

LOCATIONS: ("Y" = Yes)

West:	Southwest:	Midwest:	Southeast:	Northeast:	International:
					Y

NRG ENERGY INC

www.nrgenergy.com

Industry Group Code: 221 **Ranks within this company's industry group:** Sales: 19 Profits: 15

Exploration/Production:		Refining/Retailing:		Utilities:		Alternative Energy:		Specialty Services:		Energy Mktg./Other Svcs.	
Exploration:		Refining:		Electric Utility:	Y	Waste/Solar/Other:	Y	Consulting/Eng.:		Energy Marketing:	Y
Production:		Retailing:		Gas Utility:		Thermal/Steam:	Y	Seismic:		Equipment/Machinery:	
Coal Production:		Convenience Stores:		Pipelines:		Wind:	Y	Drilling:		Oil Field Services:	
		Chemicals:		Water:		Hydro:	Y	InfoTech:		Air/Shipping Transportation:	
						Fuel Cells:		Specialty Services:	Y		

TYPES OF BUSINESS:

Electricity Generation
Operating & Maintenance Services
Energy Trading
Hydroelectric Generation
Electricity Retail

BRANDS/DIVISIONS/AFFILIATES:

NRG Thermal LLC
NRG Solar LLC
Bluewater Wind
Northwind Phoenix LLC
Padoma Wind Power LLC

CONTACTS:

Note: Officers with more than one job title may be intentionally listed here more than once.

David Crane, CEO
Mauricio Gutierrez, COO/Exec. VP
David Crane, Pres.
Christian Schade, CFO/Exec. VP
Denise Wilson, Chief Admin. Officer/Exec. VP
Michael Bramnick, General Counsel/Exec. VP
Meredith Moore, Sr. VP-Corp. Comm.
Nahla Azmy, Sr. VP-Investor Rel.
James Ingoldsby, Chief Acct. Officer/VP
John Ragan, Exec. VP/Regional Pres., Texas
J. Andrew Murphy, Exec. VP/Regional Pres., Northwest
Steve Hoffman, Sr. VP/Regional Pres., West
Jeff Baudier, Sr. VP/Regional Pres., South Central
Howard E. Cosgrove, Chmn.

Phone: 609-524-4500	**Fax:** 609-524-4501
Toll-Free:	
Address: 211 Carnegie Center, Princeton, NJ 08540-6213 US	

GROWTH PLANS/SPECIAL FEATURES:

NRG Energy, Inc. is an independent wholesale power generation company engaged in the ownership, development, construction and operation of power generation facilities; the transacting in and trading of fuel and transportation services; the trading of energy, capacity and related products in the U.S. and internationally; and the supply of electricity in Texas. NRG has a global portfolio of approximately 187 active operating fossil fuel and nuclear generation units as 44 power generation plants, with an aggregate generation capacity of approximately 24.1 gigawatts (GW) and 400 megawatts (MW) under construction. About 1 GW of its power comes from power generation projects in Australia and Germany. The company also operates three wind farms and a solar facility with a total generation capacity of 365 MW. Domestically, NRG has approximately 23.1 GW of generation capacity in 179 active generation units at 42 plants. These plants are located in primarily in Texas, as well as the Northeast, South Central and Western regions of the U.S. Additionally, the firm receives approximately 115 MW from its thermal assets. NRG's principal domestic power plants consist of natural gas-fired facilities, representing approximately 46% of its total domestic generation capacity; coal-fired facilities, representing 32%; oil-fired facilities, representing 16%; nuclear facilities, representing 5%; and renewable facilities representing 1%. In 2009, the company acquired Bluewater Wind, an offshore wind development business; and acquired the largest utility-scale solar project in California. In January 2010, the company sold subsidiary Padoma Wind Power LLC. In June 2010, NRG acquired the 101-MW South Trent wind farm in Texas; acquired Northwind Phoenix LLC; and agreed to acquire nine solar development projects in California and Arizona. In August 2010, the firm agreed to acquire 3.8 GW of assets in California and Maine from Dyergy, Inc. In September 2010, the company agreed to acquire Green Mountain Energy Company.

FINANCIALS:

Sales and profits are in thousands of dollars—add 000 to get the full amount. 2010 Note: Financial information for 2010 was not available for all companies at press time.

2010 Sales: $	2010 Profits: $	**U.S. Stock Ticker: NRG**
2009 Sales: $8,952,000	2009 Profits: $942,000	**Int'l Ticker:** Int'l Exchange:
2008 Sales: $6,885,000	2008 Profits: $1,225,000	Employees: 4,607
2007 Sales: $5,989,000	2007 Profits: $573,000	Fiscal Year Ends: 12/31
2006 Sales: $5,585,000	2006 Profits: $621,000	Parent Company:

SALARIES/BENEFITS:

Pension Plan:	ESOP Stock Plan:	Profit Sharing:	Top Exec. Salary: $1,100,000	Bonus: $2,320,800
Savings Plan:	Stock Purch. Plan:		Second Exec. Salary: $573,692	Bonus: $

OTHER THOUGHTS:

Apparent Women Officers or Directors: 5
Hot Spot for Advancement for Women/Minorities: Y

LOCATIONS: ("Y" = Yes)

West:	Southwest:	Midwest:	Southeast:	Northeast:	International:
Y	Y	Y	Y	Y	Y

NSTAR

www.nstar.com

Industry Group Code: 221 **Ranks within this company's industry group:** Sales: 38 Profits: 33

Exploration/Production:		Refining/Retailing:		Utilities:		Alternative Energy:		Specialty Services:		Energy Mktg./Other Svcs.	
Exploration:		Refining:		Electric Utility:	Y	Waste/Solar/Other:		Consulting/Eng.:		Energy Marketing:	Y
Production:		Retailing:		Gas Utility:	Y	Thermal/Steam:	Y	Seismic:		Equipment/Machinery:	
Coal Production:		Convenience Stores:		Pipelines:		Wind:		Drilling:		Oil Field Services:	
		Chemicals:		Water:		Hydro:		InfoTech:		Air/Shipping Transportation:	
						Fuel Cells:		Specialty Services:			

TYPES OF BUSINESS:

Utilities-Electricity & Natural Gas
Telecommunications Services
Steam Sales & Marketing
Liquefied Natural Gas

BRANDS/DIVISIONS/AFFILIATES:

NSTAR Electric
NSTAR Gas
Advanced Energy Systems
NSTAR Com
Northeast Utilities

CONTACTS:

Note: Officers with more than one job title may be intentionally listed here more than once.

Tom May, CEO
Tom May, Pres.
Jim Judge, CFO/Sr. VP
Christine Carmody, Sr. VP-Human Resources
Kathy Kountze-Tatum, VP-IT
Larry Gelbien, VP-Eng.
Doug Horan, General Counsel/Sr. VP-Law & Policy/Corp. Sec.
Werner Schweiger, Sr. VP-Oper.
Doug Horan, Sr. VP-Strategy
Joe Nolan, Jr., Sr. VP-Customer & Corp. Rel.
John M. Moreira, Dir.-Investor Rel. & Financial Reporting
Bob Weafer, Jr., Controller/VP/Chief Acct. Officer
Phil Limbo, Treas./VP
Craig Hallstrom, VP-Electric Field Oper.
Penni Conner, VP-Customer Care
Geoff Lubbock, VP-Financial Strategic Planning & Policy
Tom May, Chmn.
Ellen Angley, VP-Energy Supply & Supply Chain Mgmt.

Phone: 617-424-2000	**Fax:** 617-424-4032
Toll-Free:	
Address: 800 Boylston St., 3rd Fl., Boston, MA 02199 US	

GROWTH PLANS/SPECIAL FEATURES:

NSTAR is a holding company engaged, through its subsidiaries, in the energy delivery business. The firm serves approximately 1.4 million customers in Massachusetts, including approximately 1.1 million electric customers in 81 communities and approximately 300,000 natural gas customers in 51 communities. Utility operations account for approximately 99% of NSTAR's consolidated operating revenue, with the remainder generated from its unregulated operations. NSTAR Electric supplies electricity at retail to an area of 1,702 square miles, including Boston and 80 surrounding cities and towns. Commercial and industrial customers generate approximately 57% of NSTAR Electric's operating revenues; residential customers generate approximately 42%; and other customers generate approximately 1%. NSTAR Gas distributes natural gas in a 1,067 square mile area of central and eastern Massachusetts. Residential gas sales and transportation customers generate approximately 62% of NSTAR Gas' operating revenues; commercial and industrial customers generate approximately 28%; other customers generate approximately 5%; and the remaining 5% is generated by off-system and contract sales. NSTAR's unregulated operations segment engages in businesses that include district energy operations, telecommunications and liquefied natural gas service. District energy operations are provided through subsidiary Advanced Energy Systems, which sells chilled water, steam and electricity to hospitals and teaching facilities located in Boston's Longwood Medical Area. Telecommunications are provided through NSTAR Com, which installs, owns, operates and maintains a wholesale transport network for other telecommunications service providers in the metropolitan Boston area. In June 2010, NSTAR sold its district energy operations subsidiary Medical Area Total Energy Plant to a joint venture between Veolia Energy North America and Morgan Stanley Infrastructure Partners for $343.7 million. In October 2010, the company agreed to be acquired by and merged into electric utility firm Northeast Utilities for $4.3 billion.

NSTAR offers its employees 401(k), dependent care and pension plans; tuition assistance; medical, dental, vision, life, discounted auto and discounted homeowner's insurance.

FINANCIALS:

Sales and profits are in thousands of dollars—add 000 to get the full amount. 2010 Note: Financial information for 2010 was not available for all companies at press time.

2010 Sales: $	2010 Profits: $	**U.S. Stock Ticker: NST**
2009 Sales: $3,050,044	2009 Profits: $253,248	**Int'l Ticker:** Int'l Exchange:
2008 Sales: $3,208,321	2008 Profits: $237,547	Employees: 3,000
2007 Sales: $3,261,784	2007 Profits: $221,515	Fiscal Year Ends: 12/31
2006 Sales: $3,577,702	2006 Profits: $206,774	Parent Company:

SALARIES/BENEFITS:

Pension Plan: Y	ESOP Stock Plan:	Profit Sharing:	Top Exec. Salary: $1,021,667	Bonus: $1,800,000
Savings Plan: Y	Stock Purch. Plan: Y		Second Exec. Salary: $451,667	Bonus: $550,000

OTHER THOUGHTS:

Apparent Women Officers or Directors: 5
Hot Spot for Advancement for Women/Minorities: Y

LOCATIONS: ("Y" = Yes)

West:	Southwest:	Midwest:	Southeast:	Northeast:	International:
				Y	

NUSTAR ENERGY LP

www.nustarenergy.com

Industry Group Code: 424710 **Ranks within this company's industry group:** Sales: 4 Profits: 2

Exploration/Production:		Refining/Retailing:		Utilities:		Alternative Energy:		Specialty Services:		Energy Mktg./Other Svcs.	
Exploration:		Refining:		Electric Utility:		Waste/Solar/Other:		Consulting/Eng.:		Energy Marketing:	
Production:		Retailing:		Gas Utility:		Thermal/Steam:		Seismic:		Equipment/Machinery:	
Coal Production:		Convenience Stores:		Pipelines:	Y	Wind:		Drilling:		Oil Field Services:	
		Chemicals:		Water:		Hydro:		InfoTech:		Air/Shipping Transportation:	
						Fuel Cells:		Specialty Services:	Y		

TYPES OF BUSINESS:

Petroleum Pipeline Transportation
Anhydrous Ammonia Transportation
Refined Products Transportation

BRANDS/DIVISIONS/AFFILIATES:

Aves Oil
S-Oil
Pettus South Pipeline
NuStar Logistics LP
Kaneb Pipe Line Operating Partnership LP

CONTACTS: *Note: Officers with more than one job title may be intentionally listed here more than once.*

Curtis Anastasio, CEO
Curtis Anastasio, Pres.
Steve Blank, CFO/Sr. VP
Paul Brattlof, Sr. VP-Mktg.
Mary Rose Brown, Sr. VP-Admin.
Brad Barron, General Counsel/Sr. VP/Sec.
James R. Bluntzer, Sr. VP-Oper.
Mary Morgan, Sr. VP-Bus. Dev. & Mktg.
Mary Rose Brown, Sr. VP-Corp. Comm.
Steven A. Blank, Treas.
Mike Hoeltzel, Sr. VP-Strategic Planning
Bill Greehey, Chmn.
Paul Brattlof, VP-Supply & Trading

Phone: 210-918-2000	**Fax:**
Toll-Free: 800-866-9060	
Address: 2330 N. Loop 1604 W., San Antonio, TX 78248 US	

GROWTH PLANS/SPECIAL FEATURES:

NuStar Energy L.P. is one of the largest terminal and independent petroleum liquids pipeline operators in the U.S. The company engages in the terminaling and storage of petroleum products, the transportation of petroleum products and anhydrous ammonia; and asphalt and fuels marketing. The company conducts its operations through its subsidiaries, NuStar Logistics L.P. and Kaneb Pipe Line Operating Partnership, L.P. NuStar operates in three business segments: storage, transportation and asphalt and fuels marketing. The storage segment owns 49 terminals in the U. S.; one terminal on the island of St. Eustatius, Netherlands Antilles; one terminal in Amsterdam, the Netherlands; one terminal in Point Tupper, Nova Scotia; six terminals in the U.K.; and one terminal in Nuevo Laredo, Mexico. In addition, the company owns 60 crude oil and intermediate feedstock storage tanks in Texas and California. The transportation segment consists of the transportation of refined petroleum products and crude oil. The firm owns refined product pipelines in Texas, Oklahoma, Colorado, New Mexico, Kansas, Nebraska, Iowa, South Dakota, North Dakota and Minnesota, which span a total of approximately 5,679 miles. In addition, the company owns a 2,000-mile anhydrous ammonia pipeline located in Louisiana, Arkansas, Missouri, Illinois, Indiana, Iowa and Nebraska. Nustar holds an ownership interest in 11 crude oil pipelines in Texas, Oklahoma, Kansas, Colorado and Illinois. The asphalt and fuels marketing segment includes its asphalt refining operations and fuels marketing operations. It refines crude oil to produce asphalt and certain other refined products from its asphalt operations. NuStar also purchases gasoline and other refined petroleum products for resale.

The company offers its employees a health and wellness program; adoption assistance; and tuition reimbursement.

FINANCIALS: **Sales and profits are in thousands of dollars—add 000 to get the full amount. 2010 Note: Financial information for 2010 was not available for all companies at press time.**

2010 Sales: $	2010 Profits: $	**U.S. Stock Ticker: NS**
2009 Sales: $3,855,871	2009 Profits: $224,875	**Int'l Ticker:** Int'l Exchange:
2008 Sales: $4,828,770	2008 Profits: $254,018	Employees: 1,379
2007 Sales: $1,475,014	2007 Profits: $150,298	Fiscal Year Ends: 12/31
2006 Sales: $1,137,261	2006 Profits: $149,530	Parent Company:

SALARIES/BENEFITS:

Pension Plan: Y	ESOP Stock Plan:	Profit Sharing:	Top Exec. Salary: $466,900	Bonus: $284,300
Savings Plan: Y	Stock Purch. Plan:		Second Exec. Salary: $335,950	Bonus: $127,800

OTHER THOUGHTS:

Apparent Women Officers or Directors: 2
Hot Spot for Advancement for Women/Minorities:

LOCATIONS: ("Y" = Yes)

West:	Southwest:	Midwest:	Southeast:	Northeast:	International:
Y	Y	Y	Y	Y	Y

NV ENERGY INC

www.nvenergy.com

Industry Group Code: 221 **Ranks within this company's industry group:** Sales: 32 Profits: 38

Exploration/Production:		**Refining/Retailing:**		**Utilities:**		**Alternative Energy:**		**Specialty Services:**		**Energy Mktg./Other Svcs.**	
Exploration:		Refining:		Electric Utility:	Y	Waste/Solar/Other:		Consulting/Eng.:		Energy Marketing:	
Production:		Retailing:		Gas Utility:	Y	Thermal/Steam:		Seismic:		Equipment/Machinery:	
Coal Production:		Convenience Stores:		Pipelines:	Y	Wind:		Drilling:		Oil Field Services:	
		Chemicals:		Water:		Hydro:		InfoTech:		Air/Shipping Transportation:	
						Fuel Cells:		Specialty Services:			

TYPES OF BUSINESS:

Utilities-Electricity & Natural Gas
Pipelines
Communications Services

BRANDS/DIVISIONS/AFFILIATES:

Lands of Sierra
Sierra Pacific Communications
Sierra Pacific Energy Co
Sierra Pacific Power Company
Nevada Power Company
NVE Insurance Company Inc.
SPPC Electric
NV Electric

CONTACTS:

Note: Officers with more than one job title may be intentionally listed here more than once.

Michael W. Yackira, CEO
Michael W. Yackira, Pres.
Dilek Samil, CFO/Sr. VP-Finance/Treas.
Robert E. Stewart, VP-Mktg.
Punam Mather, VP-People Resources
Stephen R. Wood, Sr. VP-Admin.
Paul J. Kaleta, General Counsel/Sr. VP-Shared Svcs./Corp. Sec.
Mary O. Simmons, VP-External Affairs
E. Kevin Bethel, Controller/VP/Chief Acct. Officer
Jeffry L. Ceccarelli, Sr. VP-Energy Supply
Robert E. Stewart, Sr. VP-Customer Relationship
Robert R. Denis, Sr. VP-Energy Delivery
Thomas R. Fair, VP-Renewable Energy
Philip G. Satre, Chmn.

Phone: 702-402-5000	**Fax:** 775-834-3815
Toll-Free:	
Address: 6226 W. Sahara Ave., Las Vegas, NV 89146 US	

GROWTH PLANS/SPECIAL FEATURES:

NV Energy, Inc. (NV), formerly Sierra Pacific Resources, is a holding company of several electric utilities and natural gas companies. The firm operates primarily through its subsidiaries Nevada Power Company (NPC) and Sierra Pacific Power Company (SPPC), which do business as NV Energy. NV operates in three business segments: SPPC electric, NV Electric and SPPC natural gas. SPPC Electric serves roughly 367,000 electric customers in a 50,000 square mile service territory in parts of Nevada and California. NV electric provides service to approximately 827,000 customers in Las Vegas and surrounding Clark County; northern Nevada; and the Lake Tahoe area of California. Together, SPPC Electric and NV Electric operate a transmission system that delivers over 29.4 million megawatt hours of electricity to its customers each year. SPPC natural gas provides natural gas services to 151,000 customers in the Reno-Sparks area. NV generating facilities include Lenzie Generating Station, Silverhawk Generating Station and Higggins Generating Station. In addition, the firm is financing new projects, which include the Carson Lake project and Goodsprings Waste Heat Recovery project. Both projects are scheduled for commercial operation within the next few years. NV Energy meets its customers' energy needs through company-owned generation and purchased power. The company also operates through four other subsidiaries: Sierra Pacific Communications, which develops business opportunities in telecommunications services and infrastructure; Lands of Sierra, which manages NV Energy's non-utility properties in Nevada and California; Sierra Pacific Energy Company; and NVE Insurance Company, Inc.

The company offers its employees medical, dental, vision, disability, life, child life and AD&D insurance; a 401(k) plan; flexible spending accounts; an employee stock purchase plan; an employee assistance program; adoption assistance; and tuition reimbursement.

FINANCIALS:

Sales and profits are in thousands of dollars—add 000 to get the full amount. 2010 Note: Financial information for 2010 was not available for all companies at press time.

2010 Sales: $	2010 Profits: $	**U.S. Stock Ticker: NVE**
2009 Sales: $3,585,798	2009 Profits: $182,936	**Int'l Ticker:** Int'l Exchange:
2008 Sales: $3,528,113	2008 Profits: $208,887	Employees: 3,087
2007 Sales: $3,600,960	2007 Profits: $197,295	Fiscal Year Ends: 12/31
2006 Sales: $3,355,950	2006 Profits: $277,451	Parent Company:

SALARIES/BENEFITS:

Pension Plan: Y	ESOP Stock Plan:	Profit Sharing:	Top Exec. Salary: $730,000	Bonus: $556,962
Savings Plan: Y	Stock Purch. Plan: Y		Second Exec. Salary: $435,000	Bonus: $

OTHER THOUGHTS:

Apparent Women Officers or Directors: 5
Hot Spot for Advancement for Women/Minorities: Y

LOCATIONS: ("Y" = Yes)

West:	Southwest:	Midwest:	Southeast:	Northeast:	International:
Y					

OAO TATNEFT

www.tatneft.ru

Industry Group Code: 211111 **Ranks within this company's industry group:** Sales: 43 Profits: 31

Exploration/Production:		Refining/Retailing:		Utilities:		Alternative Energy:		Specialty Services:		Energy Mktg./Other Svcs.	
Exploration:	Y	Refining:	Y	Electric Utility:		Waste/Solar/Other:		Consulting/Eng.:	Y	Energy Marketing:	
Production:	Y	Retailing:		Gas Utility:		Thermal/Steam:		Seismic:		Equipment/Machinery:	
Coal Production:		Convenience Stores:		Pipelines:		Wind:		Drilling:		Oil Field Services:	Y
		Chemicals:	Y	Water:		Hydro:		InfoTech:		Air/Shipping Transportation:	
						Fuel Cells:		Specialty Services:			

TYPES OF BUSINESS:

Oil & Natural Gas Exploration & Production
Petrochemicals
Crude Oil & Oil Product Sales
Oilfield Equipment Sales
Drilling Services
Tire Sales

BRANDS/DIVISIONS/AFFILIATES:

AZS-Zapad

CONTACTS:

Note: Officers with more than one job title may be intentionally listed here more than once.

Shafagat Fakhrazovich Takhautdinov, CEO
Nail Gabdulbarievich Ibragimov, Chief Engineer/General Dir.-Production
Evgeny Aleksandrovich Tikhturov, Head-Finance
Nail Ulfatovich Maganov, Head-Crude Oil & Oil Products
Iksandar G. Garifullin, Chief Accountant
Vladimir Pavlovich Lavushchenko, Deputy Gen. Dir.-Economics
Rustam Nurgalievich Minnikhanov, Chmn.

Phone: 8553-371-111 **Fax:** 8553-376-151
Toll-Free:
Address: 75, Lenin St., Almetyevsk, Tatarstan, 423400 Russia

GROWTH PLANS/SPECIAL FEATURES:

OAO Tatneft is an oil exploration and production firm operating primarily in the Republic of Tatarstan. Tatneft operates through three primary divisions: exploration and production; refining and marketing; and petrochemicals. The company has 862.2 million tons of proved developed, undeveloped, and undrilled reserves. The annual production is approximately 26 million tons of oil and 671.7 million cubic meters of natural gas. The company has operations in approximately 82 oil fields in the Republic of Tatarstan, with an average oil production of 4.2 tons a day. The firm's primary activities include exploration and drilling; oil production; oil service; refining and gas processing; crude oil and oil product sales; petrochemistry; and research and development. Additionally, the petrochemical segment sells tires, as well as the materials and refined products to make tires. Tatneft also earns revenues from the sale of oilfield equipment and drilling services. Furthermore, the company has more than 600 service stations in the regions of the Russian Federation and the CIS countries. The company's subsidiary, AZS-Zapad, operates 190 of the filling stations in the Moscow region. The company is also involved a number of other industries through its subsidiaries such as banking service, road construction, cultural facilities and transportation. In September 2010, the company announced an agreement with global tire producer Continental AG for the manufacturing of solid steel cord tires under the off-take system at TATNEFT's Nizhnekamsk SSC Tire Factory.

FINANCIALS:

Sales and profits are in thousands of dollars—add 000 to get the full amount. 2010 Note: Financial information for 2010 was not available for all companies at press time.

2010 Sales: $	2010 Profits: $	**U.S. Stock Ticker: AOTTF.PK**
2009 Sales: $12,349,400	2009 Profits: $1,765,600	**Int'l Ticker:** Int'l Exchange:
2008 Sales: $15,263,000	2008 Profits: $289,200	Employees:
2007 Sales: $13,649,200	2007 Profits: $1,658,060	Fiscal Year Ends: 12/31
2006 Sales: $12,193,700	2006 Profits: $1,115,570	Parent Company:

SALARIES/BENEFITS:

Pension Plan:	ESOP Stock Plan:	Profit Sharing:	Top Exec. Salary: $	Bonus: $
Savings Plan:	Stock Purch. Plan:		Second Exec. Salary: $	Bonus: $

OTHER THOUGHTS:

Apparent Women Officers or Directors:
Hot Spot for Advancement for Women/Minorities:

LOCATIONS: ("Y" = Yes)

West:	Southwest:	Midwest:	Southeast:	Northeast:	International:
					Y

OCCIDENTAL PETROLEUM CORP

www.oxy.com

Industry Group Code: 211111 **Ranks within this company's industry group:** Sales: 38 Profits: 25

Exploration/Production:		Refining/Retailing:		Utilities:		Alternative Energy:		Specialty Services:		Energy Mktg./Other Svcs.	
Exploration:	Y	Refining:		Electric Utility:		Waste/Solar/Other:		Consulting/Eng.:		Energy Marketing:	
Production:	Y	Retailing:		Gas Utility:		Thermal/Steam:		Seismic:		Equipment/Machinery:	
Coal Production:		Convenience Stores:		Pipelines:		Wind:		Drilling:		Oil Field Services:	
		Chemicals:	Y	Water:		Hydro:		InfoTech:		Air/Shipping Transportation:	
						Fuel Cells:		Specialty Services:			

TYPES OF BUSINESS:

Oil & Natural Gas Exploration & Production
Basic Chemicals
Vinyls

BRANDS/DIVISIONS/AFFILIATES:

OxyChem
Phibro LLC

CONTACTS:

Note: Officers with more than one job title may be intentionally listed here more than once.

Ray R. Irani, CEO
Stephen I. Chazen, Pres.
Stephen I. Chazen, CFO
Martin A. Cozyn, Exec. VP-Human Resources
Anita Powers, Exec. VP-Oxy Oil & Gas, Worldwide Exploration
Donald P. de Brier, General Counsel/Exec. VP/Sec.
James M. Lienert, Exec. VP-Planning & Finance
Richard S. Kline, VP-Comm. & Public Affairs
Christopher G. Stavros, VP-Investor Rel.
Roy Pineci, Chief Acct. Officer/VP/Controller
B. Chuck Anderson, Pres., Occidental Chemical Corp.
William E. Albrecht, Pres., Oxy Oil & Gas US
Robert J. Williams, Treas./VP
Ray R. Irani, Chmn.
Edward A. Lowe, VP/Pres., Int'l Prod., Oxy Oil and Gas

Phone: 310-208-8800	**Fax:** 310-443-6690
Toll-Free:	
Address: 10889 Wilshire Blvd., Los Angeles, CA 90024-4201 US	

GROWTH PLANS/SPECIAL FEATURES:

Occidental Petroleum Corp. (OPC) explores for, develops, produces and markets crude oil and natural gas. The company also manufactures and markets basic chemicals, vinyls and specialty chemicals. The firm operates in three segments: oil and gas; chemical; and midstream, marketing and other. The oil and gas segment has proven reserves of oil totaling approximately 2.37 billion barrels and roughly 5.16 billion cubic feet of natural gas reserves. OPC's primary domestic oil and gas operations are in California; Colorado; the Hugoton field in Kansas and Oklahoma; and the Permian field in west Texas and New Mexico. International operations are principally located in Colombia, Libya, the United Arab Emirates, Argentina, Bahrain, Bolivia, Oman, Qatar and Yemen. The firm's chemicals business, run by Occidental Chemical Corporation (OxyChem), owns and operates 22 chemical manufacturing plants in the U.S. and two internationally in Chile and Canada. The segment produces chlorine; caustic soda; potassium chemicals for use in glass, fertilizer, cleaning products and rubber; chlorinated isocyanurates, resorcinol; calcium chloride; and sodium silicates. OxyChem is also a leading producer of vinyls for piping, medical, building and automotive products, focusing on polyvinyl chloride (PVC) resins and vinyl chloride monomers (VCM). The midstream, marketing and other segment gathers, treats, processes and trades crude oil, natural gas, NGLs, power, condensate and carbon dioxide. In December 2009, OPC acquired commodity investor Phibro LLC from Citigroup, Inc.

OPC offers employees medical/dental insurance, matches contributions to a personal savings account, educational assistance and employee retirement accounts.

FINANCIALS:

Sales and profits are in thousands of dollars—add 000 to get the full amount. 2010 Note: Financial information for 2010 was not available for all companies at press time.

2010 Sales: $	2010 Profits: $	**U.S. Stock Ticker: OXY**
2009 Sales: $15,403,000	2009 Profits: $2,927,000	**Int'l Ticker:** Int'l Exchange:
2008 Sales: $24,217,000	2008 Profits: $6,857,000	Employees: 10,100
2007 Sales: $18,784,000	2007 Profits: $5,400,000	Fiscal Year Ends: 12/31
2006 Sales: $17,175,000	2006 Profits: $4,191,000	Parent Company:

SALARIES/BENEFITS:

Pension Plan: Y	ESOP Stock Plan:	Profit Sharing:	Top Exec. Salary: $1,170,000	Bonus: $3,752,550
Savings Plan: Y	Stock Purch. Plan:		Second Exec. Salary: $720,000	Bonus: $1,452,240

OTHER THOUGHTS:

Apparent Women Officers or Directors: 2
Hot Spot for Advancement for Women/Minorities: Y

LOCATIONS: ("Y" = Yes)

West:	Southwest:	Midwest:	Southeast:	Northeast:	International:
Y	Y	Y	Y	Y	Y

OCEANEERING INTERNATIONAL INC

www.oceaneering.com

Industry Group Code: 213112 **Ranks within this company's industry group:** Sales: 12 Profits: 8

Exploration/Production:		Refining/Retailing:		Utilities:		Alternative Energy:		Specialty Services:		Energy Mktg./Other Svcs.	
Exploration:		Refining:		Electric Utility:		Waste/Solar/Other:		Consulting/Eng.:	Y	Energy Marketing:	
Production:		Retailing:		Gas Utility:		Thermal/Steam:		Seismic:		Equipment/Machinery:	Y
Coal Production:		Convenience Stores:		Pipelines:		Wind:		Drilling:	Y	Oil Field Services:	Y
		Chemicals:		Water:		Hydro:		InfoTech:		Air/Shipping Transportation:	
						Fuel Cells:		Specialty Services:	Y		

TYPES OF BUSINESS:

Oil & Gas Drilling Support Services
Subsea Construction
Engineered Services & Hardware
Maintenance & Repair Services
Production Systems
Remotely Operated Vehicles
Robotic Systems

BRANDS/DIVISIONS/AFFILIATES:

Oceaneering Intervention Engineering
Grayloc Products
Oceaneering Multiflex
Oceaneering Rotator
Advanced Technologies
Deepwater Technical Solutions

CONTACTS:

Note: Officers with more than one job title may be intentionally listed here more than once.

T. Jay Collins, CEO
M. Kevin McEvoy, COO/Exec. VP
T. Jay Collins, Pres.
Marvin J. Migura, CFO/Sr. VP
Janet G. Charles, VP-Human Resources
Gregg K. Farris, VP-IT
F. Richard Frisbie, Sr. VP-Deepwater Tech.
George R. Haubenreich, Jr., General Counsel/Sr. VP/Sec.
Stephen E. Bradshaw, VP-Bus. Dev.
Jack Jurkoshek, Dir.-Investor Rel.
W. Cardon Gerner, Chief Acct. Officer/VP
M. Kevin McEvoy, Exec. VP
Kevin Kerins, Sr. VP-Remotely Operated Vehicles
Robert P. Mingoia, Treas./VP
Robert P. Moschetta, VP-Health Safety Environment
John R. Huff, Chmn.
Todd Hoefler, VP-Supply Chain Mgmt.

Phone: 713-329-4500	**Fax:** 713-329-4951
Toll-Free:	
Address: 11911 FM 529, Houston, TX 77041 US	

GROWTH PLANS/SPECIAL FEATURES:

Oceaneering International, Inc. primarily provides oilfield products and services worldwide to the oil and gas industry. The oil and gas business of the company has five segments: Remotely Operated Vehicles (ROVs), Subsea Products, Subsea Projects, Inspection and Mobile Offshore Production Systems (MOPS). The company uses submersible ROVs to support drilling and construction; pipeline inspection; and subsea production facility operation and maintenance. It designs and builds ROVs, owning a total of 248, one of the largest ROV fleets worldwide. The firm is an industry leader in providing ROV services on deepwater wells, a highly technically demanding operation. Its Subsea Products segment manufactures typically built-to-order items including hydraulic hoses, ROV tooling, control valves, production control equipment and pipeline repair systems. These products are manufactured mainly by the Oceaneering Intervention Engineering; Grayloc Products; Oceaneering Multiflex; and Oceaneering Rotator divisions. The Subsea Projects segment primarily operates in the Gulf of Mexico, offering subsea installation, inspection, maintenance and repair services. The Inspection segment provides nondestructive testing and inspection services, including to the power generation, engineering and petrochemical industries. The MOPS segment functions through the Ocean Legend unit, which operates offshore Western Australia. Oceaneering's non-oilfield business is accomplished by its Advanced Technologies unit, which manufactures remotely operated diving vessels used extensively by the U.S. Navy, as well as life-support and robotic systems for use in government space programs. In December 2009, the company sold one of its MOPS units, the Ocean Producer, which had previously operated off West Africa. In August 2010, the firm acquired SMX International Canada, Inc., which specializes in manufacturing clamp connectors, check valves and universal ball joints.

Oceaneering offers its employees medical, dental and vision coverage, life and AD&D insurance; flexible spending accounts; an employee assistance program; and a 401(k) program.

FINANCIALS:

Sales and profits are in thousands of dollars—add 000 to get the full amount. 2010 Note: Financial information for 2010 was not available for all companies at press time.

2010 Sales: $	2010 Profits: $	**U.S. Stock Ticker: OII**
2009 Sales: $1,822,081	2009 Profits: $292,116	**Int'l Ticker:** Int'l Exchange:
2008 Sales: $1,977,421	2008 Profits: $317,558	Employees: 7,900
2007 Sales: $1,743,080	2007 Profits: $180,374	Fiscal Year Ends: 12/31
2006 Sales: $1,280,198	2006 Profits: $124,494	Parent Company:

SALARIES/BENEFITS:

Pension Plan:	ESOP Stock Plan:	Profit Sharing:	Top Exec. Salary: $625,000	Bonus: $2,525,000
Savings Plan: Y	Stock Purch. Plan:		Second Exec. Salary: $400,000	Bonus: $1,175,000

OTHER THOUGHTS:

Apparent Women Officers or Directors: 1
Hot Spot for Advancement for Women/Minorities:

LOCATIONS: ("Y" = Yes)

West:	Southwest:	Midwest:	Southeast:	Northeast:	International:
Y	Y		Y	Y	Y

OGE ENERGY CORP

www.oge.com

Industry Group Code: 221 **Ranks within this company's industry group:** Sales: 40 Profits: 32

Exploration/Production:		Refining/Retailing:		Utilities:		Alternative Energy:		Specialty Services:		Energy Mktg./Other Svcs.	
Exploration:		Refining:	Y	Electric Utility:	Y	Waste/Solar/Other:		Consulting/Eng.:		Energy Marketing:	Y
Production:		Retailing:		Gas Utility:	Y	Thermal/Steam:		Seismic:		Equipment/Machinery:	
Coal Production:		Convenience Stores:		Pipelines:	Y	Wind:		Drilling:		Oil Field Services:	
		Chemicals:		Water:		Hydro:		InfoTech:		Air/Shipping Transportation:	
						Fuel Cells:		Specialty Services:			

TYPES OF BUSINESS:

Utilities-Electricity
Energy Marketing
Pipelines
Natural Gas Processing
Electric Generation

BRANDS/DIVISIONS/AFFILIATES:

Oklahoma Gas & Electric Co.
Enogex, Inc.
OG&E Electric Services
Ozark Gas Transmission System
OGE Energy Resources

CONTACTS: *Note: Officers with more than one job title may be intentionally listed here more than once.*

Peter B. Delaney, CEO
Danny P. Harris, COO/Sr. VP
Peter B. Delaney, Pres.
Sean Trauschke, CFO/VP
Craig Johnston, VP-Mktg.
Stephen E. Merrill, VP-Human Resources
Reid V. Nuttall, CIO/VP-IT
Patricia D. Horn, Corp. Sec.
Max J. Myers, Managing Dir.-Corp. Dev.
Craig Johnston, VP-Strategy
Paul L. Renfrow, VP-Public Affairs
H. Scott Forbes, Chief Acct. Officer/Controller
Gary D. Huneryager, VP-Internal Audits
Cristina F.McQuistion, VP-Process & Performance Improvement
Max J. Meyers, Treas.
Jerry A. Peace, Chief Risk Officer
Peter B. Delaney, Chmn.

Phone: 405-553-3000	**Fax:** 405-553-3760
Toll-Free:	
Address: 321 N. Harvey, Oklahoma City, OK 73101 US	

GROWTH PLANS/SPECIAL FEATURES:

OGE Energy Corp. is an energy and energy services provider offering physical delivery and related services for both electricity and natural gas primarily in the south central U.S. The company conducts these activities through four business segments: electric utility, natural gas transportation and storage, natural gas gathering and processing and natural gas marketing. The electric utility segment generates, transmits, distributes and sells electric energy in Oklahoma and western Arkansas. The three remaining segments consist of the transportation and storage of natural gas; the gathering and processing of natural gas; and the marketing of natural gas. OGE Energy operates through subsidiaries Oklahoma Gas and Electric Co. (OG&E); Enogex, LLC; and OGE Energy Resources. OG&E is an electric utility company that serves more than 765,000 retail customers in Oklahoma and western Arkansas; owns and operates natural gas, low-sulfur Wyoming and wind power plants, with a total generating capacity of 6,800 megawatts; and transmits electricity through an interconnected transmission and distribution system covering 30,000 square miles. Enogex transports, stores, gathers, processes, markets and trades natural gas. Enogex owns a controlling interest in and operates the Ozark Gas Transmission LLC, a regulated interstate pipeline that extends from southeastern Oklahoma through Arkansas to southeastern Missouri. OGE Energy Resources is a national energy marketing company offering commodity products and related services, including marketing, trading, transportation and risk management.

FINANCIALS: **Sales and profits are in thousands of dollars—add 000 to get the full amount. 2010 Note: Financial information for 2010 was not available for all companies at press time.**

2010 Sales: $	2010 Profits: $	**U.S. Stock Ticker: OGE**
2009 Sales: $2,869,700	2009 Profits: $258,300	**Int'l Ticker:** Int'l Exchange:
2008 Sales: $4,070,700	2008 Profits: $462,100	Employees: 3,363
2007 Sales: $3,797,600	2007 Profits: $244,200	Fiscal Year Ends: 12/31
2006 Sales: $4,005,600	2006 Profits: $262,100	Parent Company:

SALARIES/BENEFITS:

Pension Plan:	ESOP Stock Plan:	Profit Sharing:	Top Exec. Salary: $783,193	Bonus: $895,252
Savings Plan:	Stock Purch. Plan:		Second Exec. Salary: $516,866	Bonus: $486,557

OTHER THOUGHTS:

Apparent Women Officers or Directors: 2
Hot Spot for Advancement for Women/Minorities: Y

LOCATIONS: ("Y" = Yes)

West:	Southwest:	Midwest:	Southeast:	Northeast:	International:
	Y		Y		

OGX PETROLEO E GAS PARTICIPACOES SA

www.ogx.com.br

Industry Group Code: 211111 **Ranks within this company's industry group:** Sales: 104 Profits: 71

Exploration/Production:		Refining/Retailing:		Utilities:		Alternative Energy:		Specialty Services:		Energy Mktg./Other Svcs.	
Exploration:	Y	Refining:		Electric Utility:		Waste/Solar/Other:		Consulting/Eng.:		Energy Marketing:	
Production:	Y	Retailing:		Gas Utility:		Thermal/Steam:		Seismic:		Equipment/Machinery:	
Coal Production:		Convenience Stores:		Pipelines:		Wind:		Drilling:		Oil Field Services:	
		Chemicals:		Water:		Hydro:		InfoTech:		Air/Shipping Transportation:	
						Fuel Cells:		Specialty Services:			

TYPES OF BUSINESS:

Oil & Natural Gas Exploration
Natural Gas Refining
Petroleum Transportation

BRANDS/DIVISIONS/AFFILIATES:

EBX Group
OGX Petroleo e Gas Ltd

CONTACTS:

Note: Officers with more than one job title may be intentionally listed here more than once.

Eike Fuhrken Batista, CEO
Paulo Mendonca, COO
Marcelo Faber Torres, CFO
Reinaldo Belotti, Prod. Dev. Officer
Marcelo Faber Torres, Investor Rel. Officer
Francisco Gros, Vice Chmn.
Eike Fuhrken Batista, Chmn.

Phone: 55-21-25555248 **Fax:** 55-21-25555202
Toll-Free:
Address: Praia do Flamengo, 154 7 Andar, Flamengo, Rio de Janeiro, 22210-030 Brazil

GROWTH PLANS/SPECIAL FEATURES:

OGX Petroleo e Gas Participacoes SA is one of the largest oil and natural gas companies in Brazil. The firm is a leader in Brazilian oil and natural gas exploration and production and focuses on the acquisition of exploration blocks. The company maintains 22 concession blocks spanning approximately 1.7 million acres and containing 20.2 billion barrels of oil. It currently has concession rights to seven exploration blocks in the Campos Basin in Rio de Janeiro, covering 290,843 acres; five exploration blocks in the Santos Basin, south east of Sao Paulo, covering 247, 105 acres; five exploration blocks in the Espirito Santo basin, covering 894,521 acres; and five blocks in the Para-Maranhao Basin covering 237,221 acres. The firm also has a 70% participating interest in seven blocks in the Parnaiba Basin in northeast Brazil. Subsidiary, OGX Petroleo e Gas Ltda, is focused on natural gas refining and petroleum transportation. The firm is part of Brazilian holding company, EBX Group.

FINANCIALS:

Sales and profits are in thousands of dollars—add 000 to get the full amount. 2010 Note: Financial information for 2010 was not available for all companies at press time.

2010 Sales: $	2010 Profits: $	**U.S. Stock Ticker:**
2009 Sales: $127,500	2009 Profits: $6,380	**Int'l Ticker: OGXP3** Int'l Exchange: Sao Paulo-SAO
2008 Sales: $116,820	2008 Profits: $212,550	Employees:
2007 Sales: $	2007 Profits: $	Fiscal Year Ends: 12/31
2006 Sales: $	2006 Profits: $	Parent Company: EBX GROUP

SALARIES/BENEFITS:

Pension Plan:	ESOP Stock Plan:	Profit Sharing:	Top Exec. Salary: $	Bonus: $
Savings Plan:	Stock Purch. Plan:		Second Exec. Salary: $	Bonus: $

OTHER THOUGHTS:

Apparent Women Officers or Directors:
Hot Spot for Advancement for Women/Minorities:

LOCATIONS: ("Y" = Yes)

West:	Southwest:	Midwest:	Southeast:	Northeast:	International:
					Y

Note: Financial information, benefits and other data can change quickly and may vary from those stated here.

OIL & NATURAL GAS CORP LTD

www.ongcindia.com

Industry Group Code: 211111 **Ranks within this company's industry group:** Sales: 30 Profits: 19

Exploration/Production:		Refining/Retailing:		Utilities:		Alternative Energy:		Specialty Services:		Energy Mktg./Other Svcs.	
Exploration:	Y	Refining:	Y	Electric Utility:		Waste/Solar/Other:		Consulting/Eng.:		Energy Marketing:	
Production:	Y	Retailing:		Gas Utility:		Thermal/Steam:		Seismic:		Equipment/Machinery:	
Coal Production:		Convenience Stores:		Pipelines:	Y	Wind:	Y	Drilling:		Oil Field Services:	
		Chemicals:		Water:		Hydro:		InfoTech:		Air/Shipping Transportation:	
						Fuel Cells:		Specialty Services:			

TYPES OF BUSINESS:

Oil & Gas Exploration & Production
Refining
Pipelines
Coal Bed Methane
Wind Farms

BRANDS/DIVISIONS/AFFILIATES:

Mangalore-Hassan-Bangalore Product Pipeline
ONGC Videsh, Ltd.
Mangalore Refinery & Petrochemicals, Ltd.
Sagar Samriddhi Deepwater Exploration

CONTACTS: *Note: Officers with more than one job title may be intentionally listed here more than once.*

Radhey S. Sharma, Managing Dir.
D. K. Sarraf, Dir.-Finance
A. K. Balyan, Dir.-Human Resources
D. K. Pande, Dir.-Exploration
U. N. Bose, Dir.-Tech. & Field Svcs.
N. K. Sinha, Corp. Sec.
S. Vasudeva, Dir.-Offshore
A. K. Hazarika, Dir.-Onshore
Radhey S. Sharma, Chmn.

Phone: 91-135-275-9561 **Fax:** 91-135-275-5298
Toll-Free:
Address: Tel Bhavan, Dehradun, 248 003 India

GROWTH PLANS/SPECIAL FEATURES:

Oil & Natural Gas Corp., Ltd. (ONGC), majority owned by the Indian government, is among India's largest exploration and production companies. The company has a total of 227 million tons of proved reserves (roughly 60% of India's reserves) and owns more than 9,300 miles of pipeline, including more than 2,300 miles of undersea pipeline, more than twice the extent of any other Indian company's pipelines. ONGC's network includes 240 onshore product installations, 69 onshore drilling rigs, 59 onshore work-over rigs, 34 seismic units, 32 logging units, 160 offshore well platforms, 29 offshore drilling rigs, 73 offshore supply vessels and one offshore seismic vessel. The firm's wholly-owned subsidiary ONGC Videsh, Ltd. (OVL) has over 40 active exploration operations in 15 countries across Africa, Eastern Europe, the Middle East, Latin America and Southeast Asia. The company also owns 72% of Mangalore Refinery and Petrochemicals Limited, which operates a refinery that processes some 12.6 million metric tons annually, and a 23% share of the Mangalore-Hassan-Bangalore Product Pipeline. ONGC also has interests in coal bed methane operations and underground coal gasification. The company's on-going Sagar Samriddhi Deepwater Exploration campaign includes several deepwater drill ships operating on different prospects in Krishna-Godavari Basin. The company is also interested in expanding outside of upstream operations and participating in petrochemicals, power generation, crude oil and gas shipping and research in alternative fuels. In February 2010, a consortium of international oil companies led by OVL and including Indian Oil Corporation Ltd.; Oil India Ltd.; Repsol YPF; and Petronas was selected by the Venezuelan government to take a 40% ownership in Empresa Mixta to develop several blocks on the Orinoco Heavy Oil Belt.

FINANCIALS: **Sales and profits are in thousands of dollars—add 000 to get the full amount. 2010 Note: Financial information for 2010 was not available for all companies at press time.**

2010 Sales: $	2010 Profits: $	**U.S. Stock Ticker:**
2009 Sales: $22,143,300	2009 Profits: $4,163,670	**Int'l Ticker: 500312** Int'l Exchange: Bombay-BSE
2008 Sales: $22,725,000	2008 Profits: $4,302,000	Employees: 33,035
2007 Sales: $18,900,000	2007 Profits: $4,110,000	Fiscal Year Ends: 3/31
2006 Sales: $19,237,400	2006 Profits: $3,929,200	Parent Company:

SALARIES/BENEFITS:

Pension Plan:	ESOP Stock Plan:	Profit Sharing:	Top Exec. Salary: $	Bonus: $
Savings Plan:	Stock Purch. Plan:		Second Exec. Salary: $	Bonus: $

OTHER THOUGHTS:

Apparent Women Officers or Directors: 4
Hot Spot for Advancement for Women/Minorities: Y

LOCATIONS: ("Y" = Yes)

West:	Southwest:	Midwest:	Southeast:	Northeast:	International:
					Y

OIL SEARCH LTD

www.oilsearch.com

Industry Group Code: 211111 **Ranks within this company's industry group:** Sales: 95 Profits: 62

Exploration/Production:		Refining/Retailing:		Utilities:		Alternative Energy:		Specialty Services:		Energy Mktg./Other Svcs.	
Exploration:	Y	Refining:		Electric Utility:		Waste/Solar/Other:		Consulting/Eng.:		Energy Marketing:	
Production:	Y	Retailing:		Gas Utility:		Thermal/Steam:		Seismic:		Equipment/Machinery:	
Coal Production:		Convenience Stores:		Pipelines:		Wind:		Drilling:		Oil Field Services:	
		Chemicals:		Water:		Hydro:		InfoTech:		Air/Shipping Transportation:	
						Fuel Cells:		Specialty Services:			

TYPES OF BUSINESS:

Oil & Gas Exploration & Production

BRANDS/DIVISIONS/AFFILIATES:

PNG LNG Project
Esso Highlands Limited
Independent Public Business Corporation
Nippon Oil Exploration
Santos Limited
Mineral Resources Development Company
Petromin PNG Holdings Limited.

CONTACTS:

Note: Officers with more than one job title may be intentionally listed here more than once.

Peter R. Botten, Managing Dir.
Paul Crute, Exec. Gen. Mgr.-Human Resources
Philip Baibridge, Exec. Gen. Mgr.-Gas Dev.
Zlatko Todorcevski, Exec. Gen. Mgr.-Admin.
Richard Robinson, Exec. Gen. Mgr.-Oil Oper.
Austin Miller, Exec. Gen. Mgr.-Strategy & Investment
Zlatko Todorcevski, Exec. Gen. Mgr.-Finance
Gerea Aopi, Exec. Gen. Mgr.-PNG
Nigel Hartley, Exec. Gen. Mgr.-PNG & LNG Finance
Philip Caldwell, Exec. Gen. Mgr.-PNG & LNG
B.F. Horwood, Chmn.

Phone: 675-322-5599 **Fax:** 675-322-5566
Toll-Free:
Address: 7th Fl., Credit House, Cuthbertson St., Port Moresby, Papua New Guinea

GROWTH PLANS/SPECIAL FEATURES:

Oil Search Ltd. is engaged in oil and gas exploration and development in Papua New Guinea and the Middle East. The firm operates international offices in Sydney and Brisbane, Australia; Sana'a, Yemen; Dubai, U.A.E.; Tunis, Tunisia; and Cairo, Egypt. The company is one of Papua New Guinea's largest producers of oil and gas, operating the entirety of the country's producing fields. The firm has proven reserves of over 344.5 million barrels of oil equivalent (mmboe) and proven plus probable reserves of approximately 566.9 mmboe. The company owns approximately 7,954 square miles of exploration fields in the country, much of which Oil Search has yet to explore. Internationally, the firm has interests in two concession areas in Yemen; two in Tunisia; and two in Iraq. Oil Search places high priority on commercializing its gas resources, and so it is developing a gas export pipeline from the PNG highlands to Australia in partnership with ExxonMobil subsidiary Esso Highland Ltd.; as well as constructing a world-class petrochemical facility in PNG and exporting compressed natural gas to New Zealand by tanker. In March 2010, the PNG LNG Project, in which Oil Search owns 29% interest, began full operations. The project includes gas production and processing facilities; a liquefaction facility with an annual capacity of 6.6 million tons; and onshore and offshore pipelines. Other owners of the project include operator Esso Highlands Limited, Independent Public Business Corporation, Nippon Oil Exploration, Santos Limited, Mineral Resources Development Company and Petromin PNG Holdings Limited.

FINANCIALS:

Sales and profits are in thousands of dollars—add 000 to get the full amount. 2010 Note: Financial information for 2010 was not available for all companies at press time.

2010 Sales: $	2010 Profits: $	**U.S. Stock Ticker: OISHY.PK**
2009 Sales: $512,200	2009 Profits: $133,700	**Int'l Ticker:** Int'l Exchange:
2008 Sales: $814,300	2008 Profits: $313,400	Employees: 976
2007 Sales: $718,800	2007 Profits: $137,200	Fiscal Year Ends: 12/31
2006 Sales: $644,534	2006 Profits: $411,982	Parent Company:

SALARIES/BENEFITS:

Pension Plan:	ESOP Stock Plan:	Profit Sharing:	Top Exec. Salary: $	Bonus: $528,225
Savings Plan:	Stock Purch. Plan:		Second Exec. Salary: $	Bonus: $

OTHER THOUGHTS:

Apparent Women Officers or Directors:
Hot Spot for Advancement for Women/Minorities:

LOCATIONS: ("Y" = Yes)

West:	Southwest:	Midwest:	Southeast:	Northeast:	International:
					Y

OIL STATES INTERNATIONAL INC

www.oilstatesintl.com

Industry Group Code: 213112 **Ranks within this company's industry group:** Sales: 11 Profits: 16

Exploration/Production:		Refining/Retailing:		Utilities:		Alternative Energy:		Specialty Services:		Energy Mktg./Other Svcs.	
Exploration:		Refining:		Electric Utility:		Waste/Solar/Other:		Consulting/Eng.:	Y	Energy Marketing:	
Production:		Retailing:		Gas Utility:		Thermal/Steam:		Seismic:		Equipment/Machinery:	Y
Coal Production:		Convenience Stores:		Pipelines:		Wind:		Drilling:	Y	Oil Field Services:	Y
		Chemicals:		Water:		Hydro:		InfoTech:		Air/Shipping Transportation:	
						Fuel Cells:		Specialty Services:	Y		

TYPES OF BUSINESS:

Oil & Gas Drilling Support Services
Offshore Products
Well Site Services
Tubular Services
Drilling Services
Catering & Logistics Services
Construction Services
Equipment Rental

BRANDS/DIVISIONS/AFFILIATES:

Oil States Industries, Inc.
HWC Energy Services, Inc.
PTI Group, Inc.

CONTACTS:

Note: Officers with more than one job title may be intentionally listed here more than once.

Cindy B. Taylor, CEO
Cindy B. Taylor, Pres.
Bradley J. Dodson, CFO/Treas./Sr. VP
Lias J. Steen, VP-Human Resources
Lias J. Steen, VP-Legal
Christopher E. Cragg, Sr. VP-Oper.
Robert W. Hampton, Sr. VP-Acct.
Ron R. Green, CEO/Pres., PTI Group, Inc.
Charles Moses, VP-Offshore Products
Robert W. Hampton, Corp. Sec.
Stephen A. Wells, Chmn.

Phone: 713-652-0582 **Fax:** 713-652-0499
Toll-Free:
Address: 333 Clay St., 3 Allen Ctr., Ste. 4620, Houston, TX 77002 US

GROWTH PLANS/SPECIAL FEATURES:

Oil States International, Inc., is a leading provider of specialty products and services to oil and gas drilling/production companies worldwide. Areas of operation include West Africa, the North Sea, South America, Central Asia, Southeast Asia and onshore U.S. It operates in three principal business segments: Offshore products, tubular services and well site services. Its offshore products segment designs and manufactures products for the offshore energy industry, such as flexible bearings and connector products; subsea pipeline products; marine winches, mooring and lifting systems and rig equipment; drilling riser repair; and blowout preventer stack assembly, integration, testing and repair services. Oil States' tubular services segment offers casing, premium tubing and line pipe, which are purchased from manufacturers and sold to oil/gas companies and drilling contractors. It has also developed an e-commerce portal for pricing, ordering and tracking tubular products, operating under Sooner, Inc. The firm's well site services segment provides worker services, drilling services, rental equipment, remote site accommodations, catering and logistics services and modular building construction services. Subsidiary HWC Energy Services, Inc. provides worldwide well control services, drilling services and rental equipment to the oil and gas industry, while subsidiary PTI Group, Inc. is a supplier of integrated housing, food, site management and logistics support services to remote sites.

Oil States offers its employees medical, dental and vision coverage; a 401(k) plan; flexible spending accounts; life and AD&D insurance; an employee assistance plan; disability income; a 529 college savings plan; and educational assistance.

FINANCIALS:

Sales and profits are in thousands of dollars—add 000 to get the full amount. 2010 Note: Financial information for 2010 was not available for all companies at press time.

2010 Sales: $	2010 Profits: $	**U.S. Stock Ticker: OIS**
2009 Sales: $2,108,250	2009 Profits: $59,612	**Int'l Ticker:** Int'l Exchange:
2008 Sales: $2,948,457	2008 Profits: $222,710	Employees: 5,474
2007 Sales: $2,088,235	2007 Profits: $203,372	Fiscal Year Ends: 12/31
2006 Sales: $1,923,357	2006 Profits: $197,634	Parent Company:

SALARIES/BENEFITS:

Pension Plan:	ESOP Stock Plan:	Profit Sharing:	Top Exec. Salary: $480,000	Bonus: $442,030
Savings Plan: Y	Stock Purch. Plan:		Second Exec. Salary: $316,800	Bonus: $308,611

OTHER THOUGHTS:

Apparent Women Officers or Directors: 1
Hot Spot for Advancement for Women/Minorities:

LOCATIONS: ("Y" = Yes)

West:	Southwest:	Midwest:	Southeast:	Northeast:	International:
Y	Y	Y	Y		Y

OMV AKTIENGESELLSCHAFT

www.omv.com

Industry Group Code: 211111 **Ranks within this company's industry group:** Sales: 29 Profits: 43

Exploration/Production:		Refining/Retailing:		Utilities:		Alternative Energy:		Specialty Services:		Energy Mktg./Other Svcs.	
Exploration:	Y	Refining:	Y	Electric Utility:		Waste/Solar/Other:		Consulting/Eng.:		Energy Marketing:	
Production:	Y	Retailing:	Y	Gas Utility:		Thermal/Steam:		Seismic:		Equipment/Machinery:	
Coal Production:		Convenience Stores:		Pipelines:	Y	Wind:		Drilling:		Oil Field Services:	
		Chemicals:	Y	Water:		Hydro:		InfoTech:		Air/Shipping Transportation:	
						Fuel Cells:		Specialty Services:	Y		

TYPES OF BUSINESS:

Oil & Gas Exploration & Production
Chemicals
Geotextiles
Gas Stations
Refining
Pipelines
Fertilizers

BRANDS/DIVISIONS/AFFILIATES:

SNP Petrom SA
Petrol Ofisi
Borealis AG
OMV Future Energy Fund
OMV Exploration & Production
OMV Refining & Marketing
OMV Gas & Power
OMV Solutions

CONTACTS:

Note: Officers with more than one job title may be intentionally listed here more than once.

Wolfgang Ruttenstorfer, CEO
David C. Davies, CFO
Gerhard Roiss, Head-Mktg.
Helmut Langanger, Head-Exploration & Prod.
Michaela Huber, Head-Media Rel.
Angelika Altendorf-Zwerenz, Head-Investor Rel.
Gerhard Roiss, Head-Refining
Werner Auli, Head-Gas & Power
Peter Michaelis, Chmn.

Phone: 43-1-40-440-0	**Fax:** 43-1-40-440-20091
Toll-Free:	
Address: 6-8 Trabrennstrasse, Vienna, 1020 Austria	

GROWTH PLANS/SPECIAL FEATURES:

OMV Aktiengesellschaft is an oil and natural gas exploration and production company. The firm is based in Austria, with active exploration and production projects in 20 countries on four continents. OMV operates in three business segments: Exploration and Production; Refining and Marketing; and Gas and Power. The company extracts approximately 115.5 million barrels of oil equivalent (BOE) per year and distributes oil products in 13 countries through a network of gas stations and distributors. OMV also manufactures jet fuels, heating oil, lubricants and chemicals including bitumen, butadiene, ethylene and propylene. The company operates two of its own refineries with a total refining capacity of approximately 317,000 BOE per day. Subsidiary OMV Gas GmbH operates a 1,250-mile natural gas pipeline network as well as three gas storage facilities, which serve Austria as well as Germany, Italy, France, Slovakia, Croatia and Hungary. OMV holds a 36% stake in Borealis AG, one of the world's largest polyolefin producers; a 59% stake in EconGas GmbH; 50% of SNP Petrom SA; a 10% stake in Pearl Petroleum Limited; a 45% stake in the Bayneroil-Raffinerieverbund GmbH refining network, which adds 250,000 barrels per day to the firm's refining capacity; and a 42% stake in Turkish company Petrol Ofisi, among other investments. In December 2009, the company sold its Italian subsidiary OMV Italia to San Marco Petroli, a northern Italian petroleum company. In February and June 2010, OMV drilled successful exploration wells in southern Tunisia as part of ongoing exploration with the development of a full-scale oilfield operation in mind.

FINANCIALS:

Sales and profits are in thousands of dollars—add 000 to get the full amount. 2010 Note: Financial information for 2010 was not available for all companies at press time.

2010 Sales: $	2010 Profits: $	**U.S. Stock Ticker: OMVKY**
2009 Sales: $22,565,900	2009 Profits: $720,030	**Int'l Ticker: OMV** Int'l Exchange: Vienna-VSX
2008 Sales: $35,893,740	2008 Profits: $2,148,560	Employees: 34,676
2007 Sales: $25,030,000	2007 Profits: $1,820,000	Fiscal Year Ends: 12/31
2006 Sales: $25,534,680	2006 Profits: $2,232,040	Parent Company:

SALARIES/BENEFITS:

Pension Plan:	ESOP Stock Plan:	Profit Sharing:	Top Exec. Salary: $	Bonus: $
Savings Plan:	Stock Purch. Plan:		Second Exec. Salary: $	Bonus: $

OTHER THOUGHTS:

Apparent Women Officers or Directors: 2
Hot Spot for Advancement for Women/Minorities:

LOCATIONS: ("Y" = Yes)

West:	Southwest:	Midwest:	Southeast:	Northeast:	International:
					Y

Note: Financial information, benefits and other data can change quickly and may vary from those stated here.

ONCOR ELECTRIC DELIVERY COMPANY www.txuelectricdelivery.com

Industry Group Code: 2211 **Ranks within this company's industry group:** Sales: 33 Profits: 27

Exploration/Production:		Refining/Retailing:		Utilities:		Alternative Energy:		Specialty Services:		Energy Mktg./Other Svcs.	
Exploration:		Refining:		Electric Utility:	Y	Waste/Solar/Other:		Consulting/Eng.:		Energy Marketing:	
Production:		Retailing:		Gas Utility:		Thermal/Steam:		Seismic:		Equipment/Machinery:	
Coal Production:		Convenience Stores:		Pipelines:		Wind:		Drilling:		Oil Field Services:	
		Chemicals:		Water:		Hydro:		InfoTech:		Air/Shipping Transportation:	
						Fuel Cells:		Specialty Services:	Y		

TYPES OF BUSINESS:

Electric Utility
Management Services
Broadband Enabled Power Distribution

BRANDS/DIVISIONS/AFFILIATES:

Energy Future Holdings Corp
AskOncor.com

CONTACTS:

Note: Officers with more than one job title may be intentionally listed here more than once.

Bob S. Shapard, CEO
Charles Jenkins, COO/Sr. VP
Rob D. Trimble, Pres.
David Davis, CFO/VP
Debbi Elmer, Sr. VP-Human Resources
Jim Greer, Sr. VP-Eng. & Asset Mgmt.
Jim O'Brien, General Counsel
Brenda Pulis, Sr. VP/Chief Customer Officer
Don Clevenger, Sr. VP-External Affairs
Bob S. Shapard, Chmn.
Brenda Pulis, Sr. VP-Dist.

Phone: 214-486-2000	**Fax:**
Toll-Free: 888-313-6862	
Address: 1601 Bryan St., Energy Plz., Dallas, TX 75201 US	

GROWTH PLANS/SPECIAL FEATURES:

Oncor Electric Delivery Company, an 80%-owned subsidiary of Energy Future Holdings Corp., is one of the nation's largest electric distribution and transmission companies. The firm provides power to 3 million electric delivery points over more than 117,000 miles of distribution and transmission lines. The company supplies electricity to over 7 million customers. Oncor is one of three independently managed businesses of Energy Future Holdings Corp., the others being Luminant Energy and TXU Energy. Oncor Electric Delivery operates in a service area in east, west and north central Texas with 401 incorporated municipalities and 91 counties, serving cities that include the Dallas-Fort Worth area and surrounding cities, Odessa, Midland, Killeen, Waco, Wichita Falls and Tyler. The firm operates within the ERCOT market, which represents approximately 85% of electricity consumption in Texas. The company also provides transmission grid connections to merchant generation plants and interconnections to other transmission grids in Texas. In May 2010, Oncor Electric Delivery added real-time weather and outage information on its web site. In July 2010, the firm began construction on a 20-mile, 345-kilovolt transmission line in the area of Northwest Carrollton - Roanoke Junction in Highland Village, Texas. Also in July 2010, the company established a new web site, AskOncor.com, and a corresponding hotline through which customers can request information about the Texas electric industry, electricity in general and Oncor Electric Delivery. The company offers answers from its representatives within two business days.

FINANCIALS:

Sales and profits are in thousands of dollars—add 000 to get the full amount. 2010 Note: Financial information for 2010 was not available for all companies at press time.

2010 Sales: $	2010 Profits: $	**U.S. Stock Ticker: Subsidiary**
2009 Sales: $2,690,000	2009 Profits: $320,000	**Int'l Ticker:** Int'l Exchange:
2008 Sales: $2,580,000	2008 Profits: $-487,000	Employees:
2007 Sales: $2,500,000	2007 Profits: $327,000	Fiscal Year Ends: 12/31
2006 Sales: $2,449,000	2006 Profits: $344,000	Parent Company: ENERGY FUTURE HOLDINGS CORP

SALARIES/BENEFITS:

Pension Plan:	ESOP Stock Plan:	Profit Sharing:	Top Exec. Salary: $	Bonus: $450,000
Savings Plan:	Stock Purch. Plan:		Second Exec. Salary: $	Bonus: $

OTHER THOUGHTS:

Apparent Women Officers or Directors: 4
Hot Spot for Advancement for Women/Minorities: Y

LOCATIONS: ("Y" = Yes)

West:	Southwest:	Midwest:	Southeast:	Northeast:	International:
	Y				

ONEOK INC

www.oneok.com

Industry Group Code: 221210 **Ranks within this company's industry group:** Sales: 4 Profits: 3

Exploration/Production:		Refining/Retailing:		Utilities:		Alternative Energy:		Specialty Services:		Energy Mktg./Other Svcs.	
Exploration:	Y	Refining:		Electric Utility:		Waste/Solar/Other:		Consulting/Eng.:		Energy Marketing:	Y
Production:	Y	Retailing:		Gas Utility:	Y	Thermal/Steam:		Seismic:		Equipment/Machinery:	
Coal Production:		Convenience Stores:		Pipelines:	Y	Wind:		Drilling:		Oil Field Services:	
		Chemicals:		Water:		Hydro:		InfoTech:		Air/Shipping Transportation:	
						Fuel Cells:		Specialty Services:			

TYPES OF BUSINESS:

Utilities-Natural Gas
Wholesale Gas Marketing & Trading
Oil & Natural Gas Production
Gas Transportation & Storage
Natural Gas Liquids

BRANDS/DIVISIONS/AFFILIATES:

ONEOK Partners LP
ONEOK Leasing Company
ONEOK Parking Company LLC
ONEOK Plaza
Overland Pass Pipeline Company LLC

CONTACTS: *Note: Officers with more than one job title may be intentionally listed here more than once.*

John W. Gibson, CEO
Robert F. Martinovich, COO
John W. Gibson, Pres.
Curtis L. Dinan, CFO/Sr. VP/Treas.
Steve Guy, Sr. VP-Tech. Svcs.
Daniel Walker, VP-Eng.
David Roth, Sr. VP-Admin. Svcs.
John R. Barker, General Counsel/Sr. VP
Daniel Walker, VP-Oper.
Caron A. Lawhorn, Sr. VP-Corp. Planning & Dev.
Dan Harrison, VP-Public Affairs
Dan Harrison, VP-Investor Rel.
Derek S. Reiners, Chief Acct. Officer/Sr. VP
Eric Grimshaw, VP/Corp. Sec.
Patrick J. McDonie, Pres., ONEAK Energy Svcs.
Terry K. Spencer, COO-ONEOK Partners
Pierce H. Norton, Pres., ONEOK Distribution Companies
David L. Kyle, Chmn.

Phone: 918-588-7000	**Fax:** 918-588-7273
Toll-Free:	
Address: 100 W. 5th St., Tulsa, OK 74103 US	

GROWTH PLANS/SPECIAL FEATURES:

ONEOK, Inc. purchases, transports, stores and distributes natural gas in the south central areas of the U.S. The firm's largest distribution markets are Oklahoma City and Tulsa, Oklahoma; Kansas City, Wichita, and Topeka, Kansas; and Austin and El Paso, Texas. The company operates in three segments: ONEOK Partners; Distribution and Energy Services. ONEOK is the sole general partner and owns 42.8% of ONEOK Partners, L.P., which is engaged in gathering, processing, storing and transporting natural gas in the U.S.; the fractionation of natural gas liquids (NGLs), primarily in the Rocky Mountain regions covering Oklahoma, Kansas, Montana, North Dakota and Wyoming; and the gathering of unprocessed natural gas produced from crude oil and natural gas wells. ONEOK's Distribution segment provides natural gas distribution services to more than 2 million customers in Oklahoma, Kansas and Texas through Oklahoma Natural Gas, Kansas Gas Service and Texas Gas Service, respectively. It serves residential, commercial, industrial and transportation customers in all three states. In addition, the firm's distribution companies in Oklahoma and Kansas serve wholesale customers and in Texas its distribution companies serve public authority customers, such as cities, governmental agencies and schools. ONEOK's Energy Services segment delivers physical natural gas products and risk management services through its network of contracted transportation and storage capacity and natural gas supply. These services include meeting its customers' baseload, swing and peaking natural gas commodity requirements on a year-round basis. Other subsidiaries include ONEOK Leasing Company and ONEOK Parking Company LLC, through which the company owns a parking garage and an office building (ONEOK Plaza) in downtown Tulsa, Oklahoma. In September 2010, the firm sold 49% of its ownership of Overland Pass Pipeline Company LLC to Williams Partners L.P. for $434 million.

The company offers employees medical, dental and vision insurance; flexible spending accounts; life insurance; an employee assistance program; and employee discounts.

FINANCIALS: **Sales and profits are in thousands of dollars—add 000 to get the full amount. 2010 Note: Financial information for 2010 was not available for all companies at press time.**

2010 Sales: $	2010 Profits: $	**U.S. Stock Ticker: OKE**
2009 Sales: $11,111,600	2009 Profits: $894,600	**Int'l Ticker:** Int'l Exchange:
2008 Sales: $16,157,433	2008 Profits: $917,004	Employees: 4,758
2007 Sales: $13,488,027	2007 Profits: $304,921	Fiscal Year Ends: 12/31
2006 Sales: $11,913,529	2006 Profits: $306,312	Parent Company:

SALARIES/BENEFITS:

Pension Plan: Y	ESOP Stock Plan:	Profit Sharing: Y	Top Exec. Salary: $825,000	Bonus: $1,125,000
Savings Plan:	Stock Purch. Plan: Y		Second Exec. Salary: $600,000	Bonus: $750,000

OTHER THOUGHTS:

Apparent Women Officers or Directors: 3
Hot Spot for Advancement for Women/Minorities: Y

LOCATIONS: ("Y" = Yes)

West:	Southwest:	Midwest:	Southeast:	Northeast:	International:
	Y	Y			

ONEOK PARTNERS LP

www.oneokpartners.com

Industry Group Code: 486 **Ranks within this company's industry group:** Sales: 8 Profits: 7

Exploration/Production:		**Refining/Retailing:**		**Utilities:**		**Alternative Energy:**		**Specialty Services:**		**Energy Mktg./Other Svcs.**	
Exploration:		Refining:	Y	Electric Utility:		Waste/Solar/Other:		Consulting/Eng.:		Energy Marketing:	
Production:		Retailing:		Gas Utility:		Thermal/Steam:		Seismic:		Equipment/Machinery:	
Coal Production:		Convenience Stores:		Pipelines:	Y	Wind:		Drilling:		Oil Field Services:	
		Chemicals:		Water:		Hydro:		InfoTech:		Air/Shipping Transportation:	
						Fuel Cells:		Specialty Services:			

TYPES OF BUSINESS:

Pipelines-Natural Gas
Natural Gas Processing

BRANDS/DIVISIONS/AFFILIATES:

Midwestern Gas Transmission Company
Northwest Border Pipeline Company
ONEOK Inc
OkTex
Viking Gas Transmission Company
Guardian Pipeline
Sycamore Gas System

CONTACTS:

Note: Officers with more than one job title may be intentionally listed here more than once.

John W. Gibson, CEO
Terry K. Spencer, COO
John W. Gibson, Pres.
Curtis L. Dinan, CFO/Sr. VP/Treas.
John R. Barker, General Counsel/Sr. VP/Sec.
Wesley J. Christensen, Sr. VP-Natural Gas Liquids Oper.
Caron A. Lawhorn, Sr. VP-Corp. Planning & Dev.
Derek S. Reiners, Chief Acct. Officer/Sr. VP
Sheridan C. Swords, Pres., Natural Gas Liquids
Robert S. Mareburger, Pres., Natural Gas
Roger G. Thorpe, Pres., Natural Gas Liquid Pipelines
Randy L. Jordan, VP-Natural Gas Liquids Optimization
John W. Gibson, Chmn.

Phone: 918-588-7000 **Fax:** 918-588-7971
Toll-Free: 877-208-7318
Address: 100 W. 5th St., Tulsa, OK 74103 US

GROWTH PLANS/SPECIAL FEATURES:

ONEOK Partners, LP owns and manages natural gas gathering, processing and intrastate pipeline assets and natural gas liquids (NGL) gathering and distribution pipelines, storage and fractionators, connecting much of the natural gas and NGL supply in the mid-continent region. The company also owns a 50% equity interest in a transporter of natural gas imported from Canada and the U.S. The firm operates in three segments: natural gas gathering and processing, which primarily gathers and processes raw natural gas; natural gas pipelines, which operates regulated interstate and intrastate natural gas transmission pipelines and storage facilities; and natural gas liquids, which gathers, treats, fractionates, stores and markets NGL and operates interstate natural gas liquids gathering/distribution pipelines. The company owns a 50% interest in Northern Border Pipeline Company, which owns and operates a 1,249-mile natural gas pipeline system that transports over approximately 18% of all natural gas imported from Canada to the U.S.; and a 48% interest in Sycamore Gas System, a gathering system with compression located in south central Oklahoma. The firm also owns Midwestern Gas Transmission Company, which owns a 350-mile interstate natural gas pipeline system that runs from Tennessee to Illinois; and Viking Gas Transmission Company, which serves markets in Minnesota, Wisconsin and North Dakota. Other pipeline properties include OkTex Pipeline, operating in Oklahoma, Texas, New Mexico and Mexico; and Guardian Pipeline, operating in Illinois and Wisconsin. ONEOK Partners is approximately 42.8%-owned by ONEOK, Inc., a diversified energy firm that is also its general partner.

The firm offers employees benefits including life, medical, dental, vision, prescription drug and long-term care insurance; paid time off; an assistance program; a profit sharing plan; a 401(k); a stock purchase plan; flexible spending accounts; computer and cell phone discounts; and educational assistance.

FINANCIALS:

Sales and profits are in thousands of dollars—add 000 to get the full amount. 2010 Note: Financial information for 2010 was not available for all companies at press time.

2010 Sales: $	2010 Profits: $	**U.S. Stock Ticker: OKS**
2009 Sales: $6,474,491	2009 Profits: $434,356	**Int'l Ticker:** Int'l Exchange:
2008 Sales: $7,720,206	2008 Profits: $625,616	Employees:
2007 Sales: $5,831,558	2007 Profits: $407,747	Fiscal Year Ends: 12/31
2006 Sales: $4,738,248	2006 Profits: $445,186	Parent Company:

SALARIES/BENEFITS:

Pension Plan:	ESOP Stock Plan:	Profit Sharing: Y	Top Exec. Salary: $472,539	Bonus: $644,372
Savings Plan: Y	Stock Purch. Plan: Y		Second Exec. Salary: $343,665	Bonus: $429,581

OTHER THOUGHTS:

Apparent Women Officers or Directors: 2
Hot Spot for Advancement for Women/Minorities:

LOCATIONS: ("Y" = Yes)

West:	Southwest:	Midwest:	Southeast:	Northeast:	International:
Y	Y	Y			Y

ONTARIO POWER GENERATION INC

www.opg.com

Industry Group Code: 2211 **Ranks within this company's industry group:** Sales: 27 Profits: 21

Exploration/Production:		Refining/Retailing:		Utilities:		Alternative Energy:		Specialty Services:		Energy Mktg./Other Svcs.	
Exploration:		Refining:		Electric Utility:	Y	Waste/Solar/Other:	Y	Consulting/Eng.:		Energy Marketing:	Y
Production:		Retailing:		Gas Utility:		Thermal/Steam:		Seismic:		Equipment/Machinery:	
Coal Production:		Convenience Stores:		Pipelines:		Wind:	Y	Drilling:		Oil Field Services:	
		Chemicals:		Water:		Hydro:	Y	InfoTech:	Y	Air/Shipping Transportation:	
						Fuel Cells:		Specialty Services:	Y		

TYPES OF BUSINESS:

Electricity Generation
Nuclear Hydro & Wind Power
Venture Capital
Financial Services
Software

BRANDS/DIVISIONS/AFFILIATES:

OPG Evergreen
Bruce Power L.P.
Lower Mattagami Project

CONTACTS:

Note: Officers with more than one job title may be intentionally listed here more than once.

Tom Mitchell, CEO
Tom Mitchel, Pres.
Donn Hanbidge, CFO/Sr. VP
Barb Keenan, Sr. VP-Human Resources/Chief Ethics Officer
Robert Boguski, Sr. VP-IT & Bus. Svcs.
David Brennan, General Counsel/Sr. VP-Law
Pat McNeil, Exec. VP-Corp. Bus. Dev.
Bruce Boland, Sr. VP-Corp. Affairs
Colleen M. Sidford, VP-Treas.
Pat McNeil, Chief Risk Officer
John Murphy, Exec. VP-Hydro
Frank Chiarotto, Sr. VP-Thermal
Catriona King, VP/Corp. Sec.
Jake Epp, Chmn.

Phone: 416-592-2555	**Fax:**
Toll-Free: 877-592-2555	
Address: 700 University Ave., Toronto, ON M5G 1X6 Canada	

GROWTH PLANS/SPECIAL FEATURES:

Ontario Power Generation, Inc. (OPG) is principally engaged in the generation and sale of electricity to customers in Ontario and in interconnected markets. OPG operates three nuclear power plants, with a generating capacity of 6,606 MW; five thermal generating stations, 6,327 MW; 65 hydroelectric stations, 6,963 MW; and two wind power turbines with a capacity of 2 MW. Of the 92.5 terawatt hours of electricity the firm generates, nuclear power generated approximately 51%; hydroelectric power, 39%; and thermal generating stations, 10%. OPG's green power and renewable energy facilities are run by OPG-Evergreen, which also buys power from green power generators and invests in green power projects. The firm sells its power primarily to businesses that have average electricity needs of at least 1 MW, as well as to local utilities. OPG also owns two additional nuclear generating stations which are leased on a long-term basis to Bruce Power L.P. In October 2010, OPG ceased the operations of four of its coal fired electricity generator located in Southern Ontario. In June 2010, the firm began construction on the Lower Mattagami Project, a 440 MW hydroelectric generating plant.

Ontario Power Generation, Inc. offers its employees benefits including an employee assistance program; pregnancy and parental leave; sick leave and long-term disability plans; and daycare facilities at certain sites.

FINANCIALS:

Sales and profits are in thousands of dollars—add 000 to get the full amount. 2010 Note: Financial information for 2010 was not available for all companies at press time.

2010 Sales: $	2010 Profits: $	**U.S. Stock Ticker: Government-Owned**
2009 Sales: $5,599,060	2009 Profits: $621,450	**Int'l Ticker:** Int'l Exchange:
2008 Sales: $5,972,740	2008 Profits: $82,650	Employees: 12,100
2007 Sales: $5,042,070	2007 Profits: $452,280	Fiscal Year Ends: 12/31
2006 Sales: $4,903,930	2006 Profits: $419,730	Parent Company:

SALARIES/BENEFITS:

Pension Plan:	ESOP Stock Plan:	Profit Sharing:	Top Exec. Salary: $	Bonus: $
Savings Plan:	Stock Purch. Plan:		Second Exec. Salary: $	Bonus: $

OTHER THOUGHTS:

Apparent Women Officers or Directors: 3
Hot Spot for Advancement for Women/Minorities: Y

LOCATIONS: ("Y" = Yes)

West:	Southwest:	Midwest:	Southeast:	Northeast:	International:
					Y

OSAKA GAS CO LTD

www.osakagas.co.jp

Industry Group Code: 221210 **Ranks within this company's industry group:** Sales: 3 Profits: 6

Exploration/Production:		Refining/Retailing:		Utilities:		Alternative Energy:		Specialty Services:		Energy Mktg./Other Svcs.	
Exploration:	Y	Refining:		Electric Utility:		Waste/Solar/Other:		Consulting/Eng.:	Y	Energy Marketing:	Y
Production:	Y	Retailing:	Y	Gas Utility:	Y	Thermal/Steam:		Seismic:		Equipment/Machinery:	
Coal Production:		Convenience Stores:		Pipelines:	Y	Wind:	Y	Drilling:		Oil Field Services:	
		Chemicals:		Water:		Hydro:		InfoTech:		Air/Shipping Transportation:	
						Fuel Cells:		Specialty Services:	Y		

TYPES OF BUSINESS:

Natural Gas Utility
Natural Gas Development
Real Estate & Property
Pipeline Construction
Electric Power Generation

BRANDS/DIVISIONS/AFFILIATES:

Brown Hill North Pty Ltd.

CONTACTS:

Note: Officers with more than one job title may be intentionally listed here more than once.

Hiroshi Ozaki, Pres.
Noriyuki Nakajima, Chief Dir.-Tech. Dev.
Shigeki Hirano, Dir.-Gas Mfg. & Power Generation
Takahiko Kawagishi, Sec.
Masato Kitamae, Chief Dir.-Bus. Planning
Tetsuo Setoguchi, Dir.-Metropolitan Energy Sales
Koji Kono, Dir.-Pipe Bus.
Hirofumi Kyutoku, Dir.-Energy Bus.
Kazuo Kakehashi, Dir.-Overseas Bus.

Phone: 81-6-6205-4737 **Fax:** 81-6-6222-5831
Toll-Free:
Address: 4-1-2, Hiranomachi, Chuo-ku, Osaka, 541-0046 Japan

GROWTH PLANS/SPECIAL FEATURES:

Osaka Gas Co., Ltd. (OGC), a leading Japanese natural gas distributor, supplies gas to approximately 6.9 million customers. Its Kansai region service territory includes some 75 cities and 30 municipalities in six prefectures. The company is primarily involved in the manufacture, supply and sale of gas; the sale of gas appliances, as well as associated installation and construction work; and the installation of pipelines. OGC imports approximately 7 million tons of LNG (Liquefied Natural Gas) annually from Brunei, Indonesia, Australia, Malaysia, Qatar and Oman. OGC operates through five business segments. The gas segment acquires and distributes the firm's natural gas. Residential sales represented approximately 27.6% of OGC's 2009 gas sales; commercial and industrial sales, 66.8%; and wholesale sales, 5.6%. The LNG, electricity and other energies segment transports LNG, generates electric power and provides services related to cogeneration systems. The gas appliances and house-pipe installation segment installs exterior and interior gas pipes. The real estate segment offers real estate management and development. Lastly, the other segment includes companies providing software development; security; and sport facility and restaurant operation, among other services. The firm manages a transmission and distribution pipeline network totaling nearly 36,000 miles. OGC maintains interests in sic LNG carriers, used to meet company demand as well as for trading purposes. In October 2009, OGC, acting with a consortium of other energy firms, purchased Brown Hill North Pty Ltd., including interest in a 63-turbine wind farm in Southern Australia, scheduled to begin power generation in mid-2011. In May 2010, the company acquired a 20% stake in an LNG terminal near Valencia, Spain, from Endesa S.A.

FINANCIALS:

Sales and profits are in thousands of dollars—add 000 to get the full amount. 2010 Note: Financial information for 2010 was not available for all companies at press time.

2010 Sales: $
2009 Sales: $14,726,890
2008 Sales: $13,743,010
2007 Sales: $13,036,090
2006 Sales: $9,064,900

2010 Profits: $
2009 Profits: $400,040
2008 Profits: $447,130
2007 Profits: $587,500
2006 Profits: $686,400

U.S. Stock Ticker: OSGSF
Int'l Ticker: 9532 Int'l Exchange: Tokyo-TSE
Employees:
Fiscal Year Ends: 3/31
Parent Company:

SALARIES/BENEFITS:

Pension Plan: Y
Savings Plan:
ESOP Stock Plan:
Stock Purch. Plan:
Profit Sharing:
Top Exec. Salary: $
Second Exec. Salary: $
Bonus: $
Bonus: $

OTHER THOUGHTS:

Apparent Women Officers or Directors:
Hot Spot for Advancement for Women/Minorities:

LOCATIONS: ("Y" = Yes)

West:	Southwest:	Midwest:	Southeast:	Northeast:	International:
					Y

OXBOW CORPORATION

www.oxbow.com

Industry Group Code: 21211 **Ranks within this company's industry group:** Sales: 6 Profits:

Exploration/Production:		**Refining/Retailing:**		**Utilities:**		**Alternative Energy:**		**Specialty Services:**		**Energy Mktg./Other Svcs.**	
Exploration:		Refining:	Y	Electric Utility:		Waste/Solar/Other:		Consulting/Eng.:	Y	Energy Marketing:	
Production:		Retailing:		Gas Utility:		Thermal/Steam:	Y	Seismic:		Equipment/Machinery:	
Coal Production:	Y	Convenience Stores:		Pipelines:		Wind:		Drilling:		Oil Field Services:	
		Chemicals:		Water:		Hydro:	Y	InfoTech:	Y	Air/Shipping Transportation:	Y
						Fuel Cells:		Specialty Services:	Y		

TYPES OF BUSINESS:

Petroleum Coke
Coal Mining
Shipping & Logistics
Metals Production
Electric Power Generation
Real Estate
Logistics Software
Geothermal & Hydroelectric Generation

BRANDS/DIVISIONS/AFFILIATES:

Gunnison Energy Corporation
xOrigins

CONTACTS:

Note: Officers with more than one job title may be intentionally listed here more than once.

William I. Koch, Pres.
Zachary K. Shipley, CFO
Kathy Flaherty, VP-Human Resources
Richard P. Callahan, General Counsel/Exec. VP
Steve Fried, Exec. VP-Oper.
Steve Fried, Exec. VP-Corp. Dev.
David Nestler, Exec. VP-Petcoke Supply & Optimization
Jim Cooper, Pres., Oxbow Mining
Eric Johnson, Exec. VP-Calcined Petcoke Bus.
Larry Black, Exec. VP-Worldwide Fuel Grade Petcoke & Gypsum
Patrick Bruning, VP-Dist.

Phone: 561-697-4300	**Fax:** 561-697-1876
Toll-Free:	
Address: 1601 Forum Pl., Ste. 1400, West Palm Beach, FL 33401 US	

GROWTH PLANS/SPECIAL FEATURES:

Oxbow Corporation is a diversified energy company that encompasses over two dozen subsidiaries. It manages one of the most diversified solid fuel portfolios in the world, supplying over 11 million tons of petroleum coke and 8.82 million steam tons of coal to customers in more than 35 countries each year. The company's Elk Creek longwall mining technology produces over 6 million tons of D-Seam coal annually. Coke products provided by Oxbow include petroleum coke, calcined petroleum coke and metallurgical coke. Oxbow also provides ferroalloys, including ferrosilicon, ferromolybdenum, metallurgical process materials, nickel, ferromanganese and fluorspar. Oxbow also operates a blending and bagging facility in Aurora, Indiana, manufacturing specialty blends used by the North American steel industry for extracting sulfur from steel and slag. Industrial minerals provided by the company include gypsum, limestone, fly ash, bed ash and mill scale. Subsidiary Gunnison Energy Corporation has natural gas leases in excess of 100,000 acres located in Delta, Mesa and Gunnison counties of Colorado. The company's shipping operations include four petroleum coke shipping terminals located in Long Beach, California; Texas City, Texas; and St. Croix, Virgin Islands. Oxbow delivers over 9 million tons of coal, petroleum and metallurgical coke, gypsum, steel and ferroalloys annually worldwide by barge, vessel, rail and truck, tracking deliveries with its proprietary xOrigins software.

FINANCIALS:

Sales and profits are in thousands of dollars—add 000 to get the full amount. 2010 Note: Financial information for 2010 was not available for all companies at press time.

2010 Sales: $	2010 Profits: $	**U.S. Stock Ticker: Private**
2009 Sales: $3,700,000	2009 Profits: $	**Int'l Ticker:** Int'l Exchange:
2008 Sales: $4,500,000	2008 Profits: $	Employees: 1,200
2007 Sales: $	2007 Profits: $	Fiscal Year Ends: 12/31
2006 Sales: $1,600,000	2006 Profits: $	Parent Company:

SALARIES/BENEFITS:

Pension Plan:	ESOP Stock Plan:	Profit Sharing:	Top Exec. Salary: $	Bonus: $
Savings Plan:	Stock Purch. Plan:		Second Exec. Salary: $	Bonus: $

OTHER THOUGHTS:

Apparent Women Officers or Directors: 1
Hot Spot for Advancement for Women/Minorities:

LOCATIONS: ("Y" = Yes)

West:	Southwest:	Midwest:	Southeast:	Northeast:	International:
Y	Y	Y	Y	Y	Y

PAA NATURAL GAS STORAGE LP

www.pnglp.com

Industry Group Code: 424710 **Ranks within this company's industry group:** Sales: 8 Profits: 6

Exploration/Production:		Refining/Retailing:		Utilities:		Alternative Energy:		Specialty Services:		Energy Mktg./Other Svcs.	
Exploration:		Refining:		Electric Utility:		Waste/Solar/Other:		Consulting/Eng.:		Energy Marketing:	
Production:		Retailing:		Gas Utility:		Thermal/Steam:		Seismic:		Equipment/Machinery:	
Coal Production:		Convenience Stores:		Pipelines:		Wind:		Drilling:		Oil Field Services:	
		Chemicals:		Water:		Hydro:		InfoTech:		Air/Shipping Transportation:	
						Fuel Cells:		Specialty Services:	Y		

TYPES OF BUSINESS:

Natural Gas Storage Facilities

BRANDS/DIVISIONS/AFFILIATES:

Plains All American Pipeline
Pine Prairie
Bluewater

CONTACTS:

Note: Officers with more than one job title may be intentionally listed here more than once.

Greg L. Armstrong, CEO
Dean Liollio, Pres.
Al Swanson, CFO/Sr. VP
Richard Tomaski, VP-Mktg.
Richard McGee, VP-Legal/Sec.
Dan Noack, VP-Oper.
Richard McGee, VP-Bus. Dev.
Roy I. Lamoreaux, Dir.-Investor Rel.
Donald C. O'Shea, Chief Acct. Officer
Benjamin J. Reese, Sr. VP-Commercial
Todd Brown, VP-Optimization
Greg L. Armstrong, Chmn.

Phone: 713-6464100	Fax:
Toll-Free: 877-707-6457	
Address: 333 Clay St., Ste. 1500, Houston, TX 77002 US	

GROWTH PLANS/SPECIAL FEATURES:

PAA Natural Gas Storage L.P. is a fee-based, growth-oriented partnership. The firm owns, acquires, develops and manages natural gas storage facilities. Currently, the company owns and operates two facilities located in Michigan and Louisiana. PAA Natural Gas Storage was formed in January 2010 to handle the natural gas storage operations of diversified energy firm Plains All American Pipeline, L.P. Plains All American Pipeline owns roughly 77 % equity interest, including a 2% general partner interest, in PAA Natural Gas Storage. The company's Louisiana facility, Pine Prairie, has a total working gas storage capacity of approximately 24 billion cubic feet (bcf) located in three caverns. The facility has an aggregate peak injection and withdrawal capacity of 1.7 bcf per day. The firm's Michigan facility, Bluewater, is a depleted reservoir natural gas storage complex located approximately 50 miles from Detroit in St. Clair County. Bluewater has a total working gas storage capacity of roughly 26 bcf in two depleted reservoirs. It has an aggregate peak injection and withdrawal capacity of 3.2 bcf per day. In May 2010, PAA Natural Gas Storage began operating its third well cavern at Pine Prairie, which increased the facility's working gas storage capacity by roughly 70% and increased the firm's aggregate working capacity by 25%. In June 2010, the company formed a commercial optimization group. In October 2010, PAA Natural Gas Storage announced plans to expand its Pine Prairie facility by adding two new 12 bcf caverns and expanding its capacity in four caverns by 2 bcf each. This expansion will add 32 bcf of working gas to the facility's production.

FINANCIALS:

Sales and profits are in thousands of dollars—add 000 to get the full amount. 2010 Note: Financial information for 2010 was not available for all companies at press time.

2010 Sales: $	2010 Profits: $	**U.S. Stock Ticker: PNG**
2009 Sales: $72,200	2009 Profits: $24,000	**Int'l Ticker:** Int'l Exchange:
2008 Sales: $49,200	2008 Profits: $19,600	Employees:
2007 Sales: $	2007 Profits: $	Fiscal Year Ends: 12/31
2006 Sales: $	2006 Profits: $	Parent Company: PLAINS ALL AMERICAN PIPELINE

SALARIES/BENEFITS:

Pension Plan:	ESOP Stock Plan:	Profit Sharing:	Top Exec. Salary: $	Bonus: $
Savings Plan:	Stock Purch. Plan:		Second Exec. Salary: $	Bonus: $

OTHER THOUGHTS:

Apparent Women Officers or Directors:
Hot Spot for Advancement for Women/Minorities:

LOCATIONS: ("Y" = Yes)

West:	Southwest:	Midwest:	Southeast:	Northeast:	International:
	Y	Y	Y		

PACIFICORP

www.pacificorp.com

Industry Group Code: 2211 **Ranks within this company's industry group:** Sales: 28 Profits: 22

Exploration/Production:		Refining/Retailing:		Utilities:		Alternative Energy:		Specialty Services:		Energy Mktg./Other Svcs.	
Exploration:		Refining:		Electric Utility:	Y	Waste/Solar/Other:		Consulting/Eng.:		Energy Marketing:	Y
Production:		Retailing:		Gas Utility:		Thermal/Steam:	Y	Seismic:		Equipment/Machinery:	
Coal Production:	Y	Convenience Stores:		Pipelines:		Wind:	Y	Drilling:		Oil Field Services:	
		Chemicals:		Water:		Hydro:	Y	InfoTech:		Air/Shipping Transportation:	
						Fuel Cells:		Specialty Services:			

TYPES OF BUSINESS:

Electric Utility
Hydroelectric, Wind & Geothermal Power
Coal Mining
Energy Marketing

BRANDS/DIVISIONS/AFFILIATES:

MidAmerican Energy Holdings Co
Pacific Power
Rocky Mountain Power
PacifiCorp Energy
High Plains
McFadden Ridge I

CONTACTS:

Note: Officers with more than one job title may be intentionally listed here more than once.

Gregory E. Abel, CEO
Micheal Dunn, Pres.
Douglas K. Stuver, CFO
Mark C. Moench, General Counsel/Sr. VP
A. Richard Walje, Pres., Rocky Mountain Power
Patrick Reiten, Pres., Pacific Power
Gregory E. Abel, Chmn.

Phone: 503-813-5000	**Fax:**
Toll-Free: 888-221-7070	
Address: 825 NE Multnomah St., Portland, OR 97232 US	

GROWTH PLANS/SPECIAL FEATURES:

PacifiCorp, a subsidiary of Mid-American Energy Holdings Co., is an electric utility that generates, distributes and markets electricity. PacifiCorp serves business, residential and industrial customers in Oregon, Washington and California through its Pacific Power subsidiary; its Rocky Mountain Power subsidiary serves customers in Utah, Wyoming and Idaho. Its PacifiCorp Energy subsidiary controls the firm's electric generation, commercial and energy trading functions, as well as the coal-mining operations. Combined, PacifiCorp's subsidiaries provide electricity to approximately 1.7 million customers. It also operates roughly 15,900 miles of transmission lines, over 62,000 miles of overhead distribution lines and over 14,000 miles of underground distribution lines, with 908 substations and 80 generating plants across the West. PacifiCorp has a generating capacity of over 8,400 megawatts (MW), largely from coal-fired and gas-fired generating plants, but also from hydroelectric, geothermal and wind power plants. Roughly 63% of the company's power supply is derived from coal; 12% is derived from natural gas; 5% from hydroelectric resources; and 4% from other energy sources. The remaining 16% of PacifiCorp's energy is purchased from third parties. The firm operates 47 hydroelectric generation facilities; 11coal-fueled plants; six natural gas plants; 12 wind plants; and two geothermal facilities. In October 2009, the company's wind projects, High Plains and McFadden Ridge I, located in Albany County and Carbon County, Wyoming began operations.

PacifiCorp offers employees flexible spending accounts; an employee assistance program; and medical, dental and vision insurance.

FINANCIALS:

Sales and profits are in thousands of dollars—add 000 to get the full amount. 2010 Note: Financial information for 2010 was not available for all companies at press time.

2010 Sales: $	2010 Profits: $	**U.S. Stock Ticker: Subsidiary**
2009 Sales: $4,457,000	2009 Profits: $542,000	**Int'l Ticker:** Int'l Exchange:
2008 Sales: $4,498,000	2008 Profits: $458,000	Employees:
2007 Sales: $4,258,000	2007 Profits: $439,000	Fiscal Year Ends: 12/31
2006 Sales: $3,896,700	2006 Profits: $360,700	Parent Company: MIDAMERICAN ENERGY HOLDINGS CO

SALARIES/BENEFITS:

Pension Plan:	ESOP Stock Plan:	Profit Sharing:	Top Exec. Salary: $351,900	Bonus: $583,217
Savings Plan: Y	Stock Purch. Plan:		Second Exec. Salary: $265,740	Bonus: $623,417

OTHER THOUGHTS:

Apparent Women Officers or Directors:
Hot Spot for Advancement for Women/Minorities:

LOCATIONS: ("Y" = Yes)

West:	Southwest:	Midwest:	Southeast:	Northeast:	International:
Y					

PAKISTAN STATE OIL CO LTD

www.psopk.com

Industry Group Code: 324110 **Ranks within this company's industry group:** Sales: 21 Profits: 19

Exploration/Production:		Refining/Retailing:		Utilities:		Alternative Energy:		Specialty Services:		Energy Mktg./Other Svcs.	
Exploration:		Refining:		Electric Utility:		Waste/Solar/Other:		Consulting/Eng.:		Energy Marketing:	
Production:		Retailing:	Y	Gas Utility:		Thermal/Steam:		Seismic:		Equipment/Machinery:	
Coal Production:		Convenience Stores:	Y	Pipelines:	Y	Wind:		Drilling:		Oil Field Services:	
		Chemicals:		Water:		Hydro:		InfoTech:		Air/Shipping Transportation:	Y
						Fuel Cells:		Specialty Services:	Y		

TYPES OF BUSINESS:

Oil Marketing
Oil & Gas Storage & Distribution
Service Stations
Lube Shops
Petrochemical Import & Distribution
Convenience Stores

BRANDS/DIVISIONS/AFFILIATES:

New Vision
PSO Club
Kuwait Petroleum Corporation
United Bank Limited
E10 Gasoline
Northern Power Generation Company Limited
Karachi Electric Supply Corp.
Petrosin

CONTACTS: *Note: Officers with more than one job title may be intentionally listed here more than once.*

Irfan K. Qureshi, Managing Dir.
S. Aijazuddin Ahmed, Gen. Mgr.-Mktg. Svcs.
Babar H. Chaudhary, Gen. Mgr.-Human Resources
Irfan U. Qidwai, Gen. Mgr.-IT
Abu K. M. Arif, Deputy Gen. Mgr.-Admin.
Faiz M. K. Durrani, Mgr.-Legal Affairs
Syed Z. Hasan, Gen. Mgr.-Oper.
S. Tariq Hassan Razvi, Gen. Mgr.-New Bus. Dev.
Naimatullah Behan, Deputy Gen. Mgr.-Public Rel.
Yacoob Suttar, Exec. Dir.-Finance & IT
Shahzad Manzoor, Gen. Mgr.-Aviation, Marine & Exports
Zafar A. Khan, Gen. Mgr.-Logistics
Tariq Akber, Gen. Mgr.-Construction & Retail Fuel Facilities
Vaqar A. Khan, Gen. Mgr.-Training & Organizational Dev.
Nazim F. Haji, Chmn.
Naved A. Zubairi, Exec. Dir.-Supply Chain

Phone: 92-21-111-111776 **Fax:**
Toll-Free:
Address: PSO House, Khayaban-e-Iqbal, Clifton, Karachi, 75600 Pakistan

GROWTH PLANS/SPECIAL FEATURES:

Pakistan State Oil Co., Ltd. (PSO), 54% owned by the Pakistani government, is Pakistan's largest oil marketing company, serving approximately 2.8 million fuel and non-fuel customers daily. The firm owns approximately 88.3% of the country's black oil market (crude oil, low-grade oil, and non-fluid oils) and a 55.4% share of the white oils market (clear, refined oils such as kerosene and jet fuel). It imports, stores, distributes and markets a large variety of petroleum products, including motor gasoline, high-speed diesel, furnace oil, jet fuel, kerosene, LPG (liquefied petroleum gas), petrochemicals and lubricants. PSO serves customers in every oil-consuming industry in Pakistan, including automotive, aviation, railways, power projects, armed forces, marine, agriculture industrial and government markets. At nine Pakistani airports, the firm supplies refueling stations with jet fuel, in addition to supplying three of the country's ports with fuel. PSO currently has a 30-year contract with Kuwait Petroleum Corporation for the purchase of high-speed diesel (HSD) and furnace oil (FO), which protects the company from frequent price fluctuations. The firm supplies approximately 7 million tons of FO annually. The company's marketing and distribution segment operates approximately 3,481 retail outlets, in addition to 53 outlets that serve the agriculture industry and 145 outlets that handle bulk customers. Additionally, the firm imports about 8.4 million tons of HSD, high sulfur furnace oil (HSFO), low sulfur furnace oil (LSFO) and others. PSO also provides corporate, fleet and pre-paid cards. The company has been modernizing its dispensing stations to upgraded retail outlets, called New Vision outlets. In March 2010, PSO entered a partnership with Petrosin through which Petrosin will provide LPG to the firm's gas stations. In April 2010, the firm signed a fuel supply agreement with Karachi Electric Supply Corp. to provide up to 33,000 tons of FO per month for 10 years.

FINANCIALS: **Sales and profits are in thousands of dollars—add 000 to get the full amount. 2010 Note: Financial information for 2010 was not available for all companies at press time.**

2010 Sales: $	2010 Profits: $	**U.S. Stock Ticker:**
2009 Sales: $7,150,060	2009 Profits: $-78,170	**Int'l Ticker: PSO** Int'l Exchange: Karachi-KSE
2008 Sales: $7,322,010	2008 Profits: $80,050	Employees:
2007 Sales: $5,918,820	2007 Profits: $167,950	Fiscal Year Ends: 6/30
2006 Sales: $5,862,300	2006 Profits: $125,100	Parent Company:

SALARIES/BENEFITS:

Pension Plan:	ESOP Stock Plan:	Profit Sharing:	Top Exec. Salary: $	Bonus: $
Savings Plan:	Stock Purch. Plan:		Second Exec. Salary: $	Bonus: $

OTHER THOUGHTS:

Apparent Women Officers or Directors:
Hot Spot for Advancement for Women/Minorities:

LOCATIONS: ("Y" = Yes)

West:	Southwest:	Midwest:	Southeast:	Northeast:	International:
					Y

PARKER DRILLING COMPANY

www.parkerdrilling.com

Industry Group Code: 213111 **Ranks within this company's industry group:** Sales: 13 Profits: 12

Exploration/Production:		Refining/Retailing:		Utilities:		Alternative Energy:		Specialty Services:		Energy Mktg./Other Svcs.	
Exploration:		Refining:		Electric Utility:		Waste/Solar/Other:		Consulting/Eng.:		Energy Marketing:	
Production:		Retailing:		Gas Utility:		Thermal/Steam:		Seismic:		Equipment/Machinery:	
Coal Production:		Convenience Stores:		Pipelines:		Wind:		Drilling:	Y	Oil Field Services:	
		Chemicals:		Water:		Hydro:		InfoTech:		Air/Shipping Transportation:	
						Fuel Cells:		Specialty Services:	Y		

TYPES OF BUSINESS:

Oil & Gas Drilling Support Services
Tool Rental Services

BRANDS/DIVISIONS/AFFILIATES:

Quail Tools, LP

CONTACTS:

Note: Officers with more than one job title may be intentionally listed here more than once.

David C. Mannon, CEO
David C. Mannon, Pres.
W. Kirk Brassfield, CFO/Sr. VP
Denis Graham, VP-Eng.
Jon-Al Duplantier, General Counsel/VP
Philip Schlom, Corp. Controller/Principal Acct. Officer
J. Daniel Chapman, Chief Compliance Officer
David W. Tucker, Treas.
Robert L. Parker Jr., Chmn.

Phone: 281-406-2000	**Fax:** 281-406-2001
Toll-Free:	
Address: 5 Greenway Plz., Ste. 100, Houston, TX 77046 US	

GROWTH PLANS/SPECIAL FEATURES:

Parker Drilling Company is a worldwide provider of contract drilling and drilling-related services. Parker derives its revenues from five segments: U.S. drilling; international drilling; project management and engineering services; rental tools; and construction contract services. Its core U.S. barge drilling operations include 13 barge drilling and workover rigs in the U.S. Gulf of Mexico and one land rig in New Iberia, Louisiana. The firm's international land drilling operations consist of nine land rigs in Kazakhstan and Turkmenistan; eight land rigs in Asian Pacific region; nine land rigs in Latin America (Mexico and Colombia) region; two land rigs in Africa and the Middle East region; and the world's largest arctic-class barge rig in the Caspian Sea. Project management and engineering services such as Front End Engineering and Design (FEED), Engineering, Procurement, Construction and Installation (EPCI) and project management services provide technical expertise to third-party companies. Its subsidiary, Quail Tools, provides rental tools that are used for land and offshore oil and gas drilling and workover activities. Quail Tools has four offices that are located in the Gulf of Mexico, West Texas and Rocky Mountain regions. The company also provides international rentals to Trinidad and Tobago, Mexico, Russia, Singapore, Nigeria, Brazil and Chad.

FINANCIALS:

Sales and profits are in thousands of dollars—add 000 to get the full amount. 2010 Note: Financial information for 2010 was not available for all companies at press time.

2010 Sales: $	2010 Profits: $	**U.S. Stock Ticker: PKD**
2009 Sales: $752,910	2009 Profits: $9,267	**Int'l Ticker:** Int'l Exchange:
2008 Sales: $829,842	2008 Profits: $22,728	Employees: 2,372
2007 Sales: $654,573	2007 Profits: $104,078	Fiscal Year Ends: 12/31
2006 Sales: $586,435	2006 Profits: $81,026	Parent Company:

SALARIES/BENEFITS:

Pension Plan:	ESOP Stock Plan:	Profit Sharing:	Top Exec. Salary: $638,817	Bonus: $319,356
Savings Plan: Y	Stock Purch. Plan:		Second Exec. Salary: $524,768	Bonus: $262,088

OTHER THOUGHTS:

Apparent Women Officers or Directors:
Hot Spot for Advancement for Women/Minorities:

LOCATIONS: ("Y" = Yes)

West:	Southwest:	Midwest:	Southeast:	Northeast:	International:
Y	Y		Y		Y

PATTERSON-UTI ENERGY INC

www.patenergy.com

Industry Group Code: 213111 **Ranks within this company's industry group:** Sales: 12 Profits: 13

Exploration/Production:		Refining/Retailing:		Utilities:		Alternative Energy:		Specialty Services:		Energy Mktg./Other Svcs.	
Exploration:	Y	Refining:		Electric Utility:		Waste/Solar/Other:		Consulting/Eng.:		Energy Marketing:	
Production:	Y	Retailing:		Gas Utility:		Thermal/Steam:		Seismic:		Equipment/Machinery:	
Coal Production:		Convenience Stores:		Pipelines:		Wind:		Drilling:	Y	Oil Field Services:	Y
		Chemicals:		Water:		Hydro:		InfoTech:		Air/Shipping Transportation:	
						Fuel Cells:		Specialty Services:			

TYPES OF BUSINESS:

Oil & Gas Services
Onshore Contract Drilling Services
Drilling & Completion Fluid Services
Pressure Pumping Services
Oil & Gas Production

BRANDS/DIVISIONS/AFFILIATES:

CONTACTS:

Note: Officers with more than one job title may be intentionally listed here more than once.

Douglas J. Wall, CEO
Douglas J. Wall, Pres.
John E. Vollmer, III, CFO/Treas.
Seth D. Wexler, General Counsel/Sec.
John E. Vollmer, III, Sr. VP-Corp. Dev.
Greg Pipkin, Chief Acct. Officer
Kenneth N. Berns, Sr. VP
Mark S. Siegel, Chmn.

Phone: 281-765-7100	**Fax:** 281-765-7175
Toll-Free:	
Address: 450 Gears Rd., Ste. 500, Houston, TX 77067 US	

GROWTH PLANS/SPECIAL FEATURES:

Patterson-UTI Energy, Inc. serves land-based oil and natural gas exploration and production companies. The company operates in Texas, New Mexico, Oklahoma, Arkansas, Louisiana, Mississippi, Colorado, Utah, Wyoming, Montana, North Dakota, Pennsylvania, West Virginia and western Canada through three business segments: contract drilling; pressure pumping; and oil and natural gas. The firm operates 341 currently marketable contract drilling rigs, with a maximum drilling depth capacity ranging from 5,000 to 30,000 feet; of these rigs, 234 are mechanical and 107 silicon-controlled rectifier (SCR) electric. Under turnkey contracts, the company will drill a well to a certain depths under specified conditions for a fixed fee. Patterson-UTI dug 1,534 wells in 2009, each dug on average in about 20 days. It operates 323 trucks and 417 trailers used to transport and support its rigs. Pressure pumping services includes stimulation, which enhances well flow by pumping corrosive acid, nitrogen gas or highly pressurized fracturing fluid into a well; and cementing, which involves inserting a substance between a wellbore and its casing to add support. The oil and gas segment operates in Texas, New Mexico, Mississippi and Louisiana as a working interest owner. Contract drilling provided 76% of the company's 2009 revenue; pressure pumping, 21%; and oil and natural gas, 3%. In January 2010, Patterson-UTI sold its drilling and completion fluid business to National Oilwell Varco LP for about $48 million. In July 2010, the firm entered into an agreement to acquire the pressure pumping and wireline business of Key Energy Services for $237.7 million.

FINANCIALS:

Sales and profits are in thousands of dollars—add 000 to get the full amount. 2010 Note: Financial information for 2010 was not available for all companies at press time.

2010 Sales: $	2010 Profits: $	**U.S. Stock Ticker: PTEN**
2009 Sales: $781,946	2009 Profits: $-38,290	**Int'l Ticker:** Int'l Exchange:
2008 Sales: $2,063,880	2008 Profits: $347,069	Employees: 4,200
2007 Sales: $1,986,096	2007 Profits: $438,639	Fiscal Year Ends: 12/31
2006 Sales: $2,546,586	2006 Profits: $673,254	Parent Company:

SALARIES/BENEFITS:

Pension Plan:	ESOP Stock Plan:	Profit Sharing:	Top Exec. Salary: $600,000	Bonus: $396,347
Savings Plan: Y	Stock Purch. Plan:		Second Exec. Salary: $350,000	Bonus: $528,462

OTHER THOUGHTS:

Apparent Women Officers or Directors:
Hot Spot for Advancement for Women/Minorities:

LOCATIONS: ("Y" = Yes)

West:	Southwest:	Midwest:	Southeast:	Northeast:	International:
Y	Y	Y	Y	Y	Y

PEABODY ENERGY CORP

www.peabodyenergy.com

Industry Group Code: 21211 **Ranks within this company's industry group:** Sales: 4 Profits: 6

Exploration/Production:		**Refining/Retailing:**		**Utilities:**		**Alternative Energy:**		**Specialty Services:**		**Energy Mktg./Other Svcs.**	
Exploration:		Refining:		Electric Utility:		Waste/Solar/Other:		Consulting/Eng.:		Energy Marketing:	Y
Production:		Retailing:		Gas Utility:		Thermal/Steam:		Seismic:		Equipment/Machinery:	
Coal Production:	Y	Convenience Stores:		Pipelines:		Wind:		Drilling:		Oil Field Services:	
		Chemicals:		Water:		Hydro:		InfoTech:		Air/Shipping Transportation:	Y
						Fuel Cells:		Specialty Services:			

TYPES OF BUSINESS:

Coal Production
Energy Trading & Marketing
Transportation Services
Carbon Capture
Coal Conversion Technologies

BRANDS/DIVISIONS/AFFILIATES:

Peabody-Winsway Resources

CONTACTS:

Note: Officers with more than one job title may be intentionally listed here more than once.

Gregory H. Boyce, CEO
Eric Ford, COO/Exec. VP
Richard A. Navarre, Pres.
Michael C. Crews, CFO/Exec. VP
Sharon D. Fiehler, Exec. VP-Admin.
Alexander C. Scoch, Chief Legal Officer/Exec. VP-Law/Sec.
Vic Svec, Sr. VP-Corp. Comm.
Vic Svec, Sr. VP-Investor Rel.
Richard A. Navarre, Chief Commercial Officer
Gregory H. Boyce, Chmn.
Michael J. Flannigan, VP-Int'l Rel.

Phone: 314-342-3400	**Fax:** 314-342-7799
Toll-Free:	
Address: 701 Market St., St. Louis, MO 63101 US	

GROWTH PLANS/SPECIAL FEATURES:

Peabody Energy Corp. is a private-sector coal company with operations worldwide. The firm sells approximately 244 million tons of coal annually to a clientele of nearly 345 electricity generating and industrial plants in 23 countries. It has 28 coal mining operations in the U.S. and Australia. In 2009, the firm produced 210 million tons of coal. The company has approximately 9 billion tons of proven and probable coal reserves. The mining operations consist of three principal operating segments: western U.S. mining, midwestern U.S. mining and Australian mining. In addition to mining operations, the firm markets, brokers and trades coal through a trading and brokerage operations segment. Peabody Energy has international trading locations in London, U.K.; Newcastle, Australia; Beijing, China; Jakarta, Indonesia; and Singapore. Other energy-related commercial activities include the development of mine-mouth coal-fueled generating plants; the management of vast coal reserve and real estate holdings; the advancement of carbon capture sequestration initiatives; and Btu conversion technologies, which are designed to convert coal to natural gas and transportation fuels. In July 2010, the company formed a joint venture in Mongolia with Winsway Coking Coal Holdings Ltd called Peabody-Winsway Resources. This joint venture maintains uranium and coal licenses in Mongolia and is currently heading an exploration program in the country.

FINANCIALS:

Sales and profits are in thousands of dollars—add 000 to get the full amount. 2010 Note: Financial information for 2010 was not available for all companies at press time.

2010 Sales: $	2010 Profits: $	**U.S. Stock Ticker: BTU**
2009 Sales: $6,012,400	2009 Profits: $463,000	**Int'l Ticker:** Int'l Exchange:
2008 Sales: $6,593,400	2008 Profits: $953,500	Employees: 7,300
2007 Sales: $4,574,712	2007 Profits: $264,285	Fiscal Year Ends: 12/31
2006 Sales: $4,108,396	2006 Profits: $600,697	Parent Company:

SALARIES/BENEFITS:

Pension Plan:	ESOP Stock Plan:	Profit Sharing:	Top Exec. Salary: $1,075,000	Bonus: $2,227,052
Savings Plan:	Stock Purch. Plan:		Second Exec. Salary: $730,000	Bonus: $1,138,806

OTHER THOUGHTS:

Apparent Women Officers or Directors: 7
Hot Spot for Advancement for Women/Minorities: Y

LOCATIONS: ("Y" = Yes)

West:	Southwest:	Midwest:	Southeast:	Northeast:	International:
Y		Y			Y

PENN VIRGINIA CORP

www.pennvirginia.com

Industry Group Code: 211111 **Ranks within this company's industry group:** Sales: 84 Profits: 84

Exploration/Production:		Refining/Retailing:		Utilities:		Alternative Energy:		Specialty Services:		Energy Mktg./Other Svcs.	
Exploration:	Y	Refining:		Electric Utility:		Waste/Solar/Other:		Consulting/Eng.:		Energy Marketing:	
Production:	Y	Retailing:		Gas Utility:		Thermal/Steam:		Seismic:		Equipment/Machinery:	
Coal Production:	Y	Convenience Stores:		Pipelines:		Wind:		Drilling:		Oil Field Services:	
		Chemicals:		Water:		Hydro:		InfoTech:		Air/Shipping Transportation:	
						Fuel Cells:		Specialty Services:	Y		

TYPES OF BUSINESS:

Oil & Gas Exploration & Production
Coal Properties
Natural Gas Processing

BRANDS/DIVISIONS/AFFILIATES:

Penn Virginia Resource Partners LP

CONTACTS:

Note: Officers with more than one job title may be intentionally listed here more than once.

A. James Dearlove, CEO
H. Baird Whitehead, COO/Exec. VP
A. James Dearlove, Pres.
A. James Dearlove, Interim CFO
Nancy M. Snyder, Chief Admin. Officer/Exec. VP
Nancy M. Snyder, General Counsel/Corp. Sec.
Jim Dean, VP-Corp. Dev.
Forrest W. McNair, Controller/VP
Dana Wright, VP-Planning
Steven A. Hartman, VP/Treas.
Robert Garrett, Chmn.

Phone: 610-687-8900 **Fax:** 610-687-3688
Toll-Free:
Address: 100 Matsonford Rd., 4 Radnor Corp. Ctr., Ste. 200, Radnor, PA 19087 US

GROWTH PLANS/SPECIAL FEATURES:

Penn Virginia Corp. is an independent oil and gas firm. The company is engaged in the exploration, development and production of crude oil and natural gas primarily in the Appalachian, Mississippi and Mid-continent areas of the U.S. The firm is also indirectly involved in the business of Penn Virginia Resources Partners, L.P. (PVR). Penn Virginia operates in three segments: oil and gas; coal and natural resource management; and natural gas midstream. The oil and gas segment explores for, develops, produces and sells crude oil, condensate and natural gas. The company has proved oil and natural gas reserves of approximately 935 billion cubic feet equivalent, of which 83% is natural gas and 47% is proved developed. PVR operates the coal and natural resource management and natural gas midstream segments. The PVR coal and natural resource management segment involves the management and leasing of coal properties and the subsequent collection of royalties. PVR owns or controls approximately 829 million tons of proven and probable coal reserves in Central and Northern Appalachia, the Illinois Basin and the San Juan Basin. Divisional revenue comes from oil and gas royalty interests, coal transportation rights and the sale of standing timber on its properties. The natural gas midstream segment is engaged in providing natural gas processing, gathering and other related services. PVR owns and operates natural gas midstream assets located in Oklahoma and Texas, including five natural gas processing facilities having 400 millions of cubic feet equivalent a day of total capacity and approximately 4,118 miles of natural gas gathering pipelines. In February 2010, Penn Virginia Corp. disposed of its southern Texas and southern Louisiana Gulf Coast assets for $38 million; and acquired roughly 1,300 acres in Mississippi for $6 million. In May 2010, the company acquired approximately 10,000 acres in Pennsylvania for $19.5 million.

FINANCIALS:

Sales and profits are in thousands of dollars—add 000 to get the full amount. 2010 Note: Financial information for 2010 was not available for all companies at press time.

2010 Sales: $	2010 Profits: $	**U.S. Stock Ticker: PVA**
2009 Sales: $815,137	2009 Profits: $-77,368	**Int'l Ticker:** Int'l Exchange:
2008 Sales: $1,220,851	2008 Profits: $124,168	Employees: 382
2007 Sales: $852,950	2007 Profits: $50,754	Fiscal Year Ends: 12/31
2006 Sales: $753,929	2006 Profits: $75,909	Parent Company:

SALARIES/BENEFITS:

Pension Plan:	ESOP Stock Plan:	Profit Sharing:	Top Exec. Salary: $450,000	Bonus: $500,000
Savings Plan:	Stock Purch. Plan:		Second Exec. Salary: $325,000	Bonus: $325,000

OTHER THOUGHTS:

Apparent Women Officers or Directors: 2
Hot Spot for Advancement for Women/Minorities:

LOCATIONS: ("Y" = Yes)

West:	Southwest:	Midwest:	Southeast:	Northeast:	International:
	Y		Y	Y	

PENN WEST ENERGY TRUST

www.pennwest.com

Industry Group Code: 211111 **Ranks within this company's industry group:** Sales: 69 Profits: 93

Exploration/Production:		Refining/Retailing:		Utilities:		Alternative Energy:		Specialty Services:		Energy Mktg./Other Svcs.	
Exploration:	Y	Refining:		Electric Utility:		Waste/Solar/Other:		Consulting/Eng.:		Energy Marketing:	
Production:	Y	Retailing:		Gas Utility:		Thermal/Steam:		Seismic:		Equipment/Machinery:	
Coal Production:		Convenience Stores:		Pipelines:		Wind:		Drilling:		Oil Field Services:	
		Chemicals:		Water:		Hydro:		InfoTech:		Air/Shipping Transportation:	
						Fuel Cells:		Specialty Services:	Y		

TYPES OF BUSINESS:

Oil & Gas Exploration & Production
Carbon Sequestration

BRANDS/DIVISIONS/AFFILIATES:

China Investment Corporation
Canetic Resources Trust

CONTACTS:

Note: Officers with more than one job title may be intentionally listed here more than once.

William E. Andrew, CEO
Murray R. Nunns, COO
Murray R. Nunns, Pres.
Todd Takeyasu, CFO/Exec. VP
Bob Shepherd, Sr. VP-Exploration & Dev.
David W. Middleton, Exec. VP-Eng.
Mark Fitzgerald, Sr. VP-Prod.
Keith Luft, General Counsel/Sr. VP
Thane A. E. Jensen, Sr. VP-Oper. Eng.
David W. Middleton, VP-Corp. Dev.
Keith Luft, Sr. VP-Stakeholder Rel.
Hilary Foulkes, Sr. VP-Bus. Dev
John A. Brussa, Chmn.

Phone: 403-777-2500 **Fax:** 403-777-2699
Toll-Free: 866-693-2707
Address: 207 9th Ave. SW, Ste. 200, Calgary, AB T2P 1K3 Canada

GROWTH PLANS/SPECIAL FEATURES:

Penn West Energy Trust, formerly Penn West Petroleum, Ltd., is an independent Canadian oil and natural gas company headquartered in Calgary, Alberta. It is one of the largest conventional oil and natural gas producing income trusts in North America. In total, it produces an average of 164,141 boe (barrels of oil equivalent) per day, of which approximately 41% is natural gas and approximately 59% is crude oil. The firm operates in three core areas: Northern, Central and Plains. The Plains area yields heavy oil and shallow natural gas. The Central area contains light oil and multi-zone natural gas as well as Cardium oil reserves. The Northern area is expected to be an abundant source of natural gas. The company also has 6.5 million acres (net) of undeveloped land, creating a source of additional value through land monetization, farm-outs and exploration joint ventures. The firm has roughly 368 million barrels (mmbbls) of proved plus probable reserves of light and medium oil; 71 mmbbls of heavy oil; 33 mmbbls of natural gas liquid; and 1.292 trillion cubic feet of natural gas. In total, the company has roughly 687 million proved plus provable boe. In recent years, Penn West combined with Canetic Resources Trust to form one of the largest conventional oil and gas energy trusts in North America. In June 2010, the firm formed a joint venture with China Investment Corporation to develop the company's Peace River bitumen assets located in northern Alberta; Penn West owns 55% of the venture. In September 2010, Penn West announced plans to convert from an income trust to a corporation; and formed a 50-50 joint venture with a subsidiary of Mitsubishi Corporation to develop some of Penn West's conventional gas assets in the Wildboy area of northeastern British Columbia and its shale gas assets in the Cordova Embayment area.

FINANCIALS:

Sales and profits are in thousands of dollars—add 000 to get the full amount. 2010 Note: Financial information for 2010 was not available for all companies at press time.

2010 Sales: $	2010 Profits: $	**U.S. Stock Ticker: PWE**
2009 Sales: $2,280,510	2009 Profits: $-138,910	**Int'l Ticker: PWT.UN** Int'l Exchange: Toronto-TSX
2008 Sales: $3,906,000	2008 Profits: $1,177,880	Employees:
2007 Sales: $1,927,700	2007 Profits: $168,500	Fiscal Year Ends: 12/31
2006 Sales: $1,579,900	2006 Profits: $639,000	Parent Company:

SALARIES/BENEFITS:

Pension Plan:	ESOP Stock Plan:	Profit Sharing:	Top Exec. Salary: $519,537	Bonus: $346,394
Savings Plan:	Stock Purch. Plan:		Second Exec. Salary: $435,467	Bonus: $346,394

OTHER THOUGHTS:

Apparent Women Officers or Directors: 2
Hot Spot for Advancement for Women/Minorities:

LOCATIONS: ("Y" = Yes)

West:	Southwest:	Midwest:	Southeast:	Northeast:	International:
					Y

PEPCO HOLDINGS INC

www.pepcoholdings.com

Industry Group Code: 221 **Ranks within this company's industry group:** Sales: 18 Profits: 34

Exploration/Production:		Refining/Retailing:		Utilities:		Alternative Energy:		Specialty Services:		Energy Mktg./Other Svcs.	
Exploration:		Refining:		Electric Utility:	Y	Waste/Solar/Other:		Consulting/Eng.:		Energy Marketing:	Y
Production:		Retailing:		Gas Utility:	Y	Thermal/Steam:		Seismic:		Equipment/Machinery:	
Coal Production:		Convenience Stores:		Pipelines:		Wind:		Drilling:		Oil Field Services:	
		Chemicals:		Water:		Hydro:		InfoTech:		Air/Shipping Transportation:	
						Fuel Cells:		Specialty Services:			

TYPES OF BUSINESS:

Utilities-Electricity & Natural Gas
Gas & Electricity Marketing
Energy Investments

BRANDS/DIVISIONS/AFFILIATES:

Potomac Electric Power Company
Pepco Energy Services, Inc.
Delmarva Power and Light Company
Atlantic City Electric Company

CONTACTS: *Note: Officers with more than one job title may be intentionally listed here more than once.*

Joseph M. Rigby, CEO
Joseph M. Rigby, Pres.
Anthony J. Kamerick, CFO/Sr. VP
Kirk J. Emge, General Counsel/Sr. VP
Ronald K. Clark, Controller/VP
John U. Huffman, CEO/Pres., Pepco Energy Svcs.
Gary J. Morsches, CEO/Pres., Conectiv Energy
Beverly L. Perry, Sr. VP
Joseph M. Rigby, Chmn.

Phone: 202-872-2000	**Fax:** 202-331-6750
Toll-Free:	
Address: 701 9th St. NW, Washington, DC 20068 US	

GROWTH PLANS/SPECIAL FEATURES:

Pepco Holdings, Inc. (PHI) is a diversified energy company engaged in two principal business operations: electricity and natural gas delivery (Power Delivery); and competitive energy generation, marketing and supply. Power delivery, consisting of the distribution of electricity and natural gas, comprises the bulk of PHI's business. Power delivery is undertaken by subsidiaries Potomac Electric Power Company (Pepco); Delmarva Power and Light Company (DPL); and Atlantic City Electric Company (ACE). All three of these subsidiaries provide electricity to their customers, and DPL also delivers natural gas. Over 1.8 million customers use these services in Delaware, Washington, D.C., Maryland, New Jersey and Virginia. Pepco, DPL and ACE are members of the PJM Regional Transmission Organization. Subsidiary Pepco Energy Services, Inc. (PES) undertakes competitive energy generation, marketing and supply. It offers retail energy supply (including electricity and natural gas) and energy management services to commercial, industrial and government customers. In July 2010, the company sold power generation subsidiary, Conective Energy, to Calpine Corporation for $1.63 billion.

The firm offers employees medical, dental and vision insurance; a 401(k) plan; a pension plan; life insurance; disability coverage; travel insurance; healthcare and dependent care spending accounts; transportation spending accounts; and an educational assistance plan.

FINANCIALS: **Sales and profits are in thousands of dollars—add 000 to get the full amount. 2010 Note: Financial information for 2010 was not available for all companies at press time.**

2010 Sales: $	2010 Profits: $	**U.S. Stock Ticker: POM**
2009 Sales: $9,259,000	2009 Profits: $235,000	**Int'l Ticker:** Int'l Exchange:
2008 Sales: $10,700,000	2008 Profits: $300,000	Employees: 5,110
2007 Sales: $9,366,400	2007 Profits: $334,200	Fiscal Year Ends: 12/31
2006 Sales: $8,362,900	2006 Profits: $248,300	Parent Company:

SALARIES/BENEFITS:

Pension Plan: Y	ESOP Stock Plan:	Profit Sharing:	Top Exec. Salary: $796,669	Bonus: $
Savings Plan: Y	Stock Purch. Plan:		Second Exec. Salary: $446,295	Bonus: $

OTHER THOUGHTS:

Apparent Women Officers or Directors: 4
Hot Spot for Advancement for Women/Minorities: Y

LOCATIONS: ("Y" = Yes)

West:	Southwest:	Midwest:	Southeast:	Northeast:	International:
				Y	

PETROBRAS DISTRIBUIDORA SA

www.br.com.br

Industry Group Code: 486 **Ranks within this company's industry group:** Sales: Profits:

Exploration/Production:		**Refining/Retailing:**		**Utilities:**		**Alternative Energy:**		**Specialty Services:**		**Energy Mktg./Other Svcs.**	
Exploration:		Refining:		Electric Utility:		Waste/Solar/Other:		Consulting/Eng.:		Energy Marketing:	
Production:		Retailing:	Y	Gas Utility:		Thermal/Steam:		Seismic:		Equipment/Machinery:	
Coal Production:		Convenience Stores:		Pipelines:		Wind:		Drilling:		Oil Field Services:	
		Chemicals:		Water:		Hydro:		InfoTech:		Air/Shipping Transportation:	
						Fuel Cells:		Specialty Services:			

TYPES OF BUSINESS:

Fuel Distribution

BRANDS/DIVISIONS/AFFILIATES:

Petroleo Brasileiro SA (Petrobras)

CONTACTS:

Note: Officers with more than one job title may be intentionally listed here more than once.

Dilma Vana Rousseff, Chmn.

Phone: 55-21-3876-4477	**Fax:**
Toll-Free:	
Address: Rua General Canabarro 500, Maracana, Rio de Janeiro, 20271 Brazil	

GROWTH PLANS/SPECIAL FEATURES:

Petrobras Distribuidora S.A., a subsidiary of Brazilian energy giant Petroleo Brasileiro S.A. (Petrobras), is a distributor of oil products, ethanol, biodiesel and vehicular natural gas to retail, commercial and industrial customers. The products distributed by the firm are primarily supplied by Petrobras. Petrobras Distribuidora provides roughly 698 million barrels a day (mbbl/d) of oil products to wholesale and retail customers, of which the largest portion (39.6%) was diesel. The firm supplies products to a network of 6,782 BR-branded service stations in Brazil. Most company stations are owned by franchisees that use the BR brand name under license and purchase exclusively from Petrobras. Petrobras owns 656 of the BR stations and are required by law to subcontract the operation of these owned stations to third parties. The firm also distributes oil products and biofuels under the BR brand to commercial and industrial customers. Petrobras Distribuidora's customers include aviation, transportation and industrial companies, as well as utilities and government entities.

FINANCIALS:

Sales and profits are in thousands of dollars—add 000 to get the full amount. 2010 Note: Financial information for 2010 was not available for all companies at press time.

2010 Sales: $	2010 Profits: $	**U.S. Stock Ticker: Subsidiary**
2009 Sales: $	2009 Profits: $	**Int'l Ticker:** Int'l Exchange:
2008 Sales: $	2008 Profits: $	Employees:
2007 Sales: $	2007 Profits: $	Fiscal Year Ends: 12/31
2006 Sales: $	2006 Profits: $	Parent Company: PETROLEO BRASILEIRO SA (PETROBRAS)

SALARIES/BENEFITS:

Pension Plan:	ESOP Stock Plan:	Profit Sharing:	Top Exec. Salary: $	Bonus: $
Savings Plan:	Stock Purch. Plan:		Second Exec. Salary: $	Bonus: $

OTHER THOUGHTS:

Apparent Women Officers or Directors: 1

Hot Spot for Advancement for Women/Minorities:

LOCATIONS: ("Y" = Yes)

West:	Southwest:	Midwest:	Southeast:	Northeast:	International:
					Y

PETROBRAS ARGENTINA SA

www.petrobrasenergia.com

Industry Group Code: 211111 **Ranks within this company's industry group:** Sales: 65 Profits: 56

Exploration/Production:		Refining/Retailing:		Utilities:		Alternative Energy:		Specialty Services:		Energy Mktg./Other Svcs.	
Exploration:	Y	Refining:	Y	Electric Utility:	Y	Waste/Solar/Other:		Consulting/Eng.:		Energy Marketing:	Y
Production:	Y	Retailing:		Gas Utility:	Y	Thermal/Steam:		Seismic:		Equipment/Machinery:	
Coal Production:		Convenience Stores:		Pipelines:		Wind:		Drilling:		Oil Field Services:	
		Chemicals:	Y	Water:		Hydro:		InfoTech:		Air/Shipping Transportation:	Y
						Fuel Cells:		Specialty Services:			

TYPES OF BUSINESS:

Oil & Gas Exploration & Production
Electricity, Production & Distribution
Refining
Petrochemicals & Fertilizer
Transportation, Shipping & Storage
Gas Stations

BRANDS/DIVISIONS/AFFILIATES:

Perez Companc
Petrobras Energia S.A.
EBR Refinery
Ricardo Elicabe Refinery
Innova
Petroquimica Cuyo
Refinor

CONTACTS:

Note: Officers with more than one job title may be intentionally listed here more than once.

Carlos Alberto da Costa, CEO
Luis Miguel Sas, CFO
Adelson da Silca, Exec. Mgr.-Human Resources
Gustavo Fernandez Martinez, Dir.-Oil & Gas Exploration & Prod.
Daniel Casal, Dir.-Legal Affairs
Alfredo Guia Y Diaz, Exec. Mgr.-Planning & Mgmt. Control
Juan Zadjman, Exec. Mgr.-Comm.
Clovis Correa de Queiroz, Dir.-Commercial
Moreira Valdison, Dir.-Industrial
Juan Martin D'Agostino, Exec. Mgr.-Quality, Safety, Environment & Health
Jose Carlos Vilar Amigo, Chmn.

Phone: 54-11-4344-6000 **Fax:** 54-11-4344-6315
Toll-Free:
Address: Maipu 1, 22 Fl., Buenos Aires, C1084 ABA Argentina

GROWTH PLANS/SPECIAL FEATURES:

Petrobras Argentina S.A., formerly Petrobras Energia S.A., is an energy company focused on oil and gas exploration; production, refining and petrochemicals; electricity generation, transmission and distribution; and oil and gas transportation, storage and shipping. Petrobras, based in Argentina, has subsidiaries in Peru, Venezuela and Ecuador, with partial holdings in energy, petrochemical and transportation companies throughout South America. The company has proven oil reserves of approximately 758 million barrels oil equivalent, the majority coming from Argentina. Approximately 75% of these reserves are comprised of crude oil, while natural gas accounts for roughly 24.9%. Petrobras's refineries are located in Argentina and Bolivia. The firm operates two refineries and maintains approximately 644 gas stations in Argentina. In addition to gasoline, most stations offer compressed natural gas. Petrobras's petrochemical branch is operated through Brazilian subsidiary Innova, a producer of styrene and polystyrene. Additionally, the company operates in the electricity business, through interests in generation, transmission and distribution. In May 2010, Petrobras announced the sale of its San Lorenzo refining business for $74 million to Oil Combustibles S.A.

FINANCIALS:

Sales and profits are in thousands of dollars—add 000 to get the full amount. 2010 Note: Financial information for 2010 was not available for all companies at press time.

2010 Sales: $	2010 Profits: $	**U.S. Stock Ticker: PZE**
2009 Sales: $3,021,500	2009 Profits: $233,450	**Int'l Ticker: PBE** Int'l Exchange: Buenos Aires-BCBA
2008 Sales: $3,978,390	2008 Profits: $203,440	Employees:
2007 Sales: $3,528,520	2007 Profits: $199,770	Fiscal Year Ends: 12/31
2006 Sales: $3,745,735	2006 Profits: $310,736	Parent Company:

SALARIES/BENEFITS:

Pension Plan: ESOP Stock Plan: Profit Sharing: Top Exec. Salary: $ Bonus: $
Savings Plan: Stock Purch. Plan: Second Exec. Salary: $ Bonus: $

OTHER THOUGHTS:

Apparent Women Officers or Directors:
Hot Spot for Advancement for Women/Minorities:

LOCATIONS: ("Y" = Yes)

West:	Southwest:	Midwest:	Southeast:	Northeast:	International:
					Y

PETROCHINA COMPANY

www.petrochina.com.cn

Industry Group Code: 211111 **Ranks within this company's industry group:** Sales: 10 Profits: 7

Exploration/Production:		Refining/Retailing:		Utilities:		Alternative Energy:		Specialty Services:		Energy Mktg./Other Svcs.	
Exploration:	Y	Refining:	Y	Electric Utility:		Waste/Solar/Other:		Consulting/Eng.:		Energy Marketing:	
Production:	Y	Retailing:	Y	Gas Utility:		Thermal/Steam:		Seismic:		Equipment/Machinery:	
Coal Production:		Convenience Stores:	Y	Pipelines:	Y	Wind:		Drilling:		Oil Field Services:	
		Chemicals:	Y	Water:		Hydro:		InfoTech:		Air/Shipping Transportation:	
						Fuel Cells:		Specialty Services:			

TYPES OF BUSINESS:

Oil & Gas Exploration & Production
Chemicals, Lubricants & Petroleum Products
Oil Refining, Transportation & Marketing
Gas Stations

BRANDS/DIVISIONS/AFFILIATES:

China National Petroleum Company
Shell Energy Holdings Australia Ltd.
Jilin Chemical Industrial Company Ltd
PetroChina International Investment Australia Ltd.
Singapore Petroleum Company Ltd.
PetroChina International (Singapore) Pte Ltd

CONTACTS:

Note: Officers with more than one job title may be intentionally listed here more than once.

Zhou Jiping, Pres./Vice Chmn.
Zhou Mingchun, CFO
Liu Hongbin, VP/Gen. Mgr.-Mktg. Dept.
Wang Daofu, Chief Geologist
Lin Aiguo, Chief Engineer
Li Hualin, Sec./VP/Gen. Mgr.-China Petroleum Hongkong Holding
Zhou Mingchun, Gen. Mgr.-Finance Dept.
Shen Diancheng, VP/Gen. Mgr.-Refining & Chemicals Co.
Huang Weihe, Gen. Mgr.-PetroChina Natural Gas & Pipelines Co.
Zhao Zhengzhang, VP/Gen. Mgr.-Exploration & Prod. Co.
Jiang Jiemen, Chmn.
Bo Qilang, VP/Gen. Mgr.-PetroChina Int'l Ltd.

Phone: 86-10-5998-6223 **Fax:** 86-10-6209-9557
Toll-Free:
Address: 9 Dongzhimen N. St., Dongcheng District, Beijing, 100007 China

GROWTH PLANS/SPECIAL FEATURES:

PetroChina Company, headquartered in Beijing, is one of the largest oil and gas producers and distributors in China. The company is involved in a broad range of crude oil and natural gas operations, including the exploration, development, production and sale of crude oil and natural gas; crude oil and petroleum product refining, marketing and trading; basic petrochemical product, derivative chemical and other chemical production and marketing; and natural gas, crude oil and refined oil transmission. The company operates in four business segments: exploration and production; refining and chemicals; marketing; and natural gas and pipeline. The firm produces approximately 843.5 million barrels of crude oil a year and 2,112.2 billion cubic feet of natural gas, representing 2.31 barrels of crude oil and 5.79 billion cubic feet of natural gas per day. The firm also produces approximately 3.2 million tons of gasoline, diesel and kerosene annually. PetroChina markets refined petroleum products through roughly16,607 owned and operated retail service stations and 655 franchise service stations. The company also produces and sells chemical products, including ethylene, polyethylene and polypropylene. PetroChina has proven oil reserves of approximately 11.3 billion barrels of oil and 63,243.8 billion cubic feet of natural gas. The company is roughly 86.28%-owned by China National Petroleum Company (CNPC). In May 2009, the firm's indirect wholly-owned subsidiary, PetroChina International (Singapore) Pte. Ltd., agreed to acquire 45.51% of Singapore Petroleum Company Limited from Keppel Oil and Gas Services Pte. Ltd. for approximately $1 billion. In February 2010, PetroChina agreed to acquire certain oil sands assets in Canada from Athabasca Oil Sands Corp. In August 2010, subsidiary PetroChina International Investment Australia Ltd. and Shell Energy Holdings Australia Ltd. agreed to acquire, through their joint venture, Australia-based Arrow Energy Limited.

FINANCIALS:

Sales and profits are in thousands of dollars—add 000 to get the full amount. 2010 Note: Financial information for 2010 was not available for all companies at press time.

2010 Sales: $	2010 Profits: $	**U.S. Stock Ticker: PTR**
2009 Sales: $149,107,000	2009 Profits: $15,124,200	**Int'l Ticker: 0857** Int'l Exchange: Hong Kong-HKEX
2008 Sales: $156,490,000	2008 Profits: $18,503,200	Employees:
2007 Sales: $122,188,000	2007 Profits: $22,670,600	Fiscal Year Ends: 12/31
2006 Sales: $89,221,840	2006 Profits: $18,417,270	Parent Company:

SALARIES/BENEFITS:

Pension Plan:	ESOP Stock Plan:	Profit Sharing:	Top Exec. Salary: $	Bonus: $
Savings Plan:	Stock Purch. Plan:		Second Exec. Salary: $	Bonus: $

OTHER THOUGHTS:

Apparent Women Officers or Directors:
Hot Spot for Advancement for Women/Minorities:

LOCATIONS: ("Y" = Yes)

West:	Southwest:	Midwest:	Southeast:	Northeast:	International:
					Y

PETROLEO BRASILEIRO SA (PETROBRAS) www.petrobras.com.br

Industry Group Code: 211111 **Ranks within this company's industry group:** Sales: 12 Profits: 5

Exploration/Production:		Refining/Retailing:		Utilities:		Alternative Energy:		Specialty Services:		Energy Mktg./Other Svcs.	
Exploration:	Y	Refining:	Y	Electric Utility:		Waste/Solar/Other:		Consulting/Eng.:		Energy Marketing:	Y
Production:	Y	Retailing:	Y	Gas Utility:		Thermal/Steam:		Seismic:		Equipment/Machinery:	
Coal Production:		Convenience Stores:	Y	Pipelines:	Y	Wind:		Drilling:		Oil Field Services:	
		Chemicals:		Water:		Hydro:		InfoTech:		Air/Shipping Transportation:	Y
						Fuel Cells:		Specialty Services:			

TYPES OF BUSINESS:

Oil & Gas Exploration & Production
Oil Refineries
Service Stations
Transportation & Pipelines
Energy Trading

BRANDS/DIVISIONS/AFFILIATES:

Petrobras
Petrobras de Valores Internacional de Espana SL
Petrobras Participaciones SL
Petrobras Venezuela Investments & Services BV
Petrobras Energia Participaciones SA
Chevron Chile SAC

CONTACTS: *Note: Officers with more than one job title may be intentionally listed here more than once.*

Jose S. G. de Azevedo, CEO
Almir G. Barbassa, CFO
Guilherme de O. Estrella, Chief Exploration & Prod. Officer
Almir G. Barbassa, Chief Investor Rel. Officer
Paulo R. Costa, Chief Downstream Officer
Maria das G.S. Foster, Chief Gas & Energy Officer
Renato de S. Duque, Chief Svcs. Officer
Dilma V. Rousseff, Chmn.
Jorge L. Zelada, Chief Int'l Officer

Phone: 55-21-3224-2040 **Fax:**
Toll-Free:
Address: 65 Ave. Republica do Chile, Rio de Janeiro, 20031-912 Brazil

GROWTH PLANS/SPECIAL FEATURES:

Petroleo Brasileiro S.A., known as Petrobras, is owned primarily by the Brazilian government and is one of the country's largest energy companies. It refines, produces and distributes oil and oil-based products both nationally and internationally. The firm divides company activities into five business sectors: exploration and production; supply; distribution; gas and energy; and international. Petrobas' exploration and production unit researches, identifies, develops, produces and incorporates oil and natural gas reserves in Brazil. It currently produces roughly 2.4 million barrels of oil per day equivalent. The company's supply business includes 11 oil refineries and roughly 8,595 miles of pipeline that operate approximately 98.4% of Brazil's total refining capacity. Petrobras distributes approximately 34.9% of the demand for petroleum byproducts in Brazil through nearly 6,800 service stations. The gas and energy segment markets domestic and imported natural gas and implements project with the private sector to guarantee fuel throughout Brazil. This division also develops/invests in alternative energy sources, including wind, solar and biofuel energy. Internationally, Petrobras operates in 23 countries, maintaining international operations including exploration and petroleum procurement. Subsidiary Petrobras Transporte S.A. is responsible for the transportation and storage of the firm's oil and gas. The firm sells fuels and lubricants for the auto, aviation, marine, railroad, and other industries. Petrobras has a research staff of more than 1,800 people and a massive exploration budget. It will invest $174.5 billion from 2009 through 2013 in improvements and new fields, concentrating on finds in deep offshore waters, including the new Tupi field, which may contain as many as 8 billion barrels of oil. In April 2009, the company acquired the remaining 60% interest in now wholly-owned subsidiary Petrobras de Valores Internacional de Espana S.L.; and subsidiaries Petrobras Participaciones, S.L. and Petrobras Venezuela Investments & Services B.V. acquired the Chilean distribution/logistics operations of ExxonMobil. In November 2009, Petrobas acquired Chevron Chile S.A.C.

FINANCIALS: **Sales and profits are in thousands of dollars—add 000 to get the full amount. 2010 Note: Financial information for 2010 was not available for all companies at press time.**

2010 Sales: $	2010 Profits: $	**U.S. Stock Ticker: PBR**
2009 Sales: $103,523,000	2009 Profits: $16,421,100	**Int'l Ticker: PETR3** Int'l Exchange:
2008 Sales: $118,257,000	2008 Profits: $18,879,000	Employees:
2007 Sales: $87,735,000	2007 Profits: $13,138,000	Fiscal Year Ends: 12/31
2006 Sales: $93,893,000	2006 Profits: $12,826,000	Parent Company:

SALARIES/BENEFITS:

Pension Plan:	ESOP Stock Plan:	Profit Sharing:	Top Exec. Salary: $	Bonus: $
Savings Plan:	Stock Purch. Plan:		Second Exec. Salary: $	Bonus: $

OTHER THOUGHTS:

Apparent Women Officers or Directors: 2
Hot Spot for Advancement for Women/Minorities:

LOCATIONS: ("Y" = Yes)

West:	Southwest:	Midwest:	Southeast:	Northeast:	International:
	Y			Y	Y

PETROLEOS DE VENEZUELA SA (PDVSA)

www.pdvsa.com.ve

Industry Group Code: 211111 **Ranks within this company's industry group:** Sales: 15 Profits:

Exploration/Production:		Refining/Retailing:		Utilities:		Alternative Energy:		Specialty Services:		Energy Mktg./Other Svcs.	
Exploration:	Y	Refining:	Y	Electric Utility:		Waste/Solar/Other:		Consulting/Eng.:		Energy Marketing:	
Production:	Y	Retailing:	Y	Gas Utility:		Thermal/Steam:		Seismic:		Equipment/Machinery:	
Coal Production:		Convenience Stores:	Y	Pipelines:		Wind:		Drilling:		Oil Field Services:	
		Chemicals:	Y	Water:		Hydro:		InfoTech:		Air/Shipping Transportation:	Y
						Fuel Cells:		Specialty Services:	Y		

TYPES OF BUSINESS:

Oil & Gas-Exploration & Production
Petroleum Refining
Petrochemicals Manufacturing
Asphalt Refining
Gas Stations
Crude Oil Distribution
Financial Services

BRANDS/DIVISIONS/AFFILIATES:

CITGO Petroleum Corporation
PDV America Inc
Orinoco Belt

CONTACTS:

Note: Officers with more than one job title may be intentionally listed here more than once.

Rafael Ramirez Carreno, CEO
Rafael Ramirez Carreno, Pres.
Hercilio Rivas, Dir.-R&D
Ricardo Coronado, Dir.-Prod. & Svcs.
Fadi Kabboul, Dir.-Planning & Control
Eudomario Carruyo, Dir.-Finance
Asdrubal Chavez, VP-Refining, Commerce & Supply
Carlos Vallejo, Dir.-Gas
Eulogio Del Pino, VP-Exploration & Prod.
Luis Pulido, Dir.-Logistics & Prod.

Phone: 58-212-708-4111 **Fax:** 58-212-708-4661
Toll-Free:
Address: Avenida Libertado, La Camina, Apdo. 169, Caracas, 1010-A Venezuela

GROWTH PLANS/SPECIAL FEATURES:

Petroleos de Venezuela S.A. (PDVSA), the national oil company of Venezuela, is one of the world's top exporters of crude oil. Within Venezuela, the company conducts exploration and harvesting of oil reserves, along with light refining activities. The company has a daily production of over 3 million barrels and over 77 billion barrels of proven reserves. In the U.S., where most of its crude oil is shipped, the company works through a number of subsidiaries, including CITGO Petroleum Corporation. Owned through PDVSA subsidiary PDV America, Inc., CITGO has some of the largest refining operations in the U.S., with a combined crude oil refining capacity of roughly 203 million barrels per year. Its refineries, which mainly process Venezuelan oil, are located in Lemont, Illinois; Lake Charles, Louisiana; and Corpus Christi, Texas. CITGO also operates a national chain of roughly 8,000 branded gas stations, which sell over 12 billion gallons of gasoline annually. PDVSA hopes to actively promote the economic integration of the oil industry in Latin America, an integration that it has already established throughout the Caribbean with the Petrocaribe agreement. Since Venezuela belongs to and, indeed, helped found OPEC (the Organization of Petroleum Exporting Countries) in 1960, OPEC's agreements and mandates strongly affect PDVSA's policies. After nationalizing all 32 companies operating in the area of Venezuela known as the Orinoco Belt, the company is the dominant player in the Venezuelan oil industry. In April 2010, PDVSA agreed to establish joint venture (through Venezuelan Petroleum Corporation) Petromiranda with the Russian National Oil Consortium. Petromiranda, which will operate in Block Junin 6 of the Orinoco Oil Belt, will be 60% owned by PDVSA.

FINANCIALS:

Sales and profits are in thousands of dollars—add 000 to get the full amount. 2010 Note: Financial information for 2010 was not available for all companies at press time.

2010 Sales: $	2010 Profits: $	**U.S. Stock Ticker: Government-Owned**
2009 Sales: $90,000,000	2009 Profits: $	**Int'l Ticker:** Int'l Exchange:
2008 Sales: $126,364,000	2008 Profits: $7,451,000	Employees: 78,739
2007 Sales: $120,000,000	2007 Profits: $	Fiscal Year Ends: 12/31
2006 Sales: $100,000,000	2006 Profits: $	Parent Company:

SALARIES/BENEFITS:

Pension Plan:	ESOP Stock Plan:	Profit Sharing:	Top Exec. Salary: $	Bonus: $
Savings Plan:	Stock Purch. Plan:		Second Exec. Salary: $	Bonus: $

OTHER THOUGHTS:

Apparent Women Officers or Directors:
Hot Spot for Advancement for Women/Minorities:

LOCATIONS: ("Y" = Yes)

West:	Southwest:	Midwest:	Southeast:	Northeast:	International:
	Y			Y	Y

PETROLEOS MEXICANOS (PEMEX)

www.pemex.com

Industry Group Code: 211111 **Ranks within this company's industry group:** Sales: 16 Profits:

Exploration/Production:		Refining/Retailing:		Utilities:		Alternative Energy:		Specialty Services:		Energy Mktg./Other Svcs.	
Exploration:	Y	Refining:	Y	Electric Utility:		Waste/Solar/Other:		Consulting/Eng.:		Energy Marketing:	
Production:	Y	Retailing:	Y	Gas Utility:		Thermal/Steam:		Seismic:		Equipment/Machinery:	
Coal Production:		Convenience Stores:		Pipelines:		Wind:		Drilling:		Oil Field Services:	
		Chemicals:	Y	Water:		Hydro:		InfoTech:		Air/Shipping Transportation:	
						Fuel Cells:		Specialty Services:	Y		

TYPES OF BUSINESS:

Oil & Gas Exploration & Production
Oil & Gas Transportation & Storage
Gas Stations
Refining
Petrochemicals

BRANDS/DIVISIONS/AFFILIATES:

PMI Comercio Internacional
Pemex Exploration and Production
Pemex Refining
Pemex Gas and Basic Petrochemicals
Pemex Petrochemicals

CONTACTS:

Note: Officers with more than one job title may be intentionally listed here more than once.

Juan Jose Suarez Coppel, CEO
Carlos Murrieta Cummings, Dir.-Oper.
Carlos Trevino Medina, CFO
Carlos Arnoldo Morales Gil, Dir.-Exploration & Prod.
Mauricio Abraham Galan Ramirez, Dir.-IT & Bus. Processes
Jordy Herrera Flores, Dir.-Gas & Basic Petrochemicals
Jose Antonio Ceballos Soberanis, Dir.-Refining Unit
Rafael Beverido Lomelin, Dir.-Petrochemicals Unit
Georgina K. Martinez, Chmn.
Maria del Rocio Cardenas Zubieta, CEO-PMI Comercio Internacional S.A. de C.V.

Phone: 52-55-1944--2500 **Fax:** 52-55-1944-8768
Toll-Free:
Address: Avenida Marina Nacional 329, Mexico City, 11311 Mexico

GROWTH PLANS/SPECIAL FEATURES:

Petroleos Mexicanos (Pemex) is Mexico's national petroleum company and an essential source of revenue for the country's government. Pemex, under Mexican Law, has the exclusive right to explore, exploit, refine/produce, transport and sell crude oil, natural gas and other petroleum derivatives in Mexico. The company operates through four subsidiaries: Pemex Exploration and Production; Pemex Refining; Pemex Gas and Basic Petrochemicals; and Pemex Petrochemicals. The exploration and production segment has operations throughout Mexico and produces roughly 2.9 million barrels of crude oil daily. Pemex Refining converts crude oil into gasoline, jet fuel, diesel, fuel oil, asphalts and lubricants at its six refineries and petrochemical plants. This segment also markets and distributes these products through Petroleos Mexicanos gas stations, with thousands of franchised locations. Pemex Gas and Basic Petrochemicals subsidiary processed wet natural gas into dry natural gas, LPG and other natural gas liquids. It also transports, distributes and sells natural gas, LPG and basic petrochemical feedstock, used by Pemex Refining and Pemex Petrochemicals, throughout Mexico. Pemex Petrochemicals manufactures petrochemical products including methane derivatives, such as ammonia and methanol; ethane derivatives, such as ethylene; aromatics and their derivatives; propylene and its derivatives; and oxygen, nitrogen and other products. The company's PMI Comercio Internacional subsidiary (Pemex International) provides administrative and commercial services for the international sale of oil and for cooperation with foreign companies. The U.S. purchases approximately 80% of the total of the company's crude oil exports.

FINANCIALS:

Sales and profits are in thousands of dollars—add 000 to get the full amount. 2010 Note: Financial information for 2010 was not available for all companies at press time.

2010 Sales: $	2010 Profits: $	**U.S. Stock Ticker: Government-Owned**
2009 Sales: $85,000,000	2009 Profits: $	**Int'l Ticker:** Int'l Exchange:
2008 Sales: $98,200,000	2008 Profits: $-8,100,000	Employees:
2007 Sales: $104,548,000	2007 Profits: $-1,685,000	Fiscal Year Ends: 12/31
2006 Sales: $105,115,540	2006 Profits: $4,201,160	Parent Company:

SALARIES/BENEFITS:

Pension Plan:	ESOP Stock Plan:	Profit Sharing:	Top Exec. Salary: $	Bonus: $
Savings Plan:	Stock Purch. Plan:		Second Exec. Salary: $	Bonus: $

OTHER THOUGHTS:

Apparent Women Officers or Directors: 2
Hot Spot for Advancement for Women/Minorities:

LOCATIONS: ("Y" = Yes)

West:	Southwest:	Midwest:	Southeast:	Northeast:	International:
	Y				Y

PETROLEUM DEVELOPMENT CORPORATION

www.petd.com

Industry Group Code: 211111 **Ranks within this company's industry group:** Sales: 99 Profits: 85

Exploration/Production:		Refining/Retailing:		Utilities:		Alternative Energy:		Specialty Services:		Energy Mktg./Other Svcs.	
Exploration:	Y	Refining:		Electric Utility:		Waste/Solar/Other:		Consulting/Eng.:		Energy Marketing:	Y
Production:	Y	Retailing:		Gas Utility:		Thermal/Steam:		Seismic:		Equipment/Machinery:	
Coal Production:		Convenience Stores:		Pipelines:		Wind:		Drilling:		Oil Field Services:	
		Chemicals:		Water:		Hydro:		InfoTech:		Air/Shipping Transportation:	
						Fuel Cells:		Specialty Services:			

TYPES OF BUSINESS:

Oil & Gas Production
Gas Marketing

BRANDS/DIVISIONS/AFFILIATES:

Riley Natural Gas
PDC Energy

CONTACTS:

Note: Officers with more than one job title may be intentionally listed here more than once.

Richard W. McCullough, CEO
Gysle R. Shellum, CFO
Tina R. Smith, VP-Natural Gas & Oil Mktg.
John A. DeLawder, VP-Human Resources
Karen S. Griffin, Dir.-IT
Susan A. Foster, Dir.-Reserve Eng.
John A. DeLawder, VP-Admin.
Daniel W. Amidon, General Counsel
Scott J. Reasoner, VP-Oper.
Lance A. Lauck, Sr. VP-Bus. Dev.
Marti Dowling, Mgr.-Investor Rel.
Peter G. Schreck, VP-Finance/Treas.
Barton R. Brookman, Sr. VP-Exploration & Prod.
Celesta M. Miracle, VP-Strategic Planning
R. Scott Meyers, Chief Acct. Officer
James R. Schaff, VP-Land
Richard W. McCullough, Chmn.

Phone: 303-860-5800	**Fax:** 303-860-5838
Toll-Free:	
Address: 1775 Sherman St., Ste. 3000, Denver, CO 80203 US	

GROWTH PLANS/SPECIAL FEATURES:

Petroleum Development Corporation, doing business as PDC Energy, is an independent energy company engaged in the exploration, acquisition, development, production and marketing of natural gas and oil. The company owns interest in approximately 5,000 wells located in the Rocky Mountain Region and the Appalachian Basin. PDC Energy's wells have net proved reserves of roughly 717 billion cubic feet equivalent. About 82% of the company's production consists of natural gas; 87% of its total production is generated by the Rocky Mountain Region properties, and 9.4% by its Appalachian Basin properties. The firm operates in two segments: natural gas and oil sales; and natural gas marketing. The natural gas and oil sales segment primarily constitutes revenues and expenses from the production and sale of natural gas and oil. The natural gas marketing segment operates through Riley Natural Gas (RNG), which purchases, aggregates and resells natural gas developed by the firm and other producers. During 2009, PDC Energy drilled about 80 wells, with plans to drill an additional 250 wells during 2010. In 2009, the firm moved its corporate headquarters to Denver, Colorado. In November 2009, the company and Lime Rock Partners formed a joint venture, PDC Mountaineer LLC, in the Appalachian region for the development of the Marcellus Shale resource play. In May 2010, PDC Energy acquired certain producing assets in the Wolfberry oil trend in Texas in exchange for its fully-developed producing Michigan Gas assets. In June 2010, the firm agreed to increase its ownership in the Wattenberg Niobrara area in Colorado to 70,000 acres. In July 2010, the company announced that it would begin doing business as PDC Energy.

FINANCIALS:

Sales and profits are in thousands of dollars—add 000 to get the full amount. 2010 Note: Financial information for 2010 was not available for all companies at press time.

2010 Sales: $	2010 Profits: $	**U.S. Stock Ticker: PETD**
2009 Sales: $254,800	2009 Profits: $-79,300	**Int'l Ticker:** Int'l Exchange:
2008 Sales: $473,900	2008 Profits: $113,300	Employees: 326
2007 Sales: $305,235	2007 Profits: $33,209	Fiscal Year Ends: 12/31
2006 Sales: $286,503	2006 Profits: $237,772	Parent Company:

SALARIES/BENEFITS:

Pension Plan:	ESOP Stock Plan:	Profit Sharing:	Top Exec. Salary: $450,000	Bonus: $788,000
Savings Plan:	Stock Purch. Plan:		Second Exec. Salary: $270,000	Bonus: $235,000

OTHER THOUGHTS:

Apparent Women Officers or Directors: 5
Hot Spot for Advancement for Women/Minorities: Y

LOCATIONS: ("Y" = Yes)

West:	Southwest:	Midwest:	Southeast:	Northeast:	International:
Y				Y	

PETROLEUM GEO SERVICES ASA

www.pgs.com

Industry Group Code: 213112 **Ranks within this company's industry group:** Sales: 17 Profits: 10

Exploration/Production:		Refining/Retailing:		Utilities:		Alternative Energy:		Specialty Services:		Energy Mktg./Other Svcs.	
Exploration:		Refining:		Electric Utility:		Waste/Solar/Other:		Consulting/Eng.:	Y	Energy Marketing:	
Production:		Retailing:		Gas Utility:		Thermal/Steam:		Seismic:	Y	Equipment/Machinery:	Y
Coal Production:		Convenience Stores:		Pipelines:		Wind:		Drilling:		Oil Field Services:	Y
		Chemicals:		Water:		Hydro:		InfoTech:	Y	Air/Shipping Transportation:	
						Fuel Cells:		Specialty Services:	Y		

TYPES OF BUSINESS:

Oil & Gas Drilling Support Services
Seismic Data Acquisition & Analysis
Marine Survey Services

BRANDS/DIVISIONS/AFFILIATES:

PGS Data Processing & Technology
GeoStreamer
HD3D
HD4D
PGS Reservoir

CONTACTS:

Note: Officers with more than one job title may be intentionally listed here more than once.

Jon Erik Reinhardsen, CEO
Jon Erik Reinhardsen, Pres.
Gottfred Langseth, CFO/Exec. VP
Terje Bjolseth, Sr. VP-Human Resources
Guillaume Cambois, Exec. VP-Data Processing
Guillaume Cambois, Exec. VP-Tech.
Espen Sandvik, General Counsel
Magne Reiersgard, Exec. VP-Oper.
Jostein Ueland, Sr. VP-Bus. Dev.
Tore Langballe, Sr. VP-Group Comm.
Bard Stenberg, Mgr.-Investor Rel.
Per Arild Reksnes, Exec. VP-New Ventures
Sverre Strandenes, Exec VP-Multi-Client Svcs. & Marine Contract
Francis Gugen, Chmn.

Phone: 47-67-52-64-00	**Fax:** 47-67-52-64-64
Toll-Free:	
Address: Strandveien 4, Lysaker, N-1326 Norway	

GROWTH PLANS/SPECIAL FEATURES:

Petroleum Geo-Services ASA (PGS), based in Norway, develops technological solutions for geophysical and reservoir surveying, analysis and data acquisition, supporting the oil exploration and production industry from offices on six continents and in nearly 25 countries. The firm's two business units are the marine geophysical group and the data processing and technology group. The marine geophysical group acquires, processes, markets and sells seismic data to companies and government agencies worldwide. The group maintains a fleet of vessels including two classic streamer ships, which are able to tow six streamers, and eight Ramform ships, which are able to tow up to 22 streamers. Additionally, the company operates three 2D vessels equipped with the PGS GeoStreamer, a dual sensor streamer technology, and a 3D vessel equipped with GeoStreamer. PGS also utilizes HD3D and 4D (Higher Density) seismic data products used for exploration, detailed reservoir description and time-lapse reservoir monitoring. The data processing and technology group, operated as a discrete organization, maintains over 23 processing centers, from which it offers a myriad of technological and applied geophysical services. A list of its offerings includes depth processing solutions; reservoir interpretation; Multi Transient EM (MTEM), a technology that can identify the presents of hydrocarbons prior to engaging in drilling projects; seismic modeling and survey design; and a data library. The company also offers interpretation services through PGS Reservoir, a geophysical, reservoir engineering and petroleum economics team. In February 2010, the firm completed the sale of its onshore operating group to Geokinetics for a combination of $185 million in cash and 2.15 million shares of Geokinetics. In June 2010, PGS and Shell announced a collaboration agreement to develop an ultra-high channel count fiber-optic seismic sensing system that will cancel image noise and increase image resolution on reservoir data.

FINANCIALS:

Sales and profits are in thousands of dollars—add 000 to get the full amount. 2010 Note: Financial information for 2010 was not available for all companies at press time.

2010 Sales: $	2010 Profits: $	**U.S. Stock Ticker:**
2009 Sales: $1,350,200	2009 Profits: $165,800	**Int'l Ticker: PGS** Int'l Exchange: Oslo-OBX
2008 Sales: $1,647,400	2008 Profits: $417,400	Employees: 2,680
2007 Sales: $1,519,900	2007 Profits: $470,000	Fiscal Year Ends: 12/31
2006 Sales: $1,308,500	2006 Profits: $298,600	Parent Company:

SALARIES/BENEFITS:

Pension Plan:	ESOP Stock Plan:	Profit Sharing:	Top Exec. Salary: $	Bonus: $
Savings Plan:	Stock Purch. Plan:		Second Exec. Salary: $	Bonus: $

OTHER THOUGHTS:

Apparent Women Officers or Directors:
Hot Spot for Advancement for Women/Minorities:

LOCATIONS: ("Y" = Yes)

West:	Southwest:	Midwest:	Southeast:	Northeast:	International:
	Y				Y

PETRON CORP

www.petron.com

Industry Group Code: 324110 **Ranks within this company's industry group:** Sales: 24 Profits: 15

Exploration/Production:		Refining/Retailing:		Utilities:		Alternative Energy:		Specialty Services:		Energy Mktg./Other Svcs.	
Exploration:		Refining:	Y	Electric Utility:		Waste/Solar/Other:		Consulting/Eng.:		Energy Marketing:	Y
Production:		Retailing:	Y	Gas Utility:		Thermal/Steam:		Seismic:		Equipment/Machinery:	
Coal Production:		Convenience Stores:	Y	Pipelines:		Wind:		Drilling:		Oil Field Services:	
		Chemicals:		Water:		Hydro:		InfoTech:		Air/Shipping Transportation:	
						Fuel Cells:		Specialty Services:	Y		

TYPES OF BUSINESS:

Petroleum Refining
Fuel Retailing
Jet Fuels
Lubricants
Convenience Stores
Lube & Tire Shops

BRANDS/DIVISIONS/AFFILIATES:

Ashmore Group Inc
Treats
Gasul
XCS Plus
DieselMax
Blaze
Petrochemical Asia (HK) Ltd.
Limay Energen Corp.

CONTACTS: *Note: Officers with more than one job title may be intentionally listed here more than once.*

Ramon S. Ang, CEO
Eric O. Recto, Pres.
Emmanuel E. Erana, CFO/Sr. VP
Ramon V. Del Rosario, VP-Retail Mktg.
Peter Paul V. Shotwell, VP-Depot & Plant Oper.
Concepcion F. De Claro, VP-Corp. Planning
Christina M. Menorca, Controller/VP
Lubin B. Nepomuneco, Sr. VP/Gen. Mgr.
Miguel V. Angeles, VP-Commercial Mktg.
Susan Y. Yu, VP-Procurement
Albert S. Sarte, Treas./VP
Ramon S. Ang, Chmn.
Rowena O. Cortez, VP-Supply

Phone: 63-2-886-3888 **Fax:** 63-2-884-0945
Toll-Free:
Address: 40 San Miguel Ave., SMC Head Office Complex, Manila, 1550 Philippines

GROWTH PLANS/SPECIAL FEATURES:

Petron Corp. is one of the largest oil refining and marketing companies in the Philippines. Supplying nearly 40% of the country's oil requirements, Petron's Limay, Bataan refinery has a capacity of 180,000 barrels per day, processing crude oil into a variety of petroleum products, including liquid petroleum gas (LPG), gasoline, diesel, jet fuel, kerosene, industrial fuel oil, solvents, asphalts and mixed xylene and propylene. The company also operates a fully automated lube oil blending plant in Pandacan, where it manufactures lubes and greases that are sold through service stations and sales centers. In addition, the firm operates a blending plant in Subic Bay that produces additives for its fuels brands Blaze, XCS Plus, Xtra Unleaded and DieselMax. Petron transports its petroleum products from the refinery in Limay to 32 depots and terminals throughout the Philippines, supplying fuel oil, diesel and LPG to industrial customers, including companies in the power generation, construction, land and marine transports, fishing and manufacturing sectors. Petron also supplies jet fuel at key airports to international and domestic carriers. The company also markets its Gasul brand of LPG to household customers. Petron markets gasoline, diesel, and kerosene to motorists and public transport operators through its 1,400 service stations, as well as its Treats-brand convenience stores. Private equity firm the Ashmore Group owns a majority stake in the company. In July 2010, the firm announced plans to construct a 70-megawatt (MW) power plant at its Limay refinery; and acquired a 40% stake in Petrochemical Asia (HK) Ltd. In October 2010, the company formed a joint venture, Limay Energen Corp., with Two San Isidro SIAI Assets, Inc. to engage in power generation.

FINANCIALS: **Sales and profits are in thousands of dollars—add 000 to get the full amount. 2010 Note: Financial information for 2010 was not available for all companies at press time.**

2010 Sales: $	2010 Profits: $	**U.S. Stock Ticker:**
2009 Sales: $4,149,660	2009 Profits: $99,620	**Int'l Ticker: PCOR** Int'l Exchange: Pasig-PSE
2008 Sales: $5,608,300	2008 Profits: $-82,130	Employees: 1,347
2007 Sales: $4,210,400	2007 Profits: $127,500	Fiscal Year Ends: 12/31
2006 Sales: $4,234,500	2006 Profits: $120,200	Parent Company:

SALARIES/BENEFITS:

Pension Plan:	ESOP Stock Plan:	Profit Sharing:	Top Exec. Salary: $	Bonus: $
Savings Plan:	Stock Purch. Plan:		Second Exec. Salary: $	Bonus: $

OTHER THOUGHTS:

Apparent Women Officers or Directors: 4
Hot Spot for Advancement for Women/Minorities: Y

LOCATIONS: ("Y" = Yes)

West:	Southwest:	Midwest:	Southeast:	Northeast:	International:
					Y

PETRONAS (PETROLIAM NASIONAL BERHAD) www.petronas.com.my

Industry Group Code: 211111 **Ranks within this company's industry group:** Sales: 18 Profits: 6

Exploration/Production:		Refining/Retailing:		Utilities:		Alternative Energy:		Specialty Services:		Energy Mktg./Other Svcs.	
Exploration:	Y	Refining:	Y	Electric Utility:		Waste/Solar/Other:		Consulting/Eng.:		Energy Marketing:	Y
Production:	Y	Retailing:	Y	Gas Utility:		Thermal/Steam:		Seismic:		Equipment/Machinery:	
Coal Production:		Convenience Stores:	Y	Pipelines:	Y	Wind:		Drilling:		Oil Field Services:	
		Chemicals:	Y	Water:		Hydro:		InfoTech:		Air/Shipping Transportation:	Y
						Fuel Cells:		Specialty Services:			

TYPES OF BUSINESS:

Oil & Gas Exploration & Production
Oil & Gas Refining, Marketing & Distribution
Oil & Gas Transportation & Storage
Gasoline Retailing
Petrochemical Manufacturing & Marketing
Shipping
Methanol

BRANDS/DIVISIONS/AFFILIATES:

PETRONAS

CONTACTS: *Note: Officers with more than one job title may be intentionally listed here more than once.*

Shamsul Azhar Abbas, CEO
Shamsul Azhar Abbas, Pres.
Juniwait Rahmat Hussin, VP-Human Resource Mgmt.
Colin Wong Hee Huing, VP-Research
Colin Wong Hee Huing, VP-Tech. Div.
Azhar Osman Khairuddin, VP-Legal
Mohammed Arif Mahmood, VP-Corp. Strategic Planning
George Ratilal, Exec. VP-Finance
Wee Yiaw Hin, Exec. VP-Exploration & Production Bus.
Anuar Ahmad, Exec VP-Gas & Power Bus.
Wan Zulkiflee Wan Ariffin, Exec. VP-Downstream
Nasarudin Mohammad Idris, Pres./CEO-Misc. Berhad
Shamsul Azhar Abbas, Chmn.

Phone: 603-2051-5000 **Fax:** 603-2026-5050
Toll-Free:
Address: Twr. 1, Petronas Twin Twrs., Kuala Lumpur City Ctr, Kuala Lumpur, 50088 Malaysia

GROWTH PLANS/SPECIAL FEATURES:

PETRONAS (Petroliam Nasional Berhad) is the national petroleum company of Malaysia. It is engaged in the exploration and production of oil and gas; oil refining; marketing and distributing petroleum products; trading; gas processing and liquefaction; gas transmission pipeline network operations; marketing of liquefied natural gas; petrochemical manufacturing and marketing; shipping; and property investment. It operates through approximately 42 wholly-owned subsidiaries, 20 partly-owned subsidiaries and 25 associated companies. Domestic exploration and production is conducted through contracts with various international companies, including ExxonMobile, Shell and ChevronTexaco. The company has 53 productive oil fields and 22 gas fields in Malaysia, producing approximately 1.75 million barrels of oil equivalent (BOE) every day; and other production facilities in 33 countries with proved reserves of 27.1 billion BOE. PETRONAS owns and runs two refineries and operates several petrochemical complexes. It operates a fleet of tankers ships and has international pipeline interests in several countries; and also owns and operates over 700 gasoline service stations in Malaysia. PETRONAS maintains a production sharing contract with ExxonMobil Exploration, Production Malaysia Inc., and PETRONAS Carigali Sdn Bhd which allows the partners to continue participation in seven oil fields offshore Peninsular Malaysia. PETRONAS also has a 40% interest in Santos Limited of Australia's integrated liquefied natural gas project. In May 2010, the company announced a joint venture agreement with Repsol YPF, ONGC Videsh Ltd., Indian Oil Corporation Ltd., and Oil India Limited in coordination with Venezuelan company Petroleos De Venezuela S.A. for the development of a hydrocarbons project in Venezuela. In September 2010, PETRONAS signed an agreement with British Petroleum to acquire BP's 15% interest in Ethylene Malaysia and its 60% interest in Polyethylene Malaysia.

PETRONAS offers its employees housing and vehicle loans; medical and dental care; and transfer allowances. Employees working in Sabah, Sarawak or the Wilayah Persekutuan Labuan areas are paid additional wages, called the East Malaysia Allowance.

FINANCIALS: **Sales and profits are in thousands of dollars—add 000 to get the full amount. 2010 Note: Financial information for 2010 was not available for all companies at press time.**

2010 Sales: $	2010 Profits: $	**U.S. Stock Ticker: Government-Owned**
2009 Sales: $79,590,800	2009 Profits: $15,815,700	**Int'l Ticker:** Int'l Exchange:
2008 Sales: $76,965,000	2008 Profits: $15,309,000	Employees:
2007 Sales: $50,984,000	2007 Profits: $14,446,000	Fiscal Year Ends: 3/31
2006 Sales: $44,425,000	2006 Profits: $12,719,000	Parent Company:

SALARIES/BENEFITS:

Pension Plan: Y	ESOP Stock Plan:	Profit Sharing:	Top Exec. Salary: $	Bonus: $
Savings Plan:	Stock Purch. Plan:		Second Exec. Salary: $	Bonus: $

OTHER THOUGHTS:

Apparent Women Officers or Directors: 3
Hot Spot for Advancement for Women/Minorities: Y

LOCATIONS: ("Y" = Yes)

West:	Southwest:	Midwest:	Southeast:	Northeast:	International:
					Y

PETROQUEST ENERGY INC

www.petroquest.com

Industry Group Code: 211111 **Ranks within this company's industry group:** Sales: 100 Profits: 86

Exploration/Production:		**Refining/Retailing:**		**Utilities:**		**Alternative Energy:**		**Specialty Services:**		**Energy Mktg./Other Svcs.**	
Exploration:	Y	Refining:		Electric Utility:		Waste/Solar/Other:		Consulting/Eng.:		Energy Marketing:	
Production:	Y	Retailing:		Gas Utility:		Thermal/Steam:		Seismic:		Equipment/Machinery:	
Coal Production:		Convenience Stores:		Pipelines:		Wind:		Drilling:		Oil Field Services:	
		Chemicals:		Water:		Hydro:		InfoTech:		Air/Shipping Transportation:	
						Fuel Cells:		Specialty Services:			

TYPES OF BUSINESS:

Oil & Gas Exploration & Production

BRANDS/DIVISIONS/AFFILIATES:

CONTACTS:

Note: Officers with more than one job title may be intentionally listed here more than once.

Charles T. Goodson, CEO
W. Todd Zehnder, COO
Charles T. Goodson, Pres.
J. Bond Clement, CFO/Exec. VP
Janine Hebert, Mgr.-Human Resources
Stephen H. Green, Sr. VP-Exploration
Daniel G. Fournerat, Chief Admin. Officer
Daniel G. Fournerat, General Counsel/Exec. VP/Sec.
Art M. Mixon, Exec. VP-Oper. & Prod.
Dalton F. Smith, III, Sr. VP-Bus. Dev.
Matt Quantz, Mgr.-Corp. Comm.
J. Bond Clement, Treas.
James S. Blair, VP-Bus. Dev.
Mark K. Stover, Exec. VP-Exploration & Dev.
Charles T. Goodson, Chmn.

Phone: 337-232-7028	**Fax:** 337-232-0044
Toll-Free:	
Address: 400 E. Kaliste Saloom Rd., Ste. 6000, Lafayette, LA 70508 US	

GROWTH PLANS/SPECIAL FEATURES:

PetroQuest Energy, Inc. is an independent oil and gas company involved in the generation, exploration, development, acquisition and operation of oil and gas properties on- and offshore in Oklahoma, Texas, Arkansas and the Gulf Coast Basin, including areas in Louisiana. The company's proved reserves total 1.9 million barrels of oil and 167.4 million cubic feet of natural gas. The firm's Oklahoma properties account for 73% of its proved undeveloped reserves. The firm is continually engaged in drilling projects. These exploration endeavors are largely based on three-dimensional models of seismic data, which PetroQuest uses to identify potentially lucrative properties that have generally been under-exploited. Such projects exist in the east Texas region, the Fayetteville Shale region in Arkansas, the Gulf of Mexico region, the South Louisiana region and the Woodford Shale region in Oklahoma. Over a six-year period, PetroQuest drilled approximately 551 gross wells with a 97% drilling success rate. In 2009, the firm drilled 66 gross exploratory wells and 16 gross development wells with an overall success rate of 98%. In May 2010, the company sold a 50% interest in its undeveloped Woodford Shale acreage and a 50% interest in its proved undeveloped reserves in that region to NextEra Energy Resources subsidiaries, WSGP Gas Producing, LLC and NextEra Gas Producing, LLC.

FINANCIALS:

Sales and profits are in thousands of dollars—add 000 to get the full amount. 2010 Note: Financial information for 2010 was not available for all companies at press time.

2010 Sales: $	2010 Profits: $	**U.S. Stock Ticker: PQ**
2009 Sales: $218,875	2009 Profits: $-90,190	**Int'l Ticker:** Int'l Exchange:
2008 Sales: $313,958	2008 Profits: $-96,960	Employees: 99
2007 Sales: $262,334	2007 Profits: $40,619	Fiscal Year Ends: 12/31
2006 Sales: $200,544	2006 Profits: $23,986	Parent Company:

SALARIES/BENEFITS:

Pension Plan:	ESOP Stock Plan:	Profit Sharing:	Top Exec. Salary: $500,000	Bonus: $300,000
Savings Plan:	Stock Purch. Plan:		Second Exec. Salary: $327,850	Bonus: $302,800

OTHER THOUGHTS:

Apparent Women Officers or Directors: 1
Hot Spot for Advancement for Women/Minorities:

LOCATIONS: ("Y" = Yes)

West:	Southwest:	Midwest:	Southeast:	Northeast:	International:
	Y		Y		

PG&E CORPORATION

www.pgecorp.com

Industry Group Code: 221 **Ranks within this company's industry group:** Sales: 11 Profits: 5

Exploration/Production:		Refining/Retailing:		Utilities:		Alternative Energy:		Specialty Services:		Energy Mktg./Other Svcs.	
Exploration:		Refining:		Electric Utility:	Y	Waste/Solar/Other:	Y	Consulting/Eng.:		Energy Marketing:	
Production:		Retailing:		Gas Utility:	Y	Thermal/Steam:		Seismic:		Equipment/Machinery:	
Coal Production:		Convenience Stores:		Pipelines:	Y	Wind:		Drilling:		Oil Field Services:	
		Chemicals:		Water:		Hydro:	Y	InfoTech:		Air/Shipping Transportation:	
						Fuel Cells:		Specialty Services:			

TYPES OF BUSINESS:

Utilities-Electricity & Natural Gas
Energy Trading
Electricity Generation
Pipelines
Hydroelectric & Nuclear Generation
Natural Gas

BRANDS/DIVISIONS/AFFILIATES:

Pacific Gas and Electric Co

CONTACTS:

Note: Officers with more than one job title may be intentionally listed here more than once.

Peter A. Darbee, CEO
John S. Keenan, COO/Sr. VP-Pacific Gas & Electric Co.
Peter A. Darbee, Pres.
Kent M. Harvey, CFO/Sr. VP
John R. Simon, Sr. VP-Human Resources
Patricia Lawicki, CIO/Sr. VP-Pacific Gas & Electric Co.
Edward A. Salas, Sr. VP-Eng., Pacific Gas & Electric Co.
Hyun Park, General Counsel/Sr. VP
Edward A. Salas, Sr. VP-Oper., Pacific Gas & Electric Co.
Rand L. Rosenberg, Sr. VP-Corp. Strategy & Dev.
Greg S. Pruett, Sr. VP-Corp. Affairs
Gabriel B. Togneri, VP-Investor Rel.
Dinyar B. Mistry, Controller/VP
Christopher P. Johns, Pres., Pacific Gas & Electric Co.
Nancy E. McFadden, Sr. VP
Linda Y.H. Cheng, VP-Corp. Governance/Corp. Sec.
Steven L. Kline, VP-Corp. Environmental & Federal Affairs
Peter A. Darbee, Chmn.
Roy M. Kuga, VP-Energy Supply Mgmt., Pacific Gas & Electric Co.

Phone: 415-267-7000 **Fax:** 415-267-7268
Toll-Free: 800-719-9056
Address: 1 Market, Spear Tower, Ste. 2400, San Francisco, CA 94105 US

GROWTH PLANS/SPECIAL FEATURES:

PG&E Corporation is a holding company that markets energy services and products in northern and central California through subsidiary Pacific Gas and Electric Co. The subsidiary is one of the largest electric and natural gas utilities in the U.S., serving roughly 5.1 million electric and 4.3 million natural gas customers. With approximately 141,213 circuit miles of distribution lines, the company's electricity distribution network extends through most of northern and central California. Pacific owns and operates power plants producing nearly half of the power it sells, including 110 hydroelectric, two nuclear and four fossil fuel facilities. The company's hydroelectric generation system covers 16 counties in northern and central California. It includes 99 reservoirs; 44 miles of flumes; 170 dams; 184 miles of canals; 56 diversions; 19 miles of pipe; 135 miles of tunnels; and five miles of natural waterways. The company's natural gas operations consist of an integrated transportation, storage and distribution system throughout 39 counties, including most of northern and central California. This system consists of approximately 6,438 miles of backbone and local transmission pipelines; 42,142 miles of distribution pipelines; and three storage facilities. Through interconnections with various interstate pipelines, the company receives gas from every major natural gas basin in western North America, including basins in Canada, the southwestern U.S. and the Rocky Mountains.

The company offers employees supplemental life, medical, dental and vision insurance; health care and dependent care reimbursement accounts; paid time off; a retirement savings plan; adoption reimbursement; and tuition refund opportunities.

FINANCIALS:

Sales and profits are in thousands of dollars—add 000 to get the full amount. 2010 Note: Financial information for 2010 was not available for all companies at press time.

2010 Sales: $	2010 Profits: $	**U.S. Stock Ticker: PCG**
2009 Sales: $13,399,000	2009 Profits: $2,299,000	**Int'l Ticker:** Int'l Exchange:
2008 Sales: $14,628,000	2008 Profits: $2,261,000	Employees: 19,425
2007 Sales: $13,237,000	2007 Profits: $1,006,000	Fiscal Year Ends: 12/31
2006 Sales: $12,539,000	2006 Profits: $2,108,000	Parent Company:

SALARIES/BENEFITS:

Pension Plan: Y	ESOP Stock Plan:	Profit Sharing:	Top Exec. Salary: $1,135,633	Bonus: $1,871,524
Savings Plan: Y	Stock Purch. Plan:		Second Exec. Salary: $593,866	Bonus: $684,431

OTHER THOUGHTS:

Apparent Women Officers or Directors: 11
Hot Spot for Advancement for Women/Minorities: Y

LOCATIONS: ("Y" = Yes)

West:	Southwest:	Midwest:	Southeast:	Northeast:	International:
Y				Y	

PHI INC

www.phihelico.com

Industry Group Code: 481211 **Ranks within this company's industry group:** Sales: 2 Profits: 2

Exploration/Production:		Refining/Retailing:		Utilities:		Alternative Energy:		Specialty Services:		Energy Mktg./Other Svcs.	
Exploration:		Refining:		Electric Utility:		Waste/Solar/Other:		Consulting/Eng.:		Energy Marketing:	
Production:		Retailing:		Gas Utility:		Thermal/Steam:		Seismic:		Equipment/Machinery:	
Coal Production:		Convenience Stores:		Pipelines:		Wind:		Drilling:		Oil Field Services:	
		Chemicals:		Water:		Hydro:		InfoTech:		Air/Shipping Transportation:	Y
						Fuel Cells:		Specialty Services:			

TYPES OF BUSINESS:

Helicopter Services
Oil & Gas Drilling Support
Aero Medical Support
Aircraft Maintenance Services

BRANDS/DIVISIONS/AFFILIATES:

CONTACTS:

Note: Officers with more than one job title may be intentionally listed here more than once.

Al A. Gonsoulin, CEO
Lance Bospflug, COO
Michael J. McCann, CFO
Richard A. Rovinelli, Dir.-Human Resources
Richard A. Rovinelli, Chief Admin. Officer
Michael J. McCann, Sec.
Pat Attaway, Dir.-Oper.
William P. Sorenson, Dir.-Corp. Bus. Dev.
Michael J. McCann, Treas.
Robert DesRosiers, Dir.-Materials
Manuel (Tony) Gonzalez, Jr., Dir.-Maintenance
Robert Bouillion, Dir.-Health, Safety & Environment
David Motzkin, Dir.-Air Medical Group
Al A. Gonsoulin, Chmn.

Phone: 337-235-2452 **Fax:** 337-232-6537
Toll-Free: 800-235-2452
Address: 2001 SE Evangeline Thruway, Lafayette, LA 70508 US

GROWTH PLANS/SPECIAL FEATURES:

PHI, Inc. offers helicopter transportation of personnel, parts and equipment to and from offshore platforms for customers engaged in oil and gas exploration, development and production, primarily in the Gulf of Mexico. Founded in 1949, the firm is also one of the world's leading helicopter services companies. In addition to providing helicopter services to the oil and gas industry, PHI provides services to clients in the health care industry and to U.S. governmental agencies, including the National Science Foundation. PHI owns and operates 255 helicopters and other aircraft, with flight ranges of up to 495 miles with a 30-minute fuel reserve, making them capable of flying to locations as far as 200 miles offshore in international waters. PHI operates through three segments: domestic oil and gas, which generates approximately 65% of its revenue; air medical services, which generates approximately 33%; and technical services, which generates approximately 2%. The firm's oil and gas segment operates 164 aircraft and provides helicopter services to offshore platforms in the Gulf of Mexico and the Democratic Republic of Congo. Its air medical services segment provides air medical transportation services and operates as an independent provider of medical services in 17 states using approximately 85 aircraft. The technical services segment provides helicopter repair and overhaul services and operates six aircraft for the National Science Foundation in Antarctica.

FINANCIALS:

Sales and profits are in thousands of dollars—add 000 to get the full amount. 2010 Note: Financial information for 2010 was not available for all companies at press time.

2010 Sales: $	2010 Profits: $	**U.S. Stock Ticker: PHII**
2009 Sales: $487,175	2009 Profits: $12,968	**Int'l Ticker:** Int'l Exchange:
2008 Sales: $509,514	2008 Profits: $23,515	Employees: 2,299
2007 Sales: $446,406	2007 Profits: $28,218	Fiscal Year Ends: 12/31
2006 Sales: $413,118	2006 Profits: $- 667	Parent Company:

SALARIES/BENEFITS:

Pension Plan:	ESOP Stock Plan:	Profit Sharing:	Top Exec. Salary: $569,520	Bonus: $
Savings Plan: Y	Stock Purch. Plan:		Second Exec. Salary: $264,420	Bonus: $

OTHER THOUGHTS:

Apparent Women Officers or Directors:
Hot Spot for Advancement for Women/Minorities:

LOCATIONS: ("Y" = Yes)

West:	Southwest:	Midwest:	Southeast:	Northeast:	International:
Y	Y	Y	Y	Y	

PIEDMONT NATURAL GAS COMPANY INC

www.piedmontng.com

Industry Group Code: 221210 **Ranks within this company's industry group:** Sales: 15 Profits: 13

Exploration/Production:		Refining/Retailing:		Utilities:		Alternative Energy:		Specialty Services:		Energy Mktg./Other Svcs.	
Exploration:		Refining:		Electric Utility:		Waste/Solar/Other:		Consulting/Eng.:		Energy Marketing:	Y
Production:		Retailing:		Gas Utility:	Y	Thermal/Steam:		Seismic:		Equipment/Machinery:	
Coal Production:		Convenience Stores:		Pipelines:	Y	Wind:		Drilling:		Oil Field Services:	
		Chemicals:		Water:		Hydro:		InfoTech:		Air/Shipping Transportation:	
						Fuel Cells:		Specialty Services:	Y		

TYPES OF BUSINESS:

Utilities-Natural Gas
Pipelines
Gas Transportation & Storage
Natural Gas Marketing

BRANDS/DIVISIONS/AFFILIATES:

SouthStar Energy Services

CONTACTS:

Note: Officers with more than one job title may be intentionally listed here more than once.

Thomas E. Skains, CEO
Thomas E. Skains, Pres.
David J. Dzuricky, CFO/Sr. VP
Jane R. Lewis-Raymond, General Counsel/VP/Sec./Chief Compliance Officer
Franklin H. Yoho, Sr. VP-Commercial Oper.
Karl W. Newlin, Sr. VP-Bus. Dev. & Corp. Planning
Kevin M.O'Hara, Sr. VP-Corp. & Community Affairs
Robert O. Pritchard, Treas./VP/Chief Risk Officer
June B. Moore, VP-Enterprise Quality Mgmt.
Michael H. Yount, Sr. VP-Utility Oper.
Thomas E. Skains, Chmn.

Phone: 704-364-3120	**Fax:** 704-365-3849
Toll-Free:	
Address: 4720 Piedmont Row Dr., Charlotte, NC 28210 US	

GROWTH PLANS/SPECIAL FEATURES:

Piedmont Natural Gas Company, Inc. is an energy services company primarily engaged in the distribution of natural gas to residential, commercial and industrial customers in North Carolina, South Carolina and Tennessee. The company is one of the largest natural gas utilities in the Southeast with over 1 million customers, including 61,000 wholesale customers that are served by municipalities. Piedmont owns approximately 2,600 miles of transmission pipelines and approximately 28,900 miles of distribution mains. The company is also invested in several of non-utility, energy related businesses including unregulated retail natural gas marketing and interstate and intrastate natural gas storage and transportation. Piedmont has interest in SouthStar Energy Services, which offers a combination of unregulated energy products and services to industrial, commercial and residential customers in the southeastern U.S. Business strategies for Piedmont include focusing on core-utility businesses, pursuing new construction markets and converting existing homes and businesses to natural energy. Recently, the firm announced plans to design, construct, own and operate a liquefied natural gas peak (LNG) storage facility in Robeson County, North Carolina. The plant will have the capacity to store approximately 1.25 billion cubic feet of natural gas. The LNG facility will be a part of its regulated utility segment and is expected to be in service by early 2013. In October 2009, Piedmont announced an agreement with Progress Energy Carolinas to construct 38-miles of pipeline along with an additional compression facilities to provide natural gas delivery service to the Progress Energy Carolina plant in Wayne County, North Carolina. The pipeline and compression facility has an estimated cost of $85 million and is expected to be operational by 2012. In January 2010, the firm sold 15% of its ownership interest in SouthStar Energy Services to AGL Resources for $57.5 million. The company maintains a 15% interest in SouthStar Energy Services.

FINANCIALS:

Sales and profits are in thousands of dollars—add 000 to get the full amount. 2010 Note: Financial information for 2010 was not available for all companies at press time.

2010 Sales: $	2010 Profits: $	**U.S. Stock Ticker: PNY**
2009 Sales: $1,638,116	2009 Profits: $122,824	**Int'l Ticker:** Int'l Exchange:
2008 Sales: $2,089,108	2008 Profits: $110,007	Employees: 1,821
2007 Sales: $1,711,292	2007 Profits: $104,387	Fiscal Year Ends: 10/31
2006 Sales: $1,924,628	2006 Profits: $97,189	Parent Company:

SALARIES/BENEFITS:

Pension Plan: Y	ESOP Stock Plan: Y	Profit Sharing:	Top Exec. Salary: $740,385	Bonus: $742,367
Savings Plan: Y	Stock Purch. Plan:		Second Exec. Salary: $395,192	Bonus: $336,194

OTHER THOUGHTS:

Apparent Women Officers or Directors: 4
Hot Spot for Advancement for Women/Minorities: Y

LOCATIONS: ("Y" = Yes)

West:	Southwest:	Midwest:	Southeast:	Northeast:	International:
			Y	Y	

PINNACLE WEST CAPITAL CORPORATION www.pinnaclewest.com

Industry Group Code: 2211 **Ranks within this company's industry group:** Sales: 30 Profits: 42

Exploration/Production:		Refining/Retailing:		Utilities:		Alternative Energy:		Specialty Services:		Energy Mktg./Other Svcs.	
Exploration:		Refining:		Electric Utility:	Y	Waste/Solar/Other:	Y	Consulting/Eng.:		Energy Marketing:	
Production:		Retailing:		Gas Utility:		Thermal/Steam:		Seismic:		Equipment/Machinery:	
Coal Production:		Convenience Stores:		Pipelines:		Wind:		Drilling:		Oil Field Services:	
		Chemicals:		Water:		Hydro:		InfoTech:		Air/Shipping Transportation:	
						Fuel Cells:		Specialty Services:	Y		

TYPES OF BUSINESS:

Utilities-Electricity & Natural Gas
Real Estate Development
Venture Capital Investments
Energy Services
Electricity Generation
Nuclear Generation

BRANDS/DIVISIONS/AFFILIATES:

Arizona Public Service Company
SunCor Development Company
Pinnacle West Energy
APS Energy Services Company
Palo Verde Nuclear Power Plant

CONTACTS:

Note: Officers with more than one job title may be intentionally listed here more than once.

Donald E. Brandt, CEO
Donald E. Brandt, Pres.
James R. Hatfield, CFO/Sr. VP
Lori Sundberg, VP-Human Resources, Arizona Public Service Co.
Kenneth C. Bohlen, CIO/VP-Arizona Public Service Co.
David P. Falck, General Counsel/Exec. VP/Corp. Sec.
Bob Bement, VP-Oper., Palo Verde Nuclear Generating Station
Rebecca L. Hickman, Dir.-Investor Rel.
Denise R. Danner, Chief Acct. Officer/Controller/VP
Robert S. Aiken, VP-Federal Affairs
Donald G. Robinson, Pres./COO-Arizona Public Service Co.
Martin L. Shultz, VP-Gov't Affairs
Lee R. Nickloy, VP/Treas.
Donald E. Brandt, Chmn.
Barbara M. Gomez, VP-Supply Chain Mgmt., Arizona Public Service Co.

Phone: 602-250-1000	**Fax:**
Toll-Free: 800-824-8101	
Address: 400 N. 5th St., Phoenix, AZ 85004 US	

GROWTH PLANS/SPECIAL FEATURES:

Pinnacle West Capital Corporation (PWCC) is engaged, through its subsidiaries, in the generation and distribution of electricity, in real estate development and in venture capital investment. The company currently has consolidated assets of approximately $11 billion and around 6,000 megawatts (MW) of plant generation capacity. PWCC's major subsidiary is Arizona Public Service Company (APS), one of Arizona's largest electric utility companies with over 1.1 million customers. Founded in 1920, APS provides wholesale or retail electric service to 11 of the 15 counties in Arizona. APS's sources of energy are comprised of approximately 36.3% coal; 25.9% nuclear; 20.6% purchased power; and 17.2% gas. The company's coal-fired power plants include Cholla in northeastern Arizona; Four Corners in northwestern New Mexico; and the Navajo Generating Station in northern Arizona. The coal requirements for these stations are purchased from a number of sources, including coal suppliers that mine the coal under long-term leases of coal reserves with the Navajo Nation, the Hopi Tribe, the federal government and private landholders. Palo Verde Nuclear Generation is APS' jointly owned nuclear power plant located about 50 miles west of Phoenix, Arizona. In addition to its own generating capacity, APS purchases electricity under various arrangements, one of the most important of which is a long-term contract with Salt River Project. PWCC's other primary subsidiaries are SunCor Development Company, a developer of residential, commercial and industrial real estate projects focusing on planned communities; APS Energy Services Company, providing administrative services to the company; and El Dorado Investment Company, a venture capital and investment firm. In May 2010, APS Energy Services agreed to sell its district cooling operations to NRG Thermal LLC.

Employees are offered life, disability, medical and dental insurance; healthcare and dependent care spending accounts; a 401(k) plan; tuition reimbursement; a pension plan; and a stock purchase plan.

FINANCIALS:

Sales and profits are in thousands of dollars—add 000 to get the full amount. 2010 Note: Financial information for 2010 was not available for all companies at press time.

2010 Sales: $	2010 Profits: $	**U.S. Stock Ticker: PNW**
2009 Sales: $3,297,101	2009 Profits: $68,330	**Int'l Ticker:** Int'l Exchange:
2008 Sales: $3,310,558	2008 Profits: $242,125	Employees: 7,200
2007 Sales: $3,523,620	2007 Profits: $307,143	Fiscal Year Ends: 12/31
2006 Sales: $3,401,748	2006 Profits: $327,255	Parent Company:

SALARIES/BENEFITS:

Pension Plan: Y	ESOP Stock Plan:	Profit Sharing:	Top Exec. Salary: $890,568	Bonus: $1,232,136
Savings Plan: Y	Stock Purch. Plan: Y		Second Exec. Salary: $800,000	Bonus: $908,625

OTHER THOUGHTS:

Apparent Women Officers or Directors: 7
Hot Spot for Advancement for Women/Minorities: Y

LOCATIONS: ("Y" = Yes)

West:	Southwest:	Midwest:	Southeast:	Northeast:	International:
Y	Y				

PIONEER NATURAL RESOURCES COMPANY www.pioneernrc.com

Industry Group Code: 211111 **Ranks within this company's industry group:** Sales: 74 Profits: 80

Exploration/Production:		Refining/Retailing:		Utilities:		Alternative Energy:		Specialty Services:		Energy Mktg./Other Svcs.	
Exploration:	Y	Refining:		Electric Utility:		Waste/Solar/Other:		Consulting/Eng.:		Energy Marketing:	
Production:	Y	Retailing:		Gas Utility:		Thermal/Steam:		Seismic:		Equipment/Machinery:	
Coal Production:		Convenience Stores:		Pipelines:		Wind:		Drilling:		Oil Field Services:	
		Chemicals:		Water:		Hydro:		InfoTech:		Air/Shipping Transportation:	
						Fuel Cells:		Specialty Services:			

TYPES OF BUSINESS:

Oil & Gas Exploration & Production

BRANDS/DIVISIONS/AFFILIATES:

Spraberry
Hugoton
Oooguruk
Raton
Pawnee
Eagle Ford Shale

CONTACTS:

Note: Officers with more than one job title may be intentionally listed here more than once.

Scott D. Sheffield, CEO
Timothy L. Dove, COO
Timothy L. Dove, Pres.
Richard P. Dealy, CFO/Exec. VP
Thomas C. Halbouty, CIO/CTO/VP
Chris J. Cheatwood, Exec. VP-Tech.
Larry N. Paulsen, VP-Admin. & Risk Mgmt.
Mark S. Berg, General Counsel/Exec. VP
Jay P. Still, Exec. VP-Domestic Oper.
Chris J. Cheatwood, Exec. VP-Bus. Dev.
Susan A. Spratlen, Sr. Dir.-Corp. Comm. & Public Affairs
Frank E. Hopkins, VP-Investor Rel.
Frank W. Hall, Chief Acct. Officer/VP
Danny L. Kellum, Exec. VP-Permian Oper.
William F. Hannes, Exec. VP-South Texas Oper.
Roger W. Wallace, VP-Gov't Affairs
Mark H. Kleinman, VP/Corp. Sec./Chief Compliance Officer
Scott D. Sheffield, Chmn.
David McManus, VP-Int'l Oper.

Phone: 972-444-9001	**Fax:** 972-969-3576
Toll-Free:	
Address: 5205 N. O'Connor Blvd., Ste. 200, Irving, TX 75039 US	

GROWTH PLANS/SPECIAL FEATURES:

Pioneer Natural Resources Company is one of the largest independent exploration and production companies in the U.S. The company owns interests in oil, natural gas liquids (NGL) and gas properties located in the U.S., South Africa and Tunisia. The firm has total proved reserves of about 898.6 million barrels of oil equivalent (boe), and produces approximately 115,000 boe per day. It owns over 9,100 producing wells and controls approximately $8.9 billion in assets. Pioneer Natural Resources' operations are spread between domestic and international divisions. The domestic division includes the Spraberry field in west Texas; the Hugoton gas field in southwest Kansas and Oklahoma; the West Panhandle gas field in Texas; the Raton field gas operations in southern Colorado; the Pawnee gas field production and exploration wells in the Edwards Reef expansion in southern Texas; and a 70% interest in the Oooguruk project on Alaska's north slope. The firm's international operations are centered in Africa, with exploration projects in Tunisia and offshore South Africa. Pioneer Natural Resources focuses its production efforts toward increasing its average daily production of oil and gas through development drilling, production enhancement activities and acquisitions of producing properties. Pioneer's drilling activities seek to increase its oil/gas reserves, production and cash flow by concentrating on drilling low-risk development wells and by conducting additional development activities such as well recompletions. In August 2009, the company sold certain properties in Spraberry Field to Pioneer Energy Southwest Partners L.P. for approximately $171 million. In June 2010, Pioneer Natural Resources sold 45% ownership of roughly 212,000 net acres leased by in the Eagle Ford Shale play to a subsidiary of Reliance Industries Limited for roughly $1.15 billion. The land is now operated by both firms through a joint venture arrangement.

FINANCIALS:

Sales and profits are in thousands of dollars—add 000 to get the full amount. 2010 Note: Financial information for 2010 was not available for all companies at press time.

2010 Sales: $	2010 Profits: $	**U.S. Stock Ticker: PXD**
2009 Sales: $1,711,516	2009 Profits: $-52,106	**Int'l Ticker:** Int'l Exchange:
2008 Sales: $2,284,841	2008 Profits: $210,020	Employees: 1,888
2007 Sales: $1,785,018	2007 Profits: $372,728	Fiscal Year Ends: 12/31
2006 Sales: $1,500,871	2006 Profits: $739,700	Parent Company:

SALARIES/BENEFITS:

Pension Plan:	ESOP Stock Plan:	Profit Sharing:	Top Exec. Salary: $956,000	Bonus: $1,051,600
Savings Plan: Y	Stock Purch. Plan:		Second Exec. Salary: $531,000	Bonus: $573,480

OTHER THOUGHTS:

Apparent Women Officers or Directors: 1
Hot Spot for Advancement for Women/Minorities:

LOCATIONS: ("Y" = Yes)

West:	Southwest:	Midwest:	Southeast:	Northeast:	International:
Y	Y	Y			Y

PLAINS ALL AMERICAN PIPELINE

www.paalp.com

Industry Group Code: 486 **Ranks within this company's industry group:** Sales: 5 Profits: 6

Exploration/Production:		Refining/Retailing:		Utilities:		Alternative Energy:		Specialty Services:		Energy Mktg./Other Svcs.	
Exploration:		Refining:		Electric Utility:		Waste/Solar/Other:		Consulting/Eng.:		Energy Marketing:	Y
Production:		Retailing:		Gas Utility:		Thermal/Steam:		Seismic:		Equipment/Machinery:	
Coal Production:		Convenience Stores:		Pipelines:	Y	Wind:		Drilling:		Oil Field Services:	
		Chemicals:		Water:		Hydro:		InfoTech:		Air/Shipping Transportation:	Y
						Fuel Cells:		Specialty Services:			

TYPES OF BUSINESS:

Crude Oil Pipelines
Terminals & Storage Activities
Gathering & Marketing Activities
Truck & Barge Transportation
Natural Gas Storage

BRANDS/DIVISIONS/AFFILIATES:

Plains All American Pipeline LP
Plains Marketing GP Inc
PAA Natural Gas Storage LLC
Settoon Towing LLC
PAA Finance Corp
PMC (Nova Scotia) Company
Plains Midstream Canada ULC
PAA Natural Gas Storage LP

CONTACTS:

Note: Officers with more than one job title may be intentionally listed here more than once.

Greg L. Armstrong, CEO
Harry N. Pefanis, COO
Harry N. Pefanis, Pres.
Al Swanson, CFO/Exec. VP
Roger D. Everett, VP-Human Resources
Alfred A. Lindseth, Sr. VP-Tech., Process & Risk Mgmt.
Daniel J. Nerbonne, VP-Eng.
Tim Moore, General Counsel/Sec./VP
Mark J. Gorman, Sr. VP-Oper.
Mark J. Gorman, Sr. VP-Bus. Dev.
Roy I. Lamoreaux, Dir.-Investor Rel.
Chris Herbold, VP-Acct./Chief Acct. Officer
John R. Keffer, VP-Terminals
Troy E. Valenzuela, VP-Environmental, Health & Safety
Phil D. Kramer, Exec. VP
Charles Kingswell-Smith, VP/Treas.
Greg L. Armstrong, Chmn.
W. Dave Duckett, Pres., PMC (Nova Scotia) Company
James B. Fryfogle, VP-Refinery Supply

Phone: 713-646-4100 **Fax:** 713-646-4572
Toll-Free: 800-564-3036
Address: 333 Clay St., Ste. 1600, Houston, TX 77002 US

GROWTH PLANS/SPECIAL FEATURES:

Plains All American Pipeline (PAA) is a limited partnership. The firm is engaged in crude oil pipeline transportation, gathering and marketing; and oil, liquefied petroleum gas (LPG) and natural gas storage. The company operates through three business segments: transportation, facilities and marketing. Through its transportation division, PAA owns and operates approximately 16,000 miles of crude oil pipelines throughout the U.S. and Canada. Additionally, the firm owns 353 trailers and 84 trailers; and 65 transport/storage barges and 39 transport tugs through its interest in Settoon Towing. The facilities segment is capable of storing 51 million barrels of crude oil/refined products, 6 million barrels of LPG and 40 billion cubic feet of natural gas. This segment includes a fractionation plant in Canada with a processing capacity of 4,400 barrels per day and a fractionation/isomerization plant in California with an aggregate processing capacity of 22,500 barrels per day. The firm's supply and logistics segment purchases crude oil; purchases refined products and LPG; stores inventory; resells and exchanges crude oil, refined products and LPG; and arranges the transportation of crude oil, refined products and LPG via trucks, pipelines, ocean-going vessels, barges and railcars. This segment includes pipelines with 12 million (10 million owned) barrels of crude oil and LPG; 522 trucks; 630 trailers; and 1,473 railcars. PAA's subsidiaries include Plains All American Pipeline, L.P.; Plains Marketing GP, Inc.; PAA Natural Gas Storage, LLC; Settoon Towing, LLC; PAA Finance Corp.; Plains Midstream Canada ULC; PMC (Nova Scotia) Company; and Plains Marketing Canada, L.P. In October 2009, PAA acquired 400,000 barrels of crude oil storage capacity from Holly Corporation. In April 2010, the company established PAA Natural Gas Storage, L.P. In October 2010, PAA acquired various assets, including 34% ownership of White Cliffs Pipeline L.L.C.

PAA offers its employees medical, dental, long-term disability and life insurance.

FINANCIALS:

Sales and profits are in thousands of dollars—add 000 to get the full amount. 2010 Note: Financial information for 2010 was not available for all companies at press time.

2010 Sales: $	2010 Profits: $	**U.S. Stock Ticker: PAA**
2009 Sales: $18,520,000	2009 Profits: $580,000	**Int'l Ticker:** Int'l Exchange:
2008 Sales: $30,061,000	2008 Profits: $437,000	Employees: 3,400
2007 Sales: $20,394,000	2007 Profits: $365,000	Fiscal Year Ends: 12/31
2006 Sales: $22,444,400	2006 Profits: $285,100	Parent Company:

SALARIES/BENEFITS:

Pension Plan:	ESOP Stock Plan:	Profit Sharing:	Top Exec. Salary: $375,000	Bonus: $3,000,000
Savings Plan: Y	Stock Purch. Plan:		Second Exec. Salary: $300,000	Bonus: $2,900,000

OTHER THOUGHTS:

Apparent Women Officers or Directors: 1
Hot Spot for Advancement for Women/Minorities:

LOCATIONS: ("Y" = Yes)

West:	Southwest:	Midwest:	Southeast:	Northeast:	International:
Y	Y	Y	Y	Y	Y

PLAINS EXPLORATION AND PRODUCTION COMPANY

www.plainsxp.com

Industry Group Code: 211111 **Ranks within this company's industry group:** Sales: 77 Profits: 61

Exploration/Production:		Refining/Retailing:		Utilities:		Alternative Energy:		Specialty Services:		Energy Mktg./Other Svcs.	
Exploration:	Y	Refining:		Electric Utility:		Waste/Solar/Other:		Consulting/Eng.:		Energy Marketing:	
Production:	Y	Retailing:		Gas Utility:		Thermal/Steam:		Seismic:		Equipment/Machinery:	
Coal Production:		Convenience Stores:		Pipelines:		Wind:		Drilling:		Oil Field Services:	
		Chemicals:		Water:		Hydro:		InfoTech:		Air/Shipping Transportation:	
						Fuel Cells:		Specialty Services:			

TYPES OF BUSINESS:

Oil & Gas Exploration & Production

BRANDS/DIVISIONS/AFFILIATES:

CONTACTS:

Note: Officers with more than one job title may be intentionally listed here more than once.

James C. Flores, CEO
James C. Flores, Pres.
Winston M. Talbert, CFO/Exec. VP
Doss R. Bourgeois, Exec. VP-Exploration & Prod.
John F. Wombwell, General Counsel/Exec. VP/Sec.
Scott Winters, VP-Corp. Comm.
Hance Myers, VP-Investor Rel.
Joanna Pankey, Mgr.-Investor Rel. & Shareholder Svcs.
Steven P. Rusch, VP-Environmental, Health & Safety
James C. Flores, Chmn.

Phone: 713-579-6000 **Fax:** 713-579-6611
Toll-Free: 800-934-6083
Address: 700 Milam St., Ste. 3100, Houston, TX 77002 US

GROWTH PLANS/SPECIAL FEATURES:

Plains Exploration and Production Company (PXP) is an independent upstream energy company that acquires, develops, exploits, explores for and produces oil and gas in the U.S. Its principal operations in the U.S. are in the Los Angeles and San Joaquin Basins and the Arroyo Grande Field in California; the Santa Maria Basin offshore California; the Gulf Coast region, including the Haynesville Shale and areas of South and East Texas; the Gulf of Mexico, including areas of Louisiana; the Mid-Continent region, including parts of northern Texas and western Oklahoma; and the Wind River Basin in the Wyoming Rocky Mountains. It also has interest in an exploration block offshore Vietnam. The company's focus areas include mature properties with long-lived reserves, as well as newer properties with development, exploitation and exploration potential. The firm has estimated proved reserves of 359.5 million barrels of oil equivalent, of which 60% is proved developed, with additional estimated resource potential of 2 billion barrels of oil equivalent. The firm has oil marketing arrangements with ConocoPhillips under which ConocoPhillips purchases the majority of the company's net oil production. In September 2010, PXP agreed to sell its properties located in Gulf of Mexico shallow water to McMoRan Exploration Co. In October 2010, the firm agreed to acquire about 60,000 acres in South Texas, part of the Eagle Ford oil and gas condensate area.

FINANCIALS:

Sales and profits are in thousands of dollars—add 000 to get the full amount. 2010 Note: Financial information for 2010 was not available for all companies at press time.

2010 Sales: $	2010 Profits: $	**U.S. Stock Ticker: PXP**
2009 Sales: $1,187,130	2009 Profits: $136,305	**Int'l Ticker:** Int'l Exchange:
2008 Sales: $2,403,471	2008 Profits: $-709,094	Employees: 808
2007 Sales: $1,272,840	2007 Profits: $158,751	Fiscal Year Ends: 12/31
2006 Sales: $1,018,503	2006 Profits: $597,528	Parent Company:

SALARIES/BENEFITS:

Pension Plan:	ESOP Stock Plan:	Profit Sharing:	Top Exec. Salary: $1,200,000	Bonus: $1,200,000
Savings Plan:	Stock Purch. Plan:		Second Exec. Salary: $650,000	Bonus: $650,000

OTHER THOUGHTS:

Apparent Women Officers or Directors: 1
Hot Spot for Advancement for Women/Minorities:

LOCATIONS: ("Y" = Yes)

West:	Southwest:	Midwest:	Southeast:	Northeast:	International:
Y	Y		Y		

PNM RESOURCES INC

www.pnm.com

Industry Group Code: 221 **Ranks within this company's industry group:** Sales: 47 Profits: 42

Exploration/Production:		Refining/Retailing:		Utilities:		Alternative Energy:		Specialty Services:		Energy Mktg./Other Svcs.	
Exploration:		Refining:		Electric Utility:	Y	Waste/Solar/Other:		Consulting/Eng.:		Energy Marketing:	Y
Production:		Retailing:		Gas Utility:	Y	Thermal/Steam:		Seismic:		Equipment/Machinery:	
Coal Production:		Convenience Stores:		Pipelines:		Wind:		Drilling:		Oil Field Services:	
		Chemicals:		Water:		Hydro:		InfoTech:		Air/Shipping Transportation:	
						Fuel Cells:		Specialty Services:	Y		

TYPES OF BUSINESS:

Utilities-Electricity & Natural Gas
Energy & Technology Services

BRANDS/DIVISIONS/AFFILIATES:

Public Service Company of New Mexico (PNM)
Texas-New Mexico Power Co.
First Choice Power L.P.
Optim Energy

CONTACTS: *Note: Officers with more than one job title may be intentionally listed here more than once.*

Pat Vincent-Collawn, CEO
Pat Vincent-Collawn, Pres.
Charles Eldred, CFO/Exec. VP
Kevin Judice, CIO/VP
Alice A. Cobb, Chief Admin. Officer/Sr. VP
Patrick Apodaca, General Counsel/Sr. VP
Tom Sategna, Corp. Controller/VP
Patrick Themig, VP-Generation
Terry Horn, Treas./VP
Ernie C'de Baca, VP-Gov't Affairs
Jeff Sterba, Chmn.

Phone: 505-241-2700 **Fax:** 505-241-2367
Toll-Free:
Address: Alvarado Sq., Albuquerque, NM 87158 US

GROWTH PLANS/SPECIAL FEATURES:

PNM Resources, Inc. is an investor-owned holding company of energy and energy-related businesses. The company delivers electricity to approximately 859,000 businesses and homes in Texas and New Mexico. PNM Resources, Inc. has a current production capacity of 2,706 Megawatts of energy; of this, 40% is coal, 37% is natural gas, 15% is nuclear and 8% is comprised of renewable energy. The firm's primary subsidiaries are Public Service Company of New Mexico (PNM), Texas-New Mexico Power Co. (TNMP) and First Choice Power L.P. PNM is an integrated public utility divided between utility operations and wholesale operations. Its electric services department consists of the generation and distribution of electricity to retail customers in New Mexico, in particular, to residents of Santa Fe and Albuquerque. PNM Wholesale consists of the generation and sale of electricity into the wholesale market based on two product lines, long-term contracts and short-term sales. PNM owns or leases approximately 3,170 miles of electric transmission lines interconnected with other utility firms in New Mexico, Arizona, Texas, Colorado and Utah. TNMP is a regulated utility operating in Texas where it provides regulated transmission and distribution services. PNM Resources, Inc. owns a 50% stake in Optim Energy, a company involved in the development, operation and ownership of unregulated electric operations. First Choice is a retail electric provider in Texas. In January 2009, the firm sold its natural gas segment to New Mexico Gas Company.

Employees are offered medical, dental and vision insurance; an employee assistance plan; flexible spending accounts; life insurance; disability coverage; credit union membership; educational assistance' a pension plan; a 401(k) plan; and a stock purchase plan.

FINANCIALS: **Sales and profits are in thousands of dollars—add 000 to get the full amount. 2010 Note: Financial information for 2010 was not available for all companies at press time.**

2010 Sales: $
2009 Sales: $1,647,744
2008 Sales: $1,959,522
2007 Sales: $1,914,029
2006 Sales: $1,963,360

2010 Profits: $
2009 Profits: $124,316
2008 Profits: $-270,644
2007 Profits: $74,874
2006 Profits: $120,818

U.S. Stock Ticker: PNM
Int'l Ticker: Int'l Exchange:
Employees: 660
Fiscal Year Ends: 12/31
Parent Company:

SALARIES/BENEFITS:

Pension Plan: Y ESOP Stock Plan: Profit Sharing: Top Exec. Salary: $847,067 Bonus: $1,487,422
Savings Plan: Y Stock Purch. Plan: Y Second Exec. Salary: $456,926 Bonus: $565,422

OTHER THOUGHTS:

Apparent Women Officers or Directors: 4
Hot Spot for Advancement for Women/Minorities: Y

LOCATIONS: ("Y" = Yes)

West:	Southwest:	Midwest:	Southeast:	Northeast:	International:
	Y				

POLSKI KONCERN NAFTOWY ORLEN SA (PKN ORLEN GROUP)

www.orlen.pl

Industry Group Code: 211111 **Ranks within this company's industry group:** Sales: 32 Profits: 52

Exploration/Production:		Refining/Retailing:		Utilities:		Alternative Energy:		Specialty Services:		Energy Mktg./Other Svcs.	
Exploration:		Refining:	Y	Electric Utility:		Waste/Solar/Other:		Consulting/Eng.:		Energy Marketing:	
Production:		Retailing:	Y	Gas Utility:		Thermal/Steam:		Seismic:		Equipment/Machinery:	
Coal Production:		Convenience Stores:	Y	Pipelines:	Y	Wind:		Drilling:		Oil Field Services:	
		Chemicals:		Water:		Hydro:		InfoTech:		Air/Shipping Transportation:	Y
						Fuel Cells:		Specialty Services:			

TYPES OF BUSINESS:

Crude Oil Refining
Plastics
Petrochemicals
Petrochemical Storage
Petrochemical Transport
Oil Product Retailing

BRANDS/DIVISIONS/AFFILIATES:

ORLEN
Petrochemia Plock
Bliska
Star
ORLEN Lietuva
ORLEN Ventus
Benzina
Benzina Plus

CONTACTS:

Note: Officers with more than one job title may be intentionally listed here more than once.

Darius Jacek Krawiec, CEO
Darius Jacek Krawiec, Pres.
Slawomir Jedrzejczyk, CFO/VP
Wojciech Robert Kotlarek, Dir.-Sales
Marek Serafin, Dir.-Petrochemical Oper.
Krystian Pater, Dir.-Refinery Oper.
Maciej Mataczyski, Chmn.

Phone: 48-24-365-0000	**Fax:** 48-24-365-4040
Toll-Free:	
Address: ul. Chemikow 7, Plock, 09-411 Poland	

GROWTH PLANS/SPECIAL FEATURES:

Polski Koncern Naftowy Orlen S.A. (PKN Orlen Group) is a Polish company engaged in the refining of crude oil and sale of petroleum products. The company's offerings include unleaded gasoline, diesel, heating oil and aviation fuel as well as petrochemicals, plastics and other petroleum related products. The firm operates seven refineries located in Plock, Trzebinia and Jedlicze, Poland; Litvinov, Kralupy and Paramo, Czech Republic; and Mazeikiu, Lithuania. The total deep processing capacity of the refineries is approximately 31.7 million tons annually; in 2009 the firm processed 27.4 million tons of crude oil. The firm's retail network comprises approximately 2,700 service stations in Poland, Germany, the Czech Republic and Lithuania. PKN ORLEN Group operates under ORLEN, Petrochemia Plock and Bliska in Poland; the ORLEN and Star brands in Germany; Benzina and Benzina Plus in the Czech Republic; and ORLEN Lietuva and Ventus in Lithuania. The company controls a network of storage depots, pipelines and sea reloading facilities to support its operations.

FINANCIALS:

Sales and profits are in thousands of dollars—add 000 to get the full amount. 2010 Note: Financial information for 2010 was not available for all companies at press time.

2010 Sales: $	2010 Profits: $	**U.S. Stock Ticker: PSKZF**
2009 Sales: $20,809,900	2009 Profits: $400,860	**Int'l Ticker: PKN** Int'l Exchange: Warsaw-WSE
2008 Sales: $27,843,200	2008 Profits: $-877,000	Employees: 22,535
2007 Sales: $22,332,180	2007 Profits: $844,520	Fiscal Year Ends:
2006 Sales: $	2006 Profits: $	Parent Company:

SALARIES/BENEFITS:

Pension Plan:	ESOP Stock Plan:	Profit Sharing:	Top Exec. Salary: $	Bonus: $
Savings Plan:	Stock Purch. Plan:		Second Exec. Salary: $	Bonus: $

OTHER THOUGHTS:

Apparent Women Officers or Directors: 1
Hot Spot for Advancement for Women/Minorities:

LOCATIONS: ("Y" = Yes)

West:	Southwest:	Midwest:	Southeast:	Northeast:	International:
					Y

Note: Financial information, benefits and other data can change quickly and may vary from those stated here.

PORTLAND GENERAL ELECTRIC COMPANY www.portlandgeneral.com

Industry Group Code: 221111 **Ranks within this company's industry group:** Sales: 4 Profits: 4

Exploration/Production:		Refining/Retailing:		Utilities:		Alternative Energy:		Specialty Services:		Energy Mktg./Other Svcs.	
Exploration:		Refining:		Electric Utility:	Y	Waste/Solar/Other:		Consulting/Eng.:		Energy Marketing:	Y
Production:		Retailing:		Gas Utility:		Thermal/Steam:		Seismic:		Equipment/Machinery:	
Coal Production:		Convenience Stores:		Pipelines:	Y	Wind:	Y	Drilling:		Oil Field Services:	
		Chemicals:		Water:		Hydro:	Y	InfoTech:		Air/Shipping Transportation:	
						Fuel Cells:		Specialty Services:			

TYPES OF BUSINESS:

Electric Utility
Energy Marketing
Natural Gas Pipeline
Hydroelectric Plants
Wind Power Generation

BRANDS/DIVISIONS/AFFILIATES:

Biglow Canyon Wind Farm
Kelso-Beaver Natural Gas Pipeline
enXco

CONTACTS:

Note: Officers with more than one job title may be intentionally listed here more than once.

Jim Piro, CEO
Jim Piro, Pres.
Maria Pope, CFO
Cam Henderson, CIO/VP-IT
Arleen Barnett, VP-Admin.
Jay Dudley, General Counsel/VP/Corp. Compliance Officer
James Lobdell, VP-Power Oper. & Resource Planning
Maria Pope, Sr. VP-Finance/Treas.
Stephen R. Hawke, Sr. VP-Customer Service, Transmission & Dist.
Carol Dillin, VP-Customers & Economic Dev.
Dave Robertson, VP-Public Policy
Stephen Quennoz, VP-Nuclear & Power Supply/Generation
Corbin A. McNeill, Jr., Chmn.

Phone: 503-464-8000 **Fax:** 503-464-2676
Toll-Free: 800-542-8818
Address: 121 SW Salmon St., Portland, OR 97204 US

GROWTH PLANS/SPECIAL FEATURES:

Portland General Electric Company (PGE) generates, purchases, transmits and distributes electricity, serving over 815,700 customers in Oregon, as well as wholesale customers throughout the western U.S. The company's service territory covers more than 4,000 square miles and includes 52 Oregon cities. The firm's service area has a population of more than 1.7 million people (roughly 43% of the state's population). The firm's total generating capacity of 2,609 megawatts (MW) is provided by its five wholly-owned hydroelectric plants, two wholly-owned fossil fuel plants and two wind power facilities, along with two jointly-owned hydroelectric plants and two jointly-owned fossil fuel plants. With regards to energy transmission, PGE owns or has access to 25,700 miles of transmission and distribution lines, and delivers approximately 22 million MWh (megawatt-hours) of electricity annually. PGE also owns approximately 79% of the Kelso-Beaver Natural Gas Pipeline, which connects its Beaver and Port Westward generating plants to the Northwest Pipeline, an interstate natural gas pipeline operating between British Columbia and New Mexico. In February 2010, PGE agreed to sell the Bull Run Powerhouse, a hydroelectric powerhouse that began operation in 1913, to Powerhouse Re Gen LLC for its future preservation. In August 2010, the company opened the first public-use, quick-charge station for electric vehicles in North America. In September 2010, the firm announced the completion of Phase II of the Biglow Canyon Wind Farm project, located in Sherman County, Oregon. Also in September 2010, PGE and enXco formed a power purchase agreement related to certain solar power installations near Salem, Oregon.

The company offers its employees medical insurance, paid vacations, training and development programs and gym access.

FINANCIALS:

Sales and profits are in thousands of dollars—add 000 to get the full amount. 2010 Note: Financial information for 2010 was not available for all companies at press time.

2010 Sales: $	2010 Profits: $	**U.S. Stock Ticker: POR**
2009 Sales: $1,804,000	2009 Profits: $89,000	**Int'l Ticker:** Int'l Exchange:
2008 Sales: $1,745,000	2008 Profits: $87,000	Employees: 2,753
2007 Sales: $1,743,000	2007 Profits: $145,000	Fiscal Year Ends: 12/31
2006 Sales: $1,520,000	2006 Profits: $71,000	Parent Company:

SALARIES/BENEFITS:

Pension Plan: Y	ESOP Stock Plan:	Profit Sharing:	Top Exec. Salary: $550,008	Bonus: $103,301
Savings Plan: Y	Stock Purch. Plan:		Second Exec. Salary: $416,508	Bonus: $50,179

OTHER THOUGHTS:

Apparent Women Officers or Directors: 4
Hot Spot for Advancement for Women/Minorities: Y

LOCATIONS: ("Y" = Yes)

West:	Southwest:	Midwest:	Southeast:	Northeast:	International:
Y					

POWER FINANCE CORPORATION LIMITED

www.pfcindia.com

Industry Group Code: 522220 **Ranks within this company's industry group:** Sales: 1 Profits: 1

Exploration/Production:		Refining/Retailing:		Utilities:		Alternative Energy:		Specialty Services:		Energy Mktg./Other Svcs.	
Exploration:		Refining:		Electric Utility:		Waste/Solar/Other:		Consulting/Eng.:		Energy Marketing:	
Production:		Retailing:		Gas Utility:		Thermal/Steam:		Seismic:		Equipment/Machinery:	
Coal Production:		Convenience Stores:		Pipelines:		Wind:		Drilling:		Oil Field Services:	
		Chemicals:		Water:		Hydro:		InfoTech:		Air/Shipping Transportation:	
						Fuel Cells:		Specialty Services:	Y		

TYPES OF BUSINESS:

Commercial Finance
Consulting
Leasing
Electric Industry Financing

BRANDS/DIVISIONS/AFFILIATES:

Chhattisgarh Surguja Power Ltd.
Coastal Karnataka Power Limited
Coastal Maharashtra Mega Power Limited
Orissa Integrated Power Limited
Coastal Tamil Nadu Power Limited
Bokaro Kodarma Maithon Transmission Co Ltd
PFC Consulting Ltd
National Power Exchange Limited

CONTACTS:

Note: Officers with more than one job title may be intentionally listed here more than once.

Satnam Singh, Managing Dir.
J.S. Amitabh, Company Sec.
Shri R. Nagarajan, Dir.-Finance
Rajeev Sharma, Dir.-Projects
Satnam Singh, Chmn.

Phone: 91-11-2345-6000	**Fax:** 91-11-2341-2545
Toll-Free:	
Address: Urjanidhi 1 Barakhamba Ln., Connaught Place, New Delhi, 110 001 India	

GROWTH PLANS/SPECIAL FEATURES:

Power Finance Corporation Limited (PFC) is a non-banking financial company focused on providing financing to power sector and related industries in India. Products and services offered by the company include project term loans, lease financing, direct discounting of bills, short-term working capital loans and consulting services. PFC's loan portfolio includes projects within a variety of power sector sub-disciplines, including thermal generation; hydro generation; wind and solar power; renovation and modernization of thermal power stations; renovation and up-rating of hydro power projects; transmission; and distribution. The firm has a particular focus on funding the development of power projects with power generation capacities in the range of 4000 megawatts (MW) and the ability to serve a number of Indian states through both regional and national power grids. The firm also awards grants, primarily to fund studies related to the power sector and power industry optimization and modernization. The company has recently been increasing its focus on expanding its investments in alternative and renewable energy sources, including solar, wind farms, small hydro-electric projects and bio-mass projects. Subsidiaries of the company include Chhattisgarh Surguja Power Ltd. ; Coastal Karnataka Power Limited; Coastal Maharashtra Mega Power Limited; Orissa Integrated Power Limited; Coastal Tamil Nadu Power Limited; PFC Consulting Ltd.; Jharkhand Integrated Power Limited; and Bhopal Dhule Transmission Company Limited. The firm also maintains a joint venture, National Power Exchange Limited, with partners NTPC Limited; NHPC Limited; and Tata Consultancy Services Ltd. Power Finance Corporation Limited is approximately 90% government-owned.

FINANCIALS:

Sales and profits are in thousands of dollars—add 000 to get the full amount. 2010 Note: Financial information for 2010 was not available for all companies at press time.

2010 Sales: $	2010 Profits: $	**U.S. Stock Ticker:**
2009 Sales: $506,390	2009 Profits: $425,470	**Int'l Ticker: 532810** Int'l Exchange: Bombay-BSE
2008 Sales: $409,980	2008 Profits: $259,350	Employees: 316
2007 Sales: $322,650	2007 Profits: $211,940	Fiscal Year Ends: 3/31
2006 Sales: $270,730	2006 Profits: $197,680	Parent Company:

SALARIES/BENEFITS:

Pension Plan:	ESOP Stock Plan:	Profit Sharing:	Top Exec. Salary: $	Bonus: $
Savings Plan:	Stock Purch. Plan:		Second Exec. Salary: $	Bonus: $

OTHER THOUGHTS:

Apparent Women Officers or Directors:
Hot Spot for Advancement for Women/Minorities:

LOCATIONS: ("Y" = Yes)

West:	Southwest:	Midwest:	Southeast:	Northeast:	International:
					Y

POWER GRID CORPORATION OF INDIA LTD www.powergridindia.com

Industry Group Code: 2211 **Ranks within this company's industry group:** Sales: 39 Profits: 24

Exploration/Production:		Refining/Retailing:		Utilities:		Alternative Energy:		Specialty Services:		Energy Mktg./Other Svcs.	
Exploration:		Refining:		Electric Utility:	Y	Waste/Solar/Other:		Consulting/Eng.:	Y	Energy Marketing:	
Production:		Retailing:		Gas Utility:		Thermal/Steam:		Seismic:		Equipment/Machinery:	Y
Coal Production:		Convenience Stores:		Pipelines:		Wind:		Drilling:		Oil Field Services:	
		Chemicals:		Water:		Hydro:		InfoTech:		Air/Shipping Transportation:	
						Fuel Cells:		Specialty Services:			

TYPES OF BUSINESS:

Electric Power Transmission, Control & Distribution
Telecommunications Services
Internet Service
Consulting

BRANDS/DIVISIONS/AFFILIATES:

POWERTEL

CONTACTS:

Note: Officers with more than one job title may be intentionally listed here more than once.

S.K. Chaturvedi, Managing Dir.
V.M. Kaul, Dir.-Personnel
Divya Tandon, Corp. Sec./Chief Compliance Officer
R.N. Nayak, Dir.-Oper.
J. Sridharan, Dir.-Finance
I.S. Jha, Dir.-Projects
T. Venkatesh, Chief Vigilance Officer
S.K. Chaturvedi, Chmn.

Phone: 91-124-257-1700 **Fax:** 91-124-257-1760
Toll-Free:
Address: Saudamini, Plot No. 2, Sector 29, Gurgaon, 122 001 India

GROWTH PLANS/SPECIAL FEATURES:

Power Grid Corporation of India, Ltd. (PGCI), is a public sector company engaged in the construction, operation and maintenance of inter-state power transmission infrastructure, as well as the operation of regional power grids throughout India. The company operates and maintains a power transmission network comprised of approximately 44,490 miles of power cable, through which about 45% of total power in the country is transmitted. PGCI also operates approximately 122 power substations in support of its transmission network. As part of its rural electrification program, the firm has recently completed infrastructure to bring power to over 22,000 additional villages. The company also maintains a broadband telecommunications fiber optic cable network of approximately 13,670 miles, connecting over 110 Indian cities and towns. Through its telecom business, operating as POWERTEL, PGCI provides national long distance, Internet service, Ethernet private lines, leased lines and infrastructure services. In addition, PGCI offers consulting services in areas such as transmission line and substation operation and maintenance, load dispatch center construction, tower and foundation design, substation upgrade, equipment testing, project reports, distribution management systems, contract and procurement services, project management services and training services. Clients include both domestic power companies and international clients in such countries as Afghanistan, Bangladesh, Bhutan, Dubai, Nepal, Nigeria and Sri Lanka. PGCI is approximately 86% government-owned. In June 2010, the firm announced plans to begin leasing space on its power transmission towers to tower firms and mobile service providers.

FINANCIALS:

Sales and profits are in thousands of dollars—add 000 to get the full amount. 2010 Note: Financial information for 2010 was not available for all companies at press time.

2010 Sales: $	2010 Profits: $	**U.S. Stock Ticker:**
2009 Sales: $1,444,270	2009 Profits: $365,750	**Int'l Ticker: 532898** Int'l Exchange: Bombay-BSE
2008 Sales: $1,422,340	2008 Profits: $360,200	Employees:
2007 Sales: $985,010	2007 Profits: $308,610	Fiscal Year Ends: 3/31
2006 Sales: $	2006 Profits: $	Parent Company:

SALARIES/BENEFITS:

Pension Plan:	ESOP Stock Plan:	Profit Sharing:	Top Exec. Salary: $	Bonus: $
Savings Plan:	Stock Purch. Plan:		Second Exec. Salary: $	Bonus: $

OTHER THOUGHTS:

Apparent Women Officers or Directors: 2
Hot Spot for Advancement for Women/Minorities:

LOCATIONS: ("Y" = Yes)

West:	Southwest:	Midwest:	Southeast:	Northeast:	International:
					Y

POWERSECURE INTERNATIONAL INC

www.powersecure.com

Industry Group Code: 335 **Ranks within this company's industry group:** Sales: 9 Profits: 9

Exploration/Production:		**Refining/Retailing:**		**Utilities:**		**Alternative Energy:**		**Specialty Services:**		**Energy Mktg./Other Svcs.**	
Exploration:		Refining:		Electric Utility:		Waste/Solar/Other:		Consulting/Eng.:	Y	Energy Marketing:	
Production:		Retailing:		Gas Utility:		Thermal/Steam:		Seismic:		Equipment/Machinery:	Y
Coal Production:		Convenience Stores:		Pipelines:		Wind:		Drilling:		Oil Field Services:	
		Chemicals:		Water:		Hydro:		InfoTech:	Y	Air/Shipping Transportation:	
						Fuel Cells:		Specialty Services:	Y		

TYPES OF BUSINESS:

Energy Metering Products & Services
Data Management Systems
Wireless Devices
Energy Analysis & Consulting

BRANDS/DIVISIONS/AFFILIATES:

WaterSecure Holdings Inc
PowerSecure Inc
Southern Flow Companies Inc
Interactive Distributed Generation
Innovative Electronic Solutions Lighting LLC

CONTACTS:
Note: Officers with more than one job title may be intentionally listed here more than once.

Sidney Hinton, CEO
Sidney Hinton, Pres.
Chris Hutter, CFO/Exec. VP/Treas.
Gary J. Zuiderveen, Corp. Sec.
Gary J. Zuiderveen, VP-Financial Reporting
Gary J. Zuiderveen, Controller/Chief Acct. Officer
Anthony Pell, Chmn.

Phone: 919-556-3056 **Fax:** 919-556-3596
Toll-Free: 866-347-5455
Address: 1609 Heritage Commerce Court, Wake Forest, NC 27587 US

GROWTH PLANS/SPECIAL FEATURES:

PowerSecure International, Inc. (PSII) is an energy holding company. The firm provides energy technology measurement products, services and data management systems to industrial/commercial consumers and suppliers of natural gas and electricity. PSII conducts business in two segments through three subsidiaries: Energy/Smart Grid Solutions through PowerSecure, Inc.; and Energy Services through Southern Flow Companies, Inc. and WaterSecure Holdings, Inc. PowerSecure engineers, sells and manages distributed generation systems marketed primarily to industrial and commercial users of electricity; it also provides energy management, engineering and consulting services. PowerSecure's Interactive Distributed Generation systems provide on-site power generation that supplements or bypasses the public power grid by generating power at the customer's site, in order to take advantage of peak-shaving and load interruption incentives. The subsidiary's turnkey program provides system design; generator and switch gear acquisition and installation; financing; operation; rate analysis; and contract negotiation with utilities. Southern Flow provides measurement, calibration and analytical services to natural gas producers, gas gathering, pipeline and transmission companies as well as oil, gas and petrochemical companies. Its services include meter installation, calibration, inspection, repair and maintenance; chart integration and processing; flow computer data acquisition and validation; independent auditing of measurement data; and laboratory analysis of natural gas, liquids and plant products. WaterSecure operates water processing facilities in northeastern Colorado. PSII also offers a utility infrastructure unit, which provides utilities with power system engineering/construction, regulatory consulting and rate design services. In April 2010, the company acquired majority ownership of Innovative Electronic Solutions Lighting, LLC an LED lighting development firm.

FINANCIALS:
Sales and profits are in thousands of dollars—add 000 to get the full amount. 2010 Note: Financial information for 2010 was not available for all companies at press time.

2010 Sales: $	2010 Profits: $	**U.S. Stock Ticker: POWR**
2009 Sales: $102,540	2009 Profits: $2,793	**Int'l Ticker:** Int'l Exchange:
2008 Sales: $135,440	2008 Profits: $10,658	Employees: 411
2007 Sales: $111,112	2007 Profits: $-1,608	Fiscal Year Ends: 12/31
2006 Sales: $115,702	2006 Profits: $11,705	Parent Company:

SALARIES/BENEFITS:

Pension Plan:	ESOP Stock Plan:	Profit Sharing:	Top Exec. Salary: $485,000	Bonus: $
Savings Plan:	Stock Purch. Plan:		Second Exec. Salary: $300,000	Bonus: $

OTHER THOUGHTS:

Apparent Women Officers or Directors:
Hot Spot for Advancement for Women/Minorities:

LOCATIONS: ("Y" = Yes)

West:	Southwest:	Midwest:	Southeast:	Northeast:	International:
	Y		Y	Y	

PPL CORPORATION

www.pplweb.com

Industry Group Code: 221 **Ranks within this company's industry group:** Sales: 24 Profits: 23

Exploration/Production:		Refining/Retailing:		Utilities:		Alternative Energy:		Specialty Services:		Energy Mktg./Other Svcs.	
Exploration:		Refining:		Electric Utility:	Y	Waste/Solar/Other:	Y	Consulting/Eng.:		Energy Marketing:	Y
Production:		Retailing:		Gas Utility:	Y	Thermal/Steam:		Seismic:		Equipment/Machinery:	
Coal Production:		Convenience Stores:		Pipelines:		Wind:	Y	Drilling:		Oil Field Services:	
		Chemicals:		Water:		Hydro:	Y	InfoTech:		Air/Shipping Transportation:	
						Fuel Cells:		Specialty Services:			

TYPES OF BUSINESS:

Utilities-Electricity & Natural Gas
Wholesale & Retail Energy Marketing
Power Generation
Generation Development Projects
Hydroelectric Generation
Nuclear Plant

BRANDS/DIVISIONS/AFFILIATES:

PPL Generation
PPL EnergyPlus
PPL Global
Western Power Distribution
PPL Electric
PPL Energy Supply

CONTACTS: *Note: Officers with more than one job title may be intentionally listed here more than once.*

James H. Miller, CEO
William H. Spence, COO/Exec. VP
James H. Miller, Pres.
Paul A. Farr, CFO/Exec. VP
James Schinski, CIO/VP
Robert J. Grey, General Counsel/Corp. Sec./Sr. VP
Joanne H. Raphael, VP-External Affairs
James E. Abel, Treas./VP-Finance
William H. Spence, Pres., PPL Generation
David G. DeCampli, Pres., PPL Electric Utilities
Victor N. Lopiano, Pres., PPL Nuclear Dev.
Robert D. Gabbard, Pres., PPL EnergyPlus
James H. Miller, Chmn.
Rick L. Klingensmith, Pres., PPL Global/Pres., PPL Energy Svcs.

Phone: 610-774-5151 **Fax:**
Toll-Free: 800-342-5775
Address: 2 N. 9th St., Allentown, PA 18101 US

GROWTH PLANS/SPECIAL FEATURES:

PPL Corporation (PPL) is an energy and utility holding company. The company's business operations are divided into three segments: supply, Pennsylvania delivery and international delivery. The supply segment owns and operates power plants; markets electricity in the deregulated wholesale and retail markets; and acquires and develops generation projects. PPL Energy Supply has generation assets focused on the eastern and western markets. PPL Generation owns and operates power plants in Pennsylvania, Montana, Illinois, Connecticut, New York and Maine. The firm's power plants have a total capacity of 9,583 MW and are fueled by uranium, coal, gas, oil and water. PPL EnergyPlus markets the electricity produced by PPL Generation subsidiaries. A subsidiary of PPL Energy Supply develops renewable energy plants using technology such as small turbines, reciprocating engines and photovoltaic solar panels. The Pennsylvania delivery segment includes the delivery operations of PPL Electric, which provides service to 1.4 million customers in 29 eastern and central Pennsylvania. PPL's international delivery segment is composed of PPL Global, the parent company of Western Power Distribution, which provides electricity to 2.6 million customers in the U.K. In February 2010, the firm's generating subsidiary sold its Long Island generation business to an affiliate of J-POWER USA Development Co., Ltd. for approximately $125 million. In April 2010, the company agreed to acquire the regulated U.S. business E.ON U.S. LLC, from German company, E.ON AG for $7.6 billion. In September 2010, the firm agreed to sell interests in some of its non-core generating stations to LS Power Equity Advisors.

FINANCIALS: **Sales and profits are in thousands of dollars—add 000 to get the full amount. 2010 Note: Financial information for 2010 was not available for all companies at press time.**

2010 Sales: $	2010 Profits: $	**U.S. Stock Ticker: PPL**
2009 Sales: $7,556,000	2009 Profits: $426,000	**Int'l Ticker:** Int'l Exchange:
2008 Sales: $8,007,000	2008 Profits: $930,000	Employees: 10,489
2007 Sales: $6,498,000	2007 Profits: $1,288,000	Fiscal Year Ends: 5/31
2006 Sales: $6,131,000	2006 Profits: $865,000	Parent Company:

SALARIES/BENEFITS:

Pension Plan:	ESOP Stock Plan:	Profit Sharing:	Top Exec. Salary: $1,189,039	Bonus: $2,519,000
Savings Plan:	Stock Purch. Plan:		Second Exec. Salary: $685,385	Bonus: $1,122,000

OTHER THOUGHTS:

Apparent Women Officers or Directors: 3
Hot Spot for Advancement for Women/Minorities: Y

LOCATIONS: ("Y" = Yes)

West:	Southwest:	Midwest:	Southeast:	Northeast:	International:
Y		Y		Y	Y

PRECISION DRILLING CORPORATION

www.precisiondrilling.com

Industry Group Code: 213111 **Ranks within this company's industry group:** Sales: 10 Profits: 10

Exploration/Production:		Refining/Retailing:		Utilities:		Alternative Energy:		Specialty Services:		Energy Mktg./Other Svcs.	
Exploration:		Refining:		Electric Utility:		Waste/Solar/Other:		Consulting/Eng.:		Energy Marketing:	
Production:		Retailing:		Gas Utility:		Thermal/Steam:		Seismic:		Equipment/Machinery:	Y
Coal Production:		Convenience Stores:		Pipelines:		Wind:		Drilling:	Y	Oil Field Services:	Y
		Chemicals:		Water:		Hydro:		InfoTech:		Air/Shipping Transportation:	
						Fuel Cells:		Specialty Services:	Y		

TYPES OF BUSINESS:

Oil Field Services
Drilling Services
Equipment Rental
Drilling Rig Component Manufacturing
Service Rigs
Wastewater Treatment
Onsite Catering Services
Oilfield Supply Services

BRANDS/DIVISIONS/AFFILIATES:

Precision Drilling Trust
LRG Catering
Gray Wolf International, Inc.
Precision Well Servicing
Precision Drilling Directional Services

CONTACTS:

Note: Officers with more than one job title may be intentionally listed here more than once.

Kevin A. Neveu, CEO
Kevin A. Neveu, Pres.
Rob McNally, CFO/Exec. VP
Joanne I. Alexander, General Counsel/VP/Corp. Sec.
Gene Stahl, Pres., Drilling Oper.
Ken Haddad, VP-Bus. Dev.
Darren Ruhr, VP-Corp. Svcs.
David W. Wehlmann, Exec. VP-Investor Rel.
Doug Strong, Pres., Completion & Prod. Svcs.
Robert L. Phillips, Chmn.
David Crowley, Pres., U.S. Oper.

Phone: 403-716-4500	**Fax:** 403-264-0251
Toll-Free:	
Address: 150 6th Ave. SW, Ste. 4200, Calgary, AB T2P 3Y7 Canada	

GROWTH PLANS/SPECIAL FEATURES:

Precision Drilling Corporation, formerly Precision Drilling Trust, is a provider of oilfield drilling, well servicing, energy services and wastewater treatment services in Canada, the U.S. and internationally. The firm operates 203 land drilling rigs in Canada, 146 drilling rigs in the U.S., as well as two in Mexico and one in Chile through Gray Wolf International, Inc. It also provides well servicing solutions in Canada with 199 service rigs, operated through Precision Well Servicing. The company also operates 85 camps, which it provides with catering through LRG Catering, as well as planning, set-up, site management and tear-down services. The company operates in two business segments: contract drilling services and completion and production services. The contract drilling services segment consists of the firm's drilling rig operations in North America and Chile, as well as its camp operation and catering services. This segment also contains the operations of Precision Drilling Directional Services, which provides experienced crews and 24-hour technical support for the drilling of vertical monitoring, directional and horizontal wells in Canada and the U.S.; and turnkey drilling services, which has completed projects in South Louisiana, Gulf Coast, South and East Texas and Mississippi. The completion and production segment consists of the company's service rig operations, in addition to its snubbing services, designed to enhance production and increase recoverable reserves; its equipment rental activities, including the rental of surface, tubular and well-control equipment; and its wastewater treatment services, primarily provided at industrial campsites. Precision Drilling also provides oilfield supplies, marketing over 2,600 types of consumables and materials in Canada and the U.S. The firm's business support activities include drilling rig, service rig and component manufacture, repair, procurement and distribution. In June 2010, the company converted from a trust to a corporation and changed its name to Precision Drilling Corporation.

FINANCIALS:

Sales and profits are in thousands of dollars—add 000 to get the full amount. 2010 Note: Financial information for 2010 was not available for all companies at press time.

2010 Sales: $	2010 Profits: $	**U.S. Stock Ticker: PDS**
2009 Sales: $1,171,830	2009 Profits: $158,240	**Int'l Ticker: PD** Int'l Exchange: Toronto-TSX
2008 Sales: $1,024,310	2008 Profits: $281,390	Employees:
2007 Sales: $989,000	2007 Profits: $338,900	Fiscal Year Ends: 12/31
2006 Sales: $1,408,800	2006 Profits: $568,000	Parent Company:

SALARIES/BENEFITS:

Pension Plan:	ESOP Stock Plan:	Profit Sharing:	Top Exec. Salary: $500,000	Bonus: $590,520
Savings Plan:	Stock Purch. Plan:		Second Exec. Salary: $231,911	Bonus: $385,892

OTHER THOUGHTS:

Apparent Women Officers or Directors: 1
Hot Spot for Advancement for Women/Minorities:

LOCATIONS: ("Y" = Yes)

West:	Southwest:	Midwest:	Southeast:	Northeast:	International:
	Y				Y

PREMIER OIL PLC

www.premier-oil.com

Industry Group Code: 211111 **Ranks within this company's industry group:** Sales: 90 Profits: 63

Exploration/Production:		Refining/Retailing:		Utilities:		Alternative Energy:		Specialty Services:		Energy Mktg./Other Svcs.	
Exploration:	Y	Refining:		Electric Utility:		Waste/Solar/Other:		Consulting/Eng.:		Energy Marketing:	
Production:	Y	Retailing:		Gas Utility:		Thermal/Steam:		Seismic:		Equipment/Machinery:	
Coal Production:		Convenience Stores:		Pipelines:		Wind:		Drilling:		Oil Field Services:	
		Chemicals:		Water:		Hydro:		InfoTech:		Air/Shipping Transportation:	
						Fuel Cells:		Specialty Services:			

TYPES OF BUSINESS:

Oil & Gas Exploration & Production

BRANDS/DIVISIONS/AFFILIATES:

Premier Oil UK Limited
Premier Oil Natuna Sea BV
Premier Oil Norge AS
Premier Oil Pakistan Holdings BV
Premier Oil Far East Ltd Singapore
Premier Oil Vietnam Offshore BV
Antrim Energy Inc
Oilexco North Sea Ltd

CONTACTS: *Note: Officers with more than one job title may be intentionally listed here more than once.*

Simon Lockett, CEO
Andrew Lodge, Dir.-Exploration
Neil Hawkings, Dir.-Oper.
Mary Pert, Coordinator-External Rel.
Mary Pert, Contact-Investor Rel.
Tony Durrant, Dir.-Finance
Mike Welton, Chmn.
Robin Allan, Dir.-Asia

Phone: 44-20-7730-1111	**Fax:** 44-20-7730-4696
Toll-Free:	
Address: 23 Lower Belgrave St., London, SW1W ONR UK	

GROWTH PLANS/SPECIAL FEATURES:

Premier Oil PLC is a U.K.-based, independent oil and gas exploration and production company. It operates producing fields in offshore Indonesia, on- and offshore Pakistan, offshore Mauritania and in the U.K. The company is also exploring areas in Norway, Pakistan, Congo, Egypt, Vietnam, Indonesia and the Sahrawi Arab Democratic Republic. These projects are all in different stages of development, from land acquisition to seismic mapping to exploratory drilling. The firm's average production rate is about 100,000 barrels of oil equivalent per day. Production and exploration subsidiary offices include Premier Oil U.K. Limited; Premco Abu Dhabi; Premier Oil Natuna Sea BV; Premier Oil Pakistan Holdings BV; Premier Oil Far East Limited Singapore; Premier Oil Vietnam Offshore BV; and Premier Oil Norge A.S. The company has proven plus probable reserves of approximately 400 million barrels of oil equivalent. In mid 2009, Premier Oil plc acquired Oilexco North Sea Limited, an oil and gas exploration and development firm that operates in the U.K. North Sea; and Delek Energy (Vietnam) LLC, the holding company for its 25% stake in a Vietnamese field, from Delek Energy Systems Ltd. In December 2009, Premier Oil sold its 10% ownership in Egypt's Northwest Gemsa permit to Sea Dragon Energy Inc. for approximately $14.8 million. In October 2010, the company agreed to form a joint venture with Antrim Energy, Inc., to investigate development options for the Fyne Area, which is located in the U.K.'s Central North Sea.

FINANCIALS: **Sales and profits are in thousands of dollars—add 000 to get the full amount. 2010 Note: Financial information for 2010 was not available for all companies at press time.**

2010 Sales: $	2010 Profits: $	**U.S. Stock Ticker: PMOIY.PK**
2009 Sales: $617,900	2009 Profits: $113,000	**Int'l Ticker: PMO** Int'l Exchange: London-LSE
2008 Sales: $651,200	2008 Profits: $98,300	Employees: 508
2007 Sales: $578,200	2007 Profits: $39,000	Fiscal Year Ends: 12/31
2006 Sales: $402,200	2006 Profits: $67,600	Parent Company:

SALARIES/BENEFITS:

Pension Plan:	ESOP Stock Plan:	Profit Sharing:	Top Exec. Salary: $	Bonus: $
Savings Plan:	Stock Purch. Plan:		Second Exec. Salary: $	Bonus: $

OTHER THOUGHTS:

Apparent Women Officers or Directors: 2
Hot Spot for Advancement for Women/Minorities:

LOCATIONS: ("Y" = Yes)

West:	Southwest:	Midwest:	Southeast:	Northeast:	International:
					Y

PRIDE INTERNATIONAL INC

www.prideinternational.com

Industry Group Code: 213111 **Ranks within this company's industry group:** Sales: 9 Profits: 7

Exploration/Production:		Refining/Retailing:		Utilities:		Alternative Energy:		Specialty Services:		Energy Mktg./Other Svcs.	
Exploration:		Refining:		Electric Utility:		Waste/Solar/Other:		Consulting/Eng.:		Energy Marketing:	
Production:		Retailing:		Gas Utility:		Thermal/Steam:		Seismic:		Equipment/Machinery:	
Coal Production:		Convenience Stores:		Pipelines:		Wind:		Drilling:	Y	Oil Field Services:	Y
		Chemicals:		Water:		Hydro:		InfoTech:		Air/Shipping Transportation:	
						Fuel Cells:		Specialty Services:			

TYPES OF BUSINESS:

Contract Drilling Services
Oil Rig Management Services

BRANDS/DIVISIONS/AFFILIATES:

GP Investments, Ltd.
Ferncliff TIH AS
Blake International LLC

CONTACTS:

Note: Officers with more than one job title may be intentionally listed here more than once.

Louis A. Raspino, CEO
Louis A. Raspino, Pres.
Brian C. Voegele, CFO/Sr. VP
Kevin C. Robert, VP-Mktg.
Lonnie D. Bane, Sr. VP-Human Resources
Jenny M. Rub, CIO/VP
Mark Diehl, VP-Tech. Support
Mark Diehl, VP-Eng.
W. Gregory Looser, Chief Admin. Officer/Sr. VP
Brady K. Long, General Counsel/Sec./VP
Imran Toufeeq, Sr. VP-Oper.
Kevin C. Robert, Sr. VP-Bus. Dev.
Jeffrey L. Chastain, VP-Comm.
Jeffrey L. Chastain, VP-Investor Rel.
Steven D. Oldham, Treas./VP
Robert E. Warren, VP-Industry
Leonard Travis, Chief Acct. Officer/VP
Lonnie D. Bane, Sr. VP-Admin.
Michael G. O'Reilly, VP-Risk Mgmt.
David A. B. Brown, Chmn.
Tony Seeliger, VP/Managing Dir.-Europe, Africa & Asia
Ann Ackerson, VP-Supply Chain

Phone: 713-789-1400	**Fax:** 713-789-1430
Toll-Free:	
Address: 5847 San Felipe St., Ste. 3300, Houston, TX 77057 US	

GROWTH PLANS/SPECIAL FEATURES:

Pride International, Inc. is a leading international provider of offshore contract drilling and related services to oil and natural gas companies worldwide, operating in approximately 15 countries and marine provinces. Pride owns a fleet of 23 rigs, consisting of two deepwater drillships, 12 semisubmersible rigs and seven jackup rigs, as well as four ultra-deepwater drillships under construction. Pride's operations are conducted in many of the most active oil and natural gas basins of the world, including South America, the Gulf of Mexico, the Mediterranean Sea, West Africa, the Middle East and Asia Pacific. Pride's customers consist of large multinational oil and natural gas companies, government-owned oil and natural gas companies and independent oil and natural gas producers. The company also provides rig management services, such as technical drilling assistance, personnel, repair and maintenance services and drilling operation management services for a variety of rigs.

Employees receive a full benefits package that includes medical, vision and dental insurance; a flexible spending account; and an employee assistance program.

FINANCIALS:

Sales and profits are in thousands of dollars—add 000 to get the full amount. 2010 Note: Financial information for 2010 was not available for all companies at press time.

2010 Sales: $	2010 Profits: $	**U.S. Stock Ticker: PDE**
2009 Sales: $1,594,200	2009 Profits: $285,800	**Int'l Ticker:** Int'l Exchange:
2008 Sales: $1,702,600	2008 Profits: $851,100	Employees: 4,020
2007 Sales: $1,329,000	2007 Profits: $778,300	Fiscal Year Ends: 12/31
2006 Sales: $2,495,400	2006 Profits: $295,300	Parent Company:

SALARIES/BENEFITS:

Pension Plan:	ESOP Stock Plan:	Profit Sharing:	Top Exec. Salary: $986,538	Bonus: $867,500
Savings Plan: Y	Stock Purch. Plan: Y		Second Exec. Salary: $441,346	Bonus: $225,279

OTHER THOUGHTS:

Apparent Women Officers or Directors: 2
Hot Spot for Advancement for Women/Minorities:

LOCATIONS: ("Y" = Yes)

West:	Southwest:	Midwest:	Southeast:	Northeast:	International:
	Y		Y		Y

PRIMEENERGY CORPORATION

www.primeenergy.com

Industry Group Code: 211111 **Ranks within this company's industry group:** Sales: 109 Profits: 76

Exploration/Production:		Refining/Retailing:		Utilities:		Alternative Energy:		Specialty Services:		Energy Mktg./Other Svcs.	
Exploration:	Y	Refining:		Electric Utility:		Waste/Solar/Other:		Consulting/Eng.:	Y	Energy Marketing:	
Production:	Y	Retailing:		Gas Utility:		Thermal/Steam:		Seismic:		Equipment/Machinery:	
Coal Production:		Convenience Stores:		Pipelines:		Wind:		Drilling:		Oil Field Services:	Y
		Chemicals:		Water:		Hydro:		InfoTech:		Air/Shipping Transportation:	
						Fuel Cells:		Specialty Services:			

TYPES OF BUSINESS:

Oil & Gas Exploration & Production
Oil Field Services & Construction

BRANDS/DIVISIONS/AFFILIATES:

PrimeEnergy Management Corporation
Prime Operating Company
Southwest Oilfield Construction Company
EOWS Midland Company
Eastern Oil Well Service Company

CONTACTS:
Note: Officers with more than one job title may be intentionally listed here more than once.

Charles E. Drimal, Jr., CEO
Charles E. Drimal, Jr., Pres.
Beverly A. Cummings, CFO
James F. Gilbert, Corp. Sec.
Beverly A. Cummings, Treas./Exec. VP

Phone: 203-358-5700	**Fax:** 203-358-5786
Toll-Free:	
Address: 1 Landmark Sq., Ste. 100, Stamford, CT 06901 US	

GROWTH PLANS/SPECIAL FEATURES:

PrimeEnergy Corporation is engaged in the acquisition, exploration, development and production of crude oil and natural gas. The company currently operates oil and gas wells primarily located in Texas, Oklahoma, the Gulf of Mexico, New Mexico, Colorado, Louisiana and West Virginia. Subsidiary PrimeEnergy Management Corporation (PEMC) acts as the managing general partner in 18 oil and gas limited partnerships and as the managing trustee of two asset and income business trusts. As such, PEMC is responsible for all partnership and trust activities, including the review and analysis of oil and gas properties for acquisition, the drilling of development wells and the production and sale of oil and gas from producing wells. PrimeEnergy provides well servicing support operations and acts as operator for many of the onshore oil and gas wells in which the company has an interest, as well as for third parties, through its wholly-owned subsidiaries, Prime Operating Company; Southwest Oilfield Construction Company; EOWS Midland Company; and Eastern Oil Well Service Company. The firm also acquires producing oil and gas properties through joint ventures with industry partners and private investors. Southwest Oilfield Construction Company serves both PrimeEnergy and third parties with site preparation and construction services for oil and gas drilling and re-working operations. The firm has proved reserves of approximately 82 billion cubic feet equivalent of natural gas, 80% of which was developed, while 20% was still undeveloped. At present, the company does not own any refineries or marketing or bulk storage facilities and the only owned pipelines are those used in connection with producing wells and the interests in certain gas gathering systems.

FINANCIALS:
Sales and profits are in thousands of dollars—add 000 to get the full amount. 2010 Note: Financial information for 2010 was not available for all companies at press time.

2010 Sales: $	2010 Profits: $	**U.S. Stock Ticker: PNRG**
2009 Sales: $89,992	2009 Profits: $-22,665	**Int'l Ticker:** Int'l Exchange:
2008 Sales: $169,338	2008 Profits: $ 541	Employees: 213
2007 Sales: $146,455	2007 Profits: $7,920	Fiscal Year Ends: 12/31
2006 Sales: $92,059	2006 Profits: $18,300	Parent Company:

SALARIES/BENEFITS:

Pension Plan:	ESOP Stock Plan:	Profit Sharing:	Top Exec. Salary: $360,500	Bonus: $
Savings Plan:	Stock Purch. Plan:		Second Exec. Salary: $360,500	Bonus: $

OTHER THOUGHTS:

Apparent Women Officers or Directors: 1
Hot Spot for Advancement for Women/Minorities:

LOCATIONS: ("Y" = Yes)

West:	Southwest:	Midwest:	Southeast:	Northeast:	International:
Y	Y	Y	Y	Y	

PROGRESS ENERGY INC

www.progress-energy.com

Industry Group Code: 2211 **Ranks within this company's industry group:** Sales: 21 Profits: 18

Exploration/Production:		Refining/Retailing:		Utilities:		Alternative Energy:		Specialty Services:		Energy Mktg./Other Svcs.	
Exploration:		Refining:		Electric Utility:	Y	Waste/Solar/Other:	Y	Consulting/Eng.:		Energy Marketing:	
Production:	Y	Retailing:		Gas Utility:		Thermal/Steam:		Seismic:		Equipment/Machinery:	
Coal Production:	Y	Convenience Stores:		Pipelines:		Wind:		Drilling:		Oil Field Services:	
		Chemicals:		Water:		Hydro:	Y	InfoTech:		Air/Shipping Transportation:	
						Fuel Cells:		Specialty Services:	Y		

TYPES OF BUSINESS:

Utilities-Electricity
Energy Services

BRANDS/DIVISIONS/AFFILIATES:

Progress Energy Carolinas Inc
Progress Energy Florida Inc
Customized Home Energy Report
Home Energy Improvement Program
Methane Power, Inc.
SunSense

CONTACTS: *Note: Officers with more than one job title may be intentionally listed here more than once.*

William D. Johnson, CEO
William D. Johnson, Pres.
Mark F. Mulhern, CFO/Sr. VP
John R. McArthur, Exec. VP-Admin.
John R. McArthur, General Counsel/Corp. Sec.
Paula J. Sims, Sr. VP-Corp. Dev. & Improvement
John R. McArthur, Exec. VP-Corp. Rel.
Bob Drennan, VP-Investor Rel.
Jeffrey M. Stone, Chief Acct. Officer/Controller
Vincent Dolan, CEO/Pres., Progress Energy Florida
Lloyd M. Yates, CEO/Pres., Progress Energy Carolinas
James Scarola, Sr. VP/Chief Nuclear Officer
Michael L. Lewis, Sr. VP-Energy Delivery, Progress Energy Florida
William D. Johnson, Chmn.

Phone: 919-546-6111	**Fax:** 919-546-7678
Toll-Free:	
Address: 410 S. Wilmington St., Raleigh, NC 27601 US	

GROWTH PLANS/SPECIAL FEATURES:

Progress Energy, Inc. is a public utility holding company. Through utility subsidiaries Progress Energy Carolinas, Inc. (PEC) and Progress Energy Florida, Inc. (PEF), the company is engaged in the generation, transmission, distribution and sale of electricity in the southeastern U.S. The utilities have over 22,000 megawatts (MW) of regulated electric generation capacity and serve roughly 3.1 million retail electric customers. PEC serves North and South Carolina customers in a 34,000-square-mile territory; PEF serves customers in west central Florida, with a service area encompassing approximately 20,000 square miles, including the cities of St. Petersburg, Clearwater and Orlando. PEC's consumption of various fuels includes 44% coal, 44% nuclear, 6% oil and gas, 5% purchased power and 1% hydro. PEF's consumption includes 44% oil/gas, 25% coal, 20% purchased power and 11% nuclear. In June 2009, the firm launched SunSense, a program aimed at increasing solar power use in Florida and the Carolinas by over 100 MW over 10 years. In 2009, PEC agreed to purchase power derived from two future solar plants and agreed to shut down three coal-fired factories. In July 2009, the company launched Customized Home Energy Report, an online program to help customers reduce power usage; and Home Energy Improvement Program, which gives rebates to customers who improve their homes' efficiency. In December 2009, PEC announced its intention to close 11 coal-fired units at four sites in North Carolina; and filed plans to construct a 600-MW natural gas-fueled power plant. In September 2010, PEC signed an agreement with Methane Power, Inc. for the construction of a 3-MW landfill gas-to-energy facility, whose generated electricity PEC will purchase.

The company offers its employees benefits such as medical, dental, vision, life and disability insurance; flexible and alternate work schedules; and a 401(k) plan and retirement plans.

FINANCIALS: **Sales and profits are in thousands of dollars—add 000 to get the full amount. 2010 Note: Financial information for 2010 was not available for all companies at press time.**

2010 Sales: $	2010 Profits: $	**U.S. Stock Ticker: PGN**
2009 Sales: $9,885,000	2009 Profits: $761,000	**Int'l Ticker:** Int'l Exchange:
2008 Sales: $9,167,000	2008 Profits: $830,000	Employees: 11,000
2007 Sales: $9,153,000	2007 Profits: $504,000	Fiscal Year Ends: 12/31
2006 Sales: $8,724,000	2006 Profits: $571,000	Parent Company:

SALARIES/BENEFITS:

Pension Plan: Y	ESOP Stock Plan:	Profit Sharing:	Top Exec. Salary: $979,231	Bonus: $950,000
Savings Plan: Y	Stock Purch. Plan:		Second Exec. Salary: $450,846	Bonus: $235,000

OTHER THOUGHTS:

Apparent Women Officers or Directors: 13
Hot Spot for Advancement for Women/Minorities: Y

LOCATIONS: ("Y" = Yes)

West:	Southwest:	Midwest:	Southeast:	Northeast:	International:
				Y	

PT PERTAMINA (PERSERO)

www.pertamina.com

Industry Group Code: 211111 **Ranks within this company's industry group:** Sales: Profits:

Exploration/Production:		Refining/Retailing:		Utilities:		Alternative Energy:		Specialty Services:		Energy Mktg./Other Svcs.	
Exploration:	Y	Refining:	Y	Electric Utility:		Waste/Solar/Other:	Y	Consulting/Eng.:	Y	Energy Marketing:	Y
Production:	Y	Retailing:	Y	Gas Utility:		Thermal/Steam:	Y	Seismic:		Equipment/Machinery:	
Coal Production:		Convenience Stores:		Pipelines:	Y	Wind:		Drilling:		Oil Field Services:	Y
		Chemicals:	Y	Water:		Hydro:		InfoTech:		Air/Shipping Transportation:	Y
						Fuel Cells:		Specialty Services:	Y		

TYPES OF BUSINESS:

Oil & Gas Exploration & Production
Oil & Gas Refining, Marketing & Distribution
Petrochemicals
Pipelines
Tankers
Biodiesel Fuel
Aviation Services

BRANDS/DIVISIONS/AFFILIATES:

Dana Pensiun Pertamina
PT Elnusa
Pertamina Energy Trading Limited
PT Pelita Air Service
PT Pertamina Retail
PT Pertamina Drilling Services Indonesia
Pertamina Energy Services Pte Limited
PT Pertamina Bina Medika

CONTACTS:

Note: Officers with more than one job title may be intentionally listed here more than once.

Karen Agustiawan, CEO
Karen Agustiawan, Pres.
Djailani Sutomo, Dir.-Mktg. & Trading
Rukmi Hadihartini, Dir.-Human Resources
Ferederick ST Siahaan, Dir-Investment Planning
M. Afdal Bahaudin, Dir.-Finance
Ferederick ST Siahaan, Dir.-Risk Mgmt.
Bagus Setiardja, Dir.-Upstream
Edi Setianto, Dir.-Refinery

Phone: 62-21-381-5111	**Fax:** 62-21-363-3585
Toll-Free:	
Address: Jalan Merdeka Timur, 1A, Jakarta, 10110 Indonesia	

GROWTH PLANS/SPECIAL FEATURES:

PT Pertamina (Persero) is a petroleum company owned by the Indonesian government. The company's upstream activities cover the exploration for and production of oil, gas and geothermal power. It maintains 33 oil contracts, 15 geothermal production areas and numerous gas and other energy activities; and operates 28 drilling rigs. Pertamina's downstream activities include oil and gas refining and the distribution and marketing of refined products. The company operates six fuel refineries, two liquid petroleum gas (LPG) plants and two liquid natural gas (LNG) plants. It also operates a fleet of owned and chartered tankers to transport oil and gas. Pertamina markets gasoline, kerosene, diesel and jet fuels; lube oils; LPG and LNG; petrochemicals including green cokes, benzene, waxes, propylene and toluene; and other non-fuels such as naphtha, sulfur and lean gas. In addition, the company has 22 subsidiaries and 10 joint ventures in the hotel, business support, shipping, airlines, dockyard, marketing, hospital, management, contractor, insurance and manufacturing industries. The firm's subsidiaries include Dana Pensiun Pertamina; PT Elnusa; PT Pelita Air Service; PT Patra Jasa; PT Patra Niaga; PT Pertamina Geothermal Energy; PT Pertamina EP Cepu; PT Usayana; PT Pertamina Dana Ventura; PT Pertamina Training & Consulting; PT Pertamina Retail; PT Pertamina Drilling Services Indonesia; Pertamina Energy Trading Limited; PT Pertamina Bina Medika; and Pertamina Energy Services Pte Limited.

FINANCIALS:

Sales and profits are in thousands of dollars—add 000 to get the full amount. 2010 Note: Financial information for 2010 was not available for all companies at press time.

2010 Sales: $	2010 Profits: $	**U.S. Stock Ticker: Government-Owned**
2009 Sales: $	2009 Profits: $	**Int'l Ticker:** Int'l Exchange:
2008 Sales: $	2008 Profits: $	Employees:
2007 Sales: $	2007 Profits: $	Fiscal Year Ends: 3/31
2006 Sales: $	2006 Profits: $	Parent Company:

SALARIES/BENEFITS:

Pension Plan:	ESOP Stock Plan:	Profit Sharing:	Top Exec. Salary: $	Bonus: $
Savings Plan:	Stock Purch. Plan:		Second Exec. Salary: $	Bonus: $

OTHER THOUGHTS:

Apparent Women Officers or Directors: 2
Hot Spot for Advancement for Women/Minorities:

LOCATIONS: ("Y" = Yes)

West:	Southwest:	Midwest:	Southeast:	Northeast:	International:
					Y

PTT AROMATICS AND REFINING PCL

www.pttar.com

Industry Group Code: 324110 **Ranks within this company's industry group:** Sales: 20 Profits: 7

Exploration/Production:		Refining/Retailing:		Utilities:		Alternative Energy:		Specialty Services:		Energy Mktg./Other Svcs.	
Exploration:		Refining:	Y	Electric Utility:		Waste/Solar/Other:		Consulting/Eng.:		Energy Marketing:	
Production:		Retailing:		Gas Utility:		Thermal/Steam:		Seismic:		Equipment/Machinery:	
Coal Production:		Convenience Stores:		Pipelines:		Wind:		Drilling:		Oil Field Services:	
		Chemicals:		Water:		Hydro:		InfoTech:		Air/Shipping Transportation:	
						Fuel Cells:		Specialty Services:			

TYPES OF BUSINESS:

Petroleum Refineries
Refined Petroleum Products
Aromatics Products

BRANDS/DIVISIONS/AFFILIATES:

PTT PCL
PTT Phenol Co., Ltd.
PTT Utilities Co., Ltd.
PTT ICT Solutions Co., Ltd.
PTT Group

CONTACTS:

Note: Officers with more than one job title may be intentionally listed here more than once.

Bowon Vongsinudom, CEO
Chainoi Puankosoom, Pres.
Varit Namwong, Exec. VP-Human Resources
Jeeranee Pimthanothai, VP-Tech.
Kun Patumraj, Sr. Exec. VP-Tech. Eng. & Maintenance
Varit Namwong, Exec. VP-Admin
Monwipa Choopiban, Sec.
Pomtemp Butniphant, Exec. VP-Refinery Oper.
Monwipa Choopiban, VP-Corp. Comm.
Nitima Thepvanangkul, Exec. VP-Finance & Acct.
Prachum Oneiam, Exec. VP-Aromatics Oper.
Dumrong Pinpuvadol, VP-Corp. Strategy
Norkun Sitthiphong, Chmn.
Vanchai Tadadoltip, Exec. VP-Supply Planning

Phone: 66-2937-1099 **Fax:** 66-2937-1088-9
Toll-Free:
Address: 555 Rasa Tower 2, 18th Fl., Phaholyothin Rd., Bangkok, 10900 Thailand

GROWTH PLANS/SPECIAL FEATURES:

PTT Aromatics and Refining PCL (PTTAR), part of the PTT Group, also known as PTT PCL, is one of Thailand's largest integrated petroleum refining companies and a top manufacturer of aromatics products. The firm operates through two segments, petrochemicals and refinery, and divides its operations into four lines of business: petroleum refining and refined petroleum product supply; the manufacture and sale of aromatics products; intermediate products; and joint venture business. The refinery business produces light products, such as liquefied petroleum gas, light naphtha and reformate; middle distillates, including diesel and jet fuel, which constitute the majority of the company's products; and heavy products, such as fuel oil. PTTAR has a refining capacity of 280,000 barrels of oil per day (BOPD), consisting of 145,000 BOPD of crude and 135,000 BOPD of condensate, and a refined petroleum products capacity of 228,000 BOPD. The aromatics business is a manufactures and distributes aromatics such as benzene, paraxylene, orthoxylene, toluene, mixed xylenes and cyclohexane. The company has an aromatics production capacity of 2.26 million tons per year. The intermediate product business, also called the derivative product business, primarily manufactures cyclohexane products. The firm's joint ventures include PTT Phenol Co., Ltd., a phenol and acetone production company in which PTTAR owns a 30% stake; PTT Utilities Co., Ltd., an electricity, steam and water utility production company of which PTTAR owns 20%; and PTT ICT Solutions Co., Ltd., which provides information technology services to the PTT Group and of which PTTAR owns 20%.

FINANCIALS:

Sales and profits are in thousands of dollars—add 000 to get the full amount. 2010 Note: Financial information for 2010 was not available for all companies at press time.

2010 Sales: $	2010 Profits: $	**U.S. Stock Ticker: Subsidiary**
2009 Sales: $7,587,240	2009 Profits: $308,150	**Int'l Ticker: PTTAR** Int'l Exchange: Bangkok-BAK
2008 Sales: $7,429,410	2008 Profits: $-249,950	Employees:
2007 Sales: $2,421,980	2007 Profits: $233,130	Fiscal Year Ends:
2006 Sales: $	2006 Profits: $	Parent Company: PTT PCL

SALARIES/BENEFITS:

Pension Plan:	ESOP Stock Plan:	Profit Sharing:	Top Exec. Salary: $	Bonus: $
Savings Plan:	Stock Purch. Plan:		Second Exec. Salary: $	Bonus: $

OTHER THOUGHTS:

Apparent Women Officers or Directors: 1
Hot Spot for Advancement for Women/Minorities:

LOCATIONS: ("Y" = Yes)

West:	Southwest:	Midwest:	Southeast:	Northeast:	International:
					Y

PTT EXPLORATION AND PRODUCTION PCL

www.pttep.com

Industry Group Code: 211111 **Ranks within this company's industry group:** Sales: 62 Profits: 41

Exploration/Production:		Refining/Retailing:		Utilities:		Alternative Energy:		Specialty Services:		Energy Mktg./Other Svcs.	
Exploration:	Y	Refining:		Electric Utility:		Waste/Solar/Other:		Consulting/Eng.:		Energy Marketing:	
Production:	Y	Retailing:		Gas Utility:		Thermal/Steam:		Seismic:		Equipment/Machinery:	
Coal Production:		Convenience Stores:		Pipelines:		Wind:		Drilling:		Oil Field Services:	
		Chemicals:		Water:		Hydro:		InfoTech:		Air/Shipping Transportation:	
						Fuel Cells:		Specialty Services:			

TYPES OF BUSINESS:

Oil Exploration & Production
Natural Gas Production & Transportation
LNG Production
Condensate Production

BRANDS/DIVISIONS/AFFILIATES:

PTT ICT Services Solutions Co. Ltd.
PTTEP Petroleum Development Support Base
Coogee Resources Limited

CONTACTS:

Note: Officers with more than one job title may be intentionally listed here more than once.

Anon Sirisaengtaksin, CEO
Anon Sirisaengtaksin, Pres.
Luechai Wongsirasawad, Exec. VP-Human Resources & Bus. Svcs.
Somkiet Janmaha, Exec. VP-Geosciences & Exploration
Pramote Phloi-montri, VP-Prod. Tech. & Well Eng.
Phongsthorn Thavisin, VP-Prod. Dev. Div.
Prisdapunt Pojanapreecha, Exec. VP-Eng.
Pranot Tirasai, Sr. VP-Legal Div.
Prisdapunt Pojanapreecha, Exec. VP-Oper. Support Div.
Kesara Limmeechokchai, VP-Strategic Planning
Sidhichai Jayant, VP-External Rel.
Chatchawal Eimsiri, Exec. VP-Finance & Acct.
Suraphong Iamchula, Exec. VP-Domestic Assets
Phongsthorn Thavisin, Sr. VP-Eng. & Construction
Suchitra Suwansinpan, VP-Petroleum Economics & Commercial
Vinit Hansamuit, VP-Reservoir Eng.
Prasert Bunsumpun, Chmn.
Somporn Vongvuthipornchai, VP-Int'l Assets
Pornthip Uyakul, Sr. Mgr.-Procurement

Phone: 660-2537-4000 | **Fax:** 660-2537-4444
Toll-Free:
Address: 555 Vibhavadi-Rangsit Rd., PTTEP Office Bldg., Bangkok, 10900 Thailand

GROWTH PLANS/SPECIAL FEATURES:

PTT Exploration and Production pcl (PTTEP), 65.46% owned by PTT Plc, is a Thailand-based petroleum exploration and production company, with over 1 billion barrels of oil equivalent in proved reserves. The firm generates about 53% of its revenue from natural gas sales, 26% from crude oil, 20% from gas condensate and 1% from liquefied petroleum gas. In 2009, it produced 263,000 barrels of oil equivalent per day. PTTEP operates on 42 exploration and production projects in 13 countries (including Thailand) spanning from Algeria in Africa to the Middle East, Southeast Asia, Australia and New Zealand. While some of these projects are wholly-owned by the company, many others are operated in conjunction with foreign energy companies such as Chevron and Hess. The company also draws revenue from its natural gas pipelines. Beyond exploration and production operations, the firm invests in energy-related projects. Inside Thailand, the Energy Complex Development Project develops office space for government agencies involved in the energy industry. The PTT Information and Communication Technology Services Solutions Company Limited (PTT ICT) is a consolidated project designed to promote synergies between a handful of Thai companies, including PTTEP and Thai Oil Public Co. Ltd. PTTEP's Petroleum Development Support Base explores viable options for resource exploitation outside of the immediate areas around Thailand. In the international arena, the company is developing a floating liquefied natural gas production scheme and investing in a natural gas pipeline in Myanmar.

FINANCIALS:

Sales and profits are in thousands of dollars—add 000 to get the full amount. 2010 Note: Financial information for 2010 was not available for all companies at press time.

2010 Sales: $	2010 Profits: $	**U.S. Stock Ticker:**
2009 Sales: $4,031,900	2009 Profits: $744,580	**Int'l Ticker: PTTEP** Int'l Exchange: Bangkok-BAK
2008 Sales: $4,102,920	2008 Profits: $1,230,600	Employees:
2007 Sales: $2,806,630	2007 Profits: $840,250	Fiscal Year Ends: 12/31
2006 Sales: $	2006 Profits: $	Parent Company:

SALARIES/BENEFITS:

Pension Plan: Y	ESOP Stock Plan: Y	Profit Sharing:	Top Exec. Salary: $	Bonus: $
Savings Plan:	Stock Purch. Plan:		Second Exec. Salary: $	Bonus: $

OTHER THOUGHTS:

Apparent Women Officers or Directors: 11
Hot Spot for Advancement for Women/Minorities: Y

LOCATIONS: ("Y" = Yes)

West:	Southwest:	Midwest:	Southeast:	Northeast:	International:
					Y

PTT PCL

www.pttplc.com

Industry Group Code: 211111 **Ranks within this company's industry group:** Sales: 23 Profits: 30

Exploration/Production:		Refining/Retailing:		Utilities:		Alternative Energy:		Specialty Services:		Energy Mktg./Other Svcs.	
Exploration:	Y	Refining:	Y	Electric Utility:		Waste/Solar/Other:		Consulting/Eng.:		Energy Marketing:	
Production:	Y	Retailing:		Gas Utility:		Thermal/Steam:		Seismic:		Equipment/Machinery:	
Coal Production:		Convenience Stores:		Pipelines:		Wind:		Drilling:		Oil Field Services:	
		Chemicals:		Water:		Hydro:		InfoTech:		Air/Shipping Transportation:	
						Fuel Cells:		Specialty Services:			

TYPES OF BUSINESS:

Oil Exploration, & Production & Marketing
Natural Gas Exploration, & Production & Marketing
Petroleum Refining & Petrochemical Production
International Petroleum Trading

BRANDS/DIVISIONS/AFFILIATES:

PTT Exploration & Production PCL (PTTEP)
PTT Aromatics and Refining PCL

CONTACTS: *Note: Officers with more than one job title may be intentionally listed here more than once.*

Prasert Bunsumpun, CEO
Prasert Bunsumpun, Pres.
Tevin Vongvanich, CFO
Pitipan Tepartimagorn, Sr. Exec. VP-Human Resources
Nuttachat Charuchinda, Sr. Exec. VP-Corp. Strategy
Sukrit Surabotsopon, Sr. Exec. VP-Petrochemicals & Refining Business
Wichai Pornkeratiwat, Sr. Exec. VP-Gas Business
Prajya Phinyawat, COO-Downstream Petroleum Business
Prajya Phinyawat, Sr. Exec. VP-Oil Business
Norkun Sitthiphong, Chmn.
Sarakorn Kulatham, Sr. Exec. VP-Int'l Trading Business

Phone: 66-2-537-2000	**Fax:** 66-2-537-3498-9
Toll-Free:	
Address: 555 Vibhavadi Rangsit Rd., Chatuchak, Bangkok, 10900 Thailand	

GROWTH PLANS/SPECIAL FEATURES:

PTT PCL, founded as part of the corporatization of the Petrochemical Authority of Thailand, operates in the petroleum and petrochemical industry. The company is 51% government-owned. It has four primary businesses: Gas Unit (generating 18% of 2009 sales revenues), Oil Unit (23%), International Trading Unit (49%) and Petrochemical & Refining Unit (2%). Subsidiary PTT Exploration & Production PCL (PTTEP), which conducts most of PTT's petroleum exploration and production, generates 7%, while the firm's coal business accounts for 1%. The Gas Unit explores for and produces natural gas; separates natural gas products like ethane and propane; operates onshore and offshore natural gas pipelines; and markets and trades natural gas and gas products. Besides producing its own gas, this unit procures natural gas through contracts from 10 fields in Thailand and two in Myanmar. Besides exporting petroleum products, the Oil Unit operates 1,146 gas stations throughout Thailand. Many stations sell biodiesel, including purified palm diesel, as well as gas-ethanol mixtures (commonly called gasohol) in addition to petroleum-based fuels. This unit also markets other petroleum products, including lubricants for cars, airplanes, ships and industrial applications. Besides its gas stations, the Oil Unit sells petroleum products, including fuel and lubricants, directly to larger customers like government agencies. The International Trading Unit engages in all aspects of petroleum trading, including procuring, importing and exporting crude oil, natural gas condensate and petrochemical products. The Petrochemical & Refining unit focuses on downstream petrochemical products such as polymer, resin, ethylene oxide and oleo-chemicals and bio-based chemicals. Its petrochemical business also involves maintenance and engineering services, as well as safety and environmental services. The unit's refining business has a total refining capacity of 1.04 million barrels per day. The company owns a 49% stake in Thai Oil, one of Thailand's largest refining companies.

FINANCIALS: **Sales and profits are in thousands of dollars—add 000 to get the full amount. 2010 Note: Financial information for 2010 was not available for all companies at press time.**

2010 Sales: $	2010 Profits: $	**U.S. Stock Ticker:**
2009 Sales: $48,814,700	2009 Profits: $1,832,580	**Int'l Ticker: PTT** Int'l Exchange: Bangkok-BAK
2008 Sales: $59,081,520	2008 Profits: $1,526,780	Employees:
2007 Sales: $44,533,120	2007 Profits: $2,888,020	Fiscal Year Ends:
2006 Sales: $	2006 Profits: $	Parent Company:

SALARIES/BENEFITS:

Pension Plan:	ESOP Stock Plan:	Profit Sharing:	Top Exec. Salary: $	Bonus: $
Savings Plan:	Stock Purch. Plan:		Second Exec. Salary: $	Bonus: $

OTHER THOUGHTS:

Apparent Women Officers or Directors: 3
Hot Spot for Advancement for Women/Minorities: Y

LOCATIONS: ("Y" = Yes)

West:	Southwest:	Midwest:	Southeast:	Northeast:	International:
					Y

PUBLIC POWER CORPORATION SA

www.dei.gr

Industry Group Code: 2211 **Ranks within this company's industry group:** Sales: 22 Profits: 15

Exploration/Production:		Refining/Retailing:		Utilities:		Alternative Energy:		Specialty Services:		Energy Mktg./Other Svcs.	
Exploration:		Refining:		Electric Utility:	Y	Waste/Solar/Other:	Y	Consulting/Eng.:		Energy Marketing:	
Production:		Retailing:		Gas Utility:		Thermal/Steam:		Seismic:		Equipment/Machinery:	
Coal Production:	Y	Convenience Stores:		Pipelines:		Wind:	Y	Drilling:		Oil Field Services:	
		Chemicals:		Water:		Hydro:	Y	InfoTech:		Air/Shipping Transportation:	
						Fuel Cells:		Specialty Services:			

TYPES OF BUSINESS:

Electric Utility
Power Generation
Telecommunications Services
Hydroelectric Generation
Wind & Solar Generation
Coal Mining

BRANDS/DIVISIONS/AFFILIATES:

PPC Telecommunications SA
PPC Renewable Sources SA
PPC Rhodes SA
PPC Crete SA
Telas SA
Larco SA
PPC Crete SA
Sencap SA

CONTACTS:

Note: Officers with more than one job title may be intentionally listed here more than once.

Arthouros Zervos, CEO
Georgios Angelopoulos, CFO
Georgios Triantafillis, Gen. Mgr.-Human Resources & Organization
Ourania Ekaterinari, Deputy CEO/Head-Finance
Evangelos Petropoulos, Vice Chmn.
Apostolos Baratsis, Deputy CEO/Head-Mines, Generation & Supply
Nikolaos Hatziargyriou, Deputy CEO/Head-Transmission & Dist.
Dimitrios Lathouris, Gen. Mgr.-Dist.
Arthouros Zervos, Chmn.
Christos Poseidon, Gen. Mgr.-Supply Div.

Phone: 30-210-52-30-501	**Fax:** 30-210-52-34-379
Toll-Free:	
Address: 30 Chalkokondyli St., Athens, 104 32 Greece	

GROWTH PLANS/SPECIAL FEATURES:

Public Power Corporation S.A. (PPC) is Greece's major power provider, supplying more than 97% of the country's electricity to 7.6 million customers. The firm owns and operates 98 generating facilities, using hydroelectric, thermal, wind and solar generation, with a current installed capacity of 12,814 megawatts (MW). The company's eight lignite power plants represent 42% of Greece's total installed capacity and generate nearly 56% of the country's electrical energy. PPC's power generation mix is split between lignite (61%), fuel oil (13%), natural gas (15.5%), hydroelectric (10%) and other renewable sources (.5%). PPC is the sole operator of transmission and distribution networks within Greece. Its network includes over 7,400 miles of transmission lines and over 134,000 miles of distribution lines. Duties of the company's distribution technical services unit include new services, power failure recovery, maintenance and inspection of the network. The firm has multiple subsidiaries, including PPC Telecommunications, a joint venture with Wind SPA, which provides standard telephony services, multimedia and Internet applications. The firm's subsidiary PPC Renewable Sources S.A. produces renewable energy; PPC Rhodes S.A. develops, constructs and operates the firm's power station in Rhodes; and PPC Crete S.A. manages the generating facilities on Crete. Telas S.A., which works under PPC Telecommunications, offers international long-distance telephone and Internet service. Other subsidiaries include Larco S.A.; PPC Crete S.A.; and Sencap S.A., which is 50% owned by PPC.

FINANCIALS:

Sales and profits are in thousands of dollars—add 000 to get the full amount. 2010 Note: Financial information for 2010 was not available for all companies at press time.

2010 Sales: $	2010 Profits: $	**U.S. Stock Ticker:**
2009 Sales: $8,550,930	2009 Profits: $983,080	**Int'l Ticker: PPC** Int'l Exchange: Athens-ATHEX
2008 Sales: $8,646,380	2008 Profits: $-454,180	Employees: 22,582
2007 Sales: $7,652,650	2007 Profits: $330,060	Fiscal Year Ends: 12/31
2006 Sales: $6,947,950	2006 Profits: $32,070	Parent Company:

SALARIES/BENEFITS:

Pension Plan:	ESOP Stock Plan:	Profit Sharing:	Top Exec. Salary: $	Bonus: $
Savings Plan:	Stock Purch. Plan:		Second Exec. Salary: $	Bonus: $

OTHER THOUGHTS:

Apparent Women Officers or Directors: 1
Hot Spot for Advancement for Women/Minorities:

LOCATIONS: ("Y" = Yes)

West:	Southwest:	Midwest:	Southeast:	Northeast:	International:
					Y

PUBLIC SERVICE ENTERPRISE GROUP (PSEG) www.pseg.com

Industry Group Code: 221 **Ranks within this company's industry group:** Sales: 14 Profits: 6

Exploration/Production:		Refining/Retailing:		Utilities:		Alternative Energy:		Specialty Services:		Energy Mktg./Other Svcs.	
Exploration:		Refining:		Electric Utility:	Y	Waste/Solar/Other:	Y	Consulting/Eng.:		Energy Marketing:	Y
Production:		Retailing:		Gas Utility:	Y	Thermal/Steam:		Seismic:		Equipment/Machinery:	
Coal Production:		Convenience Stores:		Pipelines:	Y	Wind:		Drilling:		Oil Field Services:	
		Chemicals:		Water:		Hydro:		InfoTech:		Air/Shipping Transportation:	
						Fuel Cells:		Specialty Services:	Y		

TYPES OF BUSINESS:

Utilities-Electricity & Natural Gas
Nuclear Generating Stations
Energy-Related Investments
Energy Distribution Systems
International Power Generation
Electricity & Gas Trading

BRANDS/DIVISIONS/AFFILIATES:

Public Service Electric & Gas Company
PSEG Power
PSEG Energy Holdings
PSEG Fossil
PSEG Global
PSEG Nuclear
PSEG Services
PSEG Solar Source

CONTACTS:

Note: Officers with more than one job title may be intentionally listed here more than once.

Ralph Izzo, CEO
Ralph Izzo, Pres.
Caroline Dorsa, CFO/Exec. VP
Margaret M. Pego, Sr. VP-Human Resources, PSEG Svcs. Corp.
J.A. Bouknight, Jr., General Counsel/Exec. VP
Anne E. Hoskins, Sr. VP-Public Affairs & Policy, PSEG Svcs. Corp.
Kathleen A. Lally, VP-Investor Rel.
Morton A. Plawner, Treas.
Randall E. Mehrberg, Pres., PSEG Energy Holdings
Ralph A. LaRossa, Pres./COO-Public Service Electric & Gas Co.
William Levis, COO/Pres., PSEG Power
Richard P. Lopriore, Pres., PSEG Fossil
Ralph Izzo, Chmn.

Phone: 973-430-7000 **Fax:** 973-824-7056
Toll-Free:
Address: 80 Park Plz., Newark, NJ 07101-1171 US

GROWTH PLANS/SPECIAL FEATURES:

Public Service Enterprise Group (PSEG) is a public utility holding company. The firm has three principal operating subsidiaries: PSEG Power, Public Service Electric and Gas Company (PSE&G) and PSEG Energy Holdings, Inc. PSEG Power, through subsidiaries PSEG Fossil, PSEG Nuclear and PSEG Energy Resources and Trade LLC (ER&T), is engaged in the generation, wholesale marketing and trading of electric energy. This division controls approximately 15,500 megawatts (MW) of installed capacity. PSEG Fossil has interests in 19 natural gas, coal and oil-fired electric generating stations in New York, New Jersey, Connecticut, Pennsylvania and Texas. PSEG Nuclear has ownership interests in three nuclear generating stations and operates two of them. PSE&G is a regulated public utility engaged primarily in the transmission, distribution and sale of electric energy and gas service in New Jersey. The subsidiary supplies electric and gas service to 2.1 million electric customers and 1.7 million gas customers in an area of approximately 2,600 square miles. PSEG Energy Holdings, through subsidiaries PSEG Global and PSEG Resources, participates in energy-related businesses which develop, acquire, own, operate and invest in independent power generation and distribution facilities throughout the world. In late 2009, PSEG's subsidiary, PSEG Solar Source, acquired two utility-scale solar projects, located in Florida and Ohio, from Juwi Solar, Inc. The firm also announced plans for a third solar project to be built in New Jersey. Its Florida project, with a 15 MW solar capacity, was completed in October 2010.

The company offers its employees medical, dental, vision, disability and life insurance; a health and wellness program; a 401(k); an employee stock purchase plan; a pension plan; referral and resource services; an employee assistance program; and tuition aid.

FINANCIALS:

Sales and profits are in thousands of dollars—add 000 to get the full amount. 2010 Note: Financial information for 2010 was not available for all companies at press time.

2010 Sales: $	2010 Profits: $	**U.S. Stock Ticker: PEG**
2009 Sales: $12,406,000	2009 Profits: $1,592,000	**Int'l Ticker:** Int'l Exchange:
2008 Sales: $13,322,000	2008 Profits: $1,188,000	Employees: 10,352
2007 Sales: $12,853,000	2007 Profits: $1,335,000	Fiscal Year Ends: 12/31
2006 Sales: $11,762,000	2006 Profits: $739,000	Parent Company:

SALARIES/BENEFITS:

Pension Plan: Y	ESOP Stock Plan:	Profit Sharing:	Top Exec. Salary: $946,450	Bonus: $1,345,000
Savings Plan: Y	Stock Purch. Plan: Y		Second Exec. Salary: $543,960	Bonus: $374,000

OTHER THOUGHTS:

Apparent Women Officers or Directors: 5
Hot Spot for Advancement for Women/Minorities: Y

LOCATIONS: ("Y" = Yes)

West:	Southwest:	Midwest:	Southeast:	Northeast:	International:
		Y		Y	

PUERTO RICO ELECTRIC POWER AUTHORITY www.prepa.com

Industry Group Code: 2211 **Ranks within this company's industry group:** Sales: Profits:

Exploration/Production:		Refining/Retailing:		Utilities:		Alternative Energy:		Specialty Services:		Energy Mktg./Other Svcs.	
Exploration:		Refining:		Electric Utility:	Y	Waste/Solar/Other:		Consulting/Eng.:		Energy Marketing:	
Production:		Retailing:		Gas Utility:		Thermal/Steam:		Seismic:		Equipment/Machinery:	
Coal Production:		Convenience Stores:		Pipelines:		Wind:		Drilling:		Oil Field Services:	
		Chemicals:		Water:		Hydro:		InfoTech:		Air/Shipping Transportation:	
						Fuel Cells:		Specialty Services:			

TYPES OF BUSINESS:

Electric Utility

BRANDS/DIVISIONS/AFFILIATES:

GROWTH PLANS/SPECIAL FEATURES:

Puerto Rico Electric Power Authority (PREPA) is the government-owned electric utility in Puerto Rico. The firm produces, transmits and distributes nearly all of the electric power used in Puerto Rico, supplying electricity to 1.5 million residential and business customers. PREPA operates through 33 client service offices, 29 technical service offices and 38 local offices, located throughout seven main regions. With a combined capacity of 5,839 megawatts (MW), the firm produces electricity at six fossil fuel-based generation plants, 21 hydroelectric facilities and purchases additional capacity from two natural gas and coal cogenerators. PREPA's fuel mix is split between 82% oil, 8% coal, 9% natural gas and 1% hydro and other renewable sources. The transmission system is composed of 2,444 miles of transmission lines, 51 transmission centers, more than 31,000 miles of distribution lines, 293 substations and 27 technical offices. In recent years, the Puerto Rican government began allowing independent power producers to build cogeneration plants on the island to sell power to PREPA in order to keep up with the increasing demand for energy.

CONTACTS:

Note: Officers with more than one job title may be intentionally listed here more than once.

Miguel A. Cordero, Exec. Dir.
Martin V. Arroyo Feliciano, Dir.-Finance
Astrid Rodriguez Cruz, Dir.-Human Resources & Labor Affairs
Elisa A. Fumero Perez, Dir.-Legal Affairs
Angel L. Rivera, Dir.-Planning & Environmental Protection
Josue A. Colon Ortiz, Dir.-Generation, Transmission & Dist.
Otoniel Cruz Carrillo, Dir.-Customer Svcs.
Jose A. Del Valle-Vazquez, Chmn.

Phone: 787-289-3434 **Fax:** 787-289-4120
Toll-Free: 800-981-2434
Address: P.O. Box 364267, San Juan, 00936-4267 Puerto Rico

FINANCIALS:

Sales and profits are in thousands of dollars—add 000 to get the full amount. 2010 Note: Financial information for 2010 was not available for all companies at press time.

2010 Sales: $	2010 Profits: $	**U.S. Stock Ticker: Government-Owned**
2009 Sales: $	2009 Profits: $	**Int'l Ticker:** Int'l Exchange:
2008 Sales: $	2008 Profits: $	Employees:
2007 Sales: $	2007 Profits: $	Fiscal Year Ends: 6/30
2006 Sales: $	2006 Profits: $	Parent Company:

SALARIES/BENEFITS:

Pension Plan:	ESOP Stock Plan:	Profit Sharing:	Top Exec. Salary: $	Bonus: $
Savings Plan:	Stock Purch. Plan:		Second Exec. Salary: $	Bonus: $

OTHER THOUGHTS:

Apparent Women Officers or Directors: 2
Hot Spot for Advancement for Women/Minorities:

LOCATIONS: ("Y" = Yes)

West:	Southwest:	Midwest:	Southeast:	Northeast:	International:
					Y

PUGET HOLDINGS LLC

Industry Group Code: 221 **Ranks within this company's industry group:** Sales: Profits:

Exploration/Production:		Refining/Retailing:		Utilities:		Alternative Energy:		Specialty Services:		Energy Mktg./Other Svcs.	
Exploration:		Refining:		Electric Utility:	Y	Waste/Solar/Other:	Y	Consulting/Eng.:		Energy Marketing:	
Production:		Retailing:		Gas Utility:	Y	Thermal/Steam:		Seismic:		Equipment/Machinery:	
Coal Production:		Convenience Stores:		Pipelines:		Wind:	Y	Drilling:		Oil Field Services:	
		Chemicals:		Water:		Hydro:	Y	InfoTech:		Air/Shipping Transportation:	
						Fuel Cells:		Specialty Services:			

TYPES OF BUSINESS:

Utilities-Electricity & Natural Gas
Hydroelectric Generation
Wind Generation
Solar Generation

BRANDS/DIVISIONS/AFFILIATES:

Puget Sound Energy Inc
Puget Energy
Puget Equico LLC
Macquarie Infrastructure Partners I
Canada Pension Plan Investment Board
Alberta Investment Management Corporation
Macquarie Capital Group Limited

CONTACTS:

Note: Officers with more than one job title may be intentionally listed here more than once.

Stephen P. Reynolds, CEO-Puget Energy & Puget Sound Energy
William Ayers, Chmn.-Puget Energy & Puget Sound Energy
Kimberly Harris, Pres., Puget Sound Energy
Eric M. Markell, CFO/Exec. VP-Puget Sound Energy

Phone: 425-454-6363	Fax:
Toll-Free:	
Address: 10885 NE 4th St., Ste. 1200, Bellevue, WA 98004 US	

GROWTH PLANS/SPECIAL FEATURES:

Puget Holdings LLC is a public utility holding company that operates exclusively through Puget Energy and its subsidiary, Puget Sound Energy, Inc. (PSE), a regulated electric and gas utility company in Washington. PSE provides electric and natural gas energy services for a territory covering approximately 6,000 square miles in Washington. The firm serves over approximately 1 million electric customers consisting of 949,900 residential, 118,400 commercial, 3,700 industrial and 3,400 other customers; and over 748,900 natural gas customers consisting of 691,900 residential, 54,300 commercial, 2,500 industrial and 200 transportation customers. In 2009, approximately 375,000 customers purchased both electricity and natural gas from PSE. The company's owned and contracted power resources total nearly 5,044 megawatts and are generated by hydroelectric, coal-fired, and gas/oil-fired plants, as well as wind generation. Approximately 37.4% of the electricity distributed by PSE comes from company-owned generation facilities and 62.6% comes from other utilities and power producers. PSE owns eight natural gas-fired power plants, three hydroelectric projects and two wind powered electric generation facility. PSE also distributes natural gas, including a limited amount of liquefied natural gas (LNG) and propane-air gas. All of the company's natural gas products are distributed through the facilities of Williams Northwest Pipeline Corporation (NWP). The firm maintains natural gas storage facilities in Washington and Utah, and stores LNG in facilities owned by NWP in Washington. Puget Equico LLC, an indirect wholly-owned subsidiary of Puget Holdings LLC. Puget Holdings was created in 2009 by a group of infrastructure investors to acquire and hold Puget Energy and its subsidiary, Puget Sound Energy. Puget Holdings is a consortium of long-term infrastructure investors including Macquarie Infrastructure Partners I, Macquarie Infrastructure Partners II, Macquarie Capital Group Limited, Macquarie-FSS Infrastructure Trust, the Canada Pension Plan Investment Board, the British Columbia Investment Management Corporation and the Alberta Investment Management Corporation.

FINANCIALS:

Sales and profits are in thousands of dollars—add 000 to get the full amount. 2010 Note: Financial information for 2010 was not available for all companies at press time.

2010 Sales: $	2010 Profits: $	**U.S. Stock Ticker: Private**
2009 Sales: $	2009 Profits: $	**Int'l Ticker:** Int'l Exchange:
2008 Sales: $3,357,773	2008 Profits: $154,929	Employees: 2,800
2007 Sales: $3,220,147	2007 Profits: $184,464	Fiscal Year Ends: 12/31
2006 Sales: $2,907,063	2006 Profits: $219,216	Parent Company:

SALARIES/BENEFITS:

Pension Plan:	ESOP Stock Plan:	Profit Sharing:	Top Exec. Salary: $819,792	Bonus: $788,906
Savings Plan:	Stock Purch. Plan:		Second Exec. Salary: $390,836	Bonus: $266,625

OTHER THOUGHTS:

Apparent Women Officers or Directors:
Hot Spot for Advancement for Women/Minorities:

LOCATIONS: ("Y" = Yes)

West:	Southwest:	Midwest:	Southeast:	Northeast:	International:
Y					

QATAR PETROLEUM

www.qp.com.qa

Industry Group Code: 211111 **Ranks within this company's industry group:** Sales: Profits:

Exploration/Production:		Refining/Retailing:		Utilities:		Alternative Energy:		Specialty Services:		Energy Mktg./Other Svcs.	
Exploration:	Y	Refining:	Y	Electric Utility:		Waste/Solar/Other:		Consulting/Eng.:		Energy Marketing:	
Production:	Y	Retailing:	Y	Gas Utility:		Thermal/Steam:		Seismic:		Equipment/Machinery:	
Coal Production:		Convenience Stores:		Pipelines:		Wind:		Drilling:	Y	Oil Field Services:	
		Chemicals:	Y	Water:		Hydro:		InfoTech:		Air/Shipping Transportation:	Y
						Fuel Cells:		Specialty Services:	Y		

TYPES OF BUSINESS:

Oil Exploration & Production
Oil Refining
Oil Transportation
Fertilizer Production
Fuel Additives
Liquefied Natural Gas
Petrochemical Production
Helicopter Transportation

BRANDS/DIVISIONS/AFFILIATES:

Qatar Fertiliser Company (QAFCO)
Qatar Petrochemical Company Ltd. (QAPCO)
Al-Shaheen Energy Services (ASES)
Qatar Liquefied Gas Company(Qatargas)
RasGas Companies
Qatar Vinyl Company (QVC)
Qatar Fuel Additives Company Ltd. (QAFAC)
Qatar Chemical Company (Q-Chem)

CONTACTS:

Note: Officers with more than one job title may be intentionally listed here more than once.

Abdullah Bin Hamad Al-Attiyah, Managing Dir.
Sheikh Kalid Bin Khalifa Al-Thani, CEO-Qatargas
Mohamed Yousef Al-Mulla, Gen. Mgr.-QAPCO
Ahmed Saif Al Sulaiti, Chmn.-Al-Shaheen Energy Services
Hamad Rashid Al Mohannadi, CEO-RasGas
Abdullah Bin Hamad Al-Attiyah, Chmn.

Phone: 974-440-2000	**Fax:** 974-483-1125
Toll-Free:	
Address: P.O. Box 3212, Doha, Qatar	

GROWTH PLANS/SPECIAL FEATURES:

Qatar Petroleum (QP) is the state oil company of Qatar. Through its subsidiaries, the firm manages the entire oil industry in Qatar, including exploration and drilling, refining, transportation, distribution and export of oil and natural gas. Some of its many subsidiaries include Qatar Fertilizers Co. (QAFCO), one of the world's largest single-site producers of urea and ammonia; Qatar Petrochemicals Co. (QAPCO), a joint venture with Atofina of France, which manufactures ethylene, sulfur and low-density polyethylene (LDPE); Qatar Liquefied Gas Co. (Qatargas), one of the world's largest producers of liquefied natural gas (LNG) and a supplier of LNG and condensate ; Ras Laffan Liquefied Natural Gas Co. (RasGas), which extracts, stores, processes and transports LNG and related products; and Qatar Vinyl Company (QVC), which produces ethylene dichloride, vinyl chloride monomer and caustic soda, products that are sold to clients in India, Pakistan, Australia and South East Asia. Qatar Fuel Additives Co. (QAFAC) owns and operates facilities that produce methanol and gasoline additive methyl tertiary butyl ether (MTBE). Qatar Chemical Company (Q-Chem), a joint venture between Chevron Phillips Chemical Company and International Qatar Holdings, LLC, operates a petrochemical plant that produces high-density polyethylene, 1-Hexene and associated byproducts. Qatar Vinyl Company (QVC) makes ethylene dichloride, vinyl chloride monomer and caustic soda. Lastly, Gulf Helicopters Company (GHC) provides helicopter transportation in six countries. Al-Shaheen Energy services (ASES) was created in 2006 to further explore joint venture projects. In January 2010, QP announced a joint venture with ExxonMobil Chemical to build a world-scale petrochemical complex in Ras Laffan Industrial City, Qatar. This complex will include one of the world's largest steam crackers, a polyethylene plant and an ethylene glycol plant.

Employees of QP receive salaries free of local taxes; education assistance; free medical and dental care; transport allowances; and annual leave with paid air fares to the employee's home country.

FINANCIALS:

Sales and profits are in thousands of dollars—add 000 to get the full amount. 2010 Note: Financial information for 2010 was not available for all companies at press time.

2010 Sales: $	2010 Profits: $	**U.S. Stock Ticker: Government-Owned**
2009 Sales: $	2009 Profits: $	**Int'l Ticker:** Int'l Exchange:
2008 Sales: $	2008 Profits: $	Employees:
2007 Sales: $17,902,000	2007 Profits: $	Fiscal Year Ends: 12/31
2006 Sales: $	2006 Profits: $	Parent Company:

SALARIES/BENEFITS:

Pension Plan:	ESOP Stock Plan:	Profit Sharing:	Top Exec. Salary: $	Bonus: $
Savings Plan:	Stock Purch. Plan:		Second Exec. Salary: $	Bonus: $

OTHER THOUGHTS:

Apparent Women Officers or Directors:
Hot Spot for Advancement for Women/Minorities:

LOCATIONS: ("Y" = Yes)

West:	Southwest:	Midwest:	Southeast:	Northeast:	International:
					Y

QUESTAR CORPORATION

www.questar.com

Industry Group Code: 211111 **Ranks within this company's industry group:** Sales: 64 Profits: 53

Exploration/Production:		Refining/Retailing:		Utilities:		Alternative Energy:		Specialty Services:		Energy Mktg./Other Svcs.	
Exploration:		Refining:		Electric Utility:		Waste/Solar/Other:		Consulting/Eng.:		Energy Marketing:	Y
Production:		Retailing:	Y	Gas Utility:		Thermal/Steam:		Seismic:		Equipment/Machinery:	
Coal Production:		Convenience Stores:		Pipelines:	Y	Wind:		Drilling:		Oil Field Services:	
		Chemicals:		Water:		Hydro:		InfoTech:		Air/Shipping Transportation:	
						Fuel Cells:		Specialty Services:			

TYPES OF BUSINESS:

Natural Gas Distribution
Energy Marketing & Trading
Pipelines

BRANDS/DIVISIONS/AFFILIATES:

Wexpro Co.
Questar Pipeline Co.
Questar Gas Co.
QEP Resources, Inc.
Questar Market Resources

CONTACTS: *Note: Officers with more than one job title may be intentionally listed here more than once.*

Ronald W. Jobson, CEO
Ronald W. Jobson, Pres.
Martin H. Craven, CFO
Kelly B. Maxfield, VP-IT
Kelly B. Maxfield, VP-Admin.
Thomas C. Jepperson, General Counsel/Exec. VP/Sec.
C. Scott Brown, VP-Oper., Questar Gas
Martin H. Craven, Treas./VP
R. Allan Bradley, Sr. VP/Pres./CEO-Questar Pipeline
James R. Livsey, Exec. VP/Gen. Mgr.-Wexpro
Craig C. Wagstaff, VP/Gen. Mgr.-Questar Gas
Shahad Saeed, COO-Questar Energy Services
Keith O. Rattie, Chmn.

Phone: 801-324-5000	**Fax:** 801-324-5483
Toll-Free:	
Address: 180 E. 100 S., Salt Lake City, UT 84145-0433 US	

GROWTH PLANS/SPECIAL FEATURES:

Questar Corporation is a natural gas-focused energy company that operates in the Rocky Mountain regions of the U.S. The firm's primary operations include retail gas distribution, interstate gas transportation and gas production. The company conducts its operations through three principal subsidiaries: Wexpro Company; Questar Pipeline Company; and Questar Gas Company. Wexpro develops and produces natural gas for Questar Gas in Utah and Wyoming. Questar Pipeline provides natural gas transport and underground storage services in Utah, Wyoming and Colorado. The subsidiary operates more than 2,500 miles of interstate pipelines, through which it transports gas to other major pipeline systems for delivery to additional markets, including Utah, southwest Wyoming and southern Idaho. Through subsidiaries, Questar Pipeline also owns and operates the Overthrust Pipeline in Wyoming and the eastern segment of Southern Trails Pipeline, a 488-mile line that extends from the Blanco hub in the San Juan basin to inside the California state line. Questar Pipeline also owns the Clay Basin storage facility on the Wyoming-Utah border and owns 50% of the White River Hub in western Colorado. Questar Gas provides retail natural gas distribution service to 900,000 customers in Utah, southwestern Wyoming and southeastern Idaho. In July 2010, Questar spun off subsidiary QEP Resources, Inc. (formerly Questar Market Resources), consisting of Questar's former natural gas and oil exploration and production and midstream field services businesses.

FINANCIALS: **Sales and profits are in thousands of dollars—add 000 to get the full amount. 2010 Note: Financial information for 2010 was not available for all companies at press time.**

2010 Sales: $	2010 Profits: $	**U.S. Stock Ticker: STR**
2009 Sales: $3,038,000	2009 Profits: $395,900	**Int'l Ticker:** Int'l Exchange:
2008 Sales: $3,465,100	2008 Profits: $683,800	Employees: 2,457
2007 Sales: $2,726,600	2007 Profits: $507,400	Fiscal Year Ends: 12/31
2006 Sales: $2,835,600	2006 Profits: $444,100	Parent Company:

SALARIES/BENEFITS:

Pension Plan:	ESOP Stock Plan:	Profit Sharing:	Top Exec. Salary: $900,000	Bonus: $1,718,548
Savings Plan: Y	Stock Purch. Plan:		Second Exec. Salary: $700,000	Bonus: $1,285,699

OTHER THOUGHTS:

Apparent Women Officers or Directors: 2
Hot Spot for Advancement for Women/Minorities: Y

LOCATIONS: ("Y" = Yes)

West:	Southwest:	Midwest:	Southeast:	Northeast:	International:
Y	Y	Y	Y		

QUICKSILVER RESOURCES INC

www.qrinc.com

Industry Group Code: 211111 **Ranks within this company's industry group:** Sales: 82 Profits: 105

Exploration/Production:		Refining/Retailing:		Utilities:		Alternative Energy:		Specialty Services:		Energy Mktg./Other Svcs.	
Exploration:	Y	Refining:		Electric Utility:		Waste/Solar/Other:		Consulting/Eng.:		Energy Marketing:	
Production:	Y	Retailing:		Gas Utility:		Thermal/Steam:		Seismic:		Equipment/Machinery:	
Coal Production:		Convenience Stores:		Pipelines:		Wind:		Drilling:		Oil Field Services:	
		Chemicals:		Water:		Hydro:		InfoTech:		Air/Shipping Transportation:	
						Fuel Cells:		Specialty Services:			

TYPES OF BUSINESS:

Oil & Gas Exploration & Production
Fractured Shale Gas
Coal Bed Methane
Tight Sand Gas

BRANDS/DIVISIONS/AFFILIATES:

Quicksilver Resources Canada, Inc.

CONTACTS:

Note: Officers with more than one job title may be intentionally listed here more than once.

Glenn Darden, CEO
Glenn Darden, Pres.
Philip W. Cook, CFO/Sr. VP
Anne D. Self, VP-Human Resources
Chris M. Mundy, VP-Eng.
John C. Cirone, General Counsel/Corp. Sec./Sr. VP
Jeff Cook, Exec. VP-Oper.
Richard C. Buterbaugh, VP-Corp. Planning
Richard C. Buterbaugh, VP-Investor Rel.
John C. Regan, Chief Acct. Officer/Controller/VP
Stan Page, Sr. VP-US Oper.
C. Clay Blum, VP-Land
Vanessa Gomez LaGatta, VP/Treas.
Robert N. Wagner, VP-Special Projects
Thomas F. Darden, Chmn.
David Rushford, VP/COO-Quicksilver Resources Canada Inc.

Phone: 817-665-5000	**Fax:** 817-665-5005
Toll-Free: 877-665-5000	
Address: 801 Cherry St., Ste. 3700, Unit 19, Fort Worth, TX 76102 US	

GROWTH PLANS/SPECIAL FEATURES:

Quicksilver Resources, Inc. is an independent energy company engaged in the exploration, development and production of oil, natural gas and natural gas liquids (NGLs) in North America. The company's efforts are focused on unconventional reservoirs found in fractured shales, coal seams and tight sands. Quicksilver's operations are concentrated in Texas, Colorado, Wyoming and Montana, as well as Alberta and British Columbia in Canada. Its principal areas of operation are the Horn River Basin of Northeast British Columbia; the Western Canadian Sedimentary Basin of Alberta; the Fort Worth Basin in Texas; and the Green River Basin of Colorado. The company has estimated proved reserves of 2.4 trillion cubic feet equivalent, of which approximately 99% is natural gas and NGLs and approximately 68% is proved developed. Its average production is approximately 325 million cubic feet equivalents per day (MMcfe/d). The company's Fort Worth Basin operations consist of 163,000 leased acres in the Barnett Shale formation, which is currently approximately 40% developed. The firm has three rigs operating in this area, and plans to drill 100 wells and complete another 125 wells during 2010. Quicksilver conducts its Canadian operations through subsidiary Quicksilver Resources Canada, Inc. (QRCI). In the Western Canadian Sedimentary Basin of Alberta, QRCI has a land position of approximately 342,000 acres. In the Horn River Basin of British Columbia, it has leased 130,000 net acres. In May 2009, Quicksilver entered a strategic alliance with Eni concerning acquisition, development and exploitation operations in the Fort Worth Basin. In June 2009, the firm sold 27.5% of certain natural gas leasehold interests to Eni. In May 2010, the company acquired additional interests in its operated Lake Arlington project in Texas. In October 2010, Quicksilver sold its entire interest stake, constituting about 61% of the partnership interest, in Quicksilver Gas Services, a midstream services company.

FINANCIALS:

Sales and profits are in thousands of dollars—add 000 to get the full amount. 2010 Note: Financial information for 2010 was not available for all companies at press time.

2010 Sales: $	2010 Profits: $	**U.S. Stock Ticker: KWK**
2009 Sales: $832,725	2009 Profits: $-545,239	**Int'l Ticker:** Int'l Exchange:
2008 Sales: $800,641	2008 Profits: $-373,994	Employees: 596
2007 Sales: $561,258	2007 Profits: $479,378	Fiscal Year Ends: 12/31
2006 Sales: $390,362	2006 Profits: $93,719	Parent Company:

SALARIES/BENEFITS:

Pension Plan:	ESOP Stock Plan:	Profit Sharing:	Top Exec. Salary: $440,000	Bonus: $706,200
Savings Plan:	Stock Purch. Plan:		Second Exec. Salary: $440,000	Bonus: $706,200

OTHER THOUGHTS:

Apparent Women Officers or Directors: 2
Hot Spot for Advancement for Women/Minorities:

LOCATIONS: ("Y" = Yes)

West:	Southwest:	Midwest:	Southeast:	Northeast:	International:
Y	Y				Y

Note: Financial information, benefits and other data can change quickly and may vary from those stated here.

RANGE RESOURCES CORP

www.rangeresources.com

Industry Group Code: 211111 **Ranks within this company's industry group:** Sales: 79 Profits: 81

Exploration/Production:		Refining/Retailing:		Utilities:		Alternative Energy:		Specialty Services:		Energy Mktg./Other Svcs.	
Exploration:	Y	Refining:		Electric Utility:		Waste/Solar/Other:		Consulting/Eng.:		Energy Marketing:	
Production:	Y	Retailing:		Gas Utility:		Thermal/Steam:		Seismic:		Equipment/Machinery:	
Coal Production:		Convenience Stores:		Pipelines:		Wind:		Drilling:		Oil Field Services:	
		Chemicals:		Water:		Hydro:		InfoTech:		Air/Shipping Transportation:	
						Fuel Cells:		Specialty Services:			

TYPES OF BUSINESS:

Oil & Gas Exploration & Production
Gas Processing & Transportation

BRANDS/DIVISIONS/AFFILIATES:

CONTACTS:

Note: Officers with more than one job title may be intentionally listed here more than once.

John H. Pinkerton, CEO
Jeffrey L. Ventura, COO
Jeffrey L. Ventura, Pres.
Roger S. Manny, CFO/Exec. VP
Carol Culpepper, VP-Human Resources
Mark D. Whitley, Sr. VP-Eng. Tech.
Alan W. Farquharson, Sr. VP-Reservoir Eng.
David P. Poole, General Counsel/Corp. Sec./Sr. VP
Chad L. Stephens, Sr. VP-Corp. Dev.
Ray N. Walker, Jr., Sr. VP-Marcellus Shale
Mark D. Whitley, Sr. VP-Southwest
Rodney L. Waller, Sr. VP/Assistant Sec.
John H. Pinkerton, Chmn.

Phone: 817-870-2601 **Fax:** 817-869-9100
Toll-Free:
Address: 100 Throckmorton St., Ste. 1200, Fort Worth, TX 76102 US

GROWTH PLANS/SPECIAL FEATURES:

Range Resources Corp. is an independent natural gas company engaged in the exploration, development and acquisition of oil and natural gas properties, primarily in the Southwestern and Appalachian regions of the U.S. The Southwestern region includes the Barnett Shale of North Central Texas; the Permian Basin of West Texas and eastern New Mexico; the East Texas Basin; the Texas Panhandle; and the Anadarko Basin of Western Oklahoma. The Appalachian region includes shale, coal bed methane and conventional oil and gas resources in Pennsylvania, Virginia, Ohio, New York and West Virginia. Currently, the firm's proven reserves are 3.1 trillion cubic feet, of which 84% are natural gas, 55% are proved developed and 79% are operated. The firm has an estimated reserve life of 18.6 years. The company produces approximately 435.9 million cubic feet of natural gas daily. In June 2009, the firm sold its West Texas Fuhrman Mascho properties located in Andrews County for $182 million, which included its interests in 445 producing wells and 54 water injection wells located on approximately 13,200 acres. In late 2009, the company sold natural gas properties in New York. In March 2010, Range Resources sold its tight gas sand properties in Ohio for $300 million. In June 2010, the firm purchased proved and unproved natural gas properties in Virginia for $135 million. In September 2010, the firm announced plans for the development and expansion of its regional headquarters near Pittsburgh, Pennsylvania.

The company offers employees a 401(k) plan; health, dental, vision, prescription, disability, critical illness and life insurance; equity ownership; health club memberships; accident assistance; and educational assistance.

FINANCIALS:

Sales and profits are in thousands of dollars—add 000 to get the full amount. 2010 Note: Financial information for 2010 was not available for all companies at press time.

2010 Sales: $	2010 Profits: $	**U.S. Stock Ticker: RRC**
2009 Sales: $907,341	2009 Profits: $-53,870	**Int'l Ticker:** Int'l Exchange:
2008 Sales: $1,322,947	2008 Profits: $351,040	Employees: 787
2007 Sales: $862,091	2007 Profits: $230,569	Fiscal Year Ends: 12/31
2006 Sales: $744,812	2006 Profits: $158,702	Parent Company:

SALARIES/BENEFITS:

Pension Plan:	ESOP Stock Plan:	Profit Sharing:	Top Exec. Salary: $641,346	Bonus: $1,022,000
Savings Plan: Y	Stock Purch. Plan:		Second Exec. Salary: $481,539	Bonus: $767,000

OTHER THOUGHTS:

Apparent Women Officers or Directors:
Hot Spot for Advancement for Women/Minorities:

LOCATIONS: ("Y" = Yes)

West:	Southwest:	Midwest:	Southeast:	Northeast:	International:
	Y		Y	Y	

RATCHABURI ELECTRICITY GENERATING HOLDING PCL

www.ratch.co.th

Industry Group Code: 2211 **Ranks within this company's industry group:** Sales: 42 Profits: 32

Exploration/Production:		Refining/Retailing:		Utilities:		Alternative Energy:		Specialty Services:		Energy Mktg./Other Svcs.	
Exploration:		Refining:		Electric Utility:	Y	Waste/Solar/Other:		Consulting/Eng.:		Energy Marketing:	
Production:		Retailing:		Gas Utility:		Thermal/Steam:		Seismic:		Equipment/Machinery:	Y
Coal Production:	Y	Convenience Stores:		Pipelines:		Wind:		Drilling:		Oil Field Services:	
		Chemicals:		Water:		Hydro:		InfoTech:		Air/Shipping Transportation:	
						Fuel Cells:		Specialty Services:			

TYPES OF BUSINESS:

Electricity Generation
Mining
Equipment Repair & Maintenance

BRANDS/DIVISIONS/AFFILIATES:

Ratchaburi Electricity Generating Company Limited
Ratchaburi Energy Company Limited
Ratchaburi Gas Company Limited
Ratch Udom Company Limited
Ratchaburi Alliances Company Limited
Ratchaburi Power Company Limited
SouthEast Asia Energy Limited
Chubu Ratchaburi Electric Services Company Limited

CONTACTS:

Note: Officers with more than one job title may be intentionally listed here more than once.

Noppol Milinthanggoo, Pres.
Prayut Thongsuwan, Exec. VP-Corp. Admin.
Boontiva Dansamasatid, Sec./VP
Thawat Vimolsarawong, Sr. Exec. VP-Bus. Dev.
Charusuda Boonkerd, Dir.-Corp. Rel.
Polagorn Kheosiplard, Dir.-Investor Rel.
Darunee Abhinoraseth, Sr. Exec. VP-Finance
Prachuab Ujjin, Sr. Exec. VP-Planning & Portfolio Mgmt.
Peerawat Pumthong, Exec. VP-Bus. Dev.
Ni-run Wongchanglor, Exec. VP-Planning & Portfolio Mgmt.
Suchart Avusosakul, Exec. VP-Finance
Sombat Sarntijaree, Chmn.

Phone: 66-2978-5000	**Fax:** 66-2937-9321
Toll-Free:	
Address: 19SCB Park Plz., 3 E., Fl. 20, Ratchadaphisek Rd., Bangkok, 10900 Thailand	

GROWTH PLANS/SPECIAL FEATURES:

Ratchaburi Electricity Generating Holding PCL (REGH), based in Thailand, is an investment holding company with primary interests in power generating companies. REGH currently operates through six 99.99%-owned subsidiaries with a combined installed capacity of 4,346 megawatts. These six subsidiaries include the following companies. Ratchaburi Electricity Generating Company Limited manages the Ratchaburi Power Plant, which has an installed capacity of 3,645 megawatts (MW). Ratchaburi Energy Company Limited focuses on the development of renewable power sources. Ratchaburi Gas Company Limited owns a 50% interest in Tri Energy Company Limited, a joint venture with Texaco Thailand Energy Company that operates a 700 MW combined cycle power plant. Ratch Udom Company Limited is a holding company for power businesses. Ratchaburi Alliances Company Limited runs two combined cycle power plants. RATCH-LAO Services Co., Ltd. operates a hydroelectric power plant in the Lao People's Deomcratic Republic (Laos). The company is also a minority stakeholder in the Ratchaburi Power Company, an independent power producer that has two combined cycle power facilities with a total capacity of 1,400 MW; and SouthEast Asia Energy Limited, a hydroelectric power plant operator. Other investments include a 50% interest in Chubu Ratchaburi Electric Services Company Limited, which operates and maintains various power plants on a contract basis; a 37.5% interest in Phu Fai Mining Co.; and a 10% interest in EGAT Diamond Service Co., which offers repair and maintenance on hot gas path parts and equipment. In July 2010, subsidiary Ratchaburi Energy Company Limited purchased a 60% stake in a solar power project being developed by Yanhee Solar Power Co. Ltd. In September 2010, the company established RH International Corporation Ltd. in order to invest in international power businesses in Mauritius and Singapore.

FINANCIALS:

Sales and profits are in thousands of dollars—add 000 to get the full amount. 2010 Note: Financial information for 2010 was not available for all companies at press time.

2010 Sales: $	2010 Profits: $	**U.S. Stock Ticker:**
2009 Sales: $1,188,130	2009 Profits: $226,520	**Int'l Ticker: RATCH** Int'l Exchange: Bangkok-BAK
2008 Sales: $1,246,410	2008 Profits: $191,730	Employees:
2007 Sales: $1,293,970	2007 Profits: $172,140	Fiscal Year Ends: 6/30
2006 Sales: $	2006 Profits: $	Parent Company:

SALARIES/BENEFITS:

Pension Plan:	ESOP Stock Plan:	Profit Sharing:	Top Exec. Salary: $	Bonus: $
Savings Plan:	Stock Purch. Plan:		Second Exec. Salary: $	Bonus: $

OTHER THOUGHTS:

Apparent Women Officers or Directors: 3
Hot Spot for Advancement for Women/Minorities: Y

LOCATIONS: ("Y" = Yes)

West:	Southwest:	Midwest:	Southeast:	Northeast:	International:
					Y

RED APPLE GROUP INC

Industry Group Code: 324110 **Ranks within this company's industry group:** Sales: 25 Profits:

Exploration/Production:		Refining/Retailing:		Utilities:		Alternative Energy:		Specialty Services:		Energy Mktg./Other Svcs.	
Exploration:		Refining:	Y	Electric Utility:		Waste/Solar/Other:		Consulting/Eng.:		Energy Marketing:	
Production:		Retailing:	Y	Gas Utility:		Thermal/Steam:		Seismic:		Equipment/Machinery:	
Coal Production:		Convenience Stores:	Y	Pipelines:		Wind:		Drilling:		Oil Field Services:	
		Chemicals:		Water:		Hydro:		InfoTech:		Air/Shipping Transportation:	
						Fuel Cells:		Specialty Services:	Y		

TYPES OF BUSINESS:

Oil Refining
Gas Stations
Convenience Stores
Grocery Stores

BRANDS/DIVISIONS/AFFILIATES:

United Refining Company
Kwik-Fill
Citgo
Red Apple Foot Marts
Country Fair
Gristede's Foods, Inc.
United Refining Energy Corp
Hellenic Times

CONTACTS: *Note: Officers with more than one job title may be intentionally listed here more than once.*

John A. Catsimatidis, CEO
John A. Catsimatidis, Pres.
John A. Catsimatidis, CEO-Gristede's Foods & United Refining Co.
John A. Catsimatidis, CEO/Chmn.-United Refining Energy Corp.
John A. Catsimatidis, Chmn.

Phone: 212-956-5803	**Fax:** 212-247-4509
Toll-Free:	
Address: 823 11th Ave., New York, NY 10019 US	

GROWTH PLANS/SPECIAL FEATURES:

Red Apple Group, Inc. (RAG) is a private holding company owned by CEO John A. Catsimatidis. The firm has operations in refining, supermarkets and convenience stores, real estate, aviation and publishing. Its main subsidiary is United Refining Company, acquired by RAG in 1986, which operates a 92-acre refinery in Warren, Pennsylvania. The refinery processes 70,000 barrels a day of crude oil. Its retail business sells petroleum products under the brand names Kwik-Fill, Citgo and Keystone and operates combined gasoline stations and convenience stores under the names Red Apple Food Mart and Country Fair. In all, the retail segment operates approximately 367 stores, in New York, Pennsylvania and Ohio. United Refining Energy Corp., is a blank check company formed for the purpose of acquiring, merging with, engaging in a capital stock exchange with, purchasing all or substantially all of the assets of, or engaging in any other similar business combination of an unidentified operating business. Gristede's Foods, Inc. is RAG's supermarket subsidiary, operating primarily in New York, New York. The firm's stores typically offer basic grocery items, meat, dairy, produce, seafood and frozen foods, as well as a bakery, deli, floral department and pharmacy. Aside from megastores, many of Gristede's items are sold online, shipping mainly in Manhattan but also across the continental U.S. and Canada. RAG's real estate subsidiary is Red Apple Real Estate, which owns properties in New York and New Jersey. The firm also has an aircraft leasing company that formerly controlled aviation management assets but currently only maintains small aircraft. Hellenic Times, RAG's publishing subsidiary, is one of the largest Greek-American newspapers in the country.

FINANCIALS: **Sales and profits are in thousands of dollars—add 000 to get the full amount. 2010 Note: Financial information for 2010 was not available for all companies at press time.**

2010 Sales: $	2010 Profits: $	**U.S. Stock Ticker: Private**
2009 Sales: $4,020,000	2009 Profits: $	**Int'l Ticker:** Int'l Exchange:
2008 Sales: $3,950,000	2008 Profits: $	Employees: 7,600
2007 Sales: $	2007 Profits: $	Fiscal Year Ends: 2/28
2006 Sales: $3,630,000	2006 Profits: $	Parent Company:

SALARIES/BENEFITS:

Pension Plan:	ESOP Stock Plan:	Profit Sharing:	Top Exec. Salary: $	Bonus: $
Savings Plan:	Stock Purch. Plan:		Second Exec. Salary: $	Bonus: $

OTHER THOUGHTS:

Apparent Women Officers or Directors:
Hot Spot for Advancement for Women/Minorities:

LOCATIONS: ("Y" = Yes)

West:	Southwest:	Midwest:	Southeast:	Northeast:	International:
				Y	Y

RELIANCE INDUSTRIES LTD (RELIANCE GROUP)

www.ril.com

Industry Group Code: 325110 **Ranks within this company's industry group:** Sales: 2 Profits: 1

Exploration/Production:		Refining/Retailing:		Utilities:		Alternative Energy:		Specialty Services:		Energy Mktg./Other Svcs.	
Exploration:		Refining:		Electric Utility:		Waste/Solar/Other:		Consulting/Eng.:		Energy Marketing:	
Production:		Retailing:		Gas Utility:		Thermal/Steam:		Seismic:		Equipment/Machinery:	
Coal Production:		Convenience Stores:		Pipelines:		Wind:		Drilling:		Oil Field Services:	
		Chemicals:	Y	Water:		Hydro:		InfoTech:		Air/Shipping Transportation:	
						Fuel Cells:		Specialty Services:			

TYPES OF BUSINESS:

Petrochemicals Refining & Manufacturing
Textiles & Fabrics
Oil & Gas Exploration
Power Generation
Supermarkets
Mall Development

BRANDS/DIVISIONS/AFFILIATES:

Recrylon
Vimal
Harmony
Reance
Hualon Corporation Sdn Bhd
Indian Petrochemicals Corporation Limited
GAIL, Ltd.
Reliance Group

CONTACTS: *Note: Officers with more than one job title may be intentionally listed here more than once.*

Mukesh D. Ambani, Managing Dir.
Vinod M. Ambani, Sec./Compliance Officer
Hital R. Meswani, Exec. Dir.-Petroleum Div.
Nikhil R. Meswani, Exec. Dir.-Petrochemicals Div.
Mukesh D. Ambani, Chmn.

Phone: 91-22-2278-5000 **Fax:**
Toll-Free:
Address: Makers Chambers IV, Nariman Point, Mumbai, 400 021 India

GROWTH PLANS/SPECIAL FEATURES:

Reliance Industries, Ltd. (Reliance Group or RIL) is a conglomerate that operates in several business sectors, including energy, textiles, retail and petrochemicals. RIL produces and distributes plastics and intermediates, polyester filament yarn, polymer intermediates, chemicals, textiles, retail, oil and natural gas. It is one of the largest producers of polyester fiber and yarn in the world. RIL has one of the largest marketing networks in India with textile products sold under the the labels, Vimal, the firm's flagship brand, and V2. Its latest textile products include anti-microbial and anti-bacterial work-wear fabrics; heavy-duty textiles for home furnishing and automobiles; silk-amino suiting materials; fire-retardant and water-repellent tent fabrics; and insect and mosquito repellent nets in compliance with World Health Organization standards. RIL's petroleum exploration and production segment provides crude oil and natural gas to refining, power, fertilizer, petrochemical and other industries, and the company also conducts its own refining and marketing under the Reliance Gas brand name. The firm's petrochemicals, chemicals, acrylics and polyesters division, through brands such as Repol, Relene and Recron, supplies a wide variety of products and materials to domestic and international technology partners. The polyester division holds roughly 120 polyester patents. RIL's retail segment includes grocery stores under the Reliancefresh brand name; hypermarkets such as RelianceSuper and RelianceMart; Reliancetrends apparel retailers; Reliancedigital electronics stores; Reliancewellness pharmacies; Reliancefootprint shoe stores; and iStore an exclusive Apple products store. In April 2009, Reliance Industries, Ltd. merged with subsidiary Reliance Petroleum Limited.

FINANCIALS: **Sales and profits are in thousands of dollars—add 000 to get the full amount. 2010 Note: Financial information for 2010 was not available for all companies at press time.**

2010 Sales: $45,590,800	2010 Profits: $5,483,010	**U.S. Stock Ticker:**
2009 Sales: $33,819,500	2009 Profits: $3,350,120	**Int'l Ticker: 500325** Int'l Exchange: Bombay-BSE
2008 Sales: $30,689,300	2008 Profits: $4,378,690	Employees:
2007 Sales: $25,510,000	2007 Profits: $2,510,000	Fiscal Year Ends: 3/31
2006 Sales: $19,976,000	2006 Profits: $2,033,000	Parent Company:

SALARIES/BENEFITS:

Pension Plan: Y	ESOP Stock Plan:	Profit Sharing:	Top Exec. Salary: $	Bonus: $
Savings Plan:	Stock Purch. Plan:		Second Exec. Salary: $	Bonus: $

OTHER THOUGHTS:

Apparent Women Officers or Directors:
Hot Spot for Advancement for Women/Minorities:

LOCATIONS: ("Y" = Yes)

West:	Southwest:	Midwest:	Southeast:	Northeast:	International:
					Y

RELIANCE INFRASTRUCTURE LTD

www.rinfra.com

Industry Group Code: 2211 **Ranks within this company's industry group:** Sales: 32 Profits: 28

Exploration/Production:		Refining/Retailing:		Utilities:		Alternative Energy:		Specialty Services:		Energy Mktg./Other Svcs.	
Exploration:		Refining:		Electric Utility:	Y	Waste/Solar/Other:		Consulting/Eng.:	Y	Energy Marketing:	
Production:		Retailing:		Gas Utility:		Thermal/Steam:		Seismic:		Equipment/Machinery:	Y
Coal Production:		Convenience Stores:		Pipelines:		Wind:		Drilling:		Oil Field Services:	
		Chemicals:		Water:		Hydro:		InfoTech:		Air/Shipping Transportation:	
						Fuel Cells:		Specialty Services:			

TYPES OF BUSINESS:

Utilities, Electric
Power Generation, Transmission and Distribution
Construction Services
Cement Production

BRANDS/DIVISIONS/AFFILIATES:

Reliance Power Transmission Limited
Reliance Infraprojects Limited
Reliance Projects Finance Private Limited
Reliance Power Infrastructure Limited
Reliance Energy Trading Limited

CONTACTS: *Note: Officers with more than one job title may be intentionally listed here more than once.*

Ramesh Shenoy, Company Sec./Compliance Officer
S.C. Gupta, Dir.-Oper.
Satish Seth, Vice Chmn.
Lalit Jalan, Dir.-Energy Transmission, Dist. & Trading
Anil D. Ambani, Chmn.

Phone: 91-22-3009-9311 **Fax:** 91-22-3009-9763
Toll-Free: 800-200-3030
Address: Reliance Energy Centre, Santacruz E, Mumbai, 400 055 India

GROWTH PLANS/SPECIAL FEATURES:

Reliance Infrastructure Ltd., formerly Reliance Energy Limited, is a private sector power utility and an infrastructure company, and a part of the Reliance Anil Dhirubhai Ambani Group, one of India's largest business houses. The firm is active in the power sector through its 45% interest in Reliance Power, whose activities include the generation, transmission, distribution and trading of electricity. Reliance Power serves approximately 5.2 million electricity customers throughout India, including two-thirds of the homes in Mumbai and Delhi. The company generates over 940 megawatts (MW) of electricity through its mix of combined cycle and wind generating power stations located in the Indian states of Maharashtra, Andhra Pradesh, Kerala, Karnataka and Goa. The company's infrastructure business focuses on the construction of roads, urban infrastructure and rapid transit systems, airports, business districts, skyscrapers, convention centers and special economic zones (SEZs). Current projects include a 14-mile high-speed metro rail line connecting New Delhi's railway station and the city's international airport; 5 airfield construction projects; and 11 road projects, including a freeway sea link connecting Haji Ali, Worli and Bandra. This division also oversees the production of cement. Reliance EPC (Engineering, Procurement and Construction) manages the company's power plant constriction projects internally for Reliance Power and for external businesses. It is currently actively engaged in the construction of 7,500 MW of power projects and about 75 miles of road construction. Wholly-owned subsidiaries of the company include Reliance Power Transmission Limited, Reliance Infraprojects Limited, Reliance Projects Finance Private Limited, Reliance Power Infrastructure Limited and Reliance Energy Trading Limited.

FINANCIALS: **Sales and profits are in thousands of dollars—add 000 to get the full amount. 2010 Note: Financial information for 2010 was not available for all companies at press time.**

2010 Sales: $
2009 Sales: $2,721,170
2008 Sales: $1,694,640
2007 Sales: $1,398,270
2006 Sales: $823,480

2010 Profits: $
2009 Profits: $292,761
2008 Profits: $239,230
2007 Profits: $170,370
2006 Profits: $132,770

U.S. Stock Ticker:
Int'l Ticker: 500390 Int'l Exchange: Bombay-BSE
Employees:
Fiscal Year Ends: 3/31
Parent Company:

SALARIES/BENEFITS:

Pension Plan: ESOP Stock Plan: Profit Sharing: Top Exec. Salary: $ Bonus: $
Savings Plan: Stock Purch. Plan: Second Exec. Salary: $ Bonus: $

OTHER THOUGHTS:

Apparent Women Officers or Directors: 1
Hot Spot for Advancement for Women/Minorities:

LOCATIONS: ("Y" = Yes)

West:	Southwest:	Midwest:	Southeast:	Northeast:	International:
					Y

RELIANCE PETROLEUM LTD

www.ril.com

Industry Group Code: 324110 **Ranks within this company's industry group:** Sales: 29 Profits: 17

Exploration/Production:		Refining/Retailing:		Utilities:		Alternative Energy:		Specialty Services:		Energy Mktg./Other Svcs.	
Exploration:		Refining:	Y	Electric Utility:		Waste/Solar/Other:		Consulting/Eng.:		Energy Marketing:	
Production:		Retailing:		Gas Utility:		Thermal/Steam:		Seismic:		Equipment/Machinery:	
Coal Production:		Convenience Stores:		Pipelines:		Wind:		Drilling:		Oil Field Services:	
		Chemicals:		Water:		Hydro:		InfoTech:		Air/Shipping Transportation:	
						Fuel Cells:		Specialty Services:			

TYPES OF BUSINESS:

Petroleum Refining
Petrochemicals Production

BRANDS/DIVISIONS/AFFILIATES:

Reliance Group
Reliance Industries Ltd.

CONTACTS:

Note: Officers with more than one job title may be intentionally listed here more than once.

Shri Mukesh D. Ambani, Managing Dir./Chmn.-Reliance Industries Ltd.

Phone: 91-22-2278-5000	**Fax:** 91-22-2204-2268
Toll-Free:	
Address: Makers Chamber IV, Nariman Point, Mumbai, 400 021 India	

GROWTH PLANS/SPECIAL FEATURES:

Reliance Petroleum Ltd. (RPL) is an India-based petroleum refining company. The firm was established in 2006 by Reliance Industries Ltd., a Fortune Global 500 company and is one of India's largest private sector conglomerates, for the express purpose of establishing a petroleum refinery and polypropylene plant within a special economic zone (SEZ) in the western Indian state of Gujarat. The petroleum refinery, which recently commenced operations, has a crude processing capacity of approximately 580,000 barrels per stream day (BPSD), a measuring unit that represents a plant's maximum capacity for a 24-hour-a-day period of continuous operations under optimal production conditions. The refinery's capacity places it among the largest in the world. The polypropylene plant has the capacity to produce approximately 900,000 metric tons annually. RPL's facility is adjacent to an existing refinery and petrochemicals complex operated by the founding company and the new facility will share in some aspects of the established infrastructure. The refinery's location on India's west coast allows for expedited sourcing from crude oil reserves in the Middle East. In January 2009, the company announced that it was ready to begin exporting products from the refinery, though certain secondary processing units at the facility were still being brought on line. Reliance Industries Ltd. holds approximately 70% of Reliance Petroleum Ltd. In April 2010, the firm's parent company entered into a joint venture with U.S. based Atlas Energy, Inc. to acquired 40% interest in the Marcellus Shale region in southwestern Pennsylvania. The acquisition will be for $339 million up front and an additional $1.36 billion arrangement for 75% of Atlas's capital costs over an anticipated seven and a half year development.

FINANCIALS:

Sales and profits are in thousands of dollars—add 000 to get the full amount. 2010 Note: Financial information for 2010 was not available for all companies at press time.

2010 Sales: $	2010 Profits: $	**U.S. Stock Ticker: Subsidiary**
2009 Sales: $783,630	2009 Profits: $17,900	**Int'l Ticker: 532743** Int'l Exchange: Bombay-BSE
2008 Sales: $	2008 Profits: $	Employees:
2007 Sales: $	2007 Profits: $	Fiscal Year Ends: 3/31
2006 Sales: $	2006 Profits: $	Parent Company: RELIANCE INDUSTRIES LTD (RELIANCE GROUP)

SALARIES/BENEFITS:

Pension Plan:	ESOP Stock Plan:	Profit Sharing:	Top Exec. Salary: $	Bonus: $
Savings Plan:	Stock Purch. Plan:		Second Exec. Salary: $	Bonus: $

OTHER THOUGHTS:

Apparent Women Officers or Directors:
Hot Spot for Advancement for Women/Minorities:

LOCATIONS: ("Y" = Yes)

West:	Southwest:	Midwest:	Southeast:	Northeast:	International:
					Y

RELIANCE POWER LIMITED

www.reliancepower.co.in

Industry Group Code: 237 **Ranks within this company's industry group:** Sales: 10 Profits: 5

Exploration/Production:		Refining/Retailing:		Utilities:		Alternative Energy:		Specialty Services:		Energy Mktg./Other Svcs.	
Exploration:		Refining:		Electric Utility:		Waste/Solar/Other:		Consulting/Eng.:		Energy Marketing:	
Production:		Retailing:		Gas Utility:		Thermal/Steam:		Seismic:		Equipment/Machinery:	Y
Coal Production:		Convenience Stores:		Pipelines:		Wind:		Drilling:		Oil Field Services:	
		Chemicals:		Water:		Hydro:		InfoTech:		Air/Shipping Transportation:	
						Fuel Cells:		Specialty Services:			

TYPES OF BUSINESS:

Power Plant Construction
Power Generation

BRANDS/DIVISIONS/AFFILIATES:

Reliance ADA Group
Rosa Power Supply Company Limited
Coastal Andhra Power Limited
Vidharbha Industries Power Limited
Tato Hydro Power Private Limited
Siyom Hydro Power Private Limited
Reliance Natural Resources Limited
Sasan Power Limited

CONTACTS:

Note: Officers with more than one job title may be intentionally listed here more than once.

K.H. Mankad, CEO
Paresh Rathod, Company Sec./Compliance Officer
Anil Dhirubhai Ambani, Chmn.

Phone: 91-22-3038-6010	Fax: 91-22-3037-6633
Toll-Free:	
Address: H Block, 1st Fl., Dhirubhai Ambani Knowledge City, Navi Mumbai, 400 710 India	

GROWTH PLANS/SPECIAL FEATURES:

Reliance Power Limited (RPL) is a private sector company and a member of the Reliance Anil Dhirubhai Ambani Group (Reliance ADA Group), one of India's largest business houses. The firm is focused on the development, construction and operation of power generation projects. The company, on its own and through its subsidiaries, has a portfolio of nearly 35,000 megawatts (MW) power generation capacity, consisting of about 1,000 MW from operational projects and the remaining capacity linked to projects under development. RPL's operational projects include Samalkot IPP, a 220 MW gas-based project; and Goa Power Station, a gas-based project with 48 MW capacity. The firm is developing 16 medium and large-sized power projects of varied fuel types and sources. Project sites include six coal-fired projects, with a combined planned capacity of 19,060 MW; one gas-fired project, with a planned capacity of 7,000 MW; and seven hydroelectric projects, with a combined planned capacity of 4,620 MW. The firm also has tentative plans to develop coal bed methane (CBM) power generation projects. Wholly-owned subsidiaries of the company include Sasan Power Limited; Rosa Power Supply Company Limited; Vidharbha Industries Power Limited; Coastal Andhra Power Limited; Chitrangi Power Private Limited; Jharkhand Integrated Power Limited; Tato Hydro Power Private Limited; Siyom Hydro Power Private Limited; Urthing Sobla Hydro Power Private Limited; Kalai Power Pvt Ltd; Amulin Hydro Power Pvt Ltd; Emini Hydro Power Pvt Ltd; and Mihundon Hydro Power Pvt Ltd. In August 2009, RPL acquired Jharkhand Integrated Power Limited from Power Finance Corporation Ltd. In December 2009, the firm's 1,200 MW capacity Rosa Power Project commenced power generation with its 300 MW Unit 1; 300 MW Unit 2 commenced power generation in June 2010. In July 2010, the company announced an agreement to merge with Reliance Natural Resources Limited, another Reliance ADA Group company.

FINANCIALS:

Sales and profits are in thousands of dollars—add 000 to get the full amount. 2010 Note: Financial information for 2010 was not available for all companies at press time.

2010 Sales: $	2010 Profits: $	**U.S. Stock Ticker:**
2009 Sales: $85,970	2009 Profits: $64,010	**Int'l Ticker: 532939** Int'l Exchange: Bombay-BSE
2008 Sales: $65,990	2008 Profits: $50,570	Employees: 500
2007 Sales: $	2007 Profits: $	Fiscal Year Ends: 3/31
2006 Sales: $	2006 Profits: $	Parent Company:

SALARIES/BENEFITS:

Pension Plan:	ESOP Stock Plan:	Profit Sharing:	Top Exec. Salary: $	Bonus: $
Savings Plan:	Stock Purch. Plan:		Second Exec. Salary: $	Bonus: $

OTHER THOUGHTS:

Apparent Women Officers or Directors:
Hot Spot for Advancement for Women/Minorities:

LOCATIONS: ("Y" = Yes)

West:	Southwest:	Midwest:	Southeast:	Northeast:	International:
					Y

REPSOL YPF SA

www.repsol.com

Industry Group Code: 325110 **Ranks within this company's industry group:** Sales: 1 Profits: 2

Exploration/Production:		**Refining/Retailing:**		**Utilities:**		**Alternative Energy:**		**Specialty Services:**		**Energy Mktg./Other Svcs.**	
Exploration:	Y	Refining:	Y	Electric Utility:	Y	Waste/Solar/Other:		Consulting/Eng.:		Energy Marketing:	Y
Production:	Y	Retailing:	Y	Gas Utility:	Y	Thermal/Steam:		Seismic:		Equipment/Machinery:	
Coal Production:		Convenience Stores:		Pipelines:	Y	Wind:		Drilling:		Oil Field Services:	
		Chemicals:	Y	Water:		Hydro:		InfoTech:		Air/Shipping Transportation:	Y
						Fuel Cells:		Specialty Services:			

TYPES OF BUSINESS:

Petrochemical Manufacturing
Oil & Gas Exploration & Production
Refining & Retailing
Service Stations
Electric Generation
Transportation

BRANDS/DIVISIONS/AFFILIATES:

YPF International Ltd
Canaport LNG
Orisol
IBIL Gestor de Carga de Vehiculo Electrico SA

CONTACTS: *Note: Officers with more than one job title may be intentionally listed here more than once.*

Antonio Brufau Niubo, CEO
Miguel Martinez San Martin, COO
Cristina Sanz Mendiola, Exec. Dir.-People & Organization
Luis Suarez de Lezo Mantilla, General Counsel/Corp. Sec.
Begona Elices Garcia, Corp. Dir.-Comm. & External Rel.
Fernando Ramirez Mazarredo, Exec. Dir.-Finance & Corp. Svcs.
Pedro Fernandez Frial, Exec. Dir.-Downstream
Nemesio Fernandez-Cuesta Luca de Tena, Exec. Dir.-Upstream
Antonio Brufau Niubo, Chmn.
Antonio Gomis, Exec. Dir.-YPF Int'l Ltd.

Phone: 34-9175-38100 **Fax:** 34-91-314-2821
Toll-Free:
Address: Paseo de la Castellana, 278-280, Madrid, 28046 Spain

GROWTH PLANS/SPECIAL FEATURES:

Repsol YPF SA is a leading private energy company that explores, produces, refines, markets and distributes petroleum products, with operations in over 30 countries. It divides its operations into five business units: Upstream, Downstream, LNG, YPF International Ltd. and Gas Natural Fenosa. Upstream handles the firm's exploration and production activities in 25 countries; it produces over a million barrels of oil per day. The Downstream unit handles the petro-chemistry, refining, marketing and trading of oil derived products such as Liquefied Natural Gas (LNG). It owns six refineries, including five in the Iberian peninsula and one in Peru; owns 30% interest in a Brazilian refinery; has over 4,400 service stations; and sells its products to over 10 million butane and propane gas customers worldwide. Repsol's LNG division specializes in integrated LNG projects that involve LNG marketing; natural gas prospecting and production; and the building of liquefaction and regasification facilities. Subsidiary YPF International, which operates primarily in Argentina, explores, produces, refines and markets hydrocarbons and chemicals. The company's Gas Natural Fenosa segment explores, produces, liquefies, transports and wholesale markets LNG. It serves over 20 million customers in 23 countries, including 5.42 million in Latin America. In September 2009, the Canaport LNG terminal in Canada, in which Repsol owns 75% interest, began operations. In April 2010, the firm launched a new energy business unit to research new energy solutions. In June 2010, the company opened a new LNG plant in Peru. In September 2010, Repsol acquired 47% interest in international renewable energy developer Orisol. In October 2010, the firm sold 40% of subsidiary Repsol Brazil to Sinopec; and formed joint venture IBIL, Gestor de Carga de Vehiculo Electrico SA with EVE to develop electric vehicle technologies.

Repsol offers its employees benefits including pension and savings plans; medical insurance; and food vouchers.

FINANCIALS: **Sales and profits are in thousands of dollars—add 000 to get the full amount. 2010 Note: Financial information for 2010 was not available for all companies at press time.**

2010 Sales: $	2010 Profits: $	**U.S. Stock Ticker: REP**
2009 Sales: $60,084,800	2009 Profits: $1,981,350	**Int'l Ticker: REP** Int'l Exchange: Madrid-MCE
2008 Sales: $79,177,000	2008 Profits: $3,968,000	Employees:
2007 Sales: $61,800,000	2007 Profits: $4,360,000	Fiscal Year Ends: 12/31
2006 Sales: $72,722,120	2006 Profits: $3,923,930	Parent Company:

SALARIES/BENEFITS:

Pension Plan: Y	ESOP Stock Plan:	Profit Sharing:	Top Exec. Salary: $	Bonus: $
Savings Plan: Y	Stock Purch. Plan:		Second Exec. Salary: $	Bonus: $

OTHER THOUGHTS:

Apparent Women Officers or Directors: 3
Hot Spot for Advancement for Women/Minorities: Y

LOCATIONS: ("Y" = Yes)

West:	Southwest:	Midwest:	Southeast:	Northeast:	International:
					Y

RHINO RESOURCE PARTNERS

www.rhinolp.com

Industry Group Code: 21211 **Ranks within this company's industry group:** Sales: Profits:

Exploration/Production:		Refining/Retailing:		Utilities:		Alternative Energy:		Specialty Services:		Energy Mktg./Other Svcs.	
Exploration:		Refining:		Electric Utility:		Waste/Solar/Other:		Consulting/Eng.:		Energy Marketing:	
Production:		Retailing:		Gas Utility:		Thermal/Steam:		Seismic:		Equipment/Machinery:	
Coal Production:	Y	Convenience Stores:		Pipelines:		Wind:		Drilling:		Oil Field Services:	
		Chemicals:		Water:		Hydro:		InfoTech:		Air/Shipping Transportation:	
						Fuel Cells:		Specialty Services:	Y		

TYPES OF BUSINESS:

Coal Mining
Coal Hauling
Mine-Related Construction
Roadway Maintenance

BRANDS/DIVISIONS/AFFILIATES:

Tug River Mining Complex
Rob Fork Mining Complex
Deane Mining Complex
Rhino Easter Mining Complex
McClane Canyon Mine
Hopedale Mining Complex
Sands Hill Mining Complex

CONTACTS:

Note: Officers with more than one job title may be intentionally listed here more than once.

David G. Zatezalo, CEO
David G. Zatezalo, Pres.
Richard A. Boone, CFO/Sr. VP
Andrew W. Cox, VP-Sales
Joseph R. Miller, General Counsel/Corp. Sec./VP
Christopher N. Moravec, Exec. VP
Mark D. Zand, Chmn.

Phone: 859-389-6500 **Fax:**
Toll-Free:
Address: 424 Lewis Hargett Cir., Ste. 250, Lexington, KY 40503 US

GROWTH PLANS/SPECIAL FEATURES:

Rhino Resource Partners, LP, produces and markets coal primarily to electric utilities. The company produces steam coal for electricity generation and metallurgical coal for the production of steel. Through asset bases in Colorado, Utah, Ohio, Kentucky and West Virginia, the firm holds approximately 285.4 million tons of proved and probable coal reserves, as well as approximately 122.2 million tons of non-reserve coal deposits. Through a joint venture with an affiliate of Patriot, it also controls an additional 22.4 million tons of metallurgical coal reserves and an additional 34.3 million tons of non-reserve deposits. The firm divides its operations into four primarily geographical business units: Central Appalachia, Northern Appalachia, Western Bituminous and Other Non-Mining. Rhino's holdings in Central Appalachia include the Tug River, Rob Fork, Deane and Rhino Eastern Mining Complexes, consisting of five active underground mines producing approximately 1.9 million tons of steam coal and 400,000 tons of metallurgical coal annually. Northern Appalachia interests include two mining complexes, Hopedale and Sands Hill, with three active mines producing about 2.2 million tons of steam coal annually. In the Western Bituminous region of Colorado, the company owns one mine, the McClane Canyon Mine. McClane Canyon produces roughly 300,000 tons of coal a year, which Rhino sells to Xcel Energy, Inc. The Other Non-Mining business unit consists of several subsidiaries that provide support services for Rhino's mining operations: Rhino Trucking, which provides coal hauling services in Kentucky; and Rhino Services, which manages mine-related construction, site and roadway maintenance and post-mining reclamation operations. The firm also owns certain mining assets in Utah, including coal reserves and non-reserve deposits, underground mining equipment, an overland belt conveyor system, a loading facility and support facilities, which it acquired in August 2010. In October 2010, Rhino filed for its initial public offering (IPO).

FINANCIALS:

Sales and profits are in thousands of dollars—add 000 to get the full amount. 2010 Note: Financial information for 2010 was not available for all companies at press time.

2010 Sales: $	2010 Profits: $	**U.S. Stock Ticker: RNO**
2009 Sales: $	2009 Profits: $	**Int'l Ticker:** Int'l Exchange:
2008 Sales: $	2008 Profits: $	Employees:
2007 Sales: $	2007 Profits: $	Fiscal Year Ends: 12/31
2006 Sales: $	2006 Profits: $	Parent Company:

SALARIES/BENEFITS:

Pension Plan:	ESOP Stock Plan:	Profit Sharing:	Top Exec. Salary: $	Bonus: $
Savings Plan:	Stock Purch. Plan:		Second Exec. Salary: $	Bonus: $

OTHER THOUGHTS:

Apparent Women Officers or Directors:
Hot Spot for Advancement for Women/Minorities:

LOCATIONS: ("Y" = Yes)

West:	Southwest:	Midwest:	Southeast:	Northeast:	International:
Y		Y		Y	

RIO TINTO GROUP

www.riotinto.com

Industry Group Code: 212 **Ranks within this company's industry group:** Sales: 1 Profits: 1

Exploration/Production:		Refining/Retailing:		Utilities:		Alternative Energy:		Specialty Services:		Energy Mktg./Other Svcs.	
Exploration:	Y	Refining:		Electric Utility:		Waste/Solar/Other:		Consulting/Eng.:	Y	Energy Marketing:	Y
Production:		Retailing:		Gas Utility:		Thermal/Steam:		Seismic:		Equipment/Machinery:	Y
Coal Production:	Y	Convenience Stores:		Pipelines:		Wind:		Drilling:		Oil Field Services:	
		Chemicals:		Water:		Hydro:		InfoTech:		Air/Shipping Transportation:	
						Fuel Cells:		Specialty Services:	Y		

TYPES OF BUSINESS:

Mining
Coal & Uranium Mining
Industrial Minerals
Aluminum
Copper
Iron Ore
Diamonds
Exploration

BRANDS/DIVISIONS/AFFILIATES:

Rio Tinto plc
Rio Tinto, Ltd.
Rio Tinto Alcan
Diavik Diamonds
Kennecott Utah Copper
Rio Tinto Minerals
Rio Tinto Coal Australia
Ironore Company of Canada

CONTACTS: *Note: Officers with more than one job title may be intentionally listed here more than once.*

Tom Albanese, CEO
Guy Elliot, CFO
Hugo Bague, Group Exec.-People & Organization
Preston Chiaro, Group. Exec.-Tech. & Innovation
Debra Valentine, Group Exec.-Legal & External Affairs
Bret Clayton, Group Exec.-Oper. & Bus. Support
Nick Cobban, Dir.-Media Rel., London
Jason Combes, Dir.-Investor Rel., North America
Sam Walsh, CEO-Iron Ore
Doug Ritchie, CEO-Energy
Jacynthe Cote, CEO-Rio Tinto Alcan
Henry Kenyon-Slaney, CEO-Diamonds & Minerals
Jan du Plessis, Chmn.
Ian Bauert, Managing Dir.-China

Phone: 44-20-7930-2399 **Fax:** 44-20-7930-3249
Toll-Free:
Address: 6 St. James's Sq., London, SW1Y 4LD UK

GROWTH PLANS/SPECIAL FEATURES:

Rio Tinto Group comprises two companies, Rio Tinto, Ltd. (RTL) and Rio Tinto plc (RTP), which trade separately but operate as a single company. The company operates through six principal businesses: Aluminum, which represented 27% of the firm's 2009 gross revenue; Copper (along with) gold, molybdenum, silver and nickel), 14%; Diamonds & Minerals, 6%; Energy, 15%; Iron Ore, 29%; and Global Functions, which includes the firm's exploration and technology & innovation activities. The Aluminum group comprises mining operations in Australia, New Zealand, Europe and Guinea. The Rio Tinto Copper group includes Kennecott Utah Copper in the U.S. and joint-venture interests in Chile, Indonesia, Australia and South Africa. The Diamonds & Minerals operations consist of Argyle Diamonds in Australia, Diavik Diamonds in Canada and the Murowa project in Zimbabwe, as well as Rio Tinto Minerals and Rio Tinto Iron & Titanium. The Rio Tinto Energy group includes uranium, thermal coal and coking coal operations, with coal interests located primarily in Australia and the U.S. Rio Tinto supplies uranium through Rossing in Namibia and Energy Resources of Australia. The iron ore group is responsible for the management of iron ore mines and salt complexes in Australia. Rio Tinto Exploration discovers and identifies mineral resources for the product groups, and the Technology & Innovation segment develops practices and equipment that enhance operational efficiencies. In February 2010, the firm sold its Alcan Packaging global Pharmaceuticals, global Tobacco, Food Europe and Food Asia divisions to Amcor for $1.94 billion. In the following month, Rio Tinto divested its Alcan Packaging Food Americas division for approximately $1.2 billion. In July 2010, it completed the divestment of the Alcan Packaging business, selling Medical Flexibles and Alcan Beauty Packaging. In October 2010, the company began trial operations of a new excavation system developed by its technology department in conjunction with Aker Wirth.

FINANCIALS: **Sales and profits are in thousands of dollars—add 000 to get the full amount. 2010 Note: Financial information for 2010 was not available for all companies at press time.**

2010 Sales: $	2010 Profits: $	**U.S. Stock Ticker: RTP**
2009 Sales: $41,825,000	2009 Profits: $4,872,000	**Int'l Ticker: RIO** Int'l Exchange: Sydney-ASX
2008 Sales: $54,264,000	2008 Profits: $3,676,000	Employees:
2007 Sales: $29,700,000	2007 Profits: $7,746,000	Fiscal Year Ends: 12/31
2006 Sales: $22,465,000	2006 Profits: $7,867,000	Parent Company:

SALARIES/BENEFITS:

Pension Plan:	ESOP Stock Plan:	Profit Sharing:	Top Exec. Salary: $	Bonus: $1,288,000
Savings Plan:	Stock Purch. Plan:		Second Exec. Salary: $	Bonus: $

OTHER THOUGHTS:

Apparent Women Officers or Directors: 2
Hot Spot for Advancement for Women/Minorities:

LOCATIONS: ("Y" = Yes)

West:	Southwest:	Midwest:	Southeast:	Northeast:	International:
Y					Y

ROCHESTER GAS AND ELECTRIC CORP

www.rge.com

Industry Group Code: 221 **Ranks within this company's industry group:** Sales: Profits:

Exploration/Production:		**Refining/Retailing:**		**Utilities:**		**Alternative Energy:**		**Specialty Services:**		**Energy Mktg./Other Svcs.**	
Exploration:		Refining:		Electric Utility:	Y	Waste/Solar/Other:		Consulting/Eng.:		Energy Marketing:	
Production:		Retailing:		Gas Utility:	Y	Thermal/Steam:		Seismic:		Equipment/Machinery:	
Coal Production:		Convenience Stores:		Pipelines:	Y	Wind:	Y	Drilling:		Oil Field Services:	
		Chemicals:		Water:		Hydro:	Y	InfoTech:		Air/Shipping Transportation:	
						Fuel Cells:		Specialty Services:	Y		

TYPES OF BUSINESS:

Utilities-Electricity & Natural Gas
Pipelines
Energy Technology
Hydroelectric Generation
Online Services
SafeGuard Lighting
CASHBACK Programs
Construction Resources

BRANDS/DIVISIONS/AFFILIATES:

IBERDROLA SA
NewWind Energy
Catch the Wind
Community Energy, Inc.
Russell Station

CONTACTS: *Note: Officers with more than one job title may be intentionally listed here more than once.*

James P. Lauritto, CEO
Mark S. Lynch, Pres.
Joseph J. Syta, VP

Phone: 585-546-2700	**Fax:** 585-771-2895
Toll-Free: 800-743-2110	
Address: 89 East Ave., Rochester, NY 14649 US	

GROWTH PLANS/SPECIAL FEATURES:

Rochester Gas and Electric Corp. (RGE), a subsidiary of IBERDROLA S.A., generates, purchases and distributes electricity; and purchases and distributes natural gas. The company provides its services in parts of nine New York counties, including and surrounding the city of Rochester. RGE supplies regulated electric and gas service to approximately 650,000 residential, commercial and industrial customers within its 2,700-square-mile service area. The company generates electricity from one coal-fired plant, three gas turbine plants and several smaller hydroelectric stations. RGE's Catch the Wind program allows customers the option to have some or all of their electricity supplied by renewable wind energy generated in New York through the purchase of NewWind Energy, a product of Community Energy, Inc. The company's energy technology group is involved in aquaculture, erosion control and greenhouse vegetable cultivation projects and uses optical methane detectors to quickly and efficiently detect leaks on its natural gas system. RGE's aquaculture project includes a 10,000-square-foot indoor fish farm, with an additional three facilities in various stages of development. RGE utilizes a computer system to control plant nutrients, pH and the oxygen and carbon dioxide content of ponds used to grow the plants.

RGE offers its employees comprehensive benefits plans including: traditional healthcare coverage; HMOS; point-of-sale service plans; dental, vision and life insurance; a 401(k) and pension plan; pre-tax flexible spending accounts for dependent and medical care; competitive wages and salaries; and positions eligible for incentive compensation programs.

FINANCIALS: **Sales and profits are in thousands of dollars—add 000 to get the full amount. 2010 Note: Financial information for 2010 was not available for all companies at press time.**

2010 Sales: $	2010 Profits: $	**U.S. Stock Ticker: Subsidiary**
2009 Sales: $	2009 Profits: $	**Int'l Ticker:** Int'l Exchange:
2008 Sales: $	2008 Profits: $	Employees:
2007 Sales: $	2007 Profits: $	Fiscal Year Ends: 12/31
2006 Sales: $	2006 Profits: $	Parent Company: IBERDROLA SA

SALARIES/BENEFITS:

Pension Plan: Y	ESOP Stock Plan:	Profit Sharing:	Top Exec. Salary: $	Bonus: $
Savings Plan: Y	Stock Purch. Plan:		Second Exec. Salary: $	Bonus: $

OTHER THOUGHTS:

Apparent Women Officers or Directors:
Hot Spot for Advancement for Women/Minorities:

LOCATIONS: ("Y" = Yes)

West:	Southwest:	Midwest:	Southeast:	Northeast:	International:
				Y	

ROSNEFT (OAO)

www.rosneft.com

Industry Group Code: 211111 **Ranks within this company's industry group:** Sales: 24 Profits: 13

Exploration/Production:		Refining/Retailing:		Utilities:		Alternative Energy:		Specialty Services:		Energy Mktg./Other Svcs.	
Exploration:	Y	Refining:	Y	Electric Utility:		Waste/Solar/Other:		Consulting/Eng.:		Energy Marketing:	
Production:	Y	Retailing:		Gas Utility:		Thermal/Steam:		Seismic:		Equipment/Machinery:	
Coal Production:		Convenience Stores:		Pipelines:		Wind:		Drilling:		Oil Field Services:	
		Chemicals:		Water:		Hydro:		InfoTech:		Air/Shipping Transportation:	
						Fuel Cells:		Specialty Services:			

TYPES OF BUSINESS:

Oil Production & Exploration
Refineries

BRANDS/DIVISIONS/AFFILIATES:

East Siberia-Pacific Ocean Pipeline
Kuibyshev Refinery
Novokuibyshev Refinery
Syzran Refinery
Achinsk Refinery
Angarsk Petrochemical Company
Neft-Aktiv
OJSC Tomskneft

CONTACTS:

Note: Officers with more than one job title may be intentionally listed here more than once.

Eduard Khudainatov, Pres.
Viktor Ploskina, Head-Sales Dept.
Pavel Federov, First VP
Sergey Tregub, VP
Larisa Kalanda, VP
Riso Tursunov, VP
Igor Sechin, Chmn.

Phone: 7-495-777-44-22 **Fax:** 7-495-777-44-44
Toll-Free:
Address: Sofiskaya Embankment, 26/1, Moscow, 117997 Russia

GROWTH PLANS/SPECIAL FEATURES:

Rosneft (OAO) is a 75% state-owned oil and gas producer in Russia, with operations in European Russia, Siberia, Kazakhstan and Algeria and over 20,000 wells in operation. Rosneft's reserves total approximately 47 billion barrels of proved, probable and possible oil and gas reserves. Daily crude oil production by Rosneft totals over 2 million barrels annually. West Siberia holds 77% of Rosneft's crude oil reserves as well as 90% of the company's gas reserves, while East Siberia counts for 10% of crude oil reserves. The firm also owns an extensive hydrocarbon reserve base in the provinces of southern Russia, east and west Siberia, central Russia, Timan-Pechora and the Far East. The company is continuing to increase its resource base through geological research at existing fields and through acquisitions of additional fields. Rosneft owns and operates seven major refineries in Russia including: the Komsomosk refinery in the Russian Far East; the Kuibyshev, Novokuibyshevsk and the Syzran refineris in the Volga-Urals region; the Achinsk and Angarsk refineries in Eastern Siberia; and the Tuapse refinery on the Black Sea Coast. The refineries produce approximately 391 million barrels of crude oil annually. The coastal location of these refineries provides ease of exporting petroleum products to Europe and Asia. In October 2010, Rosneft announced the acquisition of a 50% stake in Ruhr Oel GmbH, a German petrochemical company.

FINANCIALS:

Sales and profits are in thousands of dollars—add 000 to get the full amount. 2010 Note: Financial information for 2010 was not available for all companies at press time.

2010 Sales: $	2010 Profits: $	**U.S. Stock Ticker: Government-Owned**
2009 Sales: $35,431,000	2009 Profits: $6,514,000	**Int'l Ticker:** Int'l Exchange:
2008 Sales: $55,054,000	2008 Profits: $11,120,000	Employees:
2007 Sales: $39,032,000	2007 Profits: $12,862,000	Fiscal Year Ends: 12/31
2006 Sales: $17,670,000	2006 Profits: $4,160,000	Parent Company:

SALARIES/BENEFITS:

Pension Plan: Y	ESOP Stock Plan:	Profit Sharing:	Top Exec. Salary: $	Bonus: $
Savings Plan:	Stock Purch. Plan:		Second Exec. Salary: $	Bonus: $

OTHER THOUGHTS:

Apparent Women Officers or Directors: 1
Hot Spot for Advancement for Women/Minorities:

LOCATIONS: ("Y" = Yes)

West:	Southwest:	Midwest:	Southeast:	Northeast:	International:
					Y

ROWAN COMPANIES INC

www.rowancompanies.com

Industry Group Code: 213111 **Ranks within this company's industry group:** Sales: 8 Profits: 6

Exploration/Production:		Refining/Retailing:		Utilities:		Alternative Energy:		Specialty Services:		Energy Mktg./Other Svcs.	
Exploration:		Refining:		Electric Utility:		Waste/Solar/Other:		Consulting/Eng.:		Energy Marketing:	
Production:		Retailing:		Gas Utility:		Thermal/Steam:		Seismic:		Equipment/Machinery:	Y
Coal Production:		Convenience Stores:		Pipelines:		Wind:		Drilling:	Y	Oil Field Services:	Y
		Chemicals:		Water:		Hydro:		InfoTech:		Air/Shipping Transportation:	
						Fuel Cells:		Specialty Services:	Y		

TYPES OF BUSINESS:

Drilling-Offshore & Land
Steel Production
Heavy Equipment Manufacturing

BRANDS/DIVISIONS/AFFILIATES:

LeTourneau Technologies, Inc.

CONTACTS:

Note: Officers with more than one job title may be intentionally listed here more than once.

W. Matt Ralls, CEO
W. Matt Ralls, Pres.
William H. Wells, CFO/Sr. VP-Finance/Treas.
Terry Woodall, VP-Human Resources
Lisa Gauthier, CIO/VP
Mike Dowdy, VP-Eng.
John L. Buvens, Exec. VP-Legal
David P. Russell, Exec. VP-Drilling Oper.
Mark A. Keller, Exec. VP-Bus. Dev.
Suzanne M. McLeod, Dir.-Investor Rel.
Gregory M. Hatfield, Controller/VP
Thomas P. Burke, Pres./CEO-LeTourneau Technologies, Inc.
J. Kevin Bartol, VP-Corp. Dev.
Barbara Carroll, VP-Health, Safety & Environment
Melanie M. Trent, Corp. Sec./VP
H.E. Lentz, Chmn.

Phone: 713-621-7800 **Fax:** 713-960-7660
Toll-Free:
Address: 2800 Post Oak Blvd., Ste. 5450, Houston, TX 77056 US

GROWTH PLANS/SPECIAL FEATURES:

Rowan Companies, Inc. is a provider of international and domestic contract drilling services. The company also manufactures equipment for the drilling, mining and timber industries. Rowan operates through three segments: Drilling Services, Drilling Products and Systems, and Mining, Forestry and Steel Products. Drilling Services, the firm's largest segment, provides contract drilling services utilizing a fleet of 23 self-elevating mobile offshore drilling platforms (called jack-up rigs) and 29 deep-well land drilling rigs. The offshore drilling fleet includes 20 premium cantilever jack-up rigs, featuring three harsh environment Gorilla class rigs, four enhanced Super Gorilla class rigs, four Tarzan Class rigs, seven 116-C class rigs and two 240C class rigs; and three conventional jack-up rigs, with skid-off capability. Rowan operates larger, deep-water type jack-up rigs capable of drilling to depths of up to 35,000 feet in maximum water depths range from 250-550 feet. Rowan's drilling operations are conducted primarily in the Gulf of Mexico, Texas, Oklahoma, Louisiana and Alaska, as well as internationally primarily in the Middle East, the North Sea, West Africa, Canada, Mexico and Egypt. The Drilling Products and Systems and Mining, Forestry and Steel Products segments operate through subsidiary LeTourneau Technologies, Inc. The Drilling Products segment manufactures jack-up rigs, rig kits and related components, mud pumps, drawworks, top drives, rotary tables, variable-speed motors, drives and other electrical components for the drilling industry. The Mining, Forestry and Steel Products segment manufactures heavy equipment such as large-wheeled front-end loaders, diesel-electric powered log stackers and steel plate products. In July 2010, Rowan announced its intention to acquire Norwegian company Skeie Drilling & Production ASA, an owner and manufacturer of high-spec jack-up rigs.

Employees are offered medical, dental, vision and prescription drug coverage; life and AD&D insurance; disability coverage; an employee assistance program; a 401(k) plan; and a pension plan.

FINANCIALS:

Sales and profits are in thousands of dollars—add 000 to get the full amount. 2010 Note: Financial information for 2010 was not available for all companies at press time.

2010 Sales: $	2010 Profits: $	**U.S. Stock Ticker: RDC**
2009 Sales: $1,770,180	2009 Profits: $367,504	**Int'l Ticker:** Int'l Exchange:
2008 Sales: $2,212,736	2008 Profits: $427,628	Employees: 4,846
2007 Sales: $2,095,021	2007 Profits: $483,800	Fiscal Year Ends: 12/31
2006 Sales: $1,510,734	2006 Profits: $318,246	Parent Company:

SALARIES/BENEFITS:

Pension Plan: Y	ESOP Stock Plan:	Profit Sharing:	Top Exec. Salary: $800,000	Bonus: $1,134,440
Savings Plan: Y	Stock Purch. Plan:		Second Exec. Salary: $400,000	Bonus: $365,000

OTHER THOUGHTS:

Apparent Women Officers or Directors: 3
Hot Spot for Advancement for Women/Minorities: Y

LOCATIONS: ("Y" = Yes)

West:	Southwest:	Midwest:	Southeast:	Northeast:	International:
Y	Y		Y		Y

ROYAL DUTCH SHELL (SHELL GROUP)

www.shell.com

Industry Group Code: 211111 **Ranks within this company's industry group:** Sales: 2 Profits: 8

Exploration/Production:		Refining/Retailing:		Utilities:		Alternative Energy:		Specialty Services:		Energy Mktg./Other Svcs.	
Exploration:	Y	Refining:	Y	Electric Utility:		Waste/Solar/Other:	Y	Consulting/Eng.:	Y	Energy Marketing:	Y
Production:	Y	Retailing:	Y	Gas Utility:		Thermal/Steam:	Y	Seismic:		Equipment/Machinery:	
Coal Production:		Convenience Stores:	Y	Pipelines:	Y	Wind:	Y	Drilling:		Oil Field Services:	
		Chemicals:	Y	Water:		Hydro:	Y	InfoTech:		Air/Shipping Transportation:	
						Fuel Cells:	Y	Specialty Services:			

TYPES OF BUSINESS:

Oil & Gas-Exploration & Production
Gas Stations
Refineries
Solar & Wind Power
Chemicals
Consulting & Technology Services
Hydrogen & Fuel Cell Technology

BRANDS/DIVISIONS/AFFILIATES:

Shell Oil Co
Shell Canada Limited
Shell Chemicals Limited
Shell WindEnergy BV
CRI Catalyst Companay
CRI Asia Pacific Pte Ltd
PetroChina Company
Arrow Energy Limited

CONTACTS: *Note: Officers with more than one job title may be intentionally listed here more than once.*

Peter Voser, CEO
Simon Henry, CFO
Hugh Mitchell, Chief Human Resources Officer
Matthias Bichsel, Dir.-Projects & Tech.
Beat Hess, Dir.-Legal
Malcom Brinded, Exec. Dir.-Upstream Int'l
Mark Williams, Dir.-Downstream
Jorma Ollila, Chmn.
Marvin Odum, Dir.-Upstream Americas

Phone: 31-70-377-9111 **Fax:** 31-70-377-3115
Toll-Free:
Address: Carel van Bylandtlaan 16, The Hague, 2596 HR The Netherlands

GROWTH PLANS/SPECIAL FEATURES:

Royal Dutch Shell (Shell) is one of the world's largest oil and gas groups, with operations in over 90 countries. The company's business segments include Upstream International; Upstream Americas; Downstream; and Projects & Technology. The Upstream International segment searches for and recovers crude oil and natural gas, liquefies and transports gas and operates the upstream and midstream infrastructure necessary to deliver oil and gas to market. This segment also manages Shell's global liquefied natural gas business, as well as its European wind energy business. The firm's Upstream Americas segment oversees exploration activities in North and South America, including the extraction of bitumen from oil sands for conversion into synthetic crude oil. This segment also oversees Shell's wind energy business in the U.S. The upstream segments together produce roughly 3.1 million barrels of oil equivalent (BOE) daily. The Downstream segment, representing more than 80% of 2009 revenues, manages Shell's manufacturing, distribution and marketing activities for oil products and chemicals, including the refining, supply and shipping of crude oil. This segment oversees the sale a range of products including fuels, lubricants, bitumen and liquefied petroleum gas for home, transport and industrial use, as well as petrochemicals for industrial customers, including raw materials for plastics, coatings and detergents used in the manufacture of textiles, medical supplies and computers. In addition, the downstream segment trades hydrocarbons and other energy related products, supplies the downstream businesses and provides shipping services, while also overseeing Shell's interests in non-wind alternative energy and carbon dioxide emissions management. Shell's worldwide retail network includes approximately 44,000 gasoline stations. The Projects & Technology segment conducts research and provides technical services to both the upstream and downstream segments. In March 2010, Shell announced a partnership with PetroChina International Investment Company to acquire Australia-based Arrow Energy Limited for approximately $3.2 billion.

FINANCIALS: **Sales and profits are in thousands of dollars—add 000 to get the full amount. 2010 Note: Financial information for 2010 was not available for all companies at press time.**

2010 Sales: $	2010 Profits: $	**U.S. Stock Ticker: RDSA**
2009 Sales: $278,188,000	2009 Profits: $12,718,000	**Int'l Ticker: RDSA** Int'l Exchange: Amsterdam-Euronext
2008 Sales: $458,361,000	2008 Profits: $26,476,000	Employees: 101,000
2007 Sales: $355,782,000	2007 Profits: $31,926,000	Fiscal Year Ends: 12/31
2006 Sales: $318,845,000	2006 Profits: $26,311,000	Parent Company:

SALARIES/BENEFITS:

Pension Plan: Y	ESOP Stock Plan:	Profit Sharing:	Top Exec. Salary: $	Bonus: $
Savings Plan:	Stock Purch. Plan: Y		Second Exec. Salary: $	Bonus: $

OTHER THOUGHTS:

Apparent Women Officers or Directors: 1
Hot Spot for Advancement for Women/Minorities:

LOCATIONS: ("Y" = Yes)

West:	Southwest:	Midwest:	Southeast:	Northeast:	International:
Y	Y	Y	Y	Y	Y

ROYAL VOPAK NV

www.vopak.com

Industry Group Code: 486 **Ranks within this company's industry group:** Sales: 18 Profits: 8

Exploration/Production:		Refining/Retailing:		Utilities:		Alternative Energy:		Specialty Services:		Energy Mktg./Other Svcs.	
Exploration:		Refining:		Electric Utility:		Waste/Solar/Other:		Consulting/Eng.:		Energy Marketing:	
Production:		Retailing:		Gas Utility:		Thermal/Steam:		Seismic:		Equipment/Machinery:	
Coal Production:		Convenience Stores:		Pipelines:		Wind:		Drilling:		Oil Field Services:	
		Chemicals:		Water:		Hydro:		InfoTech:		Air/Shipping Transportation:	Y
						Fuel Cells:		Specialty Services:	Y		

TYPES OF BUSINESS:

Oil Transportation
Oil Storage
Logistics Services

BRANDS/DIVISIONS/AFFILIATES:

HAL Holding
Alpetrol
Fos Faster LNG Terminal SAS
Vopak-Oxiquim Terminal Mejillones SA
Sealink Storage Company

CONTACTS:

Note: Officers with more than one job title may be intentionally listed here more than once.

John P. Broeders, Chmn.-Exec. Board
Jack de Kreij, CFO
Ans Knape, Dir.-Human Resources
Ton van Dijk, Dir.-Info. & Comm. Tech.
Tjeerd Wassenaar, Dir.-Legal Affairs/Company Sec.
Niek Verbree, Dir.-Oper. Excellence
Chris Badenhorst, Dir.-Strategic Projects & Commercial Excellence
Bas Rutgers, Dir.-Comm.
Bas Rutgers, Dir.-Investor Rel.
Cees Vletter, Treas.
Frits Eulderink, Exec. Dir.
Jos Steeman, Pres., Latin America
Frank Erkelens, Pres., Oil EMEA Div.
Dick Richelle, Pres., North America Div.
A. van Rossum, Chmn.
Kees van Seventer, Pres., Chemicals EMEA Div.

Phone: 31-10-400-2911 **Fax:** 31-10-413-9829
Toll-Free:
Address: Westerlaan 10, Rotterdam, 3016 CK The Netherlands

GROWTH PLANS/SPECIAL FEATURES:

Royal Vopak N.V. is a global independent tank terminal group. HAL Holding N.V., an investment firm based in Holland, owns about 48.15% of the company. The firm's divisions are organized by market regions: Chemicals in EMEA (Europe, the Middle East and Africa), which accounts for roughly 15% of Vopak's terminal capacity; Oil in EMEA, which accounts for 40%; North America, which accounts for 20%; Asia, which accounts for 22%; and Latin America, which accounts for 3%. Its clients include oil companies, oil traders, and chemical manufacturers. Vopak operates approximately 80 terminals, with a storage capacity of over 1 billion cubic feet (bcf). These terminals are located in 31 countries throughout Africa, Asia, the Americas, Australia, Europe and the Middle East. The firm provides complementary logistics services to its customers through third-party providers. These services include air, land, and sea transportation; short- and deep-sea tanker shipping; barging; and port and hub services. Vopak recently announced its intent to expand into liquefied natural gas (LNG) storage. Construction on the company's first LNG storage facility is forecast to be completed by 2011. In November 2009, Vopak agreed to sell a terminal in Switzerland to Fluvia Holding BV and North Sea Petroleum Holding BV; and joint venture Vopak-Oxiquim Terminal Mejillones S.A. (with Oxiquim S.A.) began constructing a new storage terminal for bulk liquid chemicals in Chile. In April 2010, the company acquired 80% interest in Spain-based Alpetrol from Novaro Invest S.A. In May 2010, Vopak acquired 50% ownership of China-based Sealink Storage Company from Merit. Both of these companies will build new bulk liquid storage terminals for Vopak. In June 2010, the firm formed joint ventures with Bohai & Tianjin Lingang Port and Tianjin Bohai Chemical Industry Group to build/operate a bulk liquid storage terminal and two jetties in China.

FINANCIALS:

Sales and profits are in thousands of dollars—add 000 to get the full amount. 2010 Note: Financial information for 2010 was not available for all companies at press time.

2010 Sales: $	2010 Profits: $	**U.S. Stock Ticker:**
2009 Sales: $1,426,470	2009 Profits: $385,930	**Int'l Ticker: VPK** Int'l Exchange: Amsterdam-Euronext
2008 Sales: $1,371,160	2008 Profits: $316,550	Employees: 3,669
2007 Sales: $1,266,480	2007 Profits: $271,560	Fiscal Year Ends: 12/31
2006 Sales: $1,030,900	2006 Profits: $193,800	Parent Company:

SALARIES/BENEFITS:

Pension Plan: Y	ESOP Stock Plan:	Profit Sharing:	Top Exec. Salary: $	Bonus: $561,787
Savings Plan:	Stock Purch. Plan:		Second Exec. Salary: $	Bonus: $

OTHER THOUGHTS:

Apparent Women Officers or Directors:
Hot Spot for Advancement for Women/Minorities:

LOCATIONS: ("Y" = Yes)

West:	Southwest:	Midwest:	Southeast:	Northeast:	International:
Y	Y		Y	Y	Y

RPC INC

www.rpc.net

Industry Group Code: 213112 **Ranks within this company's industry group:** Sales: 22 Profits: 22

Exploration/Production:		Refining/Retailing:		Utilities:		Alternative Energy:		Specialty Services:		Energy Mktg./Other Svcs.	
Exploration:		Refining:		Electric Utility:		Waste/Solar/Other:		Consulting/Eng.:		Energy Marketing:	
Production:		Retailing:		Gas Utility:		Thermal/Steam:		Seismic:		Equipment/Machinery:	Y
Coal Production:		Convenience Stores:		Pipelines:		Wind:		Drilling:		Oil Field Services:	Y
		Chemicals:		Water:		Hydro:		InfoTech:		Air/Shipping Transportation:	
						Fuel Cells:		Specialty Services:	Y		

TYPES OF BUSINESS:

Oil & Gas Technical & Support Services
Equipment Rental
Oilfield Services

BRANDS/DIVISIONS/AFFILIATES:

Bronco Oilfield Services
Patterson Rental & Fishing Tools
Well Control School
Cudd Energy Services
Thru Tubing Solutions

CONTACTS:

Note: Officers with more than one job title may be intentionally listed here more than once.

Richard A. Hubbell, CEO
Richard A. Hubbell, Pres.
Ben M. Palmer, CFO/VP/Treas.
Linda H. Graham, Sec./VP
Sharon A. Lennon, Mgr.-Corp. Comm.
Sharon A. Lennon, Mgr.-Investor Rel.
Jim Landers, VP-Corp. Finance
R. Randall Rollins, Chmn.

Phone: 404-321-2140 **Fax:** 404-321-5483
Toll-Free:
Address: 2801 Buford Hwy., Ste. 520, Atlanta, GA 30329 US

GROWTH PLANS/SPECIAL FEATURES:

RPC, Inc. is an energy holding company whose operating units provide specialized oilfield services and equipment. The firm primarily serves independent and major oil and gas companies engaged in the exploration, production and development of oil and gas properties. Its clients operate in the Gulf of Mexico, mid-continent, southwest, Rocky Mountain and Appalachian regions, and in certain international markets including Canada, Cameroon, Egypt, Gabon, South Africa, Bolivia, Mexico, New Zealand, Oman and the United Arab Emirates. RPC services and equipment offered include pressure pumping services; coiled tubing services; snubbing services; nitrogen services; drill pipe and other specialized oilfield equipment rental services; downhole tool rental services; and firefighting and well control. The company operates in two segments: technical services and support services. The technical services segment handles the firm's oil and gas service lines, which perform value-added completion, production and maintenance services directly to customer wells. This segment's equipment and services offerings include pressure pumping, coiled tubing, snubbing, nitrogen, well control, downhole tools, wireline and fishing. RPC's support services division includes the company's oil and gas service lines that primarily provide equipment for customer use or services to assist client operations. Equipment and service offerings include drill pipe and related tools; pipe handling; pipe inspection; storage services; and oilfield training services. Both technical services and support services division customers primarily include certain nationally owned oil companies and domestic producers of major multi-national and independent oil and gas firms. RPC operates through units including Cudd Energy Services; Patterson Rental and Fishing Tools; Bronco Oilfield Services; Thru Tubing Solutions; and Well Control School.

FINANCIALS:

Sales and profits are in thousands of dollars—add 000 to get the full amount. 2010 Note: Financial information for 2010 was not available for all companies at press time.

2010 Sales: $	2010 Profits: $	**U.S. Stock Ticker: RES**
2009 Sales: $587,863	2009 Profits: $-22,745	**Int'l Ticker:** Int'l Exchange:
2008 Sales: $876,977	2008 Profits: $83,403	Employees: 1,980
2007 Sales: $690,226	2007 Profits: $87,049	Fiscal Year Ends: 12/31
2006 Sales: $596,630	2006 Profits: $110,794	Parent Company:

SALARIES/BENEFITS:

Pension Plan:	ESOP Stock Plan:	Profit Sharing:	Top Exec. Salary: $625,624	Bonus: $
Savings Plan:	Stock Purch. Plan:		Second Exec. Salary: $536,250	Bonus: $

OTHER THOUGHTS:

Apparent Women Officers or Directors: 2
Hot Spot for Advancement for Women/Minorities:

LOCATIONS: ("Y" = Yes)

West:	Southwest:	Midwest:	Southeast:	Northeast:	International:
Y	Y		Y	Y	

RRI ENERGY INC

www.rrienergy.com

Industry Group Code: 221 **Ranks within this company's industry group:** Sales: 46 Profits: 24

Exploration/Production:		**Refining/Retailing:**		**Utilities:**		**Alternative Energy:**		**Specialty Services:**		**Energy Mktg./Other Svcs.**	
Exploration:		Refining:		Electric Utility:	Y	Waste/Solar/Other:	Y	Consulting/Eng.:		Energy Marketing:	Y
Production:		Retailing:		Gas Utility:		Thermal/Steam:		Seismic:		Equipment/Machinery:	
Coal Production:		Convenience Stores:		Pipelines:		Wind:		Drilling:		Oil Field Services:	
		Chemicals:		Water:		Hydro:		InfoTech:		Air/Shipping Transportation:	
						Fuel Cells:		Specialty Services:			

TYPES OF BUSINESS:

Utilities-Electricity
Power Generation
Wholesale Energy Trading & Marketing

BRANDS/DIVISIONS/AFFILIATES:

CONTACTS:

Note: Officers with more than one job title may be intentionally listed here more than once.

Mark M. Jacobs, CEO
Mark M. Jacobs, Pres.
Rick Dobson, CFO/Exec. VP
Karen D. Taylor, Sr. VP-Human Resources/Chief Diversity Officer
Michael L. Jines, General Counsel/Exec. VP/Sec.
David Brast, Sr. VP-Commercial Oper. & Organization
Rogers Herndon, Exec. VP-Strategic Planning & Bus. Dev.
Albert Myres, Sr. VP-Gov't & Public Affairs
Thomas C. Livengood, Controller/Sr. VP
Dave Freysinger, Sr. VP-Generation Oper.
Michael L. Jines, Chief Compliance Officer
Steven L. Miller, Chmn.

Phone: 713-497-3000	**Fax:**
Toll-Free:	
Address: 1000 Main St., Houston, TX 77002 US	

GROWTH PLANS/SPECIAL FEATURES:

RRI Energy, Inc. formerly Reliant Energy, Inc., provides electricity and energy services to wholesale customers. The company is one of the largest independent power producers in the U.S., with a power generation capacity of approximately 14,581 megawatts (MW). The firm operates primarily through four segments: East Coal, East Gas, West and Other. The East Gas, West and Other segments consist primarily of gas plants, while the East Coal segment includes the company's coal plants. In 2009, the firm owned, had an interest in or leased 37 operating electric power generation facilities in eight states. These facilities run on coal, gas and oil power, as well as utilize circulating fluidized bed (CFB) coal technology. The net generating capacity of plants by segment consists of 32% East Coal, 28% East Gas, 23% West (gas) and 17% other. RRI's commercial operations division sells electricity, generation capacity and ancillary service products to independent power producers; power grids and ISOs (independent system operators; investor-owned utilities; municipalities; cooperatives; banks and trading companies; and other companies that serve end users. In March 2009, the firm agreed to sell its Texas retail electricity business to NRG Energy, which provides power to about 1.8 million Texas customers. In May 2009, in conjunction with the completion of this sale, the company changed its name to RRI Energy, Inc. In April 2010, the company agreed to merge with Mirant Corp., with the combined company called GenOn Energy.

The firm offers employees medical, dental and vision coverage; participation in discount fitness program; a 401(k) plan; and profit sharing programs.

FINANCIALS:

Sales and profits are in thousands of dollars—add 000 to get the full amount. 2010 Note: Financial information for 2010 was not available for all companies at press time.

2010 Sales: $	2010 Profits: $	**U.S. Stock Ticker: RRI**
2009 Sales: $1,825,000	2009 Profits: $403,000	**Int'l Ticker:** Int'l Exchange:
2008 Sales: $3,394,000	2008 Profits: $-740,000	Employees: 2,239
2007 Sales: $3,203,000	2007 Profits: $365,000	Fiscal Year Ends: 12/31
2006 Sales: $10,877,000	2006 Profits: $-328,000	Parent Company:

SALARIES/BENEFITS:

Pension Plan:	ESOP Stock Plan:	Profit Sharing: Y	Top Exec. Salary: $910,000	Bonus: $527,838
Savings Plan: Y	Stock Purch. Plan:		Second Exec. Salary: $515,000	Bonus: $209,127

OTHER THOUGHTS:

Apparent Women Officers or Directors: 2
Hot Spot for Advancement for Women/Minorities: Y

LOCATIONS: ("Y" = Yes)

West:	Southwest:	Midwest:	Southeast:	Northeast:	International:
Y		Y	Y	Y	

RWE AG

www.rwe.com

Industry Group Code: 221 **Ranks within this company's industry group:** Sales: 2 Profits: 2

Exploration/Production:		Refining/Retailing:		Utilities:		Alternative Energy:		Specialty Services:		Energy Mktg./Other Svcs.	
Exploration:	Y	Refining:		Electric Utility:	Y	Waste/Solar/Other:	Y	Consulting/Eng.:		Energy Marketing:	Y
Production:	Y	Retailing:		Gas Utility:	Y	Thermal/Steam:		Seismic:		Equipment/Machinery:	
Coal Production:		Convenience Stores:		Pipelines:	Y	Wind:	Y	Drilling:		Oil Field Services:	
		Chemicals:		Water:	Y	Hydro:	Y	InfoTech:		Air/Shipping Transportation:	
						Fuel Cells:		Specialty Services:	Y		

TYPES OF BUSINESS:

Utilities-Electricity, Natural Gas & Water
Wind Energy Generation
Gas Pipelines & Distribution
Waste & Wastewater Management Services
Construction Services
Water Utility
Nuclear Power Generation
Energy Marketing

BRANDS/DIVISIONS/AFFILIATES:

RWE Power AG
RWE-DEA
RWE Gas Midstream
RWE npower
RWE Systems
RWE Energy
Essent
RWE Innogy

CONTACTS: *Note: Officers with more than one job title may be intentionally listed here more than once.*

Jurgen Grossmann, CEO
Rolf Martin Schmitz, COO
Jurgen Grossmann, Pres.
Rolf Pohlig, CFO
Alwin Fitting, Exec. VP-Human Resources
Leonhard Birnbaum, Exec. Dir.-Group Strategy & Bus. Dev.
Jurgen Frech, Head-Group Press Rel.
Manfred Schneider, Chmn.-Supervisory Board

Phone: 49-201-12-15025	**Fax:** 49-201-12-15265
Toll-Free:	
Address: Opernplatz 1, Essen, 45128 Germany	

GROWTH PLANS/SPECIAL FEATURES:

RWE AG is an international energy company that provides electricity, natural gas, water and waste management services in Europe and the U.S. The company is one of the world's leading electricity utilities, providing electricity to over 20 million customers and gas to 10 million. The firm's electricity subsidiary, RWE Power, uses various types of energy production: nuclear, hard coal, lignite, gas, oil and hydropower. The company's RWE-DEA subsidiary explores for and produces natural gas in Germany, Norway, Egypt, the U.A.E., Poland and Kazakhstan. RWE Supply & Trading comprises the operations of the former RWE Trading and RWE Gas Midstream divisions and trades electricity, gas, coal and mineral oil as well as energy derivatives. The division uses the Netherlands, the U.K., Russia and Norway for its major sources of gas supplies. RWE Energy is the firm's sales and grid company for customers in continental Europe. RWE npower is a leading electricity and gas supplier in England and Wales. One of the company's newest subsidiaries is RWE Innogy, which consolidates the firm's renewable and alternative energy assets. These include wind farms, hydro power stations and biomass power plants. In September 2009, the firm acquired Essent N.V. In September 2010, RWE announced the reorganization of its business, effective January 2011, which will see the reduction of departments and staff, particularly in the RWE Holding division and among its executive board. In October 2010, RWE Innogy announced plans to construct a biomass cogeneration plant in Italy.

FINANCIALS: **Sales and profits are in thousands of dollars—add 000 to get the full amount. 2010 Note: Financial information for 2010 was not available for all companies at press time.**

2010 Sales: $	2010 Profits: $	**U.S. Stock Ticker: RWEOY**
2009 Sales: $59,530,700	2009 Profits: $4,538,420	**Int'l Ticker: RWE** Int'l Exchange: Frankfurt-Euronext
2008 Sales: $60,839,700	2008 Profits: $3,250,990	Employees: 73,807
2007 Sales: $56,170,000	2007 Profits: $3,640,000	Fiscal Year Ends: 12/31
2006 Sales: $64,903,391	2006 Profits: $5,885,242	Parent Company:

SALARIES/BENEFITS:

Pension Plan:	ESOP Stock Plan:	Profit Sharing:	Top Exec. Salary: $	Bonus: $
Savings Plan:	Stock Purch. Plan:		Second Exec. Salary: $	Bonus: $

OTHER THOUGHTS:

Apparent Women Officers or Directors: 2
Hot Spot for Advancement for Women/Minorities:

LOCATIONS: ("Y" = Yes)

West:	Southwest:	Midwest:	Southeast:	Northeast:	International:
Y	Y	Y	Y	Y	Y

RWE NPOWER

www.rwenpower.com

Industry Group Code: 221 **Ranks within this company's industry group:** Sales: Profits:

Exploration/Production:		Refining/Retailing:		Utilities:		Alternative Energy:		Specialty Services:		Energy Mktg./Other Svcs.	
Exploration:		Refining:		Electric Utility:	Y	Waste/Solar/Other:		Consulting/Eng.:	Y	Energy Marketing:	Y
Production:		Retailing:		Gas Utility:	Y	Thermal/Steam:		Seismic:		Equipment/Machinery:	
Coal Production:		Convenience Stores:		Pipelines:		Wind:	Y	Drilling:		Oil Field Services:	
		Chemicals:		Water:		Hydro:	Y	InfoTech:		Air/Shipping Transportation:	
						Fuel Cells:		Specialty Services:			

TYPES OF BUSINESS:

Utilities
Electricity Generation & Trading
Energy Retail
Wind Power
Consulting & Technical Services
Hydroelectric Power

BRANDS/DIVISIONS/AFFILIATES:

RWE AG
npower
npower Cogen
RWE Power International
RE GmbH

CONTACTS: *Note: Officers with more than one job title may be intentionally listed here more than once.*

Volker Beckers, CEO
Frank Weigand, CFO
Chris Pilgrim, Dir.-Human Resources
Kevin McCullough, CTO
Guy Johnson, General Counsel/Corp. Sec./Dir.-Regulation
Alison Cole, Dir.-Comm.
Kevin Miles, CEO-Retail
Andrew Duff, Chmn.

Phone: 44-1793-87-77-77 **Fax:** 44-1793-89-39-55
Toll-Free:
Address: Windmill Hill Bus. Park, Whitehill Way, Swindon, SN5 6PB UK

GROWTH PLANS/SPECIAL FEATURES:

RWE npower, a subsidiary of RWE AG, is an integrated energy generation and trading business based in the U.K. RWE npower conducts its operations through five distinct business units: npower; generation; npower Cogen; renewable energy; and RWE Power International. The firm's retail business, known simply as npower, is one of the U.K.'s largest suppliers of electricity and natural gas, serving approximately 6.7 million residential and business customers. The generation division operates power stations in the U.K., using a variety of fuels including coal, gas and oil, with a combined generating capacity of over 10,000 megawatts (MW). npower Cogen is the cogeneration division and a leading developer of industrial CHP (Combined Heat and Power) in the U.K. With 16 plants in the U.K. and Ireland, npower Cogen has more than 2,000 MW of heat and power capacity. npower Renewables is a leader in wind and hydroelectric power in the U.K. It develops and operates onshore and offshore wind farms and hydro plants. The division operates 22 onshore wind farms with a combined capacity of 423 MW, two offshore wind farms, 18 hydroelectric power plants with a combined capacity of 67 MW and three co-firing biomass stations with a combined capacity of 35 MW. RWE Power International, a partnership with RE GmbH, is active in the construction, commissioning, operation, maintenance and decommissioning of power plants.

FINANCIALS: **Sales and profits are in thousands of dollars—add 000 to get the full amount. 2010 Note: Financial information for 2010 was not available for all companies at press time.**

2010 Sales: $	2010 Profits: $	**U.S. Stock Ticker: Subsidiary**
2009 Sales: $	2009 Profits: $	**Int'l Ticker:** Int'l Exchange:
2008 Sales: $	2008 Profits: $	Employees:
2007 Sales: $938,646	2007 Profits: $	Fiscal Year Ends: 12/31
2006 Sales: $553,800	2006 Profits: $	Parent Company: RWE AG

SALARIES/BENEFITS:

Pension Plan:	ESOP Stock Plan:	Profit Sharing:	Top Exec. Salary: $	Bonus: $
Savings Plan:	Stock Purch. Plan:		Second Exec. Salary: $	Bonus: $

OTHER THOUGHTS:

Apparent Women Officers or Directors: 1
Hot Spot for Advancement for Women/Minorities:

LOCATIONS: ("Y" = Yes)

West:	Southwest:	Midwest:	Southeast:	Northeast:	International:
					Y

SAIPEM SPA

www.saipem.it

Industry Group Code: 213112 **Ranks within this company's industry group:** Sales: 3 Profits: 4

Exploration/Production:		Refining/Retailing:		Utilities:		Alternative Energy:		Specialty Services:		Energy Mktg./Other Svcs.	
Exploration:		Refining:		Electric Utility:		Waste/Solar/Other:		Consulting/Eng.:	Y	Energy Marketing:	
Production:	Y	Retailing:		Gas Utility:		Thermal/Steam:		Seismic:		Equipment/Machinery:	
Coal Production:		Convenience Stores:		Pipelines:	Y	Wind:		Drilling:	Y	Oil Field Services:	Y
		Chemicals:		Water:		Hydro:		InfoTech:		Air/Shipping Transportation:	Y
						Fuel Cells:		Specialty Services:	Y		

TYPES OF BUSINESS:

Pipeline Installation
Drilling Services
Oil Field Services
Engineering & Construction Services
Remotely Operated Vehicles

BRANDS/DIVISIONS/AFFILIATES:

Eni SpA
Snamprogetti S.p.A.
Snamprogetti Netherlands BV
Saipem s.a.
Saipem FPSO S.p.A.
Saipem International B.V.
Intermare Sarda S.p.A.
Saipem Energy International S.p.A.

CONTACTS: *Note: Officers with more than one job title may be intentionally listed here more than once.*

Pietro Franco Tali, CEO
Hugh J. O'Donnell, COO
Giulio Bozzini, CFO
D. Gallinari, Human Resources
P. Galizzi, General Counsel
G. Caselli, COO-Drilling
P. Varone, COO-Onshore
Yves Inbona, COO-Offshore
Pietro Franco Tali, Deputy Chmn.
Marco Mangiagalli, Chmn.
P. Daleffe, VP-Procurement

Phone: 39-2-5201 **Fax:** 39-2-5205-4295
Toll-Free:
Address: Via Martiri di Cefalonia 67, San Donato, Milan, 20097 Italy

GROWTH PLANS/SPECIAL FEATURES:

Saipem S.p.A. is a provider of contracting services to oil and gas companies worldwide. The firm operates in three primary business units: offshore, onshore and drilling. The offshore unit specializes in laying large-diameter pipelines, especially in challenging environmental conditions. The offshore fleet consists of a range of vessels ranging from cargo barges capable of hauling structures up to 14,000 tons, to the Saipem 7000 semi-submersible derrick vessel capable of laying pipe in depths greater than 9,800 feet. The onshore unit offers a diverse array of project definition and executions services, which includes upstream oil and gas production and processing; liquefied natural gas; land pipelines design and construction; oil refining; gas monetization into chemicals; power plant construction and design; infrastructures and environmental activities; and equipment such as mobile cranes, pay welders, rock drills and more. The drilling unit specializes in contractor drilling operations in hostile on and offshore locations. The company has completed more than 7,100 wells. The firm also owns, either directly or indirectly, several subsidiaries: Saipem S.A.; Snamprogetti Netherlands BV; Saipem International B.V; Intermare Sarda S.p.A.; Saipem Energy International S.p.A.; and Energy Maintenance Services S.p.A.

FINANCIALS: **Sales and profits are in thousands of dollars—add 000 to get the full amount. 2010 Note: Financial information for 2010 was not available for all companies at press time.**

2010 Sales: $	2010 Profits: $	**U.S. Stock Ticker: Subsidiary**
2009 Sales: $14,365,200	2009 Profits: $1,021,700	**Int'l Ticker: SPMI** Int'l Exchange: Milan-BI
2008 Sales: $15,001,800	2008 Profits: $1,357,050	Employees: 36,468
2007 Sales: $14,958,800	2007 Profits: $1,365,000	Fiscal Year Ends: 12/31
2006 Sales: $11,792,000	2006 Profits: $599,000	Parent Company: ENI SPA

SALARIES/BENEFITS:

Pension Plan:	ESOP Stock Plan:	Profit Sharing:	Top Exec. Salary: $	Bonus: $
Savings Plan:	Stock Purch. Plan:		Second Exec. Salary: $	Bonus: $

OTHER THOUGHTS:

Apparent Women Officers or Directors:
Hot Spot for Advancement for Women/Minorities:

LOCATIONS: ("Y" = Yes)

West:	Southwest:	Midwest:	Southeast:	Northeast:	International:
	Y				Y

SAN DIEGO GAS & ELECTRIC COMPANY

www.sdge.com

Industry Group Code: 221 **Ranks within this company's industry group:** Sales: Profits:

Exploration/Production:		Refining/Retailing:		Utilities:		Alternative Energy:		Specialty Services:		Energy Mktg./Other Svcs.	
Exploration:		Refining:		Electric Utility:	Y	Waste/Solar/Other:	Y	Consulting/Eng.:		Energy Marketing:	
Production:		Retailing:		Gas Utility:	Y	Thermal/Steam:		Seismic:		Equipment/Machinery:	
Coal Production:		Convenience Stores:		Pipelines:		Wind:	Y	Drilling:		Oil Field Services:	
		Chemicals:		Water:		Hydro:		InfoTech:		Air/Shipping Transportation:	
						Fuel Cells:		Specialty Services:			

TYPES OF BUSINESS:

Utilities-Electricity & Natural Gas
Online Services
Online Bill Payment
Rebates
Financial Assistance
Workshops
Training
Incentives

BRANDS/DIVISIONS/AFFILIATES:

Sempra Energy
Southern California Gas Co
Sempra Generation
Sempra LNG
Sempra Pipelines Storage

CONTACTS: *Note: Officers with more than one job title may be intentionally listed here more than once.*

Jessie J. Knight, Jr., CEO
Michael R. Niggli, COO
Michael R. Niggli, Pres.
Robert M. Schlax, CFO
Vicki L. Zeiger, VP-Human Resources
J. Chris Baker, CIO/Sr. VP-Support Svcs.
Richard R. Morrow, VP-Eng.
W. Davis Smith, General Counsel/Sr. VP
Richard R. Morrow, VP-Oper.
Michelle M. Mueller, VP-External Affairs
Robert M. Schlax, Treas./Controller/VP
James P. Avery, Sr. VP-Power Supply
Lee Schavrien, Sr. VP-Finance/Regulatory & Legislative Affairs
Hal D. Snyder, VP-Customer Solutions
David L. Geier, VP-Electric Oper.
Jessie J. Knight, Jr., Chmn.

Phone: 619-696-2000	**Fax:** 858-541-5737
Toll-Free: 800-411-7343	
Address: 8326 Century Park Ct., San Diego, CA 92123-4150 US	

GROWTH PLANS/SPECIAL FEATURES:

San Diego Gas & Electric Company (SDGE), a subsidiary of Sempra Energy Utilities, is a regulated public utility that has a 4,100-square-mile service area covering San Diego County and southern Orange County, stretching to the Mexican border. The company serves 3.4 million customers through 1.4 million electric, 840,000 natural gas, 1,217,200 residential, 147,600 commercial, 500 industrial, 2,000 street and highway lighting and 5,000 direct access meters. The firm's electric facilities are located in San Diego, Imperial and southern Orange counties in California. SDGE generates power via its Palomar and Miramar natural gas-fired generation facilities, and owns 20% interest in San Onofre Nuclear Generating Station. The remainder of its power supply is obtained through primarily long-term purchase agreements. Natural gas purchased and delivered by SDGE is obtained primarily in the southwestern U.S., U.S. Rockies and Canada. To fulfill California renewable energy requirements, SDGE has entered into a number of energy purchase agreements that include hydroelectric, wind and renewable biomass generated energy. The firm also has a program that provides energy savings as well as cash incentives for customers who incorporate energy-efficient design into new homes.

The firm's employee benefits include: medical, life and accident insurance; vision care; domestic partnership benefits; pension and retirement savings plan; a wellness program; gym and volunteer incentive program; telecommuting; Employee Assistance and scholarship program; education assistance; paid vacation; subsidized transportation; a career development center; and leadership ability reward/recognition.

FINANCIALS: **Sales and profits are in thousands of dollars—add 000 to get the full amount. 2010 Note: Financial information for 2010 was not available for all companies at press time.**

2010 Sales: $	2010 Profits: $	**U.S. Stock Ticker: Subsidiary**
2009 Sales: $	2009 Profits: $	**Int'l Ticker:** Int'l Exchange:
2008 Sales: $	2008 Profits: $	Employees:
2007 Sales: $	2007 Profits: $	Fiscal Year Ends: 12/31
2006 Sales: $	2006 Profits: $	Parent Company: SEMPRA ENERGY

SALARIES/BENEFITS:

Pension Plan: Y	ESOP Stock Plan:	Profit Sharing:	Top Exec. Salary: $	Bonus: $803,500
Savings Plan:	Stock Purch. Plan:		Second Exec. Salary: $	Bonus: $

OTHER THOUGHTS:

Apparent Women Officers or Directors: 5
Hot Spot for Advancement for Women/Minorities: Y

LOCATIONS: ("Y" = Yes)

West:	Southwest:	Midwest:	Southeast:	Northeast:	International:
Y					

SANDRIDGE ENERGY INC

www.sandridgeenergy.com

Industry Group Code: 211111 **Ranks within this company's industry group:** Sales: 92 Profits: 107

Exploration/Production:		Refining/Retailing:		Utilities:		Alternative Energy:		Specialty Services:		Energy Mktg./Other Svcs.	
Exploration:	Y	Refining:		Electric Utility:		Waste/Solar/Other:		Consulting/Eng.:		Energy Marketing:	
Production:	Y	Retailing:		Gas Utility:		Thermal/Steam:		Seismic:		Equipment/Machinery:	
Coal Production:		Convenience Stores:		Pipelines:		Wind:		Drilling:	Y	Oil Field Services:	Y
		Chemicals:		Water:		Hydro:		InfoTech:		Air/Shipping Transportation:	
						Fuel Cells:		Specialty Services:	Y		

TYPES OF BUSINESS:

Oil & Gas Exploration & Production
Oil Well Drilling Services
Oilfield Services
Natural Gas Gathering & Compression
Carbon Dioxide Treatment
Oil Recovery Services

BRANDS/DIVISIONS/AFFILIATES:

Lariat Services, Inc.
SandRidge Midstream, Inc.
SandRidge Tertiary LLC
Arena Resources Inc

CONTACTS:

Note: Officers with more than one job title may be intentionally listed here more than once.

Tom L. Ward, CEO
Matthew K. Grubb, COO/Exec. VP
Tom L. Ward, Pres.
Dirk M. Van Doran, CFO/Exec. VP
Mary L. Whitson, Sr. VP-Human Resources
Todd N. Tipton, Exec. VP-Exploration
Thomas L. Winton, CIO/Sr. VP-IT
Kevin R. White, Sr. VP-Bus. Dev.
Randall D. Cooley, Sr. VP-Acct.
Wayne C. Chang, Sr. VP/Pres., SandRidge Midstream Inc.
Rodney E. Johnson, Exec. VP-Reservoir Exploration
Tom L. Ward, Chmn.

Phone: 405-429-5500	**Fax:** 405-429-5977
Toll-Free:	
Address: 123 Robert S. Kerr, Oklahoma City, OK 73102-6406 US	

GROWTH PLANS/SPECIAL FEATURES:

SandRidge Energy, Inc., based in Oklahoma City, is an oil and gas company. The company operates in three business segments: exploration and production, drilling and oilfield services and midstream gas services. The exploration and production segment comprises the firm's exploration, development and production activities, with areas of operation primarily concentrated in west Texas, although it also has interests in the Cotton Valley Trend in east Texas, the Permian Basin and the Mid-Continent, Gulf Coast and Gulf of Mexico regions of the U.S. SandRidge has estimated proved reserves of over 1,312 billion cubic feet of oil equivalent (Bcfe), with an average daily production of approximately 296.2 million cfe. This segment also conducts tertiary oil recovery operations. The drilling and oilfield services segment operates through wholly-owned subsidiary Lariat Services, Inc., which owns and operates drilling rigs primarily in West Texas. Lariat Services drills wells for both SandRidge and third parties. Its fleet comprises 44 rigs. Lariat Services also provides oilfield services, including pulling unit provision, trucking, rental tools, location and road construction and roustabout services. Finally, the midstream gas services segment provides natural gas gathering, compression, processing and treating services in West Texas through subsidiary SandRidge Midstream, Inc.; and operates carbon dioxide treating and transportation facilities. Subsidiary SandRidge Tertiary LLC conducts the company's carbon dioxide treatment and oil recovery operations. In July 2009, the firm sold natural gas gathering and compression assets in Texas. In December 2009, SandRidge acquired certain properties in the Permian Basin from Forest Oil Company. Also in July 2010, the company merged with Arena Resources, Inc., with SandRidge as the surviving entity. Following the merger, SandRidge's holdings in the Permian Basin increased to over 200,000 acres.

SandRidge offers its employees medical, dental and vision coverage, flexible spending accounts, life and disability insurance, a 401(k) plan and restricted stock benefits.

FINANCIALS:

Sales and profits are in thousands of dollars—add 000 to get the full amount. 2010 Note: Financial information for 2010 was not available for all companies at press time.

2010 Sales: $	2010 Profits: $	**U.S. Stock Ticker: SD**
2009 Sales: $591,044	2009 Profits: $-1,773,332	**Int'l Ticker:** Int'l Exchange:
2008 Sales: $1,181,814	2008 Profits: $-1,440,425	Employees: 1,694
2007 Sales: $	2007 Profits: $	Fiscal Year Ends: 12/31
2006 Sales: $	2006 Profits: $	Parent Company:

SALARIES/BENEFITS:

Pension Plan:	ESOP Stock Plan:	Profit Sharing:	Top Exec. Salary: $1,212,894	Bonus: $1,350,000
Savings Plan: Y	Stock Purch. Plan:		Second Exec. Salary: $589,586	Bonus: $735,000

OTHER THOUGHTS:

Apparent Women Officers or Directors: 1
Hot Spot for Advancement for Women/Minorities:

LOCATIONS: ("Y" = Yes)

West:	Southwest:	Midwest:	Southeast:	Northeast:	International:
	Y				

SANTOS LTD

www.santos.com.au

Industry Group Code: 211111 **Ranks within this company's industry group:** Sales: 70 Profits: 48

Exploration/Production:		Refining/Retailing:		Utilities:		Alternative Energy:		Specialty Services:		Energy Mktg./Other Svcs.	
Exploration:	Y	Refining:	Y	Electric Utility:		Waste/Solar/Other:		Consulting/Eng.:		Energy Marketing:	Y
Production:	Y	Retailing:		Gas Utility:		Thermal/Steam:		Seismic:		Equipment/Machinery:	
Coal Production:		Convenience Stores:		Pipelines:		Wind:		Drilling:		Oil Field Services:	
		Chemicals:		Water:		Hydro:		InfoTech:		Air/Shipping Transportation:	
						Fuel Cells:		Specialty Services:			

TYPES OF BUSINESS:

Oil & Gas Exploration & Production

BRANDS/DIVISIONS/AFFILIATES:

Santos Offshore Pty Ltd
Santos Brantas Pty Ltd

CONTACTS:

Note: Officers with more than one job title may be intentionally listed here more than once.

David Knox, CEO/Managing Dir.
Peter Wasow, CFO/Exec. VP
Petrina Coventry, Chief Human Resources Officer
Trevor Brown, VP-Exploration & Subsurface
Ray Betros, Exec. VP-Tech.
Roger Kennett, VP-GLNG Oper.
Peter Cleary, VP-Strategy & Corp. Dev.
John Anderson, VP-Western Australia & Northern Territory
James Baulderstone, VP-Eastern Australia
Martyn Eames, VP-Asia
Peter Roland Coates, Chmn.
Martyn Eames, VP-Asia

Phone: 61-8-8116-5000	**Fax:** 61-8-8116-5050
Toll-Free:	
Address: Santos Ctr., 60 Flinders St., Ground Fl., Adelaide, 5000 Australia	

GROWTH PLANS/SPECIAL FEATURES:

Santos Ltd. is one of Australia's largest oil and gas exploration and production companies. The firm is mainly involved in the production, treatment and marketing of crude oil, liquid petroleum gas, condensate, naphtha and natural gas; petroleum exploration; and the pipeline transportation of crude oil. The firm maintains interests in every major Australian petroleum province as well as in India, Vietnam and Indonesia. The company produces approximately 54.4 million barrels of oil equivalent annually, and has proved plus probable reserves of over 1 billion barrels. Santos Ltd. is organized in four geographic business units: Western Australia and Northern Territory; Eastern Australia; Asia; and Santos Gladstone Liquefied Natural Gas (GLNG). GLNG, located in Papa New Guinea, is a project that involves the exploration/development of coal seam gas (CSG) in the Surat and Bowen Basin gas fields, as well as the conversion of CGS to liquefied natural gas by a 3.5 million ton annual LNG liquefaction plant (currently under construction). Santos Ltd. operates the upstream operations of the GLNG project. In December 2009, Santos announced an agreement for the sale and purchase of 1.5 million tons per year of liquefied natural gas to Osaka Gas.

FINANCIALS:

Sales and profits are in thousands of dollars—add 000 to get the full amount. 2010 Note: Financial information for 2010 was not available for all companies at press time.

2010 Sales: $	2010 Profits: $	**U.S. Stock Ticker: STOSY**
2009 Sales: $2,214,500	2009 Profits: $440,670	**Int'l Ticker: STO** Int'l Exchange: Sydney-ASX
2008 Sales: $2,492,860	2008 Profits: $1,489,410	Employees:
2007 Sales: $2,160,000	2007 Profits: $420,000	Fiscal Year Ends: 12/31
2006 Sales: $2,160,200	2006 Profits: $507,800	Parent Company:

SALARIES/BENEFITS:

Pension Plan:	ESOP Stock Plan:	Profit Sharing:	Top Exec. Salary: $	Bonus: $864,074
Savings Plan: Y	Stock Purch. Plan:		Second Exec. Salary: $	Bonus: $

OTHER THOUGHTS:

Apparent Women Officers or Directors: 1
Hot Spot for Advancement for Women/Minorities:

LOCATIONS: ("Y" = Yes)

West:	Southwest:	Midwest:	Southeast:	Northeast:	International:
					Y

SAUDI ARAMCO (SAUDI ARABIAN OIL CO) www.saudiaramco.com

Industry Group Code: 211111 **Ranks within this company's industry group:** Sales: 5 Profits:

Exploration/Production:		Refining/Retailing:		Utilities:		Alternative Energy:		Specialty Services:		Energy Mktg./Other Svcs.	
Exploration:	Y	Refining:	Y	Electric Utility:		Waste/Solar/Other:		Consulting/Eng.:	Y	Energy Marketing:	
Production:	Y	Retailing:		Gas Utility:		Thermal/Steam:		Seismic:		Equipment/Machinery:	
Coal Production:		Convenience Stores:		Pipelines:	Y	Wind:		Drilling:		Oil Field Services:	
		Chemicals:	Y	Water:		Hydro:		InfoTech:		Air/Shipping Transportation:	Y
						Fuel Cells:		Specialty Services:			

TYPES OF BUSINESS:

Oil & Gas-Exploration & Production
Oil Refining
Crude Oil Distribution
Pipelines
Oil Tankers

BRANDS/DIVISIONS/AFFILIATES:

CONTACTS:

Note: Officers with more than one job title may be intentionally listed here more than once.

Khalid A. Al-Falih, CEO
Khalid A. Al-Falih, Pres.
Khalid G. Al-Buainain, Sr. VP-Mktg. & Refining
Amin H. Nasser, Sr. VP-Exploration & Prod.
Salim S. Al-Aydh, Sr. VP-Eng. & Project Mgmt.
David B. Kultgen, General Counsel/Sec.
Adbulrahman F. Al-Wuhaib, Sr. VP-Oper. Svcs.
Abdulaziz F. Al-Khayyal, Sr. VP-Industrial Rel.
Abdullatif A. Al-Othman, Sr. VP-Finance
Ali I. Al-Naimi, Chmn.
Khalid G. Al-Buainain, Sr. VP-Int'l

Phone: 966-3-872-0115 **Fax:** 966-3-873-8190
Toll-Free:
Address: R-2220 E. Administration Bldg., P.O. Box 5000, Dhahran, 31311 Saudi Arabia

GROWTH PLANS/SPECIAL FEATURES:

Saudi Aramco (Saudi Arabian Oil Co.) is among the world's largest holders and producers of crude oil and natural gas, with reserves of 260.1 billion barrels of oil and 275.2 trillion cubic feet of gas. Saudi Aramco's 2009 oil production averaged approximately 7.9 million barrels per day (bpd), totaling 2.9 billion barrels; natural gas production averaged 8.6 billion cubic feet per day, totaling 3.2 trillion cubic feet; and natural gas liquids production averaged 1.1 million bpd, totaling 410.2 million barrels. The company conducts extensive surveying and exploration activities while harvesting oil from some of the largest oil fields in the world, such as the Dhahran, Khurais, Shaybah, Ghawar and Safaniya fields. The company also operates an extensive network of pipelines, refineries and oil tankers. Annually, over 3,700 tankers make port at Saudi Aramco's Ras Tanura and Ju'aymah ports on the Arabian Gulf; and at Yanbu', Jiddah and Rabigh on the Red Sea. Its main domestic refineries include Ras Tanura, processing 550,000 bpd; Yanbu', 170,000 bpd; Jiddah, 85,000 bpd; and Riyadh, 122,000 bpd. It also owns 50% or less of three domestic refineries, which together process 1.1 million bpd; and owns primarily minority interests in four international refineries that collectively process 2.2 million bpd. Saudi Aramco mainly exports its oil through overseas refineries and distribution hubs in New York, Houston, London, Leiden, Beijing, Tokyo and Hong Kong. Most of its crude oil (52.7%) goes to the Far East, followed by the U.S. (20%), the Mediterranean (7%), Europe (5.2%) and other regions (15.1%).

Employees of Saudi Aramco receive free health care at company-owned or -designated hospitals; suburban-style low-cost housing; and 30 days of vacation annually.

FINANCIALS:

Sales and profits are in thousands of dollars—add 000 to get the full amount. 2010 Note: Financial information for 2010 was not available for all companies at press time.

2010 Sales: $	2010 Profits: $	**U.S. Stock Ticker: Government-Owned**
2009 Sales: $190,000,000	2009 Profits: $	**Int'l Ticker:** Int'l Exchange:
2008 Sales: $280,000,000	2008 Profits: $	Employees:
2007 Sales: $240,000,000	2007 Profits: $	Fiscal Year Ends: 12/31
2006 Sales: $200,000,000	2006 Profits: $	Parent Company:

SALARIES/BENEFITS:

Pension Plan:	ESOP Stock Plan:	Profit Sharing:	Top Exec. Salary: $	Bonus: $
Savings Plan:	Stock Purch. Plan:		Second Exec. Salary: $	Bonus: $

OTHER THOUGHTS:

Apparent Women Officers or Directors:
Hot Spot for Advancement for Women/Minorities:

LOCATIONS: ("Y" = Yes)

West:	Southwest:	Midwest:	Southeast:	Northeast:	International:
	Y			Y	Y

Note: Financial information, benefits and other data can change quickly and may vary from those stated here.

SCANA CORPORATION

www.scana.com

Industry Group Code: 221 **Ranks within this company's industry group:** Sales: 30 Profits: 28

Exploration/Production:		Refining/Retailing:		Utilities:		Alternative Energy:		Specialty Services:		Energy Mktg./Other Svcs.	
Exploration:		Refining:		Electric Utility:	Y	Waste/Solar/Other:		Consulting/Eng.:		Energy Marketing:	Y
Production:		Retailing:		Gas Utility:	Y	Thermal/Steam:		Seismic:		Equipment/Machinery:	
Coal Production:		Convenience Stores:		Pipelines:	Y	Wind:		Drilling:		Oil Field Services:	
		Chemicals:		Water:		Hydro:		InfoTech:		Air/Shipping Transportation:	
						Fuel Cells:		Specialty Services:			

TYPES OF BUSINESS:

Electricity & Natural Gas
Telecommunications Services
Ethernet Services & Data Center Facilities
Communications Towers Management
Management & Maintenance Services
Service Contracts
Risk Management Services

BRANDS/DIVISIONS/AFFILIATES:

South Carolina Electric & Gas Co.
South Carolina Generating Co., Inc.
South Carolina Fuel Co., Inc.
Public Service Co. of North Carolina, Inc.
Carolina Gas Transmission Corp.
SCANA Communications, Inc.
SCANA Energy Marketing, Inc.
ServiceCare, Inc.

CONTACTS: *Note: Officers with more than one job title may be intentionally listed here more than once.*

William B. Timmerman, CEO
William B. Timmerman, Pres.
Jimmy Addison, CFO/Sr. VP
George J. Bullwinkel, Jr., Pres./COO-Scana Energy Mktg.
Ronald Lindsey, General Counsel/Sr. VP
Mark R. Cannon, Treas./Risk Mgmt. Officer
Kevin B. Marsh, Pres./COO-South Carolina Electric & Gas Co.
Charles McFadden, Sr. VP-Gov't Affairs & Economic Dev.
Paul V. Fant, Pres./COO-Carolina Gas Transmission
Gina S. Champion, Corp. Sec./Associate General Counsel
William B. Timmerman, Chmn.
Sarena D. Burch, Sr. VP-Fuel Procurement & Asset Mgmt.

Phone: 803-217-9000	**Fax:** 803-217-8119
Toll-Free: 800-763-5891	
Address: 1426 Main St., Columbia, SC 29201 US	

GROWTH PLANS/SPECIAL FEATURES:

SCANA Corporation is an energy-based holding company that operates through wholly-owned subsidiaries. South Carolina Electric & Gas Company (SCE&G) generates, transmits, distributes and sells electricity to about 655,000 retail and wholesale customers, as well as purchasing, selling and transporting natural gas to about 310,000 customers. South Carolina Generating Company, Inc. owns and operates Williams Station and sells electricity exclusively to SCE&G. South Carolina Fuel Company, Inc. acquires, owns and provides financing for SCE&G's nuclear fuel, fossil fuel and emission allowances. Public Service Company of North Carolina, Inc. purchases, sells and transports natural gas for residential, commercial and industrial customers. Carolina Gas Transmission Corp. (CGTC) transports natural gas in southeastern Georgia and South Carolina. SCANA Communications, Inc. (SCI) provides fiber optic communications, Ethernet services and data center facilities through a 500-mile fiber optic and Ethernet telecommunications network. SCI also provides communication tower site construction, management and rental services in South Carolina, North Carolina and Georgia. SCANA Energy Marketing, Inc. (SEMI) markets natural gas, primarily in the Southeast, and provides energy-related risk management services. Through its SCANA Energy division, SEMI markets natural gas in Georgia's retail market. ServiceCare, Inc. provides service contracts on home appliances and heating and air conditioning units. SCANA Services, Inc. provides administrative and management services to SCANA's subsidiaries. The firm also owns three smaller energy-related companies. SCANA's electrical service operations primarily serve the chemicals, educational services, textile manufacturing, paper products, food products, lumber and wood products, health services, food and retail industries; the company markets natural gas to automobile manufacturers and the pharmaceuticals, chemicals, ceramics, food products and steel industries. The firm's natural gas operations include liquefied natural gas liquefaction and storage facilities.

The company offers its employees medical, dental and vision insurance; a retirement plan; and a 401(k) plan.

FINANCIALS: **Sales and profits are in thousands of dollars—add 000 to get the full amount. 2010 Note: Financial information for 2010 was not available for all companies at press time.**

2010 Sales: $	2010 Profits: $	**U.S. Stock Ticker: SCG**
2009 Sales: $4,237,000	2009 Profits: $348,000	**Int'l Ticker:** Int'l Exchange:
2008 Sales: $5,319,000	2008 Profits: $346,000	Employees: 5,828
2007 Sales: $4,621,000	2007 Profits: $320,000	Fiscal Year Ends: 12/31
2006 Sales: $4,563,000	2006 Profits: $310,000	Parent Company:

SALARIES/BENEFITS:

Pension Plan: Y	ESOP Stock Plan:	Profit Sharing:	Top Exec. Salary: $1,099,000	Bonus: $700,613
Savings Plan: Y	Stock Purch. Plan:		Second Exec. Salary: $580,000	Bonus: $282,750

OTHER THOUGHTS:

Apparent Women Officers or Directors: 5
Hot Spot for Advancement for Women/Minorities: Y

LOCATIONS: ("Y" = Yes)

West:	Southwest:	Midwest:	Southeast:	Northeast:	International:
				Y	

SCHLUMBERGER LIMITED

www.slb.com

Industry Group Code: 213112 **Ranks within this company's industry group:** Sales: 1 Profits: 1

Exploration/Production:		Refining/Retailing:		Utilities:		Alternative Energy:		Specialty Services:		Energy Mktg./Other Svcs.	
Exploration:		Refining:		Electric Utility:		Waste/Solar/Other:		Consulting/Eng.:	Y	Energy Marketing:	
Production:		Retailing:		Gas Utility:		Thermal/Steam:		Seismic:	Y	Equipment/Machinery:	
Coal Production:		Convenience Stores:		Pipelines:		Wind:		Drilling:	Y	Oil Field Services:	Y
		Chemicals:		Water:		Hydro:		InfoTech:	Y	Air/Shipping Transportation:	
						Fuel Cells:		Specialty Services:			

TYPES OF BUSINESS:

Oil & Gas Drilling Support Services
Seismic Services
Reservoir Imaging
Data & IT Consulting Services
Outsourcing
Stimulation Services

BRANDS/DIVISIONS/AFFILIATES:

Schlumberger Oilfield Services
WesternGeco
Framo Engineering
M-I Drilling Fluids
IntelliServ
Nexus Geosciences Inc
IGEOSS
Techsia SA

CONTACTS: *Note: Officers with more than one job title may be intentionally listed here more than once.*

Andrew Gould, CEO
Paal Kibsgaard, COO
Simon Ayat, CFO/Exec. VP
Stephanie Cox, VP-Personnel
Ashok Belani, CTO/VP
Charles Woodburn, VP-Eng.
Charles Woodburn, VP-Mfg. & Sustaining
Alexander Juden, General Counsel/Sec.
Satish Pai, VP-Oper.
Rod Nelson, VP-Corp. Comm.
Malcolm Theobald, VP-Investor Rel.
Hatem Soliman, Pres., Latin America
Aaron Gatt Floridia, Pres., Middle East & Asia
Steve Fulgham, Pres., North America
Maurice Dijols, Pres., Russia
Andrew Gould, Chmn.
Mark Corrigan, Pres., Europe & Africa

Phone: 713-513-2000 **Fax:**
Toll-Free:
Address: 5599 San Felipe St., Fl. 17, Houston, TX 77056 US

GROWTH PLANS/SPECIAL FEATURES:

Schlumberger Limited (SLB) is a leading oil field service company offering technology, project management and information solutions for customers in the international oil and gas industry. Schlumberger operates in 80 countries throughout North America, Latin America, Europe, Africa, the Middle East and Asia. It also maintains 25 research and engineering facilities worldwide. The SLB Oilfield Services segment is divided into eight technology-based service lines, which include wireline; drilling and measurements; well testing; well services; completions; artificial lift; data and consulting services; and SLB information solutions. The overall purpose of the Oilfield Services sector is to provide proper exploration with production services and technologies throughout the entire life cycle of a reservoir. Another SLB service is its Integrated Project Management (IPM) line, which provides consulting, project management and engineering services for well construction using SLB technology. The company owns 40% of M-I SWACO, which offers drilling and completion fluids to stabilize rock and minimize formation damage. In addition, the firm owns a majority stake in Framo Engineering, a Norwegian-based company that provides multiphase booster pumps, flow metering equipment and swivel stack systems. Another subsidiary of SLB, WesternGeco, offers worldwide marine and seismic reservoir imaging, data processing centers and a multi-client seismic library for monitoring and development services. In May 2009, Schlumberger acquired Techsia SA. In September 2009, the firm and National Oilwell Varco formed joint venture IntelliServ to expand the use of the IntelliServ Broadband Network. In October 2009, the company opened a reservoir completions manufacturing center in Saudi Arabia. In December 2009, Schlumberger opened new offices in Rio de Janeiro, Beijing, New Delhi and Abu Dhabi. In February 2010, the company agreed to acquire Smith International, Inc. for $11 billion in stock. In March 2010, the firm acquired Nexus Geosciences, Inc. In April 2010, Schlumberger acquired IGEOSS.

FINANCIALS: **Sales and profits are in thousands of dollars—add 000 to get the full amount. 2010 Note: Financial information for 2010 was not available for all companies at press time.**

2010 Sales: $	2010 Profits: $	**U.S. Stock Ticker: SLB**
2009 Sales: $22,702,000	2009 Profits: $3,134,000	**Int'l Ticker:** Int'l Exchange:
2008 Sales: $27,163,000	2008 Profits: $5,435,000	Employees: 77,000
2007 Sales: $23,277,000	2007 Profits: $5,177,000	Fiscal Year Ends: 12/31
2006 Sales: $19,230,000	2006 Profits: $3,710,000	Parent Company:

SALARIES/BENEFITS:

Pension Plan: Y	ESOP Stock Plan:	Profit Sharing:	Top Exec. Salary: $2,500,000	Bonus: $1,787,500
Savings Plan: Y	Stock Purch. Plan: Y		Second Exec. Salary: $1,178,927	Bonus: $783,981

OTHER THOUGHTS:

Apparent Women Officers or Directors: 2
Hot Spot for Advancement for Women/Minorities:

LOCATIONS: ("Y" = Yes)

West:	Southwest:	Midwest:	Southeast:	Northeast:	International:
Y	Y	Y		Y	Y

SCHNEIDER ELECTRIC SA

www.schneider-electric.com

Industry Group Code: 335 **Ranks within this company's industry group:** Sales: 5 Profits: 5

Exploration/Production:		**Refining/Retailing:**		**Utilities:**		**Alternative Energy:**		**Specialty Services:**		**Energy Mktg./Other Svcs.**	
Exploration:		Refining:		Electric Utility:		Waste/Solar/Other:		Consulting/Eng.:		Energy Marketing:	
Production:		Retailing:		Gas Utility:		Thermal/Steam:		Seismic:		Equipment/Machinery:	Y
Coal Production:		Convenience Stores:		Pipelines:		Wind:		Drilling:		Oil Field Services:	
		Chemicals:		Water:		Hydro:		InfoTech:		Air/Shipping Transportation:	
						Fuel Cells:		Specialty Services:	Y		

TYPES OF BUSINESS:

Electrical Distribution Products
Infrastructure Products
Building Automation & Control Products

BRANDS/DIVISIONS/AFFILIATES:

BEI Technologies, Inc.
Systron Donner Inertial
American Power Conversion Corp
Merlin Gerin
Square D
Telemecanique
Wessen

CONTACTS: *Note: Officers with more than one job title may be intentionally listed here more than once.*

Jean-Pascal Tricoire, CEO
Jean-Pascal Tricoire, Pres.
Pierre Bouchut, CFO
Aaron Davis, Chief Mktg. Officer
Karen Ferguson, Exec. VP-Human Resources
Herve Coureil, CIO
Eric Pilaud, Exec. VP-Strategy
Eric Pilaud, Exec. VP-Custom Sensors & Technologies
Michel Crochon, Exec. VP-Industry Bus.
Chris Curtis, Exec. VP-Buildings Bus.
Laurent Vernerey, Exec. VP-IT Bus.
Julio Rodriguez, Exec. VP-Power Global & EMEAS Bus.
Hal Grant, Exec. VP-Supply Chain

Phone: 33-1-41-29-70-00	**Fax:** 33-1-41-29-71-00
Toll-Free:	
Address: 35 rue Joseph Monier, Rueil-Malmaison, 92500 France	

GROWTH PLANS/SPECIAL FEATURES:

Schneider Electric S.A. manufactures and markets a range of products and services for the energy and infrastructure markets in residential buildings and industry areas. Schneider Electric has operations in nearly 200 countries worldwide, with approximately 15,000 sales outlets; 25 research and development sites; 205 manufacturing facilities; and 60 logistics centers. The company works through three core business segments: electrical distribution; automation & control; and critical power & cooling services. The firm's electrical distribution segment, accounting for 63% of annual revenues, offers products, equipment and systems covering all phases of transmission and electrical distribution, classified according to their voltage level. Low-voltage products, including circuit breakers, switches, security lighting, prefabricated electrical wiring, modular switchgear and communication products, are used in the building market. Medium-voltage equipment is designed to transform electricity and then deliver it to an end user. The company's electrical distribution segment has two primary brand names: Merlin Gerin and Square D. The Merlin Gerin brand supplies intermediaries with modular and autonomous components that are organized as systems designed to increase and optimize distribution. The Square D brand aids companies in meeting market requirements for products that must comply with NEMA (National Electrical Manufacturers Association) standards. The company's automation & control segment, accounting for 29% of annual revenues, specializes in developing platforms and products for human-machine interaction including contractors, overload relays, soft starters, speed drives, sensors and operator terminals. This segment includes company Telemecanique, which develops products and systems for automation that include abilities in detection, man-machine dialogue and process supervision. The recently-created critical power and cooling services segment, accounting for a growing portion of annual revenues, focuses on providing solutions for energy-critical applications, such as data centers and hospitals.

FINANCIALS: **Sales and profits are in thousands of dollars—add 000 to get the full amount. 2010 Note: Financial information for 2010 was not available for all companies at press time.**

2010 Sales: $	2010 Profits: $	**U.S. Stock Ticker:**
2009 Sales: $21,457,000	2009 Profits: $1,157,560	**Int'l Ticker: SU** Int'l Exchange: Paris-Euronext
2008 Sales: $24,395,700	2008 Profits: $2,240,930	Employees: 116,065
2007 Sales: $23,060,800	2007 Profits: $2,109,030	Fiscal Year Ends: 12/31
2006 Sales: $18,113,600	2006 Profits: $1,776,600	Parent Company:

SALARIES/BENEFITS:

Pension Plan:	ESOP Stock Plan:	Profit Sharing:	Top Exec. Salary: $	Bonus: $
Savings Plan:	Stock Purch. Plan:		Second Exec. Salary: $	Bonus: $

OTHER THOUGHTS:

Apparent Women Officers or Directors: 1
Hot Spot for Advancement for Women/Minorities:

LOCATIONS: ("Y" = Yes)

West:	Southwest:	Midwest:	Southeast:	Northeast:	International:
					Y

SCOTTISH AND SOUTHERN ENERGY PLC www.scottish-southern.co.uk

Industry Group Code: 221 **Ranks within this company's industry group:** Sales: 4 Profits: 8

Exploration/Production:		**Refining/Retailing:**		**Utilities:**		**Alternative Energy:**		**Specialty Services:**		**Energy Mktg./Other Svcs.**	
Exploration:		Refining:		Electric Utility:	Y	Waste/Solar/Other:		Consulting/Eng.:		Energy Marketing:	
Production:		Retailing:		Gas Utility:	Y	Thermal/Steam:		Seismic:		Equipment/Machinery:	Y
Coal Production:		Convenience Stores:		Pipelines:		Wind:	Y	Drilling:		Oil Field Services:	
		Chemicals:		Water:		Hydro:	Y	InfoTech:		Air/Shipping Transportation:	
						Fuel Cells:		Specialty Services:	Y		

TYPES OF BUSINESS:

Electric Utilities
Power Distribution & Transmission
Hydroelectric Generation
Wind Generation
Utility Contracting Services
Telecommunications Services
Natural Gas Utility

BRANDS/DIVISIONS/AFFILIATES:

SSE Telecom
Scottish Hydro
Southern Electric
SWALEC
SSE Gas Storage
SSE Power Distribution
SSE Contracting Group
Airtricity

CONTACTS: *Note: Officers with more than one job title may be intentionally listed here more than once.*

Ian Marchant, CEO
Colin Hood, COO
Gregor Alexander, Dir.-Finance
Vincent Donnelly, Sec.
Alistair Phillips-Davies, Dir.-Energy Supply
Robert Smith, Chmn.

Phone: 44-1738-456-000 **Fax:**
Toll-Free:
Address: Inveralmond House, 200 Dunkeld Rd., Perth, Scotland PH1 3AQ UK

GROWTH PLANS/SPECIAL FEATURES:

Scottish and Southern Energy plc (SSE), based in Perth, Scotland, is one of the U.K.'s largest energy companies and a major generator of renewable energy. Through its subsidiaries, SSE generates, transmits, distributes and supplies electricity to industrial, commercial and domestic customers; markets, stores and supplies natural gas; offers environmental, electrical and utility contracting services; retails domestic appliances; and offers telecommunications services. In the U.K., the company serves approximately 10 million gas and electricity customers, supplying power through Scottish Hydro, Southern Electric, SWALEC, Airtricity and Atlantic, and distributing through SSE Power Distribution Limited. Its transmission and distribution network comprises over 78,914 miles of line and extends across a third of the U.K. The firm has a combined generating capacity of about 11,330 megawatts (MW). In addition, SSE, through SSE Renewables, owns 12 operational wind farms with a total capacity of 840 MW and has 26 under construction. The company also operates through affiliates including SSE Gas Storage, which owns nearly 11.5 billion cubic feet of gas storage capacity; SSE Telecom, which manages one of the U.K.'s largest private telecoms networks; and SSE Contracting Group, which provides mechanical and electrical contracting solutions. In November 2009, SEE acquired Ireland-based ESB Contracts Limited and opened a new regional head office in Havant, U.K. In December 2009, the firm and DONG Energy agreed to form a joint venture to build three wind farms in the Dutch North Sea region; and established a new 50%-owned 840MW combined cycle gas turbine power station in the U.K. In March 2010, the company agreed to acquire the six business park ATLAS Connect fiber telecommunications network from Scottish Enterprise. In September 2010, SSE sold its Butendiek wind farm project to wpd AG. In October 2010, SSE Renewables acquired the 32MW Calliachar wind farm project from I & H Brown Ltd.

FINANCIALS: **Sales and profits are in thousands of dollars—add 000 to get the full amount. 2010 Note: Financial information for 2010 was not available for all companies at press time.**

2010 Sales: $	2010 Profits: $	**U.S. Stock Ticker:**
2009 Sales: $25,424,200	2009 Profits: $1,503,310	**Int'l Ticker: SSE** Int'l Exchange: London-LSE
2008 Sales: $22,579,300	2008 Profits: $1,291,900	Employees: 18,795
2007 Sales: $17,150,800	2007 Profits: $1,200,270	Fiscal Year Ends: 3/31
2006 Sales: $14,662,250	2006 Profits: $928,278	Parent Company:

SALARIES/BENEFITS:

Pension Plan:	ESOP Stock Plan:	Profit Sharing:	Top Exec. Salary: $	Bonus: $336,447
Savings Plan:	Stock Purch. Plan:		Second Exec. Salary: $	Bonus: $

OTHER THOUGHTS:

Apparent Women Officers or Directors: 1
Hot Spot for Advancement for Women/Minorities:

LOCATIONS: ("Y" = Yes)

West:	Southwest:	Midwest:	Southeast:	Northeast:	International:
					Y

SCOTTISHPOWER UK PLC

www.scottishpower.com

Industry Group Code: 221 **Ranks within this company's industry group:** Sales: Profits:

Exploration/Production:		**Refining/Retailing:**		**Utilities:**		**Alternative Energy:**		**Specialty Services:**		**Energy Mktg./Other Svcs.**	
Exploration:		Refining:		Electric Utility:	Y	Waste/Solar/Other:	Y	Consulting/Eng.:		Energy Marketing:	Y
Production:		Retailing:		Gas Utility:	Y	Thermal/Steam:		Seismic:		Equipment/Machinery:	
Coal Production:		Convenience Stores:		Pipelines:	Y	Wind:	Y	Drilling:		Oil Field Services:	
		Chemicals:		Water:		Hydro:	Y	InfoTech:		Air/Shipping Transportation:	
						Fuel Cells:		Specialty Services:			

TYPES OF BUSINESS:

Utilities-Electricity & Natural Gas
Wind & Hydroelectric Power
Alternative Energy
Gas Distribution

BRANDS/DIVISIONS/AFFILIATES:

Iberdrola SA
ScottishPower Renewables
ScottishPower Power Systems Ltd.
SP Transmission Ltd.
SP Distribution Ltd.
SP Manweb Ltd.
SP Dataserve Ltd.

CONTACTS:

Note: Officers with more than one job title may be intentionally listed here more than once.

Amparo Moraleda, Acting CEO
Raymond Jack, Dir.-Energy Retail
Sheila Duncan, Dir.-Human Resources
Marion Venman, Head-Legal/Gen. Sec.
Ramon Fernandez, Dir.-Finance
John Campbell, Dir.-Energy Wholesale
Rupert Steele, Dir.-Regulation
Frank Mitchell, Dir.-Energy Networks
Keith Anderson, Managing Dir.-ScottishPower Renewables

Phone: 34-944-151-411	**Fax:** 34-944-154-579
Toll-Free:	
Address: Iberdola, Cardenal Gardoqui, 8, Bilbao, 48008 Spain	

GROWTH PLANS/SPECIAL FEATURES:

ScottishPower UK plc, a subsidiary of Iberdrola S.A., is an international energy company. ScottishPower has four main businesses: energy networks; energy wholesale; energy retail; and ScottishPower Renewables. The energy networks division owns and operates the firm's transmission and distribution lines, serving 3.3 million customers. Subsidiary ScottishPower Power Systems Ltd. handles the day-to-day operations of the firm's nearly 69,600-mile network. Subsidiaries SP Transmission Ltd.; SP Distribution Ltd.; and SP Manweb Ltd. own ScottishPower's distribution and transmission licenses and assets. The energy wholesale division operates hydroelectric, wind farm, coal and gas power generating stations with a combined capacity of over 6,800 megawatts (MW); a fuel pellet manufacturing facility near Glasgow; trades coal, gas, power and other commodities; assists in setting U.K. energy policies; and is responsible for the firm's acquisitions and other developments. The firm's energy retail division supplies electricity and gas, serving 5.2 million U.K. customers. The division's billing and settlement data is processed by subsidiary SP Dataserve Ltd. ScottishPower Renewables is a leading operator of wind power plants in the U.K., with over 20 wind farms fully operational and a current generating capacity of roughly 800 MW. It is also conducting feasibility studies for the potential development of wave and tidal power generating activities in Scottish waters. In July 2010, the firm completed construction on a new wind farm, the Clachan Flats, with an output capacity of 15 MW. In September 2010, ScottishPower Renewables received approval to expand its Whitelee Wind Farm by adding 75 wind turbines and increasing its capacity to 539 MW.

FINANCIALS:

Sales and profits are in thousands of dollars—add 000 to get the full amount. 2010 Note: Financial information for 2010 was not available for all companies at press time.

2010 Sales: $	2010 Profits: $	**U.S. Stock Ticker: Subsidiary**
2009 Sales: $	2009 Profits: $	**Int'l Ticker:** Int'l Exchange:
2008 Sales: $	2008 Profits: $	Employees:
2007 Sales: $	2007 Profits: $	Fiscal Year Ends: 3/31
2006 Sales: $10,390,670	2006 Profits: $2,945,240	Parent Company: IBERDROLA SA

SALARIES/BENEFITS:

Pension Plan: Y	ESOP Stock Plan:	Profit Sharing:	Top Exec. Salary: $	Bonus: $
Savings Plan:	Stock Purch. Plan:		Second Exec. Salary: $	Bonus: $

OTHER THOUGHTS:

Apparent Women Officers or Directors: 2
Hot Spot for Advancement for Women/Minorities: Y

LOCATIONS: ("Y" = Yes)

West:	Southwest:	Midwest:	Southeast:	Northeast:	International:
					Y

SEACOR HOLDINGS INC

www.seacorholdings.com

Industry Group Code: 483111 **Ranks within this company's industry group:** Sales: 3 Profits: 2

Exploration/Production:		Refining/Retailing:		Utilities:		Alternative Energy:		Specialty Services:		Energy Mktg./Other Svcs.	
Exploration:		Refining:		Electric Utility:		Waste/Solar/Other:		Consulting/Eng.:		Energy Marketing:	
Production:		Retailing:		Gas Utility:		Thermal/Steam:		Seismic:		Equipment/Machinery:	Y
Coal Production:		Convenience Stores:		Pipelines:		Wind:		Drilling:		Oil Field Services:	Y
		Chemicals:		Water:		Hydro:		InfoTech:		Air/Shipping Transportation:	Y
						Fuel Cells:		Specialty Services:	Y		

TYPES OF BUSINESS:

Offshore Oil Platform Logistics
Inland Shipping
Aviation Services
Environmental Services
Helicopter Services

BRANDS/DIVISIONS/AFFILIATES:

V&A Commodity Traders, Inc.
EraMed LLC
National Response Corp.
SCF Marine Inc.
O'Brien Response Management, Inc.
Era Helicopters LLC
SEACOR Commodity Trading LLC
SEACOR Marine LLC

CONTACTS: *Note: Officers with more than one job title may be intentionally listed here more than once.*

Charles Fabrikant, CEO
Charles Fabrikant, Pres.
Richard Ryan, CFO/Sr. VP
Paul Robinson, General Counsel/Sr. VP/Corp. Sec.
Dick Fagerstal, Sr. VP-Corp. Dev. & Finance
Molly Hottinger, VP-Corp. Comm.
Molly Hottinger, VP-Investor Rel.
Matthew Cenac, Chief Acct. Officer/VP
John Gellert, Sr. VP-Offshore Marine Svcs.
Randall Blank, Sr. VP/Pres./CEO-Environmental Svcs.
Timothy Power, Pres., SCF Marine, Inc.
Peter Coxon, Pres., SEACOR Energy, Inc.
Charles Fabrikant, Chmn.

Phone: 954-523-2200	**Fax:** 954-524-9185
Toll-Free:	
Address: 2200 Eller Dr., Ft. Lauderdale, FL 33316 US	

GROWTH PLANS/SPECIAL FEATURES:

SEACOR Holdings, Inc. owns, operates, invests in and markets equipment primarily in the offshore oil and gas, industrial aviation and marine transportation industries, as well as providing environmental remediation and crisis response services. The company's operations are divided into six business segments. The firm's principal business segment, offshore marine services, operates a diversified fleet of support vessels primarily servicing offshore oil and gas exploration, development and production facilities worldwide. This segment accounts for about 33% of the firm's annual revenue. The marine transportation services segment (5% of revenue) operates a fleet of eight U.S.-flag tankers providing marine transportation services for petroleum products and chemicals moving in the U.S. domestic coastwise trade. The inland river services division (9%), operating as SCF Marine, Inc., operates a fleet of 1,200 dry cargo vessels, which dry and liquid bulk cargo on U.S. inland waterways, including the Mississippi River, its tributaries and Gulf Intracoastal Waterways. The aviation services segment (14%) operates 145 helicopters providing transportation services to the offshore oil and gas exploration, development and production industry, through Era Helicopters LLC; aircraft leasing; transportation services to hospitals, through EraMED LLC; and flightseeing tours in Alaska. The firm's commodity trading and logistics services (28%) subsidiary, SEACOR Commodity Trading LLC, has operations in the purchase, storage, transportation and sale of agricultural and energy commodities, such as rice, sugar, ethanol and clean blendstocks. Finally, the environmental services group (8%), which comprises various subsidiaries including National Response Corporation and O'Brien Response Management, Inc., provides emergency preparedness and response services to oil, chemical, industrial and marine transportation customers and government agencies. In May 2009, the company acquired V&A Commodity Traders, Inc., a sugar trading business.

SEACOR offers its employees medical, dental, life and AD&D insurance; short- and long-term disability coverage; a 401(k) plan; and a stock purchase plan.

FINANCIALS: **Sales and profits are in thousands of dollars—add 000 to get the full amount. 2010 Note: Financial information for 2010 was not available for all companies at press time.**

2010 Sales: $	2010 Profits: $	**U.S. Stock Ticker: CKH**
2009 Sales: $1,711,338	2009 Profits: $145,103	**Int'l Ticker:** Int'l Exchange:
2008 Sales: $1,655,956	2008 Profits: $219,423	Employees: 4,956
2007 Sales: $1,359,230	2007 Profits: $236,819	Fiscal Year Ends: 12/31
2006 Sales: $1,323,445	2006 Profits: $234,394	Parent Company:

SALARIES/BENEFITS:

Pension Plan:	ESOP Stock Plan:	Profit Sharing:	Top Exec. Salary: $700,000	Bonus: $2,800,000
Savings Plan: Y	Stock Purch. Plan: Y		Second Exec. Salary: $365,000	Bonus: $750,000

OTHER THOUGHTS:

Apparent Women Officers or Directors: 1
Hot Spot for Advancement for Women/Minorities:

LOCATIONS: ("Y" = Yes)

West:	Southwest:	Midwest:	Southeast:	Northeast:	International:
Y	Y	Y	Y	Y	Y

SEADRILL LIMITED

www.seadrill.com

Industry Group Code: 213111 **Ranks within this company's industry group:** Sales: 6 Profits: 3

Exploration/Production:		Refining/Retailing:		Utilities:		Alternative Energy:		Specialty Services:		Energy Mktg./Other Svcs.	
Exploration:		Refining:		Electric Utility:		Waste/Solar/Other:		Consulting/Eng.:	Y	Energy Marketing:	
Production:		Retailing:		Gas Utility:		Thermal/Steam:		Seismic:		Equipment/Machinery:	
Coal Production:		Convenience Stores:		Pipelines:		Wind:		Drilling:	Y	Oil Field Services:	Y
		Chemicals:		Water:		Hydro:		InfoTech:		Air/Shipping Transportation:	
						Fuel Cells:		Specialty Services:	Y		

TYPES OF BUSINESS:

Oil & Gas Drilling Support Services
Drilling Rigs & Drillships
Well Services
Well Construction
Engineering Services

BRANDS/DIVISIONS/AFFILIATES:

Seadrill Management AS
Wellbore Solutions AS
Eastern Drilling AS
Varia Perdana Bhd
Seawell Limited

CONTACTS:

Note: Officers with more than one job title may be intentionally listed here more than once.

John Fredriksen, Pres.
Anton Dibowitz, VP-Mktg.
Derek Massie, Sr. VP-Human Resources
Hilde Waaler, VP-Corp. Comm. & Public Affairs
Jim Datland, VP-Investor Rel.
Alf C. Thorkildsen, CEO/Pres., Seadrill Management AS
Tim Juran, Exec. VP-Deepwater Western Hemisphere
Trond Brandsrud, CFO/Sr. VP-Seadril Management AS
Svend Anton Maier, VP-Deepwater Eastern Hemisphere
John Fredriksen, Chmn.
Sveinung Lofthus, Sr. VP-Europe

Phone: 441-295-9500 **Fax:** 441-295-3494
Toll-Free:
Address: 14 Par-la-Ville Rd., Par-la-Ville Pl., Hamilton, HM 08 Bermuda

GROWTH PLANS/SPECIAL FEATURES:

Seadrill Limited is a Bermuda-based company with holdings in offshore drilling companies. The firm's main holding is Seadrill Management AS, a company employing a fleet of drilling units specifically designed for offshore oil and gas exploration and development in harsh environments. The firm's mobile drilling fleet consists of 10 semi-submersible rigs, 10 jack-up rigs, four ultra-deepwater drillships and 12 self-erecting tender rigs. In total, Seadrill Limited has 36 units, of which eight are under construction. In addition, the company provides well services on fixed installations in the Norwegian and U.K. sectors of the North Sea, as well as holding contracts for production drilling, wireline operations and engineering services. The firm anticipates that demand for its offshore drilling units will increase as the global demand for oil increases. Seadrill maintains long-term contracts that minimize its exposure to market volatility. The company's biggest customers include Statoil A.S., which accounts for approximately 17% of its revenues; Total S.A. Group, which accounts for 13%; Exxon Mobil Corp., which accounts for 12%; Petroleo Brasileiro S.A., which accounts for 10%; and Royal Dutch Shell, which accounts for 10%. Seadrill Limited is the majority shareholder of Wellbore Solutions AS and Eastern Drilling AS, two other Norwegian drilling companies; and owns 49% interest in Varia Perdana Bhd, an Indonesian drilling company. It also has operating subsidiaries in Bermuda, the U.S., the U.K., Singapore, Brazil, the Cayman Islands, the British Virgin Islands, Cyprus, Nigeria, Liberia, Hungary, Hong Kong, Panama, Denmark, Malaysia and Brunei. In August 2010, Seadrill subsidiary Seawell Limited agreed to acquire Allis-Chalmers Energy, Inc. for roughly $890 million.

FINANCIALS:

Sales and profits are in thousands of dollars—add 000 to get the full amount. 2010 Note: Financial information for 2010 was not available for all companies at press time.

2010 Sales: $	2010 Profits: $	**U.S. Stock Ticker: SDRL**
2009 Sales: $3,253,900	2009 Profits: $1,353,100	**Int'l Ticker: SDRL** Int'l Exchange: Oslo-OBX
2008 Sales: $2,105,800	2008 Profits: $-164,400	Employees: 7,600
2007 Sales: $1,552,100	2007 Profits: $502,000	Fiscal Year Ends: 12/31
2006 Sales: $1,151,500	2006 Profits: $214,100	Parent Company:

SALARIES/BENEFITS:

Pension Plan:	ESOP Stock Plan:	Profit Sharing:	Top Exec. Salary: $	Bonus: $
Savings Plan:	Stock Purch. Plan:		Second Exec. Salary: $	Bonus: $

OTHER THOUGHTS:

Apparent Women Officers or Directors: 3
Hot Spot for Advancement for Women/Minorities: Y

LOCATIONS: ("Y" = Yes)

West:	Southwest:	Midwest:	Southeast:	Northeast:	International:
	Y				Y

SEITEL INC

www.seitel-inc.com

Industry Group Code: 541360 **Ranks within this company's industry group:** Sales: Profits:

Exploration/Production:		Refining/Retailing:		Utilities:		Alternative Energy:		Specialty Services:		Energy Mktg./Other Svcs.	
Exploration:		Refining:		Electric Utility:		Waste/Solar/Other:		Consulting/Eng.:		Energy Marketing:	
Production:		Retailing:		Gas Utility:		Thermal/Steam:		Seismic:	Y	Equipment/Machinery:	
Coal Production:		Convenience Stores:		Pipelines:		Wind:		Drilling:		Oil Field Services:	
		Chemicals:		Water:		Hydro:		InfoTech:	Y	Air/Shipping Transportation:	
						Fuel Cells:		Specialty Services:			

TYPES OF BUSINESS:

Seismic Data Acquisition
Seismic Data Library
Software

BRANDS/DIVISIONS/AFFILIATES:

Seitel Solutions
Seitel Matrix
Olympic Seismic
Seitel Data
ValueAct Capital Master Fund LP
Seitel Holdings Inc

CONTACTS: *Note: Officers with more than one job title may be intentionally listed here more than once.*

Robert D. Monson, CEO
Kevin P. Callaghan, COO/Exec. VP
Robert D. Monson, Pres.
Marcia H. Kendrick, CFO/Exec. VP
Marcia H. Kendrick, Corp. Sec.
Robert J. Simon, Sr. VP-Bus. Dev.
Marcia H. Kendrick, Treas.
Randall A. Sides, Pres., Seitel Data, Ltd.
David A. Richard, Pres., Olympic Seismic, Ltd.
Peter H. Kamin, Chmn.

Phone: 832-295-8300 **Fax:** 832-295-8301
Toll-Free:
Address: 10811 S. Westview Cir. Dr., Ste. 100, Bldg. C, Houston, TX 77043 US

GROWTH PLANS/SPECIAL FEATURES:

Seitel, Inc. provides seismic data and related geophysical technology and expertise to the oil and gas industries. The firm is a wholly-owned subsidiary of Seitel Holdings, Inc., which is 99.5%-owned by ValueAct Capital Master Fund L.P. The company owns one of the largest offshore and onshore seismic data libraries in North America, which assists in the identification of new geographical areas for oil and gas exploration. Seitel's seismic library is constantly expanding through new seismic data creation programs and through the addition of seismic surveys or entire seismic libraries from oil/gas companies that have discontinued exploration and production in particular geographical areas. Seitel currently claims ownership of approximately 1.1 million linear miles of two-dimensional data and over 35,000 square miles of three-dimensional seismic data; this covers the majority of all the major onshore U.S. sites, the transition zone, offshore U.S., Gulf of Mexico and Canada. The library serves a market of over 1,600 oil and gas companies. Through its subsidiary, Seitel Solutions, the company offers the ability to access and interact with its seismic data through the Internet. Its other company subsidiaries, Seitel Data, Seitel Matrix and Olympic Seismic, are dedicated to data processing and storage of seismic data. Its proprietary display and inventory software stores, manages, accesses and delivers data, tapes and graphic cross-sections to its licensees. The firm sells its proprietary information technology to petroleum companies either for cash or in exchange for working equity interests in exploration, development and ownership of natural gas and crude oil reserves. These customers use seismic surveys and analysis of seismic data for the identification and definition of underground geological structures to determine the existence and location of subsurface hydrocarbons.

FINANCIALS: **Sales and profits are in thousands of dollars—add 000 to get the full amount. 2010 Note: Financial information for 2010 was not available for all companies at press time.**

2010 Sales: $	2010 Profits: $	**U.S. Stock Ticker: Subsidiary**
2009 Sales: $	2009 Profits: $	**Int'l Ticker:** Int'l Exchange:
2008 Sales: $	2008 Profits: $	Employees:
2007 Sales: $148,812	2007 Profits: $-93,456	Fiscal Year Ends: 12/31
2006 Sales: $191,919	2006 Profits: $47,214	Parent Company: VALUE ACT CAPITAL MASTER FUND LP

SALARIES/BENEFITS:

Pension Plan:	ESOP Stock Plan:	Profit Sharing:	Top Exec. Salary: $588,000	Bonus: $
Savings Plan:	Stock Purch. Plan:		Second Exec. Salary: $436,800	Bonus: $

OTHER THOUGHTS:

Apparent Women Officers or Directors: 1
Hot Spot for Advancement for Women/Minorities:

LOCATIONS: ("Y" = Yes)

West:	Southwest:	Midwest:	Southeast:	Northeast:	International:
Y	Y		Y		Y

SEMBCORP INDUSTRIES LTD

www.sembcorp.com.sg

Industry Group Code: 237 **Ranks within this company's industry group:** Sales: 4 Profits: 2

Exploration/Production:		Refining/Retailing:		Utilities:		Alternative Energy:		Specialty Services:		Energy Mktg./Other Svcs.	
Exploration:		Refining:		Electric Utility:	Y	Waste/Solar/Other:		Consulting/Eng.:		Energy Marketing:	Y
Production:		Retailing:		Gas Utility:	Y	Thermal/Steam:	Y	Seismic:		Equipment/Machinery:	Y
Coal Production:		Convenience Stores:		Pipelines:		Wind:		Drilling:		Oil Field Services:	
		Chemicals:		Water:	Y	Hydro:		InfoTech:		Air/Shipping Transportation:	
						Fuel Cells:		Specialty Services:	Y		

TYPES OF BUSINESS:

Heavy Construction
Marine Construction & Shipbuilding
Utilities Services
Environmental Engineering & Waste Management
Industrial Parks
Internet Service Provider
Floating Oil Production Platforms
Pipelines

BRANDS/DIVISIONS/AFFILIATES:

Sembcorp Marine
Sembcorp Environment
Sembcorp Utilities
Sembcorp Gas
Sembcorp Cogen
Singapore Mint
Singapore Precision Industries
Sembcorp Design and Production

CONTACTS: *Note: Officers with more than one job title may be intentionally listed here more than once.*

Tang Kin Fei, CEO
Tang Kin Fei, Pres.
Koh Chiap Khiong, CFO
Tan Cheng Guan, Exec. VP-Group Bus. & Strategic Dev.
Wong Weng Sun, Pres./CEO-SembCorp Marine
Paul Gavens, Exec. VP-Sembcorp Utilities (U.K.)

Phone: 65-6723-3113	**Fax:** 65-6822-3254
Toll-Free:	
Address: 30 Hill St., 05-04, Singapore, 179360 Singapore	

GROWTH PLANS/SPECIAL FEATURES:

Sembcorp Industries, Ltd. is one of Singapore's leading utilities and marine groups. The firm's primary businesses include Sembcorp Utilities; Sembcorp Marine; Sembcorp Environment; and Sembcorp Industrial Parks. Sembcorp Utilities provides integrated utilities, energy and water solutions to the chemical and petrochemical industry in Singapore, the U.K. and China. In addition, the firm operates power a desalination plants in Vietnam and the United Arab Emirates (U.A.E.). The firm offers a variety of industrial utilities services including water supply and wastewater treatment; power generation; process stream production and distribution; chemical feedstock; and asset protection. The utility segment's operation has a generation capacity of 5,600 megawatts. Sembcorp Marine has one of the largest ship repair, shipbuilding and ship conversion operations in East Asia. The company offers a full range of marine and offshore engineering solutions including container ships, chemical tankers, production platforms; and converts Floating Production, Storage and Offloading units (FPSO) for the oil and gas industry. Sembcorp Environment provides treatment methods and waste-to-resource technologies to 1.2 million households, 47,000 industrial and commercial customers and government agencies, plus 9,000 healthcare establishments in Singapore, India and Australia. The Sembcorp Industrial Parks segment owns, develops, markets and manages multinational industrial parks predominately located in China, Indonesia and Vietnam. Sembcorp Industries operates numerous subsidiaries including Sembcorp Gas; Sembcorp Cogen; Sembcorp Power; Singapore Mint; SembCorp Design and Production; and Singapore Precision Industries. In January 2010, the firm began construction on a new industrial park in Hai Phong, Vietnam; and Sembcorp Utilities formed 80%-owned joint venture Qinzhou Sembcorp Water Co. (with partner Guangxi Qinzhou Linhai Industrial Investment Co.) to build, own and operate a wastewater treatment facility in Qinzhou Economic Development Zone. In August 2010, through Sembcorp Utilities, Sembcorp increased its ownership of Cascal to roughly 96.43%.

Sembcorp offers employees health benefits; loan/interest subsidy; and bonus and job development programs.

FINANCIALS: **Sales and profits are in thousands of dollars—add 000 to get the full amount. 2010 Note: Financial information for 2010 was not available for all companies at press time.**

2010 Sales: $	2010 Profits: $	**U.S. Stock Ticker: SCRPF**
2009 Sales: $6,870,650	2009 Profits: $490,010	**Int'l Ticker: U96** Int'l Exchange: Singapore-SIN
2008 Sales: $6,548,910	2008 Profits: $482,170	Employees:
2007 Sales: $5,990,000	2007 Profits: $370,000	Fiscal Year Ends: 12/31
2006 Sales: $4,880,000	2006 Profits: $670,000	Parent Company:

SALARIES/BENEFITS:

Pension Plan:	ESOP Stock Plan: Y	Profit Sharing:	Top Exec. Salary: $	Bonus: $1,165,529
Savings Plan:	Stock Purch. Plan:		Second Exec. Salary: $	Bonus: $

OTHER THOUGHTS:

Apparent Women Officers or Directors:
Hot Spot for Advancement for Women/Minorities:

LOCATIONS: ("Y" = Yes)

West:	Southwest:	Midwest:	Southeast:	Northeast:	International:
					Y

SEMPRA ENERGY

www.sempra.com

Industry Group Code: 221 **Ranks within this company's industry group:** Sales: 22 Profits: 13

Exploration/Production:		Refining/Retailing:		Utilities:		Alternative Energy:		Specialty Services:		Energy Mktg./Other Svcs.	
Exploration:		Refining:		Electric Utility:	Y	Waste/Solar/Other:		Consulting/Eng.:		Energy Marketing:	Y
Production:		Retailing:		Gas Utility:	Y	Thermal/Steam:		Seismic:		Equipment/Machinery:	
Coal Production:		Convenience Stores:		Pipelines:		Wind:		Drilling:		Oil Field Services:	
		Chemicals:		Water:		Hydro:		InfoTech:		Air/Shipping Transportation:	
						Fuel Cells:		Specialty Services:	Y		

TYPES OF BUSINESS:

Utilities-Electricity & Natural Gas
Energy Management
Energy Marketing
Power Generation-Natural Gas Plants
LNG Pipelines, Storage & Terminals
Power Generation-Solar Power Plants
Power Generation-Wind Farms

BRANDS/DIVISIONS/AFFILIATES:

Southern California Gas Company
San Diego Gas & Electric Company
Sempra Generation
Sempra LNG
Sempra Pipeline & Storage

CONTACTS: *Note: Officers with more than one job title may be intentionally listed here more than once.*

Donald E. Felsinger, CEO
Neal E. Schmale, COO
Neal E. Schmale, Pres.
Mark A. Snell, CFO/Exec. VP
G. Joyce Rowland, Sr. VP-Human Resources
Javade Chaudhri, General Counsel/Exec. VP
Monica Haas, VP-Corp. Planning
Steven D. Davis, VP-Investor Rel.
Joseph A. Householder, Chief Acct. Officer/Controller/Sr. VP
Jessie J. Knight, Jr., Exec. VP-External Affairs
Amy Chiu, VP-Risk Analysis & Mgmt.
Paul Young, Chief Tax Counsel/VP-Tax
Lisa Urick, VP-Audit Svcs.
Donald E. Felsinger, Chmn.

Phone: 619-696-2000	**Fax:** 619-696-2374
Toll-Free: 877-866-2066	
Address: 101 Ash St., San Diego, CA 92101-3017 US	

GROWTH PLANS/SPECIAL FEATURES:

Sempra Energy provides electric, natural gas and other energy products and services primarily in California and internationally. The company operates through two main branches: Sempra Utilities and Sempra Global. Sempra Utilities is comprised of two main companies: Southern California Gas Co., which is a natural gas distribution utility that supplies natural gas to a population of 20 million in a 20,000-square-mile service territory in southern and central California; and San Diego Gas and Electric, which provides electricity distribution and transmission and natural gas distribution services to more than 1.4 million customers across 4,100 square miles in southern Orange County and San Diego, California. The division also includes Pacific Enterprises, the holding company for Southern California Gas Co. The Sempra Global is primarily composed of subsidiaries not subject to California utility regulations, including Sempra Generation; Sempra Pipelines and Storage; and Sempra LNG. Sempra Generation develops, owns and operates electric power plants in the U.S. and Mexico, including one of the largest thin-film solar power facilities in North America. Sempra Pipeline and Storage develops and operates natural gas pipelines and storage facilities in Mexico and the U.S. Sempra LNG develops liquefied natural gas (LNG) receipt terminals in North America. In December 2009, Sempra Generation and BP Wind Energy unveiled a new wind farm in Benton County, Indiana, with a power generation capacity of 200 MW. In July 2010, the company sold parts of its interest in RBS Sempra Commodities to J.P Morgan for about $1.6 billion. The firm was previously involved in RBS Sempra Commodities as a joint venture with the Royal Bank of Scotland to sell commodity products.

Sempra offers its employees medical, dental and vision care; life and AD&D insurance; a pension plan; tuition reimbursement; an employee assistance program; a health club membership subsidy; volunteer/giving incentive programs; and a mass-transit/parking subsidy.

FINANCIALS: **Sales and profits are in thousands of dollars—add 000 to get the full amount. 2010 Note: Financial information for 2010 was not available for all companies at press time.**

2010 Sales: $	2010 Profits: $	**U.S. Stock Ticker: SRE**
2009 Sales: $8,106,000	2009 Profits: $1,119,000	**Int'l Ticker:** Int'l Exchange:
2008 Sales: $10,758,000	2008 Profits: $1,113,000	Employees: 13,839
2007 Sales: $11,438,000	2007 Profits: $1,099,000	Fiscal Year Ends: 12/31
2006 Sales: $11,761,000	2006 Profits: $1,406,000	Parent Company:

SALARIES/BENEFITS:

Pension Plan: Y	ESOP Stock Plan:	Profit Sharing:	Top Exec. Salary: $1,184,300	Bonus: $2,136,500
Savings Plan: Y	Stock Purch. Plan:		Second Exec. Salary: $833,900	Bonus: $1,094,100

OTHER THOUGHTS:

Apparent Women Officers or Directors: 4
Hot Spot for Advancement for Women/Minorities: Y

LOCATIONS: ("Y" = Yes)

West:	Southwest:	Midwest:	Southeast:	Northeast:	International:
Y	Y		Y		Y

SHAW GROUP INC (THE)

www.shawgrp.com

Industry Group Code: 237 **Ranks within this company's industry group:** Sales: 3 Profits: 8

Exploration/Production:		**Refining/Retailing:**		**Utilities:**		**Alternative Energy:**		**Specialty Services:**		**Energy Mktg./Other Svcs.**	
Exploration:		Refining:		Electric Utility:		Waste/Solar/Other:		Consulting/Eng.:	Y	Energy Marketing:	
Production:		Retailing:		Gas Utility:		Thermal/Steam:		Seismic:		Equipment/Machinery:	Y
Coal Production:		Convenience Stores:		Pipelines:		Wind:		Drilling:		Oil Field Services:	
		Chemicals:		Water:		Hydro:		InfoTech:		Air/Shipping Transportation:	
						Fuel Cells:		Specialty Services:	Y		

TYPES OF BUSINESS:

Pipe Manufacturing
Construction & Engineering
Consulting Services
Environmental Services
Facilities Management
Power Plant Construction
Nuclear Power Plant Construction

BRANDS/DIVISIONS/AFFILIATES:

Westinghouse

CONTACTS:

Note: Officers with more than one job title may be intentionally listed here more than once.

James M. Bernhard, Jr., CEO
Gary P. Graphia, COO/Exec. VP
James M. Bernhard, Jr., Pres.
Brian K. Ferraioli, CFO/Exec. VP
Gentry Brann, Dir.-Mktg.
David L. Chapman, Sr., Pres., Fabrication & Mfg. Group
John Donofrio, General Counsel/Exec. VP/Corp. Sec.
Lee Elder, Sr. VP-Bus. Dev., Power Group
Gentry Brann, Dir.-Corp. Comm.
Michael J. Kershaw, Chief Acct. Officer/Sr. VP
Frederick W. Buckman, Pres., Power Group
Louis J. Pucher, Pres., Energy & Chemicals Group
George P. Bevan, Pres., Environmental & Infrastructure Group
Ron Barnes, Pres., Fossil, Renewables & Nuclear Div.
James M. Bernhard, Jr., Chmn.
Ronald W. Oakley, Managing Dir.-Europe

Phone: 225-932-2500	**Fax:** 225-987-3328
Toll-Free:	
Address: 4171 Essen Ln., Baton Rouge, LA 70809 US	

GROWTH PLANS/SPECIAL FEATURES:

The Shaw Group, Inc. is a construction and engineering contractor firm. It is involved in engineering; technology; construction; fabrication; and environmental and industrial services. The company operates in six segments: fossil, renewables & nuclear (FR&N); energy & chemicals (E&C); environmental & infrastructure (E&I); maintenance; fabrication & manufacturing (F&M); investment in Westinghouse; and corporate. The FR&N segment provides a range of project-related services, primarily to the global fossil and nuclear power generation industries. The E&C division's offerings include design, engineering, construction, procurement, technology and consulting services, primarily to the oil and gas, refinery, petrochemical and chemical industries. The E&I segment designs and executes remediation solutions involving contaminants in soil, air and water. It also provides project/facilities management for non-environmental construction, watershed restoration, emergency response services, program management and solutions to support and enhance domestic and global land, water and air transportation systems. The maintenance segment performs routine and outage/turnaround maintenance, engineering, construction, recovery and specialty services. The maintenance sector' services include fossil/nuclear maintenance and turbine generator repair. The F&M segment supplies fabricated piping systems. Shaw's Investment in Westinghouse division includes its 20% equity interest in Westinghouse, which offers advanced licensing, nuclear plant designs, engineering services, equipment, fuel and other products and services to the international nuclear electric power industry. The corporate segment includes the corporate management and expenses associated with managing the firm. The company's customer base includes multinational oil companies and industrial corporations; regulated utilities; independent and merchant power producers; government agencies; and other equipment manufacturers. In March 2009, Shaw opened a new office in United Arab Emirates.

FINANCIALS:

Sales and profits are in thousands of dollars—add 000 to get the full amount. 2010 Note: Financial information for 2010 was not available for all companies at press time.

2010 Sales: $	2010 Profits: $	**U.S. Stock Ticker: SGR**
2009 Sales: $7,279,690	2009 Profits: $14,995	**Int'l Ticker:** Int'l Exchange:
2008 Sales: $6,998,011	2008 Profits: $140,717	Employees: 28,000
2007 Sales: $5,723,712	2007 Profits: $-19,000	Fiscal Year Ends: 8/31
2006 Sales: $4,775,649	2006 Profits: $50,226	Parent Company:

SALARIES/BENEFITS:

Pension Plan:	ESOP Stock Plan:	Profit Sharing:	Top Exec. Salary: $1,767,617	Bonus: $2,376,000
Savings Plan: Y	Stock Purch. Plan:		Second Exec. Salary: $759,449	Bonus: $996,050

OTHER THOUGHTS:

Apparent Women Officers or Directors:
Hot Spot for Advancement for Women/Minorities:

LOCATIONS: ("Y" = Yes)

West:	Southwest:	Midwest:	Southeast:	Northeast:	International:
Y	Y	Y	Y	Y	Y

SHELL CANADA LIMITED

www.shell.ca

Industry Group Code: 211111 **Ranks within this company's industry group:** Sales: Profits:

Exploration/Production:		Refining/Retailing:		Utilities:		Alternative Energy:		Specialty Services:		Energy Mktg./Other Svcs.	
Exploration:	Y	Refining:	Y	Electric Utility:		Waste/Solar/Other:		Consulting/Eng.:		Energy Marketing:	
Production:	Y	Retailing:	Y	Gas Utility:		Thermal/Steam:		Seismic:		Equipment/Machinery:	
Coal Production:		Convenience Stores:	Y	Pipelines:		Wind:		Drilling:		Oil Field Services:	
		Chemicals:	Y	Water:		Hydro:		InfoTech:		Air/Shipping Transportation:	
						Fuel Cells:		Specialty Services:			

TYPES OF BUSINESS:

Oil Refineries
Oil & Natural Gas Exploration & Production
Service Stations
Bitumen & Sulfur
Oil Sands Operations
Lubricants

BRANDS/DIVISIONS/AFFILIATES:

Peace River Bitumen Recovery Complex
Sable Offshore Energy Project
Shell Canada Products Lubricants Division
Shell Rotella Energized Protection
Athabasca Oils Sands Project
Royal Dutch Shell (Shell Group)

CONTACTS: *Note: Officers with more than one job title may be intentionally listed here more than once.*

Lorraine Mitchelmore, Pres.
David R. Brinley, General Counsel/VP
John Broadhurst, VP-Dev.
John Abbott, Exec. VP-Heavy Oil
Peter Voser, CEO-Royal Dutch Shell plc
Jorma Ollila, Chmn.-Royal Dutch Shell plc

Phone: 403-691-3111 **Fax:** 403-269-7462
Toll-Free: 800-661-1600
Address: 400 4th Ave. SW, Shell Ctr., Calgary, AB T2P 0J4 Canada

GROWTH PLANS/SPECIAL FEATURES:

Shell Canada Limited is one of the largest integrated petroleum companies in Canada. The company is a wholly-owned subsidiary of oil giant Royal Dutch Shell, plc, and accounts for approximately 4.6% of its total revenues. The firm produces natural gas, natural gas liquids and bitumen and is a leading manufacturer, distributor and marketer of refined petroleum products as well as a major producer of sulfur. Shell Canada is divided into three major business units: exploration and production; oil sands; and oil products. The exploration and production segment explores for and produces natural gas and related liquids. It operates four natural gas processing facilities and a bitumen facility in Alberta, in addition to a 31.3% ownership of the Sable Offshore Energy Project off the coast of Nova Scotia. The oil sands segment has operations in three major oil sands deposits, as well as the firm's Peace River bitumen recovery complex. Shell Canada has a 60% interest in the Athabasca Oils Sands Project, which produces roughly 255,000 barrels of bitumen per day. The oil products division manufactures, distributes and markets refined petroleum products. It operates the company's various refineries, manufacturing and processing facilities. These include one crude oil refinery; one refined gasoline and jet fuel products facility; one hydrocarbon processing site; one grease manufacturer; and one lubricant oils blending and packaging plant. In addition, the company owns and operates over 1,600 branded retail gasoline service stations in Canada, many of which feature a Select convenience store and a car wash. Shell Canada Products' oil products business offers a variety of branded products at its service stations including nitrogen enriched gasoline and Shell Rotella Energized Protection engine oil products. In mid 2009, the firm began to market a 10% cellulosic ethanol gasoline, which is produced from non-food raw materials.

FINANCIALS: **Sales and profits are in thousands of dollars—add 000 to get the full amount. 2010 Note: Financial information for 2010 was not available for all companies at press time.**

2010 Sales: $
2009 Sales: $
2008 Sales: $
2007 Sales: $
2006 Sales: $12,705,000

2010 Profits: $
2009 Profits: $
2008 Profits: $
2007 Profits: $
2006 Profits: $1,491,400

U.S. Stock Ticker: Subsidiary
Int'l Ticker: Int'l Exchange:
Employees:
Fiscal Year Ends: 12/31
Parent Company: ROYAL DUTCH SHELL (SHELL GROUP)

SALARIES/BENEFITS:

Pension Plan: ESOP Stock Plan: Profit Sharing: Top Exec. Salary: $ Bonus: $
Savings Plan: Stock Purch. Plan: Second Exec. Salary: $ Bonus: $

OTHER THOUGHTS:

Apparent Women Officers or Directors:
Hot Spot for Advancement for Women/Minorities:

LOCATIONS: ("Y" = Yes)

West:	Southwest:	Midwest:	Southeast:	Northeast:	International:
					Y

SHELL OIL CO

www.shell.us

Industry Group Code: 211111 **Ranks within this company's industry group:** Sales: 13 Profits:

Exploration/Production:		Refining/Retailing:		Utilities:		Alternative Energy:		Specialty Services:		Energy Mktg./Other Svcs.	
Exploration:	Y	Refining:	Y	Electric Utility:	Y	Waste/Solar/Other:		Consulting/Eng.:		Energy Marketing:	Y
Production:	Y	Retailing:	Y	Gas Utility:	Y	Thermal/Steam:		Seismic:		Equipment/Machinery:	
Coal Production:		Convenience Stores:	Y	Pipelines:	Y	Wind:		Drilling:		Oil Field Services:	
		Chemicals:	Y	Water:		Hydro:		InfoTech:		Air/Shipping Transportation:	
						Fuel Cells:		Specialty Services:			

TYPES OF BUSINESS:

Oil & Gas Exploration & Production
Chemicals
Power Generation
Nanocomposites
Nanocatalysts
Refineries
Pipelines & Shipping
Hydrogen Storage Technology

BRANDS/DIVISIONS/AFFILIATES:

Shell Oil Products US
Shell Chemicals Limited
Shell Gas and Power
Shell Exploration and Production
Royal Dutch Shell (Shell Group)
Motiva Enterprises LLC
Shell Hydrogen
Shell Renewables

CONTACTS: *Note: Officers with more than one job title may be intentionally listed here more than once.*

Marvin E. Odum, Pres.
Bill Lowrey, General Counsel/Sr. VP/Corp. Sec.
Curtis R. Frasier, Exec. VP-Americas Shell Gas & Power
Marvin E. Odum, Dir.-Shell-Upstream Americas
Mark Quartermain, Pres., Shell Energy North America (US) L.P.

Phone: 713-241-6161 **Fax:** 713-241-4044
Toll-Free:
Address: 910 Louisiana St., Houston, TX 77002 US

GROWTH PLANS/SPECIAL FEATURES:

Shell Oil Co., an affiliate of the Shell Group, is a chemical, oil and natural gas producer in the U.S., with operations in all 50 states. Shell Oil has a number of divisions, joint ventures and operations, including Shell Oil Products U.S., Motiva Enterprises, Shell Chemicals, Shell Gas and Power, Shell Exploration and Production (SEPCo) and others. These companies discover, develop, manufacture, transport and market crude oil, natural gas and chemical products. Specifically, Shell Oil Products has four refineries which produce a total of 753,000 barrels of oil per day, as well as a network of approximately 6,000 branded gasoline stations in the western U.S. Shell Oil Products' sister company is Motiva Enterprises LLC, with whom the firm refines and ships gasoline to approximately 7,700 Shell-branded stations in the eastern and southern U.S. Shell Chemicals is involved in manufacturing chemicals, including ethylene and propylene, for use in cars, computers, packaging and paints. SEPCo explores and develops natural gas in the U.S, with interests in five states and the Gulf of Mexico. Shell Oil's Gas and Power business is involved in power generation, gas pipeline transmission, receiving terminals, liquefied natural gas (LNG), shipping and coal gasification. Other divisions include Shell Hydrogen, focused on the development of hydrogen and fuel cell technologies from regional bases in Houston and Tokyo; and Shell Renewables, which invests heavily in wind and solar power research.

Employees are offered medical and vision insurance; flexible spending accounts; disability coverage; group auto and home insurance; a group legal plan; a pension plan; a savings plan; and an employee assistance program.

FINANCIALS: **Sales and profits are in thousands of dollars—add 000 to get the full amount. 2010 Note: Financial information for 2010 was not available for all companies at press time.**

2010 Sales: $
2009 Sales: $100,000,000
2008 Sales: $100,818,000
2007 Sales: $87,548,000
2006 Sales: $80,974,000

2010 Profits: $
2009 Profits: $
2008 Profits: $
2007 Profits: $
2006 Profits: $

U.S. Stock Ticker: Subsidiary
Int'l Ticker: Int'l Exchange:
Employees: 24,008
Fiscal Year Ends: 12/31
Parent Company: ROYAL DUTCH SHELL (SHELL GROUP)

SALARIES/BENEFITS:

Pension Plan: Y ESOP Stock Plan: Profit Sharing: Top Exec. Salary: $ Bonus: $
Savings Plan: Y Stock Purch. Plan: Y Second Exec. Salary: $ Bonus: $

OTHER THOUGHTS:

Apparent Women Officers or Directors:
Hot Spot for Advancement for Women/Minorities:

LOCATIONS: ("Y" = Yes)

West:	Southwest:	Midwest:	Southeast:	Northeast:	International:
Y	Y	Y	Y	Y	Y

SHIKOKU ELECTRIC POWER COMPANY INC

www.yonden.co.jp

Industry Group Code: 2211 **Ranks within this company's industry group:** Sales: 24 Profits: 26

Exploration/Production:		Refining/Retailing:		Utilities:		Alternative Energy:		Specialty Services:		Energy Mktg./Other Svcs.	
Exploration:		Refining:		Electric Utility:	Y	Waste/Solar/Other:	Y	Consulting/Eng.:	Y	Energy Marketing:	Y
Production:		Retailing:		Gas Utility:		Thermal/Steam:	Y	Seismic:		Equipment/Machinery:	Y
Coal Production:		Convenience Stores:		Pipelines:		Wind:	Y	Drilling:		Oil Field Services:	
		Chemicals:		Water:		Hydro:	Y	InfoTech:		Air/Shipping Transportation:	
						Fuel Cells:		Specialty Services:	Y		

TYPES OF BUSINESS:

Electric Utility
Telecommunications Services
Engineering Services
Equipment Manufacturing
Real Estate Management
Technology Research
Manufacturing
Nursing Homes

BRANDS/DIVISIONS/AFFILIATES:

Yondenko Corporation
Yonden Engineering Company, Inc.
Yonden Consultants Company, Inc.
Shikoku Instrumentation Co., Ltd.
STNet, Inc.
Yonden Energy Services Co, Inc.
Yonden Business Co., Inc.
Yonden Life Care Co., Inc.

CONTACTS: *Note: Officers with more than one job title may be intentionally listed here more than once.*

Akira Chiba, Pres.
Mikio Kawai, Managing Dir.-Mktg. & Customer Rel.
Toru Sunouchi, Exec. VP-Human Resources/Public Rel.
Shozo Manabe, Exec. VP/Mgr.-Info. Div.
Susumu Nakamura, Dir.-Civil & Architectural Eng.
Kunio Takei, Managing Dir.-System Oper. & Transmission Div.
Junichi Ietaka, Managing Dir.-Gen. Planning Div.
Shozo Manabe, Exec. VP-Comm. Div.
Shozo Manabe, Exec. VP-Finance & Acct. Dept.
Yukihito Ishizaki, Exec. VP-Nuclear Power Div.
Koji Yamaji, Gen. Mgr.-Transmission & Substation Dept.
Tomizo Tsuda, Managing Dir.-Thermal Power Div.
Seiki Sakida, Gen Mgr.-Ikata Nuclear Power Station
Momoki Tokiwa, Chmn.
Amu Nakamura, Managing Dir.-Purchasing & Materials Dept.

Phone: 81-87-821-5061	**Fax:**
Toll-Free:	
Address: 2-5, Marunouchi, Takamatsu, 760-8573 Japan	

GROWTH PLANS/SPECIAL FEATURES:

Shikoku Electric Power Company, Inc. generates, transmits, distributes and sells electricity. Headquartered in Takamatsu City, the capitol of Japan's Kagawa Prefecture, the firm serves more than 4 million residential and industrial customers in four prefectures on the island of Shikoku: Tokushima, Kochi, Ehime and Kagawa. Shikoku has 65 generating facilities with a total capacity of roughly 6,665 megawatts (MW); of that capacity, hydroelectric plants account for approximately 17% (58 facilities); nuclear plants account for 30% (one facility); and thermal plants (coal- and oil-fired) account for roughly 53% (four facilities). Shikoku also operates a solar plant in Ehime and a wind-driven plant in Kochi that together account for less than 1 MW of the firm's total capacity. The firm sells approximately 31 million megawatt hours of electricity annually, including sales to electricity distributors in other regions. Roughly 30% of the electricity it sells goes to residential customers; 58% to industrial and commercial customers; and 12% to other customer types, including accommodation sales to other power companies. The company operates about 3,950 miles of transmission lines and almost 103,000 miles of distribution lines. It has 26 subsidiaries and affiliates across various lines of business, including the following. Shikoku Research Institute, Inc. conducts research and development operations concerning electric utility-related technologies. Yondenko Corporation and Yonden Engineering Company, Inc. provide engineering and maintenance services for power supply facilities. Yonden Consultants Company, Inc. studies, plans and designs civil works. Shikoku Instrumentation Co., Ltd., designs, manufactures, engineers and sells automatic gauging control systems and information transmission systems. STNet, Inc. provides telecommunications and information systems services. Yonden Energy Services Co, Inc. designs and engineers electric water heaters and air conditioning systems. Yonden Business Co., Inc. provides real estate services, including buildings management and maintenance and office services. Lastly, Yonden Life Care Co., Inc. operates nursing care facilities.

FINANCIALS: **Sales and profits are in thousands of dollars—add 000 to get the full amount. 2010 Note: Financial information for 2010 was not available for all companies at press time.**

2010 Sales: $	2010 Profits: $	**U.S. Stock Ticker:**
2009 Sales: $7,043,240	2009 Profits: $322,750	**Int'l Ticker: 9507** Int'l Exchange: Tokyo-TSE
2008 Sales: $7,049,760	2008 Profits: $323,050	Employees:
2007 Sales: $4,907,136	2007 Profits: $239,483	Fiscal Year Ends: 3/31
2006 Sales: $4,445,692	2006 Profits: $237,709	Parent Company:

SALARIES/BENEFITS:

Pension Plan:	ESOP Stock Plan:	Profit Sharing:	Top Exec. Salary: $	Bonus: $
Savings Plan:	Stock Purch. Plan:		Second Exec. Salary: $	Bonus: $

OTHER THOUGHTS:

Apparent Women Officers or Directors:
Hot Spot for Advancement for Women/Minorities:

LOCATIONS: ("Y" = Yes)

West:	Southwest:	Midwest:	Southeast:	Northeast:	International:
					Y

SHOWA SHELL SEKIYU KK

www.showa-shell.co.jp

Industry Group Code: 324110 **Ranks within this company's industry group:** Sales: 13 Profits: 27

Exploration/Production:		Refining/Retailing:		Utilities:		Alternative Energy:		Specialty Services:		Energy Mktg./Other Svcs.	
Exploration:		Refining:	Y	Electric Utility:		Waste/Solar/Other:	Y	Consulting/Eng.:		Energy Marketing:	Y
Production:		Retailing:	Y	Gas Utility:		Thermal/Steam:		Seismic:		Equipment/Machinery:	
Coal Production:		Convenience Stores:	Y	Pipelines:		Wind:		Drilling:		Oil Field Services:	
		Chemicals:		Water:		Hydro:		InfoTech:		Air/Shipping Transportation:	
						Fuel Cells:		Specialty Services:			

TYPES OF BUSINESS:

Petroleum Product Sales
Service Stations
Aviation Fuel
Solar Power Research & Development
Liquid Petroleum Gas (LPG)

BRANDS/DIVISIONS/AFFILIATES:

Royal Dutch Shell (Shell Group)
Niigata Yukigunigata Megasolar
Solar Frontier

CONTACTS: *Note: Officers with more than one job title may be intentionally listed here more than once.*

Jun Arai, Pres.
Richard A. Carruth, CFO/VP
Atsuhiko Hirano, Exec. Officer-Domestic Mktg.
Hitoshi Satou, Managing Dir.-Human Resources
Hitoshi Satou, Managing Dir.-IT Planning
Misao Hamamoto, Exec. Officer-Mfg., Oil Bus. Center
Yuri Inoue, Exec. Officer-Legal
Kaoru Shiraki, Exec. Officer-Oper. & Dist., Oil Bus. Center
Hiroto Tamai, Exec. Officer-Corp. Planning
Hitoshi Satou, Managing Dir.-General Affairs
Kiyotaka Yamada, Exec. Officer-Finance & Control
Yukimichi Ikemura, Sr. Exec. Officer-Oil Bus., Lubricants & Bitumen
Shigeaki Kameda, Pres., Solar Frontier KK
Kazunori Yamamoto, Corp. Exec. Officer-Oil Prod., Crude Oil & Marine
Atsuhiko Hirano, Exec. Officer-Solar Power Project
Shigeya Kato, Chmn.
Brooks Herring, Exec. Officer-Int'l Sales, Solar Bus. Center
Richard A. Carruth, VP-Procurement

Phone: 81-3-5531-5591 **Fax:** 81-3-5531-5598
Toll-Free:
Address: Daiba Frontier Bldg., 2-3-2, Daiba, Minato-ku, Tokyo, 135-8074 Japan

GROWTH PLANS/SPECIAL FEATURES:

Showa Shell Sekiyu K.K. (SSS) is a Japanese company that primarily sells gasoline, liquid petroleum gas (LPG) and other petroleum products. The firm operates in two primary business divisions: oil and non-oil. The operations of its oil business include crude oil refining and the manufacture of oil products; the sale of gasoline, diesel, heating oil and automotive lubricants to service stations, as well as the sale of liquid natural gas (LNG) and industrial lubricants to the industry; the production and sale of LPG to residential, commercial, automotive and industrial customers; the production and sale of lubricants, greases, jet and vessel fuels and lubricants, compounds and bitumen for road paving; the production and sale of mixed xylene, benzene and propane; and the export of diesel and other refined oil products. SSS operates two lubricants blending plants, two LPG terminals, two asphalt terminals and five depots. The non-oil business includes the production and sale of CIS solar powered cells; and the retail and wholesale of electric power. At 33%, the Shell Group is the firm's largest single shareholder. In August 2009, the firm announced a partnership with Nissan Motor Company to develop advanced car battery charging technology. In November 2009, the company announced plans to construct a 900-megawatt solar power generation plant powered by CIS thin-film photovoltaic modules in Miyazaki Prefecture. In February 2010, SSS announced its intention to close the Toa Keihin Refinery Ohgimachi Factory. In August 2010, the firm began operations at the Niigata Yukigunigata Megasolar power plant in Niigata Prefecture, which has a generation capacity of 1,000 kilowatts. In October 2010, subsidiary Solar Frontier and IBM formed a joint development agreement concerning thin film solar cell technology.

FINANCIALS: **Sales and profits are in thousands of dollars—add 000 to get the full amount. 2010 Note: Financial information for 2010 was not available for all companies at press time.**

2010 Sales: $	2010 Profits: $	**U.S. Stock Ticker:**
2009 Sales: $21,865,900	2009 Profits: $-622,930	**Int'l Ticker: 5002** Int'l Exchange: Tokyo-TSE
2008 Sales: $31,664,000	2008 Profits: $-157,000	Employees:
2007 Sales: $27,560,000	2007 Profits: $390,000	Fiscal Year Ends: 12/31
2006 Sales: $24,540,000	2006 Profits: $390,000	Parent Company:

SALARIES/BENEFITS:

Pension Plan: Y	ESOP Stock Plan:	Profit Sharing:	Top Exec. Salary: $	Bonus: $
Savings Plan:	Stock Purch. Plan:		Second Exec. Salary: $	Bonus: $

OTHER THOUGHTS:

Apparent Women Officers or Directors: 2
Hot Spot for Advancement for Women/Minorities:

LOCATIONS: ("Y" = Yes)

West:	Southwest:	Midwest:	Southeast:	Northeast:	International:
					Y

SHV HOLDINGS NV

www.shv.nl

Industry Group Code: 486 **Ranks within this company's industry group:** Sales: Profits:

Exploration/Production:		Refining/Retailing:		Utilities:		Alternative Energy:		Specialty Services:		Energy Mktg./Other Svcs.	
Exploration:	Y	Refining:	Y	Electric Utility:		Waste/Solar/Other:		Consulting/Eng.:		Energy Marketing:	
Production:	Y	Retailing:	Y	Gas Utility:		Thermal/Steam:		Seismic:		Equipment/Machinery:	
Coal Production:		Convenience Stores:		Pipelines:		Wind:		Drilling:		Oil Field Services:	
		Chemicals:		Water:		Hydro:		InfoTech:		Air/Shipping Transportation:	
						Fuel Cells:		Specialty Services:	Y		

TYPES OF BUSINESS:

Liquid Petroleum Gas (LPG) Trading & Distribution
Oil & Gas Exploration & Production
Wholesale Distribution-Food & Consumer Goods
Scrap Collection, Brokerage & Processing
Retail Sales-Food & Consumer Goods
Private Equity
Recycling
Used Auto Parts

BRANDS/DIVISIONS/AFFILIATES:

SHV Gas
Makro
NPM Capital
ERIKS NV
Kubra Plastics
Dyas
Clean Energy Company (The)
Kramp

CONTACTS:

Note: Officers with more than one job title may be intentionally listed here more than once.

P.J. Kennedy, Chmn.-Exec. Board
W. van der Woerd, Dir.-Personnel Affairs
M. J. de Hoop, Dir.-IT
F. H. Rebel, Dir.-Legal Affairs
C.G.M. van der Drift, Dir.-Financial & Economic Affairs
W. N. Pals, Dir.-Treasury
G.Y.B. Kruisinga, Dir.-Fiscal Affairs
C. Dekker, Dir.-Internal Audit
J. van Klink, Corp. Sec.
A.M. Fentener van Vlissingen, Chmn.

Phone: 31-30-233-8833 **Fax:** 31-30-233-8304
Toll-Free:
Address: Rijnkade 1, Utrecht, 3511 LC The Netherlands

GROWTH PLANS/SPECIAL FEATURES:

SHV Holdings NV is a holding company based in the Netherlands. With roughly $11.56 billion in assets, the company is involved in activities in 48 countries related to liquid petroleum gas (LPG); cash and carry wholesale; oil/gas exploration and production; renewable energy; and heavy lifting and transport. The firm also provides private equity to firms that develop and produce oil and gas in the North Sea through its subsidiary NPM Capital. The company's oil and gas businesses are operated by Dyas, which invests in the production of oil and gas in the Netherlands and the North Sea. Dyas functions as a non-operator of its joint venture investments. SHV Gas, a main subsidiary of the firm, operates in 27 countries on three continents. It offers retail LPG services through brands such as Liquigas, Ipragaz, Supergasbras, Minasgas, Super Gas, Primagaz, Calor Gas, Gaspol, Probugas and Butan Plin. The firm provides wholesale distribution through its 184 Makro brand stores in Thailand and South America. Makro is a cash-and-carry wholesaler, selling high volumes retail products to registered professional customers. Subsidiary ERIKS NV supplies mechanical engineering components and associated technical/logistics services in 21 countries. The Clean Energy Company distributes wood pellets and heat contracting with the aim of producing renewable energy on a worldwide scale. Mammoet provides heavy lifting and transport services to the petrochemical, power generation and civil and offshore sectors. In March 2010, ERIKS acquired plastics technology manufacturer and marketer Kubra Plastics. In April 2010, NPM Capital acquired 40% ownership of Kramp, an international technical wholesaler. In August 2010, ERIKS agreed to acquire U.S.-based flow control solutions provider Rawson LP.

FINANCIALS:

Sales and profits are in thousands of dollars—add 000 to get the full amount. 2010 Note: Financial information for 2010 was not available for all companies at press time.

2010 Sales: $	2010 Profits: $	**U.S. Stock Ticker: Private**
2009 Sales: $	2009 Profits: $	**Int'l Ticker:** Int'l Exchange:
2008 Sales: $	2008 Profits: $	Employees:
2007 Sales: $	2007 Profits: $	Fiscal Year Ends: 12/31
2006 Sales: $	2006 Profits: $	Parent Company:

SALARIES/BENEFITS:

Pension Plan:	ESOP Stock Plan:	Profit Sharing:	Top Exec. Salary: $	Bonus: $
Savings Plan:	Stock Purch. Plan:		Second Exec. Salary: $	Bonus: $

OTHER THOUGHTS:

Apparent Women Officers or Directors: 2
Hot Spot for Advancement for Women/Minorities:

LOCATIONS: ("Y" = Yes)

West:	Southwest:	Midwest:	Southeast:	Northeast:	International:
					Y

SIEMENS AG

www.siemens.com

Industry Group Code: 335 **Ranks within this company's industry group:** Sales: 1 Profits: 2

Exploration/Production:		**Refining/Retailing:**		**Utilities:**		**Alternative Energy:**		**Specialty Services:**		**Energy Mktg./Other Svcs.**	
Exploration:		Refining:		Electric Utility:		Waste/Solar/Other:	Y	Consulting/Eng.:	Y	Energy Marketing:	
Production:		Retailing:		Gas Utility:		Thermal/Steam:		Seismic:		Equipment/Machinery:	Y
Coal Production:		Convenience Stores:		Pipelines:		Wind:	Y	Drilling:		Oil Field Services:	
		Chemicals:		Water:		Hydro:		InfoTech:		Air/Shipping Transportation:	
						Fuel Cells:		Specialty Services:	Y		

TYPES OF BUSINESS:

Electrical Equipment Manufacturing
Energy & Power Plant Systems & Consulting
Medical and Health Care Services and Equipment
Lighting & Optical Systems
Automation Systems
Transportation & Logistics Systems
Photovoltaic Equipment

BRANDS/DIVISIONS/AFFILIATES:

CTI Molecular Imaging
Siemens Building Technologies
Siemens Canada
Siemens Corporate Technology
Siemens Energy & Automation Inc
Siemens Energy Services
Siemens Healthcare
Solel Solar Systems

CONTACTS:

Note: Officers with more than one job title may be intentionally listed here more than once.

Peter H. Loscher, CEO
Peter H. Loscher, Pres.
Joe Kaeser, Head-Finance
Brigitte Ederer, Head-Corp. Human Resources
Joe Kaeser, Head-IT Solutions & Svcs.
Hermann Requardt, Head-Corp. Tech.
Peter Y. Solmssen, Head-Legal & Compliance
Joe Kaeser, Controller
Hermann Requardt, Sector CEO-Healthcare
Siegfried Russwurm, Sector CEO-Industry
Wolfgang Dehen, Sector CEO-Energy/Dir.-Asia & Australia
Eric Spiegel, CEO/Pres., Siemens Corp.
Gerhard Cromme, Chmn.
Peter Y. Solmssen, Dir.-The Americas
Barbara Kux, Head-Supply Chain Mgmt. & Sustainability

Phone: 49-69-797-6660	**Fax:**
Toll-Free:	
Address: Wittelsbacherplatz 2, Munich, 80333 Germany	

GROWTH PLANS/SPECIAL FEATURES:

Siemens AG is one of the largest electrical engineering and manufacturing companies in the world. Based in Germany, the firm sells products and services to approximately 190 countries around the globe, including all 50 states in the U.S. The company is organized in three primary sectors: industry, energy and healthcare. The industry sector's offerings range from industry automation products and services to building, lighting and mobility systems and services, as well as system integration for plant businesses. Additionally, this sector provides networking technology for transportation systems, including airport logistics, postal automation and railway electrification. The energy sector offers a broad range of products and services related to the generation, transmission and distribution of power, as well as for the extraction, conversion and transportation of oil and gas. The healthcare sector develops, manufactures and markets diagnostic and therapeutic systems, devices and consumables, as well as information technology systems for clinical and healthcare administration settings. Besides these activities, subsidiaries Siemens IT Solutions & Services (SIS) as well as Siemens Financial Services support sector activities as business partners, meanwhile continuing to build up their own business with external customers. In July 2009, the firm sold its 50% stake in Fujitsu Siemens Computers, an IT infrastructure provider, to Fujitsu Limited for roughly $670 million. In October 2009, Siemens announced that it would acquire Israel-based Solel Solar Systems Limited for $418 million. In October 2010, the company announced the further establishment of SIS as an independent limited liability company, operating under the Siemens IT Solutions and Services GmbH name. Later that month, Siemens also announced a strategic partnership with Masdar, Abu Dhabi's renewable energy company, in order to research and develop future energy technologies.

FINANCIALS:

Sales and profits are in thousands of dollars—add 000 to get the full amount. 2010 Note: Financial information for 2010 was not available for all companies at press time.

2010 Sales: $	2010 Profits: $	**U.S. Stock Ticker: SI**
2009 Sales: $113,842,000	2009 Profits: $3,404,080	**Int'l Ticker: SIE** Int'l Exchange: Frankfurt-Euronext
2008 Sales: $107,580,000	2008 Profits: $8,189,070	Employees: 427,000
2007 Sales: $115,406,000	2007 Profits: $3,535,760	Fiscal Year Ends: 9/30
2006 Sales: $113,740,000	2006 Profits: $3,950,360	Parent Company:

SALARIES/BENEFITS:

Pension Plan:	ESOP Stock Plan:	Profit Sharing:	Top Exec. Salary: $4,618,982	Bonus: $
Savings Plan:	Stock Purch. Plan: Y		Second Exec. Salary: $2,098,621	Bonus: $

OTHER THOUGHTS:

Apparent Women Officers or Directors: 5
Hot Spot for Advancement for Women/Minorities: Y

LOCATIONS: ("Y" = Yes)

West:	Southwest:	Midwest:	Southeast:	Northeast:	International:
Y	Y	Y	Y	Y	Y

SIEMENS METERING SERVICES LTD

www.siemensenergy.co.uk

Industry Group Code: 3345 **Ranks within this company's industry group:** Sales: Profits:

Exploration/Production:		**Refining/Retailing:**		**Utilities:**		**Alternative Energy:**		**Specialty Services:**		**Energy Mktg./Other Svcs.**	
Exploration:		Refining:		Electric Utility:		Waste/Solar/Other:		Consulting/Eng.:		Energy Marketing:	
Production:		Retailing:		Gas Utility:		Thermal/Steam:		Seismic:		Equipment/Machinery:	Y
Coal Production:		Convenience Stores:		Pipelines:		Wind:		Drilling:		Oil Field Services:	
		Chemicals:		Water:		Hydro:		InfoTech:	Y	Air/Shipping Transportation:	
						Fuel Cells:		Specialty Services:	Y		

TYPES OF BUSINESS:

Utility Meters
Meter Reading

BRANDS/DIVISIONS/AFFILIATES:

Siemens AG
Siemens PLC
National Quantum Gas Pre-payment System

CONTACTS:

Note: Officers with more than one job title may be intentionally listed here more than once.

Andreas. J. Goss, CEO
Roland Jaksch, CFO
Martin Pollock, Dir.-Mktg.
Gordon Lovell-Read, CIO
Woflgang Dehen, CEO-Siemens Energy Sector

Phone: 44-1276-696-000 **Fax:**
Toll-Free:
Address: Sir. William Siemens Sq., Frimley, Camberley, GU16 8QD UK

GROWTH PLANS/SPECIAL FEATURES:

Siemens Metering Services Ltd. (SMS) is a wholly-owned subsidiary of Siemens PLC that, through contracts with energy suppliers, installs, maintains and collects data from meters. The company's products and services consist of data collection; data retrieval; data processing and data aggregation; prepayment; asset provision; and asset maintenance and management. The company supplies its services and products to nearly 14 million residences and business throughout the U.K. and parts of New Zealand. It also provides 25,000 private and public organizations within the U.K. with metering and data services that help to manage cost and consumption. The firm operates the National Quantum Gas Pre-payment System, a system that tracks customer usage and pre-payment on behalf of all U.K. gas companies. SMS has installed its Quantum technology smart meters in approximately 1.3 million residential homes in New Zealand. SMS also provides its services to the water utility market, serving two of the largest water utilities in the U.K.: Southern Water and United Utilities.

The company sets a global labor and social policy standard for all of its employees through which it attempts to provide all employees with training and education programs, and sets universal workplace health and safety standards.

FINANCIALS:

Sales and profits are in thousands of dollars—add 000 to get the full amount. 2010 Note: Financial information for 2010 was not available for all companies at press time.

2010 Sales: $	2010 Profits: $	**U.S. Stock Ticker: Subsidiary**
2009 Sales: $	2009 Profits: $	**Int'l Ticker:** Int'l Exchange:
2008 Sales: $31,414,000	2008 Profits: $1,995,000	Employees: 83,500
2007 Sales: $	2007 Profits: $	Fiscal Year Ends:
2006 Sales: $	2006 Profits: $	Parent Company: SIEMENS AG

SALARIES/BENEFITS:

Pension Plan:	ESOP Stock Plan:	Profit Sharing:	Top Exec. Salary: $	Bonus: $
Savings Plan:	Stock Purch. Plan:		Second Exec. Salary: $	Bonus: $

OTHER THOUGHTS:

Apparent Women Officers or Directors:
Hot Spot for Advancement for Women/Minorities:

LOCATIONS: ("Y" = Yes)

West:	Southwest:	Midwest:	Southeast:	Northeast:	International:
					Y

SILVER SPRING NETWORKS

www.silverspringnet.com

Industry Group Code: 33411 **Ranks within this company's industry group:** Sales: Profits:

Exploration/Production:		Refining/Retailing:		Utilities:		Alternative Energy:		Specialty Services:		Energy Mktg./Other Svcs.	
Exploration:		Refining:		Electric Utility:		Waste/Solar/Other:		Consulting/Eng.:		Energy Marketing:	
Production:		Retailing:		Gas Utility:		Thermal/Steam:		Seismic:		Equipment/Machinery:	Y
Coal Production:		Convenience Stores:		Pipelines:		Wind:		Drilling:		Oil Field Services:	
		Chemicals:		Water:		Hydro:		InfoTech:		Air/Shipping Transportation:	
						Fuel Cells:		Specialty Services:	Y		

TYPES OF BUSINESS:

Utility Network Management Systems
Smart Grid Equipment

BRANDS/DIVISIONS/AFFILIATES:

Smart Energy Platform
Access Point
UtilityIQ
CustomerIQ
Demand Response
Silver Spring Relay

CONTACTS: *Note: Officers with more than one job title may be intentionally listed here more than once.*

Scott Lang, CEO
Warren Jenson, COO
Scott Lang, Pres.
John R. Joyce, CFO
Eric Dresselhuys, Chief Mktg. Officer/Exec. VP
Amy Cappellanti-Wolf, Chief Human Resources Officer
George Flammer, Chief Scientist
Raj Vaswani, CTO
Lisa Magnuson, Contact-Media
Scott Lang, Chmn.
Gary Gysin, Exec. VP-Worldwide Sales

Phone: 650-298-4200 **Fax:** 650-363-5240
Toll-Free: 866-204-0200
Address: 555 Broadway St., Redwood City, CA 94063 US

GROWTH PLANS/SPECIAL FEATURES:

Silver Spring Networks is a builder of networks for utility companies. The firm seeks to aid utilities in improving efficiency, reliability and customer service while reducing operating costs. Silver Spring Networks offers several network solutions, including improved outage management; advanced metering services, which reduce field service and support costs; a secure distribution automation solution, a unified infrastructure that allows multiple applications to run on it; credit and collection services, which lessen a utility's number of accounts receivable and bad debt write-offs; electric car metering and communications systems; and Demand Response, a program that allows customers to receive automated current, hour-ahead or day-ahead pricing signals. The firm's software products include the Smart Energy Platform, which allows a utility company to use any IP-enabled device, perform intelligent load shedding, deploy IP-based consumer energy portals and more; The CustomerIQ web portal, which allows utilities to directly communicate pricing, usage and recommendations to consumers; and the UtilityIQ suite of smart energy applications. The company's Access Point device links endpoint devices and mission-critical systems to improve intelligent network control and monitoring. Another device, Silver Spring Relay, links the Access Point and Smart Energy Platform endpoint devices. Silver Spring Networks also offers network interface cards, which communicate with in-home devices and can be applied to gas, water and electrical meters, as well as automate load-control devices. The firm's many technology partners include GE Energy, Oracle, Carrier Corporation, Cisco, Digi International, ClipperCreek, S&C Electric Company and ABB.

The firm offers employee benefits including life, disability, medical, dental and vision insurance; a 401(k); an assistance program; paid time off; onsite dry cleaning and fitness center; and flexible spending accounts.

FINANCIALS: **Sales and profits are in thousands of dollars—add 000 to get the full amount. 2010 Note: Financial information for 2010 was not available for all companies at press time.**

2010 Sales: $	2010 Profits: $	**U.S. Stock Ticker: Private**
2009 Sales: $	2009 Profits: $	**Int'l Ticker:** Int'l Exchange:
2008 Sales: $	2008 Profits: $	Employees:
2007 Sales: $	2007 Profits: $	Fiscal Year Ends:
2006 Sales: $	2006 Profits: $	Parent Company:

SALARIES/BENEFITS:

Pension Plan:	ESOP Stock Plan:	Profit Sharing:	Top Exec. Salary: $	Bonus: $
Savings Plan: Y	Stock Purch. Plan:		Second Exec. Salary: $	Bonus: $

OTHER THOUGHTS:

Apparent Women Officers or Directors: 3
Hot Spot for Advancement for Women/Minorities: Y

LOCATIONS: ("Y" = Yes)

West:	Southwest:	Midwest:	Southeast:	Northeast:	International:
Y					Y

SINCLAIR OIL CORP

www.sinclairoil.com

Industry Group Code: 324110 **Ranks within this company's industry group:** Sales: Profits:

Exploration/Production:		Refining/Retailing:		Utilities:		Alternative Energy:		Specialty Services:		Energy Mktg./Other Svcs.	
Exploration:	Y	Refining:	Y	Electric Utility:		Waste/Solar/Other:		Consulting/Eng.:		Energy Marketing:	
Production:	Y	Retailing:	Y	Gas Utility:		Thermal/Steam:		Seismic:		Equipment/Machinery:	
Coal Production:		Convenience Stores:	Y	Pipelines:	Y	Wind:		Drilling:		Oil Field Services:	
		Chemicals:		Water:		Hydro:		InfoTech:		Air/Shipping Transportation:	Y
						Fuel Cells:		Specialty Services:	Y		

TYPES OF BUSINESS:

Service Stations & Convenience Stores
Refining
Pipelines
Trucking & Fleet Management
Hotels & Ski Resorts
Lubricants
Oil & Gas Exploration & Production

BRANDS/DIVISIONS/AFFILIATES:

Little America
Snowbasin Resort
Sun Valley Resort
Grand America
Sinclair Trucking Company
Fleet Track Card

CONTACTS: *Note: Officers with more than one job title may be intentionally listed here more than once.*

Ross B. Matthews, CEO
Peter M. Johnson, Pres.
Bud Blackmore, Sr. VP-Mktg.
Bud Blackmore, Sr. VP-Supply

Phone: 801-524-2700 **Fax:** 801-524-2880
Toll-Free:
Address: 550 E. South Temple, Salt Lake City, UT 84130 US

GROWTH PLANS/SPECIAL FEATURES:

Sinclair Oil Company, based in Salt Lake City, Utah, is an oil/gas production and distribution company. The company is a subsidiary of The Sinclair Companies, which is owned by R. Earl Holding. The firm owns a network of more than 2,600 convenience stores, service stations and truck stops across Arizona, Arkansas, Colorado, Idaho, Illinois, Iowa, Kansas, Minnesota, Missouri, Mississippi, Montana, Nebraska, Nevada, New Mexico, North Dakota, Oklahoma, Oregon, South Dakota, Utah, Wisconsin and Wyoming. Sinclair also owns 11 product terminals; a crude oil and refined petroleum pipeline network; two refineries; and trucking operations used in the refining, distribution and marketing of oil and gas products. The company engages in several areas of the oil and gas industry, including exploration and production; fleet services, including fleet fueling and fuel management; and manufacturing of lubricants. Its refineries refine approximately 80,000 barrels of petroleum product per day. Sinclair operates more than 1,000 miles of pipeline extending through the Rocky Mountains to regional marketing terminals, as well as a pipeline control center in Sinclair, Wyoming. Sinclair Trucking Company offers a distribution network for products including liquid petroleum gases, gas, diesel, jet fuel, fuel oils and asphalts. Sinclair's Fleet Track Card provides spending limits and fuel management services. Sinclair also owns and operates eight hotel and travel centers under various names. These properties include the Snowbasin Resort in Huntsville, Utah; the Westgate Hotel in San Diego, California; the Sun Valley Resort in Sun Valley, Idaho; the Grand America Hotel in Salt Lake City, Utah; and the Little America chain, located in Arizona, Wyoming and Utah. The firm recently sold its Tulsa, Oklahoma, refinery to Holly Energy Partners and the refinery's inventory to Holly Corporation. In 2009, Sinclair Oil announced plans to discontinue its retail fuel operations and sell its 90 directly-operated convenience stores.

FINANCIALS: **Sales and profits are in thousands of dollars—add 000 to get the full amount. 2010 Note: Financial information for 2010 was not available for all companies at press time.**

2010 Sales: $	2010 Profits: $	**U.S. Stock Ticker: Subsidiary**
2009 Sales: $	2009 Profits: $	**Int'l Ticker:** Int'l Exchange:
2008 Sales: $7,750,000	2008 Profits: $	Employees: 7,000
2007 Sales: $	2007 Profits: $	Fiscal Year Ends: 12/31
2006 Sales: $6,800,000	2006 Profits: $	Parent Company: SINCLAIR COMPANIES (THE)

SALARIES/BENEFITS:

Pension Plan:	ESOP Stock Plan:	Profit Sharing:	Top Exec. Salary: $	Bonus: $
Savings Plan:	Stock Purch. Plan:		Second Exec. Salary: $	Bonus: $

OTHER THOUGHTS:

Apparent Women Officers or Directors:
Hot Spot for Advancement for Women/Minorities:

LOCATIONS: ("Y" = Yes)

West:	Southwest:	Midwest:	Southeast:	Northeast:	International:
Y	Y	Y			Y

SINOPEC SHANGHAI PETROCHEMICAL

www.spc.com.cn

Industry Group Code: 325110 **Ranks within this company's industry group:** Sales: 4 Profits: 4

Exploration/Production:		Refining/Retailing:		Utilities:		Alternative Energy:		Specialty Services:		Energy Mktg./Other Svcs.	
Exploration:		Refining:	Y	Electric Utility:		Waste/Solar/Other:		Consulting/Eng.:		Energy Marketing:	
Production:		Retailing:	Y	Gas Utility:		Thermal/Steam:		Seismic:		Equipment/Machinery:	
Coal Production:		Convenience Stores:		Pipelines:		Wind:		Drilling:		Oil Field Services:	
		Chemicals:	Y	Water:		Hydro:		InfoTech:		Air/Shipping Transportation:	
						Fuel Cells:		Specialty Services:			

TYPES OF BUSINESS:

Petrochemical Manufacturing
Plastics
Synthetic Resins & Fibers
Electrical Generation
Refining

BRANDS/DIVISIONS/AFFILIATES:

China Petroleum & Chemical (Sinopec)

CONTACTS:

Note: Officers with more than one job title may be intentionally listed here more than once.

Rong Guangdao, Pres.
Ye Guohua, CFO/Exec. Dir.
Zhang Jingming, General Counsel/Company Sec.
Du Chongjun, Vice Chmn./VP
Gao Jinping, Chmn.-Trade Union/Exec. Dir.
Wu Haijun, VP/Exec. Dir.
Shi Wei, VP/Exec. Dir.
Rong Guangdao, Chmn.

Phone: 86-21-5794-3143	**Fax:** 86-21-5794-0050
Toll-Free:	
Address: 48 Jinyi Rd., Jinshan District, Shanghai, 200540 China	

GROWTH PLANS/SPECIAL FEATURES:

Sinopec Shanghai Petrochemical (SPC), 55.6%-owned by state-run China Petroleum & Chemical Corporation (Sinopec Corp.), is a leading Chinese petrochemical company. SPC manufactures over 60 different products across a number of product categories, including petroleum derivatives, such as gasoline, generating approximately 40.0% of the firm's sales; intermediate petrochemicals, including ethylene, 17.8%; resins and plastics, 25.9%; synthetic fibers, 5.9%; and other products and trading, 10.4%. SPC is one of China's largest producers of ethylene for use in the production of synthetic fibers, resins and plastics. The firm has its own utilities to supply electricity, gas and water for its facilities. In 2009, it produced roughly 806,000 tons of gasoline; 2.8 million tons of diesel; 679,000 tons of jet fuel; 927,700 tons of ethylene; 487,600 tons of propylene; 1 million tons of synthetic resins and co-polymers; 902,700 tons of synthetic fiber monomers; 599,700 tons of synthetic fiber polymers; 241,300 tons of synthetic fibers; and approximately 2.4 billion kilowatt-hours of generated electricity. The firm also processed 8.8 million tons of crude oil. Most of the company's products other than petroleum products are permitted to be sold at market prices. However, four types of petroleum products (gasoline, diesel and jet fuel, and liquefied petroleum gas) that it sells are subject to varying degrees of government pricing control and are, accordingly, sold at prices set by the Chinese government. In 2009, approximately 47.7%, of SPC's sales were from products subject to price controls. The company has established a joint venture with BP Chemicals East China Investments Ltd. and Sinopec Corp., which manufactures and markets intermediate petrochemicals and other petroleum products; provides related after-sales services and technical advice concerning its products; and engages in polymers application development.

FINANCIALS:

Sales and profits are in thousands of dollars—add 000 to get the full amount. 2010 Note: Financial information for 2010 was not available for all companies at press time.

2010 Sales: $	2010 Profits: $	**U.S. Stock Ticker: SHI**
2009 Sales: $7,759,160	2009 Profits: $234,260	**Int'l Ticker: 600688** Int'l Exchange: Shanghai-SHE
2008 Sales: $9,047,470	2008 Profits: $-936,900	Employees: 17,131
2007 Sales: $7,451,192	2007 Profits: $230,758	Fiscal Year Ends: 12/31
2006 Sales: $6,435,674	2006 Profits: $108,973	Parent Company:

SALARIES/BENEFITS:

Pension Plan:	ESOP Stock Plan:	Profit Sharing:	Top Exec. Salary: $	Bonus: $
Savings Plan:	Stock Purch. Plan:		Second Exec. Salary: $	Bonus: $

OTHER THOUGHTS:

Apparent Women Officers or Directors:
Hot Spot for Advancement for Women/Minorities:

LOCATIONS: ("Y" = Yes)

West:	Southwest:	Midwest:	Southeast:	Northeast:	International:
					Y

SK HOLDINGS CO LTD

www.sk.com

Industry Group Code: 324110 **Ranks within this company's industry group:** Sales: 2 Profits: 11

Exploration/Production:		Refining/Retailing:		Utilities:		Alternative Energy:		Specialty Services:		Energy Mktg./Other Svcs.	
Exploration:	Y	Refining:	Y	Electric Utility:	Y	Waste/Solar/Other:	Y	Consulting/Eng.:		Energy Marketing:	Y
Production:	Y	Retailing:	Y	Gas Utility:	Y	Thermal/Steam:	Y	Seismic:		Equipment/Machinery:	
Coal Production:	Y	Convenience Stores:	Y	Pipelines:		Wind:		Drilling:		Oil Field Services:	
		Chemicals:	Y	Water:		Hydro:		InfoTech:		Air/Shipping Transportation:	Y
						Fuel Cells:		Specialty Services:	Y		

TYPES OF BUSINESS:

Oil Refining
Oil Exploration & Production
Lubricants
Chemicals
Pharmaceuticals
Mobile Phone Technology
Batteries & Hydrogen Energy
Marketing

BRANDS/DIVISIONS/AFFILIATES:

SK Corporation
SK Energy
SKC
SK E&S
K-Power
SK Telecom Co Ltd
SK Networks
SK Shipping

CONTACTS:

Note: Officers with more than one job title may be intentionally listed here more than once.

Tae Won Chey, Co-CEO
Young-Ho Park, Pres./Co-CEO
Katharine Junghae Kho, Head-Global Public Rel.
Jin-Won Jang, Internal Acct. & Control Officer
Jae-Won Chey, Vice Chmn./Co-CEO
Heon-Cheol Shin, Co-CEO/Pres., SK Energy
Joon-Ho Kim, Exec. VP-Ethics Mgmt. Office, SK Energy
Tae Won Chey, Chmn.

Phone: 82-2-2121-5114	**Fax:** 82-2-2121-7001
Toll-Free:	
Address: 99 Seorin-dong, Jongno-gu, Seoul, 110-728 Korea	

GROWTH PLANS/SPECIAL FEATURES:

SK Holdings Co. Ltd., a Korean holding company, operates through subsidiaries in the energy and chemicals; telecommunications; and trading and services industries. In the energy and chemicals industry, subsidiaries include SK Energy, SKC, SK E&S, SK Gas and K-Power. SK Energy, Korea's first oil refining company, is involved in the production of energy and petrochemicals. Chemical products produced by SK Energy include olefin, aromatics, solvents, polymers, special polymers, EPDM (ethylene propylene diene monomer) rubber and lithium ion batteries, using the world's third lithium ion battery separator. SKC produces chemicals including PO and polyol; polyester, polyamide and biodegradable film; and display materials. SK E&S produces and supplies liquefied petroleum gases (LPG) to all of Korea's major cities; it also runs a heat absorption generator that produces both electricity and steam and a polyurethane manufacturing plant in Covington, Georgia. SK Gas supplies over half of Korea's consumed LPG's through roughly 260 charging stations. K-Power operates the Gwangyang Composite Power Generator; produces and distributes electricity; and imports LNG. Other subsidiaries of SK Holdings include SK Telecom, providing mobile telephone service, wireless and fixed-line service, corporate client services and ubiquitous/convergence service; SK Networks, a global integrated marketing company; and SK Shipping, a leading global shipping company specializing in the transport of natural resources. In February 2010, the firm purchased the remaining 35% interest in K-Power held by Korea Energy Investment Holdings, making K-Power a wholly-owned subsidiary of SK. In September 2010, the company acquired all the outstanding shares of SK Shipping Co. Also in September, SK C&C announced a partnership with First Data Corporation to introduce mobile commerce services, including mobile wallet applications that allow consumers to complete transactions using mobile phones, into the U.S. In October 2010, SK Holdings announced plans to spin off its medical and healthcare division, SK Life Sciences, into a separate entity.

FINANCIALS:

Sales and profits are in thousands of dollars—add 000 to get the full amount. 2010 Note: Financial information for 2010 was not available for all companies at press time.

2010 Sales: $	2010 Profits: $	**U.S. Stock Ticker:**
2009 Sales: $68,720,100	2009 Profits: $224,950	**Int'l Ticker: 003600** Int'l Exchange: Seoul-KRX
2008 Sales: $70,636,157	2008 Profits: $1,381,315	Employees:
2007 Sales: $52,258,036	2007 Profits: $2,518,864	Fiscal Year Ends: 12/31
2006 Sales: $	2006 Profits: $	Parent Company:

SALARIES/BENEFITS:

Pension Plan:	ESOP Stock Plan:	Profit Sharing:	Top Exec. Salary: $	Bonus: $
Savings Plan:	Stock Purch. Plan:		Second Exec. Salary: $	Bonus: $

OTHER THOUGHTS:

Apparent Women Officers or Directors: 1
Hot Spot for Advancement for Women/Minorities:

LOCATIONS: ("Y" = Yes)

West:	Southwest:	Midwest:	Southeast:	Northeast:	International:
	Y			Y	Y

SM ENERGY COMPANY

www.sm-energy.com

Industry Group Code: 211111 **Ranks within this company's industry group:** Sales: 83 Profits: 87

Exploration/Production:		Refining/Retailing:		Utilities:		Alternative Energy:		Specialty Services:		Energy Mktg./Other Svcs.	
Exploration:	Y	Refining:		Electric Utility:		Waste/Solar/Other:		Consulting/Eng.:		Energy Marketing:	
Production:	Y	Retailing:		Gas Utility:		Thermal/Steam:		Seismic:		Equipment/Machinery:	
Coal Production:		Convenience Stores:		Pipelines:		Wind:		Drilling:		Oil Field Services:	
		Chemicals:		Water:		Hydro:		InfoTech:		Air/Shipping Transportation:	
						Fuel Cells:		Specialty Services:			

TYPES OF BUSINESS:

Oil & Gas Exploration & Production

BRANDS/DIVISIONS/AFFILIATES:

St. Mary Land & Exploration Company

CONTACTS:

Note: Officers with more than one job title may be intentionally listed here more than once.

Tony J. Best, CEO
Jay D. Ottoson, COO/Exec. VP
Tony J. Best, Pres.
Wade Pursell, CFO/Exec. VP
David J. Whitcomb, VP-Mktg.
John Monark, VP-Human Resources
Dennis A. Zubieta, VP-Eng. & Evaluation
Kenneth Knott, VP-Bus. Dev. & Land
Newt Newton, Sr. VP/Regional Mgr.-Permian
Stephen Pugh, VP/Regional Mgr.-ArkLaTex
Mark D. Mueller, Sr. VP/Regional Mgr.-Rocky Mountain
Greg Leyendecker, Sr. VP/Regional Mgr.-South Texas & Gulf Coast
William D. Sullivan, Chmn.

Phone: 303-861-8140 **Fax:** 303-861-0934
Toll-Free:
Address: 1775 Sherman St., Ste. 1200, Denver, CO 80203 US

GROWTH PLANS/SPECIAL FEATURES:

SM Energy Company, formerly St. Mary Land & Exploration Company, is an independent oil and gas company engaged in the exploration, exploitation, development, acquisition and production of natural gas, natural gas liquids and crude oil in North America. The firm is based in Denver, Colorado, with regional offices in Montana, Oklahoma, Texas and Louisiana. It has diversified exploration, development and production holdings in the Williston Basin in the Rocky Mountain region; the Anadarko and Arkoma Basins in the Mid-Continent region; the Permian Basin; productive formations in East Texas and North Louisiana; north central Pennsylvania; the Maverick Basin in South Texas; and the onshore Gulf Coast. SM Energy's assets include proved reserves of 53.8 million barrels of oil and 449.5 billion cubic feet of oil equivalent of natural gas. About 82% of its reserves are proved developed. The company controls about 2,046 gross productive oil wells and 3,154 gross productive gas wells. In February 2010, the firm sold certain non-core properties in Wyoming to Legacy Reserves Operating LP; in March, it divested similar properties in North Dakota. In May 2010, the company changed its name to SM Energy. In July 2010, SM Energy and Eagle Ford Gathering LLC announced an agreement under which Eagle Ford Gathering will provide gather, transport, and production services from SM Energy's Eagle Ford shale assets in southern Texas. In August 2010, the firm announced plans to divest a number of non-strategic assets and joint venture agreements over the next year, potentially including its interest in the Marcellus shale position in Pennsylvania.

SM Energy offers its employees medical, dental, vision, life and disability insurance; flexible spending accounts; flexible schedules; a 401(k) plan and pension plan; and employee stock purchase plan; tuition reimbursement; and relocation assistance.

FINANCIALS:

Sales and profits are in thousands of dollars—add 000 to get the full amount. 2010 Note: Financial information for 2010 was not available for all companies at press time.

2010 Sales: $	2010 Profits: $	**U.S. Stock Ticker: SM**
2009 Sales: $832,201	2009 Profits: $-99,370	**Int'l Ticker:** Int'l Exchange:
2008 Sales: $1,301,301	2008 Profits: $87,348	Employees: 560
2007 Sales: $990,094	2007 Profits: $189,712	Fiscal Year Ends: 12/31
2006 Sales: $787,701	2006 Profits: $190,015	Parent Company:

SALARIES/BENEFITS:

Pension Plan: Y	ESOP Stock Plan:	Profit Sharing:	Top Exec. Salary: $513,000	Bonus: $287,280
Savings Plan: Y	Stock Purch. Plan: Y		Second Exec. Salary: $345,000	Bonus: $169,050

OTHER THOUGHTS:

Apparent Women Officers or Directors: 1
Hot Spot for Advancement for Women/Minorities:

LOCATIONS: ("Y" = Yes)

West:	Southwest:	Midwest:	Southeast:	Northeast:	International:
Y	Y		Y		

SMF ENERGY CORPORATION

www.mobilefueling.com

Industry Group Code: 486 **Ranks within this company's industry group:** Sales: 23 Profits: 19

Exploration/Production:		**Refining/Retailing:**		**Utilities:**		**Alternative Energy:**		**Specialty Services:**		**Energy Mktg./Other Svcs.**	
Exploration:		Refining:		Electric Utility:		Waste/Solar/Other:		Consulting/Eng.:		Energy Marketing:	
Production:		Retailing:	Y	Gas Utility:		Thermal/Steam:		Seismic:		Equipment/Machinery:	
Coal Production:		Convenience Stores:		Pipelines:		Wind:		Drilling:		Oil Field Services:	
		Chemicals:	Y	Water:		Hydro:		InfoTech:		Air/Shipping Transportation:	Y
						Fuel Cells:		Specialty Services:	Y		

TYPES OF BUSINESS:

Fuel Distribution
Transportation Logistics Services
Emergency Response Services
Lubricants & Chemicals Distribution

BRANDS/DIVISIONS/AFFILIATES:

H & W Petroleum Co, Inc.
SMF Services, Inc.
Streicher Realty, Inc.

CONTACTS: *Note: Officers with more than one job title may be intentionally listed here more than once.*

Richard E. Gathright, CEO
Richard E. Gathright, Pres.
Michael S. Shore, CFO/Sr. VP
Robert W. Beard, Sr. VP-Mktg. & Sales
Timothy E. Shaw, CIO/Sr. VP-Info. Svcs.
Timothy E. Shaw, Sr. VP-Admin.
Louise P. Lungaro, Sec.
Gary G. Williams, Sr. VP-Commercial Oper.
Robert W. Beard, Investor Rel. Officer
Michael S. Shore, Treas.
Richard E. Gathright, Chmn.

Phone: 954-308-4200 **Fax:**
Toll-Free: 800-383-5734
Address: 200 W. Cypress Creek Rd., Ste. 400, Fort Lauderdale, FL 33309 US

GROWTH PLANS/SPECIAL FEATURES:

SMF Energy Corporation is a provider of petroleum product distribution services, transportation logistics and emergency response services to the trucking, manufacturing, construction, shipping, utility, chemical, telecommunication and government services industries. The company provides its services and products through 34 locations in Georgia, Nevada, North Carolina, Louisiana, Alabama, California, Florida, Mississippi, South Carolina, Tennessee and Texas. Services offered include commercial mobile and bulk fueling; the packaging, distribution and sale of lubricants; integrated outsourced fuel management; transportation logistics; and emergency response services. The company's fleet of custom specialized vehicles delivers diesel fuel and gasoline to customers' locations on a regularly scheduled or as-needed basis, refueling vehicles and equipment, re-supplying fixed-site and temporary bulk storage tanks and emergency power generation systems. The fleet also distributes a variety of specialized petroleum products, lubricants and chemicals and provides heavy haul transportation services to customers requiring the movement of over-sized or over-weight equipment and manufactured products. SMF Energy operates a fleet of more than 200 specialized commercial vehicles, including fueling and lubricant tank wagons; tractor-trailer fuel and lubricant transports; lubricant delivery box trucks; flatbed vehicles; and special heavy haul tractor-trailer units. The custom commercial mobile fueling trucks have fuel carrying capacities ranging from 2,800 to 4,500 gallons and are equipped with multi-compartmented tanks. The company also owns over 800 fuel and lubricant storage tanks with a capacity of more than 1.7 million gallons. The firm operates three subsidiaries, SMF Services, Inc.; H & W Petroleum Company, Inc.; and Streicher Realty, Inc.

FINANCIALS: **Sales and profits are in thousands of dollars—add 000 to get the full amount. 2010 Note: Financial information for 2010 was not available for all companies at press time.**

2010 Sales: $	2010 Profits: $	**U.S. Stock Ticker: FUEL**
2009 Sales: $199,249	2009 Profits: $-2,339	**Int'l Ticker:** Int'l Exchange:
2008 Sales: $260,689	2008 Profits: $-6,769	Employees: 248
2007 Sales: $229,769	2007 Profits: $-6,589	Fiscal Year Ends: 6/30
2006 Sales: $248,699	2006 Profits: $-4,878	Parent Company:

SALARIES/BENEFITS:

Pension Plan:	ESOP Stock Plan:	Profit Sharing:	Top Exec. Salary: $323,000	Bonus: $
Savings Plan:	Stock Purch. Plan:		Second Exec. Salary: $200,307	Bonus: $

OTHER THOUGHTS:

Apparent Women Officers or Directors: 1
Hot Spot for Advancement for Women/Minorities:

LOCATIONS: ("Y" = Yes)

West:	Southwest:	Midwest:	Southeast:	Northeast:	International:
Y	Y		Y	Y	

Note: Financial information, benefits and other data can change quickly and may vary from those stated here.

SMITH INTERNATIONAL INC

www.smith.com

Industry Group Code: 213112 **Ranks within this company's industry group:** Sales: 6 Profits: 13

Exploration/Production:		Refining/Retailing:		Utilities:		Alternative Energy:		Specialty Services:		Energy Mktg./Other Svcs.	
Exploration:		Refining:		Electric Utility:		Waste/Solar/Other:		Consulting/Eng.:		Energy Marketing:	
Production:		Retailing:		Gas Utility:		Thermal/Steam:		Seismic:		Equipment/Machinery:	Y
Coal Production:		Convenience Stores:		Pipelines:		Wind:		Drilling:	Y	Oil Field Services:	Y
		Chemicals:		Water:		Hydro:		InfoTech:		Air/Shipping Transportation:	
						Fuel Cells:		Specialty Services:	Y		

TYPES OF BUSINESS:

Oil & Gas Drilling Support Services
Waste Management Services
Drilling Equipment
Supply Chain Services

BRANDS/DIVISIONS/AFFILIATES:

M-I SWACO
Smith Oilfield
Wilson International, Inc.
At Balance B.V.
CE Franklin, Ltd.

CONTACTS:

Note: Officers with more than one job title may be intentionally listed here more than once.

John Yearwood, CEO
John Yearwood, COO
John Yearwood, Pres.
William J. Restrepo, CFO/Treas.
Malcolm W. Anderson, Sr. VP-Human Resources
Richard E. Chandler, Jr., General Counsel/Sr. VP/Corp. Sec.
Peter J. Pintar, VP-Corp. Strategy & Bus. Dev.
Shawn Housley, Dir.-Investor Rel.
Geraldine Wilde, VP-Taxes/Assistant Treas.
Bryan L. Dudman, Exec. VP/Pres., Smith Drilling & Evaluation
Norman (Norrie) McKay, Exec. VP/Pres., Smith Technologies
John J. Kennedy, Pres./CEO-Wilson
Lee A. Turner, VP-Quality, Health, Safety & Environmental
Douglas L. Rock, Chmn.

Phone: 281-443-3370	**Fax:** 281-233-5996
Toll-Free: 800-877-6484	
Address: 1310 Rankin Rd., Houston, TX 77073 US	

GROWTH PLANS/SPECIAL FEATURES:

Smith International, Inc. is a leading worldwide supplier of premium products and services to the oil and gas exploration and production industry. The company operates through three segments: M-I SWACO, which generated 51% of the firm's 2009 revenues; Smith Oilfield, 27%; and Distribution, 22%. M-I SWACO, a 60% owned joint-venture, provides drilling and completion fluid systems, solids-control and separation equipment, engineering and technical services, waste management and oil field production chemicals. Key products include the MUD D-GASSER and SUPER CHOKE pressure controllers. Smith Oilfield designs, manufactures and sells three-cone and diamond drill bits, turbines and borehole enlargement tools, in addition to planning software and specialty services. The segment is also a leading supplier of drilling tools and services, tubulars, completion services and other related downhole solutions. It sells and rents impact drilling tools such as Hydra-Jar and Accelerator, as well as selling drill collars, subs, stabilizers, kellys and the Hevi-Wate DrillPipe. Smith Oilfield also provides complete fishing, remedial and thru-tubing services. Smith International's Distribution segment consists of the supply chain management company Wilson International, Inc, as well as a majority interest in CE Franklin, Ltd. The company markets pipe, valves and fittings as well as mill, safety and other maintenance products to energy and industrial markets. In February 2010, the company agreed to be purchased by Schlumberger Ltd. for $11 billion in stock. In May 2010, the company completed the acquisition of At Balance B.V., a provider of managed pressure drilling. In July 2010, the company announced that it had received approval for its merger with Schlumberger from the European Commission and the U.S. Department of Justice.

Smith International offers its employees medical and dental coverage; life and AD&D insurance; paid time off; a 401(k) plan; educational assistance; dependent scholarships; and an employee assistance program.

FINANCIALS:

Sales and profits are in thousands of dollars—add 000 to get the full amount. 2010 Note: Financial information for 2010 was not available for all companies at press time.

2010 Sales: $	2010 Profits: $	**U.S. Stock Ticker: SII**
2009 Sales: $8,218,559	2009 Profits: $148,469	**Int'l Ticker:** Int'l Exchange:
2008 Sales: $10,770,838	2008 Profits: $767,284	Employees: 21,931
2007 Sales: $8,764,330	2007 Profits: $647,051	Fiscal Year Ends: 12/31
2006 Sales: $7,333,559	2006 Profits: $502,006	Parent Company:

SALARIES/BENEFITS:

Pension Plan: Y	ESOP Stock Plan:	Profit Sharing:	Top Exec. Salary: $1,300,000	Bonus: $240,240
Savings Plan: Y	Stock Purch. Plan:		Second Exec. Salary: $942,308	Bonus: $154,000

OTHER THOUGHTS:

Apparent Women Officers or Directors: 2
Hot Spot for Advancement for Women/Minorities: Y

LOCATIONS: ("Y" = Yes)

West:	Southwest:	Midwest:	Southeast:	Northeast:	International:
Y	Y	Y	Y	Y	Y

SNAM RETE GAS SPA

www.snamretegas.it

Industry Group Code: 221210 **Ranks within this company's industry group:** Sales: 6 Profits: 2

Exploration/Production:		Refining/Retailing:		Utilities:		Alternative Energy:		Specialty Services:		Energy Mktg./Other Svcs.	
Exploration:		Refining:		Electric Utility:		Waste/Solar/Other:		Consulting/Eng.:	Y	Energy Marketing:	
Production:		Retailing:		Gas Utility:		Thermal/Steam:		Seismic:		Equipment/Machinery:	
Coal Production:		Convenience Stores:		Pipelines:	Y	Wind:		Drilling:		Oil Field Services:	
		Chemicals:		Water:		Hydro:		InfoTech:		Air/Shipping Transportation:	Y
						Fuel Cells:		Specialty Services:	Y		

TYPES OF BUSINESS:

Natural Gas Pipelines & Distribution
Gas Storage
Fiber-Optic Network
Consulting Services
Construction Services

BRANDS/DIVISIONS/AFFILIATES:

Eni SPA
GNL Italia S.p.A.
Stogit S.p.A.
Italgas S.p.A.

CONTACTS:

Note: Officers with more than one job title may be intentionally listed here more than once.

Carlo Malacarne, CEO
Antonio Paccioretti, CFO
Fabrizio Barbieri, Dir.-Human Resources & Organization
Marco Reggiani, General Counsel/Dir.-Corp. Affairs
Francesco Iovane, Managing Dir.-Oper.
Eduardo Di Benedetto, Dir.-Bus. Dev. & Commercial
Patrizia Rutigliano, Dir.-Public Affairs & Comm.
Marco Porro, Head-Investor Rel.
Geatano Mazzitelli, Dir.-Regulatory Affairs
Silvio Bianchi, Head-Internal Audit
Paolo Mosa, CEO-Italgas
Paolo Bacchetta, CEO-Stogit
Salvatore Sardo, Chmn.
Salvatore De Gaetano, Dir.-Supply Chain

Phone: 39-02-520-1	**Fax:** 39-02-520-38227
Toll-Free:	
Address: Piazza Santa Barbara, 7, San Donato Milanese, Milan, 20097 Italy	

GROWTH PLANS/SPECIAL FEATURES:

Snam Rete Gas S.p.A., a publicly-traded subsidiary of Eni S.p.A., provides transportation, storage and distribution of natural gas, as well as regasification of liquid natural gas (LNG), in Italy. The company operates a network of more than 19,573 miles of natural gas pipeline and transports over 3 trillion cubic feet of natural gas annually, which represents around 94% of Italy's entire transportation business. The network is overseen by eight supervisory districts, 55 local management centers, 11 compressor stations and one dispatch center. Snam Rete Gas' pipeline is directly connected to the production fields, import lines and storage centers that feed the Italian gas system. With the acquisition of Stogit in 2009, the firm became a leading operator of natural gas storage facilities in Italy. Stogit oversees natural gas storage activities at eight storage fields across Italy, with a combined capacity of 45.6 billion cubic feet. Italgas, another acquisition in 2009, is responsible for the distribution of natural gas to third-party marketers of gas to end users. The firm has a pipeline distribution network spanning over 31,000 miles. Through its wholly-owned subsidiary GNL Italia S.p.A., the company owns and manages a LNG regasification plant in Panigaglia, Italy, which has a production capacity of 57,415 cubic feet per day. The firm also provides leasing space on its fiber-optic network, as well as consulting, construction, maintenance and operation services for retail gas sellers. n June 2009, the company acquired Stogit S.p.A. and Italgas S.p.A., an Italian gas distribution company, for a combined $6.67 billion.

FINANCIALS:

Sales and profits are in thousands of dollars—add 000 to get the full amount. 2010 Note: Financial information for 2010 was not available for all companies at press time.

2010 Sales: $	2010 Profits: $	**U.S. Stock Ticker: Subsidiary**
2009 Sales: $3,447,690	2009 Profits: $1,026,730	**Int'l Ticker: SRG** Int'l Exchange: Milan-BI
2008 Sales: $2,673,430	2008 Profits: $743,400	Employees: 6,187
2007 Sales: $2,626,900	2007 Profits: $873,200	Fiscal Year Ends: 12/31
2006 Sales: $2,581,300	2006 Profits: $658,600	Parent Company: ENI SPA

SALARIES/BENEFITS:

Pension Plan:	ESOP Stock Plan:	Profit Sharing:	Top Exec. Salary: $	Bonus: $
Savings Plan:	Stock Purch. Plan:		Second Exec. Salary: $	Bonus: $

OTHER THOUGHTS:

Apparent Women Officers or Directors:
Hot Spot for Advancement for Women/Minorities:

LOCATIONS: ("Y" = Yes)

West:	Southwest:	Midwest:	Southeast:	Northeast:	International:
					Y

S-OIL CORPORATION

www.s-oil.com

Industry Group Code: 324110 **Ranks within this company's industry group:** Sales: 16 Profits: 12

Exploration/Production:		Refining/Retailing:		Utilities:		Alternative Energy:		Specialty Services:		Energy Mktg./Other Svcs.	
Exploration:		Refining:	Y	Electric Utility:		Waste/Solar/Other:		Consulting/Eng.:		Energy Marketing:	
Production:		Retailing:		Gas Utility:		Thermal/Steam:		Seismic:		Equipment/Machinery:	
Coal Production:		Convenience Stores:		Pipelines:		Wind:		Drilling:		Oil Field Services:	
		Chemicals:		Water:		Hydro:		InfoTech:		Air/Shipping Transportation:	
						Fuel Cells:		Specialty Services:			

TYPES OF BUSINESS:

Oil Refining & Marketing

BRANDS/DIVISIONS/AFFILIATES:

Ultra-S
STX Corporation

CONTACTS:

Note: Officers with more than one job title may be intentionally listed here more than once.

Ahmed A. Al-Subaey, CEO
Yeol Ryu, CFO/VP
Dong Cheol Kim, Exec. VP
Bong Su Park, Exec. VP
Seong Gi Ha, Exec. VP
Yong Hui Lee, VP
Yang Ho Cho, Chmn.

Phone: 82-2-3772-5151 **Fax:**
Toll-Free:
Address: 63rd Fl. Bldg., 60 Yoido-dong, Yeongdungpo-Gu, Seoul, 150-607 Korea

GROWTH PLANS/SPECIAL FEATURES:

S-Oil Corporation is a Korean firm involved in the oil refining and marketing business. It operates in three segments: oil refining, petrochemical and lube oil. The oil refining segment produces gasoline for automobiles; premium gasoline; diesel and kerosene used as heating fuel; and bunker-C oil used as fuel for industries and marine transportation. The company's bunker-C oil cracking center is able to convert the petroleum products into light and low-sulfur products. This helps the firm cope with the changes in circumstances such as increased demand for light oils in the domestic and overseas markets and strengthened environmental regulation. The petrochemical segment offers xylene, para-xylene, benzene and toluene. The lube oil division provides automotive oils such as gasoline engine oil, diesel engine oil, transmission oil and gear oil; and industrial oils, including hydraulic oil, compressor oil and gear oil. This division markets products under the Ultra-S brand name. Facilities under the firm's management include a crude oil refinery with a 580,000 barrels per day (b/d) capacity; a bunker-C cracking center with capacity of 292,000 b/d; a BTX (benzene-toluene-xylene) production plant with an annual capacity of nearly 1 million tons; a para-xylene plant with 650,000 tons of annual production capacity; and a lube oil plant with output levels of 24,000 b/d. In October 2010, the firm signed a partnership agreement with fellow Korean company STX Corporation to collaborate on new business opportunities related to domestic and international energy operations.

FINANCIALS:

Sales and profits are in thousands of dollars—add 000 to get the full amount. 2010 Note: Financial information for 2010 was not available for all companies at press time.

2010 Sales: $	2010 Profits: $	**U.S. Stock Ticker:**
2009 Sales: $14,029,200	2009 Profits: $183,540	**Int'l Ticker: 010950** Int'l Exchange: Seoul-KRX
2008 Sales: $19,477,160	2008 Profits: $376,140	Employees:
2007 Sales: $12,838,380	2007 Profits: $629,300	Fiscal Year Ends:
2006 Sales: $	2006 Profits: $	Parent Company:

SALARIES/BENEFITS:

Pension Plan:	ESOP Stock Plan:	Profit Sharing:	Top Exec. Salary: $	Bonus: $
Savings Plan:	Stock Purch. Plan:		Second Exec. Salary: $	Bonus: $

OTHER THOUGHTS:

Apparent Women Officers or Directors:
Hot Spot for Advancement for Women/Minorities:

LOCATIONS: ("Y" = Yes)

West:	Southwest:	Midwest:	Southeast:	Northeast:	International:
					Y

SONATRACH

www.sonatrach-dz.com

Industry Group Code: 211111 **Ranks within this company's industry group:** Sales: Profits:

Exploration/Production:		Refining/Retailing:		Utilities:		Alternative Energy:		Specialty Services:		Energy Mktg./Other Svcs.	
Exploration:	Y	Refining:	Y	Electric Utility:		Waste/Solar/Other:	Y	Consulting/Eng.:		Energy Marketing:	
Production:	Y	Retailing:	Y	Gas Utility:		Thermal/Steam:		Seismic:		Equipment/Machinery:	
Coal Production:		Convenience Stores:		Pipelines:	Y	Wind:		Drilling:		Oil Field Services:	
		Chemicals:	Y	Water:		Hydro:		InfoTech:		Air/Shipping Transportation:	Y
						Fuel Cells:		Specialty Services:	Y		

TYPES OF BUSINESS:

Oil & Gas Exploration & Production
Renewable Energy
Water Desalination
Refineries
Petrochemicals
Oil & Gas Transportation

BRANDS/DIVISIONS/AFFILIATES:

Endesa SA
Compania Espanola de Petroleos SA
Iberdrola SA
GDF Suez SA

CONTACTS:

Note: Officers with more than one job title may be intentionally listed here more than once.

Nourredine Cherouati, CEO
Ali Rezaiguia, Exec. Dir.-Finance
Shawki M. Rahal, VP-Mktg.
Malika Belkahla, Exec. Dir.-Human Resources
Abdelmalek Zitouni, Sec. Gen.
Fatma-Zohra Benoughlis, Exec. Dir.-Strategy, Planning & Economics
Boumediene Belkacem, VP-Upstream
Benamar Zenasni, VP-Pipeline Transportation
Abdelhafid Feghouli, VP-Downstream
Abdelaziz Abdelouahab, Exec. Dir.-Central Activities
Mohamed Meziane, Chmn.

Phone: 213-2154-7000	**Fax:** 213-2154-7700
Toll-Free:	
Address: Djenane El Malik, Hydra, Algiers, Algeria	

GROWTH PLANS/SPECIAL FEATURES:

Sonatrach, wholly-owned by the Algerian government, researches, explores, refines, transports and markets hydrocarbons and refined hydrocarbon derivatives, including oil and gas variations. The firm is also involved in electrical power, renewable energies and the desalination of seawater. Sonatrach is a leading oil producer on the African continent and is a world leader in natural gas exports, with operations in West and North Africa, western Europe, the U.S. and Peru. The company's activities represent about 30% of the gross national product of Algeria. The company divides its activities into four segments: upstream, downstream, transportation and marketing. The upstream segment manages the company's hydrocarbon research, development and production. The downstream segment primarily includes the firm's liquefied natural gas (LNG) and liquefied petroleum gas (LPG) separation and refining operations; its petrochemicals activities; five crude oil refineries; and its industrial gases activities. Sonatrach's downstream operations include four LNG refineries, two petroleum refineries, two petrochemical facilities, one helium extracting facility and five refineries. The transportation segment includes the company's activities related to the transport of liquid and gaseous hydrocarbons by pipeline. Sonatrach maintains a 4,600-mile gas and oil pipeline network, including two transcontinental gas pipelines. The marketing segment manages the firm's sales operations and shipping activities. In August 2010, the firm commenced operations of the Medgaz pipeline connecting Algeria and Spain. The pipeline is managed by Sonatrach in conjunction with Endesa; Compania Espanola de Petroleos; Iberdrola; and GDF Suez.

FINANCIALS:

Sales and profits are in thousands of dollars—add 000 to get the full amount. 2010 Note: Financial information for 2010 was not available for all companies at press time.

2010 Sales: $	2010 Profits: $	**U.S. Stock Ticker: Government-Owned**
2009 Sales: $	2009 Profits: $	**Int'l Ticker:** Int'l Exchange:
2008 Sales: $	2008 Profits: $	Employees:
2007 Sales: $	2007 Profits: $	Fiscal Year Ends: 12/31
2006 Sales: $	2006 Profits: $	Parent Company:

SALARIES/BENEFITS:

Pension Plan:	ESOP Stock Plan:	Profit Sharing:	Top Exec. Salary: $	Bonus: $
Savings Plan:	Stock Purch. Plan:		Second Exec. Salary: $	Bonus: $

OTHER THOUGHTS:

Apparent Women Officers or Directors: 2
Hot Spot for Advancement for Women/Minorities:

LOCATIONS: ("Y" = Yes)

West:	Southwest:	Midwest:	Southeast:	Northeast:	International:
				Y	Y

SOUTHERN CALIFORNIA EDISON COMPANY

www.sce.com

Industry Group Code: 2211 **Ranks within this company's industry group:** Sales: 20 Profits: 8

Exploration/Production:		Refining/Retailing:		Utilities:		Alternative Energy:		Specialty Services:		Energy Mktg./Other Svcs.	
Exploration:		Refining:		Electric Utility:	Y	Waste/Solar/Other:		Consulting/Eng.:		Energy Marketing:	
Production:		Retailing:		Gas Utility:		Thermal/Steam:		Seismic:		Equipment/Machinery:	
Coal Production:		Convenience Stores:		Pipelines:		Wind:		Drilling:		Oil Field Services:	
		Chemicals:		Water:		Hydro:	Y	InfoTech:		Air/Shipping Transportation:	
						Fuel Cells:		Specialty Services:			

TYPES OF BUSINESS:

Electric Utility
Nuclear Generation
Hydroelectric Generation

BRANDS/DIVISIONS/AFFILIATES:

Edison International

CONTACTS:

Note: Officers with more than one job title may be intentionally listed here more than once.

Alan J. Fohrer, CEO
John R. Fielder, Pres.
Linda G. Sullivan, CFO/Sr. VP
Stephen E. Pickett, General Counsel/Sr. VP
Cecil R. House, Sr. VP-Oper. Support
Barbara J. Parsky, Sr. VP-Corp. Comm.
Richard M. Rosenblum, Sr. VP-Generation
Pedro J. Pizarro, VP-Power Procurement
Alan J. Fohrer, Chmn.
Cecil R. House, Chief Procurement Officer

Phone: 626-302-1212	**Fax:** 626-302-2517
Toll-Free: 800-655-4555	
Address: 2244 Walnut Grove Ave., Rosemead, CA 91770 US	

GROWTH PLANS/SPECIAL FEATURES:

Southern California Edison Company (SCE) is one of the largest electric utilities in the U.S. The firm is the largest subsidiary of Edison International, an electric power generator, distributor and investor in infrastructure and renewable energy projects. SCE serves more than 13 million individuals in over 400 cities and communities in a 50,000-square-mile service area within central, coastal and southern California, excluding Los Angeles. The firm operates the following generating facilities: a 78.21% interest in San Onofre Units 2 and 3, pressurized water nuclear units with 1,760 MW capacity; the natural-gas fueled Mountainview plant, 1,050 MW capacity; 36 hydroelectric plants located in surrounding mountain passes, 1,179 MW; a 15.8% interest in Palo Verde, 591 MW; a 48% in Units 4 and 5 at Four Corners Generating Station, 720 MW; and other smaller generating facilities. SCE has a total capacity of 42.7% nuclear, 21.4% hydroelectric, 19.1% natural gas, 16.6% coal and less than 1% diesel, with power generation in California, Nevada, Arizona and New Mexico. The firm's transmission network consists of approximately 12,000 circuit miles of lines and 858 substations, while its distribution network consists of approximately 60,000 circuit miles of overhead lines, 39,000 miles of underground lines, 1.5 million poles and 588 distribution substations. Approximately 42% of the company's revenues are derived from commercial customers; 39% residential customers; 2% resale sales; 6% industrial customers; 6% public authorities; and 5% agricultural and other customers. In mid 2009, the firm and First Solar, Inc. agreed to build two large-scale solar power facilities in San Bernardino and Riverside, California. In September 2009, the firm installed 5 million smart meters, new digital, secure, two-way communication meters that measure electricity usage up to the minute.

Employee benefits include medical, dental, and vision benefits; 401(k) with company match; employee assistance program; retirement pension plan; and educational reimbursements.

FINANCIALS:

Sales and profits are in thousands of dollars—add 000 to get the full amount. 2010 Note: Financial information for 2010 was not available for all companies at press time.

2010 Sales: $	2010 Profits: $	**U.S. Stock Ticker: Subsidiary**
2009 Sales: $9,965,000	2009 Profits: $1,371,000	**Int'l Ticker:** Int'l Exchange:
2008 Sales: $11,248,000	2008 Profits: $904,000	Employees: 17,348
2007 Sales: $10,233,000	2007 Profits: $1,063,000	Fiscal Year Ends: 12/31
2006 Sales: $10,312,000	2006 Profits: $827,000	Parent Company: EDISON INTERNATIONAL

SALARIES/BENEFITS:

Pension Plan: Y	ESOP Stock Plan:	Profit Sharing:	Top Exec. Salary: $	Bonus: $1,936,000
Savings Plan: Y	Stock Purch. Plan:		Second Exec. Salary: $	Bonus: $

OTHER THOUGHTS:

Apparent Women Officers or Directors: 3
Hot Spot for Advancement for Women/Minorities: Y

LOCATIONS: ("Y" = Yes)

West:	Southwest:	Midwest:	Southeast:	Northeast:	International:
Y	Y				

SOUTHERN CALIFORNIA GAS COMPANY

www.socalgas.com

Industry Group Code: 221210 **Ranks within this company's industry group:** Sales: Profits:

Exploration/Production:		Refining/Retailing:		Utilities:		Alternative Energy:		Specialty Services:		Energy Mktg./Other Svcs.	
Exploration:		Refining:		Electric Utility:		Waste/Solar/Other:		Consulting/Eng.:		Energy Marketing:	
Production:		Retailing:		Gas Utility:	Y	Thermal/Steam:		Seismic:		Equipment/Machinery:	
Coal Production:		Convenience Stores:		Pipelines:	Y	Wind:		Drilling:		Oil Field Services:	
		Chemicals:		Water:		Hydro:		InfoTech:		Air/Shipping Transportation:	
						Fuel Cells:		Specialty Services:			

TYPES OF BUSINESS:

Natural Gas Utility
Pipelines

BRANDS/DIVISIONS/AFFILIATES:

Sempra Energy
FAR OFF
San Diego Gas and Electric Company
Sempra Pipelines and Storage
Sempra LNG

CONTACTS:

Note: Officers with more than one job title may be intentionally listed here more than once.

Michael W. Allman, CEO
Anne Shen Smith, COO
Michael W. Allman, Pres.
Robert M. Schlax, CFO/Controller/VP
Jimmie I. Cho, VP-Human Resources, Diversity & Inclusion
Pamela J. Fair, VP-Environmental, Safety & Facilities
J. Chris Baker, CIO/Sr. VP-Support Svcs.
Richard M. Morrow, VP-Eng. & Oper. Staff
Erbin B. Keith, General Counsel/Sr. VP-External Affairs
Michael P. Gallagher, Sr. VP-Oper.
Lee Schavrien, Sr. VP-Finance, Regulatory & Legislative Affairs
Lee M. Stewart, Sr. VP-Gas Oper.
James P. Harrigan, VP-Gas Acquisition
J. Bret Lane, VP-Field Svcs.
Margot A. Kyd, VP-Supply Mgmt.

Phone: 213-244-1200	**Fax:** 213-244-3897
Toll-Free:	
Address: 555 W. 5th St., Los Angeles, CA 90013 US	

GROWTH PLANS/SPECIAL FEATURES:

Southern California Gas Company (SoCalGas) is one of the nation's largest natural gas distribution utilities. Its main activity is the management of its pipeline system, along with compressor stations and underground storage facilities. The firm serves approximately 20.5 million customers through 5.7 million gas meters in over 500 communities. The company is a subsidiary of Sempra Energy, a natural gas and electricity distributor and generator with multiple subsidiaries in addition to SoCalGas, including San Diego Gas and Electric Company; Sempra Pipelines and Storage; and Sempra LNG. Customers include residential, commercial, industrial, utility electric generation and wholesale clients. SoCalGas has a territory of approximately 20,000 square miles that covers the majority of southern and central California, including the cities of Los Angeles, Palm Springs, Ventura, Santa Barbara, Bakersfield and San Luis Obispo. The commercial division offers builder services, events and training at the Energy Resource Center, as well as the FAR OFF (Firm Access Receipt Rights And Off-System Delivery) product. The FAR OFF system enables customers, gas suppliers and producers access receipt point rights. Holders of these rights can hold firm and/or interruptible access rights at receipt points into the SoCalGas/SDG&E integrated gas transmission system with the option to trade their rights or exchange receipt points electronically.

The firm offers its employees benefits including health, life, AD&D and vision coverage; domestic partnership benefits; pension and retirement plans; subsidized transportation; an employee assistance program; education assistance; a scholarship program; and a wellness program.

FINANCIALS:

Sales and profits are in thousands of dollars—add 000 to get the full amount. 2010 Note: Financial information for 2010 was not available for all companies at press time.

2010 Sales: $	2010 Profits: $	**U.S. Stock Ticker: Subsidiary**
2009 Sales: $	2009 Profits: $	**Int'l Ticker:** Int'l Exchange:
2008 Sales: $	2008 Profits: $	Employees:
2007 Sales: $	2007 Profits: $	Fiscal Year Ends: 12/31
2006 Sales: $4,181,000	2006 Profits: $224,000	Parent Company: SEMPRA ENERGY

SALARIES/BENEFITS:

Pension Plan: Y	ESOP Stock Plan:	Profit Sharing:	Top Exec. Salary: $	Bonus: $
Savings Plan: Y	Stock Purch. Plan:		Second Exec. Salary: $	Bonus: $

OTHER THOUGHTS:

Apparent Women Officers or Directors: 3
Hot Spot for Advancement for Women/Minorities: Y

LOCATIONS: ("Y" = Yes)

West:	Southwest:	Midwest:	Southeast:	Northeast:	International:
Y					

SOUTHERN COMPANY (THE)

www.southerncompany.com

Industry Group Code: 2211 **Ranks within this company's industry group:** Sales: 10 Profits: 6

Exploration/Production:		Refining/Retailing:		Utilities:		Alternative Energy:		Specialty Services:		Energy Mktg./Other Svcs.	
Exploration:		Refining:		Electric Utility:	Y	Waste/Solar/Other:	Y	Consulting/Eng.:	Y	Energy Marketing:	
Production:		Retailing:		Gas Utility:	Y	Thermal/Steam:		Seismic:		Equipment/Machinery:	
Coal Production:		Convenience Stores:		Pipelines:		Wind:		Drilling:		Oil Field Services:	
		Chemicals:		Water:		Hydro:		InfoTech:		Air/Shipping Transportation:	
						Fuel Cells:		Specialty Services:	Y		

TYPES OF BUSINESS:

Utilities-Electricity & Natural Gas
Wireless Communications Services
Fiber Optic Solutions
Nuclear Power Operating Services
Consulting Services

BRANDS/DIVISIONS/AFFILIATES:

Alabama Power Company
Georgia Power Company
Mississippi Power Company
Gulf Power Company
Southern Power
SEGCO
Southern Nuclear
Nacogdoches Power LLC

CONTACTS: *Note: Officers with more than one job title may be intentionally listed here more than once.*

Thomas A. Fanning, CEO
Anthony J. Topazi, COO/Exec. VP
Thomas A. Fanning, Pres.
Art P. Beattie, CFO/Exec. VP
Chris Womack, Pres., External Affairs
Michael D. Garrett, CEO/Pres., Georgia Power
Susan N. Story, Pres./CEO-Gulf Power Company
Charles D. McCrary, CEO/Pres., Alabama Power
James H. Miller, III, Chmn./CEO/Pres., Southern Nuclear
Thomas A. Fanning, Chmn.

Phone: 404-506-5000	**Fax:** 404-506-0455
Toll-Free:	
Address: 30 Ivan Allen Jr. Blvd. NW, Atlanta, GA 30308 US	

GROWTH PLANS/SPECIAL FEATURES:

The Southern Company, through its subsidiaries, is a producer and distributor of electricity in the U.S. Its four main subsidiaries (Alabama Power Company; Georgia Power Company; Mississippi Power Company; and Gulf Power Company) have a combined service territory of 120,000 square miles. It also owns Southern Power, which constructs, acquires and manages power generation assets and sells electricity. Southern Power owns almost 7,800 megawatts (MW) of generating capacity, through a total of 10 power plants, and serves investor-owned utilities, Independent Power Producers, municipalities and electric cooperatives across five states. Alabama Power and Georgia Power each own 50% of SEGCO, which operates a power generation plant and 230,000 miles of transmission lines in Alabama, supplying electricity to both Alabama and Georgia. Combined, the company's utility subsidiaries have a generating capacity of roughly 42,000 MW and serve more than 4.4 million residential, commercial and industrial electricity customers in the southeastern U.S. through 73 fossil and hydro generation plants. Its sources of generation consist of 57% coal; 23% oil and gas; 16% nuclear; and 4% hydro. The firm also owns Southern Nuclear, which operates the company's nuclear power plants; SouthernLINC Wireless, which provides digital wireless communications and wholesale fiber optic solutions; and Southern Renewable Energy, formed in January 2010 to acquire, own and construct renewable generation assets. In October 2009, Southern Power acquired Nacogdoches Power LLC and announced plans to construct a biomass power plant in Texas; and agreed to acquire West Georgia Generating Company LLC, which owns a 600 MW plant in Georgia. In March 2010, the firm and Turner Renewable Energy acquired a 30 MW solar power plant.

The Southern Company offers its employees medical, dental and prescription drug coverage; an employee assistance program; life insurance; flexible spending accounts; tuition reimbursement; adoption assistance; a pension plan; and a savings plan.

FINANCIALS: **Sales and profits are in thousands of dollars—add 000 to get the full amount. 2010 Note: Financial information for 2010 was not available for all companies at press time.**

2010 Sales: $	2010 Profits: $	**U.S. Stock Ticker: SO**
2009 Sales: $15,743,000	2009 Profits: $1,643,000	**Int'l Ticker:** Int'l Exchange:
2008 Sales: $17,127,000	2008 Profits: $1,742,000	Employees: 26,112
2007 Sales: $15,353,000	2007 Profits: $1,734,000	Fiscal Year Ends: 12/31
2006 Sales: $14,356,000	2006 Profits: $1,573,000	Parent Company:

SALARIES/BENEFITS:

Pension Plan: Y	ESOP Stock Plan:	Profit Sharing:	Top Exec. Salary: $1,172,908	Bonus: $5,019,745
Savings Plan: Y	Stock Purch. Plan:		Second Exec. Salary: $722,149	Bonus: $847,998

OTHER THOUGHTS:

Apparent Women Officers or Directors: 3
Hot Spot for Advancement for Women/Minorities: Y

LOCATIONS: ("Y" = Yes)

West:	Southwest:	Midwest:	Southeast:	Northeast:	International:
			Y		

SOUTHERN UNION COMPANY

www.sug.com

Industry Group Code: 221210 **Ranks within this company's industry group:** Sales: 10 Profits: 9

Exploration/Production:		Refining/Retailing:		Utilities:		Alternative Energy:		Specialty Services:		Energy Mktg./Other Svcs.	
Exploration:		Refining:	Y	Electric Utility:		Waste/Solar/Other:		Consulting/Eng.:		Energy Marketing:	Y
Production:		Retailing:		Gas Utility:	Y	Thermal/Steam:		Seismic:		Equipment/Machinery:	Y
Coal Production:		Convenience Stores:		Pipelines:	Y	Wind:		Drilling:		Oil Field Services:	
		Chemicals:		Water:		Hydro:		InfoTech:		Air/Shipping Transportation:	
						Fuel Cells:		Specialty Services:	Y		

TYPES OF BUSINESS:

Utilities-Electricity & Natural Gas
Natural Gas Pipelines
Gas Appliances & Appliance Service
Electricity Generation

BRANDS/DIVISIONS/AFFILIATES:

Panhandle Eastern Pipeline Co. LP
Citrus Corp.
Florida Gas Transmission Co., LLC
Missouri Gas Energy
New England Gas Co.
Southern Union Gas Services

CONTACTS: *Note: Officers with more than one job title may be intentionally listed here more than once.*

George L. Lindemann, CEO
Eric D. Herschmann, COO/Vice Chmn.
Eric D. Herschmann, Pres.
Richard N. Marshall, CFO/Sr. VP
Monica M. Gaudiosi, General Counsel/Sr. VP
Robert O. Bond, Sr. VP-Pipeline Oper.
John Barnett, Dir.-External Affairs
Jack Walsh, VP-Investor Rel.
Robert O. Bond, Pres./COO-Panhandle Energy
George L. Lindemann, Chmn.

Phone: 713-989-2000 **Fax:**
Toll-Free:
Address: 5444 Westheimer Rd., Houston, TX 77056 US

GROWTH PLANS/SPECIAL FEATURES:

Southern Union Company (SUG) owns and operates assets in the regulated and unregulated natural gas industry and gathers, processes, transports, stores and distributes natural gas in the U.S. The company operates in three reportable segments: transportation and storage; gathering and processing; and distribution. The transportation and storage segment's operations include interstate transportation and storage of natural gas to Midwest, Southwest and Florida markets; and liquefied natural gas terminalling and regasification services. This segment operates through Panhandle Eastern Pipe Line Company, LP and its subsidiaries (Panhandle) and its 50% interest in Florida Gas Transmission Company LLC through Citrus Corp. The gathering and processing segment is primarily engaged in the gathering, treating, processing and redelivery of natural gas and natural gas liquids (NGLs) in Texas and New Mexico. Its operations are conducted through Southern Union Gas Services (SUGS), which controls a network of approximately 5,500 miles of natural gas and NGL pipelines; four cryogenic processing plants, with a combined capacity of 410 million cubic feet per day (MMcf/d); and five natural gas treating plants, with a combined capacity of 585 MMcf/d. SUGS activities include connecting natural gas wells to its gathering system; treating natural gas to remove impurities and NGL; and redelivering natural gas and NGLs to various markets. SUGS's primary resources are located in the Permian Basin of Texas and New Mexico. The distribution segment primarily distributes natural gas locally in Missouri and Massachusetts, serving over 550,000 residential, commercial and industrial customers through 9,140 miles of mains, 6,185 miles of service lines and 45 miles of transmission lines. It operates through Missouri Gas Energy and New England Gas Company.

SUG offers its employees health, dental, vision and group term and dependent life insurance; an employee assistance program; dependent care and medical care pre-tax plans; long-term disability coverage; and a 401(k) plan.

FINANCIALS: **Sales and profits are in thousands of dollars—add 000 to get the full amount. 2010 Note: Financial information for 2010 was not available for all companies at press time.**

2010 Sales: $	2010 Profits: $	**U.S. Stock Ticker: SUG**
2009 Sales: $2,179,018	2009 Profits: $170,897	**Int'l Ticker:** Int'l Exchange:
2008 Sales: $3,070,154	2008 Profits: $279,412	Employees: 2,446
2007 Sales: $2,616,665	2007 Profits: $211,346	Fiscal Year Ends: 12/31
2006 Sales: $2,340,144	2006 Profits: $64,131	Parent Company:

SALARIES/BENEFITS:

Pension Plan:	ESOP Stock Plan:	Profit Sharing:	Top Exec. Salary: $1,038,462	Bonus: $2,560,000
Savings Plan: Y	Stock Purch. Plan:		Second Exec. Salary: $986,538	Bonus: $2,560,000

OTHER THOUGHTS:

Apparent Women Officers or Directors: 1
Hot Spot for Advancement for Women/Minorities:

LOCATIONS: ("Y" = Yes)

West:	Southwest:	Midwest:	Southeast:	Northeast:	International:
Y	Y	Y	Y	Y	

Note: Financial information, benefits and other data can change quickly and may vary from those stated here.

SOUTHWEST GAS CORP

www.swgas.com

Industry Group Code: 221210 **Ranks within this company's industry group:** Sales: 14 Profits: 15

Exploration/Production:		Refining/Retailing:		Utilities:		Alternative Energy:		Specialty Services:		Energy Mktg./Other Svcs.	
Exploration:		Refining:		Electric Utility:		Waste/Solar/Other:		Consulting/Eng.:		Energy Marketing:	
Production:		Retailing:		Gas Utility:	Y	Thermal/Steam:		Seismic:		Equipment/Machinery:	
Coal Production:		Convenience Stores:		Pipelines:	Y	Wind:		Drilling:		Oil Field Services:	
		Chemicals:		Water:		Hydro:		InfoTech:		Air/Shipping Transportation:	
						Fuel Cells:		Specialty Services:	Y		

TYPES OF BUSINESS:

Utilities-Natural Gas
Pipeline Construction Services

BRANDS/DIVISIONS/AFFILIATES:

Northern Pipeline Construction Co

CONTACTS:

Note: Officers with more than one job title may be intentionally listed here more than once.

Jeffrey W. Shaw, CEO
James P. Kane, Pres.
George C. Biehl, CFO/Exec. VP/Corp. Sec.
James F. Wunderlin, Sr. VP-Tech. Support
James F. Wunderlin, Sr. VP-Eng.
Karen S. Haller, General Counsel/VP/Chief Compliance Officer
James F. Wunderlin, Sr. VP-Bus. Oper.
Edward A. Janov, Sr. VP-Finance
Kenneth J. Kenny, VP/Treas.
Roy R. Centrella, VP/Controller/Chief Acct. Officer
John P. Hester, Sr. VP-Regulatory Affairs & Energy Resources
Donald L. Soderberg, VP-Pricing
James J. Kropid, Chmn.

Phone: 702-876-7011 **Fax:**
Toll-Free: 800-331-1119
Address: 5241 Spring Mountain Rd., Las Vegas, NV 89150-0002 US

GROWTH PLANS/SPECIAL FEATURES:

Southwest Gas Corp. purchases, transports and distributes natural gas to approximately 1.82 million residential, commercial and industrial customers in Arizona, Nevada and California. Approximately 86% of the firm's customers are residential and small business customers; 10% are transportation companies; and 4% are industrial or other customers. The company operates in two segments: natural gas operations and construction services. The natural gas segment is one of the largest distributors in Arizona, selling and transporting natural gas in most of central and southern Arizona, including the Phoenix and Tucson metropolitan areas. It is also one of the largest suppliers of natural gas in Nevada, serving the Las Vegas metropolitan area and northern Nevada. In California, the company serves regions such as the Lake Tahoe area and the high desert and mountain areas in San Bernardino County. The company acquires its gas supplies from about 47 suppliers. The firm transports much of its gas through the pipelines of El Paso Natural Gas Company; Northwest Pipeline Corp.; Kern River Gas Transmission Company; Tuscarora Gas Pipeline Company.; Transwestern Pipeline Company; Southern California Gas Co.; and Paiute. The construction services segment, through Northern Pipeline Construction Co. (NPL), is an underground piping contractor that provides utility companies with trenching and installation, replacement and maintenance services for energy distribution systems. NPL contracts primarily with local distribution companies to install, repair and maintain energy distribution systems from the town border station to the end-user. Construction operations are conducted from 17 field locations, with sales to Southwest Gas accounting for 19% of NPL's revenues.

FINANCIALS:

Sales and profits are in thousands of dollars—add 000 to get the full amount. 2010 Note: Financial information for 2010 was not available for all companies at press time.

2010 Sales: $	2010 Profits: $	**U.S. Stock Ticker: SWX**
2009 Sales: $1,893,824	2009 Profits: $87,482	**Int'l Ticker:** Int'l Exchange:
2008 Sales: $2,144,743	2008 Profits: $60,973	Employees: 2,423
2007 Sales: $2,152,088	2007 Profits: $83,246	Fiscal Year Ends: 12/31
2006 Sales: $2,024,758	2006 Profits: $83,860	Parent Company:

SALARIES/BENEFITS:

Pension Plan:	ESOP Stock Plan:	Profit Sharing:	Top Exec. Salary: $654,521	Bonus: $352,176
Savings Plan:	Stock Purch. Plan:		Second Exec. Salary: $417,893	Bonus: $195,530

OTHER THOUGHTS:

Apparent Women Officers or Directors: 3
Hot Spot for Advancement for Women/Minorities: Y

LOCATIONS: ("Y" = Yes)

West:	Southwest:	Midwest:	Southeast:	Northeast:	International:
Y	Y				

SOUTHWESTERN ENERGY CO

www.swn.com

Industry Group Code: 211111 **Ranks within this company's industry group:** Sales: 71 Profits: 78

Exploration/Production:		Refining/Retailing:		Utilities:		Alternative Energy:		Specialty Services:		Energy Mktg./Other Svcs.	
Exploration:	Y	Refining:		Electric Utility:		Waste/Solar/Other:		Consulting/Eng.:		Energy Marketing:	Y
Production:	Y	Retailing:		Gas Utility:		Thermal/Steam:		Seismic:		Equipment/Machinery:	
Coal Production:		Convenience Stores:		Pipelines:		Wind:		Drilling:		Oil Field Services:	
		Chemicals:		Water:		Hydro:		InfoTech:		Air/Shipping Transportation:	
						Fuel Cells:		Specialty Services:			

TYPES OF BUSINESS:

Oil & Gas Exploration & Production
Gas Utility

BRANDS/DIVISIONS/AFFILIATES:

SEECO Inc
Southwestern Energy Production Co
Southwestern Energies Services Co
DeSoto Gathering Co LLC
DeSoto Drilling Inc
Angelina Gathering Company LLC

CONTACTS: *Note: Officers with more than one job title may be intentionally listed here more than once.*

Steven L. Mueller, CEO
Steven L. Mueller, Pres.
Greg D. Kerley, CFO/Exec. VP
Jennifer N. McCauley, Sr. VP-Human Resources
Dee W. Hency, CIO
Dee W. Hency, Sr. VP-Admin.
Mark K. Boling, General Counsel/Exec. VP/Sec.
Sonny H. Bryan, VP-Oper., SEECO, Inc.
Jim R. Dewbre, Sr. VP-Bus. & Land Dev., SEECO, Inc.
Timothy J. O'Donnell, VP-Corp. Affairs
Bradley D. Sylvester, VP-Investor Rel.
Robert C. Owen, Controller/Chief Acct. Officer
Gene A. Hammons, Pres., Southwestern Midstream Services Co.
William N. Banks, VP/Treas.
Danny W. Ferguson, VP-Gov't & Community Rel.
James L. Bolander, Jr., VP-Health, Safety & Environmental
Harold M. Korell, Chmn.

Phone: 281-618-4700 **Fax:** 281-618-4818
Toll-Free:
Address: 2350 N. Sam Houston Pkwy. E., Ste. 125, Houston, TX 77032 US

GROWTH PLANS/SPECIAL FEATURES:

Southwestern Energy Co. is an integrated energy company. The firm is primarily engaged in the exploration, development and production of crude oil and natural gas. The company also focuses on creating and capturing additional value through its drilling and gathering businesses. Southwestern Energy operates in two segments: exploration and production; and midstream services. Southwestern Energy conducts the majority of its exploration and production operations in the Arkoma Basin of Arkansas (called Fayetteville Shale play), Texas, Pennsylvania and Oklahoma. The exploration and production segment engages in natural gas and oil exploration and production through its wholly-owned subsidiaries SEECO, Inc., and Southwestern Energy Production Co. (SEPCO). SEECO operates exclusively in Arkansas, holds a large base of both developed and undeveloped gas reserves and conducts both the ongoing conventional drilling program in the Arkansas part of the Arkoma Basin and the drilling program for the Fayetteville Shale play. SEPCO conducts development drilling and exploration programs in Oklahoma's Arkoma basin, Texas and Pennsylvania. DeSoto Drilling, Inc., a wholly-owned subsidiary of SEPCO, operates drilling rigs in East Texas and in the Fayetteville Shale play. The midstream services segment markets and transports the firm's gas production and some third-party natural gas. The segment operates through Southwestern Energies Services, Co., a marketing subsidiary; and gathering subsidiaries Angelina Gathering Company, L.L.C. and DeSoto Gathering Co., LLC. In March 2010, Southwestern Energy acquired an exclusive exploration license to over 2.519 million acres in New Brunswick, Canada, to test new hydrocarbon basins. In June 2010, the firm agreed to sell the oil and gas production rights to 20,063 net acres in East Texas to EXCO Resources, Inc. for roughly $355 million.

The company offers employee benefits such as life, long-term disability, health, dental and vision insurance; an employee assistance program; a 401(k); paid vacation and holidays; and educational assistance.

FINANCIALS: **Sales and profits are in thousands of dollars—add 000 to get the full amount. 2010 Note: Financial information for 2010 was not available for all companies at press time.**

2010 Sales: $	2010 Profits: $	**U.S. Stock Ticker: SWN**
2009 Sales: $2,145,779	2009 Profits: $-35,792	**Int'l Ticker:** Int'l Exchange:
2008 Sales: $2,311,552	2008 Profits: $567,946	Employees: 1,702
2007 Sales: $1,255,131	2007 Profits: $221,174	Fiscal Year Ends: 12/31
2006 Sales: $763,112	2006 Profits: $162,636	Parent Company:

SALARIES/BENEFITS:

Pension Plan: Y	ESOP Stock Plan:	Profit Sharing:	Top Exec. Salary: $672,916	Bonus: $3,339,000
Savings Plan: Y	Stock Purch. Plan:		Second Exec. Salary: $440,000	Bonus: $1,447,000

OTHER THOUGHTS:

Apparent Women Officers or Directors: 2
Hot Spot for Advancement for Women/Minorities:

LOCATIONS: ("Y" = Yes)

West:	Southwest:	Midwest:	Southeast:	Northeast:	International:
	Y		Y		

SPECTRA ENERGY CORP

www.spectraenergy.com

Industry Group Code: 486 **Ranks within this company's industry group:** Sales: 13 Profits: 4

Exploration/Production:		**Refining/Retailing:**		**Utilities:**		**Alternative Energy:**		**Specialty Services:**		**Energy Mktg./Other Svcs.**	
Exploration:		Refining:	Y	Electric Utility:		Waste/Solar/Other:		Consulting/Eng.:		Energy Marketing:	
Production:		Retailing:	Y	Gas Utility:		Thermal/Steam:		Seismic:		Equipment/Machinery:	
Coal Production:		Convenience Stores:		Pipelines:	Y	Wind:		Drilling:		Oil Field Services:	Y
		Chemicals:		Water:		Hydro:		InfoTech:		Air/Shipping Transportation:	
						Fuel Cells:		Specialty Services:	Y		

TYPES OF BUSINESS:

Natural Gas Pipelines & Storage
Natural Gas Distribution
Natural Gas Processing
Field Services

BRANDS/DIVISIONS/AFFILIATES:

BC Pipeline
BC Field Services
Algonquin Gas Transmission LLC
Union Gas Limited
DCP Midstream
Ozark Gas Transmission LLC
East Tennessee Natural Gas LLC
Maritimes & Northeast Pipeline LP

CONTACTS:

Note: Officers with more than one job title may be intentionally listed here more than once.

Gregory L. Ebel, CEO
Alan N. Harris, COO
Gregory L. Ebel, Pres.
John Patrick Reddy, CFO
Dorothy Ables, Chief Admin. Officer
Reginald D. Hedgebeth, General Counsel
Alan N. Harris, Chief Dev. Officer
John R. Arensdorf, Chief Comm. Officer
Thomas C. O'Connor, CEO/Pres./Chmn.-DCP Midstream
Julie A. Dill, Pres., Union Gas Limited
Douglas P. Bloom, Pres., Spectra Energy Transmission West
R. Mark Fiedorek, VP-U.S. Transmission & Storage Southeast
William T. Esrey, Chmn.

Phone: 713-627-5400	**Fax:**
Toll-Free:	
Address: 5400 Westheimer Ct., Houston, TX 77056 US	

GROWTH PLANS/SPECIAL FEATURES:

Spectra Energy Corp. is a leading North American midstream natural gas firm. It operates in four segments: U.S. Transmission; Western Canada Transmission and Processing; Distribution; and Field Services. Spectra Energy's U.S. pipeline systems includes over 14,300 miles of transmission pipelines with seven primary transmission systems: Algonquin Gas Transmission, LLC; Ozark Gas Transmission, LLC; Texas Eastern Transmission, LP; East Tennessee Natural Gas, LLC; Maritimes & Northeast Pipeline, LLC; Maritimes & Northeast Pipeline LP; Gulfstream Natural Gas System, LLC; and Southeast Supply Header, LLC. The Western Canada Transmission and Processing segment includes four divisions: BC Pipeline, BC Field Services, Canadian midstream and natural gas liquids (NGL) marketing operations. BC Pipeline and BC Field Services provide natural gas transportation and gas gathering and processing services. The BC Pipeline has approximately 1,800 miles of transmission pipeline in British Columbia and Alberta; it includes 18 mainline compressor stations. The BC Field Services business include five gas processing plants located in British Columbia, 17 field compressor stations and roughly 1,500 miles of gathering pipelines. Its Canadian midstream operations unit includes 11 natural gas processing plants and approximately 600 miles of gathering pipelines. Its NGL division owns majority interest in assets including an NGL extraction facility; an integrated NGL fractionation plant; an NGL transmission pipeline; seven terminals; and two NGL storage plants. Spectra Energy's Field Services segment includes its 50%-interest in DCP Midstream, which owns/operates 58 storage/compression facilities; and approximately 60,000 miles of gathering and transmission pipeline with 36,000 active receipt points. The Distribution segment operates through subsidiary Union Gas Limited, which owns 37,300 miles of pipelines. It serves more than 1.3 million Canadian customers with a transmission system of 3,000 miles. In August 2010, the firm acquired the operations of Bobcat Gas Storage from GE Energy Financial Services and Haddington Energy Partners III LP.

FINANCIALS:

Sales and profits are in thousands of dollars—add 000 to get the full amount. 2010 Note: Financial information for 2010 was not available for all companies at press time.

2010 Sales: $	2010 Profits: $	**U.S. Stock Ticker: SE**
2009 Sales: $4,552,000	2009 Profits: $923,000	**Int'l Ticker:** Int'l Exchange:
2008 Sales: $5,074,000	2008 Profits: $1,129,000	Employees: 5,400
2007 Sales: $4,742,000	2007 Profits: $957,000	Fiscal Year Ends: 12/31
2006 Sales: $4,532,000	2006 Profits: $1,244,000	Parent Company:

SALARIES/BENEFITS:

Pension Plan: Y	ESOP Stock Plan:	Profit Sharing:	Top Exec. Salary: $850,000	Bonus: $926,893
Savings Plan: Y	Stock Purch. Plan:		Second Exec. Salary: $500,000	Bonus: $462,938

OTHER THOUGHTS:

Apparent Women Officers or Directors: 3
Hot Spot for Advancement for Women/Minorities: Y

LOCATIONS: ("Y" = Yes)

West:	Southwest:	Midwest:	Southeast:	Northeast:	International:
Y	Y			Y	Y

STATOIL ASA

www.statoil.com

Industry Group Code: 211111 **Ranks within this company's industry group:** Sales: 19 Profits: 24

Exploration/Production:		**Refining/Retailing:**		**Utilities:**		**Alternative Energy:**		**Specialty Services:**		**Energy Mktg./Other Svcs.**	
Exploration:	Y	Refining:	Y	Electric Utility:		Waste/Solar/Other:		Consulting/Eng.:		Energy Marketing:	Y
Production:	Y	Retailing:	Y	Gas Utility:		Thermal/Steam:		Seismic:		Equipment/Machinery:	
Coal Production:		Convenience Stores:		Pipelines:	Y	Wind:		Drilling:		Oil Field Services:	
		Chemicals:		Water:		Hydro:		InfoTech:		Air/Shipping Transportation:	
						Fuel Cells:		Specialty Services:			

TYPES OF BUSINESS:

Oil & Gas Exploration & Production
Refining
Pipelines
Energy Marketing
Oil Sands Production
Wind Turbine Production

BRANDS/DIVISIONS/AFFILIATES:

CONTACTS:

Note: Officers with more than one job title may be intentionally listed here more than once.

Helge Lund, CEO
Eldar Sætre, CFO
Jon Arnt Jacobsen, Exec. VP-Mktg.
Margareth Ovrum, Exec. VP-Tech. & New Energy
Jon Arnt Jacobsen, Exec. VP-Mfg.
Jannik Lindbaek, Jr., Head-Corp. Comm.
Oystein Michelsen, Exec. VP-Exploration & Prod., Norway
Helga Nes, Exec. VP-Staff Functions & Corp. Svcs.
Rune Bjornson, Exec. VP-Natural Gas
Gunnar Myreboe, Exec. VP-Projects & Procurement
Svein Rennemo, Chmn.
Peter Mellbye, Exec. VP-Int'l Exploration & Prod.

Phone: 47-51-99-0000 **Fax:** 47-51-99-0050
Toll-Free:
Address: Forusbeen 50, Stavanger, N-4035 Norway

GROWTH PLANS/SPECIAL FEATURES:

Statoil ASA, formerly StatoilHydro ASA, is a Norwegian oil and gas company that operates in roughly 40 countries. The company has proved reserves of approximately 2.174 billion barrels of oil and 18.1 trillion cubic feet (cf) of natural gas, which represents an aggregate of 5.408 billion barrels of oil equivalent (boe). The firm operates through six divisions: exploration and production in Norway (E&P Norway); international exploration and production (International E&P); natural gas; manufacturing and marketing; projects and procurement; and technology and new energy. E&P Norway explores, develops and produces petroleum products on the Norwegian continental shelf. It currently operates 42 fields and has an average daily production of oil and natural gas liquids (NGL) of 784,000 boe and 3.7 billion cf of natural gas. Statoil's pipelines extend from the offshore outposts to locations in Norway and other countries. International E&P includes all exploration, development and production operations outside Norway, with interests in fields in 12 countries in North America, South America, Europe, Africa and Asia. The company's natural gas segment transports, processes and sells roughly 2.62 trillion cf of natural gas from upstream positions offshore of Norway and abroad. The manufacturing and marketing segment includes the group's operations in transporting oil, processing, sale of crude oil and refined products and retailing. The division operates roughly 2,000 service stations, two refineries, one methanol plant and three crude oil terminals in 13 countries. The projects and procurement division handles project and operational procurement; and the planning and executing of all major development and modification projects. The technology and new energy segment develops distinct technology positions and strengthens project execution. It operates three research and development centers in Norway and one in Canada. In July 2010, Statoil sold subsidiary Tampnet AS to HitecVision.

Statoil offers employees benefits including profit sharing and pension plans.

FINANCIALS:

Sales and profits are in thousands of dollars—add 000 to get the full amount. 2010 Note: Financial information for 2010 was not available for all companies at press time.

2010 Sales: $	2010 Profits: $	**U.S. Stock Ticker: STO**
2009 Sales: $79,003,700	2009 Profits: $3,004,650	**Int'l Ticker: STL** Int'l Exchange: Oslo-OBX
2008 Sales: $98,337,900	2008 Profits: $6,530,720	Employees:
2007 Sales: $89,000,000	2007 Profits: $7,520,000	Fiscal Year Ends: 12/31
2006 Sales: $71,295,100	2006 Profits: $6,810,630	Parent Company:

SALARIES/BENEFITS:

Pension Plan: Y	ESOP Stock Plan: Y	Profit Sharing:	Top Exec. Salary: $	Bonus: $
Savings Plan:	Stock Purch. Plan:		Second Exec. Salary: $	Bonus: $

OTHER THOUGHTS:

Apparent Women Officers or Directors: 6
Hot Spot for Advancement for Women/Minorities: Y

LOCATIONS: ("Y" = Yes)

West:	Southwest:	Midwest:	Southeast:	Northeast:	International:
	Y			Y	Y

STONE ENERGY CORPORATION

www.stoneenergy.com

Industry Group Code: 211111 **Ranks within this company's industry group:** Sales: 86 Profits: 98

Exploration/Production:		Refining/Retailing:		Utilities:		Alternative Energy:		Specialty Services:		Energy Mktg./Other Svcs.	
Exploration:	Y	Refining:		Electric Utility:		Waste/Solar/Other:		Consulting/Eng.:		Energy Marketing:	
Production:	Y	Retailing:		Gas Utility:		Thermal/Steam:		Seismic:		Equipment/Machinery:	
Coal Production:		Convenience Stores:		Pipelines:		Wind:		Drilling:		Oil Field Services:	
		Chemicals:		Water:		Hydro:		InfoTech:		Air/Shipping Transportation:	
						Fuel Cells:		Specialty Services:			

TYPES OF BUSINESS:

Oil & Gas Exploration & Production

BRANDS/DIVISIONS/AFFILIATES:

Bois d'Arc Energy Inc

CONTACTS:

Note: Officers with more than one job title may be intentionally listed here more than once.

David H. Welch, CEO
David H. Welch, Pres.
Kenneth H. Beer, CFO/Sr. VP
Florence M. Ziegler, VP-Human Resources
Florence M. Ziegler, VP-Admin.
Andrew L. Gates, III, General Counsel/Sr. VP/Sec.
Jerome F. Wenzel, Jr., Sr. VP-Oper. & Exploitation
Richard L. Smith, Sr. VP-Bus. Dev. & Exploration
Florence M. Ziegler, VP-Corp. Comm.
J. Kent Pierret, Treas./Chief Acct. Officer/Sr. VP
E. J. Louviere, Sr. VP-Land
Richard L. Toothman, Jr., VP-Appalachia
Richard A. Pattarozzi, Chmn.

Phone: 337-237-0410	**Fax:** 337-237-0426
Toll-Free:	
Address: 625 E. Kaliste Saloom Rd., Lafayette, LA 70508 US	

GROWTH PLANS/SPECIAL FEATURES:

Stone Energy Corporation is an independent oil and natural gas firm. The company acquires, explores, develops and operates oil and gas properties located in the conventional/deep shelf and the deepwater of the Gulf of Mexico. Stone Energy also operates in the Appalachia regions of West Virginia and Pennsylvania. The firm owns approximately 71 active properties and 100 primary term leases in the Gulf Coast Basin; and five active properties in the Appalachia region. It serves as operator on 83% of its active properties. Stone Energy has estimated proved reserves of 32.33 million barrels of oil and 216.69 billion cubic feet of natural gas, total roughly 410.7 billion cubic feet equivalent. The company produces roughly 6.2 million barrels of oil and 41.33 billion cubic feet of natural gas annually. The firm's oil and natural gas production is sold under short-term contracts to larger companies. Sales to Shell Trading (US) Company account for roughly 34% of Stone Energy's revenues; sales to Conoco, Inc. account for approximately 27%; sales to Sequent Energy Management LP account for 13%; and sales to Hess Corporation account for roughly 11%. Stone Energy's continuing business strategy is to increase production, cash flow and reserves through the acquisition, exploration, exploitation, development and operation of properties within its current operating areas.

FINANCIALS:

Sales and profits are in thousands of dollars—add 000 to get the full amount. 2010 Note: Financial information for 2010 was not available for all companies at press time.

2010 Sales: $	2010 Profits: $	**U.S. Stock Ticker: SGY**
2009 Sales: $714,356	2009 Profits: $-211,708	**Int'l Ticker:** Int'l Exchange:
2008 Sales: $801,042	2008 Profits: $-1,137,231	Employees: 313
2007 Sales: $753,252	2007 Profits: $181,436	Fiscal Year Ends: 12/31
2006 Sales: $688,988	2006 Profits: $-254,222	Parent Company:

SALARIES/BENEFITS:

Pension Plan:	ESOP Stock Plan:	Profit Sharing:	Top Exec. Salary: $520,000	Bonus: $540,000
Savings Plan:	Stock Purch. Plan:		Second Exec. Salary: $330,000	Bonus: $345,000

OTHER THOUGHTS:

Apparent Women Officers or Directors: 2
Hot Spot for Advancement for Women/Minorities:

LOCATIONS: ("Y" = Yes)

West:	Southwest:	Midwest:	Southeast:	Northeast:	International:
	Y		Y	Y	

SUBSEA 7 INC

www.subsea7.com

Industry Group Code: 213112 **Ranks within this company's industry group:** Sales: 10 Profits: 6

Exploration/Production:		Refining/Retailing:		Utilities:		Alternative Energy:		Specialty Services:		Energy Mktg./Other Svcs.	
Exploration:		Refining:		Electric Utility:		Waste/Solar/Other:		Consulting/Eng.:	Y	Energy Marketing:	
Production:		Retailing:		Gas Utility:		Thermal/Steam:		Seismic:		Equipment/Machinery:	Y
Coal Production:		Convenience Stores:		Pipelines:		Wind:		Drilling:		Oil Field Services:	Y
		Chemicals:		Water:		Hydro:		InfoTech:	Y	Air/Shipping Transportation:	
						Fuel Cells:		Specialty Services:	Y		

TYPES OF BUSINESS:

Oil & Gas Production Support Services
Subsea Engineering Services
Pipelay Services
Subsea Construction
Remotely Operated Vehicles
Survey & Positioning Services

BRANDS/DIVISIONS/AFFILIATES:

i-Tech
Centurion QX
Veripos
Acergy SA

CONTACTS:

Note: Officers with more than one job title may be intentionally listed here more than once.

Mel Fitzgerald, CEO
John Evans, COO
Barry Mahon, CFO
Russell Stewart, VP-Human Resources
Stuart N Smith, VP-Tech. & Asset Dev.
Dave Adams, VP-Project Mgmt. & Eng.
Graeme Murray, VP-Legal & Insurance
Craig Broussard, Regional VP-Asia Pacific
Steve Wisely, Exec. VP-Commercial
Ian Cobban, Regional VP-North America
David Cassie, VP-Client Rel.
Kristian Siem, Chmn.
Steph McNeill, Regional VP-U.K.

Phone: 44-1224-344-300	**Fax:** 44-1224-344-600
Toll-Free:	
Address: Ugland House, S. Church St., Georgetown, KY1-1104 Cayman Islands	

GROWTH PLANS/SPECIAL FEATURES:

Subsea 7, Inc. is an offshore petroleum services company that specializes in all products and services necessary for subsea field development, including design and engineering, project management, procurement, fabrication and installation, as well as commissioning facilities on seabeds and the tie-back of seabed facilities. The i-Tech division delivers remote operated vehicles (ROV) and intervention tooling support services to the offshore exploration and production industries. It operates over 70 ROV systems and has co-designed a purpose-built drill support system, the Centurion QX work-class ROV, to enhance its fleet. Subsea 7's fleet of construction, survey and multi-purpose support vessels provide construction and IRM services, including the design and installation of flexible and rigid flowlines; facilities design and installation; pipeline design, construction, installation and commission; remote intervention technology and robotics services; subsea well intervention; diving and survey services; and well abandonment services. Subsea 7's navigation and positioning division, Veripos, provides services such as surface and sub-surface positioning solutions such as offshore construction support to pipelines, structures and field development; seabed mapping route and site surveys; AUV services; precision underwater metrology; pipeline inspections; and structural inspection. The company's deepwater services and technology division includes a fleet of 21 multi-purpose vessels equipped to install deepwater systems and facilities, several of which are permanently fitted with deepwater-work-class ROV systems rated for roughly 3-mile water depth. Subsea Engineering Solutions Inc. provides specialist engineering support to its ROV services and construction activities. In August 2009, Subsea opened a new pipeline fabrication spoolbase in Port Isabel, Texas at a cost of over $30 million. In June 2010, the firm and another offshore services company, Acergy S.A., agreed to merge under the Subsea 7 name.

FINANCIALS:

Sales and profits are in thousands of dollars—add 000 to get the full amount. 2010 Note: Financial information for 2010 was not available for all companies at press time.

2010 Sales: $	2010 Profits: $	**U.S. Stock Ticker: SUB**
2009 Sales: $2,439,278	2009 Profits: $412,200	**Int'l Ticker:** Int'l Exchange:
2008 Sales: $2,373,252	2008 Profits: $394,503	Employees:
2007 Sales: $2,187,354	2007 Profits: $314,780	Fiscal Year Ends: 12/31
2006 Sales: $1,670,358	2006 Profits: $207,152	Parent Company:

SALARIES/BENEFITS:

Pension Plan:	ESOP Stock Plan:	Profit Sharing:	Top Exec. Salary: $	Bonus: $
Savings Plan:	Stock Purch. Plan:		Second Exec. Salary: $	Bonus: $

OTHER THOUGHTS:

Apparent Women Officers or Directors:
Hot Spot for Advancement for Women/Minorities:

LOCATIONS: ("Y" = Yes)

West:	Southwest:	Midwest:	Southeast:	Northeast:	International:
			Y		Y

Note: Financial information, benefits and other data can change quickly and may vary from those stated here.

SUNCOR ENERGY INC

www.suncor.com

Industry Group Code: 211111 **Ranks within this company's industry group:** Sales: 27 Profits: 38

Exploration/Production:		**Refining/Retailing:**		**Utilities:**		**Alternative Energy:**		**Specialty Services:**		**Energy Mktg./Other Svcs.**	
Exploration:	Y	Refining:	Y	Electric Utility:		Waste/Solar/Other:	Y	Consulting/Eng.:		Energy Marketing:	Y
Production:	Y	Retailing:	Y	Gas Utility:		Thermal/Steam:		Seismic:		Equipment/Machinery:	
Coal Production:		Convenience Stores:	Y	Pipelines:		Wind:	Y	Drilling:		Oil Field Services:	
		Chemicals:	Y	Water:		Hydro:		InfoTech:		Air/Shipping Transportation:	
						Fuel Cells:		Specialty Services:	Y		

TYPES OF BUSINESS:

Oil & Gas Exploration & Production
Wind Power
Oil Sands Production
Oil Refining & Transportation
Energy Marketing

BRANDS/DIVISIONS/AFFILIATES:

Petro-Canada

CONTACTS:

Note: Officers with more than one job title may be intentionally listed here more than once.

Rick George, CEO
Steve W. Williams, COO
Rick George, Pres.
Bart Demosky, CFO
Boris J. Jackman, Exec. VP-Mktg. & Refining
Sue Lee, Sr. VP-Human Resources
Terry Hopwood, General Counsel/Sr. VP
Eric Axford, Sr. VP-Operations Support
Jay Thornton, Exec. VP-Dev.
Sue Lee, Sr. VP-Comm.
Mike MacSween, Sr. VP-In-Situ
Neil Camarta, Exec. VP-Natural Gas
Kevin Nabholz, Exec. VP-Major Projects
Kirk Bailey, Exec. VP-Oil Sands
John Ferguson, Chmn.
Mark Little, Sr. VP-Int'l & Offshore
Jay Thornton, Exec. VP-Energy Supply & Trading

Phone: 403-296-8000 **Fax:** 403-296-3030
Toll-Free:
Address: 112 4th Ave. SW, Calgary, AB T2P 3E3 Canada

GROWTH PLANS/SPECIAL FEATURES:

Suncor Energy, Inc. is a Canadian energy company. It explores, acquires, develops, produces and markets crude oil and natural gas; transports and refines crude oil; and markets petroleum and petrochemical products. Once recovered, the firm upgrades it to refinery-ready feedstock and diesel oil. The company's mining and in-situ leases have the potential to produce over 18 billion barrels. The natural gas unit develops and acquires natural gas in western Canada, and the U.S. Rocky Mountain region. It also explores long-term supplies in the Mackenzie Delta and Corridor in the Northwest Territories, Alaska and Canada's Arctic Islands. Suncor has projects throughout northern Canada with its two largest assets being in Canada's Arctic Islands. Internationally and offshore, the company operates in the North Sea and the east coast of Canada. It has additional interest in Libya, Syria, and Trinidad and Tobago. The refining operations include refineries in Alberta, at 135,000-barrels-per-day; Ontario, at 85,000-barrels-per-day; Quebec, at 130,000-barrels-per-day and Colorado, 93,000-barrels-per-day. The firm's products include bitumen blends, sweet and sour crude oil, diesel, gasoline, jet fuel, asphalt, chemicals, heavy fuel and home heating oils, petroleum coke and sulphur. The company's desulphurization plant in Ontario produces gasoline, kerosene and jet and diesel fuels. The company has long term goals to continue investing in renewable resources such as wind power and biofuels. Its four wind power plants currently have a total generating capacity of 147 megawatts. In mid 2009, Suncor acquired Petro-Canada. In 2010, the firm agreed to divest several non-core assets, including its oil and gas producing operations in the U.S. Rocky Mountains; several offshore assets in the U.K.; certain natural gas properties in Western Canada; and all of its operations in Trinidad and Tobago. In June 2010, the firm agreed to sell Petro-Canada Netherlands B.V. to Dana Petroleum plc for approximately $568 million.

FINANCIALS:

Sales and profits are in thousands of dollars—add 000 to get the full amount. 2010 Note: Financial information for 2010 was not available for all companies at press time.

2010 Sales: $	2010 Profits: $	**U.S. Stock Ticker: SU**
2009 Sales: $24,559,700	2009 Profits: $1,104,610	**Int'l Ticker: SU** Int'l Exchange: Toronto-TSX
2008 Sales: $27,680,000	2008 Profits: $2,004,000	Employees: 12,978
2007 Sales: $18,080,000	2007 Profits: $2,850,000	Fiscal Year Ends: 12/31
2006 Sales: $13,582,900	2006 Profits: $2,536,500	Parent Company:

SALARIES/BENEFITS:

Pension Plan: Y	ESOP Stock Plan:	Profit Sharing:	Top Exec. Salary: $1,270,406	Bonus: $1,757,421
Savings Plan: Y	Stock Purch. Plan:		Second Exec. Salary: $1,276,529	Bonus: $1,221,159

OTHER THOUGHTS:

Apparent Women Officers or Directors: 3
Hot Spot for Advancement for Women/Minorities: Y

LOCATIONS: ("Y" = Yes)

West:	Southwest:	Midwest:	Southeast:	Northeast:	International:
Y					Y

SUNOCO INC

www.sunocoinc.com

Industry Group Code: 324110 **Ranks within this company's industry group:** Sales: 6 Profits: 24

Exploration/Production:		Refining/Retailing:		Utilities:		Alternative Energy:		Specialty Services:		Energy Mktg./Other Svcs.	
Exploration:		Refining:	Y	Electric Utility:		Waste/Solar/Other:		Consulting/Eng.:		Energy Marketing:	
Production:		Retailing:		Gas Utility:		Thermal/Steam:		Seismic:		Equipment/Machinery:	
Coal Production:	Y	Convenience Stores:		Pipelines:		Wind:		Drilling:		Oil Field Services:	
		Chemicals:	Y	Water:		Hydro:		InfoTech:		Air/Shipping Transportation:	Y
						Fuel Cells:		Specialty Services:			

TYPES OF BUSINESS:

Petroleum Refiner & Chemicals Manufacturer
Petrochemicals & Lubricants
Coke Manufacturing
Retail Gasoline & Middle Distillate Sales

BRANDS/DIVISIONS/AFFILIATES:

SunCoke Energy, Inc.
Sunoco Logistic Partners L.P.
Sunoco Chemicals
Sunoco A-Plus
Sunoco Ultra Service Center

CONTACTS: *Note: Officers with more than one job title may be intentionally listed here more than once.*

Lynn L. Elsenhans, CEO
Lynn L. Elsenhans, Pres.
Brian P. MacDonald, CFO/Sr. VP
Robert W. Owens, Sr. VP-Mktg.
Dennis Zeleny, Chief Human Resources Officer/Sr. VP
Vincent J. Kelley, Sr. VP-Tech.
Vincent J. Kelley, Sr. VP-Eng
Stacy L. Fox, General Counsel/Sr. VP
Bruce G. Fischer, Sr. VP-Strategy & Portfolio
Thomas Golembeski, Contact-Corp. Comm.
Clare McGrory, Contact-Investor Rel.
Charmain Uy, VP/Treas.
Michael J. Thomson, Sr. VP/Pres., SunCoke Energy, Inc.
Joseph P. Krott, Comptroller
Ann C. Mule, Chief Governance Officer/Corp. Sec.
Anne-Marie Ainsworth, Sr. VP-Refining
Lynn L. Elsenhans, Chmn.

Phone: 215-977-3000 **Fax:** 215-977-3409
Toll-Free: 800-786-6261
Address: 1735 Market St., Ste. LL, Philadelphia, PA 19103-7583 US

GROWTH PLANS/SPECIAL FEATURES:

Sunoco, Inc., through its subsidiaries, is principally a petroleum refiner and chemicals manufacturer with interests in logistics and cokemaking. Sunoco operates five segments: Refining and supply; retail marketing; chemicals; logistics; and coke. Additionally, the firm has a holding company and a professional services group. The holding company is a non-operating parent company and the professional services group consists of a number of staff functions including finance, risk management, human resources, information systems and engineering services. The refining and supply business manufactures petroleum products, including gasoline, middle distillates and residual fuel oil; commodity petrochemicals including olefins and olefin derivatives; and aromatics and derivates. The retail marketing business consists of the retail sale of gasoline and middle distillates and the operation of convenience stores in 23 states. The chemicals segment, operating through Sunoco Chemicals, manufactures, distributes and markets commodity and intermediate petrochemicals. The logistics division, including Sunoco Logistic Partners L.P., operates refined product and crude oil pipelines and terminals and conducts crude oil acquisition and marketing activities. The coke segment operates metallurgical coke plants and metallurgical coal mines through SunCoke Energy, Inc. Sunoco also owns and operates facilities in Pennsylvania and Ohio, which produce phenol and acetone. The firm operates three refineries and markets gasoline, middle distillates and other convenience store merchandise through 4,720 retail outlets. In June 2009, the company completed the purchase of an ethanol manufacturing plant in Volney, New York for $8.5 million. In September 2009, Sunoco sold its retail heating oil and propane distribution concern to Superior Plus Corporation for approximately $86 million. In April 2010, Sunoco sold its polypropylene business to Braskem S.A., a Brazilian petrochemical company, for $350 million.

Sunoco, Inc. offers its employees medical and dental insurance; an employee assistance program; flexible spending accounts; and an educational assistance plan.

FINANCIALS: **Sales and profits are in thousands of dollars—add 000 to get the full amount. 2010 Note: Financial information for 2010 was not available for all companies at press time.**

2010 Sales: $	2010 Profits: $	**U.S. Stock Ticker: SUN**
2009 Sales: $31,312,000	2009 Profits: $-329,000	**Int'l Ticker:** Int'l Exchange:
2008 Sales: $51,076,000	2008 Profits: $776,000	Employees: 11,200
2007 Sales: $42,569,000	2007 Profits: $891,000	Fiscal Year Ends: 12/31
2006 Sales: $38,636,000	2006 Profits: $979,000	Parent Company:

SALARIES/BENEFITS:

Pension Plan: Y	ESOP Stock Plan:	Profit Sharing: Y	Top Exec. Salary: $1,240,000	Bonus: $
Savings Plan: Y	Stock Purch. Plan:		Second Exec. Salary: $510,450	Bonus: $

OTHER THOUGHTS:

Apparent Women Officers or Directors: 7
Hot Spot for Advancement for Women/Minorities: Y

LOCATIONS: ("Y" = Yes)

West:	Southwest:	Midwest:	Southeast:	Northeast:	International:
Y	Y	Y	Y	Y	Y

SUNOCO LOGISTICS PARTNERS LP

www.sunocologistics.com

Industry Group Code: 424710 **Ranks within this company's industry group:** Sales: 3 Profits: 1

Exploration/Production:		Refining/Retailing:		Utilities:		Alternative Energy:		Specialty Services:		Energy Mktg./Other Svcs.	
Exploration:		Refining:	Y	Electric Utility:		Waste/Solar/Other:		Consulting/Eng.:		Energy Marketing:	Y
Production:		Retailing:		Gas Utility:		Thermal/Steam:		Seismic:		Equipment/Machinery:	
Coal Production:		Convenience Stores:		Pipelines:	Y	Wind:		Drilling:		Oil Field Services:	
		Chemicals:		Water:		Hydro:		InfoTech:		Air/Shipping Transportation:	
						Fuel Cells:		Specialty Services:			

TYPES OF BUSINESS:

Pipelines
Crude Oil Refining & Marketing
Terminal & Storage Facilities

BRANDS/DIVISIONS/AFFILIATES:

Sunoco Inc
Mid-Valley Pipeline Company
Excel Pipeline LLC
Wolverine Pipe Line Co
Yellowstone Pipe Line Co
West Shore Pipe Line Co
West Texas Gulf Pipe Line Company

CONTACTS:

Note: Officers with more than one job title may be intentionally listed here more than once.

Lynn L. Elsenhans, CEO
Michael J. Hennigan, COO
Michael J. Hennigan, Pres.
Neal E. Murphy, CFO/VP
Scott W. McCord, VP-Lease Mktg. & Acquisition
Dennis Zeleny, Chief Human Resources Officer
Kathleen Shea-Ballay, General Counsel/VP/Sec.
David A. Justin, VP-Oper.
Michael D. Galtman, Controller/Chief Acct. Officer
Lynn L. Elsenhans, Chmn.

Phone: 215-977-6350	**Fax:**
Toll-Free: 866-248-4344	
Address: 1818 Market St., Ste. 1500, Philadelphia, PA 19103 US	

GROWTH PLANS/SPECIAL FEATURES:

Sunoco Logistics Partners, L.P., formed by Sunoco, Inc., is an energy logistics company. The firm is principally engaged in the transport, terminalling and storage of refined products and crude oil; and the purchase and sale of crude oil in 13 states located in the Midwest, northeast and southwest regions of the U.S. The company operates in three segments: the refined products pipeline system, the crude oil pipeline system and terminal facilities. The refined products pipeline system primarily serves the northeast and Midwest U.S. and includes roughly 2,200 miles of refined product pipelines; about 140 miles of crude oil pipelines; 31.5% interest in Wolverine Pipe Line Co.; 14% interest in Yellowstone Pipe Line Co.; and 12.3% interest in West Shore Pipe Line Co. The crude oil pipeline system gathers, purchases, sells and transports crude oil principally in Oklahoma and Texas and consists of roughly 3,350 miles of crude oil trunk pipelines. Through this segment, Sunoco Logistics owns 55.3% of Mid-Valley Pipeline Company; and 43.8% of West Texas Gulf Pipe Line Company. The terminal facilities segment includes 41 refined product terminals with an aggregate storage capacity of 7.0 million barrels, primarily serving the refined product pipeline system; the Nederland terminal, a 19.6 million marine crude oil terminal on the Texas Gulf Coast; two marine and one inland crude oil terminals with a combined capacity of 3.4 million barrels; a liquefied petroleum gas terminal near Michigan with a capacity of 1 million barrels; and a 2 million barrel refined product terminal in Pennsylvania. Sunoco, Inc. owns roughly 33.2% of the company and accounts for roughly 13.1% of the firm's revenues. In September 2009, Sunoco Logistics Partners acquired Excel Pipeline LLC from Gary-Williams Energy Corporation. In June 2010, the firm agreed to acquire certain butane blending operations from Texon L.P. for roughly $140 million.

FINANCIALS:

Sales and profits are in thousands of dollars—add 000 to get the full amount. 2010 Note: Financial information for 2010 was not available for all companies at press time.

2010 Sales: $	2010 Profits: $	**U.S. Stock Ticker: SXL**
2009 Sales: $5,429,677	2009 Profits: $250,362	**Int'l Ticker:** Int'l Exchange:
2008 Sales: $10,136,618	2008 Profits: $214,480	Employees: 1,340
2007 Sales: $7,405,836	2007 Profits: $120,875	Fiscal Year Ends: 12/31
2006 Sales: $5,854,550	2006 Profits: $90,341	Parent Company:

SALARIES/BENEFITS:

Pension Plan:	ESOP Stock Plan:	Profit Sharing:	Top Exec. Salary: $515,000	Bonus: $412,000
Savings Plan:	Stock Purch. Plan:		Second Exec. Salary: $306,400	Bonus: $148,221

OTHER THOUGHTS:

Apparent Women Officers or Directors: 4
Hot Spot for Advancement for Women/Minorities: Y

LOCATIONS: ("Y" = Yes)

West:	Southwest:	Midwest:	Southeast:	Northeast:	International:
	Y	Y		Y	

SUPERIOR ENERGY SERVICES INC

www.superiorenergy.com

Industry Group Code: 213112 **Ranks within this company's industry group:** Sales: 15 Profits: 23

Exploration/Production:		Refining/Retailing:		Utilities:		Alternative Energy:		Specialty Services:		Energy Mktg./Other Svcs.	
Exploration:		Refining:		Electric Utility:		Waste/Solar/Other:		Consulting/Eng.:	Y	Energy Marketing:	
Production:		Retailing:		Gas Utility:		Thermal/Steam:		Seismic:		Equipment/Machinery:	Y
Coal Production:		Convenience Stores:		Pipelines:		Wind:		Drilling:		Oil Field Services:	Y
		Chemicals:		Water:		Hydro:		InfoTech:		Air/Shipping Transportation:	
						Fuel Cells:		Specialty Services:	Y		

TYPES OF BUSINESS:

Oil & Gas Drilling Support Services
Drilling Tool Rental
Field Management Services
Engineering Services

BRANDS/DIVISIONS/AFFILIATES:

International Snubbing Services
Meridian International Services
Fastorq
Warrior Energy Services
Stabil Drill

CONTACTS:

Note: Officers with more than one job title may be intentionally listed here more than once.

David Dunlap, CEO
Ken Blanchard, COO
Ken Blanchard, Pres.
Robert Taylor, CFO/Exec. VP
Patrick Campbell, Exec. VP-Tech. Solutions Group
Bill Masters, General Counsel/Exec. VP
Greg Rosenstein, VP-Investor Rel.
Robert Taylor, Treas.
Guy Cook, Exec. VP-Rental Tools
Danny Young, Exec. VP-Corp. Svcs.
James Holleman, Exec VP-Well Solutions
Charlie Hardy, Exec. VP-Marine Svcs.
Terry Hall, Chmn.
Patrick Zuber, Exec. VP-Int'l

Phone: 504-587-7374 **Fax:** 504-362-1818
Toll-Free:
Address: 601 Poydras St., Ste. 2400, New Orleans, LA 70130 US

GROWTH PLANS/SPECIAL FEATURES:

Superior Energy Services, Inc. provides specialized oil field services and equipment for oil and gas companies. The company offers post-wellhead products and services necessary to maintain offshore wells, as well as plug and abandonment services once the well is no longer productive. The firm operates in three segments: subsea and well enhancement; drilling products and services; and marine services. Superior Energy's subsea and well enhancement services include engineering and well evaluation; coiled tubing; plug and abandonment; electric line; gas lift; well control; snubbing; pumping; stimulation; recompletion; offshore oil/gas tank and vessel cleaning; decommissioning; and mechanical wireline. This division includes 142 offshore wireline units; 24 offshore electric line units; 43 land wireline units; seven offshore coiled tubing units; 68 land electric line units; 32 land coiled tubing units; and 10 dedicated liftboats configured specifically for wireline services. The drilling products and services segment manufactures, sells and rents specialized equipment for onshore and offshore drilling; it maintains rental locations in the U.S. (including the Gulf of Mexico), Venezuela, West Africa, Trinidad, Canada, Asia Pacific, Europe, the U.K., the Netherlands and the Middle East. The company's rental tools include stabilizers, handling tools, specialty tubular goods, connecting iron, pressure control equipment, torquing tools and drill collars. The marine services segment owns and operates 26 liftboats (self-propelled, self-elevating work platforms with legs), which it contracts to drilling companies. Combined, Superior Energy's major customers (Chevron Corporation, BP plc and Apache Corporation) account for roughly 39% of the company's revenues. The firm's subsidiaries include International Snubbing Services, Meridian International Services, Fastorq, Warrior Energy Services and Stabil Drill. In January 2010, Superior Energy Services acquired integrated subsea services and engineering solutions provider Hallin Marine Subsea Plc. In July 2010, the company agreed to acquire the Gulf of Mexico stimulation and sand control operations of Baker Hughes, Inc.

FINANCIALS:

Sales and profits are in thousands of dollars—add 000 to get the full amount. 2010 Note: Financial information for 2010 was not available for all companies at press time.

2010 Sales: $	2010 Profits: $	**U.S. Stock Ticker: SPN**
2009 Sales: $1,449,300	2009 Profits: $-102,323	**Int'l Ticker:** Int'l Exchange:
2008 Sales: $1,881,124	2008 Profits: $361,722	Employees: 4,800
2007 Sales: $1,572,467	2007 Profits: $281,120	Fiscal Year Ends: 12/31
2006 Sales: $1,093,821	2006 Profits: $188,241	Parent Company:

SALARIES/BENEFITS:

Pension Plan:	ESOP Stock Plan:	Profit Sharing:	Top Exec. Salary: $722,949	Bonus: $1,755,066
Savings Plan:	Stock Purch. Plan:		Second Exec. Salary: $441,510	Bonus: $810,994

OTHER THOUGHTS:

Apparent Women Officers or Directors:
Hot Spot for Advancement for Women/Minorities:

LOCATIONS: ("Y" = Yes)

West:	Southwest:	Midwest:	Southeast:	Northeast:	International:
Y	Y		Y	Y	Y

SURGUTNEFTEGAS (OJSC)

www.surgutneftegas.ru

Industry Group Code: 211111 **Ranks within this company's industry group:** Sales: 35 Profits: 20

Exploration/Production:		**Refining/Retailing:**		**Utilities:**		**Alternative Energy:**		**Specialty Services:**		**Energy Mktg./Other Svcs.**	
Exploration:	Y	Refining:	Y	Electric Utility:	Y	Waste/Solar/Other:		Consulting/Eng.:		Energy Marketing:	
Production:	Y	Retailing:	Y	Gas Utility:		Thermal/Steam:		Seismic:		Equipment/Machinery:	
Coal Production:		Convenience Stores:	Y	Pipelines:		Wind:		Drilling:		Oil Field Services:	
		Chemicals:	Y	Water:		Hydro:		InfoTech:		Air/Shipping Transportation:	
						Fuel Cells:		Specialty Services:	Y		

TYPES OF BUSINESS:

Exploration & Production-Oil & Natural Gas
Hydrocarbon, Diesel & Jet Fuel Refining
Natural Gas Processing
Gas Stations
Storage Facilities

BRANDS/DIVISIONS/AFFILIATES:

Kirishinefteorgsintez, Ltd.
Izoflex
Surgutpolimer OJSC
Pskovnefteprodukt, Ltd.
Kaliningradnefteprodukt, Ltd.
Novgorodnefteprodukt, Ltd.
Tvernefteprodukt, Ltd.
Lennefteprodukt

CONTACTS:

Note: Officers with more than one job title may be intentionally listed here more than once.

Vladimir Leonidovich Bogdanov, Gen. Dir.
Aleksandr Nikolaevich Bulanov, Chief Eng./First Deputy Gen. Dir.
Sergei Alexeevich Ananiev, Head-Drilling Div./Deputy Gen. Dir.
Igor Nikolaevich Gorbunov, Head-Oil & Gas Prod. Div., Bystrinskneft
Alexander Filippovich Resyapov, Deputy Gen. Dir.-Capital Construction
Vladimir Petrovich Erokhin, Chmn.

Phone: 7-346-240-10-07 **Fax:** 7-346-240-10-18
Toll-Free:
Address: 1 Kukuevitskogo St., Surgut, Tyumenskaya, 628415 Russia

GROWTH PLANS/SPECIAL FEATURES:

Surgutneftegas (OJSC), based in the city of Surgut in Siberia, is one of the largest oil companies in Russia. Activities of the firm include exploration; gas and oil field construction and development; oil and gas production and marketing; and oil and petrochemical products refining and marketing. The firm has recoverable oil and gas reserves of approximately 2.5 billion tons of oil equivalent. Surgutneftegas' share in overall Russian oil production is approximately 12%, with 59.6 million tons of crude oil produced in 2009. The company produces around 50 billion cubic feet (Bcf) of natural gas annually, representing 24% of gas produced in the country. OJSC also implements its own energy program to carry out production works, and constructs power stations to provide nearby regions with electric power. The firm owns and operates 17 gas turbine power plants and seven gas piston power plants with total capacity of 605 megawatts, which provide nearly 30% of the firm's energy needs. Surgutneftegas' refining and petrochemical operations, under Kirishinefteorgsintez, Ltd., take place in the city of Kirishi. A division of Kirishinefteorgsintez, Izoflex, produces a bituminous-polymeric surfaced material used for roofing and hydro-insulation works. The firm's marketing companies include Kaliningradnefteprodukt, Kirishiavtoservis, Lennefteprodukt, Novgorodnefteprodukt, Pskovnefteprodukt, and Tvernefteprodukt. The marketing segment of Surgutneftegas comprises over 300 retail outlets and service stations and 28 tank farms. In addition, the firm's marketing subsidiary Novgorodnefteprodukt operates five liquefied petroleum gas filling stations.

FINANCIALS:

Sales and profits are in thousands of dollars—add 000 to get the full amount. 2010 Note: Financial information for 2010 was not available for all companies at press time.

2010 Sales: $ | 2010 Profits: $
2009 Sales: $17,117,700 | 2009 Profits: $3,779,160
2008 Sales: $21,976,000 | 2008 Profits: $5,785,000
2007 Sales: $19,010,000 | 2007 Profits: $2,930,000
2006 Sales: $14,920,000 | 2006 Profits: $3,980,000

U.S. Stock Ticker: SGTZY
Int'l Ticker: CJSC Int'l Exchange: St. Petersburg-SPBEX
Employees:
Fiscal Year Ends: 12/31
Parent Company:

SALARIES/BENEFITS:

Pension Plan: | ESOP Stock Plan: | Profit Sharing: | Top Exec. Salary: $ | Bonus: $
Savings Plan: | Stock Purch. Plan: | | Second Exec. Salary: $ | Bonus: $

OTHER THOUGHTS:

Apparent Women Officers or Directors:
Hot Spot for Advancement for Women/Minorities:

LOCATIONS: ("Y" = Yes)

West:	Southwest:	Midwest:	Southeast:	Northeast:	International:
					Y

SUSSER HOLDINGS CORPORATION

www.susser.com

Industry Group Code: 447110 **Ranks within this company's industry group:** Sales: 1 Profits: 1

Exploration/Production:		Refining/Retailing:		Utilities:		Alternative Energy:		Specialty Services:		Energy Mktg./Other Svcs.	
Exploration:		Refining:		Electric Utility:		Waste/Solar/Other:		Consulting/Eng.:		Energy Marketing:	
Production:		Retailing:	Y	Gas Utility:		Thermal/Steam:		Seismic:		Equipment/Machinery:	
Coal Production:		Convenience Stores:	Y	Pipelines:		Wind:		Drilling:		Oil Field Services:	
		Chemicals:		Water:		Hydro:		InfoTech:		Air/Shipping Transportation:	
						Fuel Cells:		Specialty Services:			

TYPES OF BUSINESS:

Gas Stations & Convenience Stores
Restaurants
Environmental Consulting

BRANDS/DIVISIONS/AFFILIATES:

Susser Petroleum Company
Stripes
Laredo Taco Company
Applied Petroleum Technologies Ltd
Monkey Loco
Town & Country
Country Cookin
Cafe de La Casa

CONTACTS: *Note: Officers with more than one job title may be intentionally listed here more than once.*

Sam L. Susser, CEO
Sam L. Susser, Pres.
Mary E. Sullivan, CFO/Exec. VP/Treas.
Rod Martin, VP-Mktg.
Otis Peaks, Sr. VP-Human Resources
George Mrvos, VP-IT
Kevin J. Mahany, VP-Merch.
E. V. Bonner, Jr., General Counsel/Exec. VP
Richard Sebastian, Sr. VP-Retail Oper.
Cal McIntosh, VP-Bus. Dev., Wholesale
Otis Peaks, Contact-Media Rel.
Cathy Hauslein, Corp. Controller
Steve DeSutter, CEO/Pres., Retail
Rocky B. Dewbre, COO/Pres., Wholesale
Jerry L. Susser, VP-Real Estate
Patrick Albro, VP-Dealer Oper.
Bruce W. Krysiak, Chmn.
Les Phelps, VP-Supply & Transportation

Phone: 361-884-2463 **Fax:** 361-884-2494
Toll-Free: 800-569-3585
Address: 4525 Ayers St., Corpus Christi, TX 78415 US

GROWTH PLANS/SPECIAL FEATURES:

Susser Holdings Corporation is a non-refining operator of convenience stores and non-refining motor fuel distributor based in Texas. The company operates in two divisions: retail convenience stores and wholesale motor fuel distribution. The retail division operates over 521 convenience stores in Texas, New Mexico and Oklahoma under the Stripes (427 locations) and Town & Country (88 locations) banners. Over the next few years, Susser Holdings plans to rebrand all of its Town & Country locations under the Stripes brand. The stores carry an average of 2,300 to 3,000 individual items that include candy, food service, motor fuel, newspaper, magazines, health and beauty aids and other services. In certain stores, the company operates its proprietary Laredo Taco Company restaurants that offer breakfast and lunch tacos, rotisserie chickens and other hot food prepared on site; Slush Monkey frozen carbonated beverages; Quake energy drinks; Thunderstick meat snacks; Smokin' Barrel beef jerky; Monkey Loco candies; Monkey juice; Country Cookin', a restaurant which features breakfast burritos, fried chicken, hamburgers and other various finger foods; Cafe de la Casa custom blended coffee; and Royal brand cigarettes. The wholesale motor fuel segment purchases over 1.2 billion gallons of branded and unbranded motor fuel from refiners and distributes it to the firm's retail convenience stores, contracted independent operators of convenience stores, unbranded convenience stores and commercial users. The wholesale division consists of Susser Petroleum Company (SPC). SPC purchases CITGO, Chevron, Exxon, Conoco, Phillips 66, Texaco, Valero, Shamrock, Shell and other unbranded motor fuels. Susser owns Applied Petroleum Technologies, Ltd., an environmental consulting, maintenance and construction operation. In 2009, the company acquired 23 Texas and two Louisiana convenience stores from Jack in the Box, Inc.

Employees are offered health, life, AD&D, dental and short-term disability insurance; a 401(k) plan; bereavement leave; tuition reimbursement; paid time off; and credit union membership.

FINANCIALS: **Sales and profits are in thousands of dollars—add 000 to get the full amount. 2010 Note: Financial information for 2010 was not available for all companies at press time.**

2010 Sales: $	2010 Profits: $	**U.S. Stock Ticker: SUSS**
2009 Sales: $3,307,308	2009 Profits: $2,068	**Int'l Ticker:** Int'l Exchange:
2008 Sales: $4,240,645	2008 Profits: $16,477	Employees: 7,211
2007 Sales: $2,717,362	2007 Profits: $16,252	Fiscal Year Ends: 12/31
2006 Sales: $2,265,159	2006 Profits: $-3,746	Parent Company:

SALARIES/BENEFITS:

Pension Plan:	ESOP Stock Plan:	Profit Sharing:	Top Exec. Salary: $519,231	Bonus: $
Savings Plan: Y	Stock Purch. Plan:		Second Exec. Salary: $467,308	Bonus: $

OTHER THOUGHTS:

Apparent Women Officers or Directors: 7
Hot Spot for Advancement for Women/Minorities: Y

LOCATIONS: ("Y" = Yes)

West:	Southwest:	Midwest:	Southeast:	Northeast:	International:
	Y				

SWIFT ENERGY CO

www.swiftenergy.com

Industry Group Code: 211111 **Ranks within this company's industry group:** Sales: 97 Profits: 79

Exploration/Production:		Refining/Retailing:		Utilities:		Alternative Energy:		Specialty Services:		Energy Mktg./Other Svcs.	
Exploration:	Y	Refining:		Electric Utility:		Waste/Solar/Other:		Consulting/Eng.:		Energy Marketing:	
Production:	Y	Retailing:		Gas Utility:		Thermal/Steam:		Seismic:		Equipment/Machinery:	
Coal Production:		Convenience Stores:		Pipelines:		Wind:		Drilling:		Oil Field Services:	
		Chemicals:		Water:		Hydro:		InfoTech:		Air/Shipping Transportation:	
						Fuel Cells:		Specialty Services:			

TYPES OF BUSINESS:

Oil & Gas Exploration & Production

BRANDS/DIVISIONS/AFFILIATES:

Lake Washington
Horseshoe Bayou
Bayou Penchant
Masters Creek
Sun TSH
Las Tiendas
AWP Olmos
Brookeland

CONTACTS:

Note: Officers with more than one job title may be intentionally listed here more than once.

Terry E. Swift, CEO
Robert J. Banks, COO/Exec. VP
Bruce H. Vincent, Pres./Sec.
Alton D. Heckaman, Jr., CFO/Exec. VP
John C. Branca, VP-Exploration & Dev.
Randy A. Bailey, VP-Prod.
Steven L. Tomberlin, VP-Eng.
Steven B. Yakle, VP-Corp. Admin.
Laurent A. Baillargeon, General Counsel/VP
James M. Kitterman, Sr. VP-Oper.
Paul Vincent, Mgr.-Investor Rel.
Adrian D. Shelley, Treas.
James P. Mitchell, Sr. VP-Commercial Transactions & Land
Barry S. Turcotte, VP-Acct./Controller
Terry E. Swift, Chmn.
Robert J. Banks, VP-Int'l Oper., Swift Energy Int'l

Phone: 281-874-2700 **Fax:** 281-874-2726
Toll-Free: 800-777-2412
Address: 16825 Northchase Dr., Ste. 400, Houston, TX 77060-6098 US

GROWTH PLANS/SPECIAL FEATURES:

Swift Energy Co., headquartered in Houston, Texas, is an independent exploration company. The firm develops, explores, acquires and operates oil and gas properties, focusing particularly on oil and natural gas reserves onshore and in the inland waters of Louisiana and Texas. The company has interests in several domestic wells. Swift Energy Co. is currently focused on exploring and developing 15 fields in four areas: Lake Washington and Bay de Chene in southeastern Louisiana; Sun TSH, Briscoe, Las Tiendas, Other South Texas and AWP in southern Texas; High Island, Bayou Penchant, Cote Blanche Island, Horseshoe Bayou and Jeanerette in southern Louisiana; and Masters Creek, South Bearhead Creek and Brookeland in central Louisiana and eastern Texas. The firm has estimated proved reserves from continuing operations of 112.9 million barrels of oil equivalent. Of the company's total proved reserves, approximately 39% is crude oil, 43% is natural gas and 18% is made up of natural gas liquids. Roughly half of Swift Energy's total reserves are proved developed. Nearly all of these proved reserves are in Louisiana (56%) and Texas (43%). In recent years, Swift Energy Co. sold its New Zealand assets to subsidiaries of Origin Energy Limited.

FINANCIALS:

Sales and profits are in thousands of dollars—add 000 to get the full amount. 2010 Note: Financial information for 2010 was not available for all companies at press time.

2010 Sales: $	2010 Profits: $	**U.S. Stock Ticker: SFY**
2009 Sales: $370,445	2009 Profits: $-39,076	**Int'l Ticker:** Int'l Exchange:
2008 Sales: $820,815	2008 Profits: $-257,130	Employees: 295
2007 Sales: $654,121	2007 Profits: $21,287	Fiscal Year Ends: 12/31
2006 Sales: $550,836	2006 Profits: $161,565	Parent Company:

SALARIES/BENEFITS:

Pension Plan:	ESOP Stock Plan:	Profit Sharing:	Top Exec. Salary: $609,000	Bonus: $822,150
Savings Plan: Y	Stock Purch. Plan:		Second Exec. Salary: $476,700	Bonus: $579,191

OTHER THOUGHTS:

Apparent Women Officers or Directors: 1
Hot Spot for Advancement for Women/Minorities:

LOCATIONS: ("Y" = Yes)

West:	Southwest:	Midwest:	Southeast:	Northeast:	International:
	Y		Y		

SYNCRUDE CANADA LTD

www.syncrude.com

Industry Group Code: 211111 **Ranks within this company's industry group:** Sales: Profits:

Exploration/Production:		Refining/Retailing:		Utilities:		Alternative Energy:		Specialty Services:		Energy Mktg./Other Svcs.	
Exploration:		Refining:	Y	Electric Utility:		Waste/Solar/Other:		Consulting/Eng.:		Energy Marketing:	
Production:	Y	Retailing:		Gas Utility:		Thermal/Steam:		Seismic:		Equipment/Machinery:	
Coal Production:		Convenience Stores:		Pipelines:		Wind:		Drilling:		Oil Field Services:	
		Chemicals:		Water:		Hydro:		InfoTech:		Air/Shipping Transportation:	
						Fuel Cells:		Specialty Services:	Y		

TYPES OF BUSINESS:

Oil Sands Production
Crude Oil Production & Refining
Bitumen Refining & Treatment
Synthetic Crude Oil

BRANDS/DIVISIONS/AFFILIATES:

Syncrude Project
Syncrude Crude Oil
Canadian Oil Sands Trust
Imperial Oil Resources
Suncor Energy Oil and Gas Partnership
Canadian Oil Sands Limited
ConocoPhillips Company
Nexen Oil Sands Partnership

CONTACTS:

Note: Officers with more than one job title may be intentionally listed here more than once.

Tom Katinas, CEO
Tom Katinas, Pres.
Maggie Grant, Mgr.-Community Investment
Marcel R. Coutu, Chmn.

Phone: 780-790-5911 | **Fax:** 780-790-6270
Toll-Free: 800-667-9494
Address: 200-9911 MacDonald Ave., Fort McMurray, AB T9H 3H5 Canada

GROWTH PLANS/SPECIAL FEATURES:

Syncrude Canada, Ltd. is a producer of crude oil from oil sands. The firm operates the Syncrude Project, which produces Syncrude Crude Oil and is the top source of oil in Canada, producing approximately 105.8 million barrels per year and satisfying roughly 15% of Canada's total oil needs. The Syncrude Project is a joint-venture operated by the company and owned by seven oil and gas entities: Canadian Oil Sands Limited, the largest shareholder with approximately 36.74% ownership; Imperial Oil Resources (25%); Suncor Energy Oil and Gas Partnership (12%); Sinopec Oil Sands Partnership (9.03%); Nexen Oil Sands Partnership (7.23%); Mocal Energy Limited (5%); and Murphy Oil Company Limited (5%). As the operator of the Syncrude Project, the firm is responsible for managing all the oil sands operations of the joint-venture, including the mining, extraction, upgrading and utilities facilities at both the Mildred Lake and Aurora sites; and managing the research center in Edmonton, Alberta. Alberta's oil sand deposits are estimated to contain approximately 1.7 trillion barrels of bitumen, through which over 315 billion barrels of crude oil are projected to be recoverable in the future. Syncrude Canada is currently in the midst of a three-stage expansion plan called Syncrude 21, which is scheduled to end in 2015, by which time the company hopes to be producing 500,000 barrels of oil per day. At present, the production from the Syncrude Project is about 350,000 barrels per day. In June 2010, ConocoPhillips sold its 9% in Syncrude to Sinopec International Petroleum Exploration and Production Company (SIPC) for $4.65 billion.

Employees receive benefits including tuition reimbursement; scholarships for dependents; employee development programs; vacation time; relocation assistance; the Impact 21 bonus program; a company-matched savings program; pension plan options; and life, accident, disability, health and dental insurance.

FINANCIALS:

Sales and profits are in thousands of dollars—add 000 to get the full amount. 2010 Note: Financial information for 2010 was not available for all companies at press time.

2010 Sales: $ | 2010 Profits: $
2009 Sales: $ | 2009 Profits: $
2008 Sales: $ | 2008 Profits: $
2007 Sales: $ | 2007 Profits: $
2006 Sales: $ | 2006 Profits: $

U.S. Stock Ticker: Private
Int'l Ticker: Int'l Exchange:
Employees:
Fiscal Year Ends: 12/31
Parent Company:

SALARIES/BENEFITS:

Pension Plan: Y | ESOP Stock Plan: | Profit Sharing: | Top Exec. Salary: $ | Bonus: $
Savings Plan: | Stock Purch. Plan: | | Second Exec. Salary: $ | Bonus: $

OTHER THOUGHTS:

Apparent Women Officers or Directors: 1
Hot Spot for Advancement for Women/Minorities:

LOCATIONS: ("Y" = Yes)

West:	Southwest:	Midwest:	Southeast:	Northeast:	International:
					Y

TALISMAN ENERGY INC

www.talisman-energy.com

Industry Group Code: 211111 **Ranks within this company's industry group:** Sales: 56 Profits: 51

Exploration/Production:		Refining/Retailing:		Utilities:		Alternative Energy:		Specialty Services:		Energy Mktg./Other Svcs.	
Exploration:	Y	Refining:		Electric Utility:		Waste/Solar/Other:		Consulting/Eng.:		Energy Marketing:	
Production:	Y	Retailing:		Gas Utility:		Thermal/Steam:		Seismic:		Equipment/Machinery:	
Coal Production:		Convenience Stores:		Pipelines:		Wind:		Drilling:		Oil Field Services:	
		Chemicals:		Water:		Hydro:		InfoTech:		Air/Shipping Transportation:	
						Fuel Cells:		Specialty Services:			

TYPES OF BUSINESS:

Oil & Gas Exploration & Production

BRANDS/DIVISIONS/AFFILIATES:

Talisman Energy Norge AS
Talisman Energy (UK) Limited
Talisman (Asia) Ltd.
Ecopetrol SA
BP Exploration Company (Columbia) Ltd.
Statoil ASA

CONTACTS:

Note: Officers with more than one job title may be intentionally listed here more than once.

John Manzoni, CEO
John Manzoni, Pres.
Scott Thomson, CFO/Exec. VP
Richard Herbert, Exec. VP-Exploration
Robert Rooney, General Counsel/Exec. VP-Legal
Paul Smith, Exec. VP-North American Oper.
Helen Wesley, Exec. VP-Corp. Svcs.
David Mann, VP-Corp. & Investor Comm.
Christopher LeGallais, VP-Investor Rel.
Scott Thomson, Exec. VP-Finance
Paul Blakeley, Exec. VP-Int'l Oper., East
Charles Williamson, Chmn.
Nick Walker, Exec. VP-Int'l Oper., West

Phone: 403-237-1234 **Fax:** 403-237-1902
Toll-Free:
Address: 888 Third St. SW, Ste. 2000, Calgary, AB T2P 5C5 Canada

GROWTH PLANS/SPECIAL FEATURES:

Talisman Energy, Inc., with approximately $24 billion in assets, produces oil and gas in three geographic regions: North America; the North Sea; and Southeast Asia. The North American segment comprises the firm's operations in the U.S. and Canada. Total North American oil production was approximately 27,000 barrels of oil per day (bbls/d) in 2009; natural gas production was approximately 788 million cubic feet per day (mmcf/d). The North Sea segment, comprising U.K. and Scandinavian operations, controls approximately 39 fields. In the U.K., the firm's total production was 86,000 bbls/d of oil and 19 mmcf/d of natural gas, while its Scandinavian production totals were 34,000 bbls/d of oil and 58 mmcf/d of natural gas. The Southeast Asia segment comprises the firm's activities in Malaysia, Indonesia, Vietnam and Papua New Guinea, which produced 41,000 bbls/d of oil and 403 mmcf/d of natural gas. The firm gathered an additional 14,000 bbls/d of oil from other parts of the world. Talisman's 2009 total worldwide production was approximately 425,000 barrels of oil equivalent per day (boe/d), consisting of approximately 50% oil and liquids and 50% natural gas. Talisman's gross proved reserves in 2009 were just over 1.4 billion boe. The firm is currently conducting exploration activities in South America (Peru and Columbia) and in the Kurdistan region of northern Iraq. In April 2010, through a series of five transactions, the company disposed of 1 million net acres of non-core, producing assets located in Canada. In August 2010, Talisman and Ecopetrol agreed to acquire jointly the operations of BP Exploration Company (Columbia) Ltd. for total cash considerations of $1.9 billion. In October 2010, the firm acquired material positions in the Eagle Ford Shale play in south Texas through a joint venture agreement with Statoil ASA.

FINANCIALS:

Sales and profits are in thousands of dollars—add 000 to get the full amount. 2010 Note: Financial information for 2010 was not available for all companies at press time.

2010 Sales: $	2010 Profits: $	**U.S. Stock Ticker: TLM**
2009 Sales: $6,179,580	2009 Profits: $416,930	**Int'l Ticker: TLM** Int'l Exchange: Toronto-TSX
2008 Sales: $9,115,500	2008 Profits: $3,271,210	Employees: 3,000
2007 Sales: $7,020,220	2007 Profits: $1,931,680	Fiscal Year Ends: 12/31
2006 Sales: $6,816,800	2006 Profits: $1,647,600	Parent Company:

SALARIES/BENEFITS:

Pension Plan:	ESOP Stock Plan:	Profit Sharing:	Top Exec. Salary: $1,238,674	Bonus: $2,229,612
Savings Plan:	Stock Purch. Plan:		Second Exec. Salary: $613,494	Bonus: $662,574

OTHER THOUGHTS:

Apparent Women Officers or Directors: 3
Hot Spot for Advancement for Women/Minorities: Y

LOCATIONS: ("Y" = Yes)

West:	Southwest:	Midwest:	Southeast:	Northeast:	International:
Y	Y			Y	Y

TAMPA ELECTRIC COMPANY

www.tampaelectric.com

Industry Group Code: 2211 **Ranks within this company's industry group:** Sales: Profits:

Exploration/Production:		Refining/Retailing:		Utilities:		Alternative Energy:		Specialty Services:		Energy Mktg./Other Svcs.	
Exploration:		Refining:		Electric Utility:	Y	Waste/Solar/Other:	Y	Consulting/Eng.:		Energy Marketing:	
Production:		Retailing:		Gas Utility:	Y	Thermal/Steam:		Seismic:		Equipment/Machinery:	
Coal Production:		Convenience Stores:		Pipelines:		Wind:		Drilling:		Oil Field Services:	
		Chemicals:		Water:		Hydro:		InfoTech:		Air/Shipping Transportation:	Y
						Fuel Cells:		Specialty Services:	Y		

TYPES OF BUSINESS:

Utilities-Electricity & Natural Gas
Electric Generation
Solar Power
Coal Mining & Preparation
Synthetic Fuel
Ocean & River Shipping

BRANDS/DIVISIONS/AFFILIATES:

TECO Energy Inc
Peoples Gas System
M.TampaElectric.com
Tampa Electric

CONTACTS: *Note: Officers with more than one job title may be intentionally listed here more than once.*

Gordon L. Gillette, Pres.
Bruce Narzissenfeld, VP-Customer Care & Fuels Mgmt.
William T. Whale, VP-Electric & Gas Delivery
Thomas L. Hernandez, VP-Energy Supply

Phone: 813-228-1111 **Fax:** 813-228-1670
Toll-Free:
Address: 702 N. Franklin St., TECO Plz., Tampa, FL 33602 US

GROWTH PLANS/SPECIAL FEATURES:

Tampa Electric Company is the principal subsidiary of TECO Energy, Inc. The firm is a public utility that generates, purchases, transmits, distributes, markets and sells electric energy and natural gas in Florida. Founded in 1899, the company operates through two divisions: Tampa Electric and Peoples Gas System. Tampa Electric, with a total generating capacity of 4,719 megawatts, generates, transmits and distributes electric energy. The company serves approximately 666,747 customers in a 2,000 square mile operating service territory including all of Hillsborough County and parts of Pasco, Polk and Pinellas counties in Florida. Tampa Electric derives roughly 46.2% of its revenue from residential sales; 33.4% from commercial sales; 10.6% from industrial sales; and 9.8% from other sales, including bulk power sales for resale. The company operates four generating plants with approximately 54% of energy produced coming from its coal fired plants, approximately 45% coming from its gas fired plants and approximately 1% coming from its oil fired plant. Peoples Gas System operates fossil-fueled power plants and distributes natural gas for more than 334,000 residential, commercial and industrial customers. In early 2009, Tampa Electric Company agreed to purchase solar power for 25 years (beginning in 2011) from a facility to be built by Energy 5.0, a Florida-based firm that develops, finances and operates renewable energy projects. In September 2009, the firm completed construction of five new 60-megawatt natural gas-fired peaking units located at two of its power plants; and launched a new mobile web site, M.TampaElectric.com. In June 2010, Tampa Electric Company installed nitrogen oxide emissions equipment at its Big Bend Power Station Unit 1.

The company offers its employees benefits including life, long-term disability, medical, dental and vision insurance; a pension plan; flexible spending accounts; tuition reimbursement; and paid time off.

FINANCIALS: **Sales and profits are in thousands of dollars—add 000 to get the full amount. 2010 Note: Financial information for 2010 was not available for all companies at press time.**

2010 Sales: $	2010 Profits: $	**U.S. Stock Ticker: Subsidiary**
2009 Sales: $	2009 Profits: $	**Int'l Ticker:** Int'l Exchange:
2008 Sales: $	2008 Profits: $	Employees:
2007 Sales: $	2007 Profits: $	Fiscal Year Ends: 12/31
2006 Sales: $2,661,900	2006 Profits: $165,600	Parent Company: TECO ENERGY INC

SALARIES/BENEFITS:

Pension Plan: Y	ESOP Stock Plan:	Profit Sharing:	Top Exec. Salary: $455,500	Bonus: $284,694
Savings Plan: Y	Stock Purch. Plan:		Second Exec. Salary: $245,640	Bonus: $135,102

OTHER THOUGHTS:

Apparent Women Officers or Directors:
Hot Spot for Advancement for Women/Minorities:

LOCATIONS: ("Y" = Yes)

West:	Southwest:	Midwest:	Southeast:	Northeast:	International:
			Y		

TARGA RESOURCES PARTNERS LP

www.targaresources.com

Industry Group Code: 211111 **Ranks within this company's industry group:** Sales: 63 Profits: 66

Exploration/Production:		Refining/Retailing:		Utilities:		Alternative Energy:		Specialty Services:		Energy Mktg./Other Svcs.	
Exploration:		Refining:		Electric Utility:		Waste/Solar/Other:		Consulting/Eng.:		Energy Marketing:	
Production:	Y	Retailing:		Gas Utility:	Y	Thermal/Steam:		Seismic:		Equipment/Machinery:	
Coal Production:		Convenience Stores:		Pipelines:	Y	Wind:		Drilling:		Oil Field Services:	
		Chemicals:		Water:		Hydro:		InfoTech:		Air/Shipping Transportation:	
						Fuel Cells:		Specialty Services:	Y		

TYPES OF BUSINESS:

Natural Gas Gathering & Compression
Natural & Gas Liquids Processing & Selling

BRANDS/DIVISIONS/AFFILIATES:

Targa Resources Inc
Venice Energy Services Company LLC
Versado System

CONTACTS:

Note: Officers with more than one job title may be intentionally listed here more than once.

Rene R. Joyce, CEO
Michael A. Heim, COO/Exec. VP
Joe Bob Perkins, Pres.
Jeffrey J. McParland, CFO/Exec. VP
James W. Whalen, Pres., Admin.
Paul W. Chung, General Counsel/Exec. VP/Sec.
James W. Whalen, Pres., Finance
Roy E. Johnson, Exec. VP

Phone: 713-584-1000 **Fax:** 713-584-1100
Toll-Free:
Address: 1000 Louisiana St., Ste. 4300, Houston, TX 77002 US

GROWTH PLANS/SPECIAL FEATURES:

Targa Resources Partners LP owns, operates, acquires and develops a diversified portfolio of complementary midstream energy assets. The firm was formed in recent years by its former parent company, Targa Resources, Inc. The company currently operates in Southwest Louisiana, the Fort Worth Basin in north Texas and the Permian Basin in West Texas. It is engaged in the business of gathering, compressing, treating, processing and selling natural gas; and fractioning and selling natural gas liquids (NGL) and NGL products. The firm has two divisions: the natural gas gathering/processing division and the NGL logistics/marketing division. The firm's operations consist of an extensive network of roughly 6,500 miles of natural gas and 750 miles of NGL pipe lines. It also operates 13,500 miles integrated gathering pipelines that gather and compress natural gas received from receipt points in the Fort Worth Basin, Permian Basin, the onshore region of the Louisiana Gulf Coast and the Gulf of Mexico.; and seven natural gas processing plants that compress, treat and process the natural gas. Targa Resources Partners' assets include the Chico system, located in the northeast part of the Fort Worth Basin; the Shackelford system, located on the western side of the Fort Worth Basin; a 165-mile, 10-inch diameter natural gas pipeline connecting the Shackelford and Chico systems used to send extra natural gas of the Shackelford system to the Chico plant; and the Gillis and Acadia systems in Louisiana. Targa Resources, Inc. still owns roughly 32% of the company. In September 2009, the firm acquired Targa Resources' NGL operations. In 2010, Targa Resources Partners acquired several additional assets from Targa Resources, including certain natural gas gathering and processing operations in Texas and Louisiana; its 63% interest in the Versado System for $24.7 million; and 76.8% interest in Venice Energy Services Company, L.L.C.

FINANCIALS:

Sales and profits are in thousands of dollars—add 000 to get the full amount. 2010 Note: Financial information for 2010 was not available for all companies at press time.

2010 Sales: $	2010 Profits: $	**U.S. Stock Ticker: NGLS**
2009 Sales: $3,950,000	2009 Profits: $54,200	**Int'l Ticker:** Int'l Exchange:
2008 Sales: $7,370,300	2008 Profits: $49,700	Employees: 1,000
2007 Sales: $1,661,500	2007 Profits: $40,300	Fiscal Year Ends: 12/31
2006 Sales: $1,738,500	2006 Profits: $11,600	Parent Company:

SALARIES/BENEFITS:

Pension Plan:	ESOP Stock Plan:	Profit Sharing:	Top Exec. Salary: $337,500	Bonus: $510,000
Savings Plan:	Stock Purch. Plan:		Second Exec. Salary: $303,750	Bonus: $459,000

OTHER THOUGHTS:

Apparent Women Officers or Directors:
Hot Spot for Advancement for Women/Minorities:

LOCATIONS: ("Y" = Yes)

West:	Southwest:	Midwest:	Southeast:	Northeast:	International:
	Y	Y	Y	Y	Y

TATA POWER

www.tatapower.com

Industry Group Code: 2211 **Ranks within this company's industry group:** Sales: 29 Profits: 30

Exploration/Production:		Refining/Retailing:		Utilities:		Alternative Energy:		Specialty Services:		Energy Mktg./Other Svcs.	
Exploration:		Refining:		Electric Utility:	Y	Waste/Solar/Other:	Y	Consulting/Eng.:	Y	Energy Marketing:	Y
Production:		Retailing:		Gas Utility:		Thermal/Steam:	Y	Seismic:		Equipment/Machinery:	
Coal Production:		Convenience Stores:		Pipelines:		Wind:	Y	Drilling:		Oil Field Services:	
		Chemicals:		Water:		Hydro:	Y	InfoTech:		Air/Shipping Transportation:	
						Fuel Cells:		Specialty Services:	Y		

TYPES OF BUSINESS:

Electricity Generation
Electricity Transmission & Distribution
Strategic Defense Electronics
Electricity Power Project Consulting

BRANDS/DIVISIONS/AFFILIATES:

Nelco Limited
Chemical Terminal Trombay Limited
Tata Power Trading Company Limited
Maithon Power Limited
Tata Power (Cyprus) Limited
Tata Power (Mauritius) Limited
Tata Power International Holdings Limited
Korea East West Power Company Ltd.

CONTACTS:

Note: Officers with more than one job title may be intentionally listed here more than once.

Prasad R. Menon, Managing Dir.
B.J. Shroff, VP/Company Sec.
S. Padmanabhan, Exec. Dir.-Oper.
Banmali Agrawala, Exec. Dir.-Strategy & Bus. Dev.
Shalini Singh, Head-Corp. Comm.
S. Ramakrishnan, Exec. Dir.
Ratan Naval Tata, Chmn.

Phone: 91-22-6665-8282 **Fax:** 91-22-6665-8801
Toll-Free:
Address: Bombay House, 24, Homi Mody St., Mumbai, 400 001 India

GROWTH PLANS/SPECIAL FEATURES:

Tata Power (TPC) is an India-based power and energy firm, as well as a member of the Tata Group. The company operates in two business segments: Power and Other. The power segment is focused on the generation, transmission and distribution of electricity. The other business segment offers products and services such as strategic electronic equipment and project consultancy. The firm has an installed generation capacity of approximately 2,976 megawatts (MW), including thermal power stations at Jojobera, Trombay and Belgaum; hydroelectric power stations at Bhivpuri, Khopoli and Bhira; and wind farms at Maharashtra, Gujarat and Karnataka. Projects currently under development include a 1,050 MW thermal plant in Maithon, in northeastern India, and a 4,000 MW ultra mega power project (UMPP) in the west-Indian state of Gujarat, as well as a solar and wind project in Maharashtra. The firm has also participated in the erection and commissioning of power plants outside of India, in locations such as Saudi Arabia, Bangladesh, Kuwait, Algeria, Myanmar and Thailand. Subsidiaries of the company include Nelco Limited, Chemical Terminal Trombay Limited, Af-Taab Investment Company Limited, Tata Power Trading Company Limited, Tatanet Services Limited, Maithon Power Limited, Powerlinks Transmission Limited, Coastal Gujrat Power Limited, Industrial Energy Limited, Tata Power (Cyprus) Limited, Tata Power (Mauritius) Limited, Tata Power International Holdings Limited, Veltina Holdings Limited, Industrial Power Infrastructure Limited, Industrial Power Utility Limited and North Delhi Power Limited. In October 2009, the firm signed a partnership agreement with the Norwegian firm SN Power to develop hydropower projects in India and Nepal. In February 2010, the company signed an agreement with Korea's East West Power Company Ltd. to cooperate in the field of operation and maintenance of electricity generation assets.

FINANCIALS:

Sales and profits are in thousands of dollars—add 000 to get the full amount. 2010 Note: Financial information for 2010 was not available for all companies at press time.

2010 Sales: $	2010 Profits: $	**U.S. Stock Ticker:**
2009 Sales: $3,713,330	2009 Profits: $257,320	**Int'l Ticker: 500400** Int'l Exchange: Bombay-BSE
2008 Sales: $2,299,440	2008 Profits: $222,760	Employees: 3,541
2007 Sales: $1,367,230	2007 Profits: $160,380	Fiscal Year Ends: 3/31
2006 Sales: $1,171,000	2006 Profits: $152,590	Parent Company:

SALARIES/BENEFITS:

Pension Plan:	ESOP Stock Plan:	Profit Sharing:	Top Exec. Salary: $	Bonus: $
Savings Plan:	Stock Purch. Plan:		Second Exec. Salary: $	Bonus: $

OTHER THOUGHTS:

Apparent Women Officers or Directors:
Hot Spot for Advancement for Women/Minorities:

LOCATIONS: ("Y" = Yes)

West:	Southwest:	Midwest:	Southeast:	Northeast:	International:
					Y

TEAM INC

www.teamindustrialservices.com

Industry Group Code: 213112 **Ranks within this company's industry group:** Sales: 24 Profits: 19

Exploration/Production:		Refining/Retailing:		Utilities:		Alternative Energy:		Specialty Services:		Energy Mktg./Other Svcs.	
Exploration:		Refining:		Electric Utility:		Waste/Solar/Other:		Consulting/Eng.:	Y	Energy Marketing:	
Production:		Retailing:		Gas Utility:		Thermal/Steam:		Seismic:		Equipment/Machinery:	Y
Coal Production:		Convenience Stores:		Pipelines:		Wind:		Drilling:		Oil Field Services:	
		Chemicals:		Water:		Hydro:		InfoTech:		Air/Shipping Transportation:	
						Fuel Cells:		Specialty Services:	Y		

TYPES OF BUSINESS:

Piping System Maintenance & Construction Services

BRANDS/DIVISIONS/AFFILIATES:

Team Industrial Services, Inc.
Team Industrial Services International, Inc.
Team Industrial Services Asia (PTE) Ltd.
TISI Canada, Inc.

CONTACTS:

Note: Officers with more than one job title may be intentionally listed here more than once.

Philip J. Hawk, CEO
Pete W. Wallace, COO/Exec. VP
Ted W. Owen, CFO/Exec. VP
John P. Kearns, Sr. VP-Eng.
John P. Kearns, Sr. VP-Mfg.
Andre C. (Butch) Bouchard, Sr. VP-Admin.
Andre C. (Butch) Bouchard, General Counsel/Sec.
David C. Palmore, Sr. VP-TMS Div.
Art Victorson, Sr. VP-TCM Div.
Philip J. Hawk, Chmn.

Phone: 281-331-6154	**Fax:**
Toll-Free: 800-662-8326	
Address: 200 Hermann Dr., Alvin, TX 77511 US	

GROWTH PLANS/SPECIAL FEATURES:

Team, Inc. is a provider of specialty maintenance and construction services related primarily to the maintenance of high temperature and high pressure piping systems utilized in heavy industries. The company's offerings encompass a range of services, including leak repair, hot tapping, fugitive emissions control, field machining, technical bolting, field valve repair, non-destructive testing and field heat treating. Team's services are available 24-hour-a-day, seven-days-a-week, and are marketed to companies in a broad range of industries, including petrochemicals, refining, power, pipeline, pulp and paper, steel, shipbuilding, original equipment manufacturers (OEMs), municipalities and large engineering and construction firms. Team's leak repair services consist of on-stream repairs of leaks in pipes, valves, flanges and other parts of piping systems and related equipment, utilizing both standard and custom-designed clamps and enclosures for piping systems. The company's hot tapping services involve utilizing special equipment to cut holes in pressurized pipelines so that new branch pipes can be connected without interrupting operations. Emissions control services are focused on volatile organic chemical leaks, and include identification, monitoring, data management and reporting services primarily for the chemical, refining and natural gas processing industries. Field machining services include flange facing, pipe cutting, line boring, journal turning, drilling and milling, while technical bolting services help to maintain leak-free connections. Field valve services encompass on-site repairs for a variety of valves, as well as diagnostics and repair for specialty valve actuators. The company maintains over 100 locations throughout the U.S., as well as international locations in Canada, Aruba, Belgium, Singapore, the Netherlands, Trinidad and Venezuela. In 2009, 71% of the firm's revenues were generated by business in the U.S., while Canada accounted for approximately 20% and Europe 5%, with the remaining 4% coming from other foreign locations.

FINANCIALS:

Sales and profits are in thousands of dollars—add 000 to get the full amount. 2010 Note: Financial information for 2010 was not available for all companies at press time.

2010 Sales: $	2010 Profits: $	**U.S. Stock Ticker: TISI**
2009 Sales: $497,559	2009 Profits: $22,911	**Int'l Ticker:** Int'l Exchange:
2008 Sales: $478,475	2008 Profits: $23,623	Employees: 3,400
2007 Sales: $318,348	2007 Profits: $15,515	Fiscal Year Ends: 5/31
2006 Sales: $259,838	2006 Profits: $10,636	Parent Company:

SALARIES/BENEFITS:

Pension Plan:	ESOP Stock Plan:	Profit Sharing:	Top Exec. Salary: $550,000	Bonus: $220,000
Savings Plan: Y	Stock Purch. Plan:		Second Exec. Salary: $300,000	Bonus: $105,000

OTHER THOUGHTS:

Apparent Women Officers or Directors:
Hot Spot for Advancement for Women/Minorities:

LOCATIONS: ("Y" = Yes)

West:	Southwest:	Midwest:	Southeast:	Northeast:	International:
Y	Y	Y	Y	Y	Y

Note: Financial information, benefits and other data can change quickly and may vary from those stated here.

TECHNIP

www.technip.com

Industry Group Code: 213112 **Ranks within this company's industry group:** Sales: 5 Profits: 9

Exploration/Production:		**Refining/Retailing:**		**Utilities:**		**Alternative Energy:**		**Specialty Services:**		**Energy Mktg./Other Svcs.**	
Exploration:		Refining:		Electric Utility:		Waste/Solar/Other:		Consulting/Eng.:	Y	Energy Marketing:	
Production:		Retailing:		Gas Utility:		Thermal/Steam:		Seismic:		Equipment/Machinery:	
Coal Production:		Convenience Stores:		Pipelines:		Wind:		Drilling:		Oil Field Services:	Y
		Chemicals:		Water:		Hydro:		InfoTech:		Air/Shipping Transportation:	
						Fuel Cells:		Specialty Services:	Y		

TYPES OF BUSINESS:

Construction Services-Oil & Gas Wells
Marine & Subsea Construction
Refinery Construction
Pipeline Construction
Petrochemical Plant Construction
Maintenance Services
Metallurgical Facility Construction
Power Generation Systems

BRANDS/DIVISIONS/AFFILIATES:

Technip USA, Inc.
Angoflex
Technip Angola Engenharia, Limitada
Flexibras Tubos Flexiveis Ltda
Technip KTI SpA
Duco Ltd
Technip Seiffert GmbH
RJ Brown Deepwater, Inc.

CONTACTS: *Note: Officers with more than one job title may be intentionally listed here more than once.*

Thierry Pilenko, CEO
Bernard di Tullio, COO
Bernard di Tullio, Pres.
Julian Waldron, CFO
Thierry Parmentier, Dir.-Human Resources
John Harrison, General Counsel
Philippe Barril, Sr. VP-Offshore
Dominique de Soras, Sr. VP-Subsea
Nello Uccelletti, Sr. VP-Onshore
Thierry Pilenko, Chmn.

Phone: 33-1-47-78-21-21 **Fax:** 33-1-47-78-33-40
Toll-Free:
Address: 6-8 Allee de l'Arche, Paris, 92973 France

GROWTH PLANS/SPECIAL FEATURES:

Technip is a Paris-based oil, gas and petrochemical engineering and construction services company with global operations. It is active in the subsea, offshore and onshore industry sectors. The firm's subsea services include development solutions; subsea transportation and control systems; design, manufacturing, installation and commissioning of pipeline systems; and flowlines, riser systems, umbilicals and subsea construction. The offshore segment's activities include offshore oil field development, fixed and floating platform construction, maintenance and mooring services. Technip's proprietary technologies are offered under the Spar, TPG 500, MOSS Unideck, EDP, IDV and Jackdeck brand names. The onshore segment develops onshore oil fields and constructs pipeline systems. Its services include field development, gas treatment and liquefaction, oil refining, pipelines, petrochemicals and advanced systems engineering. The types of facilities available include gathering systems and pipelines; well test facilities; multiphase and triphase pumping; gas-lift; secondary recovery and assisted recovery; crude storage; and power plants. The firm's main industrial assets included 16 operating pipelay and subsea construction vessels. Additional assets include flexible pipe manufacturing plants in Le Trait, France and Vitoria, Brazil; umbilical plants in England, the US and Angola; and rigid steel pipe spoolbases in Scotland, Norway, the US and Angola. The main engineering and project management operations are located in Paris, Aberdeen, Pori, Oslo, Houston, Abu Dhabi, Kuala Lumpur, Rio de Janeiro and Perth. In November 2009, Technip and Schlumberger announced a joint development agreement to collaborate on the development of subsea integrity and surveillance solutions for flexible pipes used in deep offshore oil and gas production. In August 2010, the firm agreed to establish a long-term strategic collaboration with two subsidiaries of Petroliam Nasional Berhad (PETRONAS) for on and offshore development projects.

FINANCIALS: **Sales and profits are in thousands of dollars—add 000 to get the full amount. 2010 Note: Financial information for 2010 was not available for all companies at press time.**

2010 Sales: $	2010 Profits: $	**U.S. Stock Ticker: TKP**
2009 Sales: $8,773,380	2009 Profits: $231,510	**Int'l Ticker: TECF** Int'l Exchange: Paris-Euronext
2008 Sales: $9,898,940	2008 Profits: $592,770	Employees: 23,000
2007 Sales: $10,434,940	2007 Profits: $167,110	Fiscal Year Ends: 12/31
2006 Sales: $11,082,400	2006 Profits: $320,200	Parent Company:

SALARIES/BENEFITS:

Pension Plan:	ESOP Stock Plan:	Profit Sharing:	Top Exec. Salary: $	Bonus: $
Savings Plan:	Stock Purch. Plan:		Second Exec. Salary: $	Bonus: $

OTHER THOUGHTS:

Apparent Women Officers or Directors:
Hot Spot for Advancement for Women/Minorities:

LOCATIONS: ("Y" = Yes)

West:	Southwest:	Midwest:	Southeast:	Northeast:	International:
Y	Y		Y		Y

TECO ENERGY INC

www.tecoenergy.com

Industry Group Code: 221 **Ranks within this company's industry group:** Sales: 36 Profits: 37

Exploration/Production:		Refining/Retailing:		Utilities:		Alternative Energy:		Specialty Services:		Energy Mktg./Other Svcs.	
Exploration:		Refining:		Electric Utility:	Y	Waste/Solar/Other:		Consulting/Eng.:	Y	Energy Marketing:	Y
Production:		Retailing:		Gas Utility:	Y	Thermal/Steam:		Seismic:		Equipment/Machinery:	
Coal Production:	Y	Convenience Stores:		Pipelines:	Y	Wind:		Drilling:		Oil Field Services:	
		Chemicals:		Water:		Hydro:		InfoTech:		Air/Shipping Transportation:	Y
						Fuel Cells:		Specialty Services:	Y		

TYPES OF BUSINESS:

Utilities-Electricity & Natural Gas
Natural Gas Distribution
Bulk Commodities Shipping
Coal Mining
Engineering & Energy Services

BRANDS/DIVISIONS/AFFILIATES:

Tampa Electric Company
TECO Coal Corp
TECO Transport Corp
TECO Guatemala Inc
Tampa Electric
Peoples Gas System (The)

CONTACTS:

Note: Officers with more than one job title may be intentionally listed here more than once.

John B. Ramil, CEO
John B. Ramil, Pres.
Sandra W. Callahan, CFO/VP-Finance & Acct.
Clinton E. Childress, Chief Human Resources Officer/Sr. VP-Corp. Svcs.
Karen Mincey, CIO/VP-IT
Charles A. Attal, III, General Counsel/Chief Legal Officer/VP
Phil Barringer, VP-Oper.
Deidre A. Brown, VP-Bus. Strategy & Compliance
Gordon L. Gillette, Pres., Tampa Electric & People Gas
J. J. Shackleford, Pres., TECO Coal
Phil Barringer, VP-Human Resources
Sherrill W. Hudson, Chmn.
Phil Barringer, Pres., TECO Guatemala

Phone: 813-228-1111	Fax:
Toll-Free:	
Address: 702 N. Franklin St., Tampa, FL 33602 US	

GROWTH PLANS/SPECIAL FEATURES:

TECO Energy, Inc. is a holding company for regulated utilities and other unregulated businesses. The company's largest subsidiary is Tampa Electric Company, which operates through divisions Tampa Electric and The Peoples Gas System. The Tampa Electric division provides retail electric service to more than 667,000 customers in west central Florida with a generating capability of 4,719 megawatts (MW). The Peoples Gas System division purchases, distributes and sells natural gas for residual, commercial, industrial and electric power generation customers in Florida. With over 334,000 customers, the gas division has operations in Florida's major metropolitan areas. Its annual gas throughput is roughly 1.4 billion therms. Subsidiary TECO Coal Corp. has 13 subsidiaries located in eastern Kentucky, Tennessee and Virginia. These entities own interests in coal processing and loading facilities; synthetic fuel production facilities; mineral rights; and surface and underground mines. TECO Coal uses two distinct extraction techniques: dozer/front-end loader surface mining and continuous underground mining. Annually, TECO Coal sells about 8.75 million tons of coal, all of which is sold to customers other than Tampa Electric. TECO Transport Corp. owns nine subsidiaries that provide waterborne transportation, storage and transfer service of coal and other dry-bulk commodities. TECO Guatemala, Inc. primarily has investments in unconsolidated subsidiaries that participate in independent power plant projects and electric distribution in Guatemala. Currently, it operates two power plants in Guatemala: the San Jose Power Station, a 120 MW plant, and Alborada Power Station, a 78 MW plant. In August 2009, Tampa Electric completed construction on a $190 million expansion project of the H. L. Culbreath Bayside Power Station, a 240 MW plant in Tampa, Florida.

The firm offers its employees life, long-term disability, medical, dental, vision and prescription drug insurance; profit sharing; retirement plans; an assistance plan; paid time off; paid time off; and tuition reimbursement.

FINANCIALS:

Sales and profits are in thousands of dollars—add 000 to get the full amount. 2010 Note: Financial information for 2010 was not available for all companies at press time.

2010 Sales: $	2010 Profits: $	**U.S. Stock Ticker: TE**
2009 Sales: $3,310,500	2009 Profits: $213,900	**Int'l Ticker:** Int'l Exchange:
2008 Sales: $3,375,300	2008 Profits: $162,400	Employees: 4,073
2007 Sales: $3,536,100	2007 Profits: $413,200	Fiscal Year Ends: 12/31
2006 Sales: $3,448,100	2006 Profits: $246,300	Parent Company:

SALARIES/BENEFITS:

Pension Plan: Y	ESOP Stock Plan:	Profit Sharing: Y	Top Exec. Salary: $826,189	Bonus: $579,628
Savings Plan: Y	Stock Purch. Plan:		Second Exec. Salary: $534,000	Bonus: $328,742

OTHER THOUGHTS:

Apparent Women Officers or Directors: 4
Hot Spot for Advancement for Women/Minorities: Y

LOCATIONS: ("Y" = Yes)

West:	Southwest:	Midwest:	Southeast:	Northeast:	International:
		Y	Y	Y	Y

TENAGA NASIONAL BERHAD (TNB)

www.tnb.com.my

Industry Group Code: 2211 **Ranks within this company's industry group:** Sales: 23 Profits: 29

Exploration/Production:		Refining/Retailing:		Utilities:		Alternative Energy:		Specialty Services:		Energy Mktg./Other Svcs.	
Exploration:		Refining:		Electric Utility:	Y	Waste/Solar/Other:		Consulting/Eng.:	Y	Energy Marketing:	
Production:		Retailing:		Gas Utility:		Thermal/Steam:		Seismic:		Equipment/Machinery:	Y
Coal Production:	Y	Convenience Stores:		Pipelines:		Wind:		Drilling:		Oil Field Services:	
		Chemicals:		Water:		Hydro:		InfoTech:		Air/Shipping Transportation:	
						Fuel Cells:		Specialty Services:	Y		

TYPES OF BUSINESS:

Electric Utility
Manufacturing-Electrical Transmission Equipment
Engineering & Consulting Services
Repair & Maintenance
Fuel Distribution
Property Development
Research & Project Management
University Education

BRANDS/DIVISIONS/AFFILIATES:

TBN Engineering Corporation
Universiti Tenaga Nasional
Sabah Electricity
Malaysia Transformer Manufacturing
TNB Coal International Limited
Tenaga Cable Industries
TNB Liberty Power Limited
Sultan Ahmad Shah Training Institute

CONTACTS: *Note: Officers with more than one job title may be intentionally listed here more than once.*

Che Khalib bin Mohamad Noh, CEO
Azman Mohd, COO
Che Khalib bin Mohamad Noh, Pres.
Mohd Rafique Merican Mohd Wahiduddin, CFO
Muhammad Razif bin Abdul Rahman, VP-Human Resources
Razali bin Awang, CIO
Nor Zakiah binti Abdul Ghani, Corp. Sec.
Roslina Zainal, VP-Planning
Adelina Iskandar, VP-Corp. Affairs
Mohd Rafique Merican Mohd Wahiduddin, VP-Finance
Rozimi Remeli, VP-Transmission
Mohd Nazri bin Shahruddin, VP-Generation
Hussin Othamn, VP-Dist.
Md. Jailani Abas, Sr. Gen. Mgr.-Corp. Svcs.
Leo Moggie, Chmn.
Nor Azmi Ramli, Chief Procurement Officer

Phone: 603-2296-5566 **Fax:** 603-2283-3686
Toll-Free:
Address: 129 Jalan Bangsar, Kuala Lumpur, 59200 Malaysia

GROWTH PLANS/SPECIAL FEATURES:

Tenaga Nasional Berhad (TNB), with over $23 billion in assets, is one of the largest electricity companies in Malaysia. The firm serves over 7.5 million customers throughout mainland Malaysia and Sabah, on Borneo; and has a generation capacity of approximately 12,233 megawatts (MW). In 2009, hydroelectric generation accounted for approximately 15% of this capacity; conventional coal-fired plants, 26%; and various gas-fired plants, 59%. TNB also supports a complete power supply system, including the national grid, customer service centers, call management centers and administrative offices. The company has numerous subsidiaries, many of which have additional subsidiaries under them. These subsidiaries are involved in a diverse mix of industrial and professional industries, including the manufacture of transformers, high voltage switchgears and cables; repair and maintenance services for power plant equipment; consultancy for architectural, civil and electrical engineers; and research and development, property development and project management services. These subsidiaries include TNB Engineering Corporation, Sabah Electricity, Malaysia Transformer Manufacturing, TNB Coal International Limited, Tenaga Cable Industries, TNB Liberty Power Limited and Universiti Tenaga Nasional. Through its Sultan Ahmad Shah Training Institute (ILSAS), TNB provides training services for power companies in emerging countries, including Vietnam, Yemen, Mongolia, Laos, Indonesia, Thailand, Nepal, Egypt and Pakistan.

TNB offers its employees higher education classes through its Universiti Tenaga Nasional, which has graduated 7,000 students in its decade of operations, and other technical training through another institution. The firm is a sponsor of sports throughout the country and hosts a bi-annual sports carnival for its entire workforce.

FINANCIALS: **Sales and profits are in thousands of dollars—add 000 to get the full amount. 2010 Note: Financial information for 2010 was not available for all companies at press time.**

2010 Sales: $
2009 Sales: $8,426,700
2008 Sales: $7,507,920
2007 Sales: $6,660,000
2006 Sales: $5,540,000

2010 Profits: $
2009 Profits: $268,700
2008 Profits: $756,320
2007 Profits: $1,160,000
2006 Profits: $580,000

U.S. Stock Ticker:
Int'l Ticker: 5347 Int'l Exchange: Kuala Lumpur-KLSE
Employees: 29,210
Fiscal Year Ends: 8/31
Parent Company:

SALARIES/BENEFITS:

Pension Plan: ESOP Stock Plan: Profit Sharing: Top Exec. Salary: $ Bonus: $
Savings Plan: Stock Purch. Plan: Second Exec. Salary: $ Bonus: $

OTHER THOUGHTS:

Apparent Women Officers or Directors: 2
Hot Spot for Advancement for Women/Minorities: Y

LOCATIONS: ("Y" = Yes)

West:	Southwest:	Midwest:	Southeast:	Northeast:	International:
					Y

Note: Financial information, benefits and other data can change quickly and may vary from those stated here.

TENARIS SA

www.tenaris.com

Industry Group Code: 331210 **Ranks within this company's industry group:** Sales: 1 Profits: 1

Exploration/Production:		**Refining/Retailing:**		**Utilities:**		**Alternative Energy:**		**Specialty Services:**		**Energy Mktg./Other Svcs.**	
Exploration:		Refining:		Electric Utility:		Waste/Solar/Other:		Consulting/Eng.:		Energy Marketing:	
Production:		Retailing:		Gas Utility:		Thermal/Steam:		Seismic:		Equipment/Machinery:	Y
Coal Production:		Convenience Stores:		Pipelines:		Wind:		Drilling:		Oil Field Services:	
		Chemicals:		Water:		Hydro:		InfoTech:		Air/Shipping Transportation:	
						Fuel Cells:		Specialty Services:			

TYPES OF BUSINESS:

Steel Pipe Manufacturing

BRANDS/DIVISIONS/AFFILIATES:

Seamless Pipe Indonesia Jaya
Tenaris Pipeline Services
Tenaris Process and Power Plant Services
Tenaris Industrial and Automotive Services

CONTACTS:

Note: Officers with more than one job title may be intentionally listed here more than once.

Paolo Rocca, CEO
Ricardo Soler, CFO
Marco Radnic, Dir.-Human Resources
Carlos Pappier, CIO
Marcelo Ramos, Dir.-Tech.
Guillermo Moreno, Dir.-Planning
Alejandro Lammertyn, Mgr.-Eastern Hemisphere
Sergio Tosato, Dir.-Industrial Coordination
Vincenzo Crapanzano, Mgr.-Europe
Sergio de la Maza, Mgr.-Central America
Paolo Rocca, Chmn.
German Cura, Mgr.-North America
Renato Catallini, Dir.-Supply Chain

Phone: 352-26-478-978	**Fax:** 352-26-478978
Toll-Free: 888-300-5432	
Address: 46A, John F. Kennedy Ave., 2nd Fl., Luxembourg, 1855 Luxembourg	

GROWTH PLANS/SPECIAL FEATURES:

Tenaris S.A. is a manufacturer and supplier of steel pipe products and related services for the energy industry. The firm's customers include oil/gas and engineering companies engaged in constructing oil and gas gathering, transportation and processing facilities. Tenaris' principal products include casing, tubing, line pipe, coiled tubing, premium joints/couplings, and mechanical/structural pipes. Other products include welded steel pipes for electric conduits used in the construction industry; sucker rods used in oil extraction activities; and industrial equipment of various specifications and diverse applications, including liquid and gas storage equipment. The company operates in 25 countries through three business units: Tenaris Pipeline Services; Tenaris Process and Power Plant Services; and Tenaris Industrial and Automotive Services. Tenaris Pipeline Services provides products and services for the transmission of fluids and gases from the well head to processing and distribution facilities for oil/gas and other energy companies. The Tenaris Process and Power Plant Services division offers products and services for construction and maintenance purposes to oil and gas processing facilities, refineries, petrochemical companies and energy generating plants. Tenaris Industrial and Automotive Services provides tubular products and services for automobile and other industrial manufacturers. In early 2009, the firm acquired 77.45% ownership of Seamless Pipe Indonesia Jaya, an Indonesian OCTG processing company, from Green Pipe International Limited, Bakrie & Brothers TbK and Cakrawala Baru for $72.5 million. In August 2009, the Venezuelan government took over operational control of former Tenaris subsidiary Matesi Materiales Siderurgicos S.A. In November 2009, Venezuela nationalized former Tenaris subsidiary Tavsa, Tubos de Acero de Venezuela S.A. In July 2010, the company dissolved its Tenaris Oilfield Services division into its other three divisions.

FINANCIALS:

Sales and profits are in thousands of dollars—add 000 to get the full amount. 2010 Note: Financial information for 2010 was not available for all companies at press time.

2010 Sales: $	2010 Profits: $	**U.S. Stock Ticker: TS**
2009 Sales: $8,149,320	2009 Profits: $1,207,599	**Int'l Ticker:** Int'l Exchange:
2008 Sales: $11,987,760	2008 Profits: $2,275,620	Employees: 22,591
2007 Sales: $10,042,008	2007 Profits: $2,076,059	Fiscal Year Ends: 12/31
2006 Sales: $7,727,745	2006 Profits: $2,059,404	Parent Company:

SALARIES/BENEFITS:

Pension Plan:	ESOP Stock Plan:	Profit Sharing:	Top Exec. Salary: $	Bonus: $
Savings Plan:	Stock Purch. Plan:		Second Exec. Salary: $	Bonus: $

OTHER THOUGHTS:

Apparent Women Officers or Directors:
Hot Spot for Advancement for Women/Minorities:

LOCATIONS: ("Y" = Yes)

West:	Southwest:	Midwest:	Southeast:	Northeast:	International:
Y	Y	Y	Y	Y	Y

TENASKA INC

www.tenaska.com

Industry Group Code: 523140 **Ranks within this company's industry group:** Sales: 1 Profits:

Exploration/Production:		Refining/Retailing:		Utilities:		Alternative Energy:		Specialty Services:		Energy Mktg./Other Svcs.	
Exploration:		Refining:		Electric Utility:	Y	Waste/Solar/Other:		Consulting/Eng.:	Y	Energy Marketing:	Y
Production:		Retailing:		Gas Utility:		Thermal/Steam:		Seismic:		Equipment/Machinery:	Y
Coal Production:		Convenience Stores:		Pipelines:		Wind:		Drilling:		Oil Field Services:	
		Chemicals:		Water:		Hydro:		InfoTech:		Air/Shipping Transportation:	
						Fuel Cells:		Specialty Services:	Y		

TYPES OF BUSINESS:

Energy Trading & Marketing
Electric Generation Plants
Engineering & Construction Services

BRANDS/DIVISIONS/AFFILIATES:

Tenaska Power Services Co
Tenaska Marketing Ventures
Tenaska Marketing Canada
Tenaska BioFuels LLC
Voyager Midstream LLC
Tenaska Capital Management LLC
Tenaska Resources LLC
Tenaska Midstream Services LLC

CONTACTS:

Note: Officers with more than one job title may be intentionally listed here more than once.

Jerry K. Crouse, CEO
Gregory A. Van Dyke, CFO/Treas.
Michael C. Lebens, CEO/Pres., Eng. Group
Drew J. Fossum, General Counsel/VP
Michael C. Lebens, CEO/Pres., Oper. Group
David G. Fiorelli, CEO/Pres., Bus. Dev. Group
Jana Martin, Dir.-Gov't & Public Affairs
Tim Kudron, Corp. Controller/Sr. VP
Thomas E. Hendricks, Exec. VP
Michael F. Lawler, Exec. VP-Corp. Investments
Trudy A. Harper, Pres., Tenaska Power Svcs. Co.
Paul G. Smith, CEO/Sr. Managing Dir.-Tenaska Capital Mgmt. LLC
Howard L. Hawks, Chmn.
Fred R. Hunzeker, Pres., Tenaska Mktg. Canada

Phone: 402-691-9500 **Fax:** 402-691-9526
Toll-Free:
Address: 1044 N. 115th St., Ste. 400, Omaha, NE 68154-4446 US

GROWTH PLANS/SPECIAL FEATURES:

Tenaska, Inc. is involved in natural gas and electric power marketing, fuel procurement and generation asset development and acquisition. The firm provides development, engineering, construction, financing and operating management services; it also owns and operates its own cogeneration and non-utility electric generation power plants. Tenaska has developed about 9,000 megawatts (MW) of generating facilities and currently operates and manages roughly 6,700 MW at eight generating facilities. In addition, Tenaska's power marketing subsidiary, Tenaska Power Services (TPS), develops custom power supply strategies and sells roughly 7,000 gigawatt-hours per year in the U.S. and Canada. TPS also manages 17,500 MW of electricity, part of which is in the form of installed wind capacity in Texas. Through subsidiary Tenaska Marketing Ventures (which also operates as Tenaska Marketing Canada), the firm sells and/or manages 2 trillion cubic feet of gas annually. The firm's Tenaska BioFuels, LLC subsidiary provides marketing, transportation and financial services to the ethanol and biodiesel industries. Other subsidiaries and affiliates include Tenaska Resources, LLC, a gas exploration and production firm with leases in Pennsylvania and West Virginia; Tenaska Drilling Services, LLC, which purchases and operates the drilling rigs used by Tenaska Resources; Tenaska Midstream Services, LLC, a developer and operator of midstream facilities for Tenaska Resources; and Tenaska Capital Management, LLC, which manages private equity funds Tenaska Power Fund, L.P. and TPF II, L.P. In August 2009, Tenaska Capital Management, LLC and Energy Spectrum Partners V LP formed joint venture Frontier Gas Services, LLC.

FINANCIALS:

Sales and profits are in thousands of dollars—add 000 to get the full amount. 2010 Note: Financial information for 2010 was not available for all companies at press time.

2010 Sales: $	2010 Profits: $
2009 Sales: $7,904,000	2009 Profits: $
2008 Sales: $16,027,000	2008 Profits: $
2007 Sales: $11,600,000	2007 Profits: $
2006 Sales: $8,700,000	2006 Profits: $

U.S. Stock Ticker: Private
Int'l Ticker: Int'l Exchange:
Employees: 688
Fiscal Year Ends: 12/31
Parent Company:

SALARIES/BENEFITS:

Pension Plan:	ESOP Stock Plan:	Profit Sharing:	Top Exec. Salary: $	Bonus: $
Savings Plan: Y	Stock Purch. Plan:		Second Exec. Salary: $	Bonus: $

OTHER THOUGHTS:

Apparent Women Officers or Directors: 5
Hot Spot for Advancement for Women/Minorities: Y

LOCATIONS: ("Y" = Yes)

West:	Southwest:	Midwest:	Southeast:	Northeast:	International:
Y	Y	Y			Y

TENNESSEE VALLEY AUTHORITY (TVA)

www.tva.gov

Industry Group Code: 2211 **Ranks within this company's industry group:** Sales: 18 Profits: 19

Exploration/Production:		Refining/Retailing:		Utilities:		Alternative Energy:		Specialty Services:		Energy Mktg./Other Svcs.	
Exploration:		Refining:		Electric Utility:	Y	Waste/Solar/Other:	Y	Consulting/Eng.:		Energy Marketing:	
Production:		Retailing:		Gas Utility:		Thermal/Steam:		Seismic:		Equipment/Machinery:	
Coal Production:		Convenience Stores:		Pipelines:		Wind:	Y	Drilling:		Oil Field Services:	
		Chemicals:		Water:		Hydro:	Y	InfoTech:		Air/Shipping Transportation:	
						Fuel Cells:		Specialty Services:	Y		

TYPES OF BUSINESS:

Electric Utility
Power Generation
Renewable Energy
Hydroelectric Facilities
Nuclear Facilities
Hydrological & Public Lands Management

BRANDS/DIVISIONS/AFFILIATES:

Green Power Switch
TVA Renewable Standard Offer

CONTACTS: *Note: Officers with more than one job title may be intentionally listed here more than once.*

Tom Kilgore, CEO
William R. McCollum, Jr., COO
Tom Kilgore, Pres.
John M. Thomas III, CFO
Janet C. Herrin, Exec. VP-People & Performance
Anda A. Ray, Environment & Sustainability Officer
Daniel Traynor, CIO
Anda A. Ray, CTO
Ralph Rodgers, Acting General Counsel
Robin E. Manning, Exec. VP-Power Systems Oper.
Van M. Wardlaw, Exec. VP-Strategy & Bus. Planning
David R. Mould, Sr. VP-Comm.
John Hoskins, Sr. VP-Treas.
Emily J. Reynolds, Sr. VP-Gov't Rel.
John McCormick, Sr. VP-River Oper.
Robert Fisher, Exec. VP-Fossil Power Group
William B. Sansom, Chmn.

Phone: 865-632-2101 **Fax:** 865-633-0372
Toll-Free: 888-882-4967
Address: 400 W. Summit Hill Dr., Knoxville, TN 37902-1499 US

GROWTH PLANS/SPECIAL FEATURES:

Tennessee Valley Authority (TVA) is a government-owned corporation and the largest public power company in the U.S. TVA operates in almost all of Tennessee and parts of Mississippi, Kentucky, Alabama, Georgia, North Carolina and Virginia. TVA operates three nuclear, 11 fossil, 29 hydro-electric, nine combustion-turbine and one pumped-storage plant. Fossil fuel plants produce about 46% of TVA's total generation, while 32% comes from nuclear power; 7% from hydropower; 2% from combustion turbines, diesel, and renewable sources; and 13% is purchased from third parties. TVA's renewable energy program, Green Power Switch, includes 15 solar sites, one wind-energy site and a methane gas facility. The group supplies energy to approximately 9 million people through wholesale power given to 155 distributors; it also directly serves about 60 large industrial and government installations. Its total generating capacity is approximately 33,716 megawatts and it maintains over15,900 miles of transmission lines. The company also manages one of nation's largest river systems in order to minimize flood risk, maintain navigation, provide recreational opportunities and oversee the responsible management of public land. In early 2009, the company announced plans to construct a 880-megawatt gas-fired power plant in northeast Tennessee. In June 2010, the firm added two sulfur dioxide emission reducing scrubbers to its Kingston Fossil Plant. In October 2010, TVA introduced TVA Renewable Standard Offer, which provides long-term price contracts to mid-size renewable developers producing between 201 kilowatts and 20 megawatts of electricity per project.

TVA offers its employees onsite fitness centers, transportation assistance, banking discounts, tuition reimbursement and legal services.

FINANCIALS: **Sales and profits are in thousands of dollars—add 000 to get the full amount. 2010 Note: Financial information for 2010 was not available for all companies at press time.**

2010 Sales: $	2010 Profits: $	**U.S. Stock Ticker: Government-Owned**
2009 Sales: $11,300,000	2009 Profits: $726,000	**Int'l Ticker:** Int'l Exchange:
2008 Sales: $10,382,000	2008 Profits: $817,000	Employees:
2007 Sales: $9,269,000	2007 Profits: $423,000	Fiscal Year Ends: 9/30
2006 Sales: $9,185,000	2006 Profits: $329,000	Parent Company:

SALARIES/BENEFITS:

Pension Plan: Y	ESOP Stock Plan:	Profit Sharing:	Top Exec. Salary: $	Bonus: $334,152
Savings Plan: Y	Stock Purch. Plan:		Second Exec. Salary: $	Bonus: $

OTHER THOUGHTS:

Apparent Women Officers or Directors: 4
Hot Spot for Advancement for Women/Minorities: Y

LOCATIONS: ("Y" = Yes)

West:	Southwest:	Midwest:	Southeast:	Northeast:	International:
			Y	Y	

TESCO CORPORATION

www.tescocorp.com

Industry Group Code: 33313 **Ranks within this company's industry group:** Sales: 5 Profits: 6

Exploration/Production:		Refining/Retailing:		Utilities:		Alternative Energy:		Specialty Services:		Energy Mktg./Other Svcs.	
Exploration:		Refining:		Electric Utility:		Waste/Solar/Other:		Consulting/Eng.:		Energy Marketing:	
Production:		Retailing:		Gas Utility:		Thermal/Steam:		Seismic:		Equipment/Machinery:	Y
Coal Production:		Convenience Stores:		Pipelines:		Wind:		Drilling:		Oil Field Services:	Y
		Chemicals:		Water:		Hydro:		InfoTech:		Air/Shipping Transportation:	
						Fuel Cells:		Specialty Services:			

TYPES OF BUSINESS:

Oil & Gas Drilling Equipment
Equipment Maintenance
Casing Drilling Technology

BRANDS/DIVISIONS/AFFILIATES:

TESCO CASING DRILLING

CONTACTS:

Note: Officers with more than one job title may be intentionally listed here more than once.

Julio M. Quintana, CEO
Julio M. Quintana, Pres.
Robert Kayl, CFO/Sr. VP
Fernando Assing, Sr. VP-Mktg.
Jonathan B. O'Blenes, VP-Surface Prod. Eng.
Jonathan B. O'Blenes, VP-Mfg.
Dean Ferris, General Counsel/Sr. VP/Corp. Sec.
Jeffrey L. Foster, Sr. VP-Oper.
Fernando Assing, Sr. VP-Bus. Dev.
John M. Dodson, Corp. Controller/VP
Norman W. Robertson, Chmn.

Phone: 713-359-7000 **Fax:** 713-359-7001
Toll-Free:
Address: 3993 W. Sam Houston Pkwy. N., Ste. 100, Houston, TX 77043 US

GROWTH PLANS/SPECIAL FEATURES:

Tesco Corporation is a global design, manufacture and service delivery of technology-based solutions for the upstream energy industry. The company operates in four segments: top drives; tubular services; casing drilling; and research and engineering. The top drive segment sells equipment and provides services to drilling contractors and oil and gas operating companies throughout the world. The division primarily manufactures top drives, which are used in drilling operations to rotate the drill string while suspended from the derrick above the rig floor. The segment also provides rental top drives on a day-rate basis for land and offshore drilling rigs. In addition, the segment provides after-market top drive sales and support services to customers on an ongoing basis and maintains regional stocks of high-demand parts, as well as trained field and shop service personnel to support both its own rental units and units owned by customers. The tubular services segment offers conventional and proprietary casing and tubing running services under the Azimuth Tubular Services brand name. Casing is steel pipe installed in the well bore to maintain structural integrity; isolate water-bearing surface sands; and provide structural support of the wellhead and other casing and tubing strings in the well. The segment provides specialized equipment and personnel to operators and drilling contractors. The casing drilling segment is focused on the firm's technology-based proprietary casing running solution, TESCO CASING DRILLING, which uses conventional oil well casing in well drilling but reduces drilling time and uncertainties. The company's research and engineering segment comprises the firm's research and development activities. Its portfolio includes approximately 114 issued patents and 137 pending patent applications. Tesco has operations in 23 countries.

FINANCIALS:

Sales and profits are in thousands of dollars—add 000 to get the full amount. 2010 Note: Financial information for 2010 was not available for all companies at press time.

2010 Sales: $ | 2010 Profits: $
2009 Sales: $356,478 | 2009 Profits: $-5,265
2008 Sales: $543,942 | 2008 Profits: $49,923
2007 Sales: $462,378 | 2007 Profits: $32,302
2006 Sales: $386,180 | 2006 Profits: $30,550

U.S. Stock Ticker: TESO
Int'l Ticker: TEO Int'l Exchange: Toronto-TSX
Employees: 1,301
Fiscal Year Ends: 12/31
Parent Company:

SALARIES/BENEFITS:

Pension Plan: ESOP Stock Plan: Profit Sharing: Top Exec. Salary: $415,386 Bonus: $134,400
Savings Plan: Stock Purch. Plan: Second Exec. Salary: $230,769 Bonus: $69,600

OTHER THOUGHTS:

Apparent Women Officers or Directors:
Hot Spot for Advancement for Women/Minorities:

LOCATIONS: ("Y" = Yes)

West:	Southwest:	Midwest:	Southeast:	Northeast:	International:
	Y				Y

TESORO CORP

www.tsocorp.com

Industry Group Code: 324110 **Ranks within this company's industry group:** Sales: 14 Profits: 22

Exploration/Production:		Refining/Retailing:		Utilities:		Alternative Energy:		Specialty Services:		Energy Mktg./Other Svcs.	
Exploration:		Refining:	Y	Electric Utility:		Waste/Solar/Other:		Consulting/Eng.:		Energy Marketing:	
Production:		Retailing:	Y	Gas Utility:		Thermal/Steam:		Seismic:		Equipment/Machinery:	
Coal Production:		Convenience Stores:	Y	Pipelines:		Wind:		Drilling:		Oil Field Services:	
		Chemicals:		Water:		Hydro:		InfoTech:		Air/Shipping Transportation:	
						Fuel Cells:		Specialty Services:	Y		

TYPES OF BUSINESS:

Petroleum Refining
Gas Stations
Aviation & Heavy Fuels

BRANDS/DIVISIONS/AFFILIATES:

Mirastar
Tesoro Alaska
Shell
USA Gasoline

CONTACTS:

Note: Officers with more than one job title may be intentionally listed here more than once.

Greg J. Goff, CEO
Everett Lewis, COO/Exec. VP
Greg J. Goff, Pres.
G. Scott Spendlove, CFO/Treas./Sr. VP
Claude P. Moreau, Sr. VP-Mktg.
Susan A. Lerette, Sr. VP-Admin.
Charles S. Parrish, General Counsel/Sr. VP/Sec.
Louie Rubiola, Dir.-Investor Rel.
Arlen Glenewinkel Jr., Controller
C.A. Flagg, Sr. VP-System Optimization
Joseph M. Monroe, Sr. VP-Logistics & Marine
Frank Wheeler, Sr. VP-Refining
Lynn D. Westfall, VP-External Affairs
Steven H. Grapstein, Chmn.
Joseph G. McCoy, Sr. VP-Supply & Training

Phone: 210-626-6000	**Fax:**
Toll-Free: 800-299-0570	
Address: 19100 Ridgewood Pkwy., San Antonio, TX 78259 US	

GROWTH PLANS/SPECIAL FEATURES:

Tesoro Corp. formerly known as Tesoro Petroleum Corp., is a U.S. independent petroleum refiner. The company operates in two segments: refining; and marketing and distribution. Through the refining segment, the firm owns and operates seven petroleum refineries located in California, Alaska, Washington, Hawaii, North Dakota and Utah and sells refined products to a wide variety of customers in the western and mid-continental U.S. Tesoro's refineries produce a high proportion of its refined product sales volumes, and the company purchases the remainder from its other refiners and suppliers. The firm's seven refineries have a combined crude oil capacity of 665,000 barrels per day. Through the marketing and distribution segment, the company sells refined products including gasoline and gasoline blendstocks, jet fuel, diesel fuel, heavy fuel oils and residual products in both the bulk and wholesale markets. The majority of its wholesale volumes are sold in 15 states to independent unbranded distributors that sell refined products through the firm's owned and third-party terminals. Tesoro's bulk volumes are primarily sold to independent and other oil companies; electric power producers; railroads; airlines; and marine and industrial end-users, which are distributed by pipelines, ships, railcars and trucks. In addition, the company sells refined products that it manufactures, purchases or receives on exchange from third parties. Tesoro's retail marketing operations include about 886 branded retail locations in the western U.S., Alaska and Hawaii, including Tesoro, Tesoro Alaska, Shell, USA Gasoline and 34 Mirastar-brand stations at Wal-Mart locations in the western U.S. Roughly 385 of these locations are company-operated.

Employees of the firm are offered health coverage; life and AD&D insurance; a savings plan; flexible spending accounts; education assistance; long-term disability; and long-term care insurance.

FINANCIALS:

Sales and profits are in thousands of dollars—add 000 to get the full amount. 2010 Note: Financial information for 2010 was not available for all companies at press time.

2010 Sales: $	2010 Profits: $	**U.S. Stock Ticker: TSO**
2009 Sales: $16,872,000	2009 Profits: $-140,000	**Int'l Ticker:** Int'l Exchange:
2008 Sales: $28,416,000	2008 Profits: $278,000	Employees: 5,500
2007 Sales: $21,976,000	2007 Profits: $566,000	Fiscal Year Ends: 12/31
2006 Sales: $18,104,000	2006 Profits: $801,000	Parent Company:

SALARIES/BENEFITS:

Pension Plan: Y	ESOP Stock Plan:	Profit Sharing:	Top Exec. Salary: $1,300,000	Bonus: $
Savings Plan: Y	Stock Purch. Plan:		Second Exec. Salary: $700,000	Bonus: $

OTHER THOUGHTS:

Apparent Women Officers or Directors: 2
Hot Spot for Advancement for Women/Minorities: Y

LOCATIONS: ("Y" = Yes)

West:	Southwest:	Midwest:	Southeast:	Northeast:	International:
Y	Y	Y			Y

TETRA TECHNOLOGIES INC

www.tetratec.com

Industry Group Code: 213112 **Ranks within this company's industry group:** Sales: 20 Profits: 15

Exploration/Production:		**Refining/Retailing:**		**Utilities:**		**Alternative Energy:**		**Specialty Services:**		**Energy Mktg./Other Svcs.**	
Exploration:		Refining:		Electric Utility:		Waste/Solar/Other:		Consulting/Eng.:		Energy Marketing:	
Production:		Retailing:		Gas Utility:		Thermal/Steam:		Seismic:		Equipment/Machinery:	
Coal Production:		Convenience Stores:		Pipelines:		Wind:		Drilling:		Oil Field Services:	Y
		Chemicals:	Y	Water:		Hydro:		InfoTech:		Air/Shipping Transportation:	
						Fuel Cells:		Specialty Services:	Y		

TYPES OF BUSINESS:

Oil & Gas Drilling Support Services
Specialty Chemicals & Fluids
Abandonment & Decommissioning Services
Oil & Gas Development & Production
Production Testing Services
Calcium Chloride & Brominated Products

BRANDS/DIVISIONS/AFFILIATES:

Maritech Resources, Inc.
Compressco, Inc.

CONTACTS: *Note: Officers with more than one job title may be intentionally listed here more than once.*

Stuart M. Brightman, CEO
Stuart M. Brightman, Pres.
Joseph M. Abell III, CFO/Sr. VP
Linden H. Price, VP-Admin.
Bass C. Wallace, Jr., General Counsel/Corp. Sec.
Eileen Price, Mgr.-Investor Rel.
Bruce A. Cobb, VP-Finance/Treas.
Edgar A. Anderson, Pres., Maritech Resources, Inc.
Ronald J. Foster, Pres., Compressco, Inc.
Ben C. Chambers, VP-Acct./Controller
Dennis R. Mathews, Sr. VP
Ralph S. Cunningham, Chmn.

Phone: 281-367-1983 **Fax:** 281-364-4398
Toll-Free:
Address: 24955 I-45 N., The Woodlands, TX 77380 US

GROWTH PLANS/SPECIAL FEATURES:

TETRA Technologies, Inc. is an oil and gas services company. The firm markets, produces and distributes calcium chloride and brominated products as feedstocks for its completion fluids business. The company operates in three segments: fluids, offshore and production enhancement. The fluids division manufactures and markets clear brine fluids, additives and other associated products and services to the oil and gas industry; these are used in well drilling, completion and workover operations in the U.S., Latin America, Europe, Asia, and Africa. This division also markets certain fluids and dry calcium chloride to non-energy industries. The offshore segment consists of two operating subdivisions: offshore services and Maritech. The offshore services subdivision provides downhole and subsea services, such as plugging and abandonment, workover and wireline services; construction and decommissioning services, including hurricane damage remediation; and diving services. The Maritech subdivision consists of subsidiary Maritech Resources, Inc., a producer of oil and gas from properties in the offshore, inland waters, and onshore U.S. Gulf of Mexico region. The production enhancement segment also consists of two subdivisions: production testing and Compressco. The production testing subdivision provides production testing services to the U.S., onshore Mexico, Brazil, Northern Africa, Middle Eastern and other international markets. The Compressco division, through subsidiary Compressco, Inc., provides wellhead compression-based production enhancement services, which can improve the value of natural gas and oil wells by increasing daily production and total recoverable reserves. These services are offered in onshore producing regions of the U.S., as well as in Canada, Mexico, South America, Europe, Asia and other international markets. In July 2009, TETRA Technologies completed a construction project that increased its Galveston, Texas, facility's clear brine fluids blending capacity by 35% and its overall storage capacity by over 80%.

The company offers its employees life, medical, dental and vision insurance; and a 401(k) plan.

FINANCIALS: **Sales and profits are in thousands of dollars—add 000 to get the full amount. 2010 Note: Financial information for 2010 was not available for all companies at press time.**

2010 Sales: $	2010 Profits: $	**U.S. Stock Ticker: TTI**
2009 Sales: $878,877	2009 Profits: $68,804	**Int'l Ticker:** Int'l Exchange:
2008 Sales: $1,009,065	2008 Profits: $-12,136	Employees: 2,837
2007 Sales: $982,483	2007 Profits: $28,771	Fiscal Year Ends: 12/31
2006 Sales: $767,795	2006 Profits: $101,878	Parent Company:

SALARIES/BENEFITS:

Pension Plan:	ESOP Stock Plan:	Profit Sharing:	Top Exec. Salary: $442,353	Bonus: $240,000
Savings Plan: Y	Stock Purch. Plan:		Second Exec. Salary: $430,769	Bonus: $150,000

OTHER THOUGHTS:

Apparent Women Officers or Directors:
Hot Spot for Advancement for Women/Minorities:

LOCATIONS: ("Y" = Yes)

West:	Southwest:	Midwest:	Southeast:	Northeast:	International:
Y	Y		Y	Y	Y

TEXAS GAS TRANSMISSION LLC

www.txgt.com

Industry Group Code: 486 **Ranks within this company's industry group:** Sales: Profits:

Exploration/Production:		Refining/Retailing:		Utilities:		Alternative Energy:		Specialty Services:		Energy Mktg./Other Svcs.	
Exploration:		Refining:		Electric Utility:		Waste/Solar/Other:		Consulting/Eng.:		Energy Marketing:	
Production:		Retailing:		Gas Utility:		Thermal/Steam:		Seismic:		Equipment/Machinery:	
Coal Production:		Convenience Stores:		Pipelines:	Y	Wind:		Drilling:		Oil Field Services:	
		Chemicals:		Water:		Hydro:		InfoTech:		Air/Shipping Transportation:	
						Fuel Cells:		Specialty Services:			

TYPES OF BUSINESS:

Pipelines-Natural Gas

BRANDS/DIVISIONS/AFFILIATES:

Loews Corporation
Boardwalk Pipeline Partners, L.P.
Texas Gas
GasQuest

CONTACTS: *Note: Officers with more than one job title may be intentionally listed here more than once.*

Rolf A. Gafvert, CEO/Pres., Boardwalk GP, LLC
Brian A. Cody, COO-Boardwalk GP, LLC
Jamie L. Buskill, CFO-Boardwalk GP, LLC
Michael E. McMahon, General Counsel-Boardwalk GP, LLC

Phone: 270-926-8686 **Fax:** 270-688-5872
Toll-Free: 800-626-1948
Address: 3800 Frederica St., Owensboro, KY 42301 US

GROWTH PLANS/SPECIAL FEATURES:

Texas Gas Transmission, LLC, is one of three wholly-owned subsidiaries of Boardwalk Pipeline Partners, LP, which is itself 80% owned by Loews Corporation, a holding company. Texas Gas is an interstate natural gas transmission company headquartered in Owensboro, Kentucky that owns and operates a 6,110-mile pipeline. The pipeline provides storage services and transports natural gas from the Gulf Coast, Louisiana and East Texas to U.S. markets in the South, Midwest and Northeast. The firm also has indirect market access to other states through interconnections with unaffiliated pipelines. Currently, Texas Gas provides services to urban utilities, rural utility districts and power generators. Texas Gas is able to deliver about 4.3 billion cubic feet (bcf). The 31 compressor stations set on the pipeline have a moving capacity of 552,700 horsepower. The firm also has nine natural gas storage fields in Indiana and Kentucky for approximately 180 billion cubic feet of gas. Texas Gas operates GasQuest, an Internet-based computer application used to conduct interactive transactions and provide informational postings relating to transportation services. Recent developments of the firm were the Fayetteville Lateral expansion project, which will carry gas from the Fayetteville Shale at Grandview, Arkansas to Lulla, Mississippi with total of 165 miles of 36-inch pipe and a peak capacity of 1.3 bcf a day. The Greenville lateral will carry gas from Greeneville, Mississippi to Kosciusko, Mississippi with 95 miles of 36-inch pipe and a capacity of 1.0 bcf of gas a day. Texas Gas constructed two new compressor stations, the Bald Knob Compressor Station (in White County, Arkansas) and the Isola Compressor Station (in Humphreys County, Mississippi) part of the Fayetteville Lateral expansion project. In addition, the firm made modifications at its existing Greenville Compressor Station in order to meet the increased demands. The pipelines were completed in January 2010.

FINANCIALS: **Sales and profits are in thousands of dollars—add 000 to get the full amount. 2010 Note: Financial information for 2010 was not available for all companies at press time.**

2010 Sales: $	2010 Profits: $	**U.S. Stock Ticker: Subsidiary**
2009 Sales: $	2009 Profits: $	**Int'l Ticker:** Int'l Exchange:
2008 Sales: $	2008 Profits: $	Employees:
2007 Sales: $	2007 Profits: $	Fiscal Year Ends: 12/31
2006 Sales: $	2006 Profits: $	Parent Company: BOARDWALK PIPELINE PARTNERS LP

SALARIES/BENEFITS:

Pension Plan:	ESOP Stock Plan:	Profit Sharing:	Top Exec. Salary: $292,500	Bonus: $150,000
Savings Plan:	Stock Purch. Plan:		Second Exec. Salary: $	Bonus: $

OTHER THOUGHTS:

Apparent Women Officers or Directors:
Hot Spot for Advancement for Women/Minorities:

LOCATIONS: ("Y" = Yes)

West:	Southwest:	Midwest:	Southeast:	Northeast:	International:
	Y	Y	Y		

THAI OIL PCL

www.thaioil.co.th

Industry Group Code: 324110 **Ranks within this company's industry group:** Sales: 18 Profits: 6

Exploration/Production:		Refining/Retailing:		Utilities:		Alternative Energy:		Specialty Services:		Energy Mktg./Other Svcs.	
Exploration:	Y	Refining:	Y	Electric Utility:		Waste/Solar/Other:		Consulting/Eng.:		Energy Marketing:	
Production:	Y	Retailing:		Gas Utility:		Thermal/Steam:		Seismic:		Equipment/Machinery:	
Coal Production:		Convenience Stores:		Pipelines:	Y	Wind:		Drilling:		Oil Field Services:	
		Chemicals:	Y	Water:		Hydro:		InfoTech:		Air/Shipping Transportation:	Y
						Fuel Cells:		Specialty Services:			

TYPES OF BUSINESS:

Petroleum Refineries
Petrochemical Products
Lube Base Oil
Petrochemical Transportation
Power Generation

BRANDS/DIVISIONS/AFFILIATES:

Thai Parazylene
Thai Lube Base
Thai Oil Marine
Thappline
Thai Oil Power
Independent Power

CONTACTS:

Note: Officers with more than one job title may be intentionally listed here more than once.

Surong Bulakul, CEO
Somkeirt Hudthagosol, Pres.
Wirat Uanarumit, Deputy Managing Dir.-Finance
Phongphet Sarakun, Mgr.-Commerce
Kosol Pimthanothai, Mgr.-Human Resources
Bandhit Thamprajamchit, Mgr.-Tech.
Suchart Monyanont, Mgr.-Eng.
Yuthana Pasurapunya, Mgr.-Oper.
Duangporn Teerapabpaisit, Mgr.-Bus. Dev.
Somchai Wongwattanasan, Asst. Managing Dir.-Corp. Affairs
Prapin Thongnium, Mgr.-Acct.
Chaiwat Damrongmongkolgul, Deputy Managing Dir.-Refinery
Pattaralada Sangasang, Mgr.-Strategic Planning
Athavuth Vikitsreth, Mgr.-Oper. Support
Siriporn Mahajchariyawong, Treas.
Pichai Chunhavajira, Chmn.

Phone: 66-2-299-0000 **Fax:** 66-2-299-0024
Toll-Free:
Address: 123 Suntowers Bldg B, Fl. 16, Vibhavadi Rangsit Rd, Bangkok, 10900 Thailand

GROWTH PLANS/SPECIAL FEATURES:

Thai Oil PCL is a Thailand-based oil company involved in the refining, distribution and derivative production of petrochemicals. While refining operations are the firm's primary task, it has expanded into creating lube base products, generating energy, and transporting oil through its network of pipelines. The company divides its business into five segments: oil refining, petrochemicals, lube base oils, transportation, and power generation. The oil refining segment produces 275,000 barrels per day, representing a quarter of the country's total processing capacity. The majority of the product remains in the domestic market, while a small amount is exported. The petrochemical business (Thai Paraxylene, or TPX) specializes in upstream production. The process begins with naphtha and ends with benzene, toluene, mixed-xylene, paraxylene and gasoline blending as a byproduct. The lube base oil business (Thai Lube Base) produces yearly amounts of 270,000 tons of lube base, 400,000 tons of bitumen and 270,000 tons of other byproducts. The transportation sector is responsible for moving petroleum and petrochemical products, employing a fleet of six tankers in its marine segment (Thaioil Marine) and a 26,000 million liter per year capacity in its pipelines (Thappline) for unleaded gasoline, regular gasoline, jet fuel and diesel. Finally, the power generation segment works with two plants: a small power producer, operated by Thaioil Power, creates 118 megawatts (MW) for the Thai market; and a natural gas cogeneration plant, operated by Independent Power, produces 700 MW.

FINANCIALS:

Sales and profits are in thousands of dollars—add 000 to get the full amount. 2010 Note: Financial information for 2010 was not available for all companies at press time.

2010 Sales: $	2010 Profits: $	**U.S. Stock Ticker:**
2009 Sales: $9,427,690	2009 Profits: $400,130	**Int'l Ticker: TOP** Int'l Exchange: Bangkok-BAK
2008 Sales: $11,915,700	2008 Profits: $6,670	Employees:
2007 Sales: $7,793,670	2007 Profits: $570,700	Fiscal Year Ends: 12/31
2006 Sales: $	2006 Profits: $	Parent Company:

SALARIES/BENEFITS:

Pension Plan: Y	ESOP Stock Plan:	Profit Sharing:	Top Exec. Salary: $	Bonus: $
Savings Plan:	Stock Purch. Plan:		Second Exec. Salary: $	Bonus: $

OTHER THOUGHTS:

Apparent Women Officers or Directors: 6
Hot Spot for Advancement for Women/Minorities: Y

LOCATIONS: ("Y" = Yes)

West:	Southwest:	Midwest:	Southeast:	Northeast:	International:
					Y

TIDEWATER INC

www.tdw.com

Industry Group Code: 213112 **Ranks within this company's industry group:** Sales: 16 Profits: 7

Exploration/Production:		Refining/Retailing:		Utilities:		Alternative Energy:		Specialty Services:		Energy Mktg./Other Svcs.	
Exploration:		Refining:		Electric Utility:		Waste/Solar/Other:		Consulting/Eng.:		Energy Marketing:	
Production:		Retailing:		Gas Utility:		Thermal/Steam:		Seismic:		Equipment/Machinery:	
Coal Production:		Convenience Stores:		Pipelines:		Wind:		Drilling:		Oil Field Services:	
		Chemicals:		Water:		Hydro:		InfoTech:		Air/Shipping Transportation:	Y
						Fuel Cells:		Specialty Services:	Y		

TYPES OF BUSINESS:

Offshore Drilling Support Vessels
Supply Vessels
Marine Services
Shipbuilding

BRANDS/DIVISIONS/AFFILIATES:

Quality Shipyards, LLC

CONTACTS: *Note: Officers with more than one job title may be intentionally listed here more than once.*

Dean E. Taylor, CEO
Jeffrey M. Platt, COO
Dean E. Taylor, Pres.
Quinn P. Fanning, CFO/Exec. VP
Chris Orth, VP-Sales, Western Hemisphere
Debbie Willingham, Chief Human Resources Officer/VP
Matthew Mancheski, CIO/VP
William R. Brown, IV, Mgr.-Eng. & Tech. Svcs. Group
Bruce D. Lundstrom, General Counsel/Exec. VP/Sec.
Matthew Mancheski, Chief Strategic Planning Officer
Joseph M. Bennett, Chief Investor Rel. Officer/Exec. VP
Craig J. Demarest, Principal Acct. Officer/Controller/VP
Stephen W. Dick, Exec. VP-Domestic Div.
Kevin Carr, VP-Taxation
William R. Brown, IV, VP/Gen. Mgr.-Quality Shipyards LLC
Monty Orr, VP-Int'l Sales, Eastern Hemisphere
Dean E. Taylor, Chmn.
Gerard P. Kehoe, Sr. VP/Regional Mgr.-Latin America

Phone: 504-568-1010	**Fax:** 504-566-4559
Toll-Free: 800-678-8433	
Address: 601 Poydras St., Ste. 1900, New Orleans, LA 70130 US	

GROWTH PLANS/SPECIAL FEATURES:

Tidewater, Inc., through its subsidiaries and joint ventures, provides offshore service vessels and marine support services to the international offshore energy industry through the operation of one of the world's largest fleets of offshore marine service vessels. The company operates in two reportable segments: U.S. and International. Principal areas of international operation include the Persian Gulf, the Arabian Gulf, and areas offshore Australia, Brazil, Egypt, India, Indonesia, Malaysia, Mexico, Trinidad and West Africa. Through offices in over 30 countries, Tidewater's international operations provide approximately 89% of the company's revenue. The firm's fleet of 398 vessels includes deepwater vessels; towing supply and supply vessels; crewboats and utility vessels; platform supply vessels; offshore and inshore tugs; and production, line-handling, platform maintenance, diving support and various other special purpose vessels. The vessels provide services supporting all phases of offshore exploration, development and production, including towing and anchor handling for mobile offshore drilling units; transporting supplies and personnel necessary to sustain drilling, workover and production activities; offshore construction and seismic support; and a variety of specialized services, such as pipe and cable laying. Subsidiary Quality Shipyards LLC constructs, modifies and repairs vessels for Tidewater's own operations and third-party operations though two shipyards in Houma, Louisiana. The shipyard operation delivered two 266-foot platform supply vessels to Tidewater in December 2009 and March 2010, and is currently constructing one additional 266-foot platform supply vessel, expected to be delivered in February 2012.

Tidewater offers its employees medical and dental coverage, disability insurance, life insurance, business travel accident coverage, a 401(k) plan and a retirement plan.

FINANCIALS: **Sales and profits are in thousands of dollars—add 000 to get the full amount. 2010 Note: Financial information for 2010 was not available for all companies at press time.**

2010 Sales: $	2010 Profits: $	**U.S. Stock Ticker: TDW**
2009 Sales: $1,390,835	2009 Profits: $406,898	**Int'l Ticker:** Int'l Exchange:
2008 Sales: $1,270,171	2008 Profits: $348,763	Employees: 8,500
2007 Sales: $1,125,260	2007 Profits: $256,646	Fiscal Year Ends: 3/31
2006 Sales: $877,617	2006 Profits: $235,756	Parent Company:

SALARIES/BENEFITS:

Pension Plan: Y	ESOP Stock Plan:	Profit Sharing:	Top Exec. Salary: $615,940	Bonus: $493,477
Savings Plan: Y	Stock Purch. Plan:		Second Exec. Salary: $332,072	Bonus: $189,231

OTHER THOUGHTS:

Apparent Women Officers or Directors: 3
Hot Spot for Advancement for Women/Minorities: Y

LOCATIONS: ("Y" = Yes)

West:	Southwest:	Midwest:	Southeast:	Northeast:	International:
Y	Y		Y		Y

TNK-BP

www.tnk-bp.com

Industry Group Code: 211111 **Ranks within this company's industry group:** Sales: 25 Profits: 16

Exploration/Production:		Refining/Retailing:		Utilities:		Alternative Energy:		Specialty Services:		Energy Mktg./Other Svcs.	
Exploration:	Y	Refining:	Y	Electric Utility:		Waste/Solar/Other:		Consulting/Eng.:		Energy Marketing:	
Production:	Y	Retailing:	Y	Gas Utility:		Thermal/Steam:		Seismic:		Equipment/Machinery:	
Coal Production:		Convenience Stores:		Pipelines:		Wind:		Drilling:		Oil Field Services:	
		Chemicals:		Water:		Hydro:		InfoTech:		Air/Shipping Transportation:	
						Fuel Cells:		Specialty Services:			

TYPES OF BUSINESS:

Oil & Gas-Exploration & Production
Petroleum Refining
Retail Gasoline Sales

BRANDS/DIVISIONS/AFFILIATES:

BP plc
Alfa, Access/Renova group (AAR)
RUSIA Petroleum
Vik Oil

CONTACTS: *Note: Officers with more than one job title may be intentionally listed here more than once.*

Mikhail M. Fridman, Interim CEO
Bill Schrader, COO
Jonathan Muir, CFO
Francis Sommer, Exec. VP-Tech.
Igor Maidannik, Exec. VP-Legal Support
Stan Miroshnik, Exec. VP-Strategy & Bus. Dev.
Anatoly Tyomkin, Exec. VP-Bus. Support
Vadim Ogar, Exec. VP-Security
Sergey Brezitsky, Exec. VP-Upstream
Didier Baudrand, Exec. VP-Downstream
Mikhail M. Fridman, Chmn.

Phone: 7-495-777-77-07 **Fax:** 7-495-777-77-08
Toll-Free:
Address: 1 Arbat St., Moscow, 119019 Russia

GROWTH PLANS/SPECIAL FEATURES:

TNK-BP, a 50-50 joint venture between BP and Alfa, Access/Renova group (AAR), is a leading vertically integrated Russian oil company. The company's upstream operations are located primarily in West Siberia, East Sibera and Volga-Urals, with an average production of 1.69 million barrels of oil equivalent (BOEs) per day and total proved reserves of 8.586 billion BOEs. TNK-BP operates r refining assets in Russia and the Ukraine with a combined refining capacity of 675,000 barrels per day. The company also operates a retail network of roughly 1,400 filling stations throughout Russia and the Ukraine under the BP and TNK brands. While TNK-BP has no proven gas reserves, it does extract roughly 13 billion cubic meters of associated gas per year. The company owns 63% of RUSIA Petroleum, a company that holds the exploration licenses for the Kovykta field in East Siberia, with a potential gas production of as much as 40-45 billion cubic meters per year. In May2010, the company acquired the Vik Oil group of companies in Ukraine, consisting of118 fuel stations, eight oil depots, 49 petrol tankers and 122 land plots. Also in 2010, the firm agreed to form a joint venture with Iraq Oil Company Investments for the purpose of developing oil and gas fields in Iraq.

FINANCIALS: **Sales and profits are in thousands of dollars—add 000 to get the full amount. 2010 Note: Financial information for 2010 was not available for all companies at press time.**

2010 Sales: $	2010 Profits: $	**U.S. Stock Ticker: Joint Venture**
2009 Sales: $34,753,000	2009 Profits: $4,973,000	**Int'l Ticker:** Int'l Exchange:
2008 Sales: $51,886,000	2008 Profits: $5,284,000	Employees:
2007 Sales: $38,926,000	2007 Profits: $4,233,000	Fiscal Year Ends: 12/31
2006 Sales: $24,450,000	2006 Profits: $2,060,000	Parent Company: BP PLC

SALARIES/BENEFITS:

Pension Plan:	ESOP Stock Plan:	Profit Sharing:	Top Exec. Salary: $	Bonus: $
Savings Plan:	Stock Purch. Plan:		Second Exec. Salary: $	Bonus: $

OTHER THOUGHTS:

Apparent Women Officers or Directors:
Hot Spot for Advancement for Women/Minorities:

LOCATIONS: ("Y" = Yes)

West:	Southwest:	Midwest:	Southeast:	Northeast:	International:
					Y

TOHOKU ELECTRIC POWER CO INC

www.tohoku-epco.co.jp

Industry Group Code: 2211 **Ranks within this company's industry group:** Sales: 9 Profits: 47

Exploration/Production:		**Refining/Retailing:**		**Utilities:**		**Alternative Energy:**		**Specialty Services:**		**Energy Mktg./Other Svcs.**	
Exploration:		Refining:		Electric Utility:	Y	Waste/Solar/Other:	Y	Consulting/Eng.:	Y	Energy Marketing:	Y
Production:		Retailing:		Gas Utility:		Thermal/Steam:	Y	Seismic:		Equipment/Machinery:	
Coal Production:		Convenience Stores:		Pipelines:		Wind:		Drilling:		Oil Field Services:	
		Chemicals:		Water:		Hydro:	Y	InfoTech:		Air/Shipping Transportation:	
						Fuel Cells:		Specialty Services:	Y		

TYPES OF BUSINESS:

Electric Utility
Thermal, Hydroelectric & Nuclear Generation
Engineering & Construction
Wholesale Energy Marketing
Manufacturing
Fuel
Real Estate
Telecommunications

BRANDS/DIVISIONS/AFFILIATES:

Tousei Kougyo Co., Inc.
Sakata Kyodo Power Co., Ltd.
Joban Joint Power Co., Ltd.
Tohoku Hydropower & Geothermal Energy Co., Inc.
Nihonkai LNG Co., Ltd.
Tohoku Intelligent Telecommunication Co., Inc.
Kitanihon Electric Cable Co., Ltd.
Yurtec Corp.

CONTACTS:

Note: Officers with more than one job title may be intentionally listed here more than once.

Makoto Kaiwa, Pres.
Hiroshi Kato, Exec. VP
Fumio Ube, Exec. VP
Nobuaki Abe, Exec. VP
Takeo Umeda, Exec. VP
Hiroaki Takahashi, Chmn.

Phone: 81-22-225-2111 **Fax:** 81-22-225-2550
Toll-Free:
Address: 1-7-1 Honcho, Aoba-ku, Sendai, Miyagi, 980-8550 Japan

GROWTH PLANS/SPECIAL FEATURES:

Tohoku Electric Power Co., Inc. (Tohoku EPCO) supplies electricity to approximately 7.7 million customers in the Tohoku region, the northern part of Japan's main island, Honshu. Tohoku EPCO operates 227 hydroelectric power plants with a combined generating capacity of 2.5 gigawatts (GW); 14 thermal power plants with generating capacity of 11.3 GW; two nuclear power plants with a capacity of 3.27 GW; and six renewable, geothermal energy facilities with a capacity of 262 megawatts. The firm also owns over 9,300 miles of transmission lines, 90,600 miles of distribution lines and 612 substations. In total, the firm has 11 affiliates and operates 48 subsidiaries, of which it considers 14 as its main subsidiaries. Of these main operating subsidiaries, five generate and supply electricity; three perform construction services to upgrade or expand facilities; one supplies liquefied natural gas (LNG) used in power generation; two provide information processing and telecommunication services utilizing the firm's communication technology and equipment; and three more are involved in other industries. These main subsidiaries are Tousei Kougyo Co., Inc.; Sakata Kyodo Power Co., Ltd.; Tohoku Hydropower & Geothermal Energy Co., Inc.; Joban Joint Power Co., Ltd.; Soma Kyodo Power Co., Ltd.; Yurtec Corp.; Tohoku Electric Power Engineering & Construction Co., Inc.; Tohoku Ryokka Kankyohozen Co., Ltd.; Nihonkai LNG Co., Ltd.; Tohoku Intelligent Telecommunication Co., Inc.; Tohoku Information Systems Co., Ltd.; Tsuken Electric Ind Co., Ltd.; Higashi Nihon Kougyou Co., Ltd.; and Kitanihon Electric Cable Co., Ltd. Approximately 89% of the firm's revenues were generated from electricity sales in 2009. Besides its main headquarters in Sendai, the firm has eight other branches in Aomori, Iwate, Akita, Miyagi, Yamagata, Fukushima, Niigata and Tokyo.

FINANCIALS:

Sales and profits are in thousands of dollars—add 000 to get the full amount. 2010 Note: Financial information for 2010 was not available for all companies at press time.

2010 Sales: $	2010 Profits: $	**U.S. Stock Ticker: TEPCF**
2009 Sales: $20,420,980	2009 Profits: $-352,090	**Int'l Ticker: 9506** Int'l Exchange: Tokyo-TSE
2008 Sales: $19,971,030	2008 Profits: $191,600	Employees:
2007 Sales: $14,635,413	2007 Profits: $450,275	Fiscal Year Ends: 3/31
2006 Sales: $14,131,650	2006 Profits: $461,147	Parent Company:

SALARIES/BENEFITS:

Pension Plan: Y	ESOP Stock Plan:	Profit Sharing:	Top Exec. Salary: $	Bonus: $
Savings Plan:	Stock Purch. Plan:		Second Exec. Salary: $	Bonus: $

OTHER THOUGHTS:

Apparent Women Officers or Directors:
Hot Spot for Advancement for Women/Minorities:

LOCATIONS: ("Y" = Yes)

West:	Southwest:	Midwest:	Southeast:	Northeast:	International:
					Y

TOKYO ELECTRIC POWER COMPANY INC (THE) www.tepco.co.jp

Industry Group Code: 2211 **Ranks within this company's industry group:** Sales: 2 Profits: 12

Exploration/Production:		Refining/Retailing:		Utilities:		Alternative Energy:		Specialty Services:		Energy Mktg./Other Svcs.	
Exploration:	Y	Refining:		Electric Utility:	Y	Waste/Solar/Other:	Y	Consulting/Eng.:	Y	Energy Marketing:	
Production:	Y	Retailing:	Y	Gas Utility:	Y	Thermal/Steam:	Y	Seismic:		Equipment/Machinery:	Y
Coal Production:		Convenience Stores:		Pipelines:		Wind:	Y	Drilling:		Oil Field Services:	
		Chemicals:		Water:		Hydro:	Y	InfoTech:	Y	Air/Shipping Transportation:	Y
						Fuel Cells:		Specialty Services:	Y		

TYPES OF BUSINESS:

Electric Utilities
Thermal, Hydro, Wind & Nuclear Generation
Fuel Supply
Construction
Oil & Gas Transportation
Real Estate
Consulting
Telecommunications

BRANDS/DIVISIONS/AFFILIATES:

Japan Atomic Power Company, Ltd.
Family Net Japan
Kawagoe Cable Vision Co., Ltd.
AT Tokyo Corp.
Tokyo Electric Generation Co., Inc. (The)
Star Buck Power Corporation
TEPCO Cable Television, Inc.
Tokyo Heat Energy Co., Ltd.

CONTACTS:

Note: Officers with more than one job title may be intentionally listed here more than once.

Masataka Shimizu, Pres.
Makio Fujiwara, Exec. VP/Gen. Mgr.-Mktg. & Sales Div.
Masao Yamazaki, Exec. VP-Employee Rel. & Human Resources Dept.
Hiroaki Takatsu, Deputy Gen. Mgr.-R&D Div.
Hiroaki Takatsu, Deputy Gen. Mgr.-Eng. Dept.
Toshio Nishizawa, Managing Dir.-Corp. Planning Dept.
Toshio Nishizawa, Managing Dir.-Corp. Comm. Dept.
Masaru Takei, Exec. VP-Acct. & Treas. Dept.
Takashi Fujimoto, Exec. VP/Gen. Mgr.-Power Network Div.
Norio Tsuzumi, Exec. VP-Nuclear Power & Plant Siting Div.
Hiroshi Yamaguchi, Deputy Gen. Mgr.-Power Network Div.
Fumiaki Miyamoto, Managing Dir.-Corp. Systems Dept. & Telecomm Dept.
Tsunehisa Katsumata, Chmn.
Naomi Hirose, Managing Dir.-Int'l Affairs Dept.
Yoshihiro Naito, Managing Dir.-Materials & Procurement Dept.

Phone: 81-3-6373-1111 **Fax:**
Toll-Free:
Address: 1-1-3, Uchisaiwai-cho, Chiyoda-ku, Tokyo, 100-8560 Japan

GROWTH PLANS/SPECIAL FEATURES:

The Tokyo Electric Power Company, Inc. (TEPCO) produces and distributes electric power in 10 provinces in and around Tokyo, Japan, supplying 28.3 million customers with electricity. Its total generating capacity is 64.3 gigawatts. TEPCO maintains a diverse mix of electric generation sources, including nuclear generation facilities, which represented 28% of its 2009 production. Other sources include hydroelectric plants, 5%; coal-fired plants, 12%; gas-fired plants, 46%; and oil burning facilities, 9%. The company has over 240 affiliates, including The Tokyo Electric Generation Co., Inc.; Soma Kyodo Power Co., Ltd.; Japan Atomic Power Company, Ltd.; Family Net Japan Corp.; Kawagoe Cable Vision Co., Ltd; AT Tokyo Corp.; Japan Digital Serve Corp.; Kandenko Co., Ltd.; Toko Electric Corp.; TEPCO Systems Corp.; TEPCO Cable Television, Inc.; Gas Business Company; Toden Kokoku Co., Ltd.; Dream Tran Internet, Inc.; CELT, Inc.; Tokyo Heat Energy Co., Ltd.; ReBITA, Inc.; and TM Energy Australia Pty Ltd. Six of these affiliate businesses generate electrical power; 13 focus on information communication, including telecommunications, cable television broadcasting and IT software and services; 10 are involved in facilities construction and maintenance; four offer materials and equipment; 22 supply and transport fuel; 17 offer energy and environmental solutions; seven are involved in real estate; 17 offer other services, including hotel and golf course management, nursing home operation, city planning and construction contracting; and 14 operate overseas in Indonesia, Taiwan, Australia and elsewhere. In March 2010, the firm, along with a group of companies that includes Toyota Motor Corp.; Nissan Motor Co.; and Mitsubishi Motors Corp., established CHAdeMO Association to increase quick-charger installations for electric vehicles worldwide. In September 2010, Eurus Energy Holdings Corp., a subsidiary of TEPCO, began construction of photovoltaic power plant in California. In October 2010, TEPCO and 12 other Japanese companies formed the International Nuclear Energy Development of Japan Co., Ltd., with the purpose of supporting nuclear power projects in emerging countries.

FINANCIALS:

Sales and profits are in thousands of dollars—add 000 to get the full amount. 2010 Note: Financial information for 2010 was not available for all companies at press time.

2010 Sales: $	2010 Profits: $	**U.S. Stock Ticker: TKECF**
2009 Sales: $52,356,100	2009 Profits: $1,103,720	**Int'l Ticker: 9501** Int'l Exchange: Tokyo-TSE
2008 Sales: $58,605,000	2008 Profits: $-841,000	Employees:
2007 Sales: $44,960,000	2007 Profits: $2,540,000	Fiscal Year Ends: 3/31
2006 Sales: $41,631,800	2006 Profits: $2,639,500	Parent Company:

SALARIES/BENEFITS:

Pension Plan:	ESOP Stock Plan:	Profit Sharing:	Top Exec. Salary: $	Bonus: $
Savings Plan:	Stock Purch. Plan:		Second Exec. Salary: $	Bonus: $

OTHER THOUGHTS:

Apparent Women Officers or Directors: 1
Hot Spot for Advancement for Women/Minorities:

LOCATIONS: ("Y" = Yes)

West:	Southwest:	Midwest:	Southeast:	Northeast:	International:
Y				Y	Y

TOKYO GAS CO LTD

www.tokyo-gas.co.jp

Industry Group Code: 221210 **Ranks within this company's industry group:** Sales: 2 Profits: 5

Exploration/Production:		**Refining/Retailing:**		**Utilities:**		**Alternative Energy:**		**Specialty Services:**		**Energy Mktg./Other Svcs.**	
Exploration:		Refining:		Electric Utility:	Y	Waste/Solar/Other:		Consulting/Eng.:		Energy Marketing:	Y
Production:		Retailing:		Gas Utility:	Y	Thermal/Steam:		Seismic:		Equipment/Machinery:	
Coal Production:		Convenience Stores:		Pipelines:	Y	Wind:		Drilling:		Oil Field Services:	
		Chemicals:		Water:		Hydro:		InfoTech:		Air/Shipping Transportation:	Y
						Fuel Cells:		Specialty Services:	Y		

TYPES OF BUSINESS:

Gas Utility
Air Conditioning & Heating Services
Real Estate Management
Construction
Gas Appliance Sales
Liquid Natural Gas Conversion
Electricity Supply

BRANDS/DIVISIONS/AFFILIATES:

Kawasaki Natural Gas Power Generation Co., Ltd.
North West Shelf LNG Project
Gorgon LNG Project

CONTACTS: *Note: Officers with more than one job title may be intentionally listed here more than once.*

Tsuyoshi Okamoto, Pres.
Hirokazu Hayashi, Exec. VP-Regional Dev. Mktg.
Toshiyuki Kanisawa, Exec. VP-Personnel
Hisao Watanabe, Sr. Exec. Officer-IT
Hisao Watanabe, Sr. Exec. Officer-Tech. Dev.
Toshiyuki Kanisawa, Exec. VP-Admin.
Toshiyuki Kanisawa, Corp. Sec.
Michiaki Hirose, Exec. Dir.-Corp. Planning & Project Mgmt.
Michiaki Hirose, Exec. Dir.-Corp. Comm.
Kazuo Yoshino, Sr. Exec. Officer-Investor Rel.
Kazuo Yoshino, Sr. Exec. Officer-Finance & Acct.
Tsutomu Oya, Exec. Dir./CEO-Energy Prod. Div.
Shigeru Muraki, Exec. VP/CEO-Energy Solutions Div.
Tadaaki Maeda, Exec. Dir./Vice Chmn.
Mikio Itazawa, Exec. Dir./Sr. Exec. Officer-Pipeline Network Div.
Mitsunori Torihara, Chmn.
Manabu Fukumoto, Sr. Exec. Officer-Purchasing & Real Estate Mgmt.

Phone: 81-3-5400-3888 **Fax:** 81-3-3437-2668
Toll-Free:
Address: 1-5-20, Kaigan, Minato-ku, Tokyo, 105-8527 Japan

GROWTH PLANS/SPECIAL FEATURES:

Tokyo Gas Co., Ltd., is one of Japan's leading gas suppliers, serving over 10.6 million customers in the Kanto region through a 35,000-mile pipeline network. The firm supplies gas primarily to the Tokyo metropolitan area, as well as to Kanagawa, Saitama, Chiba, Ibaraki, Tochigi and Gunma. Approximately 25% of its gas sales are to residential customers, 22% are to commercial customers, 40% are to industrial customers and 13% are to wholesale customers, including other gas companies. The company operates in five segments: Gas sales, gas appliances, installation work, real estate rentals and other business. The gas sales segment includes the sale of gas, as well as the conversion of liquefied natural gas (LNG) to city gas through three LNG terminals in Tokyo Bay. The gas appliance sales segment markets gas cook-tops, water heaters, gas air conditioning systems and residential cogeneration systems. The installation work system performs construction related to its gas business, such as gas pipe and valve installation. The real estate rental segment performs leasing, management and other activities for the Shinjuku Park Tower and other office buildings. The other business segment includes Tokyo Gas's energy services; facility construction and engineering; industry gas sales; system integration services; electric power; and shipping operations. Gas sales account for about 67% of the company's sales; gas appliance sales, 8%; installation work, 3%; real estate rental, 2%; and other business, 20%. In June 2010, the firm acquired a total ownership interest in companies holding five gas-fired combined cycle power stations in Mexico, with aggregate generating capacity of 2,233 megawatts.

FINANCIALS: **Sales and profits are in thousands of dollars—add 000 to get the full amount. 2010 Note: Financial information for 2010 was not available for all companies at press time.**

2010 Sales: $	2010 Profits: $
2009 Sales: $16,940,428	2009 Profits: $425,591
2008 Sales: $14,874,970	2008 Profits: $424,875
2007 Sales: $11,669,137	2007 Profits: $853,389
2006 Sales: $9,402,250	2006 Profits: $482,270

U.S. Stock Ticker: TKGSF
Int'l Ticker: 9531 Int'l Exchange: Tokyo-TSE
Employees:
Fiscal Year Ends: 3/31
Parent Company:

SALARIES/BENEFITS:

Pension Plan: ESOP Stock Plan: Profit Sharing: Top Exec. Salary: $ Bonus: $
Savings Plan: Stock Purch. Plan: Second Exec. Salary: $ Bonus: $

OTHER THOUGHTS:

Apparent Women Officers or Directors:
Hot Spot for Advancement for Women/Minorities:

LOCATIONS: ("Y" = Yes)

West:	Southwest:	Midwest:	Southeast:	Northeast:	International:
					Y

TONENGENERAL SEKIYU KK

www.tonengeneral.co.jp

Industry Group Code: 324110 **Ranks within this company's industry group:** Sales: 11 Profits: 23

Exploration/Production:		Refining/Retailing:		Utilities:		Alternative Energy:		Specialty Services:		Energy Mktg./Other Svcs.	
Exploration:		Refining:	Y	Electric Utility:		Waste/Solar/Other:		Consulting/Eng.:		Energy Marketing:	
Production:		Retailing:	Y	Gas Utility:		Thermal/Steam:		Seismic:		Equipment/Machinery:	
Coal Production:		Convenience Stores:	Y	Pipelines:		Wind:		Drilling:		Oil Field Services:	
		Chemicals:	Y	Water:		Hydro:		InfoTech:		Air/Shipping Transportation:	Y
						Fuel Cells:		Specialty Services:	Y		

TYPES OF BUSINESS:

Petroleum Refining & Production
Petroleum Distribution & Marketing
Lubricants & Chemicals
Marine Transportation
Research & Development
Service Stations

BRANDS/DIVISIONS/AFFILIATES:

Exxon Mobil Corporation (ExxonMobil)
TonenGeneral Kaiun Y.K.
Tonen Technology K.K.
Chuo Sekiyu Hanbai K.K.
Tonen Chemical Corp.
ExxonMobil Research & Engineering Co.
Toray Industries, Inc.
Toray Tonen Specialty Separator Godo Kaisha

CONTACTS: *Note: Officers with more than one job title may be intentionally listed here more than once.*

J. Mutoh, Managing Dir.
Philippe P. Ducom, Pres.
Kyoji Yoshida, Exec. Officer
M. J. Aguiar, Chmn.

Phone: 81-3-5495-6000 **Fax:**
Toll-Free:
Address: 1-8-15, Kohnan, Kaigan Minato-ku, Tokyo, 108-8005 Japan

GROWTH PLANS/SPECIAL FEATURES:

TonenGeneral Sekiyu K.K., 50%-owned subsidiary of ExxonMobil Corp., produces oil and chemical products, including gasoline, naphtha, jet fuel, kerosene, diesel fuel, fuel oils, liquid propane gas (LPG), ethylene, propylene, benzene, toluene, paraxylene and micro-porous film. A vertically integrated company, TonenGeneral has four direct subsidiaries: TonenGeneral Kaiun Y.K.; Tonen Technology K.K.; Chuo Sekiyu Hanbai K.K.; and Tonen Chemical Corp. It also has two subsidiaries through Tonen Chemical Corp., Tonen Chemical Nasu Co., Ltd., which is wholly-owned; and Nippon Unicar Corp., which is 50%-owned. The firm divides its petroleum activities into importing, refining and production, distribution and marketing. It also has a lubricant and chemicals development business and a research and development arm. TonenGeneral imports crude oil to Japan for processing using its marine transportation units, which is then unloaded and refined at the company's three refineries (Kawasaki, Sakai and Wakayama). Together these refineries have a total crude oil processing capacity of more than 660,000 barrels of oil per day. Products include liquefied petroleum gas, naphtha, gasoline, jet fuel, kerosene, diesel oil, fuel oils and lubricants. The petroleum and petrochemical products produced at the refineries are then transported to oil terminals by tankers and distributed to customers through service stations. TonenGeneral has approximately 4,200 independently run service stations throughout Japan under the Esso, General and Mobil brands, as well as an additional 850 Express self-service stations. The chemicals business, through Tonen Chemical, manufactures petrochemical products, including ethylene and propylene, and sells them as the raw materials for polymers such as polyethylene. The research and development arm offers technical services based on technologies of ExxonMobil Research and Engineering Co., ExxonMobil's research organization. In February 2010, a joint venture between TonenGeneral and Toray Industries, Inc. to produce battery separator film, Toray Tonen Specialty Separator Godo Kaisha, began operations.

FINANCIALS: **Sales and profits are in thousands of dollars—add 000 to get the full amount. 2010 Note: Financial information for 2010 was not available for all companies at press time.**

2010 Sales: $	2010 Profits: $	**U.S. Stock Ticker:**
2009 Sales: $22,708,900	2009 Profits: $-233,550	**Int'l Ticker: 5012** Int'l Exchange: Tokyo-TSE
2008 Sales: $36,254,890	2008 Profits: $878,390	Employees:
2007 Sales: $33,788,870	2007 Profits: $77,710	Fiscal Year Ends: 12/31
2006 Sales: $29,556,200	2006 Profits: $382,300	Parent Company:

SALARIES/BENEFITS:

Pension Plan:	ESOP Stock Plan:	Profit Sharing:	Top Exec. Salary: $	Bonus: $
Savings Plan:	Stock Purch. Plan:		Second Exec. Salary: $	Bonus: $

OTHER THOUGHTS:

Apparent Women Officers or Directors:
Hot Spot for Advancement for Women/Minorities:

LOCATIONS: ("Y" = Yes)

West:	Southwest:	Midwest:	Southeast:	Northeast:	International:
					Y

TOTAL SA

www.total.com

Industry Group Code: 211111 **Ranks within this company's industry group:** Sales: 8 Profits: 9

Exploration/Production:		Refining/Retailing:		Utilities:		Alternative Energy:		Specialty Services:		Energy Mktg./Other Svcs.	
Exploration:	Y	Refining:	Y	Electric Utility:		Waste/Solar/Other:	Y	Consulting/Eng.:		Energy Marketing:	Y
Production:	Y	Retailing:	Y	Gas Utility:		Thermal/Steam:		Seismic:		Equipment/Machinery:	
Coal Production:		Convenience Stores:		Pipelines:		Wind:		Drilling:		Oil Field Services:	
		Chemicals:	Y	Water:		Hydro:		InfoTech:		Air/Shipping Transportation:	
						Fuel Cells:		Specialty Services:			

TYPES OF BUSINESS:

Oil & Gas Exploration & Production
Petrochemicals
Specialty Chemicals
Hydrocarbons
Service Stations
Photovoltaic Cells

BRANDS/DIVISIONS/AFFILIATES:

Total
Elan
Elf
Bostik Inc
Total Petrochemicals
Total UK Limited

CONTACTS:

Note: Officers with more than one job title may be intentionally listed here more than once.

Christophe de Margerie, CEO
Patrick de la Chevardiere, CFO
Michel Benezit, Pres., Mktg. & Refining
Francois Viaud, Sr. VP-Human Resources
Marc Blaizot, Sr. VP-Geosciences Exploration & Prod.
Jean-Jacques Guilbaud, Chief Admin. Officer
Peter Herbel, General Counsel
Jean-Jacques Mosconi, VP-Strategic Planning
Yves-Marie Dalibard, VP-Corp. Comm.
Alain Champeaux, Sr. VP-Overseas
Francois Cornelis, Pres., Chemicals
Philippe Boisseau, Pres., Gas & Power
Thierry Desmarest, Chmn.
Jacques Marraud des Grottes, Sr. VP-Exploration & Prod., Africa

Phone: 33-1-47-44-45-46	**Fax:** 33-1-47-44-49-44
Toll-Free:	
Address: 2 Place Jean Miller, La Defense 6, Courbevoie, 92400 France	

GROWTH PLANS/SPECIAL FEATURES:

Total S.A. is one of the world's largest energy companies, with operations in more than 130 countries. The firm's activities are divided into three segments: Upstream, Downstream and Chemicals. The Upstream sector handles oil and gas exploration, development and production. Total produces 2.34 million barrels of oil (BOE) per day, with proven reserves of 10.48 billion BOE. The company has exploration and production activities in more than forty countries and produces oil or gas in thirty countries. The Downstream segment does trading, shipping, refining and marketing of petroleum and other fuels; it is a leader in Europe and Africa in the refining and service station market. Total has a worldwide network of over 16,000 service stations under the Total, Elf and Elan brand names. The Chemicals division prepares petrochemicals and fertilizers for the industrial/commercial markets; it is also involved in rubber processing, resins, adhesives and electroplating. The company is focusing on high-growth zones (such as Africa, the Mediterranean Basin and Asia) as well as specialty products such as liquefied petroleum gas, aviation fuel, lubricants, waxes, bitumens and solvents. Total, Electrabel and IMEC have collaborated to form a company called Photovoltech for the production of photovoltaic cells and modules. In December 2009, the company signed an agreement with PetroChina and Petronas to develop the Halfaya oil field. In January 2010, Total and ERG signed a joint venture agreement to create TotalErg. TotalErg will operate under both brands and will become an Italy-based marketing firm. In February 2010, the company announced plans to build a Refining Training Center and Technical Support Center at the Flandres Refinery in France. In April 2010, Total sold Mapa Spontex, its consumer specialty chemicals business, to U.S.-based Jarden Corporation. In July of the same year, the company agreed to buy Canada-based UTS Energy Corp. for $1.42 billion.

FINANCIALS:

Sales and profits are in thousands of dollars—add 000 to get the full amount. 2010 Note: Financial information for 2010 was not available for all companies at press time.

2010 Sales: $	2010 Profits: $	**U.S. Stock Ticker: TOT**
2009 Sales: $152,376,000	2009 Profits: $11,476,400	**Int'l Ticker: FP** Int'l Exchange: Paris-Euronext
2008 Sales: $213,742,000	2008 Profits: $14,117,800	Employees: 96,959
2007 Sales: $182,404,000	2007 Profits: $17,572,000	Fiscal Year Ends: 12/31
2006 Sales: $208,359,000	2006 Profits: $16,439,500	Parent Company:

SALARIES/BENEFITS:

Pension Plan:	ESOP Stock Plan:	Profit Sharing:	Top Exec. Salary: $	Bonus: $1,457,656
Savings Plan:	Stock Purch. Plan:		Second Exec. Salary: $	Bonus: $

OTHER THOUGHTS:

Apparent Women Officers or Directors: 2
Hot Spot for Advancement for Women/Minorities:

LOCATIONS: ("Y" = Yes)

West:	Southwest:	Midwest:	Southeast:	Northeast:	International:
Y	Y				Y

TOTAL UK LIMITED

www.total.co.uk

Industry Group Code: 324110 **Ranks within this company's industry group:** Sales: Profits:

Exploration/Production:		Refining/Retailing:		Utilities:		Alternative Energy:		Specialty Services:		Energy Mktg./Other Svcs.	
Exploration:		Refining:	Y	Electric Utility:		Waste/Solar/Other:		Consulting/Eng.:		Energy Marketing:	
Production:		Retailing:	Y	Gas Utility:		Thermal/Steam:		Seismic:		Equipment/Machinery:	
Coal Production:		Convenience Stores:	Y	Pipelines:	Y	Wind:		Drilling:		Oil Field Services:	
		Chemicals:	Y	Water:		Hydro:		InfoTech:		Air/Shipping Transportation:	
						Fuel Cells:		Specialty Services:			

TYPES OF BUSINESS:

Oil Refineries
Lubricants & Solvents
Aviation, Industrial & Heating Fuels
Gas Stations & Convenience Stores

BRANDS/DIVISIONS/AFFILIATES:

Total SA
Air Total
Total Bulter
Fina-Line
Lindsey Oil Refinery
Milford Haven Refinery
Elf
Bonjour Convenience Stores

CONTACTS: *Note: Officers with more than one job title may be intentionally listed here more than once.*

Malcome Jones, Managing Dir.
Michael Crane, Mktg. Exec.
Pierre Hutchison, Dir.-Info.
Peter Hollister, Mgr.-Retail Fuels Dev.
Iain Cracknell, Mgr.-Corp. Comm.

Phone: 44-1923-694-000	**Fax:** 44-1923-694-400
Toll-Free:	
Address: 40 Clarendon Rd., Watford, Hertfordshire WD17 1TQ UK	

GROWTH PLANS/SPECIAL FEATURES:

TOTAL UK Limited is the British refining and marketing subsidiary of French fuel giant Total S.A., one of the largest oil and gas companies in the world, with operations in 130 countries. The firm owns the Lindsey Oil Refinery in Lincolnshire, which produces 220,000 barrels of petroleum and related products a day. In addition, the company owns the Milford Haven Refinery in West Wales; a lubricant blending plant at Ferrybridge, West Yorkshire that produces Elf brand lubricants; and a bitumen plant at Preston, Lancashire. The products are distributed throughout the UK by road, rail, sea and underground pipelines, including the Fina-Line, a 140-mile joint pipeline that runs from the Lindsey Oil Refinery to a terminal in Hertfordshire and connects to Heathrow Airport in London. TOTAL UK also supplies jet fuel through the Air Total brand and agricultural, industrial and home heating fuels through Total Butler. The firm has a specialty division, which manufactures and sells automotive and industrial lubricants, bitumen products and solvents to customers in the transport, building and manufacturing sectors. Furthermore, the firm owns the Bonjour convenience stores and over 850 TOTAL service stations located throughout the UK and a network of approximately 3,000 service stations located in Europe and Africa.

FINANCIALS: **Sales and profits are in thousands of dollars—add 000 to get the full amount. 2010 Note: Financial information for 2010 was not available for all companies at press time.**

2010 Sales: $	2010 Profits: $	**U.S. Stock Ticker: Subsidiary**
2009 Sales: $	2009 Profits: $	**Int'l Ticker:** Int'l Exchange:
2008 Sales: $	2008 Profits: $	Employees:
2007 Sales: $	2007 Profits: $	Fiscal Year Ends: 12/31
2006 Sales: $	2006 Profits: $	Parent Company: TOTAL SA

SALARIES/BENEFITS:

Pension Plan:	ESOP Stock Plan:	Profit Sharing:	Top Exec. Salary: $	Bonus: $
Savings Plan:	Stock Purch. Plan:		Second Exec. Salary: $	Bonus: $

OTHER THOUGHTS:

Apparent Women Officers or Directors: 1
Hot Spot for Advancement for Women/Minorities:

LOCATIONS: ("Y" = Yes)

West:	Southwest:	Midwest:	Southeast:	Northeast:	International:
					Y

TRACTEBEL ENERGIA SA

www.tractebelenergia.com.br

Industry Group Code: 221121 **Ranks within this company's industry group:** Sales: 3 Profits: 2

Exploration/Production:		**Refining/Retailing:**		**Utilities:**		**Alternative Energy:**		**Specialty Services:**		**Energy Mktg./Other Svcs.**	
Exploration:		Refining:		Electric Utility:	Y	Waste/Solar/Other:		Consulting/Eng.:		Energy Marketing:	
Production:		Retailing:		Gas Utility:		Thermal/Steam:	Y	Seismic:		Equipment/Machinery:	
Coal Production:		Convenience Stores:		Pipelines:		Wind:	Y	Drilling:		Oil Field Services:	
		Chemicals:		Water:		Hydro:	Y	InfoTech:		Air/Shipping Transportation:	
						Fuel Cells:		Specialty Services:			

TYPES OF BUSINESS:

Electricity Generation

BRANDS/DIVISIONS/AFFILIATES:

SUEZ SA
SUEZ Energy International

CONTACTS:

Note: Officers with more than one job title may be intentionally listed here more than once.

Manoel A.Z. Torres, CEO
Luciano F. Andriani, Dir.-Admin.
Jose L.J. Laydner, Dir.-Bus. Dev.
Eduardo A.G. Sattamini, Dir.-Investor Rel.
Eduardo A.G. Sattamini, Dir.-Finance
Jose C.C. Minuzzo, Dir.-Energy Prod.
Miroel M. Wolowski, Dir.-Project Implementation
Marco A.A. Sureck, Dir.-Planning & Control
Mauricio S. Bahr, Chmn.

Phone: 55-48-3221-7000	**Fax:** 55-48-3221-7001
Toll-Free:	
Address: 366 Antonio Dib Mussi Rd., Florianopolis, SC 88015-110 Brazil	

GROWTH PLANS/SPECIAL FEATURES:

Tractebel Energia S.A. is a Brazilian electric energy generation company. The firm is part of GDF SUEZ Group, which specializes in energy production and is a division of SUEZ Energy International. Tractebel Energia produces approximately 8% of the electricity generated in Brazil. The company operates 19 wind, hydroelectric and thermoelectric power plants with an installed capacity of approximately 6,432 megawatts (MW). These facilities are located in the states of Santa Catarina, Mato Grosso, Parana, Rio Grande do Sul, Mato Grosso do Sul, Goias, Tocantins, Piaui and Ceara. Tractebel Energia primarily markets its electricity to distributors and traders, in addition to large industries. The firm also offers services such as cogeneration, electricity/steam generation and energy consumption monitoring services. The company is in the process of building a sugarcane bagasse-fired thermal electricity plant in Sao Paulo that is expected to have a generation capacity of 33MW. In 2009, Tractebel Energia opened its 18th and 19th power plants.

FINANCIALS:

Sales and profits are in thousands of dollars—add 000 to get the full amount. 2010 Note: Financial information for 2010 was not available for all companies at press time.

2010 Sales: $	2010 Profits: $	**U.S. Stock Ticker: TBLEY**
2009 Sales: $2,083,230	2009 Profits: $675,840	**Int'l Ticker:** Int'l Exchange:
2008 Sales: $2,025,800	2008 Profits: $664,400	Employees:
2007 Sales: $	2007 Profits: $	Fiscal Year Ends: 12/31
2006 Sales: $	2006 Profits: $	Parent Company: SUEZ SA

SALARIES/BENEFITS:

Pension Plan:	ESOP Stock Plan:	Profit Sharing:	Top Exec. Salary: $	Bonus: $
Savings Plan:	Stock Purch. Plan:		Second Exec. Salary: $	Bonus: $

OTHER THOUGHTS:

Apparent Women Officers or Directors:
Hot Spot for Advancement for Women/Minorities:

LOCATIONS: ("Y" = Yes)

West:	Southwest:	Midwest:	Southeast:	Northeast:	International:
					Y

TRANSALTA CORP

www.transalta.com

Industry Group Code: 2211 **Ranks within this company's industry group:** Sales: 34 Profits: 33

Exploration/Production:		Refining/Retailing:		Utilities:		Alternative Energy:		Specialty Services:		Energy Mktg./Other Svcs.	
Exploration:		Refining:		Electric Utility:		Waste/Solar/Other:	Y	Consulting/Eng.:		Energy Marketing:	Y
Production:	Y	Retailing:		Gas Utility:		Thermal/Steam:	Y	Seismic:		Equipment/Machinery:	
Coal Production:	Y	Convenience Stores:		Pipelines:		Wind:	Y	Drilling:		Oil Field Services:	
		Chemicals:		Water:		Hydro:	Y	InfoTech:		Air/Shipping Transportation:	
						Fuel Cells:		Specialty Services:			

TYPES OF BUSINESS:

Electrical Power Generation
Wholesale Energy Marketing
Gas Production
Coal Mining

BRANDS/DIVISIONS/AFFILIATES:

TransAlta Utilities
TransAlta Energy Corporation
Keephills 3
TransAlta Generation Ltd.
Canadian Hydro Developers
CE Generation LLC

CONTACTS: *Note: Officers with more than one job title may be intentionally listed here more than once.*

Stephen G. Snyder, CEO
Dawn Farrell, COO
Stephen G. Snyder, Pres.
Brett Gellner, CFO
Stephen W. Foster, VP-Human Resources & Labor Svcs.
Mark B. Mackay, VP-Tech. & Innovation
Parviz Mohamed, VP-IT
William D.A. Bridge, CTO
Robert Emmott, Chief Eng. Officer/VP
Mike Williams, Chief Admin. Officer
Ken S. Stickland, Chief Legal Officer
Doug Jackson, VP-Coal & Mining Oper.
Rob Schaefer, VP-Bus. & Customer Dev.
Jennifer Pierce, VP-Comm.
Jennifer Pierce, VP-Investor Rel.
Hume Kyle, VP-Finance/Controller
Maryse C.C. St.-Laurent, VP/Corp. Sec.
Frank Hawkins, Treas./VP
Richard P. Langhammer, Chief Productivity Officer
Donna S. Kaufman, Chmn.
Aron Willis, Country Mgr.-TransAlta Energy (Australia) Pty Ltd.
Dawn da Lima, VP-Procurement & Materials Mgmt.

Phone: 403-267-7110 **Fax:**
Toll-Free:
Address: 110 12th Ave. SW, Box 1900, Station M, Calgary, AB T2P 2M1 Canada

GROWTH PLANS/SPECIAL FEATURES:

TransAlta Corp. is among Canada's largest non-regulated electric generation and energy marketing companies. The company generates electricity in Canada, the U.S. and Australia through biomass, coal, gas, hydroelectric, wind and geothermal plants with a total generating capacity of approximately 10,578 megawatts (MW). The firm is organized into two business segments: Generation; and Corporate Development and Marketing. The Generation group is responsible for constructing, operating and maintaining electricity generation facilities. The Corporate Development and Marketing group is responsible for managing the sale of production, natural gas purchasing, transmission capacity and market risks associated with TransAlta's generation assets and non-asset backed trading activities. In Canada, the company holds approximately 6,461 MW of electrical generating capacity in thermal, gas-fired, wind-powered, biomass and hydroelectric facilities. In the U.S., TransAlta's principal facilities include a 1,376 MW thermal facility and a 248 MW gas-fired facility, both located in Centralia, Washington. The firm also owns 50% of CE Generation LLC, which operates geothermal facilities in California and gas-fired facilities in Texas, Arizona and New York. TransAlta owns facilities with approximately 300 MW of net electrical generating capacity in Australia. In November 2009, TransAlta acquired Canadian Hydro Developers, a developer, owner, and operator of 21 renewable energy generation facilities in Canada, with a net total of 694 MW of capacity through water, wind and biomass facilities. In April 2010, the firm ceased operations at its Wabamun power plant in Alberta.

FINANCIALS: **Sales and profits are in thousands of dollars—add 000 to get the full amount. 2010 Note: Financial information for 2010 was not available for all companies at press time.**

2010 Sales: $	2010 Profits: $	**U.S. Stock Ticker: TAC**
2009 Sales: $2,684,340	2009 Profits: $175,400	**Int'l Ticker: TA** Int'l Exchange: Toronto-TSX
2008 Sales: $2,888,430	2008 Profits: $218,260	Employees: 2,228
2007 Sales: $2,800,000	2007 Profits: $310,000	Fiscal Year Ends: 12/31
2006 Sales: $2,399,700	2006 Profits: $34,700	Parent Company:

SALARIES/BENEFITS:

Pension Plan: Y	ESOP Stock Plan: Y	Profit Sharing:	Top Exec. Salary: $953,062	Bonus: $349,945
Savings Plan:	Stock Purch. Plan:		Second Exec. Salary: $602,791	Bonus: $168,781

OTHER THOUGHTS:

Apparent Women Officers or Directors: 7
Hot Spot for Advancement for Women/Minorities: Y

LOCATIONS: ("Y" = Yes)

West:	Southwest:	Midwest:	Southeast:	Northeast:	International:
Y	Y				Y

TRANSAMMONIA INC

www.transammonia.com

Industry Group Code: 486 **Ranks within this company's industry group:** Sales: 10 Profits:

Exploration/Production:		Refining/Retailing:		Utilities:		Alternative Energy:		Specialty Services:		Energy Mktg./Other Svcs.	
Exploration:		Refining:		Electric Utility:		Waste/Solar/Other:		Consulting/Eng.:		Energy Marketing:	Y
Production:	Y	Retailing:		Gas Utility:		Thermal/Steam:		Seismic:		Equipment/Machinery:	
Coal Production:		Convenience Stores:		Pipelines:		Wind:		Drilling:		Oil Field Services:	
		Chemicals:	Y	Water:		Hydro:		InfoTech:		Air/Shipping Transportation:	Y
						Fuel Cells:		Specialty Services:			

TYPES OF BUSINESS:

Liquefied Petroleum Gas (LPG) Distribution
Marketing & Trading Operations
Distribution & Transport
Crude Oil & Oil Products
Methanol
Fertilizer Materials
Petrochemicals
Propane

BRANDS/DIVISIONS/AFFILIATES:

Transammonia Group
Trammochem
Trammo Gas
Sea-3
Transammonia DMCC
Trammo Gas International Inc
Trammochem Asia PTE
Transammonia Shanghai

CONTACTS:

Note: Officers with more than one job title may be intentionally listed here more than once.

Ronald P. Stanton, CEO
Edward G. Weiner, CFO/Sr. VP
Ronald P. Stanton, Chmn.

Phone: 212-223-3200	**Fax:** 212-759-1410
Toll-Free:	
Address: 320 Park Ave., New York, NY 10022 US	

GROWTH PLANS/SPECIAL FEATURES:

Transammonia, Inc., known as the Transammonia Group, is a marketer, trader, distributor and transporter of fertilizer materials, liquefied petroleum gas (LPG), petrochemicals (chiefly aromatics), methanol, crude oil and oil products internationally. The firm works through its five subsidiaries: Transammonia; Trammochem; Trammo Gas; Sea-3; and Trammo Petroleum. The company has international offices in 31 cities worldwide. The firm began as a producer and transporter of fertilizers, raw materials and ammonia and continues operations in these markets through the Transammonia subsidiary. Petrochemicals are created, bought and sold for the firm through subsidiary Trammochem. Through Trammochem, the firm trades methyl tertiary-butyl ether (MTBE), benzene, methanol, olefins, gasoline blend components, styrene monomers, toluene, ethanol, xylenes and isomers internationally, with annual traded volumes at about 2.7 million tons in 2009. Trammo Gas, headquartered in Houston, Texas, is focused solely on the U.S. and sells LPG, including propane, ethane, butane, iso butane and natural gas. In 2009, Trammo Gas traded approximately 8.0 million metric tons of all its products. Trammo Gas International, Inc., part of Trammo Gas, operates three gas carriers under long term time charters and provides international transportation of LPG for third parties. The Sea-3 subsidiary is a leading importer and distributor of liquefied propane in the northeastern U.S. and parts of Florida, and also participates in gas marketing on the Gulf Coast and other areas of the U.S. Its customers include thousands of homes, businesses, industries, schools and hospitals. Recently, the firm established Trammochem Asia PTE in Singapore for trading and selling petrochemicals in Asia. In 2009, the company established Transammonia DMCC in Dubai UAE and Transammonia Shanghai in China. In 2010, TA Bulk Carriers, a wholly-owned division of Transammonia AG enters the fertilizer shipping business.

FINANCIALS:

Sales and profits are in thousands of dollars—add 000 to get the full amount. 2010 Note: Financial information for 2010 was not available for all companies at press time.

2010 Sales: $	2010 Profits: $	**U.S. Stock Ticker: Private**
2009 Sales: $5,490,000	2009 Profits: $	**Int'l Ticker:** Int'l Exchange:
2008 Sales: $11,200,000	2008 Profits: $	Employees: 390
2007 Sales: $8,300,000	2007 Profits: $	Fiscal Year Ends: 12/31
2006 Sales: $5,430,000	2006 Profits: $	Parent Company:

SALARIES/BENEFITS:

Pension Plan:	ESOP Stock Plan:	Profit Sharing:	Top Exec. Salary: $	Bonus: $
Savings Plan:	Stock Purch. Plan:		Second Exec. Salary: $	Bonus: $

OTHER THOUGHTS:

Apparent Women Officers or Directors:
Hot Spot for Advancement for Women/Minorities:

LOCATIONS: ("Y" = Yes)

West:	Southwest:	Midwest:	Southeast:	Northeast:	International:
	Y	Y	Y	Y	Y

TRANSCANADA CORP

www.transcanada.com

Industry Group Code: 221 **Ranks within this company's industry group:** Sales: 20 Profits: 10

Exploration/Production:		**Refining/Retailing:**		**Utilities:**		**Alternative Energy:**		**Specialty Services:**		**Energy Mktg./Other Svcs.**	
Exploration:		Refining:		Electric Utility:		Waste/Solar/Other:	Y	Consulting/Eng.:		Energy Marketing:	Y
Production:		Retailing:		Gas Utility:		Thermal/Steam:		Seismic:		Equipment/Machinery:	
Coal Production:		Convenience Stores:		Pipelines:	Y	Wind:	Y	Drilling:		Oil Field Services:	
		Chemicals:		Water:		Hydro:	Y	InfoTech:		Air/Shipping Transportation:	
						Fuel Cells:		Specialty Services:	Y		

TYPES OF BUSINESS:

Power & Natural Gas Distribution
Pipelines
Power Plants
Alternative Power Generation
Small-Scale Hydroelectric Generation
Biomass Generation

BRANDS/DIVISIONS/AFFILIATES:

Tamazunchale Pipeline (The)
TransCanada Energy, Ltd.
Iroquois Gas Transmission System
TransCanada PipeLines, Ltd.
Northern Border Pipeline Company
Tuscarora Gas Transmission Company
Exxon Mobil Corporation
Alaska Pipeline Project

CONTACTS: *Note: Officers with more than one job title may be intentionally listed here more than once.*

Russell K. Girling, CEO
Russell K. Girling, Pres.
Donald R. Marchand, CFO/Exec. VP
Sean McMaster, General Counsel/Exec. VP
Don Wishart, Exec. VP-Oper. & Major Projects
Dennis McConaghy, Exec. VP-Corp. Dev.
G. Glenn Menuz, VP/Controller
Alexander J. Pourbaix, Pres., Energy & Oil Pipelines
Sarah E. Raiss, Exec. VP-Corp. Svcs.
Gregory A. Lohnes, Pres., Natural Gas Pipelines
Garry E. Lamb, VP-Risk Mgmt.
S. Barry Jackson, Chmn.

Phone: 403-920-2000 **Fax:** 403-920-2200
Toll-Free: 800-661-3805
Address: 450 1st St. SW, Calgary, AB T2P 5H1 Canada

GROWTH PLANS/SPECIAL FEATURES:

TransCanada Corp. is an energy holding company that focuses on natural gas transmission, power generation, marketing and trading. The company's transmission business has several wholly-owned pipelines including the Alberta system, 14,646 miles; Canadian Mainline, 8,762 miles; Foothills system, 771 miles; GTN system, 1,351 miles; ANR pipeline, 10,500 miles; the Keystone Oil Pipeline, 2,147 miles; and Tamazunchale pipeline, 81 miles. It has ownership interests in the affiliate pipelines of Great Lakes Gas Transmission Company (2,115 miles) and Iroquois Gas Transmission system (414 miles). In addition, the company has interest in and operates North Baja, 80 miles; Portland Natural Gas Transmission system, 295 miles; and Trans Quebec and Maritimes Pipeline, 355 miles. Furthermore, through its general partner TC PipeLines, LP, TransCanada owns interests in the U.S. pipelines of Northern Border Pipeline Company, which extend 1,398 miles, and the Tuscarora Gas Transmission Company, 305 miles. The firm transports roughly 20% of the natural gas consumed in North America. The power segment of TransCanada's business includes the construction, ownership, operation and management of power plants and the marketing of electricity. The company owns or has interests in 20 power plants in the U.S. and Canada, which have the capacity to service nearly 12 million homes with more than 11,700 megawatts (MW) of power. TransCanada generates its power utilizing natural gas, nuclear, coal, hydro and wind generation primarily located in Alberta, Ontario, Quebec and the northeastern U.S. Marketed and trading activities are handled through subsidiaries TransCanada Power Marketing and TransCanada Energy. In October 2009, the company began operations at the Kibby Wind Power Project in northern Maine, with half of the 44 wind turbines fully operational. In July 2010, TransCanada, in partnership with ExxonMobil, closed the initial open season on its Alaska Pipeline Project, a proposed pipeline system for natural gas transport in Alaska's North Slope.

FINANCIALS: **Sales and profits are in thousands of dollars—add 000 to get the full amount. 2010 Note: Financial information for 2010 was not available for all companies at press time.**

2010 Sales: $
2009 Sales: $8,688,740
2008 Sales: $8,352,470
2007 Sales: $8,900,000
2006 Sales: $5,146,000

2010 Profits: $
2009 Profits: $1,337,330
2008 Profits: $1,395,470
2007 Profits: $1,230,000
2006 Profits: $325,000

U.S. Stock Ticker: TRP
Int'l Ticker: TRP Int'l Exchange: Toronto-TSX
Employees: 4,000
Fiscal Year Ends: 12/31
Parent Company:

SALARIES/BENEFITS:

Pension Plan: ESOP Stock Plan: Profit Sharing: Top Exec. Salary: $1,221,875 Bonus: $1,612,875
Savings Plan: Stock Purch. Plan: Second Exec. Salary: $733,125 Bonus: $879,750

OTHER THOUGHTS:

Apparent Women Officers or Directors: 2
Hot Spot for Advancement for Women/Minorities:

LOCATIONS: ("Y" = Yes)

West:	Southwest:	Midwest:	Southeast:	Northeast:	International:
Y				Y	Y

TRANSMONTAIGNE INC

www.transmontaigne.com

Industry Group Code: 486 **Ranks within this company's industry group:** Sales: Profits:

Exploration/Production:		Refining/Retailing:		Utilities:		Alternative Energy:		Specialty Services:		Energy Mktg./Other Svcs.	
Exploration:		Refining:		Electric Utility:		Waste/Solar/Other:		Consulting/Eng.:		Energy Marketing:	
Production:		Retailing:		Gas Utility:		Thermal/Steam:		Seismic:		Equipment/Machinery:	
Coal Production:		Convenience Stores:		Pipelines:	Y	Wind:		Drilling:		Oil Field Services:	
		Chemicals:		Water:		Hydro:		InfoTech:		Air/Shipping Transportation:	Y
						Fuel Cells:		Specialty Services:	Y		

TYPES OF BUSINESS:

Oil & Gas Transportation & Marketing
Terminals & Storage Services
Marketing Services
Tugboats & Barges
Risk Management Services

BRANDS/DIVISIONS/AFFILIATES:

Morgan Stanley Capital Group
Coastal Fuels Marketing, Inc.
TransMontaigne Product Services, Inc.

CONTACTS:

Note: Officers with more than one job title may be intentionally listed here more than once.

Randall Larson, CEO
Randall Larson, Pres.
Ronald A. Majors, Sr. VP-Bus. Dev.
Deborah A. Davis, Chief Acct. Officer
Stephen Mugner, Chmn.

Phone: 303-626-8200	**Fax:** 303-626-8228
Toll-Free:	
Address: 1670 Broadway, Ste. 3100, Denver, CO 80202 US	

GROWTH PLANS/SPECIAL FEATURES:

TransMontaigne, Inc., a subsidiary of Morgan Stanley, gathers, transports, stores, distributes and markets refined petroleum products, chemicals and crude oil; delivering approximately 300,000 barrels per day throughout the U.S. to independent wholesalers and industrial and commercial end users. Its operations are primarily located in the Gulf Coast, Southeast and Midwest regions. TransMontaigne owns, operates, builds and manages pipeline and terminal assets; owns and operates a fleet of tugboats and barges; and provides transportation services via railway cars and trucks. It also offers budget and risk management services; retail and supply chain services, such as product delivery, inventory management, environmental monitoring and services and technical services; and e-supply chain services, such as supply, storage, distribution, transportation, pricing and consumption data. Florida-based Coastal Fuels Marketing, Inc. conducts supply, distribution and marketing operations principally to marine vessels and power generation plants. Its other subsidiary is TransMontaigne Product Services, Inc.

FINANCIALS:

Sales and profits are in thousands of dollars—add 000 to get the full amount. 2010 Note: Financial information for 2010 was not available for all companies at press time.

2010 Sales: $	2010 Profits: $	**U.S. Stock Ticker: Subsidiary**
2009 Sales: $	2009 Profits: $	**Int'l Ticker:** Int'l Exchange:
2008 Sales: $15,950,000	2008 Profits: $	Employees: 800
2007 Sales: $	2007 Profits: $	Fiscal Year Ends: 6/30
2006 Sales: $	2006 Profits: $	Parent Company: MORGAN STANLEY

SALARIES/BENEFITS:

Pension Plan:	ESOP Stock Plan:	Profit Sharing:	Top Exec. Salary: $	Bonus: $75,000
Savings Plan:	Stock Purch. Plan:		Second Exec. Salary: $	Bonus: $

OTHER THOUGHTS:

Apparent Women Officers or Directors: 1
Hot Spot for Advancement for Women/Minorities:

LOCATIONS: ("Y" = Yes)

West:	Southwest:	Midwest:	Southeast:	Northeast:	International:
Y	Y	Y	Y	Y	

TRANSOCEAN INC

www.deepwater.com

Industry Group Code: 211111 **Ranks within this company's industry group:** Sales: 45 Profits: 21

Exploration/Production:		Refining/Retailing:		Utilities:		Alternative Energy:		Specialty Services:		Energy Mktg./Other Svcs.	
Exploration:	Y	Refining:		Electric Utility:		Waste/Solar/Other:		Consulting/Eng.:		Energy Marketing:	
Production:	Y	Retailing:		Gas Utility:		Thermal/Steam:		Seismic:		Equipment/Machinery:	
Coal Production:		Convenience Stores:		Pipelines:		Wind:		Drilling:	Y	Oil Field Services:	Y
		Chemicals:		Water:		Hydro:		InfoTech:		Air/Shipping Transportation:	
						Fuel Cells:		Specialty Services:			

TYPES OF BUSINESS:

Oil & Gas Exploration & Production
Mobile Offshore Production Units
Offshore Drilling & Production
Drilling Management Services
Dual-Activity Drilling
High-Specification Drillships

BRANDS/DIVISIONS/AFFILIATES:

Applied Drilling Technology Inc.
ADT International
Transocean, Inc.

CONTACTS: *Note: Officers with more than one job title may be intentionally listed here more than once.*

Steven L. Newman, CEO
Steven L. Newman, Pres.
Ricardo H. Rosa, CFO/Sr. VP
Terry B. Bonno, Sr. VP-Mktg.
Ian M. Clark, VP-Human Resources
John L. Truschinger, CIO/VP
N. Pharr Smith, VP-Tech. Svcs.
N. Pharr Smith, VP-Eng.
Eric B. Brown, General Counsel/Sr. VP
Gregory S. Panagos, VP-Comm.
Gregory S. Panagos, VP-Investor Rel.
John H. Briscoe, Controller/VP
Adrian P. Rose, VP-Quality, Health, Safety & Environment
Arnaud A.Y. Bobillier, Exec. VP-Asset & Performance
Michael F. Munro, Chief Compliance Officer/VP
Ihab Toma, Exec. VP-Global Bus.
Robert E. Rose, Chmn.
David A. Tonnel, Sr. VP-Europe & Africa Unit
Gary B. Eshenroder, VP-Global Supply Chain

Phone: 41-22-930-9000 **Fax:**
Toll-Free:
Address: Chemin de Blandonnet 2, Vernier, CH-1214 Switzerland

GROWTH PLANS/SPECIAL FEATURES:

Transocean, Inc., together with its subsidiaries, is a leading international provider of deepwater and harsh environment offshore contract drilling services for oil and gas wells. The company owns, partially owns or operates 139 mobile offshore drilling units, consisting of 45 high-specification floaters (ultra-deepwater, deepwater and harsh environment semisubmersibles and drillships); 26 mid-water floaters; 10 high-specification jackups; 55 standard jackups; and three other rigs, comprised of two barge drilling rigs and one coring drillship. These units operate worldwide, with 25 units in the Asia Pacific and Southeast Asia, 12 units in India, 16 units in the Middle East, 15 units in the U.S. Gulf of Mexico, 16 units in the U.K.'s North Sea, 10 units in Brazil, seven units in Nigeria, six units in Angola, 14 units in other West African countries, five units in Norway, four units in the Mediterranean, two units in Trinidad and Tobago, two units in Australia, two units in Canada, and one unit each in the Caspian Sea and the Netherlands. The company also has three ultra-deepwater drillships under construction or contracted for construction. The firm contracts its drilling rigs, related equipment and work crews primarily on a day-rate basis to drill oil and gas wells. Transocean also provides oil and gas drilling management services, drilling engineering and drilling project management services through Applied Drilling Technology, Inc., a wholly-owned subsidiary, and ADT International, a division of one of its U.K. subsidiaries. In April 2010, a Transocean rig that was completing a deepwater well in the Gulf of Mexico, on which BP is the operator and majority owner, blew out, creating a massive oil spill.

FINANCIALS: **Sales and profits are in thousands of dollars—add 000 to get the full amount. 2010 Note: Financial information for 2010 was not available for all companies at press time.**

2010 Sales: $	2010 Profits: $	**U.S. Stock Ticker: RIG**
2009 Sales: $11,556,000	2009 Profits: $3,170,000	**Int'l Ticker:** Int'l Exchange:
2008 Sales: $12,674,000	2008 Profits: $4,031,000	Employees: 21,600
2007 Sales: $6,377,000	2007 Profits: $3,131,000	Fiscal Year Ends: 12/31
2006 Sales: $3,882,000	2006 Profits: $1,385,000	Parent Company:

SALARIES/BENEFITS:

Pension Plan: Y	ESOP Stock Plan:	Profit Sharing:	Top Exec. Salary: $1,212,663	Bonus: $
Savings Plan: Y	Stock Purch. Plan: Y		Second Exec. Salary: $636,405	Bonus: $

OTHER THOUGHTS:

Apparent Women Officers or Directors: 1
Hot Spot for Advancement for Women/Minorities:

LOCATIONS: ("Y" = Yes)

West:	Southwest:	Midwest:	Southeast:	Northeast:	International:
	Y				Y

TRANSPORTADORA DE GAS DEL SUR SA

www.tgs.com.ar

Industry Group Code: 486 **Ranks within this company's industry group:** Sales: 22 Profits: 16

Exploration/Production:		Refining/Retailing:		Utilities:		Alternative Energy:		Specialty Services:		Energy Mktg./Other Svcs.	
Exploration:		Refining:	Y	Electric Utility:		Waste/Solar/Other:		Consulting/Eng.:		Energy Marketing:	Y
Production:		Retailing:		Gas Utility:		Thermal/Steam:		Seismic:		Equipment/Machinery:	
Coal Production:		Convenience Stores:		Pipelines:	Y	Wind:		Drilling:		Oil Field Services:	
		Chemicals:		Water:		Hydro:		InfoTech:		Air/Shipping Transportation:	
						Fuel Cells:		Specialty Services:	Y		

TYPES OF BUSINESS:

Pipelines
Gas Processing & Marketing
Telecommunications Services
Natural Gas Liquids Production

BRANDS/DIVISIONS/AFFILIATES:

MetroGas
Gas Natural Ban
Camuzzi Gas Pampeana
Camuzzi Gas del Sur
General Cerri Processing Complex
Telcosur

CONTACTS: *Note: Officers with more than one job title may be intentionally listed here more than once.*

Carlos Seijo, CEO
Gonzalo Castro Olivera, CFO
Jorge Garcia, VP-Mktg.
Juan Martin Encina, VP-Human Resources
Nicolas Mordeglia, VP-Legal Affairs
Jorge Bonetto, VP-Oper.
Javier Sato, VP-Bus.
Francisco Vila, Mgr.-Investor Rel.
Leandro Perez Castano, Mgr.-Finance & Corp. Info.
Daniel Perrone, VP-Regulatory & Institutional Affairs
Oscar Sardi, VP-Service
Alejandro Bass, VP-Mgmt. Control & Corp. Regulations
Ricardo Isidro Monge, Chmn.

Phone: 54-11-4865-9050 | **Fax:** 54-11-4865-7154
Toll-Free:
Address: Don Bosco 3672, 6th Fl., Buenos Aires, C1206ABF Argentina

GROWTH PLANS/SPECIAL FEATURES:

Transportadora De Gas Del Sur S.A. (TGS) is one of the largest gas transportation companies in Argentina and operates one of the most extensive gas pipeline systems in South America. Covering over 5,500 miles (4,713 of which are owned by TGS), the system has a transportation capacity of nearly 2.6 billion cubic feet per day (Bcf/d). The firm delivers approximately 60% of all the gas consumed in Argentina, serving roughly 4.6 million users; and connects the main gas reserves in southern and western Argentina with the gas distributors in those areas. Direct service is rendered to customers through four gas distribution companies: MetroGas, Gas Natural Ban, Camuzzi Gas Pampeana and Camuzzi Gas del Sur. TGS is one of the country's largest natural gas processors and one of the largest marketers of liquid petroleum gas, operating the General Cerri Processing Complex located in the Buenos Aires Province. TGS provides services in the midstream sector, consisting primarily of treatment, separation of impurities and compression of gas and other services related to the construction, operation and maintenance of gas pipelines. The primary activity of its non-regulated segment is the production and processing of NGLs (Natural Gas Liquids) such as propane, butane and ethane, which accounts for approximately 50% of the firm's revenues. Its production facilities can process on average 1.7 Bcf/d of NGLs. Telcosur, a communications subsidiary, was formed to take advantage of the firm's existing telecommunications assets and infrastructure, as well as expansion in response to the deregulation of the Argentinean telecommunications market. Telcosur's customers include Global Crossing, Silica Networks, CTI, Telemex, Comsat, Ertach, Transener, Oldeval and Pan American Energy. Compania de Inversiones de Energia S.A. owns 55.3% of the firm.

TGS offers employees medical and dental coverage; it also offers leave time for new parents.

FINANCIALS: **Sales and profits are in thousands of dollars—add 000 to get the full amount. 2010 Note: Financial information for 2010 was not available for all companies at press time.**

2010 Sales: $	2010 Profits: $	**U.S. Stock Ticker: TGS**
2009 Sales: $403,890	2009 Profits: $45,020	**Int'l Ticker: TGSU** Int'l Exchange: Buenos Aires-BCBA
2008 Sales: $371,553	2008 Profits: $45,840	Employees:
2007 Sales: $416,840	2007 Profits: $48,900	Fiscal Year Ends: 12/31
2006 Sales: $434,140	2006 Profits: $118,690	Parent Company:

SALARIES/BENEFITS:

Pension Plan:	ESOP Stock Plan:	Profit Sharing:	Top Exec. Salary: $	Bonus: $
Savings Plan:	Stock Purch. Plan:		Second Exec. Salary: $	Bonus: $

OTHER THOUGHTS:

Apparent Women Officers or Directors:
Hot Spot for Advancement for Women/Minorities:

LOCATIONS: ("Y" = Yes)

West:	Southwest:	Midwest:	Southeast:	Northeast:	International:
					Y

TRICO MARINE SERVICES INC

www.tricomarine.com

Industry Group Code: 213112 **Ranks within this company's industry group:** Sales: 21 Profits: 24

Exploration/Production:		**Refining/Retailing:**		**Utilities:**		**Alternative Energy:**		**Specialty Services:**		**Energy Mktg./Other Svcs.**	
Exploration:		Refining:		Electric Utility:		Waste/Solar/Other:		Consulting/Eng.:		Energy Marketing:	
Production:		Retailing:		Gas Utility:		Thermal/Steam:		Seismic:		Equipment/Machinery:	Y
Coal Production:		Convenience Stores:		Pipelines:		Wind:		Drilling:		Oil Field Services:	Y
		Chemicals:		Water:		Hydro:		InfoTech:		Air/Shipping Transportation:	Y
						Fuel Cells:		Specialty Services:			

TYPES OF BUSINESS:

Oil & Gas Drilling Support Services
Marine Drilling Support Services
Transportation Services

BRANDS/DIVISIONS/AFFILIATES:

DeepOcean ASA
Eastern Marine Services Ltd.
CTC Marine Project Ltd.

CONTACTS:

Note: Officers with more than one job title may be intentionally listed here more than once.

Richard A. Bachmann, Interim CEO
Rishi A. Varma, COO
Rishi A. Varma, Pres.
Geoff A. Jones, CFO/Sr. VP
Ray Hoover, Global Dir.-Tech. Svcs.
Geoff A. Jones, Chief Admin. Officer/Sr. VP
Sue Kean, General Counsel/VP/Sec.
D. Michael Wallace, VP-Bus. Dev.
Jeff Favret, Chief Acct. Officer
Tomas Salazar, VP-Americas & West Africa
Daryl Lynch, Pres., CTC Marine
Mads Bardsen, Pres., DeepOcean
Richard A. Bachmann, Chmn.
Gerald Gray, VP-Int'l Oper. (Trico U.K.)

Phone: 713-780-9926 **Fax:** 713-780-0062
Toll-Free: 800-259-3833
Address: 10001 Woodloch Forest Dr., Ste. 610, The Woodlands, TX 77380 US

GROWTH PLANS/SPECIAL FEATURES:

Trico Marine Services, Inc. provides marine and subsea support vessels to the oil and gas industry. The firm is most active in West Africa, Mexico, the North Sea, Southeast Asia and Brazil. In addition, Trico Marine Services has master service agreements with some major and independent oil companies in the Gulf of Mexico. The firm operates in three divisions: Subsea services; subsea trenching and protection; and towing and supply. The services provided by Trico's subsea services segment, managed by DeepOcean AS, span the entire life-cycle of a well; beginning with the initial survey of the sea floor to construction and installation of subsea infrastructure, and finally to disassembly once the well is depleted. Subsea trenching and protection operations, offered through subsidiary CTC Marine, include solutions for the burial of subsea transmission systems, such as pipelines, flowlines and cables, as well as the installation of subsea infrastructure and subsea flexible products. Towing and supply services provide for the transportation of materials and crew to drilling rigs and offshore facilities, as well as towing support and support for the construction, installation, repair and maintenance of offshore facilities. Trico has a total fleet of 60 vessels, including 26 supply ships; six subsea platform supply vessels; one multi-purpose platform supply vessel; five subsea trenching and protection vessels; five large-capacity platform supply ships; nine multi-purpose service vessels; four crew/line-handling vessels; and four large anchor-handling, towing and supply vessels. The company's vessels are typically contracted on a day-rate basis, even for very long contracts. Trico Marine Services owns 49% interest in Eastern Marine Services Limited, a limited liability company based in Hong Kong that develops and provides marine support services for the oil and gas industry in Asia and Australia.

Trico provides its employees with life, AD&D, cancer, disability, medical, dental and vision insurance; a flexible spending account; and a 401(k) savings plan.

FINANCIALS:

Sales and profits are in thousands of dollars—add 000 to get the full amount. 2010 Note: Financial information for 2010 was not available for all companies at press time.

2010 Sales: $	2010 Profits: $	**U.S. Stock Ticker: TRMA**
2009 Sales: $642,200	2009 Profits: $-145,266	**Int'l Ticker:** Int'l Exchange:
2008 Sales: $556,131	2008 Profits: $-113,655	Employees: 1,780
2007 Sales: $256,108	2007 Profits: $62,931	Fiscal Year Ends: 12/31
2006 Sales: $248,717	2006 Profits: $58,724	Parent Company:

SALARIES/BENEFITS:

Pension Plan:	ESOP Stock Plan:	Profit Sharing:	Top Exec. Salary: $600,000	Bonus: $240,000
Savings Plan: Y	Stock Purch. Plan:		Second Exec. Salary: $325,000	Bonus: $174,625

OTHER THOUGHTS:

Apparent Women Officers or Directors: 1
Hot Spot for Advancement for Women/Minorities:

LOCATIONS: ("Y" = Yes)

West:	Southwest:	Midwest:	Southeast:	Northeast:	International:
	Y				Y

TRUMAN ARNOLD COMPANIES

www.trumanarnoldcompanies.com

Industry Group Code: 486 **Ranks within this company's industry group:** Sales: 15 Profits:

Exploration/Production:		Refining/Retailing:		Utilities:		Alternative Energy:		Specialty Services:		Energy Mktg./Other Svcs.	
Exploration:		Refining:		Electric Utility:		Waste/Solar/Other:		Consulting/Eng.:	Y	Energy Marketing:	Y
Production:		Retailing:		Gas Utility:		Thermal/Steam:		Seismic:		Equipment/Machinery:	
Coal Production:		Convenience Stores:	Y	Pipelines:		Wind:		Drilling:		Oil Field Services:	
		Chemicals:		Water:		Hydro:		InfoTech:		Air/Shipping Transportation:	Y
						Fuel Cells:		Specialty Services:	Y		

TYPES OF BUSINESS:

Petroleum Marketing & Distribution
Trucking
Aviation Facilities
Convenience Stores
Real Estate Services
Construction Services

BRANDS/DIVISIONS/AFFILIATES:

Road Runner
TAC Energy
TAC Air
TAC Terminals

CONTACTS:

Note: Officers with more than one job title may be intentionally listed here more than once.

Gregory A. Arnold, CEO
Gregory A. Arnold, Pres.
John Rettiger, VP-TAC Energy
Christian Sasfai, COO/VP-TAC Air
Daniel Walsh, Dir.-Fixed Base Operations Svcs.
Truman Arnold, Chmn.

Phone: 903-794-3835	**Fax:** 903-831-4056
Toll-Free: 800-235-5343	
Address: 701 S. Robison Rd., Texarkana, TX 75501 US	

GROWTH PLANS/SPECIAL FEATURES:

Truman Arnold Companies (TAC) is an international petroleum marketing and distribution company with an annual volume of more than 1 billion gallons. TAC is organized into three major divisions: TAC Energy, TAC Terminals and TAC Air. TAC Energy handles the bulk of TAC's interests including refined products marketing, transportation and branded dealer sales. It sells over 2 billion gallons per year of wholesale-refined products to government entities, industrial end-users and retailers. TAC Energy provides services including inventory management, custom invoicing, bulk supply, custom reports and complete supply chain management. TAC Terminals has two major storage terminals located in Texas and Arkansas, which together store roughly 1.3 million barrels and offer pipeline and loading services. TAC Air operates 13 locations across the U.S., offering hangers and conference rooms for business customers. These aviation Fixed Base Operation (FBO) facilities also include amenities such as aircraft maintenance, weather information centers, ground transportation and catering. TAC serves customers including government, bus lines, railroads, airlines, truck lines, grocery and service stations in the continental U.S. and in Canada. In addition, TAC operates convenience stores under the Road Runner brand and has interests in real estate, ranching and banking. The company operates a sales office in Mobile, Alabama, responsible for spot and long-term sales activities in all refined product markets in the region. In July 2010, TAC Air opened a new 12,000 square foot executive terminal at its Blue Grass Airport (LEX) location in Lexington, Kentucky.

The firm offers its employees life, AD&D, long-term disability, medical, dental and vision insurance; a retirement plan; paid time off; and flexible spending accounts.

FINANCIALS:

Sales and profits are in thousands of dollars—add 000 to get the full amount. 2010 Note: Financial information for 2010 was not available for all companies at press time.

2010 Sales: $	2010 Profits: $	**U.S. Stock Ticker: Private**
2009 Sales: $2,300,000	2009 Profits: $	**Int'l Ticker:** Int'l Exchange:
2008 Sales: $	2008 Profits: $	Employees: 450
2007 Sales: $	2007 Profits: $	Fiscal Year Ends: 9/30
2006 Sales: $2,130,000	2006 Profits: $	Parent Company:

SALARIES/BENEFITS:

Pension Plan: Y	ESOP Stock Plan:	Profit Sharing:	Top Exec. Salary: $	Bonus: $
Savings Plan:	Stock Purch. Plan:		Second Exec. Salary: $	Bonus: $

OTHER THOUGHTS:

Apparent Women Officers or Directors:
Hot Spot for Advancement for Women/Minorities:

LOCATIONS: ("Y" = Yes)

West:	Southwest:	Midwest:	Southeast:	Northeast:	International:
Y	Y	Y	Y	Y	

TSAKOS ENERGY NAVIGATION LTD

www.tenn.gr

Industry Group Code: 483111 **Ranks within this company's industry group:** Sales: 5 Profits: 5

Exploration/Production:		Refining/Retailing:		Utilities:		Alternative Energy:		Specialty Services:		Energy Mktg./Other Svcs.	
Exploration:		Refining:		Electric Utility:		Waste/Solar/Other:		Consulting/Eng.:		Energy Marketing:	
Production:		Retailing:		Gas Utility:		Thermal/Steam:		Seismic:		Equipment/Machinery:	
Coal Production:		Convenience Stores:		Pipelines:		Wind:		Drilling:		Oil Field Services:	
		Chemicals:		Water:		Hydro:		InfoTech:		Air/Shipping Transportation:	Y
						Fuel Cells:		Specialty Services:			

TYPES OF BUSINESS:

Petroleum Tankers
Maritime Training Centers

BRANDS/DIVISIONS/AFFILIATES:

Tsakos Group
Tsakos Shipping & Trading SA
Tsakos Columbia Shipmanagement SA

CONTACTS:

Note: Officers with more than one job title may be intentionally listed here more than once.

Nikolas P. Tsakos, CEO
George V. Saroglou, COO/VP
Nikolas P. Tsakos, Pres.
Paul Durham, CFO
Michael G. Jolliffe, Deputy Chmn.
Vladimir Jadro, Chief Marine Officer
D. John Stavropoulos, Chmn.

Phone: 30-210-940771013 **Fax:** 30-210-94-07-716

Toll-Free:

Address: 367, Syngrou Ave., 175 64 P. Faliro, Athens, 175 64 P Greece

GROWTH PLANS/SPECIAL FEATURES:

Tsakos Energy Navigation, Ltd. (TEN) is an international energy transporter. The firm ships crude oil/petroleum and liquefied natural gas (LNG) products for oil companies and refiners. Its largest major oil customers include ExxonMobil, FLOPEC, Trafigura, Glencore, Shell, BP, Houston Refining, PDVSA, Sunoco, Tesoro, Petrobras and Neste Oil. The company operates a fleet of 45 ships, including one chartered-in vessel; and has an additional four ships currently under construction. TEN's fleet is relatively young, with an average age of approximately seven years, compared to the world tanker average of nine years; 23 of its ships have ice-class qualifications. The firm is controlled by the Tsakos Group. Its fleet is managed by Group member Tsakos Shipping & Trading S.A., a leading global independent ship management company. Tsakos Shipping's immense size allows TEN to benefit from economies of scale in procuring supplies and underwriting insurance. The company also has access to Tsakos Shipping's network of worldwide offices and its pool of more than 2,500 seafarers. Approximately 24.4% of the company's fleet operate on fixed-rate time charters, with contracts lasts from months to years; approximately 51.2% are on variable rate time charters; 13.3% are on spot voyages, a charter that lasts for a single voyage often with duration of several weeks; and 11.1% are on variable rate period employment, often in a pool or working under contract of affreightment with a specific charterer. In November 2009, TEN sold three of its vessels. In January 2010, the firm sold its Marathon and Parthenon tankers. In February 2010, Tsakos Shipping and Schoeller Holdings Ltd. formed joint venture Tsakos Columbia Shipmanagement SA to offer technical management of Tsakos Shipping's fleet. In July 2010, the company agreed to sell one and acquire four ships; upon completion of these transactions, TEN's fleet will be an average of 6.5 years.

FINANCIALS:

Sales and profits are in thousands of dollars—add 000 to get the full amount. 2010 Note: Financial information for 2010 was not available for all companies at press time.

2010 Sales: $	2010 Profits: $	**U.S. Stock Ticker: TNP**
2009 Sales: $444,926	2009 Profits: $30,175	**Int'l Ticker:** Int'l Exchange:
2008 Sales: $623,040	2008 Profits: $202,931	Employees: 850
2007 Sales: $500,617	2007 Profits: $183,171	Fiscal Year Ends: 12/31
2006 Sales: $427,654	2006 Profits: $196,404	Parent Company:

SALARIES/BENEFITS:

Pension Plan:	ESOP Stock Plan:	Profit Sharing:	Top Exec. Salary: $	Bonus: $
Savings Plan:	Stock Purch. Plan:		Second Exec. Salary: $	Bonus: $

OTHER THOUGHTS:

Apparent Women Officers or Directors:
Hot Spot for Advancement for Women/Minorities:

LOCATIONS: ("Y" = Yes)

West:	Southwest:	Midwest:	Southeast:	Northeast:	International:
	Y			Y	Y

UGI CORP

www.ugicorp.com

Industry Group Code: 454312 **Ranks within this company's industry group:** Sales: 1 Profits: 1

Exploration/Production:		Refining/Retailing:		Utilities:		Alternative Energy:		Specialty Services:		Energy Mktg./Other Svcs.	
Exploration:		Refining:		Electric Utility:	Y	Waste/Solar/Other:		Consulting/Eng.:		Energy Marketing:	Y
Production:		Retailing:		Gas Utility:	Y	Thermal/Steam:		Seismic:		Equipment/Machinery:	
Coal Production:		Convenience Stores:		Pipelines:		Wind:		Drilling:		Oil Field Services:	
		Chemicals:		Water:		Hydro:		InfoTech:		Air/Shipping Transportation:	
						Fuel Cells:		Specialty Services:	Y		

TYPES OF BUSINESS:

Utilities-Electricity & Natural Gas
Propane Distribution
Energy Marketing

BRANDS/DIVISIONS/AFFILIATES:

AmeriGas Partners, L.P.
UGI Utilities, Inc.
AmeriGas Propane, Inc.
GASMARK
POWERMARK
Antargaz
FLAGA GmbH
UGI Central Penn Gas, Inc.

CONTACTS: *Note: Officers with more than one job title may be intentionally listed here more than once.*

Lon R. Greenberg, CEO
John L. Walsh, COO
John L. Walsh, Pres.
Peter Kelly, CFO
Robert H. Knauss, General Counsel/VP
Bradley C. Hall, VP-New Bus. Dev.
Peter Kelly, VP-Finance
Eugene Bissell, Pres./CEO-AmeriGas Propane, Inc.
Davinder Athwal, Chief Risk Officer/Chief Acct. Officer
Francois Varagne, Chmn./CEO-Antargaz
Margaret M. Calabrese, Corp. Sec.
Lon R. Greenberg, Chmn.

Phone: 610-337-1000	**Fax:** 610-992-3259
Toll-Free:	
Address: 460 N. Gulph Rd., King of Prussia, PA 19406 US	

GROWTH PLANS/SPECIAL FEATURES:

UGI Corp. is a holding company that distributes and markets energy products and related services through subsidiaries and venture affiliates. The firm offers propane and butane retail distribution domestically and internationally; provides natural gas and electric service through regulated local distribution utilities; generates electricity; markets energy commodities regionally; and provides heating and cooling services. The company operates in five segments: AmeriGas propane, international propane, gas utility, electric utility and energy services. The AmeriGas propane segment consists of the propane distribution business of AmeriGas Partners, L.P. whose sole general partner is subsidiary AmeriGas Propane, Inc. The international propane segment consists of the liquefied petroleum gases distribution businesses of wholly-owned subsidiaries Antargaz, a French corporation, and FLAGA GmbH, an Austrian company; and of the firm's joint venture in China. The gas utility segment consists of the regulated natural gas distribution businesses of subsidiary UGI Utilities, Inc. and its subsidiary UGI Penn Natural Gas, Inc. Gas Utility serves roughly 563,000 customers in eastern and northeastern Pennsylvania. The electric utility segment consists of the regulated electric distribution business of UGI Utilities, serving approximately 62,000 customers in northeastern Pennsylvania. The energy services segment consists of energy-related businesses conducted by a number of subsidiaries. These businesses market energy in the eastern region of the U.S. under the trade names GASMARK and POWERMARK; operate or own interests in electric generation assets in Pennsylvania; operate liquefied natural gas and propane storage and peak-shaving facilities in eastern Pennsylvania; and operate a propane import and storage facility in Virginia. UGI also owns and operates heating, ventilation, air conditioning, refrigeration and electrical contracting service businesses serving customers in the Mid-Atlantic region. In August 2010, the firm agreed to acquire BP's Denmark-based liquefied petroleum gas distribution business. In September 2010, FLAGA GmbH acquired Shell Gas Hungary Zrt.'s liquefied petroleum gas distribution business.

FINANCIALS: **Sales and profits are in thousands of dollars—add 000 to get the full amount. 2010 Note: Financial information for 2010 was not available for all companies at press time.**

2010 Sales: $	2010 Profits: $	**U.S. Stock Ticker: UGI**
2009 Sales: $5,737,800	2009 Profits: $258,500	**Int'l Ticker:** Int'l Exchange:
2008 Sales: $6,648,200	2008 Profits: $215,500	Employees: 5,950
2007 Sales: $5,476,900	2007 Profits: $204,300	Fiscal Year Ends: 9/30
2006 Sales: $5,221,000	2006 Profits: $176,200	Parent Company:

SALARIES/BENEFITS:

Pension Plan:	ESOP Stock Plan:	Profit Sharing:	Top Exec. Salary: $1,067,975	Bonus: $1,591,643
Savings Plan:	Stock Purch. Plan:		Second Exec. Salary: $648,202	Bonus: $821,800

OTHER THOUGHTS:

Apparent Women Officers or Directors:
Hot Spot for Advancement for Women/Minorities:

LOCATIONS: ("Y" = Yes)

West:	Southwest:	Midwest:	Southeast:	Northeast:	International:
Y	Y	Y	Y	Y	Y

UIL HOLDINGS CORPORATION

www.uil.com

Industry Group Code: 2211 **Ranks within this company's industry group:** Sales: 45 Profits: 43

Exploration/Production:		Refining/Retailing:		Utilities:		Alternative Energy:		Specialty Services:		Energy Mktg./Other Svcs.	
Exploration:		Refining:		Electric Utility:	Y	Waste/Solar/Other:		Consulting/Eng.:	Y	Energy Marketing:	
Production:		Retailing:		Gas Utility:		Thermal/Steam:		Seismic:		Equipment/Machinery:	
Coal Production:		Convenience Stores:		Pipelines:		Wind:		Drilling:		Oil Field Services:	
		Chemicals:		Water:		Hydro:		InfoTech:	Y	Air/Shipping Transportation:	
						Fuel Cells:		Specialty Services:	Y		

TYPES OF BUSINESS:

Utilities-Electricity
Electricity Generation & Distribution
Electrical Systems Design

BRANDS/DIVISIONS/AFFILIATES:

United Illuminating Co (The)
Xcel Services Inc
United Capital Investments Inc
Ironbridge Mezzanine Fund
GenConn Energy LLC

CONTACTS: *Note: Officers with more than one job title may be intentionally listed here more than once.*

James P. Torgerson, CEO
James P. Torgerson, Pres.
Richard J. Nicholas, CFO/Exec. VP
Linda Randell, General Counsel/Sr. VP/Corp. Sec.
Al Carbone, Contact-Media
Susan E. Allen, VP-Investor Rel.
Susan E. Allen, Treas.
Steven P. Favuzza, Controller/VP
Deborah C. Hoffman, VP-Audit Svcs./Chief Compliance Officer
Betsy Henley-Cohn, Chmn.

Phone: 203-499-2000	**Fax:** 203-4993626
Toll-Free:	
Address: 157 Church St., New Haven, CT 06506 US	

GROWTH PLANS/SPECIAL FEATURES:

UIL Holdings Corporation is a holding company that primarily operates in the regulated utility business. The utility business consists of the electric transmission and distribution operations of The United Illuminating Company (UI). UI is a regional distribution utility that provides electricity to a 335-square-mile area in the greater New Haven and Bridgeport areas of Connecticut. It purchases, transmits, distributes and sells electricity for residential, commercial and industrial purposes. UI has approximately 325,000 customers, representing nearly half of the residents in its service area. Approximately 60% of UI's retail electric revenues are derived from residential sales; 34% from commercial sales; 5% from industrial sales; and 1% from street lighting and other sales. UI also maintains a 50-50 joint venture with NRG Energy, Inc. called GenConn Energy, LLC, which was created to build power plants in Connecticut. UIL Holdings also has non-utility businesses consisting of an operating lease and passive minority ownership interests in two investment funds, collectively held at United Capital Investments, Inc. (UCI), a heating and cooling facility and a mechanical contracting business. UCI invests in projects that earn above-average returns and form logical extensions to its current energy and subsidiary businesses. Investments include Ironwood Mezzanine Fund, a small business investment fund that partially invests in minority-owned and women-owned businesses, as well as in companies located in low to moderate income areas. In December 2009, UIL Holdings divested the operations of mechanical contracting subsidiary Xcel Services, Inc. In May 2010, the firm agreed to acquire The Southern Connecticut Gas Company, The Berkshire Gas Company and Connecticut Natural Gas Corporation from Iberdrola USA, Inc. for roughly $1.3 billion.

FINANCIALS: **Sales and profits are in thousands of dollars—add 000 to get the full amount. 2010 Note: Financial information for 2010 was not available for all companies at press time.**

2010 Sales: $	2010 Profits: $	**U.S. Stock Ticker: UIL**
2009 Sales: $896,550	2009 Profits: $54,317	**Int'l Ticker:** Int'l Exchange:
2008 Sales: $948,720	2008 Profits: $48,148	Employees: 1,066
2007 Sales: $981,999	2007 Profits: $44,697	Fiscal Year Ends: 12/31
2006 Sales: $845,950	2006 Profits: $-65,164	Parent Company:

SALARIES/BENEFITS:

Pension Plan:	ESOP Stock Plan:	Profit Sharing:	Top Exec. Salary: $625,000	Bonus: $485,625
Savings Plan:	Stock Purch. Plan:		Second Exec. Salary: $390,000	Bonus: $259,740

OTHER THOUGHTS:

Apparent Women Officers or Directors: 5
Hot Spot for Advancement for Women/Minorities: Y

LOCATIONS: ("Y" = Yes)

West:	Southwest:	Midwest:	Southeast:	Northeast:	International:
				Y	

UK COAL PLC

www.ukcoal.com

Industry Group Code: 21211 **Ranks within this company's industry group:** Sales: 13 Profits: 12

Exploration/Production:		**Refining/Retailing:**		**Utilities:**		**Alternative Energy:**		**Specialty Services:**		**Energy Mktg./Other Svcs.**	
Exploration:		Refining:		Electric Utility:		Waste/Solar/Other:	Y	Consulting/Eng.:		Energy Marketing:	
Production:		Retailing:		Gas Utility:		Thermal/Steam:		Seismic:		Equipment/Machinery:	
Coal Production:	Y	Convenience Stores:		Pipelines:		Wind:	Y	Drilling:		Oil Field Services:	
		Chemicals:		Water:		Hydro:		InfoTech:		Air/Shipping Transportation:	
						Fuel Cells:		Specialty Services:			

TYPES OF BUSINESS:

Coal Production
Property Development
Power Generation-Waste Gas
Wind Generation

BRANDS/DIVISIONS/AFFILIATES:

Harworth Estates
Peel Energy

CONTACTS:

Note: Officers with more than one job title may be intentionally listed here more than once.

Jon Lloyd, CEO
David Brocksom, Group Dir.-Finance
Richard Cole, Sec.
Gareth Williams, Managing Dir.-Mining Div.
Owen Michaelson, Managing Dir.-Property Div.
David Jones, Chmn.

Phone: 44-1302-751751 **Fax:** 44-1302-752420
Toll-Free:
Address: Harworth Park, Blyth Rd., Harworth, Doncaster, South Yorkshire DN11 8DB UK

GROWTH PLANS/SPECIAL FEATURES:

UK Coal PLC is one of Britain's largest producers of coal, with land and property interests throughout the U.K. It is the supplier of approximately 15% of all the coal burned within the U.K. The firm divides its operations into two divisions: Mining and property. UK Coal's mining division oversees the operation of three deep mines in central and northern England with reserves that total over 98 million tons and four surface mines with reserves topping 50 million tons. More than 80% of the firm's coal production is generated at its producing deep mines operations at Daw Mill, Kellingley, Thoresby and Welbeck (which ceased production in 2010). Over 85% of the coal mined by the firm is sold to the country's power generators. The remaining portion is sold to customers in the industrial sector for household and other uses. UK Coal generates electricity from the methane it extracts from operating mines in an effort to utilize it as a fuel source and to minimize the environmental impact of its mining activities. The company generates over 165 megawatts per hour using extracted methane, which provides 60% of its deep mining electrical needs. The company's property division, operating as Harworth Estates, manages a land holdings portfolio of approximately 43,500 acres, with plans to develop about 4,000 acres into residential and business sites over the next decade. Harworth Estates also has a collaboration agreement with Peel Energy to develop wind power opportunities.

FINANCIALS:

Sales and profits are in thousands of dollars—add 000 to get the full amount. 2010 Note: Financial information for 2010 was not available for all companies at press time.

2010 Sales: $	2010 Profits: $	**U.S. Stock Ticker: UKCLF**
2009 Sales: $511,250	2009 Profits: $-206,280	**Int'l Ticker: UKC** Int'l Exchange: London-LSE
2008 Sales: $642,260	2008 Profits: $-25,690	Employees: 3,152
2007 Sales: $537,540	2007 Profits: $153,820	Fiscal Year Ends: 12/31
2006 Sales: $676,000	2006 Profits: $34,800	Parent Company:

SALARIES/BENEFITS:

Pension Plan: Y	ESOP Stock Plan:	Profit Sharing:	Top Exec. Salary: $591,562	Bonus: $56,790
Savings Plan:	Stock Purch. Plan:		Second Exec. Salary: $370,199	Bonus: $33,316

OTHER THOUGHTS:

Apparent Women Officers or Directors:
Hot Spot for Advancement for Women/Minorities:

LOCATIONS: ("Y" = Yes)

West:	Southwest:	Midwest:	Southeast:	Northeast:	International:
					Y

ULTRA PETROLEUM CORP

www.ultrapetroleum.com

Industry Group Code: 211111 **Ranks within this company's industry group:** Sales: 88 Profits: 102

Exploration/Production:		Refining/Retailing:		Utilities:		Alternative Energy:		Specialty Services:		Energy Mktg./Other Svcs.	
Exploration:	Y	Refining:		Electric Utility:		Waste/Solar/Other:		Consulting/Eng.:		Energy Marketing:	
Production:	Y	Retailing:		Gas Utility:		Thermal/Steam:		Seismic:		Equipment/Machinery:	
Coal Production:		Convenience Stores:		Pipelines:		Wind:		Drilling:		Oil Field Services:	
		Chemicals:		Water:		Hydro:		InfoTech:		Air/Shipping Transportation:	
						Fuel Cells:		Specialty Services:			

TYPES OF BUSINESS:

Oil & Gas Exploration & Production

BRANDS/DIVISIONS/AFFILIATES:

GROWTH PLANS/SPECIAL FEATURES:

Ultra Petroleum Corp. is an independent oil and gas company. The firm is engaged in the development, production, operation, exploration and acquisition of oil and natural gas properties. The company's properties are primarily in the Green River Basin of southwest Wyoming. Ultra Petroleum Corp. has interests in over 56,000 net (112,000 gross) acres in Wyoming, covering roughly 190 square miles. The firm is in the process of drilling more wells in the upper Cretaceous Lance Pool in the Pinedale and Jonah fields. Ultra Petroleum Corp. plans to drill delineation, step-out and exploration wells on its Green River Basin acreage positions in an ongoing attempt to further define and expand the current known producing limits of the two fields' areas. The firm owns working interests in roughly 600 net (1,270 gross) producing wells and operates about 50% of them. The company also owns interests in approximately 225,000 net acres in Pennsylvania. Ultra Petroleum Corp. sells all of its natural gas production to a diverse group of third-party, non-affiliated entities in a portfolio of transactions of various durations. The majority of the firm's customers are located in the western, eastern and Midwestern U.S. Ultra Petroleum Corp. has offices in Texas, Colorado, Pennsylvania and Wyoming.

The firm offers employees benefits including life, medical, dental, vision, AD&D and long-term disability insurance; a 401(k); flexible spending accounts; paid vacation; and an employee assistance program.

CONTACTS: *Note: Officers with more than one job title may be intentionally listed here more than once.*

Michael D. Watford, CEO
Michael D. Watford, Pres.
Marshall D. Smith, CFO
Stuart E. Nance, VP-Mktg.
William R. Picquet, VP-Oper.
Kelly Whitley, Mgr.-Investor Rel.
Garland R. Shaw, Controller/Chief Acct. Officer
Michael D. Watford, Chmn.

Phone: 281-876-0120 **Fax:** 281-876-2831
Toll-Free:
Address: 363 N. Sam Houston Pkwy. E., Ste. 1200, Houston, TX 77060 US

FINANCIALS: **Sales and profits are in thousands of dollars—add 000 to get the full amount. 2010 Note: Financial information for 2010 was not available for all companies at press time.**

2010 Sales: $	2010 Profits: $	**U.S. Stock Ticker: UPL**
2009 Sales: $666,762	2009 Profits: $-451,053	**Int'l Ticker:** Int'l Exchange:
2008 Sales: $1,084,400	2008 Profits: $414,275	Employees: 94
2007 Sales: $567,725	2007 Profits: $263,036	Fiscal Year Ends: 12/31
2006 Sales: $510,600	2006 Profits: $231,195	Parent Company:

SALARIES/BENEFITS:

Pension Plan:	ESOP Stock Plan:	Profit Sharing:	Top Exec. Salary: $725,000	Bonus: $2,000,000
Savings Plan: Y	Stock Purch. Plan:		Second Exec. Salary: $300,000	Bonus: $600,000

OTHER THOUGHTS:

Apparent Women Officers or Directors:
Hot Spot for Advancement for Women/Minorities:

LOCATIONS: ("Y" = Yes)

West:	Southwest:	Midwest:	Southeast:	Northeast:	International:
Y	Y			Y	

ULTRAPAR PARTICIPACOES SA

www.ultra.com.br

Industry Group Code: 486 **Ranks within this company's industry group:** Sales: 4 Profits: 10

Exploration/Production:		Refining/Retailing:		Utilities:		Alternative Energy:		Specialty Services:		Energy Mktg./Other Svcs.	
Exploration:		Refining:		Electric Utility:		Waste/Solar/Other:		Consulting/Eng.:		Energy Marketing:	
Production:	Y	Retailing:	Y	Gas Utility:	Y	Thermal/Steam:		Seismic:		Equipment/Machinery:	
Coal Production:		Convenience Stores:	Y	Pipelines:		Wind:		Drilling:		Oil Field Services:	
		Chemicals:	Y	Water:		Hydro:		InfoTech:		Air/Shipping Transportation:	Y
						Fuel Cells:		Specialty Services:	Y		

TYPES OF BUSINESS:

Liquefied Petroleum Gas Production & Distribution
Petrochemical Production
Ethylene Oxide Production
Transportation & Logistics Services
Fuel Service Stations
Convenience Stores

BRANDS/DIVISIONS/AFFILIATES:

Ultragaz
Oxiteno
Ultracargo
Ipiranga
am/pm
Jet Oil

CONTACTS: *Note: Officers with more than one job title may be intentionally listed here more than once.*

Pedro Wongtschowski, CEO
Andre Covre, CFO
Andre Covre, Investor Rel. Officer
Ricardo Isaac Catran, CEO-Ultracargo
Joao Benjamin Parolin, CEO-Oxiteno
Pedro J. Filho, CEOO-Ultragaz
Leocadio de Almeida Antunes Filho, CEO-Ipiranga
Paulo G. A. Cunha, Chmn.

Phone: 55-11-3177-6695 **Fax:** 55-11-3177-6107
Toll-Free:
Address: 1343 Ave. Brigaderio Luiz Antonio, Sao Paulo, 01350-900 Brazil

GROWTH PLANS/SPECIAL FEATURES:

Ultrapar Participacoes S.A., based in Brazil, is a holding company that produces, sells, distributes and transports liquefied petroleum gas (LPG) and other chemical compounds through its subsidiaries: Ipiranga, Ultragaz, Oxiteno and Ultracargo. Through Ipiranga, the firm operates fuel service stations, totaling some 5,500 outlets throughout the country. Ipiranga is one of the largest fuel distributors in Brazil, with a total market share just over 20%. Fuels distributed at its retail locations include diesel, gasoline, ethanol, natural gas for vehicles (NGV), fuel oil and kerosene, as well as vehicle lubricants. Also included in Ipiranga's operations is the network of nearly 1,500 franchise am/pm convenience stores and Jet Oil lube shops. Ultragaz is a leader in LPG distribution in Brazil, with an approximate 24% market share. It delivers LPG to an estimated 10 million households and approximately 4,500 independent retailers using the firm's vehicle fleet. Oxiteno produces chemical compounds and is the largest manufacturer of ethylene oxide and its derivatives in Brazil, Argentina, Paraguay or Uruguay. The subsidiary supplies petrochemicals to more than 30 market segments, primarily agricultural chemicals, food, cosmetics, leather, detergents, packaging for beverages, thread and polyester filaments, brake fluids, petroleum, paints and varnishes. Ultracargo offers integrated multimodal transportation of chemicals and fuels, loading and unloading services and the management of third-party fleets. It is also the leading logistics operator in the chemical and fuel products segments in Brazil. In March 2010, the firm entered into a sale and purchase agreement with Aqces Logística Internacional Ltda. to sell its in-house logistics, solid bulk storage and road transportation businesses, which will allow Ultracargo to focus entirely on its liquid bulk storage business.

FINANCIALS: Sales and profits are in thousands of dollars—add 000 to get the full amount. 2010 Note: Financial information for 2010 was not available for all companies at press time.

2010 Sales: $	2010 Profits: $	**U.S. Stock Ticker: UGP**
2009 Sales: $19,379,000	2009 Profits: $250,420	**Int'l Ticker: UGPA3** Int'l Exchange: Sao Paulo-SAO
2008 Sales: $16,308,020	2008 Profits: $225,170	Employees: 9,400
2007 Sales: $11,952,800	2007 Profits: $109,100	Fiscal Year Ends: 12/31
2006 Sales: $2,876,400	2006 Profits: $169,200	Parent Company:

SALARIES/BENEFITS:

Pension Plan:	ESOP Stock Plan:	Profit Sharing:	Top Exec. Salary: $	Bonus: $
Savings Plan:	Stock Purch. Plan:		Second Exec. Salary: $	Bonus: $

OTHER THOUGHTS:

Apparent Women Officers or Directors: 1
Hot Spot for Advancement for Women/Minorities:

LOCATIONS: ("Y" = Yes)

West:	Southwest:	Midwest:	Southeast:	Northeast:	International:
					Y

UNISOURCE ENERGY CORPORATION

www.uns.com

Industry Group Code: 221 **Ranks within this company's industry group:** Sales: 50 Profits: 44

Exploration/Production:		**Refining/Retailing:**		**Utilities:**		**Alternative Energy:**		**Specialty Services:**		**Energy Mktg./Other Svcs.**	
Exploration:		Refining:		Electric Utility:	Y	Waste/Solar/Other:		Consulting/Eng.:		Energy Marketing:	
Production:		Retailing:		Gas Utility:	Y	Thermal/Steam:		Seismic:		Equipment/Machinery:	
Coal Production:		Convenience Stores:		Pipelines:		Wind:		Drilling:		Oil Field Services:	
		Chemicals:		Water:		Hydro:		InfoTech:		Air/Shipping Transportation:	
						Fuel Cells:		Specialty Services:	Y		

TYPES OF BUSINESS:

Utilities-Electricity & Natural Gas
Investments

BRANDS/DIVISIONS/AFFILIATES:

Tucson Electric Power Co
UniSource Energy Services Inc
Millennium Energy Holdings Inc
UniSource Energy Development Co
Southwest Energy Solutions Inc
UNS Electric
UNS Gas

CONTACTS:

Note: Officers with more than one job title may be intentionally listed here more than once.

Paul J. Bonavia, CEO
Michael J. DeConcini, COO/Sr. VP
Paul J. Bonavia, Pres.
Kevin P. Larson, CFO/Sr. VP/Treas.
Lou Boltik, Dir.-Mktg. Comm.
Catherine E. Ries, VP-Human Resources
Thomas A. McKenna, VP-Eng.
Raymond S. Heyman, General Counsel/Sr. VP
Joe Salkowski,, Dir.-Corp. Comm.
Jo Smith, Dir.-Investor Rel.
Kentton C. Grant, VP-Finance & Rates
Philip J. Dion, VP-Public Policy
David G. Hutchens, VP-Energy Efficiency & Resource Planning
Herlinda H. Kennedy, Corp. Sec.
Karen G. Kissinger, Controller/VP/Chief Compliance Officer
Paul J. Bonavia, Chmn.

Phone: 520-571-4000	**Fax:** 520-884-3602
Toll-Free:	
Address: 1 S. Church Ave., Ste. 100, Tucson, AZ 85702 US	

GROWTH PLANS/SPECIAL FEATURES:

UniSource Energy Corporation is a diverse energy company. It is the holding company for UniSource Energy Services, Inc. (UES) and Tucson Electric Power Co. (TEP). The firm conducts its business in three primary business segments: TEP, UNS Gas and UNS Electric. TEP, which generates roughly 79% of the firm's revenue, is an electric utility that provides electric service to approximately 402,000 customers in the Tucson, Arizona, metropolitan area. Its principal fuel for electric generation is low-sulfur, bituminous or sub-bituminous coal from mines in Arizona, New Mexico and Colorado. The majority of the coal supplies are purchased under long-term contracts. TEP also holds a franchise to provide electric distribution service to customers in the city of Tucson and south Tucson. UES, through its subsidiaries UNS Gas, Inc. and UNS Electric, Inc., provides gas and electric service to 30 communities in Northern and Southern Arizona. UNS Gas has approximately 145,000 retail customers and UNS Electric has approximately 91,000 retail customers. UES subsidiary Millennium Energy Holdings, Inc. invests in unregulated businesses and emerging technology companies. Another UES subsidiary, UniSource Energy Development Co., develops generating resources and other project development activities, including the expansion of the Springerville Generating Station. Southwest Energy Solutions, Inc., a wholly-owned subsidiary of Millennium, provides UNS Electric and TEP with services such as line locating, facilities maintenance, meter reading, transmitting, distributing, dusk to dawn lighting and general supplemental support. In September 2009, TEP announced plans to open a new 25 megawatt (MW) photovoltaic array and a 5 MW concentrating solar power plant in Tucson by early 2012.

FINANCIALS:

Sales and profits are in thousands of dollars—add 000 to get the full amount. 2010 Note: Financial information for 2010 was not available for all companies at press time.

2010 Sales: $	2010 Profits: $	**U.S. Stock Ticker: UNS**
2009 Sales: $1,394,424	2009 Profits: $104,258	**Int'l Ticker:** Int'l Exchange:
2008 Sales: $1,397,511	2008 Profits: $14,021	Employees: 1,358
2007 Sales: $1,381,373	2007 Profits: $58,373	Fiscal Year Ends: 12/31
2006 Sales: $1,308,141	2006 Profits: $67,447	Parent Company:

SALARIES/BENEFITS:

Pension Plan:	ESOP Stock Plan:	Profit Sharing:	Top Exec. Salary: $593,327	Bonus: $599,800
Savings Plan:	Stock Purch. Plan:		Second Exec. Salary: $348,448	Bonus: $204,300

OTHER THOUGHTS:

Apparent Women Officers or Directors: 5
Hot Spot for Advancement for Women/Minorities: Y

LOCATIONS: ("Y" = Yes)

West:	Southwest:	Midwest:	Southeast:	Northeast:	International:
	Y				

UNISTAR NUCLEAR ENERGY LLC

www.unistarnuclear.com

Industry Group Code: 221113 **Ranks within this company's industry group:** Sales: Profits:

Exploration/Production:		Refining/Retailing:		Utilities:		Alternative Energy:		Specialty Services:		Energy Mktg./Other Svcs.	
Exploration:		Refining:		Electric Utility:		Waste/Solar/Other:		Consulting/Eng.:	Y	Energy Marketing:	
Production:		Retailing:		Gas Utility:		Thermal/Steam:		Seismic:		Equipment/Machinery:	
Coal Production:		Convenience Stores:		Pipelines:		Wind:		Drilling:		Oil Field Services:	
		Chemicals:		Water:		Hydro:		InfoTech:		Air/Shipping Transportation:	
						Fuel Cells:		Specialty Services:			

TYPES OF BUSINESS:

Nuclear Power Projects
Evolutionary Power Reactor (EPR) Support

BRANDS/DIVISIONS/AFFILIATES:

EDF Group
Constellation Energy Group
ELECTRICITE DE FRANCE SA (EDF)

CONTACTS: *Note: Officers with more than one job title may be intentionally listed here more than once.*

George Vanderheyden, CEO
George Vanderheyden, Pres.
Patrick Blandin, CFO
Debbie Hendell, Chief Counsel
Michael McGough, Sr. VP-Commercial Oper.
Joe Turnage, Sr. VP-Strategy
Patrick Blandin, Treas.
Jean-Pierre West, Exec. VP
Chris Colbert, Sr. VP-UNE Services Co. & Project Holdings

Phone: 410-470-4400	**Fax:** 410-470-5607
Toll-Free:	
Address: 750 E. Pratt Street, Baltimore, MD 21202 US	

GROWTH PLANS/SPECIAL FEATURES:

UniStar Nuclear Energy LLC, a joint venture between Constellation Energy Group and the EDF Group, is engaged in the development, construction and eventual operation of nuclear power plants in the U.S. The company's prime technology is AREVA SA's Evolutionary Power Reactor (EPR), a 1.6 gigawatt pressurized water reactor. The company has four planned projects currently under review by the U.S. Nuclear Regulatory Commission (NRC) and other government agencies: Calvert Cliffs Unit 3 in Maryland; Callaway Unit 2 in Missouri; Bell Bend Unit 1 in Pennsylvania; and Nine Mile Point Unit 3 in New York. The Calvert Cliffs project is a project planned in Calvert County near Lusby, Maryland. The company has received approval from the Maryland Public Service Commission (PSC) for its application for a Certificate of Public Convenience and Necessity (CPCN). If built, the new reactor would supply 1,600 megawatts (MW) of electricity upon completion. The planned projects have yet to receive all of the required application approvals from the various government agencies, including the U.S. Nuclear Regulatory Commission (NRC) and the Department of Energy, requisite to begin construction. Constellation announced in the fall of 2010 that it is pulling out of a federal loan guarantee program for the partnership's first project, stating that fees charged by the government were far too high. EDF hopes to acquire Constellation's interest in Unistar and move ahead with the project, which would be located in Maryland.

FINANCIALS: **Sales and profits are in thousands of dollars—add 000 to get the full amount. 2010 Note: Financial information for 2010 was not available for all companies at press time.**

2010 Sales: $	2010 Profits: $	**U.S. Stock Ticker: Joint Venture**
2009 Sales: $	2009 Profits: $	**Int'l Ticker:** Int'l Exchange:
2008 Sales: $	2008 Profits: $	Employees:
2007 Sales: $	2007 Profits: $	Fiscal Year Ends:
2006 Sales: $	2006 Profits: $	Parent Company: ELECTRICITE DE FRANCE SA (EDF)

SALARIES/BENEFITS:

Pension Plan:	ESOP Stock Plan:	Profit Sharing:	Top Exec. Salary: $	Bonus: $
Savings Plan:	Stock Purch. Plan:		Second Exec. Salary: $	Bonus: $

OTHER THOUGHTS:

Apparent Women Officers or Directors: 1
Hot Spot for Advancement for Women/Minorities:

LOCATIONS: ("Y" = Yes)

West:	Southwest:	Midwest:	Southeast:	Northeast:	International:
				Y	

UNIT CORP

www.unitcorp.com

Industry Group Code: 213111 **Ranks within this company's industry group:** Sales: 15 Profits: 14

Exploration/Production:		Refining/Retailing:		Utilities:		Alternative Energy:		Specialty Services:		Energy Mktg./Other Svcs.	
Exploration:	Y	Refining:		Electric Utility:		Waste/Solar/Other:		Consulting/Eng.:		Energy Marketing:	
Production:	Y	Retailing:		Gas Utility:		Thermal/Steam:		Seismic:		Equipment/Machinery:	
Coal Production:		Convenience Stores:		Pipelines:		Wind:		Drilling:	Y	Oil Field Services:	
		Chemicals:		Water:		Hydro:		InfoTech:		Air/Shipping Transportation:	
						Fuel Cells:		Specialty Services:	Y		

TYPES OF BUSINESS:

Oil & Gas Exploration & Production
Contract Drilling Services
Natural Gas Wholesales

BRANDS/DIVISIONS/AFFILIATES:

Unit Petroleum Co
Unit Drilling Co
Unit Texas Drilling LLC
Superior Pipeline Company LLC

CONTACTS: *Note: Officers with more than one job title may be intentionally listed here more than once.*

Larry D. Pinkston, CEO
Larry D. Pinkston, Pres.
David T. Merrill, CFO
Brad Guidry, Sr. VP-Exploration, Unit Petroleum Co.
Mark E. Schell, General Counsel/Sr. VP/Corp. Sec.
John Cromling, Sr. VP-Drilling Oper.
David T. Merrill, Treas.
Richard E. Heck, VP-Safety, Health & Environment
Mark Colclasure, Sr. VP-Oper., Unit Petroleum Co.
Mike Fankhouser, VP-Land & Prod. Admin., Unit Petroleum Co.
John G. Nikkel, Chmn.

Phone: 918-493-7700 **Fax:** 918-493-7711
Toll-Free:
Address: 7130 S. Lewis Ave., Ste. 1000, Tulsa, OK 74136 US

GROWTH PLANS/SPECIAL FEATURES:

Unit Corp. is a diversified energy company. The firm contracts to drill onshore oil and natural gas wells; explores, develops, acquires and produces oil and natural gas properties; and buys, sells, processes and treats natural gas. The company's contract drilling business is conducted through subsidiary Unit Drilling Co. and its subsidiary Unit Texas Drilling, L.L.C. Through these companies, Unit Corp. drills onshore natural gas and oil wells for its own account as well as for other oil and gas companies. Its operations are mainly located in the Texas and Louisiana Gulf Coast; East Texas; the Oklahoma and Texas areas of the Anadarko and Arkoma Basins; the North Texas Barnett Shale; and the Rocky Mountain regions of Wyoming, Colorado, Utah and Montana. Subsidiary Unit Petroleum Company conducts the exploration and production activities. Its producing oil and natural gas properties, undeveloped leaseholds and related assets are located mainly in Oklahoma, Texas, Louisiana and New Mexico. It also operates in 11 other states and a small portion in Canada. Through this subsidiary, Unit Corp. owns over 576.9 billion cubic feet of oil equivalent of reserves. The company owns about 121 drilling rigs, three natural gas treatment plants, eight operating processing plants and 33 active natural gas gathering systems. It also has interests in roughly 7,851 wells. Its rig fleet is leveraged towards natural gas drilling, with one of the largest percentage of deep rated premium rigs in the industry. Unit Corp.'s rigs have maximum drilling capacities from 5,000 to 40,000 feet. Another subsidiary, Superior Pipeline, L.L.C., buys, sells, gathers, processes and treats natural gas for the company's own account, as well as for third parties. In 2010, the firm sold eight drilling rigs. In June 2010, Unit Petroleum Company acquired 45,000 acres and 11 producing oil wells in Oklahoma for $75 million.

FINANCIALS: **Sales and profits are in thousands of dollars—add 000 to get the full amount. 2010 Note: Financial information for 2010 was not available for all companies at press time.**

2010 Sales: $
2009 Sales: $709,898
2008 Sales: $1,358,093
2007 Sales: $1,158,754
2006 Sales: $1,162,385

2010 Profits: $
2009 Profits: $-55,500
2008 Profits: $143,625
2007 Profits: $266,258
2006 Profits: $312,177

U.S. Stock Ticker: UNT
Int'l Ticker: Int'l Exchange:
Employees: 1,094
Fiscal Year Ends: 12/31
Parent Company:

SALARIES/BENEFITS:

Pension Plan:
Savings Plan: Y
ESOP Stock Plan:
Stock Purch. Plan:
Profit Sharing:
Top Exec. Salary: $600,000 Bonus: $450,000
Second Exec. Salary: $300,000 Bonus: $150,000

OTHER THOUGHTS:

Apparent Women Officers or Directors:
Hot Spot for Advancement for Women/Minorities:

LOCATIONS: ("Y" = Yes)

West:	Southwest:	Midwest:	Southeast:	Northeast:	International:
Y	Y		Y		

UNITED REFINING COMPANY

www.urc.com

Industry Group Code: 324110 **Ranks within this company's industry group:** Sales: Profits:

Exploration/Production:		Refining/Retailing:		Utilities:		Alternative Energy:		Specialty Services:		Energy Mktg./Other Svcs.	
Exploration:		Refining:	Y	Electric Utility:		Waste/Solar/Other:		Consulting/Eng.:		Energy Marketing:	
Production:		Retailing:	Y	Gas Utility:		Thermal/Steam:		Seismic:		Equipment/Machinery:	
Coal Production:		Convenience Stores:	Y	Pipelines:	Y	Wind:		Drilling:		Oil Field Services:	
		Chemicals:		Water:		Hydro:		InfoTech:		Air/Shipping Transportation:	Y
						Fuel Cells:		Specialty Services:			

TYPES OF BUSINESS:

Oil Refining
Convenience Stores
Service Stations
Pipelines
Trucking

BRANDS/DIVISIONS/AFFILIATES:

Kwik Fill
Keystone
Citgo
Country Fair
Red Apple Food Mart
Country Fair
Kiantone Pipeline

CONTACTS: *Note: Officers with more than one job title may be intentionally listed here more than once.*

John A. Catsimatidis, CEO
Myron L. Turfitt, COO
Myron L. Turfitt, Pres.
James E. Murphy, CFO/VP
Ashton L. Ditka, Sr. VP-Mktg.
Thomas E. Skarada, VP-Refining
John A. Catsimatidis, Chmn.

Phone: 814-723-1500	**Fax:** 814-726-4709
Toll-Free:	
Address: 15 Bradley St., Warren, PA 16365 US	

GROWTH PLANS/SPECIAL FEATURES:

United Refining Company, a subsidiary of Red Apple Group, is a leading integrated a petroleum refiner and marketer, with operations centered in Pennsylvania and parts of New York and Ohio. United Refining owns and operates a 70,000 barrel-per-day petroleum refinery in Warren, Pennsylvania, where it produces various grades of gasoline, ultra low sulfur diesel fuel, kerosene, No. 2 heating oil (a low-viscosity product often used in boilers and furnaces) and asphalt. The company's operations are organized into two business segments, wholesale and retail. The wholesale segment is responsible for the acquisition of crude oil, petroleum refining, supplying petroleum products to the retail segment and the marketing of petroleum products to wholesale and industrial customers. The retail segment sells petroleum products under the Kwik Fill, Citgo, Keystone and Country Fair brand names at a network of company-operated retail units, and also sells convenience and grocery items through convenience stores operated under the Red Apple Food Mart and Country Fair brand names. United Refining has some 367 retail outlets, of which it owns approximately 184 units, leases 120 units and operates the remaining units under management agreements. Gasoline sales generate approximately 51% of United Refining's annual revenues and other petroleum products generate approximately 39%, while merchandise and other miscellaneous sources generate the remainder. The company owns and operates the Kiantone Pipeline, a 78-mile crude oil pipeline connecting the company's Pennsylvania refinery to Canadian, U.S. and world crude oil sources and capable of transporting up to 70,000 barrels per day. United Refining utilizes the storage capacity of its pipeline to blend various grades of crude oil from different suppliers. The company's products are used to fuel cars, trucks, airplanes and farm and construction equipment, as well as to heat homes and industrial facilities.

FINANCIALS: **Sales and profits are in thousands of dollars—add 000 to get the full amount. 2010 Note: Financial information for 2010 was not available for all companies at press time.**

2010 Sales: $	2010 Profits: $	**U.S. Stock Ticker: Subsidiary**
2009 Sales: $	2009 Profits: $	**Int'l Ticker:** Int'l Exchange:
2008 Sales: $	2008 Profits: $	Employees:
2007 Sales: $	2007 Profits: $	Fiscal Year Ends: 8/31
2006 Sales: $	2006 Profits: $	Parent Company: RED APPLE GROUP INC

SALARIES/BENEFITS:

Pension Plan:	ESOP Stock Plan:	Profit Sharing:	Top Exec. Salary: $	Bonus: $
Savings Plan:	Stock Purch. Plan:		Second Exec. Salary: $	Bonus: $

OTHER THOUGHTS:

Apparent Women Officers or Directors:
Hot Spot for Advancement for Women/Minorities:

LOCATIONS: ("Y" = Yes)

West:	Southwest:	Midwest:	Southeast:	Northeast:	International:
		Y	Y	Y	Y

UNITED UTILITIES GROUP PLC

www.unitedutilities.com

Industry Group Code: 2213 **Ranks within this company's industry group:** Sales: 1 Profits: 1

Exploration/Production:		Refining/Retailing:		Utilities:		Alternative Energy:		Specialty Services:		Energy Mktg./Other Svcs.	
Exploration:		Refining:		Electric Utility:		Waste/Solar/Other:		Consulting/Eng.:		Energy Marketing:	
Production:		Retailing:		Gas Utility:		Thermal/Steam:		Seismic:		Equipment/Machinery:	
Coal Production:		Convenience Stores:		Pipelines:	Y	Wind:		Drilling:		Oil Field Services:	
		Chemicals:		Water:	Y	Hydro:		InfoTech:		Air/Shipping Transportation:	
						Fuel Cells:		Specialty Services:			

TYPES OF BUSINESS:

Utilities-Water
Natural Gas Distribution
Water Management & Sewage Treatment

BRANDS/DIVISIONS/AFFILIATES:

United Utilities plc
United Utilities Water plc
United Utilities Property Solutions Limited
United Utilities Electricity Services, Ltd.
United Utilities Energy Services, Ltd.
United Utilities International, Ltd.
United Utilities Waste Management, Ltd.
United Utilities Australia Pty Ltd.

CONTACTS: *Note: Officers with more than one job title may be intentionally listed here more than once.*

Philip Green, CEO
Russ Houlden, CFO
Alison Clarke, Dir.-Human Resources
Paul Worthington, CIO
Tom Keevil, General Counsel/Corp. Sec.
Steve Fraser, Managing Dir.-Oper.
Gaynor Kenyon, Dir.-Comm.
Darren Jameson, Head-Investor Rel.
Phil Aspin, Treas.
Matthew Wright, Managing Dir.-Asset Mgmt. & Delivery
John McAdam, Chmn.

Phone: 441-92-523-7000 **Fax:** 441-92-237-066
Toll-Free:
Address: Haweswater House, Lingley Mere Business Park, Great Sankey, Warrington WA5 3LP UK

GROWTH PLANS/SPECIAL FEATURES:

United Utilities Group PLC, formerly United Utilities plc, offers public utilities including the collection and treatment of wastewater; the collection, treatment and distribution of water; and the distribution of natural gas to customers in northwest England. The company provides about 500 million gallons of water to 3.2 million homes and businesses daily; maintains 26,000 miles of water main; and manages 575 wastewater treatment plants and 100 impounding reservoirs in the U.K. United Utilities operates in three divisions: regulated activities, non-regulated activities and other. The regulated activities division includes the firm's water transportation and wastewater collection and treatment operations, conducted through United Utilities Water plc. The company treats 336 million gallons of wastewater daily through a 27,000-mile sewer network. The non-regulated activities division includes the firm's outsourced utility contracts, under which it transports natural gas for third parties. Its gas operations serve 2.5 million customers in Yorkshire, the North East and part of Cumbria. The other division includes administrative activities and the company's property business, which operates through United Utilities Property Solutions Limited. Other subsidiaries include United Utilities Electricity Services, Ltd.; United Utilities Energy Services, Ltd.; United Utilities International, Ltd.; United Utilities Waste Management, Ltd.; and a number of subsidiaries operating internationally. While United Utilities' operations are concentrated in the U.K., it also operates in select international markets, including India, the Middle East, Central and Eastern Europe. In late 2009, United Utilities sold its interests in Northern Gas Networks Holdings Limited and the Manila Water Company. In May 2010, the firm agreed to sell its Australian subsidiary, United Utilities Australia Pty Ltd., to a consortium led by Mitsubishi Corporation.

FINANCIALS: **Sales and profits are in thousands of dollars—add 000 to get the full amount. 2010 Note: Financial information for 2010 was not available for all companies at press time.**

2010 Sales: $
2009 Sales: $4,014,360
2008 Sales: $3,895,970
2007 Sales: $3,284,760
2006 Sales: $4,467,660

2010 Profits: $
2009 Profits: $295,800
2008 Profits: $1,499,100
2007 Profits: $714,760
2006 Profits: $389,700

U.S. Stock Ticker: UUGRY
Int'l Ticker: UU Int'l Exchange: London-LSE
Employees: 8,966
Fiscal Year Ends: 3/31
Parent Company:

SALARIES/BENEFITS:

Pension Plan: Y ESOP Stock Plan: Profit Sharing: Top Exec. Salary: $1,258,845 Bonus: $1,459,029
Savings Plan: Stock Purch. Plan: Second Exec. Salary: $731,960 Bonus: $951,548

OTHER THOUGHTS:

Apparent Women Officers or Directors: 3
Hot Spot for Advancement for Women/Minorities: Y

LOCATIONS: ("Y" = Yes)

West:	Southwest:	Midwest:	Southeast:	Northeast:	International:
					Y

Note: Financial information, benefits and other data can change quickly and may vary from those stated here.

US VENTURE INC

www.usventure.com

Industry Group Code: 486 **Ranks within this company's industry group:** Sales: Profits:

Exploration/Production:		**Refining/Retailing:**		**Utilities:**		**Alternative Energy:**		**Specialty Services:**		**Energy Mktg./Other Svcs.**	
Exploration:		Refining:		Electric Utility:		Waste/Solar/Other:		Consulting/Eng.:		Energy Marketing:	
Production:		Retailing:	Y	Gas Utility:		Thermal/Steam:		Seismic:		Equipment/Machinery:	Y
Coal Production:		Convenience Stores:	Y	Pipelines:		Wind:		Drilling:		Oil Field Services:	
		Chemicals:		Water:		Hydro:		InfoTech:		Air/Shipping Transportation:	
						Fuel Cells:		Specialty Services:	Y		

TYPES OF BUSINESS:

Petroleum Equipment Installation
HVAC Equipment, Wholesale
Refurbished Petroleum Equipment
Convenience Stores
Automotive Parts & Tires
Petroleum & Lubricant Distribution
Heavy Equipment Maintenance
Oil Analysis and Testing Services

BRANDS/DIVISIONS/AFFILIATES:

U.S. Oil
U.S. Petroleum Equipment
Express Convenience Centers
U.S. Oil Lubricants
Oil Chek
U.S. AutoForce
U.S. Custom Manufacturing
Design Air

CONTACTS:

Note: Officers with more than one job title may be intentionally listed here more than once.

John Schmidt, CEO
John Schmidt, Pres.
Lori Hoersch, Dir.-Human Resources

Phone: 920-739-6101 **Fax:** 920-788-0531
Toll-Free: 800-876-4526
Address: 425 Better Way, Appleton, WI 54915 US

GROWTH PLANS/SPECIAL FEATURES:

U.S. Venture, Inc., formerly U.S. Oil Co., Inc. is a marketer of petroleum products, including gasoline and diesel fuel, primarily in Wisconsin and Michigan. The company operates through seven divisions. The first, U.S. Oil formerly, U.S. Petroleum Operations, focuses on the wholesale petroleum industry and operates a number of bulk storage terminals throughout Wisconsin; the division is also involved in the distribution of wholesale and branded petroleum and bio-fuel products. The petroleum equipment division markets and installs petroleum tanks, pumps and other related equipment in both industrial and retail settings; the division also offers used and rebuilt gasoline pumps and dispensers. The Express Convenience Centers division operates 19 retail locations in Wisconsin, selling gasoline and diesel for cars and trucks, with adjacent convenience stores offering sundry goods. U.S. Oil Lubricants markets a variety of automotive and industrial lubricants, including engine oils, hydraulic oils, metal processing fluids and gear oils. The Oil Chek program is designed to spot abnormalities in a lubrication system by offering a range of oil analysis services and related system maintenance. U.S. AutoForce sells a range of coolants, lubricants, greases, shop supplies, exhaust system components, shop chemicals, tires, under-the-hood components and related products to automobile repair shops, dealers and specialty outlets. The Design Air division operates as a heating, ventilation and air conditioning (HVAC) wholesaler, with a focus on forced air and hydraulic heating and cooling systems and HVAC supplies. Finally, the U.S. Custom Manufacturing division produces and sells metal tubing in a range of shapes and sizes, serving customers in sectors such as automotive, furniture, lawn products and garden equipment.

Employees are offered benefits that include medical, dental and vision insurance; life and disability insurance; a 401(k) plan; a family and medical leave program; a matching charitable gifts program; and educational assistance.

FINANCIALS:

Sales and profits are in thousands of dollars—add 000 to get the full amount. 2010 Note: Financial information for 2010 was not available for all companies at press time.

2010 Sales: $	2010 Profits: $	**U.S. Stock Ticker: Private**
2009 Sales: $	2009 Profits: $	**Int'l Ticker:** Int'l Exchange:
2008 Sales: $	2008 Profits: $	Employees:
2007 Sales: $	2007 Profits: $	Fiscal Year Ends: 7/31
2006 Sales: $1,590,000	2006 Profits: $	Parent Company:

SALARIES/BENEFITS:

Pension Plan:	ESOP Stock Plan:	Profit Sharing:	Top Exec. Salary: $	Bonus: $
Savings Plan: Y	Stock Purch. Plan:		Second Exec. Salary: $	Bonus: $

OTHER THOUGHTS:

Apparent Women Officers or Directors: 1
Hot Spot for Advancement for Women/Minorities:

LOCATIONS: ("Y" = Yes)

West:	Southwest:	Midwest:	Southeast:	Northeast:	International:
		Y			

USEC INC

www.usec.com

Industry Group Code: 325188 **Ranks within this company's industry group:** Sales: 1 Profits: 1

Exploration/Production:		Refining/Retailing:		Utilities:		Alternative Energy:		Specialty Services:		Energy Mktg./Other Svcs.	
Exploration:		Refining:		Electric Utility:		Waste/Solar/Other:	Y	Consulting/Eng.:	Y	Energy Marketing:	
Production:		Retailing:		Gas Utility:		Thermal/Steam:		Seismic:		Equipment/Machinery:	Y
Coal Production:		Convenience Stores:		Pipelines:		Wind:		Drilling:		Oil Field Services:	
		Chemicals:		Water:		Hydro:		InfoTech:		Air/Shipping Transportation:	
						Fuel Cells:		Specialty Services:	Y		

TYPES OF BUSINESS:

Uranium Enrichment
Spent Fuel Transportation & Storage Systems
Fuel Cycle Consulting Services
Centrifuge Manufacturing

BRANDS/DIVISIONS/AFFILIATES:

United States Enrichment Corp
American Centrifuge
NAC International Inc

CONTACTS:

Note: Officers with more than one job title may be intentionally listed here more than once.

John K. Welch, CEO
John K. Welch, Pres.
John C. Barpoulis, CFO/Sr. VP
John M. A. Donelson, VP-Mktg. & Sales
W. Lance Wright, Sr. VP-Human Resources
Paul E. Sullivan, Chief Engineer
W. Lance Wright, Sr. VP-Admin.
Peter B. Saba, General Counsel/Sr. VP/Corp. Sec.
Paul Jacobson, VP-Corp. Comm.
Steven Wingfield, Dir.-Investor Rel.
Stephen S. Greene, VP-Finance/Treas.
Robert Van Namen, Sr. VP-Uranium Enrichment
Philip G. Sewell, Sr. VP-American Centrifuge
J. Tracy Mey, Chief Acct. Officer/Controller
Christine M. Ciccone, Sr. VP-External Rel.
James R. Mellor, Chmn.
Philip G. Sewell, Sr. VP-Russian HEU

Phone: 301-564-3200 **Fax:** 301-564-3201
Toll-Free:
Address: 6903 Rockledge Dr., Bethesda, MD 20817 US

GROWTH PLANS/SPECIAL FEATURES:

USEC, Inc. is an international energy company that supplies low enriched uranium (LEU) for approximately 150 commercial nuclear power plants worldwide. Through its subsidiaries, including United States Enrichment Corp., USEC operates one of the only uranium enrichment facilities in the U.S., a gaseous diffusion plant in Paducah, Kentucky. The firm's customers are domestic and international electric utilities that generate electricity through nuclear power and independent nuclear power plants. USEC is the executive agent for the U.S. government for the Megatons to Megawatts program with Russia, which purchases low enriched uranium units derived from the highly enriched uranium found in decommissioned nuclear warheads. USEC has spent several years on perfecting its proprietary American Centrifuge next-generation uranium enrichment technology, intended to be one of the world's most efficient uranium enrichment processes. The majority of construction on the American Centrifuge Plant in Piketon, Ohio, has been temporarily suspended until the company receives more financing. The firm's facility in Oak Ridge, Tennessee, is involved in the design, development, manufacturing and testing of centrifuge machines. USEC's subsidiary NAC International, Inc. is a provider of transportation and storage systems for spent nuclear fuel and fuel cycle consulting services. The subsidiary also utilizes its proprietary MAGNASTOR system, a high capacity design, fabrication and implementation system for spent nuclear fuel technologies. Sales of LEU account for roughly 87.1% of the firm's revenues, while U.S. government contracts comprise the remaining 12.9%. Approximately 68.8% of USEC's revenues are derived form the U.S., while the remaining 31.2% is derived from international clients. Nearly half of its international revenues are derived from Japan.

The company offers employees benefits such as disability, health and life insurance; paid time off; flexible spending accounts; a 401(k) plan; tuition reimbursement; an employee stock purchase plan; and an assistance program.

FINANCIALS:

Sales and profits are in thousands of dollars—add 000 to get the full amount. 2010 Note: Financial information for 2010 was not available for all companies at press time.

2010 Sales: $	2010 Profits: $
2009 Sales: $2,036,800	2009 Profits: $58,500
2008 Sales: $1,614,600	2008 Profits: $48,700
2007 Sales: $1,928,000	2007 Profits: $96,600
2006 Sales: $1,848,600	2006 Profits: $106,200

U.S. Stock Ticker: USU
Int'l Ticker: Int'l Exchange:
Employees: 2,908
Fiscal Year Ends: 12/31
Parent Company:

SALARIES/BENEFITS:

Pension Plan:	ESOP Stock Plan:	Profit Sharing:	Top Exec. Salary: $934,615	Bonus: $544,500
Savings Plan: Y	Stock Purch. Plan: Y		Second Exec. Salary: $505,928	Bonus: $228,655

OTHER THOUGHTS:

Apparent Women Officers or Directors: 2
Hot Spot for Advancement for Women/Minorities: Y

LOCATIONS: ("Y" = Yes)

West:	Southwest:	Midwest:	Southeast:	Northeast:	International:
		Y	Y	Y	

VAALCO ENERGY INC

www.vaalco.com

Industry Group Code: 211111 **Ranks within this company's industry group:** Sales: 105 Profits: 75

Exploration/Production:		Refining/Retailing:		Utilities:		Alternative Energy:		Specialty Services:		Energy Mktg./Other Svcs.	
Exploration:	Y	Refining:		Electric Utility:		Waste/Solar/Other:		Consulting/Eng.:		Energy Marketing:	Y
Production:	Y	Retailing:		Gas Utility:		Thermal/Steam:		Seismic:		Equipment/Machinery:	
Coal Production:		Convenience Stores:		Pipelines:		Wind:		Drilling:		Oil Field Services:	
		Chemicals:		Water:		Hydro:		InfoTech:		Air/Shipping Transportation:	
						Fuel Cells:		Specialty Services:			

TYPES OF BUSINESS:

Oil & Gas-Exploration & Production
Acquisition, Exploration, Development Crude Oil & Natural Gas
Production of Crude Oil & Natural Gas

BRANDS/DIVISIONS/AFFILIATES:

VAALCO Energy (USA) Inc
VAALCO International Inc
VAALCO Gabon (Etame) Inc
VAALCO Production (Gabon) Inc
VAALCO Angola (Kwanza) Inc
VAALCO UK (North Sea) Limited

CONTACTS: *Note: Officers with more than one job title may be intentionally listed here more than once.*

Robert L. Gerry, III, CEO
W. Russell Scheirman, COO
W. Russell Scheirman, Pres.
Gregory R. Hullinger, CFO
Gayla M. Cutrer, Corp. Sec./VP
Robert L. Gerry, III, Chmn.

Phone: 713-623-0801	**Fax:** 713-623-0982
Toll-Free:	
Address: 4600 Post Oak Place, Ste. 309, Houston, TX 77027 US	

GROWTH PLANS/SPECIAL FEATURES:

VAALCO Energy, Inc. is an independent energy company. The firm is engaged in the acquisition, exploration, development and production of crude oil and natural gas. The company owns producing properties and conducts exploration activities as operator in Gabon, West Africa, and conducts exploration activities in Angola. VAALCO Energy primarily sells its oil and gas at the well head at posted or indexed prices under short-term contracts. In Gabon, the company sells oil under a contract with Total Oil Trading SA. Additionally, the firm has organized a British subsidiary focused on exploration activities in the British North Sea. Domestically, VAALCO has minor interests in the Texas Gulf Coast area and offshore Louisiana. The company's primary source of revenue is from the Etame Production Sharing Contract related to the Etame Marin block located offshore Gabon. The company produces from the Etame, Avouma and South Tchibala fields on the license. This block produces approximately 8.3 million barrels of oil annually, with the company's share equaling roughly 1.9 million barrels. VAALCO's international subsidiaries include VAALCO Gabon (Etame), Inc.; VAALCO Production (Gabon), Inc.; VAALCO Angola (Kwanza), Inc.; VAALCO UK (North Sea), Ltd; and VAALCO International, Inc. Through VAALCO Gabon and VAALCO Production, the firm owns an approximate 30% interest in the 750,000-acre Etame Marin Block offshore Gabon. Through VAALCO Angola, VAALCO has a 40% interest in Block 5 offshore Angola, totaling approximately 1.4 million acres. In Gabon, in addition to the Etame, Avouma and South Tchibala fields, the company is developing the Ebouri field, where it commenced production on three development wells in early 2009.

FINANCIALS: **Sales and profits are in thousands of dollars—add 000 to get the full amount. 2010 Note: Financial information for 2010 was not available for all companies at press time.**

2010 Sales: $	2010 Profits: $	**U.S. Stock Ticker: EGY**
2009 Sales: $115,298	2009 Profits: $-4,144	**Int'l Ticker:** Int'l Exchange:
2008 Sales: $169,525	2008 Profits: $29,722	Employees: 77
2007 Sales: $125,044	2007 Profits: $19,052	Fiscal Year Ends: 12/31
2006 Sales: $98,325	2006 Profits: $40,343	Parent Company:

SALARIES/BENEFITS:

Pension Plan:	ESOP Stock Plan:	Profit Sharing:	Top Exec. Salary: $495,720	Bonus: $371,790
Savings Plan: Y	Stock Purch. Plan:		Second Exec. Salary: $408,240	Bonus: $306,180

OTHER THOUGHTS:

Apparent Women Officers or Directors: 1
Hot Spot for Advancement for Women/Minorities:

LOCATIONS: ("Y" = Yes)

West:	Southwest:	Midwest:	Southeast:	Northeast:	International:
	Y				Y

VALERO ENERGY CORP

www.valero.com

Industry Group Code: 324110 **Ranks within this company's industry group:** Sales: 3 Profits: 25

Exploration/Production:		Refining/Retailing:		Utilities:		Alternative Energy:		Specialty Services:		Energy Mktg./Other Svcs.	
Exploration:		Refining:	Y	Electric Utility:		Waste/Solar/Other:		Consulting/Eng.:		Energy Marketing:	
Production:		Retailing:	Y	Gas Utility:		Thermal/Steam:		Seismic:		Equipment/Machinery:	
Coal Production:		Convenience Stores:	Y	Pipelines:		Wind:		Drilling:		Oil Field Services:	
		Chemicals:		Water:		Hydro:		InfoTech:		Air/Shipping Transportation:	
						Fuel Cells:		Specialty Services:			

TYPES OF BUSINESS:

Petroleum Refineries & Retail Marketing
Convenience Stores
Home Heating Fuels
Wholesale Fuel Marketing
Asphalt
Marine Transportation
Ethanol Production

BRANDS/DIVISIONS/AFFILIATES:

Diamond Shamrock
Corner Store
Stop N Go

CONTACTS:

Note: Officers with more than one job title may be intentionally listed here more than once.

William R. Klesse, CEO
Richard J. Marcogliese, COO/Exec. VP
William R. Klesse, Pres.
Michael S. Ciskowski, CFO/Exec. VP
Joseph W. Gorder, Exec. VP-Mktg.
Mike Crownover, Sr. VP-Human Resources
Hal Zesch, CIO/Sr. VP
Kim Bowers, General Counsel/Exec. VP
S. Eugene Edwards, Exec. VP-Corp. Dev. & Strategic Planning
Eric Fisher, VP-Corp. Comm.
Eric Fisher, VP-Investor Comm.
Donna Titzman, Treas./VP
Gary Arthur, Jr., Sr. VP-Retail Mktg.
Jay D. Browning, Sec./Sr. VP-Corp. Law
Clay Killinger, Sr. VP/Controller
William R. Klesse, Chmn.
Joseph W. Gorder, Exec. VP-Supply

Phone: 210-345-2000 **Fax:** 210-345-2646
Toll-Free: 800-531-7911
Address: 1 Valero Way, San Antonio, TX 78249 US

GROWTH PLANS/SPECIAL FEATURES:

Valero Energy Corp. is a refiner and retailer of gasoline and other oil related products. Valero owns and operates 15 refineries located in the U.S., Canada and Aruba that produce refined products such as conventional gasolines, distillates, jet fuel, asphalt, petrochemicals and lubricants; and a slate of premium products including low-sulfur/ultra-low-sulfur diesel fuel and oxygenates (liquid hydrocarbon compounds containing oxygen). The firm markets branded and unbranded refined products on a wholesale basis in the U.S. and Canada through an extensive bulk and rack marketing network. Valero also sells refined products through a network of about 5,800 retail and wholesale branded outlets in the U.S., Canada and Aruba. The company's business is organized into two reportable segments: refining and retail. The refining segment offers refining and transportation operations; wholesale marketing; and product supply. The segment has a total throughput capacity of approximately 2.8 million barrels per day. Valero's retail segment sells transportation fuels at retail stores and unattended, self-service cardlocks; convenience store merchandise in retail stores; and home heating oil to residential customers. The segment is separated into two groups: Retail-U.S., which owns or leases about 1,000 stores under the names Corner Store and Stop N Go and sells transportation fuel under the Valero and Diamond Shamrock brands; and Retail-Canada, which owns or leases 396 retail stores, distributes gasoline to 428 dealers/jobbers and sells transportation fuels under the Ultramar brand through a network of 824 outlets. In early 2009, the firm agreed to acquire most of the ethanol production assets of bankrupt VeraSun, which will give Valero 780 million gallons of ethanol capacity yearly.

FINANCIALS:

Sales and profits are in thousands of dollars—add 000 to get the full amount. 2010 Note: Financial information for 2010 was not available for all companies at press time.

2010 Sales: $	2010 Profits: $	**U.S. Stock Ticker: VLO**
2009 Sales: $68,144,000	2009 Profits: $-352,000	**Int'l Ticker:** Int'l Exchange:
2008 Sales: $113,136,000	2008 Profits: $-1,012,000	Employees: 20,920
2007 Sales: $89,987,000	2007 Profits: $4,377,000	Fiscal Year Ends: 12/31
2006 Sales: $87,640,000	2006 Profits: $5,463,000	Parent Company:

SALARIES/BENEFITS:

Pension Plan:	ESOP Stock Plan:	Profit Sharing:	Top Exec. Salary: $1,500,000	Bonus: $
Savings Plan:	Stock Purch. Plan:		Second Exec. Salary: $955,000	Bonus: $450,000

OTHER THOUGHTS:

Apparent Women Officers or Directors: 3
Hot Spot for Advancement for Women/Minorities: Y

LOCATIONS: ("Y" = Yes)

West:	Southwest:	Midwest:	Southeast:	Northeast:	International:
Y	Y	Y	Y	Y	Y

VATTENFALL AB

www.vattenfall.com

Industry Group Code: 2211 **Ranks within this company's industry group:** Sales: 8 Profits: 3

Exploration/Production:		Refining/Retailing:		Utilities:		Alternative Energy:		Specialty Services:		Energy Mktg./Other Svcs.	
Exploration:	Y	Refining:		Electric Utility:	Y	Waste/Solar/Other:	Y	Consulting/Eng.:		Energy Marketing:	Y
Production:	Y	Retailing:		Gas Utility:	Y	Thermal/Steam:		Seismic:		Equipment/Machinery:	
Coal Production:	Y	Convenience Stores:		Pipelines:		Wind:	Y	Drilling:		Oil Field Services:	
		Chemicals:		Water:		Hydro:	Y	InfoTech:		Air/Shipping Transportation:	
						Fuel Cells:		Specialty Services:			

TYPES OF BUSINESS:

Utilities-Electricity & Natural Gas
Electricity Supplier
Wind Power Generation
Biomass Power Generation
Nuclear Power Generation

BRANDS/DIVISIONS/AFFILIATES:

AMEC Wind Energy Limited
N.V. Nuon Energy
Thanet Offshore Wind Farm

CONTACTS:

Note: Officers with more than one job title may be intentionally listed here more than once.

Oystein Loseth, CEO
Oystein Loseth, Pres.
Jonas Florinus, Acting CFO
Lars Gejrot, Sr. VP-Human Resources
Helmar Rendez, Sr. VP-Group Strategy
Elisabeth Strom, Sr. VP-Comm.
Klaus Aurich, Head-Investor Rel.
Anders Dahl, Acting Head-Pan-Europe Bus. Group
Torbjorn Wahlborg, Sr. Exec. VP/Head-Nordic Bus. Group
Huib Morelisse, Sr. Exec. VP/Head-Benelux Bus. Group
Harald von Heyden, Sr. VP/Head-Trading & Generation Mgmt.
Lars Westerberg, Chmn.
Frederic de Maneville, Country Mgr.-France

Phone: 46-8-739-50-00	**Fax:** 46-8-17-85-06
Toll-Free:	
Address: SE-162 87, Stockholm, Sweden	

GROWTH PLANS/SPECIAL FEATURES:

Vattenfall AB generates, distributes, trades and sells electricity and gas used for heating residential and commercial areas. The majority of its electricity sales are made to industrial customers and energy companies. The company is completely owned by the Swedish government, has approximately 4.8 million customers and generates roughly 20% of the electricity used in the Nordic countries of Norway, Sweden, Finland and Denmark. Vattenfall divides its operations between its Nordic Group, which includes operations in Norway, Sweden, Finland and Denmark; the Central Europe Group, overseeing the firm's activities in Germany and Poland; the Pan Europe Group, which includes the wind, nuclear and engineering business groups across Europe; the Benelux Group, which incorporates the acquisition of Nuon Energy; and other miscellaneous business activities, including energy trading and finance operations. In 2009, Vattenfall generated approximately 158.7 terawatt hours (TWh) of electricity and 38 TWh of heat. The 2009 electricity generation, broken down by source, included 80.5 TWh of fossil-fuel power; 41.5 TWh of nuclear-generated power; 33.6 TWh of hydro-electric power; 1.7 TWh of wind-generated power; and 1.4 TWh of electricity generated from biomass and waste products. The company is one of the largest generators of wind power in Northern Europe, with about 700 turbines spread throughout Denmark, Sweden, Germany, Poland, the Netherlands, Belgium and the U.K. In October 2009, the company announced plans for an ocean wave electricity generation project off the western coast of Ireland. The firm planned to open nine new wind farms in six nations between 2009 and 2011. In September 2010, Vattenfall opened a major offshore wind turbine farm off the coast of southeast England. Dubbed the Thanet Offshore Wind Farm, it has 100 turbines and a total generating capacity of 300 megawatts.

FINANCIALS:

Sales and profits are in thousands of dollars—add 000 to get the full amount. 2010 Note: Financial information for 2010 was not available for all companies at press time.

2010 Sales: $	2010 Profits: $	**U.S. Stock Ticker: Government-Owned**
2009 Sales: $26,515,400	2009 Profits: $3,606,430	**Int'l Ticker:** Int'l Exchange:
2008 Sales: $22,212,700	2008 Profits: $3,172,200	Employees: 40,026
2007 Sales: $19,257,900	2007 Profits: $2,773,410	Fiscal Year Ends: 12/31
2006 Sales: $18,207,200	2006 Profits: $2,662,400	Parent Company:

SALARIES/BENEFITS:

Pension Plan: Y	ESOP Stock Plan:	Profit Sharing:	Top Exec. Salary: $	Bonus: $
Savings Plan:	Stock Purch. Plan:		Second Exec. Salary: $	Bonus: $

OTHER THOUGHTS:

Apparent Women Officers or Directors: 5
Hot Spot for Advancement for Women/Minorities: Y

LOCATIONS: ("Y" = Yes)

West:	Southwest:	Midwest:	Southeast:	Northeast:	International:
					Y

VECTREN CORPORATION

www.vectren.com

Industry Group Code: 221 **Ranks within this company's industry group:** Sales: 45 Profits: 40

Exploration/Production:		Refining/Retailing:		Utilities:		Alternative Energy:		Specialty Services:		Energy Mktg./Other Svcs.	
Exploration:		Refining:		Electric Utility:	Y	Waste/Solar/Other:	Y	Consulting/Eng.:		Energy Marketing:	Y
Production:		Retailing:		Gas Utility:	Y	Thermal/Steam:		Seismic:		Equipment/Machinery:	
Coal Production:	Y	Convenience Stores:		Pipelines:	Y	Wind:		Drilling:		Oil Field Services:	
		Chemicals:		Water:		Hydro:		InfoTech:		Air/Shipping Transportation:	
						Fuel Cells:		Specialty Services:	Y		

TYPES OF BUSINESS:

Utilities-Electricity & Natural Gas
Energy Infrastructure Services
Energy Marketing
Coal Mining

BRANDS/DIVISIONS/AFFILIATES:

Indiana Gas Co., Inc.
Southern Indiana Gas and Electric Co.
Vectren Energy Delivery of Ohio
Vectren Utility Holdings, Inc.
Vectren Fuels, Inc.
Miller Pipeline Corp.
Vectren Energy Delivery of Indiana
Energy Systems Group, LLC

CONTACTS: *Note: Officers with more than one job title may be intentionally listed here more than once.*

Carl L. Chapman, CEO
Carl L. Chapman, Pres.
Jerome A. Benkert, Jr., CFO/Exec. VP
Ellis Redd, VP-Human Resources
Jon Luttrell, VP-IT
Bob Heidorn, General Counsel/VP/Chief Compliance Officer
William S. Doty, Exec. VP-Utility Oper.
Elizabeth I. Witte, VP-Planning & Corp. Dev.
Michael Roeder, VP-Comm. & Gov't Affairs
Robert L. Goocher, VP-Investor Rel.
Robert L. Goocher, Treas.
M. Susan Hardwick, VP/Controller
Jon Luttrell, VP-Customer Svcs.
Ronald E. Christian, Exec. VP/Chief Legal & External Affairs Officer
Niel C. Ellerbrook, Chmn.

Phone: 812-491-4000	**Fax:** 812-491-4706
Toll-Free: 800-227-1376	
Address: 1 Vectren Sq., Evansville, IN 47708 US	

GROWTH PLANS/SPECIAL FEATURES:

Vectren Corporation is an energy holding company with $4 billion in assets. Wholly-owned subsidiary Vectren Utility Holdings, Inc. (Utility Holdings) serves as the intermediate holding company for three operating public utilities: Indiana Gas Co., Inc.; Southern Indiana Gas & Electric Co. (SIGECO); and the Ohio operations. Utility Holdings also has other assets that provide information technology and various services to the three utilities. Indiana Gas provides energy delivery services to 567,000 natural gas customers in Indiana. SIGECO provides energy delivery services to 141,000 electric customers and about 111,000 gas customers in Indiana. In addition, SIGECO owns six gas turbines and three active underground gas storage fields in Indiana. Indiana Gas and SIGECO do business as Vectren Energy Delivery of Indiana. The Ohio operations, doing business as Vectren Energy Delivery of Ohio, provide energy delivery services to 315,000 natural gas customers. The Ohio operations are owned by Vectren Energy Delivery of Ohio, Inc. and Indiana Gas. Non-utilities operations, managed through Vectren Enterprises, Inc., include energy marketing and services; coal mining; and energy infrastructure services. The energy marketing and services are conducted through ProLiance, a management company that provides services to municipalities, industrial operations, schools and health care institutions, and Vectren Source, which provides natural gas and other related products and services. The coal mining group, through Vectren Fuels, Inc., mines and sells coal to Vectren's utility operations and to third parties. In 2009, Vectren Fuels operated two mines in Indiana, producing 3.55 million tons of coal. The energy infrastructure services segment provides energy performance contracting operations through Energy Systems Group, LLC; and natural gas and water distribution, transmission, construction repair and rehabilitation and other services through Miller Pipeline Corp.

The company offers its employees a 401(k) plan; a pension plan; life and long-term disability insurance; an employee assistance program; and educational assistance.

FINANCIALS: **Sales and profits are in thousands of dollars—add 000 to get the full amount. 2010 Note: Financial information for 2010 was not available for all companies at press time.**

2010 Sales: $	2010 Profits: $	**U.S. Stock Ticker: VVC**
2009 Sales: $2,088,900	2009 Profits: $133,100	**Int'l Ticker:** Int'l Exchange:
2008 Sales: $2,484,700	2008 Profits: $129,000	Employees: 3,700
2007 Sales: $2,281,900	2007 Profits: $143,100	Fiscal Year Ends: 12/31
2006 Sales: $2,041,600	2006 Profits: $108,800	Parent Company:

SALARIES/BENEFITS:

Pension Plan: Y	ESOP Stock Plan:	Profit Sharing:	Top Exec. Salary: $778,847	Bonus: $358,079
Savings Plan: Y	Stock Purch. Plan: Y		Second Exec. Salary: $456,924	Bonus: $151,719

OTHER THOUGHTS:

Apparent Women Officers or Directors: 2
Hot Spot for Advancement for Women/Minorities:

LOCATIONS: ("Y" = Yes)

West:	Southwest:	Midwest:	Southeast:	Northeast:	International:
		Y			

VIRGINIA ELECTRIC AND POWER COMPANY

www.dom.com

Industry Group Code: 2211 **Ranks within this company's industry group:** Sales: Profits:

Exploration/Production:		Refining/Retailing:		Utilities:		Alternative Energy:		Specialty Services:		Energy Mktg./Other Svcs.	
Exploration:		Refining:		Electric Utility:	Y	Waste/Solar/Other:		Consulting/Eng.:		Energy Marketing:	Y
Production:		Retailing:		Gas Utility:		Thermal/Steam:		Seismic:		Equipment/Machinery:	
Coal Production:		Convenience Stores:		Pipelines:		Wind:		Drilling:		Oil Field Services:	
		Chemicals:		Water:		Hydro:		InfoTech:		Air/Shipping Transportation:	
						Fuel Cells:		Specialty Services:			

TYPES OF BUSINESS:

Electric Utility
Energy Trading & Marketing

BRANDS/DIVISIONS/AFFILIATES:

Dominion Resources Inc
Dominion Virginia Power
Dominion North Carolina Power

CONTACTS: *Note: Officers with more than one job title may be intentionally listed here more than once.*

Thomas F. Farrell II, CEO
Thomas F. Farrell II, Pres.
Mark F. McGettrick, CFO/Exec. VP
James F. Stutts, General Counsel/Sr. VP
Robert M. Blue, Sr. VP-Corp. Comm. & Public Policy
Ashwini Sawhney, Controller/VP
David A. Christian, CEO-Dominion Generation
Paul D. Koonce, CEO-Dominion Virginia Power
Carter M. Reid, Corp. Sec./VP-Governance
David A. Heacock, Pres., Dominion Nuclear
Thomas F. Farrell II, Chmn.

Phone: 804-819-2000	**Fax:** 804-819-2233
Toll-Free: 888-667-3000	
Address: 120 Tredegar St., Richmond, VA 23219 US	

GROWTH PLANS/SPECIAL FEATURES:

Virginia Electric and Power Company is a regulated public utility that generates, transmits and distributes electricity for sale in Virginia and northeastern North Carolina. The company does business as Dominion Virginia Power (DVP) in Virginia and Dominion North Carolina Power in North Carolina. The firm is a subsidiary of Dominion Resources, which has more than $42.5 billion in assets and transmits and distributes electricity and gas to nearly 12 million customers in nine states. The Virginia service area comprises about 65% of Virginia's total land area, but accounts for over 80% of its population. DVP includes regulated electric transmission, distribution and customer service operations. Its electric transmission and distribution operations serve residential, commercial, industrial and governmental customers in Virginia and northeastern North Carolina. The firm served approximately 2.4 million retail customer accounts, including governmental agencies, as well as, wholesale customers such as rural electric cooperatives and municipalities. DVP has approximately 6,000 miles of electric transmission lines of 69 kilovolt or more located in the states of North Carolina, Virginia and West Virginia. The generation segment includes the electric generation facilities, power purchase agreements and energy supply operations. The electric generation operations serve customers in Virginia and northeastern North Carolina. Through its Dominion Retail division, the firm also serves roughly 1.9 million non-regulated customers in 12 states. Virginia Electric and Power accounts for roughly 59% of Dominion Resources' revenues.

The firm offers its employees medical, dental vision and basic life insurance; a 401(k) plan; flexible work arrangements; tuition and book reimbursement; adoption assistance; and an employee assistance program.

FINANCIALS: **Sales and profits are in thousands of dollars—add 000 to get the full amount. 2010 Note: Financial information for 2010 was not available for all companies at press time.**

2010 Sales: $	2010 Profits: $	**U.S. Stock Ticker: Subsidiary**
2009 Sales: $	2009 Profits: $	**Int'l Ticker:** Int'l Exchange:
2008 Sales: $	2008 Profits: $	Employees:
2007 Sales: $	2007 Profits: $	Fiscal Year Ends: 12/31
2006 Sales: $	2006 Profits: $	Parent Company: DOMINION RESOURCES INC

SALARIES/BENEFITS:

Pension Plan:	ESOP Stock Plan:	Profit Sharing:	Top Exec. Salary: $452,833	Bonus: $2,559,300
Savings Plan:	Stock Purch. Plan:		Second Exec. Salary: $327,253	Bonus: $1,061,894

OTHER THOUGHTS:

Apparent Women Officers or Directors: 3
Hot Spot for Advancement for Women/Minorities: Y

LOCATIONS: ("Y" = Yes)

West:	Southwest:	Midwest:	Southeast:	Northeast:	International:
				Y	

W&T OFFSHORE INC

www.wtoffshore.com

Industry Group Code: 211111 **Ranks within this company's industry group:** Sales: 91 Profits: 95

Exploration/Production:		Refining/Retailing:		Utilities:		Alternative Energy:		Specialty Services:		Energy Mktg./Other Svcs.	
Exploration:	Y	Refining:		Electric Utility:		Waste/Solar/Other:		Consulting/Eng.:		Energy Marketing:	
Production:	Y	Retailing:		Gas Utility:		Thermal/Steam:		Seismic:		Equipment/Machinery:	
Coal Production:		Convenience Stores:		Pipelines:		Wind:		Drilling:		Oil Field Services:	
		Chemicals:		Water:		Hydro:		InfoTech:		Air/Shipping Transportation:	
						Fuel Cells:		Specialty Services:			

TYPES OF BUSINESS:

Oil Exploration & Production

BRANDS/DIVISIONS/AFFILIATES:

W&T Energy VI LLC
W&T Energy VII LLC
N.O. Properties LLC
White Shoal Pipeline Corporation
Total E&P USA Inc

CONTACTS:

Note: Officers with more than one job title may be intentionally listed here more than once.

Tracy W. Krohn, CEO
Stephen L. Schroeder, COO/Sr. VP
Jamie L. Vazquez, Pres.
J. Daniel Gibbons, CFO/Sr. VP
W. Allen Tate, VP-Mktg. & Midstream
Jeffrey M. Durrant, Sr. VP-Exploration & Geosciences
Gregory E. Percival, VP-IT
Paul R. Baker, VP-Prod.
Clifford J. Williams, VP-Reservoir Eng.
Thomas F. Getten, General Counsel
Joseph P.Slattery, Sr. VP-Oper.
Karen S. Acree, Controller
Kenneth F. Fagan, VP-Acquisitions
Todd E. Grabois, VP/Treas.
Jerome F. Freel, Corp. Sec.
Daniel P. Huffman, VP-Exploitation
Tracy W. Krohn, Chmn.

Phone: 713-626-8525	**Fax:** 713-626-8527
Toll-Free:	
Address: 9 Greenway Plz., Ste. 300, Houston, TX 77046 US	

GROWTH PLANS/SPECIAL FEATURES:

W&T Offshore, Inc. is an independent energy company. The firm is engaged in the acquisition, exploitation, exploration and production of oil and natural gas. W&T Offshore is focused on higher impact capital projects primarily in the Gulf of Mexico area, including the deepwater (water depths in excess of 500 feet) and the deep shelf (well depths in excess of 15,000 feet) areas. The company has approximately 371.0 billion cubic feet equivalent (Bcfe) of proved reserves, 45% of which are oil/natural gas liquids and 45% of which are natural gas. Of these reserves, 76% are proved developed and 24% are undeveloped. W&T Offshore owns interests in approximately 72 fields located in federal and state waters, covering approximately nine million acres. A significant portion of the company's acreage is explored between the depths of 10 to 4,200 feet. The company owns interests in roughly 288 offshore structures, 163 of which are located in fields that the firm operates. Wholly-owned energy subsidiaries of the company include: N.O. Properties LLC; W&T Energy VI, LLC; W&T Energy VII, LLC; and in addition the firm owns 73.4% of White Shoal Pipeline Corporation. In 2009, the company sold one of its fields in Louisiana state waters, and 36 non-core oil and natural gas fields in the Gulf of Mexico for approximately $32.2 million. In May 2010, W&T Offshore acquired W&T Energy VI, LLC, and all of the interests of Total E&P USA, Inc., for $150 million. In addition to this transaction, the firm acquired Mississippi Canyon block 243 (Matterhorn) and a 64% working interest in Viosca Knoll blocks 822 and 823 (Virgo).

FINANCIALS:

Sales and profits are in thousands of dollars—add 000 to get the full amount. 2010 Note: Financial information for 2010 was not available for all companies at press time.

2010 Sales: $	2010 Profits: $	**U.S. Stock Ticker: WTI**
2009 Sales: $610,996	2009 Profits: $-187,919	**Int'l Ticker:** Int'l Exchange:
2008 Sales: $1,215,609	2008 Profits: $-558,819	Employees: 286
2007 Sales: $1,113,749	2007 Profits: $144,300	Fiscal Year Ends: 12/31
2006 Sales: $800,466	2006 Profits: $199,104	Parent Company:

SALARIES/BENEFITS:

Pension Plan:	ESOP Stock Plan:	Profit Sharing:	Top Exec. Salary: $1,038,462	Bonus: $
Savings Plan:	Stock Purch. Plan:		Second Exec. Salary: $529,615	Bonus: $

OTHER THOUGHTS:

Apparent Women Officers or Directors: 3
Hot Spot for Advancement for Women/Minorities: Y

LOCATIONS: ("Y" = Yes)

West:	Southwest:	Midwest:	Southeast:	Northeast:	International:
	Y		Y		

WEATHERFORD INTERNATIONAL LTD

www.weatherford.com

Industry Group Code: 213111 **Ranks within this company's industry group:** Sales: 2 Profits: 8

Exploration/Production:		**Refining/Retailing:**		**Utilities:**		**Alternative Energy:**		**Specialty Services:**		**Energy Mktg./Other Svcs.**	
Exploration:		Refining:		Electric Utility:		Waste/Solar/Other:		Consulting/Eng.:		Energy Marketing:	
Production:		Retailing:		Gas Utility:		Thermal/Steam:		Seismic:		Equipment/Machinery:	
Coal Production:		Convenience Stores:		Pipelines:		Wind:		Drilling:	Y	Oil Field Services:	Y
		Chemicals:		Water:		Hydro:		InfoTech:		Air/Shipping Transportation:	
						Fuel Cells:		Specialty Services:			

TYPES OF BUSINESS:

Oil & Gas Drilling Support Services
Artificial Lift Systems
Completion Systems
Research & Development

BRANDS/DIVISIONS/AFFILIATES:

International Logging Inc

CONTACTS:

Note: Officers with more than one job title may be intentionally listed here more than once.

Bernard J. Duroc-Danner, CEO
Bernard J. Duroc-Danner, Pres.
Andrew P. Becnel, CFO/Sr. VP
William B. Jacobson, Co-General Counsel/Chief Compliance Officer/VP
Keith R. Morley, Sr. VP-Well Construction & Oper. Support
M. Jessica Abarca, Chief Acct. Officer/VP-Acct.
Joseph C. Henry, Co-General Counsel/Sec.
Kyle Chapman, Mgr.-Latin America Oper. Bus. Unit
M. David Colley, VP-Artificial Lift Global Bus. Unit
James M. Hudgins, VP-Tax
Bernard J. Duroc-Danner, Chmn.
Wolfgang Puennel, VP-Europe & West Africa

Phone: 41-22-816-1500	**Fax:**
Toll-Free:	
Address: 4-6 Rue Jean-Francois Bartholoni, Geneva, 1204 Switzerland	

GROWTH PLANS/SPECIAL FEATURES:

Weatherford International, Ltd. provides equipment and services for the oil and natural gas industry. The firm operates throughout the U.S. and in over 100 countries around the world, with more than 800 service, sales and manufacturing locations. The company offers oil/natural gas well drilling, evaluation, completion, production, intervention and industrial products/services. Weatherford International's drilling offerings include controlled pressure drilling systems; well installation services; cementing products; and measurement-while-drilling systems. With regard to evaluation, the company provides testing, data, geoscience, cased-hole and open-hole services; surface logging systems; and micro-seismic monitoring. The firm's completion system activities include hydraulic intelligent, open-hole, cased-hole and expandable completion systems, as well as intelligent well, liner, packer and flow control systems. The firm's artificial lift system activities provide all forms of artificial lift primarily used for the production of oil. This operation also provides production optimization services and automation and monitoring of well head production. Weatherford's intervention services are intended to extend the production capacity of oil and natural gas wells; these include fishing services, multilateral systems, casing exit systems and thru-tubing packers. The firm's industrial operations focus primarily on pumping technologies, including multiplex pumps, horizontal surface pumping units and progressing cavity pumps. These are used in a variety of applications related to industries such as pulp and paper; oil and gas; poultry and dairy; petrochemical; and automotives and aircrafts. The firm has 34 research, development and engineering facilities and Weatherford spent a total of $195 million for research and development in 2009. Wholly-owned subsidiary International Logging, Inc., is a provider of surface logging and formation evaluation and drilling related services at the well site. In February 2009, Weatherford International moved its corporate headquarters from the U.S. to Switzerland. In July 2009, the company acquired the Oil Field Services unit of TNK-BP, a Russian oil firm.

FINANCIALS:

Sales and profits are in thousands of dollars—add 000 to get the full amount. 2010 Note: Financial information for 2010 was not available for all companies at press time.

2010 Sales: $	2010 Profits: $	**U.S. Stock Ticker: WFT**
2009 Sales: $8,826,933	2009 Profits: $253,766	**Int'l Ticker:** Int'l Exchange:
2008 Sales: $9,600,564	2008 Profits: $1,353,903	Employees: 52,000
2007 Sales: $7,832,062	2007 Profits: $1,070,606	Fiscal Year Ends: 12/31
2006 Sales: $6,578,928	2006 Profits: $896,369	Parent Company:

SALARIES/BENEFITS:

Pension Plan:	ESOP Stock Plan:	Profit Sharing:	Top Exec. Salary: $1,640,000	Bonus: $1,750,000
Savings Plan:	Stock Purch. Plan:		Second Exec. Salary: $829,121	Bonus: $525,000

OTHER THOUGHTS:

Apparent Women Officers or Directors: 1
Hot Spot for Advancement for Women/Minorities:

LOCATIONS: ("Y" = Yes)

West:	Southwest:	Midwest:	Southeast:	Northeast:	International:
Y	Y	Y	Y	Y	Y

WESTAR ENERGY

www.westarenergy.com

Industry Group Code: 2211 **Ranks within this company's industry group:** Sales: 37 Profits: 34

Exploration/Production:		Refining/Retailing:		Utilities:		Alternative Energy:		Specialty Services:		Energy Mktg./Other Svcs.	
Exploration:		Refining:		Electric Utility:	Y	Waste/Solar/Other:	Y	Consulting/Eng.:		Energy Marketing:	Y
Production:		Retailing:		Gas Utility:		Thermal/Steam:		Seismic:		Equipment/Machinery:	
Coal Production:		Convenience Stores:		Pipelines:		Wind:	Y	Drilling:		Oil Field Services:	
		Chemicals:		Water:		Hydro:		InfoTech:		Air/Shipping Transportation:	
						Fuel Cells:		Specialty Services:			

TYPES OF BUSINESS:

Utilities-Electricity & Natural Gas
Nuclear Power Plants

BRANDS/DIVISIONS/AFFILIATES:

Kansas Gas & Electric Co.
Wolf Creek Generating Station
Wolf Creek Nuclear Operating Corp.

CONTACTS: *Note: Officers with more than one job title may be intentionally listed here more than once.*

William B. Moore, CEO
Doug Sterbenz, COO/Exec. VP
William B. Moore, Pres.
Mark A. Ruelle, CFO/Exec. VP
Jerl Banning, VP-Human Resources
Larry Irick, General Counsel/VP/Corp. Sec.
Kelly B. Harrison, VP-Transmission Oper. & Environmental Svcs.
Bruce Akin, VP-Oper. Strategy & Support
James Ludwig, Exec. VP-Public Affairs & Consumer Svcs.
Bruce Burns, Dir.-Investor Rel.
Tony Somma, Treas./VP
Leroy P. Wages, VP/Controller
Jeff Beasley, VP-Corp. Compliance & Internal Audit
Greg A. Greenwood, VP-Major Construction Projects
Michael Lennen, VP-Regulatory Affairs
Charles Q. Chandler, IV, Chmn.

Phone: 785-575-6300 **Fax:** 785-575-1796
Toll-Free:
Address: 818 Kansas Ave., Topeka, KS 66612 US

GROWTH PLANS/SPECIAL FEATURES:

Westar Energy is an electric utility providing electric generation, transmission and distribution services to approximately 685,000 customers in central and northeastern Kansas, including the cities of Topeka, Lawrence, Manhattan, Salina and Hutchinson. Wholly-owned subsidiary Kansas Gas and Electric Co. (KGE) provides the same services for south-central and southeastern Kansas areas, including the Wichita metropolitan area. Both Westar Energy and KGE conduct business under the Westar Energy name. Westar also supplies wholesale electric energy to electric distribution systems in 55 Kansas cities and four rural electric cooperatives and has contracts for the sale, purchase or exchange of wholesale electricity with other utilities. Along with utility supplies, KGE owns a 47% interest in the Wolf Creek Generating Station, a nuclear power plant located near Burlington, Kansas, and a 47% interest in Wolf Creek Nuclear Operating Corp., the operating company for the generating station. Westar owns 92% interest in three coal-fired units at Jeffrey Energy Center and a 50% interest in the two coal-fired units at LaCygne Generating Station. Approximately 50% of the company's total energy capacity comes from coal, and 42% from natural gas or oil, with the remainder comprised of nuclear energy. The firm also provides energy generating capacity to other companies, including four energy businesses in Oklahoma and Kansas. The company has two wind farms at Jeffrey Energy Center in Kansas. In January 2010, the firm purchased development rights for the Ironwood wind energy site in Kansas from Infinity Wind Power. The site is expected to have a generating capacity of 500 megawatts upon completion.

The company offers its employees medical and dental insurance; flexible spending accounts; life and disability insurance; a retirement plant; a 401(k) plan; tuition reimbursement and an employee assistance program.

FINANCIALS: **Sales and profits are in thousands of dollars—add 000 to get the full amount. 2010 Note: Financial information for 2010 was not available for all companies at press time.**

2010 Sales: $	2010 Profits: $	**U.S. Stock Ticker: WR**
2009 Sales: $1,858,231	2009 Profits: $175,075	**Int'l Ticker:** Int'l Exchange:
2008 Sales: $1,838,996	2008 Profits: $177,170	Employees: 2,397
2007 Sales: $1,726,834	2007 Profits: $167,384	Fiscal Year Ends: 12/31
2006 Sales: $1,605,743	2006 Profits: $164,339	Parent Company:

SALARIES/BENEFITS:

Pension Plan: Y	ESOP Stock Plan:	Profit Sharing:	Top Exec. Salary: $630,000	Bonus: $
Savings Plan: Y	Stock Purch. Plan:		Second Exec. Salary: $435,000	Bonus: $

OTHER THOUGHTS:

Apparent Women Officers or Directors: 2
Hot Spot for Advancement for Women/Minorities: Y

LOCATIONS: ("Y" = Yes)

West:	Southwest:	Midwest:	Southeast:	Northeast:	International:
	Y	Y			Y

WESTERNGECO

www.westerngeco.com

Industry Group Code: 213112 **Ranks within this company's industry group:** Sales: Profits:

Exploration/Production:		Refining/Retailing:		Utilities:		Alternative Energy:		Specialty Services:		Energy Mktg./Other Svcs.	
Exploration:		Refining:		Electric Utility:		Waste/Solar/Other:		Consulting/Eng.:		Energy Marketing:	
Production:		Retailing:		Gas Utility:		Thermal/Steam:		Seismic:	Y	Equipment/Machinery:	
Coal Production:		Convenience Stores:		Pipelines:		Wind:		Drilling:		Oil Field Services:	
		Chemicals:		Water:		Hydro:		InfoTech:	Y	Air/Shipping Transportation:	
						Fuel Cells:		Specialty Services:			

TYPES OF BUSINESS:

Seismic Services
Seismic Surveys
Reservoir Imaging, Monitoring & Development
Seismic Data Software
Seismic Data Library

BRANDS/DIVISIONS/AFFILIATES:

Schlumberger Limited
WesternGeco Electromagnetics
Q-Technology
IndigoPool
WesternGeco Oslo Technology Center
Nexus Geosciences, Inc.
Integra Group

CONTACTS:

Note: Officers with more than one job title may be intentionally listed here more than once.

Carl Trowell, Pres.
Ginger Hildebrand, VP-Seismic Data Processing
Thomas Scoulios, Mgr.-North American Region
Andrew Gould, Chmn./CEO-Schlumberger
Wadii El Karkouri, Mgr.-Africa Region

Phone: 44-1293-55-66-55 **Fax:** 44-1293-55-69-40
Toll-Free:
Address: Schlumberger House, Buckingham Gate, Gatwick Airport, West Sussex RH6 0NZ UK

GROWTH PLANS/SPECIAL FEATURES:

WesternGeco, the seismic business unit of Schlumberger, Ltd., is a leading geophysical services company that provides worldwide reservoir imaging, monitoring and development services for its parent company and third party oil exploration companies. The company's solutions are based on Q-Technology, a proprietary suite of advanced seismic services and technologies for both on- and offshore enhanced reservoir delineation, characterization and monitoring. Schlumberger provides a full range of oil and gas services, including seismic surveys, multi-component and electromagnetic surveys, land and marine seismic acquisition and processing services, reservoir location and monitoring services, data processing and controlled-source electromagnetic and magneto-telluric data acquisition surveys. The company divides its solutions into two sectors: geophysical services and additional services. Geophysical services include marine acquisition services, such as conventional marine seismic services, 2D and 3D surveys over shelf and deepwater areas, seabed multi-component surveys and time-lapse 4D surveys; land and transition zone (TZ) data acquisition services, including reservoir characterization and 4D production monitoring studies; seismic data processing services, including reservoir seismic technologies, algorithms, and workflows, reservoir property description, and Q-Technology data processing; and electromagnetics services, offered through subsidiary WesternGeco Electromagnetics, which include controlled-source electromagnetics (CSEM) and marine magnetotelluric (MMT) solutions, initial modeling, survey design, acquisition, integrated data processing and interpretation. WesternGeco also offers acquisition and divestiture services through subsidiary IndigoPool. Additionally, the firm manages the world's largest multiclient seismic data library. In March 2010, Schlumberger acquired Nexus Geosciences, Inc., a provider of seismic software, and combined its operations into WesternGeco. In May 2010, the firm inaugurated the new WesternGeco Oslo Technology Center in Norway, which will house a marine testing laboratory and an interactive operations center. In July of the same year, WesternGeco established a joint venture with Integra Group to provide land seismic acquisition services and data processing in Russia, Kazakhstan, Uzbekistan and Turkmenistan.

FINANCIALS:

Sales and profits are in thousands of dollars—add 000 to get the full amount. 2010 Note: Financial information for 2010 was not available for all companies at press time.

2010 Sales: $	2010 Profits: $	**U.S. Stock Ticker: Subsidiary**
2009 Sales: $	2009 Profits: $	**Int'l Ticker:** Int'l Exchange:
2008 Sales: $	2008 Profits: $	Employees:
2007 Sales: $	2007 Profits: $	Fiscal Year Ends: 12/31
2006 Sales: $	2006 Profits: $	Parent Company: SCHLUMBERGER LIMITED

SALARIES/BENEFITS:

Pension Plan:	ESOP Stock Plan:	Profit Sharing:	Top Exec. Salary: $	Bonus: $
Savings Plan:	Stock Purch. Plan:		Second Exec. Salary: $	Bonus: $

OTHER THOUGHTS:

Apparent Women Officers or Directors: 1
Hot Spot for Advancement for Women/Minorities:

LOCATIONS: ("Y" = Yes)

West:	Southwest:	Midwest:	Southeast:	Northeast:	International:
	Y				Y

WESTINGHOUSE ELECTRIC COMPANY LLC

www.westinghousenuclear.com

Industry Group Code: 335 **Ranks within this company's industry group:** Sales: Profits:

Exploration/Production:		Refining/Retailing:		Utilities:		Alternative Energy:		Specialty Services:		Energy Mktg./Other Svcs.	
Exploration:		Refining:		Electric Utility:		Waste/Solar/Other:		Consulting/Eng.:	Y	Energy Marketing:	
Production:		Retailing:		Gas Utility:		Thermal/Steam:		Seismic:		Equipment/Machinery:	Y
Coal Production:		Convenience Stores:		Pipelines:		Wind:		Drilling:		Oil Field Services:	
		Chemicals:		Water:		Hydro:		InfoTech:		Air/Shipping Transportation:	
						Fuel Cells:		Specialty Services:	Y		

TYPES OF BUSINESS:

Nuclear Power Plant Equipment
Nuclear Power Plant Repair Services
Nuclear Fuel
Nuclear Power Plant Design & Engineering

BRANDS/DIVISIONS/AFFILIATES:

Toshiba Corporation
Westinghouse Nuclear Fuel
KW Nuclear Components Company, Ltd.
CS Innovations LLC
NuCrane Manufacturing LLC
Advance Uranium Asset Management, Ltd.

CONTACTS:

Note: Officers with more than one job title may be intentionally listed here more than once.

Aris Candris, CEO
Aris Candris, Pres.
Masayoshi Hirada, CFO/Sr. VP
Anthony D. Greco, Sr. VP-Human Resources
Kathryn J. Jackson, CTO/Sr. VP
F. Ramsey Coates, General Counsel/Sr. VP-Legal & Contracts
Ricardo Perez, Pres., Oper.
Anthony D. Greco, Sr. VP-Corp. Rel.
Jim Ferland, Pres., Americas
Anders Jackson, Pres., EMEA
Deva Chari, Sr. VP-Nuclear Power Plants
Michael Sweeney, VP/Deputy General Counsel
Shigenori Shiga, Chmn.
Jack Allen, Pres./CEO-Westinghouse Electric Japan

Phone: 412-374-4111 **Fax:** 412-374-3272
Toll-Free:
Address: 4350 Northern Pike, Monroeville, PA 15146-2886 US

GROWTH PLANS/SPECIAL FEATURES:

Westinghouse Electric Company LLC is a wholly-owned subsidiary of Toshiba Corp. The firm provides plant design, services, fuel, technology and equipment to utility, government and industrial clients in the international commercial nuclear electric power market. The firm operates in three segments: nuclear services, nuclear fuel and nuclear power plants. The nuclear services division provides field services such as outage support, component services and training; engineering services that improve plant reliability, including plant analyses and management programs; and installation and modification services, including plant engineering, welding and machining, site installation and decommissioning and dismantling services. The nuclear fuel division, which operates as Westinghouse Nuclear Fuel, offers fuel products, materials and components, services and technology for pressurized water reactors (PWRs), boiling water reactors (BWRs), VVERs, advanced gas-cooled reactors (AGRs) and Magnox reactors. The nuclear power plants division supplies plant design expertise, equipment and component manufacturing for nuclear power plants. Westinghouse has locations in the U.S., the U.K., Europe, South Africa, China and Japan. In February 2009, Westinghouse Electric and Korea Nuclear Fuel Company formed joint venture KW Nuclear Components Company, Ltd. In April 2009, the firm agreed to form a joint venture with State Nuclear Baoti Zirconium Industry Company, Ltd. In August 2009, the company acquired nuclear product supplier CS Innovations LLC and opened a new plant in Tennessee. In September 2009, subsidiary PaR Nuclear and Hutchinson Manufacturing formed joint venture NuCrane Manufacturing LLC. In January 2010, the company opened its European Pump and Motor Maintenance and Repair Center in Belgium. In March 2010, Westinghouse and Toshiba announced a joint venture, Advance Uranium Asset Management, Ltd., a nuclear front end business based in the U.K.

Employee benefits include medical, dental and vision insurance; flexible spending accounts; a savings plan; a pension plan; short and long-term disability coverage; and flexible schedules.

FINANCIALS:

Sales and profits are in thousands of dollars—add 000 to get the full amount. 2010 Note: Financial information for 2010 was not available for all companies at press time.

2010 Sales: $	2010 Profits: $	**U.S. Stock Ticker: Subsidiary**
2009 Sales: $	2009 Profits: $	**Int'l Ticker:** Int'l Exchange:
2008 Sales: $	2008 Profits: $	Employees:
2007 Sales: $	2007 Profits: $	Fiscal Year Ends: 3/31
2006 Sales: $	2006 Profits: $	Parent Company: TOSHIBA CORPORATION

SALARIES/BENEFITS:

Pension Plan: Y	ESOP Stock Plan:	Profit Sharing:	Top Exec. Salary: $	Bonus: $
Savings Plan: Y	Stock Purch. Plan:		Second Exec. Salary: $	Bonus: $

OTHER THOUGHTS:

Apparent Women Officers or Directors: 1
Hot Spot for Advancement for Women/Minorities:

LOCATIONS: ("Y" = Yes)

West:	Southwest:	Midwest:	Southeast:	Northeast:	International:
Y	Y	Y	Y	Y	Y

WESTMORELAND COAL CO

www.westmoreland.com

Industry Group Code: 21211 **Ranks within this company's industry group:** Sales: 14 Profits: 11

Exploration/Production:		Refining/Retailing:		Utilities:		Alternative Energy:		Specialty Services:		Energy Mktg./Other Svcs.	
Exploration:		Refining:		Electric Utility:		Waste/Solar/Other:		Consulting/Eng.:	Y	Energy Marketing:	Y
Production:		Retailing:		Gas Utility:		Thermal/Steam:		Seismic:		Equipment/Machinery:	
Coal Production:	Y	Convenience Stores:		Pipelines:		Wind:		Drilling:		Oil Field Services:	
		Chemicals:		Water:		Hydro:		InfoTech:		Air/Shipping Transportation:	
						Fuel Cells:		Specialty Services:	Y		

TYPES OF BUSINESS:

Coal Mining
Power Plants
Technical Services
Property & Casualty Insurance

BRANDS/DIVISIONS/AFFILIATES:

Westmoreland Mining LLC
Westmoreland Resources Inc
Westmoreland Energy LLC
Westmoreland Technical Services
Absaloka Mine
Westmoreland Coal Sales Company
ROVA

CONTACTS: *Note: Officers with more than one job title may be intentionally listed here more than once.*

Keith E. Alessi, CEO
Keith E. Alessi, Pres.
Kevin A. Paprzycki, CFO
Mary A. Hauck, VP-Human Resources
Thomas G. Durham, VP-Eng.
Mark K. Seglem, VP-Admin.
Morris W. Kegley, General Counsel/Sec.
John V. O'Laughlin, VP-Coal Oper.
Kevin A. Paprzycki, Treas.
Douglas P. Kathol, Exec. VP
Diane S. Kathol, VP-Power & Mining
Richard M. Klingaman, Chmn.

Phone: 719-442-2600 **Fax:** 719-219-2594
Toll-Free:
Address: 2 N. Cascade Ave., 2nd Fl., Colorado Springs, CO 80903 US

GROWTH PLANS/SPECIAL FEATURES:

Westmoreland Coal Co. is an energy company that mines coal and owns power-generating plants. The company produces approximately 30 million tons of coal and generates roughly 1.6 million megawatt-hours (MWH) of electric power annually. Westmoreland Coal sells approximately 24.3 million tons of coal per year. The firm is divided into coal and power operations. The coal operations are headed by Westmoreland Mining, LLC, which through its subsidiaries owns four mining complexes (the Rosebud, Jewett, Savage and Beulah mines) in Montana, North Dakota and Texas; and Westmoreland Resources, Inc., which owns the Absaloka Mine on Montana's Crow Indian Reservation. The firm conducts power operations through its Westmoreland Energy, LLC subsidiary, owner and manager of the Roanoke Valley (ROVA) independent project, which consists of two coal-fired units with 230 megawatts of total generating capacity. These plants deliver based load power to Dominion North Carolina Power. Subsidiary Westmoreland Technical Services provides fuel handling, electrical, mechanical, welding and emergency services to power plants and industrial facilities. The company's wholly-owned subsidiary Westmoreland Coal Sales Company offers market analysis, contract management and the selling of coal to base-load clients.

The firm offers its employees benefits including life, AD&D, health, dental, vision and disability insurance; health savings and flexible spending accounts; a 401(k); an employee assistance program; and a nurse advice line.

FINANCIALS: **Sales and profits are in thousands of dollars—add 000 to get the full amount. 2010 Note: Financial information for 2010 was not available for all companies at press time.**

2010 Sales: $	2010 Profits: $	**U.S. Stock Ticker: WLB**
2009 Sales: $443,368	2009 Profits: $-29,162	**Int'l Ticker:** Int'l Exchange:
2008 Sales: $509,696	2008 Profits: $-48,567	Employees: 1,068
2007 Sales: $504,217	2007 Profits: $-21,793	Fiscal Year Ends: 12/31
2006 Sales: $444,407	2006 Profits: $-12,698	Parent Company:

SALARIES/BENEFITS:

Pension Plan:	ESOP Stock Plan:	Profit Sharing:	Top Exec. Salary: $588,461	Bonus: $720,731
Savings Plan: Y	Stock Purch. Plan:		Second Exec. Salary: $233,287	Bonus: $83,983

OTHER THOUGHTS:

Apparent Women Officers or Directors: 2
Hot Spot for Advancement for Women/Minorities: Y

LOCATIONS: ("Y" = Yes)

West:	Southwest:	Midwest:	Southeast:	Northeast:	International:
Y	Y	Y		Y	

WGL HOLDINGS INC

www.wglholdings.com

Industry Group Code: 221 **Ranks within this company's industry group:** Sales: 41 Profits: 43

Exploration/Production:		Refining/Retailing:		Utilities:		Alternative Energy:		Specialty Services:		Energy Mktg./Other Svcs.	
Exploration:		Refining:		Electric Utility:		Waste/Solar/Other:		Consulting/Eng.:		Energy Marketing:	Y
Production:		Retailing:		Gas Utility:	Y	Thermal/Steam:		Seismic:		Equipment/Machinery:	Y
Coal Production:		Convenience Stores:		Pipelines:		Wind:		Drilling:		Oil Field Services:	
		Chemicals:		Water:		Hydro:		InfoTech:		Air/Shipping Transportation:	
						Fuel Cells:		Specialty Services:	Y		

TYPES OF BUSINESS:

Natural Gas Utility
Energy Marketing
Residential & Light Commercial Services
Energy Systems Design & Engineering
Energy Systems Upgrading

BRANDS/DIVISIONS/AFFILIATES:

Washington Gas Light Co.
Hampshire Gas Co.
Crab Run Gas Co.
Washington Gas Resources Corp.
Washington Gas Energy Services, Inc.
Washington Gas Energy Systems, Inc.
Washington Gas Credit Corp.

CONTACTS: *Note: Officers with more than one job title may be intentionally listed here more than once.*

Terry McCallister, CEO
Adrian P. Chapman, COO
Adrian P. Chapman, Pres.
Vincent L. Ammann, Jr., CFO/VP
Beverly J. Burke, General Counsel/VP
Gautam Chandra, VP-Bus. Dev., Strategy & Bus. Process Outsourcing
Eric C. Grant, Dir.-Corp. Comm.
Robert L. Dennis, Dir.-Investor Rel.
Mark P. O'Flynn, VP-Finance
Anthony Nee, Treas.
Arden T. Phillips, Sec./Corp. Governance. Officer
William R. Ford, Controller
Terry McCallister, Chmn.

Phone: 703-750-2000 **Fax:**
Toll-Free:
Address: 101 Constitution Ave. NW, Washington, DC 20080 US

GROWTH PLANS/SPECIAL FEATURES:

WGL Holdings, Inc. is a public utility holding company that, through its subsidiaries, sells and delivers natural gas and provides a variety of energy-related products and services to customers primarily in Washington, D.C. and the surrounding metropolitan areas in Maryland and Virginia. The firm operates in three business segments: regulated utility; retail energy marketing; and design-build energy systems, through subsidiaries Washington Gas Light Co.; Washington Gas Resources Corp.; Hampshire Gas Co.; and Crab Run Gas Co. Washington Gas is a regulated public utility that delivers and sells natural gas to more than one million customers in Washington, D.C., Maryland and Virginia. Washington Gas Resources owns most of the company's unregulated subsidiaries, including Washington Gas Energy Services, Inc. (WGE Services); Washington Gas Energy Systems, Inc. (WGE Systems); and Washington Gas Credit Corp. WGE Services is engaged solely in the sale of natural gas and electricity to residential, commercial and industrial customers; it does not own or operate any natural gas or electric generation, production, transmission or distribution assets. WGE Services serves approximately 190,000 customers. WGE Systems is a provider of design-build energy efficient and sustainable solutions to government and commercial clients. It focuses on upgrading the mechanical, electrical, water and energy-related systems of large government and commercial facilities in Maryland, Virginia and Washington, D.C. Hampshire Gas is a regulated utility that operates underground natural gas storage facilities, including pipeline delivery facilities, in West Virginia. Crab Run is an exploration and production company. In January 2010, WGE Services announced it would expand its operations into the Pennsylvania market.

FINANCIALS: **Sales and profits are in thousands of dollars—add 000 to get the full amount. 2010 Note: Financial information for 2010 was not available for all companies at press time.**

2010 Sales: $
2009 Sales: $2,706,856
2008 Sales: $2,628,194
2007 Sales: $2,646,008
2006 Sales: $2,637,883

2010 Profits: $
2009 Profits: $120,373
2008 Profits: $116,523
2007 Profits: $107,900
2006 Profits: $87,578

U.S. Stock Ticker: WGL
Int'l Ticker: Int'l Exchange:
Employees: 1,410
Fiscal Year Ends: 9/30
Parent Company:

SALARIES/BENEFITS:

Pension Plan: ESOP Stock Plan: Profit Sharing: Top Exec. Salary: $760,000 Bonus: $821,940
Savings Plan: Y Stock Purch. Plan: Second Exec. Salary: $485,000 Bonus: $449,595

OTHER THOUGHTS:

Apparent Women Officers or Directors: 3
Hot Spot for Advancement for Women/Minorities: Y

LOCATIONS: ("Y" = Yes)

West:	Southwest:	Midwest:	Southeast:	Northeast:	International:
				Y	

WILLBROS GROUP INC

www.willbros.com

Industry Group Code: 541330 **Ranks within this company's industry group:** Sales: 3 Profits: 3

Exploration/Production:		Refining/Retailing:		Utilities:		Alternative Energy:		Specialty Services:		Energy Mktg./Other Svcs.	
Exploration:		Refining:		Electric Utility:		Waste/Solar/Other:		Consulting/Eng.:	Y	Energy Marketing:	
Production:		Retailing:		Gas Utility:		Thermal/Steam:		Seismic:		Equipment/Machinery:	
Coal Production:		Convenience Stores:		Pipelines:		Wind:		Drilling:		Oil Field Services:	Y
		Chemicals:		Water:		Hydro:		InfoTech:		Air/Shipping Transportation:	Y
						Fuel Cells:		Specialty Services:	Y		

TYPES OF BUSINESS:

Oil Industry Engineering
Construction & Engineering Services
Pipeline & Infrastructure Construction
Project Management
Transport Services
Procurement Services
Electricity & Natural Gas Transmission & Distribution

BRANDS/DIVISIONS/AFFILIATES:

Willbros USA, Inc.
Willbros Construction
Willbros Engineering
InServ
Oman Construction Company LLC (The)
Willbros Canada Inc.
Wink Companies LLC
InfrastruX Group, Inc.

CONTACTS: *Note: Officers with more than one job title may be intentionally listed here more than once.*

Randy Harl, CEO
Randy Harl, COO
Randy Harl, Pres.
Van Welch, CFO/Sr. VP
Michael W. Collier, VP-Mktg. & Sales
Gordon Hagendorf, VP-Human Resources
Ed Wiegele, Pres., Willbros Eng.
Peter W. Arbour, General Counsel/Sr. VP/Corp. Sec.
Connie Dever, Dir.-Strategic Planning
Michael W. Collier, VP-Investor Rel.
Ronald A. Lefaive, Controller
James R. Beasley, Sr. VP-Willbros USA
Kevin Kox, Pres., Willbros US Construction
Jerrit M. Coward, Pres., Upstream Oil & Gas
James L. Gibson, Pres., Willbros Downstream
John T. McNabb, II, Chmn.
Kevin Fleury, Pres., Willbros Canada
Rafael Marrero, VP-Global Procurement

Phone: 713-403-8000	**Fax:**
Toll-Free:	
Address: 4400 Post Oak Pkwy., Ste. 1000, Houston, TX 77027 US	

GROWTH PLANS/SPECIAL FEATURES:

Willbros Group, Inc. is an independent contractor serving the oil and gas, refinery and petrochemical industries. The firm provides engineering; construction; engineering, procurement and construction (EPC); and specialty services to industry and governmental entities worldwide, specializing in pipelines and associated facility services. The company operates in two segments: upstream oil and gas; and downstream oil and gas. The upstream segment provides full EPC services, as well as individual engineering, procurement and construction services, for the design and construction of large-diameter pipelines, engineered structures, process modules and facilities. The downstream segment provides specialty construction, turnaround, repair and maintenance services primarily to refineries and petrochemical facilities. This segment also builds oil and gas production facilities, pump stations, flow stations, gas compressor stations, gas processing facilities, gathering lines and related facilities. The company has completed numerous landmark projects around the world and has been employed by more than 400 clients to carry out work in 60 countries. In Canada, services are provided by Willbros Canada, Inc. In Oman, The Oman Construction Company provides oil field maintenance; field gathering and processing construction; and mainline pipeline construction services. In the U.S., through Willbros Construction, Willbros Engineering and InServ, the company provides project management, engineering, procurement and construction services on a stand-alone basis or through collaboration with other Willbros units or third parties. In July 2010, the company acquired InfrastruX Group, Inc., a leading national provider of electric power and natural gas transmission and distribution infrastructure services in the South Central, Midwest and East Coast energy corridors. The newly acquired company will operate as a discrete segment of Willbros' operations.

Willbros offers its employees medical, dental and prescription drug plans; flexible spending accounts; voluntary life insurance; a 401(k) plan; and flexible work schedules.

FINANCIALS: **Sales and profits are in thousands of dollars—add 000 to get the full amount. 2010 Note: Financial information for 2010 was not available for all companies at press time.**

2010 Sales: $	2010 Profits: $	**U.S. Stock Ticker: WG**
2009 Sales: $1,259,818	2009 Profits: $19,640	**Int'l Ticker:** Int'l Exchange:
2008 Sales: $1,912,704	2008 Profits: $46,487	Employees: 3,714
2007 Sales: $947,691	2007 Profits: $-48,964	Fiscal Year Ends: 12/31
2006 Sales: $543,259	2006 Profits: $-105,437	Parent Company:

SALARIES/BENEFITS:

Pension Plan: Y	ESOP Stock Plan:	Profit Sharing:	Top Exec. Salary: $700,000	Bonus: $
Savings Plan: Y	Stock Purch. Plan:		Second Exec. Salary: $409,008	Bonus: $

OTHER THOUGHTS:

Apparent Women Officers or Directors: 1
Hot Spot for Advancement for Women/Minorities:

LOCATIONS: ("Y" = Yes)

West:	Southwest:	Midwest:	Southeast:	Northeast:	International:
	Y	Y	Y		Y

WILLIAMS COMPANIES INC (THE)

www.williams.com

Industry Group Code: 211111 **Ranks within this company's industry group:** Sales: 53 Profits: 54

Exploration/Production:		Refining/Retailing:		Utilities:		Alternative Energy:		Specialty Services:		Energy Mktg./Other Svcs.	
Exploration:	Y	Refining:		Electric Utility:		Waste/Solar/Other:		Consulting/Eng.:		Energy Marketing:	
Production:	Y	Retailing:		Gas Utility:		Thermal/Steam:		Seismic:		Equipment/Machinery:	
Coal Production:		Convenience Stores:		Pipelines:	Y	Wind:		Drilling:		Oil Field Services:	
		Chemicals:		Water:		Hydro:		InfoTech:		Air/Shipping Transportation:	
						Fuel Cells:		Specialty Services:			

TYPES OF BUSINESS:

Gas Exploration & Production
Natural Gas Transportation
Pipelines
Wholesale Power

BRANDS/DIVISIONS/AFFILIATES:

Williams Production Co LLC
Williams Production RMT Co
Williams Gas Pipeline Co LLC
Williams Field Services Group LLC
Laurel Mountain Midstream LLC
Williams Partners LP
Williams Natural Gas Liquids Inc
Midstream Gas & Liquids

CONTACTS:

Note: Officers with more than one job title may be intentionally listed here more than once.

Steven J. Malcomb, CEO
Steven J. Malcomb, Pres.
Don R. Chappel, CFO/Sr. VP
Ralph A. Hill, Pres., Exploration
Ralph A. Hill, Pres., Prod.
Robyn L. Ewing, Chief Admin. Officer/Sr. VP-Admin.
James J. Bender, General Counsel/Sr. VP
Robyn L. Ewing, Sr. VP-Strategic Svcs.
Chris Stockton, Contact-Media Rel.
Richard George, Contact-Investor Rel.
Alan Armstrong, Pres., Midstream Gathering & Processing
Phillip D. Wright, Pres., Gas Pipeline
Sharna Reingold, Contact-Investor Rel.
Steven J. Malcolm, Chmn.

Phone: 918-573-2000 **Fax:** 918-573-6714
Toll-Free: 800-945-5426
Address: 1 Williams Ctr., Tulsa, OK 74172 US

GROWTH PLANS/SPECIAL FEATURES:

The Williams Companies, Inc., finds, produces, gathers, processes and transports natural gas. The firm operates in five segments: exploration and production; gas pipeline; midstream gas and liquids; gas marketing services; and other. The exploration and production segment produces, develops and manages natural gas reserves primarily located in the Rocky Mountain and Mid-Continent regions of the U.S. It is operated through subsidiaries such as Williams Production RMT Company and Williams Production Company LLC. The gas pipeline segment includes natural gas pipelines and pipeline joint venture investments organized under subsidiaries Williams Gas Pipeline Co., LLC, and Williams Pipeline Partners L.P. The midstream and gas liquids segment includes its natural gas gathering, treating and processing business; it is comprised of several subsidiaries, including Williams Natural Gas Liquids, Inc.; Midstream Gas & Liquids; Williams Field Services Group LLC; and Williams Partners L.P. The gas marketing services segment manages the firm's natural gas commodity risk through purchases, sales and other related transactions through subsidiary Williams Gas Marketing, Inc. The other segment primarily consists of corporate operations. The company owns holdings in several production basins, including the Piceance Basin in Colorado, the San Juan Basin in New Mexico, Barnett Shale in Texas, the Powder River Basin in Wyoming and the Arkoma Basin in Arkansas and Oklahoma. In June 2009, Williams and Atlas Pipeline Partners L.P. formed joint venture Laurel Mountain Midstream LLC. In April 2009, the company agreed to build a new pipeline in Alberta, Canada. In August 2009, the firm agreed to buy 21,800 additional acres in the Piceance Valley for $258 million. In September 2009, the company sold Longhorn Partners Pipeline, L.P., to Magellan Midstream Partners, L.P., for $250 million. In May 2010, the firm announced the signing of a merger agreement between subsidiaries Williams Partners L.P. and Williams Pipeline Partners L.P.

FINANCIALS:

Sales and profits are in thousands of dollars—add 000 to get the full amount. 2010 Note: Financial information for 2010 was not available for all companies at press time.

2010 Sales: $	2010 Profits: $	**U.S. Stock Ticker: WMB**
2009 Sales: $8,255,000	2009 Profits: $361,000	**Int'l Ticker:** Int'l Exchange:
2008 Sales: $11,890,000	2008 Profits: $1,418,000	Employees: 4,801
2007 Sales: $10,239,000	2007 Profits: $990,000	Fiscal Year Ends: 12/31
2006 Sales: $9,376,000	2006 Profits: $309,000	Parent Company:

SALARIES/BENEFITS:

Pension Plan: Y	ESOP Stock Plan:	Profit Sharing:	Top Exec. Salary: $1,142,308	Bonus: $1,903,360
Savings Plan: Y	Stock Purch. Plan:		Second Exec. Salary: $623,077	Bonus: $765,047

OTHER THOUGHTS:

Apparent Women Officers or Directors: 5
Hot Spot for Advancement for Women/Minorities: Y

LOCATIONS: ("Y" = Yes)

West:	Southwest:	Midwest:	Southeast:	Northeast:	International:
Y	Y	Y	Y	Y	Y

WINTERSHALL AG

www.wintershall.de

Industry Group Code: 211111 **Ranks within this company's industry group:** Sales: Profits:

Exploration/Production:		Refining/Retailing:		Utilities:		Alternative Energy:		Specialty Services:		Energy Mktg./Other Svcs.	
Exploration:	Y	Refining:		Electric Utility:	Y	Waste/Solar/Other:		Consulting/Eng.:		Energy Marketing:	
Production:	Y	Retailing:		Gas Utility:		Thermal/Steam:		Seismic:		Equipment/Machinery:	
Coal Production:		Convenience Stores:		Pipelines:		Wind:		Drilling:		Oil Field Services:	
		Chemicals:		Water:		Hydro:		InfoTech:		Air/Shipping Transportation:	
						Fuel Cells:		Specialty Services:			

TYPES OF BUSINESS:

Oil & Gas Exploration & Production
Oil & Gas Trading
Oil & Gas Storage & Transportation
Electric Utilities

BRANDS/DIVISIONS/AFFILIATES:

BASF AG
Wintershall Erdgas Handelshaus GmbH
Wintershall Erdgas Handelshaus Zug AG
WINGAS GmbH
Nord Stream

CONTACTS: *Note: Officers with more than one job title may be intentionally listed here more than once.*

Andreas Priefler, Dir.-Comm. & Gov't Rel.
Reinhard Solter, Mgr.-Wintershall Oil AG
Michael Sasse, Head-Public Rel.
Rainer Seele, Chmn.

Phone: 49-561-301-0	**Fax:** 49-561-301-1702
Toll-Free:	
Address: Friedrich-Ebert-Strasse 160, Kassel, 34119 Germany	

GROWTH PLANS/SPECIAL FEATURES:

Wintershall AG, a wholly-owned subsidiary of BASF AG, is a major crude oil and natural gas producer in Germany. The firm is active in exploration, production and trading of crude oil and natural gas. The firm operates crude oil and natural gas storage facilities and offers natural gas transportation. Wintershall conducts oil and natural gas exploration and production in Germany, North Africa and South America; as well as hydrocarbons production and exploration in Russia and the Caspian Sea. The firm has two electric utility joint ventures with OAO Gazprom: Wintershall Erdgas Handelshaus GmbH and Wintershall Erdgas Handelshaus Zug AG. Additionally, Wintershall owns a majority stake in natural gas transportation subsidiary WINGAS GmbH, which operates nearly 1,250 miles of natural gas pipeline. Wintershall has a cooperation agreement with Hydro, Inc. for the exploration of oil and gas in Libya. The two companies also intend to cooperate on exploration in parts of the Norwegian continental shelf. Wintershall has a 24% interest in the Nord Stream pipeline project, which will provide gas imports for Germany and Western Europe. In April 2009, the firm opened a new office in Abu Dhabi, U.A.E. In November 2009, the company invested $7.1 million to build a 45 million kilowatt-per-year heat and power generator at its Emlichheim site in Germany.

Wintershall offers employees mentoring, professional development, career advancement and reintegration programs; child care assistance; flexible working hours; legal assistance; and a stock option plan established by BASF.

FINANCIALS: **Sales and profits are in thousands of dollars—add 000 to get the full amount. 2010 Note: Financial information for 2010 was not available for all companies at press time.**

2010 Sales: $	2010 Profits: $	**U.S. Stock Ticker: Subsidiary**
2009 Sales: $	2009 Profits: $	**Int'l Ticker:** Int'l Exchange:
2008 Sales: $	2008 Profits: $	Employees:
2007 Sales: $	2007 Profits: $	Fiscal Year Ends: 12/31
2006 Sales: $	2006 Profits: $	Parent Company: BASF SE

SALARIES/BENEFITS:

Pension Plan:	ESOP Stock Plan:	Profit Sharing:	Top Exec. Salary: $	Bonus: $
Savings Plan:	Stock Purch. Plan:		Second Exec. Salary: $	Bonus: $

OTHER THOUGHTS:

Apparent Women Officers or Directors:
Hot Spot for Advancement for Women/Minorities:

LOCATIONS: ("Y" = Yes)

West:	Southwest:	Midwest:	Southeast:	Northeast:	International:
					Y

WISCONSIN ENERGY CORP

www.wisconsinenergy.com

Industry Group Code: 221 **Ranks within this company's industry group:** Sales: 31 Profits: 26

Exploration/Production:		Refining/Retailing:		Utilities:		Alternative Energy:		Specialty Services:		Energy Mktg./Other Svcs.	
Exploration:		Refining:		Electric Utility:	Y	Waste/Solar/Other:		Consulting/Eng.:		Energy Marketing:	Y
Production:		Retailing:		Gas Utility:	Y	Thermal/Steam:		Seismic:		Equipment/Machinery:	
Coal Production:		Convenience Stores:		Pipelines:		Wind:		Drilling:		Oil Field Services:	
		Chemicals:		Water:	Y	Hydro:		InfoTech:		Air/Shipping Transportation:	
						Fuel Cells:		Specialty Services:	Y		

TYPES OF BUSINESS:

Utilities-Electricity & Natural Gas
Non-utility Energy
Real Estate Development

BRANDS/DIVISIONS/AFFILIATES:

Wisconsin Gas LLC
Wisconsin Electric Power Company
Blue Sky Green
We Energies
WE Power LLC
Wispark LLC
American Transmission Company
Power the Future

CONTACTS: *Note: Officers with more than one job title may be intentionally listed here more than once.*

Gale E. Klappa, CEO
Gale E. Klappa, Pres.
Allen L. Leverett, CFO/Exec. VP
Kristine Rappe, Chief Admin. Officer/Sr. VP
James C. Fleming, General Counsel/Exec. VP
Jeffrey P. West, Treas./VP
Frederick D. Kuester, Exec. VP
Susan H. Martin, VP/Corp. Sec./Associate General Counsel
Stephen P. Dickson, Controller/VP
Darnell DeMasters, VP-Federal Policy
Gale E. Klappa, Chmn.

Phone: 414-221-2345 **Fax:** 414-221-2554
Toll-Free:
Address: 231 W. Michigan St., Milwaukee, WI 53201 US

GROWTH PLANS/SPECIAL FEATURES:

Wisconsin Energy Corp. is a diversified energy holding company. The firm conducts operations primarily in two operating segments: Utility energy and non-utility energy. The utility energy segment consists of Wisconsin Electric Power Company and Wisconsin Gas LLC. Wisconsin Electric and Wisconsin Gas operate under the trade name We Energies. The segments serves roughly 1.117 million electric customers in Wisconsin and Michigan's Upper Peninsula; 465 steam customers in Metro Milwaukee, Wisconsin; and more than 1 million gas customers throughout Wisconsin. The non-utility energy segment consists primarily of W.E. Power, LLC, which designs, constructs, owns and leases to Wisconsin Electric generating capacity. Another operating subsidiary, Wispark, LLC, develops and invests in real estate. Business affiliates of the company include American Transmission Company, which owns, operates and maintains electric transmission assets in Wisconsin, Illinois and Michigan. Wisconsin Energy Corp. owns approximately 26.2% of American Transmission Company. Power the Future, the company's created strategy, aims to improve the supply and reliability of electricity in Wisconsin through investments and upgrades in generation facilities and distribution over several years. Wisconsin Energy's Blue Sky Green field wind project consists of 88 Vestas Wind Systems turbines that cover 10,600 acres and are able to generate roughly 145 emission-free megawatt hours annually. In May 2010, Wisconsin Energy Corp. sold subsidiary Edison Sault Electric Company to Cloverland Electric Cooperative for roughly $63 million.

FINANCIALS: **Sales and profits are in thousands of dollars—add 000 to get the full amount. 2010 Note: Financial information for 2010 was not available for all companies at press time.**

2010 Sales: $
2009 Sales: $4,127,900
2008 Sales: $4,427,800
2007 Sales: $4,237,800
2006 Sales: $3,996,400

2010 Profits: $
2009 Profits: $382,400
2008 Profits: $359,100
2007 Profits: $335,600
2006 Profits: $316,400

U.S. Stock Ticker: WEC
Int'l Ticker: Int'l Exchange:
Employees: 4,692
Fiscal Year Ends: 12/31
Parent Company:

SALARIES/BENEFITS:

Pension Plan: ESOP Stock Plan: Profit Sharing: Top Exec. Salary: $1,129,008 Bonus: $2,286,241
Savings Plan: Stock Purch. Plan: Second Exec. Salary: $657,000 Bonus: $1,064,340

OTHER THOUGHTS:

Apparent Women Officers or Directors: 5
Hot Spot for Advancement for Women/Minorities: Y

LOCATIONS: ("Y" = Yes)

West:	Southwest:	Midwest:	Southeast:	Northeast:	International:
		Y			

WOODSIDE PETROLEUM LTD

www.woodside.com.au

Industry Group Code: 211111 **Ranks within this company's industry group:** Sales: 60 Profits: 29

Exploration/Production:		Refining/Retailing:		Utilities:		Alternative Energy:		Specialty Services:		Energy Mktg./Other Svcs.	
Exploration:	Y	Refining:		Electric Utility:		Waste/Solar/Other:		Consulting/Eng.:		Energy Marketing:	
Production:	Y	Retailing:		Gas Utility:		Thermal/Steam:		Seismic:		Equipment/Machinery:	
Coal Production:		Convenience Stores:		Pipelines:		Wind:		Drilling:		Oil Field Services:	
		Chemicals:		Water:		Hydro:		InfoTech:		Air/Shipping Transportation:	
						Fuel Cells:		Specialty Services:	Y		

TYPES OF BUSINESS:

Oil & Gas Exploration & Production
LNG Processing

BRANDS/DIVISIONS/AFFILIATES:

North West Shelf Project
Pluto-Xena Project
Neptune Project
Woodside Natural Gas, Inc.

CONTACTS: *Note: Officers with more than one job title may be intentionally listed here more than once.*

Don R. Voelte, CEO/Managing Dir.
Mark Chatterji, CFO/Exec. VP
Reinhardt Matisons, Pres., Mktg.
Tina Thomas, VP-Human Resources
Peter Moore, Sr. VP-Exploration
Vince Santostefano, Exec. VP-Production
Rob Cole, General Counsel/Exec. VP-Corp. Center
Mike Lynn, VP-Investor Rel.
Feisal Ahmed, Exec. VP-Project Dev.
Lucio Della Martina, Exec. VP-Pluto
Eve Howell, Exec. VP-Health, Safety & Security
Michael A. Chaney, Chmn.

Phone: 61-8-9348-4000 **Fax:** 61-8-9214-2777
Toll-Free:
Address: 240 St. Georges Terrace, Perth, 6000 Australia

GROWTH PLANS/SPECIAL FEATURES:

Woodside Petroleum Ltd. is an oil and gas exploration and production company based in Australia. The company produces natural gas, crude oil, liquefied natural gas (LNG), condensate and liquefied petroleum gas (LPG). Woodside's primary region of focus is Australia, with additional operations in Africa and the U.S. The firm is currently conducting exploration activities in Western Australia, the Timor Sea and Victoria, as well as in Libya, Sierra Leone, Liberia, Brazil and Korea. The company's major customer centers are located in India, China, Korea and Japan, with new market expansion in Pakistan, Thailand and Singapore. The company produced about 80 million barrels of oil equivalent (Mmboe) in 2009, of which 54% was natural gas, 32% was oil and the remaining 14% was condensate. The firm's proved plus probable reserves total roughly 1.65 billion barrels of oil equivalent, of which approximately 83% is natural gas. In 2009, oil accounted for approximately 45% of the company's total revenue; natural gas accounted for 38% of revenue; and condensate, 17%. Woodside owns the North West Shelf Project (NWSP), which explores, develops and manages gas, oil and condensate reserves off the northeast shore of Australia, producing natural gas and liquefied natural gas that account for more than 40% of Australia's hydrocarbon production. The NWSP includes proved plus probable reserves of 700 Mmboe. A second major project, the Pluto-Xena LNG Project in Australia, is expected to begin producing by the end of 2010. The Pluto-Xena Project has proved plus probable reserves of 780 Mmboe. In March 2010, the firm sold its operating interest in the Otway Gas Project in Victoria to Origin Energy Resources Ltd.

FINANCIALS: **Sales and profits are in thousands of dollars—add 000 to get the full amount. 2010 Note: Financial information for 2010 was not available for all companies at press time.**

2010 Sales: $	2010 Profits: $	**U.S. Stock Ticker: WOPEY**
2009 Sales: $4,418,850	2009 Profits: $1,852,020	**Int'l Ticker: WPL** Int'l Exchange: Sydney-ASX
2008 Sales: $5,503,670	2008 Profits: $1,641,000	Employees: 3,124
2007 Sales: $3,529,150	2007 Profits: $946,370	Fiscal Year Ends: 12/31
2006 Sales: $2,840,000	2006 Profits: $1,120,000	Parent Company:

SALARIES/BENEFITS:

Pension Plan:	ESOP Stock Plan:	Profit Sharing:	Top Exec. Salary: $501,775	Bonus: $
Savings Plan:	Stock Purch. Plan:		Second Exec. Salary: $254,570	Bonus: $

OTHER THOUGHTS:

Apparent Women Officers or Directors: 3
Hot Spot for Advancement for Women/Minorities: Y

LOCATIONS: ("Y" = Yes)

West:	Southwest:	Midwest:	Southeast:	Northeast:	International:
	Y		Y		Y

WORLD FUEL SERVICES CORP

www.wfscorp.com

Industry Group Code: 424710 **Ranks within this company's industry group:** Sales: 1 Profits: 3

Exploration/Production:		Refining/Retailing:		Utilities:		Alternative Energy:		Specialty Services:		Energy Mktg./Other Svcs.	
Exploration:		Refining:		Electric Utility:		Waste/Solar/Other:		Consulting/Eng.:		Energy Marketing:	
Production:		Retailing:	Y	Gas Utility:		Thermal/Steam:		Seismic:		Equipment/Machinery:	
Coal Production:		Convenience Stores:		Pipelines:		Wind:		Drilling:		Oil Field Services:	
		Chemicals:		Water:		Hydro:		InfoTech:		Air/Shipping Transportation:	
						Fuel Cells:		Specialty Services:	Y		

TYPES OF BUSINESS:

Aviation & Marine Fuel Products
Fuel-Related Services
Price Risk Management
Logistics Services
Aviation Services

BRANDS/DIVISIONS/AFFILIATES:

World Fuel
Trans-Tec
Bunkerfuels
Oil Shipping
Marine Energy
Norse Bunker
Casa Petro
Tramp Oil

CONTACTS: *Note: Officers with more than one job title may be intentionally listed here more than once.*

Paul H. Stebbins, CEO
Michael J. Kasbar, COO
Michael J. Kasbar, Pres.
Ira M. Birns, CFO/Exec. VP
Francis X. Shea, Chief Admin. Officer/Exec. VP
R. Alexander Lake, General Counsel/Corp. Sec.
Paul M. Nobel, Chief Acct. Officer/Sr. VP
Michael S. Clementi, Pres., World Fuel Svcs., Inc.
Francis X. Shea, Chief Risk Officer
Paul H. Stebbins, Chmn.

Phone: 305-428-8000	**Fax:** 305-392-5600
Toll-Free:	
Address: 9800 NW 41st St., Ste. 400, Miami, FL 33178 US	

GROWTH PLANS/SPECIAL FEATURES:

World Fuel Services Corp. markets and sells fuel products and related services worldwide. The company operates in three segments: marine, aviation and land. The marine segment markets fuel and related services to a broad base of customers, including international container and tanker fleets; time-charter operators; and U.S. and foreign governments. Marine-related services include management services for the procurement of fuel, cost control through the use of price hedging instruments, quality control and claims management. The division offers its products and services under the brand names Norse Bunker, Bunkerfuels, Oil Shipping, World Fuel, Trans-Tec, Marine Energy, Casa Petro and Tramp Oil. The aviation segment markets fuel and related services to major commercial airlines; regional and low cost carriers; the U.S. and foreign governments; second- and third-tier airlines; cargo carriers; corporate fleets; fractional operators; private aircraft; and military fleets. Aviation related services include fuel and price risk management; and arranging ground handling and international trip planning, including flight plans, weather reports and overflight permits. Its trade brands include World Fuel, PetroServicios de Costa Rica, Tramp Oil, Baseops, PAFCO, PetroServicios de Mexico Airdata and AVCARD. The land segment markets fuel and related services to petroleum distributors operating in the land transportation market. Land-related services include management services for the procurement of fuel, price risk management and financing. The land division also operates a small number of retail gas stations and offers branded/unbranded gasoline and diesel fuel to retail petroleum operators and industrial, commercial and government clients. Its trade names are Tobras, World Fuel, Henty Oil and Texor. World Fuel Services has offices in North America, South America, Europe, Asia, Africa and the Middle East. In July 2010, the firm acquired certain assets of Lakeside Oil Company, including its wholesale motor fuel distribution operations. In October 2010, the company acquired the assets of Western Petroleum Company.

FINANCIALS: **Sales and profits are in thousands of dollars—add 000 to get the full amount. 2010 Note: Financial information for 2010 was not available for all companies at press time.**

2010 Sales: $	2010 Profits: $	**U.S. Stock Ticker: INT**
2009 Sales: $11,295,177	2009 Profits: $117,139	**Int'l Ticker:** Int'l Exchange:
2008 Sales: $18,509,403	2008 Profits: $105,039	Employees:
2007 Sales: $13,729,555	2007 Profits: $64,773	Fiscal Year Ends: 12/31
2006 Sales: $10,785,136	2006 Profits: $63,948	Parent Company:

SALARIES/BENEFITS:

Pension Plan:	ESOP Stock Plan:	Profit Sharing:	Top Exec. Salary: $575,000	Bonus: $580,616
Savings Plan: Y	Stock Purch. Plan:		Second Exec. Salary: $575,000	Bonus: $580,616

OTHER THOUGHTS:

Apparent Women Officers or Directors:
Hot Spot for Advancement for Women/Minorities:

LOCATIONS: ("Y" = Yes)

West:	Southwest:	Midwest:	Southeast:	Northeast:	International:
Y	Y		Y	Y	Y

XCEL ENERGY INC

www.xcelenergy.com

Industry Group Code: 221 **Ranks within this company's industry group:** Sales: 16 Profits: 17

Exploration/Production:		**Refining/Retailing:**		**Utilities:**		**Alternative Energy:**		**Specialty Services:**		**Energy Mktg./Other Svcs.**	
Exploration:		Refining:		Electric Utility:	Y	Waste/Solar/Other:	Y	Consulting/Eng.:		Energy Marketing:	Y
Production:		Retailing:		Gas Utility:	Y	Thermal/Steam:		Seismic:		Equipment/Machinery:	
Coal Production:		Convenience Stores:		Pipelines:	Y	Wind:	Y	Drilling:		Oil Field Services:	
		Chemicals:		Water:		Hydro:	Y	InfoTech:		Air/Shipping Transportation:	
						Fuel Cells:		Specialty Services:			

TYPES OF BUSINESS:

Utilities-Electricity & Natural Gas
Natural Gas Pipelines
Wind Power
Broadband Telecommunications Services
Hydroelectricity
Rental Property Investment

BRANDS/DIVISIONS/AFFILIATES:

Northern States Power Company Minnesota
Northern States Power Company Wisconsin
Public Service Company of Colorado
Southwestern Public Service Company
WestGas InterState, Inc.
Eloigne Company

CONTACTS:

Note: Officers with more than one job title may be intentionally listed here more than once.

Richard C. Kelly, CEO
Benjamin G.S. Fowke, III, COO
Benjamin G.S. Fowke III, Pres.
David M. Sparby, CFO
Dennis L. Koehl, Chief Nuclear Officer/VP
Marvin McDaniel, Jr., Chief Admin. Officer/VP
Michael C. Connelly, General Counsel/VP
Cathy J. Hart, VP-Corp. Svcs. & Corp. Comm./Corp. Sec.
Paul A. Johnson, Managing Dir.-Investor Rel./Assistant Treas.
Teresa S. Madden, Controller/VP
Judy M. Poferl, Pres./CEO-Northern States Power Co. (Minnesota)
David L. Eves, Pres./CEO-Public Service Co. of Colorado
Riley Hill, Pres./CEO-Southwestern Public Service Co.
Michael L. Swenson, Pres./CEO-Northern States Power Co. (Wisconsin)
Richard C. Kelly, Chmn.

Phone: 612-330-5500	**Fax:** 612-330-5878
Toll-Free: 800-328-8226	
Address: 414 Nicollet Mall, Minneapolis, MN 55401 US	

GROWTH PLANS/SPECIAL FEATURES:

Xcel Energy, Inc. is a holding company primarily engaged in the utility business. The firm owns more than 34,500 miles of natural gas pipelines and services 3.4 million electricity customers and 1.9 million natural gas customers. The firm operates primarily through the following subsidiaries: Northern States Power Company Minnesota (NSP-Minnesota); Northern States Power Company Wisconsin (NSP-Wisconsin); Public Service Company of Colorado (PSCo); Southwestern Public Service Company (SPS); and WestGas Interstate, Inc., a Colorado corporation operating an interstate natural gas pipeline. Together, these subsidiaries serve electric and natural gas customers in eight states: Colorado, Michigan, Minnesota, New Mexico, North Dakota, South Dakota, Texas and Wisconsin. NSP-Minnesota generates, purchases, transmits, distributes and sells electricity in Minnesota, North Dakota and South Dakota. NSP-Wisconsin generates, transmits and distributes electricity in portions of northwestern Wisconsin and the western portion of the Upper Peninsula in Michigan. It also purchases, transports, distributes and sells natural gas to retail customers and transports customer-owned natural gas within the same territory. PSCo provides electricity and natural gas in Colorado and transports customer-owned natural gas. SPS provides electric utility services in portions of Texas and New Mexico. The firm also owns or has an interest in a number of non-regulated businesses, such as Eloigne Company, which invests in rental housing projects qualifying for low-income housing tax credits. The company has been working to develop reliance on sustainable energy sources, and is currently among the largest providers of wind energy in the U.S. In April 2010, PSCo announced intentions to purchase two power plant currently operated by Calpine Corp.

Xcel Energy offers employee benefits that include medical, dental and vision coverage; life and disability insurance; long term disability insurance; health care and dependent care reimbursement accounts; transportation reimbursement accounts; a pension plan; and a 401(k) savings plan with a company match.

FINANCIALS:

Sales and profits are in thousands of dollars—add 000 to get the full amount. 2010 Note: Financial information for 2010 was not available for all companies at press time.

2010 Sales: $	2010 Profits: $	**U.S. Stock Ticker: XEL**
2009 Sales: $9,644,303	2009 Profits: $680,887	**Int'l Ticker:** Int'l Exchange:
2008 Sales: $11,203,156	2008 Profits: $645,554	Employees: 11,351
2007 Sales: $10,034,000	2007 Profits: $577,000	Fiscal Year Ends: 12/31
2006 Sales: $9,840,304	2006 Profits: $571,754	Parent Company:

SALARIES/BENEFITS:

Pension Plan: Y	ESOP Stock Plan:	Profit Sharing:	Top Exec. Salary: $1,175,000	Bonus: $1,933,808
Savings Plan: Y	Stock Purch. Plan:		Second Exec. Salary: $650,000	Bonus: $509,439

OTHER THOUGHTS:

Apparent Women Officers or Directors: 4
Hot Spot for Advancement for Women/Minorities: Y

LOCATIONS: ("Y" = Yes)

West:	Southwest:	Midwest:	Southeast:	Northeast:	International:
Y	Y	Y			

XSTRATA PLC

www.xstrata.com

Industry Group Code: 21211 **Ranks within this company's industry group:** Sales: 1 Profits: 3

Exploration/Production:		Refining/Retailing:		Utilities:		Alternative Energy:		Specialty Services:		Energy Mktg./Other Svcs.	
Exploration:	Y	Refining:		Electric Utility:		Waste/Solar/Other:		Consulting/Eng.:		Energy Marketing:	
Production:	Y	Retailing:		Gas Utility:		Thermal/Steam:		Seismic:		Equipment/Machinery:	
Coal Production:	Y	Convenience Stores:		Pipelines:		Wind:		Drilling:		Oil Field Services:	
		Chemicals:		Water:		Hydro:		InfoTech:		Air/Shipping Transportation:	
						Fuel Cells:		Specialty Services:	Y		

TYPES OF BUSINESS:

Mining
Mineral Processing
Coal Production
Copper, Lead, Zinc & Vanadium Production

BRANDS/DIVISIONS/AFFILIATES:

Xstrata Alloys
Xstrata Coal
Xstrata Copper
Xstrata Nickel
Xstrata Zinc
Xstrata Technology

CONTACTS:

Note: Officers with more than one job title may be intentionally listed here more than once.

Michael (Mick) Davis, CEO
Trevor Reid, CFO
Phil Jones, Gen. Mgr.-Human Resources
Jason Wilkins, Head-IT
Benny Levene, Chief Legal Counsel
Thras Moraitis, Exec. Gen. Mgr.-Group Strategy & Corp. Affairs
Claire Divver, Gen. Mgr.-Corp. Affairs
Hanre Rossouw, Gen. Mgr.-Investor Rel.
Ian Wall, Group Treas.
Charlie Sartain, CEO-Xstrata Copper
Santiago Zaldumbide, CEO-Xstrata Zinc
Peter Freyberg, CEO-Xstrata Coal
Peet Nienaber, CEO-Xstrata Alloys
Willy R. Strothotte, Chmn.
Andile Sangqu, Exec. Dir.-Xstrata South Africa

Phone: 41-41-726-60-70 **Fax:** 41-41-726-60-89
Toll-Free:
Address: Bahnhofstrasse 2, P.O. Box 102, Zug, 6301 Switzerland

GROWTH PLANS/SPECIAL FEATURES:

Xstrata PLC is among the largest diversified metals and mining companies in the world, with operations in 19 countries and mineral extraction activities across seven major categories: copper, coking coal, thermal coal, ferrochrome, vanadium, nickel and zinc. Xstrata's operations are organized into six separate business units, each of which in set up to function fairly autonomously within the larger group structure. Xstrata Alloys is a leading global producer of ferrochrome and primary vanadium, and also owns carbon and platinum operations. Headquartered in Sydney, Australia, Xstrata Coal is a leading global exporter of thermal coal, premium quality hard coking coal and semi-soft coal, with operations in Australia, Colombia, Canada and South Africa. Xstrata Copper, headquartered in Brisbane, Australia, operates mines and mineral processing plants in Australia, Chile, Peru, Argentina and Canada. Xstrata Nickel is a leading global nickel and cobalt producer, with operations including five mines and processing facilities in Canada; a ferronickel mine and processing facility in the Dominican Republic; and a refinery in Norway, as well as additional operations in Australia, Brazil and Tanzania. Xstrata Zinc is a leading global miner and producer of zinc, with operations in Spain, Germany, Australia, the U.K. and Canada and an interest in the Antamina copper-zinc mine in Peru. Xstrata Technology develops and supports technologies for mining, mineral processing and metals extraction, including its IsaProcess, IsaSmelt, IsaMill, Jameson Cell and Albion Process technologies. In February 2010, the firm sold its 70% interest in El Morro SCM, which held the El Morro copper-gold project, to New Gold, Inc. for approximately $463 million. In July 2010, Xstrata began construction of the Bracemac-McLeod zinc and copper mine in Canada. In August 2010, the firm made an offer to purchase the operations of Sphere Minerals, which holds interests in three iron ore projects in Mauritania, West Africa.

FINANCIALS:

Sales and profits are in thousands of dollars—add 000 to get the full amount. 2010 Note: Financial information for 2010 was not available for all companies at press time.

2010 Sales: $	2010 Profits: $	**U.S. Stock Ticker:**
2009 Sales: $22,732,000	2009 Profits: $661,000	**Int'l Ticker: XTA** Int'l Exchange: London-LSE
2008 Sales: $27,952,000	2008 Profits: $3,595,000	Employees: 37,845
2007 Sales: $28,542,000	2007 Profits: $5,543,000	Fiscal Year Ends: 12/31
2006 Sales: $18,570,000	2006 Profits: $2,050,000	Parent Company:

SALARIES/BENEFITS:

Pension Plan:	ESOP Stock Plan:	Profit Sharing:	Top Exec. Salary: $2,051,460	Bonus: $2,083,293
Savings Plan:	Stock Purch. Plan:		Second Exec. Salary: $1,352,180	Bonus: $1,347,864

OTHER THOUGHTS:

Apparent Women Officers or Directors: 2
Hot Spot for Advancement for Women/Minorities:

LOCATIONS: ("Y" = Yes)

West:	Southwest:	Midwest:	Southeast:	Northeast:	International:
Y					Y

XTO ENERGY INC

www.xtoenergy.com

Industry Group Code: 211111 **Ranks within this company's industry group:** Sales: 48 Profits: 27

Exploration/Production:		Refining/Retailing:		Utilities:		Alternative Energy:		Specialty Services:		Energy Mktg./Other Svcs.	
Exploration:	Y	Refining:		Electric Utility:		Waste/Solar/Other:		Consulting/Eng.:		Energy Marketing:	
Production:	Y	Retailing:		Gas Utility:		Thermal/Steam:		Seismic:		Equipment/Machinery:	
Coal Production:		Convenience Stores:		Pipelines:		Wind:		Drilling:		Oil Field Services:	
		Chemicals:		Water:		Hydro:		InfoTech:		Air/Shipping Transportation:	
						Fuel Cells:		Specialty Services:			

TYPES OF BUSINESS:

Oil & Gas Exploration & Production

BRANDS/DIVISIONS/AFFILIATES:

Exxon Mobil Corporation (Exxonmobil)

CONTACTS:

Note: Officers with more than one job title may be intentionally listed here more than once.

Jack Williams, Pres.
Louis G. Baldwin, CFO/Exec. VP
Vaughn O. Vennerberg, II, Exec. VP-Admin.
Keith Hutton, Exec. VP-Oper.
Bennie G. Kniffen, Sr. VP/Controller
Timothy L. Petrus, Exec. VP-Acquisitions
Brent W. Clum, Sr. VP/Treas.

Phone: 817-870-2800	**Fax:** 817-870-1671
Toll-Free: 800-299-2800	
Address: 810 Houston St., Fort Worth, TX 76102-6298 US	

GROWTH PLANS/SPECIAL FEATURES:

XTO Energy, Inc., a wholly-owned subsidiary of Exxon Mobil Corporation, is engaged in the acquisition, development, exploitation and exploration of unconventional resources, as well as in the production, processing, marketing and transportation of oil and natural gas. The firm's proved reserves are concentrated in several regions that the company groups as follows: the Eastern Region, which includes the East Texas Basin, the Haynesville Shale, and northwester Louisiana and Mississippi; the North Texas Region, which includes the Barnett Shale; the Mid-Continent and Rocky Mountain Region, including the Fayetteville Shale, the Woodford Shale and the Bakken Shale; the San Juan Region, spanning parts of New Mexico, Colorado and Utah; the Permian Region, centered in West Texas; the South Texas and Gulf Coast Region, including reserves located offshore in the Gulf of Mexico; and other properties that including reserves in the Marcellus Shale in Pennsylvania and in the North Sea. In 2009, the firm's estimated proven reserves included 294.4 million barrels of oil, 12.5 trillion cubic feet of natural gas and 93 million barrels of natural gas liquids. Average daily production during 2009 was 2.34 billion cubic feet of natural gas, 20,600 barrels of natural gas liquids and approximately 66,300 barrels of oil. In June 2010, the firm was acquired by Exxon Mobil Corp. The new organization will focus on the global development and production of unconventional natural gas resources.

XTO Energy offers its employees benefits including medical, dental and vision coverage; life and accidental death and dismemberment insurance; long-term disability insurance; and a 401(k) plan with a company match up to 10% of pre-tax earnings.

FINANCIALS:

Sales and profits are in thousands of dollars—add 000 to get the full amount. 2010 Note: Financial information for 2010 was not available for all companies at press time.

2010 Sales: $	2010 Profits: $	**U.S. Stock Ticker: Subsidiary**
2009 Sales: $9,064,000	2009 Profits: $2,019,000	**Int'l Ticker:** Int'l Exchange:
2008 Sales: $7,695,000	2008 Profits: $1,912,000	Employees:
2007 Sales: $5,513,000	2007 Profits: $1,691,000	Fiscal Year Ends: 12/31
2006 Sales: $4,576,000	2006 Profits: $1,860,000	Parent Company: EXXON MOBIL CORPORATION (EXXONMOBIL)

SALARIES/BENEFITS:

Pension Plan:	ESOP Stock Plan:	Profit Sharing:	Top Exec. Salary: $3,600,000	Bonus: $
Savings Plan: Y	Stock Purch. Plan:		Second Exec. Salary: $1,400,000	Bonus: $3,125,000

OTHER THOUGHTS:

Apparent Women Officers or Directors:
Hot Spot for Advancement for Women/Minorities:

LOCATIONS: ("Y" = Yes)

West:	Southwest:	Midwest:	Southeast:	Northeast:	International:
Y	Y	Y	Y	Y	Y

YANZHOU COAL MINING CO LTD

www.yanzhoucoal.com.cn

Industry Group Code: 21211 **Ranks within this company's industry group:** Sales: 7 Profits: 4

Exploration/Production:		Refining/Retailing:		Utilities:		Alternative Energy:		Specialty Services:		Energy Mktg./Other Svcs.	
Exploration:	Y	Refining:		Electric Utility:		Waste/Solar/Other:		Consulting/Eng.:		Energy Marketing:	Y
Production:		Retailing:		Gas Utility:		Thermal/Steam:		Seismic:		Equipment/Machinery:	
Coal Production:	Y	Convenience Stores:		Pipelines:		Wind:		Drilling:		Oil Field Services:	
		Chemicals:	Y	Water:		Hydro:		InfoTech:		Air/Shipping Transportation:	Y
						Fuel Cells:		Specialty Services:			

TYPES OF BUSINESS:

Coal Mining
Coal Transportation
Methanol Production
Electricity Generation
Heat Generation

BRANDS/DIVISIONS/AFFILIATES:

Yancoal Australia Pty Limited
Yanzhou Coal Shanxi Nenghua Co. Ltd.
Yanmei Heze Nenghua Co. Ltd.
Hua Ju Energy
Felix Resources Ltd.
Ordos Nenghua
Inner Mongolia Rongxin Chemical Co., Ltd.
Inner Mongolia Daxin Industrial Gas Co., Ltd.

CONTACTS:

Note: Officers with more than one job title may be intentionally listed here more than once.

Yang Deyu, Gen. Mgr./Vice Chmn.
Wu Yuxiang, CFO
Ni Xinghua, Chief Engineer
Zhang Baocai, Sec.
Geng Jiahuai, Vice Chmn.
He Ye, Deputy Gen. Mgr.
Jin Tai, Deputy Gen. Mgr.
Zhang Yingmin, Exec. Deputy Gen. Mgr.
Wang Xin, Chmn.

Phone: 86-537-538-2319 **Fax:** 86-537-538-3311
Toll-Free:
Address: 298 Fushan S. Rd., Zoucheng, 273500 China

GROWTH PLANS/SPECIAL FEATURES:

Yanzhou Coal Mining Co., Ltd. is engaged primarily in the underground mining, preparation and sale of coal, as well as the railway transportation of coal. A majority-owned subsidiary of Yankuang Group Corporation, Ltd., Yanzhou has six domestic company-owned mines, as well as mines owned by subsidiaries Yancoal Australia Pty Limited and Yanzhou Coal Shanxi Nenghua Co. Ltd. During 2009, the firm produced approximately 36.3 million tons of raw coal, including 1.9 million tons from Yancoal Australia and 1.1 million tons from Shanxi Nenghua. Yanzhou's proven and probable reserves total roughly 1.87 billion tons; and Yancoal Australia and Shanxi Nenghua have an additional 48 million tons and 28.5 million tons of coal reserves, respectively. Roughly 30% of the firm's coal sales are to Chinese electric utility customers, including sales to its electricity and heat generating subsidiary Hua Ju Energy. Other industry customers include metallurgical companies, chemical manufacturing companies, construction material manufacturers and fuel supply companies. Some coal is also sold to provincial and municipal fuel trading companies, which distribute it to personal-use customers. Approximately 95% of Yanzhou's coal sales are made in the domestic Chinese market, with international sales to Japan, Korea, Australia and other countries totaling 5%. In October 2009, Yanzhou acquired, through subsidiary Yancoal Australia, Australian-based coal producer Felix Resources Ltd., which has coal reserves totaling 1.42 billion tons. In December 2009, the company formed Ordos Nenghua to manage its coal assets in the Inner Mongolia Autonomous Region. In April 2010, Ordos Nenghua acquired Inner Mongolia Rongxin Chemical Co., Ltd.; Inner Mongolia Daxin Industrial Gas Co., Ltd.; and Inner Mongolia Yize Mining Investment Co., Ltd. with the intention of establishing a methanol project in Mongolia.

FINANCIALS:

Sales and profits are in thousands of dollars—add 000 to get the full amount. 2010 Note: Financial information for 2010 was not available for all companies at press time.

2010 Sales: $
2009 Sales: $2,967,100
2008 Sales: $3,820,030
2007 Sales: $1,660,000
2006 Sales: $1,538,500

2010 Profits: $
2009 Profits: $605,400
2008 Profits: $948,090
2007 Profits: $300,000
2006 Profits: $30,830

U.S. Stock Ticker: YZC
Int'l Ticker: 1171 Int'l Exchange: Hong Kong-HKEX
Employees: 49,663
Fiscal Year Ends: 12/31
Parent Company:

SALARIES/BENEFITS:

Pension Plan: ESOP Stock Plan: Profit Sharing: Top Exec. Salary: $ Bonus: $
Savings Plan: Stock Purch. Plan: Second Exec. Salary: $ Bonus: $

OTHER THOUGHTS:

Apparent Women Officers or Directors:
Hot Spot for Advancement for Women/Minorities:

LOCATIONS: ("Y" = Yes)

West:	Southwest:	Midwest:	Southeast:	Northeast:	International:
					Y

YPF SA

www.ypf.com

Industry Group Code: 211111 **Ranks within this company's industry group:** Sales: 49 Profits: 44

Exploration/Production:		**Refining/Retailing:**		**Utilities:**		**Alternative Energy:**		**Specialty Services:**		**Energy Mktg./Other Svcs.**	
Exploration:	Y	Refining:	Y	Electric Utility:		Waste/Solar/Other:		Consulting/Eng.:		Energy Marketing:	
Production:	Y	Retailing:	Y	Gas Utility:		Thermal/Steam:		Seismic:		Equipment/Machinery:	
Coal Production:		Convenience Stores:	Y	Pipelines:		Wind:		Drilling:		Oil Field Services:	
		Chemicals:	Y	Water:		Hydro:		InfoTech:		Air/Shipping Transportation:	
						Fuel Cells:		Specialty Services:			

TYPES OF BUSINESS:

Oil & Gas Production
Refining
Petrochemicals
Gas Stations

BRANDS/DIVISIONS/AFFILIATES:

Yacimientos Petroliferos Fiscales
Refineria del Norte S.A.
YPF International S.A.
YPF Holdings, Inc.
Petersen Energia Inversora S.A.

CONTACTS:

Note: Officers with more than one job title may be intentionally listed here more than once.

Sebastian Eskenazi, CEO
Ignacio Cruz Moran, COO
Guillermo Reda, CFO
Alfredo Pochintesta, Chief Commercial Officer
Fernando Dasso, Dir.-Human Resources
Angel Ramos Sanchez, Chief Admin. Officer
Mauro Renato Jose Dacom, Dir.-Legal Svcs.
Carlos Jimenez, Dir.-Oper.
Carlos Jimenez, Dir.-Planning & Control Mgmt.
Sergio Resumil, Dir.-Comm.
Gabriel Abalos, Contact-Investor Rel.
Enrique Eskenazi, Vice Chmn.
Carlos Alfonsi, Dir.-Downstream
Antonio Gomis Saez, Deputy CEO/Dir. Gen.-Repsol Argentina
Tomas Garcia Blanco, Dir.-Exploration & Production
Antonio Brufau Niubo, Chmn.
Carlos Alfonsi, Dir.-Logistics & Refining

Phone: 54-11-4329-2000 **Fax:** 54-11-5071-2113
Toll-Free:
Address: Avenida Pte. R. Saenz Pena 777, Buenos Aires, C1035AAC Argentina

GROWTH PLANS/SPECIAL FEATURES:

YPF S.A., which stands for Yacimientos Petroliferos Fiscales, is a leading integrated oil and gas company in Argentina and is majority-owned by Repsol YPF, one of Spain's largest oil companies. YPF is active in more than 30 countries. The company's upstream operations consist of the exploration, development and production of crude oil, natural gas and liquefied petroleum gas (LPG). Its downstream operations include the refining, marketing, transportation and distribution of oil and a range of petroleum products, petroleum derivatives, petrochemicals, LPG and bio-fuels. In addition, YPF is active in the gas separation and natural gas distribution sectors, both directly and through investments in several affiliated companies. The company has proved reserves of approximately 538 million barrels of crude oil, along with some 2.67 trillion cubic feet (Tcf) of natural gas, totaling in an estimated 1 billion barrels of oil equivalent (boe). More than 99% of YPF's reserves are located in Argentina, where, during 2009, it produced 111 million barrels of crude oil, condensate and lateral gas liquids, and 533 billion cubic feet of natural gas. The firm's total production for 2009 equaled 39% of Argentina's crude oil and natural gas production. YPF operates more than 70 oil and gas fields in Argentina. The company's domestic refining operations are conducted at three refineries with a combined annual refining capacity of approximately 116 million barrels, as well as through its 50% interest in Refineria del Norte S.A., which has a refinery with a capacity of approximately 26,000 barrels per day. YPF's retail distribution network for automotive petroleum products consists of approximately 1,632 YPF-branded service stations, roughly 31% of the country's total. The company's international operations are conducted through its subsidiaries, including Bolivia-based YPF International S.A. and U.S.-headquartered YPF Holdings, Inc.

FINANCIALS:

Sales and profits are in thousands of dollars—add 000 to get the full amount. 2010 Note: Financial information for 2010 was not available for all companies at press time.

2010 Sales: $	2010 Profits: $	**U.S. Stock Ticker: YPF**
2009 Sales: $9,032,000	2009 Profits: $686,000	**Int'l Ticker:** Int'l Exchange:
2008 Sales: $10,109,000	2008 Profits: $1,055,000	Employees: 12,140
2007 Sales: $9,175,570	2007 Profits: $1,288,190	Fiscal Year Ends: 12/31
2006 Sales: $8,195,704	2006 Profits: $1,172,367	Parent Company: REPSOL YPF SA

SALARIES/BENEFITS:

Pension Plan: Y	ESOP Stock Plan:	Profit Sharing:	Top Exec. Salary: $	Bonus: $
Savings Plan:	Stock Purch. Plan:		Second Exec. Salary: $	Bonus: $

OTHER THOUGHTS:

Apparent Women Officers or Directors:
Hot Spot for Advancement for Women/Minorities:

LOCATIONS: ("Y" = Yes)

West:	Southwest:	Midwest:	Southeast:	Northeast:	International:
					Y

Note: Financial information, benefits and other data can change quickly and may vary from those stated here.

ADDITIONAL INDEXES

Contents:

INDEX OF FIRMS NOTED AS HOT SPOTS FOR ADVANCEMENT FOR WOMEN & MINORITIES

SCOTTISHPOWER UK PLC
SEADRILL LIMITED
SEMPRA ENERGY
SIEMENS AG
SILVER SPRING NETWORKS
SMITH INTERNATIONAL INC
SOUTHERN CALIFORNIA EDISON COMPANY
SOUTHERN CALIFORNIA GAS COMPANY
SOUTHERN COMPANY (THE)
SOUTHWEST GAS CORP
SPECTRA ENERGY CORP
STATOIL ASA
SUNCOR ENERGY INC
SUNOCO INC
SUNOCO LOGISTICS PARTNERS LP
SUSSER HOLDINGS CORPORATION
TALISMAN ENERGY INC
TECO ENERGY INC
TENAGA NASIONAL BERHAD (TNB)
TENASKA INC
TENNESSEE VALLEY AUTHORITY (TVA)
TESORO CORP
THAI OIL PCL
TIDEWATER INC
TRANSALTA CORP
UIL HOLDINGS CORPORATION
UNISOURCE ENERGY CORPORATION
UNITED UTILITIES GROUP PLC
USEC INC
VALERO ENERGY CORP
VATTENFALL AB
VIRGINIA ELECTRIC AND POWER COMPANY
W&T OFFSHORE INC
WESTAR ENERGY
WESTMORELAND COAL CO
WGL HOLDINGS INC
WILLIAMS COMPANIES INC (THE)
WISCONSIN ENERGY CORP
WOODSIDE PETROLEUM LTD
XCEL ENERGY INC

INDEX OF SUBSIDIARIES, BRAND NAMES AND AFFILIATIONS

Brand or subsidiary, followed by the name of the related corporation

INDEX OF SUBSIDIARIES, BRAND NAMES AND AFFILIATIONS, CONT.

INDEX OF SUBSIDIARIES, BRAND NAMES AND AFFILIATIONS, CONT.

INDEX OF SUBSIDIARIES, BRAND NAMES AND AFFILIATIONS, CONT.

INDEX OF SUBSIDIARIES, BRAND NAMES AND AFFILIATIONS, CONT.

INDEX OF SUBSIDIARIES, BRAND NAMES AND AFFILIATIONS, CONT.

INDEX OF SUBSIDIARIES, BRAND NAMES AND AFFILIATIONS, CONT.

INDEX OF SUBSIDIARIES, BRAND NAMES AND AFFILIATIONS, CONT.

INDEX OF SUBSIDIARIES, BRAND NAMES AND AFFILIATIONS, CONT.

INDEX OF SUBSIDIARIES, BRAND NAMES AND AFFILIATIONS, CONT.

INDEX OF SUBSIDIARIES, BRAND NAMES AND AFFILIATIONS, CONT.

INDEX OF SUBSIDIARIES, BRAND NAMES AND AFFILIATIONS, CONT.

INDEX OF SUBSIDIARIES, BRAND NAMES AND AFFILIATIONS, CONT.

INDEX OF SUBSIDIARIES, BRAND NAMES AND AFFILIATIONS, CONT.

INDEX OF SUBSIDIARIES, BRAND NAMES AND AFFILIATIONS, CONT.

INDEX OF SUBSIDIARIES, BRAND NAMES AND AFFILIATIONS, CONT.

INDEX OF SUBSIDIARIES, BRAND NAMES AND AFFILIATIONS, CONT.

INDEX OF SUBSIDIARIES, BRAND NAMES AND AFFILIATIONS, CONT.

INDEX OF SUBSIDIARIES, BRAND NAMES AND AFFILIATIONS, CONT.

INDEX OF SUBSIDIARIES, BRAND NAMES AND AFFILIATIONS, CONT.

INDEX OF SUBSIDIARIES, BRAND NAMES AND AFFILIATIONS, CONT.

INDEX OF SUBSIDIARIES, BRAND NAMES AND AFFILIATIONS, CONT.

INDEX OF SUBSIDIARIES, BRAND NAMES AND AFFILIATIONS, CONT.

INDEX OF SUBSIDIARIES, BRAND NAMES AND AFFILIATIONS, CONT.

INDEX OF SUBSIDIARIES, BRAND NAMES AND AFFILIATIONS, CONT.

INDEX OF SUBSIDIARIES, BRAND NAMES AND AFFILIATIONS, CONT.

INDEX OF SUBSIDIARIES, BRAND NAMES AND AFFILIATIONS, CONT.

LaVergne, TN
03 April 2011
222653LV

USA

00003B/1/P

9 781593 921866